EXCEPTIONAL CHILDREN

EXCEPTIONAL CHILDREN

An Introductory Survey of Special Education
FOURTH EDITION

WILLIAM L. HEWARD
The Ohio State University

MICHAEL D. ORLANSKY
United States Information Agency

Merrill, an imprint of Macmillan Publishing Company
New York

Maxwell Macmillan Canada
Toronto

Maxwell Macmillan International
New York ◆ *Oxford* ◆ *Singapore* ◆ *Sydney*

To Kieu, the Wokmaster of Chinese Village,
and his creations: Snow Cabbage,
Tai Lo Mein, and Beef Stew Noodle (thick)

Cover Photo: Arthur Sirdufsky
Editor: Ann Castel
Developmental Editor: Linda Kauffman Peterson
Production Editor: Mary M. Irvin
Art Coordinator: Lorraine Woost
Photo Editor: Gail Meese
Text Designer: Debra A. Fargo
Production Buyer: Patricia A. Tonneman
Electronic Publishing Coordinator: Marilyn Wilson Phelps

This book was set in Garamond Light by Clarinda Company and was printed and bound by R. R. Donnelley/Willard.
The cover was printed by Lehigh Press.

Macmillan Publishing Company
866 Third Avenue
New York, NY 10022

Macmillan Publishing Company is part of the
Maxwell Communication Group of Companies.

Maxwell Macmillan Canada, Inc.
1200 Eglington Avenue East, Suite 200
Don Mills, Ontario M3C 3N1

Library of Congress Cataloging-in-Publication Data
Heward, William L., 1949–
  Exceptional children: an introductory survey of special education/William L. Heward, Michael D. Orlansky.—4th ed.
      p.   cm.
  Includes bibliographical references (p.   ) and index.
  ISBN 0–675–22200–1
  1. Special education—United States.   2. Exceptional children—Education—United States.   I. Orlansky , Michael D.   II. Title.
  LC3981.H49   1992
  371.9—dc20   91-18865
                                                                               CIP

Printing: 3 4 5 6 7 8 9   Year: 2 3 4 5

Photo credits: See page 670

Preface

Special education is the story of people. It is the story of the parents and teachers who work together to meet the needs of a preschool child with multiple handicaps. It is the story of the third-grader with learning disabilities who encounters both regular and special teachers in her public school. It is the story of the gifted child who brings new insights to old problems, the high school student with cerebral palsy who is learning English as his second language, and the woman who has recently moved into a group home after spending most of her life in a large institution. Special education is their story.

Special education is a young and rapidly evolving field; we have never found it to be dry, dull, or pedantic. In writing the first edition of *Exceptional Children* more than 12 years ago, we sought to convey the diversity and excitement of special education and to tell the story of the many people who participate in it. Our objectives remain unchanged. We hope, in this book, to present a comprehensive, current, and up-to-date survey of professional research, practice, and trends in the education of people with special needs. We believe the human perspective is essential to a meaningful description of special education, and to this end, we have again incorporated several special features—Focus inserts—into each chapter. We think they add a useful and inviting dimension to the study of special education.

Attitudes are at least as important as the content, research, and laws that shape the field of special education, and we believe that language can influence the ways in which exceptional individuals are viewed. To the extent possible in a text of this kind, we have used terminology that consistently respects the individuality and dignity of persons with special needs. Impersonal terms such as "the handicapped," "the mentally retarded," and "the cerebral palsied" create the impression of a group that is somehow very different from normal people, and mistakenly imply that all persons within a given category are alike. Rather than use such terms extensively, we refer to individuals with disabilities in a straightforward, realistic, and humanistic way—they are children, students, adults, and people.

We hope you will find the Fourth Edition of *Exceptional Children* an informative, readable, and challenging introduction to special education. Whether you are a beginner or a person with years of experience, we hope you continue your study and involvement with children and adults who have special needs. For you, too, can make a worthwhile contribution to the still-unfinished story of special education.

■ ORGANIZATION AND STRUCTURE

We begin the book with Our Personal View of Special Education—seven statements summarizing our views of the purpose, responsibilities, and future outlook of education for exceptional children—which sets the stage for the chapters that follow. The book's 15 chapters are organized into three parts. Part One—Introduction—presents an overview of terminology, and a discussion of laws, policies, and practices that are consistent with the exceptional child's right to receive an education in the least restrictive and most appropriate environment. Part Two—Exceptional Children—surveys nine specific categories of exceptionality, introducing definitions, prevalence, causes, historical background, assessment techniques, education and treatment strategies, and current and future trends. It is our experience that the most effective presentation for the introductory course in special education is a categorical one. We treat most instructional issues and strategies, however, in a generic or cross-categorical manner, reflecting contemporary special education practice. Part Three—Cultural, Family, and Life-Span Issues in Special Education—considers four topics of general importance to all special educators: cultural and linguistic differences, parent and family involvement, early intervention, and transition to adulthood.

■ FEATURES OF THE TEXT

Focus Questions

Each chapter begins with five questions that provide a framework for studying the chapter and its implications. These Focus Questions can serve as discussion starters for introducing, overviewing, concluding, or reviewing. Points to consider in discussing these questions can be found in both the Instructor's Manual and Student Study Guide, thus helping integrate this feature with the core content of each chapter, as well as with the broad scope of special education.

Margin Notes

Margin notes offer parenthetical comments and perspectives on chapter content and frequently direct students to related material in other chapters or professional resources.

Key Terms/Glossary

Each of the more than 240 key terms appears in **boldface** the first time it is presented in the text. These terms are included in the Glossary, which serves as a convenient guide to the professional terminology of special education. The key terms also appear in the charts that accompany both the Instructor's Manual and Student Study Guide, allowing for a quick overview of the sections in which they appear.

Special Features

The text continues the tradition of using Focus inserts to highlight and personalize the people of special education—students, teachers, parents, and families. Some inserts describe innovative programs and interventions, thus expanding the horizons of the book's scope. In this edition, we have divided these features into two types: Focus Essays and Focus on Intervention.

Chapter Summaries

Chapter summaries, now organized by the main headings from the chapter, use a bulleted list to overview the major principles and key points for each chapter. When used with the Chapter Overviews in the Instructor's Manual and Student Study Guide, these Summaries provide succinct review packages for students and offer checkpoints (for students and professors) for coverage of chapter contents.

For More Information

These end-of-chapter sections provide additional resources for students and professors: journals, books, organizations, and special services. These are particularly helpful for outside assignments, extended research, graduate-level projects, and professional contacts once students become practicing professionals. The items in this section complement the references that appear at the end of the text.

References

Over 1,600 references to the professional literature are cited in the book, and a complete list appears at the end of the text. This reference list provides a compendium of recent research and up-to-date work in the field of special education and reflects the more than 650 new citations added to this Fourth Edition.

■ NEW TO THIS EDITION

Recent Research and Development in the Field

♦ **Research.** Special education does not stand still for long. Since the appearance of the previous edition, the field has been changed by many new research studies, theoretical contributions, significant laws and judicial cases, and innovative approaches to education and training. In an effort to accurately reflect this growth in the field, we have included over 650 new references in this edition.

♦ **Technology.** Technology has been increasingly utilized in virtually all areas of special education, as it holds great promise for enhancing the learning, development, and independence of children and adults with special needs. Many of our new four-color photographs reflect the great strides the field has made in technological advancements, and several new Focus inserts also reveal the contribution of technology.

♦ **Legislation.** Almost two decades after the passage of Public Law 94-142, the Individuals with Disabilities Education Act, there is much discussion of the ways in which special educators and regular educators can interact with each other most effectively. Public Law 99-457, more recent legislation, focuses a great deal of attention on the importance of identifying and serving infants and preschool children who may have disabilities. All of these, and many other recent developments, are incorporated into this Fourth Edition.

Special Features

♦ **Focus Questions.** To provide a framework for approaching and synthesizing chapter content, we begin each chapter with a set of focusing questions. These questions encourage discussion and reflection and move students from rote learning to analysis and application of content. Answers to the questions appear in the Instructor's Manual and the Student Study Guide.

♦ **Focus Essays.** In previous editions, we presented essays highlighting some of the personal struggles, triumphs, and stories of persons with disabilities. We have continued that tradition in this edition. To reinforce our philosophy of "people first, disability second," several new vignettes have been added, ranging from interviews with the student leaders of the Gallaudet University uprising to hire a president who is deaf to two pieces contributed by Stephen W. Hawking, the world-renowned theoretical physicist whose severe disabilities are paled by his scholarly accomplishments.

♦ **Focus on Intervention.** New Focus on Intervention inserts explore the learning environment and the relationships between students, teachers, and parents. These features describe a wide range of effective interventions—from classroom performance and classroom management, to organizational checklists and communication tips. We highlight some innovative strategies for improving the achievement and independence of students with disabilities—from using guided notes to help students with learning disabilities to teaching students who are blind to cook with tape-recorded recipes. We present sound and practical techniques that teachers have found successful in their classrooms.

■ SUPPLEMENTS TO ACCOMPANY THE TEXT

Instructor's Manual

An expanded and improved Instructor's Manual is fully integrated with the text and includes numerous recommendations for presenting and extending the content of the chapters. The Manual consists of recommendations for using overhead projectors, a section on audiovisual supplements, lists of introductory or enrichment activities, and chapter-by-chapter sections. Individual chapter guides include answers to Focus Questions, Chapter Overviews, Chapter-at-a-Glance charts, Chapter Outlines, "To Focus Your Teaching" sections, and an in-class quiz. Each of these features assists the instructor in enhancing the text and its presentation to students.

Student Study Guide

The Student Study Guide, a new feature with this edition, is based on a newly developed prototype that takes an interactive approach to reinforcing the content of the text. Individual chapter sections include answers to Focus Questions; Chapter Overviews; Chapter-at-a-Glance charts; an Interactive Chapter Review that walks students through the contents, invites reflection, presents study tips and explanations of content—all in a conversational and personal tone; and a chapter Self-Check Quiz with answers.

Test Bank

A print Test Bank of approximately 1,000 items also accompanies the text. True/false, multiple choice, and essay/short answer items are available for every chapter.

Overhead Transparency Package

A package of 136 full-color acetate transparencies is available with the text. The transparencies highlight key concepts, summaries of content, and important figures from the core text.

Additional Teaching and Management Aids

Computerized test banks, available in Apple, Macintosh, and IBM versions, assist in customizing assessment tools for individual classrooms. **Grading software** is also available for constructing electronic grade books.

Acknowledgments

Many people contributed ideas, suggestions, insights, and constructive criticism during the preparation of *Exceptional Children*. The Fourth Edition has been enhanced by the combined efforts of a talented team of professionals at Macmillan Publishing Company. Our Editor, Ann Castel, displayed unwavering support and enthusiasm for the Fourth Edition, which we greatly appreciated. Linda Kauffman Peterson deserves special thanks as our Developmental Editor. She worked patiently and effectively with us throughout the year we spent researching, writing, and revising the Fourth Edition. The overall consistency and cohesiveness of the new edition is due in large part to Linda's professionalism, her sensitivity to our approach, and her commitment to quality. Molly Kyle and Beth Harcum copyedited the manuscript with superb technical skill and respect for our writing style. The Fourth Edition was greatly enhanced by the combined talents and creativity of Production Editor Mary Irvin, Text Designer Debra Fargo, Photo Editor Gail Meese, and Art Coordinator Lorry Woost.

The following professors—all of whom have served as instructors of introductory special education courses at other colleges and universities—provided timely and helpful reviews of the manuscript: Bruce Baum, State University at Buffalo; Jim Burns, The College of St. Rose; Peter Carullias, II, University of Cincinnati; Carol Chase-Thomas, University of North Carolina at Wilmington; Alice E. Christie, University of Akron; Sheila Drake, Kansas Wesleyan University; Pamela J. Gent, Clarion University of Pennsylvania; Joan M. Goodship, University of Richmond; Sheldon Maron, Portland State University; James M. Patton, College of William and Mary; Leonila P. Rivera, Southwest Missouri State University; James A. Siders, University of Southern Mississippi; and Scott Sparks, Ohio University. Their perspectives and experiences were of much value to us.

Other special educators contributed material and information that greatly improved the currency and quality of the Fourth Edition. This group of dedicated professionals includes: Martin Agran, Utah State University; Nancy L.

Cooke, University of North Carolina at Charlotte, Jerry C. Eyer, Oklahoma Department of Human Services; Marsha Forst, Centre for Integrated Education and Community, Toronto, Canada; Michael F. Giangreco, University of Vermont; Ronni Hochman, Upper Arlington Schools; Carolyn Hughes, Arizona State University; Sandy Letham and Dennis Higgins, Zuni Elementary School, Albuquerque, NM; James R. Patton, University of Hawaii; Frank R. Rusch, University of Illinois, Sandie Trask, Ohio State School for the Blind; and David W. Test, University of North Carolina at Charlotte. We are especially grateful to Professor Stephen W. Hawking of Cambridge University and to Bridgetta Bourne and Jerry Covell, students at Gallaudet University for sharing their stories with us.

We are grateful for the assistance of each of these special educators who arranged photo shoots: Don Cantrell, Debra Edwards, and Anne Gibson, Columbus Public Schools; Ronni Hochman, Upper Arlington Schools; Sandie Trask, Ohio School for the Blind, Janelle Degn, Dahlberg Learning Center; and Susan M. Berg, Touchstone Cafe. The talents of photographer Larry Hamill are evident throughout this edition, and we appreciate his important contribution.

We appreciate the efforts of Rodney A. Cavanaugh and Patricia M. Barbetta, both doctoral students in special education at Ohio State, who co-authored the Student Study Guide that accompanies the text. Rodney also prepared the Instructor's Manual. Their work has significantly enhanced the scope and quality of the ancillary package. Teresa A. Grossi, another Ohio State University Ph.D. student, helped by tracking down some hard-to-find references. We thank our colleague, Raymond H. Swassing, for his contribution of Chapter 11, Gifted and Talented Children. We also thank our colleagues at The Ohio State University for their helpful reviews and suggestions: Gwendolyn Cartledge, Chapters 5 and 12; Ralph Gardner III, Chapters 5 and 12; Timothy E. Heron, Chapters 2 and 4; Peter V. Paul, Chapters 6 and 7; and Diane M. Sainato, Chapters 2 and 14. We continue to be grateful to Tom Hutchinson, who introduced us to each other and was the moving force behind the first edition, and to Francie Margolin, who worked closely with us on the first three editions.

We owe a great debt of thanks to our families for putting up with us (or frequently putting up without us!). Thanks, Jill, Jan, Lee, Lynn, Tamar, and Robin for your patience and support.

Perhaps most of all, we owe a great debt to our students. Over the years they have taught us a great deal about our field, and this book reflects their contributions.

Contents

Chapter 6
Communication Disorders   233

Chapter 7
Hearing Impairment   277

Chapter 8
Visual Impairment   331

PART I
Introduction

Our Personal View of Special Education

Our goal in writing this book was to give a clear and objective explanation of the history, practices, problems, and challenges that comprise the complex and dynamic field called special education. We recognize, of course, that our personal views of the field and of exceptional children are surely implicit in our words—between the lines, as they say. But we believe we owe you an explicit statement of our views, since they affect both the substance and the tone of the entire book. The statements that follow summarize our personal view of special education.

We believe that people with disabilities have a fundamental right to live and participate fully in settings and programs—in school, at home, in the workplace, and in the community—that are as normalized as possible. That is, the settings and programs in which children and adults with disabilities learn, live, work, and recreate should, to the greatest extent possible, be the same settings and programs in which people without disabilities participate. We believe a defining feature of normalized settings and programs is the integration of handicapped and nonhandicapped participants.

We believe that individuals with disabilities have the right to as much independence as we can help them achieve. The ultimate effectiveness of special education should be evaluated in terms of its success in assisting students with disabilities to maximize their independent functioning in normal environments. There is no more important teaching task than helping children and adults with disabilities learn how to use self-management and self-advocacy skills.

We believe that special education must continue to expand its efforts to recognize and respond appropriately to all learners with special needs and attributes—the gifted and talented child, the preschooler with a handicap, the infant who is at risk for a future learning problem, the exceptional child

from a different cultural background, and the adult with disabilities. In support of this belief, we have included a chapter on each of these important areas of special education.

We believe that professionals have too long ignored the needs of parents and families of exceptional children, often treating them as patients, clients, or even adversaries, instead of realizing that they are partners with the same goals. We believe that some special educators have too often given the impression (and, worse, believed it to be true) that parents are there to serve professionals, when in fact the opposite is more correct. We believe that we have long neglected to recognize parents as a child's first—and in many ways best—teachers. We believe that learning to work effectively with parents is one of the most important skills the special educator can acquire. We have devoted a chapter to the importance of the parent-professional partnership.

We believe the efforts of special educators are most effective when they incorporate the input and services of all of the disciplines in the helping professions. We see our primary responsibility as educators to be the design and implementation of effective instruction for personal, social, vocational, and academic skills. But we consider it foolish to argue over territorial rights when we can accomplish more by working together within an interdisciplinary team that includes our colleagues in psychology, medicine, social services, and vocational rehabilitation.

We believe that teachers must demand effectiveness from their instructional approaches. The belief that special educators require unending patience is a disservice to exceptional children and to the teachers whose job it is to help them learn. The special educator should not wait patiently for the exceptional child to learn, attributing his lack of progress to retardation, a learning disability, or some other label. Instead, the special educator should modify the instructional program to improve its effectiveness, using information obtained from direct observations of the child's performance of the skills being taught. Although we do not pretend that you will know how to teach exceptional children after reading this introductory text, we do hope you will gain an appreciation for the importance of direct, systematic instruction and an understanding of the kinds of teaching skills the special educator must have.

Finally, we are essentially optimistic about the futures of exceptional children. That is to say, we have enough confidence in their potential to affirm that they can succeed in building fuller and more independent lives in the community. We believe that we have only begun to discover the ways to improve teaching, increase learning, prevent handicapping conditions, encourage acceptance, and develop technology to compensate for disabilities. And, although we make no predictions for the future, we are certain that we have not come as far as we can in helping exceptional individuals to help themselves.

1
Keys to Special Education

◆ When is special education needed? How do we know?

◆ What would be the advantages and disadvantages of delivering special education services without labeling and classifying students?

◆ If categorical labels do not help a teacher decide what and how to teach, why are they used so frequently?

◆ Can a special educator provide all three kinds of intervention—preventive, remedial, and compensatory—on behalf of an individual child?

◆ What do you think are the three most important challenges facing special education today? Why? Read your answer again after completing this textbook.

Educating children with special needs or abilities presents a difficult challenge. Teachers and related professionals who have accepted that challenge—special educators—work in an exciting and rapidly changing field. In this introductory text, we have captured for you some of the action and excitement that characterize this important and dynamic field. Throughout the book, we present specific information about exceptional children, describe both proven and promising instructional techniques, share some of the accomplishments that can be attained when professionals and parents work together, and examine areas that present continuing difficulty and concern for the future. We will first talk about the background information, concepts, and perspectives that are basic to an understanding of exceptional children and special education.

■ WHO ARE EXCEPTIONAL CHILDREN?

We begin by defining four terms: *exceptional children, disability, handicap,* and *at risk*. All children exhibit differences from one another in terms of physical attributes (some are shorter, some are stronger) and learning abilities (some learn quickly and generalize what they learn to new situations; others need repeated practice and have difficulty remembering what they have been taught). The differences among most children are relatively small, enabling them to benefit from the general education program. The physical attributes and/or learning abilities of some children, however—those we call **exceptional children**—differ from the norm (either below or above) to such an extent that an individualized program of special education is required to meet their needs. The term *exceptional children* includes both children who experience difficulties in learning and children whose performance is so superior that special education is necessary to help them fulfill their potential. Thus, *exceptional children* is an inclusive term that refers to children with learning and/or behavior problems, children with physical disabilities, and children who are intellectually gifted.

Disability refers to reduced function or loss of a particular body part or organ; the term *impairment* is often used synonymously. A disability limits the ability to perform certain tasks (e.g., to see, hear, walk) in the same way that most nondisabled persons do. A disabled person is not handicapped, however, unless the physical disability leads to educational, personal, social, vocational, or other problems. If a child who has lost a leg, for example, can learn to use an artificial limb and thus function in and out of school without problems, she is not handicapped.

Handicap refers to the problems a person with a disability or impairment encounters in interacting with the environment. A disability may pose a handicap in one environment but not in another. The child with an artificial limb may be handicapped when competing against nondisabled peers on the basketball court but experience no handicap in the classroom. The term *handicapped children* is more restrictive than *exceptional children* and does not include gifted and talented children.

At risk refers to children who are not currently identified as handicapped or disabled but are considered to have a greater-than-usual chance of developing a handicap. The term is most often applied to infants and preschoolers who,

Terms in **boldface** are defined in the glossary.

Although there are technical differences between *disability* and *handicap,* most special educators use the two terms synonymously as we have in this book.

because of conditions surrounding their births or home environments, may be expected to experience developmental problems at a later time. The term also refers to students who are experiencing learning problems in the regular classroom and are therefore "at risk" of being identified as handicapped.

In separate chapters, we will examine the defining characteristics and educational implications of each of the following so-called categories of exceptional children:

- Mental retardation
- Learning disabilities
- Behavior disorders (emotional disturbance)
- Communication (speech and language) disorders
- Hearing impairments
- Visual impairments
- Physical and other health impairments
- Severe handicaps
- Gifted and talented

It is a mistake, however, to think that there are two distinct kinds of children—that is, those who are special and those who are regular. As we have said, all children differ from one another in individual characteristics along a continuum; exceptional children are those whose differences from the norm are large enough to require a specially designed instructional program if they are to benefit fully from education. *Exceptional children are more like other children than they are different.* All children are unique individuals who require individual attention, nurturing, and caring.

■ HOW MANY EXCEPTIONAL CHILDREN ARE THERE AND WHERE ARE THEY SERVED?

Each year, the U.S. Department of Education reports to Congress on the education of the country's handicapped children. As this book went to press, the most recent data available pertained to the 1988–89 school year (U.S. Department of Education, 1990).

Let's take a quick look at some of the numerical facts about special education in the United States.

- Over 4.5 million handicapped children, or 6.7% of the resident population from birth to age 21, received special education services during the 1988–89 school year.
- The number of children and youth who receive special education has grown every year since a national count was begun in 1976, with an overall increase of 24% since 1976–77.
- New early intervention programs have been major contributors to the increases since 1986. During 1988–89, 362,443 preschoolers (age 3 to 5) and 34,412 infants and toddlers (birth through age 2) were among those receiving special education.

Physicians also use the terms *at risk* or *high risk* to identify pregnancies with a greater-than-normal probability of producing babies with disabilities. For example, a pregnancy may be considered "high risk" if the pregnant woman is above or below normal child-bearing age, uses alcohol heavily, or is drug-dependent.

Handicapism refers to the negative stereotyping and unequal and unjust treatment of people with disabilities.

- Handicapped children in special education represent approximately 9.4% of the entire school-age population. (This is less than the 12% once projected by the federal government.)

- The number of children who receive special education increases from age 3 through age 9. The number served decreases gradually with each successive age year after age 9 until age 17. After age 17, the number of students receiving special education decreases sharply.

- Four types of handicaps account for 94% of all school-age children receiving special education: learning disabilities (48%), speech and language impairment (23%), mental retardation (14%), and emotional disturbance (9%).

- The number of children identified as learning disabled has grown dramatically (up 152%) since the federal government began collecting and reporting child count data in 1976–77.

- The number of students served as mentally retarded has decreased steadily; in 1988–89, there were 36% fewer students reported in the category of mental retardation than in the 1976–77 school year.

- About twice as many males as females receive special education.

- The vast majority—approximately 90%—of school-age children receiving special education are "mildly handicapped."

- Based on these data, the "typical" child receiving special education in the United States is a 9-year-old boy with learning disabilities who spends part of each school day in the regular classroom and part in a resource room.

What factors might be responsible for the huge increase in the number of children identified as learning disabled? Why do you think the number of children identified as mentally retarded has decreased in recent years? Compare your ideas with what you learn later in Chapters 3 and 4.

In 1988 Congress passed the Jacob K. Javits Gifted and Talented Students Education Act which provides federal funds in support of research, teacher training, and program development.

Although special education for children who are gifted and talented is not mandated by federal law as it is for children with disabilities, a national survey conducted during the 1986–87 school year reported that approximately 1.5 million children were served in public school programs for gifted and talented students (*State of the States: Gifted and Talented Education, 1986–87,* 1988). This number ranks gifted and talented students as the second largest group of exceptional children receiving special education services. Based on an estimate that gifted and talented children may comprise as much as 5% of the school-age population, approximately 2.5 million gifted children may need special education (Clark, 1988). This discrepancy between need and the level of service may make gifted and talented children the most underserved group of exceptional children.

To state precisely how many exceptional children live in the United States is virtually impossible for many reasons: the different criteria states and local school systems use to identify exceptional children; the relative ability of a school system to provide effective instructional support to the regular classroom teacher so that an at-risk student does not become a special education student; the imprecise nature of assessment; the large part subjective judgment plays in interpretation of assessment data; and the fact that a child may be diagnosed as disabled at one time in his school career and not disabled (or included in a different disability category) at another time.

Two-thirds of all children with handicaps received at least part of their education in regular classrooms with nonhandicapped children during the

About one-fourth of all students with disabilities are educated in separate classrooms.

1987–88 school year (Figure 1.1). This includes 29.7% who were served in the regular classroom and 38.2% who were served for part of each school day in a special setting, called a *resource room,* in which a special educator provides individualized instruction. One-fourth of all children with disabilities are educated in separate classrooms within a regular school. Slightly more than 1 in 20 school-age handicapped students, usually the student with the most severe handicaps, is educated in special schools. Residential schools serve slightly less than 1% of all children with disabilities, as do nonschool environments such as homebound or hospital programs.

The vast majority of children in the two largest groups of students with disabilities spend at least part of the school day in regular classrooms: 77% of children with learning disabilities and 94% of children with speech or language impairments (Table 1.1). In contrast, only 16% of children who are deaf-blind and 20% of children with multiple handicaps were educated in regular classrooms during the 1987–88 school year, although these figures represent increases over those of previous years.

FIGURE 1.1

Percentage of all students with handicaps ages 3 to 21 served in six educational placements. (*Source:* From *Twelfth Annual Report to Congress on the Implementation of the Education of the Handicapped Act* (p. 20), 1990, U.S. Department of Education.)

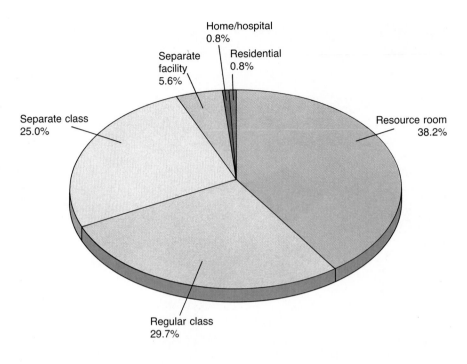

Home/hospital
0.8%

Residential
0.8%

Separate facility
5.6%

Resource room
38.2%

Separate class
25.0%

Regular class
29.7%

Note: Includes data from 50 states and Puerto Rico.

TABLE 1.1

Percentage of children and youth age 6 to 21 served in different educational placements by handicapping condition. (Slight differences in percentages from Figure 1.1 are because children under age 6 are not reported by handicapping condition.)

Handicapping Condition	Regular Class	Resource Room	Separate Class	Separate School	Residential Facility	Home/ Hospital
Learning disabled	17.6%	59.2%	21.7%	1.4%	0.1%	0.1%
Speech impaired	74.8	19.7	3.8	1.5	0.1	0.1
Mentally retarded	5.7	24.0	57.6	11.4	1.0	0.3
Emotionally disturbed	12.6	32.9	34.6	14.3	3.5	2.2
Hard of hearing and deaf	24.4	20.9	35.2	10.8	8.6	0.2
Multihandicapped	6.4	13.3	45.9	27.2	4.0	3.1
Orthopedically impaired	27.8	18.0	31.8	13.2	1.0	8.3
Other health impaired	30.6	20.8	18.7	9.5	0.8	19.6
Visually handicapped	37.7	25.6	20.8	5.4	10.0	0.6
Deaf-blind	8.9	7.2	35.1	21.0	24.2	3.7
All conditions	28.9	40.0	24.7	4.9	0.8	0.7

Notes: Totals include data from the 50 states, District of Columbia, and Puerto Rico.
Educational placements for children ages 3–5 are not reported by handicapping condition.

Source: (From *Twelfth Annual Report to Congress on the Implementation of the Education of the Handicapped Act* (p. 23), U.S. Department of Education, 1990.)

■ PROBLEMS OF LABELING AND CLASSIFYING EXCEPTIONAL CHILDREN

Centuries ago, labeling and classifying people was of little importance—survival was the main concern. Those whose disabilities prevented their full participation in the activities necessary for survival were left on their own to perish or, in some instances, were even killed. In later years, derogatory labels like "dunce," "imbecile," and "fool" were applied to people with mental retardation or behavior problems, and other demeaning words were used for persons with other disabilities or physical deformities. In each instance, however, the purpose of classification was the same—to exclude the person with disabilities from the activities, privileges, and facilities of normal society.

The Pros and Cons

Some educators argue that, even today, the classification of exceptional children functions to exclude them from normal society. Others argue that a workable system of classifying exceptional children (or their exceptional learning needs) is a prerequisite to providing the special educational programs those children require if they are to be integrated into normal society. No other aspects of special education have been more widely debated during the past two decades than classification and labeling. Classification is a complex issue involving emotional, political, and ethical considerations, in addition to scientific and educational interests. Research sheds little light on the problem; studies that have been conducted to assess the effects of labeling have produced inconclusive, often contradictory, evidence and have generally been marked by methodological weakness (MacMillan, 1982).

As with most complex questions, there are valid arguments on both sides. Here are some of the reasons for and against classification and labeling of exceptional children.

Possible Benefits of Labeling

♦ Categories can relate diagnosis to specific treatment.

♦ Labeling may lead to a "protective" response in which nonlabeled children accept certain behaviors of their handicapped peers more fully than they would accept those same behaviors in "normal" children (MacMillan, 1982).

♦ Labeling helps professionals communicate with one another and classify and assess research findings.

♦ Funding of special education programs is often based on specific categories of exceptionality.

♦ Labels allow special-interest groups to promote specific programs and spur legislative action.

♦ Labeling helps make exceptional children's special needs more visible to the public.

A protective response by a nondisabled child toward a peer with a disability can be a disadvantage if it diminishes the labeled child's chances to develop independence and learn appropriate social skills.

Possible Disadvantages of Labeling

♦ Labels usually focus on a child's negative aspects, causing others to think about the child only in terms of inadequacies or defects.

Not all labels used to classify children with handicaps are considered equally negative or stigmatizing. It is believed that one factor contributing to the large number of children identified as *learning disabled* is that many parents view "learning disabilities" as a socially acceptable classification (Algozzine & Korinek, 1985; Lieberman, 1985).

For more on culturally diverse children, see Chapter 12.

♦ Labels may cause others to react to and hold low expectations for a child based on the label, resulting in a self-fulfilling prophecy.

♦ Labels that describe a child's performance deficit often mistakenly acquire the role of explanatory constructs (e.g., "Sherry acts that way because she is emotionally disturbed.").

♦ Labels tend to suggest that learning problems are primarily the result of something wrong within the child, thereby reducing the systematic examination of instructional variables as the cause of performance deficits.

♦ A labeled child may develop a poor self-concept.

♦ Labels may lead peers to reject or ridicule the labeled child.

♦ Special education labels have a certain permanence; once labeled "retarded" or "learning disabled," a child has difficulty ever again achieving the status of being "just another kid."

♦ Labels often provide a basis for keeping children out of the regular classroom.

♦ A disproportionate number of children from minority culture groups have been inaccurately labeled "handicapped," especially as educably mentally retarded.

♦ Classification of exceptional children requires the expenditure of a great amount of professional and student time that could better be spent in planning and delivering instruction.

Clearly, there are strong reasons both for and against classification and labeling of exceptional children. In the early 1970s, the U.S. government commissioned a comprehensive study of the classification of exceptional children. This 2-year project involved 93 psychologists, educators, lawyers, and parents working on 31 different task forces. The results of this project can be found in *Issues in the Classification of Children* (Volumes 1 and 2), edited by the project's director, Nicholas Hobbs (Hobbs, 1976a, 1976b). A third book, *The Futures of Children* (Hobbs, 1975), summarizes findings and recommendations. Other reviews of labeling and classification of exceptional children can be found in MacMillan (1982) and Smith, Neisworth, and Hunt (1983). None of these discussions has produced conclusive arguments that could lead to total acceptance or absolute rejection of labeling practices.

Labeling and Services

On one level, the various labels given to children with special learning needs can be viewed as a means of organizing the funding and administration of special education services in the schools. To receive special education services, a child must be labeled as handicapped and, with few exceptions, must be further classified into one of that state's categories, such as mental retardation or learning disabilities. In practice, therefore, a student becomes eligible for various kinds of special education and related services because of membership in a given category. If losing one's label also means loss of needed services, the trade-off is not likely to be beneficial for the child. In the mid-1970s, for example, the definition of *mental retardation* was changed so that persons previously classified as having "borderline mental retardation" were no longer considered mentally retarded and were therefore no longer eligible for special education services designed for children with mental retardation. Although many of this large group of youngsters receive services under other handicapping conditions, most notably learning disabilities, some do not receive needed services (MacMillan, 1989; Zetlin & Murtaugh, 1990).

Arguing that labels are necessary for students with behavior disorders, Braaten, Kauffman, Braaten, Polsgrove, and Nelson (1988) write:

> We share the concern regarding the stigma of the label "behaviorally disordered," even more the stigma of "seriously emotionally disturbed." The label itself has little value other than channeling services. But to argue that BD students' stigma derives from their label misses the point that these students become social outcasts before they are referred for special education. . . . Serious problems must be talked about with serious language at an "official" level, else the students' difficulties are trivialized. Descriptions such as "naughty in class" (e.g., Shepard, 1987) and other euphemisms used to characterize LD and other mildly handicapped students—and by implication BD students—suggest that their problems are minor. The likely consequence of such language will be reduction in services for an already underserved group. (p. 23)

Although identification and classification of exceptional children appear necessary, no one is happy with our current system of categorical labels. Labels signify eligibility for services, but they have proven unreliable in many cases. For example, one study that examined the classification of 523 students with mild handicaps found that 24% had been given two or more labels during their school years, and 17% of those who were moved from their initial category to another category were later reassigned to their initial classification (Wolman, Thurlow, & Bruininks, 1989).

Reynolds, Wang, & Walberg (1987), who advocate strongly against the present system of identifying and labeling children for special education services, believe that "the boundaries of the categories have shifted so markedly in response to legal, economic, and political forces as to make diagnosis largely meaningless" (p. 396). Some special educators believe the classification of exceptional children by category of handicapping condition may actually interfere with the assessment and instructional planning that is directed toward each student's real learning needs. Stainback and Stainback (1984) argue that

> These categories often do not reflect the specific educational needs and interests of students in relation to such services. For example, some students categorized as visually handicapped may not need large-print books, while others who are not labeled visually impaired and thus are ineligible for large-print books could benefit from their use. Similarly, not all students labeled behaviorally disordered may need self-control training, while some students not so labeled may need self-control training as a part of their educational experience. (p. 105)

Impact on Instruction

What we *can* say about the possible benefits of classifying exceptional children is that most of the benefits are experienced not by individual children, but rather by groups of children, parents, and professionals who are associated with a certain category. On the other hand, all the negative aspects of labeling affect the

WHAT'S IN A NAME?
The Labels and Language of Special Education

Some years ago at the annual convention of the Council for Exceptional Children, hundreds of attendees were wearing a big yellow and black button that was very popular that year. The button proclaimed "Label jars, not children!" Wearers of the button were presumably making a statement about one or more of the criticisms leveled at categorizing and labeling exceptional children, such as labeling is negative, it focuses only on the child's deficits in learning or behavior; labeling makes it more likely that others (teachers, parents, peers) will expect poor performance and bad behavior from the labeled child; labels may hurt the child's self-esteem.

Labels, in and of themselves, are not the problem. The dictionary defines *label* as a "descriptive word or phrase applied to a person, group, theory, etc., as a convenient generalized classification" (Webster's New World Dictionary, 1984). Most professionals in special education agree that a common language for referring to children who share common instructional and related service needs is necessary. The kinds of words that we use as labels, and even the order in which they are spoken or written, do, however, influence the degree to which a particular label serves as an *appropriate* generalized classification for communicating variables relevant to the design and provision of educational and other human services. For example, while they may refer to a common set of educational needs, terms such as "the retarded," "the deaf," or "blind children" also imply negative connotations that are unwarranted and inappropriate. Such blanket labels imply that all persons in the group being labeled are alike; individuality has been lost. At the personal level, when we describe a child as a "physically handicapped boy," we place too much emphasis on the disability, suggesting the deficits caused by the disability are the most important thing to know about him.

How, then, should we refer to exceptional children? At the personal level we can, and should, follow Tom Lovitt's advice and call them by their names: Linda, Shawon, or Jackie. Referring to a child as "Molly, a fifth-grade student with learning disabilities" helps us focus on the individual child and her primary role as a student. Such a description does not ignore or gloss over the learning problems that challenge Molly, but it does acknowledge there are other things we should know about her.

We believe it is important for everyone, not just special educators, to speak, write, and think about exceptional children and adults in ways that respect each person's individuality and recognize strengths and abilities instead of focusing only on disabilities. But simply changing the way we talk and write about an individual with a disability will not make the needs and challenges posed by the disability go away. The following commentary, written by Michael Goldfarb, Executive Director of the Association for the Help of Retarded Children, offers some provocative and insightful thoughts on the "language of special education."

Even after it had become fashionable to use the phrase "Down syndrome," Louis Striar insisted on calling his son a mongoloid. He enjoyed the shocked look on people's faces when he stubbornly clung to the old label. He consistently refused to trade in a phrase he was used to for one that was used by others. I always thought that Louie did this simply to shock people, because he enjoyed that.

I now realize that his real goal, as a Board member of AHRC and as a parent of a disabled son, was to demonstrate that no new label, however popular, would solve his son's problem with society or society's problem with his son. No matter what label you used, Martin was retarded. Louie was attempting to teach us a very painful lesson, one which we still have not learned, namely, that linguistic reform alone can't really change the world. It has taken me a dozen years to figure out what he meant.

individual child who has been labeled. Of the possible advantages of labeling listed earlier, only the first two could be said to benefit an individual child. And the argument that labels associate diagnosis with proper treatment is tenuous, particularly when you consider the kinds of labels used in special education.

Consider the following lists of words:

crippled
handicapped
disabled
challenged

inmate
patient
resident
client
program participant

feeble minded
retarded
person with mental retardation
person

institution
state school

developmental center

Consider the words on the top of each list, the old and unfashionable ones. The names at the bottom are new and more acceptable. Many professionals in this field have made it a matter of deep personal commitment to get you to use the most up-to-date expressions.

Every one of these changes has been presented as an essential act of consciousness raising. Every one of these changes has been proposed by numbers of enlightened, progressive, and intelligent professionals with the genuine intent of changing the image and role of disabled people in this society. Every one of these linguistic reforms has been followed several years later by newer and "better" names. Every one of these changes has failed to make the world different.

Linguistic reform without systemic change conceals unhappy truths. Social problems may be reflected in the way we speak, but they are rarely, if ever, cured by changes in language. It is certainly true that liberals feel better when they use the most acceptable phrase, but this should not obscure the fact that the oppressed continue to be oppressed under any label. (Perhaps we should not call people "the oppressed"; perhaps it would be better to call them "people with oppression.")

Our real problem in this and many other societies is that we respect only intelligence, stylish good looks, and earning potential. This society denigrates people who are not intelligent, who are deemed unattractive, or who are poor. Referring to retarded people as "people with mental retardation" will not make them brighter, prettier, richer. These names leave the old prejudices intact. Society's attitudes and the values that underlie them must be changed. This will take far more than trivial linguistic changes. Can you imagine a Planning Board meeting at which a local resident says, "We don't want any retarded people living in our neighborhood! But people with mental retardation? That's different. They can move in anytime." I can't.

Changing attitudes and values is more difficult than changing language. Perhaps that is why we spend so much time changing language.

From M. Goldfarb, Executive Director's Report, AHRC Chronicle, *Spring 1990. Adapted by permission.* ◆

Changing the label used to classify this student's disability won't lessen the severity of her handicap. But referring to her as a person first, as Carla, helps us recognize her strengths and abilities—what she can do— instead of focusing on her disabilities.

The children are given various labels including deaf, blind, orthopedically handicapped, trainable mentally retarded, educable mentally retarded, autistic, socially maladjusted, perceptually handicapped, brain-injured, emotionally disturbed, disadvantaged, and those with learning disabilities. For the most part the labels are not important. They rarely tell the teacher who can be taught in what way. One could put five or six labels on the same child and still not know what to teach him or how. (Becker, Engelmann, & Thomas, 1971, pp. 435–436)

A number of special educators have proposed alternative approaches to classifying exceptional children that focus on educationally relevant variables (e.g., Iscoe & Payne, 1972; Lovitt, 1982; Quay, 1968; Sontag, Sailor, & Smith, 1977). Lovitt (1982) has suggested that exceptional children be classified according to the skills they need to learn.

"What should we call the special children who are sent to our classes?" This question might be asked by regular education teachers who are about to have special education children mainstreamed in their classes. Should they carefully study the dossiers of the children to figure out what others have called them? Should a regular teacher, for instance, try to remember that Roy, who will soon be sent to his regular class, was called emotionally disturbed by two school psychologists, a social worker, and a reading teacher (even though he was referred to as learning disabled by another school psychologist)? Should he hang onto the fact that Amy was called mentally retarded by most of the people who wrote reports for her folder? Likewise, should he make every effort to recall that Tim was most often referred to as learning disabled?

No. Those labels do not help teachers design effective programs for the special children they will teach. They won't help teachers decide where to seat the children; they certainly won't help them to design educational and management strategies.

But if we shouldn't refer to these special children by using those old labels, then how should we refer to them? For openers, call them Roy, Amy, and Tim. Beyond that, refer to them on the basis of what you're trying to teach them. For example, if a teacher wants to teach Roy to compute, read, and comprehend, he might call him a student of computation, reading, and comprehension. We do this all the time with older students. Sam, who attends Juilliard, is referred to as "the trumpet student"; Jane, who attends Harvard, is called "the law student." (Lovitt, 1979, p. 5)

In a system such as this, called **curriculum-based assessment**, students would be assessed and classified relative to the degree to which they are learning specific curriculum content (Howell & Morehead, 1987; Potter & Wamre, 1990; Tucker, 1985). The fundamental question in curriculum-based assessment is "How is the student progressing in the curriculum of the local school?" (Tucker, 1985). Educators who employ curriculum-based assessment believe it is more important to assess (and thereby classify) students in terms of acquisition of the skills and knowledge included in the school's curriculum than determining the degree to which they differ from the normative score of all children in some general physical attribute or learning characteristic.

Even though curriculum-based assessment is being used more frequently, use of the traditional labels and categories of exceptional children is likely to continue. The continued development and use of educationally relevant classification systems, however, make it more likely that diagnosis and assessment will lead to meaningful instructional programs for children, promote more educationally meaningful communication and research by professionals, and perhaps decrease some of the negative aspects of the current practice of labeling children.

■ LEGISLATION AFFECTING EXCEPTIONAL CHILDREN

The 14th Amendment to the Constitution of the United States guarantees equal protection under the law for all citizens. Yet a long series of court cases and federal legislation has been required to make equal protection with respect to education a reality for children with handicaps. A "civil rights" movement for persons with handicaps has resulted in legislation guaranteeing that exceptional children can no longer be denied appropriate educational services. (Table 2.1 in Chapter 2 outlines some of the major court cases and legislation that have affected the education of exceptional children.)

We will focus our attention on Public Law 94–142, the Individuals with Disabilities Education Act, which became law in 1975. P.L. 94–142 is a landmark piece of legislation that has changed the face of special education. Its passage marked the culmination of the efforts of a great many educators, parents, and legislators to bring together in one comprehensive bill this country's laws regarding the education of handicapped children. The law reflects society's concern for treating people with disabilities as full citizens, with the same rights and privileges that all other citizens enjoy.

P.L. 94–142 is central to many of the practices and trends in special education today. The major features of P.L. 94–142 are:

P.L. 94–142 was originally called the Education for All Handicapped Children Act. Since it became law in 1975, Congress has amended P.L. 94–142 three times, in 1983, in 1986, and again in 1990. The most recent amendments renamed the law as the Individuals with Disabilities Education Act. The basic features and requirements of the law have remained unchanged. We will examine special education legislation and each of the features of P.L. 94–142 more fully in Chapter 2.

♦ A free, appropriate public education must be provided for all children with disabilities.

♦ School systems must provide safeguards to protect the rights of children with disabilities and their parents.

♦ Children with disabilities must be educated with nondisabled children to the maximum extent possible.

♦ An individualized education program (IEP) must be developed and implemented for each child with disabilities.

♦ Parents of children with disabilities are to play an active role in the process of making any educational decisions about their children with disabilities.

♦ States meeting the requirements of P.L. 94–142 receive federal tax dollars to help offset the additional costs incurred in providing special education services.

Gifted children are not mentioned in P.L. 94–142, which deals only with the education of children with disabilities. Special education for children who are gifted and talented is not mandated by federal law, although the federal government "encourages" states to develop gifted programs. Federal monies that might be used for development and support of programs for gifted and talented children are included as part of a block grant that each state receives to fund a wide range of elementary and secondary education programs. Mitchell (1982) reports that 48 states have programs of some sort for gifted and talented students. The amount of funding available at either the federal or the state level for support of gifted programs, however, is only a tiny fraction of the dollars spent for educating children with disabilities.

■ WHAT IS SPECIAL EDUCATION?

Special education can be defined from many different perspectives. One may, for example, view special education as a legislatively governed enterprise. From this viewpoint, one would be concerned about the legal implications of informing parents of handicapped students about their right to participate in planning their children's individualized education programs. From a purely administrative point of view, special education might be seen as that part of a school system's operation that requires certain teacher-pupil ratios in the classroom and has special formulas for determining levels of funding according to the category of exceptional children served. Or, from a sociological or political perspective, special education can be seen as an outgrowth of the civil rights movement, a demonstration of society's changing attitudes about people with disabilities in general. Each perspective has some validity, and each continues to play a role in defining what special education is and how it is practiced. None of these views, however, would yield the essence of special education.

Special Education as Teaching

Ultimately, *teaching* is what special education is most about—but that is true of all of education. What then is *special* about special education? One way to try to answer that question is to look at special education in terms of the *who, what, where,* and *how* of its teaching.

Who?

Are there jobs in special education? Yes. In the 1988–89 school year, there were 297,034 special education teachers employed in the United States, with a reported 29,774 more needed (U.S. Department of Education, 1990). During the same year, 240,978 special education personnel other than teachers were employed, with a reported shortage of 15,571. All 50 states reported shortages in one or more areas.

We have already identified the most important *who* in special education—the exceptional children whose special needs or abilities necessitate an individualized program of education. In addition, exceptional children receive some or all of their instruction from teachers who have completed specialized teacher training programs in preparation for their work with students with special needs. Working with special educators and regular classroom teachers are many other professionals—including school psychologists, speech and language therapists, physical therapists, counselors, and medical specialists, to name only a few—helping to provide all the educational and related services exceptional children need. Together, this interdisciplinary team of professionals bears the primary responsibility for helping exceptional children learn despite their differences and special needs.

What?

Special education can sometimes be differentiated from regular education by its curriculum—that is, by *what* is taught. Some exceptional children need intensive, systematic instruction to learn skills that normally developing children acquire naturally. For example, self-help skills, such as dressing, eating, and

Ultimately, special education is about teaching.

toileting, are not part of the regular education curriculum, yet these skills are an important part of the curriculum for many students with severe handicaps. Also, some exceptional children are taught certain skills to compensate for or reduce the handicapping effects of a disability. A child who is blind may receive special training in reading and writing braille, whereas a seeing child does not need these skills. It can be said that in regular education the school system dictates the curriculum, but in special education the child's individual needs dictate the curriculum (Lieberman, 1985). We should not forget, however, that two-thirds of children with disabilities are educated in regular classrooms for at least part of the day—meaning that most children in special education experience the regular school curriculum.

Where?

Special education can sometimes be identified by *where* it takes place. Although two-thirds of all children with handicaps receive much of their education in regular classrooms, one-third are someplace else—mostly in separate classrooms and separate residential and day schools. And many of those in a regular classroom leave it to spend a portion of each day in a resource room, where they receive individualized instruction. Special educators also teach in many environments not usually thought of as "school." An early childhood special

We will discuss the environments where students with disabilities are taught in greater detail in Chapter 2.

educator may spend much of his time teaching parents how to work with their handicapped toddler at home. Teachers of students with severe disabilities are spending greater amounts of instructional time in community and employment settings, helping their students learn important daily living and job skills.

How?

How special educators teach can, at times, be differentiated from the methods used by regular education teachers. One special educator may use sign language to communicate with his students. Another special educator may use a carefully structured procedure for gradually withdrawing visual prompts in helping a student learn to discriminate her own name from others. But for the most part, effective special education teachers employ the same set of fundamental teaching skills that all good teachers use. There are not two distinct sets of instructional methods—one to use with special students, the other with regular students. Nor is there a certain set of teaching methods appropriate for students within a given disability category that differs significantly from effective teaching methods for students in another category. Morsink, Thomas, and Smith-Davis (1987) reviewed the literature and found no evidence that specific teaching methods are differentially effective with students labeled as learning disabled, mildly mentally retarded, and emotionally disturbed. Instead, all special educators should be skilled in the procedures for systematically designing, implementing, and evaluating instruction (e.g., Kameenui & Simmons, 1990; Mercer & Mercer, 1989; Snell, in press).

Special Education as Intervention

Intervention is a general name for all efforts on behalf of individuals with disabilities. The overall goal of intervention is to eliminate, or at least reduce, the obstacles that might keep a child or adult with disabilities from full and active participation in school and society. The three basic kinds of intervention efforts are

♦ *Preventive* (keeping possible problems from becoming a serious handicap)

♦ *Remedial* (overcoming disability through training or education)

♦ *Compensatory* (giving the individual new ways to deal with the disability)

Preventive Techniques

Early intervention with infants, toddlers, and preschoolers is the subject of Chapter 14.

Preventive efforts are most promising when they begin early—even before birth, in many cases. In later chapters, we will explore some of the exciting new methods available for preventing disabilities. We will explore, too, the efforts in social and educational programs to stimulate infants and very young children to acquire skills that most children learn normally, without special help. Unfortunately, prevention programs have only just begun to affect the number and severity of handicaps in this country. And it is likely that we will be well into the 21st century before we will achieve a significant reduction of handicaps (Hayden & Pious, 1979). In the meantime, we must count on remedial and compensatory efforts to help handicapped people achieve fuller and more independent lives.

Remedial Programs

Remedial programs are supported largely by educational institutions and social agencies. In fact, the word **remediation** is primarily an educational term; the word **rehabilitation** is used more often by social service agencies. Both have a common purpose—to teach the person with disabilities basic skills for independence. In school, those skills may be academic (reading, writing, speaking, computing), social (getting along with other children; following instructions, schedules, and other daily routines), or even personal (feeding, dressing, using the toilet without assistance). More and more, schools are also teaching career and job skills to prepare exceptional youngsters for jobs as adults in the community. In doing so, schools are sharing more of the responsibilities that social service agencies have historically accepted. Vocational training, or **vocational rehabilitation**, includes preparation to develop work habits and work attitudes, as well as specific training in a particular skill like auto mechanics, carpentry, or assembly-line work. The underlying assumption of both remedial and habilitative programs is that a person with disabilities needs special help to succeed in the normal settings.

Programs for helping secondary students with handicaps make the transition from school to adulthood are discussed in Chapter 15.

Compensatory Efforts

Still another approach is to compensate for a person's disability by giving him a kind of substitute skill or device on which to rely. For example, a child with cerebral palsy can be trained to make maximum use of her hands, but the use of a headstick and a template placed over a regular typewriter may effectively compensate for lack of muscle control by letting her type instead of write lessons by hand. (Of course, the device itself requires training—she will have to learn to type with the headstick.) The point is that compensatory efforts aim to give the individual with a disability some kind of asset that nondisabled individuals do not need—whether it be a device like a headstick or special training, like mobility instruction, for a child without vision.

What, then, is special education? At one level, it is a profession, with tools, techniques, and research efforts focused on evaluating and meeting the learning needs of exceptional children and adults. At a more practical level, special education is individually planned, systematically implemented, and carefully evaluated instruction to help exceptional learners achieve the greatest possible personal self-sufficiency and success in present and future environments.

■ SPECIAL EDUCATION: CURRENT CHALLENGES AND FUTURE PREDICTIONS

Special education has accomplished a great deal during the past 25 years, and there is legitimate reason for those in the field to feel good about the progress. Much has been accomplished in terms of making a free, appropriate education available to many handicapped children who were previously denied access to an education. Much has been learned about how to effectively teach children with severe handicaps, children who many had thought were not capable of learning. Special educators and parents have learned to work together on behalf of exceptional children. Technological advances have helped many students

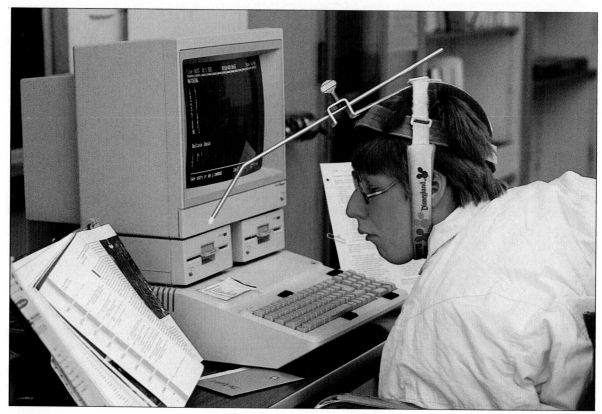

Gregory's mastery of a headstick compensates for the impaired muscular control of his hands and arms.

overcome physical disabilities or communication handicaps. Throughout the remaining chapters, we will describe many of these advances, but attempting to reveal the state of the art in a fast-changing discipline like special education is difficult.

Current Challenges

Although the beginnings of special education can be traced back several centuries, in many respects the field is still in its elementary, formative years. There is much to learn about teaching exceptional children and much to be done to make special education most useful to those who need it most. Here are four areas that most in the field consider critical.

♦ *Least restrictive environment.* We must maximize the movement of students with disabilities, particularly those with severe disabilities, into educational settings that are as normalized as possible. Even though two out of three students with disabilities do spend part of each day in a regular classroom, to many children with disabilities, a special education means a separate education. (Chapter 2 examines the concept of educating exceptional children in the least restrictive environment; various strategies and techniques for integrating students with disabilities into the regular classroom will be presented throughout the book.)

- *Early intervention.* We must make special education and related services for handicapped and at-risk infants and toddlers more available. The number of preschool children who receive special education will grow significantly during the coming years. The most recent federal law amending the Individuals with Disabilities Act requires that all preschoolers aged 3 to 5 with handicaps receive special education, and it increases the level of federal support to states for providing early intervention programs to handicapped and at-risk infants and toddlers. (Chapter 14 is devoted to early intervention.)

- *School-to-adult-life transition.* We must improve the ability of young people to leave secondary special education programs and live and work independently in their communities. (Chapter 15 is devoted to the special needs of adults with disabilities and to educational programs to promote a successful transition from school to adulthood.)

- *Special education—regular education relationship.* It has been estimated that in addition to the children with disabilities who receive special education, another 10% to 20% of the student population has mild to moderate learning problems that interfere with their ability to progress and succeed in a regular education program (Will, 1986). Both special and regular educators must develop strategies for working together and sharing their skills and resources to prevent these millions of at-risk students from becoming failures of our educational system.

These four areas are by no means the only important issues in special education today. We could easily identify other challenges that many in the field would argue are equally or even more important. For example,

- Increasing the availability and quality of special education programs for gifted and talented students

- Developing teaching strategies that enable students with severe handicaps to generalize newly learned skills to other settings

- Reducing the number of special education students who drop out of school (27% in the 1988–89 school year)

- Applying advances in high technology to greatly reduce or eliminate the handicapping effects of physical and sensory disabilities

- Combating the pervasive effects of childhood poverty on development and success in school (one in five American children under the age of 5 is living in poverty)

- Developing effective methods for providing education and related services to the growing numbers of children entering school whose development and learning are affected by prenatal exposure to drugs or alcohol

- Improving the behavior and attitudes of nonhandicapped people toward those with disabilities

- Opening up more opportunities for individuals with disabilities to participate in the full range of residential, employment, and recreational options available to nondisabled persons

Special education's effectiveness must be measured, in part, by its ability to facilitate a successful transition to adult life.

Future Predictions

We do not know how successful special education will be in meeting these challenges. And, of course, special educators do not face many of these challenges alone—general education; adult service agencies, such as vocational rehabilitation, social work, and medicine; and society as a whole must all help find the solutions to these problems. Predicting the future is always a tricky business. We can report, however, some of the results Putnam and Bruininks (1986) discovered in a study designed to forecast the future of special education. They asked people in a variety of leadership positions in special education around the country to identify the desirability of certain outcomes and to predict the probability that those outcomes would occur at a future date. Following are 10 of the 31 outcomes the respondents as a group identified as both desirable and likely to occur.

♦ Educational services for mildly handicapped learners will be moved from special education into regular education, along with other remedial programs (by 2000).

♦ Employment options for handicapped persons will increase by at least one-third as a result of advances in microtechnology (by 2000).

♦ Instruction of handicapped persons will increasingly occur in natural environments and situations, using natural cues and correction procedures (by 1996).

♦ There will be significant growth in research focusing on the cost effectiveness and efficiency of various instructional strategies (e.g., one-to-one instruction versus group instruction) in educating handicapped persons (by 1996).

- There will be greater emphasis on training that enhances functioning in extra-school settings rather than developmental learning sequences (by 1996).

- Shaping the attitudes of the next generation (today's school children) will be a major focus of those who advocate the integration and acceptance of handicapped people into society (by 1991).

- Nonhandicapped children who attend school and socially associate with severely handicapped peers will become an adult generation better capable of facilitating the social integration of handicapped persons into all community environments (by 1991).

- The cultural revolution that has increased the "valuing" of persons with handicaps will continue (by 1996).

- There will be greater understanding and acceptance of differences by nonhandicapped persons who grow up alongside handicapped persons in regular school classes (by 1991).

- Great societal willingness to support habilitative programs for handicapped people will come with more face-to-face interactions between persons with handicaps and nonhandicapped people (by 2000). (adapted from Putnam & Bruininks, 1986, pp. 58–61)

Three of the outcomes—all dealing with positive changes in the attitudes of nondisabled children and adults toward persons with disabilities—were predicted to occur by 1991. We believe there is evidence that the three "attitude" outcomes have occurred to a considerable extent, and we will cite some of that evidence throughout the book. Virtually all current approaches for integrating students with disabilities into regular classrooms (or adults into work settings, for that matter) are built around the importance of peer support and acceptance. There is also evidence of positive changes in the understanding and acceptance of differences by nonhandicapped young people who go to school with handicapped peers.

Do the remaining predictions represent the reality to come or merely a wish list? Only time will tell. But we do know there is a large and growing group of people working hard to make these predictions become reality—people with and without disabilities, people within and outside special education. Whatever professional and career goals you follow, we hope your introductory study of special education will help you make a personal commitment to be part of that group.

SUMMARY

Who Are Exceptional Children?

- *Exceptional children* are those whose physical attributes and/or learning abilities differ from the norm, either above or below, to such an extent that an individualized program of special education is indicated.

- *Disability* refers to the reduced function or loss of a particular body part or organ.

- *Handicap* refers to the problems a person with a disability or impairment encounters when interacting with the environment.
- A child who is *at risk* is not currently identified as handicapped or disabled but is considered to have a greater-than-usual chance of developing a handicap.

How Many Exceptional Children Are There and Where Are They Served?

- Handicapped children in special education represent approximately 9.4% of the school-age population.
- The four largest categories of children with disabilities receiving special education are learning disabilities, speech and language impairments, mental retardation, and emotional disturbance.
- Ninety percent of children receiving special education are "mildly handicapped."
- Two-thirds of children with disabilities receive at least part of their education in regular classrooms.

Problems of Labeling and Classifying Exceptional Children

- Some believe labels lead to exclusion of exceptional children from normal society; others believe labeling is necessary to provide appropriate programs.
- Labels can be convenient for communicating about handicapping conditions.
- Labels can also have a negative effect on the child and on others' perceptions of him.

Legislation Affecting Exceptional Children

- P.L. 94–142, the Individuals with Disabilities Education Act, reflects today's concern for treating individuals with disabilities as full citizens, with all the rights of other citizens.
- Gifted and talented children are not included in P.L. 94–142; federal legislation does not mandate special education programs for gifted children.

What Is Special Education?

- Special education is individually planned, systematically implemented, and carefully evaluated instruction to help exceptional children achieve the greatest possible personal self-sufficiency and success in present and future environments.
- There are three kinds of intervention efforts: preventive, remedial, and compensatory.

Special Education: Some Current Challenges and Some Predictions About the Future

- Four major challenges special education faces are educating children with disabilities in the least restrictive environment; making early intervention programs more widely available to infants and toddlers who are handicapped or at risk; improving the ability of young adults with disabilities to make a successful transition from school to community life; and improving the relationship with regular education to better serve the many students who have not been identified as handicapped but who are not progressing in the general education program.

Journals

Education & Treatment of Children. A quarterly journal devoted to the development and improvement of services for children and youth. Publishes original research, reviews of the literature, and descriptions of innovative intervention and treatment programs. Published by PRO-ED, 8700 Shoal Creek Boulevard, Austin, TX 78758-6897.

Exceptionality. Quarterly journal of original research on the education of exceptional learners. Published by the Council for Exceptional Children, 1920 Association Drive, Reston, VA 22091-1589.

Exceptional Children. The official journal of the Council for Exceptional Children. Publishes articles on professional issues of concern to special educators and articles on the education and development of exceptional students. Designed to assist all professionals who work with exceptional children. Published six times per year by the Council for Exceptional Children, 1920 Association Drive, Reston, VA 22091-1589.

Intervention in School and Clinic (formerly *Academic Therapy*). An interdisciplinary journal directed toward an international audience of teachers, parents, educational therapists, and specialists in all fields who deal with the day-to-day aspects of special and remedial education. Published five times per year by PRO-ED, 8700 Shoal Creek Boulevard, Austin, TX 78758-6897.

The Journal of Special Education. A quarterly journal that publishes articles from all disciplines; deals with research, theory, opinion, and reviews of the literature in special education. Published by PRO-ED, 8700 Shoal Creek Boulevard, Austin, TX 78758-6897.

Preventing School Failure (formerly *The Pointer*). Published six times per year by Pro-Ed, 8700 Shoal Creek Boulevard, Austin, TX 78758-6897.

Remedial and Special Education. Devoted to discussion of issues involving the education of persons for whom typical instruction is not effective. Emphasizes interpretation of research literature and recommendations for the practice of remedial and special education. Published six times per year by PRO-ED, 8700 Shoal Creek Boulevard, Austin, TX 78758-6897.

Teacher Education and Special Education. Quarterly journal of research, program descriptions, and discussion articles on issues and methods pertaining to the education of teachers and other educational personnel for exceptional children. Published by the Teacher Education Division of CEC, 1920 Association Drive, Reston, VA 22091-1589.

Teaching Exceptional Children. Presents articles suggesting classroom teaching strategies, reports of materials, a teacher idea exchange, and other information designed to assist the teacher of exceptional children. Published quarterly by the Council for Exceptional Children, 1920 Association Drive, Reston, VA 22091-1589.

Books

Marozas, D. S., & May, D. C. (1988). *Issues and practices in special education*. New York: Longman.

Morris, R. J., & Blatt, B. (Eds.). (1986). *Special education: Research and trends*. Elmsford, NY: Pergamon Press.

Payne, J. S., Patton, J. R., Kauffman, J. M., Brown, G. B., & Payne, R. A. (1987). *Exceptional children in focus* (4th ed.). Columbus, OH: Merrill.

Wang, M. C., Reynolds, M. C., & Walberg, H. J. (1988). *The handbook of special education: Research and practice*. Oxford, England: Pergamon Press.

Organization

Council for Exceptional Children, 1920 Association Drive, Reston, VA, 22091-1589. Includes over 50,000 teachers, teacher educators, administrators, researchers, and other professionals involved in the education of exceptional children and adults.

2

The Promise and the Challenge: Special Education in the Schools

◆ Why are court cases and legislation required to ensure that children with disabilities receive an appropriate education?

◆ Can one judge the quality of an individualized education program by examining the document itself?

◆ Is the continuum of services still an appropriate model for special education?

◆ Is the least restrictive environment always the regular classroom?

◆ How might services to exceptional children change if special and regular education merge into one educational system?

It is said that a society can be judged by the way it treats those who are different. By this criterion, our educational system has less than a distinguished history. Children who are different because of race, culture, language, gender, or exceptionality have often been denied full and fair access to educational opportunities (Banks & Banks, in press). Even worse, some children were totally neglected and hidden away; others were abused, exploited, or even put to death (S. R. Morgan, 1987).

Although exceptional children have always been with us, attention has not always been paid to their special needs. In the past, many children with disabilities were entirely excluded from any publicly supported program of education. Prior to the 1970s, many states had laws permitting public schools to deny enrollment to children with handicaps (Heward & Cavanaugh, in press). Local school officials had no legal obligation to grant students with disabilities the same educational access that nondisabled students enjoyed. One state law, for example, allowed schools to refuse to serve "children physically or mentally incapacitated for school work"; another state had a law stipulating that children with "bodily or mental conditions rendering attendance inadvisable" could be turned away. When these laws were contested, the nation's courts generally supported exclusion. In a 1919 case, for example, a 13-year-old student with physical handicaps (but normal intellectual ability) was excluded from his local school because he "produces a depressing and nauseating effect upon the teachers and school children. . . . [H]e takes up an undue portion of the teacher's time and attention, distracts attention of other pupils, and interferes generally with the discipline and progress of the school" (T. P. Johnson, 1986, p. 2). Many communities had no facilities or services whatsoever to help exceptional children and their families.

When local public schools began to accept a measure of responsibility for educating certain exceptional students, a philosophy of segregation prevailed—a philosophy that continued unchanged until recently. Integration of exceptional children into regular schools and classes is a relatively recent phenomenon. Children received labels—such as mentally retarded, crippled, or emotionally disturbed—and were confined mainly to isolated special classrooms. One special education teacher describes the sense of isolation she felt and the crude facilities in which her special class operated in the 1960s.

> I accepted my first teaching position, a special education class in a basement room next door to the furnace. Of the 15 "educable mentally retarded" children assigned to work with me, most were simply nonreaders from poor families. One child had been banished to my room because she posed a behavior problem to her fourth-grade teacher.
>
> My class and I were assigned a recess spot on the opposite side of the play yard, far away from the "normal" children. I was the only teacher who did not have a lunch break. I was required to eat with my "retarded" children while other teachers were permitted to leave their students. . . . Isolated from my colleagues, I closed my door and did my thing, oblivious to the larger educational circles in which I was immersed. Although it was the basement room, with all the negative perceptions that arrangement implies, I was secure in the knowledge that despite the ignominy of it all I did good things for children who were previously unloved and untaught. (Aiello, 1976)

Children with mild learning and behavior disorders usually remained in the regular classroom but received no special treatment. If their deportment in class exceeded the teacher's tolerance for misbehavior, they were labeled "disciplinary problems" and suspended from school. If they did not make satisfactory academic progress, they were termed "slow learners," "failures," or "ineducable." Children with more severe disabilities—including many with visual, hearing, and physical or health impairments—were usually placed in segregated schools or institutions or kept at home. Children who were gifted and talented seldom received special attention in schools. They could make it on their own, it was felt, without help.

Society's response to exceptional children has come a long way. As our concepts of equality, freedom, and justice have expanded, exceptional children and their families have moved from isolation to participation. Although the speed of these changes has been described as a "painfully slow process of integration and participation" (Cremins, 1983, p. 3), the "history of special education can be summarized quite well in two words: *progressive integration*" (Reynolds, 1989, p. 7).

Society no longer regards exceptional children as beyond the responsibility of their local public schools. No longer may a child who is different from the norm be turned away from school because someone believes he is "unable to appropriately benefit from typical instruction." Recent legislation and court decisions confirm that all exceptional children, no less than any other citizen, have the right to a *free, appropriate program of public education in the least restrictive environment*. Attempting to meet the individual needs of all students with disabilities has had enormous impact on schools.

◼ SPECIAL EDUCATION AS CIVIL RIGHTS

The provision of equal educational opportunities to exceptional children has not come about by chance. Many laws and court cases have had important effects on public education in general and on the education of children with special needs in particular. And the process of change is never finished. As Prasse (1986) notes, legal influences on special education are not fixed or static, but rather fluid and dynamic.

Table 2.1 summarizes key judicial decisions and Table 2.2 summarizes federal legislation that has had significant impact on special education and the lives of citizens with disabilities.

The recent history of special education, especially in regard to the education of children with disabilities in regular schools, is related to the civil rights movement. Special education was strongly influenced by social developments and court decisions in the 1950s and 1960s, especially the landmark case of *Brown v. Board of Education of Topeka* (1954). This case challenged the practice of segregating students according to race. In its ruling in the *Brown* case, the U.S. Supreme Court declared that education must be made available to *all* children on equal terms:

> Today, education is perhaps the most important function of state and local governments. Compulsory school attendance laws and the great expenditure for education both demonstrate our recognition of the importance of education to our democratic society. It is required in the performance of our most basic responsibilities. . . . In these days, it is doubtful that any child may reasonably be ex-

TABLE 2.1

Court cases affecting education of exceptional children.

Year	Court Case
1954	*Brown v. Board of Education of Topeka* (Kansas) Established the right of all children to an equal opportunity for an education.
1967	*Hobson v. Hansen* (Washington, D.C.) Declared the track system, which used standardized tests as a basis for special education placement, unconstitutional because it discriminated against black and poor children.
1970	*Diana v. State Board of Education* (California) Declared that children cannot be placed in special education on the basis of culturally biased tests or tests given in other than the child's native language.
1972	*Mills v. Board of Education of the District of Columbia* Established the right of every child to an equal opportunity for education; declared that lack of funds was not an acceptable excuse for lack of educational opportunity.
1972	*Pennsylvania Association for Retarded Citizens v. the Commonwealth of Pennsylvania* Class action suit that established the right to free public education for all retarded children.
1972	*Wyatt v. Stickney* (Alabama) Declared that individuals in state institutions have the right to appropriate treatment within those institutions.
1979	*Central York District v. Commonwealth of Pennsylvania Department of Education* Ruled that school districts must provide services for gifted and talented children whether or not advance guarantee of reimbursement from the state has been received.
1979	*Larry P. v. Riles* (California) First brought to court in 1972; ruled that IQ tests cannot be used as the sole basis for placing children in special classes.
1979	*Armstrong v. Kline* (Pennsylvania) Established right of some children with severe handicaps to an extension of the 180-day public school year.
1982	*Board of Education of the Hendrik Hudson Central School District v. Rowley* (New York) First case based on P.L. 94–142 to reach the U.S. Supreme Court; while denying plaintiff's specific request, upheld each handicapped child's right to a personalized program of instruction and necessary supportive services.

pected to succeed in life if he is denied the opportunity of an education. (*Brown v. Board of Education of Topeka* 1954)

The *Brown* decision, and the ensuing extension of public school education to black and white children on equal terms, began a period of intense concern and questioning among parents and handicapped children, who asked why the same principles of equal access to education did not apply to their children. Numerous court cases were initiated in the 1960s and early 1970s by parents and other advocates dissatisfied with an educational system that denied equal access to children with disabilities. Generally, the parents based their arguments on the 14th Amendment to the Constitution, which provides that no state shall deny any person within its jurisdiction the **equal protection** of the law and that no state shall deprive any person of life, liberty, or property without **due process** of law.

TABLE 2.1

continued

Year	Court Case
1983	*Abrahamson v. Hershman* (Massachusetts) Ruled that residential placement in a private school was necessary for a child with multiple handicaps who needed around-the-clock training; required the school district to pay for the private placement.
1984	*Department of Education v. Katherine D.* (Hawaii) Ruled that a homebound instructional program for a child with multiple health impairments did not meet the least-restrictive-environment standard; called for the child to be placed in a class with non-handicapped children and provided with related medical services.
1984	*Irving Independent School District v. Tatro* (Texas) Ruled that catheterization was necessary for a physically handicapped child to remain in school and that it could be performed by a nonphysician, thus obligating the school district to provide that service.
1984	*Smith v. Robinson* (Rhode Island) Ordered the state to pay a severely handicapped child's placement in a residential program and ordered the school district to reimburse the parents' attorney fees. U.S. Supreme Court later ruled that P.L. 94–142 did not entitle parents to recover such fees, but Congress subsequently passed an "Attorney's Fees" bill, leading to enactment of P.L. 99–372.
1985	*Cleburne v. Cleburne Living Center* (Texas) U.S. Supreme Court ruled unanimously that communities cannot use a discriminatory zoning ordinance to prevent establishment of group homes for persons with mental retardation.
1988	*Honig v. Doe* (California) Ruled that children with handicaps could not be excluded from school for any misbehavior that is "handicap-related" (in this case, "aggressive behavior against other students" on the part of two "emotionally handicapped" students) but that educational services could cease if the misbehavior is not related to the handicap.
1989	*Timothy W. v. Rochester School District* (New Hampshire) A U.S. Appeals Court upheld the literal interpretation that P.L. 94–142 requires that *all* handicapped children be provided with a free, appropriate public education. The three-judge Appeals Court overturned the decision of a District Court judge, who had ruled that the local school district was not obligated to educate a 13-year-old boy with multiple and severe disabilities because he could not "benefit" from special education.

The concepts of equal protection and due process are so fundamentally important in special education that we will discuss them in some detail.

Equal Protection

In the past, children with disabilities usually received differential treatment; that is, they were excluded from certain educational programs or were given special education only in segregated settings. Basically, when the courts have been asked to rule on the practice of denial and segregation, judges have examined whether such treatment is *rational* and whether it is *necessary* (Williams, 1977). One of the most historically significant cases to examine these questions was the class action suit, *Pennsylvania Association for Retarded Children v. Commonwealth of Pennsylvania* (1972). The association (PARC) challenged a state law

A class-action lawsuit is one made on behalf of a group of people. In the PARC case, the class of people was school-age children with mental retardation living in Pennsylvania.

TABLE 2.2

Legislation affecting education of exceptional children.

Year	Legislation
1958	National Defense Education Act (P.L. 85–926) Provided funds for training professionals to train teachers of children with mental retardation.
1961	Special Education Act (P.L. 87–276) Provided funds for training professionals to train teachers of deaf children.
1963	Mental Retardation Facility and Community Center Construction Act (P.L. 88–164) Extended support given in P.L. 85–926 to training teachers of children with other disabilities.
1965	Elementary and Secondary Education Act (P.L. 89–10) Provided money to states and local districts for developing programs for economically disadvantaged and handicapped children.
1966	Amendment to Title I of the Elementary and Secondary Education Act (P.L. 89–313) Provided funding for state-supported programs in institutions and other settings for handicapped children.
1966	Amendments to the Elementary and Secondary Education Act (P.L. 89–750) Created the Bureau of Education for the Handicapped.
1968	Handicapped Children's Early Assistance Act (P.L. 90–538) Established the "first chance network" of experimental programs for preschool children with handicaps (see Chapter 14).
1969	Elementary, Secondary, and Other Educational Amendments (P.L. 91–230) Defined learning disabilities; provided funds for state-level programs for children with learning disabilities.
1973	Section 504 of the Rehabilitation Act (P.L. 93–112) Declared that a person cannot be excluded on the basis of handicap alone from any program or activity receiving federal funds (adopted 1977).
1974	Education Amendments (P.L. 93–380) Extended previous legislation; provided money to state and local districts for programs for gifted and talented students for the first time. Also protected rights of handicapped children and parents in placement decisions.
1975	Developmental Disabilities Assistance and Bill of Rights Act (P.L. 94–103) Affirmed rights of citizens with mental retardation and cited areas where services must be provided for people with mental retardation and other developmental disabilities.

that denied public school education to certain children considered "unable to profit from public school attendance."

The lawyers and parents supporting PARC argued that even though the children had intellectual disabilities, it was neither rational nor necessary to assume they were ineducable and untrainable. Because the state was unable to prove the children were, in fact, ineducable and untrainable, or to demonstrate a rational basis for excluding them from public school programs, the court decided the children were entitled to receive a free, public education. In

TABLE 2.2
continued

Year	Legislation
1975	Individuals with Disabilities Education Act (P.L. 94–142) Originally named the Education for All Handicapped Children Act (EHA), P.L. 94–142 mandates free, appropriate public education for all handicapped children regardless of degree of severity of handicap; protects rights of handicapped children and parents in educational decision making; requires development of an individualized education program (IEP) for each handicapped child; states that handicapped students with disabilities must receive educational services in the least restrictive environment.
1978	Gifted and Talented Children's Education Act (P.L. 95–561) Provided financial incentives for states and local education agencies to identify and educate gifted and talented students, for in-service training, and for research (see Chapter 11).
1983	Amendments to the Education of the Handicapped Act (P.L. 98–199) Required states to collect data on the number of handicapped youth exiting their systems and to address the needs of secondary students making the transition to adulthood (see Chapter 15). Also gave incentives to states to provide services to handicapped infants and preschool children.
1984	Developmental Disabilities Assistance and Bill of Rights Act (P.L. 98–527) Mandated development of employment related training activities for adults with disabilities.
1986	Handicapped Children's Protection Act (P.L. 99–372) Provided authority for reimbursement of attorney's fees to parents who must go to court to secure an appropriate education for their child. Parents who prevail in a hearing or court case may recover the costs incurred for lawyers to represent them, retroactive to July 4, 1984.
1986	Education of the Handicapped Act Amendments of 1986 (P.L. 99–457) Encouraged states to develop comprehensive interdisciplinary services for handicapped infants and toddlers (birth through age 2) and to expand services for preschool children (aged 3 through 5). After the 1990–91 school year, states must provide free, appropriate education to all handicapped 3- to 5-year-olds to be eligible to apply for federal preschool funding (see Chapter 14).
1986	Rehabilitation Act Amendments (P.L. 99–506) Set forth regulations for development of supported employment programs for adults with disabilities (see Chapter 15).
1990	Americans with Disabilities Act (P.L. 101–336) Provides civil rights protection against discrimination to citizens with disabilities in private sector employment, access to all public services, public accommodations, transportation, and telecommunications.
1990	Education of the Handicapped Act Amendments of 1990 (P.L. 101–476) In addition to renaming the EHA as the Individuals with Disabilities Education Act, this law added autism and traumatic brain injury as two new categories of disability, required all IEPs to include a statement of needed transition services no later than age 16, and expanded the definition of related services to include rehabilitation counseling and social work services.

addition, the court maintained that parents had the right to be notified before any change was made in their children's educational program.

These and other rights are guaranteed under the equal protection clause of the 14th Amendment, which holds that people may not be deprived of their equality or liberty because of any classification (such as race, nationality, or religion). The courts have often regarded people with handicaps as belonging to a minority group that has a history of discrimination, political powerlessness, and unequal treatment (Thomas, 1985). Thus, equal protection and certain

Are the disabilities experienced by some children so severe that they should be considered ineducable? The debate continues today—see the essay in Chapter 10 entitled "Are All Children Educable?"

Jessica is learning new skills almost every day, yet not too many years ago, she would not have been allowed to go to school.

procedures known as due process of law must be provided to ensure that children with disabilities and their families are fully informed of their rights and are treated fairly and reasonably as citizens.

The wording of the PARC decision proved particularly important because of its influence on subsequent federal legislation. Not only did the court rule that all children with mental retardation were entitled to a free, appropriate public education, but the ruling also stipulated that placements in regular classrooms and regular public schools were preferable to segregated settings.

> It is the Commonwealth's obligation to place each mentally retarded child in a free, public program of education and training appropriate to the child's capacity. . . . [P]lacement in a regular public school class is preferable to placement in a special public school class and placement in a special public school is preferable to placement in any other type of program of education and training. An assignment to homebound instruction shall be re-evaluated not less than every 3 months, and notice of the evaluation and an opportunity for a hearing thereon shall be accorded to the parent or guardian. (*Pennsylvania Association for Retarded Children v. Commonwealth of Pennsylvania,* 1972)

Due Process

In the past, students with disabilities (and some nondisabled students as well) were not always considered "people" in the eyes of the law. Several recent laws and court decisions, however, have clearly established that students are, indeed, people, entitled to exercise such rights as privacy, freedom of travel, the practice of religion, and personal rights, such as choosing their own clothing and hair styles. Although school officials may enforce reasonable regulations, they may not operate unfairly or arbitrarily, and they do not have absolute authority over their students.

An important element of due process in special education is the acknowledgment of a student as a person, with important rights and responsibilities. Some people have questioned why highly specific legal safeguards are necessary to protect the rights of handicapped children—aren't they protected by the same laws and due process procedures that apply to all citizens? Reviewing how children with disabilities have been treated in the past by schools (and by society in general), we find that our laws and legal procedures were often not equally applied. Meyen (1978) cites five reasons for the necessity of specific legal safeguards for handicapped children.

1. Once placed in a special education program, many handicapped children remained there for the rest of their educational careers. This type of system permanently excluded many children from regular classrooms once they were placed elsewhere.

2. Decisions to place students in special education programs were often made primarily on the basis of teacher recommendation or the results of a single test.

3. Children with severe and profound handicaps were routinely excluded from public school programs. If they received any education at all, their parents usually had to pay for it.

4. A disproportionate number of children from minority cultural groups were placed in special education programs.

5. The level of educational services provided to residents of institutions was often extremely low or nonexistent.

These circumstances led to higher levels of activism by parents of exceptional children and by lawyers, educators, and other advocates who were concerned that these children were not being treated fairly. Many legislators and judges agreed. The concept of due process for handicapped students and their parents within the public educational system is now embodied in law. Key elements of due process as it relates to special education are the parents' right to

♦ Be notified in writing before the school takes any action that may alter the child's program (testing, reevaluation, change in placement)

♦ Give or withhold permission to have their child tested for eligibility for special education services, reevaluated, or placed in a different classroom or program

♦ See all school records about their child

♦ Have a hearing before an impartial party (not an employee of the school district) to resolve disagreements with the school system

♦ Receive a written decision following any hearing

♦ Appeal the results of a due process hearing to the state department of education (school districts may also appeal)

Ann and Rud Turnbull, who are special educators and parents of a young man with disabilities, describe due process as "the legal technique that seeks to

The following "In a Nutshell" essay shows due process guidelines written especially for parents of exceptional children. Teachers, administrators, and other service providers should also be familiar with these guidelines.

GUIDELINES ON DUE PROCESS "IN A NUTSHELL"

Here's a quick review to keep in mind the main steps involved in due process. Each of these steps reinforces your right to stay on top of decisions about your child.

1. You must receive notice in writing before the school system takes (or recommends) any action that may change your child's school program. Notice in writing is also required if a school refuses to take action to change your child's program.

2. You have the right to give—or withhold—permission for your child to be tested to determine whether or not he requires special education services (identification); evaluated by specialists to determine what his educational needs are (evaluation); placed in a specific school program to meet his needs (placement).

3. You have the right to see and examine all school records related to the identification, evaluation, and placement of your child. If you find that certain records are inaccurate or misleading, you have the right to ask that they be removed from your child's file. Once removed, they may

not be used in planning for your child's placement.

4. If you do not agree with the school's course of action at *any* point along the way, you have the right to request an impartial due process hearing. This means that you can initiate a hearing to protest any decision related to identification, evaluation or placement of your child.

5. If you fail to win your case, you have the right to appeal the results of the due process hearing to the State Department of Education; you can appeal to the courts if you lose your case at the state level.

Calling for a due process hearing is your right, but remember that it can be an exhausting process. Before going this route, be sure you have tried to settle differences through every other means—by being as persuasive as possible in meetings with teachers, the principal, special education administrators. If you know that you're up against a brick wall, and you're sure that a due process hearing must be held to resolve conflicting points of view, then you must prepare your case as thoroughly as possible. Be sure to get help from an advocacy

group or a lawyer who is familiar with education law and procedures in your state, or an experienced parent. (According to law, the school system must tell you about sources of free legal aid. Ask for this information.)

Know your rights at a hearing:

♦ The hearing officer must be impartial, may not be employed by the school district or involved in the education of your child.

♦ You have the right to legal counsel (which includes the advice and support of any advocate, not necessarily a lawyer); to examine witnesses; present evidence; ask questions of school spokespeople; obtain a record of the hearing and all of its findings.

NOTE: Write directly to the superintendent of schools in your district to request a hearing. Hearings must be held not later than 45 days after requested. State Departments of Education must review appeals within 30 days.

Source: From Closer Look *Fall 1977 (p. 4), Washington, DC: Department of Health, Education, and Welfare.* ♦

---

assure fairness among professionals, service systems, families, and students." Due process, they further note, is "a way of changing the balance of power between professionals, who have traditionally wielded power, and families, who have felt they could not affect their children's education" (Turnbull, Turnbull, Summers, Brotherson, & Benson, 1986, p. 254).

Other Important Court Cases

In addition to the PARC case, several other judicial decisions have had far-reaching effects on special education. The rulings of some of these cases have been incorporated into subsequent legislation, most notably P.L. 94–142, the Individuals with Disabilities Education Act.

Hobson v. Hansen (1967)

In this case, the court ruled against the so-called tracking system, in which children were placed into either regular or special classes according to their scores on intelligence tests. Most of the tests had been standardized on a population of white, middle-class children. *Hobson v. Hansen* involved black working-class children, who make up most of the student population of the Washington, D.C., public schools. The court decided these children were not being classified according to their ability to learn, but according to environmental and social factors irrelevant to their learning ability and potential.

Standardized intelligence tests are discussed in Chapter 3.

Diana v. State Board of Education (1970)

Based on the results of intelligence tests that were given in English, a Spanish-speaking student in California had been placed in a special class for children with mental retardation. The court ruled this placement was inappropriate and that the child must be given another evaluation in her native language.

Mills v. Board of Education (1972)

Seven children had been excluded from the public schools in Washington, D.C., because of learning and behavior problems. The school district contended that it did not have enough money to provide special education programs for them. The court held that lack of funds is no excuse for failing to educate the children and ordered the schools to readmit and serve them appropriately. Even if funds are limited (as is often the case), children with disabilities may not be denied access to public schools. Financial problems cannot be allowed to have a greater impact on exceptional children than on nonhandicapped students.

Larry P. v. Riles (1979)

This California case found the placement of black children in special classes inappropriate because of unfair testing. The IQ tests that were used failed to recognize the children's cultural background and the learning that took place in their homes and communities. When different tests were used, it was found that the children were not mentally retarded. The court ordered that IQ tests could not be used as the sole basis for placing children into special classes.

These cases and many others helped establish the schools' responsibility to provide education for handicapped children and to treat them fairly. Exceptional children, who suffered from exclusion and segregation in the past, are today moving toward greater inclusion and integration in the schools. Gilhool (1976), an attorney who was instrumental in the PARC case, aptly summarized the judicial and social developments: "Integration is a central constitutional value. Not integration that *denies* differences, but rather integration that *accommodates* difference."

■ P.L. 94–142: THE INDIVIDUALS WITH DISABILITIES EDUCATION ACT

In 1975, the United States Congress passed Public Law 94–142, originally called the Education for All Handicapped Children Act. Shortly after its passage, P.L. 94–142 was called "blockbuster legislation" (Goodman, 1976) and hailed as the

Federal legislation is identified by a numerical system. P.L. 94–142, for example, was the 142nd bill passed by the 94th Congress.

law that "will probably become known as having the greatest impact on education in history" (Stowell & Terry, 1977). This law has affected every school in the country and has changed the roles of regular and special educators, school administrators, parents, and many others who are involved in the educational process. The law clearly has had a great deal of impact, but, in our view, its ultimate effects on both special education and regular education have yet to be determined.

What Does the Law Say?

Note that P.L. 94–142 does not refer to gifted and talented children.

P.L. 94–142 states that all children with disabilities between the ages of 3 and 21, regardless of the type or severity of their disability, shall receive a "free, appropriate public education which emphasizes special education and related services designed to meet their unique needs." This education must be provided at public expense—that is, without cost to the child's parents.

Education of students with disabilities is expensive. Laws and regulations calling for special education would be of limited value if the schools lacked the necessary financial resources. Congress backed up its mandate for free, appropriate public education by providing federal funds to help school districts meet the additional costs of educating handicapped children (many of whom had not previously been served by public schools). Congress allocates funds to each state yearly to help implement the law's goals and policies. Each state then directs most of the money it receives from the federal government to local school districts to provide services to students with handicaps.

The local school district receives federal special education funds based on the number of students with handicaps served. A maximum of 12% of a state's school-aged population can be identified as handicapped for purposes of federal funding.

States and local school districts are required to pay at least the amount of money that is spent to educate a nonhandicapped child. The original intent of Congress was that approximately 40% of the total cost of educating each handicapped child would be covered by federal funds. Many state and local educational administrators, however, contend that the federal financial assistance for the education of students with disabilities has not been sufficient and that their schools are hard-pressed to meet the costs of educating exceptional children. This problem is particularly serious today, when many school districts are experiencing severe financial difficulties.

P.L. 94–142 is directed primarily at the states, which are responsible for providing education to their citizens. Each state education agency must comply with the law by

♦ Locating and identifying all children with disabilities. (This process is called *child find*.)

♦ Identifying and placing handicapped children by means of testing and evaluation procedures that do not discriminate on the basis of race, culture, or native language. All tests must be administered in the child's native language, and identification and placement decisions must not be made on the basis of a single test score.

♦ Developing an **individualized education program (IEP)** for every handicapped child in the state.

♦ Educating each handicapped child in the **least restrictive environment (LRE)**. Handicapped children are to be placed in special classes or separate schools only when their education cannot be achieved satisfactorily in the regular classroom, even with special aids and services.

♦ Protecting the rights of handicapped children and their parents by ensuring due process, confidentiality of records, and parental involvement in educational planning and placement decisions.

Other Provisions of P.L. 94–142

Two priorities were set forth in P.L. 94–142 for the expenditure of funds to educate children with disabilities. The first priority was to children who were currently unserved by any kind of educational program. The second priority was to children who were currently inadequately served. Many previously unserved and inadequately served children were those with severe and multiple handicaps; many had been kept at home or in institutions.

P.L. 94–142 also stipulates that, in cases where an appropriate education cannot be provided in the public schools, children with disabilities may be placed in private school programs at no cost to their parents. This has proven to be a particularly controversial aspect of the law. Parents and school officials have frequently disagreed over whether private school placement, at public expense, is the most appropriate way to meet the needs of an exceptional child.

Children with disabilities have sometimes been prevented from attending regular schools by circumstances other than educational performance. A child who uses a wheelchair, for example, may require a specially equipped school bus. A child with special health problems may require medication several times a day. The law calls for schools to provide any **related services**—such as special transportation, counseling, physical therapy, and other supportive assistance—that a child with disabilities may need in order to benefit from special education. This provision has also been highly controversial, with much disagreement over what kinds of related services are necessary and reasonable for the schools to provide and what services should be the responsibility of the child's parents.

In addition, each state is required to develop a *comprehensive system for personnel development,* including inservice training programs for regular education teachers, special education teachers, school administrators, and other support personnel. Finally, each state must submit to the federal government an annual plan describing how it ensures the education of all children with disabilities in the state.

Amendments to P.L. 94–142

Like other comprehensive federal laws, P.L. 94–142 periodically undergoes reauthorization and amendment in response to changing circumstances. Since its passage, P.L. 94–142 has been amended three times. In 1982, the administrative branch of the federal government initiated action to revise some of the rules and regulations of P.L. 94–142. The proposed changes, which would have softened the law in several respects, were met with overwhelming opposition by parent advocacy and professional groups. As a result, when the law was amended for the first time in 1983 (P.L. 98–199), Congress passed a strong reaffirmation of all the major provisions of P.L. 94–142, including an expansion of research and services for the transition of secondary students from school to work, and modest increases in funding levels for various programs.

P.L. 99–457: Extending Services to Handicapped Infants, Toddlers, and Preschoolers

Early intervention for handicapped and at-risk infants, toddlers, and preschoolers is the subject of Chapter 14.

A significant series of changes to P.L. 94–142 occurred with the passage of Public Law 99–457, the Education of the Handicapped Act Amendments of 1986. Noting that more than 30 states and territories still did not require preschool services for all 3- to 5-year-old children with handicaps, Congress included provisions in P.L. 99–457 to expand services for this segment of the population. Beginning with the 1990–91 school year, each state was required to serve all handicapped preschool children fully—that is, with the same services and protections available to school-age children—or lose all future federal funds for preschoolers with handicaps. P.L. 99–457 includes a formula for awarding money to each state based on the number of handicapped preschool children identified and served.

P.L. 99–457 encourages the provision of special education services to handicapped infants and toddlers; that is, children from birth through age 2 who need early intervention services because they are experiencing developmental

Early childhood special education programs such as this one prepare preschoolers for entry into the regular classroom.

delays or because they have a diagnosed physical or mental impairment with a high probability of resulting in developmental delays. The law states that Congress has found "an urgent and substantial need" to

1. enhance the development of handicapped infants and toddlers and to minimize their potential for developmental delay,

2. reduce the educational costs to our society, including our Nation's schools, by minimizing the need for special education and related services after handicapped infants and toddlers reach school age,

3. minimize the likelihood of institutionalization of handicapped individuals and maximize their potential for independent living in society, and

4. enhance the capacity of families to meet the special needs of their infants and toddlers with handicaps. (P.L. 99–457, Sec. 1471)

Rather than mandating special services for this age group, P.L. 99–457 encourages each state to "develop and implement a statewide, comprehensive, coordinated, multidisciplinary, interagency program of early intervention services for handicapped infants and toddlers and their families." The encouragement is in the form of a gradually increasing amount of federal money to be awarded to states that agree to identify and serve all handicapped infants and toddlers. Beginning with the 1990–91 school year, only states that have developed a comprehensive service delivery system for handicapped children from birth through age 2 are eligible to receive federal grants for handicapped infants and toddlers. Various education and human service agencies within each state work together to provide such services as medical and educational assessment, physical therapy, speech and language intervention, and parent counseling and training. These early intervention services are prescribed and implemented according to an **individualized family services plan (IFSP)** written by a multidisciplinary team that includes the child's parents.

P.L. 101–476: Education of the Handicapped Act Amendments of 1990

In 1990, P.L. 94–142 was amended by Congress for the third time. This law changed the title of the "Education of the Handicapped Act" to the "Individuals with Disabilities Education Act" and made the same title change in all other laws making reference to the EHA. The new law retained all of the basic provisions of P.L. 94–142 but made several important additions.

♦ *Autism* and *traumatic brain injury* were added as two new categories of disability.

♦ Schools are now required to provide transition services to students with disabilities, as dictated by individual needs. *Transition services* were defined as "a coordinated set of activities for a student, designed within an outcome-oriented process, which promotes movement from school to post-school activities, including post-secondary education, vocational training, integrated employment, continuing and adult education, adult services, independent living, or community participation." (Sec. 602(a) (19))

♦ IEPs must now contain a statement of the needed transition services for students beginning no later than age 16 (at a younger age when determined appropriate for the individual) and annually thereafter.

◆ Rehabilitation counseling and social work services were added to the definition of *related services*.

Legal Challenges Based on P.L. 94–142

Although P.L. 94–142 has resulted in dramatic increases in the numbers of students receiving special education services and in greater recognition of the legal rights of exceptional children and their families, it has also brought about an ever-increasing number of disputes concerning the education of students with disabilities. Thousands of due process hearings and numerous court cases have been brought about by parents and other advocates. Due process hearings and court cases often place parents and schools in confrontation with each other and are expensive and time-consuming. For these reasons, or perhaps because there are now fewer disagreements between parents and schools, the number of due process hearings has dropped significantly since the years immediately following passage of P.L. 94–142 (Singer & Butler, 1987).

It is difficult to generalize as to how judges and courts have resolved the various legal challenges based on P.L. 94–142. There have been many different interpretations of concepts such as *free, appropriate education,* and *least restrictive environment*. The law uses these terms repeatedly, but, in the view of many parents, educators, judges, and attorneys, does not define them with sufficient clarity. Thus, the questions of what is appropriate and least restrictive for a particular handicapped child and whether a public school district should be compelled to provide a certain service must often be decided by judges and courts, based on consideration of the evidence presented to them.

Most public school programs operate for approximately 180 school days each year. Parents and educators have argued that for some handicapped children, particularly those with severe and multiple disabilities, a 180-day school year is not sufficient to meet their needs. In the case of *Armstrong v. Kline* (1979), the parents of five severely handicapped students claimed that their children tended to regress during the usual breaks in the school year and called on the schools to provide a period of instruction longer than 180 days. The court agreed and ordered the schools to extend the school year for these students. Several states and local districts now provide year-round educational programs for some handicapped students, but there are no clear and universally accepted guidelines as to which students are entitled to free public education for a longer-than-usual school year.

The first case based on P.L. 94–142 to reach the U.S. Supreme Court was *Board of Education of the Hendrick Hudson Central School District v. Rowley* (1982). Amy Rowley was a fourth-grader who, because of her hearing impairment, needed special education and related services. The school district had originally provided Amy with a hearing aid, speech therapy, a tutor, and a sign language interpreter to accompany her in the regular classroom. The school withdrew the sign language services after the interpreter reported that Amy did not make use of her services—Amy reportedly looked at the teacher to read her lips and asked the teacher to repeat instructions rather than get the information from the interpreter. Amy's parents contended that she was missing up to 50% of the ongoing instruction (her hearing impairment was estimated to have left her with 50% residual hearing) and was therefore being denied an

Browder, Lentz, Knoster, and Wilansky (1988) discuss the extended school year.

The Rowley case marked the first time a deaf attorney had ever argued a case before the U.S. Supreme Court.

appropriate public school education. The school district's position was that Amy, with the help of the other special services she was still receiving, was passing from grade to grade without an interpreter. School personnel felt, in fact, that an interpreter might hinder Amy's interactions with her teacher and peers. It was also noted that this service would cost the school district as much as $25,000 per year. The Supreme Court ruled that Amy, who was making satisfactory progress in school without an interpreter, was receiving an adequate education and that the school district could not be compelled to hire a full-time interpreter.

The second P.L. 94–142 case to reach the Supreme Court was *Irving Independent School District v. Tatro* (1984). In this case, the Court decided that a school district was obligated to provide catheterization and other related medical services to enable a young child with physical impairments to attend school. (See Chapter 9 for further discussion of this case.)

Some cases have resulted from parents' protesting the suspension or expulsion of their handicapped child. The case of *Stuart v. Nappi* (1978), for example, concerned a high school student who spent much of her time wandering in the halls, even though she was assigned to special classes. The school sought to have the student expelled on disciplinary grounds because her conduct was considered detrimental to order in the school. The court agreed with the student's mother that expulsion would deny the student a free, appropriate public education, as called for in P.L. 94–142. In other cases, expulsion or suspension of handicapped students has been upheld if the school could show that the grounds for expulsion did not relate to the student's disability. In 1988, however, the Supreme Court ruled in *Honig v. Doe* that a handicapped student could not be expelled from school for disciplinary reasons, which meant that, for all practical purposes, schools cannot recommend expulsion nor suspend a handicapped student for more than 10 days.

Recently, the case of *Timothy W. v. Rochester School District* threatened the "zero reject" philosophy of P.L. 94–142. In July 1988, Judge Loughlin of the district court in New Hampshire ruled that a 13-year-old boy who was quadriplegic and severely handicapped was ineligible for education services because he could not "benefit" from special education. The judge ruled in favor of the Rochester School Board, which claimed that P.L. 94–142 was not intended to provide educational services to "*all* handicapped students." In his decision, the judge determined that the federal law was not explicit regarding a "rare child" with severe handicaps, and declared that special evaluations and examinations should be used to determine "qualifications for education under P.L. 94–142."

In May 1989, a court of appeals overturned the lower court's decision, ruling that public schools must educate all children with disabilities regardless of how little they might benefit or how severe their handicap. The three-judge panel concluded that "schools cannot avoid the provisions of EHA by returning to the practices that were widespread prior to the Act's passage . . . unilaterally excluding certain handicapped children from a public education on the ground that they are uneducable." In summarizing the case, Buchanan and Kochar (1989) expressed the concerns of many parents and special educators:

The National School Boards Association (NSBA) defended the Rochester School Board when the district court's decision was appealed. The NSBA stated that local schools have no obligation to serve children on the "low end of the spectrum . . .because they have no capacity to benefit from special education."

If the Loughlin decision stood, how would the language of P.L. 94–142 have changed? Would *all* have become *some*? Would the law only apply to "mildly and moderately impaired" children, and would "free appropriate public education" only be for students who were allowed to attend school? . . .If the Loughlin decision was upheld, years of research in education for new and innovative methods of teaching the handicapped may have been lost. . . . This case underscores the need for vigilance in our watch for shifts in interpretations of EHA that subtly modify the essential foundations of zero reject and protection from functional exclusion. (p. 3)

Challenges to existing services and differing views on whether a particular program is appropriate or least restrictive are certain to continue. The high costs of providing special education and related services, although clearly not a valid basis for excluding students with disabilities, will likely be more often taken into consideration by judges and courts as they determine what schools may reasonably be expected to do. In Kauffman's (1985) words, "One of the problems we are going to have to resolve in the next decade or so is what the limits of special education are, where it stops" (p. 14). Some observers predict a lack of further expansion of related services for children with disabilities; others are more optimistic. H. R. Turnbull (1986a), for example, notes that although the Supreme Court decided against the provision of related services in the Rowley case and in favor of them in the Tatro case, the decisions are consistent: The Court recognized the need for integration of handicapped children with nonhandicapped children in both cases and kept the student's individualized education program as "the focal point of appropriateness" (p. 351). Although the courts will probably grant some requests in the future and deny others, it is now a well-established principle that each student with disabilities is entitled to a personalized program of instruction and supportive services that will enable him to benefit from an education in as integrated a setting as possible.

Related Legislation

Gifted and Talented Children

Although P.L. 94–142 does not specifically apply to gifted and talented children, other federal legislation has addressed the specialized needs of this population. Public Law 95–561, the Gifted and Talented Children's Education Act of 1978, provides financial incentives for state and local education agencies to develop programs for students who are gifted and talented. P.L. 95–561 provides for the identification of gifted and talented children and includes special procedures for identifying and educating those from disadvantaged backgrounds. The law makes funding available for inservice training programs, research, and other projects aimed at meeting the needs of gifted and talented students.

In 1982, the Education Consolidation Act phased out the federal Office of Gifted and Talented and merged gifted education with 29 other programs. Federal dollars to support these 30 different and wide-ranging education programs (K–12) are sent to the states in the form of "block grants." Each state has the responsibility to determine what portion, if any, of the block grant funds will be used to support programs and services for students who are gifted and talented.

Congress passed the Jacob K. Javits Gifted and Talented Student Education Act in 1988 as part of the Elementary and Secondary Education Bill. This act

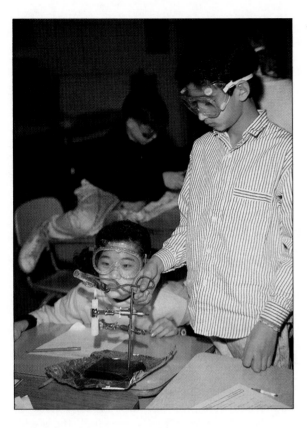

Although not required by federal law, most states have programs to identify and serve children who are gifted and talented.

provided $8 million for identification and service of gifted students, professional development and training of teachers, and the creation of a National Center for the Education of the Gifted. Although no federal legislation requires states to provide special education programs for gifted students, Sisk (1984) found that 47 states had appointed a state consultant or director of gifted programs, compared to Marland's (1972) earlier report that only 10 state departments of education had a consultant for the gifted on their staff.

Section 504 of the Rehabilitation Act of 1973

Another important law that extends civil rights to people with disabilities is Section 504 of the Rehabilitation Act of 1973. This regulation states, in part, that "no otherwise qualified handicapped individual shall, solely by reason of his handicap, be excluded from the participation in, be denied the benefits of, or be subjected to discrimination in any program or activity receiving federal financial assistance." This law, worded almost identically to the Civil Rights Act of 1964 (which prohibited discrimination based on race, color, or national origin), promises to expand opportunities to children and adults with disabilities in education, employment, and various other settings. It calls for provision of "auxiliary aids for students with impaired sensory, manual, or speaking skills"—for example, readers for blind students, interpreters for deaf students, and people to assist physically disabled students in moving from place to place. This requirement does not mean that schools, colleges, and employers must have *all* such aids available at *all* times; it simply demands that no handicapped person may be excluded from a program because of the lack of an appropriate aid.

Section 504 is not a federal grant program; unlike P.L. 94–142 and P.L. 99–457, it does not provide any federal money to assist people with disabilities. Rather, it "imposes a duty on every recipient of federal funds not to discriminate against handicapped persons" (T. P. Johnson, 1986, p. 8). This, of course, includes public school districts, virtually all of which receive federal support. Most colleges and universities have also been affected; even many students in private institutions receive federal financial aid. The Office of Civil Rights conducts periodic compliance reviews and acts on complaints when parents, disabled individuals, or others contend that a school district is violating Section 504.

Architectural accessibility for students, teachers, and others with physical and sensory impairments is an important feature of Section 504; however, the law does not call for a completely barrier-free environment. Emphasis is on accessibility to programs, not on physical modification of all existing structures. If a chemistry class is required for a premedical program of study, for example, a college might make this program accessible to a student with physical disabilities by reassigning the class to an accessible location or by providing assistance to the student in traveling to an otherwise inaccessible location. All sections of all courses need not be made accessible, but a college should not segregate students with disabilities by assigning them all to a particular section, regardless of disability. Like P.L. 94–142, Section 504 calls for nondiscriminatory placement in the "most integrated setting appropriate" and has served as the basis for many court cases over alleged discrimination against individuals with disabilities, particularly in their right to employment.

Americans with Disabilities Act

The Americans with Disabilities Act (P.L. 101–336) was signed into law on July 26, 1990. Patterned after Section 504 of the Rehabilitation Act of 1973, the Americans with Disabilities Act (ADA) extends civil rights protection to persons with disabilities in private sector employment, all public services, public accommodation, transportation, and telecommunications. A person with a disability is defined in the ADA as a person (1) with a mental or physical impairment that substantially limits that person in a major life activity (e.g., walking, talking, working, self-care); (2) with a record of such an impairment (such as a person who no longer has heart disease but is discriminated against because of that history); or (3) who is regarded as having such an impairment (a person with significant facial disfiguration due to a burn who is not limited in any major life activity but is discriminated against). The major provisions of the ADA, which go into effect between 1992 and 1994, are as follows:

♦ Employers with 15 or more employees may not refuse to hire or promote a person because of a disability if that person is qualified to perform the job. Also, the employer must make reasonable accommodations that will allow a person with a disability to perform essential functions of the job. Such modifications in job requirements or situation must be made if they will not impose undue hardship on the employer.

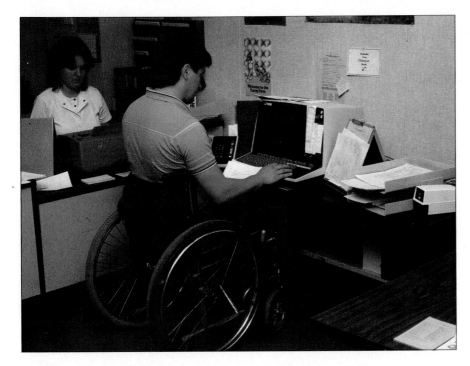

Passage of the Americans with Disabilities Act has brought wider employment opportunities for persons with disabilities.

♦ All new vehicles purchased by public transit authorities must be accessible to people with disabilities. All rail stations must be made accessible, and at least one car per train in existing rail systems must be made accessible.

♦ It is illegal for public accommodations to exclude or refuse persons with disabilities. Public accommodations are the everyday businesses and services such as hotels, restaurants, grocery stores, parks, and so on. All new buildings must be made accessible and existing facilities must remove barriers if the removal can be accomplished without much difficulty or expense.

♦ Companies offering telephone service to the general public must offer relay services to individuals who use telecommunications devices for the deaf (such as TDDs) 24 hours a day, 7 days a week.

■ SPECIAL EDUCATION IN THE SCHOOLS: MOVING BEYOND COMPLIANCE AND TOWARD EXCELLENCE

Shortly after passage of P.L. 94–142, Reynolds (1978) offered the following observation:

> Without even trying, I have been shown at least six sets of transparencies, listened to endless audio cassettes on the requirements of Public Law 94–142, and I have been guided through several versions of "sure-fire" forms to satisfy all of the new regulations.
>
> What I see and hear seems well designed to keep teachers out of jail—to comply with the law, that is—but usually I sense little vision of how people might come together creatively to design environments for better learning and living by handicapped students. (p. 60)

Indeed, creating effective learning environments for exceptional students and their peers involves far more than filling out forms and complying with the law. Regular and special educators find themselves confronted with countless new challenges and responsibilities; in effect, they are defining a new relationship with each other and with their students. Where children were formerly given a label and removed from the regular classroom, it is now recognized that exceptional children have special needs, and the services are moving to the children.

Special education may rightly be viewed as a *system* for the delivery of services to children with special needs, rather than a separate, specialized content area apart from regular education. The regular teacher who works with Sharon in her classroom, the speech-language pathologist who consults with Sharon's teacher twice each week, and the resource room teacher who works directly with Sharon and communicates with the regular teacher—all are participating in the system that delivers special education services to Sharon. We will examine three critical aspects of that system: the individualized education plan, the least restrictive environment, and the importance of teaming and collaboration among professionals.

The Individualized Education Program (IEP)

P.L. 94–142 requires that an individualized education program (IEP) be developed and maintained for every student with disabilities. The law is specific as to what an IEP must include and who is to take part in its formulation. Each

A child study team meets to develop an IEP and then reviews and revises the IEP at least once a year.

IEP must be the product of the joint efforts of the members of a *child study team,* which must include at least (1) the child's teacher(s), (2) a representative of the local school district other than the child's teacher, (3) the child's parents or guardian, and (4) whenever appropriate, the child herself. Other professionals, such as physical educators, speech-language pathologists, and physical therapists, may also be involved in the IEP conference.

The regulations written for P.L. 94–142 state that each handicapped student's IEP must include

1. A statement of the child's present levels of educational performance, including academic achievement, social adaptation, prevocational and vocational skills, psychomotor skills, and self-help skills

2. A statement of annual goals describing the educational performance to be achieved by the end of each school year

3. A statement of short-term instructional objectives presented in measurable, intermediate steps between the present level of educational performance and the annual goals

4. A statement of specific educational services needed by the child, including a description of
    a. all special education and related services needed to meet the unique needs of the child (determined without regard to the availability of those services), including the physical education program
    b. any special instructional media and materials that are needed

5. A statement of the needed transition services for students beginning no later than age 16 and annually thereafter (when determined appropriate for the individual, beginning at age 14 or younger), including, when appropriate, a statement of the interagency responsibilities or linkages (or both) before the student leaves the school setting (new IEP requirement of P.L. 101–476, Sec. 602(a)(20))

6. The date when those services will begin and the length of time the services will be given

7. A description of the extent to which the child will participate in regular education programs

8. A justification for the type of educational placement the child will have

9. A list of the individuals who are responsible for implementing the individualized education program

10. Objective criteria, evaluation procedures, and schedules of determining, at least annually, whether the short-term instructional objectives are being achieved (*Federal Register,* 1977)

Figure 2.1 shows one example of an IEP. IEP formats vary widely across school districts, and schools may go beyond the requirements of the law and include additional information. Each child's IEP must be reviewed and, if necessary, revised at least once each year. The child's parent or guardian must consent to the IEP and must receive a copy of the document.

Several systems that use computers to help produce and manage the paperwork involved in the IEP process have been created (Enell, 1983; Kellog, 1984).

INDIVIDUAL EDUCATION PROGRAM

Date _____3-1-91_____

Student	Committee	Initial
Name: Joe S. School: Adams Grade: 5 Current Placement: Regular Class/Resource Room Date of Birth: 10-1-80 Age: 11-5	Mrs. Wrens — Principal Mrs. Snow — Regular Teacher Mr. LaJoie — Counselor Mr. Thomas — Resource Teacher Mr. Ryan — School Psychologist Mrs. S. — Parent Joe S. — Student	*(initials)*

EP from ___3-15-91___ to ___3-15-92___

Present Level of Educational Functioning	Annual Goal Statements	Instructional Objectives	Objective Criteria and Evaluation
MATH Strengths 1. Can successfully compute addition and subtraction problems to two places with regrouping and zeros. 2. Knows 100 basic multiplication facts. Weaknesses 1. Frequently makes computational errors on problems with which he has had experience. 2. Does not complete seatwork. Key Math total score of 2.1 Grade Equivalent.	Joe will apply knowledge of regrouping in addition and renaming in subtraction to four-digit numbers.	1. When presented with 20 additional problems of 3-digit numbers requiring two renamings, the student will compute the answer at a rate of one problem per minute and an accuracy of 90%. 2. When presented with 20 subtraction problems of 3-digit numbers requiring two renamings, the student will compute the answer at a rate of one problem per minute with 90% accuracy. 3. When presented with 20 addition problems of 4-digit numbers requiring three renamings, the student will compute the answer at a rate of one problem per minute and an accuracy of 90%. 4. When presented with 20 subtraction problems of 4-digit numbers requiring three renamings, the student will compute the answer at a rate of one problem per minute with 90% accuracy.	Teacher-made tests (weekly) Teacher-made tests (weekly) Teacher-made tests (weekly)
READING Strengths 1. Comprehends reading material at 2nd grade level. 2. Can identify main idea of a paragraph at 2nd grade level. Weaknesses 1. Poor word attack skills and word identification. (See grade equivalents next page.) 2. Has difficulty identifying words written in cursive.	Joe will successfully identify long and short vowels.	1. When requested by the examiner, the student will correctly sound out the long and short sounds of five vowels (a, e, i, o, u) in 9 of 10 trials. 2. When presented with 3-letter words having the pattern "consonant, vowel, consonant," the student will correctly pronounce the vowel with its short sound. He will be able to perform this task for all 5 of the vowels in 9 of 10 trials. 3. When presented with one-syllable words having the pattern "consonant and final e" or "consonant, double vowel, consonant," the student will pronounce the vowel(s) with a long sound. He will be able to perform this task for all vowel sounds in 9 of 10 trials.	Brigance Diagnostic Inventory of Basic Skills (after 2 mos.)

FIGURE 2.1

Portion of a completed IEP for a fifth-grade student. (*Source:* From *Developing and Implementing Individualized Education Programs* (3rd ed.) (pp. 308, 311, 313, 316) by B. B. Strickland and A. P. Turnbull, 1990, Columbus, OH: Merrill. Reprinted by permission.)

One of the most difficult tasks is to determine how inclusive the IEP document should be. Strickland and Turnbull (1990) state that the definition of special education as "specially designed instruction" should be a key element in determining what should go into a student's IEP.

Present Level of Educational Functioning	Annual Goal Statements	Instructional Objectives	Objective Criteria and Evaluation
SOCIAL EMOTIONAL Strengths 1. Joe cooperates in group activities. 2. Attentive and cooperative in class. Weaknesses 1. Reluctant participant on playground. 2. Makes derogatory comments about himself frequently during the school day. 3. Has few friends, is ignored by peers.	Joe will speak about himself in a positive manner. Joe will participate with peers in small groups on the playground and in class.	1. In a one-to-one situation with the teacher, Joe will talk about his personal strengths for five min. a day. 2. In a one-to-one situation with the teacher, Joe will state 5 strengths he possesses for 3 days in a row. 3. After a small group activity (3–4 students), Joe will tell the teacher 3 things he did well in the group. 4. After a small group activity Joe will tell the teacher 6 things he did well in the group. 5. In a small group activity, Joe will ask a peer for help instead of asking an adult: a) With verbal reminders from an adult in 80% of opportunities. b) With nonverbal reminders in 80% of opportunities. c) With no signals in 80% of opportunities. 6. In a small group activity Joe will offer assistance to a peer: a) With verbal reminders from an adult in 80% of opportunities b) With nonverbal reminders in 80% of opportunities. c) With no signals in 80% of opportunities.	Teacher observation (daily) for 15 days. Anecdotal records (daily) Anecdotal records (daily) 3 consecutive days Anecdotal records (daily) 5 consecutive days Anecdotal records (daily) 5 consecutive days Teacher observation. Data collected 30 min. a day, 3 days a week Teacher observation. Data collected 30 min. a day, 3 days a week

Educational Services to be Provided

Services Required	Date Initiated	Duration of Service	Individual Responsible for the Service
Regular Reading-Adapted	3-15-91	3-15-92	Reading Improvement Specialist and Special Education Teacher
Resource Room	3-15-91	3-15-92	Special Education Teacher
Counselor Consultant	3-15-91	3-15-92	Counselor
Monitoring diet and general health	3-15-91	3-15-92	School Health Nurse

Extent of time in the regular education program: 60% increasing to 80%

Justification of the educational placement:

It is felt that the structure of the resource room can best meet the goals stated for Joe; especially coordinated with the regular classroom.

It is also felt that Joe could profit enormously from talking with a counselor. He needs someone with whom to talk and with whom he can share his feelings.

I have had the opportunity to participate in the development of the Individual Education Program.
I agree with the Individual Education Program (✓)
I disagree with the Individual Education Program (   )

Parent's Signature _____ *Mrs. S.* _____

FIGURE 2.1 *continued*

The determination of whether instruction is "specially designed" must be made by comparing the nature of the instruction for the student with a disability to instructional practices used with typical students at the same age and grade level. If the instructional adaptations that a student with a disability requires are (1) significantly different from adaptations normally expected or made for typical students in that setting, and if (2) the adaptations are necessary to offset or reduce the adverse effect of the disability on learning and educational performance, then these adaptations should be considered "specially designed instruction" and should be included as part of the student's IEP, regardless of the instructional setting. (p. 13)

Ideally, the IEP is a system for spelling out where the child is, where he should be going, how he will get there, how long it will take, and how to tell when he has arrived (Bierly, 1978). The legal requirement of an IEP is relatively new, but the principles of sound planning and systematic teaching are not. For many years, regular and special education teachers have been using assessment, short-range objectives leading to long-range goals, and evaluation procedures in working with their students.

The IEP is a measure of accountability for teachers and schools. Whether a particular school or educational program is effective will be judged, to some extent, by how well it is able to help children meet the goals and objectives set forth in their IEPs. Like other professionals, teachers are being called on to demonstrate effectiveness, and the IEP provides one way for them to do so. The IEP is not, however, a legally binding contract. A child's teacher and school cannot be prosecuted in the courts if the child does not achieve all the goals set forth in the IEP. Nevertheless, the teacher should be able to document that a conscientious and systematic effort was made to achieve those goals. The IEP is, however, much more than an accountability device. Its potential benefits are improved planning (including planning for the student's needs after leaving school), consistency, regular evaluation, and clearer communication between parents, teachers, and others involved in providing services to the student.

Although many educators note that "the plan for the IEP is grand and has great potential" (Morse, 1985, p. 182), inspection and evaluation of IEPs often do not reveal consistency between what is written on the document and the instruction students experience in the classroom (Nevin, McCann, & Semmel, 1983; Smith, 1990b). Of all the requirements of P.L. 94–142, the IEP is "probably the single most unpopular aspect of the law, not only because it requires a great deal of work, but because the essence of the plan itself seems to have been lost in the mountains of paperwork" (Gallagher, 1984, p. 228). Several studies of actual IEPs seem to support Gallagher's contention (Fiedler & Knight, 1986; Schenck, 1980; Smith 1990a). Smith and Simpson (1989), for example, evaluated the IEPs of 214 students with behavior disorders and found that one-third of the IEPs lacked necessary mandated components.

But even proper inclusion of all mandated components in an IEP is no guarantee the document will guide the student's learning and teachers' teaching in the classroom, as intended by P.L. 94–142. Many special and regular educators are working hard to create procedures for developing IEPs that go beyond compliance with the law and actually serve as a meaningful guide for the "specially designed instruction" a student with disabilities needs. For example, Giangreco, Cloninger, & Iverson (1990) have proposed an IEP process called C.O.A.C.H., which guides child study teams through the assessment and planning stages of IEP development in a way that results in learning goals and objectives directly related to functional skills in integrated settings. Strickland and Turnbull (1990) also provide detailed procedures for systematic development and implementation of IEPs.

Some observers have asked, "If children with disabilities must have IEPs, then why not extend this requirement to all children in the public schools?" Indeed, some states and local school districts now use individualized educational planning with both handicapped and nonhandicapped students. Utah, for example, has adopted the requirement that an "individual education plan for the projected education program [being] pursued by each student during membership in the school" (Robinson, 1982, p. 205) be developed cooperatively by teachers, parents, and the student. This requirement has reportedly led to more conferences, better career planning, and greater parental involvement. Although some teachers view IEPs as an added burden of paperwork and some parents do not wish to become involved in the planning process, the IEP seems to be gaining acceptance. All children can benefit from accurate specification of individual goals, periodic evaluation, parent involvement, and contributions from various disciplines that the IEP offers to exceptional children.

The Least Restrictive Environment

P.L. 94–142 supports each handicapped child's right to be educated in the least restrictive environment (LRE). It stipulates that

> to the maximum extent appropriate, handicapped children, including children in public or private institutions or other care facilities, are educated with children who are not handicapped, and that special classes, separate schooling, or other removal of handicapped children from the regular educational environment occurs only when the nature or severity of the handicap is such that education in regular classes with the use of supplementary aids and services cannot be achieved satisfactorily. (Section 612(5)B of P.L. 94–142)

As Bliton and Schroeder (1986) explain, if we expect students to live and work in a heterogeneous society, we must prepare them by first integrating them in schools—each school, in a sense, becomes a microcosm of the community. Thus, the *least restrictive environment* is considered to be the setting that most closely parallels a regular school program and also meets the child's special educational needs. Conversely, the *most* restrictive environment is the setting that is farthest removed from a regular public school program. A child educated at home or in a hospital, for example, would have little or no opportunity to interact with nonhandicapped children.

The least restrictive environment is a relative concept; the LRE for one child might be inappropriate for another. Since the passage of P.L. 94–142, there have been many differences of opinion over which type of setting is least restrictive and most appropriate for students with disabilities. Even though a few educators, parents, and lawyers consider any decision to place a handicapped child in a special class or school to be overly restrictive, most recognize that a regular class placement can be restrictive and inappropriate if the child's instructional and social needs are not adequately met. It is also generally accepted that there are wide individual differences among children and that there can be more than one "best" way to provide appropriate educational services to an exceptional child. As Taylor, Biklen, and Searl (1986) observe, decisions concerning a child's educational program should be based on consideration of that child's needs. Not all children with the same disability should be placed in the same setting; the goal, instead, is to find an appropriate LRE for each child.

SOMEONE'S MISSING

The Student as an Overlooked Participant in the IEP Process

Classroom teachers, specialists, administrators, and parents meet with each other once a year at the individualized education program (IEP) conference. The group meets to share progress by the student, discuss future goals and objectives, and determine needed services and placement for the student. But where is the student?

Although the regulations for P.L. 94–142 state that "the child, wherever appropriate" be included, rarely does the student play an active role in the IEP process. Gillespie (1981) found more than 90% of handicapped students and 75% of their parents had no knowledge of the student participation provision in P.L. 94–142.

Students with handicaps are often not perceived by administrators, teachers, or parents as an integral part of the IEP team, with the right (if not the responsibility) to assist in developing and implementing their own special education program. Students are more likely to be viewed as the recipients of special services. When they are empowered as active team members in all aspects of the IEP process, however, students have an opportunity to heighten their independence, self-advocacy skills, and self-esteem. Also, students may be able to offer insightful perceptions and valuable contributions. All handicapped students can and should be involved in the IEP process.

How Can Students Participate?

The IEP conference is just one part of the entire IEP process. Students may be involved at any stage. Figure A illustrates strategies that facilitate student participation in the three major stages of assessment, the IEP conference itself, and instruction.

Assessment

All students should actively participate in the assessment and evaluation of their skills and preferences.

Student Determination of Preferences. For all students, participation in the IEP process can begin with determining preferences. By sharing their likes and dislikes, students provide input from which teachers can identify objectives, goals, and potential reinforcers. Students sometimes make inappropriate or unrealistic choices. In these cases, teachers should counsel students and present them with a variety of more likely alternatives.

Student Self-Evaluation. Students can be further involved in the assessment phase by engaging in self-evaluation. They can use a teacher-made self-rating scale or checklist to determine perceived strengths, weaknesses, competencies, and successes in goal attainment. This information can help teachers devise goals that focus on the student's strong points and address deficit areas that are important to the student.

Goal Setting. Students who are trained to assess their own skills and goal achievement may be better able to set realistic expectations for themselves. Other valuable information that can contribute to the assessment phase is student identification of future goals and ambitions. A wish list can help students identify future plans, expectations, and skills they wish to acquire. Pictures, photos, checklists, or classroom activities can help students identify goals that are then incorporated into their IEPs. Computer software such as "Be A Winner: Set Your Goals" (M.C.E., Inc., 1988) offers adolescents and adults an interactive program for choosing long- and short-term goals.

The IEP Conference

The degree to which a student may participate in the IEP conference will vary. The highest degree of involvement for students is their acceptance as full team members and opportunities to act as self-advocates. There are also many opportunities for partial inclusion of students unable to be fully involved.

Preconference Preparation. Students need to be informed about the intent and significance of the meeting, the roles of each team member, and procedures that will be followed. Videotaped presentations of real or staged IEP meetings can be an excellent way to prepare students for their own conference. Role playing can also help emphasize and define the responsibilities of all team members, including those of the student. Students should rehearse appropriate and expected behaviors. These are suggested rules for student behavior during the IEP conference:

- Remain seated throughout the meeting.
- Maintain eye contact with those who are addressing you.
- Respect others as they speak by listening without interruption.
- If you don't understand, excuse yourself politely, and ask them to explain again.
- Wait your turn before offering your opinion and recommendations.
- When you disagree, state your case without being loud or impatient, and offer your own suggestions instead.
- Respond to direct questions.

Creative intervention by teachers is sometimes necessary to convince parents of the advantages of student involvement in the IEP conference. Parents may be persuaded by talking to others who have involved their child in the IEP conference. Parents can be invited to participate in or view videotapes of classroom preconference activities. In some cases, administrators may also need to be reminded of students' right to participate and be encouraged to advocate for them in this regard.

Conference Participation. Students who have been involved in other phases of the IEP process will be better prepared for the conference experience. The more active the student has been, the more likely he will be successful in the IEP meeting itself. When something should not be discussed in front of the child (e.g., controversial issues, policy decisions, disagreements), the student can enter the meeting near its conclusion to meet with team members, listen to suggested goals and objectives, and hear comments relating to his or her progress.

With parental cooperation, team commitment, prior preparation, and involvement in other phases of the IEP process, students can be successfully integrated as team members. The student might report his own progress, contribute to discussions, and help formulate goals and objectives at the conference. Once these are agreed upon, the student should cosign the completed document, just as other team members do.

Instruction

In comonitoring their progress, students participate in classroom activities that remind them of the goals they have helped set. Daily, weekly, and monthly activities can be designed to include students in the ongoing collection of data, assessment of progress, and reevaluation of goals. Teachers can help students tally stickers, tokens, points, or grades they have earned. These can be recorded on a chart or other visual representation related to identified student goals. Younger students can color bar graphs or collect small items or cards to signify their progress.

Students can also comonitor their progress in meetings with other students. These meetings should be positive, encouraging group cooperation, support, and problem-solving opportunities. Self-management, self-monitoring, and self-instruction techniques may also help students meet the goals they have helped set (Heward, 1987b; Kerr & Nelson, 1989; Lovitt, 1984).

Including students in a process designed expressly for them is often overlooked, but there are numerous possibilities for student participation in the IEP process for educators who wish to implement instruction *with* students—not just for them. ◆

(*Source: Adapted from "Someone's Missing: The Student As An Overlooked Participant in the IEP Process" by Mary T. Peters, 1990,* Preventing School Failure, *34(4), pp. 32–36. Used by permission.*)

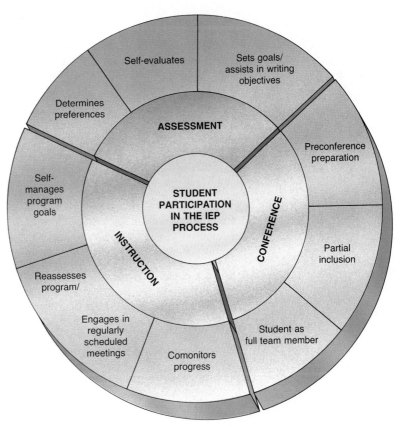

FIGURE A
Strategies to promote student involvement in three phases of the IEP process.

For many students with disabilities education in the least restrictive environment means an opportunity to learn in the mainstream alongside peers.

Recognizing the importance of the academic and social interactions the exceptional child experiences over the physical characteristics of where special education takes place, Heron and Skinner (1981) describe the least restrictive environment as

> that educational setting which maximizes the . . .student's opportunity to respond and achieve, permits the regular education teacher to interact proportionally with all the students in the classroom, and fosters acceptable social relations between nonhandicapped and [handicapped] students. (p. 116)

A Continuum of Services

Exceptional children, their teachers, and their families may need a wide range of special education and related services from time to time. Today, most schools provide a *continuum of services*—that is, a range of different placement and service options to meet students' needs. The continuum is often symbolically depicted as a pyramid, with placements ranging from least restrictive (regular classroom placement) at the bottom to most restrictive (special schools or institutions) at the top. The fact that the pyramid is widest at the bottom indicates that the greatest number of exceptional children should be served in regular classrooms, and the number of children who require more restrictive, intensive, and specialized placements gets smaller as we move up. As we have already noted, the majority of children receiving special education services have mild or moderate disabilities. The number of children with mild mental retardation, for example, is far greater than those who experience severe retardation. Likewise, children with mild or moderate behavior disorders greatly outnumber those with severe behavior disorders. As the severity of the disability increases, the need for more specialized services also increases, but the number of students involved decreases.

It is worth noting that, of the seven levels of service depicted in Figure 2.2, the first five are available in regular public school buildings. Children at Levels 1 through 4 attend regular classes with nonhandicapped peers; supportive help is given by special teachers who provide consultation to the children's regular teachers or in special resource rooms. A **resource room** usually has a specially trained teacher who provides instruction to exceptional students for part of the

Table 2.3 provides the definitions of six educational placements used by the U.S. Department of Education. Wiederholt and Chamberlain (1989) describe various types of resource room programs and review the research conducted on their effects.

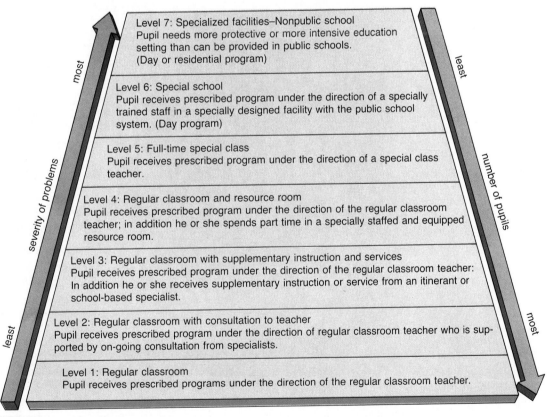

FIGURE 2.2

Continuum of educational services for students with disabilities. (*Source:* From Montgomery County Public Schools, Rockville, MD. Reprinted by permission.)

TABLE 2.3

U.S. Department of Education Definitions of six educational placements for students with handicaps.

Placement	Definition
Regular class	Students receive a majority of their education in a regular class and receive special education and related services for less than 21 percent of the school day. Includes children placed in a regular class and receiving special education within the regular class as well as children placed in a regular class and receiving special education outside the regular class.
Resource room	Students receive special education and related services for 60 percent or less of the school day and at least 21 percent of the school day. May include resource rooms with part-time instruction in the regular class.
Separate class	Students receive special education and related services for more than 60 percent of the school day and are placed in self-contained special classrooms with part-time instruction in regular class or placed in self-contained classes full-time on a regular school campus.
Separate school facility	Students receive special education and related services in separate day schools for the handicapped for greater than 50 percent of the school day.
Residential facility	Students receive education in a public or private residential facility at public expense for greater than 50 percent of the school day.
Homebound/hospital environment	Students placed in and receiving education in hospital or homebound programs.

Source: Adapted from *Twelfth Annual Report to Congress on the Implementation of the Education of the Handicapped Act,* pp. 18–19, 1990, Washington, DC: U.S. Department of Education.

school day, either individually or in small groups. Children at Level 5, who require full-time placement in a special **self-contained class**, are with other exceptional children for all or most of the school day, but they may still have the opportunity to interact with nonhandicapped children at certain times, such as during recess or on the bus to school. Although this alternative provides less integration than the regular classroom, it provides much more opportunity for interaction than placement in a residential institution or a special school attended only by children with disabilities. Self-contained classes in regular school buildings are gaining acceptance as an appropriate placement for many children with severe and multiple disabilities.

Placement of an exceptional child at any level on the continuum of services should not be regarded as permanent. Teachers, parents, and administrators should periodically review the specific goals and objectives for each child. New placement decisions can be made; in fact, the continuum concept is intended to be flexible, with children moving from one placement to another as dictated by their current educational needs. A child may be placed in a less integrated setting for a limited time; then, when a performance review shows that certain goals have been achieved, the child should return to a more normalized setting as soon as possible.

Current interpretation of the least restrictive environment, based on recent court cases, is that a child should be removed from the regular school program only to the extent that there is clear evidence that removal is necessary for the child to receive appropriate educational services. The child's parents must be properly informed if removal from the regular classroom is being considered so that they can either consent or object to the removal and can present additional information if they wish. No removal from the regular school program should be regarded as permanent; there should be a plan for returning the child to as normal a setting as possible, as soon as certain needs or conditions are met. Thus, each handicapped child must have access to educational experiences appropriate to that child's special needs and as similar as possible to those that a nonhandicapped child would have.

Implementing the least restrictive environment concept according to a continuum of services model has not been without its critics. For example, Taylor (1988) suggests that the LRE and continuum of service model

> Educators have developed other placement and service delivery alternatives not depicted on the traditional continuum. One example is the integrated classroom model, in which a teacher and a teacher aide provide all instruction to a class of handicapped and nonhandicapped students (Affleck, Madge, Adams, & Lowenbraun, 1988).

1. *Legitimates restrictive environments.* To conceptualize services in terms of restrictiveness is to legitimate more restrictive settings. As long as services are conceptualized in this manner, some people will end up in restrictive environments. Some people will continue to support institutions and other segregated settings merely by defining them as the least restrictive environment for certain people.

2. *Confuses segregation and integration with intensity of services.* As represented by the continuum, LRE equates segregation with the most intensive services and integration with the least intensive services. The principle assumes that the least restrictive, most integrated settings are incapable of providing the intensive services needed by people with severe disabilities. However, segregation and integration on the one hand and intensity of services on the other are separate dimensions.

3. *[Is] based on a "readiness model."* Implicit in LRE is the assumption that people with developmental disabilities must earn the right to move to the least restrictive environment. In other words, the person must "get ready" or "be prepared" to live, work, or go to school in integrated settings.

4. *Supports the primacy of professional decision making.* As Biklen (1988) notes, integration is ultimately a moral and philosophical issue, not a professional one. Yet LRE invariably is framed in terms of professional

judgments regarding "individual needs." The phrase "least restrictive environment" is almost always qualified with words such as "appropriate," "necessary," "feasible," and "possible" (and never with "desired" or "wanted").

5. *Sanctions infringements on people's rights.* When applied to people with disabilities, the LRE principle sanctions infringements on basic rights to freedom and community participation beyond those imposed on nondisabled people. The question imposed by LRE is not *whether* people with disabilities should be restricted, but *to what extent.*

6. *Implies that people must move as they develop and change.* As LRE is commonly conceptualized, people with disabilities are expected to move toward increasingly less restrictive environments. Even if people moved smoothly through a continuum, their lives would be a series of stops between transitional placements.

7. *Directs attention to physical settings rather than to the services and supports people need.* By its name, the principle of the least restrictive environment emphasizes facilities and environments designed specifically for people with disabilities. The field has defined the mission in terms of creating "facilities," first large ones and now smaller ones, and "programs," rather than providing the services and supports to enable people with disabilities to participate in the same settings used by other people. (pp. 45–48)

Maynard Reynolds, who was the first to propose the continuum of services concept, also believes it is time to make some changes in the model—specifically, to do away with the two most restrictive placements.

> In this writer's view, we are prepared now to lop off the top two levels of the continuum. . . . [I]t is now well demonstrated that we can deliver special education and related services within general school buildings and at a continuum level no higher than the special class. Thus, we can foresee the undoing or demise of special schools (day and residential) as delivery mechanisms for special education—at least in the United States. (1989, p. 8)

Mainstreaming

The word **mainstreaming** describes the process of integrating exceptional children into regular schools and classes. Much discussion and controversy and many misconceptions have arisen regarding the education of students with handicaps in regular classes—the so-called mainstream of our public school system. Some people view mainstreaming as placing all exceptional children into regular classrooms with no additional supportive services, whereas others have the idea that mainstreaming can mean completely segregated placement of handicapped children, as long as they interact with nonhandicapped peers in a few activities (perhaps at lunch or on the playground). Many parents have strongly supported the placement of their exceptional children in regular classes; others have resisted it just as strongly, feeling that the regular classroom does not offer the intense, individualized education that their children need.

Interestingly, the word *mainstreaming* does not appear in P.L. 94–142, which generated most of the discussion and debate. As we have seen, what the law does call for is the education of each child with disabilities in the least

Segregated day and residential schools are attended primarily by students with severe handicaps. In Chapter 10, we examine the rationale and trend toward serving students with severe handicaps in regular public schools.

Successful integration of students with disabilities into the academic and social life of the regular classroom can be accomplished in a variety of ways. One proven and increasingly popular method is *peer tutoring*. (See "Classwide Peer Tutoring" Focus in this chapter.)

restrictive appropriate educational setting, removed no further than necessary from the regular public school program.

P.L. 94–142 does not require placement of all children with handicaps in regular classes, call for handicapped children to remain in regular classes without necessary supportive services, or suggest that regular teachers should educate handicapped students without help from special educators and other specialists. It does, however, specifically call for regular and special educators to cooperate in providing an equal educational opportunity to exceptional students.

We know that simply placing a child with disabilities in a regular classroom does not mean that the child will learn and behave appropriately or will be socially accepted by nonhandicapped children (Gresham, 1982). It is important for special educators to teach appropriate social skills and behavior to the handicapped child and to educate nonhandicapped children about the differences in their handicapped classmates. But these challenges should not mean that children with disabilities are denied the right to participate in a regular classroom for all or part of the school day. Becky's main educational handicap, for example, is that she has very limited vision. It would be overly restrictive to send Becky to a residential school 200 miles from her home, where she could interact only with other visually impaired children (though this probably would have been done not too long ago). Her needs may well be met in the regular public school, through the provision of special materials and tutoring for Becky and consultation for her regular teacher.

Lewis and Doorlag (1991) provide numerous suggestions for mainstreaming students with special needs. Heron and Harris (1987) describe consultation and collaboration procedures that special educators can use in working with regular educators to deliver needed services to students with disabilities.

Assessment, Planning, and Service Delivery: The Importance of Collaboration and Teaming

Assessment and Planning

For many years, students with disabilities were tested primarily to exclude them from public school programs. Charles may have been denied entrance into his local school, for example, if he obtained a score below 50 on an IQ test, if he was unable to follow verbal directions, or if he required assistance in using the toilet. Assessment was typically conducted in a special testing room, often by an examiner who was unfamiliar with the child and who had little or no contact with the child's parents or teachers. The examiner then interpreted the results of the tests, applied a label to the child, and ruled the child eligible or ineligible to remain in the public school program.

Today, assessment should be viewed as a process of including a student on the basis of what she can do, rather than excluding her because of what she cannot do. Assessment must not be limited to defining a disability (we probably know already that the child has some difficulty before assessment even begins) but should focus instead on finding ability. What can the child *do*? How and in what situation does she learn most effectively? What materials and techniques appear to be appropriate? The answers to these and other questions can be valuable in planning a child's educational program. Assessment is virtually useless unless it leads to action, in the form of specific instruction, treatment, or other intervention given to the child.

Assessment is thus coming to be seen not as an isolated discipline, but as an inseparable part of the child's ongoing educational program. Today, assessment

Chapter 4 discusses specific instruments often used to assess children's learning problems.

CLASSWIDE PEER TUTORING
Integrating Children with Disabilities into the Regular Classroom

Including a handicapped child in classwide academic activities can present a difficult challenge. The regular classroom teacher is expected to deliver individualized instruction to the mainstreamed student, maintain effective programming for the rest of the class, and help the mainstreamed child become socially integrated into the classroom. One method that has been used successfully to individualize instruction for handicapped students without requiring them to leave the regular classroom is in-class tutoring. Certified tutors, classroom aides, parent and grandparent volunteers, and older students have all served as effective in-class tutors for handicapped children. But obtaining extra adult help or out-of-class students as tutors on a regular basis is frequently a problem.

An often-untapped and always-available source of tutoring help in every classroom is the students themselves. Although the idea of peer tutoring (same-age classmates teaching one another) is not new (Lancaster, 1806), it has recently become the focus of renewed interest and research. As peer tutoring is usually implemented, a few high-achieving students are assigned to tutor students who have not mastered a particular skill, and the handicapped or low-achieving student is singled out for special help. In contrast, a classwide peer tutoring system allows the mainstreamed student to become a full participant in an ongoing whole-class activity. Direct, individualized instruction is provided to every student in the class, and social interactions between handicapped and nonhandicapped classmates are encouraged. One classwide peer tutoring program that has been developed for teaching basic reading and math skills in the primary grades is described here.

Every student in the class has a tutoring folder containing 10 flash cards in a "GO" pocket (see page 175). Each card has one word (sound or math fact) to be taught to the child's partner. Thus, children serve as both tutor and student each day. When in the role of student, each child practices words from an individualized list of new words determined by a teacher-given pretest.

Tutor Huddle

The daily peer tutoring session begins with students getting their folders and participating in a 5-minute tutor huddle with two or three other tutors. The children take turns presenting and orally reading the sight words they will shortly be responsible for teaching to their partners. (Meanwhile, their partners are in other tutor huddles working on the words they will soon be teaching.) Fellow tutors confirm and correct responses by saying "Yes" and try to help identify words a tutor doesn't know. The teacher circulates around the room, helping tutor huddles that cannot identify or agree upon a given word.

Practice

After the tutor huddles, partners join one another to practice their words. One child begins in the role of tutor and presents the word cards as many times as possible during the 5-minute practice period. Tutors are trained to praise their students from time to time for correct responses. When a student makes an error, the tutor says, "Try again." If the student still does not read the word correctly, the tutor says, "The word is *tree; say tree.*" A timer signals the end of the first practice period, and the partners switch roles.

Testing

After the second practice period, roles are again reversed, and the first tutor tests her partner by presenting each sight word once, providing no prompts or cues. Words the student reads correctly are placed in one pile, and missed words in another. Roles are then switched again, and the first tutor is now tested on the words she practiced. The peer tutoring session ends with the tutors marking on a chart the number of words their partners said correctly during the test and praising one another for their good work. When a child correctly reads a word on the test for three consecutive sessions, that word is considered learned and is moved to the folder's STOP pocket. When all 10 words have been learned, a new set of words is placed in the GO pocket.

Results

This peer tutoring system was originally developed and evaluated over a 5-month period in a first-grade classroom of 28 children. The class included one boy with learning disabilities and one girl with mental retardation, both of whom attended a special education resource room for part of the school day. Results showed that all children in the classroom learned sight words at a rapid, consistent pace (Heward, Heron, & Cooke, 1982). The children also retained the words they had taught one another. The class average on 10-word review tests given 1 week after each set of words was learned was 8.9 words correct. Of particular interest was the performance of the two handicapped children in the class. The learning disabled boy functioned successfully both as a student and as a tutor. Although the mentally retarded child did not serve as a tutor, she participated as a student, learning at the rate of almost one new word each day. Her sight word vocabulary increased from a pretest score of 4 to a total of 51 words by the end of the study (Cooke, Heron, Heward, & Test, 1982). She, too, remembered the words she had learned, averaging 8.7 words correct out of a possible 10 on the 1-week review tests. And both she and her tutor enjoyed the daily sessions. When the long program ended, her tutor wrote, "I like peer tutoring. I liked my student vary [sic] much." The positive social interactions of a classwide peer tutoring program such as this one may, in the long run, prove to be of equal or even greater benefit to the children involved than the actual learning gains themselves.

This classwide peer tutoring system has been replicated in hundreds of classrooms with sight words, math facts, and other subject areas. (See pages 174–176 for a description of how high school students with learning disabilities used the system to teach Spanish to one another.) Interested readers may obtain a detailed description of the peer tutoring system by writing William L. Heward, College of Education, Ohio State University, Columbus, OH 43210.◆

is often accomplished in natural settings, such as the child's regular classroom or home. There is generally less reliance on standardized tests that give numerical scores and predictions of potential and more reliance on precise, structured observations of behavior. A teacher might, for example, count how many times Greg is out of his seat during a 10-minute period. A parent might observe that Jill is able to pick up small pieces of meat with a spoon but has difficulty using a fork. Observations like these, made over a period of time by people who are familiar with the child, can readily be translated into educational goals and objectives.

P.L. 94–142 reflects current concern for fair, appropriate, **multifactored assessment**. The law specifically calls for certain safeguards, including

♦ Evaluation that assesses specific areas of educational need, not merely providing a single general intelligence quotient

♦ Assessment to be made by a multidisciplinary team or group of persons

♦ Assessment of all areas in which disability may be suspected (including vision, hearing, motor abilities, health, communication, and other appropriate areas)

♦ Tests to be administered by trained personnel

♦ Evaluation that does not discriminate because of racial or cultural background or because the child speaks a language other than English

♦ A wide range of evaluation procedures, never using a single assessment as the sole criterion for determining placement

School psychologists, who have traditionally performed the majority of assessments in school settings, are finding it necessary to broaden their skills to enable them to assess children with various special needs, including such disabilities as blindness, deafness, and severe behavior handicaps (Thomas & Grimes, 1990). The problems of finding appropriate ways to measure the abilities of students with such disabilities are complex, because relatively few reliable instruments exist. If specially designed tests cannot be found, psychologists frequently adapt existing test procedures to enable the child to respond appropriately. They may also find it useful to rely on the observations of teachers, parents, and others who regularly interact with the child in a variety of environments. Assessment of an exceptional child should never be limited to the psychologist's office or testing room.

Parents have the right to obtain an independent evaluation of their child by examiners of their choice from outside the school system. The results of any such independent evaluations must be considered along with the school's assessment in determining the child's program and placement. The outcome of any evaluation process should be to obtain information that will be useful to the student, the teachers, and the parents in planning activities that will enhance the child's learning and future development.

Teams. Collaboration has become a "buzzword" for futurists' conceptualizations of the effective school in the 21st century (Benjamin, 1989). Indeed, teachers who work with handicapped students and other students who are difficult to teach have discovered they are better able to diagnose and solve learning and behavioral problems in the classroom when they work together.

Intervention assistance teams plan strategies to help children with learning problems stay in the regular classroom.

Pfeiffer (1982) concluded that team decision making was generally consistent, effective, and superior to individual decision making in the placement of exceptional children. "A cooperative work group brings to bear on a complex task differing values as well as unique professional perspectives. This enhances the problem-solving effectiveness that is required" (p. 69) when determining the most appropriate educational program for an exceptional child.

Various types of teams have been developed. Some schools use *intervention assistance teams* to help classroom teachers devise and implement adaptations for a student who is experiencing either academic or behavioral difficulties so he can remain in the regular classroom. This approach is commonly called "prereferral intervention" because successful intervention avoids the costly and time-consuming process of assessment for special education placement (Graden, Casey, & Christenson, 1985). Fuchs, Fuchs, Bahr, Fernstrom, & Stecker (1990) note that prereferral intervention

> is often "brokered" by one or more support staff, such as a special educator or school psychologist, who works indirectly with a targeted difficult-to-teach (DTT) student through consultation with the teacher. Implicit in this definition is a preventative intent; that is, (a) eliminating inappropriate referrals while increasing the legitimacy of those that are initiated and (b) reducing future student problems by strengthening the teacher's capacity to intervene effectively with a greater diversity of children. (p. 495)

Descriptions of prereferral intervention models and related research can be found in Fuchs, Fuchs, and Bahr (1990); Graden (1989); and Pugach and Johnson (1989b).

Educators are also teaming with one another to serve identified handicapped students in regular classrooms. Often called *teacher assistance teams* or *mainstream assistance teams,* these joint efforts are the subject of much research

Carter and Sugai (1989) found that 23 states required prereferral interventions for students suspected of having a handicap, and 11 additional states recommended that local school districts used prereferral systems.

(Chalfant & Pysh, 1989). Henderson (1986) describes the functioning of a "building planning and placement team," a group of full-time and part-time professionals assigned to a given school building to diagnose special needs, deliver services, and review children's placements.

Many students with disabilities need services from several different disciplines. One survey of handicapped preschool children in a noncategorical public school program found that, of the 81 children receiving services, 56 were served by four or more professionals, 16 were served by three professionals, and 9 were served by two professionals. No child was served by only one professional (Northcott & Erickson, 1977). In view of the recent expansion of services to handicapped infants, toddlers, and preschool children under P.L. 99–457 and the ongoing concern for planning transitional services for young adults after they leave programs of special education, the practice of involving professional and paraprofessional personnel as a team to assess students and plan cooperatively to meet their diverse needs is gaining even wider acceptance.

Although there are many variations of the team approach in terms of size and structure, each member of a team generally assumes certain clearly assigned responsibilities and recognizes the importance of learning from, contributing to, and interacting with the other members of the team. Many believe that the consensus and group decisions arising from a team's involvement provide a form of insurance against erroneous or arbitrary conclusions in the complex issues that face educators of exceptional students.

In practice, three different team models have emerged (Giangreco, York, & Rainforth, 1989; Woodruff & McGonigel, 1988). *Multidisciplinary teams* are composed of professionals from different disciplines who work independently of one another. Each team member conducts assessments, plans interventions, and delivers services. Teams that operate according to a multidisciplinary structure risk the danger of not providing services that recognize the child as an integrated whole; they tend to "splinter" the child into segments along disciplinary lines. (An old saying described the handicapped child as giving "his hands to the occupational therapist, his legs to the physical therapist, and his brain to the teacher" [Williamson, 1978].) Another concern is the lack of communication among team members.

An *interdisciplinary team* is characterized by formal channels of communication between members. While each professional usually conducts discipline-specific assessments, the interdisciplinary team meets to share information and develop intervention plans. Each team member is generally responsible for implementing a portion of the service plan related to his discipline.

The highest level of team involvement, but the most difficult to accomplish, is the *transdisciplinary team*. Members of transdisciplinary teams share information and expertise across discipline boundaries, enabling the selection of goals and planning of services that are discipline-free. Members of transdisciplinary teams also share roles (role release), conducting joint assessments and integrated therapy (Giangreco, York, & Rainforth, 1989). Figure 2.3 shows the relationship among professionals and the student that are likely to develop with each of the three types of teams. Regardless of the team model, team members must learn to put aside professional rivalries and work for the benefit of the student.

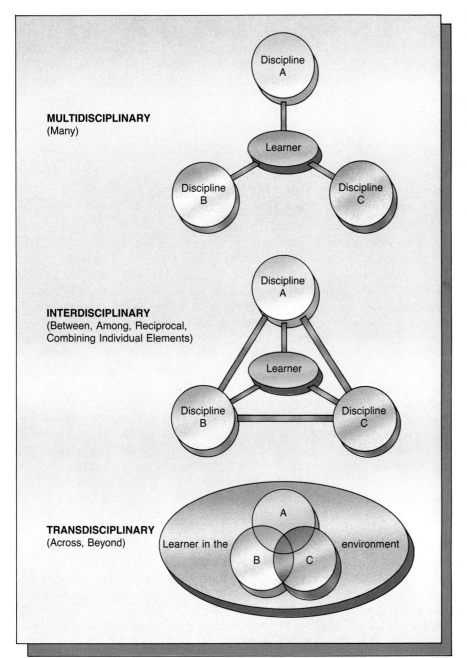

MULTIDISCIPLINARY
(Many)

INTERDISCIPLINARY
(Between, Among, Reciprocal,
Combining Individual Elements)

TRANSDISCIPLINARY
(Across, Beyond)

FIGURE 2.3
Relationships among professionals from various disciplines and the learner in three different team models. (*Source:* From "Providing Related Services to Learners with Severe Handicaps in Educational Settings: Pursuing the Least Restrictive Option" by M. F. Giangreco, J. York, and B. Rainforth, 1989, *Pediatric Physical Therapy, 1*(2), p. 57. Reprinted by permission.)

The team approach is thought to be more cost-effective, because professionals can share their expertise and serve a greater number of children through consultation. An effective team, with all members sharing their information and skills, can do much to provide an appropriate and consistent educational program for exceptional children and to enhance the individual effectiveness of each of its members. Of course, not all these advantages are realized in all cases.

It is sometimes difficult for members of an interdisciplinary team to agree on what learning objectives are most important for the child. In response to this problem, various strategies have developed to help IEP planning teams set priorities for a child's learning goals while giving equal consideration to each member's input (Dardig & Heward, 1981b; Giangreco, Cloninger, & Iverson, 1990). Recently, educators have recognized the importance of including the student with disabilities as an integral member of the team (Peters, 1990; Villa & Thousand, in press).

■ REGULAR AND SPECIAL EDUCATION: A NEW RELATIONSHIP?

How can special education and regular education work together most effectively for the benefit of all students? Every handicapped child, regardless of the service setting, must have an individualized education program (IEP) developed specially to suit his or her individual abilities and needs. Thus, special educators, regular educators, and parents should not be in an us-versus-them relationship. Instead, they must all work together to individualize instruction, manage behavior, and plan cooperatively to meet students' immediate and long-range needs.

Although not all exceptional children attend regular classes, it is generally true that regular teachers are expected to deal with a much wider variety of learning, behavioral, sensory, and physical differences among their students than was the case just a few years ago. Thus, provision of inservice training for regular educators is an important (and sometimes overlooked) requirement of P.L. 94–142. Regular educators are understandably wary of having exceptional children placed in their classes when little or no training or support is provided. The role of regular teachers is already a demanding one; they do not want their classrooms to become any larger, especially if they perceive exceptional children as unmanageable. Regular classroom teachers are entitled to be involved in decisions about children who are placed in their classes and to be offered continuous consultation and other supportive services from special educators (Heron & Harris, 1987; Idol, 1989; West & Idol, 1990).

The relationship between special education and regular education has been the subject of a great deal of debate and discussion in recent years. Stainback and Stainback (1984) were among the first to call for a merger of special and regular education, contending that the current dual system is inefficient and outdated: "It is time to stop developing criteria for who does or does not belong in the mainstream and instead turn the spotlight to increasing the capabilities of the regular school environment, the mainstream, to meet the needs of all students" (p. 110).

Proponents cite the following as major problems that indicate a merger between regular and special education is warranted:

♦ Overlapping of programs for low-achieving and mildly handicapped students

♦ High costs of assessing and placing students with disabilities in "pull-out" programs of questionable effectiveness

- Large numbers of children in regular classrooms who are failing or academically at-risk but whose needs are not being met because they do not meet the eligibility criteria for special education (e.g., Gartner & Lipsky, 1987; Wang, Reynolds, & Walberg, 1985; Will, 1986)

Most often referred to as the **regular education initiative (REI)**, it would consist of the "joining of demonstrably effective practices from special, compensatory, and general education to establish a general education system that is more inclusive and better serves all students, particularly those who require greater-than-usual educational support" (Reynolds, Wang, & Walberg, 1987, p. 394).

Lilly (1986) contends that the barriers between general and special education are gradually being broken down and that, although supportive services are needed by many students who have difficulty in learning and behaving, "we need not and should not offer these services through special education. . . . A single coordinated system of service delivery is preferable to the array of special programs currently offered in the schools" (p. 10).

For additional arguments and supportive data in favor of REI see Bilken and Zollers (1986); Stainback and Stainback (1987); and Wang and Walberg (1988).

The idea of merging general and special education is by no means universally popular. Mesinger (1985) describes Stainback and Stainback as holding "a distinctly minority viewpoint" and explains, "I am reluctant to abandon special education as a system until I see evidence of a drastic improvement in regular educational teacher training and professional practice in the public schools" (p. 512). Similarly, Lieberman (1985) calls for special education to maintain its separate identity because, among other reasons, "in regular education, the system dictates the curriculum; in special education, the child dictates the curriculum" (p. 514).

For additional arguments and supportive data questioning the wisdom of merging regular and special education without a clear base of research and practice, see Hallahan, Keller, McKinney, Lloyd, and Bryan (1988); Kauffman, Gerber, and Semmel (1988); Kauffman and Pullen (1989); Keogh (1988); and Schumaker and Deschler (1988).

Partially in response to the REI, a number of research and demonstration projects have been developed and tested to restructure the delivery of educational services to exceptional children in the regular classroom. Two of the most well-known are the Adaptive Learning Environments Model (ALEM), developed by Wang (1980) and her colleagues, and Mainstreaming Experiences for Learning Disabled Students (Project MELD), developed by Zigmond and Baker (1987). Zigmond and Baker (1990) acknowledged the difficulty of ensuring quality instructional services for students with handicaps in their report of a 2-year study of the academic progress and social behavior of 13 students with learning disabilities who participated in a Project MELD school.

> A successful alternative to pull-out (resource or self-contained) special education programs requires more than the administrative fiat to "put children back." Returning students with learning disabilities to the mainstream should be the catalyst for a schoolwide improvement effort. The current data make it clear that such students will not make progress if teachers continue with "business as usual." (p. 185)

Although Wang and Walberg (1988) claim success for most students with mild disabilities served by the ALEM model, Fuchs and Fuchs (1988a, 1988b) reviewed research on ALEM and concluded that the "jury is still out" (Fuchs & Fuchs, 1988a, p. 125).

> Before establishing a merger between special and general education, we hope parents, teachers, researchers, and policymakers insist on additional empirical

When regular and special educators work together, exceptional children can only benefit.

studies of full-time, large-scale mainstreaming and persuasive evidence that such programs indeed work as their creators claim they do. If these programs are implemented widely without sufficient validation, we fear many handicapped children and teachers may suffer. (p. 126)

Most educators, whether in regular or special education, realize that, regardless of where services are delivered, the most crucial variable is the quality of instruction that children receive. We agree with Keogh's (1990) conclusion:

It is clear that major changes are needed in the delivery of services to problem learners, and that these services need to be the responsibility of regular as well as special educators. It is also clear that teachers are the central players in bringing about change in practice. It follows, then, that our greatest and most pressing challenge in the reform effort is to determine how to improve the quality of instruction at the classroom level. (p. 190)

■ PROMISE, PROGRESS, AND PROBLEMS

The promise of a free, appropriate public education for all children with disabilities was indeed an ambitious one. The process of bringing this goal about has been described in such lofty terms as a "revolution" and a "new Bill of Rights" for exceptional persons (Goodman, 1976). Today, most observers acknowledge that substantial progress has been made toward fulfillment of that promise.

Since P.L. 94–142 was enacted more than a decade ago (the law was not fully implemented until 1980), there has been a steady increase in the number of exceptional children identified and served in public educational programs. As noted in Chapter 1, the U.S. Department of Education (1990) reported that approximately 4.5 million handicapped students received special education and related services during the 1988–89 school year. Two-thirds of those children spend at least part of each school day in regular classrooms, and only about 7% of all children with disabilities now receive their education in places other than regular school buildings. There has been an especially rapid increase in the number of adolescents and young adults with disabilities who have recently been provided with special education services.

Turnbull et al. (1986) observe that P.L. 94–142 has had far-reaching effects: "The student is no longer required to fit the school, but the school is required to fit the student" (p. 183). Schools today provide far more than academic training. In effect, they have become diversified agencies offering such services as medical support, physical therapy, vocational training, parent counseling, recreation, special transportation, and inservice education for staff members. In place of the once-prevalent practice of excluding children with disabilities from programs, schools now seek the most appropriate ways of including them. Schools are committed to providing wide-ranging services to children from different backgrounds and with different characteristics.

Many citizens—both within and outside the field of education—have welcomed the recognition of disabled children's rights in their schools and communities. Additionally, the greater involvement of parents and families in the educational process and the emphasis on team planning to meet individual needs throughout the life span are widely regarded as positive developments. Reports from teachers and students, as well as a growing number of data-based studies, indicate that many children with disabilities are being successfully educated in regular schools and that, for the most part, they are well accepted by their nondisabled schoolmates. Examples of effective mainstreaming programs can be found at age levels ranging from preschool (Esposito & Reed, 1986; Jenkins, Speltz, & Odom, 1985) to high school (Warger, Aldinger, & Okun, 1983), and they include exceptional children whose disabilities range from mild (Algozzine & Korinek, 1985; Thomas & Jackson, 1986) to severe (Brinker, 1985; Condon, York, Heal, & Fortschneider, 1986).

Despite this ample evidence of progress toward providing equal educational opportunity, it is equally true that many people—again, within and outside the field of education—have detected significant problems in the implementation of P.L. 94–142. Many school administrators maintain that the federal government has never granted sufficient financial resources to the states and local school districts to assist them in providing special services, which are often very costly. Special education teachers express dissatisfaction over excessive paperwork, unclear guidelines, and inappropriate grouping of exceptional students. Regular class teachers contend that they receive little or no training or support when exceptional children are placed in their classes. Some parents of handicapped and nonhandicapped children have voiced opposition to the integration of exceptional children in regular classes. Some observers find that the schedules and procedures used in mainstreaming programs actually allow for relatively little integration (Sansone & Zigmond, 1986). There are many other problems, real and perceived, and no "quick fix" or easy solution can be offered.

1992 marks the graduation year for many students with disabilities who began first grade when P.L. 94–142 was fully implemented.

Special education is at a crossroads. Once, the primary issue for exceptional children was that of access. Would they receive an education at all? Could they be served in their local community? Some access problems persist (for children who live in poverty or in institutions or in extremely isolated areas, for example), but now "the primary issue of contention in special education is whether students will receive a quality education in regular public schools" (Biklen, 1985, p. 174).

Special education is continually evolving and is in the process of defining its relationship with regular education. A significantly greater proportion of tomorrow's children and youth will be "educationally at risk because they will have grown up in poverty and will be racially, ethnically, and linguistically diverse" (Weintraub, 1986, p. 1). Many new technologies are becoming available, but whether they will effectively enhance the quality of instruction remains to be seen. There is room for improvement in the quality of vocational training and employment opportunities for people with disabilities, and attitudinal barriers still prohibit full acceptance of individuals with disabilities in schools, neighborhoods, and workplaces.

Can we fulfill the promise of a free, appropriate public education for all exceptional students? The answer will depend on the readiness of professionals to work together, assume new roles, communicate with each other, and involve parents, families, and exceptional individuals themselves. As Weintraub and Abeson (1974) wrote almost 20 years ago in support of the Education for All Handicapped Children Act, "At the minimum, it will make educational opportunities a reality for all handicapped children. At the maximum, it will make our schools healthier learning environments for all our children" (p. 529).

SUMMARY

Special Education as Civil Rights

♦ The move to extend educational opportunities to children with disabilities is an outgrowth of the civil rights movement.

♦ All children are now recognized to have the right to equal protection under the law, which has been interpreted to mean the right to a free public education in the least restrictive, most appropriate setting.

♦ All children and their parents have the right to due process under the law, which includes the rights to be notified of any decision affecting the child's educational placement, to have a hearing and present a defense, to see a written decision, and to appeal any decision.

♦ Court cases have also established the rights of handicapped children to fair assessment in their native language and to education at public expense, regardless of the school district's financial constraints.

P.L. 94–142: The Individuals with Disabilities Education Act

♦ P.L. 94–142 made many trends in special education part of federal law. It extends public education to all children with disabilities between the ages of 3 and 21.

- P.L. 94–142 requires that students with disabilities be educated in the least restrictive environment (LRE). LRE is a relative concept (i.e., the regular classroom is not necessarily the best placement for every student) stipulating that to the maximum extent possible handicapped students are to be educated with nonhandicapped peers in regular educational environments. The law also sets out requirements for diagnosis, nondiscriminatory assessment, individualization of programming, and personnel development.

- Court cases have challenged the way particular school districts implement specific provisions of P.L. 94–142. No trend has emerged, but rulings from the various cases have established the principle that each handicapped student is entitled to a personalized program of instruction and supportive services that will enable him to benefit from an education in as integrated a setting as possible.

- Education for the Handicapped Act Amendments of 1986 (P.L. 99–457) required states to provide special education services to all handicapped preschoolers aged 3 to 5 by 1991 or lose all future federal funds for preschoolers with handicaps. This law also makes available federal money to encourage states to develop early intervention programs for handicapped and at-risk infants and toddlers from birth to age 2. Early intervention services must be coordinated by an individualized family services plan.

- Gifted and Talented Children's Education Act (P.L. 95–561) provides financial incentives to states for developing programs for gifted and talented students.

- Section 504 of the Rehabilitation Act forbids discrimination in all federally funded programs, including educational and vocational programs, on the basis of handicap alone.

- Americans with Disabilities Act (P.L. 101–336) extends the civil rights protections to persons with disabilities to private sector employment, all public services, public accommodations, transportation, and telecommunications.

Special Education in the Schools: Moving Beyond Compliance and Toward Excellence

- The least restrictive environment remains controversial; it does not mean moving all children with disabilities into regular classrooms, but rather that each student should be placed in the most integrated setting in which he can succeed.

- A team approach, in which teachers, other professionals, and paraprofessionals share information and skills, can help make each student's education as effective and consistent as possible.

- Assessment should be an ongoing part of a child's program.

- The individualized education program (IEP), which many teachers have been using in one form or another for years, is simply a way to ensure that each child is assessed, that long-range goals and short-term objectives are established, and that the child's progress is evaluated regularly.

Regular and Special Education: A New Relationship?

- Some special educators are calling for a merger between regular and special education; this movement is called the *regular education initiative* (REI).

- Opponents of the REI are concerned that students with disabilities may not receive the services they need in the general education system.

- All agree, however, that special and regular educators must work cooperatively to improve the quality of instruction.

Promise, Progress, and Problems

♦ Schools seek to include rather than exclude children with disabilities.

♦ Studies have shown that well-planned, carefully conducted mainstreaming can be generally effective with students of all ages, types, and degrees of disability.

♦ Implementation of P.L. 94–142 has brought problems of funding, inadequate teacher training, and opposition by some to integration of children with disabilities into regular classes.

FOR MORE INFORMATION

Journals

All of the journals listed at the end of Chapter 1 are relevant to the content of Chapter 2.

Journal of Disability Policy Studies. Publishes research, discussion, and review articles addressing a broad range of topics on disability policy from the perspective of a variety of academic disciplines. Published quarterly by the Department of Rehabilitation Education and Research, University of Arkansas, 346 N. West Avenue, Fayetteville, AK 72701.

Journal of Educational and Psychological Consultation. Published quarterly by the Association for Educational and Psychological Consultants, Lawrence Erlbaum Associates, Inc., 365 Broadway, Hillsdale, NJ 07642.

Books

Biklen, D., Bogdan, R., Ferguson, D. L., Searl, S. J., & Taylor, S. J. (1985). *Achieving the complete school: Strategies for effective mainstreaming.* New York: Teachers College Press.

Gaylord-Ross, R. (Ed.). (1989). *Integration strategies for students with handicaps.* Baltimore: Paul H. Brookes.

Heron, T. E., & Harris, K. C. (1987). *The educational consultant: Helping professionals, parents and mainstreamed students* (2nd ed.). Austin, TX: Pro-Ed.

Lewis, R. B., & Doorlag, D. H. (1991). *Teaching special students in the mainstream* (3rd ed.). Columbus, OH: Merrill.

Lipsky, D. K., & Gartner, A. (Eds.). (1989). *Beyond special education: Quality education for all.* Baltimore: Paul H. Brookes.

Skrtic, T. M. (in press). *Exploring the theory/practice link in special education: A critical analysis.* Reston, VA: Council for Exceptional Children.

Skrtic, T. M. (in press). *Behind special education: A critical analysis of professional knowledge and school organization.* Denver: Love.

Slavin, R. E., Karweit, N., & Maden, N. A. (1990). *Effective programs for students at-risk.* Needham Heights, MA: Allyn & Bacon.

Stainback, S., & Stainback, W. (Eds.). (in press). *Teaching in the inclusive classroom: Curricular design, adaptation, and delivery.* Baltimore: Paul H. Brookes.

Strickland, B. B., & Turnbull, A. P. (1990). *Developing and implementing individualized education programs* (3rd ed.). Columbus, OH: Merrill.

Turnbull, H. R. (1986). *Free appropriate public education: The law and children with disabilities*. Denver: Love.

Wang, M., Reynolds, M. C., & Walberg, H. J. (Eds.). (1987). *Handbook of special education: Research and practice* (Vol 1). New York: Pergamon Press.

Weintraub, F. J. (1986). *Goals for the future of special education*. Reston, VA: Council for Exceptional Children.

Wood, J. W. (1989). *Mainstreaming: A practical approach for teachers*. Columbus, OH: Merrill.

Zins, J. E., Curtis, M., Graden, J., & Ponti, C. R. (1988). *Helping students succeed in the regular classroom: A guide for developing intervention assistance programs*. San Francisco: Jossey-Bass.

PART II
Exceptional Children

3
Mental Retardation

- ◆ Why has the definition of mental retardation changed so much over the years?

- ◆ What do you think is more important: IQ or adaptive behavior?

- ◆ How is mental retardation a socially-defined phenomenon?

- ◆ What should school programs for students with mental retardation emphasize?

- ◆ How are independent functioning and the principle of normalization interrelated?

Most people have some notion of what mental retardation is and what people with mental retardation are like. Unfortunately, although there is growing public awareness concerning mental retardation, too much of that awareness still consists of misconceptions and oversimplifications. In this chapter we examine some key factors in understanding the very complex concept known as **mental retardation**. We also describe some contemporary teaching methods and service delivery practices that are helping improve the quality of life for children and adults with mental retardation—one of the largest categories of exceptionality.

When people hear the words "special education," they usually think first of mental retardation. Mental retardation is the oldest "field" within special education in the United States. The first public school special education programs began in 1896 with classes for children with mental retardation. Of course, things have changed a great deal since then. During the past 25 years especially we have witnessed significant improvements in the education and treatment of children and adults with retarded development. After more than a century of virtually complete exclusion and segregation from everyday society, people with mental retardation are beginning to experience some of the benefits and responsibilities of participation in the mainstream.

■ HISTORY OF TREATMENT AND SERVICES FOR PEOPLE WITH MENTAL RETARDATION

The history of mental retardation is long. No doubt some people have been slower to learn than others for as long as people have populated the earth. The Greeks in 1552 B.C. and the Romans in 449 B.C. were among the first to recognize people officially as mentally retarded. There are even passages in the Bible referring to slow learners (Barr, 1913; Lindman & McIntyre, 1961).

Several special educators and historians have written detailed and interesting accounts of how philosophies about and treatment of people with mental retardation have changed over the years. For example, Hewett and Forness (1977) describe the role and importance of survival, superstition, science, and service in the treatment of people with mental retardation during different historical periods. Kolstoe and Frey (1965) describe five chronological eras of treatment: extermination, ridicule, asylum, education, and occupational adequacy. Gearheart and Litton (1975) characterize the early history of mental retardation (prior to the 1800s) as consisting primarily of superstition and extermination; the 19th century as the era that produced institutions for mentally retarded persons; the 20th century as the era of public school classes; the 1950s and 1960s as the era of legislation and national support; and the 1970s as the era of normalization, child advocacy, and litigation. Here we can only briefly describe some of the changing attitudes and significant events that have affected how persons with mental retardation have been treated over the years.

Attitudes in Early Societies

The primary goal of human beings in primitive societies was survival. The sick, physically disabled, and elderly were often abandoned or even killed to increase the chance of survival by others. The Greeks and Romans often sent mentally and physically disabled children far away from the community, where they would perish on their own. Later, as survival became less a 24-hour concern and society separated into levels, ridicule of mentally retarded people was common. Superstitions and myths developed. Words like *idiot, imbecile,* and *dunce* were used, and some kings and queens and other wealthy people kept "fools" or imbeciles as clowns or court jesters.

During the Middle Ages, as religion became a dominant force, a more humanitarian view was taken. Asylums and monasteries were opened to care for people with mental retardation. No one thought, however, that the behavior of a mentally retarded person could be altered.

Nineteenth Century Advancements

At the beginning of the 19th century, the first attempt to educate an individual with mental retardation was recorded. In 1798 three hunters found and captured an 11- or 12-year-old boy in the woods of Aveyron, France. The boy—later called Victor, the Wild Boy of Aveyron (Itard, 1894/1962)—was completely unsocialized and had no language. He was pronounced an "incurable idiot." Jean Marc Gaspard Itard, a physician working at an institution for the deaf, refused to believe that Victor was uneducable. Itard began a program of intensive training with Victor. After almost 5 years he concluded his work, deeming it a miserable failure because he did not reach his original goals for Victor. The changes that did occur with Victor, however, were significant: He was much more socialized and could read and write a few words. "The French Academy of Science encouraged Itard to publish his memoirs of his work with Victor. Itard did, which not only made Itard very famous, but may have been the single most important event in the creation of what is now viewed as a genuine field" (Blatt, 1987, p. 34).

Another Frenchman, Edouard Seguin, had tremendous influence on the creation of facilities and educational programs for mentally retarded persons in this country. Seguin, who had worked briefly with Itard prior to Itard's death in 1838 and was inspired by the work with Victor, immigrated to the United States in 1848. He later helped establish the Pennsylvania Training School, an early educational facility.

Advocacy in the United States

The first person to advocate educational programs for children with mental retardation in the United States was Samuel Gridley Howe, who had already devoted much of his life to educating children who were blind or deaf. Thanks to his powerful letter arguing for the rights of people with mental retardation in a democratic society, the Massachusetts legislature in 1848 overrode the governor's veto and provided Howe with $2,500 for the first institution for mentally retarded persons in this country. During the remainder of the 19th century, large state institutions for individuals who were mentally retarded or mentally ill (they were often viewed as the same) became the primary means of service delivery. As the institutions became overcrowded and understaffed, the optimism sparked by the educational gains produced by Itard, Seguin, and Howe began to wane. State institutions came to be considered custodial rather than educational, a view that has taken years of effort to change, extending even to the present.

See Bogdan (1986) for historical documentation of the exhibition of mentally retarded people for amusement and profit, from 1850–1940. Even the right to life itself has not always been a given for persons with mental retardation. See Hollander (1989) for a review and discussion of the *eugenics* movement and euthanasia ("mercy killing") of persons who are mentally retarded.

Many consider Itard to be the father of special education.

Readers wishing to learn more about the history of mental retardation might begin by reading Blatt (1987), MacMillan (1982), Patton, Beirne-Smith, & Payne (1990), and Scheerenberger (1983).

The first public school class for children with mental retardation was formed in 1896 in Providence, Rhode Island. Thus began the special class movement, which saw 87,030 children enrolled in special classes in 1948; 703,800 in 1969; and 1,305,000 in 1974, the year before the signing of P.L. 94–142. The great increases in the number of children being served by the public schools paralleled increases in federal aid to education, particularly to special education, in the 1950s and 1960s.

In recent years we have witnessed a move away from segregated special schools and large state-operated institutions as the most common educational and residential placements for persons with mental retardation. The trend is toward education in the least restrictive environment—which includes the regular classroom for a significant and growing number of children with mental retardation—and more normalized lifestyles for adults with mental retardation.

■ DEFINING MENTAL RETARDATION

The term *mental retardation*, when properly applied, describes performance; it is not a "thing" children are born with or possess.

Mental retardation is, above all, a label; it is a term used to identify an observed performance deficit—failure to demonstrate age-appropriate intellectual and social behavior. Numerous definitions of mental retardation have been proposed, debated, revised, and counterproposed over the years; the debate over definition continues today.

Since mental retardation is a concept that affects and is affected by people in many different disciplines, it has been defined from many different perspectives. Because physicians were the first professional group to work with people with mental retardation, it is not surprising that most early definitions emphasized biological or medical criteria. A definition used by a professional within a given discipline may be functional only from the perspective of that particular field; for example, although a definition of mental retardation based on biological or medical criteria may be useful to physicians, a medically-oriented definition is of little value to the teacher or psychologist.

Disagreements among professionals over what constitutes mental retardation are "not merely academic exercises in semantics" (MacMillan, 1982). A subtle difference between two definitions can determine whether or not the label of mental retardation will be affixed to a particular child. The critical importance of definition was noted as early as 1924 by Kuhlman, who recognized that definitions of mental deficiency are used to "decide the fate of thousands every year" (Kuhlmann, 1924).

Why is classifying someone as mentally retarded or not mentally retarded so important? Some children and adults are so clearly deficient in academic, social, and self-care skills that it is obvious to anyone who interacts with them that they require special services and educational programming. For these individuals, how mental retardation is defined is not much of an issue; they experience substantial deficits in all or most areas of development. But this group comprises a small portion of the total population of persons identified as mentally retarded. The largest segment consists of school-age children with mild retardation. Thus, how mental retardation is defined determines what special educational services many thousands of children are eligible (or ineligible) to receive.

Which one is mentally retarded? The term *mental retardation* identifies an observed performance deficit; such individuals also possess strengths and positive attributes.

In early times, only those persons with severe deficits in cognitive functioning or personal competence were identified as mentally retarded; the term *idiocy* was used (derived from a Greek word meaning "people who did not hold public office" [MacMillan, 1982]). In the 19th century, the label *imbecile* (derived from the Latin word for "weak and feeble") was applied to not-so-severely retarded people. In 1900, Ireland defined the two terms this way:

> Idiocy is mental deficiency, or extreme stupidity, depending upon malnutrition or disease of the nervous centers, occurring either before birth or before the evolution of mental faculties in childhood. The word imbecility is generally used to denote a less decided degree of mental incapacity. (p. 1)

The term *simpleton* was eventually added to identify persons who today might be considered mildly mentally retarded (Clausen, 1967).

The two definitions most widely used during the first half of this century were written by Tredgold and Doll. Tredgold's (1937) reads,

> A state of incomplete mental development of such a kind and degree that the individual is incapable of adapting himself to the normal environment of his fel-

lows in such a way to maintain existence independently of supervision, control, or external support. (p. 4)

In 1941 Doll suggested six criteria essential to the definition and concept of mental retardation:

These are (1) social incompetence, (2) due to mental subnormality, (3) which has been developmentally arrested, (4) which obtains at maturity, (5) is of constitutional origin, and (6) is essentially incurable. (p. 215)

The AAMR Definition

In 1959 the American Association on Mental Retardation (AAMR) published its first manual on terminology and classification of mental retardation that included a definition; that definition was revised slightly in 1961 to read,

Mental retardation refers to subaverage general intellectual functioning which originates during the developmental period and is associated with impairment in adaptive behavior. (Heber, 1961, p. 3)

In 1973 the AAMR made major changes in the definition that, with slight rewording, appears in the organization's most recent manual on terminology:

Mental retardation refers to significantly subaverage general intellectual functioning resulting in or associated with deficits in adaptive behavior, and manifested during the developmental period. (Grossman, 1983, p. 11)

At first glance, the two definitions may appear the same: they use the same terminology and similar word order. There are, however, important differences. First, according to the 1961 definition, mental retardation is equated with "subaverage general intellectual functioning" *associated with* adaptive behavior impairments. According to the revised definition, however, an individual must be well below average in both intellectual functioning and adaptive behavior; that is, intellectual functioning is no longer the sole defining criterion. A second important change is the degree of subaverage intellectual functioning that must be demonstrated before a person is considered mentally retarded. The word *significantly* in the current definition refers to a score of two or more standard deviations below the mean on a standardized intelligence test (which we will explain in the next section); the 1961 definition required a score of only one standard deviation below the mean. This change eliminated the category of *borderline* mental retardation. A third change, although not as important as the first two, extended the developmental period from 16 years to 18 years, to coincide with the usual span of public schooling. The definition specifies that the deficits in intellectual functioning and adaptive behavior must occur during the developmental period to help distinguish mental retardation from other disabilities (for instance, impaired performance by an adult due to head injury).

Measuring Intellectual Functioning

Intellectual functioning is most often measured by a standardized intelligence (IQ) test. An IQ test consists of a series of questions and problem-solving tasks assumed to require certain amounts of intelligence to answer or solve correctly. Although an IQ test samples only a small portion of the full range of an individual's skills and abilities, the test taker's performance on those items is used to derive a score representing his/her overall intelligence.

A *standardized* test consists of the same questions and tasks always presented in a certain, specified way, with the same scoring procedures used each time the test is administered. An IQ test has also been *normed;* that is, it has been administered to a large sample of people, selected at random from the population for whom the test is intended. Test scores of the people in the random sample are then used as norms, or averages of how people perform on the test. On the two most widely used intelligence tests, the Stanford-Binet Intelligence Scale (Thorndike, Hagen, & Sattler, 1986) and the revised Wechsler Intelligence Scale for Children (WISC-R) (Wechsler, 1974), the norm or average score is 100.

Standard deviation is a mathematical concept. It refers to the amount by which a particular score on a given test varies from the mean, or average score, of all the scores in the norm sample. (See Figure 3.1 for further information about standard deviation.) One standard deviation on the Stanford-Binet is 16 points; on the WISC-R, 15 points. (The difference stems from the difference in the distribution of scores obtained from the samples of children used to derive

The test taker's age is considered when computing an IQ. To obtain a score of 100, a 5-year-old child must respond correctly to those questions and tasks most 5-year-olds get right. A 16-year-old who responds correctly to only those test items the average 5-year-old gets right would receive a score much lower than 100.

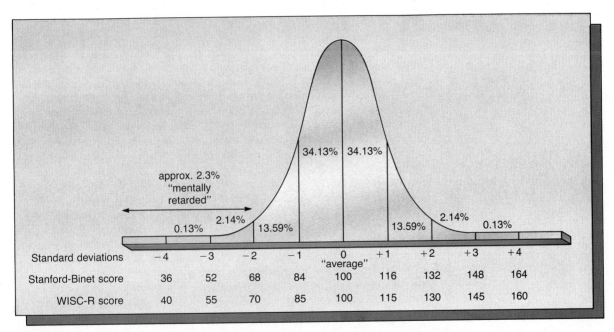

Standard deviations	−4	−3	−2	−1	0 "average"	+1	+2	+3	+4
Stanford-Binet score	36	52	68	84	100	116	132	148	164
WISC-R score	40	55	70	85	100	115	130	145	160

FIGURE 3.1

IQ scores seem to be distributed throughout the population according to a phenomenon called the normal curve, shown above. To describe how one particular score varies from the mean (average score), the population is broken into units called standard deviations. Each standard deviation includes a fixed portion of the population. For example, we know that 34.13% of the population will fall within one standard deviation above the mean, and another 34.13% will be within one standard deviation below "normal." By applying an algebraic formula to the scores achieved by the norm sample on a test, we can tell what value equals one standard deviation for that test. A person's IQ test score can then be described in terms of how many standard deviations above or below the mean it is. In this graph we can see that about 2.3% of the population falls two or more standard deviations below the mean, which the AAMR calls "significantly subaverage." That means that if IQ scores were the sole criterion, about 2.3% of the population would be considered mentally retarded.

the norms for the two tests.) Thus, according to the AAMR's earlier definition, a child could be labeled mentally retarded on the basis of an IQ score as high as 84 or 85, depending on the test used. The current AAMR definition of mental retardation requires an IQ score two standard deviations below the mean, which is 68 or 70 on the two tests.

There are a number of reasons that educators and other professionals in mental retardation advocated the revised AAMR definition, which is much more conservative than the earlier definition in terms of who is to be called mentally retarded. Four of those reasons are summarized in Figure 3.2.

Robinson and Robinson (1976), in their excellent discussion of intelligence testing, summarize some potential values and pitfalls of IQ tests.

> The development and popular utilization of the IQ as a single, simple, objective index of the rate of intellectual growth has been a mixed blessing. When properly understood and carefully used, an IQ test can be valuable in assessing a child's rate of progress, but it refers to only those aspects of mental ability tapped by a particular test. Its measurement is subject to error from a number of sources, some of them capable of drastically affecting scores. There is little doubt that IQs have been seriously misused because of persistent and erroneous notions about their supposed permanence or their magical power to predict future performance. Such a simple index of present behavior as the IQ cannot possibly reflect all the many aspects of the complex developmental phenomenon known as intelligence.
>
> Nowhere has the IQ proved to be a more mixed blessing than in matters concerning the welfare of mentally retarded children. To be sure, the development of intelligence tests provided a means for more objective assessment. Tests have been very useful in helping to identify children who need special training and in establishing more orderly methods for admissions procedures in institutions. Many retarded children have been helped to lead more productive lives because of the early identification of their problems. Other children whose school failures were not due to overall intellectual deficits have also been identified and treated accordingly.
>
> On the other hand, the apparent simplicity of the IQ led to an enthusiastic but largely misguided movement to label or classify children primarily on the basis of their scores on intelligence tests. Accurate classification of intellectual deficit was thought to be all that was required to achieve understanding of retarded children, individual characteristics being grossly underestimated. Furthermore, undue belief in IQ constancy led to a diminution in research and treatment. Professional interest in many complex problems declined over a long period, not to be rejuvenated until the mid-1960s. Fortunately, a more realistic view now prevails. (p. 343)

A recent alternative to traditional tests of intelligence is the Kaufman Assessment Battery for Children (K-ABC) (Kaufman & Kaufman, 1983). The K-ABC is based on the theory that intelligence is composed of two different information-processing abilities: sequential processing and simultaneous processing. "Sequential processing places a premium on the serial or temporal order of stimuli when solving problems; in contrast, simultaneous processing demands a gestalt-like, frequently spatial, integration of stimuli to solve problems with maximum efficiency" (Kaufman & Kaufman, 1983, p. 2). Some view the K-ABC as a significant advancement in understanding and measuring of children's intelligence, and some school psychologists use the test as part of

1. *Concern that labeling a child mentally retarded is stigmatizing.* Some educators feel that when a child is officially labeled mentally retarded, the damage done by the label itself outweighs any positive effects of special education and treatment that result from the label (Kugel & Wolfensberger, 1969; Smith & Neisworth, 1975). Although recent studies have shown that children and adults continue to hold negative misconceptions about mental retardation (e.g., Antonak, Fiedler, & Mulick, 1989; Goodman, 1989), research on whether the label *mental retardation* is itself responsible for negative stereotyping has yielded mixed results.*

2. *Intelligence tests can be culturally biased.* Both the Binet and Wechsler IQ tests have been heavily criticized for being culturally biased. The tests tend to favor children from the population on which they were normed—primarily white, middle-class children. Some of the questions on an IQ test may tap learning that only a middle-class child is likely to have experienced. Both tests, which are highly verbal, are especially inappropriate for children for whom English is a second language. Mercer (1973a) points out that when an IQ test is used to identify children for special class placement, many more black, Mexican-American, and poor children are labeled mentally retarded than are white, middle-class children.

3. *IQ scores can change significantly.* Several studies have shown that IQ scores can change, particularly in the 70–85 range that formerly constituted borderline retardation (MacMillan, 1982). Because of the misconception that mental retardation is a permanent condition even though it is intended to describe only present deficits in performance, there is hesitancy to label mentally retarded on the basis of a test score that might increase by as many as 15 to 20 points after a period of effective instruction.

4. *Intelligence testing is not an exact science.* Even though the major intelligence tests are among the most carefully developed and standardized of all psychological tests, they are still far from perfect. Among the many variables that can affect an individual's final score on an IQ test are motivation, the time and location of the test, and bias on the test giver's part in scoring responses that are not precisely covered by the test manual. Even the choice of which test to use can be critical. For example, Wechsler (1974) reports that the WISC–R and the revised Stanford-Binet correlate with each other at about the .70 level. This means that it is possible for a child to be identified as mentally retarded by one test but not by the other.

---

*See MacMillan, Jones, and Aloia (1974) and Rowitz (1981) for reviews and discussion of labeling and mental retardation. A possible negative outcome of being labeled mentally retarded is that peers may be more likely to avoid or ridicule the child. Read A. Turnbull and G. J. Bronicki (1986) and K. Turnbull and G. J. Bronicki (1989) to find out what two young researchers did to improve children's attitudes about people with mental retardation.

FIGURE 3.2
Four reasons why many professionals advocated the more conservative AAMR definition of mental retardation first published in 1973.

their battery of assessment instruments to determine eligibility for and placement in special education programs. Several authorities on special education assessment suggest, however, that complete acceptance of the new approach be deferred until a significant body of research demonstrates the validity of the K-ABC's constructs and the remedial approach it recommends (McLoughlin & Lewis, 1990; Salvia & Ysseldyke, 1988).

See the Fall 1984 issue of *The Journal of Special Education* for a series of articles on the K-ABC.

Clearly, intelligence tests have both advantages and disadvantages. Here are several more important considerations to keep in mind.

♦ *The concept of intelligence is a hypothetical construct.* No one has ever seen a thing called intelligence; it is not a precise entity, but rather something we infer from observed performance. We assume it takes more intelligence to perform some tasks than it does to perform other tasks.

- *There is nothing mysterious or all-powerful about an IQ test*. An IQ test is simply a series of questions and/or problem-solving tasks.

- *An IQ test measures only how a child performs at one point in time on the items included in one test.* We infer from that performance how a child might perform in other situations.

- *IQ tests have proven to be the best single predictor of school achievement.* Because IQ tests are composed largely of verbal and academic tasks—the same things a child must master to succeed in school—they correlate with school achievement more highly than any other single testing device.

- *In the hands of a competent school psychologist, IQ tests can provide useful information, particularly in objectively identifying an overall performance deficit.*

- *Results from an IQ test are generally not useful in planning individualized educational objectives and teaching strategies for a child.* Direct, teacher-administered, criterion-referenced assessment of a child's performance on the specific skills he needs to learn is more useful for planning instruction.

- *Results from an IQ test should never be used as the only criterion for labeling, classifying, or placing a child in a special program.*

Measuring Adaptive Behavior

> To be classified as mentally retarded, a person must be clearly subnormal in adaptive behavior. It would be pointless to identify and classify as mentally retarded a person who faces no unusual problems or whose needs are met without professional attention. Some people with an IQ below 70 do well in school and society. Such people are not mentally retarded, and should not be labeled as such. (MacMillan, 1982, p. 42)

Many children who used to be called retarded were anything but retarded outside school; they coped very well with the requirements of their homes, their neighborhoods, and their friends. In 1969 the President's Committee on Mental Retardation described the "6-hour retarded child," referring to the fact that many children are considered mentally retarded only during the 6 hours they spend in school each day; during the other 18 hours of the day they function normally and are not considered retarded by the people they interact with. In this sense, the demands of school could be said to "cause" mental retardation. In response to this problem and other criticisms of the use of an IQ score as the sole criterion for mental retardation, the definition was revised to require that a child show deficits in adaptive behavior as well as intellectual functioning.

In the most recent AAMR manual on terminology, adaptive behavior is defined as "the effectiveness or degree with which the individual meets the standards of personal independence and social responsibility expected of his age and social group" (Grossman, 1983, p. 157). AAMR further defines the areas where deficits in adaptive behavior can be found within different age groups.

During infancy and early childhood:

1. Sensorimotor skills

2. Communication skills (speech and language)

A criterion-referenced test for basic math skills, for example, might include 10 single-digit addition problems. Rather than judging the child's ability to compute single-digit math problems by comparing her performance to other children's (as in norm-referenced testing) or inferring it from her work on other types of math problems, the child's performance on the skill in question is compared to a standard criterion. For example, if the criterion is 9 and the child gets 9 or 10 correct, instruction will not be necessary on that skill; if she gets fewer than 9 correct, a teaching program for single-digit addition problems would be implemented.

3. Self-help skills

4. Socialization skills (interacting and getting along with others)

During childhood and early adolescence:

5. Application of basic academic skills in daily life activities

6. Application of appropriate reasoning and judgment in mastery of the environment

7. Social skills (participation in group activities and interpersonal relationships)

During late adolescence and adulthood:

8. Vocational and social responsibility and performance (Grossman, 1973, p. 11–12)

Adaptive Behavior Scale

The most frequently used instrument for assessing adaptive behavior is the AAMR Adaptive Behavior Scale (ABS) (Nihira, Foster, Shellhaas, & Leland, 1974). The ABS consists of two parts: Part 1 consists of 10 domains related to independent functioning and daily living skills, and Part 2 assesses the individual's level of maladaptive (inappropriate) behavior. Table 3.1 lists the areas covered by the ABS, and Figure 3.3 shows one page of Part 1.

Another version of the ABS, the AAMR Adaptive Behavior Scale, School Edition (ABS-SE), has been developed for measuring the adaptive behavior of school children with suspected mild retardation (Lambert & Windmiller, 1981). However, the ABS-SE is quite long: It has 95 items with 3 to 12 subparts per item. A shorter (75 total items) and easier-to-score adaptation of the scale, called the Classroom Adaptive Behavior Checklist, has been developed by Hunsucker, Nelson, and Clark (1986).

The ABS can be administered in several ways. Sometimes it is completed by someone familiar with the person being assessed, such as a direct care worker, teacher, or parent; sometimes an examiner completes the ABS by interviewing a direct care worker or parent; and sometimes direct observation is conducted.

Vineland Social Maturity Scale

The Vineland Social Maturity Scale (Doll, 1965) is another widely used method for assessing adaptive behavior. The Vineland has recently undergone substantial revision and is now available in three different versions under the name Vineland Adaptive Behavior Scales (Sparrow, Balla, & Cicchetti, 1984). Two of the versions, the Interview Editions in Survey Form or Expanded Form, are administered to an individual, such as a teacher or direct caregiver, who knows well the person being assessed. The Classroom Edition is designed to be completed by a teacher.

Assessment of Social Competence

One of the most recent adaptive behavior assessment instruments to be developed is the Assessment of Social Competence (ASC) (Meyer, Cole, McQuarter, & Reichle, 1990). The ASC, which is intended to measure social competence at all levels of social and intellectual functioning, consists of 252 items organized within 11 social functions (e.g., initiates interactions, follows rules, indicates preferences). Each function is further broken down into 8 levels,

Measurement of adaptive behavior is important for reasons other than identifying who will be classified as mentally retarded. The severity of maladaptive behavior emitted by persons with mental retardation is one of the most critical factors in determining their placement and success in many school, work, and residential settings (Campbell, Smith, & Wool, 1982). Because Part 2 of the ABS focuses primarily on the frequency rather than the severity of maladaptive behavior, MacDonald and Barton (1986) have developed a revision that enables an assessment of the severity of a person's maladaptive behavior.

TABLE 3.1
Areas covered by the AAMR
Adaptive Behavior Scale.

Part One	Part Two

I. Independent Functioning
  A. Eating
  B. Toilet Use
  C. Cleanliness
  D. Appearance
  E. Care of Clothing
  F. Dressing and Undressing
  G. Travel
  H. General Independent Functioning
II. Physical Development
  A. Sensory Development
  B. Motor Development
III. Economic Activity
  A. Money Handling and Budgeting
  B. Shopping Skills
IV. Language Development
  A. Expression
  B. Comprehension
  C. Social Language Development
V. Numbers and Time
VI. Domestic Activity
  A. Cleaning
  B. Kitchen Duties
  C. Other Domestic Activities
VII. Vocational Activity
VIII. Self-Direction
  A. Initiative
  B. Perseverance
  C. Leisure time
IX. Responsibility
X. Socialization
	I. Violent and Destructive Behavior
	II. Antisocial Behavior
	III. Rebellious Behavior
	IV. Untrustworthy Behavior
	V. Withdrawal
	VI. Stereotyped Behavior and Odd Mannerisms
	VII. Inappropriate Interpersonal Manners
	VIII. Unacceptable Vocal Habits
	IX. Unacceptable or Eccentric Habits
	X. Self-Abusive Behavior
	XI. Hyperactive Tendencies
	XII. Sexually Aberrant Behavior
	XIII. Psychological Disturbances
	XIV. Use of Medications

Source: From *AAMD Adaptive Behavior Scale* (pp. 6–7), by K. Nihira, R. Foster, M. Shellhaas, and H. Leland, 1974. Washington, DC: American Association on Mental Retardation.

with the highest level representing performance at an adult level of mastery. Each item is given one of three scores: "no evidence of behavior," "someone else's report of the behavior only," or "direct observation of the behavior."

The Dilemma of Accurate Measurement

Measurement of adaptive behavior has proven difficult, in large part because of the relative nature of social adjustment and competence—what is considered appropriate in one situation or by one group may not be in or by another. Nowhere is there a list that everyone would agree describes exactly those adaptive behaviors that all of us should exhibit. As with IQ tests, cultural bias can

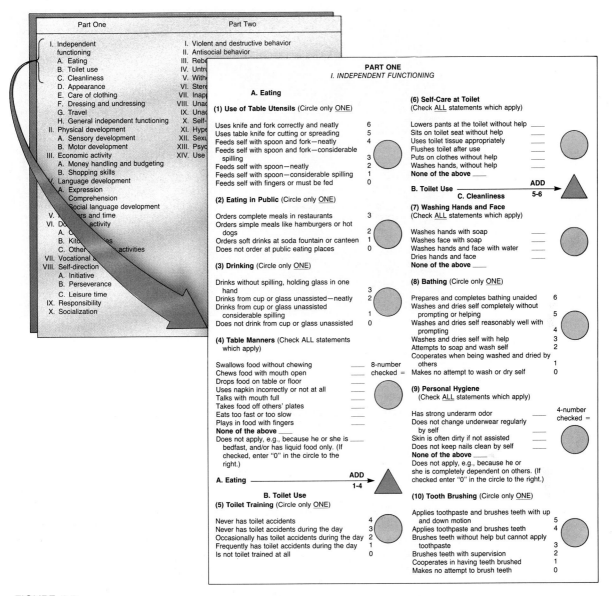

FIGURE 3.3

AAMR Adaptive Behavior Scale (*Source:* From *AAMR Adaptive Behavior Scale* (p. 3) by K. Nihira, R. Foster, M. Shellhaas, and H. Leland, 1975, Washington, DC: American Association on Mental Retardation. Reprinted by permission.)

be a problem in adaptive behavior scales; for instance, one item on some scales requires a child to tie a laced shoe, but some children have never had a shoe with laces. Ongoing research being conducted today on the measurement of adaptive behavior may help resolve these problems.

Some professionals have argued against inclusion of adaptive behavior in the definition of mental retardation (e.g., Clausen, 1972). Zigler, Balla, and Hodapp (1984) contend that mental retardation should be determined only by

Coulter and Morrow (1978) provide an excellent discussion of the many issues that surround the concept and measurement of adaptive behavior.

Adaptive behavior includes the ability to develop and maintain interpersonal relationships.

a score of less than 70 on a standardized IQ test. In a rebuttal that probably reflects the position of most professionals in the field, Barnett (1986) attacks the proposal of Zigler et al. (1984) by explaining the necessity of retaining adaptive behavior in the definition of mental retardation if the concept is to remain socially valid.

Despite the fact that most professionals view adaptive behavior as an important component of mental retardation, however, a child's IQ score remains the primary variable in determining whether she is identified as mentally retarded. A summary by Payne, Patton, and Patton (1986) of the results of two surveys of state departments of education (Huberty, Koller, & Ten Brink, 1980; Patrick & Reschly, 1982) reveals that 25 states do not require an assessment of adaptive behavior in the identification of a mentally retarded child. By contrast, these surveys found that only 6 states allow a child to be identified as mentally retarded without the use of an IQ test.

The Still-Unresolved Issue of Definition

The 1973 AAMR definition was incorporated into P.L. 94–142 as the federal definition of mental retardation and is the definition most frequently cited in the special education literature. Twice since 1973, the AAMR definition has been slightly revised in efforts to clarify the importance of clinical judgment in the diagnosis of mental retardation (Grossman, 1977, 1983). When the 1973 AAMR definition reduced the upper IQ limit from 85 to 70, the largest group of children previously considered mentally retarded could no longer be classified as such and, in some cases, were denied needed special education services. Kidd (1979) contended that many children who desperately needed the specialized instruction offered in programs for the mildly retarded were "being drowned in the mainstream" (p. 75). The most recent AAMR manual (Grossman, 1983) emphasizes that the IQ cutoff score of 70 is intended only as a guideline and should not be interpreted as a hard and fast requirement. A higher IQ score of 75 or more may be associated with mental retardation if, according to a clinician's judgment, the child exhibits deficits in adaptive behavior thought to be caused by impaired intellectual functioning.

Even though the AAMR definition of mental retardation dominates the field, numerous alternative definitions have been proposed. Four of the more prominent alternatives define mental retardation from behavioral, sociological, or instructional perspectives.

Behavioral. Sidney Bijou (1966) prefers a strictly behavioral definition that states that "a retarded individual is one who has a limited repertoire of behavior shaped by events that constitute his history" (p. 2). Bijou and Dunitz-Johnson (1981) have described an "interbehavior analysis" view of mental retardation that attributes a limited (retarded) behavioral repertoire to the hampering effects of biomedical impairment, handicapping sociocultural conditions, or both. Biomedical impairment can retard an individual's development through injury to the response equipment or to the internal or external sources of stimulation. Handicapping sociocultural conditions may include an impoverished home environment, limited educational opportunities, and negative parental practices such as indifference or abuse. This view maintains that if the environment was properly arranged, the individual might no longer act retarded. And, in fact, research is beginning to show that skill deficits of many persons with mental retardation can be replaced with more normal behavior.

Sociological. Jane Mercer, a sociologist, believes that the concept of mental retardation is a sociological phenomenon and that the label mentally retarded is "an achieved social status in a social system" (Mercer, 1973a, p. 3). Mercer's research (1973a, 1973b) shows that many children identified as mildly retarded by the school system, especially children from cultural minorities, are labeled mentally retarded because their behavior does not meet the norms of the white, middle-class social system.

She has developed a system for diagnosing mental retardation in children from minority groups. Called SOMPA (System of Multicultural Pluralistic Assessment), it is designed to eliminate cultural bias in intelligence testing. Using SOMPA, the examiner converts the child's WISC-R IQ score into what is called an estimated learning potential (ELP) score. The ELP score is affected by such variables as ethnic group membership and family size and structure. Although many school districts have begun using SOMPA, its validity and ultimate usefulness must await further research. Oakland (1980) found that WISC-R IQ scores correlated more highly with achievement than did ELP scores. As MacMillan (1982) points out, it is yet to be determined precisely how SOMPA can be used in education.

At present, the SOMPA system might reduce the number of minority children eligible for EMR [educable mentally retarded] programs, but whether this is in their best interest remains to be seen; it will probably depend on the availability of

MacMillan (1989) provides a thoughtful discussion of concerns regarding marginal learners in the 75–85 IQ range who may "reside in an educational 'DMZ', or 'no man's land' where students are ineligible for any special educational services" (p. 14).

Response equipment refers to parts of the body that produce movement or responses. It includes the brain, the eyes, the speech organs, and so forth.

For more on special education students from culturally diverse subgroups, see Chapter 12.

alternative programs to meet their learning needs when they are no longer eligible for EMR-related services. (p. 234)

A definition of mental retardation encompassing both a behavioral and a sociological perspective was proposed by Marc Gold (1980a). According to Gold, mental retardation should be viewed as society's failure to provide sufficient training and education, rather than as a deficit within the individual.

> Mental retardation refers to a level of functioning which requires from society significantly above average training procedures and superior assets in adaptive behavior, manifested throughout life. The mentally retarded person is characterized by the level of power needed in the training process for [the person] to learn, and not by limitations on what [the person] can learn. The height of a retarded person's level of functioning is determined by the availability of training technology and the amount of resources society is willing to allocate and not by significant limitations in biological potential. (p. 148)

Gold's "social responsibility" perspective is a highly optimistic one in its claim that the ultimate level of functioning of a person with mental retardation is determined by the technology available for training and the amount of resources devoted to the task.

Instructional.   Recognizing that definitions both reflect the perceptions of their developers and help shape the perceptions of people entering the field, Dever (1990) believes that mental retardation should be conceptualized from an instructional perspective. He offered the following definition to guide the efforts of personnel who work directly with persons *after* they have been identified as mentally retarded according to an "administrative" definition such as the AAMR's:

> Mental retardation refers to the need for specific training of skills that most people acquire incidentally and that enable individuals to live in the community without supervision. (p. 149)

Six corollaries derived from the definition help clarify the instructional task:

1. Persons with mental retardation can learn.
2. The need for instruction is central to mental retardation. All other services are ancillary.
3. The degree of retardation is a function of the amount and intensity of instruction required to teach individuals to live in the community without supervision.
4. Persons with mental retardation who learn to live in the community without supervision can no longer be called "retarded."
5. Some persons with retardation will never be able to acquire enough skills to live in the community without supervision.
6. The aim of the instruction for all persons with retardation is identical, despite the fact that some persons will never attain it. (Dever, 1990, pp. 149–151)

Dever (1990) argues that the aim of all instruction for persons with mental retardation should be independence.

The story of an 11-year-old with Down syndrome offers powerful support of Gold's belief in the power of systematic teaching. See essay on page 102.

Independence is exhibiting behavior patterns appropriate to the behavior settings normally frequented by others of the individual's age and social status in such a manner that the individual is not seen as requiring assistance because of his/her behavior. (p. 151)

The alternate definitions of mental retardation that Bijou, Mercer, Gold, and Dever offer are important ones. All four emphasize the fundamental notion that mental retardation represents a current level of performance; it is not something a person has in the same way one has the measles or red hair. Furthermore, performance can often be altered significantly by manipulating certain aspects of the environment (teaching nonretarded behavior or, in Mercer's view, altering one's own culturally biased perspective of what constitutes retarded behavior). All the approaches agree that mental retardation is a relative phenomenon that should not be viewed as a permanent condition.

A Proposed New AAMR Definition. As this book went to press, the AAMR at its annual meeting was voting on a new definition of mental retardation, proposed by its ad hoc Committee on Terminology and Classification. The proposed definition specified 10 areas in which deficits in adaptive skills may occur, noted that adaptive deficits often co-exist with strengths in other areas of personal competence, that mental retardation may not always be of life-long duration, and with appropriate services over sustained time life functioning will generally improve.

The debate over the definition of mental retardation is likely to continue. In the meantime, all the major professional organizations that work with children and adults who are mentally retarded use the AAMR definition and advocate its continued use because it promotes universal standards and communication to a greater degree than do other definitions.

We end this discussion of definition with the words of the late Burton Blatt—one of the field's most prolific, influential, and controversial figures—who argues that when all is said and done, mental retardation is best viewed as an administrative category. In his final book, *The Conquest of Mental Retardation* (1987), Blatt writes, "Simply stated, someone is mentally retarded when he or she is 'officially' identified as such" (p. 72).

■ CLASSIFICATION OF MENTAL RETARDATION

Many systems have been proposed for classifying mental retardation by type or degree of severity. In 1963 Gelof reported that 23 different classification systems were in use in English-speaking countries. As discussed in Chapter 1, classification of exceptional children is a difficult but necessary task. Various systems have been developed that classify mental retardation according to **etiology** (cause) or clinical type (for example, **Down syndrome**). Although these classification systems are useful to physicians, they have little utility for educators. For example, two children might be classified correctly as having Down syndrome, but one might be able to function well in a regular second grade classroom, whereas the other is unable to perform the most basic self-help tasks. The AAMR classifies mental retardation by degree or level of

DANIEL

"Hey, hey, hey, Fact Track!" The 11-year-old chose one of his favorite programs from the table next to the computer in his parents' dining room. He inserted the floppy disc, booted the system, and waited for the program to load.

"What is your name?" appeared on the monitor.

"Daniel Skandera," he typed. A menu scrolled up listing the program's possibilities. Daniel chose multiplication facts, Level 1.

"How many problems do you want to do?" the computer asked.

"20."

"Do you want to set a goal for yourself, Daniel?"

"Yes, 80 sec."

"Get ready!"

Daniel Skandera, Jr., was born with Down syndrome, a chromosomal abnormality that usually results in moderate to severe mental retardation. "A psychologist tested Daniel at 12 months and told us he was three standard deviations below normal, untestable. That assessment was the basis for Daniel's being denied enrollment in an infant stimulation pro-

gram. We knew the tests were invalid and accepted the challenge of teaching Daniel ourselves," explained Daniel's father. "Between Marie and me, we had spent about 10,000 hours working with Daniel by the time he was 5. It's paid off a million times over. He's an inspiration and joy."

"We believed that we had learned enough about how Daniel learns to work with him confidently," says his mother, Marie. "If something doesn't work, if he becomes frustrated, we are challenged to try another approach. Daniel is an only child, and we were older when he was born. When we're gone, we want him to be able to take care of himself, to be a taxpayer instead of a tax burden."

Randomly generated multiplication facts flashed on the screen: "4 × 6," "2 × 9," "3 × 3," "7 × 6." Daniel responded, deftly punching in his answers on the computer's numeric key-pad. Twice he recognized errors and corrected them before inputting his answers.

Daniel attends a regular fourth grade classroom. Academically he

performs at grade level except for two subjects. For math and spelling, his best subjects ("Hooray, I love spellin'!"), he leaves the fourth grade classroom each day—and moves to the *fifth* grade. Daniel is not a special education student; he has no IEP. His extracurricular activities are those of his classmates and neighborhood friends—riding his bicycle, working out on his regulation-size trampoline, playing along with tape recorded rock 'n' roll on his six-piece drum set, rough-housing, spending the night at a buddy's.

"Positive expectations are the key words," agreed Daniel's parents. "With Daniel it might take a little longer, but we get there."

The computer tallied the results. "You completed 20 problems in 66 seconds. You beat your goal. Problems correct = 20. Congratulations Daniel!" And with that the 11-year-old retreated hastily to the TV room. It was almost tip-off time for an NBA championship game, and Daniel wanted to see the first half before bedtime. ◆

---

severity, as measured by an IQ test. Table 3.2 lists the levels of mental retardation according to the most recent AAMR manual (Grossman, 1983). The range of scores representing the high and low ends of each level indicates an awareness of the inexactness of intelligence testing and the importance of clinical judgment in determining level of severity.

Although the AAMR classification system is the most widely cited in the professional literature, educators use different terms. In fact, Utley, Lowitzer, and Baumeister (1987) surveyed the guidelines issued by state departments of education and found that only 56% used the term *mental retardation;* the others use instead terms such as *mental disabilities* or *developmental handicaps.* For many years educators used the terms *educable mentally retarded* (EMR) and *trainable mentally retarded* (TMR) to refer to mild and moderate levels of

Level	Intelligence Test Score
Mild	50–55 to approx. 70 (+/−5)
Moderate	35–40 to 50–55
Severe	20–25 to 35–40
Profound	Below 20–25

TABLE 3.2
Levels of mental retardation according to the AAMR.

retardation respectively. Some educators and school systems still use these terms.

Mild Retardation

Children with mild retardation have traditionally been educated in self-contained classrooms in the public schools. Today, many children with mild mental retardation are being educated in regular classrooms, with a special educator helping the classroom teacher with individualized instruction for the child and providing extra tutoring in a resource room as needed. Many mildly retarded children are not identified until they enter school and sometimes not until the second or third grade, when more difficult academic work is required.

Traditionally, school programs for students with mild mental retardation stressed the basic academic subjects—reading, writing, and arithmetic—during the elementary years, with a shift in emphasis to vocational training and work-study programs in junior high and high school. Schools today are increasingly beginning career education (Brolin, 1989) and instruction on community living skills (Dever, 1989) in the elementary grades. Most mildly retarded students master academic skills up to about the sixth grade level and are able to learn job skills well enough to support themselves independently or semi-independently. Many adults with mild mental retardation develop social and communication skills similar to those of their nonretarded peers; many are not recognized as mentally retarded outside school or after they finish school.

Career education will be described in Chapter 15.

Moderate Retardation

Unlike mildly retarded children, who may not be identified as needing special education until they reach school, most children with moderate retardation show significant delays in development during their preschool years. As they grow older, discrepancies generally grow wider between these children and their nonhandicapped age-mates in overall intellectual, social, and motor development. Approximately 30% of those individuals classified as moderately retarded have Down syndrome, and about 50% have some form of brain damage (Neisworth & Smith, 1978). Additional handicapping conditions and physical abnormalities are more common in people with moderate retardation than in individuals with mild retardation.

During their school years, children with moderate mental retardation are most often taught in self-contained classrooms with highly structured instructional programs designed to teach daily living skills. Academics may be limited to development of a basic sight-word vocabulary (e.g., "survival" words such as

See Chapter 15 for more information on how adults with mental retardation live and work.

exit, don't walk, stop), some functional reading skills (such as simple recipes), and basic number concepts. In the past, most persons with moderate mental retardation were removed from society and placed in large institutions where they had little opportunity to develop and learn how to get along in the world. Today most people with moderate retardation are receiving the individualized levels of support and supervision they require to live and work in the community.

Severe and Profound Retardation

Individuals with severe and profound mental retardation are almost always identified at birth or shortly afterward. Most of these infants have significant central nervous system damage, and many have other handicapping conditions. Although the AAMR distinguishes between severe and profound retardation on the basis of IQ scores, the difference is primarily one of functional impairment. Until recently, training for individuals with severe retardation focused primarily on self-care skills—toileting, dressing, and eating and drinking—and communication development. A person with profound mental retardation may not be able to care for personal needs, may have limited or no independent mobility, and may require 24-hour nursing care. Recent developments in instructional technology, however, are showing that many persons who are severely and profoundly mentally retarded can learn skills previously thought to be beyond their capability—even to the point of becoming semi-independent adults able to live and work in the community.

Chapter 10 is devoted to the special characteristics, programming, and educational issues related to students with severe handicaps.

Until very recently, children with severe/profound mental retardation were virtually ignored by the American educational system. Fortunately, this situation is changing. Litigation and legislation assuring the rights of individuals with disabilities, regardless of the type or degree of disability, and advances in educational methods (see Snell, in press) have contributed to this change. P.L. 94–142 mandates that all children must receive an appropriate education and, furthermore, that the first priority for use of federal special education monies is to be those children currently not receiving educational services. The unserved are mostly children with severe and profound mental retardation, many of whom have additional disabilities as well. The outlook for these children is improving. A growing organization of researchers, teachers, parents, and other interested individuals—The Association for Persons with Severe Handicaps (TASH)—is working to help that future.

■ PREVALENCE

Changing definitions of mental retardation, lack of a nationwide systematic reporting system, and the changing status of mildly retarded school children (are they still considered mentally retarded after leaving school?) contribute to the difficulty of estimating the number of people with mental retardation. Historically, the federal government has estimated the prevalence of mental retardation at 3% of the general population, although recent analyses find little objective support for this figure. When prevalence figures are based on IQ scores alone, approximately 2.3% of the population theoretically scores in the retarded range—two standard deviations below the mean (see Figure 3.1). Using IQ score only as a basis for classification, Haywood (1979) estimated that

> on a population base of 222 million persons (which the United States Bureau of the Census estimates will be our population in 1980) we shall have 110,000 persons with IQs less than 20, and 444,000 with IQs between 20 and 50, but we shall have 6,693,940 individuals with IQs between 50 and 70. Thus in 1980 there will be more than 12 times as many mentally retarded persons in the IQ 50 to 70 range as there will be with IQs less than 50. (pp. 430–431)

Basing prevalence estimates on IQ scores only, however, ignores the other necessary criterion for mental retardation—deficits in adaptive behavior. Because there are as yet no universally accepted measures of adaptive behavior, no major prevalence studies have assessed it. Some professionals believe that if adaptive behavior is included with intellectual ability when estimating prevalence, the figure would drop to about 1% (Baroff, 1982; Mercer, 1973b; Tarjan, Wright, Eyman, & Keeran, 1973). The percentage of all U.S. school children receiving special education services under the disability category mental retardation was approximately 1.2% in the 1988–89 school year (U.S. Department of Education, 1990).

MacMillan (1982) and Neisworth and Smith (1978) suggest that the 3% figure probably more accurately reflects **incidence**—the percentage of people who, at some time in their lives, are diagnosed as mentally retarded—and that the **prevalence** of mental retardation—the number of persons identified at any one time—is probably closer to 1%. Two factors causing the discrepancy between incidence and prevalence are the high mortality rate of infants with severe and profound mental retardation and the fact that many mildly retarded school children are independent and self-sufficient as adults (Edgerton & Bercovici, 1976; Richardson, 1978) and so are no longer counted as mentally retarded.

Baroff (1982) has developed a formula for estimating the number of persons needing services for the mentally retarded. He suggests that there are 4 people per 1,000 population in the moderate/severe/profound ranges and 5 people per 1,000 with mild retardation. This 0.9% is about one-third the traditional 3% estimate.

■ CAUSES OF MENTAL RETARDATION

Individuals with mild mental retardation make up 80% to 85% of the people identified as mentally retarded; in the vast majority of those cases, etiology (cause) is unknown. That is, there is no demonstrable evidence of organic pathology—no brain damage or other physical problem. In general, when we can find no actual organic damage, we say the cause of the retardation is **psychosocial disadvantage**. The term suggests that the combination of a poor social and cultural environment early in the child's life can lead to retarded development. Although there is no direct proof that social and familial interactions cause mental retardation, it is generally believed that these influences cause most mild cases of retardation.

Even though more than 250 known causes of mental retardation have been identified, a recent review of 13 epidemiological studies concluded that for

In 1973 Grossman introduced the term *psychosocial disadvantage* as a suggested replacement for the term **cultural-familial retardation.** Although there are slight differences in meaning, both terms are used today to refer to mental retardation caused by environmental influences.

approximately 50% of cases of mild mental retardation and 30% of cases of severe mental retardation, the cause is unknown (McLaven & Bryson, 1987). All of the known causes of retardation are biological or medical, and these conditions are referred to as clinical or pathological (brain damage) retardation. These causes have been categorized by the AAMR (Grossman, 1983) into the following seven groups:

1. Infections and intoxications (e.g., **rubella**, syphilis, encephalitis, meningitis, exposure to drugs or poisons, blood group incompatibility)

2. Trauma and physical agents (e.g., accidents before, during, and after birth; **anoxia**)

3. Metabolic and nutritional factors (e.g., **phenylketonuria [PKU], Tay-Sachs disease**)

4. Gross postnatal brain diseases (such as tumors)

5. Other prenatal influences (e.g., **hydrocephalus, microcephalus**)

6. Chromosomal abnormalities (e.g., **Cri-du-chat syndrome**, Down syndrome, **Turner's syndrome, Fragile-X syndrome**)

7. Gestational disorders (e.g., prematurity, low birth weight)

■ EDUCATIONAL PLACEMENT, CURRICULAR GOALS, AND INSTRUCTIONAL METHODOLOGY

Where Teaching Takes Place

The regular public schools are changing their ways of providing services to students with mental retardation. Traditionally, the student with mild mental retardation (EMR) was educated in a self-contained classroom with 12 to 18 other EMR students. Children with more severe mental retardation were usually excluded from the local public school and placed in an institution or segregated special school for handicapped children only. Today P.L. 94–142 mandates that children with disabilities be educated with their nondisabled peers to the greatest extent possible. Thus, increasing numbers of students with mild-to-moderate mental retardation are spending all or part of the school day in the regular classroom, with supplemental instruction provided by a resource teacher.

See Polloway (1984) for a comprehensive review of the history and research concerning the most effective classroom placement for mildly retarded students.

But, as we saw in Chapter 2, simply putting a child with disabilities in a regular classroom does not necessarily mean that he will be accepted socially or receive the instructional programming he most needs. Many special and regular educators are, however, developing programs and methods for integrating the instruction of mentally retarded students with that of their nonhandicapped peers. Systematically planning for the student's integration into the classroom through team games and group investigation projects and directly training all students in specific skills for interacting with one another are just some of the methods for increasing the chances of a successful regular class placement (Gottlieb & Leyser, 1981; Stainback, Stainback, Raschke, & Anderson, 1981; Strain, Guralnick, & Walker, 1986). Peer tutoring programs have also proven effective in promoting the instructional and social integration of mentally retarded children into regular classrooms (Delquadri, Greenwood, Whorton,

The self-contained classroom is the most common educational placement for students with mental retardation.

Carta, & Hall, 1986; Osguthorpe & Scruggs, 1986). For example, Cooke et al. (1982) implemented a classwide peer tutoring system implemented in a first grade classroom in which a student with Down syndrome participated. Over the course of this 5-month study, the child not only interacted directly and positively with her peer tutor, but also learned more than 40 sight words from her nonhandicapped classmate.

See the Focus on Intervention box, "Classwide Peer Tutoring," pages 68–69.

The self-contained special class is the most common educational placement for students with mental retardation (U.S. Department of Education, 1990). Many students with moderate and severe mental retardation continue to attend special schools. Sometimes a number of small neighboring school districts pool their resources to offer a special school program to students in their area with moderate/severe/profound mental retardation. Many special educators believe, however, that segregated "handicapped only" schools prohibit students from obtaining an education in the least restrictive environment and that all children should attend their local neighborhood schools, regardless of the type or severity of their disability (e.g., Brown et al., 1989a).

In Chapter 10 we will examine the case for educating children with severe handicaps in their neighborhood schools.

Curriculum Goals

What do individuals with mental retardation need to learn? Not too many years ago, children with mild mental retardation were presented with a slowed down version of the general education curriculum that focused largely on traditional academic subject areas. For example, a group of EMR children might study a geography unit in which they learned the 50 states and their capitals over the course of several weeks. More severely retarded students spent many hours of instruction learning isolated skills thought to be prerequisites for other more meaningful activities. Many hundreds of students with severe mental retardation spent thousands of hours putting pegs in pegboards and sorting plastic sticks by color. Unfortunately, knowing that Boise is the capital of Idaho or being able to sort by color did not help these students become more independent.

In recent years, identifying functional curriculum goals for students with mental retardation has become a major priority for special educators. All learning activities in a functional curriculum are designed to help students acquire skills that can be used in everyday home, community, and work environments. One organized statement of functional goals that can be used as the framework around which to build a curriculum is *A Taxonomy of Community Living Skills* (Dever, 1989). The *Taxonomy* is structured around five domains that represent the person as he or she lives, works, plays, and moves through the community:

- personal maintenance and development
- homemaking and community life
- vocational
- leisure
- travel

Figure 3.4 illustrates how the five domains are related to one another, and Table 3.3 lists the major goals for each domain.

Instructional Methodology

Research in specific educational techniques for children with mental retardation began when Itard started his work with Victor, the Wild Boy of Aveyron. But only since the early 1960s has the scientific method been employed systematically in an attempt to discover effective and reliable teaching methods. Although this

FIGURE 3.4
Organization of the Taxonomy of Community Living Skills.

Learning functional vocational skills should be a major priority for all students with mental retardation.

research is far from finished—indeed, we must continually search for better teaching methods—one approach that has produced consistent educational improvements in students with mental retardation is the behavioral approach, or **applied behavior analysis**.

Applied Behavior Analysis

Applied behavior analysis can be defined as systematically arranging environmental events to produce desired changes in behavior. Behavior analysts verify the effects of their instruction by directly measuring student performance. Behavior analysis is not a single technique, but a systematic approach to teaching based on scientifically proven principles that describe how the environment affects learning.

For a detailed description of applied behavior analysis see Cooper, Heron, and Heward (1987).

Applied behavior analysis has been used effectively not only with learners who experience mental retardation (Snell, in press), it has also been successfully applied with students with other handicapping conditions (Nelson & Polsgrove, 1984; Rusch, Greenwood, & Rose, 1988). The April 1986 issue of *Exceptional Children,* which was devoted to effective instructional practices, consisted largely of articles describing behavioral teaching strategies (Anderson-Inman, 1986; Delquadri et al., 1986; Fowler, 1986; Strain & Odom, 1986; White, 1986) and indicates the significant role of applied behavior analysis in special education.

TABLE 3.3
List of major goals

Domain P Personal Maintenance and Development	

I. The learner will follow routine body maintenance procedures
  A. Maintain personal cleanliness
  B. Groom self
  C. Dress appropriately
  D. Follow appropriate sleep patterns
  E. Maintain nutrition
  F. Exercise regularly
  G. Maintain substance control
II. The learner will treat illnesses
  A. Use first aid and illness treatment procedures
  B. Obtain medical advice when necessary
  C. Follow required medication schedules
	III. The learner will establish and maintain personal relationships
	  A. Interact appropriately with family
	  B. Make friends
	  C. Interact appropriately with friends
	  D. Cope with inappropriate conduct of family and friends
	  E. Respond to sexual needs
	  F. Obtain assistance in maintaining personal relationships
	IV. The learner will handle personal "glitches"
	  A. Cope with changes in daily schedule
	  B. Cope with equipment breakdowns and material depletions

Domain H Homemaking and Community Life	

I. The learner will obtain living quarters
  A. Find appropriate living quarters
  B. Rent/ buy living quarters
  C. Set up living quarters
II. The learner will follow community routines
  A. Keep living quarters neat and clean
  B. Keep fabrics neat and clean
  C. Maintain interior living quarters
  D. Maintain exterior of living quarters
  E. Respond to seasonal changes
  F. Follow home safety procedures
  G. Follow accident/emergency procedures
  H. Maintain foodstock
  I. Prepare and serve meals
  J. Budget money appropriately
  K. Pay bills
	III. The learner will co-exist in a neighborhood and community
	  A. Interact appropriately with community members
	  B. Cope with inappropriate conduct of others
	  C. Observe requirements of the law
	  D. Carry out civic duties
	IV. The learner will handle "glitches" in the home
	  A. Cope with equipment breakdowns
	  B. Cope with depletions of household supplies
	  C. Cope with unexpected depletions of funds
	  D. Cope with disruptions in routine
	  E. Cope with sudden changes in the weather

Excellent descriptions of how to perform and validate a task analysis can be found in Bailey and Wolery (1984), Bellamy, Horner, and Inman (1979), Gold (1976), Moyer and Dardig (1978), and Snell (in press).

    An initial step in the behavioral approach to instruction is to specify exactly what skills, or behaviors, the learner is to acquire. **Task analysis,** a method in which large skills are broken down and sequenced into a series of subskills, lets a teacher break a task into small, easier-to-teach subtasks. The subtasks are then sequenced from easiest to most difficult or in the natural order in which they must be performed. Assessing a student's performance on a sequence of

TABLE 3–3
continued

<table>
<tr><td colspan="2" align="center">Domain V
Vocational</td></tr>
<tr>
<td>

I. The learner will obtain work
  A. Seek employment
  B. Accept employment
  C. Use unemployment services
II. The learner will perform the work routine
  A. Perform the job routine
  B. Follow work-related daily schedule
  C. Maintain work station
  D. Follow employer rules and regulations
  E. Use facilities appropriately
  F. Follow job safety procedures
  G. Follow accident and emergency procedures

</td>
<td>

III. The learner will co-exist with others on the job
  A. Interact appropriately with others on the job
  B. Cope with inappropriate conduct of others on the job
IV. The learner will handle "glitches" on the job
  A. Cope with changes in work routine
  B. Cope with work problems
  C. Cope with supply depletions and equipment breakdowns

</td>
</tr>
<tr><td colspan="2" align="center">Domain L
Leisure</td></tr>
<tr>
<td>

I. The learner will develop leisure activities
  A. Find new leisure activities
  B. Acquire skills for leisure activities
II. The learner will follow leisure activity routines
  A. Perform leisure activities
  B. Maintain leisure equipment
  C. Follow leisure safety procedures
  D. Follow accident and emergency procedures

</td>
<td>

III. The learner will co-exist with others during leisure
  A. Interact appropriately with others in a leisure setting
  B. Respond to the inappropriate conduct of others
IV. The learner will handle "glitches" during leisure
  A. Cope with changes in leisure routine
  B. Cope with equipment breakdowns and material depletions

</td>
</tr>
<tr><td colspan="2" align="center">Domain T
Travel</td></tr>
<tr>
<td>

I. The learner will travel routes in the community
  A. Form mental maps of frequented buildings
  B. Form mental maps of the community
II. The learner will use conveyances
  A. Follow usage procedures
  B. Make decisions preparatory to travel
  C. Follow travel safety procedures
  D. Follow accident and emergency procedures

</td>
<td>

III. The learner will co-exist with others while traveling
  A. Interact appropriately with others while traveling
  B. Respond to the inappropriate conduct of others while traveling
IV. The learner will handle "glitches"
  A. Cope with changes in travel schedule
  B. Cope with equipment breakdowns
  C. Cope with being lost

</td>
</tr>
</table>

Source: From *Community Living Skills: A Taxonomy* by R. B. Dever, 1988, Washington, DC: American Association on Mental Retardation. Copyright 1988 by American Association on Mental Retardation. Reprinted by permission.

task-analyzed subskills helps pinpoint exactly where instruction should begin. Table 3.4 shows a task analysis for eating in a fast food restaurant.

Another hallmark of the behavioral approach is direct and frequent measurement. Measurement is direct when it objectively records the learner's performance of the behavior of interest in the natural environment for that skill.

Task analysis of a seemingly simple everyday skill such as toothbrushing can reveal numerous sub-tasks for direct instruction.

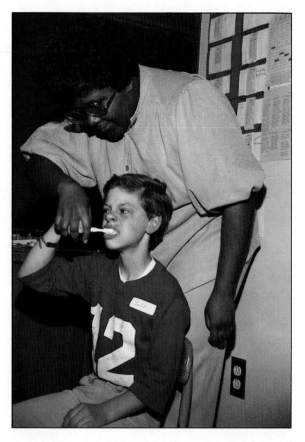

Measurement is frequent when it occurs on a regular basis; ideally, measurement should take place as often as instruction occurs. Academic achievement tests have traditionally been the major source of data for evaluating educational programs. Although achievement data have some use, they are not useful for day-to-day planning and evaluation of instruction. Achievement tests are usually given only once or twice a year, and the information they provide is too indirect, requiring that inferences be made about the student's actual classroom performance.

> Two errors of judgement are common for [teachers] who do not collect direct and frequent measurements of their student's performance. First, many ineffective intervention programs are continued. . . . Second, many effective programs are discontinued prematurely because subjective judgment finds no improvement. For example, teachers who do not use direct and frequent measures might discern little difference between a student's reading 40 words per minute with 60% accuracy and 48 words per minute with 73% accuracy. However, direct and frequent data collected on the rate and accuracy of oral reading would show an improved performance. Decision making in education must be based upon performance data; the individual's behavior must dictate the course of action. (Cooper, Heron, & Heward, 1987, p. 60)

TABLE 3.4
Task analysis of skills required to eat in a fast-food restaurant.

Skill	Appropriate Response	Inappropriate Response
1.1	Does not initiate social interaction. Does not self-stimulate.	Talks/makes manual sign to customer or trainer. Engages in motor/vocal self-stimulation so that customers differentially attend to him.
1.2	Enters double door within 2 min of start.	Uses wrong door. Does not enter within 2 min.
1.3	Goes directly to counter. Does not leave line except to get into shorter line.	Not in line or at counter within 30 sec. Gets out of line.
Ordering		
2.1	Makes ordering response within 10 sec of cue. If written, finishes within 2 min.	Does not respond within 10 sec. Responds before cue. Makes inappropriate (i.e., nonordering-related) verbalization. Not finished writing within 2 min.
2.2	Says "How much for . . .?" when giving order.	Does not inquire "How much for . . .?"
2.3	Orders food that he can afford, appropriate item combination (i.e., minimum order—sandwich & drink; maximum—sandwich, drink, side order, & any other item).	Orders more food than he can pay for. Uses inappropriate item combination.
2.4	Says "Eat here" when asked.	Does not say order is to dine in. Says "To go."
Paying		
3.1	Begins to get money within 10 sec of cue. Does not let go of money on counter before cashier cue.	Does not get money within 10 sec. Releases money before cue.
3.2	Hands cashier appropriate combination of bills.	Does not give enough money. Gives too much money so that same bill is returned.
3.3	Displays fingers on at least one hand.	Does not display fingers.
3.4	Inquires "Mistake?" if short billed.	Does not inquire if short billed. Inquires "Mistake?" when change is accurate.
3.5	Puts money in pocket.	Does not take change. Puts money on tray instead of pocket.
3.6	Requests salt, pepper, or catsup.	Does not request any condiments.
3.7	Takes a napkin from dispenser.	Does not take napkin from dispenser.
3.8	Says "Thank you."	Does not say "Thank you."
Eating and Exiting		
4.1	Sits at unoccupied, trashfree table within 1 min of availability.	Sits with other customer. Sits at a table with trash present. Does not sit down within 1 min.
4.2	Eats food placed only on paper.	Eats food off tray, table, etc.
4.3	Puts napkin in lap *and* wipes mouth or hands.	Does not put napkin in lap. Does not wipe hands or mouth on it.
4.4	Does not spill food or drink.	Drops food off tray or spills drink.
4.5	If spills occur, picks up every one, does not eat any spilled item.	Does not pick up or blot. Eats spilled food.
4.6	Puts trash in container, tray on top, within 2 min of finishing eating.	Does not put trash in container within 2 min. Uses inappropriate container. Throws tray in container.
4.7	Exits within 1 min of trash or 3 min of finishing eating.	Does not exit within time limits.

Source: From "Teaching the Handicapped to Eat in Public Places: Acquisition, Generalization, amd Maintenance of Restaurant Skills by R. A. van den Pol, B. A. Iwata, M. T. Ivancic, T. J. Page, N. A. Neef, and F. P. Whitley, 1981. *Journal of Applied Behavior Analysis, 14,* p. 63. Copyright by the Society for the Experimental Analysis of Behavior, Inc. Reprinted by permission.

HOW MANY CAN YOU DO IN ONE MINUTE?

Using Daily Time Trials to Help Students with Mental Retardation Add and Subtract with Fluency

The conventional wisdom goes something like this: Children with mental retardation can learn, but since they learn at a slower rate than children who are not handicapped, they should be given more time to complete their work. Although it is generally true that children with mental retardation acquire new skills more slowly, teachers may, instead of helping, be doing handicapped students a disservice by always providing plenty of time for them to do their work. Accuracy measures alone do not provide a complete picture of learning. Whereas two students might each complete a page of math problems with 100% accuracy, the one who finishes in 2 minutes is more accomplished than the one who needed 5 minutes to answer the same problems. To be functional, many of the skills we use everyday in the home, community, or workplace must be performed at a certain rate of speed.

Providing students with practice to build *fluency* is an important part of teaching. After the initial *acquisition stage* of learning, when a student learns *how* to perform the skill correctly, the student progresses to the *practice stage* of learning, in which the focus should shift to building fluency. "The teacher does not push fluency when the student cannot yet work the problems correctly. Similarly, when teaching a student to be fluent, techniques used to promote accuracy are not used. During fluency instruction, elaborate explanations and corrections are not needed; in fact, they might even slow the student down. Instead, the teacher talks about and rewards fluency" (Howell & Lorson-Howell, 1990, p. 21).

Daily time trials (giving students the opportunity to perform a skill as many times as they can in a brief period) are an excellent tactic for building fluency. Several studies have shown that students, nonhandicapped and handicapped alike, not only benefit from time trials, but that they like to be timed (see Van Houten, 1980). For example, 11 students with mental retardation participated in a study evaluating the effects of 1-minute time trials on the rate and accuracy of answering single-digit math facts (Miller, Hall, & Heward, 1991). During the first 2 weeks of the study, when they were told to complete as many problems as they could during an untimed 10-minute work period, the students

These journals publish examples of applied behavior analysis teaching programs for learners with mental retardation and other disabilities: *Behavior Modification, Education & Treatment of Children, Education and Treatment of the Mentally Retarded, Journal of Applied Behavior Analysis, The Journal of The Association for Persons with Severe Handicaps, Journal of Behavioral Education,* and *Research in Developmental Disabilities.*

Only through diligent direct and frequent measurement of student performance are teachers able to provide the individualized instruction so vital to the growth and progress of children with mental retardation. In addition to direct and frequent measurement, most behaviorally based teaching techniques hold the following in common:

1. They can be replicated by people other than the originator.

2. They require the student to perform the target behavior repeatedly during each session.

3. Immediate feedback, usually in the form of **positive reinforcement**, is provided to the student.

answered correctly an average of 8.4 problems per minute. During the next phase, a series of seven 1-minute time trials were conducted with 20 seconds rest period between each time trial (equaling a total of 10 minutes, as in the first phase); the students' correct rate increased to 13.2 per minute when time trials were used. Fluency improved to 16 problems per minute during a final phase, when immediate feedback and self-correction were conducted immediately after each of two consecutive time trials.

Did working faster harm the students' accuracy? Not at all: The students answered correctly 85% of all the problems they attempted during the 10-minute work period; but their accuracy improved to 89% when time trials were used. When asked which method they preferred, 10 of the 11 students indicated they liked time trials better than the untimed work period.

Guidelines for Conducting Time Trials*

- Keep the time for each trial short. One minute is sufficient for most academic skills.
- Do time trials every day. For example, a series of two or three 1-minute oral reading time trials could be conducted at the end of each day's lesson.
- Make time trials fun. Time trials should not be presented as a test; they are a learning activity that can be approached like a game.
- Use time trials only during the practice stage of learning, *after* students have learned *how* to do the skill correctly.
- Follow time trials with a more relaxed activity.
- Feedback to students should emphasize proficiency (total *number* correct), not simply accuracy (percent correct).
- Have each student try to beat his or her own best score.
- Have students keep track of their progress by self-graphing.
- Consider using a performance feedback chart to provide both individual and group feedback during a time trial program. See Van Houten (1980) for examples.

*Adapted from A. D. Miller and W. L. Heward (in press). Do your students *really* know their math facts? Using daily time trials to build fluency. *Intervention in School and Clinic.* ♦

---

4. Cues and prompts that help the student respond correctly from the very beginning of the lesson are systematically withdrawn.

5. Efforts are included to help the student generalize the newly learned skill to different, nontraining environments.

■ RESIDENTIAL ALTERNATIVES

Institutions

A survey of all 50 states and the District of Columbia found that 91,582 persons were living in 296 large state-operated institutions for individuals with mental retardation (White, Lakin, & Bruininks, 1989). This represents the lowest number of people living in mental retardation institutions since 1934. A large residential facility is defined as one serving 16 or more residents; however, the average size of most institutions today is more than 300 residents. Other key findings from this survey include the following:

♦ The number of persons with mental retardation living in state institutions has decreased steadily from a high of 228,500 in 1967.

♦ The annual cost of providing services to a person with mental retardation in a large institution in 1988 was $57,200, compared to an annual expenditure of $750 per person in 1950. Controlling for inflation, the increased cost is 15 times the 1950 level.

♦ 80% of the residents of public institutions are classified as severely or profoundly mentally retarded. Many have additional disabilities; for example, 39% have epilepsy, 12% have cerebral palsy, and 10% have visual and/or hearing impairments.

♦ Current residents in large state-operated institutions for the mentally retarded represent a wide range of abilities and disabilities: an estimated 24% can bathe or shower independently; 54% can use the toilet independently; 66% can feed themselves; 10% can use the telephone; 6% can manage money; 7% can shop for some personal items; and 7% can get around the community without assistance.

♦ Only about 25% of residents in large public facilities work for pay (5% off grounds), while an estimated 49% of residents of small residential facilities have paying jobs (47% away from where they live).

Most of our nation's public institutions were founded in the 19th or early 20th century, when it was generally believed that people with mental retardation could not be educated or trained. Large custodial institutions have kept people with mental retardation segregated from the rest of society; the institutions were never designed to train people to live in normal society. Institutions have come under severe criticism for their general inability to provide individualized services in a comfortable, humane, and normalized environment (Blatt, 1976; Blatt & Kaplan, 1966; Kugel & Wolfensberger, 1969; Wolfensberger, 1969).

The complaints are not leveled against the concept of residential programs; there will probably always be persons whose disabilities are so severe that they require the 24-hour care and supervision that only residential facilities can offer. The problem lies with the inherent inability of large institutions to provide needed services in a manner that allows a normalized lifestyle.

Over the past 25 years, tremendous improvements have been made in the abysmal living conditions in institutions that Blatt and Kaplan exposed in their book *Christmas in Purgatory* (1966). During the 1970s, the U.S. Department of Health, Education and Welfare and the Joint Commission on the Accreditation of Hospitals developed extensive standards for residential facilities for individuals with mental retardation. A residential facility must meet these standards—which cover a wide range of topics, from building construction to staffing to habilitative and educational programming—to qualify for federal and state Medicaid funding. Residential units that meet the standards are referred to as ICF-MR Medicaid facilities. Although the ICF-MR Medicaid system of rules and regulations has eliminated the inhumane, filthy conditions that were a defining feature of institutional life in the 1950s and 1960s, the system has become the target for increasing criticism:

> If Burton Blatt could spend a day in an ICF-MR today, he would likely see a smaller, more livable residence. It would be clean, well-appointed, even home-like. The people who live there would be appropriately dressed, and a few might be interacting with direct-care staff members. Professional staff members would probably be found absorbed in paperwork or in a meeting. Voluminous records would detail individualized programmatic goals and procedures, but there would be questions as to which programs are actually being implemented and working. Further observation might reveal that the staff, as a whole, is not as organized or adept in teaching as the paperwork and expertise might suggest. However, the staff members might be quite sensitive and oriented to their own ICF-MR accountability requirements, giving the impression that regulation compliance is the predominant focus in the home, whereas habilitation and enhancing the quality of life are secondary. (Holburn, 1990, p. 65)

Results of an observational study by Repp and Barton (1980) support this concern. They compared the interactions (verbal instruction, custodial guidance, no interaction, and so on) between residents and staff and the behaviors of residents (on-task, no programming, self-stimulatory, and so on) that took place in two licensed and six unlicensed cottages at a large state institution. Each of the eight cottages had from 12 to 40 residents with severe and profound mental retardation, some with additional disabilities (hearing or visual impairments, physical handicaps). The licensed cottages had resident-to-staff ratios of 4 to 1, whereas in the unlicensed cottages the resident-to-staff ratios ranged from 4 to 1 to 10 to 1. Thus, the licensed units had an advantage of more staff available to provide programming. For 16 days, four observers each recorded staff and resident behavior for more than 4 hours per day, yielding almost 160,000 individual 6-second observations.

Figure 3.5 displays the study's results. The most striking finding is the overwhelming number of observations in which no interactions between residents and staff and no programming occurred. Whether licensed or not, there were few instances of praise or encouragement directed by staff toward the residents. On the average, every resident, whether in a licensed or unlicensed cottage, spent more time engaging in self-stimulatory behaviors than in programming. In discussing the results of their study, Repp and Barton (1980) wrote,

> These data, quite objective and reliable, show that despite all the excitement over the Education for All Handicapped Children Act, 1975, that despite all the promises of court cases . . ., we still do not provide sufficient educational opportunities for many retarded citizens, even in our licensed facilities. These data cannot be interpreted too strongly, for they were recorded with the complete awareness of the administration and of the staff being observed, and they were recorded during the hours one would expect most of the educational opportunities in a resident's life to be made available. If they are biased, they are biased in a direction favorable to the facility. . . .
>
> In summary, these results are extremely discouraging. They indicate that (1) facilities can be licensed and still not provide habilitation for their clients; (2) despite the technology we have developed for teaching adaptive and reducing maladaptive behaviors, many people remain unaffected; and (3) we still do not

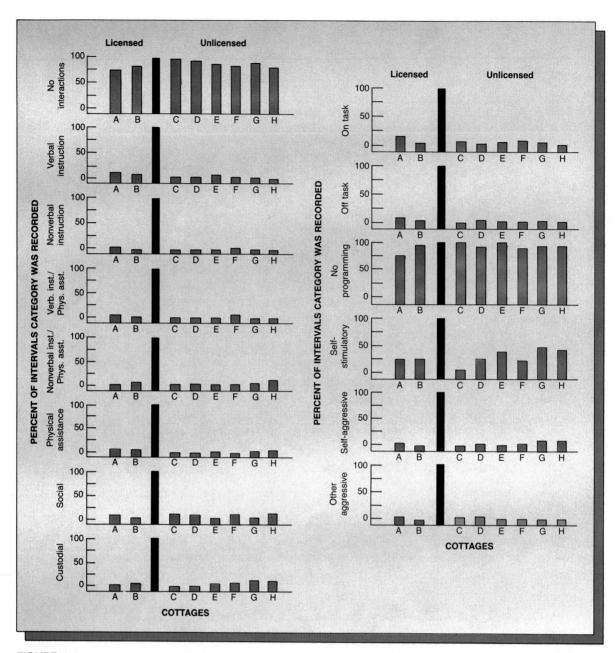

FIGURE 3.5

The mean percentage of 6-second observations in which each type of staff interaction with residents occurred (graphs on the left side) and each type of resident activity was recorded (graphs on the right side). Cottages A and B were licensed, but none of the other cottages were. (*Source:* From "Naturalistic Observation of Institutionalized Retarded Persons: A Comparison of Licensure Decisions and Behavioral Observations" by A. C. Repp and L. E. Barton, 1980, *Journal of Applied Behavior Analysis, 13,* p. 337. Copyright by the Society for the Experimental Analysis of Behavior, Inc. Reprinted by permission.)

provide habilitative opportunities for all retarded citizens, despite all that the recent judicial decisions and governmental regulations seem to promise. (pp. 339–341)

Fortunately, no new large state institutions for persons with mental retardation are on the drawing boards, and a variety of alternative residential placements are coming into reality. We will briefly describe some of these in the sections that follow. Before moving on, however, it is important to make one point. There have been, and continue to be, many caring and competent professionals working in institutions who have dedicated their careers to providing the best possible education and living conditions for the people who reside there. Many of these professionals themselves do not think large institutions are the best way to care for our citizens with severe and profound mental retardation, yet they are trying to do the best job possible under the prevailing conditions.

Regional Facilities

Regional facilities offer total-care, 24-hour residential programs like those of the large state institutions but on a much smaller basis, serving only those persons in a given geographical area within a state. The reduced distance to family and community allows for more normalized and individualized treatment programs. Hemming, Lavender, and Pill (1981) compared the quality of life of 51 adults with mental retardation who were transferred from a large institution to smaller living units and a matched control group of 50 adults who remained in the large institution. Residents who had been transferred to the smaller units showed significant improvement in adaptive behavior (as measured by the Adaptive Behavior Scale) and increased participation in culturally normative activities.

Chapter 15 provides more information on deinstitutionalization.

Group Homes

A group home usually consists of three to six persons with mental retardation living in a family-type dwelling in a residential neighborhood. Professional staff are responsible for supervision and overall programming for the residents, who typically participate in work, social, and recreational activities in the community. In recent years there has been tremendous growth in the number of group homes and other community-based residential alternatives for persons with mental retardation.

More information on group homes and other community-based residential alternatives for adults with disabilities is presented in Chapter 15.

Apartment Living

A variety of residential alternatives involve apartment living for adults with mental retardation. Alternatives include independent apartments with minimal supervision, apartment clusters, and coresidence arrangements (a resident with mental retardation and a nondisabled roommate). A follow-up study of 69 adults with mental retardation 5 years after they had been placed in independent living arrangements found 80% of the group still in their original independent housing placements (Schalock, Harper, & Carver, 1981). These adults reported that they were proud of their apartments and that they felt good about "doing their own thing."

■ CURRENT ISSUES/FUTURE TRENDS

The first President's Committee on Mental Retardation was created by John F. Kennedy in 1961. The committee was charged with conducting an intensive study of mental retardation and making recommendations for national policy. A year later, results of the many task forces, public hearings, visits to facilities, and extensive interviews with professionals, parents, and persons with mental retardation were compiled into the committee's report, *A Proposed Program for National Action to Combat Mental Retardation* (Mayo, 1962). The report contained specific recommendations related to human and legal rights, prevention, research, education, and medical and other services for individuals with mental retardation. Many of the Committee's recommendations set the stage for much of what took place in the 1960s and early 1970s, particularly in the areas of research and legislation confirming the rights of retarded citizens.

Subsequent presidents have reconvened the Committee on Mental Retardation to track the accomplishment of earlier goals and to attempt to predict future needs. In its 1976 report to the president entitled *Mental Retardation: Century of Decision,* the Committee outlined the country's major objectives in the field of mental retardation through the year 2000. Seven major goals were stated:

1. Attainment of citizenship status in law and in fact for all mentally retarded individuals in the United States, exercised to the fullest degree possible under the conditions of disability.

2. Reduction of the incidence of mental retardation from biomedical causes by at least 50% by the year 2000.

3. Reduction of the incidence and prevalence of mental retardation associated with social disadvantage to the lowest level possible by the end of this century.

4. Adequate and humane service systems for all retarded persons in need of them.

5. Attainment of a high and stable level of international relations in the cooperative resolution of the universal human problems of preventing and ameliorating mental retardation.

6. Achievement of a firm and deep public acceptance of mentally retarded persons as members in common of the social community and as citizens in their own right.

7. Equitable, coordinated, efficient, and effective use of public resources in all mental retardation programs.

The Committee went on to list specific objectives by which it thought the major goals could be obtained. Although a great deal remains to be done to realize these goals, some accomplishments have been made in each of the seven areas. We will briefly describe some recent accomplishments and current activities in three related areas: human and legal rights, prevention, and normalization.

Rights of Citizens with Mental Retardation

We have come a long way since the time when people with mental retardation were exterminated, ridiculed, or employed as court jesters—but we still have a long way to go. Of all the goals of the first President's Committee on Mental Retardation, we have the most concrete evidence of having accomplished the goal of legal rights for persons with mental retardation.

Friedman (1976, 1977) has detailed the history of the legal rights movement on behalf of people with mental retardation. Numerous court cases in recent years have advanced the position that a person with mental retardation has and should be able to exercise, with assistance from society if necessary, the same rights and freedoms as a nonhandicapped citizen. Following are the rights of persons with mental retardation as advocated by the AAMR.

> Mentally retarded citizens are entitled to enjoy and to exercise the same rights as are available to nonretarded citizens, to the limits of their ability to do so. As handicapped citizens, they are also entitled to specific extensions of, and additions to, these basic rights, in order to allow their free exercise and enjoyment. When an individual retarded citizen is unable to enjoy and exercise his or her rights, it is the obligation of the society to intervene so as to safeguard these rights, and to act humanely and conscientiously on that person's behalf.

Basic Rights

I. The basic rights that a retarded person shares with his or her nonretarded peers include, but are not limited to, those implied in "life, liberty, and the pursuit of happiness," and those specified in detail in the various documents that provide the basis for governing democratic nations.

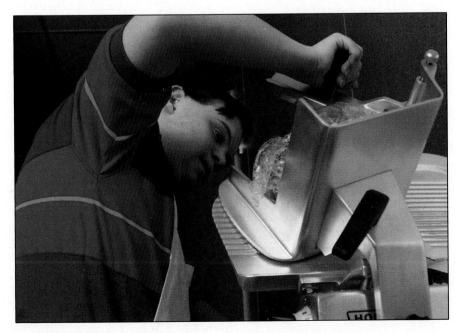

Like all citizens, people with mental retardation have the right to perform real work for real pay.

Specific rights of mentally retarded persons include, but are not limited to:

A. The right to freedom of choice within the individual's capacity to make decisions and within the limitations imposed on all persons.
B. The right to live in the least restrictive individually appropriate environment.
C. The right to gainful employment, and to a fair day's pay for a fair day's labor.
D. The right to be part of a family.
E. The right to marry and have a family of his or her own.
F. The right to freedom of movement, hence not to be interned without just cause and due process of law, including the right not to be permanently deprived of liberty by institutionalization in lieu of imprisonment.
G. The rights to speak openly and fully without fear of undue punishment, to privacy, to the practice of a religion (or the practice of no religion), and to interaction with peers.

Specific Extensions

II. Specific extensions of, and additions to, these basic rights, which are due mentally handicapped persons because of their special needs, include, but are not limited to:

A. The right to a publicly supported and administered comprehensive and integrated set of rehabilitative programs and services designed to minimize handicap or handicaps.
B. The right to a publicly supported and administered program of training and education including, but not restricted to, basic academic and interpersonal skills.
C. The right, beyond those implicit in the right to education described above, to a publicly administered and supported program of training toward the goal of maximum gainful employment, insofar as the individual is capable.
D. The right to protection against exploitation, demeaning treatment, or abuse.
E. The right, when participating in research, to be safeguarded from violations of human dignity and to be protected from physical and psychological harm.
F. The right, for a retarded individual who may not be able to act effectively in his or her own behalf, to have a responsible impartial guardian or advocate appointed by the society to protect and effect the exercise and enjoyment of these foregoing rights, insofar as this guardian, in accordance with responsible professional opinion, determines that the retarded citizen is able to enjoy and exercise these rights (American Association on Mental Deficiency, 1973).

Many states have organized citizen advocacy programs to aid individuals with mental retardation. An **advocate** is a volunteer committed to becoming personally involved with the welfare of a person with mental retardation and to becoming knowledgeable about the services available for that person. In a sense, an advocate is an informed friend who can legally take a stand to see that her client's rights are not abused and that the necessary educational and other services are in fact delivered. Being an advocate can be an excellent way to serve a citizen with mental retardation and in the process learn much about the field.

Prevention of Mental Retardation

Each week in this country more than 2,000 babies are born who are, or will at some point become, mentally retarded. As scientific research—both medical and psychological—has generated new knowledge about the causes of mental retardation, procedures and programs designed to prevent its occurrence have increased.

Probably the biggest single preventive strike against mental retardation (and many other handicapping conditions, including blindness and deafness) was the development of an effective rubella vaccine in 1962. When rubella (German measles) is contracted by mothers during the first 3 months of pregnancy, it causes severe damage in 10% to 40% of the unborn children (Krim, 1969). Fortunately, this cause of mental retardation can be eliminated if women are vaccinated for rubella before becoming pregnant.

Phenylketonuria (PKU) is a genetically inherited condition in which a child is born without an important enzyme needed to break down the amino acid phenylalanine, which is found in many common foods. Failure to break down this amino acid causes brain damage that results in severe mental retardation. By analyzing the concentration of phenylalanine in a newborn's blood plasma, doctors can diagnose PKU and treat it with a special diet. Most PKU children who receive a phenylalanine-restricted diet early enough have normal intellectual development (Berman & Ford, 1970).

Advances in medical science have enabled doctors to identify certain genetic influences strongly associated with mental retardation. One approach to prevention offered by many health service organizations is **genetic counseling**, a discussion between a specially trained medical counselor and prospective parents about the possibilities that they may give birth to a handicapped child, based on the parents' genetic backgrounds.

Amniocentesis is a procedure in which a sample of fluid is withdrawn from the amniotic sac surrounding the fetus during the second trimester of pregnancy (usually about the 14th to 17th week). Fetal cells are removed from the amniotic fluid and grown in a cell culture for about 2 weeks. At that time, a chromosome and enzyme analysis is performed to identify the presence of about 80 specific genetic disorders prior to birth. Many of these disorders, such as Down syndrome (O'Brien, 1971), are associated with mental retardation.

A new technique for prenatal diagnosis that may eventually replace amniocentesis is **chorion villus sampling (CVS)**. With CVS, a small amount of chorionic tissue (fetal component of the developing placenta) is removed and tested. The most significant advantage of CVS is that it can be performed earlier than amniocentesis (during the 8th to 10th week of pregnancy), and, because fetal cells exist in relatively large numbers in the chorion, they can be analyzed immediately without waiting for them to grow for 2–3 weeks. Although CVS is being used increasingly, it has been associated with a miscarriage rate of about 10 in 1,000 (compared to 2.5 in 1,000 with amniocentesis) and is still considered experimental.

Medical advances such as these have noticeably reduced the incidence of mental retardation caused by some of the known biological factors, but huge advancements in research are needed to reach the goal of reducing the incidence of biomedical retardation by 50% by the year 2000.

As we saw earlier, the great majority of those children labeled mentally retarded fall in the mild range and their conditions have no clear-cut etiology. These are the children whose developmental delays are thought to be primarily the result of a poor environment during their early years. The poor environment may be a result of parental neglect, poverty, disease, poor diet, and other factors—many of which are completely out of the hands of the child's parents. Two of the most well-known and long-running research and intervention programs aimed at reducing the incidence of psychosocial retardation are the Milwaukee Project and the Juniper Gardens Children's Project. The Milwaukee Project involved early identification of infants considered to be high risk (that is, children who were living in conditions associated with cultural-familial retardation). Over a 15-year period, education and family support services were provided to the children and their mothers. A recent book on this longitudinal study reports improvements in the children's cognitive and language development abilities (Garber, 1988).

In its 25-year history, the Juniper Gardens Children's Project has addressed the problems of psychosocial retardation by developing and evaluating home, school, and community-based interventions based on applied behavior analysis (Greenwood, Carta, Hart, Thurston, & Hall, 1989).

Although measuring the effects of programs that aim to prevent psychosocial retardation is much more difficult than measuring the decreased number of children suffering from a disease like PKU, the preliminary results of these projects are encouraging.

Normalization

The principle of **normalization** refers to the use of progressively more normal settings and procedures "to establish and/or maintain personal behaviors which are as culturally normal as possible" (Wolfensberger, 1972, p. 28). Normalization is not a single technique or set of procedures, but rather an overriding philosophy. That philosophy says that persons with mental retardation should, to the greatest extent possible, be both physically and socially integrated into the mainstream of society regardless of the degree or type of disability. "Such integration is maximized when all people live in a culturally normative setting in ordinary community housing, can move and communicate in age-appropriate ways and are able to use typical community services such as schools, stores, churches, and physicians" (Madle, 1978, p. 469).

Menolascino (1977) makes the following recommendations for normalizing the delivery of educational, residential, and community services to people with mental retardation.

1. Programs and facilities for mentally retarded persons should be physically and socially integrated into the community.

The November 1989, issue of *Education & Treatment of Children* was devoted to a review of the Juniper Gardens Children's Project. See Chapter 13 for more on intervention programs for young handicapped children.

Wolf Wolfensberger (1983), perhaps the most well-known champion of the normalization principle, has proposed the term *social role valorization* to replace *normalization*. He wrote: "The most explicit and highest goal of normalization must be the creation, support, and defense of *valued social roles* for people who are at risk of social devaluation" (p. 234).

2. No more mentally retarded people should be congregated in one service facility than the surrounding neighborhood can readily integrate into its resources, community social life, and so on.

3. Integration—and, therefore, normalization—can best be attained if the location of services follows population density and distribution patterns.

4. Services and facilities for retarded persons, if they are to be normalizing in their intent, must meet the same standards as other comparable services and facilities for nonretarded people; they should not be stricter or more lenient.

5. Staff personnel working with retarded persons must meet at least the same standards as those required of persons working with comparable nonretarded individuals.

6. To accomplish maximum normalization, mentally retarded persons must have maximum exposure to the nonretarded population in the community.

7. Daily routines should be comparable to those of nonretarded persons of the same age.

8. Services for children and adults should be physically separated, both because the probability that children will imitate the deviant behavior of their elders will be less and because services to adults and children tend to be separated in the mainstream of our society.

9. Mentally retarded individuals should be taught to dress and groom themselves like other persons their age; they should be taught a normal gait, normal movements, and normal expressive behavior patterns; their diet should be adjusted to assure normal weight.

10. As much as possible, the mentally retarded adult, even if severely handicapped, should be provided the opportunity to engage in work that is culturally normal in type, quantity, and setting. (Adapted from Menolascino, 1977, pp. 79–83)

As belief in normalization grows among both professionals and the public, the time draws nearer when all persons with mental retardation will experience the benefits of humane and effective treatment and educational, residential, and vocational opportunities.

SUMMARY

History of Treatment and Services for People with Mental Retardation

♦ Primitive people left individuals with mental retardation and other disabilities to die. Later, people with mental retardation became objects of superstition and ridicule.

♦ The first attempts to educate children with mental retardation came during the early 19th century in Europe and spread to the United States. Later in the century, however, large state institutions—which came to be seen as custodial rather than educational—became the primary means of service.

- The movement today is away from institutions and segregation toward normalized education in the least restrictive environment.

Defining Mental Retardation

- The current AAMR definition, used in P.L. 94–142, states that mental retardation involves both significantly subaverage general intellectual functioning and deficits in adaptive behavior manifested between birth and 18 years of age. Intellectual functioning is usually measured with a standardized intelligence test and adaptive behavior on an observation scale.

- The trend today is toward a more conservative approach in labeling children mentally retarded because of the concern over possible negative effects of labeling and the limitations of the tests.

Classification of Mental Retardation

- Children with mild mental retardation may experience substantial performance deficits only in school. Their social and communication skills may be normal or nearly so. They are likely to become independent or semi-independent adults.

- Most children with moderate mental retardation show significant developmental delays during their preschool years. Most school children with moderate mental retardation are educated in self-contained classrooms, and most live and work in the community as adults if individualized programs of support are available.

- Most persons with severe and profound mental retardation are identified in infancy. Some adults with severe and profound mental retardation can be semi-independent, but others need 24-hour care throughout their lives.

Prevalence

- Theoretically, 3% of the population would score in the retarded range on IQ tests, but this does not account for adaptive behavior, the other criterion. Many experts now cite an incidence figure of approximately 1% of the total population.

Causes of Mental Retardation

- It is difficult to determine the cause of most cases of mental retardation. About 80% to 85% of all cases involve mild retardation. In most of these cases, there is no known cause, and the terms *psychosocial disadvantage* and/or *cultural-familial retardation* are used when referring to etiology.

- All of the more than 250 known causes of mental retardation are biological.

Educational Placement, Curricular Goals, and Institutional Methodology

- Although some children with mental retardation attend special schools, more and more are being educated in their neighborhood schools—either in special classes or in regular classes where they receive special help or attend a resource room for part of the day.

- Many children with mild retardation are educated in regular classrooms with extra help provided as needed. They can generally master standard academic skills up to about a sixth grade level.

- In school, students with moderate mental retardation are usually taught communication, self-help and daily living skills, and vocational skills, along with limited academics. Most children with moderate mental retardation are educated in self-contained classrooms.

- In spite of their severe handicaps, people with severe and profound mental retardation can learn. Curricula stress functional communication and self-help skills.

- Applied behavior analysis is widely used in teaching students with mental retardation. Effective techniques include task analysis, repeated opportunities to respond, positive reinforcement, and direct and frequent measurement.

Residential Alternatives

- Today there are many different options available for residential and educational placement of children and adults with mental retardation. Institutions are seen as necessary for fewer and fewer people, and thus some are able to provide more humane and more appropriate services for their residents. Small regional residential programs help people with mental retardation live more normal lives within their own communities. Some adults with mental retardation live in supervised apartments, some with nondisabled roommates; others live in group homes with houseparents.

Current Issues/Future Trends

- Recent laws, including P.L. 94–103, P.L. 94–142, and the American with Disabilities Act have extended and affirmed the rights of persons with mental retardation. Advocates can help protect the rights of individual people with mental retardation.

- Recent scientific advances—including genetic counseling, amniocentesis, chorion villus sampling (CVS), virus vaccines, and early screening tests—are helping reduce the incidence of clinical retardation. However, there is still no widely used technique to decrease the incidence of cultural-familial mental retardation, although early identification and intensive educational services to high-risk infants show promise.

- Our current goal is to make the lives of people with mental retardation—at home, in school, and at work—as normal as possible. With this in mind, institutions are necessarily inappropriate. Thus, we must develop normalized and effective training and transition programs and community services for individuals with mental retardation and work to change public attitudes.

FOR MORE INFORMATION

Journals

American Journal on Mental Retardation. Published bimonthly by the American Association on Mental Retardation, 1719 Kalorama Road, NW, Washington, DC 20009. Publishes studies and discussions of original material dealing with the behavioral and biological aspects of retardation, as well as theoretical articles.

Education and Training of the Mentally Retarded. Published four times per school year by the Division on Mental Retardation of the Council for Exceptional Children, 1920 Association Drive, Reston, VA 22091-1589. Publishes experimental studies and discussion articles dealing with the education of mentally retarded persons.

Mental Retardation. Published bimonthly by the American Association on Mental Retardation, 1719 Kalorama Road, NW, Washington, DC 20009. Concerned with new approaches to methodology, critical summaries, essays, program descriptions, and research studies dealing with mental retardation.

Research in Developmental Disabilities. Published quarterly by Pergamon Press, Maxwell House, Fairview Park, Elmsford, New York. Publishes original behavioral research and theory on severe and pervasive developmental disabilities as well as coverage of the legal and ethical aspects of applying treatment procedures to children and adults with mental retardation.

Books

Blatt, B. (1987). *The conquest of mental retardation*. Austin, TX: Pro-Ed.

MacMillan, D. L. (1982). *Mental retardation in school and society* (2d ed.). Boston: Little, Brown.

Patton, J. R., Beirne-Smith, M., & Payne, J. S. (1990). *Mental retardation* (3rd ed.). Columbus, OH: Merrill.

Robinson, G. A., Patton, J. R., Polloway, E. A., & Sargent, L. R. (Eds.) (1989). *Best practices in mild mental disabilities*. Reston, VA: Council for Exceptional Children.

Robinson, N. M., & Robinson, H. B. (1976). *The mentally retarded child* (2nd ed.). New York: McGraw-Hill.

Organizations

American Association on Mental Retardation, 5201 Connecticut Avenue, NW, Washington, DC 20015. Primarily includes researchers, teacher educators, and psychologists interested in mental retardation.

Association for Retarded Citizens, 2709 Avenue E East, Arlington, TX 76011. An advocacy organization including parents and professionals, with active local chapters in most states.

Division on Mental Retardation, Council for Exceptional Children, 1920 Association Drive, Reston, VA 22091. Includes teachers, teacher educators, researchers, and other members of CEC working with individuals with mental retardation from preschool on.

opponents
anew
distant
boring
odd
drowsy
SCHOLASTIC NEWS
THE MYSTERIOUS RAIN FOREST

4

Learning Disabilities

♦ Why is it so difficult to define the true nature of learning disabilities?

♦ Are learning disabilities really a specific type of handicap or a school-defined phenomenon?

♦ How are methods of assessment and instructional approaches related?

♦ What are the most important skills for learning disabled students to master?

♦ Why does the area of learning disabilities continue to be so vulnerable to outlandish treatment programs?

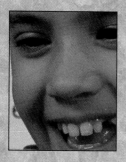

No area of special education has experienced as much rapid growth, extreme interest, and frantic activity as learning disabilities. This statement is as true today as it was a decade ago. The number of children identified as learning disabled has increased greatly in recent years, making this category the largest in special education. The increase has helped fuel an ongoing debate among professionals over the very nature of the learning disability concept. Some believe the increase in the number of children identified as learning disabled indicates the true extent of the handicapping condition. Others contend that too many low achievers—nonhandicapped children who are simply doing poorly in school—have been improperly identified as learning disabled, placing a severe strain on the limited resources available to serve the truly learning disabled student.

Learning disabilities has also been the focus of much public attention and interest, as demonstrated by countless newspaper stories, magazine articles, and television documentaries ("Does Your Child Have a Learning Disability?"). Learning disabilities, more than any other area of special education, seems to create misunderstanding and controversy. There is considerable confusion and disagreement, not just on the part of the general public but among professionals and parents as well, on such basic questions as, What is a learning disability? and How should students with learning disabilities be taught? In some ways, learning disabilities brings out both the worst and the best that special education has to offer. Learning disabilities has served as a breeding ground for fads and miracle treatments ("New Vitamin and Diet Regimen Cures Learning Disabilities!"). At the same time, some of the most innovative teachers and scholars in special education have devoted their careers to learning disabilities. Methods of assessment and instruction that were first developed for learning disabilities have influenced the entire field of education and benefited students of all kinds.

■ HISTORY OF THE AREA OF LEARNING DISABILITIES

By the 1950s, most public schools had established special education programs (or at least offered some type of special service) for students with mental retardation, physical disabilities, behavior disorders, and vision or hearing impairments. But there remained a group of children who were having serious learning problems at school, yet did not fit into any of the existing categories of exceptionality. They did not "look" handicapped; that is, the children seemed physically intact, yet they were unable to learn certain basic skills and subjects at school. In searching for help with their children's problems (remember, the public schools had no programs for these children), parents turned to other professionals—notably doctors, psychologists, and speech and language specialists. Understandably, these professionals viewed the children from the perspectives of their respective disciplines. As a result, terms such as *brain damage, minimal brain dysfunction, neurological impairment, perceptual handicap, dyslexia,* and *aphasia* were often used to describe or account for the various problems. Many of these terms are still used today, as a variety of disciplines have been and continue to be influential in the area of learning disabilities.

Although coining of the term *learning disabilities* and the focused attention to this area of special education were phenomena of the 1960s, the area is closely related to research conducted with brain-injured, mentally retarded children in the 1940s and 1950s by Werner, Strauss, Lehtinen, and Kephart. For more detailed presentations on the development of the area, see Lovitt (1989), Mercer (1987), Myers and Hammill (1990), and Wiederholt (1974a).

Origins

Most historians of special education place the official beginning of the learning disabilities movement in 1963, when Dr. Samuel Kirk delivered an address to a group of parents who were meeting in Chicago to form a national organization. The children of these parents were experiencing serious difficulties in learning to read, they were hyperactive, or they could not solve math problems. The parents did not believe their children's learning problems were the result of mental retardation or emotional disturbance, nor were they satisfied with the labels most often applied to their children. Kirk said, "Recently, I have used the term 'learning disabilities' to describe a group of children who have disorders in development in language, speech, reading, and associated communication skills" (Kirk, 1963). The parents liked the term and, that very evening, voted to form the Association for Children with Learning Disabilities (ACLD).

Today, the organization's name is the Learning Disabilities Association of America (LDA), and it is a powerful advocacy group of 50,000 members dedicated to the support of services and programs for persons with learning disabilities. Most LDA members are parents, although many teachers and other professionals are also members.

Milestones

In 1968, three more milestones were reached. First, the National Advisory Committee on Handicapped Children drafted and presented to Congress a definition of learning disabilities, which would later be incorporated into P.L. 94–142 as the definition used to govern dispersal of federal funds for support of services to learning disabled children. Second, the Council for Exceptional Children (CEC), the largest organization of educators and other professionals serving exceptional children, established the Division for Children with Learning Disabilities (DCLD). Third, Lloyd Dunn published his article "Special Education for the Mildly Retarded—Is Much of It Justifiable?" (Dunn, 1968). Dunn argued that the proliferation of self-contained classrooms at that time was not supported by evidence of their effectiveness and that the evaluation and placement procedures typically used with mildly handicapped children were questionable on many grounds. This article led many special educators to a much closer self-examination of all their practices, including those involving learning disabilities.

In 1982, the membership of DCLD left CEC to form an independent organization, the Council for Learning Disabilities (CLD). In that same year, a new Division for Learning Disabilities (DLD) was created within CEC. Many learning disabilities professionals maintain membership in both CLD and DLD.

Legislative Support

Largely because of the intense lobbying efforts of the ACLD and DCLD, legislators were made aware of learning disabled children, who were not covered under any previous legislation providing educational support for handicapped students. As a result, the Children with Learning Disabilities Act (part of P.L. 91–230) was passed by Congress in 1969. This legislation authorized a 5-year program of federal funds for teacher training and the establishment of model demonstration programs for learning disabled students. In 1975, learning disabilities was one of the handicapping conditions included in P.L. 94–142.

See Sleeter (1986) for an interesting perspective on the history of learning disabilities that is quite different from that provided by most textbooks. She contends that the category of learning disabilities was originally created to explain the failures of white middle-class children when American school achievement standards were raised following the Soviet Union's launching of Sputnik.

■ DEFINING LEARNING DISABILITIES

Since the inception of the area of learning disabilities, controversy has raged over how learning disabilities should be defined. Of the many proposed definitions, none has been universally accepted. The definition that has had the most impact was first written in 1968, when the National Advisory Committee on

Handicapped Children of the U.S. Office of Education drafted a definition that was eventually published, with only minor changes in wording, as the federal definition of learning disabilities in P.L. 94–142, the Individuals with Disabilities Education Act. It reads:

> "Specific learning disability" means a disorder in one or more of the basic psychological processes involved in understanding or in using language, spoken or written, which may manifest itself in an imperfect ability to listen, think, speak, read, write, spell, or to do mathematical calculations. The term includes such conditions as perceptual handicaps, brain injury, minimal brain dysfunction, dyslexia, and developmental aphasia. The term does not include children who have learning problems which are primarily the result of visual, hearing or motor handicaps, of mental retardation, or of environmental, cultural, or economic disadvantages. (U.S. Office of Education, 1977b, p. 65083)

When operationalizing the definition of learning disabilities, most states and school districts require that three criteria be met:

1. A discrepancy between the child's potential and actual achievement
2. An exclusion criterion
3. The need for special education services

Each factor is stated or implied in most definitions of learning disabilities.

As many as 40 different definitions have been proposed for learning disabilities (Bennett & Ragosta, 1984). In a survey of all 50 states and the District of Columbia, however, Mercer, King-Sears, and Mercer (1990) found that most states were using a definition of learning disabilities containing the key components found in the federal definition.

The student with learning disabilities experiences significant learning difficulties that cannot be explained by mental retardation, sensory impairment, emotional disturbance, or lack of educational opportunity.

A closer look at each of those criteria demonstrates even further why it is so difficult to come up with a definitive definition of learning disabilities.

Discrepancy

Children who are having minor or temporary difficulties in learning should not be identified as learning disabled. The term is meant to identify children with a true learning handicap, which, according to federal guidelines, is evidenced by a "severe discrepancy between achievement and intellectual ability" (U.S. Office of Education, 1977, p. 65083). Intellectual ability is most often measured by an IQ test, and achievement by a standardized achievement test. Even though this is a fairly well agreed-upon criterion—a survey by Mercer, King-Sears, and Mercer (1990) found that 86% of the states required that a discrepancy exist before the learning disabilities label could be applied—continual disagreement and confusion have persisted over exactly how to objectively determine a severe discrepancy (Macmann, Barnett, Lonbard, Belton-Kocher & Sharpe, 1989).

Lack of a specific definition for a severe discrepancy in the criteria published by the federal government for identifying learning disabled students has forced state and local educators to find some means of objectively identifying those children who are to receive special services.

For example, the Ohio Department of Education has issued the following rules for determining when a severe discrepancy criterion exists:

> Each child shall have a severe discrepancy between achievement and ability which adversely affects his or her educational performance to such a degree that special education and related services are required. The basis for making the determination shall be:
>
> (i) Evidence of a discrepancy score of two or greater than two between intellectual ability and achievement in one or more of the following seven areas:
> (a) Oral expression,
> (b) Listening comprehension,
> (c) Written expression,
> (d) Basic reading skills,
> (e) Reading comprehension,
> (f) Mathematics calculation, or
> (g) Mathematics reasoning.
> (ii) The following formula shall be used in computing the discrepancy score:
> (a) From:
> (i) The score obtained for the measure of intellectual ability,
> (ii) Minus the mean of the measure of intellectual ability,
> (iii) Divided by the standard deviation of the measure of intellectual ability.
> (b) Subtract:
> (i) The score obtained for the measure of achievement,
> (ii) Minus the mean of the measure of achievement,
> (iii) Divided by the standard deviation of the measure of achievement.
> (c) The result of this computation equals the discrepancy score. If the discrepancy score is two or greater than two, a severe discrepancy exists. (*Rules for the Education of Handicapped Children,* effective July 1, 1982, p. 69)

The Council for Learning Disabilities (1986) published a position statement citing eight reasons for opposing the use of discrepancy formulas. The CLD position statement also included these recommendations: (1) that discrepancy formulas be phased out as required procedure for identifying individuals with learning disabilities; (2) that when discrepancy formulas must be used, they be used with extreme caution; and (3) that the results of discrepancy formulas should never be used to dictate whether an individual has a learning disability. In lieu of discrepancy formulas, CLD recommends improved comprehensive multidisciplinary assessment of all areas of learning disabilities identified by federal rules and regulations (i.e., oral expression, listening comprehension, and writing expression in addition to reading and mathematics). After conducting two experiments evaluating the dependability of formula-based identification of learning disabled students, Macmann et al. (1989) concluded that "it appears that the severe discrepancy concept has outlived its usefulness as a viable model for service allocation" (p. 144).

Exclusion

The concept of learning disabilities is meant to identify children with significant learning problems that cannot be explained by mental retardation, sensory impairment, emotional disturbance, or lack of opportunity to learn. Kirk (1978) uses the term *specific learning disabilities* to differentiate truly learning disabled students from the larger group of children with various learning problems.

Several noted special educators have criticized the exclusion clause in the federal definition of learning disabilities because it says that children with other handicapping conditions cannot be considered learning disabled as well. For example, some children whose primary diagnosis is mental retardation do not achieve up to their expected potential (Wallace & McLoughlin, 1979). Hammill (1976) challenges the notion that only children with IQ scores in the normal range can be identified as learning disabled. He rests his criticism on two arguments. First, most IQ tests are made up of items that measure past learning. If a child with a learning disability has not learned enough of the information included on the IQ test, he will score in the retarded range. Second, there are too many sources of measurement error involved in intelligence testing to make clear-cut differential diagnosis statements such as, "This child is mildly retarded; this one is learning disabled."

Special Education

A learning disabled student needs special education that "should involve practices that are unique, uncommon, of unusual quality and that, in particular, supplement the organizational and instructional procedures used with the majority of children" (Ames, 1977, p. 328). This criterion is meant to keep children who have not had the opportunity to learn from being identified as learning disabled. These children should progress normally as soon as they are placed in a developmentally appropriate regular education program. Learning disabled children are those who show specific and severe learning problems in spite of normal educational efforts and therefore need special educational services to help remediate their achievement deficiencies.

See the Winter 1987 issue of *Learning Disabilities Research* for detailed discussion of the discrepancy concept.

The Spring 1990 issue of *Learning Disability Quarterly* is devoted to discussion of whether or not IQ scores should be considered in the concept of learning disabilities.

The NJCLD-Proposed Definition

The National Joint Committee on Learning Disabilities (NJCLD) is a group composed of official representatives from eight professional organizations involved with learning disabled students.

The NJCLD believed that the federal definition of learning disabilities had served the educational community reasonably well, but had several inherent weaknesses (Hammill, Leigh, McNutt, & Larsen, 1981). Myers and Hammill (1990) identify those elements of the P.L. 94–142 definition with which the NJCLD was not satisfied.

1. *Exclusion of adults.* Since enactment of the federal law, there has been major interest in understanding the special needs of and developing programs for adolescents and adults with learning disabilities (e.g., Alley & Deshler, 1979; Mangrum & Strichart, 1988). Because it deals with public school education, the P.L. 94–142 definition refers only to school-age children, thereby eliminating adults from consideration.

2. *Reference to basic psychological processes.* Members of the NJCLD maintain that use of the phrase "basic psychological processes" has generated extensive and perhaps unnecessary debate over how to teach learning disabled students, but that how to teach is a curricular issue, not a definitional one. The NJCLD believes the intent of the original phrase was only to show that a learning disability is intrinsic to the person affected.

3. *Inclusion of spelling as a learning disability.* Because spelling can be integrated with other areas of functioning, namely written expression, it is redundant and should be eliminated from the definition.

4. *Inclusion of obsolete terms.* The NJCLD believes that inclusion of terms such as *dyslexia, minimal brain dysfunction, perceptual handicaps,* and *developmental aphasia,* which historically have proven difficult to define, only adds confusion to the definition of learning disability.

5. *The exclusion clause.* The wording of the final clause in the P.L. 94–142 definition has led to the belief that learning disabilities cannot occur along with other handicapping conditions. A more accurate statement, according to the NJCLD, is that a person may have a learning disability along with another handicap, but not *because of* another handicap. In other words a learning disability should be considered a handicap in its own right.

In response to these problems with the federal definition, the NJCLD proposed a definition of learning disabilities in 1981, and revised it slightly in 1989:

> Learning disabilities is a generic term that refers to a heterogeneous group of disorders manifested by significant difficulties in the acquisition and use of listening, speaking, reading, writing, reasoning, or mathematical abilities. These disorders are intrinsic to the individual and presumed to be due to central nervous system dysfunction, and may appear across the life span. Problems in self-regulatory behaviors, social perception, and social interaction may exist with learning disabilities but do not themselves constitute a learning disability. Although learning disabilities may occur concomitantly with other handicapping conditions (for example, sensory impairment, mental retardation, serious emotional disturbance)

The NJCLD consists of representatives from the American Speech-Language-Hearing Association (ASHA), the Learning Disabilities Association of America (LDA), the Council for Learning Disabilities (CLD), the Division for Children with Communication Disorders (DCCD), the Division for Learning Disabilities (DLD), the International Reading Association (IRA), the National Association of School Psychologists (NASP), and the Orton-Dyslexia Society.

See the "Educational Approaches" section of this chapter.

or with extrinsic influences (such as cultural differences, insufficient or inappropriate instruction), they are not the result of those conditions or influences. (National Joint Committee on Learning Disabilities, 1989, p. 1)

After comparing and contrasting 11 different definitions of learning disabilities, Hammill (1990), one of the prime contributors to the NJCLD definition, thinks that consensus is near:

> The NJCLD never intended to write the perfect definition, only a better one. A study of the definitions discussed in this paper suggests that the committee was successful in its efforts. The NJCLD definition has obtained a high level of acceptance among multiple national associations and individuals and is arguably the best one that is presently available. None of the NJCLD members believe that their definition has settled the issue for all time. Political realities are such that the NJCLD definition may never replace the 1977 USOE definition in law. But this may not be important. What is important, however, is that professionals and parents unite around one definition so that we can say with assurance, "This is what we mean when we say *learning disabilities*." (p. 83)

For further rationale and detailed exploration of the NJCLD definition, see Hammill (1990), Hammill et al. (1981), and Myers and Hammill (1990).

It is still too early to tell what impact the NJCLD definition will have. On one level, the NJCLD definition can be seen as an effort to limit the term *learning disabilities* to the "hard-core" or truly handicapped with its statement that the disorder is "intrinsic to the individual and presumed to be due to central nervous system dysfunction."

The Debate Continues

Other special educators have proposed broader definitions of learning disabilities. For example, a definition written by an interagency committee within the National Institutes of Health includes deficits in social skills as a primary type of specific learning disability (Gresham & Elliott, 1989). Hallahan and Kauffman (1976, 1977) have suggested that a learning disabled child is simply one who is not achieving up to potential. The child may be at any intelligence level, and his learning difficulties may be caused by any number of factors. Many more children—perhaps up to one-third the population of some school districts—might be considered learning disabled with this broad definition.

We believe the most important issue, from an educator's standpoint, is not whether a student is labeled learning disabled but how to assess and remediate the specific skill deficiencies in each child's repertoire.

■ CHARACTERISTICS OF CHILDREN WITH LEARNING DISABILITIES

In describing the various categories of exceptionality, it is often useful to list the physical and psychological characteristics commonly found in the children who make up that group. The inherent danger in all such lists of characteristics is the tendency to assume, or at least look for, *each* of those characteristics in *all* the children considered to be in the category. This danger is especially acute with learning disabilities. To give you some idea of the extent of this problem—a notion of just how different from one another learning disabled children

A significant deficit in academic achievement is the most fundamental characteristic of children with learning disabilities.

are—consider this: A national task force found 99 separate characteristics of learning disabled children described in the literature (Clements, 1966).

Mercer (1987) notes that since Clements's (1966) report of the most frequently cited characteristics of learning disabled children, there has been little systematic research on the relative incidence of the various characteristics, so the list is no longer accurate. The first four characteristics on Clements's list, for example, were hyperactivity, perceptual-motor impairments, emotional ups and downs, and general coordination deficits. Specific academic difficulty, the fundamental defining characteristic of learning disabilities today, was ranked only eighth on the Clements list.

Subsequent to Clements's report, several major studies of the characteristics of students with learning disabilities have been reported (Cone, Wilson, Bradley, & Reese, 1985; Kirk & Elkins, 1975; Norman & Zigmond, 1980; Sheppard & Smith, 1981). Cone et al. (1985) examined the demographic, intellectual, and achievement data for 1,839 students enrolled in K–12 learning disabilities programs in Iowa. They found that

1. Males outnumbered females by a 3:1 ratio across primary, elementary, and secondary age levels

2. 75% of the students were initially identified as learning disabled in the elementary grades

3. The mean IQ for the sample was 95

4. Students exhibited more academic deficiencies in reading and spelling than in mathematics

5. Students' relative level of academic achievement decreased progressively as their grade level increased

Social Acceptance

Some professionals believe that deficits in social skills represent a primary type of learning disability (see Gresham & Eliot, 1989).

Other researchers have investigated the social acceptance of students labeled learning disabled, their classroom deportment, and their ability to attend to a task. The results of this research are far from conclusive, perhaps partly because of the heterogeneous nature of learning disabilities and partly because of the lack of agreement in and inconsistent application of identification criteria. Most researchers who have investigated the social status of students with learning disabilities have concluded, for example, that low social acceptance is common (Bryan & Bryan, 1978; Gresham, 1982). After reviewing the published studies on the social status of learning disabled individuals, however, Dudley-Marling and Edmiaston (1985) concluded that, as a group, learning disabled individuals may be at greater risk for attaining low social status, but that some learning disabled students are, in fact, popular. Two subsequent studies continued the contradictory findings on peer acceptance. Gresham and Reschly (1986) found significant deficits in the social skills and peer acceptance of 100 mainstreamed learning disabled children when compared to 100 nonhandicapped children. But in the same journal issue, Sabornie and Kauffman (1986) reported more optimistic findings that there was not a significant difference in the sociometric standing of 46 mainstreamed learning disabled high school students and 46 nonhandicapped peers. Moreover, they discovered that some of the learning disabled students enjoyed socially rewarding experiences in the mainstream classrooms.

One interpretation of these contradictory results is that social acceptance is not so much a characteristic of learning disabilities as it is an outcome of the different social climates created by teachers, parents, and other caregivers with whom learning disabled students interact. Toward that end, researchers have begun to identify the types of problems experienced by learning disabled

The social acceptance of students with learning disabilities can sometimes be improved through joint activities with high-status nonhandicapped classmates.

children who are ranked low in social acceptance and to discover instructional arrangements that promote the social status of students with learning disabilities in the regular classroom. For example, Stone and La Greca (1990) found that

> The subset of children with learning disabilities who experience peer problems may actually consist of two distinct subgroups, some of whom experience peer rejection, and others who are more likely to be ignored by their classmates. For instance, rejected children are more likely to demonstrate aggressive and disruptive behaviors, experience more loneliness, and be at greater risk for negative future outcome. . . . Intervention strategies for this group might be directed toward helping these children control inappropriate acting-out behaviors, as well as teaching more acceptable peer-directed behaviors. In contrast, neglected children are more likely to be shy and withdrawn and to experience social anxiety. Identification of this subgroup of children, then, might be effectively followed up with behavioral interventions for promoting social initiations as well as cognitive interventions for reducing anxiety. (p. 36)

Fox (1989) found that pairing low socially-accepted learning disabled children with popular nonhandicapped same-sex classmates in activities designed to promote the discovery and discussion of mutual interests resulted in the non-LD children rating their partners higher on a friendship rating instrument. There is also some evidence that positive social interactions are increased and negative social interactions decreased when high-status nonhandicapped children serve as academic tutors for low-status students with learning disabilities (Maheady & Sainato, 1985).

Attention Problems and Hyperactivity

Attention deficit (the inability to attend to a task) and hyperactivity (high rates of purposeless movement) are frequently cited as characteristics of learning disabled children. The term now used to describe this combination of behavioral traits is **attention deficit-hyperactivity disorder,** or **ADHD** (American Psychiatric Association, 1987). To diagnose ADHD, a physician must determine that a child consistently displays multiple examples of inattention, impulsivity, and hyperactivity. A random national sample of family practitioners found that approximately 5% of all elementary students screened received a diagnosis of ADHD (Wolraich et al., 1990).

The most commonly prescribed treatment for ADHD is drug therapy. Ritalin, a member of the amphetamine family, is the most prescribed medication. Although amphetamines are stimulants that normally increase a person's activity level, they produce a paradoxical effect in hyperactive children; that is, a reduced level of activity typically follows ingestion of the drug. The number of children on stimulant medication has increased tremendously in recent years. A survey by the Baltimore, Maryland, County Health Department found that 5.96% of all elementary-aged school children were receiving drug treatment for hyperactivity/inattentiveness (Safer & Krager, 1988). Given the results of nine previous biannual surveys, this figure represents a doubling of the rate of medication treatment for hyperactive/inattentive students every 4 to 7 years. The authors of the survey estimated that by the early 1990s, more than 1 million U.S. school children will be given daily doses of stimulant medication

Although an extended discussion of the use of psychotropic medication (behavior- and/or mood-altering drugs) is beyond the scope of this text, Gadow's book (1986) is an excellent source of information on this important topic for educators. The most common alternative to the use of drugs to treat hyperactivity is behavioral interventions. See Houlihan and Van Houten (1989) and O'Leary (1980) for reviews of these methods.

in an effort to control hyperactivity and attention deficits. Many of the children receiving prescription drugs to improve their classroom behavior are learning disabled.

Although many physicians, parents, and teachers have reported positive results with stimulant therapy for learning disabled children, results of controlled research is mixed (Gadow, 1986). Given the questionable benefits of drug therapy with school children and the fact that undesirable side effects are sometimes noted (e.g., insomnia, decreased appetite, headaches, disruption of normal growth patterns, irritability, reduced emotional affect, and increased blood pressure), many professionals now view drug treatment as an inappropriate "easy way out" that might produce short-term improvements in behavior, but result in long-term harm.

It is important to stress that ADHD is not the same as a learning disability. Although some learning disabled children are hyperactive and inattentive, many are calm and work hard at learning tasks (Samuels & Miller, 1985). Likewise, numerous children who display impulsivity, inattention, and/or hyperactivity do well in school.

See "Signaling for Help" on pages 144–145 to find out how one learning disabilities resource room teacher helps her students stay on task while working at their desks.

Behavior Problems

The type and incidence of classroom behavior problems exhibited by children with learning disabilities have been the subject of considerable research. Epstein and Cullinan have conducted a series of studies that reveal a higher-than-normal rate of behavior problems among learning disabled students (Epstein, Bursuck, & Cullinan, 1985; Epstein, Cullinan, & Lloyd, 1986; Epstein, Cullinan, & Rosemier, 1983). They point out that although their data definitely show increased behavior problems among learning disabled children, the relationships between the students' problem behavior and academic difficulty are not known. In other words, it cannot be said that either the academic deficits or the behavior problems cause the other difficulty. Also, the data from these studies summarize large groups of students. Many children with learning disabilities exhibit no behavior problems at all.

Regardless of the interrelationships of these characteristics, teachers and other caregivers responsible for planning educational programs for students with learning disabilities must be skilled in dealing with social and behavioral difficulties as well as academic skill deficits.

Subtypes of Learning Disabilities?

Because of the many learning and behavioral characteristics associated with learning disabilities and the inability to create an accurate profile of characteristics for persons labeled learning disabled, some professionals are suggesting that distinct subtypes of learning disability exist and should be classified. McKinney (1985) states that the literature, collectively, argues against a "single syndrome" theory of learning disability and that it is feasible to create more homogeneous diagnostic subgroups within this presently broad and ill-defined category of exceptional children. It is much too early to predict whether the search for subgroups among learning disabled individuals will have any legitimate implications for education and treatment.

On pages 618–619, one woman shares some of her experiences and frustrations in coping with a learning disability, both as a child and as an adult.

Life-Span Perspective

Another perspective on the characteristics of individuals with learning disabilities is the life-span view. Table 4.1 presents Mercer's (1987) summary of the

TABLE 4.1

A life span view of learning disabilities summarizing likely problem areas, purposes of assessment and treatment, and the treatments most recommended at five different age levels

	Preschool	Grades K–1	Grades 2–6	Grades 7–12	Adult
Problem Areas	Delay in developmental milestones (e.g., walking) Receptive language Expressive language Visual perception Auditory perception Short attention span Hyperactivity	Academic readiness skills (e.g., alphabet knowledge, quantitative concepts, directional concepts, etc.) Receptive language Expressive language Visual perception Auditory perception Gross and fine motor Attention Hyperactivity Social skills	Reading skills Arithmetic Skills Written expression Verbal expression Receptive language Attention span Hyperactivity Social-emotional	Reading skills Arithmetic skills Written expression Verbal expression Listening skills Study skills (metacognition) Social-emotional-delinquency	Reading skills Arithmetic skills Written expression Verbal expression Listening skills Study skills Social-emotional
Assessment	Prediction of high risk for later learning problems	Prediction of high risk for later learning problems	Identification of learning disabilities	Identification of learning disabilities	Identification of learning disabilities
Treatment Types	Preventive	Preventive	Remedial Corrective	Remedial Corrective Compensatory Learning strategies	Remedial Corrective Compensatory Learning strategies
Treatments with Most Research and/or Expert Support	Direct instruction in language skills Behavioral management Parent training	Direct instruction in academic and language areas Behavioral management Parent training	Direct instruction in academic areas Behavioral management Self-control training Parent training	Direct instruction in academic areas Tutoring in subject areas Direct instruction in learning strategies (study skills) Self-control training Curriculum alternatives	Direct instruction in academic areas Tutoring in subject (college) or job area Compensatory instruction (i.e., using aids such as tape recorder, calculator, computer, dictionary) Direct instruction in learning strategies

Source: From *Students with Learning Disabilities* (3rd ed.) (p. 44) by C. D. Mercer, 1987, Columbus, OH: Merrill. Reprinted by permission.

SIGNALING FOR HELP

A resource room for students with learning disabilities is a busy place. Students come and go throughout the day, each according to a schedule that specifies the amount of time to be spent in the resource room. Each student who comes to the resource room does so because of a need for intensive individualized instruction. The IEP objectives for any given group of students in a resource room at any one time typically cover a wide range of academic and social skills. Because of the varied skill levels and the ever-changing student groupings in the resource room, the resource room teacher is usually managing several types and levels of instruction at once. To accomplish this, students are often assigned individualized learning activities. Resource room teachers face a difficult challenge: the need to be in several places at once. While students work at their desks, the teacher moves about the room providing individual students with prompts, encouragement, praise, and/or corrective feedback as needed.

Students in a resource room are usually working on those skills in which they need the most help. Therefore an effective and efficient system with which students can signal the resource room teacher for assistance is a must. Hand-raising, the typical attention-getting signal, poses several problems. It is difficult to continue to work while holding one's hand in the air, a situation that results in a great deal of "down" time as students wait for the teacher to get to them. In addition, if several students are waving their hands in competition for the teacher's attention, it is distracting to other students and to the teacher. If unsuccessful in getting the teacher's help, students may give up trying whenever they run into difficulty. Even worse, students who are unsuccessful in obtaining the teacher's assistance may stop discriminating their need for help and simply continue to practice errors.

One solution is both simple and effective. Students need an easy, quiet means of signaling for help that allows them to keep working, with the assurance that their teacher will recognize their need for help. In Ronni Hochman's resource room for middle school students with learning disabilities, each student has a small flag made of colored felt, a dowel rod, and a 1¼ inch cube of wood. When one of Ronni's students needs assistance or wants her to check completed work, the student simply stands the flag up on his desk. While waiting for the teacher, the student can either go on to another item or work on materials in a special folder. With this simple and inexpensive system, down time is greatly reduced, and neither Ronni nor her students are distracted by hand waving or calling out. (Kerr & Nelson [1989] describe a signaling device made from an empty can wrapped with construction paper. Students turn the can on one end or the other to signal "I'm working" or "I need help.")

Ronni asked her students to write what they thought of the flag signal system after using it for about 3 months.

major problem areas most likely to occur, the purposes of assessment and treatment, and the treatments most recommended in five different age spans.

We stress that the single, fundamental characteristic of children with learning disabilities is a specific and significant achievement deficiency in the

This is one of the best way to work in sted of raising your hand you raise your flag and keep on working but if you raise you hand you can't keep working. That is special because I get more work done. If she is working with some one els you raise it and she will get to you as fast as she can.— Brent

The flags in Miss Hochmans room are used for assistance from the teacher. When Miss Hochman is working you rais you flag and she will help you as soon as she has time. But you keep on working, like going on to the next problem.— Pam ◆

Signal flags are a simple and effective way to obtain teacher assistance.

presence of adequate overall intelligence. Some learning disabled children are also hyperactive (or any of the other cited characteristics), and some are not. And children who display any of these other characteristics but who do not also have deficits in achievement should not be considered learning disabled.

■ PREVALENCE

Learning disabilities is by far the largest of all special education categories. During the 1988–89 school year, 1,998,422 children aged 6 to 21 were identified as learning disabled and received special education services (U.S. Department of Education, 1990). This figure represents 48% of all children with disabilities served in the United States. And the number has grown tremendously in recent years. The 1988–89 figure represents an increase of 152% over the 797,213 learning disabled children receiving special education in 1976–77. During this same period, the total number of children served in special education increased by only 23.7%. Among the reasons cited by the government for the growth in the number of children with learning disabilities are "eligibility criteria that permit children with a wide range of learning problems to be classified as learning disabled; social acceptance and/or preference for the learning disabled classification; the reclassification of some mentally retarded children as learning disabled; and the lack of general education alternatives for children who are experiencing learning problems in regular classes" (U.S. Department of Education, 1986, p. 5).

Because of the many ways in which the definition of learning disabilities can be interpreted, the different means of diagnosing and identifying learning disabled children from one state to the next, and the unreliable assessment instruments used to diagnose learning disabilities, it is impossible to give a true incidence rate of learning disabilities. Bryant and McLoughlin (1972) reviewed 21 incidence studies and found that children with learning disabilities were cited as comprising anywhere from 3% to 28% of a school's total enrollment. Based on P.L. 94–142 child count data reported by the states, the number of children with learning disabilities represented 4.5% of the total population of U.S. school children during the 1988–89 school year (U.S. Department of Education, 1990).

■ CAUSES OF LEARNING DISABILITIES

In almost every case, the exact cause of a child's learning disability is unknown; however, a wide variety of causes have been proposed. Three major categories of etiological factors are brain damage, biochemical imbalance, and environmental factors.

Brain Damage

The ingestion of alcohol and other drugs during pregnancy is known to cause brain damage and learning problems. These causes of learning and other disabilities are discussed in Chapter 14.

Some learning disabled individuals show definite signs of brain damage, which may well be the cause of their learning problems (Duffy & McAnulty, 1985; Geshwind & Galaburda, 1987). Spivak (1986) has estimated that as many as 20% of children with learning disabilities have sustained a prior brain injury, either before (**prenatal**), during (**perinatal**), or after birth (**postnatal**). Some professionals believe that all learning disabled children suffer from some type of brain injury or dysfunction of the central nervous system. Indeed, this belief is inherent in the NJCLD definition of learning disabilities that states that learning disorders are "presumed to be due to central nervous system dysfunction." The brain damage is not considered extensive enough to cause a generalized and severe learning problem across all kinds of intellectual development, so the individual may be referred to as minimally brain damaged.

In cases where actual evidence of brain damage cannot be shown (and this is the situation with the majority of learning disabled children), the term **minimal brain dysfunction** is often used. This phrase implies brain damage by asserting that the child's brain does not function well. The term is still used by some professionals in the area of learning disabilities, especially by physicians.

Most educators place little value on brain dysfunction as an explanation of the difficulties experienced by most learning disabled persons. As Smith and Robinson (1986) state, "The evidence linking behavioral characteristics to brain dysfunction is circumstantial, speculative, and in most cases clearly not documentable. Identifying brain damage does not lead to sets of instructional or remediation strategies that produce guaranteed or uniform results" (p. 223).

There are two major problems with current etiological theories linking learning disabilities to brain damage. The first problem is lack of evidence. Not all learning disabled children display clinical (medical) evidence of brain damage—and not all brain-damaged children are learning disabled. Boshes and Myklebust (1964) reported the results of EEG readings given to 200 normal and 200 learning disabled children. Results showed that 29% of the normal children and 42% of the learning disabled children displayed abnormal brain wave patterns. Even though more learning disabled children were rated abnormal, certainly these results show that there is not a direct, one-to-one relationship between brain injury and learning disability.

The second problem with the brain-damage assumption is that it can serve as a powerful, built-in excuse for failure to teach the child. If a child doesn't learn, it is thought to be no one's fault; after all, she has a brain injury that "prevents" her from learning. The concern that teachers do not let diagnoses of real or suspected neurological problems sway their educational judgments is shared by virtually all professionals in learning disabilities, even those who believe that a true learning disability is caused by central nervous system damage or dysfunction. Myers and Hammill (1990) conclude their discussion of etiology with these cautionary words:

> For the teacher or clinician who is not engaged in systematic research, the primary concerns are to handle the correlative symptoms . . . to teach the children to read, speak, write, and so on. Whether learning disabilities in an individual case are symptoms that result from brain injury or developmental delay will not essentially alter the methods of teaching the student. . . . Isolation of definite or presumed etiologies for the observed disabilities is of only tangential interest and value to the teacher-clinician and plays a minor role in the preparation of instructional programs. (p. 22)

Assessment of brain damage is often done with an **electroencephalograph (EEG)**, which measures and makes a graph of brain waves. Brain damage is inferred from the presence of abnormal brain waves.

Biochemical Imbalance

Some researchers claim that biochemical disturbances within a child's body are the cause of learning disabilities. Dr. Benjamin Feingold (1975a, 1975b, 1976) received much publicity for his claims that artificial colorings and flavorings in many of the foods children eat can cause learning disabilities and hyperactivity. He recommended a treatment for learning disabilities that consisted of a diet with no foods containing synthetic colors or flavors.

The Feingold Diet

In 1965, Feingold, a San Francisco allergist, treated a woman with an acute case of hives. The woman was put on a diet that removed all salicylates, a group of natural compounds found in certain fruits and vegetables. In less than 2 weeks, the hives had disappeared, and the woman reported that she did not feel as aggressive or hostile as she had before (Feingold, 1975b).

Feingold then tried the elimination diet on 25 hyperactive children in one school system and claimed that 16 of the children responded favorably. On the basis of this and several other uncontrolled studies, Feingold held a news conference and announced that "hyperactivity can be greatly reduced by the elimination of artificial food coloring and flavoring" from children's diets and that the diet "brings hope to thousands of parents who have been distressed by the need to cope with the problem of hyperactivity by giving their children prescribed drugs" (Spring & Sandoval, 1976). Newspaper and magazine articles, more press conferences, a popular book (Feingold, 1975b), and appearances on television talk shows followed. In an article in the *Journal of Learning Disabilities,* Feingold (1976) wrote,

> Artificial food colors and flavors have the capacity to induce adverse reactions affecting every system of the body. Of all these adverse reactions, the nervous system involvement, as evidenced by behavioral disturbances and learning disabilities, is the most frequently encountered and most critical, affecting millions of individuals in this country alone.
>
> The K-P diet, which eliminates all artificial food colors and flavors as well as foods with a natural salicylate radical, will control the behavioral disturbance in 30% to 50% (depending on the sample) of both normal and neurologically damaged children. (p. 558)

A number of research studies were conducted to test the Feingold diet, some claiming positive results (Connors, Goyette, Southwick, Lees, & Andrulonis, 1976; Cook & Woodhill, 1976). In a comprehensive review of diet-related studies, however, Spring and Sandoval (1976) concluded that there was very little evidence to support Feingold's theory. Many of the studies were poorly conducted, and the few experiments that were scientifically sound concluded that only a small portion of hyperactive children might be helped by the special diet. In a well-controlled study employing "double-blind" procedures, however, Rose (1978) found that two 8-year-old girls who had been on the Feingold diet for at least 11 months spent less time on-task and more time out of their seats when they had eaten cookies that contained a yellow artificial food coloring just before going to school.

In response to the controversy over diet treatments, the American Council on Science and Health (1979) issued the following statement:

> Hyperactivity will continue to be a frustrating problem until research resolves the questions of its cause, or causes, and develops an effective treatment. The reality is that we still have a great deal to learn about this condition. We do know now, however, that diet is not the answer. It is clear that the symptoms of the vast majority of the children labeled "hyperactive" are not related to salicylates, artificial food colors, or artificial flavors. The Feingold diet creates extra work for the homemakers and changes the family lifestyle . . .but it doesn't cure hyperactivity. (p. 5)

Feingold's "demonstration study" of hyperactive children was never published in a scientific journal.

The K-P diet is Feingold's name for his diet.

The girls ate a yellow cookie each day, but neither they nor the observers knew whether the cookies contained artificial coloring on any certain day. Thus, the girls' behavior and the observers' measurements could not be affected by their expectations. This is a *double-blind* control procedure.

In spite of such official rejection of Feingold's claims, many parents have continued to follow his recommendations. As Divoky (1978) writes, "Along comes Feingold. Not only is he going to get hyperactive kids off drugs, but he's going to do it with a wonderfully appealing treatment: additive-free, healthful food" (p. 56). Today the Feingold Association maintains a membership of over 10,000 people (mainly parents) in 120 local groups.

Megavitamin Therapy

Cott (1972) hypothesized that learning disabilities can be caused by the inability of a child's bloodstream to synthesize a normal amount of vitamins. Based on his contention, some physicians began megavitamin therapy with learning disabled children. Megavitamin treatment consists of massive daily doses of vitamins in an effort to overcome the suspected vitamin deficiencies.

Two studies designed to test the effects of megavitamin treatment with learning disabled and hyperkinetic children found that huge doses of vitamins did not improve the children's performance (Arnold, Christopher, Huestis, & Smeltzer, 1978; Kershner, Hawks, & Grekin, 1977). And several researchers have cautioned against the potential risks of large doses of vitamins. Toxic effects such as scurvy, cardiac arrhythmia, headaches, and abnormalities of the liver may result, especially from megadoses of certain B vitamins (Eastman, 1978; Golden, 1980).

> See Rooney (1991) for a review and critique of controversial therapies as interventions for children with learning and behavior problems.

> Vitamin therapy has also been recommended for children with mental retardation; some studies claim increases in IQ and improvements in behavior as a result of large doses of vitamin-mineral supplements (e.g., Harrell, Capp, Davis, Peerless, & Ravitz, 1981). After reviewing the Harrell et al. study and others, however, Pruess, Fewell, & Bennett (1989) concluded that "vitamin therapy is clearly not useful for young children with Down syndrome" (p. 340).

Environmental Factors

Lovitt (1978) cites three types of environmental influences that he believes are related to children's learning problems: emotional disturbance, lack of motivation, and poor instruction. Many children with learning problems have behavior disorders as well. Whether one causes the other or whether both are caused by some other factor(s) is uncertain. In addition, it is difficult to identify reinforcing activities for some learning disabled students; they may not be interested in many of the things other children like. Some studies have shown that finding a key to the child's motivational problem can sometimes solve the learning problem as well (Lovitt, 1977).

One variable that is likely to be a major contributor to children's learning problems is quality of instruction. Lovitt (1978) states it this way:

> [A] condition which might contribute to a learning disability is poor instruction. Although many children are able to learn in spite of poor teachers and inadequate techniques, others are less fortunate. Some youngsters who have experienced poor instruction in the early grades never catch up with their peers. (p. 169)

Engelmann (1977) is even more direct.

> Perhaps 90 percent or more of the children who are labeled "learning disabled" exhibit a disability not because of anything wrong with their perception, synapses, or memory, but because they have been seriously mistaught. Learning disabilities are made, not born. (pp. 46–47)

Lovitt and Engelmann are among a growing number of educators who believe that the best way to help a child with learning problems is to emphasize the assessment and training of those specific behaviors (e.g., reading and

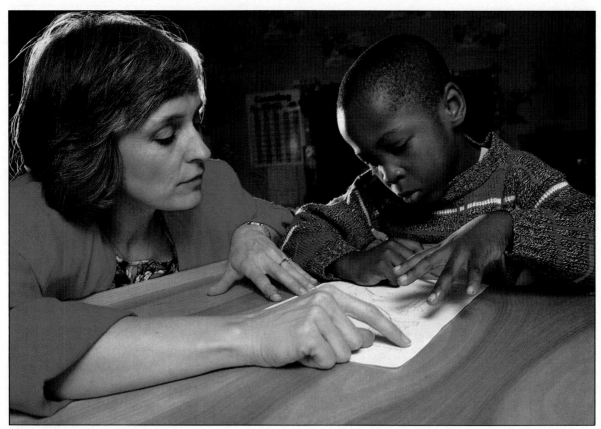

Regardless of the etiological factors responsible for this boy's learning problems, it is his teacher's responsibility to plan and deliver effective instruction.

Professionals who believe that learning disabilities are caused by central nervous system dysfunction are also concerned with environmental factors and their role in influencing the severity of the learning problem and affecting instruction.

arithmetic skills) that are troublesome for that particular child. Mounting evidence indicates that many students' learning problems can be remediated by direct, systematic instruction. It would be naive to think, however, that the learning problems of all children stem from inadequate instruction. Perhaps Engelmann's other 10% are those children whose learning disability is caused by a malfunctioning central nervous system. In any event, from an educational perspective, good, systematic instruction should be the treatment of first choice.

At present there is much more speculation than hard evidence about etiology, but the search for the real causes of children's learning problems must go on. Only when positive identification of the causes of learning disabilities has been made can prevention become a realistic alternative.

■ ASSESSMENT

In education, the word *assessment* is synonymous with *testing*. Literally hundreds of tests have been developed to measure virtually every motor, social, or academic response children make (Mitchell, 1985). Much of the testing in education is conducted primarily for the purpose of identifying children for certain special education categories and placement.

> At some point along the continuum of services provided by the school, there must be a cutoff that dictates which children will be served by special education and which will remain totally the responsibility of the general education program. Obviously, the vast majority of children who have trouble in school will have to stay in regular classes. In any event, the type of assessment that deals with identification is of the utmost importance in states where laws, policies, or traditions make it mandatory that children be classified according to type of handicap before they can qualify for special services. (Myers & Hammill, 1990, p. 66)

Because of the complex way that learning disabilities is defined, the task of identifying the true LD child guarantees that a battery of tests will be administered. One study of 14 school districts in Michigan found that, on the average, three to five different tests were given to each student referred for learning disabilities (Perlmutter & Parus, 1983). When Shepard and Smith (1981) examined how the determination of a learning disability was made in 1,000 individual cases in Colorado, they discovered that one-half of the school district funds available for services to students with learning disabilities were expended on identification alone. As a result of these assessment practices, learning disabled children have been called the "most diagnosed" of all exceptional children (Lovitt, 1982).

Even though identification and placement are appropriate and important functions of educational testing, assessment has a much more important purpose: to provide information for planning and implementing an instructional program for the child.

At least five different types of tests or methods are commonly used in assessing learning disabilities: norm-referenced tests, process tests, informal reading inventories, criterion-referenced tests, and direct daily measurement. Of these five types, norm-referenced tests and process tests are *indirect* assessment devices; that is, the child's general ability along various dimensions is measured. Informal reading inventories, criterion-referenced tests, and direct daily measurement can be classified as *direct* assessment techniques. Direct assessment measures the specific skills and behaviors that a child is to be taught. The choice between direct and indirect assessment is largely determined by the approach to instructional remediation taken by a given school program, which will be discussed later in this chapter.

Norm-Referenced Tests

Norm-referenced tests are designed so that one child's score can be compared to those of other children of the same age who have taken the same test. Because a deficit in academic achievement is the major characteristic of learning disabled children, standardized achievement tests are commonly used. Some standardized achievement tests—like the Iowa Tests of Basic Skills (Hieronymus & Lindquist, 1978), the Peabody Individual Achievement Test (Dunn & Markwardt, 1970), and the Wide Range Achievement Test (Jastak & Jastak, 1965)—are designed to measure children's overall academic achievement. Scores on these tests are reported by grade level; a score of 3.5, for example, means that the

For a critical examination of how assessment of learning disabled children is conducted, see Lovitt (1986) and Ysseldyke et al. (1983), who contend that too many tests are administered that produce too little useful data for planning instruction. These authors make a strong case for spending less time and fewer resources on assessment for classification and diagnosis and more resources on instruction.

For an excellent discussion of systematic assessment for instructional planning—that is, for using assessment to determine what to teach and how to teach—see Howell and Morehead (1987) and Zigmond and Miller (1986).

Two texts that describe special education assessment practices in detail and examine many widely used tests are McLoughlin and Lewis (1990) and Salvia and Ysseldyke (1988).

child's score equalled the average score by those students in the norm group who were halfway through the third grade. Other norm-referenced tests measure achievement in certain academic areas. Some of the frequently administered reading achievement tests are the Durrell Analysis of Reading Difficulty (Durrell, 1955), the Gates-McKillop Reading Diagnostic Test (Gates & McKillop, 1962), the Gray Oral Reading Tests (Gray, 1963), the Spache Diagnostic Reading Scales (Spache, 1963), and the Woodcock Reading Mastery Tests (Woodcock, 1974). The KeyMath Diagnostic Arithmetic Test (Connolly, Natchman, & Pritchett, 1973) and the Stanford Diagnostic Arithmetic Test (Beatty, Madden, & Gardner, 1966) are often used to test arithmetic achievement.

Process Tests

The concept of process, or ability, testing grew out of the belief that learning disabilities are caused by a basic, underlying difficulty of the child to process, or use, environmental stimuli in the same way that normal children do. These general abilities are categorized under headings such as visual perception, auditory perception, and eye-motor coordination. The developers and users of these tests believe that if the child's specific perceptual problems can be identified, treatment programs can then be designed to improve those problems, and the child's learning disability will be remediated. Of the number of process tests that have been developed, we will briefly discuss the two most widely used to diagnose and assess learning disabilities: the Illinois Test of Psycholinguistic Abilities (ITPA) (Kirk, McCarthy, & Kirk, 1968) and the Marianne Frostig Developmental Test of Visual Perception (Frostig, Lefever, & Whittlesey, 1964).

ITPA

Few tests have been as strongly associated with assessment of learning disabilities as the Illinois Test of Psycholinguistic Abilities. First published in 1961 and later revised in 1968, the ITPA consists of 12 subtests, each designed to measure some aspect of psycholinguistic ability that Kirk and his colleagues considered central to learning. Results of the test are depicted on a profile (Figure 4.1), showing in which of the 12 areas a child demonstrates weaknesses.

Many remedial education programs and activities for learning disabled children have been based on the psycholinguistic or information-processing model. Although research on the effectiveness of these training programs has not validated their effectiveness, one major contribution of the ITPA to educational assessment cannot be denied. The ITPA was developed and has been used for gathering data that can be translated directly into an educational program designed to meet the individual needs of a specific child.

For reviews of this research, see Hammill and Larsen (1974, 1978).

The Frostig

The Marianne Frostig Developmental Test of Visual Perception (Frostig et al., 1964) was developed by Dr. Frostig and her colleagues to measure certain dimensions of visual perception they considered crucial to a child's ability to learn to read. The Frostig test comprises five subtests designed to pinpoint the kinds of perceptual difficulties a child has. The five areas are eye-motor

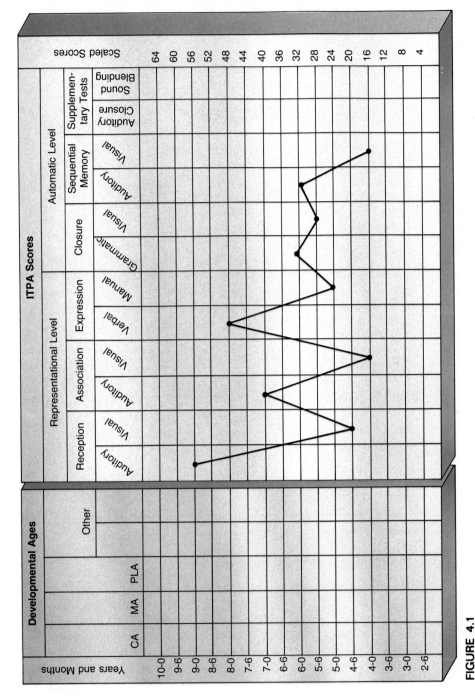

FIGURE 4.1

ITPA profile of abilities. This child was evaluated on 10 measures, involving levels of organization (representational and automatic), psycholinguistic processes (reception, association, etc.), and channels of communication (auditory, visual, etc.). In addition, some children are tested on two supplementary subtests. (*Source:* From *Illinois Test of Psycholinguistic Abilities* (rev. ed.) by S. A. Kirk, J. J. McCarthy, and W. D. Kirk, 1968, Urbana: University of Illinois Press. Copyright by the Board of Trustees of the University of Illinois. Reprinted by permission.)

FIGURE 4.2

Sample criterion-referenced
test and scoring sheet.
(*Source: Evaluating Exceptional Children: A Task Analysis Approach* (pp. 97–98) by
K. W. Howell, J. S. Kaplan, and
C. Y. O'Connell, 1979, Columbus, OH: Merrill. Reprinted by
permission.)

Task: Names each of the eight basic colors when shown.

Materials: One box of crayons (to include eight basic colors). One scoring sheet.

Directions (to student): "Say the name of each crayon as I hold it up. You have only three seconds to give me your answer, so pay close attention. (Pick up the first crayon.) What color is this?" Repeat procedure for each of the eight colors. Do not tell the subject if she is correct or incorrect. Do not let the student see what you are marking. Use a stopwatch or a sweep second hand out of the subject's field of vision. Timing should begin immediately following the word *this* in the direction.

Scoring: Wait 3 seconds for response. If the response is incorrect, put the crayon back in the box and mark "incorrect" on the scoring sheet. If the response is correct, put the crayon back in the box and mark "correct" on the scoring sheet. If the child hesitates, wait the full 3 seconds before putting the crayon back in the box and mark "incorrect."

CAP: 100% accuracy.

Skill: Knowledge of the eight basic colors.
Task: Names each of the eight basic colors when shown.

Subject _____ Age _____
Examiner _____ Date _____

Stimulus	Response (check one)	
	Correct	Incorrect
1. red	1 _____	1 _____
2. blue	2 _____	2 _____
3. yellow	3 _____	3 _____
4. green	4 _____	4 _____
5. black	5 _____	5 _____
6. orange	6 _____	6 _____
7. brown	7 _____	7 _____
8. purple	8 _____	8 _____

coordination, figure-ground discrimination, constancy of shape, position of objects in space, and spatial relationships.

Informal Reading Inventories

Teachers' growing awareness of the inability of formal achievement tests and process tests to provide truly useful information for planning instruction has led to greater use of teacher-developed and -administered informal tests, particularly in the area of reading. An informal reading inventory usually consists of a series of progressively more difficult sentences and paragraphs that a child is asked to read aloud. By directly observing and recording aspects of the child's reading skills—such as mispronounced vowels or consonants, omissions, reversals, substitutions, and comprehension—the teacher can determine the level of reading material that is most suitable for the child and the specific reading skills that require remediation.

Criterion-Referenced Tests

Criterion-referenced tests differ from norm-referenced tests in that a child's score on a criterion-referenced test is compared to a predetermined criterion, or mastery level, rather than to normed scores of other students. The value of criterion-referenced tests is that they identify the specific skills the child has already learned and the skills that require instruction. A criterion-referenced test widely used by special educators is the BRIGANCE Diagnostic Inventory of Basic Skills (Brigance, 1983), which includes 140 skill sequences in four subscales: readiness, reading, language arts, and math. Some commercially distributed curricula now include criterion-referenced test items for use both as a pretest and posttest. The pretest assesses the student's entry level, to determine what aspects of the program he is ready to learn, and the posttest evaluates the effectiveness of the program. Of course, criterion-referenced tests can be, and often are, informally developed by classroom teachers. A sample criterion-referenced test for determining a child's knowledge of the eight basic colors is shown in Figure 4.2.

Direct Daily Measurement

Direct daily measurement means observing and recording, every day, a child's performance on the specific skill that is being taught (Lovitt, 1975a, 1975b). In a program teaching multiplication facts, for example, the student's performance

Self-recording and graphing direct and daily measures of academic performance is an excellent way to motivate and involve students in their own learning.

of multiplication facts would be assessed each day that multiplication was taught. Measures such as correct rate (number of facts stated correctly per minute), error rate, and percentage correct are often recorded. Two advantages of direct daily measurement are clear. First, it gives information about the child's performance on the skill under instruction. Second, this information is available on a continuous basis, so that the teacher can adjust the child's program according to changing (or perhaps unchanging) performance, not because of intuition, guesswork, or the results of a test that measures something else. Direct and frequent measurement is the cornerstone of the behavioral approach to education introduced in Chapter 3 and is becoming an increasingly popular assessment and evaluation technique in all areas of special education (Howell, Kaplan, & O'Connell, 1979). One teaching approach of many learning disabilities teachers, based entirely on direct daily measurement, is **precision teaching**.

Precision Teaching

Precision teaching is a system of direct daily measurement of children's performances originated by Ogden R. Lindsley. Lindsley, who had worked with B. F. Skinner at Harvard, sought to translate much of the traditional operant (behavioral) terminology into language that sounded more natural in the schools. Thus, precision teachers look at behavior as *movement,* at antecedent and consequent events as *events before and after* the child's movement, at reinforcement schedules as *arrangements of the events* that follow a movement, and so on. Then, Lindsley sought to develop a set of simple but effective procedures that teachers could follow to identify, monitor, and make decisions about critical movements children need to make to succeed in school. Finally, based on data suggesting that children take bigger and bigger steps as they become more proficient at a movement, Lindsley devised the Standard Behavior Chart to show graphically the child's progress from day to day.

Since its inception, precision teaching has been refined and improved by many teachers and researchers. As presently practiced, precision teaching consists of the steps summarized here and illustrated in Figure 4.3:

1. Precisely pinpoint the movement the child must make to learn the skill required—writing digits, saying words, and so on.

2. Next, observe the child's performance of the movement, noting both accuracy and fluency (speed), and chart the results.

3. Using the information from a few days' observation, set an aim (objective) for the child—in terms of both accuracy and fluency—and note it on the chart.

4. Connect the average performance from the first few days with this aim, producing a line on the chart that represents the minimum progress the child must make each day to reach the aim in the time available.

5. As the days and weeks pass, continue to measure the child's performances every day, charting the information every day.

6. Paying careful attention to the chart, follow certain decision rules that tell when the program should be changed—to prevent the child from slipping below the line of minimum progress.

For more information about precision teaching, see issues of the *Journal of Precision Teaching;* Haring, Lovitt, Eaton, and Hansen (1978); McGreevy (1983); White (1986); and White and Haring (1980). Hasselbring and Hamlett (1983) have written a microcomputer program to help teachers implement precision teaching procedures.

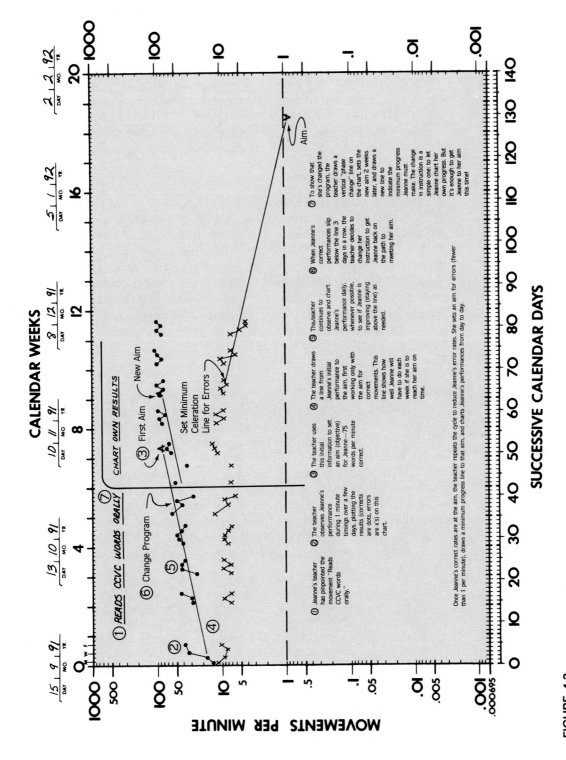

CALENDAR WEEKS

MOVEMENTS PER MINUTE

SUCCESSIVE CALENDAR DAYS

① **READS CCVC WORDS ORALLY**

③ First Aim   New Aim
CHART OWN RESULTS
⑦
⑥ Change Program
⑤
④
②

Set Minimum
Celeration
Line for Errors

① Jeanne's teacher has pinpointed the movement: "Reads CCVC words orally."

② The teacher observes Jeanne's performance during 1 minute timings over a few days, plotting the results (corrects are dots, errors are x's) on this chart.

③ The teacher uses this initial information to set an aim (objective) for Jeanne—75 words per minute correct.

④ The teacher draws a line from Jeanne's initial performance to the aim, first working only with the aim for correct movements. This line shows how well Jeanne will have to do each week if she is to reach her aim on time.

⑤ The teacher continues to observe and chart Jeanne's performance daily, whenever possible, to see if Jeanne is improving (staying above the line) as needed.

⑥ When Jeanne's correct performances slip below the line 3 days in a row, the teacher decides to change her instruction to get Jeanne back on the path to meeting her aim.

⑦ To show that she's changed the program, the teacher draws a vertical "phase change" line on the chart, sets the new aim 2 weeks later, and draws a new line to indicate the minimum progress Jeanne must make. The change in instruction is a simple one: to let Jeanne chart her own progress. But it's enough to get Jeanne to her aim this time!

Aim

Once Jeanne's correct rates are at the aim, the teacher repeats the cycle to reduce Jeanne's error rates. She sets an aim for errors (fewer than 1 per minute), draws a minimum progress line to that aim, and charts Jeanne's performances from day to day.

FIGURE 4.3

A standard behavior chart used in precision teaching. (*Source:* Adapted from *Exceptional Teaching* (p. 276) by O. White and N. Haring, 1976, Columbus, OH: Merrill. Reprinted by permission.)

7. Whenever a program change (phase change) is needed, note the change on the chart, draw a new aim and a new minimum progress line, and begin again—before the child has had a chance to fail.

In describing precision teaching, White (1986) writes:

> Essentially, in order to be responsive to the pupil's needs, the teacher must be a student of the pupil's behavior, carefully analyzing how that behavior changes from day to day and adjusting the instructional plan as necessary to facilitate continued learning. Precision Teaching offers a set of procedures designed to assist in that process. (p. 522)

Ecological Assessment

Results obtained from normative and criterion-referenced assessments are sufficient to determine instructional objectives and teaching procedures for most students. Some students' learning problems are complex enough, however, to warrant a more thorough assessment approach, known as *ecological assessment*. Ecological assessment encompasses two related perspectives: First, the learning disabled student is seen as possessing a "behavioral ecology" in the sense that changes in one behavior may affect other behaviors. Second, behavior is viewed within an environmental context whereby changes in one environmental condition may produce changes in other conditions, which, in turn, affect the child's performance (Rogers-Warren & Warren, 1977). Thus, an ecological assessment takes into account both the student and the various environments in which he lives. Heron and Heward (1988) describe six factors to consider in an ecological assessment: physiological factors (medications, health); physical aspects of the environment (e.g., amount of space provided to student, seating arrangements, lighting, noise); student-student interaction (how other children behave toward the learning disabled child); teacher-student interaction (effects that various teacher behaviors have on the child); home environment; and the student's reinforcement history. Ecological assessment data are obtained through a wide range of sources, including student records, interviews with parents and other caregivers, tests, academic products, direct observations, and behavioral checklists.

Although one can obtain a rich, descriptive data base about a student from an ecological assessment, teachers must weigh the costs and benefits of the approach.

> The key to using an ecological assessment is to know *when* to use it. Full-scale ecological assessments for their own sake are not recommendable for LD teachers charged with imparting a great number of important skills to many children in a limited amount of time. In most cases, the time and effort spent conducting an exhaustive ecological assessment would be better used in direct instruction. While the results of an ecological assessment might prove interesting, they do not always change the course of a planned intervention. Under what conditions then will an ecological assessment yield data that will significantly affect the course of treatment? Herein lies the challenge. Educators must become keen discriminators of: (1) situations in which a planned intervention has the potential for affecting student behaviors other than the behavior of concern; and (2) situations in which an intervention, estimated to be effective if the target behavior is viewed in isola-

tion, may be ineffective because other ecological variables come into play. (Heron & Heward, 1988, p. 231)

Recommendations for Assessment

The number of tests and assessment approaches available for learning disabled students is staggering. Learning disabled children are probably subjected to more testing sessions with more types of tests than any other exceptional children. It is no wonder many teachers, parents, and students become confused with the complexity of the assessment process. Lovitt (1989) offers the following recommendations for assessment:

Of course, all the assessment approaches described in this chapter are often used with other exceptional children, as well as with nonhandicapped students.

♦ *Assess directly.* In many instances, it is more sensible for teachers to measure something they are teaching than to gather inappropriate data from standardized tests. Many of the items on standardized tests are not the ones being taught.

♦ *Assess frequently.* If teachers want to know how a student is doing on a certain skill or behavior, it is important to gather pertinent data frequently, rather than rely on standardized tests, which are generally given only once or twice a year.

♦ *Assess the most important and most critical behaviors most often.* Teachers should decide which behaviors are most in need of change and then gather as much data as possible on them.

♦ *Inform pupils about the assessment process.* Teachers can help pupils by explaining not only the reasons for various measurements, but also, in many cases, the meaning of the results.

♦ *Conduct assessments in the students' classrooms or homes under normal circumstances.* When pupils are taken to testing chambers outside their familiar surroundings, they are generally not at ease, even if efforts have been made to establish rapport.

♦ *Assess skills and behaviors that are part of the pupils' IEPs.* It makes sense for teachers to rely on the IEPs for guidance on instruction and measurement. Too often, items included in IEPS are overlooked in instruction.

♦ *Become familiar with the techniques for conducting ecological assessments.* If detailed reports about certain pupils are desired, the ideas from that approach, coupled with ongoing data, blend together quite nicely.

♦ *Communicate with parents and other interested caregivers frequently and directly about the progress of their children.* Be open to suggestions from them about behaviors that should be assessed that are not being monitored. (pp. 92–93)

■ EDUCATIONAL APPROACHES

Most learning disabilities specialists believe in a diagnostic-prescriptive approach, in which the results of diagnosis (assessment) lead directly to a prescription (plan) for teaching. There is still great disagreement, however, over what is to be diagnosed and what methods of teaching should be prescribed.

Ysseldyke and Salvia (1974) outlined two major models of instructional remediation within the overall framework of the diagnostic-prescriptive approach: the ability training (or process) model and the skill training (or task-analysis) model. Although there are many variations and versions within each approach, there are fundamental differences between the two models.

Ability Training

Ability trainers believe that a child's observed performance deficit (learning problem) results from weakness in a particular ability thought necessary to perform a given task. (That is, a particular child may have failed to learn to read because of a visual-perceptual disorder.) These abilities are usually classified as perceptual-motor, sensory, or psycholinguistic. Educational remediation involves testing the child (e.g., with the ITPA or Frostig tests) to determine disabilities and then prescribing instructional activities for remediating those disabilities. If deficits in basic abilities cause the child's learning problem, remediating those deficits should result in improved achievement. The logic is sound.

Approaches to Ability Training

A number of distinct approaches can be identified within the ability-training model. The three most widely used approaches have been psycholinguistic training, based on the ITPA; the visual-perceptual approach, based on the Frostig Developmental Test of Visual Perception (Frostig & Horne, 1973); and the perceptual-motor approach (Kephart, 1971). According to Kephart, motor development precedes visual development; he believes lack of proper perceptual-motor development, such as eye-hand coordination, is often a cause of reading difficulty. Kephart's program teaches four areas of motor development: balance and posture, locomotion, contact, and receipt and propulsion.

Multisensory Approach

Another approach to teaching children with learning disabilities is the multisensory approach. Although teachers are more likely to work directly on academic skills, this approach is still based primarily on an information-processing model. As its name suggests, the multisensory approach employs as many of the child's senses as possible in an effort to help him learn. The most notable multisensory programs are those developed by Fernald (1943) and Slingerland (1971). Fernald's method is known as the VAKT technique. To learn a new letter, for example, the child would see the letter (visual), hear the letter (auditory), and trace the letter (kinesthetic and tactile). Little scientific research has been conducted on the multisensory method.

Effectiveness of Ability Training

There is little research evidence supporting the effectiveness of ability training. Hammill, Goodman, and Wiederholt (1974) reviewed the results of studies conducted on the Kephart and Frostig approaches. They concluded that 13 of the 14 studies evaluating the Frostig reading materials produced unimpressive results. Of 15 studies using Kephart's perceptual-motor training program, only 6 reported significant improvements (intelligence, school achievement, and language functioning were measured in these studies). In addition, only 4 of 11 studies measuring visual-motor functioning reported that the training significantly improved visual-motor performance. In another review, Myers and Hammill (1976) found that, in general, the Frostig materials improved children's scores on the Frostig Developmental Test of Visual Perception (Frostig et al., 1964), but it was questionable as to whether reading achievement improved. Two more comprehensive reviews have also found the effectiveness of the perceptual-motor approach wanting. Kavale and Mattison (1983) reanalyzed 180 studies that investigated the effectiveness of the perceptual-motor approach and concluded that it is "not effective and should be questioned as a feasible intervention technique for exceptional children" (p. 165). After reviewing the results of 85 perceptual-motor training studies, Myers and Hammill (1990) state,

> As a consequence of our reviews of these systems, we would recommend that perceptual-motor training in the schools be carefully reevaluated. Unlike 25 years ago, when research on the topic was sparse, one can no longer assume that these kinds of activities will be beneficial to the children who engage in them. In fact, in the long run they may even be somewhat harmful because (a) they may waste valuable time and money and (b) they may provide a child with a placebo program when the child's problems require a real remedial effort. We would suggest that when these programs are implemented in the schools, they be considered as highly experimental, nonvalidated services that require very careful scrutiny and monitoring. (p. 448)

In a major review of 38 studies of ITPA-based psycholinguistic training, Hammill and Larsen (1974, 1978) conclude that "the overwhelming consensus of research evidence concerning the effectiveness of psycholinguistic training is that it remains essentially nonvalidated" (1978, p. 412). Critics of Hammill and Larsen's ITPA review (e.g., Lund, Foster, & McCall-Perez, 1978) claim that they were not justified in their conclusions because many of the original studies were poorly controlled. Kavale (1981) reanalyzed the Hammill and Larsen studies and contends that his investigation "appears to answer affirmatively" that psycholinguistic training is effective.

In a different response to the Hammill and Larsen (1974) review, Minskoff (1975) suggests that the earlier psycholinguistic research was not a good basis on which to evaluate the approach because it tended to be incomplete and methodologically inadequate. She goes on to specify criteria for future psycholinguistic research, presumably so that its effectiveness will be more clearly understood. Sowell, Packer, Poplin, and Larsen (1979) followed Minskoff's criteria in a study designed to evaluate the effectiveness of psycholinguistic training with 63 first graders. They found the psycholinguistic training program to be unsuccessful and concluded their study with this comment:

> In summary, the amount of time, effort, and monies currently devoted in the schools to improving psycholinguistic abilities needs to be reevaluated. At best, psycholinguistic training should be viewed as experimental and not be employed extensively until its usefulness can be effectively demonstrated. In reality, the onus of documenting the value of psycholinguistic training procedures falls primarily to those individuals who produce and/or advocate them. Until such time as experimental validation for this approach is forthcoming, educators are well advised to utilize other strategies in attempting to stimulate academic and/or language skills in children under their care. (p. 76)

The CLD has published a position statement opposing the measurement and training of perceptual and perceptual-motor functions as part of educational services for individuals with learning disabilities (see *Learning Disability Quarterly,* Summer 1986, p. 247). The organization cites lack of scientific evidence in support of the claimed benefits of perceptual and perceptual-motor training.

Tomatic Listening Training Program

The attractiveness of treatment approaches that promise to reverse the academic deficiencies of learning disabled children is understandable. It seems as if every few years another esoteric therapeutic program claiming to "cure" learning disabilities is announced. Once such therapy regimen, called the Tomatic Listening Training Program, is said by its creator to increase the linguistic processing ability of the left cerebral hemisphere. During the first two phases, "Filtered Sound" and "Sonic Birth," children listen to classical music and Gregorian chants heard through filters designed to simulate how the unborn child would hear sounds passing through the amniotic fluid of the womb. During the third and longest phase, the child repeats taped messages, listens to classmates as they read, and reads and speaks into the Electronic Ear, an "audio vocal conditioning apparatus" consisting of a microphone, audio headset, and tone conductors. Tomatis (1978) claims that thousands of learning disabled children have shown remarkable improvements in auditory, linguistic, and academic deficits as a result of the program. The Tomatic listening program has received favorable coverage in the popular press in Canada, where several educational institutions have implemented it; however, both a 1-year follow-up study of 32 children and a subsequent 2-year follow-up of 26 of the same children failed to find evidence of any remedial effectiveness (Kershner, Cummings, Clarke, Hadfield, & Kershner, 1986, 1990).

Skill Training

Skill trainers believe that a child's demonstrated performance deficit is the problem. For example, if a child cannot master a complex behavior (such as

Tim's daily session in the "writing room" is spent practicing, self-evaluating, and self-editing the specific writing skills he needs to master.

reading a sentence) and has had sufficient opportunity and wants to succeed, a skill trainer would conclude that the child has not learned the necessary prerequisite skills (such as reading single words, reading letter sounds, and so on).

Skill trainers use:

1. Precise, operational definitions of the specific behaviors they intend to teach
2. Task analysis to break down complex skills into smaller units, or subskills, requiring the learner to master only one component of the task at a time
3. Direct teaching methods that require the learner to practice the new skill many times
4. Direct and frequent measurement to monitor the child's progress and evaluate instruction

Applied behavior analysis, direct instruction, and precision teaching are all skill-training approaches. All are closely related to one another, and all systematically manipulate aspects of the child's environment (materials, instructions, cues, rewards, and so on) in an attempt to facilitate the child's acquisition and retention of the new skill.

Direct Instruction

One skill-training teaching program is the Direct Instruction Model developed by Siegfried Engelmann and Wesley Becker and their colleagues at the University of Oregon. Three basic assumptions underlie the Direct Instruction Model:

1. All children can be taught
2. The learning of basic skills and their application in higher-order skills is essential to intelligent behavior and should be the main focus of a compensatory education program
3. The disadvantaged [handicapped] must be taught at a faster rate than typically occurs if they are to catch up with their middle-class [nonhandicapped] peers. (Engelmann, Becker, Carnine, & Gersten, 1988, p. 303).

Two major rules govern the selection of features in the model: "Teach more in less time" and "Control the details of what happens." DISTAR (Direct Instructional System for Teaching and Remediation) programs for arithmetic, reading, and language are commercially available .

A Direct Instruction program consists of a highly sequenced series of skills, materials, and activities to help children practice the skills and precise instructions for the teacher. The teacher works with a small group of children (4 to 10) who respond both individually and in unison to a fast-paced series of teacher-generated prompts and cues. Sometimes the teacher uses hand signals to direct and guide the children's responses. Corrective feedback for incorrect responses and praise for correct responses are also used.

Unlike the ability-training instructional approaches, the Direct Instruction Model is supported by an impressive body of research demonstrating its effectiveness. An evaluation of the Direct Instruction Model conducted by the nationwide Follow Through program and involving more than 8,000 children in

20 communities showed that children made significant gains in academic achievement (Becker & Englemann, 1976). These children caught up to or even surpassed the national norms on several arithmetic, reading, and language skills, as measured by the Wide Range Achievement Test (Jastak & Wilkinson, 1984) and the Metropolitan Achievement Tests (Balow, Farr, Hogan, & Prescott, 1978). On other skills, such as spelling, the Direct Instruction students finished a little below the national norm, but still showed significant gains. None of the other educational approaches evaluated by the Follow Through program were as effective as DISTAR.

Follow Through is a nationwide, comprehensive educational program for economically disadvantaged children, kindergarten through third grade. Many Head Start children enter Follow Through programs. See Chapter 13.

Learning Strategies Instruction

Teaching specific academic skills to students with learning disabilities is often not enough, because they often fail to use acquired knowledge and skills appropriately in novel situations. A major development during the past decade has been the emphasis on teaching students with learning disabilities *how* to learn. These *learning strategies* are taught in a direct, systematic fashion. Research on the learning strategies model, conducted by Deshler and Schumaker and their colleagues at the University of Kansas Research Institute on Learning Disabilities, has proven very promising (Deshler, Schumaker, & Lenz, 1984; Schumaker, Deshler, Alley, & Warner, 1983). They have developed, field-tested, and validated a learning strategies curriculum for learning disabled adolescents.

A student uses task-specific strategies to guide himself successfully through a learning task. The Sentence Writing Strategy (Schumaker & Sheldon, 1985), for example, provides students with a set of steps for using a variety of formulas when writing sentences, and the FIRST-Letter Mnemonic Strategy (Nagel, Schumaker, & Deshler, 1986) and the Paired-Associates Strategy (Bulgren & Schumaker, in press) give students several options for memorizing key information for tests.

FIGURE 4.4
Steps in an executive learning strategy for solving new kinds of problems.
(*Source:* From "Teaching Adolescents with Learning Disabilities to Generate and Use Task-Specific Strategies" by E. S. Ellis, D. D. Deshler, and J. B. Schumaker, 1989, *Journal of Learning Disabilities, 22,* p. 110. Reprinted by permission.)

S = Sort out the most important demand or problem

U = Unarm the problem by identifying the critical trouble spots.

C = Cash in on your old strategies, experiences, and observations of others.

C = Create a strategy for solving this problem that will work on all similar problems.

E = Echo your strategy (use substrategy ECHO)
- E = Evaluate the strategy as you try it
- C = Change the strategy to make it work better for future use
- H = Have another try and re-evaluate it
- O = Overlearn your strategy

S = See how well your strategy works in different situations.

S = Save your strategy.

After students become skilled in using task-specific strategies, they are ready to learn executive strategies to help them analyze the varying demands of the regular classroom and to adapt a previous strategy or develop a new strategy (Ellis, Deshler, & Schumaker, 1989). One such executive strategy is called SUCCESS (Ellis, 1985) (Figure 4.4).

■ EDUCATIONAL SETTINGS AND SERVICE DELIVERY OPTIONS

The Regular Classroom

Current legislation requires that children with disabilities be educated with their nondisabled peers to the maximum extent possible and that they be removed from the regular classroom only to the extent that their disability necessitates. Some children with learning disabilities spend the entire day in the regular classroom; others are there for only certain periods or activities. According to a survey conducted by the U.S. Department of Education (1989) of 60 school districts in 18 states, 100% of learning disabled students spent at least some of each school day in the regular classroom—on the average, 2.1 hours (35%) per day. Several factors combine to help make the regular classroom an effective learning environment for many children with learning disabilities. These factors include more individualized instruction, teacher aides, and peer-tutoring programs (e.g., Maheady, Sacca, & Harper, 1987, 1988) in many regular classrooms. In addition, school districts are providing teachers with more inservice training programs focusing on the identification, assessment, and remediation of children's learning problems. Although it may be unrealistic to think that the regular classroom is the best educational environment for children with severe learning disabilities (Reger, 1974), as Wallace and McLoughlin (1979) point out,

> The practice of considering the regular classroom as a realistic service delivery system is also one aspect of the intention to prevent learning disabilities. . . . [I]nstructional factors may cause or at least compound the learning difficulties of some children. By including the regular classroom setting as one of the key delivery systems, we may be channeling the necessary information and skills where they are most needed. (p. 365)

In addition to teaching students with learning disabilities problem-solving, organizational (Shields & Heron, 1989), and study skills (Hoover, 1989) to help them succeed in the regular classroom, it is often necessary to adapt various features of the instructional materials. For example, poor reading and study skills limit learning disabled students' ability to obtain needed information from assigned reading in textbooks. Lovitt and his colleagues at the University of Washington have been conducting research on how textbooks and other classroom materials can be modified to promote the mildly handicapped student's success in mainstreamed classrooms. Using graphic organizers (Horton & Lovitt, 1989; Horton, Lovitt, & Bergerud, 1990) is one of the methods they have found effective. Graphic organizers are visuospatial arrangements of

FIGURE 4.5

A graphic organizer presenting rearranged content information from an eight-page sequence in a middle school science text. (*Source:* From "Construction and Implementation of Graphic Organizers for Academically Handicapped and Regular Secondary Students" by S. V. Horton and T. C. Lovitt, 1989, *Academic Therapy,* Vol. 24, p. 630. Reprinted by permission.)

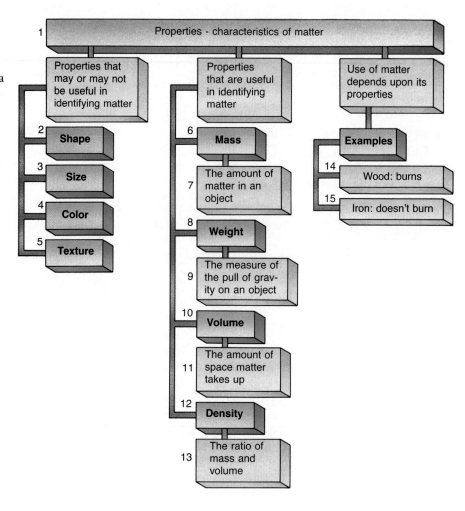

The use of guided lecture notes is another instructional adaptation that can help learning disabled students succeed in the regular classroom. See "Guided Notes" on pages 168–170.

information containing words or statements connected graphically to form meaningful diagrams. After reading and studying a passage, students fill in the various components of the diagram. Figure 4.5 shows a graphic organizer on the characteristics of matter from a middle school science text.

The Consultant Teacher

A consultant teacher provides support to regular classroom teachers and other school staff who work directly with learning disabled students. The consultant teacher helps the regular teacher select assessment devices, curriculum materials, and instructional activities. The consultant may even demonstrate teaching methods or behavior management strategies. A major advantage of this model is that the consultant teacher can work with several teachers and thus indirectly provide special education services to many children. The major drawback is that the consultant has little or no direct contact with the children. Heron and Harris (1987) describe procedures consultant teachers can use to increase their effectiveness in supporting mainstreamed children.

The Resource Room

The resource room is the most common service delivery model for educating children with learning disabilities. A resource room is a specially staffed and equipped classroom where learning disabled children come for one or several periods during the school day to receive individualized instruction (Harris & Schutz, 1986; Wiederholt, 1974b). The U.S. Department of Education (1990) reported that a resource room was the primary educational placement for 59% of all learning disabled students during the 1987–88 school year.

The resource teacher is a specially trained and certified learning disabilities specialist whose primary role is to teach needed academic skills, social skills, and learning strategies to the children who are referred to the resource room. Most of the children are in their regular classrooms for part of the school day and come to the resource room only for specialized instruction in the academic skills—usually reading or mathematics—or social skills they need to smooth their integration into the regular classroom. Other children may receive all their academic instruction in the resource room and attend the regular classroom only for such periods as art, music, and social studies. In addition to teaching learning disabled children, the resource teacher also works closely with each student's regular teacher to suggest and help plan each child's program in the regular classroom.

Ronni Hochman (1990), a middle school learning disabilities resource room teacher, offers suggestions for placing a child with learning disabilities in the regular classroom.

> I think a key to a resource room is identifying where the child's successes are and initially putting him back into the regular classroom only in the areas in which he can experience a great amount of success. I use the child's time in the resource room to build those skills he needs to learn to be completely integrated into the regular classroom—whether it's learning to read better or learning to complete a task.

Some advantages of the resource room model are that (1) the children do not lose their identity with their peer group, so there is a smaller chance they will be stigmatized as "special"; (2) the children can receive the intense, individualized instruction they need every day, which might be impossible for the regular teacher to provide; and (3) flexible scheduling allows the resource room to serve a fairly large number of students (Mayhall & Jenkins, 1977; Wiederholt, Hammill, & Brown, 1983). A typical resource room teacher serves an average of 20 students (U.S. Department of Education, 1989).

A survey of resource room teachers found that their biggest concerns were unclear role descriptions, variable expectations of administrators and regular classroom teachers, and insufficient time for planning, consulting, and observing students (McLoughlin & Kelly, 1982). Lieberman (1982) points out several disadvantages of "pull-out programs" such as resource rooms: They require students to spend time traveling between classrooms; they may result in inconsistent instructional approaches between settings; and they make it difficult to determine whether or not students should be held accountable for what they missed while out of the regular classroom.

The federal government defines a resource room as a setting outside the regular class in which a student receives special education and related services for at least 21% and not more than 60% of the school day.

GUIDED NOTES

Helping Students with Learning Disabilities (and Their Nonhandicapped Classmates) Succeed in the Regular Classroom

The lecture is widely used in middle and high school classrooms to present information to students. The teacher talks, and students are held responsible for obtaining, remembering, and later using (usually on a quiz or test) the information. Most successful students take notes during teacher lectures that they can study later. Students who take good notes and study them later consistently receive higher test scores than students who only listen to the lecture and read the text (Baker & Lombardi, 1985; Carrier, 1983).

Although various strategies and formats for effective notetaking have been identified, they are seldom taught to students (Saski, Swicegood, & Carter, 1983). The listening, linguistic, and, in some cases, motor skill deficits of many learning disabled students make it extremely difficult for them to identify what is important and write it down correctly and quickly enough during a lecture. While trying to choose and write one concept in his notebook, the learning disabled student might miss the next two points. When teachers develop guided notes to accompany their presentations, both mainstreamed handicapped and nonhandicapped students benefit.

What Are Guided Notes?

Guided notes are teacher-prepared handouts that "guide" a student through a lecture with standard cues and specific space in which to write key facts, concepts, and/or relationships (see sample in Figure A). Guided notes take advantage of one of the most consistent and important findings in recent educational research: *students who make frequent, relevant responses during a lesson learn more than students who are passive observers.*

A series of four research studies evaluating guided notes in both special and regular classrooms has been conducted by graduate students working with Bill Heward at The Ohio State University. The first study was with learning disabled secondary students studying the American constitution in a self-contained classroom (Kline, 1986). All 10 students in the class earned higher scores on the 10-item quizzes administered after lectures with guided notes than when they took their own notes during the teacher's presentations. Daily quiz scores for two of the students and the average scores and letter grades earned by the class are shown in Figure B. The next two studies produced similar results; first with oceanography in a middle-school science class (Yang, 1988), next with American history in a regular fifth-grade classroom (Pados, 1989). Students with learning disabilities were mainstreamed into both classrooms. Scores on next-day quizzes were higher for *all* students in both studies when they used guided notes, including students identified as gifted and talented. In the fourth study, Courson (1989) compared the effectiveness of two different formats of guided notes during a social studies unit in a special classroom of 19 learning disabled and academically at-risk seventh graders. Short-form guided notes required students to fill in blanks with single words or short phrases, and long-form guided notes required students to write key concepts/ideas in sentences or phrases in the open space following asterisks (*). Every student in the class earned higher scores on next-day quizzes and the review tests that were given every 2 weeks with both guided-note formats than they did when taking their own notes. There was no significant difference between the two formats.

American History   Name _____
Guided Notes   Session 16

                        Road to Revolution II
A. *New Problems and New Troubles*
   1. The French and Indian War _____ .
      a. The British thought the colonists _____
         _____ .

      b. Britain thought the colonists _____
         _____ .

   2. In 1764, Parliament decided to _____ the colonists to help pay the
      bills for the war.
      a. Colonists had to pay a tax on _____
         and _____ .
      b. _____ collected the taxes.
   3. _____ - the British lawmaking group.
   4. _____ - the people who collected the taxes. They
      were allowed to keep part of the taxes themselves.

B. *The Stamp Act (1765)*
   1. Under this law, colonists had to buy _____
      for all kinds of paper products.
      a.
      b.
      c.
C. *"Taxation without Representation"*
   1. "Taxation without Representation" means _____
      _____ by a lawmaking group in which you have no repre-
      sentation.
      a. Colonists could not _____
         _____ .
      b. Colonists also could not _____
         _____ .

   2. James Otis, a young lawyer from Massachusetts, referred to the Stamp Act
      as _____
      _____ .

D. *Protest and Repeal*
   1. _____ - a group of colonists formed to protest the taxes.
      a. It was founded by _____ .
      b.
      c.
      d.
   2. In 1766, the British Parliament *repealed* the Stamp Act (tax).
      a. Repeal - means _____ .
   3. The colonists thought _____ .

FIGURE A
Sample of guided notes
used in a fifth-grade history
lesson. (*Source:* "A Comparison of the Effects of Students'
Own Notes and Guided Notes
on the Daily Quiz Performance
of Fifth-grade Students" by
G. Pados, 1989. Unpublished
masters thesis, The Ohio State
University. Reprinted by permission.)

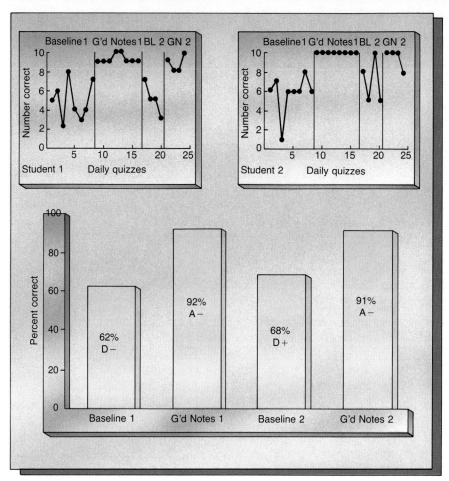

FIGURE B

Top: Daily Scores earned by two students with learning disabilities on 10-item quizzes following lectures in which students took their own notes (baseline) or used guided notes.

Bottom: Average score and letter grade equivalents earned on 10-point quizzes by 10 high school students during an American government unit with and without (baseline) guided notes. (*Source:* From "Effects of Guided Notes on Academic Achievement of Learning Disabled High School Students" by C. S. Kline, 1986. Unpublished master's thesis, The Ohio State University. Reprinted by permission.)

Although the resource room concept remains popular, its success depends on the skills of the resource teacher and the school's administrative practices. In particular, procedures must be determined that will help the child with learning disabilities generalize the skills learned in the resource room to the regular classroom (Anderson-Inman, Walker, & Purcell, 1984).

In two of the studies, data were obtained on the accuracy of students' notetaking. The two mainstreamed LD students in the Pados study correctly recorded only 18% of lecture facts/concepts when taking their own notes, compared to an overall notetaking accuracy of 89% when using guided notes. Guided notes also made a huge difference in the accuracy of notetaking for the 11 "regular" students (97% with guided notes vs. 34% when taking their own notes) and the 7 gifted and talented students in the classroom (97% vs. 38%). As a group, the students in Courson's study accurately recorded 19% of the lecture facts/concepts when taking their own notes compared to 97% and 94% accuracy with the short- and long-form guided notes, respectively.

Some Advantages of Guided Notes

♦ Students must actively respond to and interact with the lecture's content.

♦ Key concepts, facts, relationships are cued/highlighted.

♦ Students are better able to determine if they are "getting it" and are more likely to ask the teacher to clarify.

♦ Students are provided with a standard set of notes for study and review.

♦ Teachers are helped to stay "on task" with content and sequence of lecture.

♦ Teachers are required to plan the lesson/lecture carefully.

Suggestions for Using Guided Notes

♦ Include background information so student notetaking focuses on the important facts, concepts, and relationships you want them to learn.

♦ Provide consistent cues (e.g., asterisks, lines, bullets) so students know where, when, and how many concepts they should record.

♦ Don't require students to write too much.

♦ Make sure all critical facts, concepts, and relationships will be in the notes (i.e., what you want your students to be responsible for—"what will be on the test").

♦ Produce guided notes on a word processor so changes and updates are easy to do. ♦

The Self-Contained Classroom

In a self-contained classroom, the learning disabilities teacher is responsible for all educational programming for a group of about 8 to 12 learning disabled students. Some learning disabled children's academic achievement deficiencies

During the 1987–88 school year, 21.7% of students with learning disabilities were served in self-contained classrooms (U.S. Department of Education, 1990).

are so severe they need full-time placement in a learning setting with a specially trained teacher. In addition, poor work habits and inappropriate social behaviors make some learning disabled children candidates for the self-contained classroom, where distractions can be minimized and individual attention stressed. It is important, however, that placement in a self-contained (i.e., separate) class not be considered permanent. Children should be placed in a self-contained class only after unsuccessful attempts to serve them adequately in other less-restrictive environments. As Wallace and McLoughlin (1979) suggest,

> It is preferable that the basis for placing a child in a special class be diagnostic and instructional experience in the resource room model. In this way, the special class system can be used only for the child who needs the most support. Hopefully, after a period in a highly structured environment and under a consistent intervention program, the child can develop communication and social skills to a satisfactory level and be moved back into a less isolated setting. (pp. 369–370)

Although the effectiveness and appropriateness of the self-contained classroom have been the subject of much debate, some students appear to benefit from full-time separate class instruction. For example, a follow-up study of 10 high school students 5 to 6 years after they had been enrolled for a year in a self-contained learning disabilities program showed them to be performing as well as nonhandicapped students in a comparison group (Leone, Lovitt, & Hansen, 1981). Even though the students' performances varied considerably, their oral reading ability, free-time and occupational interests, and general success in high school were within the normal range. The results of this study suggest that placement in a self-contained special class because of significant academic deficits in the elementary grades does not preclude success in high school.

Secondary Programs

During the early years of the learning disabilities movement, programs and services expanded greatly, but almost exclusively at the elementary level. In 1975, a survey across 37 states found that only 9% of the districts offered educational programming for secondary-level learning disabled students (Scranton & Downs, 1975). Just 3 years later, however, McNutt and Heller (1978) surveyed 301 school districts and found that only 22.5% did not provide any programming for learning disabled adolescents. Today, virtually every public high school provides some type of special education services for students with learning disabilities.

Deshler, Lowrey, and Alley (1979) conducted a nationwide survey of junior and senior high school learning disabilities teachers and found five different models or program options predominant.

1. *Basic skills remediation model.* This model provides developmental or remedial instruction for basic academic skill deficits. Reading and mathematics deficits receive the most attention.

2. *Tutorial model.* This model emphasizes instruction in academic content areas. Areas of instruction are usually those in which the student is experiencing

These students are in a secondary learning disabilities program combining basic skills remediation and learning strategies instruction.

difficulty or failure. The teacher's major responsibility is to help keep the LD student in the regular curriculum.

3. *Functional curriculum model*. Emphasis is on equipping students to function in society. The focus of instruction is on consumer information, completion of application forms, banking and money skills, and life-care skills such as grooming. In addition, this approach often attempts to relate academic content to career concepts.

4. *Work-study model*. Instruction in job- and career-related skills and on-the-job experience is emphasized. Students typically spend half the day on the job and the remainder of the day in school studying compatible material.

5. *Learning strategies model*. Instruction is designed to teach students how to learn rather than to teach specific content. For example, the teacher might present techniques for organizing material that has to be memorized for a history test, rather than teaching the actual history content.

In their study, Deshler and colleagues (1979) found that 51% of the existing secondary learning disabilities programs followed the basic skills remediation model. Each of the five models has specific advantages and disadvantages (Alley & Deshler, 1979), and no one approach is apt to be the best for all learning disabled students.

■ CURRENT ISSUES/FUTURE TRENDS

Learning disabilities is such a dynamic and relatively new area that an entire book could easily be devoted to a discussion of current issues. Some of these

SOMOS TODOS AYUDANTES Y ESTUDIANTES!

Two years of foreign language study is an entrance requirement for many 4-year colleges, and approximately half of all colleges require second-language skills for graduation (Ganschow & Sparks, 1987). To deny a student access to foreign language study or to fail to provide a student with the opportunity to experience successful language study may unnecessarily limit his or her future educational choices. Failure to provide successful foreign language study not only limits a student's participation in the educational mainstream, but denies him or her the opportunity to experience the cultural benefits that accrue from skills in a second language. Yet students with learning disabilities are frequently discouraged from attempting a foreign language in high school. Learning disabled students are already experiencing academic difficulties, so why enroll them in a course likely to be especially difficult?

Wiig and Semel (1984) state that foreign language learning presents one of the greatest barriers to the academic career of students with learning disabilities. They cite the basic vocabulary and grammatical rules of a foreign language that are emphasized from the beginning, as well as the more abstract vocabulary and complex syntactic structures taught as study progresses. Unless special instructional modifications are made, most learning disabled students find study of a foreign language an unsuccessful struggle. Although the literature of special education in general, and learning disabilities in particular, is replete with classroom-tested methods for successfully mainstreaming handicapped students into most areas of the school curriculum, procedures for providing successful foreign language instruction for students with learning problems are virtually nonexistent. Recently, several foreign language educators have suggested methods for helping the learner with special needs (Barnett, 1989; DiGiandomenico & Carey, 1988).

The key features of systematic peer tutoring systems—many opportunities to respond, immediate feedback, praise and reinforcement, progressing at the individual student's rate, mastery learning with maintenance—are consistent with recommendations for teaching foreign language. Peer tutoring may be especially well suited for helping students with learning disabilities acquire and maintain the large amounts of vocabulary they encountered from the beginning of foreign language study.

The Peer Tutoring System

A reciprocal, classwide peer tutoring system was implemented within a second-year, "modified" Spanish class in an urban high school. The class was designed to provide an opportunity to study Spanish at a somewhat slower pace and with a focus on the most useful and practical aspects of the language for 6 students with learning disabilities and 10 students who were considered at risk for failing a foreign language class. The program was adapted from a peer tutoring model devised by Cooke, Heron, & Heward (1983). (See pages 68–69.) Students worked in pairs, each tutoring the other for 5 minutes per day on a set of 8 "Palabras para Aprender" (words to learn). Students both said and wrote the Spanish translation of words and phrases presented pictorially on flash cards and received praise or corrective feedback from their tutors after each response. When a student correctly wrote an item for 2 consecutive days on the tutor-administered test at the end of each day's session, that item went into the "Palabras para Repasar" (words to review) pocket in his peer tutoring folder. All words in that pocket were tested on a weekly maintenance test given by the teacher. See Figure A.

FIGURE A
Folder and flashcards used
by high school students
with learning disabilities
for Spanish peer tutoring
program.

Results

All the students learned Spanish vocabulary words almost as fast as the system allowed. The six learning disabled students' average rate of learning ranged from 7.0 to 7.9 new words every 2 days (the maximum rate of progress was 8 words every 2 days). To assess whether the students could learn words even faster, three tutoring pairs worked with sets of 12 words during the study's final 2 weeks. They learned new words at an average rate

FIGURE B

Cumulative records of new Spanish vocabulary items learned by two high school students during peer tutoring.

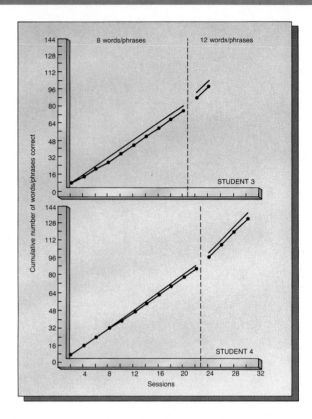

of 11.3 to 11.7 words every 2 days. Figure B shows the rate at which one tutoring pair—Student 3 (at-risk) and Student 4 (LD)—learned Spanish vocabulary items during the study.

The students not only taught each other new Spanish vocabulary, they remembered what they learned. As a group, the students averaged 87% of all words correct on the weekly tests of maintenance. When asked their opinions of the peer tutoring program, 15 of the 16 students said they would like to use it again for studying Spanish, and 14 said they wished peer tutoring was used in their other academic classes. These three comments sum up the students' opinions about the program:

> "This was about the most helpful thing I can remember for learning things you usually don't want to. The program was excellent!"

> "I think this is a program that should be used in the classroom. It causes the kids to get involved in their learning instead of just having the teacher dictate to you all day."

> "Boy, if we'd been doing this all year, I'd be acing this course!"

Based on Wright, J. E., Cavanaugh, R. A., Sainato, D. M. & Heward, W. L., (1991). Teaching each other Spanish: Evaluation of a classwide reciprocal peer tutoring program for learning disabled and at-risk high school students. *Manuscript submitted for publication.* ◆

issues include what terminology to use (is a "reading disability" the same as a "learning disability"?), where learning disabled children should be taught (the regular education initiative), what kind of training learning disabilities teachers should receive, how federal and state funds should be appropriated, and what to do about the proliferation of controversial "cures" for learning disabilities. We will briefly discuss two issues: the continuing debate over the definition of learning disabilities and the concern for the special needs of adults with learning disabilities.

Who Is Really Learning Disabled?

The widely differing findings of prevalence studies (from 5% to 30% of the school-age population) illustrate the lack of standard, operational definition of learning disabilities. Some prominent special educators believe that the trend toward expanding the learning disabilities classification to include more and more children indicates a misunderstanding of the concept and only detracts from and weakens services to children who have severe learning problems. Myers and Hammill (1990), for example, believe that far too many students are identified as learning disabled:

> A number of teachers will note readily that many, possibly most, of the "learning disabled" students enrolled in their programs do not satisfy either the 1977 USOE or the NJCLD definition. This is because, in many school districts, all students who are thought to be able to profit from tutoring or remedial education are arbitrarily called learning disabled. As a consequence of such definitional liberality, the learning disability programs have become glutted with underachieving students, culturally different students, and poorly taught students. (p. 13)

Clearly, there is no consensus regarding who is learning disabled. Two studies have shown that educators identify certain children as learning disabled even when all their evaluative data are in the normal range, and that the single most reliable variable predicting whether a child will be identified is the amount of information presented on the child (the more information, the more likely the student will be identified) rather than the type of information or its relationship to usual identification criteria (Algozzine & Ysseldyke, 1981; Ysseldyke, Algozzine, Richey, & Graden, 1982).

Although all agree that children who have any learning difficulty, major or minor, should receive help, special education services for learning disabled students should be reserved for those children with severe and specific learning difficulties (Wallace & McLoughlin, 1979). Kirk (1978) suggests one solution to this problem. He says that all regular classroom teachers should have access to consultants for assistance with the 10% of all children in any classroom that need some degree of additional help. Consultants might serve between 20 and 40 children at a given time. A second group of special educators could be highly trained learning disabilities specialists who would work with only those children who require more intensive, direct help. These teachers might serve only five or six students each day.

The discussion of what constitutes a true learning disability is likely to go on for some time. We believe that what a child's learning problem is called is not so important; what is important is that schools provide an educational program responsive to the individual needs of all children who have difficulty learning.

PERSONAL PERSPECTIVES
Tom Lovitt on Learning Disabilities

With its unending stream of claims, counterclaims, and controversy, the area of learning disabilities at times seems to lose sight of its fundamental goals and common-sense truths. Fortunately, there are a number of scholars whose work serves as a standard of good sense. Thomas C. Lovitt, professor of special education at the University of Washington, is one of those people. Although everyone in special education may not agree with him, Lovitt's views are backed by more than 25 years of classroom-based research on virtually every aspect of the education of children with learning disabilities: assessment, teaching techniques, and adapting curriculum materials, for example. He once wrote that, all things being equal, a teacher who imparts many skills to many children is good, and one who doesn't is not (Lovitt, 1977). After all, teaching is helping children learn new things. He believes the primary purpose for teachers and students coming together is the development of children's academic and social skills, and that teachers should work directly and systematically toward that end. In the
passages that follow, *Professor Lovitt shares his views on definition, placement, motivation, and remedial focus for students with learning disabilities.*

Definition

When it comes to finding the definition of learning disabilities, we should forget about it, at least for now. Far too much time, money, and space in textbooks and journals has been taken up by this futile mission. Those concerned with this goal have sought the answer by administering one test after another, giving multiple tests, and like alchemists of old, carefully selecting and combining subtests and items from many tests. The thinking is, apparently, that if *the* proper battery of tests, subtests, or items can be blended and then administered and if the proper multivariate analysis is employed, then we will be able to tell who is *really* learning disabled and who isn't (the pretenders!). And further, if our tests and measurements are highly sophisticated, we will know about the many subtypes of learning disabilities. Wrong!

Placement

We worry a great deal about where to put the learning disabled: in a self-contained room, resource room, or regular classroom. This has been going on for years. Those who advocated "mainstreaming I" in the 1960s, "mainstreaming II" in the 1970s, and now the regular education initiative argue that most, if not all, LD youngsters should be educated in regular classrooms by regular teachers. Since the data are not all in on this matter, we must take a few important issues into account as we consider the question of placement. One, placement is, to a great extent, teacher relevant. There are good and poor regular teachers, just as there are good and poor special teachers. Likewise, there are good and poor plumbers, pilots, and preachers. So to argue that LD youth should be sent to regular classes, regardless of the quality of instruction, doesn't make sense. Two, it doesn't make any difference where we learn certain things; place is rather irrelevant. Take reading for example. Students could learn to read (with a

Adults with Learning Disabilities

Discovering appropriate and effective programs and services to help young people with disabilities make a successful transition from school to adult life is one of the major challenges for special education. The task is even more difficult in the learning disabilities area because so little is known about adults with learning disabilities. As Smith and Robinson (1986) point out, "The field does not know what becomes of the LD students served in secondary schools: what percentage attend college, find successful employment, enter job training programs, or are unsuccessful in making the transition to adulthood?" (p. 242).

good teacher) in a regular or special classroom. Furthermore, they could learn to read at home, at church, at a library, or on a bus. Three, the placement options become fewer as we specify more instructional objectives, and this is where the problems over placement arise. When we list several objectives for our instruction, some of which are educational and others social, we must be realistic and be prepared to compromise, for the acquisition of certain behaviors in certain places may go counter to the learning of other behaviors in that same setting. Phrased another way, we need to evaluate the net effect.

Motivation

Skinner and other operant folk have been saying for years that we do what we were reinforced for doing. But we teachers have forgotten those lessons. Many of us believe that if we can just make the materials, the lectures, and the general environment more appealing, then youngsters will be turned on to education. Or we are of the opinion that if we offer instruction in just the "right way," our instruction will take. And of course the arguments rage as to what the right way happens to be. But all too often we forget about reinforcers and their power. We forget that there is a great chance that if we can find pupils' reinforcers, arrange them contingent on desired behaviors (or bits thereof), the desired responses will occur.

Positive Focus

Although we don't know how to *really* define LD youngsters (and heaven knows we've tried), we do know that they don't do as well as their non-LD mates in oral and silent reading, reading comprehension, spelling, mathematics, history, science, geography, industrial arts, music, or family living. Because of these many deficits and deviations, we teachers, in all good faith, set out to remediate as many of the "shortfalls" as possible so that learning disabled youth will be as normal and wonderful as we are. We should reconsider this total remedial approach to learning disabilities. One reason for considering an alternative might be obvious if we thought of a day in the life of an LD youth. First, the teacher sets out to remediate his reading, then his math, and then his language, social skills, and soccer playing. Toward the end of the day, she attempts to remediate his metacognitive deficits. That lad is in a remediation mode throughout the day. Is it any wonder that the self-concepts, self-images, self-esteems, and attributions of these youngsters are out of whack?

We should spend some time concentrating on these youngsters' positive qualities. If, for example, a girl is inclined toward mechanics, or a boy to being a chef, we teachers should nurture those skills. And if an LD child doesn't have a negotiable behavior, we should locate one and promote it. I can't help but think that if every youngster, LD or otherwise, had at least one art, trade, skill, or technique about which he or she was fairly competent, that would do more for that youngster's adjustment than would the many hours of remediation to which the child is subjected. Perhaps that accent on the positive would go a long way toward actually helping the remediation process. If children knew they could excel in something, that might help them become competent in other areas as well.

From Introduction to Learning Disabilities *(pp. 473–477) by T. C. Lovitt, 1989, Boston: Allyn & Bacon. Adapted by permission.* ♦

According to a U.S. Department of Education fact sheet, 1% of all college freshmen in 1984 reported that they were learning disabled. Recent surveys have described some of the support services that are available for college students with learning disabilities (Bursuck, Rose, Cowen, & Yahaya, 1989; Nelson & Lignugaris/Kraft, 1989).

Those studies have revealed a greater concern among adults with learning disabilities for self-perceived deficits in social and occupational skills rather than in the academic skills that caused their primary problems during their school years (Chelser, 1982; White, 1985). Kokaska and Skolnik (1986) surveyed 10 adults with learning disabilities to seek their suggestions for attaining a positive

One adult with learning disabilities tells some of her story on pages 618–619.

More important than debating what constitutes a *true* learning disability is our ability to provide each child with an education responsive to his or her needs.

employment situation. These adults were generally optimistic about future career success, although several indicated anxieties about their jobs. They suggested that adults with learning disabilities should select jobs in which personal strengths and personal initiative are emphasized, and they should accept the need to improve interpersonal skills, to work harder and longer than others to maintain good job performance, and to understand their own limitations.

We expect to witness a substantial increase in the number and range of educational, training, counseling, and other support services for adults with learning disabilities.

SUMMARY

History of the Area of Learning Disabilities

♦ Learning disabilities is a relatively new, rapidly growing field in special education.

♦ The term *learning disabilities* was first used in 1963 by S. A. Kirk to describe children who have serious learning problems in school but no other obvious handicaps.

♦ During the late 1960s two growing organizations—LDA and DLD (CEC)—helped bring about federal legislation providing funds for learning disabilities programs.

Defining Learning Disabilities

♦ There is no one, universally agreed-upon definition of learning disabilities. However, most definitions incorporate three criteria that must be met for a child to be labeled learning disabled. The learning disabled children must (1) have a severe discrepancy between potential or ability and actual achievement; (2) have learning problems that cannot be attributed to other handicapping conditions, such as blindness or mental retardation; and (3) need special educational services to succeed in school.

♦ No matter what definition is used, educators should focus on each child's specific skill deficiencies for assessment and instruction.

Characteristics of Learning Disabled Children

♦ Learning disabilities are not physically apparent. Children with learning disabilities look like all other children.

♦ The single common characteristic is a specific and significant achievement deficiency in the presence of adequate overall intelligence.

Prevalence

♦ Because definitions of learning disabilities and assessment and diagnosis procedures vary so widely, there are no reliable prevalence figures. However, children with learning disabilities are the largest category in special education, making up 48% of those served.

Causes of Learning Disabilities

♦ Although the actual cause of a specific learning disability is seldom known, the suspected causes can be grouped into three categories: brain damage, biochemical imbalance, and environmental factors such as poor instruction.

Assessment

♦ Most learning disabilities professionals take a diagnostic-prescriptive approach to assessment. That is, results of assessment should lead directly to a plan for classroom instruction.

♦ Norm-referenced tests compare a child's score with the scores of other age-mates who have taken the same test.

♦ Process tests are designed to measure a child's ability in different perceptual or psycholinguistic areas.

♦ Teachers use informal reading inventories to observe directly and record a child's reading skills.

♦ Criterion-referenced tests compare a child's score to a predetermined mastery level.

♦ Direct daily measurement involves regularly assessing a child on the specific skill being taught. One instructional system based on direct daily measurement is precision teaching.

Educational Approaches

♦ There are two basic approaches to educating learning disabled children: ability training and skill training.

- Ability training involves prescribing instructional activities designed to remediate a child's weakness in underlying basic abilities. Psycholinguistic training, the visual-perceptual approach, the perceptual-motor approach, and the multisensory approach are all types of ability training. There is little research support for the effectiveness of ability training.

- Skill training is based on the belief that a child's performance deficit is the problem, not a sign of an underlying disability. In skill training, remediation is based on direct instruction of precisely defined skills, many opportunities to practice, and direct measurement of a child's progress. Research has shown the skill-training approach—including applied behavior analysis, Direct Instruction, and precision teaching—to be effective.

Educational Settings and Service Delivery Options

- Children with learning disabilities are educated in a variety of placements and service delivery arrangements, but virtually all are educated in the regular classroom for at least part of the day.

- In some schools a consultant teacher helps regular classroom teachers work with children with learning disabilities.

- In the resource room, the most common service delivery model for educating children with learning disabilities, a specially trained teacher works with the children on particular skill deficits for one or more periods a day.

- A few children with learning disabilities attend separate, self-contained classes. This placement option, however, should be used only after attempts to serve the child in a less restrictive setting have failed, and it should not be considered permanent.

- Learning disabilities programs in the secondary schools are rapidly expanding.

Current Issues/Future Trends

- The discussion and debate over what constitutes a true learning disability are likely to continue. What is most important is for schools to respond to the individual needs of all children who have difficulty learning.

- Increasing efforts should be directed toward the development of educational, training, counseling, and other support services for adults with learning disabilities.

FOR MORE INFORMATION

Journals

Intervention in School and Clinic. Published five times a year by PRO-ED, 8700 Shoal Creek Boulevard, Austin, TX 78758-6897. An interdisciplinary journal directed to teachers, parents, educational therapists, and specialists in all fields who deal with the day-to-day aspects of special and remedial education.

Journal of Learning Disabilities. Published 10 times a year by PRO-ED, 8700 Shoal Creek Boulevard, Austin, TX 78758-6897. Publishes research and theoretical articles relating to learning disabilities.

Journal of Precision Teaching. Published by The Center for Individualized Instruction, Jacksonville State University, Jacksonville, AL 36265. A multidisciplinary journal dedicated to a science of human behavior that includes direct, continuous, and standard measurement. Publishes both formal and informal articles describing precision teaching projects.

Learning Disabilities Research and *Learning Disabilities Focus.* Each is published twice a year by the Division for Learning Disabilities, Council for Exceptional Children, 1920 Association Drive, Reston, VA 22091.

Learning Disability Quarterly. Published four times a year by the Council for Learning Disabilities. Emphasizes practical implications of research and applied research dealing with learning disability populations and settings.

Books

Alley, G., & Deshler, D. (1979). *Teaching the learning disabled adolescent: Strategies and methods.* Denver: Love.

Gearheart, B. R., & Gearheart, C. J. (1989). *Learning disabilities: Educational strategies* (5th ed.). Columbus, OH: Merrill.

Harris, W. J., & Schutz, P. N. B. (1986). *The special education resource room: Rationale and implementation.* Columbus, OH: Merrill.

Lewis, R. B., & Doorlag, D. H. (1991). *Teaching special students in the mainstream* (3rd ed.). Columbus, OH: Merrill.

Lovitt, T. C. (1989). *Introduction to learning disabilities.* Boston: Allyn & Bacon.

Mercer, C. D. (1987). *Students with learning disabilities* (3rd ed.). Columbus, OH: Merrill.

Myers, P. I., & Hammill, D. D. (1990). *Learning disabilities: Basic concepts, assessment practices, and instructional strategies* (4th ed.). Austin, TX: PRO-ED.

Smith, D. D. (1981). *Teaching the learning disabled.* Englewood Cliffs, NJ: Prentice-Hall.

Wallace, G., & Kauffman, J. M. (1986). *Teaching children with learning problems* (3rd ed.). Columbus, OH: Merrill.

Organizations

Learning Disabilities Association of America, 4156 Library Road, Pittsburgh, PA 15234. Founded in 1963, LDA is a large and active organization of parents and educators that advocates for services to learning disabled children.

Council for Learning Disabilities (CLD), P.O. Box 40303, Overland Park, KS 66204. An independent organization of professionals who work with learning disabled individuals. Publishes *Learning Disabilities Quarterly,* holds semi-annual conferences to disseminate research and information, and promotes standards for learning disabilities professionals.

Division for Learning Disabilities (DLD), Council for Exceptional Children, 1920 Association Drive, Reston, VA 22091. Includes teachers, teacher educators, researchers, and other members of CEC who work with or on behalf of individuals with learning disabilities.

Learning Disability Research Institutes

Addresses for the five federally funded learning disabilities research institutes and their primary area(s) of research interest:

Research Institute for the Study of Learning Disabilities (language comprehension)
Box 118
Teachers College, Columbia University
New York, NY 10027

Chicago Institute for Learning Disabilities (social adjustment, language)
University of Illinois at Chicago Circle
Box 4348
Chicago, IL 60680

Research Institute in Learning Disabilities (LD adolescents, learning strategies)
University of Kansas
Room 313 Carruth-O'Leary
Lawrence, KS 66045

Institute for Research on Learning Disabilities (identification, assessment, and placement)
350 Elliot Hall
75 East River Road
University of Minnesota
Minneapolis, MN 55455

Learning Disabilities Research Institute (attentional deficits, self-activated learning strategies)
University of Virginia
Department of Special Education
152 Ruffner Hall
Charlottesville, VA 22903

5

Behavior Disorders

◆ Why should a child who behaves badly be considered handicapped?

◆ Why aren't clear-cut, objective criteria used to identify children with behavior disorders?

◆ How are behavior problems and academic performance interrelated?

◆ Who is more severely handicapped: the acting-out, aggressive child or the withdrawn child?

◆ What is the most important function of the teacher of behavior disordered students?

Many nonhandicapped children act in the same ways as children with behavior disorders—but not as often or with such intensity. And, of course, behavior disordered children can be likable.

Childhood should be a happy time, a time for playing, growing, learning, and making friends—and for most children it is. But some children's lives seem to be in constant turmoil. They are in conflict, often serious, with others and themselves. Or they are so shy and withdrawn they seem to be in their own worlds. In either case, playing with others, making friends, and learning all the things a child must learn are extremely difficult for these children. They are children with behavior disorders. These children are referred to by a variety of terms—*emotionally disturbed, socially maladjusted, psychologically disordered, emotionally handicapped,* or even *psychotic* if their behavior is extremely abnormal or bizarre.

Behavior disordered children are seldom really liked by anyone—their peers, teachers, siblings, even parents. Sadder still, they often do not even like themselves. The child with behavior disorders is difficult to be around, and attempts to befriend him may lead only to rejection, verbal abuse, or even physical attack. With some emotionally withdrawn children, all overtures seem to fall on deaf ears, and yet these children are not deaf.

Although children with behavior disorders are not physically disabled, their noxious or withdrawn behavior can be as serious a handicap to their development and learning as the mentally retarded child's slowness to learn. Behavior disordered children make up a significant portion of those needing special education.

DEFINING BEHAVIOR DISORDERS

There is no generally agreed-upon definition of behavior disorders. Like their colleagues in mental retardation and learning disabilities, special educators in the area of behavior disorders have been struggling to reach consensus on a definition. The definition of a handicapping condition should provide unambiguous guidance for the reliable identification of students who need special education services because of the disability in question. Definitions that appear "theoretically sound" or "legally defensible" on paper are often found wanting in practice.

There are numerous reasons for the lack of a clear definition of behavior disorders. First, disordered behavior is a social construct; there is no clear agreement about what constitutes good mental health. Second, different theories of emotional disturbance use concepts and terminology that do little to promote meaning from one definition to another. Third, measuring and interpreting disordered behavior across time and settings is a difficult, exact, and costly endeavor. Cultural influence is another problem; expectations and norms for appropriate behavior are often quite different across ethnic and cultural groups. In addition, frequency and intensity are concerns. All children behave inappropriately at times—how often and with how much intensity must a student engage in a particular behavior before he is considered handicapped because of the behavior? Finally, disordered behavior sometimes occurs in conjunction with other handicapping conditions (most notably mental retardation and learning disabilities), making it difficult to tell whether one condition is the result or the cause of the other.

Although numerous definitions have been proposed, the one first written in 1957 by Eli Bower (1960) has had the most impact on special education. Bower's definition, with only a few changes, was adopted by the U.S. Department of Education as the definition of *seriously emotionally disturbed* children, one of the categories of handicapping conditions covered by P.L. 94–142.

Seriously emotionally disturbed is defined as follows:

(i) The term means a condition exhibiting one or more of the following characteristics over a long period of time and to a marked degree, which adversely affects educational performance.

    (a) An inability to learn which cannot be explained by intellectual, sensory, and health factors;

    (b) An inability to build or maintain satisfactory interpersonal relationships with peers and teachers;

    (c) Inappropriate types of behavior or feelings under normal circumstances;

    (d) A general pervasive mood of unhappiness or depression; or

    (e) A tendency to develop physical symptoms or fears associated with personal or school problems.

(ii) The term includes children who are schizophrenic or autistic. The term does not include children who are socially maladjusted unless it is determined that they are seriously emotionally disturbed. (*Federal Register, 42* (163), August 23, 1977, p. 42478)

This definition may at first seem straightforward enough. It specifies three conditions that must be met: *chronicity* ("over a long period of time"); *severity* ("to a marked degree"); and *difficulty in school* ("adversely affects educational performance"), and it lists five types of problems that qualify. But in fact, the definition is extremely vague and leaves much to the subjective opinion of the authorities (usually teachers) surrounding the child. How does one operationalize such terms as *satisfactory interpersonal relationships, normal, inappropriate,* and *pervasive*?

And how does one determine that some behavior problems represent social maladjustment, whereas others are indicative of true emotional disturbance? This determination is critical, because children who are socially maladjusted are not considered handicapped and are therefore ineligible for special education services under P.L. 94–142. Bower's original definition did not include any mention of social maladjustment, and the inclusion in the federal definition of this seemingly illogical criterion has been heavily criticized (Center, 1990; Cline, 1990; Kauffman, 1989; Peterson, Benson, Edwards, Rosell, & White, 1986). Bower (1982) has written that he never intended a distinction between emotional disturbance and social maladjustment, and that the five components of the definition were in fact meant to be indicators of social maladjustment. It is difficult to conceive of a child who is sufficiently socially maladjusted to have received that label but who does not display one or more of the five characteristics (especially b) included in the federal definition. As written, the definition seemingly excludes children on the same basis for which they are included.

A harsh critic of federal policy toward the education of children with behavior disorders, Kauffman has written that "the federal definition is, if not claptrap, at least dangerously close to nonsense" (1982, p. 4). Indeed, the

Children identified as autistic are no longer reported under the category of seriously emotionally disturbed. *Autism* was added as a new disability category in the 1990 amendments to P.L. 92–142. See the discussion of autism later in this chapter.

definition appears to have offered little direction to states and local school districts. Mack (1980) found that only 12 states included all the federal criteria in their definitions, and the percentages of school-age children identified varies widely from state to state.

The Council for Children with Behavior Disorders (CCBD), the major professional organization concerned with the education and treatment of children with behavior disorders, has officially adopted the position that the term **behaviorally disordered** is more appropriate than the term *seriously emotionally disturbed*. The CCBD endorses use of the term *behaviorally disordered* because (1) it does not suggest any particular theory of causation or set of intervention techniques, (2) it is more representative of the students who are handicapped by their behavior and are being served under P.L. 94–142, and (3) it is less stigmatizing (Huntze, 1985). CCBD has also emphasized the need for a revised federal definition that specifies the functional educational dimensions of this disability category, does not contain reference to the exclusion of students with social maladjustment, and focuses on the sources of data needed to determine whether a student is behaviorally disordered (Council for Children with Behavior Disorders, 1987).

Numerous other definitions of behavior disorders have been proposed (Kauffman, 1977; Ross, 1974). Although each definition differs somewhat, all agree that a child's behavior, to be considered disordered, must differ markedly (extremely) and chronically (over time) from current social or cultural norms. As we will show throughout this chapter, special education with behaviorally disordered children is most effective when it focuses on what they actually do and what the environmental conditions are when they misbehave, rather than attempting to define and classify some inner disturbance.

The Role of Teacher Tolerance in Defining Children's Behavior Disorders

Even though no definition of behavior disorders proposed so far has provided a consistent, universally agreed-upon standard for identification, diagnosis, communication, and research, they all place the concept of behavior disorders in a "conceptual ballpark" (Hewett & Taylor, 1980). And a major player in that ballpark is teacher tolerance. A number of studies show that a student's identification as behaviorally disordered is largely a function of the teacher's notion of children's expected or acceptable behavior. In a **longitudinal study**, Rubin and Balow (1978) found that 59% of all children who had received three or more annual ratings had been identified as behavior disordered by at least one teacher at some time between kindergarten and sixth grade. Of course, this study suggests another important conclusion as well—that a great many children do experience some type of behavioral problem during their early school years. Although most of these problems do go away, teachers identify problems at the time as an indication of emotional disturbance.

The role of teacher tolerance in identifying children as behavior disturbed is significant. Algozzine (1980) found that, as a group, regular classroom teachers rated certain behaviors as more disturbing than did a comparison group of special education teachers. In a subsequent study, Curran and Algozzine (1980) found teachers with varying levels of tolerance for immature

Two studies have shown that the label *behaviorally disordered* implies less negative dimensions to teachers than does the term *emotionally disturbed* (Feldman, Kinnison, Jay, & Harth, 1983; Lloyd, Kauffman, & Gansneder, 1987). Both preservice and inservice teachers indicated they thought children labeled behaviorally disordered were more teachable and likely to be successful in a regular classroom than were children identified as emotionally disturbed.

A longitudinal study follows the development of the same subjects over a period of years.

or defiant behaviors differentially rated a hypothetical child's likelihood of success in the regular classroom. These studies suggest that "emotional disturbance is a function of the perceiver . . . . What is disturbance to one teacher may not be to another" (Whelan, 1981, pp. 4–5).

PREVALENCE

Estimates vary tremendously as to how many children have behavior disorders. Morse (1975) reviewed a number of surveys and found that anywhere from 0.1% to 30% of the school-age population was considered behavior disordered. Based on his survey of California schools, Bower (1981) concluded that two or three children in the average classroom (about 10%) can be expected to show signs of emotional disturbance. In the Rubin and Balow (1978) longitudinal study, 7.4% of all the children in their sample ($n = 1,586$) were considered to have a behavior problem by every teacher who rated them over the 3-year period.

With such widely varying estimates, it is obvious that people are using different criteria to decide whether a child is behavior disordered. Wood and Zabel (1978) suggest that the difference in prevalence figures stems as much from how the figures are collected as from the use of different definitions. Most surveys ask teachers to identify students in their classes who display behavior problems at that point in time. Many children display inappropriate behavior for short periods, and such one-shot screening procedures will identify them, as in the Rubin and Balow (1978) study in which more than half of all students were identified as behavior problems by at least one teacher at some time during their elementary school careers. As Hewett and Taylor (1980) observe,

> In our experience, when you walk into any elementary classroom, you can usually pick out two or three children who are "not with it" and who are visible enough to stand out from other members of the class in terms of their problem behavior. And if you stay long enough, you can usually determine if they "fit" within the teacher's range of tolerance for behavioral differences. Whether they would be the same children a week or semester later is debatable. Thus, we get almost no meaning from incidence figures. (p. 42)

A major study of education for children with behavior disorders that investigated 26 programs in 13 states during the 1987–89 school years supports the "two to three students per classroom" figure: "Estimates suggest 10% of the child population has behavior problems serious or sustained enough to warrant intervention [and] 3% to 5% are judged to be seriously emotionally disturbed" (Knitzer, Steinberg, & Fleisch, 1990). Annual reports from the U.S. Department of Education, however, show far fewer children being served. The 377,295 children aged 6 to 21 who received special education under the seriously emotionally disturbed category during the 1988–89 school year under P.L. 94–142 represented only about .9% of the school-age population.

Although this figure marked the greatest number of children with behavior disorders ever served and ranked emotional disturbance as the fourth largest category of special education, it means that only 20% to 30% of children with behavior disorders are being served.

The number of children being served represents only one-half of the 2% estimate the federal government has traditionally used in its estimates of funding

Teachers' tolerance for deviant behavior and their expectations for classroom performance are major factors to consider in plans to integrate children with disabilities into regular classrooms—especially those with severe behavior disorders. Excellent discussions of this issue are found in Anderson-Inman, et al. (1984), Braaten, et al. (1988), and Walker and Severson (in press).

and personnel needs for children with behavior disorders. Kauffman (1989) believes that social policy and economic factors caused the government to first reduce (from 2% to 1.2%) its estimate of the prevalence of behavior disorders and then to stop publishing an estimate altogether.

> The government obviously prefers not to allow wide discrepancies between prevalence estimates and the actual number of children served. It is easier to cut prevalence estimates than to serve more students. (p. 40)

Regardless of what prevalence study one turns to, it is evident there are many thousands of school children whose disordered behavior is handicapping their educational progress but who are not presently receiving the special education they need. Although P.L. 94–142 clearly mandates that all children with disabilities receive individualized special education services, the definition included in the law may be partially responsible for the great disparity between the estimated prevalence of children with behavior disorders and the number of such children receiving special education (Bower, 1982; Kauffman, 1986, 1989; Knitzer, 1982; Wood, 1985). The uncertain meaning of many aspects of the definition allows determination of whether a child is behaviorally disordered to be more a function of a school district's available resources (i.e., its ability to provide the needed services) than a function of the child's actual needs for such services.

> If an appearance of compliance is to be maintained, it is best to work from the assumption that the number of students served is the number who need service. . . . The social policy mandate changes the question, at least for those who manage budgets, from "How many disturbed students are there in our schools?" to "How many disturbed students can we afford to serve?" And to save face and try to abide by the law, it is tempting to conclude that there are, indeed, just as many disturbed students as one is able to serve. (Kauffman, 1989, p. 41)

Sex

Boys are much more likely than girls to be identified as behavior disordered (Morse, Cutler, & Fink, 1964; Rubin & Balow, 1971; Schultz, Salvia, & Feinn, 1974; Werry & Quay, 1971). In one study, conducted in a large metropolitan school district, 82% of the children referred for evaluation for behavior disorders were boys (Mendelsohn & Jennings, 1986). Boys labeled disturbed are likely to be aggressive and act out, whereas behavior disordered girls are typically shy, anxious, and withdrawn. Among severely disturbed children (i.e., autistic and schizophrenic), boys outnumber girls anywhere from 2:1 to 5:1 (Hingtgen & Bryson, 1972; Morse, 1975).

Juvenile Delinquency

Although the word *delinquent* is a legal term, the offenses an adolescent commits to be labeled delinquent constitute a behavior disorder. Approximately 3% of all children in this country are referred to juvenile courts each year (Achenbach, 1974; Cavan & Ferdinand, 1975). In 1988 there were more than 1.6 million arrests of children under the age of 18 (U.S. Department of Commerce, 1990). The rate and seriousness of crimes committed by juveniles have been increasing. Snarr and Wolford (1985) point out that 40% of all violent crimes are

Boys are much more likely than girls to be identified as behavior disordered.

committed by juveniles, yet this age group comprises only about 20% of the total population. Persons under the age of 18 accounted for 16.1% of all arrests in 1988, but the same age group represented 28.2% of all arrests for serious crimes. Arrest rates for juveniles increase sharply during the junior high years. This pattern probably reflects both the greater harm adolescents can cause to society as a result of their inappropriate behavior and the fact that younger children are often not arrested (and therefore do not show up on the records) for committing the same acts that lead to the arrest of an older child.

Younger children are, however, being arrested; in 1988 over 600,000 arrests of children under age 15 were made. And younger children are committing more serious and violent crimes than in the past (Cavan & Ferdinand, 1975). Children under the age of 15 account for 5.2% of all arrests, but they are responsible for 11.1% of all arrests for serious crimes (U.S. Department of Commerce, 1990). Although boys have generally committed crimes involving aggression (such as assault and burglary) and girls have been associated with sex-related offenses (such as prostitution), more and more violent offenses are being committed by girls (Cavan & Ferdinand, 1975). Offenses involving the use of illegal drugs have also increased tremendously in recent years.

About half of all juvenile delinquents are *recidivists*—repeat offenders. Recidivists are more likely to begin their criminal careers at an early age (usually by age 12), commit more serious crimes, and continue a pattern of repeated antisocial behavior as adults (Tolan, 1987). The total number of criminal offenses committed by youths against others and property is, of course, impossible to determine. Many crimes go unreported or unsolved, leaving identification of the perpetrator unknown; however, Table 5.1 indicates the possible extent of the problem and the many crimes often committed by individual juvenile offenders. Originally intended to show the ability of positive peer-culture counseling groups to provide confidentiality and to generate a

TABLE 5.1
Reported and unreported crimes by juvenile offenders.

Offenses Known to Court	Offenses Not Known to Court. Discussed in Group
Student A Petty larceny; brutality (holding 9-year-old boy over burning trash barrel).	Auto theft; breaking and entering.
Student B Beyond control of parent; sexual intercourse with 12-year-old sister.	Auto theft; attempted rape; stealing; shoplifting; breaking and entering; vandalism; sexual acts with animals; incest with mother.
Student C Shoplifting; disorderly conduct; grand larceny; breaking and entering; destroying private property; truancy.	Habituation to drugs; grand larceny; petty larceny; arson; auto theft; carrying concealed weapons.
Student D Curfew violation; auto theft; breaking and entering; public intoxication; operating motor vehicle without license.	Carrying deadly weapon; robbery; arson; auto theft; multiple breaking and entering; three instances of assault and battery.
Student E Truancy; runaway; obtaining merchandise under false pretenses.	Habituation to drugs; shoplifting; auto theft; vandalism; "rolling queers" for money (assault, battery, robbery).
Student F Petty larceny; contempt of court; curfew violation; breaking and entering.	Malicious cutting and wounding; housebreaking; stealing; forgery; shoplifting.
Student G Breaking and entering; attempted safe burglary; safe burglary.	Carrying a deadly weapon; malicious cutting and wounding; burglary; concealing stolen property; fraud; stealing from automobiles.
Student H Shoplifting; runaway; violation of probation.	Breaking and entering; stealing.
Student I Public intoxication; petty larceny; carrying concealed deadly weapon; burglary; attempted safecracking.	Shoplifting; driving without license; breaking and entering.

Source: Reprinted with permission from: Vorrath, Harry H. and Larry K. Brendtro. *Positive Peer Culture.* 2nd Ed. (New York: Aldine de Gruyter) Copyright © 1985 Harry H. Vorrath and Larry K. Brendtro, p. 84.

See Nelson, Rutherford, & Wolford's (1987) book, *Special Education in the Criminal Justice System.*

feeling of trust among the youths and their adult leader, this table gives further information on the characteristics of juvenile offenders.

Although it can be argued that adjudicated delinquents are, by virtue of the behaviors that precipitated their arrest, behaviorally disordered, most juvenile offenders receive few or no special education services.

Severely Disturbed Children

The National Association for Mental Health has estimated that more than 500,000 children in the United States are severely emotionally disturbed. These children are commonly diagnosed and referred to as autistic, psychotic, or schizophrenic. It is estimated that autism occurs in approximately 5 of every 10,000 children

(National Society for Autistic Children, 1977). Although autism is quite rare, it is actually more common than blindness in children (Lotter, 1966; Rutter, 1965). Kauffman (1980) suggests that 0.5% of all children (or 1 in 200) are being served as severely disturbed.

IDENTIFICATION AND MEASUREMENT OF BEHAVIOR DISORDERS

Many school districts do not use any systematic method for identifying children with behavior disorders. Most behavior disordered children are readily identifiable. They stand out. This does not mean, however, that identification is always a sure thing. Identification of emotional disturbance is more difficult with younger children, because the behavior of all young children changes quickly and often. Also, some withdrawn children go undetected because their problem does not draw the attention of parents and teachers. Aggressive children, on the other hand, seldom go unnoticed.

Some have speculated that systematic screening and identification methods are not used because the schools would identify many more children than they could provide special education services for. Another reason may be that screening methods are not needed. If only a portion of the children with behavior problems can be served, those children with the most obvious and severe disturbances will receive the services, and they are clearly identifiable without formal methods.

Assessment of behavior disorders, as with all handicapping conditions, answers four basic questions concerning special education services: (1) who might need help? (2) who really does need help (i.e., who is eligible)? (3) what kind of help is needed? and (4) is the help benefiting the student? The first question is answered through **screening**, a process of eliminating children who are not likely to be handicapped and identifying those who show signs of behavioral disturbance or seem to be at risk for developing a behavior problem. Children identified via the screening process then undergo more complete assessment to determine their eligibility for special education and their specific educational needs.

Most screening devices consist of behavior checklists that are completed by teachers, parents, peers, and/or children themselves. One widely used screening test for behavior disorders is *A Process for In-School Screening of Children with Emotional Handicaps* (Bower & Lambert, 1962). This device employs ratings of the child's behavior by his teacher, his peers, and the child. If the child is rated negatively by the teacher and his classmates or by himself, it is suggested that he be evaluated further. The instrument has three different forms: one with rating scales and questions appropriate for kindergarten through third grade, one for fourth through seventh grade, and one for eighth through twelfth grade.

The *Child Behavior Checklist* is a screening instrument that can be used by teachers or parents of children ages 6 to 16 (Achenback & Edelrock, 1984). The teacher's form includes 112 behaviors (e.g., "cries a lot," "not liked by other pupils") on a three-point scale: "Not True," "Somewhat or Sometimes True," or "Very True or Often True."

A recently developed and promising instrument is called *Systematic Screening for Behavior Disorders* (SSBD) (Walker & Severson, 1990). The SSBD,

Many districts now require an intermediate step between screening and full-scale assessment. This step consists of interventions in the regular classroom designed to maintain the child in the regular classroom and to prevent a suspected or developing problem from getting worse.

which was normed and field-tested in school districts throughout the country, identifies students who may have increased risk for behavior disorders (Walker et al., 1988). The SSBD employs a three-step, "multiple-gating" process for narrowing down the number of children suspected of having serious behavior problems. In Stage I of the SSBD, classroom teachers rank order every student in their classrooms according to behavioral profiles on two dimensions: *externalizing* problems (acting out, aggression) or *internalizing* problems (withdrawal, anxiety, little interaction with peers). Only the top three students on each list progress to Stage II, the Critical Events Index.

> Critical events are behavioral pinpoints of high salience and intensity that do not depend on frequency to define their severity. *Any* occurrence of these target behaviors is viewed as an indicator of major disruption of social-behavioral adjustment processes in school. Critical events have been characterized as analogous to "behavioral earthquakes" in terms of their ecological disruptiveness and severity. Because of their salience and low base rates of occurrence, critical events are viewed as indicative of serious behavioral pathology and may strongly reinforce negative peer and teacher social perception biases toward students who exhibit them. (Todis, Severson, & Walker, 1990, pp. 75–76)

The 33 items that make up the Critical Events Index were developed from previous research on teachers' standards and behavioral expectations (Walker & Rankin, 1983) and include such externalizing behaviors as "is physically aggressive with other students" and "makes lewd or obscene gestures," and internalizing behaviors like "vomits after eating" and "has auditory or visual hallucinations." Students who meet normative criteria on the Critical Events Index advance to Stage III of the SSBD, which consists of direct and repeated observations during independent seatwork periods in the classroom and on the playground during recess. Children who meet or exceed cutoff criteria for either or both observational measures are referred to child study teams for further evaluation. The SSBD is the most systematic, fully developed screening instrument presently available.

Projective Tests

Traditionally, identification of children with behavior disorders has relied heavily on the results of psychological tests and interviews. The results of **projective tests** (e.g., Rorschach Ink Blot [Rorschach, 1942], Draw-A-Man Test [Goodenough & Harris, 1963]), however, have proven to be of minimal value in prescribing an appropriate intervention. Children often do not respond in a testing or interview situation in the same way they would in the classroom or at home. Also, results of these assessment procedures test an extremely limited sample of a child's behavior and, just as important, do not assess how the child typically acts over a period of time. One-time measures are not sufficient as a basis for either identifying the presence of a behavior disorder or for planning education and treatment.

Defining and Measuring Disordered Behavior

In recent years, direct and frequent measurement has been increasingly used for assessing children with behavior disorders. With this method, the actual behaviors that cause a child to be considered disturbed in the first place are clearly specified and observed in the settings where they normally occur (e.g., the classroom) every day. In this way, precise statements can be made about what problem behaviors must be weakened and what adaptive behaviors should be performed with greater frequency. In addition to providing specific information on the frequency of occurrence of the problem, direct and repeated measurement also enables the teacher to observe systematically and note what events normally occur before and after the behavior(s) of concern. As we stressed in our discussion of learning disabilities (Chapter 4), the primary purpose of assessment is not to determine whether the child has something called a behavior disorder, but to see whether the child's behavior is different enough to warrant special services and, if so, to indicate what those services should be. Kauffman (1989) makes a strong case for direct and frequent measurement with behavior disordered children.

> Disturbed students are considered to need help primarily because they exhibit behavioral excesses or deficiencies. Not to define precisely and to measure these behavioral excesses and deficiencies, then, is a fundamental error; it is akin to the malpractice of a nurse who decides not to measure vital signs (heart rate, respiration rate, temperature, and blood pressure), perhaps arguing that he/she is too busy, that subjective estimates of vital signs are quite adequate, that vital signs are only superficial estimates of the patient's health, or that vital signs do not signify the nature of the underlying pathology. The teaching profession is dedicated to the task of changing behavior—changing behavior demonstrably for the better. What can one say, then, of educational practice that does not include precise definition and reliable measurement of the behavior change induced by the teacher's methodology? I believe this: *It is indefensible.* (p. 400)

What *about* the behavior of children with behavior disorders does one measure? What dimensions of their behavior are different from those of their normal peers? We can analyze or measure several dimensions of children's behavior—its frequency, duration, topography, and magnitude.

For a detailed explanation of procedures for direct and frequent measurement of behavior, see Cooper et al. (1987).

Frequency

Frequency refers to how often a particular behavior is performed. Almost all children cry, get into fights with other children, and sulk from time to time; yet we are not apt to label them emotionally disturbed. The primary difference between behavior disordered children and normal children is the rate at which these kinds of undesirable activities occur. Although the disturbed child may not do anything that a nonhandicapped peer does not do, she does certain undesirable things much more often (e.g., crying, hitting others) and/or engages in desirable behaviors too infrequently (e.g., playing with others).

Some studies have reported a reduced frequency of inappropriate behavior following brief periods of jogging or physical exercise. See pages 200–201.

Duration

Closely related to frequency is duration. **Duration** is a measure of how long a child engages in a given activity. Again, even though normal and behavior disordered children may do the same things, the amount of time the behavior disordered child spends in certain activities is often markedly different—either longer or shorter—from that of the normal child. For example, many young children have temper tantrums, but the tantrums generally last no more than 5 or 10 minutes. A behavior disordered child may have a tantrum for an hour or more. Sometimes the problem is one of too short a duration, as with paying

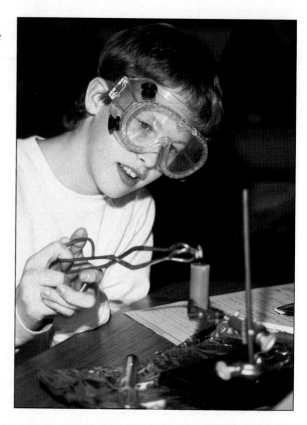

A hands-on science lesson helps this boy learn that he can exert control over his environment and his behavior.

attention or working independently. Some behavior disordered children cannot stick to one task for more than several seconds at a time.

Topography

Topography refers to the physical shape or form of behavior. For instance, throwing a baseball and rolling a bowling ball involve different topographies. Although both involve the arm, each activity requires a different movement. The responses emitted by a behavior disordered child may be of a topography seldom, if ever, seen in normal children. These behaviors may be maladaptive, bizarre, or dangerous to the child or others (e.g., twirling a small object in a bizarre manner close to the eye, or pulling out hair).

Magnitude

Finally, behavior is sometimes characterized by its **magnitude** or intensity. It may be either too soft (for example, talking in a volume so low that you cannot be heard) or too hard (such as slamming the door).

Stimulus Control

Disturbed children also have difficulty discriminating when and where certain behaviors are appropriate. Learning that kind of **stimulus control** is a major task of growing up, which most children master naturally through socialization. They pick it up from friends, siblings, parents, and other adults. Some children with behavior disorders, however, often appear unaware of their surroundings. They do not learn the proper time and place for many actions without being carefully instructed.

Clustering and Length of Intervention

There are two other important aspects of children's behavior disorders. First, these children usually exhibit a variety of problems across several different areas of functioning. Hewett and Taylor (1980) refer to this as "clustering," the exhibition of two or more types of problem behaviors that increase the chance that the child's behavior will exceed the teacher's range of tolerance. (They illustrate clustering with the case of Bobby, a child who, in one "infamous morning," destroyed school property, stole a classmate's lunch money and punched the student in the stomach, defied the teacher, and used obscene language.) Another important aspect is that behavior disordered children have long-standing problems that require extensive treatment rather than brief intervention.

Advantages of Behavioral Dimensions

The advantage of defining behavior disorders in terms of these behavioral dimensions is that identification, instructional strategies, and evaluation of the effects of treatment can all revolve around the objective measurement of these dimensions. This approach leads to a direct focus on the child's problem—the inappropriate behavior—and ways of dealing with it, as opposed to concentrating on some problem within the child. If the child can learn new, socially acceptable ways to behave, he need no longer be considered behavior disordered (Council for Children with Behavior Disorders, 1989; Sugai & Maheady, 1988).

Behaviorally oriented educators are concerned with the social significance of behavior change (Baer, Wolf, & Risley, 1968). It is not enough just to measure that a child's behavior has changed; teachers must show that the changes they bring about have **social validity** (Van Houten, 1979; Wolf, 1978). One measure of social validity is whether newly acquired behaviors are really worthwhile for the child; that is, whether the new behavior will be viewed as significant by others, by those people who deal with the child. Walker and Hops (1976) describe one approach for evaluating the effects of treatment on the classroom behavior of elementary school students referred to an experimental class because of inappropriate behavior. Instead of merely demonstrating that the children's behavior improved in the special class, Walker and Hops compared the behavior of their special students with the actual classroom behavior of their peers in the regular classroom.

The special students received a treatment program consisting of systematic social and token reinforcement in the classroom. It produced behavior that was actually better than that of the students' peers back in the regular classroom during the same period. Continued observation of the students during a 12-week follow-up period after their return to the regular classroom revealed that they maintained appropriate behavior within the normal limits defined by their peers' behavior. Walker and Hops demonstrated not only that their treatment program improved the disruptive students' behavior, but also that the improvements were socially valid (i.e., the special students now acted as well as their normal classmates) and were maintained during a 3-month follow-up.

See Figure 5.5 for another example of using the behavior of peers to evaluate the social validity of treatment gains.

THE A.M. CLUB

Jogging as Therapy for Behavior Disordered Students

The use of vigorous physical exercise has been proposed as effective therapy for children with behavior disorders, possibly resulting in reduced rates of disruptive classroom behavior and improved self-esteem. J. I. Allen (1980) found that as little as 5 minutes of jogging reduced off-task behaviors; Evans, Evans, Schmid, and Pennypacker (1985) found that 15 minutes of jogging and touch football resulted in fewer talk-outs and increased academic production in the classroom; Yell (1988) noted a reduction in the number of talk-outs and out-of-seat behaviors by six elementary students with behavior disorders; and Kern, Koegel, and Dunlap (1984) discovered that 15 minutes of vigorous jogging reduced stereotypic responding. The following story is excerpted from one teacher's description of a systematic program of running that she used with behaviorally disordered junior high school students.

The information came rushing into my head and tumbled into a box marked, "Yep, that's right!" Therapeutic jogging for behaviorally impaired kids: Whoopee—what a right idea! And A.M. Club was conceived. The administration was receptive and supportive. We began to consider the when, where, and how aspects of the program. It was suggested that we might consider running the three-story stairs in our junior high building before school each morning. But it seemed to me that I remembered my son's tennis season and how they called running the stairs the suicide run! So as a concession to myself, I did not choose the three flights as the site. How about the grassy lot across the street from the junior high each morning? But these kids have enough trouble with peer relations without adding being a spectacle. A.M. Club was having labor pains. The site finally selected was the YMCA, a new facility with a running track.

The local runners with whom I talked spoke about the joy of running, the runner's high, the inside thrill. With these kids, I might address these lofty issues later; in the meantime, they needed a tangible reward, something they could hold in their hand, carry with them, or put on the refrigerator at home. Ribbons! Any kid works for a ribbon. So design a ribbon with the club logo and for every three attendances present them with a ribbon. After eight ribbons they earn a T-shirt with the club logo on the front. We were recognizable. A.M. Club had an identity.

The biggest concern was how to structure the program to decrease inappropriate behaviors such as fighting or leaving the exercise area. How do we foster appropriate behaviors, a feeling of helping others, of being part of a team effort and giving encouragement? And how would we get kids to work on improvement of physical condition? We wrote into the IEP three rules tied to a reward that would act as an incentive.

1. No physical fighting or name-calling.
2. Stay in the designated area.
3. Continuous forward movement during the 12-minute exercise period.

If all members followed the rules for 2 weeks, we would have breakfast together at McDonald's on the second Friday on the way back to school. A.M. Club was born.

As I write this, after several months the following facts can be stated: Of the 4 original members, 3 have never missed; our group now numbers 12 students; 3 of the members have signed up for the eighth grade track team. And students are actively engaged in encouraging others in the group. They can be seen running in pairs, with one behind the other running at his shoulder saying, "Come on, one more lap."

I am not naive enough to believe a program such as A.M. Club is appropriate for every student with behavior problems, nor do I believe there is a "magic cure" that comes for those students who participate. This program is only one small part of a larger, comprehensive program tailored to the specific needs of our students. But let me tell you, there is real joy in this small group. We hear parents speak of the commitment their child shows to the group and to their own self-improvement. As a teacher I frequently follow the philosophy when working with kids, "If it looks good, try it. If it works, try it again." And that is why A.M. Club started. Physical exercise and group cohesiveness looked good as a concept, and it worked.

From "A.M. Club" by Evelyn Anderson, 1985, in *Teaching Behavioral Disordered Youth, 1,* pp. 12–16. Copyright by the Council for Children with Behavior Disorders. Reprinted by permission.

Here are some guidelines for implementing a jogging or exercise program (adapted from Anderson [1985] and Yell [1988]):

♦ Begin each session with a warm-up and stretching period.

♦ Be sure to jog only in an area clear of traffic and obstruction.

♦ End each jogging session with a cool-down period or relaxed stretching to allow heart rates to return to normal.

♦ Praise students for participating and consider using rewards such as certificates and ribbons for meeting specific accomplishments (e.g., total miles, consecutive days participating).

♦ Publicly posting each student's participation and mileage can be a good way to give feedback. Have each student try to beat his or her own best time or distance.

♦ By including group totals and setting group goals, competition between students can be replaced with peer support.

♦ Don't expect miracles. Although some students' classroom behavior may improve slightly, a jogging program does not constitute a full treatment program. ♦

■ CLASSIFICATION OF CHILDREN'S BEHAVIOR DISORDERS

As we mentioned in Chapter 1, classification of the observed phenomena within a given field is an important scientific task. A reliable and valid classification system for behavior disorders would foster accurate communication among researchers, diagnosticians, and teachers. Better communication could result, most importantly, in a child's receiving the educational placement and treatment that have been proven most effective for her specific behavior problem. Unfortunately, we have yet to develop such a workable classification system in the area of behavior disorders.

The DSM-III-R

One system of classifying behavior disorders is the *Diagnostic and Statistical Manual of Mental Disorders (Revised)* (DSM-III-R) developed by the American Psychiatric Association (1987). The DSM-III-R is an elaborate and vast classification system consisting of 230 separate diagnostic categories, or labels, to identify the various types of disordered behavior noted in clinical practice. Because of its more precise language, its use of more examples, and the greater amount of information it requires about the person being diagnosed, the DSM-III-R represents an improvement in clinical classification over earlier versions from 1952 and 1968. The DSM-III-R classification system is used quite regularly in the mental health professions; however, it suffers from a lack of reliability. Even with the more precise language, it is not uncommon for one psychiatrist or psychologist to classify a child in one category and a second examiner to place the same child in a completely different category (Epstein, Detwiler, & Reitz, 1985).

But an even greater problem is that putting a child in a given category provides no guidelines for treatment. Knowing that a child has been diagnosed as fitting a certain category in the DSM-III-R provides a teacher with virtually no useful information on what intervention or therapy is needed.

Quay's Statistical Classification

Another well-known classification system was developed by Quay and his co-workers (Quay, 1975, 1986). Quay collected a wide range of data—including behavior ratings by parents and teachers, life histories, and children's own responses on questionnaires—for hundreds of behavior disordered children. When all this information was analyzed statistically, the researchers found that children's behavior disorders tend to appear in groups, or clusters. Children who showed some of the behaviors in a given cluster had a high likelihood of also showing the other traits and behaviors in that cluster. Quay calls the four types *conduct disorder, personality disorder, immaturity,* and *socialized aggression.*

Children described as having a **conduct disorder** are likely to be disobedient and/or disruptive, get into fights, be bossy, and have temper tantrums. A **personality disorder** in children is identified by social withdrawal, anxiety, depression, feelings of inferiority, guilt, shyness, and unhappiness.

Immaturity is characterized by a short attention span, extreme passivity, daydreaming, preference for younger playmates, and clumsiness. The fourth dimension, **socialized aggression**, is marked by truancy, gang membership, theft, and a feeling of pride in belonging to a delinquent subculture. Although Quay's system has proven quite reliable—the same four clusters of behavior and personality traits have been found in many samples of behavior disordered children (Quay, 1986)—it does not provide treatment information. Therefore, its usefulness is limited primarily to describing the major types of children's behavior disorders for purposes of research and communication.

Learning Competence

Hewett and his colleagues have developed a classification scheme based on "levels of learning competence" (Hewett, 1964, 1968; Hewett & Forness, 1977; Hewett & Taylor, 1980). Hewett and Taylor (1980) describe an actual episode that led them to seek better ways of classifying behavior disorders. Donald, an 11-year-old boy, was completely immobilized—he would not walk, talk, eat, or care for himself. He was fed with a stomach tube at first, but later began to swallow juice, his only observable response. At this point, Donald's psychiatrist felt that going to school might help him. He introduced him to the teacher by saying,

> "This is Donald. He is in a catatonic schizophrenic stupor with severe psychomotor retardation. Good luck."
>
> Such a description was a bit unsettling for the teacher and is an excellent example of the alien and essentially useless contribution such labels and diagnostic terms have to make in educational settings. As long as the teacher was intimidated by this pathetic little boy in a "catatonic schizophrenic stupor," it was doubtful that any worthwhile program could be provided by the school. But once she set aside the psychiatric jargon and took a long, hard look at Donald, things got better. Here was this immobilized student. We had heard what his psychiatric problem was. Now, what was his educational problem? Simple. Donald *was a severe response problem* in educational and learning terms. He did not move. To learn you must respond. Donald was a candidate for a response curriculum. He was no longer a mysterious alien with catatonic schizophrenia. He was now a learner, and it would be the role of the school to teach him to respond as the initial educational task. (p. 96)

Hewett's classification system includes six levels of learning competence. The *attention level* has to do with children making contact with their environment; the *response level,* with active motor and verbal participation; the *order level* is concerned with teaching children to follow instructions and routines; the *exploratory level* has children accurately and thoroughly investigate their environment; the *social level* focuses on interactions with others; and the *mastery level* involves skills related to self-care, academics, and vocational interests. Table 5.2 shows how the classification scheme views behavior problems along a continuum of too little to too much in respect to the six levels of learning competence.

Hewett and Taylor (1980) contend that this classification system is both descriptive and functional, that classifying a child's behavior problem within the system "provides a direct link to the setting of curriculum goals" (p. 99). In the

TABLE 5.2

Classification of disturbed children by negative variants of six levels of learning competence.

Too Little	Optimal			Too Much
Disturbances in sensory perception	Excessive daydreaming Poor memory Short attention span In a world all his or her own	Attention	Selective attention	Fixation on particular stimuli
Immobilization	Sluggishness Passivity Drowsiness Clumsiness Depression	Response	Hyperactivity Restlessness	Self-stimulation
Failure to develop speech	Failure to use language for communication	Response	Extremely talkative	Uses profanity Verbally abusive
Self-injurious Lawlessness Destructiveness	Disruptiveness Attention seeking Irresponsibility Disobedience	Order	Overly conforming	Resistance to change Compulsive
Bizarre or stereotyped behavior Bizarre interests	Anxiety Preoccupation Doesn't know how to have fun Behaves like an adult Shyness	Exploratory	Plunges into activities	Tries to do everything at once
Preoccupation with inanimate objects Extreme self-isolation Inability to relate to people	Social withdrawal Alienates others Aloofness Prefers younger playmates Acts bossy Secretiveness Fighting Temper tantrums	Social	Hypersensitivity Jealousy Overly dependent	Inability to function alone
Blunted, uneven or fragmented intellectual development	Lacks self-care skills Lacks basic school skills Laziness in school Dislike for school Lacks vocational skills	Mastery	Preoccupation with academics	Overintellectualizing

Source: From Frank M. Hewett and Frank D. Taylor, THE EMOTIONALLY DISTURBED CHILD IN THE CLASSROOM: THE ORCHESTRATION OF SUCCESS, Second Edition. Copyright © 1980 Allyn and Bacon, Inc. Reprinted with permission.

case of Donald, for instance, his nearly total lack of response was the first order of business for the teacher. Hewett's classification system is a considerable advance over systems that provide descriptive labels only, labeling the child without relating to useful educational strategies.

It is much easier to classify behaviors objectively than to classify children. In addition, an ever-growing body of research literature indicates that certain strategies are often successful in changing certain types of behaviors. Thus, objectively pinpointing the specific inappropriate things a disturbed child does can lead to treatment strategies. And labeling behaviors rather than children is optimistic; it implies that the child will be normal as soon as he learns more socially adaptive actions to replace his disordered behavior. This attitude might help to alleviate some of the permanent stigma that often comes from labeling children.

See journals such as *Behavior Therapy, Behavioral Disorders, Education & Treatment of Children,* and *Journal of Applied Behavior Analysis.*

Degree of Severity

Another method of classifying children with behavior disorders is by degree of severity (Clarizio, 1990). Although children have sometimes been referred to as displaying mild, moderate, and severe behavior problems, at least one study suggests that this three-level distinction is not supported in practice. Olson, Algozzine, and Schmid (1980) found that teachers of emotionally handicapped children regularly identified only two levels, or degrees, of behavioral disturbance: mild and severe. Children who were viewed as mildly emotionally disturbed were those who could respond to interventions provided in regular classrooms by regular class teachers, with the support of guidance counselors or consulting teachers. Those considered severely disturbed were children who needed intense treatment programs and residential placement.

Classification by degree of severity, however, is primarily after the fact. Important decisions as to type of programming and environment for delivery should be based on an objective assessment of the child's individual needs, rather than on someone's opinion that the child is either mildly or severely disturbed.

CHARACTERISTICS OF CHILDREN WITH BEHAVIOR DISORDERS

Having looked at some of the characteristics of behavior disordered children, we can discuss these children's intellectual ability and academic achievement as well as the two general types of behavior they display—aggression/acting out and social withdrawal. We will also describe the dominant characteristics of childhood autism.

Intelligence and Achievement

Contrary to one popular myth, most emotionally disturbed children are not bright, intellectually above-average children who are bored with their surroundings. Many more behavior disordered children than normal children score in the slow learner or mildly retarded range on IQ tests. A score of about 90–95 is average for children with behavior disorders, with more scoring lower than

See Chapter 3 for a discussion of IQ tests.

higher than that average. Many severely disturbed children are untestable; for those who can be tested, the average IQ score is about 50. Occasionally, a severely disturbed child scores very high on an IQ test, but this is a rare exception.

Whether children with behavior disorders actually have any less real intelligence than normal children is difficult to say. An IQ test measures only how well a child performs certain tasks. It is possible that the disturbed child's inappropriate behavior has interfered with past opportunities to learn the tasks included on the test, but the child really has the necessary intelligence to learn them. In any event, IQ tests are good indicators of school achievement, and behavior disordered children are noted for their problems with learning and academic achievement. Based on his review of research related to the intelligence of emotionally disturbed children, Kauffman (1989) hypothesizes that, as a group, their IQ scores are distributed as shown in Figure 5.1.

Even when IQ scores are taken into account, however, children with behavior disorders achieve below the levels suggested by their scores. Overall, it is estimated that only 30% of students with behavior disorders are performing at or above grade level (Knister et al., 1990). A study by Glavin and Annesley (1971) supports this estimate: They assessed the performance of 130 behavior disordered children and found that 81% were underachieving in reading and 72% were achieving less than would be expected in math.

Data obtained by the state of Florida on a total of 193 11th grade students classified as emotionally disturbed or socially maladjusted indicated that almost 50% of the students could not read well enough to pass a functional literacy test. Approximately 75% of the sample did not have the mathematics skills necessary for a high school diploma (reported in Cawley & Webster, 1981). A survey of correctional institutions found 34% of incarcerated delinquents to be functionally illiterate (Clearinghouse for Offender Literacy Programs, 1975). Oliver (1974), in a national survey of 12- to 17-year-old public school students, found

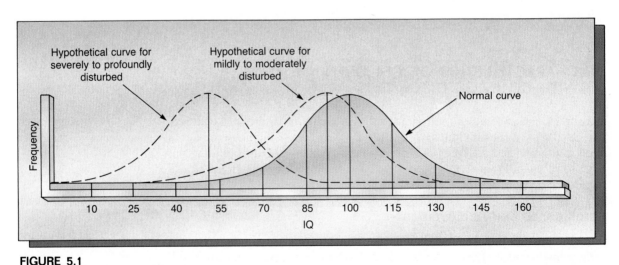

FIGURE 5.1

Hypothetical frequency distributions of IQ for children who are mildly to moderately, and severely to profoundly disturbed compared to a normal frequency distribution. (*Source:* From *Characteristics of Behavior Disorders of Children and Youth* (4th ed.) (p. 183) by J. M. Kauffman, 1989, Columbus, OH: Merrill. Reprinted by permission.)

that over 80% of those who needed frequent discipline were behind in their academic achievement.

Walker and Buckley (1973) have suggested that the behavior disordered child's academic deficits can be explained, at least in part, in terms of the large amount of time the child spends on nonacademic matters (such as running around the room or fighting), at the expense of learning. Many educators have noted the close association of learning disabilities and behavior disorders (e.g., Stephens, 1977; Wallace & McLoughlin, 1979). Many children with behavior disorders also have the problems in learning described in Chapter 4.

Aggressive/Acting Out Behavior

The most common pattern of behavior exhibited by children with behavior disorders is one of aggression and acting out, or *externalizing* behavior disorders. Hops, Beickel, and Walker (1976) list the following behaviors as characteristic of the acting-out child in the classroom.

Aggression and acting out are the major characteristics of Quay's (1975) conduct disorder and socialized aggression categories.

Is out of seat

Yells out

Runs around room

Disturbs peers

Hits or fights

Ignores teacher

Complains

Fights excessively

Steals

Destroys property

Does not comply with adult commands or directions

Argues (talks back)

Ignores other teachers

Distorts the truth

Has temper tantrums

Is excluded from activities by peers

Does not follow directions

Does not complete assignments

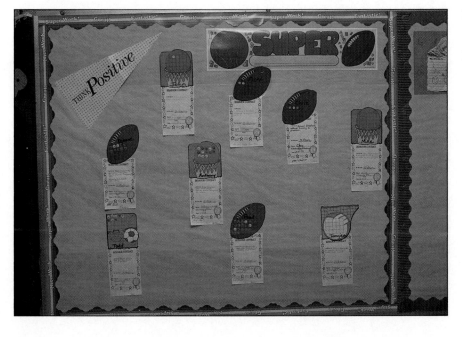

Behavior contracts provide rewards and positive recognition for performance of specified classroom behaviors.

Even though all children sometimes cry, hit others, and refuse to comply with requests of parents and teachers, children with behavior disorders do so frequently. Also, behavior disordered children's aggressive behavior often occurs with little or no provocation. Aggression takes many forms—verbal abuse toward adults and other children, destructiveness and vandalism, physical attacks on others. These children seem to be in continuous conflict with those around them. Their own aggressive outbursts often cause others to strike back in attempts to punish them. It is no wonder children with behavior disorders are seldom liked by others and find it difficult to establish friendships.

Patterson and his co-workers conducted considerable research on childhood aggression (Patterson, Reid, Jones, & Conger, 1975). Through intensive observations of many aggressive children at home and in school, they identified 14 different classes of noxious behaviors often shown by behavior disordered children. Table 5.3 shows the different rates at which behavior disordered and normal children emit these inappropriate behaviors. The data in the table were taken from observations in the homes of aggressive and nonaggressive children. Observations in the classroom indicated similar patterns (Patterson, Cobb, & Ray, 1972).

As many children with behavior disorders grow older, their aggressive behavior causes conflict in the community, leading to run-ins with law enforcement officials and arrests for criminal offenses. Teenage delinquency is a serious problem today; youth under the age of 18 are responsible for a large number of each year's criminal arrests. To add to the problem, as mentioned earlier, the incidence of serious and violent crimes committed by juveniles is increasing (Cavan & Ferdinand, 1975; U.S. Department of Commerce, 1990).

Many believe that most children who exhibit deviant behavior patterns will grow out of them with time and become normally functioning adults. Although this popular wisdom holds true for many children who exhibit problems such as withdrawal, fears, and speech impairments (Rutter, 1976), research indicates that it is not so for children who display consistent patterns of aggressive, coercive, antisocial, and/or delinquent behavior (Robins, 1979; Wahler & Dumas, 1986). Robins (1966) conducted a follow-up study of over 500 adults who as children had been seen by a clinic because of behavior problems. Robins used structured interviews to gather such information as work history, alcohol and drug use, performance in the armed services, arrest, social relationships, and marital history. A control group of 100 adults who grew up in the same communities as the subjects was used for comparison. The results were significant. Of those adults who had been referred to a clinic for behavior problems as children, 45% had five or more antisocial traits. Only 4% of those in the control group showed that many antisocial characteristics. In analyzing the results further, Robins found that those who as children had been referred to the clinic for antisocial behavior—theft, fighting, discipline problems in school, truancy, and the like—had the most difficulty adjusting as adults. Furthermore, as adults, they tended to raise children who had a higher incidence of problem behaviors than normal, thus continuing the cycle.

Withdrawn Behavior

Some behavior disordered children are anything but aggressive. Their problem is the opposite—too little social interaction with others. They are said to have

TABLE 5.3

Noxious behaviors in aggressive and nonaggressive children.

Noxious Behavior	Description	Average No. of Mins. Between Occurrences*	
		Aggressive Children	Nonaggressive Children
Disapproval	Disapproving of another's behavior by words or gestures	7	12
Negativism	Stating something neutral in content but saying it in a negative tone of voice	9	41
Noncompliance	Not doing what is requested	11	20
Yell	Shouting, yelling, or talking loudly; if carried on for sufficient time it becomes extremely unpleasant	18	54
Tease	Teasing that produces displeasure, disapproval, or disruption of current activity of the person being teased	20	51
High rate activity	Activity that is aversive to others if carried on for a long period of time (e.g., running in the house or jumping up and down)	23	71
Negative physical act	Attacking or attempting to attack another with enough intensity to potentially inflict pain (e.g., biting, kicking, slapping, hitting, spanking, throwing, grabbing)	24	108
Whine	Saying something in a slurring, nasal, high-pitched, or falsetto voice	28	26
Destructive	Destroying, damaging, or trying to damage or destroy any object	33	156
Humiliation	Making fun of, shaming, or embarrassing another intentionally	50	100
Cry	Any type of crying	52	455
Negative command	Commanding another to do something and demanding immediate compliance, plus threatening aversive consequences (explicit or implicitly) if compliance is not immediate; also directing sarcasm or humiliation at another	120	500
Dependent	Requesting help with a task the child is capable of doing alone (e.g., a 16-year-old boy asking his mother to comb his hair)	149	370
Ignore	The child appears to recognize that another has directed behavior toward him but does not respond in an active fashion	185	244

*Minutes between occurrences are expressed as approximations of reported average rates per minute (e.g., for aggressive children's whine, reported rate per minute equals 0.0360, or approximately once very 28 minutes).

Source: From *A Social Learning Approach to Family Intervention: Vol. 1. Families with Aggressive Children* (p. 5) by G. R. Patterson, J. B. Reid, R. R. Jones, and R. E. Conger, 1975. Eugene, OR: Castilia Press. Adapted by permission.

WORKING WITH DENISE
A Selective Mute

Some children become so shy and withdrawn that they refuse to speak at school, even though they use normal speech in other places or in the presence of other people. The clinical term for this behavior disorder—speaking normally in one setting and not speaking in another—is *selective mutism*.

Denise was a 5-year-old kindergarten student who spoke only to her parents and brother when at home. Throughout her first 6 months at school, no one there heard Denise talk, laugh, cry, or make any vocalizations whatsoever. Yet her speech at home was reportedly fluent. Denise's mother described her as generally happy and helpful around the house. Denise completed some school assignments at home, but she never attempted any work in school. She rarely took part in group activities and sometimes stood in one spot for long

periods, unless she was coaxed to do otherwise.

Because Denise spoke freely at home but was mute at school, it was decided to use a treatment program that united the two environments. A **token economy** was chosen for this purpose, whereby desired behaviors could be rewarded with some tangible item that could be accumulated and traded in for a variety of back-up reinforcers. Because any treatment program bridging home and school would require full cooperation from Denise's parents, a meeting was arranged. The teacher explained to the parents that when Denise did certain things at school, she would be given gold stars to take home to "buy" things with, provided she had enough stars to cover the cost of the desired item. Denise's parents then made a list of items and activities their daughter liked. In addition to vocalizations,

behaviors that would increase the likelihood of speech were also listed to be rewarded. Behaviors that required Denise to speak earned her the most stars.

A chart illustrating the available rewards and their relative cost in stars was constructed and taped to the refrigerator in Denise's house. She also got a folder in which she could save and carry home the gummed stick-on stars.

The teacher explained to Denise's classmates (in Denise's absence) that they were going to play a game, the object of which was to get Denise to talk at school. Even the promise of the possibility of Denise's talking to them was a strong incentive for her peers to cooperate. The teacher asked Denise's classmates to "try to pay more attention to Denise when she is doing one of these things," then read the list of desired

---

These children make up Quay's (1975) personality disorder and immaturity dimensions.

internalizing behavior disorders. Although children who consistently act immature and withdrawn do not present the threat to others that aggressive children do, their behavior still creates a serious impediment to development. These children seldom play with others their own age. They usually do not have the necessary social skills to make friends and have fun, and they often retreat into daydreams and fantasies. Some are fearful of things without reason, frequently complain of being sick or hurt, and go into deep bouts of depression. Obviously, these behavior patterns limit the child's chances to take part in and learn from the school and leisure activities in which normal children participate.

Because children with internalizing problems may be less disturbing to others, there is the danger of their not being identified. Happily, for the mildly or moderately disturbed child who is withdrawn and immature and who is fortunate enough to have competent teachers and other school professionals responsible for her development, the outlook is fairly good. Carefully outlining the social skills the child should learn and gradually and systematically arranging behaviors to them. They were also told to ignore her at other times.

Denise made rapid progress with this program. Whereas she had earned only one star on the first day, for joining story time, by Day 30 she took part in all group activities, said "Hi," and answered seven questions from the teacher. She had accumulated the 40 stars she needed for a new doll.

It is important to note that behaviors other than those that involve speech were rewarded. To get the token economy started, some behaviors Denise was already doing were included for reinforcement. In this case, simply waiting for Denise to speak would probably have been futile and frustrating. By increasing the frequency of behaviors that required Denise to confront other people (such as joining group activities), she had many more occasions for speaking.

Another important factor was the behavior of Denise's classmates. Before the program, they would answer questions for her, frequently ask her whether she was all right, and get things for her. She received a lot of attention for not talking. During the program, however, this attention was withheld, and Denise's classmates were very good at paying attention to her only when she was participating.

In Denise's case, the ice was broken just before the end of the school year, and it was feared that her muteness might return again in the fall. To help prevent that, Denise was enrolled in a 6-week summer school session with the same classroom teacher. During that session, social praise and special privileges (such as wiping the blackboard and feeding the class turtle) were substituted for the home reward menu and were given at school for doing the same list of behaviors. Gold stars were again used as token reinforcers until the last week and a half of the summer session. Denise's rate of speech and social activity in general continued to increase during the summer.

A year after Denise's original program, she was described by her new teacher as a child who talked "a mile a minute." She had been retained in kindergarten because her extreme withdrawal during the first 7 months of school had prevented her from acquiring most of the prerequisite skills for the first grade. At the end of her first kindergarten year, Denise could not identify shapes, colors, or numbers and knew only a few letters of the alphabet.

At the beginning of her second year, Denise would not answer a question unless she felt sure of the right answer. Her teacher dealt immediately with this temporary muteness by walking away and ignoring her. After 2 days, Denise began to answer "I don't know" to questions she did not understand. Three months later she was answering in complete sentences in front of the class, beginning conversations, initiating play with other children, and learning in school.

From a case study reported by W. L. Heward, H. T. Eachus, and J. Christopher, 1974. ♦

---

opportunities for and rewarding those behaviors often prove successful. Cartledge and Milburn (1986), Stephens (1978), and Strain, Guralnick, and Walker (1986) offer information on teaching children social skills.

Autism

Autism refers to a set of behavioral characteristics common to many profoundly disturbed children. Mildly and moderately behavior disordered children are usually not labeled as having a problem during their preschool years; many are not considered behavior disordered by anyone until they reach the middle elementary years at school. This is not true for autistic children. An autistic child often seems different from normal children even during the first 2 years. Lovaas and Newsom (1976) have described six frequently observed characteristics of children with autism.

The 1990 Amendments to P.L. 94–142 added *autism* as a new disability category under which states can report the number of children served. Professionals disagree about whether autism is a severe behavior disorder, a severe language disorder, or a health impairment. We include it here because children with autism display a variety of unusual behaviors in addition to language problems; they are most often treated with procedures similar to those used with other behavior disorders.

1. *Apparent sensory deficit*. We may move directly in front of the child, smile, and talk to him, yet he will act as if no one is there. We may not feel that the child is avoiding or ignoring us, but rather that he simply does not seem to see or hear. The mother also reports that she did, in fact, incorrectly suspect the child to be blind or deaf . . . . As we get to know the child better, we become aware of the great variability in this obliviousness to stimulation. For example, although the child may give no visible reaction to a loud noise, such as a clapping of hands directly behind his ears, he may orient to the crinkle of a candy wrapper or respond fearfully to a distant and barely audible siren.

2. *Severe affect isolation*. Another characteristic that we frequently notice is that attempts to love and cuddle and show affection to the child encounter a profound lack of interest on the child's part. Again, the parents relate that the child seems not to know or care whether he is alone or in the company of others.

3. *Self-stimulation*. A most striking kind of behavior in these children centers on very repetitive stereotyped acts, such as rocking their bodies when in a sitting position, twirling around, flapping their hands at the wrists, or humming a set of three or four notes over and over again. The parents often report that their child has spent entire days gazing at his cupped hands, staring at lights, spinning objects, etc.

4. *Tantrums and self-mutilatory behavior*. Although the child may not engage in self-mutilation when we first meet him, often the parents report that the child sometimes bites himself so severely that he bleeds, or that he beats his head against walls or sharp pieces of furniture so forcefully that large lumps rise and his skin turns black and blue. He may beat his face with his fists . . . . Sometimes the child's aggression will be directed outward against his parents or teachers in the most primitive form of biting, scratching, and kicking. Some of these children absolutely tyrannize their parents by staying awake and making noises all night, tearing curtains off the window, spilling flour in the kitchen, etc., and the parents are often at a complete loss as to how to cope with these behaviors.

5. *Echolalic and psychotic speech*. Most of these children are mute; they do not speak, but they may hum or occasionally utter simple sounds. The speech of those who do talk may be echoes of other people's attempts to talk to them. For example, if we address a child with the question, "What is your name?" the child is likely to answer, "What is your name?" (preserving, perhaps, the exact intonation of the one who spoke to him). At other times the **echolalia** is not immediate but delayed; the child may repeat statements he has heard that morning or on the preceding day, or he may repeat TV commercials or other such announcements.

6. *Behavior deficiencies*. Although the presence of the behaviors sketched above is rather striking, it is equally striking to take note of many behaviors that the autistic child does not have. At the age of 5 or 10, he may, in many ways, show the behavioral repertoire of a 1-year-old child. He has few if any self-help skills but needs to be fed and dressed by others. He may not play with toys, but put them in his mouth, or tap them repetitively with his fingers. He shows no understanding of common dangers. [From "Behavior Modification with Psy-

chotic Children" by O. I. Lovaas and C. D. Newsom, 1976, in *Handbook of Behavior Modification and Behavior Therapy* by Harold Leitenberg (Ed.) (pp. 308–309). Englewood Cliffs, NJ: Prentice-Hall. Reprinted by permission.]

Clearly, children who act as Lovaas and Newsom describe are profoundly disturbed. Their management and treatment requires intensive behavioral programming to reduce the frequency of self-injurious and/or self-stimulatory behaviors. Even after years of extensive intervention in which substantial progress has been made, unless systematic programming is continued to maintain those gains, some autistic children revert to their earlier forms of behavior (Lovaas, Koegel, Simmons, & Long, 1973).

Encouraging Research

On the brighter side, however, a great deal of exciting and promising research may lead to better futures for children with autism (Valcante, 1986). For example, the work of Lovaas (1987) and his colleagues at the University of California at Los Angeles indicates the tremendous potential of early intervention with autistic children. He reports that 50% of a group of autistic children who were provided with an early intervention program of intensive, one-to-one behavior modification for more than 40 hours per week prior to the age of 3½ made a complete recovery. That is, they were later able to advance from first to second grade in a regular classroom, attained normal IQ scores, and were considered by their teachers to be well adjusted. Another 40% of the group was said to have made substantial improvement.

Researchers are also discovering successful procedures for using sensory stimulation (e.g., movement, visual and/or auditory feedback, vibration) to reduce self-stimulation and to reinforce desired responses (Ferrari & Harris, 1981; Rincover, Cook, Peoples, & Packard, 1979). More effective methods of programming important aspects of instruction for autistic children, such as scheduling learning tasks and varying reinforcers, are being experimentally demonstrated (Dunlap & Koegel, 1980; Egel, 1981). Still other researchers are teaching autistic children to communicate through sign language (Barrera & Sulzer-Azaroff, 1983; Bonvillian & Nelson, 1976) and to use social interaction skills with nonhandicapped peers (Gaylord-Ross, Haring, Breen, & Pitts-Conway, 1984).

Russo and Koegel (1977) carried out an impressive case study showing that a child with autism could be successfully mainstreamed in a regular classroom. A 5-year-old girl with a primary diagnosis of autism was placed in a regular public school kindergarten with 20 to 30 normal children and one teacher. For the first 12 weeks (after a 3-week baseline period), a therapist was also in the classroom to provide a treatment program of token reinforcement, verbal praise, and prompts for desired behaviors. For the remaining 10 weeks of the school year, the kindergarten teacher, who had been trained by the therapist, carried out the treatment program alone and kept the autistic child in the classroom. Figure 5.2 shows the number of desirable social interactions, amount of stereotypic self-stimulatory behavior (such as rocking and rhythmic manipulation of small objects), and percent of appropriate responses to questions (such as "What color is this?") asked by the therapist or teacher.

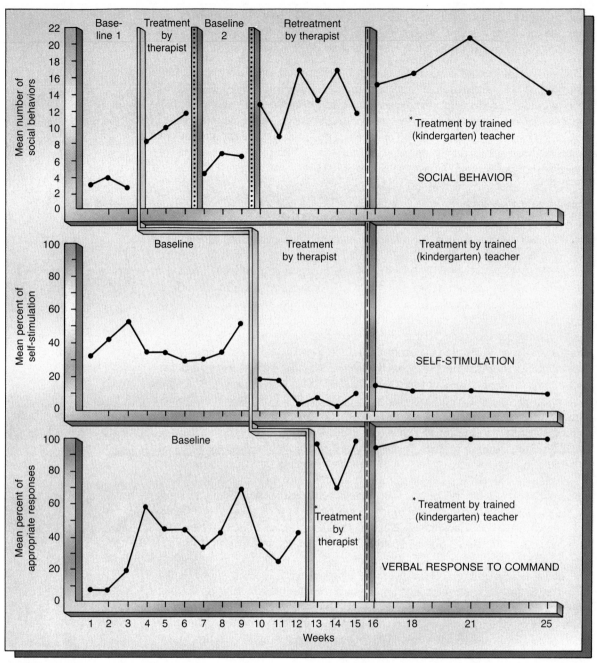

FIGURE 5.2

Social behavior, self-stimulation, and verbal response to command in the normal kindergarten classroom during baseline, treatment by the therapist, and treatment by the trained kindergarten teacher; all three behaviors were measured simultaneously. (*Source:* From "A Method for Integrating an Autistic Child in a Normal Public-School Classroom" by D. C. Russo and R. L. Koegel, 1977, *Journal of Applied Behavior Analysis, 10,* p. 585. Copyright by the Society for the Experimental Analysis of Behavior, Inc. Reprinted by permission.)

During the next school year, the girl was placed in a regular first grade classroom with another teacher. At the beginning of first grade, she was emitting fewer social behaviors and the frequency of self-stimulatory behavior had increased over the levels obtained by the end of kindergarten. In-class retreatment by the therapist and training of the first grade teacher, however, resulted in improvements similar to those of the kindergarten year. Russo and Koegel state that the school reported no further problems throughout the remainder of the first grade or during the child's second and third grade years. The researchers report that four other autistic children were also successfully placed in regular classrooms (three in kindergarten and one in the fifth grade) using the same procedures.

Studies like this one are critically important for two reasons. First, they discover at least some of the variables that can be controlled to help an autistic child function in a regular classroom. Second, the successful results offer real hope and encouragement for the many teachers and parents working to learn more about helping autistic children.

CAUSES OF BEHAVIOR DISORDERS

Several theories and conceptual models have been proposed to explain abnormal behavior. Regardless of the conceptual model from which behavior disorders are viewed, the suggested causes of disordered behavior can be grouped into two major categories—biological and psychological.

Biological Factors

For the vast majority of behavior disordered children, there is no evidence of organic injury or disease; that is, they appear to be biologically healthy and sound. Some experts believe that all children are born with a biologically determined temperament. Although a child's inborn temperament may not in itself cause a behavior problem, it may predispose the child to problems. Thus, certain events that might not produce abnormal behavior in a child with an easy-going temperament might result in disordered behavior by the child with a difficult temperament (Thomas & Chess, 1984; Thomas, Chess, & Birch, 1968).

Possible biological causes are more clearly evident in children who are severely and profoundly disturbed. Many children with autism show signs of neurochemical imbalance (Rimland, 1964, 1971), and other physiological causes of autism—including pre- and postnatal infections, chromosomal disorders, auditory impairments, and central nervous system dysfunction—have been suspected (Ciaranello, Vandenberg, & Anders, 1982; Garreau, Parthelmy, Sauvage, Leddet, & LeLord, 1984; Menolascino & Eyde, 1979; Ritvo, Ritvo, & Brothers, 1982). Genetics have been shown to play a role in childhood schizophrenia (Buss, 1966; Heston, 1970; Meehl, 1969). Even when there is a clear biological impairment, however, no one has been able to say with certainty whether the physiological abnormality actually causes the behavior problem or is just associated with it in some unknown way.

Psychological Factors

Psychological factors involve events in the child's life that affect the way she acts. Psychological factors are considered important in the development of behavior disorders in all conceptual models (except a strict physiological stance, which few adhere to). What events are important and how they are analyzed, however, are viewed differently by professionals with different approaches (e.g., a psychoanalyst and a behavior analyst). The two major settings in which these events take place are home and school.

The Influence of Home

We know that the relationship children have with their parents is critical to the way they learn to act, particularly during the early years. Observation and analysis of parent-child interaction patterns show that parents who treat their children with love, are sensitive to their children's needs, and provide praise and attention for desired behaviors tend to have normal children with positive behavioral characteristics. Aggressive, behavior-problem children often come from homes in which parents are inconsistent disciplinarians, use harsh and excessive punishment, and show little love and affection for good behavior (Becker, 1964; Martin, 1975).

Because of the research on the relationship between parental child-rearing practices and behavior problems, many mental health professionals have been quick to pin the blame for children's behavior problems on parents. But the relationship between parent and child is dynamic and reciprocal; in other words, the behavior of the child may affect the behavior of the parents just as much as the parents' actions affect the child (Patterson, 1980, 1982, 1986; Sameroff & Chandler, 1975). Therefore, it is not practical, at the least, and wrong, at the worst, to place the blame for abnormal behavior in young children on their parents. Instead, professionals must work with the parents to help them systematically change certain aspects of the parent-child relationship in an effort to prevent and modify these problems (Heward, Dardig, & Rosset, 1979).

See Chapter 13 for an in-depth discussion of working with parents.

The Influence of School

School is where children spend the largest portion of their time outside the home. Therefore, it makes sense to carefully observe what takes place in schools in an effort to identify other events that may cause problem behavior. Also, because most children with behavior disorders are not identified as such until they are in school, it seems reasonable to question whether the school actually contributes to the incidence of behavior disorders. Some professionals have gone further than simply questioning; they feel that the schools are the major cause of behavior disorders. There is, however, no evidence to support this contention. As with physiological or family causes, we cannot say for sure whether a child's school experiences are the lone cause of the behavior problems, but we can identify ways the school can influence or contribute to the child's emotional disturbance (e.g., through inappropriate expectations or inconsistent management).

Several studies have demonstrated that what takes place in the classroom can maintain and actually strengthen deviant behavior patterns, even though the teacher is trying to help the child (Bostow & Bailey, 1969; Thomas, Becker, & Armstrong, 1968; Walker & Buckley, 1973). Walker (1979) concludes,

> It is apparent that a child's behavior pattern at school is the result of a complex interaction of (1) the behavior pattern the child has been taught at home, including attitudes toward school, (2) the experiences the child has had with different teachers in the school setting, and (3) the relationship between the child and his/her current teacher(s). Trying to determine in what proportion the child's behavior pattern is attributable to each of these learning sources is an impossible and unnecessary task. Deviant child behavior can be changed very effectively without knowing the original causes for its acquisition and development. (p. 7)

INTERVENTION MODELS FOR CHILDREN WITH BEHAVIOR DISORDERS

There are several different approaches to educating emotionally disturbed children, each with its own definitions, purposes of treatment, and types of intervention. Based on the work of Rhodes and his colleagues (Rhodes & Head, 1974; Rhodes & Tracy, 1972a, 1972b), Kauffman (1989) lists six categories of models.

1. *Biogenic*. This model suggests that deviant behavior is a physical disorder with genetic or medical causes. It implies that these causes must be cured to treat the emotional disturbance. Treatment may be medical or nutritional.

2. *Psychodynamic*. Based on the idea that a disordered personality develops out of the interaction of experience and internal mental processes (ego, id, and superego) that are out of balance, this model relies on psychotherapy and creative projects for the child (and often the parents) rather than academic remediation.

3. *Psychoeducational*. This model is concerned with "unconscious motivations and underlying conflicts (hallmarks of psychodynamic models) yet also stresses the realistic demands of everyday functioning in school, home, and community" (Kauffman, 1989, p. 81). Intervention focuses on therapeutic discussions such as *life-space interviews* to allow children to understand their behavior rationally and plan to change it (Rich, Beck, & Coleman, 1982).

For a description of the life-space interview technique and a debate over its effectiveness, see Gardner (1990a, 1990b) and Long (1990).

4. *Humanistic*. This model suggests that the disturbed child is not in touch with her own feelings and cannot find self-fulfillment in traditional educational settings. Treatment takes place in an open, personalized setting where the teacher serves as a nondirective, nonauthoritarian "resource and catalyst" for the child's learning.

5. *Ecological*. This model stresses the interaction of the child with the people around him and with social institutions. Treatment involves teaching the child to function within the family, school, neighborhood, and larger community.

6. *Behavioral*. This model assumes that the child has learned disordered behavior and has not learned appropriate responses. To treat the behavior disorder, a teacher uses applied behavior analysis techniques to teach the child appropriate responses and eliminate inappropriate ones.

Few programs or teachers use only the techniques suggested by one model; most programs employ methods from several approaches. And the models themselves are not entirely discrete; they overlap in certain areas. Sometimes the difference is primarily a matter of wording; the actual classroom practices may be quite similar.

Our main purpose here is to make you aware of these different approaches. It is beyond the scope of this text to do justice to a description of each model and to compare and contrast them. We will say, however, that there is little empirical evidence to attest to the effectiveness of treatment approaches based on underlying subconscious causes of children's problems (Levitt, 1957, 1963). On the other hand, research supports the effectiveness of the ecological and behavioral models, which analyze and modify the ways a child interacts with the environment.

For reviews of some of this research, see Burchard and Harig, 1976; Hobbs, 1982; Lovaas and Newsom, 1976; Montgomery and Van Fleet, 1978; and Walker, 1979.

◼ INSTRUCTIONAL PRACTICES/TEACHER SKILLS

Teaching Self-Management Skills

See Heward (1987b) for a review of self-management procedures.

An increasing amount of research has been conducted on teaching self-control or self-management skills to children, and the results of much of this work are encouraging (Clark & McKenzie, 1989; Rhode, Morgan, & Young, 1983). Many behavior disordered children think they have little control over their lives. Things just seem to happen to them, and being disruptive is their means of reacting to a world that is inconsistent and frustrating. Children who learn self-management skills find out that they can have some control over their own behaviors and, as a result, over their environment.

When children learn to observe and record their own behavior, they can see for themselves the effects of various events on their performance. They can also be taught to influence certain events themselves. In one study, Drabman, Spitalnik, and O'Leary (1973) taught a group of eight 9- and 10-year-old emotionally disturbed children to evaluate and record their own social and academic work behaviors. Initially, when their own evaluations matched those of the teacher, they were rewarded with tokens; then, just teacher praise was given for accurate evaluations; finally, the students rated themselves and decided how many tokens they had earned during the day. A classroom token economy was operating during this study. Spot checks showed that the children evaluated themselves accurately and honestly. Disruptive behavior decreased, and academic achievement increased.

Numerous research studies have since demonstrated that children with behavior problems can effectively use self-monitoring as well as a number of other self-management techniques to help regulate their behavior. Self-monitoring can be aided by a prompt to record the target behavior; for example, a prerecorded tone from a cassette tape player might serve as the cue to monitor and record one's behavior (Abbott, 1990; Blick & Test, 1987). Lovitt (1984) describes the use of "countoons," which remind children not only what behavior to record, but also what consequence they are to self-deliver. Figure 5.3 shows a countoon that was taped to an elementary student's desk, showing her what behavior to monitor (finger snapping), how to record it (by putting an

FIGURE 5.3

A countoon that can be taped to a student's desk as a reminder of the target behavior, the need to self-record it, and the self-delivered consequence. (*Source:* From *Tactics for Teaching* (p. 202) by T. C. Lovitt, 1984, Columbus, OH: Merrill. Reprinted by permission.)

X through the next number on the countoon), and what her self-delivered consequence would be each time (solving 25 arithmetic problems).

Self-management strategies are also appealing from the standpoint of generalizing treatment gains from one setting to another. An external control agent (e.g., special education teacher in the resource room) cannot go with the student to all the settings in which he needs to exhibit newly learned behavior (e.g., staying in his seat and completing a whole workbook page). The one person who is always with the student is the student's own self (Fowler, 1986; Baer & Fowler, 1984).

Rhode et al. (1983) reported a study demonstrating the potential of self-management techniques for the generalization of improved behavior across settings. Six students with behavior disorders learned to bring their highly disruptive and off-task behaviors under control in a resource room with a combination of techniques that featured self-evaluation. Initially, the teacher rated each student and awarded points at 15-minute intervals on a scale from 5 (great) to 0 (poor) for classroom behavior and academic work. Then the students began to evaluate their own behavior with the same rating system (Figure 5.4 shows the card the students used). The teacher continued to rate each student.

Teacher and students compared their ratings: If the student's rating was within one point of the teacher's, he received the number of points he had given himself. If teacher and student matched exactly, the student earned an additional bonus point. The teacher then began to fade the number of times she also rated the students. After the students were behaving at acceptable levels and were accurately self-evaluating their behavior, they began to self-evaluate once every 30 minutes in the regular classroom. Eventually the self-evaluation cards and point system were withdrawn, and students were encouraged to continue to self-evaluate themselves "privately." Figure 5.5 shows the results of the students' behavior in both the resource room and the regular classroom.

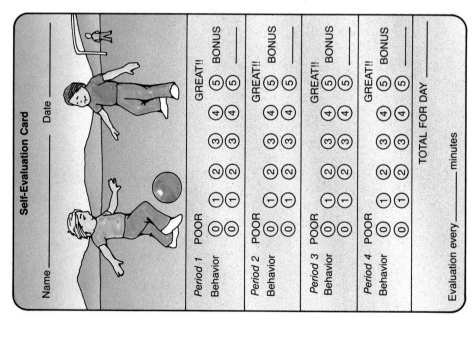

Back of Card

Front of Card

FIGURE 5.4

Card used for self-evaluation by students. (*Source:* From *Generalization and Maintenance of Treatment Gains on Behaviorally/Emotionally Handicapped Students from Resource Rooms to Regular Classrooms Using Self-Evaluation Procedures* (p. 157) by G. Rhode. Unpublished doctoral dissertation, Utah State University, 1981. Reprinted by permission.)

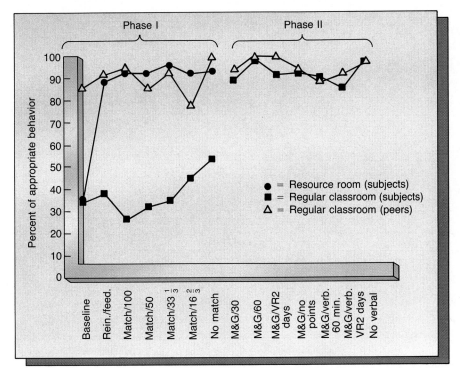

FIGURE 5.5

Appropriate behavior for six students with behavior disorders and randomly selected nonhandicapped peers. (*Source:* From "Generalization and Maintenance of Treatment Gains on Behaviorally Handicapped Students from Resource Rooms to Regular Classrooms Using Self-Evaluation Procedures" by G. Rhode, D. P. Morgan, and K. R. Young, 1983, *Journal of Applied Behavior Analysis,* Vol. 16, p. 184. Reprinted by permission.)

Self-management can also be taught as a social skill in its own right consisting of five elements: (1) self-selection and definition of the target behavior; (2) self-observation and recording of the target behavior; (3) specification of the procedures for changing the behavior; (4) implementation of those procedures; and (5) evaluation of the self-control effort (Heward, 1979; Sulzer-Azaroff & Mayer, 1991). For example, Marshall and Heward (1979) taught self-management skills to a group of eight boys in an institution for juvenile delinquents. The boys met as a group for one period each school day in a specially designed resource room. During this class period, the students were taught basic principles of behavior modification, such as defining a target behavior, recording behavior, graphing behavior, positive reinforcement, setting personal goals, and standards for behavior. Each student selected a behavior he wanted to change during the program and designed and conducted a self-management program to accomplish that goal. Students displayed their data and discussed and modified their projects as needed during the 4-week program. At the end of the study, seven of the eight students had successfully changed their behavior with the methods they had learned.

Although a great deal more research is needed, teaching behavior disordered children and adolescents to have some control over their own lives by giving them the skills to make changes in their behavior is a promising approach.

Teacher Skills

A continuing concern in the field of behavior disorders is teacher skills—that combination of professional competencies and personal characteristics that

The academic development of students with behavior disorders must not be ignored.

produces the best teaching of emotionally disturbed children. It goes without saying that a teacher of children with behavior disorders must be effective and creative, able to adapt curriculum materials and activities to the individual needs of the students. And although children with behavior disorders require the help of a specially trained teacher to work on their specific behavior problems, academic skills cannot be neglected. Most children with behavior disorders are already achieving at a rate below that of age-mates, and ignoring the three Rs would only put them at a bigger disadvantage. Reading, writing, and arithmetic are as important to children with behavior disorders as they are to any child who hopes to function normally in our society.

Improving Social Skills

The primary task of the teacher of children with behavior disorders, however, is to teach improved social skills—helping students replace maladaptive behaviors with more socially appropriate responses. This task is often difficult and demanding, particularly because the teacher seldom, if ever, knows all the factors that affect the children's behavior. There are sometimes a host of contributing factors over which the teacher can exert little or no control (e.g., the delinquent friends with whom the child associates after school). But it does little good to bemoan the child's past (which no one can alter) or to use all the things in the child's environment that cannot be changed as an excuse for failing to help the child in the classroom. Special educators should focus attention and efforts on those aspects of a child's life that they can effectively control (Kerr & Nelson, 1983; Wood, 1985). As Kauffman (1989) says,

> The focus of the special educator's concern should be on those contributing factors that the teacher can alter. Factors over which the teacher has no control may

determine how the child or youth is approached initially, but the teacher of disturbed students is called upon to begin working with specific pupils after behavior disorders have appeared. The special educator has two primary responsibilities: first, to make sure that he or she does no further disservice to the student; and second, to manipulate the student's present environment to foster development of more appropriate behavior in spite of unalterable past and present circumstances. Emphasis must be on the present and future, not the past. And although other environments may be important, the teacher's focus must be on the classroom environment. Certainly teachers may profitably extend their influence beyond the classroom, perhaps working with parents to improve the home environment or using community resources for the child's benefit. But talk of influence beyond the classroom, including such high-sounding phrases as ecological management, is patent nonsense until the teacher has demonstrated that he or she can make the classroom environment productive of improved behavior. (p. 402)

Management and Instruction

Managing the classroom environment to successfully change disturbed children's behavior patterns requires a teacher highly skilled in techniques of behavior change. Procedures such as contingency contracting; ignoring disruptive behavior (**extinction**); reinforcing any behavior except the undesirable response, which must be weakened (**differential reinforcement of other behavior**); removing the child from all chances for reward for a brief time following an inappropriate behavior (**time-out**); and requiring the child to make restitution beyond the damaging effects of her behavior (**overcorrection**), as when a child who takes another child's cookie must return it plus one of her own—these are just some of the many behavior management skills that a competent teacher of behavior disordered children needs. And these skills are not implemented as isolated events, but must be incorporated into an overall teaching and classroom management plan, such as a token economy or *level system* to help each student learn greater independence and earn more privileges (Barbetta, 1990a, 1990b; Mastropieri, Jenne, & Scruggs, 1988).

> Explanation of these behavior management techniques is beyond the scope of this book. For more information, see Alberto and Troutman, 1990; Cooper, Heron, & Heward, 1987; Sulzer-Azaroff & Mayer, 1991; Walker, 1979.

But the effective teacher of behavior disordered children must have skills beyond arranging environmental variables and measuring behavior. With behavior disordered children, the way assignments, expectations, and consequences for behavior are communicated to the child can be as important as the consequences themselves. Rothman (1977) stresses the importance of avoiding a win-lose situation, in which the teacher gains status by dominating the child. Rather, a win-win arrangement is the goal—when the child wins, the teacher wins.

Group Process

The "power" of the peer group can be an effective means of producing positive changes in students with behavior disorders (Barbetta, 1990a; Coleman & Webber, 1988). Implementing a *group process* model, however, is much more complicated than bringing together a group of children and hoping they will benefit from positive peer influence. Most children with behavior disorders have not been members of successfully functioning peer groups in which appropriate behavior is valued, nor have many such children learned to accept

In a level system, students earn greater independence and more privileges as their behavior improves.

responsibility for their actions. The teacher's first and most formidable challenge is fostering early group cohesiveness.

> There are some basic rules to help foster early group development: (1) every child is an equal member of the group, and as such is accountable and responsible to the group; (2) the group "moves" as often as possible as one; (3) all major decisions and problems the group works out together; (4) all major rewards are earned and shared by the group; (5) only in rare instances is a child "removed" from the group (i.e., no longer accountable to the group for his behavior); and (6) the teacher functions as a member of the group, but has veto power when necessary. (Barbetta, 1991)

Although group process treatment programs take many forms, most incorporate group meetings and group-oriented contingencies. Two types of group meetings are usually held daily. A planning meeting is held each morning in which the group reviews the daily schedule, each group member states a behavioral goal for the day, peers provide support and suggestions to one another for meeting their goals, and a group goal for the day is agreed upon. An evaluation meeting is held at the end of each day to discuss how well the individual and group goals were met. Each group member must give and receive positive peer comments. Problem-solving meetings are held whenever

Part II ◆ Exceptional Children

Problem-solving group meetings help students learn to discuss and solve problems appropriately.

any group member, including the teacher, feels the need to discuss a problem. The group identifies the problem, generates several solutions, discusses the likely consequences of each solution, develops a plan for the best solution, and makes verbal commitments to carry out the plan. Group-oriented contingencies specify certain rewards and privileges that are enjoyed by the group if their behavior meets certain criteria (Barbetta, 1990a). The criteria for earning the rewards, as well as the rewards themselves, are determined by the group.

Affective Traits

In addition to instructional and behavior management skills, the teacher of behavior disordered children must be able to establish healthy child-teacher relationships. Morse (1976) believes teachers must have two important affective characteristics to relate effectively and positively to emotionally disturbed children. He calls these traits differential acceptance and an empathetic relationship. *Differential acceptance* means the teacher can receive and witness frequent and often extreme acts of anger, hate, and aggression from children without responding similarly. This is much easier said than done. But the teacher of emotionally disturbed children must view disruptive behavior for what it is—behavior that reflects the child's past frustrations and conflict with himself and those around him—and try to help the child learn better ways of behaving. Acceptance should not be confused with approving of or condoning disturbed behavior—the child must learn that he is responding inappropriately. Instead, this concept calls for understanding without condemning. Having an *empathetic relationship* with a child refers to a teacher's ability to recognize and understand the many nonverbal cues that often are the keys to understanding the individual needs of emotionally disturbed children.

Kauffman (1989) stresses the importance of teachers' communicating directly and honestly with behaviorally troubled children. Many of these

MY RETURN VOYAGE
By Patricia M. Barbetta

The "power" of the peer group can be an effective means of producing positive changes in children with behavior disorders. Patricia M. Barbetta, who spent 11 years as a teacher, teacher supervisor, and education director at the Pressley Ridge School, a special school for children with severe behavior handicaps in Pittsburgh, Pennsylvania, describes some of her experiences implementing a behavior analytic group process model.

What was I doing? What could I possibly be thinking—returning to a frontline position in a classroom for children with behavior disorders after 5 years as a program supervisor? These were the common reactions of my co-workers, friends and family, and for very good reasons. They recalled my early teaching experiences with these children: The hours I spent restraining Jeremy who didn't think twice before hitting me and hitting hard; the day the fire chief threatened to fine me when Sam falsely set off the alarm "just one too many times"; the time I developed a behavioral contract for Connie to follow her mother's directions only to have her run away from home. And last but not least, they recalled my bi-annual trips to the emergency room for a tetanus shot necessitated by student bites.

My reasons for returning to the classroom were many, but I will mention just two. First of all was the progress we made that first year with our group. Don't get me wrong. We still had behavior problems right through the last day of school. But by the end of the year, the problems were less frequent and typically were resolved quickly. In our second year (we virtually had the same group), we managed to function well enough to earn money for a field trip to Washington D.C. A 3-day trip that, in spite of one time the entire group had to take a time-out at Arlington Cemetery, went without major incident. We were by far the best behaved group in the Smithsonian (much better than some of the general education groups). Witnessing our hard earned gains was very rewarding.

Second, I had an interest in directly implementing group process techniques as a new component of the treatment program at Pressley Ridge. I must admit I did not readily buy into the group model at first. The ideas of handing over "control" to a group of students with behavior disorders scared me. These students working together as a group? I simply couldn't imagine it. Most of them had never been part of a successfully functioning peer group. When they did participate in group activities, most often they were not school-related, and many times they were socially inappropriate activities like shop-lifting, hanging out on the street corner harassing passers-by, or picking on timid students in the school cafeteria.

As I had feared, things did not go well in the beginning. The students, accustomed to individualized, teacher-designed and directed classroom management systems, resented being asked to be involved in their own treatment, and they most especially resented being held accountable to each other. The students were simply not very good at working together, problem solving, or encouraging each other to behave appropriately. More to the point, they were terrible at these skills. Most did everything they could to undermine the group effort by intentionally losing points needed to earn group activities. They often refused to get involved in each other's problems, "That's his problem, Miss, not mine." Furthermore many of them intentionally encouraged inappropriate behaviors, by laughing and providing off-task friends with even more creative ways for misbehaving. And as for the teachers, we felt it was much simpler to "just do things ourselves." There were a lot of very unhappy students and teachers in that early transition period, but we since learned a lot about how we could have made that transition much smoother.

I learned three very important lessons during the transition to a group programming model. First, implementing a successful group process program is much more complicated than simply bringing together a group of students. Teachers and students alike have to work very hard to develop well-functioning groups. Second, the peer group is an extremely powerful resource—one that we cannot afford to waste. When some of the groups at our school started to "gel," we observed some powerful positive group pressure in action. I remember watching Danaire, a young man with a history of acting out problems, calmly and effectively deescalating Louie (a new group member) on many occasions when he was ready to assault a staff member. And then I recall the first time Rico, a tough inner city kid, genuinely shook Chad's hand for finally learning his multiplication facts. Why was this amazing? You see Chad was pretty much the "class nerd," and it took several weeks for Rico to even speak to Chad. They didn't become best friends, but they were able to help each other out on occasion. And finally, and maybe most important, I learned that involving the students in their treatment was not giving up "control." As teachers, we sometimes kid ourselves into thinking we are the only ones in "control." Every student in the room contributes to each other's behaviors—their influence already existed. The effective use of group process program strategies helped us guide this peer influence.

So, what was my year's return to the classroom like? Well, rewarding, frustrating, exciting, challenging, and exhausting are a few descriptors that come to mind. You might think that after 8 years in the field it would have been simple. Working with students with behavior disorders is often times rewarding, but it is never simple. The Voyagers (my group that return year) reminded me of this.

Who were the Voyagers? Well, they were 12, very different 13–15 year old boys who were referred to our program for a variety of behavior problems. Why did they decide to call themselves the Voyagers? They said it was because they would be "voyaging smoothly through their year to return quickly to their public schools." Well, not quite. Things started out great, all right (this is commonly referred to as the honeymoon period), but we quickly hit a few "meteor storms." Just a few examples. Eric, who referred to himself as "The King of Going Off," or the "Go Off Master," for short, was quite large for his age. He enjoyed staring down, shoving, and hitting students and staff, and did so often. Then there was Mark, the classroom thief, who stole anything that wasn't tied down. He would hide the stolen item in a fellow Voyager's desk to try to get him in trouble. Gary lived in a rough neighborhood and had a single mother who was an alcoholic. He often came to school tired and angry. On a bad day, even the simplest request could set him off. What did he do when he was "off"? Usually, he threw his desk across the room. Russell, the class clown, occasionally felt the need to run out into the woods, gather sticks and leaves, attach them to his clothes, and come back into the classroom acting like "Rambo." This was sometimes funny, but hardly appropriate. And don't let me forget James whose favorite activity was hanging and swinging from the doorway while making funny noises combined with the most creative variations of swear words. Imagine, I've just described five of the twelve students in the Voyagers group.

Were we ever able to function as a group? Yes, we were on many occasions, but only after a lot of disappointing moments, terribly difficult days, and many opportunities to practice pulling it together as a group. We spent many days with restricted privileges because of poor group performances, but no group was more pleased to earn top level privileges. We may not have made it to the Halloween party, but we did win the Christmas door decorating contest. And it might have taken us 55 minutes to walk back into school after we lost an intramural football game in the Fall, but no group could touch us at the Tug-of-War during Spring Field Day.

Well, was I crazy to go back into the classroom? Probably. But was I sorry? No way. That year I learned more about effective strategies for working with children with behavior disorders than ever before, and along the way I managed to help a few troubled kids. It was a rough return voyage, but a rewarding one. ◆

children have already had experience with supposedly helpful adults who have not been completely honest with them. Emotionally disturbed children can quickly detect someone who is not genuinely interested in their welfare.

The teacher of behavior disordered children must also realize that her actions serve as a powerful model. Therefore, it is critical that the teacher's actions and attitudes be mature and demonstrate self-control. Hobbs (1966) describes the kind of person he believes would make a good teacher and model for disturbed children. In his view, and ours, the effective teacher is

> A decent adult; educated, well trained; able to give and receive affection, to live relaxed, and to be firm; a person with private resources for the nourishment and refreshment of his own life; not an itinerant worker but a professional through and through; a person with a sense of the significance of time; of the usefulness of today and the promise of tomorrow; a person of hope, quiet confidence, and joy; one who has committed himself to children and to the proposition that children who are emotionally disturbed can be helped by the process of reeducation. (pp. 1106–1107)

SUMMARY

Defining Behavior Disorders

♦ There is no single, widely used definition of behavior disorders. Most definitions agree that a child's behavior must differ significantly and over time from current social or cultural norms to be considered disordered.

♦ Teacher tolerance and expectations for behavior contribute to a child's identification as behavior disordered.

Prevalence

♦ Although the U.S. Department of Education has traditionally estimated that children with behavior disorders comprise 2% of the school-age population, the number of children served is less than half the 2% estimate.

♦ Boys are much more likely to be labeled as behavior disordered than girls. Disturbed boys are likely to be aggressive and act out; girls are likely to be shy, anxious, and withdrawn.

Identification and Measurement of Behavior Disorders

♦ Although several screening tests have been developed, many school districts do not use any systematic method for identifying children with behavior disorders. Although aggressive children stand out, withdrawn children may go unnoticed.

♦ Direct and continuous observation and measurement of specific problem behaviors within the classroom is an assessment technique that indicates directly whether and for what behaviors intervention is needed.

♦ We can describe behavior disorders in terms of their rate, duration, topography, and magnitude. A child's disordered behavior may differ from his peers' behavior in one or more of these four dimensions. Improper stimulus control is also a problem for many children with behavior disorders.

Classification of Children's Behavior Disorders

- There is no widely accepted system for classifying behavior disorders. One system describes four clusters of behavior problems: conduct disorders, personality disorders, immaturity, and socialized delinquency.

- A second classification system describes six levels of learning competence, ranging from an attention level to a mastery level.

- Most children with behavior disorders have mild to moderate problems that can be treated effectively in the regular classroom and at home. Children who are severely disturbed—often called psychotic, schizophrenic, or autistic—require intensive programming, usually in a more restrictive setting.

Characteristics of Children with Behavior Disorders

- On the average, children with behavior disorders score somewhat below normal on IQ tests and have even lower achievement than their scores would predict, and many have learning problems.

- There are two general types of disordered behavior, often referred to as externalizing and internalizing.

- Children with externalizing problems are overly aggressive and frequently act out; they seem to be in constant conflict, and many become delinquents as adolescents.

- Children with internalizing problems are overly withdrawn. They do not have the social skills they need, but often they can learn those skills and can learn to be comfortable with other people.

- Children with autism usually show one or more of these characteristics: apparent sensory deficit, severe affect isolation, self-stimulation, tantrums and self-mutilation, muteness or psychotic speech, and behavior deficiencies. Behavior modification techniques can help control destructive actions, and some autistic children are being successfully mainstreamed in regular classes. Even with intensive treatment programs, some children with autism remain functionally retarded.

Causes of Behavior Disorders

- There are two groups of causes suggested for behavior disorders: biological and psychological.

- Because of its central role in a child's life, the school can also be an important contributing factor to a behavior problem.

Intervention Models for Children with Behavior Disorders

- There are at least six approaches to educating children with behavior disorders: biogenic, psychodynamic, psychoeducational, humanistic, ecological, and behavioral. Although each approach has a distinct theoretical basis and suggests types of treatment, many teachers use techniques from more than one of the models.

- A growing body of research supports the behavioral and ecological models, which analyze and modify the ways a child interacts with her environment.

Instructional Practices/Teacher Skills

- Teaching children with behavior disorders to control their own behavior with self-management skills is one new and promising approach.

♦ The primary goal of the teacher of children with behavior disorders is to help them replace inappropriate behaviors with more socially acceptable ones by modifying those factors in the teacher's control.

FOR MORE INFORMATION

Journals

Behavior Therapy. Published five times a year by Academic Press for the Association for the Advancement of Behavior Therapy.

Behavioral Disorders. Published quarterly by the Council for Children with Behavior Disorders, Council for Exceptional Children. Publishes research and discussion articles dealing with behavior disorders in children.

Education & Treatment of Children. Published quarterly by Pressley Ridge School, Pittsburgh, Pennsylvania. Includes experimental studies, discussion articles, literature reviews, and book reviews covering a wide range of education and treatment issues with children.

Journal of Applied Behavior Analysis. Published quarterly by the Society for the Experimental Analysis of Behavior, Lawrence, Kansas. Publishes original experimental studies demonstrating improvement of socially significant behaviors. Many studies involve behavior disordered children as subjects.

Journal of Autism and Developmental Disorders. A quarterly journal that publishes multidisciplinary research on all severe psychopathologies in childhood.

Books

Coleman, M. (1986). *Behavior disorders: Theory and practice*. Englewood Cliffs, NJ: Prentice-Hall.

Epanchin, B. C., & Paul, J. L. (1987). *Emotional problems of childhood and adolescence*. Columbus, OH: Merrill.

Hewett, F. M., & Taylor, F. D. (1980). *The emotionally disturbed child in the classroom: The orchestration of success* (2nd ed.). Boston: Allyn & Bacon.

Hobbs, N. (1982). *The troubled and troubling child*. San Francisco: Jossey-Bass.

Kauffman, J. M. (1989). *Characteristics of behavior disorders of children and youth* (4th ed.). Columbus, OH: Merrill.

Kazdin, A. E. (1987). *Conduct disorders in childhood and adolescence*. Beverly Hills, CA: SAGE Publications.

Kerr, M. M., & Nelson, C. M. (1989). *Strategies for managing behavior problems in the classroom* (2nd ed.). Columbus, OH: Merrill.

Koegel, R. L., Rincover, A., & Egel, A. L. (Eds.). (1982). *Educating and understanding autistic children*. San Diego: College-Hill.

Morgan, D. P., & Jenson, W. R. (1988). *Teaching behaviorally disordered students: Preferred practices*. Columbus, OH: Merrill.

Nelson, C. M., Rutherford, R. B., & Wolford, B. I. (Eds.). (1987). *Special education and the criminal justice system*. Columbus, OH: Merrill.

Quay, H. C., & Werry, J. S. (Eds.). (1986). *Psychopathological disorders of childhood* (3rd ed.). New York: John Wiley & Sons.

Reinert, H. R., & Huang, A. (1987). *Children in conflict* (3rd ed.). Columbus, OH: Merrill.

Rutherford, R. B., Nelson, C. M., & Forness, S. R. (Eds.). (1987). *Severe behavior disorders of children and youth*. Boston: College-Hill Press.

Walker, H. M. (1979). *The acting-out child: Coping with classroom disruption*. Boston: Allyn & Bacon.

Ziontz, P. (1985). *Teaching disturbed and disturbing students*. Austin, TX: PRO-ED.

Organizations

American Association for the Advancement of Behavior Therapy, 15 West 36th Street, New York, NY 10018. Includes psychologists, educational researchers, and educators (primarily at the university level).

Council for Children with Behavior Disorders, Council for Exceptional Children, 1920 Association Drive, Reston, VA 22091. Includes teachers and teacher educators interested in behavior disorders. Produces an annual publication titled *Teaching: Behaviorally Disordered Youth*.

National Society for Autistic Citizens, 621 Central Avenue, Albany, NY 12206.

6

Communication Disorders

♦ How can we differentiate a true communication disorder from a communication difference?

♦ How can the severity of a communication disorder change from situation to situation?

♦ How have changes in the treatment of communication disorders paralleled other changes in special education?

♦ When should an augmentative communication system be developed for a student?

♦ Why is professional teamwork and parent involvement especially critical in treating communication disorders?

Have you ever tried to go through an entire day without speaking? If so, you surely had a great deal of difficulty making contact with other people. And you probably experienced frustration when others did not understand your needs and feelings. By the end of the day, you may even have felt exhausted, humiliated, and incapable of functioning adequately in the world.

Even though relatively few people with communication disorders are completely unable to express themselves, an exercise such as that just described can help increase your awareness of some of the problems and frustrations faced every day by children and adults who cannot communicate effectively or acceptably. Language is central to human existence—"the most powerful, fascinating skill that humans possess" (Reed, 1986, p. vii). Children who cannot absorb information through listening and reading or who cannot express their thoughts in spoken words are virtually certain to encounter difficulties in their schools and communities. If communication disorders persist, it may be hard for children to learn, to develop, and to form satisfying relationships with other people. As Richmond and McCroskey (1985) observe, "Even though computers are playing and will continue to play a significant role in our lives, they will not replace basic human interaction . . . . [L]ive communication between humans will still be the fuel that makes our world go around" (p. 1).

Before discussing specific communication disorders, a few definitions of basic terms will be helpful.

■ COMMUNICATION, LANGUAGE, AND SPEECH

Communication

Communication is the exchange of information and ideas. Communication involves encoding, transmitting, and decoding messages. It is an interactive process requiring at least two parties to play the roles of both sender and receiver. We observe, and take part in, literally thousands of communicative interactions every day. An infant cries, and her mother reacts by picking her up. A dog barks, and its owner responds by letting it out of the house. A teacher smiles, and his student knows that an assignment has been accomplished well. Each of these interactions includes three elements needed to qualify as communication: (1) a message; (2) a sender who expresses the message; and (3) a receiver who understands the message.

Although speech and language comprise the message system most often used in human communication, spoken or written words are not necessary for true communication to occur. Both paralinguistic behaviors and nonlinguistic signs are used in human communication. *Paralinguistic phenomenon* are nonlanguage sounds (e.g., *oohh,* laugh) and speech modifications (e.g., variations in pitch, intonation, rate of delivery, pauses) that change the form and meaning of the message. *Nonlinguistic* cues include body posture, facial expressions, gestures, eye contact, head and body movement, and physical proximity.

Lindfors (1987) has enumerated several important functions that communication serves, particularly between teachers and children.

Even when no words are spoken, communication occurs in many forms of the visual and performing arts.

The study of nonlinguistic behaviors that augment language is called **kinesics**.

1. *Narrating.* Children need to be able to tell (or follow the telling of) a "story"; that is, a sequence of related events, connected in an orderly, clear, and interesting manner. Five-year-old Cindy tells her teacher, "I had a birthday party. I wore a funny hat. Mommy made a cake and Daddy took pictures." Fourteen-year-old David tells the class about the events leading up to Christopher Columbus's first voyage to America.

2. *Explaining/informing.* Teachers expect children to interpret the explanations of others in speech and in writing and also to put something they understand into words so that their listeners or readers will be able to understand it, too. In typical classroom settings, children must respond to teachers' questions frequently: "Which number is larger?" "How do you suppose the story will end?" "Why do you think George Washington was a great president?"

3. *Expressing.* It is important for children to express their personal feelings and opinions and to respond to the feelings of others. Speech and language can convey joy, fear, frustration, humor, sympathy, anger. A child writes, "I have just moved. And it is hard to find a friend because I am shy." Another tells her classmates, "Guess what? I have a new baby brother!" Through such communicative interactions, children gradually develop a sense of self and an awareness of other people.

Language

Language is a system used by a group of people for giving meaning to sounds, words, gestures, and other symbols to enable communication with one another. Lahey (1988) defines language as "a code whereby ideas about the world are expressed through a conventional system of arbitrary signals for communication" (p. 2). A child may learn to identify a familiar object, for example, by hearing the spoken word *tree,* by seeing the printed word *tree,* by viewing the sign language gesture for *tree,* or by encountering a combination of these signals. When we hear, speak, read, or write with language, we transmit information.

The symbols and the rules governing their use are essentially arbitrary in all languages, and spoken English is no exception. The arbitrariness of language means that there is usually no logical, natural, or required relationship between a set of sounds and the object, concept, or action it represents. The word *whale,* for example, brings to mind a large mammal that lives in the sea, but the sound of the word has no apparent connection with the creature. *Whale* is merely a symbol we use for this particular mammal. A small number of onomatopoeic words—such as *tinkle, buzz,* and *hiss*—are considered to sound like what they represent, but most English words have no such relationship. Likewise, there are some hand positions or movements in sign language, called iconic signs, that look like the object or event they represent (e.g., tipping an imaginary cup to one's lips is the manual sign for *drink*). It is important to remember that language is used to express descriptions of and relations between objects and events; it does not reproduce those objects and events.

Dimensions of Language

Language is often described along five dimensions: phonology, morphology, syntax, semantics, and pragmatics. *Phonology* is the study of the linguistic rules governing language's sound system. Phonological rules describe how sounds can be sequenced and combined. The English language uses approximately 45 different sound elements, called **phonemes**. Only the initial phoneme prevents the words *pear* and *bear* from being identical, for example; yet in one case we think of a fruit and in the other, a large animal.

The *morphology* of a language governs how the basic units of meaning are combined into words. Phonemes, the individual sounds, do not carry meaning. A **morpheme** is the smallest element of language that carries meaning. The word *baseball,* for example, consists of two morphemes—*base* and *ball*. The *-s* added to make *baseballs* would be a third morpheme.

Syntax is the system or rules governing the meaningful arrangement of words into sentences. If morphemes could be strung together in any order, language would be an unintelligible tangle of words. Syntactical rules are language-specific (i.e., Farsi and English have different rules), and they specify relations among the subject, verb, and object. For example, "Help my chicken eat" conveys a meaning much different from "Help eat my chicken."

Semantics is a system of rules that relate phonology and syntax to meaning; that is, semantics describes how people use language to convey meaning.

Finally, **pragmatics** is a set of rules governing how language is used. Lahey (1988) describes three kinds of pragmatic skills: (1) using language to achieve various communicative functions and goals; (2) using information from the conversational context (e.g., modifying one's message according to listener reactions); and (3) knowing how to use conversational skills effectively (e.g., beginning and ending a conversation, turn taking). "To ignore pragmatics is to concentrate on language structure and to remove language from its communicative context" (Owens, 1990, p. 43).

One model of language, developed by Bloom and Lahey (1978), describes three components of language—form, content, and use—that make up an integrated system. The *form* of the language is its surface structure that connects sound and meaning (phonology, morphology, syntax). The *content* is based on knowledge of the world and our feelings about it. Thus, the form of language allows us to express and understand content (semantics). The *use* of language refers to the ways language functions in communication (pragmatics). It includes both our purposes in communicating and how we choose a specific form to express a particular message.

> This model can be helpful in understanding and treating a child's communication disorder.

Speech

Speech is the actual behavior of producing a language code by making appropriate vocal sound patterns (Hubbell, 1985). Although it is not the only possible vehicle for expressing language (gestures, manual signing, pictures, and written symbols can also be used to convey ideas and intentions), speech is a most effective and efficient method. Speech is also one of the most complex and difficult human endeavors. Speech production requires the precise coordination of nerves and muscles in several locations to perform the important processes of *respiration* (breathing by the lungs), *phonation* (the production of sound by the larynx and vocal folds), *resonance* (vibratory response to control sound quality), and *articulation* (the formation of specific, recognizable speech sounds by the tongue, lips, teeth, and mouth). Figure 6.1 shows the normal speech organs.

Most languages start out in oral form, developed by people speaking to each other. Reading and writing are secondary language forms that attempt to represent the oral form. There is no one-to-one correspondence, however, between *graphemes* (i.e., print symbols or letters) and phonemes.

Normal Language Development

Despite the complexity of our language system, most children, without any formal instruction, learn to understand language and then to speak during the first few years of life. They integrate form, content, and use to communicate. The process of learning language is a remarkable one that is not fully understood. Parents, teachers, and scholars for centuries have been fascinated by the phenomenon of language acquisition in children.

> Whether a child grows up in a "traditional" society or in a "technological" one; whether in a large extended family or in a small nuclear one; whether on a Pacific island, in an urban ghetto, or in a tribal farm compound; whether in a villa, a straw hut, an apartment, or a tent; whether with or without formal schooling; whether in a wet, dry, hot, or cold climate—the child will acquire the language of his community. Humans vary in which languages and dialects they acquire, in how rapidly they acquire them . . . in how talkative they are, in what they use language for, and in how effectively they express themselves in speech and/or writing. But virtually all of them acquire at least one linguistic system for relating meanings. . . . Further, there is striking similarity in how all children learn their language. (Lindfors, 1987, p. 91)

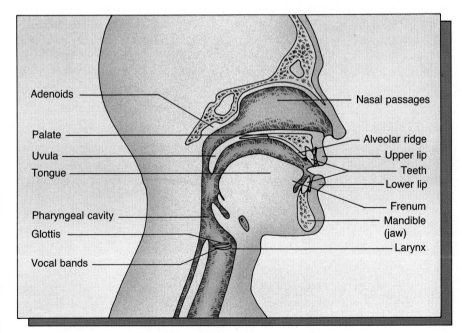

FIGURE 6.1
The normal speech organs.

Understanding how young, normally developing children acquire language is helpful to the teacher or specialist working with children who have delayed or disordered communication. Knowledge of normal language development can help the specialist determine whether a particular child is simply developing language at a slower-than-normal rate or whether the child shows an abnormal pattern of language development.

As we look at an overview of normal language development, remember that the ages at which a normal child acquires certain speech and language skills are not rigid and inflexible. Children's abilities and early environments vary widely, and all these factors affect communication. Most investigators agree, nevertheless, that most children follow a relatively predictable sequence in development of speech and language.

Birth to 6 Months

The infant first communicates by crying, which involves breath, muscles, and vocal chords. She soon learns that her crying produces a reliable consequence in the form of parental attention. Within a few months, the baby develops different types of crying—a parent can often tell from the baby's cry whether she is wet, tired, or hungry. Babies also make comfort sounds—coos, gurgles, and sighs—that contain some vowels and consonants. The comfort sounds develop into babbling, sounds that in the beginning are apparently made for the enjoyment of feeling and hearing them. Vowel sounds, such as /i/ (pronounced "ee") and /e/ (pronounced "uh") are produced earlier than consonants, such as /m/, /b/, and /f/. At this stage, the infant does not attach meaning to the words she hears from others, but may react differently to loud and soft voices. She turns her eyes and head in the direction of a sound.

6 to 12 Months

Babbling becomes differentiated before the end of the first year; a baby develops **inflection**—her voice rises and falls. She may seem to be giving you a command, asking a question, or expressing surprise. She appears to understand certain words at this stage. She may respond appropriately to "no," "bye-bye," or her own name and may perform an action, such as clapping her hands, when told to. When parents say simple sounds and words, such as "mama," the baby will repeat them.

12 to 18 Months

By 18 months, most children have learned to say several words with appropriate meaning (although their pronunciation is far from perfect). The baby may say "tup" when you point to a cup, or "goggie" when she sees a dog. She will probably be able to tell you what she wants by pointing and perhaps saying a word or two. She will respond to simple commands such as "Give me the cup" and "Open your mouth."

18 to 24 Months

Most children go through a stage of echolalia, in which they simply repeat, or echo, the speech they hear. If father says, "Do you want some milk?" the baby will repeat, "Want some milk?" Echolalia is a normal phase of language development, and most children outgrow it by about the age of 2½.

Children whose hearing is impaired have a special set of problems in learning language. See Chapter 7.

Phonemes are represented by letters or other symbols between slashes. For example, the phoneme /n/ represents the "ng" sound in *sing;* /i/ represents the long "e" as in *see*.

Although it was once believed that babbling and speech were phonetically unrelated, research shows that infant babbling at 6 to 12 months contains some of the same phonetic elements as the meaningful speech of 2 year olds (Oller, Wieman, Doyle, & Ross, 1975; Vihman, 1986).

There is a great spurt in acquisition and use of speech during this stage. Children usually begin to combine words into short sentences, such as "Daddy bye-bye" and "Want cookie." The child's receptive vocabulary—the words she understands—grows even more rapidly; by 2 years of age, she may understand more than 1,000 words. She understands such concepts as "soon" and "later" and makes more subtle distinctions between objects, such as cats and dogs, and knives, forks, and spoons.

2 to 3 Years

The 2-year-old child talks. She can say sentences like "I won't tell you" and can ask questions like "Where my daddy go?" She may have an expressive vocabulary of up to 900 different words, averaging three to four words per sentence (Weiss & Lillywhite, 1976). She is learning how to participate in conversations with the people around her. She can identify colors, use plurals, and tell simple stories about her experiences. She is able to follow compound commands such as "Pick up the doll and bring it to me." The 2-year-old child uses most of the vowel sounds and some consonant sounds correctly. The earliest consonant sounds learned are generally /p/, /b/, and /m/.

3 to 4 Years

The normal 3-year-old has lots to say, speaks rapidly, and asks many questions to obtain information. Her sentences are longer and more varied: "Cindy's playing in water"; "Mommy went to work"; "The cat is hungry." She is able to use speech to request, protest, agree, and make jokes. The 3- to 4-year-old child can understand children's stories, grasp such concepts as *funny, bigger,* and *secret,* and complete simple analogies, such as "In the daytime it is light; at night it is. . . ." She typically substitutes certain sounds, perhaps saying "baf" for "bath," or "yike" for "like." Many 3-year-olds repeat sounds or words ("b-b-ball," "l-l-little"); the repetitions and hesitations are normal and do not indicate that the child will develop a habit of stuttering.

4 to 5 Years

By age 4, children have an average vocabulary of over 1,500 words and use sentences averaging five words in length (Leonard, 1982). They are generally able to make themselves understood, even to strangers. The 4-year-old begins to show the ability to modify her speech for the listener; for example, she uses longer and more complex sentences when talking to her mother than when addressing a baby or a doll. She can define words like *hat, stove,* and *policeman* and can ask questions like "How did you do that?" or "Who made this?" She uses conjunctions such as *if, when,* and *because.* She can recite poems and sing songs from memory. Children at this age may say, "I almost fell," or "Let's do something else." They may still have difficulty with such consonant sounds as /r/, /s/, and /z/ or with blends like "tr," "gl," "sk," and "str."

After 5 Years

Language continues to develop steadily, though less dramatically, after age 5. The child acquires more vocabulary and is able to use more sophisticated grammatical forms. A 6-year-old child, in fact, normally uses most of the complex forms of adult English. Some of the consonant sounds and blends, however, are not mastered until age 7 or 8. By the time a child enters first grade, her grammar and speech patterns usually match those of her family, neighborhood, and region. An 8-year-old from rural Alabama has different pronunciation and rhythms from an 8-year-old who lives in Boston.

As these descriptions indicate, children's words and sentences often differ from adult forms while the children are learning language. Lindfors (1987) points out that children who use structures such as "All gone sticky" and "Where he is going?" or pronunciations like "cwackers" and "twuck" or word forms like "comed," "goed," or "sheeps" gradually learn to replace them with acceptable adult forms. The early developmental forms drop out as the child matures, usually without any special drilling or direct instruction.

It is also worth noting that children often produce speech sounds inconsistently. The clarity of a sound may vary according to such factors as where the sound occurs in a word and how familiar the word is to the child. Although speech sounds generally become clearer as the child grows older, there are exceptions to this rule of gradual progress. Kenney and Prather (1986), for example, found that 3½-year-old children made fewer errors on the /s/ sound than did children aged 4 to 5½. The reasons for these reversals in accuracy are not clear.

▓ DEFINING COMMUNICATION DISORDERS

As we have said, the development of speech and language is a highly individual process. No child conforms exactly to precise developmental norms; some are advanced, some are delayed, and some acquire language in an unusual sequence. Unfortunately, some children deviate from the normal to such an extent that they have serious difficulties in learning and in interpersonal relations. Children who are not able to make themselves understood or who cannot comprehend ideas that are spoken to them by others are likely to be greatly handicapped in virtually all aspects of education and adjustment. They need specialized help. These kinds of problems, called communication disorders, occur frequently among children in regular and special education classes.

When does a communication difference become a communication disorder? In making such judgments, Emerick and Haynes (1986) emphasize the impact that a communication pattern has on one's life. A communication difference would be considered a handicapping condition, they note, when

- The transmission and/or perception of messages is faulty
- The person is placed at an economic disadvantage
- The person is placed at a learning disadvantage
- The person is placed at a social disadvantage
- There is a negative impact upon the person's emotional growth
- The problem causes physical damage or endangers the health of the person (pp. 6–7)

To be considered eligible for special education services, a child's communication disorders must have an adverse effect on learning. The definition of the

Specific speech and language disorders are discussed later in this chapter.

For children whose native language is not English, the distinction between a difference and a disorder is critical. Chapter 12 offers guidelines for assessing children from multicultural backgrounds.

Matthew's physical disabilities make his speech unintelligible. Since getting his computerized speech synthesizer, however, he's discovered a whole new world of communication possibilities.

"speech or language impaired" category of disability in P.L. 94–142 reads: "a communication disorder, such as stuttering, impaired articulation, a language impairment, or voice impairment which adversely affects . . . educational performance" (U.S. General Accounting Office, 1981, p. 36).

Most specialists in the field of communication disorders make a distinction between speech disorders and language disorders. Children with *impaired speech* have difficulty producing sounds properly, maintaining an appropriate flow or rhythm in speech, or using the voice effectively. Speech disorders are impairments in language form. Children with *impaired language* have problems in understanding or expressing the symbols and rules people use to communicate with each other. A child may have difficulty with language form, content, and/or use. Speech and language are obviously closely related to each other. Some people find it helpful to view speech as the means by which language is most often conveyed. A child may have a speech impairment or a language disorder or both.

Speech Disorders

A child's speech is considered impaired if it is unintelligible, abuses the speech mechanism, or is culturally or personally unsatisfactory (Perkins, 1977). The most widely quoted definition of speech impairment is probably that of Charles Van Riper, who states that "speech is abnormal when it deviates so far from the speech of other people that it calls attention to itself, interferes with communication, or causes the speaker or his listeners to be distressed" (Van Riper & Emerick, 1984, p. 34). A general goal of professional specialists in communication disorders is to help the child speak as clearly and pleasantly as possible so that a listener's attention will focus on what the child says, rather than how she says it.

The three basic types of speech disorders are articulation, voice, and fluency. Each type is discussed later in the chapter.

It is always important to keep the speaker's age, education, and cultural background in mind when determining whether speech is impaired. A 4-year-old girl who says "Pwease weave the woom" would not be considered to have a speech impairment, but a 40-year-old woman would surely draw attention to herself with that pronunciation, because it differs markedly from the speech of most adults. A traveler unable to articulate the /l/ sound would not be clearly understood in trying to buy a bus ticket to Lake Charles, Louisiana. A male high school student with an extremely high-pitched voice might be reluctant to speak in class for fear of being mimicked and ridiculed by his classmates.

Language Disorders

Some children have serious difficulties in understanding language or in expressing themselves through language. A child with a *receptive language disorder* may be unable to learn the days of the week in proper order or may find it impossible to follow a sequence of commands, such as "Pick up the paint brushes, wash them in the sink, and then put them on a paper towel to dry." A child with an *expressive language disorder* may have a limited vocabulary for his age, be confused about the order of sounds or words ("hostipal," "aminal," "wipe shield winders"), and use tenses and plurals incorrectly ("Them throwed a balls"). Children with difficulty in expressive language may or may not also have difficulty in receptive language. For instance, a child may be able to count out six pennies when asked and shown the symbol *6,* but may not be able to say the word *six* when shown the symbol. In that case the child has an expressive difficulty, but his receptive language is adequate. He may or may not have other disorders of speech or hearing.

The American Speech-Language-Hearing Association (ASHA) defines a language disorder as "the impairment or deviant development of comprehension and/or use of a spoken, written, and/or other symbol system. The disorder may involve (1) the form of language (phonologic, morphologic, and syntactic systems), (2) the content of language (semantic system), and/or (3) the function of language in communication (pragmatic system) in any combination" (1982, p. 949).

Leonard (1986) has noted that children with impaired language frequently play a passive role in communication. They may show little tendency to initiate conversations. When language disordered children are asked questions, "their replies rarely provide new information related to the topic" (p. 114).

Children with serious language disorders are likely to have problems in school and social development. It is often difficult to detect children with language disorders; their performance may lead people to mistakenly label them as mentally retarded, hearing impaired, or emotionally disturbed, when in fact these descriptions are neither accurate nor appropriate. A recent study of peer perceptions found that an 11-year-old girl with a neurological impairment affecting her speech and language production was perceived as "frightened, nervous, tense, and unlovable" by nonhandicapped fifth and sixth grade children. These perceptions "obviously could have a negative impact on her self-concept" (Gies-Zaborowski & Silverman, 1986, p. 143).

A child may also be markedly delayed in language development. Even though a relatively wide range of language patterns and age milestones is

Language is so important in academic performance that it can be impossible to differentiate a learning disability from a language disorder. Again, the emphasis should be on remediating children's skill deficits rather than on labeling them.

considered normal, some children do not acquire speech or the ability to understand language until much later than normally expected. We would regard a 6-year-old child who cannot use such pronouns as *I, you,* and *me* as having a serious delay in language development. In rare cases, children who have no other impairment may even fail to speak at all.

Dialects and Differences

Myth: A 7-year-old black male from a working class, inner-city environment deletes the *-s* morpheme for plurality and possession. This indicates that he probably has a language disorder.

Reality: The *-s* morpheme deletion for plurality and possession are features of Black English Vernacular. The child is probably within the realm of normalcy for his speech community.

Myth: A 15-year-old black female from suburban Cleveland omits some final consonants and reduces final consonant clusters. She should not be considered for therapy since these are features of Black English Vernacular.

Reality: After consideration of the child's speech community, it is not likely that Black English Vernacular features are a part of her middle income, highly educated environment. A possible articulation disorder or hearing loss should be considered. (O. L. Taylor, 1990, pp. 126–127)

The way children speak reflects their culture. Before entering school, most children have learned patterns of speech and language appropriate to their families and neighborhoods. Every language contains a variety of forms, called *dialects,* that result from historical, geographical, and social factors. The English language, for example, includes such variations as Standard American English (as used by most teachers, employers, and public speakers), Black English, Appalachian English, Southern English, a New York dialect, and Spanish-influenced English. A child who uses these variations should not be treated as having a communication disorder. It is certainly possible, however, for a child to have a communication disorder within her dialect. The American Speech-Language-Hearing Association (1983) considers it essential for a specialist to be able to "distinguish between dialectal differences and communicative disorders" and to "treat only those features or characteristics that are true errors and not attributable to the dialect" (p. 24). A speech or language *difference* from the majority of children, then, is not necessarily a communication disorder in need of treatment. Some major factors in creating speech and language differences are race and ethnicity, social class, education, occupation, geographic region, and peer group identification (O. L. Taylor, 1990). Problems may arise in the classroom and in parent-teacher communication if the teacher does not accept natural communication differences among children and mistakenly assumes that a speech or language impairment is present (Bankson, 1982; Reed, 1986).

■ PREVALENCE

Estimates of the prevalence of communication disorders in children vary widely. Reliable figures are hard to come by, as investigators often employ different definitions of speech and language disorders and sample different populations. As Culton (1986) observes, surveys are often based on interviews of question-

DEVELOPING LANGUAGE AND LEADERSHIP

Young children with impaired speech or language are often frustrated by the difficulty they experience in asking questions, expressing their needs, or conveying their wishes to other people. When unable to make themselves understood, some children may resort to physical communication (such as pulling, pushing, or hitting classmates), whereas others become so frustrated that they stop trying to communicate.

Judith Hurvitz, Sarah Pickert, and Donna Rilla believe that teachers can help children develop language skills by encouraging them to assume leadership roles in the classroom. Activities that carry responsibility, power, and prestige, they maintain, are useful in promoting language and social interaction. Here are some suggestions developed for Karen, a hypothetical 5-year-old with a communication disorder.

♦ Ask Karen to sit on a chair while the rest of the children are seated on the floor.

♦ Allow Karen to wear a special hat or badge.

♦ Give Karen the authority to distribute rewards, such as stars or tokens, to other children.

♦ Let Karen lead circle-time activities by taking attendance, directing group songs, and greeting others ("Hi, Judy").

♦ Allow Karen to assign daily classroom jobs to other children ("Barry, mats." "Ron, get snack.").

♦ Have Karen act as class messenger, especially when the recipient of the message is familiar with the meaning to be conveyed (she might say to the librarian, "Need book.").

♦ Permit Karen to choose how class members will participate in a particular activity; for example, designating whether boys or girls will go first in line ("Boys first.").

♦ Give Karen a picture to hold up and ask her to call on a child to describe the picture ("Donna, what this?").

♦ Let Karen lead the group in a movement activity by calling out actions ("March!" "Walk!" "Sit!").

♦ Suggest words that Karen can use to solve a problem herself when she asks for teacher intervention. Say, "Go to Anthony and tell him, 'I want my block'" or "Take your puzzle to Glen and say, 'Help me.'"

♦ Encourage Karen to work with another child in such tasks as cleaning up after snack time or moving a bulky table.

♦ Invite Karen to talk with a classmate using a pair of toy telephones. (This often generates enthusiasm.)

Activities such as these can help children use language more effectively and with greater variety. They also enable children to experience the pleasure and power of using language to control their environments.

From "Promoting Children's Language Interaction" by J. A. Hurvitz, S. M. Pickert, and D. C. Rilla, 1987, Teaching Exceptional Children, *19(3), pp. 12–15. Reston, VA: Council for Exceptional Children. Adapted by permission.* ♦

able validity, and there is a likely tendency to underreport the presence of communication disorders.

Fein (1983) reviewed various prevalence studies of school-age populations and concluded that speech impairments serious enough to warrant special attention are present in approximately 4.2% of children. This represents a large population compared to other categories of exceptional children. A 4.2% prevalence rate would mean that between 2 million and 3 million American children have communication disorders. In the 1988–89 school year, 962,761 children ages 6 to 17 received special education services under the P.L. 94–142 category of "speech or language impaired." This represents about 2.3% of the school-age population and 23% of all students receiving special education services, making speech or language impaired the second largest category.

Fein reported that speech impairments tend to be more prevalent among males than females, more prevalent among nonwhite persons than white persons, and about the same in each of the major geographical regions of the United States. Similarly, the National Center for Health Statistics (1981) reported that approximately twice as many boys as girls have speech impairments.

Figures on the prevalence of language disorders are less reliable. Reed (1986) notes that about 1% of school-age children are considered to have language disorders. Because definitions of learning disabilities emphasize understanding and use of spoken and written language (see Chapter 4), however, a sizable percentage of children who are served in special education programs for learning disabled students could also be regarded as having language disorders.

Some figures are available on the incidence and prevalence of specific types of communication disorders. In the recent past, articulation disorders, which involve difficulties in producing speech sounds accurately, were by far the most common type of speech problem found in children. The American Speech-Language-Hearing Association (ASHA) estimated in 1961 that 80% of the school-age population with communication disorders had articulation disorders. Changing emphasis and improved assessment techniques, however, have led to changes in the relative number of children treated for speech and language disorders. A 1982 ASHA survey indicated that "54% of speech-language pathologists' clients were primarily exhibiting language impairments" (cited in Fein, 1983, p. 37). The speech problems of hearing impaired persons are also significant: The 1971 National Health Interview Survey found that 15.2% of the speech impaired population also had hearing impairments (National Center for Health Statistics, 1975).

The prevalence of communication disorders does not remain the same throughout the life span. As Culton (1986) observes, "Age-specific prevalence data are more meaningful than overall prevalence data" (p. 6). The percentage of children with speech and language disorders, although rather high, decreases significantly from the earlier to the later school grades. For example, Hull, Mielke, Willeford, and Timmons (1976) found that about 7% of all first grade boys were reported as having "extreme articulation deviations," but only 1% of third grade boys and 0.5% of twelfth grade boys fell into that category. Culton (1986) studied more than 30,000 college freshmen who had undergone screening tests over a 13-year period and found that 2.4% exhibited speech disorders, with an additional 2.3% reporting that they had recovered from earlier speech disorders. The largest part of the speech/language impaired population is composed of young children with articulation problems. Many of these disorders (e.g., saying *wabbit* for *rabbit* or *thith* for *this*), although significant enough to merit professional attention, are apparently not severe enough to persist into adulthood. They respond favorably to intervention and/or maturation.

■ TYPES AND CAUSES OF COMMUNICATION DISORDERS

There are many recognized types of communication disorders and numerous possible causes. A speech impairment may be *organic;* that is, attributable to a specific physical cause. Examples of physical factors that frequently result in communication disorders include cleft palate, paralysis of the speech muscles, absence of teeth, craniofacial abnormalities, enlarged adenoids, and neurological impairments. Organic speech impairments may be a child's primary disability or may be secondary to other handicapping conditions, such as delayed intellectual development, impaired hearing, and cerebral palsy.

See Chapters 3, 7, and 9 for discussions of these conditions.

Most communication disorders, however, are not considered organic, but are classified as *functional*. They cannot be ascribed to a specific physical condition, and their origin is not clearly known. McReynolds (1990) points out that decades of research on the causes of many speech and language impairments have produced few answers. A child's surroundings provide many opportunities for him to learn appropriate and inappropriate communication skills; some specialists believe that functional communication disorders derive mainly from environmental influences. It is also possible that some speech impairments are caused by disturbances in the motor control system and are not fully understood.

Regardless of whether a communication disorder is considered organic or functional, a child with speech or language that is substantially different from that of others in his age and cultural group requires special training procedures to correct or improve the impairment.

Articulation Disorders

As we have noted, articulation disorders are the most prevalent type of speech impairment among school-age children. The correct articulation, or utterance, of speech sounds requires us to activate a complicated system of muscles, nerves, and organs. Haycock (1933), who compiled a classic manual on teaching speech, describes how the speech organs are manipulated into a variety of shapes and patterns, how the breath and voice must be "molded to form words." For example, here is Haycock's description of how the /v/ sound is correctly produced.

> The lower lip must be drawn upwards and slightly inwards, so that the upper front teeth rest lightly on the lip. Breath must be freely emitted between the teeth and over the lower lip, and voice must be added to the breath.

Should any part of this process function imperfectly, a child will have difficulty articulating the /v/. Clearly, in such a complicated process, there are many different types of possible errors.

There are four basic kinds of articulation errors (Table 6.1). Children may *substitute* one sound for another, as in saying "train" for *crane* or "doze" for *those*. Children with this problem are often certain they have said the correct word and may resist correction. Substitution of sounds can cause considerable confusion for the listener. Children may *distort* certain speech sounds while attempting to produce them accurately. The /s/ sound, for example, is relatively difficult to produce; children may produce the word sleep as "schleep," "zleep," or "thleep." Some speakers have a lisp; others a whistling /s/. Distortions can cause misunderstanding, though parents and teachers often become accustomed to them. Children may *omit* certain sounds, as in saying "cool" for *school*. They may drop consonants from the ends of words, as in "pos" for *post*. Most of us leave out sounds at times, but an extensive omission problem can make speech impossible to understand. Children may also *add* extra sounds, making comprehension difficult. They may say "buhrown" for *brown* or "hamber" for *hammer*.

Dysarthria and *apraxia* refer to two groups of articulation disorders caused by neuromuscular impairments. Lack of precise motor control needed to produce and sequence sounds causes distorted and repeated sounds.

Degree of Severity

Like all communication disorders, articulation problems vary in degree of severity. Many children have mild or moderate articulation disorders. It is usually possible to understand their speech, but they may mispronounce certain sounds or use immature speech, like that of younger children. These problems often disappear as a child matures. If a mild or moderate articulation problem does not seem to be improving over an extended period or if it appears to have a negative effect on the child's interaction with others, referral to a communication disorders specialist may be indicated.

A severe articulation disorder is present when a child pronounces many sounds so poorly that his speech is unintelligible most of the time. In that case, even the child's parents, teachers, and peers cannot easily understand him. As

TABLE 6.1
Types of articulation disorders.

Error type	Definition	Example
Substitution	Replacing one sound with another	Standard: The ball is red Substitution: The ball is wed.
Distortion	Producing a sound in an unfamiliar way	Standard: Give the pencil to Sally. Distortion; Give the pencil to Sally. (the /p/ is nasalized)
Omission	Omiting a sound in a word	Standard: Play the piano Omission; P_ay the piano
Addition	Inserting an extra sound in a word	Standard: I have a black horse Addition: I have a bəlack horse

Source: From "Articulation and Phonological Disorders" by L. V. McReynolds, in *Human Communication Disorders* (3rd ed.) (p. 231) by G. H. Shames and E. H. Wiig (Eds.), 1990, Columbus, OH: Merrill.

Liebergott, Favors, von Hippel, and Needleman (1978) point out, the child with a severe articulation disorder may "chatter away and sound as though he or she is talking gibberish" (p. 17). He may say, "Yeh me yuh a wido," instead of "Let me look out the window," or perhaps "Do foop is dood" for "That soup is good." The fact that articulation disorders are prevalent does not mean that teachers, parents, and specialists should regard them as simple or unimportant. On the contrary, as Emerick and Haynes (1986) observe, "An articulation disorder severe enough to interfere significantly with intelligibility is . . . as debilitating a communication problem as many other disorders. . . . [A]rticulation disorders are not simple at all, and they are not necessarily easy to diagnose effectively" (p. 153).

Voice Disorders

Voice disorders occur when quality, loudness, or pitch is inappropriate or abnormal. Such disorders are far less common in children than in adults. Considering how often some children shout and yell without any apparent harm to their voices, it is evident that the vocal cords can withstand heavy use (Renfrew, 1972). In some cases, however, a child's voice may be difficult to understand or may be considered unpleasant. As Moore (1982) observes, a person's voice may be considered disordered if it differs markedly from what is customary in the voices of others of the same age, sex, and cultural background. Moore uses the term *dysphonia* to describe any condition of poor or unpleasant voice quality and notes that a voice—whether good, poor, or in between—is closely identified with the person who uses it.

The two basic types of voice disorders are *phonation* and *resonance*. A phonation disorder causes the voice to sound breathy, hoarse, husky, or strained most of the time. In severe cases, there is no voice at all. Phonation disorders can have organic causes, such as growths or irritations on the vocal cords, but hoarseness most frequently comes from chronic vocal abuse, such as yelling, imitating noises, or habitually talking while under tension. A breathy voice is unpleasant because it is low in volume and fails to make adequate use of the vocal cords. A voice with a resonance disorder suffers from either too many sounds coming out through the air passages of the nose (hypernasality) or, conversely, not enough resonance of the nasal passages (hyponasality). The hypernasal speaker may be perceived as talking through her nose or having an unpleasant twang. A child with hypernasality has speech that is excessively nasal, neutral, or central-sounding, rather than oral, clear, and forward-sounding (Cole & Paterson, 1986). A child with hyponasality (sometimes called denasality) may sound as though he constantly has a cold or a stuffed nose, even when he does not. As with other voice disorders, the causes of nasality may be either organic (e.g., cleft palate, swollen nasal tissues, hearing impairment) or functional (perhaps resulting from learned speech patterns or behavior problems).

Fluency Disorders

Normal speech makes use of rhythm and timing. Words and phrases flow easily, with certain variations in speed, stress, and appropriate pauses. **Fluency** disorders interrupt the natural, smooth flow of speech with inappropriate pauses, hesitations, or repetitions. One type of fluency disorder is known as *cluttering,* a condition in which speech is very rapid with extra sounds or mispronounced sounds. The clutterer's speech is garbled to the point of unintelligibility. The best known—and probably least understood—fluency disorder, however, is **stuttering**. This condition is marked by "rapid-fire repetitions of consonant or vowel sounds, especially at the beginning of words; and complete verbal blocks" (Jonas, 1976, p. 7). The cause of stuttering remains unknown, although the condition has been studied extensively with some interesting results. Stuttering is far more common among males than females. And it occurs more frequently among twins. The prevalence of stuttering is about the same in all Western countries: Regardless of what language is spoken, about 1% of the general population has a stuttering problem. Stuttering is much more commonly reported among children than adults; prevalence estimates in school-age populations are in the 5% range (Ham, 1986; Martin & Lindamood, 1986). Stuttering is considered a disorder of childhood; it rarely begins past the age of 6 (Emerick & Haynes, 1986). According to Jonas (1976), stuttering typically makes its first appearance between the ages of 3 and 5, "*after* the child has already made great strides toward fluency. . . . The trouble comes later, just as speech is becoming less of a feat and more of a habit" (p. 11).

All children experience some dysfluencies—repetitions and interruptions—in the course of developing normal speech patterns. It is important not to overreact to dysfluencies and insist on perfect speech; some specialists believe that stuttering can be caused by pressures placed on a child when parents and teachers react to normal hesitations and repetitions by labeling the child a stutterer. Lingwell (1982) explains that stuttering is not just one specific disorder but many, which may be why there are several conflicting theories about its cause. According to Lingwell, stuttering can be caused by neurological, psychological, or allergic factors or can result from rhythmic control or faulty learning patterns.

Stuttering is situational; that is, it appears to be related to the setting or circumstances of speech. A child may be likely to stutter when talking to the people whose opinions matter most to him—such as parents and teachers—and in situations like being called on to speak in front of the class. Most people who stutter are fluent about 95% of the time; a child with a fluency disorder may not stutter at all when singing, talking to his pet dog, or reciting a poem in unison with others. Parents', teachers', and peers' reactions and expectations clearly have an important effect on any child's personal and communicative development.

Several researchers and clinicians have explored the effects of social pressures on stuttering by examining its incidence in cultures other than our own. Gerald Jonas, who himself was affected by stuttering, derives insights from a comparison of American Indian tribes. He observes that certain tribes, such as the Utes and the Bannocks of the Rocky Mountain region, have an unusually permissive attitude toward children's speech and have virtually no stuttering problems. Other tribes, such as the Cowichans of the Pacific Northwest, are highly competitive, expecting children to take part in complicated rituals at a young age, and have a high incidence of stuttering. Jonas (1976) suggests that the reason the Ute and Bannock children do not stutter may be that no one ever tries to "make them speak correctly." But he acknowledges that this theory fails to explain "why in so many other cultures some children of nagging parents turn into stutterers while others do not" (p. 14). Van Riper (1972) reflects on the importance of cultural attitudes toward stuttering in the following passage:

> Once, on Fiji in the South Pacific, we found a whole family of stutterers. As our guide and translator phrased it: "Mama kaka; papa kaka; and kaka, kaka, kaka, kaka." All six persons in that family showed marked repetitions and prolongations in their speech; but they were happy people, not at all troubled by their stuttering. It was just the way they talked. We could not help but contrast their attitudes and the simplicity of their stuttering with those which would have been shown by a similar family in our own land, where the pace of living is so much faster, where defective communication is rejected, where stutterers get penalized all their lives. To possess a marked speech disorder in our society is almost as handicapping as to be a physical cripple in a nomadic tribe that exists by hunting. (p. 4)

Language Disorders

Language disorders are usually classified as either receptive or expressive. As described earlier, a receptive language disorder interferes with the understanding of language. A child may, for example, be unable to comprehend spoken sentences or to follow a sequence of directions. An expressive language disorder interferes with production of language. The child may have a very limited vocabulary, may use incorrect words and phrases, or may not even speak at all, communicating only through gestures. A child may have good receptive language when an expressive disorder is present or may have both expressive and receptive disorders in combination.

To say that a child has a language delay does not necessarily mean that she has a language disorder. As Reed (1986) explains, a language delay implies that a child is slow to develop linguistic skills but acquires them in the same sequence as normal children. Generally, all features of language are delayed at about the same rate. On the other hand, a language disorder suggests a disruption in the usual rate and sequence of specific emerging language skills. A child who consistently has difficulty in responding to who, what, and where questions but otherwise displays language skills appropriate for her age would likely be considered to have a language disorder.

Chaney and Frodyma (1982) list several factors that can contribute to spoken language disorders in children.

Some professionals view learning disabilities (see Chapter 4) and autism (see Chapter 5) primarily as language disorders.

- ◆ Cognitive limitations or retardation
- ◆ Environmental deprivation
- ◆ Hearing impairments
- ◆ Emotional deprivation or behavior disorders
- ◆ Structural abnormalities of the speech mechanism

Environmental influences are thought to play an important part in delayed, disordered, or absent language. Some children are rewarded for their efforts at communication, whereas others, unfortunately, are punished for talking, gesturing, or otherwise attempting to communicate. A child who has little stimulation at home and has few chances to speak, listen, explore, and interact with others will probably have little motivation for communication and may well develop disordered patterns of language. Children who have had little exposure to words and experiences may need the teacher's help in encouraging communication. Active participation in experiences gives children the opportunity to learn and use appropriate vocabulary.

Aphasia

Some severe disorders in expressive and receptive language result from impairments of the brain. The term **aphasia** is frequently used to describe a "breakdown in the ability to formulate, or to retrieve, and to decode the arbitrary symbols of language" (Holland & Reinmuth, 1982, p. 428). Aphasia is one of the most prevalent causes of language disorders in adults, most often occurring suddenly, following a cardiovascular accident (stroke). Aphasia can also occur in children, however, either as a congenital or an acquired condition. Head injury is considered a significant cause of aphasia in children. Aphasia may be either expressive or, less commonly, receptive. Children with mild aphasia have language patterns that are close to normal but may have difficulty retrieving certain words and tend to need more time than usual to communicate (Linebaugh, 1986). Children with severe aphasia, however, are likely to have a markedly reduced storehouse of words and language forms. They may not be able to "use language for successful communicative interchange" (Horner, 1986, p. 892).

■ DEVELOPMENT OF THE FIELD OF COMMUNICATION DISORDERS

Although there have always been people with speech and language disorders, special education and treatment for this population are relatively recent developments. The first special class for "speech defective" children in the United States was established in New York in 1908 (Hewett & Forness, 1977), whereas special education for other groups—including deaf children, blind children, and those with mental retardation—was begun much earlier, suggesting that communication disorders have historically been considered less severe and less easily recognized than other disabilities.

During the 19th century, some treatment was provided at clinics and hospitals for people with communication disorders. The earliest specialists were college and university professors who, in the course of their study of normal speech processes, became interested in people with irregular patterns of speech, particularly stuttering and articulation disorders. Although American therapists concentrated primarily on correction of speech defects, prior to World War II European specialists (largely physicians) had developed a considerable body of scientific knowledge about communication disorders (Boone, 1977). The postwar years saw a proliferation of clinical services and research efforts. Many speech pathologists became especially interested in the rehabilitation of military personnel who had developed communication disorders because of damage to the brain or to the physical speech mechanisms. Speech and hearing clinics and centers were established in many cities, often operating in cooperation with hospitals or universities.

In recent years, there has been a notable expansion of services in the regular public schools to children with speech and language disorders.

Professionals who provide remedial services to children with communication disorders are today usually called *speech-language pathologists* or *communication disorders specialists*, rather than speech therapists. In 1978, the name of the major professional organization involved with communication disorders was changed to the American Speech-Language-Hearing Association (though it is still abbreviated as ASHA). These changes in terminology reflect awareness of the interrelationships among speech, language, and other aspects of learning, communication, and behavior. Speech is no longer viewed as a narrow specialty concerned with disorders to be corrected in isolation. Increasingly, speech-language pathologists who work in school settings now function as team members concerned with children's overall education and development. The trend is increasingly for remedial procedures to be carried out in the regular classroom, rather than in a special speech room, and the speech-language pathologist often provides training and consultation for the regular teacher, who may do much of the direct work with a child with communication disorders.

ASSESSMENT AND EVALUATION

"Don't worry, she'll grow out of it."
"Speech therapists can't help a child who doesn't talk."
"He'll be all right once he starts school."

These "misguided and inaccurate remarks" are indicative of widely held attitudes toward communication disorders (Thompson, 1984). Thompson contends that such attitudes are "at best worrying and annoying, at worst positively destructive to the child's social, emotional, and intellectual development" (p. 86).

To avoid the consequences of unrecognized or untreated speech and language disorders, it is especially important for children to receive professional assessment and evaluation services. When assessing or diagnosing a child suspected of having a communication disorder, the specialist seeks to meet the following objectives:

1. *To describe the problem.* What are the dimensions of the communicative disturbance with respect to voice, fluency, language, and articulation?

2. *To estimate its severity.* How large a problem is it?

3. *To identify factors that are related to the problem.* What are the antecedents and consequences of it?

4. *To estimate prospects for improvement.* What estimate can we make of the extent of possible recovery and the time frame of treatment?

5. *To derive a plan of treatment.* What are the specific targets for therapy, and how can the client best be approached? (Emerick & Haynes, 1986, p. 50)

Case History and Examination

Most professional speech and language assessments begin with the collection of a case history from the child and the parent. This typically involves completing a biographical form that includes such diverse information as the child's birth and developmental history, illness, medications taken, scores on achievement and intelligence tests, and adjustment to school. The parent may be asked when the child first crawled, walked, and uttered words. Social skills, such as playing readily with other children, may also be considered.

The specialist examines the child's mouth carefully, noting whether there are any irregularities in the tongue, lips, teeth, palate, or other structures that may affect speech production. If the child has an organic speech problem, the specialist refers the child for possible medical intervention.

Evaluation Components

Testing procedures vary according to the suspected type of functional disorder. Often the specialist conducts broad screenings to detect areas of concern and then moves to more detailed testing in those areas. A comprehensive evaluation to detect the presence of a communication disorder would likely include the following general components.

Articulation Test

The speech errors the child is making are assessed. A record is kept of the sounds that are defective, how they are being mispronounced, and the number of errors. Examples of published tests include the Templin-Darley Test of Articulation (Templin & Darley, 1969) and the Test of Minimal Articulation Competence (Secord, 1981).

Hearing Test

Hearing is usually tested to determine whether a hearing problem is causing the speech disorder.

Auditory Discrimination Test

This test is given to determine whether the child is hearing sounds correctly. If he is unable to recognize the specific characteristics of a given sound, he will not have a good model to imitate. The Auditory Discrimination Test (Wepman, 1973) and the Washington Speech Sound Discrimination Test (Drather, Minor, Addicott, & Sunderland, 1971) are two examples.

Language Development Test

This is administered to help determine the amount of vocabulary the child has acquired, because vocabulary is generally a good indication of intelligence. Frequently used tests include the Peabody Picture Vocabulary Test (Dunn, 1965), which is a measure of receptive vocabulary, and the Carrow Elicited Language Inventory (Carrow, 1974).

Another form of evaluation used more and more frequently is an overall language test, which assesses the child's understanding and production of language structures (e.g., important syntactical elements like conjunctions showing causal relationships). An example is the Clinical Evaluation of Language Functions (Semel & Wiig, 1980).

Language Samples

An important part of any evaluation procedure is obtaining a language sample, an accurate example of the child's expressive speech and language. The effective

Assessment of communication disorders includes tests of articulation, auditory discrimination, and language development.

examiner does not merely ask, "Does the child talk?" but rather asks, "How does the child communicate?" (Ulrey, 1982, p. 123). The examiner considers such factors as intelligibility and fluency of speech, voice quality, and use of vocabulary and grammar. Some speech-language pathologists use structured tasks to evoke language samples. They may, for example, ask a child to describe a picture, tell a story, or answer a list of questions. Most specialists, however, use informal conversation as their preferred procedure to obtain language samples (Atkins & Cartwright, 1982). They believe the child's language sample will be more representative if the examiner uses natural conversation rather than highly structured tasks. Emerick and Haynes (1986) advise examiners to tape-record language samples instead of taking notes, which can be distracting to the child. Open-ended questions, such as "Tell me about your family," are suggested rather than yes-no questions or questions that can be answered with one word, such as "What color is your car?"

Behavioral observation is becoming increasingly important in assessing communication disorders. Objective recording of children's language competence in social contexts has added much to our knowledge of language acquisition. It is imperative that the observer have experience in reliably recording speech and language and to sample the child's behavior across various settings, rather than limiting it to a clinic or examining room. A parent-child observation is frequently arranged for young children. The specialist provides appropriate toys and activities and requests the parent to interact normally with the child.

McCormick and Schiefelbusch (1990) note that assessment and evaluation of intervention efforts increasingly emphasize the importance of gathering data on *both* the child and the adult's behavior in the language interaction. The extent to which the child learns and uses language effectively in the classroom depends to a large extent on the teacher's language behavior. Observational data can be obtained to guide needed changes in the adult's behavior (Blank, 1988).

Arena Assessment

When multiple members of a transdisciplinary team are involved in planning and carrying out an intervention for a child with a communication disorder, a strategy known as *arena assessment* can prove beneficial. Arena assessment is a group assessment procedure in which parents, teachers, speech-language pathologists, and other involved participants seat themselves in a circle or semicircle around the child. Wolery and Dyk (1984) claim five advantages for the arena assessment approach. First, because many similar or even identical test items appear on the tests given by different specialists, redundancy is eliminated and both the child and parents are spared responding repeatedly to the same item. Second, unnecessary handling of the child by various professionals is reduced. Third, team members observe the child perform across a wider range of performance domains and end up with a more holistic view of the child. Fourth, team members have an opportunity to observe and learn from one another. Finally, consensus regarding the child's status and intervention needs is more likely because each team member observes the same set of child behaviors.

After the assessment procedures have been completed, the speech-language pathologist reviews the results of the case history, formal and informal tests, language samples, behavioral observations, medical records, and other available data. A treatment plan is then developed in cooperation with the child's parents and teachers, to set up realistic communication objectives and to determine the methods that will be used. Kelly and Rice (1986) suggest giving parents an opportunity to question and react to the recommendations and to discuss their willingness to follow through with the treatment plans. It is also appropriate, they note, to inform parents of the frequency of therapy, the costs involved, and the availability of resources in the community.

■ TREATMENT AND REMEDIATION

Various approaches are employed in the treatment of speech and language disorders. The profession of speech-language pathology addresses both organic and nonorganic causes and encompasses practitioners with numerous points of view and a wide range of accepted intervention techniques. Medical, dental, or surgical procedures can help many children whose speech problems result from organic causes. Some specialists employ structured exercises and drills to correct speech sounds; others emphasize speech production in natural language contexts. Some prefer to work with children in individual therapy sessions; others believe that group sessions are advantageous for language modeling and peer support. Some encourage children to imitate the therapist's speech; others prefer to have the child listen to tapes of his or her own speech. Some specialists follow a highly behavioral approach, in which target speech behaviors are precisely prompted, recorded, and reinforced; others favor less structured methods. Some speech-language therapists focus exclusively on a child's expressive and receptive communication; others devote attention to other aspects of the child's behavior and environment, such as self-confidence or interactions with parents and classmates. Clearly, there are many possible options to explore in devising an appropriate treatment plan.

Articulation Disorders

Speech-language pathologists, according to Bernthal and Bankson (1986), feel more comfortable and competent when dealing with articulation disorders than with other types of speech and language impairments. This response is probably attributable, they note, to the fact that articulation disorders can be broken down into identifiable segments more readily than can disorders of voice, fluency, or language. Also, a child can logically progress from articulating simple sounds in isolation to syllables, words, phrases, sentences, and sustained conversation. A large percentage of functional articulation disorders are either treated successfully, or they simply fade away as the child matures.

Treatment Models

Four models of treatment are widely used for articulation disorders (Bernthal & Bankson, 1986; Creaghead, Newman, & Secord, 1989). In the *discrimination model,* emphasis is on developing the child's ability to listen carefully and detect the differences between similar sounds (such as the *t* in *take* and the *c* in *cake*). The child learns to match his speech to that of a standard model, using auditory, visual, and tactual feedback. The *phonologic model* seeks to identify a child's pattern of sound production and to teach her to produce gradually more acceptable sounds. A child who tends to omit final consonants, for example, might be taught to recognize the difference between word pairs like *two* and *tooth* and then to produce them more accurately. The *sensorimotor model* emphasizes the repetitive production of sounds in various contexts, with special attention to the motor skills involved in articulation; frequent exercises are employed to produce sounds with differing stress patterns. The *operant conditioning model* seeks to define antecedent events, present specific stimuli, and shape articulatory responses by providing reinforcing consequences. An instructional objective might be stated as "Wayne will say the *k* in the final position of 10 words after being shown 10 pictures by the therapist. The *k* sound must be produced correctly in 9 of the 10 words."

There is a generally consistent relationship between children's ability to recognize sounds and their ability to articulate them correctly (Creaghead et al., 1989). Whatever treatment model(s) are used, the specialist may have the child carefully watch how sounds are produced and then use a mirror to monitor his own speech production. Children are expected to accurately produce problematic sounds in syllables, words, sentences, and stories. They may tape-record their own speech and listen carefully for errors. It is sometimes helpful for children to learn to recognize the difference between the way they produce a sound and the way other people produce it. As in all communication training, it is important for the teacher, parent, or specialist to provide a good language model, to reward the child's positive performance, and to encourage the child to talk.

Voice Disorders

When a child has a voice disorder, a medical examination should always be sought. Organic causes often respond to surgery or medical treatment. In addition, communication disorders specialists sometimes recommend environmental modifications; a person who is consistently required to speak in a noisy setting, for example, may benefit from the use of a small microphone to reduce vocal straining and shouting (Moore, 1982). Most remedial techniques, however, offer direct vocal rehabilitation, which helps the child with a voice disorder gradually learn to produce more acceptable and efficient speech. Depending on the type of voice disorder and the child's overall circumstances, vocal rehabilitation may include such activities as exercises to increase breathing capacity, relaxation techniques to reduce tension, or procedures to increase or decrease the loudness of speech.

The principles of applied behavior analysis have had a major impact on the treatment of voice disorders in recent years (T. S. Johnson, 1986). Because many voice problems are directly attributable to vocal abuse, behavioral principles are frequently used to pinpoint abusive vocal behaviors and then to shape and modify them. Many children and adults have thus been able to break habitual patterns of vocal misuse. Computer technology has also been successfully applied in the treatment of voice disorders. Some instruments enable speakers to see visual representations of their voice patterns on a screen or printout; speakers are thus able to monitor their own vocalizations visually as well as auditorily and to develop new patterns of using their voices more naturally and efficiently (Bull & Rushakoff, 1987).

Visi-pitch is an example of a visual speech display. It can be used with Apple and IBM computers.

Fluency Disorders

The treatment of stuttering and other fluency disorders varies widely according to the orientation of the client and the therapist. Over the course of history, people who stutter have been subjected to countless treatments—some of them unusual, to say the least. Past treatments included holding pebbles in the mouth, sticking fingers in a light socket, talking out of one side of the mouth, eating raw oysters, speaking with the teeth clenched, taking alternating hot and cold baths, and speaking on inhaled rather than exhaled air (Ham, 1986). For many years it was widely thought that stuttering was caused by a tongue that was unable to function properly in the mouth. It was not uncommon for early physicians to prescribe ointments to blister or numb the tongue or even to remove portions of the tongue through surgery!

Today's treatment methods tend to emphasize one of two general approaches (Ham, 1986). One approach might be termed *symptom modification*. Using various techniques, the therapist takes aim at the stuttering itself and/or the stutterer's underlying emotional dimensions. The principal goal of such therapy is to develop the person's ability to control the stuttering and to behave appropriately in situations where communication is required. The other prevalent approach could be labeled *fluency reinforcement*. A therapist using this methodology would regard stuttering as a learned response and would seek to eliminate it by establishing and encouraging fluent speech.

Application of behavioral principles has strongly influenced recent practices in the treatment of fluency disorders. Hegde (1986) observes that punishing stuttering is socially undesirable as well as ineffective and tends to generate emotional side effects, but the "positive reinforcement of nonstuttered utterances can be an attractive alternative" (p. 521). Children may learn to manage their stuttering by deliberately prolonging certain sounds or by speaking slowly to get through a "block." They may increase their confidence and fluency by speaking in groups, where pressure is minimized and successful speech is positively reinforced. They may learn to monitor their own speech and reward themselves for periods of fluency. They may learn to speak to a rhythmic beat or with the aid of devices that mask or delay their ability to hear their own speech. Tape recorders are often used for drills, simulated conversations, and to document progress.

Effective Treatment

Effective treatment programs do not focus on only one aspect of stuttering, but instead identify and alter its communicative, behavioral, and emotional components (Emerick & Haynes, 1986). Hegde (1986) emphasizes the importance of generalization of the targeted speech behaviors to natural settings—that is, outside the clinic. A therapist might, for example, "accompany the stutterer to a store or a restaurant, and manage the treatment contingencies in a subtle manner" (p. 532). Parents, teachers, siblings, and peers may be invited to the treatment sessions and may be trained to reinforce stutter-free patterns of speech at home or school.

When interacting with a child who stutters, it is recommended that a teacher pay primary attention to what the child is saying, rather than to his difficulties in saying it. This focus helps the child develop a more positive attitude toward himself and toward communication with others. When the child experiences a verbal block, the teacher should be patient and calm, say nothing, and maintain eye contact with the child until he finishes what he wants to say.

Children often learn to control their stuttering and to produce increasingly fluent speech as they mature. No single method of treatment has been recognized as most effective. Stuttering frequently decreases when children enter adolescence, regardless of which treatment method was used. The problem even disappears with no treatment at all in some cases. Martin and Lindamood (1986) studied the phenomenon of spontaneous recovery from stuttering and concluded that approximately 40% to 45% of children diagnosed as stutterers apparently outgrow or get over their dysfluencies without formal intervention.

Although a variety of programs to treat stuttering are likely to continue, it is important for teachers, parents, and clients to evaluate the effectiveness of such programs. Sacco (1986) has established six essential criteria in a successful treatment of stuttering.

1. Lessens tension in the speech mechanism
2. Reduces rates of speech production
3. Eliminates accompanying struggle behaviors
4. Creates a more healthy attitude about speaking
5. Reduces the client's perception of stress
6. Produces speech that is more natural (p. 81)

Language Disorders

Treatments for language disorders are also extremely varied. Some programs center around precommunication activities that encourage the child to explore and that make the environment conducive to the development of receptive and expressive language. Clearly, children must have something they want to communicate. And because children learn through imitation, it is important for the teacher or specialist to talk clearly, use correct inflections, and provide a rich variety of words and sentences. The presence of other children in the classroom or clinical setting also appears to play a useful role in language development. Lowenthal (1981) found that preschool children with language impairments learned most effectively when they were taught in groups of three or four children. Larger groups, with 10 children, were less effective in encouraging development of vocabulary and comprehension skills.

Treatment Methods

Chaney and Frodyma (1982) describe two different methods to encourage language development in preschool children with various handicapping conditions: the precision method and the experiential method. In the *precision method,* children are placed in groups according to their ability levels in each of several areas, such as language, cognition, motor skills, self-help skills, and social skills. Group lessons and activities, about 20 minutes long, emphasize language through tasks a child has not yet learned, and extensive data on each child's performance are maintained. The *experiential method* uses groups of children with varying levels of language ability; children with higher language skills serve as models for those whose language is less well developed. Different demands and expectations are placed on each child, and each day's activities are presented around a unified theme or experience. Activities for one day, for example, might revolve around clothing. The children might discuss what clothes they are wearing, paste clothes on paper dolls, wash clothes, and learn concepts of size and color using articles of clothing.

Some specialists in language disorders do a great deal of written and verbal labeling to help the child develop language content; that is, attach meaning to important objects in the environment. In many instances, children's language skills improve when they become better able to pay attention. The specialist may reinforce the child for imitating facial expressions or body movements or simply for maintaining eye contact. Some speech-language pathologists emphasize pairing actions with words, teaching the natural gestures that go along with such expressions as "up," "look," and "goodbye." D'Angelo (1981) recommends wordless picture books as a means of building vocabulary, conversational skills, and positive attitudes with language disordered children. A parent or teacher can use questions such as "What is happening in the picture?" and "What things do you see?" to initiate conversations with a child.

Children with severe language disorders tend to require highly structured programs of intervention. The teacher's verbal or nonverbal prompts and the student's acceptable responses are defined and measured very specifically. For example, when Cindy's teacher asks, "Do you want more juice?" Cindy must clearly articulate at least the syllable *mo* (for more) within 5 seconds in order to receive a sip of juice. Sounds and partial sentences, such as "want cookie," may be regarded as suitable vocal responses. Cavallaro and Poulson (1985) defined a system of communicative prompts, ranging from least assistance to most assistance, for teachers to use to encourage language development in children with severe handicaps (Table 6.2).

No matter what the approach to treatment, it is clear that children with language disorders need to be around children and adults with something interesting to talk about. As Reed (1986) points out, it was assumed for many years that a one-to-one setting was the most effective format for language intervention. Emphasis was on eliminating distracting stimuli and focusing a child's attention on the desired communication task. Today, however, the importance of language as an interactive, interpersonal behavior is generally recognized, and small-group intervention formats can expose children with language disorders to "a variety of stimuli, experiences, contexts, and people that are not available in one-to-one situations" (Reed, 1986, p. 276).

Whether they use individual or group therapy, effective speech-language pathologists establish specific goals and objectives, keep precise records of their students' behaviors, and structure the teaching situation so that each child's efforts at communication will be rewarded and enjoyable.

Although programs for children with language disorders acknowledge the importance of oral speech, they are currently moving away from exclusive emphasis on spoken communication. Sign language has been successfully used to develop communicative skills in several children who, though their hearing was not impaired, were apparently unable to develop expressive or receptive language through normal channels. For example, Bonvillian and Nelson (1976)

TABLE 6.2
Prompts used in incidental teaching, in order of least to most assistance.

Prompt	Clarification	Used When
Nonvocal prompt	The teacher looked at the child and remained silent for at least 3 sec.	Always used as first prompt.
Question	The teacher asked a question which provided no assistance, such as "What do you want?"	When the child was able to produce the response without prompting.
Request for terminal response	"Say the whole thing," or "Tell me what you want."	When the child could produce the response without a model.
Partial model	The teacher presented a model of part of the desired response, such as "Say, want . . ."	When the child could reliably imitate a full model.
Full model	The teacher modeled the entire response, and requested imitation, such as "Say, want cookie."	When the child could not reliabily produce the response.

Source: From "Teaching Language to Handicapped Children in Natural Settings" by C. C. Cavallaro and C. L. Poulson, Winter 1985, *Education & Treatment of Children, 8*(1) p. 10. Reprinted by permission.

were able to teach sign language to an autistic child who had previously been considered mute and nonresponsive. Sign language, gestures, and symbol systems have also been successfully taught to children whose language disorders are attributed to mental retardation, aphasia, or behavior disorders. These approaches should, however, be viewed as supplements to rather than replacements for speech. Children who are able to initiate communication through signs, gestures, or symbols may be able to transfer to speech as they learn and develop their communicative abilities. Speech is always a desirable goal for children whose cognitive and physical abilities enable them to achieve it.

Augmentative Communication

For children who do not speak so others can understand, a system of augmentative communication may be devised. **Augmentative communication** refers to a total system of supplementing and enhancing an individual's communication capabilities. The system includes three components:

♦ A representational symbol set, or vocabulary

♦ A communication device for displaying messages

♦ The communication skills for effective use of the system

Augmentative communication can be both *unaided* and *aided*. Unaided techniques do not require a physical aid or device (Vanderheiden & Lloyd, 1986). They include oral speech, gestures, facial expressions, general body posture, and manual signs. Of course, nonhandicapped individuals use a wide range of unaided augmentative communication techniques.

Selection of Vocabulary and Symbol System.   Individuals who do not speak so that others can understand must have access to vocabulary that matches as nearly as possible the language they would be using and generating in various situations if they could speak. Beukelman (1988) suggests that decisions about what items to include in a student's augmentative vocabulary should be based on

♦ Vocabulary that peers in similar situations and settings use

♦ What communication partners (such as teachers and parents) think will be needed

♦ Vocabulary the student is already using in all modalities

♦ Contextual demands of specific situations

A student may have a basic communication board of common words, phrases, numbers, and so forth for use across many situations, and various situational boards, or miniboards, with specific vocabulary for certain situations (e.g., at a restaurant, in science class).

After selecting the vocabulary for an augmentative communication system, one needs a symbolic display system, such as pictures or drawings, that represent the vocabulary. There are several commercially available symbol sets, such as *The Oakland Picture Dictionary* (Kirsten, 1981) and the *Picture Communication Symbols* (Mayer-Johnson, 1986). Symbol sets may also be "homemade," consisting of photos, pictures, and perhaps words and the alphabet.

Blissymbolics, originally developed in the 1940s by Austrian chemical engineer Charles Bliss as a graphic symbol system for international communication, was adapted in the early 1970s for use by some nonspeaking, physically disabled people by the Easter Seal Communication Institute in Toronto, Canada (McDonald, 1980). Bliss symbols represent concepts through a combination of geometric shapes. The user of Blissymbolics combines multiple symbols to create new meanings (e.g., *school* is communicated by selecting the symbols *house-gives-knowledge*). The system offers a means of greatly expanded communication to the nonspeaking individual who can learn the new language of Blissymbolics. Since many of the Blissymbolics are abstract, however, and do not look like the concept they represent, some individuals have difficulty learning the system. In one study, adolescents with severe physical disabilities quickly learned to use iconic line drawings that directly represented vocabulary objects, but developed little functional use of the Bliss symbols (Hurlbut, Iwata, & Green, 1982).

Communication Displays. Once vocabulary and a symbol set have been selected, a method of displaying the symbols must be determined. The most common augmentative communication display is the language board, a flat area (often a tray or table attached to a wheelchair) on which the symbols are arranged for the user to select. Symbols can also be transported and displayed

Joshua uses his personalized language board for many purposes.

in a wallet or photo album. Electronic devices, such as computers and dedicated communication aides, are also used to display symbols.

Selection Techniques.   Symbols are selected in an augmentative communication by direct selection, scanning, or encoding responses (Vanderheiden & Lloyd, 1986). Direct selection involves pointing to the symbol one wishes to express with a finger or fist, or sometimes with a wand attached to the head or chin. With a limited number of selections widely spaced from another, the user can select symbols by "eye pointing." Scanning techniques present choices to the user one at a time and the user makes a response at the proper time to indicate which item or group of selections he wants to communicate. Scanning can be machine-assisted (as with the device physicist Stephen Hawking uses) or listener-assisted (e.g., the listener may point to symbols one at a time while watching for the user's eye-blink that signals selection). Encoding involves giving multiple signals to indicate the location of the symbol or item to be selected. Usually, the user makes a pair of responses that direct the listener to a specific printed message on a reference list. Encoding can be particularly useful for a student whose severe physical impairments prohibit reliable selection by pointing to an item, unless there are very few symbols and they are widely spaced. In a display in which symbols are organized by color and number, for example, a student can first touch one card (to select the "red" group of messages) and then make a second pointing response to indicate which number message in the red group is intended.

Patterns of Service

Although some self-contained special classes are specifically designed for children with speech or language impairments, the regular classroom is by far the most prevalent setting for school-age children with communication disorders. There is an increasing tendency for communication disorders specialists to serve as consultants for regular and special education teachers (and parents), rather than spending most of their time providing direct services to individual children. All these people are important in the development and practice of speech and language skills. The specialist concentrates on assessing communication disorders, evaluating progress, and providing materials and techniques. Teachers and parents are encouraged to follow the specialist's guidelines.

Recent surveys of members of the American Speech-Language-Hearing Association (Mansour, 1985; Shewan, 1986) have found that speech-language pathologists are employed in a wide variety of settings, with the largest single group—about 37%—working in schools. Other settings include hospitals, speech and hearing clinics, nursing homes, physicians' offices, and private practice. The caseloads of these professionals vary widely according to the setting and the types and severity of communication disorders among their clients. The most prevalent pattern of service delivery in schools is a specialist who works with a child for two sessions each week. The most prevalent communication disorders among children served by school speech-language pathologists are, in order of frequency, language disorders (52.2% of a typical caseload), articulation disorders (34.8%), hearing impairments (4.5%), fluency disorders (4.1%), and voice disorders (2.4%) (Shewan, 1986).

ASHA can provide further information about the training, qualifications, and responsibilities of speech-language pathologists. The address of ASHA appears in the listing of resources at the end of this chapter.

MY COMMUNICATION SYSTEM
By Stephen W. Hawking

Stephen W. Hawking is Lucasian Professor of Mathematics and Theoretical Physics at The University of Cambridge. He has amyotrophic lateral sclerosis (ALS). Sometimes called Lou Gehrig's disease, after one of its most famous victims, ALS is a motor neuron disease of middle or late life that involves progressive degeneration of nerve cells that control voluntary motor functions. Initial symptoms usually entail difficulty walking, clumsiness of the hands, slurred speech, and an inability to swallow normally. The muscles of the arms and legs waste away; eventually, walking is impossible and control of the hands is lost, although sensation remains normal. There is no known cause or cure for ALS. We asked Professor Hawking to tell us about the augmentative communication system he uses.

Physicist Stephen W. Hawking.

I am quite often asked: How do you feel about having ALS? The answer is, "not a lot." I try to lead as normal a life as possible, and not think about my condition, or regret the things it prevents me from doing, which are not that many. It was a great shock to me to discover that I had motor neuron disease. I had never been very well coordinated, physically, as a child. I was not good at ball games, and my handwriting was the despair of my teachers. But things seemed to change when I went to Oxford at the age of 17. I took up coxing and rowing. I was not Boat Race standard, but I got by at the level of inter-College competition.

In my third year at Oxford, however, I noticed that I seemed to be getting clumsier, and I fell over once or twice for no apparent reason. Shortly after my 21st birthday, I went into the hospital for tests. I was in for two weeks, during which I had a wide variety of tests. After all that, they didn't tell me what I had, except that it was not multiple sclerosis, and that I was an atypical case. I didn't feel like asking for more details, because they were obviously bad.

The realization that I had an incurable disease that was likely to kill me in a few years was a bit of a shock. How could something like that happen to me? Why should I be cut off like this? Not knowing what was going to happen to me, or how rapidly the disease would progress, I was at loose ends. The doctors told me to go back to Cambridge and carry on with the research I had just started, in general relativity and cosmology. But I was not making much progress with the research, and anyway, I might not live long enough to finish my Ph.D. I felt something of a tragic character. I took to listening to Wagner, but reports in magazines that I drank heavily are an exaggeration.

Before my condition had been diagnosed, I had been very bored with life. There had not seemed to be anything worth doing. But after I came out of the hospital, I dreamt several times that I would sacrifice my life to save others. After all, if I were going to die anyway, it might as well do some good.

But I didn't die. In fact, although there was a cloud hanging over my future, I found, to my surprise, that I was enjoying life in the present more than before. I began to make progress with my research, and I got engaged to Jane Wilde, a girl I had met just about the time my condition was diagnosed. Our engagement changed my life. It gave me something to live for. But it also meant that I had to get a job, if we were to get married.

Up to 1974, I was able to feed myself, and get in and out of bed. Jane managed to help me, and bring up two children, without outside help. However, things were getting more difficult, so we took to having one of my research students live with us. In return for free accommodation, and a lot of my attention, they helped me get up and go to bed. In 1980, we changed to a system of community and private nurses, who came in for an hour or two in the morning and evening. This lasted until I caught pneumonia in 1985 and had to have a tracheotomy operation. After this, I had to have 24-hour nursing care, which was made possible by grants from several foundations.

Before the operation, my speech had been getting more slurred, so that only a few people who knew me well could understand me. But at least I could communicate. I wrote scientific papers by dictating to a secretary, and I gave seminars through an interpreter, who repeated my words more clearly. However, the tracheotomy removed my ability to speak altogether. For a time, the only way I could communicate was to spell out words letter by letter, by raising my eyebrows when someone pointed to the right letter on a spelling card. It is pretty difficult to carry on a conversation like that, let alone write a scientific paper.

Today I communicate with a computer system. A computer expert in California, Walter Woltosz, sent me a program he had written called Equalizer. This program allowed me to select words from a series of menus on the screen by pressing a switch in my hand. The program could also be controlled by a switch operated by head or eye movement. When I have built up what I want to say, I can send it to a speech synthesizer. At first, I just ran the Equalizer program through a desktop computer. However, David Mason, of Cambridge Adaptive Communications, who is also the husband of one of my nurses, put together the system I now use. I have a Datavue 25 computer mounted to the back of my wheelchair that runs from a battery under the chair's seat. The screen is mounted where I can see it, though you have to view it from the right angle. I run a program called Living Center, written by a company called Words Plus of Sunnyvale, California. A cursor moves across the upper part of the screen. I can stop it by pressing a switch in my hand. In this way, I can select words that are printed on the lower part of the screen. This system allows me to communicate much better than I could before; I can manage up to 15 words a minute. I can either speak what I have written, or save it on a disk. I can then print it out, or call it back and speak it sentence by sentence, like I'm doing now. Using this system, I have written a book, and a dozen scientific papers. I have also given a number of scientific and popular talks. They have been well received. I think that is in large part due to the quality of my speech synthesizer, made by Speech Plus, also of Sunnyvale, California.

One's voice is very important. If you have a slurred voice, people are likely to treat you as mentally deficient: "Does he take sugar?" This synthesizer is by far the best I have heard, because it varies the intonation, and doesn't speak like a Dalek. The only trouble is that it gives me an American accent; however, the company is working on a British version.

I have had motor neuron disease for practically all my adult life. Yet it has not prevented me from having a very attractive family and being successful in my work. This is thanks to the help I have received from my wife, my children, and a large number of other people and organizations. I have been lucky, in that my condition has progressed more slowly than is often the case. But it shows that one need not lose hope. ◆

By direct selection with a finger or pointer the user of this voice output communication aid has said, "I want two cheeseburgers."

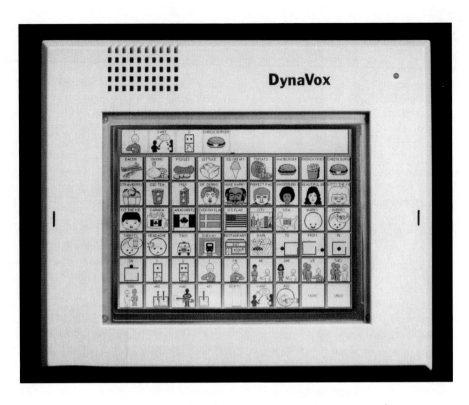

This "eyetyper" device enables the speaker to select letters, numbers, and symbols by looking at them. Note the sensor under his eye.

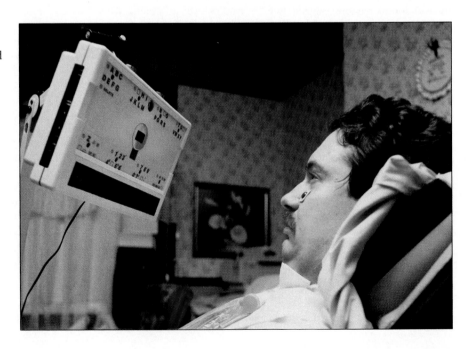

Sometimes the specialist visits schools according to a regular schedule and gives individual or group therapy to the children, but this approach is becoming somewhat less common. Communication is seen as occurring most appropriately in the natural environment rather than in the clinical setting. *Integrated therapy* is provided in the natural environment (i.e., classroom or home) in the context of ongoing routines. Consequently, some professionals believe it is impossible to adequately serve the child with a speech or language disorder with an *isolated therapy* approach (two or three 30-minute sessions each week with a specialist). In fact, this approach has been described as a futile attempt to "sweep back a river with a broom" (Hatten & Hatten, 1975). McCormick and Schiefelbusch (1990) criticize the isolated therapy model:

> The language instruction of normally developing young nonhandicapped children is not restricted to brief intervals spaced throughout the week. In fact, the language instruction of normally developing children is limited only by their waking hours. It is most difficult to justify the provisions of episodic therapy for severely language-delayed children. (p. 271)

These authors also find an isolated therapy model wanting because it impedes communication between speech-language therapists and teachers, does not promote generalization of skills learned in the therapy room to the classroom, and affords limited language-learning experiences, often focusing on pictures or objects from commercial kits that hold little interest for the child.

Tomes and Sanger (1986) surveyed the attitudes of classroom teachers toward the services provided by speech-language pathologists in their schools. Although the attitudes were generally positive, there was some confusion about the specialists' roles and responsibilities. Nietupski, Schutz, and Ockwood (1980) have suggested the following roles and functions for speech-language therapists and for classroom teachers in an integrated therapy model:

Speech-language pathologists would:

♦ Consult with the classroom teacher on the language and communication needs of all children in the class

♦ Demonstrate and model to teaching staff skills for promoting the language and communication development of children with delays and disorders

♦ Plan and develop initial programs and program modifications

♦ Assess and continuously monitor child progress and program effectiveness

Classroom teachers would:

♦ Share information with the speech-language pathologist about all aspects of each child's programming

♦ Solicit suggestions for achieving communication objectives in the context of classroom activities and routines

♦ Implement communication training recommendations in the classroom

♦ Document acquisition, mastery, and generalization of language and communication skills

♦ Revise curricula and methods in concert with input from the speech-language pathologist

COMMUNICATION PARTNERS
Strategies for Opening Doors to Communication

Effective communication requires two parties—two people who work as partners in the communication act. When one of the partners has little or no understandable speech, communication is often limited and frustrating for both. If the two persons work together and the normally speaking person learns to employ several strategies for systematic communication, however, significant information can be exchanged. June Bigge (1991) describes nine strategies that communication partners can use that will open doors to help individuals with severe speech impairments enjoy increased communication effectiveness.

Establish and Use Yes, No, and Other Fundamental Signals

A primary goal is to have the student use, or at least approximate, the spoken words or traditional head signals for *yes* and *no*. If necessary, signals may be given by using the head in a nontraditional way. An upward glance can mean *yes;* a glance to the side, *no;* a drop of the head or a shrug of shoulders might signify *I don't know*. If a student's technique is not obvious, ask for a demonstration: "Please show me how you say *yes/no*." This type of unaided communication system can go anywhere with the student. Aided signals may consist of a smiling face symbol or the word *yes* printed on one arm of a wheelchair and a frowning face or the word *no* on the opposite arm. Likewise, the teacher may write *yes* on one side of the chalkboard and *no* on the other end. To respond, the student looks at one side of the board or the other. Once reliable signals for indicating *yes, no,* and *I don't know* messages have been established, post them and tell others.

Use of *yes, no,* and *I don't know* responses should accompany other components of a student's communication system; they should not be the only components. Each student must have access to communication components that also allow access to the language she would know how to use if she could speak. Until this happens, students will not be in a position to generate their own language and must always remain in a somewhat dependent and passive role.

Provide Opportunities for Initiation

When attempting to interact with individuals with physical and speech differences, people tend to quickly take over leadership in the interaction. They inadvertently fail to wait long enough for the person to initiate requests and other communications. This leads to learned helplessness or passivity on the part of the person with the disability. Instead of anticipating students' needs and providing fillers for silence in communicative interactions, set up potential communicative opportunities and *wait* for the student to initiate.

Present a Range of Choices, Then Repeat Them One at a Time

To avoid ambiguity in asking questions, use this important listener-assisted auditory scanning strategy. Present the range of choices, "Do you want a drink of water or milk?"

Then repeat each question separately: "Water?" "Milk?" Adding the option, "neither of these" to any list of choices is a more advanced strategy for partners to use and is very helpful to the nonspeaking person.

Wait for the Expression and Expansion of Ideas

Allow students with physical and speech disabilities time to think about the content of what they want to convey, time to make the necessary motor movements to relay their message, and time after their first response to add more information. The motor response itself may be very slow for some children. They may need time to think of ways to change the direction of the conversation to more nearly reflect their original intent or to add information.

Narrow the Options to Find the Category About Which the Person Has Something to Say

Sometimes it is not clear what an individual is trying to tell or ask. What is the quickest way to find out? Use listener-assisted auditory scanning and first narrow the options by finding a category. Ask, "Are you thinking of telling something? Or asking something?" "Telling?" "Asking?" Once that is decided, ask "Do you want to talk about somebody, some place, some things, or feelings, or none of these?" If the answer is a place, for example, you could narrow the options by asking "Is it about home, or school, or some place else?" Then repeat each category one at a time to allow the individual to indicate her choice.

Clarify and Verify to Assure Messages are Received Correctly

Effectiveness of communication interactions limited to *yes* and *no* responses hinge upon a communication partner's use of the clarification strategy. It is a great temptation to ask an individual only dead-end and fact-level yes-and-no questions when they do not speak intelligibly. But speakers with unclear speech have ideas, feelings, and reactions to share with those who will listen. And these kinds of message exchanges depend very much upon clarification strategies of communication partners. To clarify and verify, communication partners repeat the perceived messages in their entirety or by segments to see if the message was received correctly. The strategy involves stating first what they think has been communicated so far. If the message was received correctly and verified by a positive answer to the question "Is this exactly right?" then the conversation may move on. If the message is not verified as correct, then more clarification is necessary. The strategy now involves repeating the message in segments and asking questions like these after each segment: "Am I close?" "Is there more to it than that?" "Do you want to change part of what I said?" "Is this too specific or too general?"

Talk "Up To" Not "Down To" the Person

It is tempting to "talk down to" a person who has an obvious disability. Be aware of your own behavior in this respect. Attempt to stimulate the student's intellect and not bore her or fill in communication silences with just anything. Finding out a student's needs, feelings, interests, and problems is an important skill. Too often, individuals who do not speak so others can understand find themselves answering questions over and over on the same topics: age, family, school, and pets. How dull and frustrating it must be to be denied the opportunity for variety and depth in conversations! Regardless of age, do the student a favor and allow her to try to experience higher levels of understanding and a greater variety of messages and information in the conversation.

Recognize Deadlocks

In conversations with students who do not speak clearly, partners often meet barriers. But partners can learn to recognize and correct barriers. In communication breakdowns, communication partners can use conversational repair strategies (Blackstone, Cassatt-James, & Bruskin, 1988). For example, the student may wish to say something, but a partner does not reflect the correct message. Sometimes the student may realize that a block has been reached over an unimportant topic and would rather drop the subject than waste time pursuing it. The opposite may also be true; the message is very important. The partner can help the speaker by saying "I'm really stuck. Do you want to go on trying?" Be certain the student does not feel pressured into changing topics. Partners should persist if the student indicates it is important to do so. If the conversation must be terminated before both partners are satisfied, they can keep the communication open by saying, "I have to leave, but I'll think about it. You think too, and maybe you'll find another way of telling me."

If communication partners try to ask questions that individuals do not wish to answer, a barrier is created. These questions might concern feelings, personal concerns, events the student is not ready to discuss, or topics that draw the conversation away from where the speaker wishes to go. Individuals have no way to say "I don't want to talk about that right now" or head the conversation in another direction. Ask, "Do you feel like going into this?"

Teach These Strategies to Other Communication Partners

Teachers and communication specialists should provide opportunities for persons to expand their conversational interactions to include new people both inside and outside of school. Signs and signals must be taught to others so that consistent procedures are used. It is advisable for parents to teach babysitters, family friends, relatives, and the neighborhood children. Teachers must teach schoolmates, classroom aides, and other teachers.

Responsibility for opening doors to communication does not lie only with communication partners. Individuals with communication disorders must learn to cue prospective communication partners, including those in the community at large. Nonspeaking students can learn to direct communication partners to the location of brief and easily accessible written cues for effecting satisfying communications for both parties.

From Teaching Students with Physical Disabilities *(3rd ed.) (pp. 231–244) by J. Bigge, 1991, Columbus, OH: Merrill. Adapted by permission.* ◆

■ CURRENT ISSUES/FUTURE TRENDS

The future will probably find specialists in communication disorders functioning even more indirectly than they do today. They will continue to work as professional team members, assisting teachers, parents, physicians, and other specialists in recognizing potential communication disorders and in facilitating communication skills. Inservice training will become an ever more important aspect of the specialist's responsibilities.

Changing Populations

Speech-language pathologists who work in schools are likely to find themselves working with an increasing percentage of children with severe and multiple disabilities who previously did not receive specialized services from communication disorders specialists. Caseloads are already growing in some school districts, along with financial restrictions that make it virtually impossible for all students with communication disorders to receive adequate services from the relatively few specialists who are employed. Even though all students with disabilities are supposed to receive all the special services they need, the schools' financial problems may necessitate difficult decisions at the local level. Some programs may choose to provide special services only to those students with the most severe speech and language impairments. Others may concentrate their professional resources on higher-functioning students who are considered to have the best potential for developing communication skills. Parents, advocates, and professional organizations will play an instrumental role in determining which children are to receive specialized speech and language services.

Paraprofessional personnel may, in the future, be more widely trained to work directly with children who have speech and language disorders, while professionals concentrate on diagnosis, prescriptive programming, evaluation, and the use of technology. Peer tutoring or therapy approaches using nonhandicapped students as language models are likely to become more prevalent. These approaches may allow more students to receive specialized help.

Currently, speech and language intervention programs are heavily oriented toward the preschool and school-age population. Though early detection and intervention will clearly remain a high priority among communication disorders specialists, there is a need for long-term studies to document the effectiveness of early intervention on later speech and language development. Professionals are also becoming increasingly aware of the special speech and language needs of adolescents and adults, many of whom have untreated communication problems. The future will likely see greater attention to the assessment and treatment of speech and language disorders caused by the aging process.

Technological Advancements

Advances in technology have already resulted in widespread use of computers and other assistive devices designed to help children with virtually every kind of speech and/or language disorder. Bull and Rushakoff (1987) report that about half of all professionals in speech and hearing currently use computers in their work. Some computers can be programmed with synthetic speech to enable previously nonspeaking children to express themselves by operating a keyboard or communication board. Other devices "understand" vocal commands. In addition, sophisticated software programs allow professionals to precisely analyze speech patterns and verbal language samples so that appropriate programs of intervention can be devised. And computers and electronic communication aids appear to have a positively reinforcing value for many students and may encourage them to communicate more effectively even when they are not using the aid directly. Applications of technology in the field of communication disorders are sure to continue.

SUMMARY

Communication, Language, and Speech

♦ Communication is any interaction that transmits information. Narrating, explaining, informing, and expressing are major communicative functions.

♦ A language is an arbitrary symbol system that enables a group of people to communicate; each language has rules of phonology, morphology, syntax, and semantics that describe how users put sounds together to convey meaning.

♦ Speech is the vocal response mode of language and the basis on which language develops.

♦ Normal language development follows a relatively predictable sequence. Most children learn to use language without direct instruction, and by the time most children enter first grade, their grammar and speech patterns match those of the adults around them.

Defining Communication Disorders

♦ A child has a speech disorder if his speech draws unfavorable attention to itself, interferes with the ability to communicate, or causes social or interpersonal problems.

♦ Some children have trouble understanding language (receptive language disorders); others have trouble using language to communicate (expressive language disorders); still other children have language delays.

♦ Speech or language differences based on cultural dialects should not be considered communication disorders; however, children with dialects may also have speech or language disorders.

Prevalence

♦ As many as 5% of school-age children may have speech impairments serious enough to warrant attention.

♦ Nearly twice as many boys as girls have speech impairments.

♦ Children with articulation problems represent the largest category of speech/language impairments.

Types and Causes of Communication Disorders

♦ Although some speech disorders have physical (organic) causes, most are functional disorders that cannot be directly attributed to physical conditions.

♦ Types of communication disorders include articulation, voice, fluency, and language disorders.

♦ The most common fluency disorder is stuttering.

Development of the Field of Communication Disorders

♦ Communication disorders have historically been considered less severe and have been less easily recognized than other disabilities.

♦ Regular public schools have recently expanded services to children with speech and language disorders.

♦ Speech is no longer a narrow specialty concerned with correcting isolated disorders; remedial procedures are often carried out in the regular classroom.

Assessment and Evaluation

♦ Assessment of a suspected communication disorder may include some or all of the following components:
Case history
Physical examination
Articulation test
Hearing test
Auditory discrimination test
Language development test
Overall language test
Conversation with the child or language sample
Behavioral observations of child's language competence in social contexts

Treatment and Remediation

♦ The different types of communication disorders call for different approaches to remediation; behavioral approaches are frequently used.

♦ Articulation disorders may be treated by one of four common models: the discrimination model, the phonological model, the sensorimotor model, or the operant conditioning model.

♦ Voice disorders can sometimes be treated medically or surgically if there is an organic cause, but the most common remediation is direct vocal rehabilitation.

♦ Treatment of fluency disorders emphasizes either symptom modification or fluency reinforcement.

♦ Language disorders are treated by either individual or group approaches.

♦ Augmentative communication may be necessary in severe situations.

♦ Most children with speech and language problems attend regular classes. The largest single group of communication disorders specialists are employed in schools.

Current Issues/Future Trends

♦ In the future, communication disorders specialists will probably provide largely consultative services and inservice training, rather than direct one-to-one therapy.

They will help train parents, teachers, and paraprofessionals to work with most children, while they concentrate on diagnosis, programming, and direct intensive services to a few children with special needs.

♦ Further service needs to be directed toward older youths and adults with untreated speech and language problems.

♦ Use of special devices to help individuals with communication disorders will expand. Electronic devices are now widely used to analyze children's speech and language and to provide instruction.

FOR MORE INFORMATION

Journals

Augmentative and Alternative Communication. Published by the International Society for Augmentative and Alternative Communication.

Communication Outlook. Emphasizes the use of augmentative communication techniques and technology. Published quarterly by Artificial Language Laboratory, Computer Science Department, Michigan State University, East Lansing, MI 48824.

Journal of Speech and Hearing Disorders. Published quarterly by the American Speech-Language-Hearing Association (ASHA). Includes articles dealing with the nature, assessment, and treatment of communication disorders.

Language, Speech, and Hearing Services in the Schools. Also published quarterly by ASHA; focuses on practical applications of speech and language training and provides activities for teachers and specialists consistent with current research and theory.

Books

Baumgart, D., Johnson, J., & Helmstetter, E. (1990). *Augmentative and alternative communication systems for persons with moderate and severe disabilities*. Baltimore, MD: Paul H. Brookes.

Blackstone, S. W. (Ed.). (1989). *Augmentative communication: Implementation strategies*. Rockville, MD: American Speech-Language-Hearing Association.

Cornett, B. S., & Chabon, S. S. (1988). *The clinical practice of speech-language pathology*. Columbus, OH: Merrill.

Costello, J. M., & Holland, A. L. (Eds.). (1986). *Handbook of speech and language disorders*. San Diego: College-Hill.

Creaghead, N. A., Newman, P. W., & Secord, W. (1989). *Assessment and remediation of articulatory and phonological disorders* (2nd ed.). Columbus, OH: Merrill.

Emerick, L. L., & Haynes, W. O. (1986). *Diagnosis and evaluation in speech pathology* (3rd ed.). Englewood Cliffs, NJ: Prentice-Hall.

Lindfors, J. W. (1987). *Children's language and learning* (2nd ed.). Englewood Cliffs, NJ: Prentice-Hall.

McCormick, L., & Schiefelbusch, R. L. (1990). *Early language intervention: An introduction* (2nd ed.). Columbus, OH: Merrill.

McLauchlin, R. M. (Ed.). (1986). *Speech-language pathology and audiology: Issues and management*. Orlando, FL: Grune & Stratton.

Reed, V. A. (1986). *An introduction to children with language disorders*. New York: Macmillan.

Shames, G. H., & Rubin, R. (1986). *Stuttering then and now*. Columbus, OH: Merrill.

Shames, G. H., & Wiig, E. H. (1990). *Human communication disorders* (3rd ed.). Columbus, OH: Merrill.

Stemple, J. C., & Holcomb, B. (1988). *Effective voice articulation*. Columbus, OH: Merrill.

Van Riper, C., & Emerick, L. L. (1984). *Speech correction: An introduction to speech pathology*. Englewood Cliffs, NJ: Prentice-Hall.

Organizations

American Speech-Language-Hearing Association, 10801 Rockville Pike, Rockville, MD 20852. The major professional organization concerned with speech and language. Serves as a certifying agency for professionals who provide speech, language, and hearing services. Publishes several journals, sponsors research in communication disorders, and provides a comprehensive Guide to Professional Services, which also includes information on accredited training programs. Also sponsors the National Student Speech, Language, Hearing Association, which has chapters on many college and university campuses.

Division for Children with Communication Disorders, Council for Exceptional Children, 1920 Association Drive, Reston, VA 22091. Includes teachers and communication disorders specialists who work with exceptional children. Sponsors sessions at state, provincial, and national conferences. Publishes the *Journal of Childhood Communication Disorders* twice yearly.

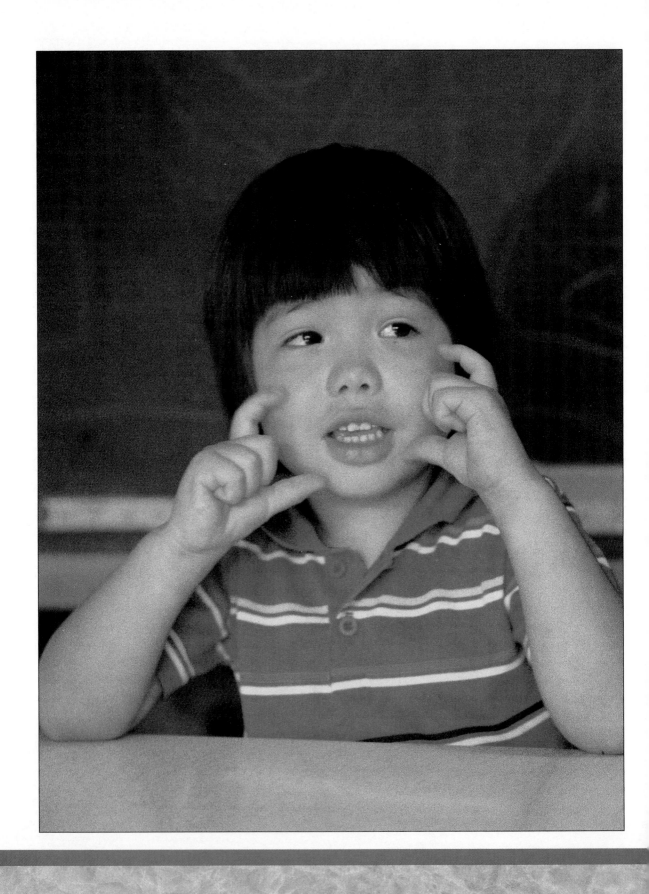

7
Hearing Impairment

♦ In what important ways do the child who is hard-of-hearing and the child who is deaf differ?

♦ Why can't reading simply replace hearing speech as a means of learning and understanding language?

♦ How do advocates of oral and total communication approaches to educating children who are deaf differ in philosophies and teaching methods?

♦ Why do you think American Sign Language (ASL) has not been a common component in education programs for children who are deaf?

♦ Is deafness a handicap in the deaf culture?

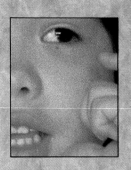

Nature attaches an overwhelming importance to hearing. As unborns we hear before we can see. Even in deep comas, people often hear what is going on around them. For most of us, when we die, the sense of hearing is the last to leave the body. (Walker 1986, p. 165)

As Lou Ann Walker, the child of deaf parents, observes in her autobiography, people who have normal hearing usually find it difficult to fully appreciate the enormous importance of the auditory sense in human development and learning. Many of us have simulated blindness by closing our eyes or donning a blindfold, but it is virtually impossible to switch off our hearing voluntarily.

From the moment of birth, children learn a great deal by using their hearing. Newborns are able to respond to sounds by startling or blinking. At a few weeks of age, infants with normal hearing can listen to quiet sounds, recognize their parents' voices, and pay attention to their own gurgling and cooing sounds. Within the first year of life, babies acquire much information by listening; they can discriminate meaningful sound from background noise and localize and imitate sounds (Lowell & Pollack, 1974).

As hearing children grow, they develop language by constantly hearing people talk and by associating these sounds with innumerable activities and events. They attach meaning to sound, quickly learning that people convey information and exchange their thoughts and feelings by speaking and hearing. By the time the typical hearing child enters school, she is likely to have a vocabulary of over 5,000 words. And she has already had perhaps 100 million meaningful contacts with language (Napierkowski, 1981).

As we saw in Chapter 6, the process of language acquisition and development, though complex, occurs naturally and spontaneously in most children. Most children with hearing impairments, however, are not able to participate in this process without special help. They may acquire a good deal of information about the world but have few symbols or patterns available to help them send and receive messages. They miss out on many early and critical opportunities for developing basic communication skills. Hans Furth (1973), a psychologist who devoted much of his career to studying the language development of hearing impaired people, suggests that a good way to approximate the experience of a child who is deaf from birth or early childhood is to watch a television program in which a foreign language is being spoken—with the sound on the TV set turned off! You would face the double problem of reading lips and understanding an unfamiliar language.

Hearing is vital to every aspect of our daily existence. If you were unable to hear, you would, at best, find it difficult to participate fully in the activities of your school or college, your job, your neighborhood, and even your own family unless some special adaptations were made. At worst, you might find that society's great reliance on speech and hearing as avenues of communication made it virtually impossible for you to function effectively.

Today, many children with impaired hearing are identified in early childhood. They are often helped to hear better through surgery or the use of hearing aids. They may learn to communicate with their families and friends by using speech, speechreading, sign language, or other techniques. Although many hearing impaired people achieve the highest levels of educational,

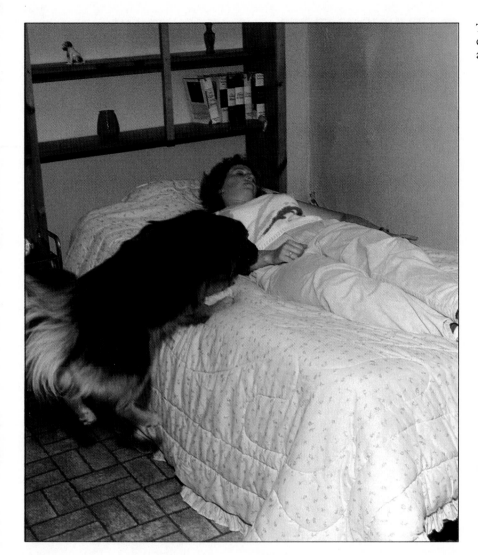

This woman's "hearing dog" wakes her when the alarm rings.

professional, and personal success, it is impossible to truly compensate for the loss of hearing. The information and understanding that come through the auditory channel can never be fully replaced.

As Paul and Quigley (1990) point out, however, the educational, vocational, and social development of a hearing impaired individual is influenced by many factors in addition to the type and degree of hearing loss. These include the age at which the hearing impairment began, the attitudes of the child's parents and siblings, the opportunities available for the child to develop oral and manual communication skills, and the presence or absence of other disabilities. A child's potential for learning can certainly not be predicted from the results of a hearing test alone.

■ DEFINITIONS, TYPES, AND MEASUREMENT

When we speak of a person with normal hearing, we generally mean that she has enough hearing to understand speech. Assuming that listening conditions are adequate, a person with normal hearing can interpret speech in everyday situations without relying on any special device or technique.

Deafness has been defined as a sensory deficiency that prevents a person from receiving the stimulus of sound in all or most of its forms (Katz, Mathis, & Merrill, 1978) and as a condition in which perceivable sounds (including speech) have no meaning for ordinary life purposes (Wolfe & Rawlings, 1986). A person who is *deaf* is not able to use his hearing to understand speech, although he may perceive some sounds. Even with a hearing aid, the hearing loss is too great to allow a deaf person to understand speech through the ears alone. A deaf person has a profound hearing impairment and is dependent on vision for language and communication, even with the use of amplification systems (Paul & Quigley, 1990).

A person who is **hard-of-hearing** has a significant hearing loss that makes some special adaptations necessary. As Berg (1986) points out, however, it is possible for a hard-of-hearing child to respond to speech and other auditory stimuli. "Communicatively, the hard-of-hearing child is more like the normal hearing child than like the deaf child, because both use audition rather than vision as the primary mode for speech and language development" (p. 3). In other words, the hard-of-hearing child's speech and language skills, though they may be delayed or deficient, are developed mainly through the auditory channel. Hard-of-hearing children are able to use their hearing to understand speech, generally with the help of a hearing aid.

Both deaf and hard-of-hearing children are said to be **hearing impaired**. This term, used mainly in education, indicates a child who needs special services because of a hearing loss. Most children in classes for the hearing impaired have some degree of **residual hearing**.

A hearing impairment may also be described in terms of age of onset. It is important to consider whether a hearing loss is **congenital** (present at birth) or **adventitious** (acquired later in life). The terms *prelinguistic hearing impairment* and *postlinguistic hearing impairment* refer to whether or not a hearing loss is sustained before or after the development of spoken language. A child who, from birth or soon after, is unable to hear the speech of other people will not learn speech and language spontaneously, as do children with normal hearing. A child who acquires a hearing impairment after speech and language are well established, usually after age 2, has educational needs very different from the prelinguistically hearing impaired child. The educational program of a prelingually deaf child usually focuses on acquisition of language and communication, whereas that of a postlingually deaf child usually emphasizes the maintenance of intelligible speech and appropriate language patterns.

When a hearing impairment goes undetected, some hard-of-hearing students are mistakenly thought to have learning disabilities or behavior disorders.

Even very slight levels of residual hearing can be useful.

How We Hear

How we hear is a complex and not completely understood process. The function of the ear is to gather sounds (acoustical energy) from the environment and transform that energy into a form (neural energy) that can be interpreted by the brain (Harris, 1986). Figure 7.1 shows the major parts of the human ear. The *outer ear* consists of the external ear and the auditory canal. The part of the ear we see, the **auricle**, functions to collect sound waves into the **auditory canal (external acoustic meatus)**. When sound waves enter the auditory canal, they are slightly amplified as they move toward the middle ear. Sounds enter the *middle ear* through the Eustachian tube, where they meet the **tympanic membrane (eardrum)**, which moves in and out in response to variations in sound pressure. These movements of the eardrum change the acoustical energy into mechanical energy, which is transferred to three tiny bones (the hammer, anvil, and stirrup). The base (called the footplate) of the third bone in the sequence, the stirrup, rests in an opening called the oval window, the path through which sound energy enters the inner ear. The vibrations of the three bones (together called the **ossicles**) transmit energy from the middle ear to the inner ear with little loss. The most critical and complex part of the entire hearing apparatus is the *inner ear,* which is covered by the temporal bone, the hardest bone in the entire body. The inner ear contains the **cochlea**, the main receptor organ for hearing, and the semicircular canals, which control the sense of balance. The cochlea, which resembles the shell of a snail, consists of two fluid-filled cavities. When energy is transmitted by the ossicles, the fluid in the cochlea moves. Tiny hairs within the cochlea change the motion of the fluid into neural impulses that are transmitted along the auditory nerve to the brain.

A person without external ears could still hear quite well, losing perhaps only 5 to 7 decibels in sound volume. The intensity or loudness of sound is measured in decibels (dB).

For more detailed discussions of the anatomy of the ear and the physiology of hearing see Davis (1978), Harris (1986), and/or Schneiderman (1984).

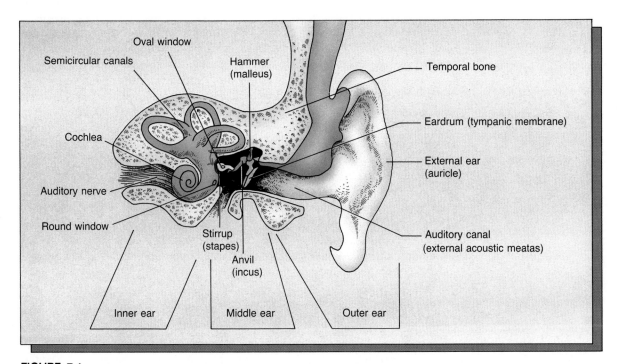

FIGURE 7.1

Parts of the human ear. The external part of the ear and the auditory canal make up the outer ear. The middle ear includes the eardrum, hammer, anvil, and stirrup. The inner ear includes the round window, the oval window, the semicircular canals, and the cochlea. Damage to any part can cause a hearing loss.

The Nature of Sound

Sound is measured in units that describe its intensity (measured in decibels [dB]) and frequency. Both are important in considering the needs of a child with impaired hearing. Zero dB represents the smallest sound a person with normal hearing can perceive. Larger dB numbers represent increasingly louder sounds. A low whisper 5 feet away registers about 10 dB, an automobile about 65 dB, and Niagara Falls about 90 dB. Conversational speech 10 to 20 feet away registers about 30 to 65 dB. A sound of about 125 dB or louder will cause pain to the average person. A person may have a loss of up to 25 dB (i.e., not be able to hear any sound of less than 25 dB) and still be considered to have hearing within the normal range (Davis & Silverman, 1970). The 25 dB level is often used in screening school children for hearing loss, although, as Berg (1986) warns, such one-shot tests may fail to identify a sizable percentage of hard-of-hearing children.

In addition to the dB loss, it is important to consider the listening environment. Northern and Lemme (1982) observe that speech needs to be only 10 to 15 dB louder than background noise for normally hearing adults to listen and understand comfortably. For children with impaired hearing, speech may need to be significantly louder than background noise for them to be able to attend to the message being transmitted.

The frequency, or pitch, of sounds is measured in cycles per second, or **hertz (Hz)**. One hertz equals one cycle per second. The lowest note on a piano has a frequency of about 30 Hz, middle C about 250 Hz, and the highest note about 4,000 Hz. Human beings are able to hear frequencies ranging from about 20 to 20,000 Hz (Davis & Silverman, 1970), but many of these audible sounds are outside the speech range, the frequency range where ordinary conversation takes place. A person who cannot hear very low sounds (such as a foghorn) or very high sounds (like a piccolo) may suffer some inconvenience but will not be handicapped in the classroom or everyday life. A person with a serious hearing loss in the speech range, however, is at a great disadvantage in communication.

The frequency range generally considered most important for hearing spoken language is 500 to 2,000 Hz. The sounds of English speech vary in their frequency level. For example, the /s/ phoneme (as in the word *sat*) is a high frequency sound, typically occurring between 4,000 and 8,000 Hz (Northern & Lemme, 1982). A child whose hearing loss is more severe at the higher frequencies will thus have particular difficulty in discriminating the /s/ sound. Conversely, phonemes such as /dj/ (the sound of the *j* in *jump*) and /m/ occur at low frequencies and will be more problematic for a person with a low-frequency hearing impairment. As you might expect, a student with a high-frequency impairment tends to hear men's voices more easily than women's voices.

Types of Hearing Impairment

The two main types of hearing impairments are conductive and sensorineural. A **conductive hearing loss** results from abnormalities or complications of the outer or middle ear. A buildup of excessive wax in the auditory canal can cause a conductive hearing loss, as can a disease that leaves fluid or debris. Some children are born with incomplete or malformed auditory canals. A hearing loss can also be caused if the eardrum or ossicles do not move properly. As its name implies, a conductive hearing impairment involves a problem with conducting, or transmitting, sound vibrations to the inner ear. Because the rest of the auditory system is generally intact, conductive hearing losses can often be corrected through surgical or medical treatment. Hearing aids are usually beneficial to persons with conductive impairments.

A **sensorineural hearing loss** refers to damage to the auditory nerve fibers or other sensitive mechanisms in the inner ear. The cochlea converts the physical characteristics of sound into corresponding neural information that the brain can process and interpret (Berg, 1986); impairment of the cochlea may mean that sound is delivered to the brain in a distorted fashion or is not delivered at all. Amplification—making the source of sound louder—may or may not help the person with a sensorineural hearing impairment. Unfortunately, most sensorineural hearing impairments cannot be corrected by surgery or medication. The combination of both conductive and sensorineural impairments is called a *mixed hearing loss*.

Hearing impairment is also described in terms of being *unilateral* (present in one ear only) or *bilateral* (present in both ears). Most children in special programs for the hearing impaired have bilateral losses, although the degree of impairment may not be the same in both ears. Children with unilateral hearing impairments generally learn speech and language without major difficulties, although they tend to have problems localizing sounds and listening in noisy or distracting settings. There is some evidence, however, that children with unilateral hearing impairments may be at a disadvantage in acquiring certain academic skills (Keller & Bundy, 1980).

■ IDENTIFICATION AND ASSESSMENT

The earlier a hearing impairment is identified, the better a child's chances are for receiving treatment and thus developing good communication ability, which is essential for learning both academic and social skills. If a child's hearing impairment goes unnoticed until the age of 5 or 6—when children usually enter school—countless opportunities for learning will surely have been lost.

Despite modern audiological techniques, hearing impairment still goes undetected in many children. All infants, hearing and deaf alike, babble, coo, and smile. Later on, deaf children tend to stop babbling and vocalizing because they cannot hear themselves or their parents, but a baby's silence may be mistakenly attributed to other causes. Unfortunately, many hearing impaired children have been erroneously labeled mentally retarded or emotionally disturbed. Some have even spent years inappropriately placed in institutions because nobody realized their problem was deafness rather than mental retardation or emotional disturbance. To avoid such misplacements in the future, efforts are continually made to conduct screening tests for hearing impairment and to educate doctors, teachers, and parents to recognize the signs of hearing loss in children. Table 7.1 offers a guide to auditory behaviors that should be present in infants with normal hearing. Failure to demonstrate these responses may mean that an infant's hearing is impaired.

TABLE 7.1
Expected auditory behaviors.

In determining whether an infant has a hearing impairment, it is helpful for parents and teachers to have a knowledge of the normal sequence of auditory development. Audiologist Linda Cleeland has provided the following guide to behaviors that may be expected at certain ages. if a young child is not displaying these behaviors, it is advisable to have the child's hearing professionally tested.

1 Month
- will jump or startle in response to loud noises
- will begin to make gurgling sounds

3 Months
- will make babbling sounds
- will be aware of voices
- may quiet down to familiar voices close to ear
- stirs or awakens from sleep when there is a loud sound relatively close

6 Months
- makes vocal sounds when alone
- turns head toward sounds out of sight or when name is called and speaker is not visible
- vocalizes when spoken to directly

9 Months
- responds differently to a cheerful versus angry voice

- turns head toward sounds out of sight or when name is called and speaker is not visible
- tries to copy the speech sounds of others

12 Months
- can locate a sound source by turning head (whether the sound is at the side, above, or below ear level)
- ceases activity when parent's voice is heard
- recognizes own name
- uses single words correctly
- vocalizes emotions
- laughs spontaneously
- disturbed by nearby noises when sleeping
- attempts imitation of sounds and words
- understands some familiar phrases or words
- responds to music or singing
- increases babbling in type and amount

24 Months
- has more than 50 words in vocabulary
- uses two words together
- responds to rhythm of music
- uses voice for a specific purpose
- shows understanding of many phrases used daily in life
- plays with sound-making objects
- uses well-inflected vocalizations
- refers to himself/herself by name

Source: From "The Function of the Auditory System in Speech and Language Development," by L. K. Cleeland, 1984, *The Hearing-Impaired Child in School,* pp. 15–16 by R. K. Hull and K. I. Dilka (Eds.). Orlando, FL: Grune & Stratton. Reprinted by permission.

Audiometry

The science of **audiology** has made many advances in recent years. The development of sophisticated instruments and techniques has enabled audiologists to detect and describe hearing impairments with increasing precision. Most instruments used to test hearing now incorporate computers into their design (Kelly, 1987).

An **audiologist** specializes in the evaluation of hearing ability and the treatment of impaired hearing.

Audiometric Assessment

Hearing is formally assessed by a testing procedure called *pure-tone audiometry*. The examiner uses an **audiometer**, an electronic device that generates sounds at different levels of intensity and frequency. The child, who receives the sound either through earphones (air conduction) or through a bone vibrator (bone conduction), is instructed to hold up a finger when he hears a sound and to lower it when he hears no sound. The test seeks to determine how loud sounds at various frequencies must be before the child is able to hear them. Most audiometers deliver tones in 5 dB increments from 0 to 120 dB, with each dB level presented in various frequencies usually starting at 125 Hz and increasing in octave intervals (doubling in frequency) to 8,000 Hz. The results of the test are plotted on a chart called an **audiogram**.

To obtain a hearing level on an audiogram, the child must be able to detect a sound at that level at least 50% of the time. A child with a hearing impairment does not begin to detect sounds until a high level of loudness is reached. For example, a child who has a 60 dB hearing loss cannot begin to detect a sound until it is at least 60 dB loud, in contrast to a child with normal hearing, who would detect that same sound at a level between 0 and 10 dB.

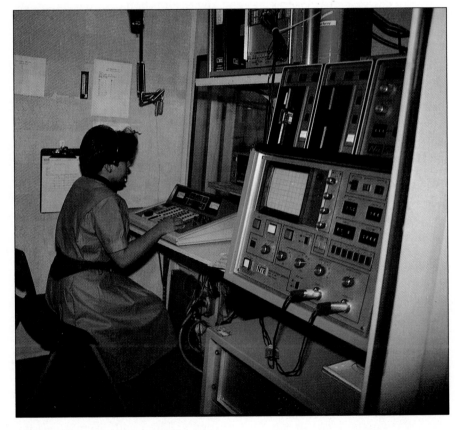

An audiometer generates tones of precise intensity and frequency.

Alternative Techniques

Alternative audiometric techniques have been developed to identify and measure hearing loss in infants and individuals who are not able to understand and follow conventional audiometry procedures (e.g., a child with severe mental retardation) (Roeser & Yellin, 1987). In **operant conditioning audiometry**, the child is reinforced with a token or small candy when he pushes a lever in the presence of a light paired with a sound. No reinforcer is given for pushing the lever when the light and sound are off. Next, the sound is presented without the light. If the child pushes the lever in response to the sound alone, the examiner knows the child can hear that sound. The intensity and frequency of the sound is then varied to determine which levels of sound the child can hear (Lloyd, Spradlin, & Reid, 1968). **Behavior observation audiometry** is a passive assessment procedure in which the child is not conditioned to make a specific response. Instead, the child's reactions to sounds are observed. A sound is presented at an increasing level of intensity until a response, such as head turning, eye blinking, or cessation of play, is reliably observed.

Two other techniques rely on physiological reactions to assess hearing. **Evoked-response audiometry** uses electrodes to sense slight electric signals that the auditory nerve generates in response to sound stimulation. Thus, the audiologist can detect hearing impairments in infants or in others who may not respond to conventional testing, because a voluntary response is not required. **Impedance audiometry** tests a child's middle ear function by inserting a small probe and pump to detect sound reflected by the eardrum. It is especially useful in detecting middle ear problems that can result in temporary or permanent conductive hearing loss (MacCarthy & Connell, 1984).

Degrees of Hearing Impairment

An individual's hearing impairment is usually described by the terms *slight, mild, moderate, severe,* and *profound,* depending on the average hearing level, in decibels, throughout the frequencies most important for understanding speech (500 to 2,000 Hz). Table 7.2 lists the decibel levels associated with these degrees of hearing impairment, some likely effects of each level of hearing impairment on children's speech and language development, and some considerations for educational programs.

No two children have exactly the same pattern of hearing, even if their responses on a hearing test are similar. Just as a single intelligence test cannot provide sufficient information to plan a child's educational program, a hearing impaired child's needs cannot be determined from an audiometric test alone. Success in communication and school achievement cannot be predicted simply by looking at an audiogram. Children hear sounds with differing degrees of clarity, and the same child's hearing ability may vary from day to day. Some children with very low levels of measurable hearing are able to benefit from hearing aids and can learn to speak. On the other hand, some children with less apparent hearing loss are not able to function well through the auditory channel and must rely on vision as their primary means of communication.

The level of hearing loss required for children to be considered deaf for educational placement purposes has changed considerably over the past decades (Connor, 1986). In the 1960s, many children with average hearing losses of 50, 60, or 70 dB were routinely enrolled in special schools and classes for deaf children. Today, however, those children are regarded as hard-of-hearing rather than deaf, thanks to improved methods of testing, amplification, and teaching. According to Connor (1986), "Only children with losses greater than 90 dB who had prelingual losses should be considered deaf in the mid-1980s" (p. 124).

Mild Loss

Figure 7.2 shows the audiogram of Vicki, a child with a *mild* hearing impairment. Vicki is able to understand face-to-face conversation with little difficulty but misses much of the discussion that goes on in her classroom—particularly if several children are speaking at once or if she cannot see the speaker clearly. Many of her friends are unaware that she has a hearing impairment. Vicki benefits from wearing a hearing aid and receives occasional speech and language assistance from a speech-language pathologist.

Moderate Loss

Figure 7.3 shows the audiogram of Raymond, a child with a *moderate* hearing impairment. Without his hearing aid, Raymond can hear conversation only if it is loud and clear. He finds male voices easier to hear than female voices, because his loss is less pronounced in the lower frequencies. Raymond's teacher attempts to arrange favorable seating for him, but most class discussions are impossible for him to follow. Raymond attends a part-time special class for hearing impaired children and is in a regular classroom for part of the day.

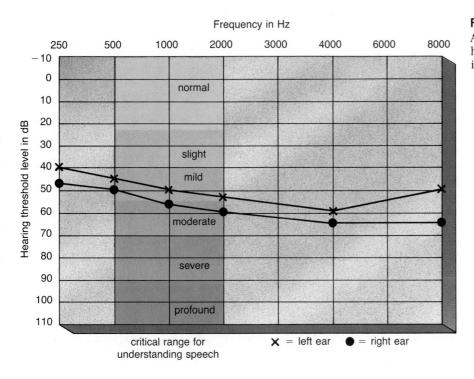

FIGURE 7.2
Audiogram for Vicki, who has a mild hearing impairment.

TABLE 7.2

Effects of different degrees
of hearing impairment.

Faintest Sound Heard	Effects on the Understanding of Language and Speech	Probable Educational Needs and Programs
27 to 40 dB (slight loss)	◆ May have difficulty hearing faint or distant speech ◆ Will not usually have difficulty in school situations	◆ May benefit from a hearing aid as loss approaches 40 dB ◆ Attention to vocabulary development ◆ Needs favorable seating and lighting ◆ May need speechreading instruction ◆ May need speech correction
41 to 55 dB (mild loss)	◆ Understands conversational speech at a distance of 3 to 5 feet (face to face) ◆ May miss as much as 50% of class discussions if voices are faint or not in line of vision ◆ May have limited vocabulary and speech irregularities	◆ Should be referred to special education for educational follow-up ◆ May benefit from individual hearing aid through evaluation and training in its use ◆ Favorable seating and possible special class placement, especially for primary-age children ◆ Attention to vocabulary and reading ◆ May need speechreading instruction ◆ Speech conservation and correction, if indicated
56 to 70 dB (moderate loss)	◆ Can understand loud conversation only ◆ Will have increasing difficulty with school group discussions ◆ Is likely to have impaired speech ◆ Is likely to have difficulty in language use and comprehension ◆ Probably will have limited vocabulary	◆ Likely to need resource teacher or special class ◆ Should have special help in language skills, vocabulary development, usage, reading, writing, grammar, etc. ◆ Can benefit from individual hearing aid through evaluation and auditory training ◆ Speechreading instruction ◆ Speech conservation and speech correction

Severe Loss

Figure 7.4 shows the audiogram of Brenda, a child with a *severe* hearing impairment. Brenda can hear voices only if they are very loud and 1 foot or less from her ear. She wears a hearing aid, but it is uncertain how much she is

TABLE 7.2
continued

Faintest Sound Heard	Effects on the Understanding of Language and Speech	Probable Educational Needs and Programs
71 to 90 dB (severe loss)	◆ May hear loud voices about 1 foot from the ear ◆ May be able to identify environmental sounds ◆ May be able to discriminate vowels but not all consonants ◆ Speech and language likely to be impaired or to deteriorate ◆ Speech and language unlikely to develop spontaneously if loss is present before 1 year of age	◆ Likely to need a special education program for hearing impaired children, with emphasis on all language skills, concept development, speechreading, and speech ◆ Needs specialized program supervision and comprehensive supporting services ◆ Can benefit from individual hearing aid through evaluation ◆ Auditory training on individual and group aids ◆ Part-time regular class placement as profitable
91 dB or more (profound loss)	◆ May hear some loud sounds but senses vibrations more than tonal pattern ◆ Relies on vision rather than hearing as primary avenue for communication ◆ Speech and language likely to be impaired or to deteriorate ◆ Speech and language unlikely to develop spontaneously if loss is prelingual	◆ Will need a special education program for children who are deaf, with emphasis on all language skills, concept development, speechreading, and speech ◆ Needs specialized program supervision and comprehensive supporting services ◆ Continuous appraisal of needs in regard to oral or manual communication ◆ Auditory training on individual and group aids ◆ Part-time regular class placement may be feasible

gaining from it. She can distinguish most vowel sounds, but hears only a few consonants. She can hear a door slamming, a vacuum cleaner, and an airplane flying overhead. She must always pay close visual attention to a person speaking with her. Brenda attends a full-time special class for hearing impaired children

FIGURE 7.3
Audiogram for Raymond, who has a moderate hearing impairment.

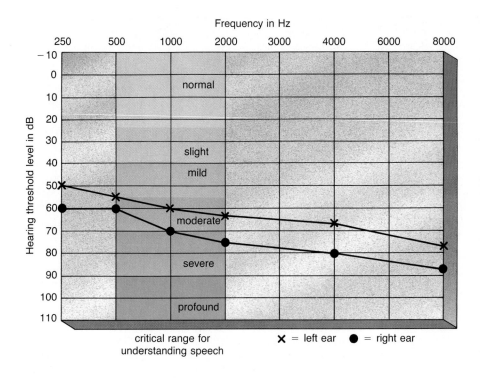

FIGURE 7.4
Audiogram for Brenda, who has a severe hearing impairment.

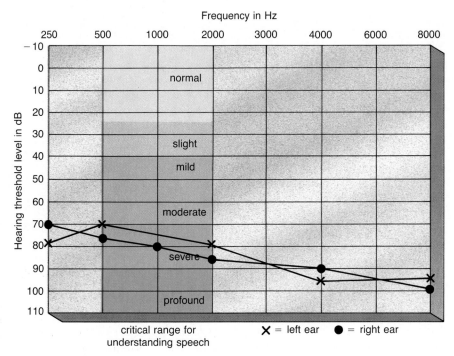

in a regular public school and interacts with nonhandicapped children in several activities.

Profound Loss

Figure 7.5 shows the audiogram for Steve, a child with a *profound* hearing impairment. Steve cannot hear conversational speech at all. His hearing aid seems to help him be aware of certain loud sounds, such as a fire alarm or a bass drum. Steve's hearing impairment is congenital, and he has not developed intelligible speech. He attends a residential school for children who are deaf and uses sign language as his principal means of communication.

■ EFFECTS OF HEARING IMPAIRMENT

The effects of hearing impairment—especially a prelinguistic loss of 90 dB or greater—are complex and pervasive. It is perhaps impossible for a person with normal hearing to fully comprehend the immense difficulties a deaf child faces trying to learn language. Hearing children typically acquire a large vocabulary and a knowledge of grammar, word order, idiomatic expressions, fine shades of meaning, and many other aspects of verbal expression by listening to others and to themselves from early infancy. A child with a hearing impairment, however, is exposed to verbal communication only partially or not at all.

Language Skills

Hearing impaired children—even those with superior intelligence and abilities—are at a great disadvantage in acquiring language skills. As Norris (1975) points out, the grammar and structure of English often do not follow logical

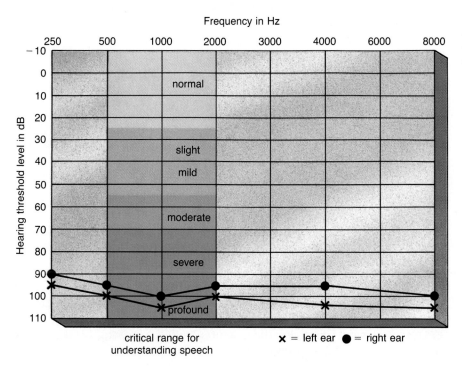

FIGURE 7.5

Audiogram for Steve, who has a profound hearing impairment.

rules, and a prelingually hearing impaired person must exert a great deal of effort to read and write with acceptable form and meaning. For example, if the past tense of *talk* is *talked,* then why doesn't *go* become *goed?* If the plural of *man* is *men,* then shouldn't the plural of *pan* be *pen?* It is far from easy to explain the difference between the expressions "He's beat" (tired) and "He was beaten" to a person who has never had normal hearing.

When standard measures of reading and writing achievement are used with deaf students, examiners typically find that the students' vocabularies are smaller and their sentence structures are simpler and more rigid than those of hearing children of the same age or grade level (Meadow, 1980). Many deaf students tend to write sentences that are short, incomplete, or improperly arranged. They may omit endings of words, such as the plural *-s, -ed,* or *-ing.* They may have difficulty in differentiating questions from statements. The following excerpts from papers written by deaf high school students illustrate some language problems directly attributable to impaired hearing.

> She is good at sewing than she is at cooking.
> Many things find in Arkansas.
> To his disappointed, his wife disgusted of what he made.
> I was happy to kiss my parents because they letted my playing football. (Fusfeld, 1958, cited in Meadow, 1980, p. 33)

Academic Performance

Not counting the obvious effects of the amount, type, and quality of instruction, five variables appear to be most closely related to the academic achievement of hearing impaired students (Moores, 1985; Paul & Quigley, 1990).

1. *The severity of the hearing impairment.* The greater the hearing loss, the more likely the child will experience difficulty in learning language and academic skills. Even a slight hearing impairment, however, has been shown to have adverse effects on academic achievement (Paul & Quigley, 1987).

2. *The age at the onset of the hearing loss.* A child who loses his hearing before acquiring speech and language (usually before age 2) is at a much greater disadvantage than a child with a postlingual hearing impairment.

3. *Intelligence.* As with hearing children, higher scores on standardized tests of intelligence are correlated with greater amounts of academic success.

4. *The socioeconomic status of the family.* A hearing impaired child whose parents are affluent and college educated is more likely to achieve academic success than a child from a low-income, less-educated family.

5. *The hearing status of the parents.* A deaf child with deaf parents is considered to have better chances for academic success than a deaf child with normally hearing parents—particularly if the deaf parents are highly educated.

Studies assessing the academic achievement of hearing impaired students have routinely found them to lag far behind their hearing peers. Several national surveys of hearing impaired students' academic achievement have been carried out and reported by the Center for Assessment and Demographic Studies (CADS) at Gallaudet University. The first three studies (involving 12,000, 17,000, and 7,000 students respectively) used a version of the Standford Achievement

Test adapted for students with hearing impairment (DiFrancesca, 1972; Gentile & DiFrancesca, 1969; Trybus & Karchmer, 1977). The results were essentially the same: Students with severe and profound hearing impairments (i.e., students who were deaf) were reading at about a fourth grade level or lower, and mathematics performance was around the fifth grade. Growth in reading achievement was between 0.2 and 0.3 grade levels per year of schooling. The most recent CADS survey repeated the findings of the earlier studies (Allen, 1986). For the oldest group of students (16 to 18 years), the median grade level for reading comprehension ranged from 2.9 to 3.2; for arithmetic computation, it ranged from 7.0 to 7.5.

One must always use caution, however, in comparing the test scores of deaf and hearing children. Geers (1985) notes that the relatively poor performance of deaf children, especially on tests normed on hearing children, has led teachers to expect too little of these children. For many deaf children, "it is more informative to define their strengths and weaknesses in relation to other hearing impaired children than in relation to their age mates with normal hearing" (Geers, 1985, p. 57). Several educators have warned that achievement tests, including the adapted version of the SAT, measure a severely or profoundly hearing impaired student's competence with the English language rather than his overall academic achievement (Moores, 1987; Quigley & Paul, 1986).

We must not, however, equate academic performance with intelligence. Most deaf children have normal intellectual capacity, and it has been repeatedly demonstrated that their scores on nonverbal intelligence tests are approximately the same as those of the general population. Deafness "imposes no limitations on the cognitive capabilities of individuals" (Moores, 1987). The problems that deaf students often experience in education and adjustment may be largely attributable to a bad fit between their perceptual abilities and the demands of spoken and written English (Hoemann & Briga, 1981). Command of English is only one indicator of a person's intelligence and ability.

Social and Psychological Factors

Impaired hearing can also influence a child's behavior and social-emotional development. Research has not provided clear insights into the effects of hearing impairment on behavior; however, it appears that the extent to which a hearing impaired child successfully interacts with family members, friends, and people in the community depends largely on others' attitudes and the child's ability to communicate in some mutually acceptable way. Deaf children of deaf parents are thought to have higher levels of social maturity, adjustment to deafness, and behavioral self-control than do deaf children of hearing parents, largely because of the early use of manual communication between parent and child that is typical in homes with deaf parents. In the opinion of Schlesinger (1985) and other psychologists, "Most deaf parents welcome their deaf children and are not rendered powerless or helpless by them" (p. 108).

Hearing impaired persons frequently express feelings of depression, withdrawal, and isolation, particularly those who experience adventitious loss of hearing (Meadow-Orlans, 1985). A study of more than 1,000 deaf adolescents who were considered disruptive in the classroom (Kluwin, 1985) found that the most frequently related factor was reading ability; that is, students who were poorer readers were more likely to exhibit problem behaviors in school. A number of deaf children do have serious behavior disorders that require treatment; unfortunately, relatively few specialists in the identification and treatment of behavior disorders are able to communicate easily and directly with deaf people, so the special needs of this population remain largely unmet.

Some observers have noted that deaf people often tend to associate primarily with other deaf people; this may be mistakenly viewed as clannishness. Certainly, communication plays a major role in anyone's adjustment. Most hearing impaired people are fully capable of developing positive relationships with their hearing peers when a satisfactory method of communication can be used.

Generalizations about how people who are deaf are supposed to act and feel should be viewed with extreme caution. Lane (1988), for example, makes a strong case against the existence of the so-called "psychology of the deaf." He shows the similarity of the traits attributed to deaf people in the professional literature to traits attributed to African people in the literature of colonialism and suggests that those traits do not "reflect the characteristics of deaf people but the paternalistic posture of the hearing experts making these attributions" (p. 8). In addition, he argues that the scientific literature on the "psychology of the deaf" is flawed in terms of test administration, test language, test scoring, test content and norms, and its description of subject populations, arguments that have been noted by other researchers as well (Moores, 1987; Paul & Quigley, 1990).

■ PREVALENCE

About 20 million Americans experience some difficulty in receiving and processing aural communication. It is estimated that about 1% of the general population are severely to profoundly hearing impaired. The incidence of hearing impairment in adults increases with age; Stein (1988) estimates that almost 40% of persons over 75 years old experience some limitations in hearing.

Like other disabilities, estimates of incidence and prevalence of hearing impairment within the school-age population vary considerably. Stein (1988) states that less than 2% of children from birth through age 14 have impaired hearing, yet other authorities have concluded that approximately 5% of all school-age children have hearing impairments (Bensberg & Sigelman, 1976; Davis & Silverman, 1970). Many of these impairments, however, are not considered severe enough to require special education services. Hoemann and Briga (1981) estimate that only about 0.2% of the school-age population (i.e., 1 child in 500) have a severe or profound hearing impairment. A 1986 report estimated that there were 129,000 school-age children in the United States who could "at best hear and understand shouted speech" and included among these 22,000 who "could not hear and understand any speech" (Ries, 1986, p. 8). Males, black students, and children aged 6 to 11 were found to be somewhat overrepresented in the hearing impaired group in comparison to their proportions in the general population.

The U.S. Department of Education (1990) reports that during the 1988–89 school year 52,783 students, or 1.4% of all students age 6 to 21 who received special education services, were served under the handicapping category of

I AM NOT DISABLED, I'M JUST DEAF

Jesse Thomas was 15 years old when he presented testimony before the National Council on Disabilities. He explained his views on the use of American Sign Language and mainstreaming. Excerpts from his testimony follow:

I think I have to explain that I am not disabled, I'm just deaf. Deaf persons are a minority group. They use American Sign Language (ASL) and are part of the Deaf Culture. One of the main reasons that mainstreaming is not good is because mainstreaming lacks Deaf Culture and ASL. I can't really explain Deaf Culture. I do know that Deaf Culture makes me proud of who I am—DEAF.

Here are reasons why I think Deaf schools should be favored over the mainstream:

♦ Learning through an interpreter is very hard. It is pretty tiring for me to keep my eyes on one "place" all day long. After watching an interpreter all morning, I find myself not paying attention in the afternoon. Also, with an interpreter, a deaf person cannot communicate with a hearing person normally, and, anyway, an interpreter is not always there. There is always SOME work or something you have to communicate with a hearing person in a hearing school ALWAYS. Not to mention, it's difficult to watch a filmstrip or a movie while watching an interpreter at the same time.

♦ It is bad socially in the mainstream situation. I communicate in SIGN, and my peers in my hearing school SPEAK.

♦ You are ALWAYS outnumbered. There are basically 25 kids in my classes—all hearing but me. That's a ratio of 25:1!

♦ You don't feel like it's YOUR school; it's like you're along for the ride. I was in one school for sixth grade and got to know some kids, and the junior high was in another town, and I knew nobody there.

♦ You never know deaf adults. Once in a while, there is one who is deaf but thinks hearing, not a deaf person proud to be deaf.

♦ You don't belong. There are still a lot of people whose faces show sympathy at the word "deaf" and gasp at the thought of a world devoid of hearing. Those people think, "My God, deaf people CAN'T HEAR, there must be something terribly astray with them!" So they don't respect deaf people and think they are inferior.

♦ You don't feel comfortable as a deaf person. I will explain.

I don't think there should be such a thing as "overcoming deafness." This implies that a person should push being deaf aside and be more hearing. That is absolutely ridiculous. Don't you think that a person should be what he is? I am deaf; I will succeed as a deaf person.

I've experienced BOTH kinds of social and educational situations, mainstream and deaf school, and I'll have to say that I favor deaf schools over mainstreaming. In deaf schools, the social situation and education is much more normal for deaf people than in hearing schools.

Jesse is now in his sophomore year at the Model Secondary School for the Deaf at Gallaudet University. He is a member of the wrestling team, assistant editor-in-chief of the school newspaper, and plans to participate in the drama program this spring.

From "Not Disabled—Just Deaf," 1991, Let's Talk, 33,(2), p. 30. *Published by the American Speech-Language-Hearing Association. Reprinted by permission.* ♦

hard of hearing and deaf. Of the students with hearing impairment receiving special education services, 90% are prelinguistically hearing impaired (Commission on Education of the Deaf, 1988).

For every child identified as deaf, there are probably six or seven children who are hard of hearing and who may need certain special education services. Surveys suggest that although over 90% of the children in the United States identified as deaf are receiving special services, the percentage of hard-of-hearing children receiving special services may be only 20% or less (Berg, 1986; Moores, 1987). It is likely, then, that a significant number of hearing impaired students in regular classes may not be receiving the special assistance they need for effective learning and adjustment. One educator describes the hard-of-hearing child as "the most neglected exceptional child in our public day school system other than the gifted" (Gonzales, 1980, p. 20).

■ CAUSES OF HEARING IMPAIRMENT

The causes of hearing impairment are usually classified as to whether they are **exogenous** or **endogenous**. Exogenous causes stem from factors outside the body (such as disease, toxicity, or injury) and reduce the auditory system's ability to receive and transmit sounds. Endogenous hearing impairments are inherited from the parents' genes. Although several hundred causes of hearing impairment have been identified, for about 30% of hearing impaired children, the exact cause is listed as "unknown" (Moores, 1987).

According to S. C. Brown (1986), four prevalent causes of deafness and severe hearing impairment in children warrant special attention.

1. *Maternal rubella.* Although rubella (also known as German measles) has relatively mild symptoms, it has been shown to cause deafness, visual impairment, heart disorders, and a variety of other serious disabilities in the developing child when it affects a pregnant woman, particularly during the first trimester. A major epidemic of rubella that took place in the United States and Canada between 1963 and 1965 accounted for more than 50% of the hearing impaired students in special education programs in the 1970s and 1980s. Maternal rubella continues to be a significant cause of hearing impairment. An effective vaccination for rubella is available, and all women of childbearing age should receive it.

2. *Heredity.* With the exception of periods of rubella epidemics, the leading cause of deafness is genetic factors (Vernon, 1987). There is strong evidence that congenital hearing impairment runs in some families. A tendency toward certain types of adventitious hearing loss may also be inherited. Even though 90% of deaf children are born to hearing parents, various surveys have found that a high percentage of deaf students have relatives who are also hearing impaired; Moores (1987) places this number at about 30% of the school-age population of deaf students. More than 200 types of hereditary or genetic deafness have been identified.

3. *Prematurity and complications of pregnancy.* These factors appear to increase the risk of deafness and other disabling conditions. It is difficult to precisely evaluate the effects of prematurity on hearing impairment, but early delivery and lower birth weight have been found to be more common among deaf children than among the general population. Complications of pregnancy arise from a variety of causes.

4. *Meningitis.* The leading cause of adventitious hearing impairment is **meningitis**. It is a bacterial or viral infection that can, among its other effects, destroy the sensitive acoustic apparatus of the inner ear. Difficulties in balance may also be present. Brown (1986) reports that children whose deafness is caused by meningitis generally have profound hearing losses but are not likely to have additional handicapping conditions.

Another significant cause of hearing impairment is **otitis media,** an infection or inflammation of the middle ear. If untreated, otitis media can result in a buildup of fluid and a ruptured eardrum, causing permanent conductive hearing impairment.

Causes of hearing impairment that appear to have declined in recent years because of improved medical treatment include blood (Rh) incompatibility between mother and child, mumps, and measles. On the other hand, the percentages of students with deafness caused by meningitis, heredity, and otitis media appear to be increasing. In addition, some factors related to people's environments and activities are regarded as growing causes of hearing loss. Noise pollution—repeated exposure to loud sounds, such as industrial noise, jet aircraft, guns, or amplified music—is increasing as a cause of hearing impairment. Damage to hearing can also result from frequent deep-sea diving; Edmonds (1985) found that more than 70% of professional divers had evidence of sensorineural high-frequency deafness.

Hearing impairment occurs more often than would be expected among certain other populations of handicapped children. Down syndrome often involves irregularities in the auditory canal and a tendency for fluid to accumulate in the middle ear; as many as 75% of children with Down syndrome may also have significant hearing impairments (Northern & Lemme, 1982). Among children with cerebral palsy, there is also a substantially higher-than-normal incidence of hearing impairment. It is always advisable to test the hearing of any child who is referred for special education services.

See Chapter 10 for more information on children with multiple handicaps.

■ BACKGROUND OF THE FIELD

Deaf children and adults have long been a source of fascination and interest. In the late 16th century, one of the first educational programs for exceptional children of any kind—a school for the deaf children of noble families—was established in Spain by Pedro Ponce de Leon (1520–1584), an Augustinian monk and scholar. At that time, for children to be recognized as persons under the law—and therefore eligible to inherit their families' titles and fortunes—it was necessary for them to be able to speak and read. Ponce de Leon reportedly achieved success in teaching speech, writing, reading, arithmetic, and foreign languages to some of his deaf students (Hewett & Forness, 1977; Sacks, 1986). During the 18th century, schools for deaf children were set up in England, France, Germany, Holland, and Scotland. Both oral and manual methods of instruction were used.

Nineteenth Century Opportunities in the United States

Deaf children were among the first groups of individuals with disabilities to receive special education in the United States, also. The American Asylum for the Education of the Deaf and Dumb opened in Hartford, Connecticut, in 1817. The original name of this institution indicates the prevailing philosophy of the early 19th century, when persons who were deaf were viewed as incapable of benefiting from oral instruction. At that time, deaf students were considered most appropriately served in asylums, special sanctuaries removed from normal society. Many of the private, public, and parochial schools for deaf students

This school, now more than 170 years old, is known today as the American School for the Deaf.

founded in the 19th century were, in fact, located in small towns, away from major centers of population. For the most part, these were residential institutions.

During the second half of the 19th century, instruction in speech and speechreading became widely available to deaf students throughout the United States. In fact, oral approaches to educating hearing impaired students came to dominate professional thought to such a great degree that the use of sign language in schools was officially prohibited at an international conference held in 1880. A particularly influential figure during this era was Alexander Graham Bell, the inventor of the telephone, who had a lifelong interest in deafness.

His mother was deaf, and his father and grandfather were teachers of speech and articulation. Bell himself married Mabel Hubbard, a deaf student whom he had tutored. Before the end of the 19th century, several day schools for deaf students were established. In general, however, the late 19th century brought about an "increasing isolation of deaf children from their families and from society at large" (Moores & Kluwin, 1986, p. 106). And it was not until many years later that most schools relaxed their restrictions against the use of sign language.

Recent Educational Opportunities

Educational opportunities for deaf children in regular public schools have only recently become widespread. In most areas of the United States, in accordance with the least-restrictive-environment concept, parents now have the option of choosing between local public school programs and residential school placement. Today, more than 60% of the deaf children in the United States attend local school programs, and many of these children are integrated into regular classrooms at least part of the time (Moores, 1987; Quigley & Paul, 1986). About one-third of the children who attend residential schools do so as day students (Schildroth, 1986); that is, they live at home with their families while attending the special school program.

Today, increasing attention is given to the needs of hearing impaired students with additional disabilities such as mental retardation, learning disabilities, behavior disorders, and physical, health, and visual impairments. Around 30% of the children currently enrolled in schools and classes for hearing impaired students are considered to be multihandicapped (Orlansky, 1986b; Schildroth, 1986). Many programs also seek to meet the needs of the sizable population of hearing impaired children from culturally diverse backgrounds. The challenge of teaching English communication skills to a deaf child when a language other than English is spoken in the home is particularly complex.

Over the years, many special methods and materials have been developed for and used with hearing impaired children, and much research has been conducted. Techniques, theories, and controversies have proliferated, often with passionate proponents. Yet we still do not fully understand the effects of hearing impairment on learning, communication, and personality, nor have we solved the most difficult problem inherent in educating deaf students: *teaching spoken language to children who cannot hear.*

Decibels are named for Alexander Graham Bell.

Chapter 12 contains further information about children from bilingual backgrounds.

The present state of special education for hearing impaired children is not a happy one. Many deaf students leave school unable to read and write English proficiently. According to Paul and Quigley (1990):

> No general improvement in achievement in most students who are severely to profoundly hearing-impaired has been observed since the . . . early years of the 20th century. The average student completing a secondary education program is still reading and writing at a level commensurate with the average 9- to 10-year-old hearing student. Achievement in mathematics is about one or two grades higher. Since the beginning of formal achievement testing, two enduring patterns above been reported: *low levels* and *small gains* in achievement despite 12 to 13 years of education. (p. 227)

Many deaf students are not able to communicate effectively, sometimes not even with normal-hearing schoolmates or members of their own families. Parents are often given confusing, contradictory information and advice when it is discovered their child has a hearing impairment; identification of a deaf child is often devastating for parents. The rate of unemployment and underemployment among deaf adults is shockingly high, and their wages are often lower than those of the hearing population.

In response to these problems Congress established the Commission on Education of the Deaf with the Education of the Deaf Act of 1986. After studying the field, the Commission began its report to Congress with these words:

> The present state of education for persons who are deaf in the United States is unsatisfactory. Unacceptably so. This is the primary and inescapable conclusion of the Commission on Education of the Deaf. (1988, p. viii)

The Commission went on to make 52 recommendations for improving the education of students with hearing impairments. Many questions remain unanswered, and many challenges remain in educating children with hearing impairments.

■ AMPLIFICATION AND AUDITORY TRAINING/LEARNING

Deafness is often mistaken to be a total lack of hearing. In years past, it was assumed that individuals who were deaf simply did not hear at all, that they were "stone deaf." This view was incorrect. Hearing loss occurs in many different degrees and patterns. Nearly all children who are deaf have some amount of residual hearing. With help, they need not grow up in a "silent world."

Modern methods of testing hearing and improved electronic technology for the amplification of sound enable many hearing impaired children today to use their residual hearing productively. Even children with severe and profound hearing impairments can benefit from hearing aids in the classroom, home, and community, regardless of whether they communicate primarily in an oral or manual mode. Ross (1986) considers residual hearing to be the "biologic birthright" of every hearing impaired child, one that "should be used and depended on to whatever extent possible" (p. 51). It is important for teachers and audiologists to cooperate with each other in reaching this goal.

Amplification Instruments

A hearing aid is an amplification instrument; that is, it functions to make sounds louder. Levitt (1985) describes the hearing aid as "the most widely used technological aid of all. . . . a low cost, acoustic amplification system that can be programmed to best match the needs of each user" (pp. 120–121). There are dozens of different kinds of hearing aids; they can be worn behind the ear, in the ear, on the body, or in eyeglasses. Children can wear hearing aids in one or both ears (monaural or binaural aids). Today's hearing aids are generally smaller and lighter than older models, yet they are also more powerful and versatile. Whatever its shape, power, or size, a hearing aid picks up sound, magnifies its energy, and delivers this louder sound to the user's ear and brain. In many ways, the hearing aid is like a miniature public address system, with a microphone, an amplifier, and controls to adjust volume and tone (Clarke & Leslie, 1980). One study found that the academic performance of students with hearing impairments was positively correlated with the length of time they had worn their hearing aids (Blair, Peterson, & Viehweg, 1985).

Hearing aids can be helpful to many children in increasing their awareness of sound. The aids make sounds louder, but not necessarily clearer. Thus, children who hear sounds with distortion will still experience distortion with hearing aids. The effect is similar to turning up the volume on an old transistor radio—you can make the music louder, but you cannot make the words clearer. And even the most powerful hearing aids generally cannot enable children with severe and profound hearing losses to hear speech sounds beyond a distance of a few feet. No hearing aid can cure a hearing loss or by itself enable a deaf child to function normally in a regular classroom. In all cases, it is the wearer of the hearing aid, not the aid itself, that does most of the work in interpreting conversation.

Teachers should check daily to see that a child's hearing aid is functioning properly. The Ling Five Sound Test is a quick and easy way to determine whether or not a child can detect the basic speech sounds (Ling, 1976). With the child's back to the teacher (to ensure that visual clues do not confound the results), the child repeats each of five sounds spoken by the teacher: /a/, /oo/, /e/, /sh/, and /s/. Ling states that these five sounds are representative of the speech energy in every English phoneme, and a child who can detect these five sounds should be able to detect every English speech sound. Absent or abnormal hearing aid function should be checked immediately; most breakdowns are due to problems with the battery.

Financial assistance from local or state agencies is often available for the purchase and maintenance of hearing aids.

The earlier in life a child can be fitted with an appropriate hearing aid, the more effectively she will learn to use hearing for communication and awareness. Today it is not at all unusual to see hearing aids on infants and preschool children; the improved listening conditions become an important part of the young child's speech and language development. A worthwhile goal is to provide for a child a sense of hearing that is "integrated into the personality" (Lowell & Pollack, 1974). To derive the maximum benefit from a hearing aid, a child should wear it throughout the day. Residual hearing cannot be effectively developed if the aid is removed or turned off outside the classroom. It is important for the child to hear sounds while eating breakfast, shopping in the supermarket, and riding the school bus.

In the classroom, problems of distance, room reverberation, and background noise often interfere with a student's ability to discriminate the desired auditory signal with a personal hearing aid (Berg, 1986). When the signal-to-noise ratio is poor, the hearing impaired child may find the auditory signal audible but not "intelligible" (Boothroyd, 1978). Group assistive listening devices can solve the problems of distance, noise, and reverberation in the classroom. They do not replace the child's personal hearing aid, but augment it in group listening situations (Zelski & Zelski, 1985). In most systems, a radio link is established between the teacher and the hearing impaired children, with the teacher wearing a small microphone-transmitter (often on the lapel, near the lips) and each child wearing a receiver that doubles as a personal hearing aid (Ross, 1986). An FM radio frequency is usually employed, and wires are not required, so teacher and students can move freely around the classroom area. The FM device creates a listening situation comparable to the teacher's "being only 6 inches away from the child's ear at all times" (Ireland, Wray, & Flexer, 1988, p. 17). Classroom amplification systems are used in both special classes and mainstream settings where hearing impaired students are integrated with nonhandicapped students.

Auditory Learning

Auditory training/learning programs help children make better use of residual hearing. All hearing impaired children, regardless of whether their preferred method of communication is oral (speech) or manual (signs), should participate in lessons and activities that help them improve their listening ability. Many hearing impaired children have much more auditory potential than they actually use, and their residual hearing can be most effectively developed in the context of actual communication and daily experiences (Ross, 1981). An auditory training program should not be limited to artificial exercises in the classroom.

A traditional **auditory training** program for a young hearing impaired child begins by teaching awareness of sound. Parents might direct the child's attention to such sounds as a doorbell ringing or water running. They might then focus on localization of sound; for example, by hiding a radio somewhere in the room and encouraging the child to look for it. Discrimination of sounds is another important part of auditory training; a child might learn to notice the differences between a man's voice and a woman's voice, between a fast song and a slow song, or between the words *rack* and *rug*. Identification of sounds comes when a child is able to recognize a sound, word, or sentence through listening.

Teachers should help parents recognize and take advantage of the many opportunities for auditory training/learning around the house.

The focus today is on *auditory learning,* that is, teaching the child to "learn to listen" and "learn by listening," instead of simply "learning to hear" (Ling, 1986). Advocates of auditory learning contend that the first three levels of auditory training—detecting, discriminating, and identifying sounds—are important but insufficient for developing the student's residual hearing. Auditory learning emphasizes a fourth and highest level of listening skills—the comprehension of meaningful sounds.

Some teachers find it helpful to conduct formal auditory training/learning sessions, in which a child is required to use only hearing—he would have to recognize sounds and words without looking at the speaker. In actual practice, however, the student gains useful information from vision and the other senses to supplement the information received from hearing. Consequently, all senses should be effectively developed and constantly used.

Speechreading

Speechreading is the process of understanding a spoken message by observing the speaker's face. Hearing impaired children, whether they have much or little residual hearing and whether they communicate primarily through oral or manual means, use their vision to help them understand speech. Some sounds are readily distinguished by watching the speaker's lips. For example, the word *pail* begins with the lips in a shut position, whereas the lips are somewhat drawn together and puckered at the corners for the word *rail*. Paying careful attention to a speaker's lips may help a hearing impaired person derive important clues—particularly if she is also able to gain some information through residual hearing, signs or gestures, facial expressions, and familiarity with the context or situation.

Speechreading is difficult and has many limitations. About half of all English words have some other word(s) that appear the same in pronunciation; that is, they may sound quite different, but they look alike on the lips. Words such as *bat, mat,* and *pat,* for example, look exactly alike and simply cannot be discriminated by watching the speaker's lips. To complicate matters, the visible sounds may be blocked by a hand or pencil, chewing gum, or a mustache. Many speakers are virtually unintelligible through speechreading; they may seem not to move their lips at all. In addition, it is extremely tiring to watch lips for a long time, and it may be impossible to do so at a distance, such as during a lecture.

Walker (1986) estimates that even the best speechreaders detect only about 25% of what is said through visual clues alone; "the rest is contextual piecing together of ideas and expected constructions" (p. 19). The average deaf child might accurately speechread only about 5% of what is said (Vernon & Koh, 1970).

The frustrations of speechreading are graphically described in this passage by Shanny Mow (1973), a teacher who is deaf.

> Like the whorls on his fingertips, each person's lips are different and move in a peculiar way of their own. When young, you build confidence as you guess correctly "ball," "fish," and "shoe" on your teacher's lips. This confidence doesn't last. As soon as you discover there are more than four words in the dictionary, it evaporates. Seventy percent of the words when appearing on the lips are no more than blurs. Lipreading is a precarious and cruel art which rewards a few who have mastered it and tortures the many who have tried and failed. (pp. 21–22)

Despite the problems inherent in speechreading, it can be a valuable adjunct in the communication of a hearing impaired person. According to Moores (1987), few new techniques have been developed recently, and little research has been done into the most effective ways of teaching speechreading. Although speechreading cannot take the place of hearing, improved methods might well enable many hearing impaired people to make better use of their vision in decoding messages.

Speechreading was traditionally called *lipreading,* but understanding speech from visual clues involves more than simply looking at the lips.

The September 1988 issue of *Volta Review* contains several articles on speechreading.

Manual signs, speechreading, and facial expressions all contribute to effective communication.

▪ EDUCATIONAL APPROACHES

Teaching hearing impaired children is one of the most "special" areas of special education.

> Special education has been defined as that education which is unique, uncommon, or of unusual quality and is in addition to the procedures used with the majority of children. The special techniques that have been developed over the years to assist deaf children in processing information without the sense of hearing are certainly unique, ingenious, and highly specialized. (Kirk, 1982, p. xi)

Educational programs and techniques for hearing impaired students are special primarily because of the many challenges involved in teaching communication to children who cannot hear normally. Educators, scientists, philosophers, and parents—both hearing and deaf—have for many years debated the most appropriate instructional methods for deaf children. Today, this controversy is as lively as ever.

The fundamental disagreement concerns the extent to which deaf children should express themselves through speech and perceive the communication of others through speechreading and residual hearing. Some educators insist that

TIPS FOR FACILITATING COMMUNICATION

People with hearing impairments are increasingly participating in community life. It is no longer unusual for a businessperson, bank teller, student, police officer, or anyone else to have the opportunity to communicate with a person who is deaf. Yet many people with normal hearing are still unsure of themselves. As a result, they may avoid deaf people altogether or use ineffective and frustrating strategies when they do attempt to communicate.

The following tips for facilitating communication with deaf people were suggested by the Community Services for the Deaf program in Akron, Ohio. These tips provide basic information about three common ways that deaf persons communicate: through speechreading, with sign language or the assistance of an interpreter, and by written communication. Usually a deaf person will indicate the approach she is most comfortable with. If the deaf person relies mainly on speechreading (lipreading), here are things you can do to help.

- Face the deaf person and stand or sit no more than 4 feet away.
- The room should have adequate illumination—but don't seat yourself in front of a strong or glaring light.
- Try to keep your whole face visible.
- Speak clearly and naturally, and not too fast.
- Don't exaggerate your mouth movements.
- Don't raise the level of your voice.
- Some words are more easily read on the lips than others. If you are having a problem being understood, try substituting different words.
- It may take a while to become used to the deaf person's speech. If at first you can't understand what he is saying, don't give up.
- Don't hesitate to write any important words that are missed.

a purely oral method is best for helping deaf students develop speech and language-related skills. These oralists often discourage the use of sign language and gestures. Other educators believe that sign language, gestures, cues, fingerspelling, and other manual means used along with speech are a more natural way of communicating and enable hearing impaired children to express themselves and to understand other people more fully.

Virtually no responsible educator today would argue that speech is unimportant or that manual communication should be used in place of speech. Speech is, of course, the principal way that people communicate; it can be of great value to a deaf person in moving into mainstream educational and living environments. We view the controversy over instructional methods as a difference of opinion over the degree to which speech should be emphasized in the education of hearing impaired children.

If the deaf person communicates best through sign language (and you do not), it will probably be necessary to use an interpreter. Here are some considerations to keep in mind.

♦ The role of the interpreter is to facilitate communication between you and the deaf person. The interpreter should not be asked to give opinions, advice, or personal feelings.

♦ Maintain eye contact with the deaf person and speak directly to her. The deaf person should not be made to take a back seat in the conversation. For example, say "How are you today?" instead of "Ask her how she is today."

♦ Remain face-to-face with the deaf person. The best place for the interpreter is behind you and a little to the side of you. Again, avoid strong or glaring light.

♦ Remember, it is the interpreter's job to communicate *everything* that you and the deaf person say. Don't say anything that you don't want interpreted.

Written messages can be helpful in exchanging information. Consider the following:

♦ Avoid the temptation to abbreviate your communication.

♦ Write in simple, direct language.

♦ The deaf person's written English may not be grammatically correct, but you will probably be able to understand it. One deaf person, for example, wrote "Pay off yesterday, finish me" to convey the message "I paid that loan off yesterday."

♦ Use visual aids, such as pictures, diagrams, and business cards.

♦ Don't be afraid to supplement your written messages with gestures and facial expressions.

♦ Written communication has limitations—but it is often more effective than no communication at all.

Remember that English is not the first language of many deaf people. They are deprived of a great deal of information because they cannot hear. Skills of spoken and written English are not an accurate reflection of a deaf person's intelligence or ability to function independently. ♦

Oral Approaches

Educational programs with an oral emphasis view speech as essential for the deaf person's integration into the hearing world. Training in producing and understanding speech and language is incorporated into virtually all aspects of the child's education. Currently, about one-third of the educational programs for hearing impaired children in the United States use a predominantly oral approach (Reagan, 1985). Connor (1986) observes that the use of speech and the development of oral receptive skills have declined markedly in recent years as more and more educational programs for hearing impaired students rely on sign language systems to transmit instructional information.

A hearing impaired child who attends a program with an oral emphasis typically uses several means to develop residual hearing and the ability to speak as intelligibly as possible. Auditory, visual, and tactual methods of input are frequently used. Much attention is given to amplification, auditory training, speechreading, the use of technological aids, and—above all—talking. Oral education tends to emphasize parent and family involvement. A few schools and classes maintain a purely oral environment and may even prohibit children from pointing, using gestures, or spelling out words to communicate. The children in these programs must express themselves and learn to understand others through speech alone. Other programs also emphasize speech, but are more flexible. They may use a variety of approaches to help students produce and understand spoken language.

Cued Speech

Cued speech is a method of supplementing oral communication. It seeks to supply a visual representation of spoken language by adding cues, in the form of hand signals near the chin, to assist the deaf person in identifying sounds that cannot be distinguished through speechreading. The hand signals must be used in conjunction with speech; they are neither signs nor manual alphabet letters and cannot be read alone. Eight different hand shapes are used to identify consonant sounds, and four different locations identify vowel sounds. A hand shape coupled with a location gives a visual indication of a syllable. See Figure 7.6 for a representation of cued speech.

According to Cornett (1974), who developed the system, cued speech can clarify the patterns of spoken English and give intensive language input to young children. It does not disrupt the natural rhythm of speech. Of course, the child's parents and teachers and preferably her peers as well must learn the cues. Reportedly, cued speech can be learned in 10 to 20 hours of instruction. Although it is advocated by a number of active parent groups, the system has not

This student is using auditory, visual, and tactual stimuli to develop his oral language skills.

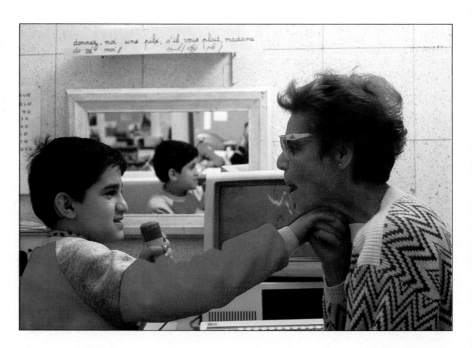

become highly popular in the United States (Calvert, 1986). Cued speech is widely used in educational programs for hearing impaired children in Australia.

Benefits of Oral Approaches

Educators who use an oral approach acknowledge that teaching speech to hearing impaired children is difficult, demanding, and time-consuming for the teacher, the parents, and—most of all—the student. Speech comes hard to the deaf child, and no recent development has made the task any easier.

> [T]here has been neither a clear record of steady improvement in teaching methods nor significant breakthroughs that have either markedly reduced the level of effort or significantly increased the quality of the result for 400 years. (Calvert, 1986, p. 167).

The rewards of successful oral communication, however, are thought to be worth all the effort. And indeed, most students with hearing losses no worse

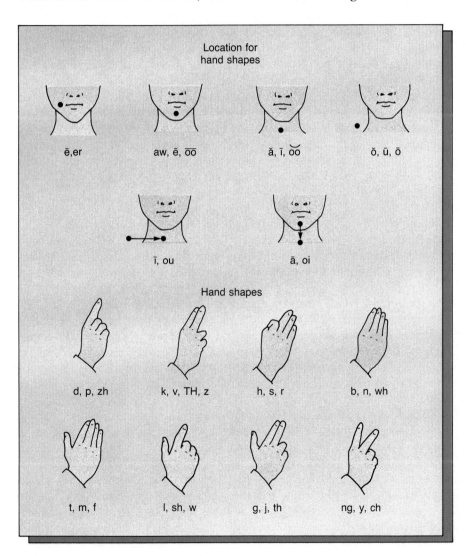

FIGURE 7.6
Hand shapes and locations used in cued speech.

than severe can learn speech well enough to communicate effectively with hearing people. Paul and Quigley (1990) point out that the best results are obtained with hearing impaired students who are enrolled in indisputably comprehensive oral programs or who are integrated most of the school day into regular education programs. They note also that most students with severe hearing impairments who develop good speech represent a select group of deaf students: They typically have above-average IQs, have parents who are highly involved in their education, and come from above-average socioeconomic status families (Geers & Moog, 1989).

Total Communication

Roy Holcomb, a deaf graduate of the Texas School for the Deaf and Gallaudet University, coined the term and is credited as the father of total communication (Gannon, 1981).

Educational programs with an emphasis on **total communication** advocate the use of a variety of forms of communication to teach language to hearing impaired students. Practitioners of total communication maintain that simultaneous presentation of manual communication (by fingerspelling and signs) and speech (through speechreading and residual hearing) makes it possible for children to use either one or both types of communication (Ling, 1984). Since its introduction as a teaching philosophy in the 1960s, total communication is now "the predominant method of instruction in schools for the deaf" (Luterman, 1986, p. 263). According to a recent survey (Wolk & Schildroth, 1986), the percentage of deaf students who both speak and sign (62.2%) is far greater than that who only speak (21.1%) or who only sign (16.7%). The communication method used may depend on the setting: Even though many hearing impaired students use sign language in their classes, they are less likely to do so outside school, because signs are not usually understood by the general public.

Sign Language

Sign language uses gestures to represent words, ideas, and concepts. Some signs are *iconic;* that is, they convey meaning through handshapes or motions that look like or appear to imitate or act out their message. In making the *cat* sign, for example, the signer seems to be stroking feline whiskers on his face; in the sign for *eat,* the hand moves back and forth into an open mouth (Figure 7.7). Most signs, however, have little or no *iconicity;* they do not resemble the objects or actions they represent. If sign language were simply a form of pantomime, then most nonsigners would be able to understand it with relatively little effort. But several studies have shown that the majority of signs cannot be guessed by people who are unfamiliar with that particular sign language (Klima & Bellugi, 1979).

Teachers who practice total communication generally speak as they sign and make a special effort to follow the form and structure of spoken English as closely as possible. Several sign language systems have been designed primarily for educational purposes, with the intention of facilitating the development of reading, writing, and other language skills in hearing impaired students. Manually Coded English is the term applied to several educationally oriented sign systems, such as Seeing Essential English (Anthony, 1971), Signing Exact English (Gustason, Pfetzing, & Zawolkow, 1980), and Signed English (Bornstein, 1974). These sign systems incorporate many features of American Sign

FIGURE 7.7
Signs for *cat* (above) and
eat (below).

Language, while also seeking to follow correct English usage and word order. Hearing impaired students often must use two or more sign language systems, depending on the person with whom they are communicating.

Fingerspelling

Fingerspelling (dactylology) is often used in conjunction with other methods of communication. Fingerspelling, or the manual alphabet, consists of 26 distinct

Rodney is learning the sign for "interpret."

hand positions, one for each English letter. A one-hand manual alphabet is used in the United States and Canada (Figure 7.8). Some manual letters—such as *C, L,* and *W*—resemble the shape of printed English letters, whereas others—such as *A, E,* and *S*—have no apparent similarity. As in typewriting, each word is spelled out letter by letter.

A user of sign language relies on fingerspelling to spell out proper names for which no sign exists and to clarify meanings. The Rochester Method uses a combination of oral communication and fingerspelling, but does not use sign language. The teacher fingerspells every letter of every word as she speaks, and the hearing impaired student learns to use the same means of expression. The Rochester Method also emphasizes reading and writing; its advocates believe that this approach facilitates the acquisition of correct language patterns.

Supporters of total communication methods believe that this approach is the best way to provide a "reliable receptive-expressive symbol system," especially in the preschool years when communication between parent and child is vitally important (Denton, 1972). Several researchers have found that children as young as 5 months of age are able to produce and understand signs effectively (e.g., Maestas y Moores & Moores, 1980; Orlansky & Bonvillian, 1985; Prinz & Prinz, 1979).

Although there is no firm evidence that deaf children's use of sign language inhibits acquisition of speech (Moores, 1987; Rooney, 1982; Sacks, 1986), some

Fingerspelling is also used by many people who are both deaf and visually impaired; the manual alphabet can be used at close distances or felt with the hand if a person is totally blind.

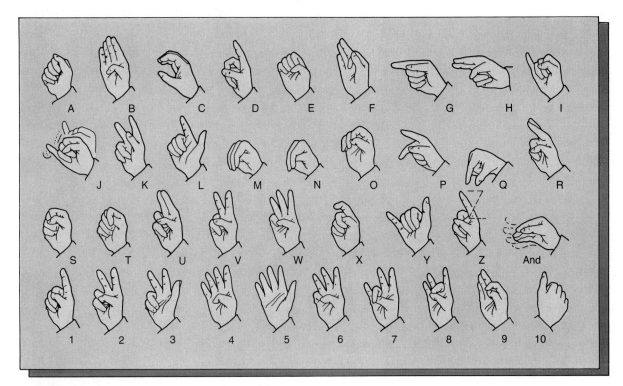

FIGURE 7.8
The manual alphabet.

specialists contend that it is difficult for hearing impaired children to process signs and speech when they are presented together. "Even for experts it is not easy to combine signs and speech effectively," writes Daniel Ling (1984, p. 11), noting that they are usually produced at different rates of speed. In Ling's view, the simultaneous use of signs and speech is likely to impair the quality of speech, signs, and/or language. It may be better, he suggests, for children to learn oral and manual skills separately, rather than at the same time.

Total communication has gained wide acceptance in educational programs for hearing impaired students. Signs were used in educational programs with over 75% of severely and profoundly hearing impaired students by the late 1980s (Gallaudet Research Institute, 1985). Luterman (1986), however, regards the effects of the movement toward total communication as unproven. Many educators consider total communication to have facilitated parent-child and teacher-child communication and to have enhanced children's self-esteem, but these supposed gains cannot be easily documented. Luterman (1986) further observes that "total communication has not made any substantial changes in the depressingly low academic achievement of deaf children" (p. 263).

American Sign Language (ASL)

American Sign Language (often referred to as ASL or Ameslan) is the language of the deaf culture in the United States and Canada. Although the sign languages used by native deaf speakers were once thought to be nonlanguages

Total communication requires the simultaneous use of signs and speech..

(alinguistic), psychologists, linguists, and educators now generally view ASL as a complex and legitimate language in its own right, rather than an imperfect variation of spoken English. ASL is a visual-gestural language with its own rules of syntax, semantics, and pragmatics (Wilbur, 1987). In ASL the shape, location, and movement pattern of the hands, the intensity of motions, and the signer's facial expressions all communicate meaning and content. As Paul and Quigley (1990) point out,

> ASL is particularly structured to accommodate the eye and motor capabilities of the body. The grammatical structure of ASL is spatially based. Space and movement play important linguistic roles. (p. 128)

Because ASL has its own vocabulary, syntax, and grammatical rules, it does not correspond exactly to spoken or written English. Articles, prepositions, tenses, plurals, and the word order may be expressed differently from those of standard English. It is difficult to make precise word-for-word translations between ASL and English, just as it is difficult to translate many foreign languages into English word for word.

Most deaf children do not learn ASL at home; only about 12% of deaf children have deaf parents (Reagan, 1985). It is often passed from children to other children (usually in residential schools), rather than the more common pattern of parents to children. ASL is seldom used within a total communication program. Although the manual communication that total communication teachers use often borrows individual signs from ASL, those signs are presented according to English syntax, resulting in a kind of "Pidgin Sign English."

Lane (1988) views hearing educators' insistence on imposing a manual form of English on deaf students as another sign of the ethnocentrism and paternalism often displayed by the hearing establishment toward students who are deaf.

> This ethnocentric misunderstanding about the nature and status of sign language leads teachers to "fix up" the children's "arbitrary gestures" to make them more like English. New signs are invented by hearing people for English function words and suffixes that have no place, of course, in American Sign Language, and the grammatical order of the signs is scrambled in an attempt to duplicate English word order. No deaf child has ever learned such a system as a native language and indeed could not, for it violates the principles of the manual-visual channel of communication. No deaf adult uses such ways of communicating. But the system is widely used in classrooms with the claim that it assists the deaf child in learning English. (p. 10)

Many members of the deaf community and some educators are calling for recognition of ASL as the deaf child's first language. They believe that English might be better learned in the context of a bilingual education approach after the child has mastered his native or first language (ASL). Among this group are Paul and Quigley (1990), who criticize the current use of various forms of manually coded English in total communication programs because (1) the codes have been contrived by a small group of persons; (2) they are not widely used outside a specific educational environment; (3) practitioners often use signs from various systems, so it is difficult for hearing impaired students to form reliable hypotheses about the rules of English; and (4) after more than 15 years of use, there is little evidence of improvements in deaf students' English literacy or academic achievement.

Language Instruction

Numerous techniques and materials have been developed to help hearing impaired children acquire and use written language. The relationship between written and spoken expression is obviously close, but there is no exact correspondence between the type of communication method a child uses (oral-only or total communication) and the method of language instruction that a particular school or class employs.

Instructional programs in language for hearing impaired students are generally classified as either structured or natural. Advocates of a structured approach believe that hearing impaired students do not acquire English naturally—they must learn the language by analyzing and categorizing its grammatical rules and relationships. A well-known structured method, developed over 60 years ago but still widely used, is the Fitzgerald Key (Fitzgerald, 1929). This method provides several labeled categories, such as who, what, where, and when. The child learns to generate correct sentences by placing words into the proper categories.

Proponents of the natural approach believe that if students are exposed to a language-rich environment, they will naturally discover the rules and principles of English. Neither grammar nor parts of speech, for example, are taught directly. An example of a natural method is Natural Language for Deaf Children (Groht, 1958). This method emphasizes language development

TEACHING IDIOMS TO CHILDREN WHO ARE DEAF

The English language is replete with idiomatic expressions and other figurative language (e.g., metaphors such as *screaming headlines*). An idiom is an idiosyncrasy of language that transgresses either the laws of grammar or the laws of logic. An idiomatic expression provides a meaning not implied by the *actual* meanings of the words that make up the expression (Boatner & Gates, 1966). Everyday conversations flow with idioms; perhaps as many as four per minute are uttered in free discourse (Pollio, Barlow, Fine, & Pollio, 1977). Instructional materials also contain many idiomatic expressions; Arter (1976) found about 10 instances of nonliteral language per 1,000 words in a sample of a fifth and sixth grade reading series.

Children with severe hearing impairments, who already have difficulty learning basic language skills, face an especially hard task in understanding the many idiomatic expressions of English (Conley, 1976; Payne & Quigley, 1987). For a child who is deaf, the meaning of an idiomatic expression becomes blurred or confusing as he tries to decipher it in terms of what each individual word is understood to mean. A more limited vocabulary, more restricted world experiences, difficulty in handling certain complex syntactic structures, and unfamiliarity with certain topics combine to make the comprehension of idioms extremely difficult for the child who is deaf (Iran-Nejad, Ortony, & Rittenhouse, 1981). Unknowingly, parents and teachers may also play a role in the deaf child's difficulty with idioms. In their efforts to converse as unambiguously as possible, adults provide deaf children with little or no practice with idiomatic expressions and other figurative language (Sanders, 1983). Consequently, teachers should make every effort to teach figurative language to deaf children.

When Kathleen Arnold, an undergraduate special education student at the University of Milwaukee, conducted her student teaching practicum with a class of deaf children, she set out to improve the students' comprehension of idioms. The teaching plan Ms. Arnold implemented provided students with many opportunities to practice and receive reinforcement and feedback. Her method for teaching idioms consists of five parts:

1. *Introduce the idiom.* The idiom to be taught can be printed on a poster board or on the blackboard, signed, and/or spoken to the class. The teacher should require each student to repeat the idiom to check on the correct pronunciation or signs.
2. *Provide examples of proper usage.* Using word phrases or short stories, the teacher gives the children as many examples as possible for each idiom. Repetition promotes retention.
3. *Have students give back examples.* To develop their understanding of the idiom, ask students to provide their own examples (e.g. "When were you fit as a fiddle?"). If they cannot come up with any examples of their own in the beginning, the teacher can give the students some personal examples. Modeling additional examples will help students think of yet other examples. Another way to check comprehension of the correct meaning of the idiom is to ask negative questions, such as "Last week Tim had chickenpox. Was he fit as a fiddle?"
4. *Use a poster board with questions.* Each idiom is presented on a poster board (an overhead projector would work equally well) with two types of sentences. The first sentence asks what the idiom means, with five examples; the second sentence asks the students five different versions of: "Are you _____ if _____ ?" Each student is required to answer "Yes" or "No" to each example.

5. *Students answer "Yes" or "No" worksheets.* The final step in instruction of idioms is a worksheet with 8 to 10 questions. It is best not to give the worksheet on the same day as the idiom has been taught with the first four steps. The worksheets give students follow-up practice.

Teaching idioms can be fun, but it requires lesson plans that are organized and prepared in advance. The key seems to be reinforcement of idiomatic expressions at every possible opportunity. Teachers should strive to use the idioms that have been taught as often as they can while teaching other subjects and skills to demonstrate that language forms are generalized outside of specific situations. It is only through exposure and use that children who are deaf will gain more understanding of idioms and other figurative language. (See Manning and Wray [1990] for additional ideas on teaching figurative language to exceptional children.)

Following are examples of how two idioms can be organized for teaching using Arnold's method.

Under the Weather

"Under the weather" means

♦ You are not feeling well.

♦ You are not doing great.

♦ You have a headache.

♦ You are tired.

♦ You have a cold and a fever.

How to Use the Idiom in a Sentence

1. Jill was invited to go skating today, but she was feeling tired and had a sore throat. She was feeling "under the weather."
2. I decided not to go because I was feeling "under the weather."
3. I feel "under the weather" today. I think I may be getting a cold.
4. She looked "under the weather" when we saw her at the store.

Posters

"Under the weather" means (YES or NO)

1. Not feeling well.
2. Feeling great.
3. Under a pile of snow.
4. Having a cold.
5. Under the sun.

Are you "under the weather" if

1. You feel fine?
2. Your stomach hurts?
3. You don't feel good?
4. You have a fever?
5. You are having fun?

Answer YES or NO

1. Are you "under the weather" if you are tired?
2. If Bill comes to school and says he feels great, is he "under the weather"?
3. Does "under the weather" mean it is raining out?
4. Jenny has a cold and does not come to school. Is she "under the weather"?
5. Are you "under the weather" if you are feeling "fit as a fiddle"?
6. If Jimmy has a headache, is he "under the weather"?
7. Sally feels good. She is in good health. Is she "under the weather"?

Call It a Day

"Call it a day" means

♦ To stop what you're doing for the day.

♦ To quit.

♦ You're finished for the day.

♦ To complete what you're doing.

♦ To take a rest from what you're doing.

How to Use the Idiom in a Sentence

1. I've been studying for my spelling test for an hour. I think I'll "call it a day."
2. The teacher said to "call it a day" when it was three o'clock.
3. Where Dad works, they say let's "call it a day" when it's five o'clock.
4. We were tired because we had been playing basketball all afternoon, so we decided to "call it a day."

through modeling and conversation; games and activities are preferred to formal drills and exercises.

Moores and Maestas y Moores (1981) provide a helpful review of methods of language instruction, noting that virtually no research has been conducted to evaluate the advantages of one approach over the other and that most educational programs today tend to use a combination of structured and natural methods.

Controversy and Choices

The debate over communication and instructional methods for hearing impaired students is likely to continue. Research has yet to provide—and perhaps never will provide—a definitive answer to the question of which communication method is best. There is general agreement, however, that our educational programs for students who are deaf leave much room for improvement.

Posters
"Call it a day" means (YES or NO)

1. To continue.
2. To stop.
3. To name the day.
4. To work 'til the end of the day.
5. To rest.

Would you "call it a day" if

1. You were falling asleep?
2. You just got out of bed?
3. You decided to stop work?
4. You decided to rest?
5. You kept working?

Answer YES or NO

1. If Alice stopped working, would she be "calling it a day"?
2. Would you "call it a day" if you said "Tuesday"?
3. Would Jenny "call it a day" if she kept working and didn't stop?
4. If Nick just ate breakfast, would he "call it a day"?
5. If Sally studied for a math test for an hour, would she "call it a day" when she stopped studying?
6. Pete got tired of working on his bike, so he took a rest. Did he "call it a day"?
7. Julie just started to study for her math test. Is she "calling it a day"?

From "Teaching Idioms to Children Who Are Deaf" by K. M. Arnold and D. Hornett, 1990, Teaching Exceptional Children, 22(4), pp. 14–17. Adapted by permission. ◆

Different children communicate in different ways. Some hearing impaired children, unfortunately, have experienced deep frustration and failure because of rigid adherence to an oral-only program. They have left oral programs without having developed a usable avenue of communication. Equally unfortunate is the fact that other hearing impaired children have not been given an adequate opportunity to develop their auditory and oral skills, because they were placed in educational programs that did not provide good oral instruction. In both cases, children have been unfairly penalized. Every hearing impaired child should have access to an educational program that uses a communication method appropriate to his unique abilities and needs.

■ EDUCATIONAL SERVICE ALTERNATIVES

Early detection of hearing loss and early intervention with the hearing impaired child and the family are critical. Many schools, speech and hearing clinics, and other agencies provide educational programs for preschool children. Usually the child's hearing is tested, an amplification aid is provided, and communication with adults and other children is emphasized. Parent groups and home visits are an important part of a preschool program; through these efforts, parents may be helped to communicate more effectively with their child. A hearing impaired child who receives no specialized assessment, amplification, or training until the age of 5 or 6 will undoubtedly be at a great disadvantage in communication and general development.

The passage of P.L. 99–457 in 1986 has led to greater emphasis on serving infants and preschoolers with disabilities (see Chapter 14).

Service Options

Educational programs for children with hearing impairments are available in residential schools, special day schools, and regular public schools. Schildroth (1986) notes that enrollment in the more than 60 public residential schools for hearing impaired children in the United States has declined sharply in the past decade, as public school programs have become more widely available and as the majority of students whose deafness was caused by the rubella epidemics of the mid-1960s have departed from the school-age population. Currently, about one-third of hearing impaired students attend residential schools, 40% of whom commute (Paul & Quigley, 1990). Over 90% of the students currently enrolled in residential schools have severe and profound prelingual hearing impairments. Nearly one-third of the hearing impaired students now served in residential schools are considered to be multihandicapped, and nearly one-third come from minority ethnic backgrounds.

Several publications (Dale, 1984; Kampfe, 1984; Lynas, 1986; Orlansky, 1979; Webster & Ellwood, 1985) provide helpful guidelines, practical suggestions, and descriptions of programs that have successfully integrated hearing impaired students into regular classes.

Educational programs for hearing impaired children in local public schools have expanded in response to federal legislation, improvements in hearing aids and other technology, and an increased demand by parents and deaf citizens for services at the local level (Davis, 1986). Hearing impaired children in regular schools may attend self-contained classes or may be integrated with nonhandicapped children for all or part of the school day. Karchmer (1984) reported that fewer than 50% of hearing impaired students are integrated into regular classrooms to some degree, and most of those who are mainstreamed have hearing losses of less than 90 dB. According to Davis (1986), the most important ingredients for the hearing impaired child's success in the regular classroom are (1) good oral communication skills, (2) strong parental support, (3) average or above-average intelligence, (4) self-confidence and other personal qualities, and (5) adequate support services, such as tutoring, audiological consultation, and speech therapy. As with all students, whether handicapped or not, we should never overlook the most fundamental factor in determining how successful a student will be in the regular classroom (or any other placement): *quality of instruction*. After studying the math achievement of 215 secondary hearing impaired students who were in either a self-contained classroom or mainstreamed into regular classes with or without an interpreter, Kluwin and Moores (1989) concluded that "quality of instruction is the prime determinant of achievement, regardless of placement" (p. 327).

The specialized needs of children with severe hearing impairments make special services necessary in virtually all cases. In an integrated public school setting, special services for a hearing impaired child may include

This Wizard's Dorothy communicates in American Sign Language.

- ◆ Smaller class size
- ◆ Regular speech, language, and auditory training instruction from a specialist
- ◆ Amplification systems
- ◆ Services of an interpreter if the child uses manual communication
- ◆ Special seating in the classroom to promote speechreading
- ◆ Captioned films
- ◆ Good acoustics and reduction of background noise
- ◆ Special tutoring or review sessions
- ◆ Someone to take notes in class so that the hearing impaired student can pay more constant attention
- ◆ Instruction for teachers and nonhandicapped students in sign language or other communication methods used by the hearing impaired student
- ◆ Counseling

It is sometimes difficult for public schools in rural areas to provide all these services. Several school districts may need to cooperate with one another.

Teacher Competencies

Teachers of hearing impaired students must complete specialized training programs and meet the certification standards established by the states and by national professional organizations. Usually, this training emphasizes the study of speech and hearing anatomy, audiology, language assessment and development, reading, curriculum, and use of audiovisual education technology. Most college and university preparation programs require the teacher to become competent in both oral and manual communication methods.

Because the teaching of communication skills dominates most university-based teacher training programs, there is concern that teachers of hearing impaired students may not be adequately trained to teach other parts of the curriculum, notably science and math (Lang, 1989). For example, a national survey of 500 science teachers of hearing impaired students found that 74% had no degree in science education, and half had never taken *any* science education courses (Lang & Propp, 1982).

Sass-Lehrer (1986) surveyed 150 supervisors of instructional programs for hearing impaired students in both regular and special schools and found that the following competencies were among those considered "most critical to the effective teaching of hearing impaired students" (p. 230):

♦ Providing language instruction

♦ Teaching small groups of hearing impaired students who function on different levels

♦ Developing and adapting instructional materials

♦ Guiding students in the development of a positive self-concept using information from various assessment procedures to formulate an IEP

♦ Dealing with crises calmly and effectively

Educational Interpreters

Interpreting—signing the speech of a teacher or other speaker for a person who is deaf—began as a profession in 1964 with the establishment of a professional organization called the Registry of Interpreters for the Deaf (RID). Many states have programs for training interpreters, who must meet certain standards of competence to be certified by the RID. The organization was initially comprised primarily of *freelance interpreters,* who interpret primarily for deaf adults in situations such as legal or medical interactions. The role of *educational interpreters* has made it possible for many hearing impaired students to enroll in and successfully complete postsecondary programs. There has also been greater use of educational interpreters in elementary and secondary classrooms (Gustason, 1985). Duties of interpreters vary across schools; they are likely to perform such tasks as tutoring, assisting regular and special education teachers, keeping records, and supervising hearing impaired students (Zawolkow & DeFiore, 1986).

Postsecondary Education

A growing number of educational opportunities are available to hearing impaired students after completion of a high-school level program. The oldest and best-known is Gallaudet University in Washington, D.C., which offers a wide range of undergraduate and graduate programs in the liberal arts, sciences, education, business, and other fields. Hearing impaired students from throughout the United States, Canada, and other countries compete for admission. All classes at Gallaudet are taught in simultaneous communication, through speech and sign language. In addition, the National Technical Institute for the Deaf (NTID), located at the Rochester (New York) Institute of Technology, provides wide-ranging programs in technical, vocational, and business-related fields such as computer science, hotel management, photography, and medical technology. Both Gallaudet and NTID are supported by the federal government and enroll approximately 1,500 hearing impaired students each.

Gallaudet also has programs to train teachers of deaf children. Both deaf and hearing students are accepted into these programs.

More than 150 other institutions of higher education have developed special programs of supportive services for students with hearing impairments. Among these are four regional postsecondary programs that enroll substantial numbers of hearing impaired students: St. Paul (Minnesota) Technical-Vocational Institute; Seattle (Washington) Central Community College; the Postsecondary Education Consortium at the University of Tennessee; and California State University at Northridge.

The percentage of hearing impaired students who attend postsecondary educational programs has risen dramatically in the past 20 years. Today, about 40% of all hearing impaired students go on to receive higher education (Connor, 1986). Enrollment has increased most sharply in areas of study related to business and office careers (Rawlings & King, 1986). It is hoped that the increase in postsecondary programs will expand vocational and professional opportunities for deaf adults.

■ CURRENT ISSUES/FUTURE TRENDS

As more hearing impaired children are educated in regular public school settings, it appears likely that oral methods of instruction will continue to be extremely important. Speech, after all, is the most widely used form of communication among teachers and students in regular classes. Manual communication, especially ASL, however, will probably become more familiar to the general public. Training in sign language is already offered to children with normal hearing in some schools, and an increasing number of people who contact the public in the course of their jobs—such as police officers, firefighters, flight attendants, and bank tellers—will learn to communicate manually with deaf individuals. Television programs, films, concerts, and other media using interpreters or printed captions are already becoming more widely available. It is no longer unusual to see a sign language interpreter standing next to a public speaker or performer.

Despite the recent expansion of postsecondary programs of education and training, many hearing impaired adults still find limited opportunities for appropriate employment and economic advancement. Recent court decisions regarding the rights of hearing impaired students have had mixed results. In one case (*Barnes v. Converse College,* 1977), a court ordered a private college to provide, at its own expense, an interpreter for a deaf student. In another case (*Southeastern Community College v. Davis,* 1979), the U.S. Supreme Court decided that a college could not be compelled to admit a hearing impaired student into its nursing program. A widely publicized Supreme Court case (*Board of Education of the Hendrick Hudson Central School District v. Rowley,*

The Rowley case was also discussed in Chapter 2. It was the first Supreme Court case to be argued by a deaf lawyer.

"DEAF PRESIDENT NOW"
A Student Protest Heard Around the World

Gallaudet University in Washington, D.C., is the world's only university dedicated exclusively to the education of deaf persons (students with normal hearing are admitted into some of its programs). A federally funded institution chartered by Congress in 1864, Gallaudet had never had a deaf president.

When a presidential vacancy occurred in 1988, many Gallaudet students, faculty, and alumni expected that a deaf person would be appointed; however, an educator with normal hearing, who was unable to use sign language, was initially selected for the position. A week of turbulent protests and demonstrations ensued, calling for a "Deaf President Now" and focusing national and international attention on Gallaudet. We asked Bridgetta Bourne and Jerry Covell, two of the protest's four primary student leaders, to tell us the dramatic story.

Bridgetta Bourne

When I identify myself as a deaf person, it's much like a black person identifying herself as black. All members of minority groups face certain challenges, and for us—the deaf—the challenge is communication. As a deaf person, I feel disabled, even among groups that include people with other disabilities. I still can't communicate with them without an interpreter. There was recently a march from the White House to the Capitol, in support of the Americans with Disabilities Act. There were many people with disabilities, but I didn't really feel like part of that community.

Bridgetta Bourne

Jerry Covell

Without an interpreter, I was basically lost. So the concept of oppression is one in which people in power are making decisions *for* me—about my life, about what I should do. Oppressed people have no voice.

Oppression is dangerous and pervasive. We even had it at Gallaudet, our own institution. Obviously, we should have a hand in running our own school, and that's why the Deaf President Now protest happened and why it was so successful. There had been so many years of struggle, so many years of deaf people being told they could not make decisions for themselves. You either have to release your anger at this oppression or just hold it in, as so many deaf people did in the past.

Jerry Covell

Prior to the Deaf President Now movement, Gallaudet had gone through six presidents, all of them hearing men. These hearing presidents served useful purposes, such as founding the college, expanding programs and services, creating new educational fields, and changing Gallaudet from college to university status. When the sixth president resigned and the board of trustees began a search for a new one, we all felt that the time was definitely right for a deaf president. Gallaudet is universally recognized and respected for its leadership in educating the deaf. Now we needed a deaf person to truly represent Gallaudet and the deaf community. We needed a deaf person who could prove to hearing people that he or she is capable of carrying out the duties and responsibilities of a university president; this would open the door to further opportunities for deaf people. There were qualified deaf people out there, with good backgrounds of education and experience.

All but four of the 21 members of the board of trustees were hearing people. Many of them had good backgrounds in business, fundraising, and public relations, and they contributed to Gallaudet in that way, but they had little or no understanding of deafness and deaf culture. They needed to be convinced! So we held rallies. We got letters of support from many well-known people, including [U.S.] presidential candidates and senators. Public awareness grew. We felt confident, especially after the three finalists in the presidential search were announced: two deaf men and a hearing woman. Then the final selection was announced by means of a press release: "Gallaudet University Appoints First Woman President." We couldn't believe our eyes! We were shocked and extremely upset. Please keep in mind, we didn't see this as a gender issue at all. It was strictly a hearing-deaf issue; a *deaf* woman president would have been great.

Bridgetta

We marched downtown to the hotel where the chairman of the board of trustees was staying. We wanted a personal explanation of why they'd selected a hearing person over a deaf person. There was a reception going on inside the hotel, to introduce the new president of Gallaudet. We hadn't planned a demonstration or a sit-in, but people were just so angry! Our sitting in the street was all spontaneous. We didn't have a permit or anything; we just marched. The police came out with police cars, barriers, and bullhorns, to try to stop us. Signs and banners appeared. I remember a deaf couple who had a dog wearing a sign: "I understand sign language better than the new president of Gallaudet."

Jerry

It was late at night by the time we got to the hotel, chanting and cheering. I remember seeing lights being turned on all over the hotel and people looking out the windows, wondering what was going on. Finally, the chairman came out. She couldn't understand sign language, either. She said, "We felt this was the best decision for Gallaudet." We went round and round asking questions. We asked, "When will a deaf person get the chance to be president of Gallaudet?" "When will you allow this?" Eventually the chairman said, "Deaf people are not ready to function in a hearing world." Ooooh, that hurt! Everyone was stunned—even the interpreter. We were ready for *real* action after that. The infamous quote really pulled us together; it lit a flame under us. So in a way, we should thank the chairman.

We set out to shut Gallaudet down. On Monday morning, we put kryptonite bike locks on the campus gates and parked cars in front of them. Students told everyone—administrators, faculty, staff, even board of trustees members— "Don't come in today. Go home. The campus is closed." When we took control of the campus, it showed how serious we were about the board's selection and the chairman's statement. The news media came in, and of course we took advantage of that.

Bridgetta

As Jerry says, the protest brought people together. Before the protest, it seemed that Gallaudet consisted of many different groups of deaf people. We came from various backgrounds. Some were interested in academics, others in sports, politics, or whatever. Some had gone to mainstream schools and others to deaf schools. Some were oral and others signed. But all rallied around the Deaf President Now movement, and our efforts were truly coordinated.

Jerry

Our chants—in sign and speech—were important to the Deaf President Now movement. One of our chants was "Four! Four! Four!" We had four demands before we would release the university back: First, the hearing president had to be replaced by a deaf person. Second, the chairman of the board of trustees had to resign because of her statement. Third, a majority of the board of trustees had to consist of deaf people. And fourth, there had to be no reprisals against faculty, staff, or students who were involved in the protest.

Toward the end of the week of protest, the new president resigned or "stepped aside," as she put it. But she hadn't yet been replaced. So we changed our chant to "Three and a half! Three and a half . . .!" That kept the motivation alive. We also chanted "Deaf and Proud!" and "Deaf Power!" We adapted that last one from the Black Power movement. We made the chant by putting one hand over an ear and raising the fist high in the air.

The media began to call us "the deaf civil rights movement." Deaf people came in from all over the country. There was a large crowd, perhaps as many as 7,000. We marched toward the Capitol to try to have Congress recognize our movement. As we marched, we chanted: "We are—

Standing tall! United, strong, and walking proud to be deaf! Shouting to the world— Time is now!"

The rest is history. Dr. I. King Jordan, a deaf man, was appointed president of Gallaudet. The chairman of the board of trustees was replaced by a deaf person. With those two demands met, we accepted a verbal agreement that the board of trustees would have a deaf majority within 5 years, and that there would be no reprisals. So we released the university. We changed our chant from "Deaf President Now" to "Deaf President Forever!" And when Dr. Jordan first appeared before a huge crowd, we chanted, "King! King! King!" It was the most inspirational and the best thing that ever happened to us when King Jordan said, "Deaf people can do anything—except hear."

Bridgetta

What happened at Gallaudet has had an international impact. And with your help, things are going to continue to get better and better for deaf people. ♦

In 1988, students at Gallaudet University were so united in their demonstration against the hiring of yet another hearing president at their school that the University is now headed by its first deaf president. Two of the student protest leaders tell their story on pages 322–324.

1982) resulted in a local school district's not being required to provide, at its expense, a sign language interpreter for a deaf child who was performing adequately without one in the regular classroom. Similar cases are certain to arise in the future, as hearing impaired people become increasingly aware of their civil rights and seek access to education, employment, and other rights.

The central role that ASL plays in the deaf culture, combined with the position taken by a number of prominent professionals in deaf education that ASL be recognized as the deaf child's first language, will probably heighten the intensity of the longstanding debate over how language should be taught to hearing impaired children. As an illustration of the intensity with which many people who are deaf view this issue, 85 students at the Tennessee School for the Deaf were suspended when they resisted a decree by the school that they sign in English word order, instead of being allowed to communicate in ASL (McCracken, 1987).

Technological advances are already having a significant impact on the educational programs of many hearing impaired students. In addition to the sophisticated techniques now used to detect hearing losses and to make use of even slight amounts of residual hearing, a number of devices known as speech production aids help deaf persons monitor and improve their own speech (Calvert, 1986). Cochlear implants have been successful in enabling even some persons with profound sensorineural hearing impairments to make use of residual hearing. (Karmody, 1986; Miller & Pfingst, 1984). Microcomputers are also being increasingly used in language and academic instruction of hearing impaired students. Prinz and Nelson (1985), for example, describe a successful microcomputer program that uses pictures and representations of ASL signs to improve deaf children's reading and writing skills; Tomlinson-Keasey, Brawley, and Peterson (1986) report that an interactive videodisc system helped enhance deaf students' language skills and motivation.

Continual progress in electronics and computer technology is making the telephone and television more accessible to people with hearing impairments. The telephone has long served as a barrier to deaf people in employment and social interaction, but acoustic couplers now make it possible to send immediate messages over conventional telephone lines in typed or digital form. Telecommunication devices for deaf persons (called TTY or TDD systems) are now widely used and relatively inexpensive. Similarly, closed captioning is used on more and more television programs; thus, a hearing impaired person who has a special decoding device is able to read captions or subtitles on the television screen. Another recent form of technology, known as *real-time graphic display,* facilitates rapid captioning of live presentations, such as public lectures.

Future technological advances may enable educators to analyze and track hearing impaired students' language development with much greater precision than is now possible and to use this information in planning appropriate language instruction for each child (Levitt, 1985). Among the most intriguing concepts is the possibility that an automatic speech recognition system may someday be perfected. Such a system could enable a deaf person to instantly decipher the speech of other people, perhaps through a small, portable printout device that would be activated by the speaker's voice. The research required to develop a speech recognition system is highly complex, as human speech patterns differ immensely. Nevertheless, improvements in technology, coupled with a concern for individual needs and rights, will enable people with impaired hearing to participate more fully in a broad range of educational, vocational, social, and recreational activities in their schools and communities.

SUMMARY

Definitions, Types, and Measurement

♦ There are many different levels of hearing ability. A deaf person is not able to understand speech through the ears alone. A hard-of-hearing person is able to use hearing to understand speech, generally with the help of a hearing aid.

♦ Hearing impairments can be classified in several ways: A *congenital* hearing impairment is present at birth; an *adventitious* hearing impairment is acquired later in life.

♦ A *prelingual* hearing impairment occurs before the child has developed speech and language; a *postlingual* hearing impairment occurs after that time.

♦ A hearing impairment can be *conductive* or *sensorineural,* depending on the type and location of the impairment.

♦ A hearing impairment can be *unilateral* (in one ear) or *bilateral* (in both ears).

Identification and Assessment

♦ A formal hearing test generates an audiogram, which graphically shows the intensity of the faintest sound an individual can hear at various frequencies.

♦ Hearing impairments are classified as slight, mild, moderate, severe, or profound, depending on the degree of hearing loss.

♦ Generally, for educational placement purposes, only children with hearing losses greater than 90 dB are considered deaf.

Prevalence

♦ Hearing impairment is a low-prevalence disability.

♦ About 5% of all school-age children have some form of hearing impairment, but most do not require special education.

♦ Although most deaf children participate in special education programs, only about 20% of hard-of-hearing children receive special services.

Causes of Hearing Impairment

♦ The four most common causes of hearing impairment are maternal rubella, heredity, prematurity and complications of pregnancy, and meningitis.

Background of the Field

♦ Traditionally, most deaf children were educated in residential schools; today, more than 60% attend classes in local public schools.

♦ Many hearing impaired students have multiple disabilities, and many are from culturally diverse backgrounds.

Amplification and Auditory Training/Learning

♦ Amplification and auditory training seek to enable hearing impaired students to use their residual hearing more effectively.

♦ Speechreading provides useful visual information but also has many limitations. Most English sounds cannot be distinguished through vision alone.

Educational Approaches

♦ Some educators use a primarily oral approach to the education of hearing impaired students, emphasizing the development of speech and related skills.

♦ Other educators use a total communication approach, using sign language and fingerspelling simultaneously with speech.

Educational Service Alternatives

♦ Early detection of hearing loss and preschool education are critical.

♦ A growing number of postsecondary educational opportunities are available. About 40% of all hearing impaired students go on to other educational programs after high school.

Current Issues/Future Trends

♦ An increasing awareness of the rights of hearing impaired individuals is positively affecting education, employment, and economic opportunities.

♦ Technology holds much promise for addressing the communication problems faced by deaf persons.

Journals

American Annals of the Deaf. Published by the Conference of Educational Administrators Serving the Deaf and the Convention of American Instructors of the Deaf, 814 Thayer Avenue, Silver Spring, MD 20910. Presents articles dealing with education of deaf and hearing impaired students.

Journal of the American Deafness and Rehabilitation Association (Formerly *Journal of Rehabilitation of the Deaf*), P. O. Box 251554, Little Rock, AR 72225. Focuses on research, innovations, patterns of service, and other topics related to deaf adults.

Sign Language Studies. Published quarterly by Linstok Press, 9306 Mintwood Street, Silver Spring, MD 20901. Contains research and practical articles related to sign language and manual communication.

The Volta Review. Published nine times a year by the Alexander Graham Bell Association for the Deaf, 3417 Volta Place, NW, Washington, DC 20007. Encourages teaching of speech, speechreading, and use of residual hearing to deaf persons. Advocates oral approach.

Books

Luterman, D. M. (Ed.). (1986). *Deafness in perspective*. San Diego: College-Hill.

Luterman, D. M. (Ed.). (1987). *Deafness in the family*. Boston: Little, Brown.

Mindel, E. D., & Vernon, M. (1987). *They grow in silence: Understanding deaf children and adults* (2nd ed.). San Diego: College-Hill.

Moores, D. F. (1987). *Educating the deaf: Psychology, principles, and practices* (3rd ed.). Boston: Houghton Mifflin.

Paul, P. V., & Quigley, S. P. (1990). *Education and deafness*. New York: Longman.

Quigley, S. P., & Paul, P. V. (1984). *Language and deafness*. San Diego: College-Hill.

Ross, M. (Ed.). (1990). *Hearing-impaired children in the mainstream*. Monkton, MD: York Press.

Schildroth, A. N., & Karchmer, M. A. (Eds.). (1986). *Deaf children in America*. San Diego: College-Hill.

Van Cleve, J. V. (Ed.). (1986). *Gallaudet encyclopedia of deaf people and deafness*. New York: McGraw-Hill.

Vernon, M., & Andrews, J. F. (1990). *The psychology of deafness*. New York: Longman.

Walker, L. A. (1986). *A loss for words: The story of deafness in a family*. New York: Harper & Row.

Organizations

Alexander Graham Bell Association for the Deaf, 3417 Volta Place, NW, Washington, DC 20007. (Voice/TDD: 202-237-5220) Provides brochures, books, software, audiovisual materials, and other information on hearing impairment, with an auditory-oral emphasis. Publishes *The Volta Review* for professionals, *Our Kids Magazine* for parents, and *Newsounds* newsletter. Sponsors organizations for teachers, parents, researchers, and oral deaf adults.

Gallaudet University, 800 Florida Avenue, NE, Washington, DC 20002. Its bookstore has one of the most complete collections of professional and popular literature about hearing impairment, communication, education, psychology, and related topics. Also has children's sign language books that appeal to many readers. Provides free catalogs of book lists; arranges tours of the Gallaudet campus for visitors.

National Association of the Deaf, 814 Thayer Avenue, Silver Spring, MD 20910. A clearinghouse for information about education, employment, legal issues, communication, technological aids, and other topics. Sponsors activities for deaf adults, children, and parents. (Voice/TDD: 301-587-1788)

National Center for Law and the Deaf. Gallaudet University, 800 Florida Avenue, NE, Washington, DC 20002. (Voice/TDD: 202-651-5373)

National Cued Speech Association, P. O. Box 31345, Raleigh, NC 27622. Provides information, training, and publications on the cued speech system of identifying sounds and supplementing speechreading skills.

National Information Center on Deafness. Gallaudet University, 800 Florida Avenue, NE, Washington, DC 20002. (Voice/TDD: 800-672-6720)

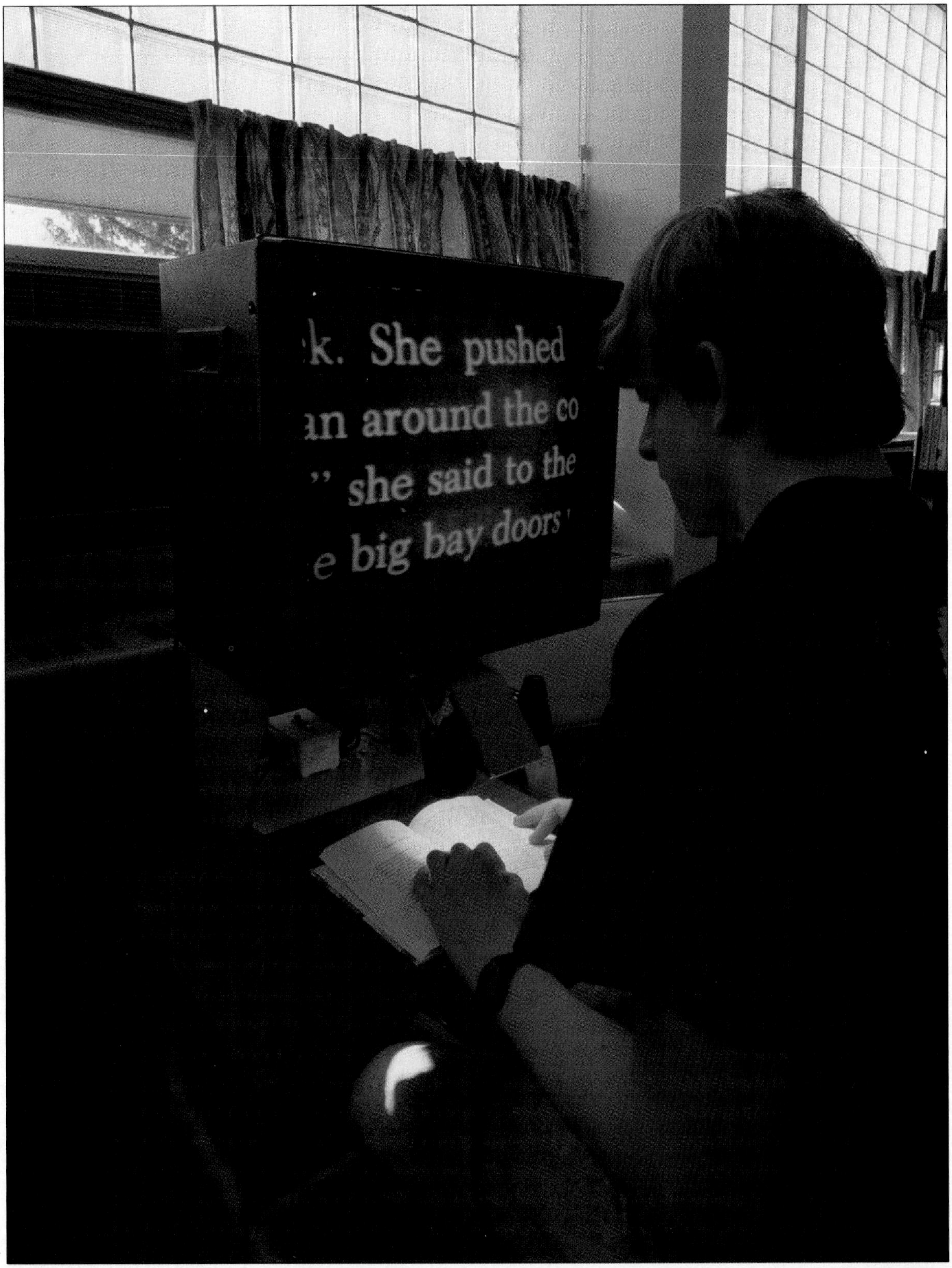
k. She pushed
an around the co
” she said to the
e big bay doors

8

Visual Impairment

◆ In what ways does loss of vision affect learning?

◆ How does the age at which vision is lost impact the student?

◆ Normally sighted children enter school with a great deal of knowledge about *trees*. How could a teacher help the young child who is congenitally blind develop the concept of *trees*?

◆ What special non-academic skills does a person with visual impairment need to learn?

◆ How do the educational needs and goals of children with low vision differ from those of children who are blind?

Sixteen-year-old Maria is a bright, college-bound student who has been totally blind since birth. She recently took a series of intellectual and psychological tests and generally performed well, scoring at about her expected age and grade level. Something unusual, however, happened on one of the test items. The examiner handed Maria an unpeeled banana and asked, "What is this?" Maria held the banana for minutes and took several guesses but could not answer correctly. The examiner was astonished, as were Maria's teachers and parents. After all, this section of the test was intended for young children. Even though Maria had eaten bananas many times, she had missed out on one important aspect of the banana experience: She had never held and peeled a banana by herself.

This true story (adapted from Swallow, 1978) illustrates the tremendous importance of vision in obtaining accurate and thorough information about the world in which we live. Visually impaired students are "a small group of handicapped pupils who are more similar to than different from their nonhandicapped peers" (Scholl, 1987, p. 36). The major difference is in the visually impaired students' need for compensatory education to help them overcome the absence of vision, an extremely important means of sensory input. Thus, teachers who work with visually impaired children find it necessary to plan and present a great many firsthand experiences. Many of the concepts that children with normal vision seem to acquire almost effortlessly may not be learned at all by visually impaired children—or may be learned incorrectly—unless someone deliberately teaches the concepts to them. Often, the best teachers are those who enable visually impaired children to learn by doing things for themselves.

Visually impaired students display a wide range of visual abilities, ranging from total blindness to relatively good residual (remaining) vision. The one characteristic all these students share is "a visual restriction of sufficient severity that it interferes with normal progress in a regular educational program without modifications" (Scholl, 1986a, p. 29).

Even when information is deliberately presented to visually impaired children, they may not learn it in exactly the same way that children with normal vision would. Visually impaired students may learn to make good use of their other senses; hearing, touch, smell, and taste can be useful channels of sensory input, but they do not totally compensate for loss of vision. Touch and taste cannot tell children much about things that are far away—or even just beyond their arms' length. Hearing can tell them a good deal about the near and distant environment, but it seldom provides information that is as complete, as continuous, or as exact as the information people obtain from seeing their surroundings.

The classroom is one important setting in which vision plays a critical role in learning. In school, normally sighted children are routinely expected to exercise several important visual skills. They must be able to see clearly; they must focus on different objects, shifting from near to far as needed; they must have good eye-hand coordination and be able to remember what they have seen; they must discriminate colors accurately; they must be able to see and interpret many things simultaneously; they must be able to maintain visual concentration. Children with visual impairments have deficits in one or more of

People who are blind are not gifted with an extraordinary sense of hearing or touch. They may learn to be more sensitive, however, to the information about the environment that they gain from their nonvisual senses.

these abilities. As a result, they may need special equipment and/or adaptation in instructional procedures or materials to function effectively in school.

■ DEFINING VISUAL IMPAIRMENT

There are both legal and educational definitions of visual impairment. The legal definition of blindness relies heavily on measurements of **visual acuity**, which is the ability to clearly distinguish forms or discriminate details at a specified distance. Most frequently, visual acuity is measured by reading letters, numbers, or other symbols from a chart 20 feet away. The familiar phrase "20/20 vision" does not, as some people think, mean "perfect vision"—it simply indicates that at a distance of 20 feet, the eye can see what a normally seeing eye should be able to see at that distance. As the bottom number increases, visual acuity decreases.

Some people, with or without correction, have visual acuity that's better than 20/20. If the vision in one of your eyes is rated as 20/10, for example, you can see from 20 feet what the "20/20" eye must close to 10 feet in order to see.

Legal Blindness

If a person's visual acuity is 20/200 or less in the better eye, *after the best possible correction* with glasses or contact lenses, then one is considered **legally blind**. If Jane has 20/200 vision while wearing her glasses, she needs to stand at a distance of 20 feet to see what most people can see from 200 feet away. In other words, Jane must get much closer than normal to see things clearly. Her legal blindness means that Jane will likely find it difficult to use her vision in many everyday situations. But many children with 20/200, or even 20/400, visual acuity succeed in the regular classroom with special help. Some students' visual acuity is so poor they are unable to perceive fine details at any distance, even while wearing glasses or contact lenses.

A person may also be considered legally blind if her **field of vision** is extremely restricted. When gazing straight ahead, a normal eye is able to see objects within a range of approximately 180 degrees. If David's field of vision is only 10 degrees, he is able to see only a limited area at any one time (even though his visual acuity in that small area may be quite good). Some people with limited fields of vision describe their perceptions as viewing the world through a narrow tube or tunnel; they may have good central vision but poor **peripheral vision** at the outer ranges of the visual field. Some eye conditions, on the other hand, make it impossible for people to see things clearly in the central visual field but allow relatively good peripheral vision.

Whether the visual field impairment is central or peripheral, one is considered legally blind if he is restricted to an area of 20 degrees or less from the normal 180-degree field. It is common for the visual field to decrease slowly over a period of years and for the decrease to go undetected in children and adults. A thorough visual examination should always include measurement of the visual field, as well as visual acuity.

Legally blind children are eligible to receive a wide variety of educational services, materials, and benefits from governmental agencies. They may, for example, obtain records (known as "Talking Books"), tapes, and record players from the Library of Congress. Their schools may be able to buy books and educational materials from the American Printing House for the Blind, because the federal quota system allots states and local school districts a certain financial allowance for each legally blind student (Chase, 1986b). A person who is legally blind is also entitled to vocational training, free U.S. mail service, and an additional income tax exemption.

Even though these services and benefits are important to know about, the legal definition of blindness is not especially useful to teachers. Some children, even though they do not meet the criteria for legal blindness, have visual impairments severe enough to require special educational techniques and materials. Other students, whose visual impairments qualify them as legally blind, find little or no use for many of these special education services. Educators differentiate between blind and low vision students. This distinction does not rely on precise measurements of visual acuity or visual field, but instead considers the extent to which a child's visual impairment affects learning and makes special methods or materials necessary.

Low Vision

A child who is **blind** is totally without sight or has so little vision that she learns primarily through the other senses. Most blind children, for example, use their sense of touch to read **braille**. A child with **low vision**, on the other hand, is able to learn through the visual channel and generally learns to read print. Although there is no universally agreed-upon definition of low vision, the definition Corn (1989) offers stresses the functional use of vision:

> Low vision is a level of vision that with standard correction hinders an individual in the visual planning and execution of tasks, but which permits enhancements of the functional vision through the use of optical or nonoptical aids and environmental modifications and/or techniques. (p. 28)

Today, the great majority of children who receive special education services for visual impairments have useful vision; students with low vision comprise between 75% and 80% of the school-age visually impaired population (Bryan & Jeffrey, 1982).

The terms **visual efficiency** (Barraga, 1983) and *functional vision* (Corn, 1989) denote how well a person uses whatever vision he has. Functional vision is the "visual ability sufficient for utilizing visual information in the planning and execution of a task" (Corn, 1989, p. 28). Functional vision cannot be determined by measuring a child's visual acuity or visual field, nor can it be predicted. Some children with severe visual impairments use what vision they have very capably. Other children with relatively minor visual impairments are unable to function as visual learners; they may even behave as though they were blind. Barraga and her colleagues have shown that systematic training in visual recognition and discrimination can help many visually impaired children use their remaining vision more efficiently.

Other Impairments

Although the most frequently mentioned visual impairments are in visual acuity and field of vision, there are several other significant ways one's vision may be impaired. **Ocular motility**, the eye's ability to move, may be impaired. This

Braille is a system of representing letters, numbers, and other symbols with combinations (patterns) of six raised dots. We'll examine braille later in the chapter.

impairment can cause problems in binocular vision, which is the ability of the two eyes to focus on one object and fuse the two images into a single clear image (Ward, 1986). **Binocular vision** is actually a complicated process, requiring good vision in each eye, normal eye muscles, and smooth functioning of the coordinating centers of the brain (Miller, 1979).

Several conditions make it difficult or impossible for a child to use her eyes together effectively. **Strabismus** describes an inability to focus on the same object with both eyes, because of an inward or outward deviation of one or both eyes. The colloquial and sometimes demeaning terms *squint, cross-eyed,* and *walleyed* have been applied to children with strabismus.

If left untreated, strabismus and other disorders of ocular motility can lead to permanent loss of vision. When the two eyes cannot focus simultaneously, the brain avoids a double image by suppressing the visual input from one eye. Thus, the weaker eye—usually the one that turns inward or outward—can actually lose its ability to see. **Amblyopia** refers to this reduction in or loss of vision in the weaker eye from lack of use, even though no disease is present. The usual treatment for amblyopia is to place a patch over the stronger eye so that the weaker eye is forced to develop better vision through training and experience. This treatment is most effective if started in early childhood. Eye muscle surgery may also help to correct the muscle imbalance and prevent further loss of vision in the weaker eye (Batshaw & Perret, 1986).

Other kinds of visual impairments include problems in **accommodation**, in which the eye cannot adjust properly for seeing at different distances. A child with difficulty in accommodation may have trouble shifting from reading a book to looking at the chalkboard and back again. Some visually impaired children have a condition known as **nystagmus**, in which there is a rapid, involuntary back-and-forth movement of the eyes in a lateral, vertical, or rotary direction. Nystagmus is generally not discernible by the person with the impairment (Chase, 1986b). Severe nystagmus can cause problems in focusing and reading.

Some children's eyes are unusually sensitive to light; this condition is known as **photophobia**. The child may need to wear tinted glasses and avoid areas of strong light or glare. Children with **albinism** almost always have photophobia because their eyes (and skin and hair) lack normal pigmentation.

Color vision can also be impaired. A child with deficient color vision is not actually color-blind; that is, he does not see only in black and white. He may find it difficult to distinguish certain colors, however; red-green confusion is most common, occurring in about 8% of all males and 0.4% of females (Ward, 1986). Deficient color vision does not get better or worse as a child gets older, and it is usually not considered an educationally significant visual impairment.

Age at Onset

Like other disabilities, visual impairment can be congenital (present at birth) or adventitious (acquired). It is useful for a teacher to know the age at which a student acquired a visual impairment. A child who has been blind since birth naturally has quite a different perception of the world than does a child who lost her vision at age 12. The first child has a background of learning through hearing, touch, and the other nonvisual senses, whereas the second child has a background of visual experiences on which to draw. Most adventitiously blind

How does someone who cannot discriminate the colors red and green drive safely? He learns to look at the position of the light on the traffic signal: red ("Stop") is always at the top, and green ("Go") is always on the bottom.

people retain a visual memory of things they formerly saw. This memory can be helpful in a child's education; an adventitiously blind child may, for instance, remember the appearance of colors, maps, and printed letters. At the same time, however, her need for emotional support and acceptance may be greater than that of the congenitally blind child, who does not have to make a sudden adjustment to the loss of vision.

■ TYPES AND CAUSES OF VISUAL IMPAIRMENT

The basic function of the eye is to collect visual information from the environment and transmit it to the brain. A simplified diagram of the eye appears in Figure 8.1. The eye is stimulated by light rays, reflected from objects in the visual field. In the normal eye, these light rays come to a clear focus on the central part of the **retina**. This multilayered sheet of nerve tissue at the back of the eye has been likened to the film in a camera: For a clear image to be transmitted to the brain, the light rays must come to a precise focus on the retina. The **optic nerve** is connected to the retina. It conducts visual images to the brain.

In the process of vision, light rays must pass through several structures and substances in the eye itself. Each of these bends the light a little bit to produce the ideal image on the retina. The light first hits the **cornea**, the curved transparent membrane that protects the eye (much as an outer crystal protects a wristwatch). It then passes through the **aqueous humor**, a watery liquid that fills the front chamber of the eye. Next, the light passes through the **pupil**, a circular hole in the center of the colored **iris**; the pupil contracts or expands to regulate the amount of light entering the eye. The light then passes through the **lens**, a transparent, elastic structure suspended by tiny muscles that adjusts its thickness so that both the near and far objects can be brought into sharp focus. Finally, the light passes through the **vitreous humor**, a jellylike substance that

FIGURE 8.1

The human eye.

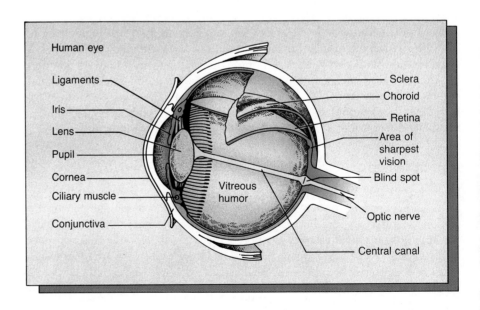

Human eye

Ligaments
Iris
Lens
Pupil
Cornea
Ciliary muscle
Conjunctiva

Vitreous humor

Sclera
Choroid
Retina
Area of sharpest vision
Blind spot
Optic nerve
Central canal

fills most of the eye's interior. Disturbances of any of these structures can prevent the clear focusing of an image on the retina.

Refractive Errors

Refraction is the process of bending light rays when they pass from one transparent structure to another. As just described, the normal eye refracts light rays so that a clear image is perceived on the retina; no special help is needed. However, for many people—perhaps half the general population (Miller, 1979)—the size and shape of the eye prevent refraction from being perfect. That is, the light rays do not focus clearly on the retina. Refractive errors can usually be corrected by glasses or contact lenses, but if severe enough, they can cause permanent visual impairment.

In **myopia,** or *nearsightedness,* the eye is larger than normal from front to back. The image conducted to the retina is thus somewhat out of focus. A child with myopia can see near objects clearly, but more distant objects—such as a blackboard or a movie—are blurred or are not seen at all. The opposite of myopia is **hyperopia,** commonly called *farsightedness.* The hyperopic eye is shorter than normal, preventing the light rays from converging on the retina. A child with hyperopia has difficulty seeing near objects clearly but is able to focus well on more distant objects. **Astigmatism** refers to distorted or blurred vision caused by irregularities in the cornea or other surfaces of the eye; both near and distant objects may be out of focus. Glasses or contact lenses can correct many refractive errors by changing the course of light rays to produce as clear a focus as possible.

Other Causes of Visual Impairment

Blindness or impaired vision can result from many causes; we will mention only a few. A **cataract** is a cloudiness in the lens of the eye that blocks the light necessary for seeing clearly. Vision may be blurred, distorted, or incomplete. Some people with cataracts liken their vision to looking through a dirty windshield. If the cataract is extremely cloudy or dense, a person may be unable to perceive any details at all.

Cataracts are common in older people, but may also occur in children. Most children born with cataracts have their cloudy lenses surgically removed. They must then wear special postcataract eyeglasses or contact lenses and usually need to wear bifocals or have one pair of glasses for distance vision and another pair for reading because the glasses or contact lenses cannot change focus as a natural lens does. A permanent lens is sometimes implanted into the eye after cataract surgery, but this procedure is not yet universally accepted by ophthalmologists.

Glaucoma is a prevalent disease marked by abnormally high pressure within the eye. There are various types of glaucoma, all related to disturbances or blockages of the fluids that normally circulate within the eye. Central and peripheral vision are impaired—or lost entirely—when the increased pressure damages the optic nerve. Although glaucoma can be extremely painful in its advanced phase, it frequently goes undetected for long periods, and children may not even be aware of the small, gradual changes in their vision. If detected in its early stages, glaucoma can often be treated successfully with medication or

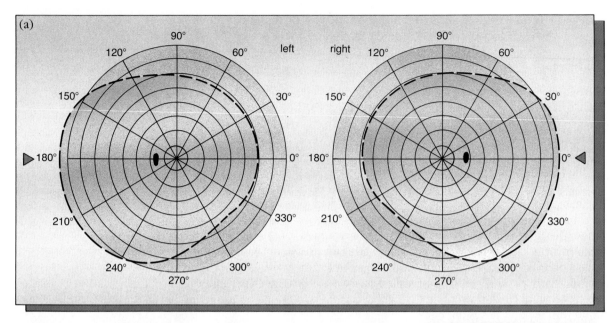

(b)

FIGURE 8.2

(a) Charts used to record field of vision. Shaded area indicates normal field of vision. Dark spot near center is the macula, or area of sharpest central vision.

(b) The same street scene as it might be viewed by a person with normal vision, advanced glaucoma, or cataracts. (*Source:* The Lighthouse, New York Association for the Blind, New York. Reprinted by permission.)

surgery. Figure 8.2 shows how the world might look to someone with cataracts or glaucoma.

Several important causes of visual impairment and blindness involve damage to the retina, the light-sensitive tissue that is so critical for clear vision. The retina is rich in blood vessels and can be affected by disorders of the circulatory system. Children and adults with diabetes frequently have impaired vision as a result of hemorrhages and the growth of new blood vessels in the area of the retina. This condition, known as **diabetic retinopathy**, is the leading cause of blindness for people between 20 and 64 years of age. Laser surgery has been helpful in some instances, but there is no effective treatment as yet. The

American Academy of Ophthalmology (1985) advises, however, that up to half of all cases of diabetic retinopathy could be prevented through early diagnosis and treatment. All children and adults with diabetes should receive regular, detailed eye examinations.

Retinitis pigmentosa (RP) is the most common of all inherited retinal disorders. This disease causes gradual degeneration of the retina. The first symptom is usually difficulty in seeing at night, followed by loss of peripheral vision. A small amount of central vision may be maintained. In most cases, RP is not treatable, although recent research has helped to identify families at high risk of having affected children (Kaiser-Kupfer & Morris, 1985). RP sometimes occurs in congenitally deaf people. The unfortunate combination of congenital deafness and gradual retinitis pigmentosa is known as **Usher's syndrome,** a significant cause of deaf-blindness among adolescents and adults.

Macular degeneration is a fairly common condition in which the central area of the retina (the macular area) gradually deteriorates. In contrast to retinitis pigmentosa, the child with macular degeneration usually retains peripheral vision but loses the ability to see clearly in the center of the visual field.

Detached retinas result when the retina becomes partially or totally separated from the outer layers of tissue in the eye. This condition may accompany several diseases of the eye or can result from trauma. Detached or torn retinas can frequently be repaired by surgery.

Retinopathy of prematurity (ROP), formerly referred to as *retrolental fibroplasia,* can result from placing low birthweight babies in incubators and administering high levels of oxygen. When the infants are later removed from the oxygen-rich incubators, the change in oxygen levels can produce an abnormally dense growth of blood vessels and scar tissue in the eyes, leading to various degrees of visual impairment and often total blindness from retinal detachment. During the 1940s, premature infants were routinely given high doses of oxygen, and approximately 25% were diagnosed with ROP. By 1952, ROP had reached epidemic proportions and was the largest single cause of childhood blindness (Newell, 1982). The amount of oxygen given to premature infants was greatly reduced in the 1950s, and the incidence of ROP decreased. It has been estimated that for each case of blindness prevented, however, 16 infants may have died because of insufficient oxygen (Lucey & Dangman, 1984).

> Since the mid-1960s, the incidence of milder ROP has risen again. Among the factors leading to this rise are modern medical techniques that allow pediatricians to save low birthweight, high-risk infants. . . . In the early 1980s, there was a resurgence of ROP. An estimated 2,100 infants were reported with some degree of ROP annually. Of these infants, approximately 23 percent became seriously visually impaired or blind. This rate was similar to that of the 1943–1953 "epidemic" years (Phelps, 1981). The birthweight of children with ROP has progressively declined. Most would have died if they had been born in earlier decades. ROP now primarily affects babies with a birthweight of less than 1,000 grams (about 2.2 lb.). (Trief, Duckman, Morse, & Silberman, 1989, p. 500)

It is seldom necessary for an educator to have detailed knowledge concerning the etiology and medical status of a child's visual impairment, but

Chapter 9 includes further information on diabetes in children.

ROP is one example of how medical technology can have both positive and negative outcomes.

familiarity with how a student's particular visual impairment affects classroom performance is important. It is useful to know, for example, that Linda has difficulty reading under strong lights, that Richard has only a small amount of central vision in his right eye, or that Ella sometimes experiences eye pain. Basic knowledge of the conditions described here can help a teacher understand some aspects of a child's learning and behavior and decide when to refer a child for professional vision care.

■ PREVALENCE

Visually impaired children constitute a small percentage of the school-age population—about 1 child in 1,000. The American Printing House for the Blind (1987), in its annual register of legally blind students who are eligible for its federally funded programs and services, reported that in 1987 there were 16,670 legally blind students enrolled in grades K–12. During the 1988–89 school year, the federal government reported that 22,743 children ages 6 to 21 received special education services under P.L. 94–142 within the category of visually handicapped. The federal government figure includes children with low vision who require special education but do not meet the criteria of legal blindness. The actual number of visually impaired students is probably somewhat higher than the government figures, because some students with visual impairments are counted under other disability categories such as deaf-blind and multihandicapped. Still, it is doubtful that visually impaired students exceed 0.1% of the entire school-age population.

Of the legally blind students in the American Printing House for the Blind census, 86% attended regular public schools and just over 12% attended residential schools for the blind. Most of the remaining 2% of visually impaired students were served in programs for multihandicapped students and in vocational rehabilitation programs.

Surveys of the reading methods that visually impaired students use give some insight into the heterogeneity and changing nature of this population. The 1987 American Printing House census identified 33% of visually impaired students as visual readers, who primarily use regular or large-print materials. The next largest group included auditory readers (17%), who use recorded or taped materials or are read to aloud, followed by braille readers (12%). Nonreaders and prereaders comprise the remaining 38%. These figures are consistent with the observation that a sizable percentage of blind and visually impaired students have other significant disabilities. According to Scholl (1986a), recent reports from the field indicate that approximately one-third of the school-age population of visually impaired students have at least one additional disability.

The prevalence of children with visual impairments within the population of handicapped children requiring special education services is also small—only 0.5% of all handicapped school-age children in 1988–89. Visual impairment is thus considered a **low-incidence disability**. Educators and parents of visually impaired children frequently express concern about this low prevalence, because they fear that when financial resources are limited, visually impaired

Nonreaders, as used here, refers to visually impaired students with additional severe disabilities, whereas prereaders are visually impaired children who are expected to follow an academic program and learn to read.

students may not receive adequate services from specially trained teachers. It may be particularly difficult for a local public school to provide comprehensive services for a visually impaired child who resides in a rural area.

Small school districts often cooperate with each other in employing special teachers for visually impaired students.

■ BACKGROUND OF THE FIELD

Blind and visually impaired people, although not a large population, have been a conspicuous group throughout history. In most countries, education of blind children is a high priority; schools and other special programs for blind children have historically been established before those for other groups of disabled children. Today, there are more than 1,000 separate organizations providing special services to visually impaired people in the United States. There are so many resources, in fact, that it is advisable for a blind person to take a special course in how to identify and use the most appropriate services, products, and information available (Winer, 1978).

In contrast, programs for disabilities that are less visible, such as learning disabilities, have a comparatively short history.

There are several possible explanations for the special attention given to people who are blind and visually impaired. Blindness is usually readily apparent to the observer and often evokes feelings of pity and sympathy. It is perhaps the most feared of any disability. There are also many widely held stereotypes and misconceptions about blind people. One study found that sighted people considered people who are blind to have "nice," "sweet," and "charming" personalities (Klinghammer, 1964). Other old but persistent assumptions are that blind children are naturally gifted in music, that they have a sixth sense enabling them to detect obstacles, that they have better-than-normal hearing, and that they have superior memory skills.

Valentin Hauy (1745–1822) is given credit for starting the first school for blind children, the *Institution des Jeunes Aveugles* in Paris, which opened in 1784. Hauy had been shocked at seeing blind people performing as jesters and beggars on the streets of Paris and resolved to teach them more dignified ways of earning a living. The subjects taught at Hauy's school included reading and writing (using embossed print), music, and vocational skills. The competence demonstrated by Hauy's students impressed citizens in France and elsewhere in Europe. By the early 19th century, residential schools for blind children had been established in several other countries, including England, Scotland, Austria, Germany, and Russia (Koestler, 1976; Roberts, 1986).

Influenced by the European institutions, American educators established private residential schools for blind children in Boston, New York, and Philadelphia around 1830. Within the next few decades, most states had opened public residential schools for visually impaired children. Such schools continued to educate the great majority of visually impaired children until the mid-20th century (Koestler, 1976).

The first American public school class for totally blind children opened in Chicago in 1900; the first class for low vision children began in Cleveland in 1909; and the first itinerant teaching program for visually impaired children attending regular classes was implemented in Oakland, California, in 1938 (Ward, 1979). Mainstreaming of visually impaired children thus has a relatively long and successful history.

Sight-Saving Classes

For a good part of this century, many children with low vision were educated in special sight-saving classes, both in regular public schools and residential schools for the blind. It was generally believed that a child's remaining vision should be conserved by not using it too much. In extreme instances, children with impaired but useful vision were even blindfolded or educated in dark rooms so that their precious vision would not be used up or lost. Today, a dramatically different approach prevails. Eye specialists agree that vision, even if imperfect, *benefits* from use; thus, educational programs for visually impaired children concentrate on helping them develop and use their visual abilities as much as possible.

This trend parallels the emphasis on teaching hearing impaired children to use their residual hearing as much as possible (see Chapter 7).

A Wave of Visually Impaired Children

As mentioned, thousands of infants became blind or severely visually impaired because of retinopathy of prematurity in the 1940s and 1950s. This unfortunate medical occurrence, however, had a beneficial side effect in expanding the educational opportunities available to visually impaired children. Because the residential schools then in existence were unable to accommodate the large, sudden influx of children affected by ROP and because many parents did not want their children to attend distant residential schools, educational programs and services for visually impaired students became much more widely available in the regular public schools during the 1950s and 1960s. Although the majority of children blinded by ROP are now adults, public school programs for visually impaired children have continued to develop and diversify. Today, in most regions of the United States and Canada, parents may choose between public and residential school education for a visually impaired child.

■ EDUCATIONAL APPROACHES

We often first think of teachers of visually impaired children in conjunction with specialized equipment and materials, such as braille, canes, tape recorders, and magnifying devices. Media and materials do play an important role in the education of children with impaired vision, but the effective teacher must know a great deal more than how to use these special devices. Because they are frequently called on to teach skills and concepts that most children acquire through vision, teachers of visually impaired students must be knowledgeable, competent, and creative. They must plan and carry out activities that will help their students gain as much information as possible through the nonvisual senses and by participation in active, practical experiences.

Many educators and psychologists have described the obstacles to learning imposed by blindness or severe visual impairment. Lowenfeld (1973), for example, observes that a blind child may hear a bird singing, but gets no concrete idea of the bird itself from this sound alone. A teacher interested in teaching such a student about birds (to follow up on Lowenfeld's example) might plan a series of activities that would have the student touch birds of various species and manipulate related objects such as eggs, nests, and feathers. The student might assume the responsibility for feeding a pet bird at home or in the classroom. Perhaps a field trip to a poultry farm could be arranged. Through experiences such as these, visually impaired children can gradually obtain a more thorough and accurate knowledge of birds than they could if their education were limited to reading books about birds, memorizing vocabulary, or feeling plastic models.

There are virtually no limits on the extent to which a visually impaired child may participate in a full, well-rounded school program. Educators should ensure that a visually impaired student's IEP "includes the full range of instructional areas: those studied with nonhandicapped peers, those that require special instruction, and those outside of the school curriculum that are essential to enable them to compete with their nonhandicapped peers when they move into the adult world" (Scholl, 1987, p. 36). Successfully accomplishing this goal, however, requires that special educators provide support, consultation, and materials to regular teachers with visually impaired students in their classes.

Of course, even though opportunities for firsthand discovery and exploration are particularly vital for visually impaired children, they are also important for children with normal vision.

Special Adaptations for Blind Students

Braille is a system of reading and writing in which letters, words, numbers, and other systems are made from arrangements of raised dots. The system was

There are virtually no limits to the kinds of activities in which visually impaired students can participate. This spelunker is totally blind.

	1 a	2 b	3 c	4 d	5 e	6 f	7 g	8 h	9 i	0 j

The six dots of the Braille cell are

arranged and numbered thus: 1● ●4 2● ●5 3● ●6

The capital sign, dot 6, placed before a letter makes it a capital. The number sign, dots 3, 4, 5, 6, placed before a character, makes it a figure and not a letter.

k	l	m	n	o	p	q	r	s	t

u	v	w	x	y	z	Capital Sign	Number Sign	Period	Comma

FIGURE 8.3

The braille system for representing numbers and letters. (*Source:* From the Division for the Blind and Physically Handicapped, Library of Congress, Washington, DC 20542.)

developed around 1830 by Louis Braille, a young Frenchman who was blind. Although the braille system is over 150 years old, it is by far the most efficient approach to reading by touch and is still an essential skill for people who have too little vision to read print. Blind students can read braille much more rapidly than they could the raised letters of the standard alphabet. Figure 8.3 shows the braille alphabet and numerals.

The braille system is complex. In many ways, it is like the shorthand secretaries use. Abbreviations, called *contractions,* help save space and permit faster reading and writing. For example, when the letter *r* stands by itself, it means rather. The word *myself* in braille is written *myf.* Frequently used words—such as *the, and, with,* and *for*—have their own special contractions. For example, the *and* symbol ( ) appears four times in the following sentence:

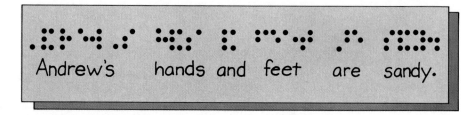

Many similar abbreviations assist in the more efficient reading and writing of braille. Mathematics, music, foreign languages, and scientific formulas all can be put into braille. When blind children attend regular public school classes, a specially trained teacher provides individual instruction in braille reading and writing. Cooperative planning with the regular classroom teacher is critical so that books can be ordered or prepared in advance. The regular classroom teacher is not usually expected to learn braille, but some teachers find it helpful and interesting to do so. The braille system is not as difficult to learn as it first appears.

Most blind children are introduced to braille at about the first grade level. The majority of teachers introduce contractions early in the program, rather than

The brailler is a six-keyed device that punches the raised dots in special paper.

having the child learn to write out every word, letter by letter, and later have to unlearn this approach. Of course, it is important for the blind child to know the full and correct spelling of words, even if every letter does not appear separately in braille. It usually takes several years for children to become thoroughly familiar with the system and its rules. The speed of braille reading varies a great deal from student to student, but it is almost always much slower than the speed of print reading.

Young children generally learn to write braille using a brailler, a six-keyed device that somewhat resembles a typewriter. Older students are usually introduced to the slate and stylus, in which the braille dots are punched out one at a time by hand, from right to left. The slate and stylus method has certain advantages in note-taking; it is much smaller and quieter than the brailler.

Technology and Other Special Aids

Typically, braille books are large, expensive, and cumbersome. It can be difficult for blind students to retrieve information quickly when they must tactually review many pages of braille books or notes. Recent technological developments are making braille more efficient, thus enabling many blind students to function more independently in regular classrooms, universities, and employment settings (Kelly, 1987; Todd, 1986).

Written Communication

One system, known as VersaBraille II+ (Telesensory System, Inc.), is a portable laptop computer on which blind students can take notes and tests in class and prepare assignments and papers at home. The keyboard has six keys that correspond to the dots in a braille cell, a numeric keypad, and a joystick. Students can check their work by reading a dynamic tactile display on the top of the VersaBraille II+ consisting of 20 braille cells, each made up of small pins that move up and down as the text progresses. Students store their work on a 3–1/2-inch floppy disc that can be used with a talking word-processing program such as the BRAILLE-EDIT Xpress (BEX) or to produce standard English print copies for teachers to read. A printer by Ohtsuki produces pages with both braille and print formats, enabling blind and sighted readers to use the same copy.

Typewriting is an important means of communication between blind children and their sighted classmates and teachers and is also a useful skill for further education and employment. Instruction in typing should begin as early as feasible in the child's school program. Today, handwriting is less widely taught to totally blind students, with the noteworthy exception that it is necessary for children to learn to sign their own names so they can assume such responsibilities as maintaining a bank account, registering to vote, and applying for a job.

A wide range of specialized materials and devices has been specially developed or modified for the instruction of blind students. Most of these educational materials are available from state instructional materials centers for the visually impaired or from the American Printing House for the Blind.

Manipulatives and Tactile Aids

Manipulatives are generally recognized as effective tools in teaching beginning mathematics skills to elementary students (Parham, 1983). When using most manipulatives, such as Cuisenaire rods, however, sighted students use length and color to distinguish the various numerical values of the rods. Belcastro (1989) has developed a set of rods that enables blind students to quickly identify different values by feeling the lengths and tactile markings associated with each number. Another mathematical aid for blind students is the Cranmer Abacus. The abacus, long used in Japan, has been adapted to assist blind students in learning number concepts and making calculations. Manipulation of the abacus beads is particularly useful in counting, adding, and subtracting. For more advanced mathematical functions, the student is likely to use the Speech-Plus talking calculator, a small electronic instrument that performs most of the operations of any standard calculator. It "talks" by voicing entries and results aloud and also presents them visually in digital form. This is only one of many instances in which the recent development of synthetic speech technology has helpful implications for blind people. Talking clocks and spelling aids are also available.

In the sciences and social studies, several adaptations encourage blind students to use their tactile and auditory senses for firsthand manipulation and discovery. Examples include embossed relief maps and diagrams, three-dimensional models, and electronic probes that give an audible signal in response to light. Curriculum modification projects such as MAVIS (Materials

A talking calculator and braille watch.

Adaptation for Visually Impaired Students in the Social Studies) and SAVI (Science Activities for the Visually Impaired) emphasize how visually impaired students can, with some modifications, participate in learning activities along with normally sighted students.

Further information about these programs is available from the organizations listed at the end of the chapter.

Technological Aids

The Optacon (optical-to-tactile converter) is a small electronic device that converts regular print into a readable vibrating form for blind people. The Optacon does not convert print into braille, but into a configuration of raised "pins" representing the letter the camera is viewing. When the tiny camera of the Optacon is held over a printed *E,* for example, the user feels on the tip of one finger a vertical line and three horizontal lines. Although extensive training and practice are required, many blind children and adults are able to read regular print effectively with the aid of the Optacon. It can allow students to work with typewriters, calculators, computer terminals, and small print.

The Kurzweil Reading Machine is another recent technological development with exciting implications for visually impaired and other disabled students. This sophisticated computer actually reads books and other printed matter aloud, using synthetic speech. The reader can regulate the speed and tone of the voice and can even have the machine spell out words letter by letter if desired. The "intelligence" of the Kurzweil Reading Machine is constantly being improved, and the machines, although costly, are currently in use at most residential schools and also in many public school programs, large public libraries, rehabilitation centers, and colleges and universities.

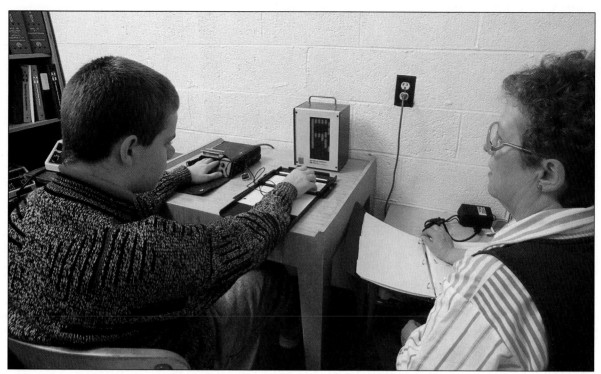

The Optacon's training monitor enables the teacher to see the letter the student must learn to feel.

Peter can adjust the speed and pitch of the Kurzweil Reading Machine's "voice."

Special Adaptations for Students with Low Vision

As noted, the great majority of children enrolled in educational programs for the visually impaired have some potentially useful vision. Their learning need not be restricted to touch, hearing, and other nonvisual senses. Currently, there is great emphasis on developing children's abilities to use their vision as effectively as possible. Recent research has shown that structured programs of visual assessment, training, and evaluation can dramatically improve these abilities; the earlier in life that such programs begin, the more likely they are to be successful (Corn, 1986; Fellows, Leguire, Rogers, & Bremer, 1986; Ferrell, 1985). Corn (1989) believes professionals must understand some basic premises about low vision and its effects on a person to guide curriculum development and instructional planning.

♦ *Those with congenital low vision view themselves as "whole"; they do not have remaining or residual vision.* While it may be proper to speak of "residual vision" in reference to those who experience adventitious low vision, those with congenital low vision do not have a "normal" vision reference. They view the world with all the vision they have ever had.

♦ *Those with low vision generally view the environment as "stationary" and "clear."* Although there are exceptions, this premise tries to dispel the misconception that people with low vision live in an impressionistic world in which they are continuously wanting to "clear" the image.

♦ *Low vision offers a different aesthetic experience.* Low vision may alter an aesthetic experience but does not necessarily produce a lesser one.

♦ *20/20 acuity is not needed for visual function for most tasks or for orientation and mobility within most environments.*

♦ *Clinical measurements do not dictate visual functioning.* Such measurements provide a "ball park" in which to anticipate visual functioning.

♦ *Those with low vision can enhance visual functioning through the use of optical aids, nonoptical aids, environmental modifications, and/or techniques.*

♦ *The use of low vision is not in all circumstances the most efficient or the preferred method of functioning.* For some individuals or for some tasks, the use of vision alone or in combination with other senses may reduce one's ability to perform. For example, using vision while pouring salt on food may not be the most efficient method for determining how much salt has been poured.

♦ *There are unique psychological aspects of low vision.* Those with low vision have life experiences not encountered by those without such a condition. There is much to be learned about the adjusting processes for those who are visually handicapped congenitally and adventitiously.

♦ *Those who have low vision may develop a sense of visual beauty, enjoy their visual abilities, and use vision to learn.* (Adapted from Corn, 1989, pp. 29–30.)

Visual Functioning

The current emphasis on utilization of low vision is largely attributable to the influential work of Natalie Barraga (1964, 1970, 1980, 1983). She demonstrated that children—even those with extremely limited visual acuity or visual field—could be helped to improve their visual functioning dramatically. Visual efficiency, as defined by Barraga, includes such skills as controlling eye movements, adapting to the visual environment, paying attention to visual stimuli, and processing visual information rapidly. The fundamental premise in developing visual efficiency is that children *learn to see* and must be actively involved in using their own vision. Merely furnishing a classroom with attractive things for children to see is not sufficient. A low vision child may, without training, be unable to derive much meaningful information through vision. Forms may be perceived as vague masses and shapeless, indistinct blobs. Training has helped many children learn to use their visual impressions intelligently and effectively, to make sense out of what they see. Downing and Bailey (1990) stress the importance of teaching the basic visual skills of attending, localizing, tracking, shifting gaze, scanning, and reaching (moving) toward an object within functional activities for the individual. For example, instead of having the child with low vision practice his visual skills by sorting miscellaneous junk objects, he could utilize those skills while learning to make a fruit and ice cream drink.

Barraga's *Program to Develop Efficiency in Visual Functioning,* including a helpful *Source Book on Low Vision* (which can be purchased separately), is available from the American Printing House for the Blind.

Corn (1989) suggests four goals around which to base instructional activities in a program in the use of low vision. Her four goals are in response to the question, "For what purposes do we use vision?"

♦ *To gain information from directed visual experience.* A four-year-old child may be asked to count the number of egg yolks in a bowl to see if more are needed to follow a recipe, or a three-year-old may be asked to repeat a dance step that has been demonstrated.

♦ *To gain information from incidental visual experiences.* A 12-year-old may notice the symbol of a plumbing company on a truck outside a friend's home and infer that there may be a plumbing problem in the house.

♦ *To gain an appreciation of visual experiences.* A child may select a video game to play for the enjoyment of watching the target move about the screen.

♦ *To utilize vision for the planning or execution of a task.* An adult may observe visually a narrow passage and determine whether it will be necessary to turn his or her body sideways to go through the opening. Through instruction, the individual may be able to enhance his or her ability to use visual observations to plan or execute the task. (pp. 31–32)

Optical Devices

Many children with low vision are able to benefit from special optical devices. These may include glasses and contact lenses, small telescopes that are held in the hand, or magnifiers placed on top of printed pages. Such aids cannot give normal vision to visually impaired children, but may help them perform better at certain tasks such as reading small print or seeing distant objects.

Optical aids are usually specialized rather than all-purpose. Juanita might, for example, use her glasses for reading large print, a magnifier stand for

Most optical aids are designed for special purposes. Juanita uses her monocular telescope for distance viewing.

reading smaller print, and a monocular (one-eye) telescope for viewing the blackboard. A usual disadvantage of corrective lenses and magnifiers is that the more powerful they are, the more they tend to distort or restrict the peripheral field of vision. Some field-widening lenses and devices are now available for students with limited visual fields. These include prisms and fish-eye lenses, designed to make objects appear smaller so that a greater area can be perceived on the unimpaired portions of a student's visual field. Instruction in vision utilization should not be taught only in isolated time blocks, but should be incorporated into all parts of the low vision student's curriculum (Corn, 1986). For example, a child learning daily living skills might be encouraged to use his vision to identify and reach for his toothbrush.

Children whose vision is extremely limited are more likely to use monocular (one-eye) than binocular (two-eye) aids, especially for seeing things at a distance. See pages 352–354 for suggestions to help children become accustomed to their optical aids.

Today, many ophthalmologists, optometrists, and clinical facilities specialize in the assessment and treatment of low vision. A professional examination can help determine which types of optical aids, if any, are appropriate for a particular student. It is usually a good idea to furnish optical aids on a trial or loan basis so the student can gradually learn to use and evaluate them in natural settings. A follow-up session should then be scheduled.

Reading Print Materials

Students with low vision use three basic approaches for reading print: approach magnification (reducing the distance between the eye and the page of print from 40 cm to 5 cm results in 8× magnification) (Jose, 1983), lenses (optical devices), and large type (Corn & Ryser, 1989). Large type was first introduced in the Cleveland Public Schools in 1913 in the form of 36-point "clear face" type (Eaken & McFarland, 1960).

Many books and other materials are available in large print for children with low vision. The American Printing House for the Blind produces books in 18-point type. Some states and other organizations produce large-type materials,

HELPING THE STUDENT WITH LOW VISION

What does a child with low vision actually see? It is difficult for us to know. We can try to obtain some idea of total blindness by wearing a blindfold, but the majority of children with visual impairments are not totally blind. Even when two children share the same cause of visual impairment, it is unlikely that they see things in exactly the same way. And each child may see things differently at different times.

We asked a few people with low vision to describe how they see. Here are some excerpts from what they told us.

> Have you ever been out camping in a strange place? When it's dark and you're trying to find your way from the tent to the bathroom, and you can't wear your glasses or contact lenses—that's like the way I see. I'm pretty much nearsighted. I can see a far object, I mean I know the image is there, but I can't distinguish it. I can see a house. It is just a white blob out there. I couldn't tell you what color is the roof trim, or where the windows are.*

> Put on a pair of sunglasses. Then rub Vaseline all around the central part of each lens. Now try reading a book. Or crossing a street. I never see blackness. . . . If I am looking at a picture, it's not like I see a hole in the middle. I fill something in there, but it wouldn't necessarily be what is really there. That's how I describe it to people—take a newspaper, hold it up, and look straight ahead. Now describe what you see here, off to the side . . . that's what I see all the time.*

Suggestions for Teachers

The following suggestions for teachers of students with low vision are from the Vision Team, a group of specialists in visual impairment who work with regular class teachers in 13 school districts in Hennepin County, Minnesota. Glenda Martin has permitted us to share the suggestions with you.

♦ Using the eyes does not harm them. The more children use their eyes, the greater their efficiency will be.

♦ Holding printed material close to the eyes may be the low vision child's way of seeing best. It will not harm the eyes.

♦ Although eyes cannot be strained from use, a low vision child's eyes may tire more quickly. A change of focus or activity helps.

♦ Copying is often a problem for low vision children. The child may need more time to do classwork or a shortened assignment.

♦ It is helpful if the teacher verbalizes as much as possible while writing on the chalkboard or using the overhead projector.

♦ Some low vision children use large print books, but many do not. As the child learns to use vision, it becomes more efficient, and the student can generally read smaller print.

♦ Dittoes can be difficult for the low vision child to read. Giving that child one of the first copies or the original from which the ditto was made can be helpful.

♦ The term *legally blind* does not mean educationally blind. Most children who are legally blind function educationally as sighted children.

Low vision aids should be portable and easily used.

♦ Contrast, print style, and spacing can be more important than the size of the print.

♦ One of the most important things a low vision child learns in school is to accept the responsibility of seeking help when necessary, rather than waiting for someone to offer help.

♦ In evaluating quality of work and applying discipline, the teacher best helps the low vision child by using the same standards that are used with other children.

Perhaps most important of all, an attitude of understanding and acceptance can help the student with low vision succeed in the regular classroom.

Using Low Vision Aids

Children who have low vision aids—such as special eyeglasses, magnifiers, and telescopes—may need instruction and assistance in learning how to use them most effectively. Here are some tips written especially for children to help them become accustomed to low vision aids.**

♦ Low vision aids take time to get used to. At first it seems like just a lot more things to take care of and carry around, but each aid you have will help you with a special job of seeing. You will get better with practice. In time, reaching for your telescope to read the blackboard will seem as natural as picking up a pencil or pen to write. It's all a matter of practice.

♦ Lighting is very important. Always work with the most effective light for you. It makes a big difference in how clear things will look. Some magnifiers come with a built-in light, but most times you will have to use another light. A desk lamp is best. (The overhead light casts a shadow on your book or paper as you get close enough to see it.) Be sure the light is along your side, coming over your shoulder.

♦ Be sure to keep your aids clean. Dust, dirt, and fingerprints are hard to see through. Clean the lenses with a clean, soft cloth (never paper). If you have contact lenses, clean them with a special solution, following your doctor's instructions carefully. Always be sure your hands are clean to begin.

♦ Keep your aids in their cases when you are not using them. They will be more protected and always ready for you to take with you wherever you go.

- Carry your low vision aids with you. Most of them are small and lightweight. That way, you will have them when you need them. If you have aids you use only at school, you may want to ask your teacher to keep them for you in a safe place.

- Experiment in new situations. Can you see the menu at McDonald's? Watch the football game? See prices on toys? Find your friend's house number? The more often you use your low vision aid, the better you will get at using it.

- Try out different combinations of aids with or without your glasses or contact lenses. This way you will find the combination that works best for you.

[Sources: *From Voices: Interviews with Handicapped People *by M. D. Orlansky and W. L. Heward, 1981, Columbus, OH: Merrill. **From* A Closer Look at Low Vision Aids *by Marybeth Dean with illustrations by Gail Feld. Available from the Connecticut State Board of Education and Services for the Blind, Division of Children's Services, 170 Ridge Road, Wethersfield, CT 06109.]* ◆

but the size and style of the print fonts, spacing, paper, and quality of production vary widely. This book is set in 10-point type. Following are four examples of different large-print type sizes.

This is 14 point type.
This is 18 point type.
This is 20 point type.
This is 24 point type.

Large-print materials have certain disadvantages. Making print very large sharply reduces the number of letters and words that can be seen at one time; it thus becomes more difficult for a student to read smoothly, with a natural sweep of eye movements. It is generally agreed that a visually impaired child should use the smallest print size that she can read comfortably. A child may be able to transfer from large print to smaller print as reading efficiency increases, just as most normally sighted children do.

A significant number of children with low vision are able to learn to read using regular-sized print, with or without the use of optical aids. Stokes (1976) believes that "large type should not be recommended by a doctor or used by a teacher unless a thorough comparison with regular type is made" (p. 346). This approach permits a much wider variety of materials and eliminates the added cost of obtaining large-print books or enlarging texts with special duplicating machines. Although print size is an important variable, other equally important factors to consider are the quality of the printed material, the contrast between print and page, the spacing between lines, and the illumination of the setting in which the child reads.

Table 8.1 compares advantages and disadvantages of large-print materials and optical devices. Corn and Ryser (1989) obtained information from the

Each of these three students at a state-run residential school for the blind uses dictionaries with different size type.

teachers of 399 students with low vision on such variables as reading speed and achievement, fatigue, and access to various materials. They concluded that, in most instances, reading regular print with an optical device is preferable to large-print materials:

> The use of optical devices (for those who can benefit from them) should be viewed as the least restrictive approach to gain access to all regular-print materials for near and distance tasks. The receipt of a prescription for a telescopic device gives the student access to chalkboards, signs, and events in the distance. . . . [O]ptical devices are individualized educational tools and are just as important to a child with a low vision as is a brace to a child with a physical handicap or a hearing aid to a hearing-impaired child. (pp. 348–349)

Some educational programs use closed-circuit television systems to enable low vision students to read regular-sized printed materials. These systems usually include a sliding table on which a book is placed, a television camera with a zoom lens mounted above the book, and a television monitor nearby. The student is able to adjust the size, brightness, and contrast of the material and can select either an ordinary black-on-white image or a negative white-on-black image, which many students prefer. The teacher may also have a television monitor that lets him see the student's work without making repeated trips to the student's desk. A disadvantage of closed-circuit television systems—in addition to cost—is that they are usually not portable, so that the student who uses television as a primary reading medium is largely restricted to the specially equipped classroom or library.

Other Classroom Modifications

Other classroom adaptations for low vision students are often minor but can be very important. Many students benefit from desks with adjustable or tilting tops so they can read and write at close range without constantly bending over and

TABLE 8.1
Advantages and disadvantages of large-type materials.

Optical Devices	Large-Type Materials
Advantages	**Advantages**
• Access to materials of various sizes, such as regular texts, newspapers, menus, and maps.	• Little or no instruction is needed to use a large-type book or other materials.
• Lower cost per child than large-type materials.	• Quota-account funds are available for large-type books.
• Lighter weight and more portable than large-type materials.	• A low vision clinical evaluation is not needed.
• No ordering or waiting time for production or availability.	• Students carry large-type "books" like other students in their classes.
• Access to distant print and objects, such as chalkboards, signs, and people.	• Funds for large-type books come from school districts that may require parental or other funding for optical devices.
Disadvantages	**Disadvantages**
• A low vision clinical evaluation must be obtained for the prescription of optical devices.	• Enlarging print by photocopy emphasizes imperfect letters.
• Funding for clinical evaluation and optical devices must be obtained.	• Pictures are in black, white, and shades of gray.
• Instruction in the use of the optical devices is needed.	• Fractions, labels on diagrams, maps, and so forth are enlarged only to a print size smaller than 18-point type.
• The cosmetics of optical devices may cause self-consciousness.	• The size and weight of large-type texts are difficult to handle.
• Optical problems associated with the optics of devices need to be tolerated.	• Large-type materials are not readily available after the school years, and students may be nonfunctional readers with regular type.

Source: From "Access to Print for Students with Low Vision" by A. Corn and G. Ryser, 1989, *Journal of Visual Impairment and Blindness, 83,* p. 341. Reprinted by permission.

See pages 352–354 for additional suggestions for helping the child with low vision succeed in the regular classroom.

casting a shadow. Most regular classrooms have adequate lighting, but special lamps may still be helpful for some children. Writing paper should have a dull finish to reduce glare; an off-white color such as buff or ivory is generally better than white. Some teachers have found it helpful to give low vision students chairs with wheels so they can easily move around the blackboard area or other places in the classroom where instruction is taking place without constantly getting up and down. Dittoed worksheets in light purple or other poorly contrasting colors are difficult for most low vision students to use; an aide or classmate could first go over the worksheet with a dark pen or marker. A teacher can make many other modifications, using common sense and considering the needs of the individual student with low vision.

Listening

Visually impaired children—both those who are totally blind and those with low vision—must obtain an enormous amount of information through the sense of hearing. A great deal of time in school is devoted to speaking and listening to others. Visually impaired students also make frequent use of recorded materials, particularly in high school. Recorded books and magazines and the equipment to use them can be obtained through the Library of Congress, the American Printing House for the Blind, the Canadian National Institute for the Blind, Recording for the Blind, and various other organizations, usually on a free-loan basis. Each state has a designated library that provides books and materials for blind readers.

Because many visually impaired students are able to process auditory information at a faster rate than that of average conversational speech, devices are available to increase the play-back rate of tapes without significantly distorting the quality of the speech. The ever-increasing use of synthetic speech equipment probably means that listening skills will become even more important to visually impaired students in the future. Rhyne (1982) investigated the ability of blind students to comprehend synthetic speech; he found that the aural (listening) mode was a generally efficient way to learn and that students' comprehension increased as they gained more experience listening to synthetic speech.

Because there are so many useful opportunities for learning through listening, an important component of the educational program of virtually every visually impaired child is the systematic development of listening skills. Children do not automatically develop the ability to listen effectively simply by being placed in a regular classroom, nor are visually impaired students necessarily better listeners than normally sighted students.

Listening involves several components, including attention to and awareness of sounds, discrimination, and assignment of meaning to sound (Heinze, 1986). Good listening skills tend to broaden a student's vocabulary and to support the development of speaking, reading, and writing abilities. Learning-to-listen approaches can take an almost unlimited variety of forms. Young children, for example, might learn to discriminate between sounds that are near and far, loud and soft, high-pitched and low-pitched. A teacher might introduce a new word into a sentence and ask the child to identify it. Older students might learn to listen for important details while there are distracting background noises, to differentiate between factual and fictional material, or to respond to verbal analogy questions. Some structured programs for developing listening skills have been developed (Alber, 1974; Stocker, 1973; Swallow & Conner, 1982). Instruction in this area can be among the most useful parts of a visually impaired student's curriculum.

Practical Living and Social Skills

Some educators of visually impaired students suggest that academic achievement has traditionally been overemphasized at the expense of important basic living skills. Hatlen (1976), for example, calls for giving "the most urgent attention" to such areas as cooking, grooming, shopping, financial management, decision making, recreational activities, personal hygiene, and social behavior. Specific instruction in these skills can facilitate a student's eventual independence as an adult. The specially trained teacher, the regular class teacher, other specialists, the parents, and the student should all participate in planning and providing instruction that will be practical and relevant to the student's needs and future objectives.

When talking with a person who is blind, don't be afraid to use words such as *look* and *see*. Individuals with visual impairments use these words too.

Tape-recorded instructions can be used as self-help devices by individuals who are blind. See "I Made It Myself, and It's Good!" on pages 358–361.

"I MADE IT MYSELF, AND IT'S GOOD!"
Blind Students Learn to Use Tape-recorded Recipes

If special education is to contribute to meaningful lifestyle changes for students, it must focus on the instruction of functional skills for postschool environments. Being able to prepare one's own food is a critical skill for independent living. Steve, Lisa, and Carl were 17 to 21 years old and enrolled in a class for multiply handicapped students at a residential school for the blind. They were living in an on-campus apartment used to teach daily living skills. Several unsuccessful attempts had been made to teach basic cooking skills to the three students. None of the students possessed any functional vision or braille skills, and their IQ scores ranged from 64 to 72 on the Perkins Binet Test of Intelligence for the Blind. To learn new skills, especially those involving long chains of responses such as food preparation, students with disabilities like Steve, Lisa, and Carl require intensive instruction over many trials. Once a particular skill sequence is learned, its generalization to other settings and situations (e.g., another recipe) and maintenance across time (2 weeks later the student has "forgotten") is often lacking. The challenge was to discover a method for teaching cooking skills to the three students that was not only initially effective but that enabled the students to successfully prepare recipes on which they had not received direct instruction and that resulted in long-term maintenance of their new skills.

A Cooking Apron with Audio Recipes

Because the three students were blind, it was not possible to use picture cookbooks or color-coded recipes that have been used successfully with learners with mental retardation and other learning handicaps (Bergstrom, Pattavina, Martella, & Marchand-Martella, in press; Book, Paul, Gwalla-Ogisi, & Test, 1990; Johnson & Cuvo, 1981). Instead, tape-recorded recipes were used. Students wore a cooking apron on which two pockets had been sewn. One pocket at the waist held a small audio cassette recorder; the second pocket, located at the chest, held a switch (sold as a foot switch and available for about $5 in any electronics store) which turned "on" the tape player for as long as it was

Carl uses his fingers to help pour and measure the milk for his cake.

depressed. Each of the steps from the task analysis for a given food item was prerecorded in sequence on a cassette tape ("Open the bag of cake mix by tearing it at the tab"). High-pitched "beeps" signaled the end of each direction.

Performance Measures

The number of steps from task-analyzed recipes that each student independently completed for trained food items was measured during preinstruction (baseline), instruction, and maintenance phases. To assess generalization effects, probes were also conducted on two classes of food items on which the students received no training. *Simple generality* items could be prepared with the same set of cooking skills learned in a related trained item. *Complex generality* recipes required the use of skills learned in two different trained items. The relationship between the trained items and the two types of items used to assess generality is shown in the accompanying table. As a measure of social validity, each trial was also scored as to whether the food prepared was edible. All training and probe trials in the study were conducted with one student at a time.

Baseline

To objectively assess whether or not learning has occurred, student performance must be measured before any instruction has begun. The first baseline trial was conducted without the tape-recorded recipes to determine which food preparation steps, if any, a student could already perform without any assistance or adaptive equipment. It was then necessary to find out whether the students could successfully prepare the food items if they were simply given the tape-recorded recipes. After showing the students how to operate the tape recorder to hear the prerecorded instructions, students were asked to prepare food items and were given no other prompts, assistance, or feedback.

Instruction

Students were told that the taped recipes told them exactly what to do and where to find the food items and utensils. They practiced using the remote switch to control the rate of instructions by stopping the tape each time they heard a "beep." Training for each step

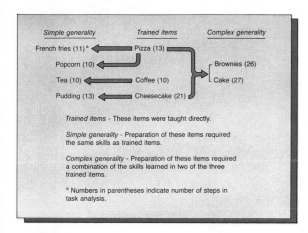

Simple generality | Trained items | Complex generality

French fries (11)[a] ← Pizza (13)
Popcorn (10) ←
Tea (10) ← Coffee (10) → Brownies (26)
Pudding (13) ← Cheesecake (21) → Cake (27)

Trained items - These items were taught directly.

Simple generality - Preparation of these items required the same skills as trained items.

Complex generality - Preparation of these items required a combination of the skills learned in two of the three trained items.

[a] Numbers in parentheses indicate number of steps in task analysis.

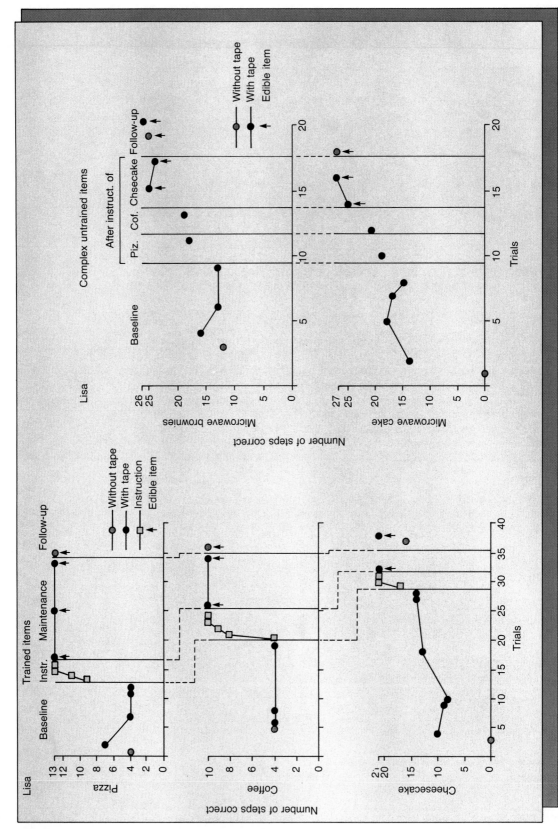

of the task analysis consisted of a three-component least-to-most prompt hierarchy (verbal, physical, and hand-over-hand guidance) following errors and verbal praise for correct responses. Training on each food item continued until a student correctly performed all steps on two consecutive trials over two sessions.

Results

All three students learned to prepare the trained food items with the tape recorded recipes. A total of 12, 20, and 36 instructional trials were needed to teach Steve, Lisa, and Carl to prepare three different recipes. Even more important, without any direct training on those items, all three students were able to prepare both the simple and the complex generality food items with tape-recorded recipes after they had mastered the trained items. The accompanying graphs show Lisa's performance throughout the study on the trained recipes and on the recipes requiring a combination of cooking skills used to make pizza and cheesecake. But lines on a graph showing how many steps were correctly performed can be misleading with a complex skill like cooking. For example, a mistake on any one of several crucial steps in the 27-step task analysis for making microwave cake (e.g., not stirring the egg into the batter) would result in a cake no one would want to eat. Before training, none of Lisa's 13 attempts to make any of the trained items could be eaten, whereas all 7 of her posttraining attempts were edible. Before she learned how to prepare the related items, Lisa was successful on only 17% (2 out of 12) of her attempts to make the simple generality recipes and on none of her 11 attempts to prepare the complex recipes. After learning how to make the related items, Lisa was able to follow tape-recorded recipes to successfully prepare 100% of both the simple (12 out of 12 tries) and complex (5 out of 5) generality items. In follow-up probes conducted 1 year after the study ended, Lisa and Carl were able to successfully prepare each of the food items.

The easy portability of the "walkman-type" tape recorder and the ease of recording taped instructions for new recipes will help the students use their newly acquired cooking skills in other settings and with other food items. As Carl remarked when sharing with his girlfriend the microwave cake he had just made, "I made it myself, and it's good!"

From "Teaching young adults who are blind and developmentally handicapped to use tape-recorded recipes: Acquisition, generalization, and maintenance of cooking skills," by S. A. Trask, T. A. Grossi, and W. L. Heward, 1991. Paper submitted for publication. ◆

Hatlen (1978) further recommends, if necessary, teaching visually impaired students how to deal with strangers, how to interpret and explain their visual impairments to other people, and how to make socially acceptable gestures in conversation. It is also important for students to be aware of the range of career opportunities available to them and to be informed about services, resources, and responsibilities in their communities.

Another area of some concern to educators is special mannerisms—repetitive body movements or other behaviors, such as rocking, eye-poking, hand-waving, and head-rolling. Although not necessarily harmful in themselves, mannerisms can place a visually impaired person at a social disadvantage, because these actions are conspicuous and call attention to the person as different or handicapped. It is not known why many visually impaired children engage in manneristic behaviors. Tooze (1981) attributes them to a child's being under stress or having a "desire to move coupled with a fear of moving forward" (p. 29). It is generally suggested that children be kept busy and active so that they will have less time to indulge in mannerisms. Applied behavioral programs have also been used with visually impaired children to modify head-drooping during conversation (Raver, 1984) and various off-task behaviors that interfere with learning (Barton & LaGrow, 1985).

Huebner (1986) provides an excellent set of guidelines for teaching social skills. She emphasizes the importance of developing socially acceptable behaviors, which in turn facilitate independence, self-confidence, and acceptance by others in school, community, and employment settings. Even though a visually impaired child may perform a task safely and independently, she may not do so in a traditional, socially acceptable manner—for example, the child who likes to eat oatmeal by scooping it up to her mouth with her fingers!

Human Sexuality

Sighted children typically learn a great deal about human sexuality through vision. They see people establish social and sexual relationships with each other; they can see their own and others' bodies. Blind children, however, may grow up with serious knowledge gaps or misconceptions about sexuality and reproduction, particularly if parents and teachers fail to provide information and explanations. "I know girls have breasts," a blind adolescent told his counselor, "but I don't know where they are!" (Elliott, 1979). Modesty makes it difficult for blind children to learn by touching others' bodies, and it is sometimes mistakenly assumed that blind people are uninterested in sex. In some European countries, live human models are used to familiarize blind students with anatomy and sexuality, but this practice has not been widely adopted in North America. In addition to providing accurate biological information, instructional programs should also consider the emotional aspects of sexual experience and the possible genetic implications of a student's visual impairment.

Some kinds of visual impairments can be passed from parents to children.

Issues in Assessment

There is a continuing concern about the use (and possible misuse) of intelligence tests with visually impaired children. Intelligence tests, standardized on sighted children, are often based largely on visual concepts. They may include questions such as "Why do people have hedges around their homes?" or "What should you do if you see a train approaching a broken track?" The results of these tests may well give an inaccurate picture of a visually impaired child's abilities and needs. Regrettably, many blind and low vision children have been placed in inappropriate educational programs because of strict reliance on standardized test performance.

Few tests have been developed for and standardized on visually impaired children; however, even if tests were more readily available, they would be of questionable value because of the diversity and small size of the population. Helpful reviews of assessment procedures and guidelines for appropriate use of tests with visually impaired learners have recently been provided by Bradley-

Johnson and Harris (1990), Chase (1986a, 1986b), and Hall, Scholl, and Swallow (1986). A number of instruments, although not specifically designed for visually impaired students, may nevertheless be useful in assessing certain aspects of performance. In gathering information that will be helpful in developing educational goals for a visually impaired child, a variety of formal and informal procedures should be used. The results of developmental or intelligence tests should always be supplemented by careful observations of the child's behavior in school and play situations (Chapman, 1978). Teachers and parents are usually in the best position to observe the child's communication, exploration, and social interaction over an extended period. Their contributions should play a major part in planning a visually impaired child's educational program.

Orientation and Mobility

The educational program of a visually impaired child could hardly be considered complete or appropriate if it failed to include instruction in orientation and mobility. **Orientation** is defined as the ability to establish one's position in relation to the environment through the use of the remaining senses. **Mobility** is the ability to move safely and efficiently from one point to another (Lowenfeld, 1973). For most students, more time and effort is spent in orientation training than in learning specific mobility techniques. It is extremely important that, from an early age, visually impaired children be taught basic concepts that will familiarize them with their own bodies and their surroundings. For example, they must be taught that the place where the leg bends is called a knee and that rooms have walls, doors, windows, corners, and ceilings.

Orientation and mobility (O&M) instruction is a well-developed subspecialty in the education and rehabilitation of individuals who are blind and visually impaired. Many specific techniques are involved in teaching visually impaired students to understand their environment and maneuver through it effectively. Training in such skills should be given by qualified *O&M specialists*. The Association for Education and Rehabilitation of the Blind and Visually Impaired (AER), the professional organization that certifies O&M specialists, also recognizes the important role of O&M assistants (Wiener et al., 1990). The O&M assistant is a paid employee who provides selected O&M services under the direction and supervision of a certified O&M specialist.

O&M specialists are called *peripatologists* in some states.

The long cane is the most common device used by visually impaired persons for independent travel. The traveler does not "tap" the cane, but sweeps it lightly in an arc while walking, to gain information about the path ahead. Properly used, the cane serves as both a *bumper* and a *probe*. The cane acts as a bumper by protecting the body from obstacles such as parking meters and doors; it is also a probe to detect in advance such things as drop-offs or changes in travel surface (e.g., from grass to concrete or from a rug to a wooden floor). Even though mastery of cane skills can do much to increase a person's independence and self-esteem, there are certain disadvantages to cane use (Tuttle, 1984). The cane cannot detect overhanging obstacles such as tree branches and provides only fragmentary information about the environment, particularly if the blind person is in new or unfamiliar surroundings. Unfortunately, many adventitiously blinded persons do not begin learning cane travel skills until 1 to 2 years after losing their sight; they mention concern about acceptance by others and the negative stigma they believe are associated with the cane (Wainapel, 1989).

Until recently, formal O&M instruction, especially for cane use, was seldom given to children younger than about 12 years; however, the importance of early development of travel skills and related concepts is now generally recognized (Pogrund & Rosen, 1989). Today, it is not at all unusual for preschool children to benefit from the services of an O&M specialist.

A small percentage of visually impaired people (about 1% to 3%) travel with the aid of guide dogs (Hill & Jacobson, 1985). Like the cane traveler, the guide dog user must have good O&M skills to select a route and to be aware of the environment. The dog wears a special harness and has been trained to follow several basic verbal commands, to avoid obstacles, and to ensure the traveler's safety. Several weeks of intensive training at special guide dog agencies are required before the person and dog can work together effectively. Misunderstandings sometimes arise if blind people with guide dogs are refused entry into restaurants, hotels, airplanes, or other places that normally do not permit animals; state and local regulations permit guide dogs to have access to these places. Guide dogs are especially helpful when a person must travel over complicated or unpredictable routes, as in large cities. They are not usually available to children under 16 years of age or to people with multiple disabilities.

In the area of mobility, most visually impaired people find it necessary to rely occasionally on the assistance of others. The *sighted guide technique* is a simple method of helping a visually impaired person travel.

♦ When offering assistance to a blind person, speak in a normal tone of voice and ask directly, "May I help you?" This helps him locate you.

♦ Do not grab the blind person's arm or body. Permit him to take your arm.

♦ The visually impaired person should lightly grasp the sighted person's arm just above the elbow and walk half a step behind in a natural manner.

♦ The sighted person should walk at a normal pace, describing curbs or other obstacles and hesitating slightly before going up or down. Never pull or push a blind person when you are serving as a sighted guide.

♦ Don't try to push a blind person into a chair. Simply place his hand on the back of the chair and he will seat himself.

When visually impaired students attend regular classes, it may be a good idea for one of the students and the O&M specialist to demonstrate the sighted guide technique to classmates. To promote independent travel, however, overreliance on the sighted guide technique should be discouraged once the student has learned to get around the classroom and school.

Several recently developed electronic travel aids may facilitate orientation and independent travel for blind and visually impaired persons. These include a laser beam cane, which emits a sound to signal objects in the traveler's path, as well as hazards overhead and drop-offs below. Other devices, designed for use in conjunction with a standard cane or guide dog, send out sound waves to bounce off objects and give the trained traveler information about the environment through auditory or tactual channels. Electronic travel aids have even been used with blind infants as young as 6 months, in an attempt to enhance their early learning and awareness by enabling them to explore their environment more thoroughly and independently (Ferrell, 1984). Disadvantages of electronic travel aids include high cost, the extensive training required, and possible problems in adverse weather conditions. Hill and Jacobson (1985) noted that users of electronic travel aids found them helpful in orienting themselves to new settings, but tended to use the aids less after they had become familiar with the environment.

Clarke (1988) describes a large number of mobility devices for preschoolers who are blind and multiply handicapped. She also provides a checklist by which parents, teachers, and O&M specialists can compare and evaluate the relative advantages and disadvantages of the different devices.

Whatever the preferred method of travel, most visually impaired students can generally learn to negotiate familiar places, such as school and home, on their own. Many visually impaired students can benefit from learning to use a systematic method for obtaining travel information and assistance with street crossing (Florence & LaGrow, 1989; LaGrow & Mulder, 1989). Good orientation and mobility skills have many positive effects. A visually impaired child who can travel independently is likely to develop more physical and social skills and more self-confidence than a child who must continually depend on other people to get around. Good travel skills also expand a student's opportunities for employment and independent living.

■ PLACEMENT ALTERNATIVES FOR STUDENTS WITH VISUAL IMPAIRMENTS

Public Schools

In the past, most children with severe visual impairments were educated in residential schools for blind children. Today, however, most visually impaired children attend regular public school classes with their normally sighted peers. Supportive help is usually given by *itinerant teacher-consultants,* sometimes called *vision specialists.* These specially trained teachers may be employed by a residential school, a school district, a regional education agency, or a state or province. Their roles and caseloads vary widely from program to program (Willoughby & Duffy, 1989). In general, however, the itinerant teacher-consultant may be expected to assume some or all of the following responsibilities:

♦ Instruct the visually impaired student directly (within the classroom and/or individually elsewhere)

♦ Obtain or prepare specialized learning materials

♦ Put reading assignments into braille, large print, or tape-recorded form or arrange for readers

♦ Interpret information about the child's visual impairment and visual functioning to other educators and parents

♦ Suggest classroom and program modifications that may be advisable because of the child's vision

♦ Help plan the child's educational goals, initiate and maintain contact with various agencies, and keep records of services provided

♦ Consult with the child's parents and other teachers

The itinerant teacher-consultant may or may not provide instruction in orientation and mobility. Some programs, particularly in rural areas, employ dually certified teachers who are also orientation and mobility specialists. Other programs employ one teacher for educational support and another for orientation and mobility training. Students on an itinerant teacher's caseload may range from infants to young adults and may include blind, low vision, and multihandicapped children. In rural areas, the itinerant teacher often spends a great deal of time on the road to visit and work with each student and has many challenging responsibilities.

Some public school programs have special resource rooms for visually impaired students. In contrast to the itinerant teacher-consultant, who travels from school to school, the resource room teacher remains in one specially equipped location and serves visually impaired students for part of their school day. Usually, only large school districts have resource rooms for visually impaired students.

The amount of time the itinerant teacher-consultant or resource room teacher spends with a visually impaired student who attends regular classes varies considerably. Some students may be seen every day because they require a great deal of specialized assistance. Others may be seen weekly, monthly, or even less frequently because they are able to function well in the regular class with less support.

Public school education for visually impaired children has many advocates. McIntire (1985) writes that "the least restrictive environment for blind children

Patrick is getting along fine in the regular classroom—thanks to the instructional adaptations jointly planned by his itinerant vision specialist and his classroom teacher.

is in the local public school regular classroom with nonhandicapped children" (p. 163); Cruickshank (1986) maintains that "the blind child is perhaps the easiest exceptional child to integrate into a regular grade in the public schools" (p. 104). To make this integration successful, however, a full program of appropriate educational and related services must be provided (Curry & Hatlen, 1988). As Griffing (1986) observes, "No category of handicap requires greater coordination and cooperation among resources than the area of the blind and visually impaired" (p. 5). The key person in the visually impaired child's program is the regular classroom teacher. An extensive study of the elements of successful mainstreaming of visually impaired children in public school classes found that the single most important factor was the regular classroom teacher's flexibility (Bishop, 1986). Other aspects of the school situation found to be highly important were peer acceptance and interaction, availability of support personnel, and adequate access to special supplies and equipment.

Residential Schools

Residential schools continue to meet the needs of a sizable number of children with visual impairments. There are 52 such schools operating in the United States today. The current population of residential schools consists largely of visually impaired children with additional disabilities, such as mental retardation, hearing impairment, behavior disorders, and cerebral palsy. Some parents are not able to care for their children adequately at home, and others prefer the greater concentration of specialized personnel, facilities, and services that the residential school usually offers.

See Chapter 10 for information on children with multiple disabilities, including those who are deaf-blind.

Parents and educators who support residential school education for visually impaired children frequently point to the leadership that such schools have provided over a long period, with their "wealth and broad range of expertise" (Miller, 1985, p. 160). These supporters argue that a residential school can be the least restrictive environment for many visually impaired and multihandicapped students. A follow-up study of visually impaired students at a state school for the blind found that parents, local education agencies, and the students themselves generally considered the residential school placement to have been appropriate and beneficial (Livingston-White, Utter, & Woodard, 1985). Among the advantages cited were specialized curriculum and equipment, participation in extracurricular activities, individualized instruction, small classes, and improved self-esteem.

Placement in a residential school program need not be regarded as permanent. Many visually impaired children move from residential schools into public schools (or vice versa) as their needs change. Some students in residential schools attend nearby public schools for all or part of their school day. Most residential schools encourage parent involvement and have recreational programs that bring visually impaired students into contact with nonhandicapped peers. Independent living skills and vocational training are important parts of the program at virtually all residential schools.

In several states and provinces, there is close cooperation between public school and residential school programs that serve visually impaired children. Thurman (1978), for example, reports that the residential school in Canada's Atlantic provinces employs a network of itinerant teacher-consultants who provide instruction, materials, and assistance to visually impaired children attending regular public schools. These professionals offer regular consultation to the various teachers who also work with visually impaired students. It is expected that most visually impaired children in this region will gradually be integrated into their local public schools and that the residential school will serve mainly multihandicapped students and young visually impaired children who require training in basic skills.

One of the oldest and best-known residential schools, Perkins School for the Blind in Watertown, Massachusetts, was chartered in 1829. Perhaps the most famous teacher-student combination in American history—Anne Sullivan and Helen Keller—spent several years at Perkins. The school also has a long history of providing training for teachers from around the world.

A residential school for the blind has an opportunity to work closely with consumers, parents, professionals, and funding agencies in developing a wide array of community-based services. Cooperative working relationships and creative short- and long-term planning efforts have the potential to generate positive and reality-based services that respond to present-day needs within the context of community integration. Residential schools, primarily because of the expertise of their staff but also because of their location, centralization of resources, and availability of facilities, have the potential to become responsive resource centers on regional and state levels.

Residential schools have long played an important role in training teachers of visually impaired children, on both a preservice and inservice basis. The residential school is usually well equipped to serve as a resource center for instructional materials and as a place where visually impaired students can receive specialized evaluation services. An increasing number of residential schools now offer short-term training to visually impaired students who attend regular public schools. One example is a summer workshop emphasizing braille, mobility, and vocational training.

■ CURRENT ISSUES/FUTURE TRENDS

As we have noted, children with visual impairments constitute only a small portion of the school-age population, but they have many unique needs. Although the current trend toward greater integration of children with visual impairments into regular public school classes is generally welcomed, some educators caution against wholesale placement of visually impaired children in regular schools without adequate support. Many vision professionals tend to resist noncategorical special education programs for visually impaired students. It is unrealistic, they argue, to expect regular teachers or teachers trained in other areas of special education to be competent in such specialized techniques as braille, mobility, and visual efficiency.

Specialization of Services

Although financial restrictions may require some public school and residential school programs for visually impaired children to close down or to consolidate with programs for children with other disabilities, there is strong support for the continuation of highly specialized services. Both public and residential programs for visually impaired children will continue to operate well into the future, occasionally challenging each other for the privilege of serving the relatively small number of available students. The results of this competition may well prove favorable if both types of schools are encouraged to improve the quality of their educational services.

As more infants and preschool children with impaired vision are identified, there will be greater emphasis on specialized programs of early intervention (Ferrell, 1986). Older students will receive more systematic instruction in skills related to employment and independent living, and there will be continuing efforts to improve coordination of services between educational programs and postschool rehabilitation agencies. The current interest in children with low vision will extend beyond the area of vision utilization and into many other aspects of education and development. Some evidence suggests that low vision children may have a more difficult time than totally blind children in gaining social acceptance by sighted children in public schools (Corn, 1986; Spenciner, 1972); thus, new programs will be designed to address the psychosocial needs of low vision children.

Technology and Research

New technological and biomedical developments will continue to aid visually impaired students, particularly in the areas of mobility, communication, and use of low vision. In the future, it may even be possible to provide a form of artificial sight to certain totally blind people, by implanting electrodes into the brain and connecting them to a miniature television camera built into an artificial eye (Dobelle, 1977; Marbach, 1982). Research in artificial sight is in the early experimental stages, but suggests much promise. Other systems of electronic vision substitution rely on tactual images projected onto an area of the body, such as the back or abdomen, enabling the blind person to perceive a visionlike sensation.

Fighting Discrimination

Like other groups of individuals with disabilities, blind and visually impaired people are becoming increasingly aware of their rights as citizens and consumers and are fighting discrimination based on their disabilities. As Willoughby (1980) observes, many people—even some who work with students who are visually impaired—tend to underestimate their students' capacities and deny them a full range of occupational and personal choices. The future will probably bring a gradual shift away from some of the vocational settings in which people with visual impairments have traditionally worked (such as piano tuning, sheltered workshops, and rehabilitation counseling) in favor of a more varied range of employment opportunities. These and other trends will be appropriately reflected in future programs of education and training for children with visual impairments.

Defining Visual Impairment

♦ Vision is a critical sense that children use to obtain information about the world. Without it, they need special materials and attention to enable them to learn and develop to their full potential.

♦ There are both legal and educational definitions of visual impairment.

♦ An educational definition considers the extent to which a visual impairment makes special education materials or methods necessary.

♦ Low vision children can learn through the visual channel and can usually learn to read print.

♦ Besides impairments in visual acuity and field of vision, a child may have problems with ocular motility or visual accommodation, photophobia, or defective color vision.

♦ The age of onset of a visual impairment may affect a child's educational and emotional needs.

Types and Causes of Visual Impairment

♦ The eye collects light reflected from objects, focuses the objects' image on the retina, and transmits the image to the brain. Difficulty with any part of this process can cause vision problems. Common types of visual impairment include:

  Myopia (nearsightedness)
  Hyperopia (farsightedness)
  Astigmatism (blurred vision caused by irregularities in the cornea or other eye surfaces)
  Cataract (blurred or distorted vision caused by cloudiness in the lens)
  Glaucoma (loss of vision caused by high pressure within the eye)
  Diabetic retinopathy, retinitis pigmentosa, macular degeneration, and retinal detachment (all caused by problems with the retina)
  Retinopathy of prematurity (retrolental fibroplasia) (caused by administration and withdrawal of high doses of oxygen to premature infants in incubators)

Prevalence

♦ Visual impairment is a low-incidence disability, affecting less than 0.1% of the school-age population. About one-third of all visually impaired students have additional disabilities.

Background of the Field

♦ Educating blind students is one of the oldest fields of special education.

♦ Hauy started the first school for blind children in Paris in 1784; by the early 19th century, several other European countries had started residential schools for blind children.

♦ The first American schools for blind children were private residential schools, established around 1830, and were soon followed by public residential schools.

♦ Until recently, children with low vision were not encouraged to use their sight so as to conserve it; today, they are taught to concentrate on developing and using their vision as much as possible.

- The influx of children whose blindness was caused by retinopathy of prematurity led to expansion of regular public school programs for visually impaired children in the 1950s and 1960s.
- Most parents can choose between public day and residential schools for their visually impaired children. Neither placement need be considered permanent.

Educational Approaches

- Teachers of visually impaired children need specialized skills along with knowledge, competence, and creativity.
- Most children who are blind learn to read braille and write with a brailler and a slate and stylus. They may also learn to type and use special equipment for mathematics, social studies, and listening to or feeling regular print.
- Children with low vision should learn to use their residual vision as efficiently as possible. Many use optical aids and large print to read regular type.
- All visually impaired children need to develop their listening skills.
- Visually impaired students also may need special instruction in practical daily living skills, in dealing with other people, and in human sexuality.
- Many visually impaired children need help to avoid developing distinctive mannerisms.
- The teacher must use observation and a variety of informal and formal procedures to assess visually impaired children. Standardized intelligence tests are often inappropriate.
- Orientation and mobility instruction is a must for blind or severely visually impaired children.

Placement Alternatives for Visually Impaired Students

- Most visually impaired children attend regular classes with sighted peers.
- In many districts, a specially trained itinerant vision specialist provides extra help for students and regular class teachers.
- Some programs also have separate orientation and mobility instructors or separate resource rooms for visually impaired students.
- Many visually impaired children—especially those with other disabilities—attend residential schools.

Current Issues/Future Trends

- Visually impaired children are likely to receive specialized services in the future in both regular and residential schools.
- There will be greater emphasis on intervention with visually impaired infants and young children and on training older students for independence.
- Low vision children will receive more attention in the coming years, and it is hoped that all visually impaired people will benefit from new technological and biomedical developments. Artificial sight may be possible in the future.
- Career opportunities for visually impaired persons will likely expand as these individuals become more aware of their legal and human rights.

Journals

Journal of Visual Impairment and Blindness. Published 10 times per year by the American Foundation for the Blind, 15 West 16th Street, New York, NY 10011. An interdisciplinary journal for practitioners and researchers concerned with the education and rehabilitation of blind and visually impaired children and adults. Includes regular updates on technological and legislative developments.

RE:view (formerly *Education of the Visually Handicapped*). Published quarterly by the Association for Education and Rehabilitation of the Blind and Visually Impaired, 206 North Washington Street, Room 320, Alexandria, VA 22314. Includes practical articles, research studies, interviews, and other features relevant to teachers of visually impaired students, orientation and mobility specialists, rehabilitation workers, administrators, and parents. Twice per year *RE:view* publishes its *Semi-annual Listing of Current Literature: Blindness, Visual Impairment, Deaf-Blindness,* an annotated bibliographic listing of articles, books, and other publications designed to "provide a fairly complete and coordinated compilation of professional literature related to serious visual impairment."

The Sight-Saving Review. Published quarterly by the National Society to Prevent Blindness, 500 East Remington Road, Schaumburg, IL 60173. Emphasizes new developments in the assessment and treatment of visual impairments, low vision aids, eye safety, and health education.

Books

Barraga, N. (1983). *Visual handicaps and learning* (rev. ed.). Austin, TX: Exceptional Resources.

Ferrell, K. A. (1985). *Reach out and teach.* New York: American Foundation for the Blind.

Heller, B. W., Flohr, L. M., & Zegans, L. S. (Eds.). (1987). *Psychosocial interventions with sensorially disabled persons.* Orlando, FL: Grune & Stratton.

Jose, R. (1983). *Understanding low vision.* New York: American Foundation for the Blind.

Scholl, G. T. (Ed.). (1986). *Foundations of education for blind and visually handicapped children and youth: Theory and practice.* New York: American Foundation for the Blind.

Tuttle, D. W. (1986). *Self-esteem and adjusting with blindness: The process of responding to life's demands.* Springfield, IL: Charles C. Thomas.

Organizations

American Foundation for the Blind, 15 West 16th Street, New York, NY 10011. Provides many publications and films about blindness. Distributes aids and appliances for people with impaired vision. Publishes the *Journal of Visual Impairment and Blindness* and *Directory of Agencies Serving the Visually Handicapped in the United States.*

American Printing House for the Blind, 1839 Frankfort Avenue, Louisville, KY 40206. Provides books, magazines, and many other publications in braille, large print, and recorded form. Distributes educational materials and aids specially designed for the blind and helpful publications for teachers. Attempts to register all legally blind U.S. children through state departments of education or residential schools. Also provides recordings and computer materials.

Association for Education and Rehabilitation of the Blind and Visually Impaired, 206 North Washington Street, Alexandria, VA 22314. Emphasizes educational, orientation, mobility, and rehabilitation services. Holds regional and national conferences in the United States and Canada. Publishes *RE:view* and a yearbook compiling recent literature in this field.

Canadian National Institute for the Blind, 1921 Bayview Avenue, Toronto, Ontario M4G 3E8. The central agency for information, materials, and supportive services for visually impaired people in Canada. Maintains regional and local offices in all provinces. Effectively depicts the growth and development of a young blind child in a film, *Shelley*.

Division for the Visually Handicapped, Council for Exceptional Children, 1920 Association Drive, Reston, VA 22091. Presents sessions of interest to educators at international, state, and provincial conferences of the Council for Exceptional Children.

National Association for Parents of the Visually Impaired, 2011 Hardy Circle, Austin, TX 78756. Provides practical information for parents. Sponsors parent groups in several areas. Holds conferences and workshops for parents and teachers.

National Federation of the Blind, 1800 Johnson Street, Baltimore, MD 21230. The largest organization of blind people in the United States, with many state and local chapters. Provides publications and films that emphasize the rights and capabilities of people who are blind. Seeks to involve blind people in education and employment and to avoid discrimination. Also sponsors activities and publications for parents of children who are blind.

9

Physical and Health Impairments

♦ How can the type and degree of handicap experienced by a child with a physical disability vary from one environment to another?

♦ How does the visibility of a physical or health impairment affect a child?

♦ How do the nature and severity of a child's physical disability affect IEP goals and objectives?

♦ To what extent should the classroom environment be modified to accommodate students with physical and health impairments?

♦ How can an adaptive or assistive device be a hindrance as well as a help?

Children with physical and health impairments are an extremely varied population. It would be impossible to describe all of them with a single set of characteristics, even if we used very general terms. Their physical disabilities may be mild, moderate, or severe. Their intellectual functioning may be normal, below normal, or above normal. A child may have a single impairment or a combination of impairments. He may have lived with his physical or health impairment since birth, or he may have suddenly acquired it. The children whose special education needs we will consider in this chapter have a great many individual differences; there is no typical case of anything. Although we can make general statements about some physical and health-related conditions, there are numerous variations in the degree and severity of the conditions and how they may affect a child.

Many students with physical and health impairments adjust to their conditions well. They present no unusual behavior problems and are fully capable of learning in the regular classroom and interacting successfully with their nondisabled peers. The sophistication of today's medical treatment enables many children with physical and health impairments to attend school regularly. Hospital stays tend to be shorter, physical therapy and many routine medical regimens can be provided in school settings, and surgery can often be scheduled during vacation periods.

Today, children with physical and health impairments are generally included in educational programs on the basis of particular learning needs, not according to their specific disability or disease. Therefore, regular classroom teachers can expect to have more students with specialized medical and physical management requirements (Mullins, 1979). It is important for teachers (and often for other students as well) to understand how a particular condition may affect a child's learning, development, and behavior. Linda, for example, has undergone long periods of hospitalization and finds it difficult to keep up with her academic work. Gary takes medication that controls his seizures most of the time, but it also tends to make him drowsy in the classroom.

Physical and health problems can give rise to special needs in the school setting. Because of their disabilities or illnesses, children with physical and health impairments may require modifications in the physical environment, in teaching techniques, in communication, or in other aspects of their educational programs. In defining the population of children with disabilities according to P.L. 94–142, the federal government emphasizes that a child's educational performance may be adversely affected by severe orthopedic impairments (including those caused by cerebral palsy, amputations, fractures, and burns) or by other serious or long-standing health problems that limit the child's strength, vitality, or alertness (such as muscular dystrophy or hemophilia).

Some children with physical and health impairments are extremely restricted in their activities and intellectual functioning, whereas others have no major limitations on what they can do and learn. Some appear entirely normal; others have highly visible disabilities. Some children must use special devices or equipment that call attention to the disability; others display behaviors that are not under voluntary control. Some disabilities are always present; others occur only from time to time. Over an extended period, the degree of disability may increase, decrease, or remain about the same.

The special problems children with physical and health impairments encounter in school also vary in kind and degree. Brian, who uses a wheelchair for mobility, is disappointed that he is unable to compete with his classmates in football, baseball, and track. Yet he participates fully in all other aspects of his high school program with no special modifications other than the addition of a few ramps in the building and a newly accessible washroom. Most of Brian's teachers and friends, in fact, do not think of him as needing special education at all.

This chapter focuses on information to help the teacher understand the nature and effects of various physical and health impairments. Many conditions, after all, can affect a child's school experience in important ways. Janice, for example, becomes tired easily and attends school for only 3 hours a day. Kenneth uses a specially designed chair to help him sit more comfortably in the classroom. Special modifications or alterations should not, however, be any more restrictive than necessary. A bright child who uses a wheelchair should not be removed from the regular school program and placed in a class where she can interact only with other children who are developmentally handicapped.

Some conditions may cause possible complications or emergencies to arise in the classroom; it is important for the teacher to know how to manage the situation effectively and when and how to seek help. Thus, general information and suggested guidelines will shape our basic approach to the topic of children with physical and health impairments.

■ TYPES AND CAUSES

There are literally hundreds of physical and health impairments that can affect children's educational performance. We will address only those that are most frequently encountered. Some conditions are congenital, meaning present at birth; other conditions are acquired during the child's development as a result of illness, accident, or unknown cause.

Orthopedic and Neurological Impairments

An **orthopedic impairment** involves the skeletal system—bones, joints, limbs, and associated muscles. A **neurologic impairment** involves the nervous system, affecting the ability to move, use, feel, or control certain parts of the body. Orthopedic and neurologic impairments are two distinct and separate types of disabilities, but they may cause similar limitations in movement (Shivers & Fait, 1985). Many of the same educational, therapeutic, or recreational activities are likely to be appropriate for students with orthopedic and neurologic impairments. And there is a close relationship between the two types; for example, a child who is unable to move his legs because of damage to the central nervous system (neurologic impairment) may also develop disorders in the bones and muscles of the legs (orthopedic impairment)—especially if he does not receive proper therapy and equipment.

Whatever their cause, orthopedic and neurologic impairments are frequently described in terms of the affected parts of the body. The term *plegia* (derived from the Greek "to strike") is often used in combination to indicate the location of limb involvement:

Quadriplegia—all four limbs (both arms and legs) are affected; movement of the trunk and face may also be impaired.

Paraplegia—motor impairment of the legs only.

Hemiplegia—only one side of the body is affected; for example, the left arm and the left leg may be impaired.

Diplegia—major involvement of the legs, with less severe involvement of the arms.

Less common forms of involvement include:

Monoplegia—only one limb is affected.

Triplegia—three limbs are affected.

Double hemiplegia—major involvement of the arms, with less severe involvement of the legs.

It is difficult to establish precise criteria for describing the degree or extent of motor involvement in orthopedic and neurologic impairments. Children's difficulties in performing motor-related tasks may vary from time to time, depending on factors such as positioning, fatigue, and medication. The terms *mild, moderate,* and *severe* are often used to describe the functioning of children with a wide variety of physical and health impairments. Jones (1983), for example, describes mild motor impairment as marked by "very little limitation of activity or incoordination." A child with moderate impairment has disabilities "severe enough to be a handicap in ambulation, self-help, and communication, but not sufficient to disable entirely," whereas a child with severe impairment has disabilities that, without treatment, are "almost totally incapacitating" (p. 43). McKee et al. (1983) suggest the criteria in Figure 9.1 as guidelines for determining level of impairment, but they also warn the chart should not be interpreted too rigidly.

Cerebral Palsy

Cerebral palsy is one of the most prevalent physical impairments in children of school age. It is a long-term condition resulting from a lesion to the brain or an abnormality of brain growth that causes a variety of disorders of movement and posture (Bleck, 1979; Gillham, 1986). "Virtually hundreds of diseases may affect the developing brain and lead to cerebral palsy" (Batshaw & Perret, 1986, p. 300). Cerebral palsy can be treated but not cured; the impairment usually does not get progressively worse as a child ages. Cerebral palsy is not fatal, it is not contagious, and, in the great majority of cases, is not inherited.

Children with cerebral palsy have disturbances of voluntary motor functions. These disturbances may include paralysis, extreme weakness, lack of coordination, involuntary convulsions, and other motor disorders. Children with cerebral palsy may have little or no control over their arms, legs, or speech, depending on the type and degree of impairment. They may also have impaired vision or hearing.

Intellectual impairments *may* accompany cerebral palsy. Nelson and Ellenberg (1986) found that 41% of the children with cerebral palsy in their

FIGURE 9.1

Guidelines for determining level of impairment. (*Source:* From *Occupational and Physical Therapy Services in School-Based Programs: Organizational Manual* (p. 24) by McKee et al., 1983, Houston, TX: Psychological Services Division, Harris County Department of Education. Adapted by permission.)

Severe Handicap

1. Total dependence in meeting physical needs.

2. Poor head control.

3. Deformities, present or potential, that limit function or produce pain.

4. Perceptual and/or sensory-integrative deficits that prevent achievement of academic and age-appropriate motor skills.

Moderate Handicap

1. Some independence in meeting physical needs.

2. Functional head control.

3. Deformities, present or potential, that limit independent function or produce pain.

4. Perceptual and/or sensory-integrative deficits that interfere with achievement of academic and age-appropriate motor skills.

Mild Handicap

1. Independence in meeting physical needs.

2. Potential to improve quality of motor and/or perceptual skills with therapy intervention.

3. Potential for regression in quality of motor and perceptual skills without intervention.

study scored below 70 on a standardized IQ test. The probability of mental retardation appears greater when a convulsive disorder is also present (Smith, 1984). Other surveys (e.g., Verhaaren & Connor, 1981) have estimated that about one-third of children with cerebral palsy have intelligence within or above the normal range. One should use caution in interpreting any such estimates, however. As Levine (1986) points out, students with cerebral palsy often have motor and/or speech impairments that limit the appropriateness of standardized intelligence tests; thus, an IQ score should never serve as the sole descriptor of a child's actual or potential ability. It is also important to bear in mind that no clear relationship exists between the degree of motor impairment and the degree of intellectual impairment (if any) in children with cerebral palsy (or other physical disabilities). A student with only mild motor impairment may experience severe developmental delays, whereas a student with severe motor impairments may be intellectually gifted.

Convulsive disorders are described later in this chapter.

The causes of cerebral palsy are varied and not clearly known. It has often been attributed to the occurrence of injuries, accidents, or illnesses that are *prenatal* (before birth), *perinatal* (at or near the time of birth), or *postnatal* (soon after birth). Recent improvements in obstetrical delivery and neonatal care, however, have not decreased the incidence of cerebral palsy, which has remained steady over the past 20 years or so at about 1.5 in every 1,000 live births (Kudrjavcev et al., 1983). An extensive study of children with cerebral palsy (Nelson & Ellenberg, 1986) found that the factors most likely to be associated with cerebral palsy were mental retardation of the mother, premature birth (i.e., gestational age of 32 weeks or less), low birth weight, and a delay of 5 minutes or more before the baby's first cry. The researchers concluded that cerebral palsy does not appear to be caused by a single factor and that complications of labor and delivery are not so important in causing cerebral palsy as was previously thought. Prevention of cerebral palsy, then, is likely to prove extremely difficult.

Types of Cerebral Palsy. Cerebral palsy is divided into several categories, according to muscle tone (hypertonia or hypotonia) and quality of motor involvement (athetosis or ataxia) (Blackburn, 1987; Gillham, 1986). Children may also be described as having mixed cerebral palsy, consisting of more than one of these types, particularly if their impairments are severe.

Approximately 60% of all individuals with cerebral palsy have **hypertonia** (commonly called *spasticity*), which is characterized by tense, contracted muscles. Their movements may be jerky, exaggerated, and poorly coordinated. They may be unable to grasp objects with their fingers. When they try to control their movements, they may become even more jerky. If they are able to walk, it may be with a scissors gait, standing on the toes with knees bent and pointed inward. Deformities of the spine, hip dislocation, and contractures of the hand, elbow, foot, and knee are common.

Most infants born with cerebral palsy have **hypotonia**, or weak, floppy muscles, particularly in the neck and trunk. When hypotonia persists throughout the child's first year without being replaced with spasticity or athetoid involvement, the condition is called *generalized hypotonia*. Hypotonic children typically have low levels of motor activity, are slow to make balancing responses, and may not walk until 30 months of age (Bleck, 1987). Severely hypotonic children must use external support to achieve and maintain an upright position.

Athetosis occurs in about 20% of all cases of cerebral palsy. Children with athetoid cerebral palsy make large, irregular, twisting movements they cannot control. When they are at rest or asleep, there is little or no abnormal motion. An effort to pick up a pencil, however, may result in wildly waving arms, facial grimaces, and extension of the tongue. These children may not be able to control the muscles of their lips, tongue, and throat and may drool. They may also seem to stumble and lurch awkwardly as they walk. At times their muscles may be tense and rigid, whereas at other times they may be loose and flaccid. Extreme difficulty in expressive oral language, mobility, and activities of daily living often accompanies this form of cerebral palsy.

Ataxia is noted as the primary type of involvement in only 1% of cases of cerebral palsy (Blackburn, 1987). Children with ataxic cerebral palsy have a poor sense of balance and hand use. They may appear to be dizzy while walking and may fall easily if not supported. Their movements tend to be jumpy and unsteady, with exaggerated motion patterns that often "overshoot" the intended objects. They seem to be constantly attempting to overcome the effect of gravity and to stabilize their bodies.

Rigidity and **tremor** are additional but much less common types of cerebral palsy. Children with the rare rigidity type of cerebral palsy display extreme stiffness in the affected limbs; they may be fixed and immobile for long periods. Tremor cerebral palsy, also rare, is marked by rhythmic, uncontrollable movements—the tremors may actually increase when the children attempt to control their actions.

The motor impairment of children with cerebral palsy often makes it frustrating, if not impossible, for them to play with toys. See pages 382–383 for ideas for simple adaptations to make commercially available toys accessible to children with cerebral palsy.

The more severe forms of cerebral palsy are often identified in the first few months of life, but in many other cases, cerebral palsy is not detected or diagnosed until later in childhood. Parents may be the first to notice that their child is having difficulty crawling, balancing, or standing. According to Bleck (1979), about 80% of children with cerebral palsy are capable of learning to walk, although many need to use wheelchairs, braces, and other assistive devices, particularly for moving around outside the home.

Complications. Infants and children with cerebral palsy may experience feeding problems. They may at first be unable to suck or swallow and may choke on food or regurgitate it. Such difficulties can be overcome with early physical therapy; the therapist can show parents how best to position the child and how to give the appropriate types and amounts of food. In this and various other areas, it is obviously important that therapy and parent education begin as early as possible. Muscle tension can sometimes be partially controlled by medications, braces, and special adaptive equipment. Orthopedic surgery may increase a child's range of motion or obviate such complications as hip dislocations and permanent muscle contractions.

Gillham (1986) describes cerebral palsy as the result of "not just a brain with a bit missing, but a reorganized brain, working to its own rules" (p. 64). Because cerebral palsy is such a complex condition, it is most effectively managed through the cooperative involvement of physicians, teachers, physical therapists, occupational therapists, communication specialists, counselors, and others who work directly with children and families. Regular exercise and careful positioning in school settings help the child with cerebral palsy to move as fully and comfortably as possible and prevent or minimize progressive damage to muscles and limbs.

Spina Bifida

About 1 in 2,000 infants is born with **spina bifida**, a congenital defect in the vertebrae that enclose the spinal cord. As a result, a portion of the spinal cord and the nerves that normally control muscles and feeling in the lower part of the body fail to develop normally. Of the three types of spina bifida, the mildest form is **spina bifida occulta**, in which only a few vertebrae are malformed, usually in the low spine. The defect is often not visible externally. If the flexible casing (*meninges*) that surrounds the spinal cord bulges through an opening in the infant's back at birth, the condition is called **meningocele**. These two forms do not usually cause any loss of function for the child. However, in the most common form of spina bifida, **myelomeningocele**, the spinal lining, spinal cord, and nerve roots all protrude. The protruding spinal cord and nerves are usually tucked back into the spinal column shortly after birth. This is the most serious condition, carrying a high risk of paralysis and infection. In general, the higher the location of the lesion on the spine, the greater the effect on the body and its functioning (Pieper, 1983). The term *neural tube defect* is sometimes used to describe spina bifida and similar impairments.

About 80% to 90% of children born with spina bifida develop hydrocephalus, the accumulation of cerebrospinal fluid in tissues surrounding the brain (Mitchell, 1983). Left untreated, this condition can lead to head enlargement and

ADAPTING TOYS FOR CHILDREN WITH CEREBRAL PALSY

Spontaneous and independent use of commercially available toys is not possible for many children with cerebral palsy. The toys often require more coordination or strength than these youngsters have. Children with uncontrolled movements may push toys out of reach or knock them over. This inability to manipulate the environment is frustrating for both children and their teachers and parents.

Lack of play experience can have a devastating effect upon a child. Continuous inability to engage in physical activity and gain mastery over the environment may cause the child to lose motivation and become passive. Because playing is an integral part of intellectual, social, perceptual, and physical development, growth in these areas may be limited when the child cannot actively play.

Toys can be adapted to make them more accessible to children with physical disabilities. Five types of modifications are most effective in promoting active, independent use of play materials. Although most of the adaptations are simple, they can make the difference between success and failure for a child.

Stabilization

Stabilizing a toy enhances its function in two ways. First, stabilizing prevents the child's uncontrolled movements and difficulty directing the hand to desired locations from moving objects out of reach or knocking them over. Second, many children with cerebral palsy have difficulty performing tasks that require holding an object with one hand while manipulating it in some way with the other hand. Toys with a base can be clamped to a table. Masking tape is an inexpensive and effective way to secure many toys. Velcro is another excellent material for stabilizing toys, by placing the hook side of the Velcro on the toy and mounting the loop side on a clean surface. Suction cups can also stabilize a toy for a short time on a clean, nonwood surface.

Boundaries

Restricting the movement of toys such as cars or trains makes it easier for some children to use and retrieve them if pushed out of reach. Boundaries can be created in various ways depending upon how the object is to be moved. For example, push toys can be placed in the top of a cardboard box or on a tray with edges to create a restricted area. Pull toys can be placed on a track, and items that require a banging motion, such as a tambourine, can be held in a wood frame with springs.

Grasping Aids

Many children with cerebral palsy have difficulty grasping objects and are therefore unable to hold and feel things independently. The ability to hold objects can be facilitated in a variety of ways. A Velcro strap can be placed around the child's hand with Velcro also placed on the materials to be held, thus creating a bond between the hand and the object. A universal cuff can be used for holding sticklike objects such as crayons or pointers. Simply enlarging an item by wrapping foam or tape around it may make it easier to hold.

Manipulation Aids

Some toys require isolated finger movements, use of a pincer grasp, and controlled movements of the wrist, which are too difficult for a child with physical disabilities. Various adaptations can help compensate for deficits in these movements. Extending and widening pieces of the toy will make swiping and pushing easier. Flat extensions, knobs, or dowels can be used to increase the surface area. A crossbar or dowel, placed appropriately, can compensate for an inability to rotate the wrist.

Switches

Some children have such limited hand function that they can operate only toys that are activated by a switch. Commercially available, battery-operated toys can be modified to operate by adapted switches. Teachers can make and adapt their own switches and toys (Burkhardt, 1981; Wright & Momari, 1985), or purchase them from a number of firms that serve the disabled community. After determining some physical action, such as moving a knee laterally, lifting a shoulder, or making a sound, that the child can perform consistently and with minimum effort, one selects the type of switch best suited to that movement. The switch is always positioned in the same place, which facilitates automatic switch activation and allows the child to give full attention to the play activity rather than concentrating on using the switch.

General Considerations

Positioning should be considered when children with cerebral palsy play with toys. Good positioning will maximize freedom of movement, improve the ability to look at a toy, and facilitate controlled, relaxed movement. An occupational or physical therapist should determine the special positioning needs of each child. Placement of the toy is crucial. It should be within easy reach and require a minimum of effort to manipulate. The child should not become easily fatigued or have to struggle. The child must be able to look at the toy while playing. Activities should be interesting and facilitate cognitive growth, yet not be beyond the child's conceptual capabilities. Toys should be sturdy and durable. Avoid toys with sharp edges or small pieces that can be swallowed.

These principles for adapting toys can be applied to other devices, such as communication aids, computers, environmental controls, and household items, to make then easier to use. Making an educational environment more accessible gives children with physical disabilities greater control of their surroundings and the opportunity to expand the scope of their learning experiences.

From "Making Toys Accessible for Children with Cerebral Palsy" by Carol Schaeffler, Spring 1988, Teaching Exceptional Children, *20, pp. 26–28. Adapted by permission.* ◆

severe brain damage. Hydrocephalus is treated by the surgical insertion of a **shunt**, a one-way valve that diverts the cerebrospinal fluid away from the brain and into the bloodstream. Replacements of the shunt are usually necessary as a child grows older. Teachers who work with children who have shunts should be aware that blockage, disconnection, or infection of the shunt may result in increased intracranial pressure; warning signs such as drowsiness, vomiting, headache, irritability, and squinting should be heeded. Shunts have become safer and more reliable in recent years and can be removed in many school-age children when the production and absorption of cerebrospinal fluid are brought into balance (Gillham, 1986).

Usually, children with spina bifida have some degree of paralysis of the lower limbs and lack full control of bladder and bowel functions. In most cases, these children have good use of their arms and upper body (although some children experience fine-motor problems). Children with spina bifida usually walk with braces, crutches, or walkers; they may use wheelchairs for longer distances. Some children need special help in dressing and toileting, whereas others are able to manage these tasks on their own. Most children with spinal bifida need to use a **catheter** (tube) or bag to collect their urine. *Intermittent catheterization* is taught to children with urinary complications so they can empty their bladders at convenient times (Tarnowski & Drabman, 1987). According to Pieper (1983), this technique is effective with both boys and girls, works best if used every 3 to 4 hours, and does not require an absolutely sterile environment.

See pages 392–394 to learn how dolls can be used to teach self-catheterization skills.

Muscular Dystrophy

Muscular dystrophy refers to a group of long-term diseases that progressively weaken and waste away the body's muscles. The most common form is *Duchenne* muscular dystrophy, which affects boys (1 in 3,500) much more frequently than girls. The child appears normal at birth, but muscle weakness is usually evident between the ages of 2 and 6, when the child begins to experience difficulty in running or climbing stairs. The child may walk with an unusual gait, showing a protruding stomach and a hollow back. The calf muscles of a child with muscular dystrophy may appear unusually large because the degenerated muscle has been replaced by fatty tissue.

Children with muscular dystrophy often have difficulty getting to their feet after lying down or playing on the floor. They may fall easily. By age 10 to 14, the child loses the ability to walk; the small muscles of the hands and fingers are usually the last to be affected. Some doctors and therapists recommend the early use of electrically powered wheelchairs, whereas others employ special braces and other devices to prolong walking as long as possible.

Unfortunately, there is no known cure for most cases of muscular dystrophy, and the disease is often fatal. A good deal of independence can be maintained, however, by regular physical therapy, exercise, and the use of appropriate aids and appliances. In school, a teacher should be careful not to lift a child with muscular dystrophy by the arms—even a gentle pull may dislocate the child's limbs. The teacher may also need to help the child deal with the gradual loss of physical abilities and the possibility of death.

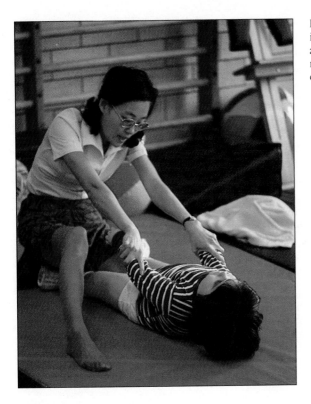

Physical therapy helps increase muscular control and range of movement for many children with orthopedic impairments.

Osteogenesis Imperfecta

Osteogenesis imperfecta is a rare (1 in 20,000 births) inherited condition marked by extremely brittle bones. The skeletal system does not grow normally, and the bones are easily fractured. Children with osteogenesis imperfecta are fragile and must be protected. Wheelchairs are usually necessary, although the children may be able to walk for short distances with the aid of braces, crutches, and protective equipment. Like other children with orthopedic impairments, the child with osteogenesis imperfecta may have frequent hospitalizations for treatment and surgery. Some children, understandably, are reluctant to be touched or handled. Usually children with osteogenesis imperfecta have adequate use of their hands and can participate in most classroom activities if they receive appropriate physical support and protection. As the children mature, their bones may become less brittle and they may require less attention.

Spinal Cord Injuries

Spinal cord injuries usually stem from accidents. Injury to the spinal column is generally described by letters and numbers indicating the site of the damage; for example, a C5–6 injury means the damage has occurred at the level of the fifth and sixth cervical vertebrae—a flexible area of the neck susceptible to injury from whiplash and diving or trampoline accidents. A T12 injury refers to the twelfth thoracic (chest) vertebra, and an L3 to the third lumbar (lower back) area. In general, there is paralysis and loss of sensation below the level of the injury. The higher the injury on the spine and the more the injury (lesion) cuts through the entire cord, the greater the paralysis (Gilgoff, 1983). Automobile accidents and falls are the most frequent causes of spinal cord injury to children.

Children who have sustained spinal cord injuries usually use wheelchairs for mobility. Motorized wheelchairs, although expensive, are recommended for those with quadriplegia, whereas paraplegic children can use self-propelled wheelchairs. Children with quadriplegia may have severe breathing problems because the muscles of the chest, which normally govern respiration, are affected. In most cases children with spinal cord injuries lack bladder and bowel control and need to follow a careful management program to maintain personal hygiene and avoid infection and skin irritation.

Rehabilitation programs for children and adolescents who have sustained spinal cord injuries usually involve physical therapy, the use of adaptive devices for mobility and independent living, and psychological support to help them adjust to a sudden disability. With supportive teachers and peers, these students can participate fully in school programs. Adolescents and adults are often particularly concerned about sexual function. Even though most spinal cord injuries do affect sexuality, with understanding partners and positive attitudes toward themselves, many individuals with spinal cord injuries are often able to enjoy satisfying sexual relationships. Some counselors now specialize in addressing the sexual concerns of people who have been disabled by spinal cord injury or other conditions.

Traumatic Head Injury

Injuries to the head are common in children and adolescents. According to Rosen and Gerring (1986), in the United States, about 20,000 persons under the age of 21 have survived a head injury severe enough to require 3 weeks or more of hospitalization. Significant causes of head trauma include automobile, motorcycle, and bicycle accidents, falls, assaults, gunshot wounds, and child abuse. Although research on the educational effects of head trauma is limited, we do know many children who have suffered serious head injury experience subsequent problems in learning, behavior, and adjustment. Temporary or lasting symptoms may include cognitive and language deficits, memory loss, seizures, and perceptual disorders. Victims may display inappropriate or exaggerated behaviors ranging from extreme aggressiveness to apathy. Children may also have difficulty paying attention and retaining new information.

A *coma* is an abnormal deep stupor that can result from severe head trauma. It may be impossible to arouse the affected individual by external stimuli for an extended period (Kleinberg, 1982). When it was originally passed, P.L. 94–142 did not specifically mention the needs of children who have experienced head trauma and/or coma; however, when the law was amended in 1990, traumatic brain injury was added as a new disability category. Although few educational programs have been specifically designed for this population, educators have recognized that many of these children may need special education services. As Rosen and Gerring (1986) observe, head-injured students reenter school with deficits from their injuries compounded by an extended absence from school. These students are likely to require academic, psychological, and family support,

Each year about 50,000 children and adults are treated in hospital emergency rooms for traumatic head injuries as a result of bicycle accidents (Stern, 1990). Most of those injuries could be avoided if riders wore an approved safety helmet (Raskin, 1990). If you know anyone who rides a bicycle, don't let him or her ride without a helmet.

and methods developed for students with other disabling conditions may not be applicable.

Limb Deficiency

Limb deficiency is the absence or partial loss of an arm or leg. Congenital limb deficiency is rare, occurring in about 1 in every 20,000 births. Acquired limb deficiency (amputations) may be the result of surgery or accident. A **prosthesis** (artificial limb) is often used to facilitate balance, to enable the child to participate in a variety of tasks, and to create a more normal appearance. Some students or their parents, however, prefer not to use artificial limbs. Most children become quite proficient at using their remaining limbs. Some children who are missing both arms, for example, learn to write, eat, and perform vocational tasks with their feet. They have a much greater feeling of being in contact with objects and people than they would if they used prosthetic limbs. Unless children have other impairments in addition to the absence of limbs, they should be able to function in a regular classroom without major modifications.

Chronic Illness and Other Health-Related Conditions

Many conditions can affect a child's health, whether permanently, temporarily, or intermittently. In general, the conditions we will discuss in this section are *chronic;* that is, they are present over long periods and tend not to get better or disappear. Children with chronic illnesses are not usually confined to beds or hospitals, except during occasional flare-ups of their diseases, but "even with good control and years of remission, the threat of a recurrent crisis is ever present" (Kleinberg, 1982, p. 5).

An *acute* illness, in contrast, is severe but of limited duration.

The usual and proper course of action for children and families affected by chronic health-related conditions is to seek medical treatment. In many instances, however, an illness or health impairment can significantly affect school performance and social acceptance; consequently, it is important for a teacher to be aware of it. Although chronic illnesses and other health-related conditions are generally less visible than orthopedic and neurologic impairments, their effects on a child may be just as great.

Convulsive Disorders (Epilepsy)

Theoretically, anyone can have a *seizure,* a disturbance of movement, sensation, behavior, and/or consciousness caused by abnormal electrical activity in the brain. It is not uncommon for seizures to occur if someone has a high fever, drinks excessive alcohol, or experiences a blow to the head. When seizures occur chronically and repeatedly, however, the condition is known as a **convulsive disorder** or, more commonly, **epilepsy**. With proper medical treatment and the support of parents, teachers, and peers, most children with convulsive disorders lead full and normal lives. Most have normal intelligence and need not be considered disabled or handicapped. Epilepsy itself constitutes a disorder only while a seizure is actually in progress.

Epileptic seizures may be largely or wholly controlled by anticonvulsant medications. Some children require such heavy doses of medication that their learning and behavior are adversely affected, and some medications have undesirable side effects, such as drowsiness, nausea, weight gain, or thickening of the gums.

The specific causes of epilepsy are not clearly known. It is believed that people become seizure-prone when a particular area of the brain becomes electrically unstable. This condition may result from an underlying lesion caused by scar tissue from a head injury, a tumor, or an interruption in blood supply to the brain (Gillham, 1986). In many cases, the origin of seizure activity cannot be traced to a particular incident. A convulsive disorder can occur at any stage of life, but most frequently begins in childhood. A wide variety of psychological, physical, and sensory factors are thought to trigger seizures in susceptible persons—for example, fatigue, excitement, anger, surprise, hyperventilation, hormonal changes (as in menstruation or pregnancy), withdrawal from drugs or alcohol, or exposure to certain patterns of light, sound, or touch. During a seizure, a dysfunction in the electrochemical activity of the brain causes a person to lose control of her muscles temporarily. Between seizures—that is, most of the time—the brain functions normally. Many unfortunate misconceptions about epilepsy have circulated in the past and are still prevalent even today. Negative public attitudes, in fact, have probably been more harmful to people with epilepsy than has the condition itself.

It is important for teachers, school health care personnel, and perhaps classmates to be aware that a child is affected by a convulsive disorder so they can be prepared to deal with a seizure if one should occur in school. There are several classifications of seizures, three of which are relatively common. The **generalized tonic-clonic seizure** (formerly called *grand mal*) is the most conspicuous and serious type of convulsive seizure. A generalized tonic-clonic seizure can be disturbing and frightening to someone who has never seen one. The affected child has little or no warning that a seizure is about to occur; the muscles become stiff; and the child loses consciousness and falls to the floor. Then the entire body shakes violently as the muscles alternately contract and relax. Saliva may be forced from the mouth; legs and arms may jerk; the bladder and bowels may be emptied. After about 2 to 5 minutes, the contractions diminish, and the child either goes to sleep or regains consciousness in a confused or drowsy state. Generalized tonic-clonic seizures may occur as often as several times a day or as seldom as once a year. They are more likely to occur during the day than at night. (See Figure 9.2 for procedures for handling seizures in the classroom.)

The **absence seizure** (previously called *petit mal*) is far less severe than the generalized tonic-clonic seizure, but may occur much more frequently—as often as 100 times per day in some children. Usually there is a brief loss of consciousness, lasting anywhere from a few seconds to half a minute or so. The child may stare blankly, flutter or blink his eyes, grow pale, or drop whatever he is holding. He may be mistakenly viewed as daydreaming or not listening. The child may or may not be aware that he has had a seizure, and no special first aid is necessary. The teacher should keep the child's parents advised of seizure activity and may also find it helpful to explain it to the child's classmates.

A **complex partial seizure** (also called *psychomotor seizure*) may appear as a brief period of inappropriate or purposeless activity. The child may smack her lips, walk around aimlessly, or shout. She may appear to be conscious, but is not actually aware of her unusual behavior. Complex partial seizures usually last

FIGURE 9.2

Procedures for handling generalized tonic-clonic seizures (*Source:* From *Epilepsy School Alert* by The Epilepsy Foundation of America, 1987, Washington, DC: Author.)

The typical seizure is not a medical emergency, but knowledgeable handling of the situation is important. When a child experiences a generalized tonic-clonic seizure in the classroom, the teacher should follow these procedures:

♦ Keep calm. Reassure the other students that the child will be fine in a minute.

♦ Ease the child to the floor and clear the area around him of anything that could hurt him.

♦ Put something flat and soft (like a folded coat) under his head so it will not bang on the floor as his body jerks.

♦ You cannot stop the seizure. Let it run its course. Do not try to revive the child and do not interfere with his movements.

♦ Turn him gently onto his side. This keeps his airway clear and allows saliva to drain away.
DON'T try to force his mouth open.
DON'T try to hold on to his tongue.
DON'T put anything in his mouth.

♦ When the jerking movements stop, let the child rest until he regains consciousness.

♦ Breathing may be shallow during the seizure, and may even stop briefly. In the unlikely event that breathing does not begin again, check the child's airway for obstruction and give artificial respiration.

Some students recover quickly after this type of seizure; others need more time. A short period of rest is usually advised. If the student is able to remain in the classroom afterwards, however, he should be encouraged to do so. Staying in the classroom (or returning to it as soon as possible) allows for continued participation in classroom activity and is psychologically less difficult for the student. If a student has frequent seizures, handling them can become routine once teacher and classmates learn what to expect.

from 2 to 5 minutes, after which the child has amnesia about the entire episode. Seizures may occur weekly, monthly, or only once or twice a year. The teacher should keep dangerous objects out of the child's way and, except in emergencies, should not try to physically restrain her. Some children may respond to spoken directions during a complex partial seizure.

In some children, absence and complex partial seizures can go undetected for long periods. An observant teacher can be instrumental in detecting the presence of a seizure disorder and in referring the child for appropriate medical help. The teacher can also assist parents and physicians by noting both the effectiveness and the side effects of any medication the child takes.

Many children experience a warning sensation, known as an *aura,* a short time before a seizure. The aura takes different forms in different people; distinctive feelings, sights, sounds, tastes, and even smells have been described. The aura can be a useful safety valve enabling the child to remove himself from a class or group before the seizure actually occurs. Some children report the warning provided by the aura helps them feel more secure and comfortable about themselves.

Today, the majority of children with convulsive disorders can be helped with medication. Drugs can sharply reduce or even eliminate seizures in many cases. All children with convulsive disorders benefit from a realistic understanding of their condition and from accepting attitudes on the part of teachers and classmates.

Diabetes

Juvenile diabetes mellitus is a disorder of metabolism; that is, it affects the way the body absorbs and breaks down the sugars and starches in foods. Diabetes is a common childhood disease, affecting about 1 in 600 school-aged children, so it is likely that most teachers will encounter students with diabetes at one time or another (Winter, 1983). Without proper medical management, the diabetic child's system is not able to obtain and retain adequate energy from food. Not only does the child lack energy, but many important parts of the body—particularly the eyes and the kidneys—can be affected by untreated diabetes. Early symptoms of diabetes include thirst, headaches, loss of weight (despite a good appetite), frequent urination, and cuts that are slow to heal.

Children with diabetes have insufficient insulin, a hormone normally produced by the pancreas that is necessary for proper metabolism and digestion of foods. To regulate the condition, insulin must be injected daily under the skin. Most children with diabetes learn to inject their own insulin—in some cases as frequently as four times per day—and to determine the amount of insulin they need by testing the level of sugar and other substances in their urine. It is important for children with diabetes to follow a specific and regular diet prescribed by a physician or nutrition specialist. A regular exercise program is also usually suggested.

Teachers should be aware of the symptoms of insulin reaction, also called *diabetic shock*. It can result from taking too much insulin, from unusually strenuous exercise, or from a missed or delayed meal (the blood sugar level is lowered by insulin and exercise and raised by food). Symptoms of insulin reaction include faintness, dizziness, blurred vision, drowsiness, and nausea. A child may appear irritable or have a marked personality change. In most cases, giving the child some form of concentrated sugar—such as a sugar cube, a glass of fruit juice, or a candy bar—ends the insulin reaction within a few minutes. The child's doctor or parents should inform the teacher and school health personnel of the appropriate foods to give in case of insulin reaction.

A *diabetic coma* is more serious. A coma indicates that too little insulin is present; that is, the diabetes is not under control. Its onset is gradual rather than sudden. The symptoms of diabetic coma include fatigue; thirst; dry, hot skin; deep, labored breathing; excessive urination; and fruity-smelling breath. A doctor or nurse should be contacted immediately if a child displays such symptoms.

Asthma

Asthma is a chronic lung disease characterized by episodic bouts of wheezing, coughing, and difficulty breathing. "Asthma is a complex disease in which inflammation of the airways is both the cause and effect of the problem"

> Diabetic retinopathy is a leading cause of blindness in adults.

(Kraemer & Bierman, 1983, p. 160). An asthmatic attack is usually triggered by allergens (e.g., pollen, certain foods, pets), irritants such as cigarette smoke or smog, exercise, or emotional stress, which result in a narrowing of the airways in the lungs. This increases the resistance to the airflow in and out of the lungs, making it harder for the individual to breathe. The severity of asthma varies greatly; the child may experience only a period of mild coughing or extreme difficulty in breathing that requires emergency treatment. Many asthmatic children experience normal lung functioning between episodes.

Asthma is the most common lung disease of children; estimates of its prevalence range from 3% to as high as 10% of school-age children (Aaronson & Rosenberg, 1985; Kraemer & Bierman, 1983). More boys are affected than girls. The causes of asthma are not completely known. Symptoms generally begin in early childhood but sometimes do not develop until late childhood or adolescence. Asthma tends to run in families, suggesting that an allergic intolerance to some stimulus may be inherited. Symptoms of asthma might also first appear following a viral infection of the respiratory system.

Primary treatment for asthma begins with a systematic effort to identify the stimuli and environmental situations that provoke attacks. The number of potential allergens and irritants is virtually limitless, and in some cases it can be extremely difficult to determine the combination of factors that results in an asthmatic episode. Changes in temperature, humidity, and season (attacks are especially common in autumn) are also related to the frequency of asthmatic symptoms. Rigorous physical exercise produces asthmatic episodes in some children. Asthma can be controlled effectively in most children with a combination of medications and limiting exposure to known allergens. Most children whose breathing attacks are induced by physical exercise can still enjoy physical exercise and sports through careful selection of activities (e.g., swimming generally provokes less exercise-asthma than running) and/or taking certain medications prior to rigorous exercise.

There is also a clear interrelationship between emotional stress and asthma. Periods of psychological stress increase the likelihood of asthmatic attacks, and asthmatic episodes produce more stress. Treatment often involves counseling or an *asthma teaching program* (Kraemer & Bierman, 1983), in which children and their families are taught ways to reduce and cope with emotional stress.

Asthma is one of the most frequently cited reasons for missing school. Chronic absenteeism makes it difficult for the child with asthma to maintain performance at grade level, and homebound instructional services may be necessary. The majority of children with asthma who receive medical and psychological support, however, successfully complete school and lead normal lives. By working cooperatively with parents and medical personnel to minimize the child's contact with provoking factors, the classroom teacher can play an important role in reducing the impact of asthma.

Cystic Fibrosis

Cystic fibrosis is a serious chronic disease of children and adolescents. The body's exocrine glands excrete a thick mucus that can block the lungs and parts of the digestive system. Children with cystic fibrosis may have difficulty

USING DOLLS TO TEACH SELF-CATHETERIZATION SKILLS TO CHILDREN WITH SPINA BIFIDA

Persons with physical and health impairments often require regular medical regimens ranging from simple procedures (such as taking prescribed oral medications) to more complex routines (injection of insulin to control diabetes). The ability to self-administer needed medical routines increases the individual's independence to function in normal environments and eliminates reliance on a caretaker. When complex procedures must be performed by children or persons with learning handicaps, direct systematic instruction is indicated. If the procedures involve invading the body or errors during practice are potentially hazardous, simulation training can be used. This program evaluated the effectiveness of simulation training with a doll.

Children and Setting

Cathy and Teresa, ages 4 and 8, two girls with spina bifida whose urinary functions were managed by intermittent catheterization performed by their parents, participated in the training program. Both girls were scheduled to attend regular schools during the fall (preschool and second grade), and their parents had requested they learn self-catheterization to promote independent functioning and adaptation in the classroom.

Task Analysis and Measurement

A task analysis of self-catheterization yielded four basic skill components, each with multiple steps: preparation (6 steps); placing and adjusting a compact magnifying mirror (6 steps); catheter insertion and removal (11 steps); and cleanup (9 steps). The children's performance on each step in the task analysis on the doll and then on themselves was observed and recorded during measurement probes before and after training of each of the four skill components. During each doll probe, the child was asked to show how to catheterize the doll; no help or feedback was given. *In vivo* (self) probes were conducted after each doll probe to determine if training with the doll generalized to self-administration of the procedure. The child was asked to show how to catheterize herself and to do the best she could, but to stop whenever she wished.

Simulation Training

Each child was taught to perform each step of the procedure on a plastic doll with female genitalia and movable arms and legs. The children were told that they were going to learn to catheterize themselves, but that a doll with the same urinary problems needed their help first. The trainer described and modeled on the doll the steps in the skill component under instruction. The child was then asked to demonstrate and verbalize the steps for that component ("Show me how you can help the doll with her catheter, and tell her what you're doing"). To simulate the performance of self-catheterization, the doll was manipulated from a sitting position on the child's lap, facing forward. If the child made an error or performed a step out of sequence, the trainer provided verbal prompts ("Where does that end of the catheter go?"), visual prompts (pointing), and manual guidance as necessary. Correct responses were praised.

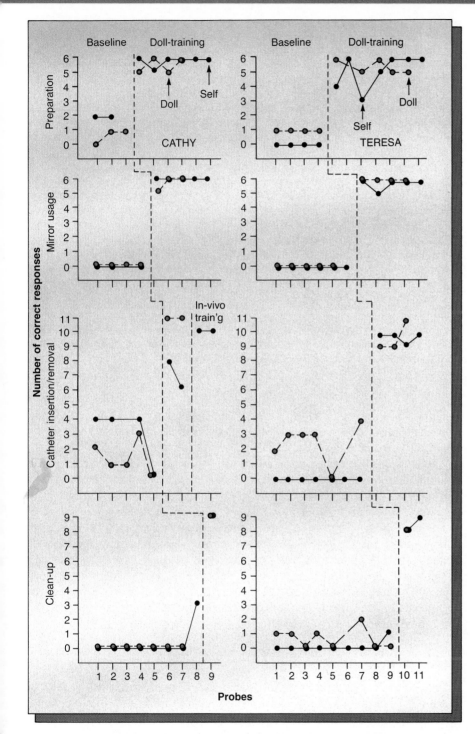

FIGURE A
Number of correct responses within skill components on simulation (doll) and in vivo (self) probes for each participant.

Results and Discussion

The number of correct responses performed by each child on both doll and self probes across each skill component is shown in the figure. During baseline (before training), the children performed few of the steps correctly on either the doll or themselves. After training and practice with the doll, their performance improved both on the doll and on themselves. Cathy required training on herself for several steps of the catheterization insertion and removal component, which she performed correctly on the doll but had trouble with on herself. Follow-up reports from the parents indicated both children were catheterizing themselves independently.

Doll training appears to offer several advantages for teaching children how to self-administer medical procedures. First, because they associated dolls with play activities, children's interest and willingness to participate in training might be increased. Second, children may be reluctant to perform an unfamiliar and intrusive procedure on themselves. Allowing children to achieve mastery on a doll before self-application may desensitize them to the process and decrease the likelihood of making potentially harmful errors while practicing on themselves. Finally, using a doll enables many more opportunities for practice than does the child's normal catheterization schedule. The use of dolls appears to be an efficient means of training. Across a 9-day period, total training time was 4 hours and 30 minutes for Cathy and 2 hours and 45 minutes for Teresa.

From "Teaching Self-Catheterization Skills to Children with Neurogenic Bladder Complications" by N. A. Neef, J. M. Parrish, K. F. Hannigan, T. J. Page, and B. A. Iwata, Fall 1990, Journal of Applied Behavior Analysis, 22, *pp. 237–243. Adapted with permission.* ◆

breathing and are susceptible to coughs and respiratory infections. They may also have large and frequent bowel movements because food passes through the system only partially digested.

Medications prescribed for children with cystic fibrosis include enzymes to facilitate digestion and solutions to thin and loosen the mucus in the lungs. During vigorous physical exercises, some children may need help from teachers, aides, or classmates to clear their lungs and air passages.

Cystic fibrosis is a hereditary disease found mainly among Caucasian children, both male and female. Medical research has not determined exactly how cystic fibrosis functions. The symptoms may be due to a missing chemical or substance in the body, but no reliable cure for cystic fibrosis has yet been found. Nonetheless, many children and young adults with this condition are able to lead active lives. With continued research and treatment techniques, the long-range outlook for children affected by cystic fibrosis is improving.

Hemophilia

Hemophilia is a rare hereditary disorder wherein the blood does not clot as quickly as it should. The most serious consequences are usually internal, rather than external, bleeding; contrary to popular opinion, minor cuts and scrapes do not usually pose a serious problem. However, internal bleeding can cause swelling, pain, and permanent damage to joints, tissues, and internal organs and may necessitate hospitalization for blood transfusions. It is thought that emotional stress may intensify episodes of bleeding (Verhaaren & Connor, 1981). A student with hemophilia may need to be excused from some physical activities and may use a wheelchair during periods of susceptibility. As with most children who have health-related impairments, however, good physical condition is important for development and well-being, so the restrictions on activities should not be any greater than necessary.

Burns

Burns are a leading type of injury in childhood. Most often, burns result from household accidents, but sometimes they are caused by child abuse. As Yurt and Pruitt (1983) point out, the skin is the largest organ of the human body and one of the most important; serious burns can cause complications in other organs, long-term physical limitations, and psychological difficulties. Children with serious burn injuries usually experience pain, scarring, limitations of motion, lengthy hospitalizations, and repeated surgery. Some children with severe burns on their faces and other areas wear sterilized elastic masks to protect and soften the skin. The disfigurement caused by severe burns can affect a child's behavior and self-image, especially if teachers and peers react negatively. When a child is returning to class after prolonged absence resulting from an extensive burn injury, it may be advisable for the teacher, parents, or other involved person (such as a social worker or physical therapist) to explain to classmates the nature of the child's injury and appearance (Yurt & Pruitt, 1983).

Acquired Immune Deficiency Syndrome (AIDS)

Persons with **acquired immune deficiency syndrome (AIDS)** are not able to resist and fight off infections because of a breakdown in the immune system. In 1983 the virus that causes AIDS was isolated and given the name **human immunodeficiency virus (HIV)**. AIDS is contracted when the HIV virus is passed from a carrier (not all persons who have the HIV virus get AIDS) to another person through sexual contact or through the blood (intravenous drug users who share needles, transfusions of unscreened contaminated blood). Pregnant women can transmit the HIV virus to their unborn children. There is no known cure or vaccine for the disease, which is fatal. As of July 1989, 99,839 cases of AIDS had been reported in the United States; 51,611 persons in the United States had died of AIDS from 1982 through 1988 (U.S. Department of Commerce, 1990). In addition, it is estimated that between 1 and 1.5 million people in the United States are infected with the HIV virus. The incidence rate for AIDS has increased alarmingly, and projections of the number of people who may contract the disease and die are staggering.

The most up-to-date data and recommendations for prevention and treatment can be obtained from the Centers for Disease Control, AIDS Division, Atlanta, Georgia.

Although only a small number of young children diagnosed with AIDS have survived to school age, the continuing development of drug treatments to counter or slow the progression of the disease means it is likely that increasing numbers of children with HIV infection and AIDS will be in the classroom. Significant neurological complications and developmental delays have been noted in children with AIDS (Barnes, 1986; Epstein, Sharer, & Goudsmit, 1988), but we do not yet know what the special education needs of these children might encompass. Based on the current knowledge of AIDS, Byers (1989) suggested the following implications and recommendations:

1. We certainly must continue with an AIDS curriculum in grades K–12 in an effort to prevent the disease from further infiltrating the pre-adolescent and adolescent populations.

2. Children harboring the virus cannot legally be excluded from schools unless they are deemed a direct health risk for other children (e.g., exhibit biting behavior, open sores). Consequently, chronic illness specialists, school psychologists, counselors, and teachers will need to make AIDS a priority issue, and be active in facilitating school/peer acceptance and the social adjustment of a child with AIDS.

3. Teachers, counselors, and other specialists will also need to be prepared to provide family therapy and broad-based support groups for parents and/or children within the school setting.

4. Pediatric AIDS patients present a particular challenge for special education professionals, due to the erratic course of neurological deterioration. The child may be stable for a number of months and then deteriorate rapidly over a period of weeks (Epstein et al., 1988), and thus requires regular monitoring of his or her educational needs.

5. Specific educational treatments for children infected with HIV await further research, and this appears to be the ultimate challenge for special educators. (p. 13)

Other Health Problems and Related Concerns

There are, of course, many other significant physical and health-related conditions that can influence a child's learning and behavior at school. Heart disease, cancer, and juvenile rheumatoid arthritis are conditions that generally do not require special teaching techniques or adaptive equipment. Yet they may cause variations in the child's performance as a direct result of not only the condition itself, but also the child's frequent absences from school and the effects of medication, fatigue, and pain.

The child with a physical or health impairment may be afraid of going to the hospital and being separated from her parents. She may look and feel different from her classmates. An older student may resent medication, therapy, prohibitions on activities, and other restrictions that limit independence and may worry about an uncertain future. The family of a child with a physical or health impairment often encounters many demands on time and energy, as well as financial problems from long-term medical care and equipment costs, which are often not covered by insurance. A teacher's concern and familiarity with a student's physical or health impairment can do much to improve the quality of the child's school experience.

■ IMPORTANT VARIABLES TO CONSIDER

In assessing the effects of a physical or health impairment on a child's development and behavior, many factors should be taken into consideration.

With a little help from a classmate, another musician joins the marching band.

Important among these are the severity and visibility of the impairment and the age at which the disabling condition was first acquired.

Severity

Most children learn by exploring their surroundings, interacting with other people, and having a wide variety of experiences in their homes, neighborhoods, schools, and communities. A minor or transient physical or health impairment, such as those most children experience while growing up, is not likely to have lasting effects—but a severe, long-standing impairment can greatly limit a child's range of experiences. Many such disabling conditions seriously restrict a child's mobility and independence, much as a severe visual or hearing impairment would. The child may not be able to travel alone at all and may have few opportunities to explore the environment by seeing, hearing, touching, smelling, or tasting things. He may spend most of the time at home or in a hospital. Some children are in virtually constant pain or become tired after any sort of physical exertion. Some take medications that decrease their alertness and responsiveness. Some may be physically fragile and afraid of injury or death.

Visibility

Some physical impairments are highly visible and conspicuous. How children think about themselves and the degree to which they are accepted by others often are affected by the visibility of a condition. Some children need to rely on a variety of special orthopedic appliances, such as wheelchairs, braces, crutches, and adaptive tables. They may ride to school with other disabled children on a specially equipped bus or van. In school they may need assistance using the toilet or may wear helmets. Although such special devices and adaptations do help children meet important needs, they often have the unfortunate side effect of making the physical impairment more visible, thus making the child look even more different from nondisabled peers. Many people with disabilities report that their hardware—wheelchairs, artificial limbs, communication devices, and other apparatus—creates a great deal of curiosity and leads to frequent, repetitive questions from strangers. For many children, learning to explain their disabilities and respond to questions can be an appropriate component of their educational programs. They may also benefit from discussing such concerns as when to ask for help from others and when to decline offers of assistance.

Age at Acquisition

As with virtually all disabilities, it is important for the teacher to be aware of the child's age at the time he or she acquired the physical or health impairment. A child who has not had the use of her legs since birth may have missed out on some important developmental experiences, particularly if early intervention services were not provided. In contrast, a teenager who suddenly loses the use of his legs in an accident has likely had a normal range of experiences throughout childhood, but may need considerable support from parents, teachers, specialists, and peers in making a successful adaptation to life with this newly acquired disability.

■ PREVALENCE

Because there are numerous different physical and health impairments and no universally accepted definition of this population, it is difficult to obtain accurate and meaningful prevalence statistics. Physical disabilities and health impairments often occur in combination with other handicapping conditions, so children may be counted under other categories, such as learning disabilities, speech impairment, or mental retardation. According to Dykes and Venn (1983), for special education placement purposes, a diagnosis of mental retardation usually takes precedence over a diagnosis of physical impairment. Also, many of the approximately 250,000 children born each year with significant birth defects are not considered disabled or handicapped by the time they reach school age, thanks to improved medical and surgical treatment or to the results of successful early intervention programs (Grove, 1982).

During the 1988–89 school year, 47,392 orthopedically impaired children and 50,349 other health-impaired children between the ages of 6 and 21 were served in special education programs (U.S. Department of Education, 1990). Together, these categories represent about 2% of all children receiving special education services; however, as noted earlier, the number of children with physical and health impairments included under other special education categories is not known but is probably sizable.

See Chapter 1 for an indication of how this prevalence rate compares with those of other areas of exceptionality.

The children most frequently placed in special education programs for physical, orthopedic, or health impairments are those with cerebral palsy. In some programs, half or more of the students considered physically impaired have cerebral palsy. Spina bifida and muscular dystrophy also account for relatively high percentages of the students who receive such services.

Current Incidence Trends

The causes of physical disabilities and health impairments have changed somewhat over the years. Medical detection, genetic counseling, and vaccination programs have significantly reduced the incidence of numerous diseases that formerly affected many children. Additionally, it is now possible to correct or control a variety of orthopedic, neurologic, and health impairments—through early surgery, physical therapy, medication, and the use of artificial internal or external body parts—to the point where many conditions formerly regarded as crippling, disabling, or disfiguring are no longer so.

On the other hand, medical and technological advances (particularly in neonatal and emergency care) mean more infants and children with serious physical and health impairments are surviving. Many of these children require special education services. The number of children and young adults who suffer physical and health impairments as the result of motor vehicle accidents, child abuse and neglect, and drug and alcohol abuse is also increasing. Many individuals and families affected by these factors are likely to need specialized educational and emotional support.

■ HISTORICAL BACKGROUND

Perhaps because there are so many different types of physical and health impairments, it is difficult to trace the development of services for this population with any precision. Before there were public school educational opportunities, which began around the turn of this century, most children with severely disabling conditions were kept at home, in hospitals, or in institutions. If local public schools were willing to accept them and make any necessary modifications, some physically disabled children probably attended regular classes, especially if their handicaps were less severe and their intellectual functioning was not impaired.

The first special public school class for children with physical handicaps in the United States was established in Chicago around 1900. Two American physicians, Winthrop Phelps and Earl Carlson, made noteworthy contributions to the understanding and acceptance of physically disabled children. Phelps demonstrated that children could be helped through physical therapy and the effective use of braces, whereas Carlson (who himself had cerebral palsy) was a strong advocate of developing the intellectual potential of physically disabled children through appropriate education (Hewett & Forness, 1977).

As the 20th century progressed, the educational needs of children with physical and health impairments were gradually recognized. A dual system of special education prevailed for many handicapped children throughout most of this century—that is, virtually all children with disabilities such as blindness, deafness, and mental retardation were served either in state-run residential schools or in separate classes in local schools. However, this dual system did not apply to children with physical impairments; hardly any state residential schools were established for them. Instead, emphasis has long been placed on making services available at the community level. Children who were kept at home or in hospitals for reasons of health or accessibility were served by homebound or hospital teachers, who traveled from place to place. Special self-contained classes for children with physical impairments were set up in many regular public schools. Large school districts sometimes operated special schools solely for children with physical impairments. These special classes or schools typically had modifications such as ramps, adapted toilets, special gymnasiums, and space for wheelchairs in school cafeterias.

Many special classes and schools still exist for children with physical and health impairments. Today, however, there is a trend toward greater integration of these students in regular public school classes. The implementation of P.L. 94–142 and Section 504 of the Rehabilitation Act of 1973—as well as numerous court cases requiring architectural accessibility, appropriate educational programs for children in the least restrictive environment, and an end to discrimination against persons with disabilities—have had a positive impact on this integration. No longer may a child be denied the right to attend the local public school simply because there is a flight of stairs at the entrance, or bathroom or locker facilities are not suitable, or school buses are not equipped to transport wheelchairs. The local public school district now has the responsibility of providing suitable programs, facilities, and services to meet each child's educational needs. Today, many thousands of children with physical and health impairments are successfully attending regular classes.

See Chapter 2 for a description of these laws.

■ EDUCATIONAL IMPLICATIONS AND INTERVENTION

Alternative Settings

Children with physical and health impairments are served in a wide variety of educational settings, ranging from regular classrooms to homes and hospitals. Special educators address the needs of these students from infancy to young adulthood in cooperation with parents, other educators, and specialists.

Early intervention programs are important for all exceptional children, especially those with physical and health impairments. Programs for infants and preschool children are increasingly available through local school districts—in part as a response to P.L. 99–457, the Education of the Handicapped Act Amendments of 1986—as well as in hospitals, clinics, university-affiliated facilities, and specialized community agencies (such as United Cerebral Palsy). The services may be directed exclusively to at-risk or disabled children or may include nondisabled children as well. Usually, early intervention programs for children with physical and health impairments emphasize assessment of a child's performance in many areas and seek to systematically develop the child's motor, self-help, social, and communication skills. A good early intervention program can be of enormous help to the child and family in providing information and support.

The regular public school classroom, in which the school-age child with physical and health impairments is educated along with nondisabled children, is

Chapter 14 provides further information on P.L. 99–457.

the educational setting that most parents and educators prefer. As Pieper (1983) observes, "Just as the concept that children with disabilities should be dependent on charity for their education is fast giving way, so too are we questioning the belief that medical settings and medically oriented staff are appropriate to foster academic learning, life skills or social behaviors" (p. 21). The amount of supportive help that may be required to enable a physically impaired student to function effectively in a regular class varies greatly, according to each child's condition, needs, and level of functioning. Many children with physical and health impairments require only minor modifications, such as ramps and altered seating arrangements, whereas some need special equipment and considerable assistance in mobility, eating, using the toilet, administering medication, and performing other daily activities. An effective program in an integrated school setting can encourage independence, communication, and social development and can make nondisabled students more aware of their peers with disabilities.

Special classes for children with physical disabilities are also offered in many public schools. Some districts have entire schools designed especially for physically disabled students, whereas in others self-contained special classrooms are housed within regular elementary or secondary school buildings. Special classes usually provide smaller class size, more adapted equipment, and easier access to the services of professionals such as physicians, physical and occupational therapists, and specialists in communication disorders and therapeutic recreation.

The continuum of educational services, as described in Chapter 2, is especially applicable to children with physical and health impairments.

Homebound or hospital education programs are available to children with especially severe physical and health impairments. If a child's medical condition necessitates hospitalization or treatment at home for a lengthy period (generally 30 days or more), the local school district is obligated to draw up an individualized education program and provide appropriate educational services to the child through a qualified teacher. Some children need home- or hospital-based instruction because their life-support equipment cannot be made portable. Such *technologically assisted* students are in need of "both a medical device to compensate for the loss of a vital body function and substantial and ongoing nursing care to avoid death or further disability" (Office of Technology Assessment, 1987, p. 3). This is usually regarded as the most restrictive level of special education service, because little or no interaction with nondisabled students is possible in a home or hospital setting. Most large hospitals and medical centers employ educational specialists who cooperate with the hospitalized student's home school district in planning and delivering instruction. Homebound children are visited regularly by itinerant teachers or tutors hired by the school district. Some school programs used a closed-circuit TV system to enable children to see, hear, and participate in class discussions and demonstrations from their beds (Kleinberg, 1984).

The Interdisciplinary Approach

Children with physical and health impairments usually come into contact with a great many teachers, physicians, therapists, and other specialists, both in and out of school. It is important that both regular and special educators make informed decisions about each child's needs, in cooperation with parents and other professionals. There are many opportunities for members of an interdisciplinary team to share information about a child from their individual vantage points. The team approach has special relevance to a child with a physical or health impairment. Medical, educational, therapeutic, vocational, and social needs are important and complex and frequently affect each other. Communication and cooperation among educational and health care personnel are especially crucial if each child's diverse needs are to be met. For example, in devising appropriate toileting procedures for Richard, a pediatrician may recommend a diet and a schedule, following a medical examination of bowel and bladder functioning. A biomedical technician may then design an adaptive device to facilitate Richard's transfer from wheelchair to toilet, and a physical therapist may help him use the device, while demonstrating proper bracing and muscle-strengthening techniques to Richard's parents and teachers.

Sirvis (1982) suggests that an interdisciplinary team of professionals and parents should work toward achieving four general goals in the educational program of a student with a physical or health impairment.

1. Physical independence, including mastery of daily living skills

2. Self-awareness and social maturation

3. Academic growth

4. Career education, including constructive leisure activities

Two particularly important specialists for many children with physical and health impairments are the physical therapist and the occupational therapist. Each is a licensed health professional who must complete a specialized training program and meet rigorous standards. Their work frequently brings them into contact with physically and health impaired children, and they are often called on to provide practical suggestions and training to teachers and parents.

Physical therapists, or PTs, use specialized knowledge to plan and oversee a child's program in making correct and useful movements. They may prescribe specific exercises to help a child increase control of muscles and use specialized equipment, such as braces, effectively. Massage and prescriptive exercises are perhaps the most frequently applied procedures, but physical therapy can also include swimming, heat treatment, special positioning for feeding and toileting, and other techniques. PTs encourage children to be as motorically independent as possible, help develop muscular function, and reduce pain, discomfort, or long-term physical damage. They may also suggest dos and don'ts for sitting positions and activities in the classroom and may suggest exercise or play programs that a disabled child can enjoy along with other children.

Occupational therapists, or OTs, are concerned with a child's participation in activities, especially those that will be useful in self-help, employment, recreation, communication, and other aspects of daily living. They may help a child learn (or relearn) such diverse motor behaviors as drinking from a modified cup, buttoning clothes, tying shoes, pouring liquids, cooking, and typing on a computer keyboard. These activities can enhance a child's physical development, independence, vocational potential, and self-concept. Occupational therapists conduct specialized assessments and make recommendations to parents and teachers regarding the effective use of appliances, materials, and activities at home and school. Many occupational therapists also work with vocational rehabilitation specialists in helping students find opportunities for work and independent living after completion of an educational program.

PTs and OTs provide three types of school-based services:

> Indirect treatment consisting of consultation, inservice education, and monitoring; in-class management where the therapist facilitates the student's performance during class activities; and direct treatment in which the student's attention is diverted from classroom activities to those that comprise a therapy session (Cusick, 1991, p. 18).

Additional specialists who frequently offer services to children with physical and health impairments include *prosthetists,* who make and fit artificial limbs; *orthotists,* who design and fit braces and other assistive devices; *biomedical engineers,* who develop or adapt technology to meet a student's specialized needs; and *medical social workers,* who assist students and families in adjusting to disabilities.

Positioning, Seating, and Mobility Devices

Importance of Positioning

The positioning of a physically disabled child can often have significant effects on how the child is perceived and accepted by others. Simple adjustments contribute to improved appearance and greater comfort and increased health for the disabled child (Wright & Bigge, 1991, p. 135):

Incidentally, a student should not be described as being "confined to a wheelchair." This expression suggests the person is restrained, or even imprisoned. Actually, most students leave their wheelchairs from time to time to exercise or lie down. It is preferable to say that a student "has a wheelchair" or "uses a wheelchair to get around." A working knowledge of techniques associated with wheelchair use can be helpful to a teacher in reducing problems and in making classrooms and school buildings accessible. See pages 406–407.

♦ Good positioning results in alignment and proximal support of the body.

♦ Stability positively affects use of the upper body.

♦ Stability promotes feelings of physical security and safety.

♦ Good positioning can reduce deformity.

♦ Positions must be changed frequently.

Proper Seating

Proper seating helps combat poor circulation, muscle tightness, and pressure sores, and contributes to digestion, respiration, and physical development. Be attentive to the following:

♦ Pelvic position; hips as far back in the chair as possible and weight distributed evenly on both sides of the buttocks.

♦ Foot support: both feet level and supported on the floor or wheelchair pedals.

♦ Shoulder/upper trunk support: seat belt, pummel or leg separator, and/or shoulder and chest straps may be necessary for upright positions.

Mobility

Many students are unable to move freely from place to place without the assistance of a mobility device. Mobility devices should be selected with the following variables in mind (Clarke, 1988):

♦ Motor capabilities

♦ Physical strength and endurance

♦ Cost of the device

♦ Physical layout of the home, school, and community

♦ Educational and therapy goals

Environmental Modifications

See pages 382–383 for an excellent example of how objects (in this case toys) can be modified to improve their accessibility to students with physical impairments.

Teachers frequently find it necessary to modify the environment to enable a student with physical and health impairments to participate more fully in the classroom. An environmental modification may involve adapting the equipment or materials used for a given task or changing the manner in which the task is done (Sowers, Jenkins, & Powers, 1988). Wright and Bigge (1991) describe four types of environmental modifications: (1) changes in location of materials and equipment, (2) work surface modifications, (3) object modifications, and (4) manipulation aids.

Although barrier-free architecture is the most publicly visible type of environmental modification for making community buildings and services more accessible, some of the most functional adaptations require little or no cost.

♦ Changing desk- and tabletops to appropriate heights for students who are very short or who use wheelchairs.

A barrier-free environment is the only modification needed for the full inclusion of some students with physical disabilities.

- Providing a wooden pointer to enable a student to reach the upper buttons on an elevator control panel.

- Installing paper-cup dispensers near water fountains so they can be used by students in wheelchairs.

- Moving a class or activity to an accessible part of a school building so that a student with a physical impairment can be included.

Adaptive Devices and Assistive Technology

Both "low technology" adaptive devices and "high tech" assistive equipment is used by children with physical and health impairments in many everyday activities. Special eating utensils, such as forks and spoons with custom-designed handles or straps, may enable children to feed themselves more independently. Simple switches are common parts of homemade environmental control systems to enable persons with disabilities to operate electric appliances such as a TV, stereo, computer, or electric wheelchair (Levin & Scherfenberg, 1987; Wright & Momari, 1985).

New technological aids for communication are used increasingly with children whose physical impairments prevent them from speaking clearly. For students who are able to speak but have limited motor function, there are voice input/output products that enable them to access computers (Esposito & Campbell, 1987). Such developments allow students with physical impairments to communicate expressively and receptively with others and to take part in a wide range of instructional programs.

See section on augmentative communication in Chapter 6.

Attitudes

How parents, teachers, classmates, and others react to a child with physical disabilities is at least as important as the disability itself. Many children with disabilities suffer from excessive pity, sympathy, and overprotection, whereas others are cruelly rejected, stared at, teased, and excluded from participation in activities with nondisabled children. All children, whether or not disabled, need to develop respect for themselves and to feel they have a rightful place in their family, school, and community.

Children with physical disabilities should have chances to participate in activities and to experience success and accomplishment. Effective parents and teachers accept these children as worthwhile individuals, rather than as disability cases. They encourage the children to develop a positive, realistic view of themselves and their physical conditions. They expect the children to meet reasonable standards of performance and behavior. They help them cope with their disabilities wherever possible and realize that, beyond their physical impairments, these children have many qualities that make them unique individuals.

Many nondisabled people tend to feel uncomfortable in the presence of a person with a visible disability and react with tension and withdrawal (Allsop, 1980). This response is probably attributable to lack of previous contact with disabled individuals; people may fear that they will say or do the wrong thing. A study by Belgrave and Mills (1981) found that when disabled people specifically mentioned their disabilities in connection with a request for help

CHECKLISTS FOR THE CLASSROOM

John Venn, Linda Morganstern, and Mary K. Dykes have prepared information and checklists that are helpful to teachers who work with children using braces, prostheses, or wheelchairs in the classroom. Here is a portion of their material on wheelchairs.

Wheelchairs

A physician prescribes wheelchair locomotion for individuals who are unable to ambulate or for those whose ambulation is unsteady, unsafe, or too strenuous. A wheelchair may also be needed by those who can ambulate but cannot rise unassisted from sitting to standing. Those who need crutches to ambulate but have to carry things from one place to another may also require the use of a wheelchair (Hirschberg, Lewis, & Thomas, 1964).

The most common type of wheelchair is made of metal and upholstery and has four wheels. The two large back wheels have a separate rim that can be grasped to propel the chair, while the two small front wheels are casters that pivot freely. The casters are attached to the wheelchair by a fork and stem assembly that allows them to pivot 360°. Wheelchairs are fitted to individuals, so the special parts and features are numerous. Special features include detachable armrests, which are fitted with a locking device to secure them in place; footrests, which often have nylon heel loops to hold the foot on the footrest; leg rest panels to support the leg in proper position; and a folding device that allows the wheelchair to be folded for easier storage (Ellwood, 1971). After it has been decided that a wheelchair is needed, the wheelchair dealer, often in conjunction with a physical therapist, measures the child to ensure an individual prescription that will properly fit the child. The dealer also provides instruction in use and care of the wheelchair.

Recent wheelchair developments include lighter weight, adaptive wheelchairs, as well as motorized wheelchairs. The lightweight chairs are primarily designed for children. Features include such things as a travel chair with a unique folding mechanism that allows it to double as a stroller and a car seat. Accessories include adjustable Velcro fasteners for lap belts, pads, attachable trays, and head restraints. In addition, motorized wheelchairs of various designs may be prescribed for individuals unable to propel themselves independently. Wheelchair transporters such as modified golf carts are also available (Peizer, 1975).

The Teacher's Role

The primary role of the teacher regarding ambulation devices is daily observation of the student's use and care of his or her equipment. Teachers should keep parents apprised of special problems and needs as they arise. The teacher, along with other special education support personnel, is responsible for designing a barrier-free classroom and also for obtaining the special equipment and materials that will allow the student to participate in classroom activities. In conjunction with the physical therapist and the family, the teacher should develop a program to encourage maximum use of ambulation devices in the classroom, the school, the home, and the community. The teacher's role therefore extends beyond the school's boundaries and into the home and the community.

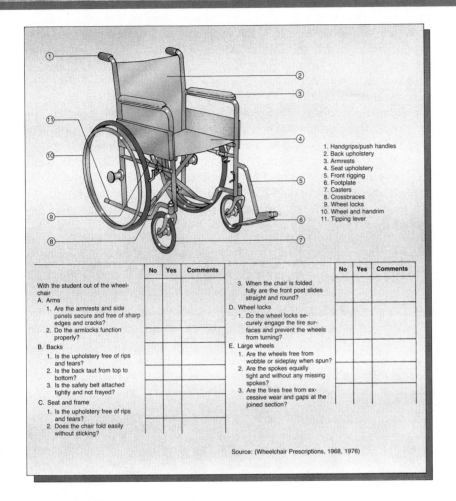

1. Handgrips/push handles
2. Back upholstery
3. Armrests
4. Seat upholstery
5. Front rigging
6. Footplate
7. Casters
8. Crossbraces
9. Wheel locks
10. Wheel and handrim
11. Tipping lever

	No	Yes	Comments		No	Yes	Comments
With the student out of the wheel-chair				3. When the chair is folded fully are the front post slides straight and round?			
A. Arms				D. Wheel locks			
1. Are the armrests and side panels secure and free of sharp edges and cracks?				1. Do the wheel locks securely engage the tire surfaces and prevent the wheels from turning?			
2. Do the armlocks function properly?				E. Large wheels			
B. Backs				1. Are the wheels free from wobble or sideplay when spun?			
1. Is the upholstery free of rips and tears?				2. Are the spokes equally tight and without any missing spokes?			
2. Is the back taut from top to bottom?				3. Are the tires free from excessive wear and gaps at the joined section?			
3. Is the safety belt attached tightly and not frayed?							
C. Seat and frame							
1. Is the upholstery free of rips and tears?							
2. Does the chair fold easily without sticking?							

Source: (Wheelchair Prescriptions, 1968, 1976)

Use of Checklists

A checklist for classroom use enables the teacher to monitor the condition and function of wheelchairs. The items on each checklist are marked with "yes" and "no" answers. If the device is in proper working condition and fitted correctly, all items should be marked in the "yes" column. "No" answers indicate problems with the device that require attention. A section for comments about specific needs is provided for each item.

The classroom teacher may use these checklists for preliminary evaluations, but should refer the child to a physical therapist for reassessment or request that parents seek physical therapist assistance/reassessment before assuming that the teacher's evaluation is correct or referring the child to a specialist.

From "Checklists for Evaluating the Fit and Function of Orthoses, Prostheses, and Wheelchairs in the Classroom" by J. Venn, L. Morganstern, & M. K. Dykes, 1979, Teaching Exceptional Children, 11, pp. 51–56. Copyright by the Council for Exceptional Children. Reprinted by permission. Drawing courtesy of Everest and Jennings. ◆

("Would you mind sharpening my pencil for me? There are just some things you can't do from a wheelchair"), they were perceived more favorably than they were when no mention was made of the disability.

The classroom can be a useful place to discuss disabilities and to encourage understanding and acceptance of a child with a physical or health impairment. Some teachers find that simulation or role-playing activities are helpful. Nondisabled children might, for example, have the opportunity to use wheelchairs, braces, or crutches to expand their awareness of some barriers a disabled classmate faces. Pieper (1983) notes that most children with physical and health impairments are "neither saintly creatures nor pitiable objects" (p. 8). She suggests that teachers emphasize cooperation rather than competition by choosing tasks that require students to work together. It is important to give praise when earned but not to make the child with a physical impairment a teacher's pet who will be resented by other students. Factual information can also help build a general understanding of an impairment. Classmates should learn to use accurate terminology and to offer the correct kind of assistance when needed.

CURRENT ISSUES/FUTURE TRENDS

Children with physical and health impairments are being integrated into regular educational programs as much as possible today. No longer is it believed that the regular classroom is an inappropriate environment for a child with physical limitations. Although architectural and attitudinal barriers still exist in some areas, integrated public school programs are gradually becoming more accessible.

Service Environments

Integrating students with physical and health impairments, however, has raised several controversial issues. Many questions center on the extent of responsibility properly assumed by teachers and schools in caring for a child's physical and health needs. In a well-publicized case (*Irving Independent School District v. Tatro,* 1984), the U.S. Supreme Court decided that a school district was obligated to provide intermittent catheterization service to a young child with spina bifida. The Court considered catheterization to be a related service, necessary for the child to remain in the least restrictive educational setting and able to be performed by a trained layperson. Some educators and school administrators believe that services such as catheterization are more medical than educational and should not be the school's responsibility. The expense of such services and the availability of insurance pose potential problems for school personnel. Nevertheless, the Tatro case probably means that "handicapped children with medical problems who were once excluded from school programs may now be provided access since certain medical services can be provided by qualified personnel who are not physicians" (Vitello, 1986, p. 356). Similar questions have been raised with regard to the equipment and special services that physically or health impaired children may need in regular schools. For example, who should bear the cost of an expensive computerized communication system for a child with cerebral palsy—the parents, the school, both, or some other agency?

We will likely see a continuation of the present trend to serve children with physical and health impairments in regular classrooms as much as possible. Therapists and other support personnel will come into the classroom to assist the teacher, child, and classmates. This appears to be a more effective and economical use of professional time and skill than removing a child with disabilities from the classroom and providing services in an isolated setting.

Technology and Research

Recent developments in technology and biomedical engineering hold exciting implications for many children with physical disabilities. People with paralysis resulting from spinal cord injury and other causes are already benefiting from sophisticated microcomputers that can stimulate paralyzed muscles by bypassing damaged nerves. In 1982, Nan Davis became the first human being to walk with permanently paralyzed muscles; she was able to control a computer with her brain and transmit impulses to sensors placed on her paralyzed muscles. Such systems are likely to become more efficient and widespread in the future, helping many people with various kinds of physical impairments. Improved medical treatment will also alleviate some physical and health-related conditions.

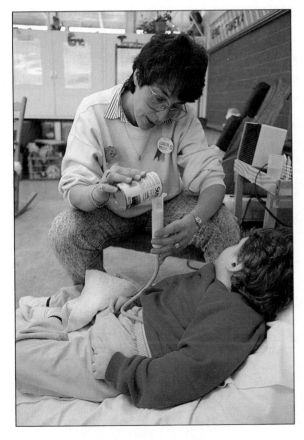

School personnel are being required to provide an increasing range of related services to students with disabilities.

Animal Assistance

Using animals to assist people with physical disabilities has also generated much recent interest. There are many ways animals can help children and adults with disabilities. Nearly everyone is familiar with guide dogs, which can help people who are blind travel independently, and some agencies train hearing dogs to assist people who are deaf by alerting them to sounds. Another recent and promising approach to the use of animals by people with disabilities is that of a "helping" or "service dog." Depending on a person's needs, dogs can be trained to carry books and other objects (in saddlebags), pick up telephone receivers, turn light switches on or off, and open doors. Dogs can also be used for balance and support—for example, to help a person propel a wheelchair up a steep ramp or to help a person stand up from a seated position. And dogs can be trained to contact family members or neighbors if the disabled person needs help. Frequently, people report that dogs serve as an ice-breaker in opening up conversations and contacts with nondisabled people in the school and community.

Monkeys have been trained to perform such complex tasks as preparing food, operating record and tape players, and turning the pages of books (MacFadyen, 1986). Sometimes technological and animal assistance are combined, as when a person uses a laser beam (emitted from a device held in the mouth) to show a monkey which light switch to turn on. In addition to providing practical assistance and enhancing the independence of people with disabilities, animals also appear to have social value as companions, and the responsibilities of caring for an animal are a worthwhile experience for many people, with or without disabilities.

Students with physical limitations should be encouraged to develop as much independence as possible. Often, well-meaning teachers, classmates, and

Helper monkeys have been trained to assist with numerous daily living and work related tasks.

parents tend to do too much for a child with a physical or health impairment. It may be difficult, frustrating, and/or time-consuming for the child to learn to care for his own needs, but the confidence and skills gained from independent functioning are well worth the effort in the long run. Nevertheless, most persons with physical disabilities find it necessary to rely on others for assistance at certain times, in certain situations. Effective teachers can help students cope with their disabilities, set realistic expectations, and accept help gracefully when it is needed.

Education, Employment, and Life Skills

The future will need to focus on several areas where progress has been made but improvement is still needed. Even though physical education is an important need of most disabled people—and specifically required by P.L. 94–142 for inclusion in the educational program of every child with disabilities—some schools still do not provide adapted physical education programs for their physically disabled students, thus excluding them from participation in most athletic and recreational activities.

Another area of concern is employment, which is one of the most critical aspects of adult life. Many studies show that successful and remunerative work is among the most important variables in enabling people with disabilities to lead satisfying, productive, and independent lives. Yet negative attitudes persist on the part of many employers. Vocational and professional opportunities must be expanded to include disabled individuals more adequately. While children are in school, their education should help them investigate practical avenues of future employment, and there should be ongoing contact between educators and vocational rehabilitation specialists.

There is also a need for improved programs of education and counseling for students with terminal illnesses. These programs should give realistic support to the child and family in dealing with death and in making the best possible use of the time available. When a child dies, teachers and classmates may also be seriously affected, and their needs should also be considered and talked about.

There are many self-help groups of people with disabilities. These groups can help provide information and support to children affected by similar disabilities. It is usually encouraging for a child and parent to meet and observe capable, independent adults who have severe disabilities, and worthwhile, helping relationships can be established. Some groups operate centers for independent living, which emphasize adaptive devices, financial benefits, access to jobs, and provision of personal care attendants. Other groups are active as advocates for social change, countering instances in which people with disabilities are excluded from meaningful participation in society.

There is every indication that the years ahead will find children and adults with physical and health impairments participating more fully in schools, colleges, and virtually all other facets of everyday community life. However, we still need better physical access to public buildings, improved public attitudes, and greater support to parents early in the lives of their disabled children. As these needs are met, the opportunities open to people with physical and health impairments will greatly expand.

- Children with physical and health impairments are a widely varied population. Some are extremely restricted in activities; others have few limitations.
- Teachers must understand how a physical or health impairment may affect a child's learning, development, or behavior.

Types and Causes

- Many types of physical and health conditions make special education services necessary.
- An orthopedic impairment involves the skeletal system; a neurologic impairment involves the nervous system.
- Physical impairments are described in terms of type of limb involvement.
- Impairments can also be described in terms of severity.
- Cerebral palsy is a long-term condition arising from impairment to the brain and causing disturbances in voluntary motor functions.
- Spina bifida is a congenital condition that may cause loss of sensation and severe muscle weakness in the lower part of the body. Children with spina bifida can usually participate in most classroom activities but need assistance in toileting.
- Muscular dystrophy is a long-term condition; most children gradually lose the ability to walk independently.
- Other conditions that can affect a child's classroom performance include osteogenesis imperfecta, spinal cord injuries, and amputations or missing limbs.
- Head injuries are a significant cause of neurologic impairments and learning problems.
- Seizure disorders produce disturbances of movement, sensation, behavior, and/or consciousness.
- Diabetes is a disorder of metabolism that can often be controlled with injections of insulin.
- Children with cystic fibrosis, asthma, hemophilia, severe burns, or other health conditions may need modifications in their education or activities or other special services, such as counseling.

Important Variables to Consider

- Variables to consider in providing appropriate services include severity, visibility, and age at acquisition of a physical or health impairment.

Prevalence

- There is no universal definition of the physically and health impaired population, and many children counted under other categories of exceptionality also have physical or health impairments.
- Cerebral palsy accounts for the largest single group of children with physical impairments.

Historical Background

- Public school programs for children with physical disabilities began around the turn of the century.

Educational Implications and Intervention

♦ Early intervention programs are important for the child and family. They are becoming increasingly available.

♦ Serving students with physical and health impairments in regular classes encourages independence, social development, and communication with nondisabled peers.

♦ Children with physical and health impairments typically require interdisciplinary services from a team of professionals.

♦ Treatment of physical and health impairments usually includes one or more of the following approaches: hands-on therapy, assistive devices, medication, and surgery.

♦ Many children with physical and health impairments need special devices, such as braces, wheelchairs, prostheses, modified eating appliances, and other equipment.

♦ Adaptations to the physical environment and to classroom activities can enable students with physical and health impairments to participate more fully in the school program.

Current Issues/Future Trends

♦ The current trend toward educating children with physical and health impairments in the regular classroom is likely to continue.

♦ The use of animals to assist people with physical needs is also increasing.

♦ Generally, programs for students with physical and health impairments seek to develop as much independence as possible.

FOR MORE INFORMATION

Journals

ACCENT on Living, P.O. Box 700, Bloomington, IL 61701. A quarterly journal of practical information, with articles on varied topics, including employment, aids to independent living, architectural barriers, and family concerns. Primarily written by and about people with physical and health impairments. Also sponsors an extensive catalog of assistive devices and a computerized information retrieval system.

The Disability Rag, P.O. Box 145, Louisville, KY 40201. Described as "a spicy, irreverent journal." A bimonthly publication tackling controversial issues affecting people with disabilities and serving as a forum for opinion and debate. Features articles on such topics as telethons, legal battles, sexuality, and media portrayals of people with disabilities.

Disability Studies Quarterly. Published by the Department of Sociology, Brandeis University, Waltham, MA 02254. Regularly prints abstracts of current research projects, book reviews, announcements of conferences, resources, and grants. Focuses on social and psychological issues, as well as advocacy, economics, and attitudes of and toward persons with physical and other disabilities.

Disabled USA. Published quarterly by the President's Committee on Employment of the Handicapped, 1111 20th Street, NW, Suite 600, Washington, DC 20036. Reports on current developments in employment, rehabilitation, and independent living. Seeks to document progress in employment and to encourage new opportunities for workers with disabilities.

Rehabilitation Literature. Published monthly by the National Easter Seal Society, 2023 West Ogden Avenue, Chicago, IL 60612. An interdisciplinary publication containing abstracts of current research and practice, with an emphasis on children and adults with orthopedic, neurological, and other physical and health-related impairments. Regularly features reviews of recent books.

Books

Batshaw, M. L., & Perret, Y. M. (1986). *Children with handicaps: A medical primer* (2nd ed.). Baltimore, MD: Paul H. Brookes.

Bigge, J. L. (1991). *Teaching individuals with physical and multiple disabilities* (3rd ed.). Columbus, OH: Merrill.

Bleck, E. E., & Nagel, D. A. (Eds.). (1981). *Physically handicapped children: A medical atlas for teachers* (2nd ed.). Orlando, FL: Grune & Stratton.

Goldfarb, L. A., Brotherson, M. J., Summers, J. A., & Turnbull, A. P. (1986). *Meeting the challenge of disability or chronic illness: A family guide.* Baltimore, MD: Paul H. Brookes.

Hanson, M. J., & Harris, S. R. (1986). *Teaching the young child with motor delays: A guide for parents and professionals.* Austin, TX: PRO-ED.

Kleinberg, S. B. (1982). *Educating the chronically ill child.* Rockville, MD: Aspen.

Pieper, E. (1983). *The teacher and the child with spina bifida* (2nd ed.). Rockville, MD: Spina Bifida Association of America.

Rosen, C. D., & Gerring, J. P. (1986). *Head trauma: Educational reintegration.* San Diego: College-Hill.

Sowers, J. & Powers, L. (1991). *Vocational preparation and employment of students with physical and multiple disabilities.* Baltimore, MD: Paul H. Brookes.

Zacharkow, D. (1984). *Wheelchair posture and pressure sores.* Springfield, IL: Charles C. Thomas.

Organizations

A large number of national agencies and organizations provide information, educational programs, and community services to children and adults with specific physical and health impairments and to their parents and teachers. Many of these have state and local chapters. Listed here are some of the largest organizations that disseminate publications and encourage research into the causes and treatment of physical and health impairments.

Cystic Fibrosis Foundation, 6000 Executive Boulevard, Rockville, MD 20852.

Epilepsy Foundation of America, 4531 Garden City Drive, Landover, MD 20785.

Juvenile Diabetes Association, 23 East 26th Street, New York, NY 10010.

Muscular Dystrophy Association, 810 Seventh Avenue, New York, NY 10019.

National Easter Seal Society, 2023 West Ogden Avenue, Chicago, IL 60612.

Spina Bifida Association of America, 343 South Dearborn Street, Chicago, IL 60604.

United Cerebral Palsy Associations, Inc., 66 East 34th Street, New York, NY 10016.

10
Severe Handicaps

◆ Why is a curriculum based on the developmental stages of nonhandicapped children inappropriate for students with severe handicaps?

◆ What are the benefits for students with severe handicaps who are educated in regular, integrated schools?

◆ What are the likely effects on the education of students who are not disabled if they share a regular classroom with peers who are severely handicapped?

◆ How can the principle of partial participation contribute to the quality of life of a student with severe handicaps?

◆ Does teaching with structure and precision make it more difficult for students with severe handicaps to make choices and express their individuality?

Are all children educable, regardless of the severity of their handicaps? See pages 424–425 for several viewpoints.

Five-year-old Zack is learning to feed himself with a spoon. A teacher is showing 13-year-old Toni that it is more appropriate to shake hands than to hug a person when first introduced. Martha, who is 20, is learning to ride a city bus to her afternoon job at a cafeteria, where she clears tables and sorts silverware. Zack, Toni, and Martha have severe handicaps. But except for their dependence on other people and their need for instruction in skills that nonhandicapped children usually acquire at a younger age, they have little in common. The behaviors and skills of students with severe disabilities are highly diverse.

Because of their intense intellectual, physical, and behavioral limitations, children with severe disabilities tend to learn much more slowly than any other group of children (including other children who are considered disabled or handicapped). Indeed, without direct instruction, some persons with severe handicaps are not able to perform the most basic, everyday behaviors we take for granted, such as eating, toileting, and communicating our needs and feelings to others.

Children with severe handicaps often have combinations of obvious and not-so-obvious disabilities that require special additions or adaptations in their education. But a severe handicap does not necessarily preclude meaningful achievements. Despite the severity and multiplicity of their disabilities, it has been shown conclusively that students with severe handicaps *can* and *do learn.* Today, many students with severe handicaps are learning useful skills and are interacting with nonhandicapped peers in schools, neighborhoods, and workplaces. Appropriate programs of instruction are helping many students with severe handicaps to engage in and enjoy a wide variety of useful, worthwhile, and personally satisfying activities.

But large-scale efforts to develop effective methods of instruction for students with severe handicaps is a relatively recent phenomenon. In the not-too-distant past, children with severe handicaps were a neglected population; it was widely believed that they were incapable of acquiring useful skills. They were usually placed in institutions as infants or young children and were considered beyond the responsibility of the public educational system. They usually received no education or training at all and were provided with only basic, custodial-level care.

Although students with severe handicaps were excluded from educational programs—and from mainstream society in general—in the past, a philosophy of inclusion now prevails. Laws requiring free, appropriate programs of public education for all handicapped students; the rapidly growing body of evidence indicating that individuals with severe handicaps can learn and function effectively in integrated school, work, and community settings; and the belief that inclusion is the "right thing to do" all support the new philosophy.

■ DEFINITION AND CHARACTERISTICS

Throughout this book, we have prefaced discussions of the various handicapping conditions by pointing out how definitions and lists of characteristics used to describe a group have limited meaning at the level of the individual child. And, of course, it is at the level of the individual child where special education takes place, where decisions about what and how to teach are made. As we consider the various ways of defining severe handicaps, we must keep in mind that students with severe handicaps constitute an extremely heterogeneous group. As Guess and Mulligan (1982) point out, the differences among students with severe handicaps are greater than their similarities.

Students with **severe handicaps** exhibit extreme deficits in intellectual functioning and may also need special services because of motor impediments, communication, visual, and auditory impairments, and medical conditions such as seizure disorders. Many have medical and physical problems that require frequent attention. The population referred to as severely handicapped encompasses students with severe and profound mental retardation, autism, and/or physical/sensory impairments combined with marked developmental delay. The term is not generally used to refer to individuals with physical or sensory impairments who do not also have mental retardation (Wolery & Haring, 1990).

Many students with severe handicaps have more than one disability. Even with the best available methods of diagnosis and assessment, it is often difficult to identify the nature and intensity of a child's multiple handicaps or to determine how combinations of disabilities affect a child's behavior. Some children, for example, do not respond in any observable way to visual stimuli, such as bright lights or moving objects. Is this because the child is blind as a result of eye damage, or is he unresponsive because of brain damage? Such

In the not-too-distant past, students with disabilities as severe and complex as Phillip's were denied the right to attend their neighborhood public school.

questions arise frequently in planning educational programs for students with severe handicaps of all types.

No single, widely accepted definition of severe handicaps has yet emerged. Most definitions have been based on tests of intellectual functioning, developmental progress, or the extent of educational need. According to the system of classifying levels of mental retardation used by the American Association on Mental Retardation, persons receiving IQ scores of 35–40 and below are considered to have *severe* mental retardation; scores of 20–25 and below result in a classification of *profound* mental retardation. In practice, however, many individuals who score in the moderate level of mental retardation (i.e., IQ scores of 40–55) are sometimes considered to have severe handicaps (Wolery & Haring, 1990).

Traditional methods of intelligence testing, however, are virtually useless with many children who have severe handicaps. If tested, they tend to be assigned IQ scores at the extreme lower end of the continuum. Knowing that a particular student has an IQ of 25, however, is of no value in designing an appropriate educational program. Educators of students with severe handicaps tend to focus on the specific skills a child needs to learn, rather than on intellectual level.

It was once common to take a developmental approach to the definition of severe handicaps. Justen (1976), for example, proposed that "those individuals age 21 and younger who are functioning at a general developmental level of half or less than the level which would be expected on the basis of chronological age" (p. 5) be considered severely handicapped. Most educators now maintain that developmental levels have little relevance to this population and instead emphasize that a severely handicapped student—regardless of age—is one who needs instruction in basic skills, such as getting from place to place independently, communicating with others, controlling bowel and bladder functions, and self-feeding. Most children without disabilities are able to acquire these basic skills in the first 5 years of life, but the student with severe handicaps needs special instruction to do so. The basic-skills definition makes it clear that education for students with severe handicaps must not be restricted to traditional academic instruction.

The definition of severe handicaps used by the U.S. Department of Education refers to the need for educational and related services that go "beyond" what is typically available in regular and special education programs.

> Severely handicapped children are those who because of the intensity of their physical, mental, or emotional problems, or a combination of such problems, need educational, social, psychological, and medical services beyond those which are traditionally offered by regular and special education programs, in order to maximize their potential for useful and meaningful participation in society and for self-fulfillment. (*Federal Register*, 1988, p. 118)

Two additional paragraphs in the federal definition provide examples of various handicapping conditions ("profoundly and severely mentally retarded," "cerebral-palsied deaf") or behavioral characteristics ("self-mutilation") that are considered severe handicaps. As Wolery and Haring (1990) point out, the inclusion of extremely challenging problems, such as self-injurious behavior, in the federal definition is not intended to imply that all children with severe

See Chapter 3 for discussion of IQ testing and classification of intellectual functioning.

Imagine the difficulty, as well as the inappropriateness, of giving an IQ test to a student who cannot hold his head up straight or point, let alone talk.

handicaps exhibit such characteristics—most do not. The intention of including such examples was to make it clear that every child is entitled to a free, public education in the least restrictive environment no matter how complicated or challenging the learning, behavioral, or medical problems.

Perhaps the best definition of severe handicaps to date is the definition drafted by The Association for Persons with Severe Handicaps.

> These people include individuals of all ages who require extensive ongoing support in more than one major life activity in order to participate in integrated community settings and to enjoy a quality of life that is available to citizens with fewer or no disabilities. Support may be required for life activities such as mobility, communication, self-care, and learning, as necessary for independent living, employment and self-sufficiency. (Lindley, 1990, p. 1)

The TASH definition not only refers to the level, duration, and focus of support needed by persons who are labeled as severely disabled, but it specifies the goals and expected outcomes of that support.

Compared to some other areas of special education—mental retardation, learning disabilities, and behavior disorders in particular—there has been less concern and debate over the definition of severe handicaps. This is not an indication that professionals are not interested in defining the population of students they serve, but rather a reflection of two features inherent in severe handicaps. First, there is little need for a definition that precisely describes who is and who is not to be identified as severely handicapped. The specific criteria a school district uses to define learning disabilities have major impact on who will be eligible for special education services, but whether or not a student who may be labeled severely handicapped needs special education is seldom an issue. Second, because of the tremendous diversity of learning and physical challenges such students experience, a single descriptor such as "severe handicaps" is inadequate. Complex statements that specify the particular disabilities and needs of individual students are more meaningful (Sontag, Sailor, & Smith, 1977).

Behavioral Characteristics

Screening, the initial step in assessing whether a child is likely to have a disability, is seldom necessary for students who are severely handicapped. The one defining characteristic of students with severe handicaps is that they exhibit obvious deficits in multiple life-skill or developmental areas (Sailor & Guess, 1983). No specific set of behaviors is common to all children with severe handicaps. Each child presents a unique combination of physical, intellectual, and social characteristics. Educators generally agree, however, that the following behaviors are frequently observed.

♦ *Severe deficits in communication skills.* Almost all children with severe handicaps are limited in their ability to express themselves and to understand others. Many cannot talk or gesture meaningfully; they might not respond when communication is attempted. Of course, this makes education and social interaction extremely difficult—some children are not able to follow even the simplest commands.

- *Impaired physical and motor development.* Most children with severe handicaps have limited physical mobility. Many cannot walk; some cannot stand or sit up without support. They are slow to perform such basic tasks as rolling over, grasping objects, or holding their heads up. Physical deformities are common and may worsen without consistent physical therapy.

- *Deficits in self-help skills.* Some children with severe handicaps are unable to independently care for their most basic needs, such as dressing, eating, exercising bowel and bladder control, and maintaining personal hygiene. To learn these basic skills, they usually require special training involving prosthetic devices and/or adapted skill sequences.

- *Infrequent constructive behavior and interaction.* Nonhandicapped children and those whose handicaps are less severe typically play with other children, interact with adults, and seek out information about their surroundings. Many children with severe handicaps do not. They may appear to be completely out of touch with reality and may not show normal human emotions. It may be difficult to capture the attention of or to evoke any observable response from a child with profound handicaps.

- *Frequent inappropriate behavior.* Many children with severe handicaps do things that appear to have no constructive purpose. These activities may take the form of ritualistic (e.g., rocking back and forth, waving fingers in front of the face, twirling the body), self-stimulatory (e.g., grinding the teeth, patting the body), and/or self-injurious behaviors (e.g., head banging, hair pulling, eye poking, hitting, or scratching or biting oneself). Although some of these behaviors may not be considered abnormal in and of themselves, the high frequency with which some children perform these activities is a serious concern, because the behaviors interfere with teaching and with social acceptance.

Supportive social relationships between disabled students and their nondisabled peers are more likely to develop in the students' home school.

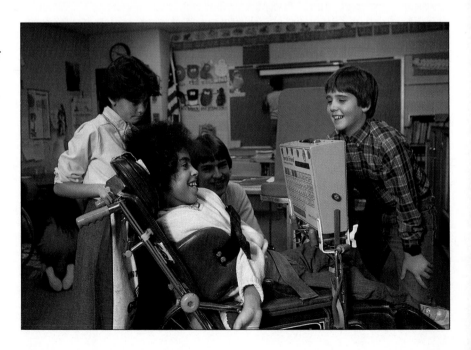

The combined effects of dual sensory impairments make it especially difficult to obtain information from the environment.

Descriptions of behavioral characteristics, such as those just mentioned, can easily give an overly negative impression. Despite the intense challenges their disabilities impose upon them, students with severe handicaps may also have many positive characteristics—including warmth, persistence, determination, sense of humor, sociability, and various other desirable traits (Forest & Lusthaus, 1990; Stainback & Stainback, 1991). Many teachers find great satisfaction in working with students who have severe handicaps and in observing their progress in school, home, and community settings.

Learning to perform a simple task that would be taken for granted by a person who is not disabled can have tremendous impact on the life of a child with severe handicaps. See page 446.

Students with Dual Sensory Impairments

A particularly challenging group of children with severe handicaps are those with dual sensory impairments. "There is perhaps no condition as disabling as deaf-blindness, the loss of part or all of one's vision and hearing" (Bullis & Otos, 1988, p. 110). Many of the several thousand children in the United States and Canada who are deaf-blind were born with visual, hearing, and other impairments after an epidemic of rubella affected thousands of pregnant women in the mid-1960s. Deaf-blind children were the first group of exceptional children to receive special education under federal mandate when the government established a special network of regional and state centers in 1968. When P.L. 94–142 was passed in 1975, the law included a section on deaf-blind children, defined as those who have

ARE ALL CHILDREN EDUCABLE?

Some educators, other professionals, and citizens question the wisdom of spending large amounts of money, time, and human resources attempting to train children with severe handicaps, many of whom have such serious disabilities that they may never be able to function independently. Some people would prefer to see our resources spent on children who have higher apparent potential—especially when economic conditions limit the availability of educational services for all children in the public schools. "Why bother with children who fail to make meaningful progress?" they ask.

> Accelerating a response rate may indeed be a worthy first goal in an educational program if there is reasonable hope of shaping the response into a meaningful skill. Nevertheless, after concerted and appropriate effort by highly trained behavior therapists, for a reasonable period of time, a child's failure to make significant progress toward acquisition of a meaningful skill could reasonably be taken as an indication that the child is ineduca-

ble. . . . Granted, all children probably are educable if education is defined as acceleration of any operant response. But such a definition trivializes the meaning of the term education and, even without consideration of benefit, moots the question of educability. Formulating consensual definitions of *education, meaningful skill,* and *significant progress* will be difficult, but it is a task we cannot avoid. . . . We suggest that public response to the questions "What is education?" "What skills are meaningful?" "What rate of progress is significant?" and "What cost/benefit ratios are acceptable?" sampled with sufficient care, could be invaluable in deciding who is educable and who is not. (Kauffman & Krouse, 1981, pp. 55–56)

A special educator who is also the parent of a daughter with severe handicaps disagrees.

> If anyone were to be the judge of whether a particular behavior change is "meaningful," it should certainly not be only the general taxpayer, who has no idea how rewarding it is to see your retarded 19-year-old acquire the skill of toilet

flushing on command or pointing to food when she wants a second helping. I suspect that the average taxpayer would not consider it "meaningful" to him or her for Karrie to acquire such skills. But in truth, it is "meaningful" to that taxpayer whether he recognizes it or not, in the sense that it is saving him or her the cost of Karrie's being institutionalized, which she certainly would have been by now if she never showed any progress; thus it is functional for the taxpayer even though his or her answer to the question "Is this meaningful?" might well be "No" or "Not enough to pay for."

> The complexity, cost, and hopelessness of evaluating fairly the "meaningfulness" of various behavior changes leads me to conclude that no one should be denied an education. . . . I would be very resistant to the idea that we should now, at this infant stage of the science and technology of education for severely retarded students, give up intensive skill training for anyone. (Hawkins, 1984, p. 285)

In many ways our knowledge of the learning and developmental pro-

both auditory and visual handicaps, the combination of which causes such severe communication and other developmental and educational problems that they cannot properly be accommodated in special education programs solely for the hearing handicapped child or for the visually handicapped child. (U.S. Office of Education, 1977a, p. 42478)

An educational program for deaf children is often inappropriate for a child who also has limited vision, because many methods of instruction and communication rely heavily on the use of sight. Programs for visually impaired students, on the other hand, usually require good hearing, because much instruction is auditory. Although 94% of individuals labeled deaf-blind have some functional hearing and/or vision (Fredericks & Baldwin, 1987), the combined effects of the dual impairments severely impede the development of communication and social skills, especially when mental retardation is also involved.

cesses of children with severe handicaps is still primitive and incomplete. We do know, however, that children with severe handicaps are capable of benefiting significantly from appropriate and carefully implemented educational programs. Even in cases where little or no progress has been observed, it would be wrong to conclude that the student is incapable of learning. It may instead be that our teaching methods are imperfect and that the future will bring improved methods and materials to enable that student to learn useful skills. Children, no matter how severe their disabilities, have the right to the best possible public education and training we can offer them.

Virtually every parent of a child with severe handicaps has heard a host of negative predictions from educators, doctors, and concerned friends and family. Parents are often offered such discouraging forecasts as "Your child will never talk" or "Your child will never be toilet-trained." Yet in many instances those children make gains that far exceed the original predictions of the professionals. Despite predictions to the contrary, many children have learned to walk, talk, toilet themselves, and perform other "impossible" tasks.

There are still many unanswered questions in the education of children with severe handicaps (Sailor, Gee, Goetz, & Graham, 1988). Even though their opportunities for education and training are rapidly expanding, nobody really knows their true learning potential or the extent to which they can be successfully integrated into the nondisabled population. What we do know is that students with the most severe disabilities will go no further than we let them; it is up to us to open doors and raise our sights, instead of creating additional barriers.

Don Baer, professor of human development at the University of Kansas and a pioneer in the development of effective instructional interventions for persons with severe disabilities, offers this wise perspective on the question of educability.

Some of us have ignored both the thesis that all retarded persons are educable and the thesis that some retarded persons are ineducable, and instead have experimented with ways to teach some previously unteachable people. Over a few centuries, those experiments have steadily reduced the size of the apparently ineducable group relative to the obviously educable group. Clearly, we have not finished that adventure. Why predict its outcome, when we could simply pursue it, and just as well without a prediction? Why not pursue it to see if there comes a day when there is such a small class of apparently ineducable persons left that it consists of one elderly institution resident who is put forward as ineducable. If it comes, that will be a very nice day, and the next day will be even better. (Baer, 1984, p. 299)

Readers wishing to learn more about the educability debate are referred to these additional references: Baer (1981b); Kauffman (1981); Noonan, Brown, Mulligan, and Rettig (1982); Orelove (1984); Tawney (1984); and Ulicny, Thompson, Favell, and Thompson (1985). ♦

The intellectual level of students who are deaf-blind ranges from giftedness (as in the famous case of Helen Keller, who lost her sight and hearing at about 16 months of age) to severe mental retardation. The majority of children who have both visual and hearing impairments at birth experience major difficulties in acquiring communication and motor skills, mobility, and appropriate social behavior.

Because these individuals do not receive clear and consistent information from either sensory modality, a tendency exists to turn inward to obtain the desired level of stimulation. The individual therefore may appear passive, nonresponsive, and/or noncompliant. Students with dual sensory impairments may not respond to or initiate appropriate interactions with others and often exhibit behavior that is considered socially inappropriate (e.g., hand flapping, finger flicking, head rocking). (Downing & Eichinger, 1990, pp. 98–99)

Educational programs for deaf-blind children who require instruction in basic skills are generally similar to those for other children with severe

See Van Dijk (1983, 1985) for descriptions of approaches to assessment, curriculum, and skill development for students who are deaf-blind.

handicaps. Although most students with dual sensory impairments can make use of information presented in these modalities, the visual and auditory stimuli used in instruction must be enhanced and the students' attention must be directed toward those stimuli. Tactile teaching techniques involving the sense of touch are used to supplement the information obtained through visual and auditory modes.

Robert Smithdas (1981), a man who is deaf-blind, vividly describes the importance of supplementing information about the world with other sensory modes.

> The senses of sight and hearing are unquestionably the two primary avenues by which information and knowledge are absorbed by an individual, providing a direct access to the world in which he lives. . . . When these senses are lost or severely limited, the individual is drastically limited to a very small area of concepts, most of which must come to him through his secondary senses or through indirect information supplied by others. The world literally shrinks; it is only as large as he can reach with his fingertips or by using his severely limited sight and hearing, and it is only when he learns to use his remaining secondary senses of touch, taste, smell, and kinesthetic awareness that he can broaden his field of information and gain additional knowledge. (p. 38)

In 1968, fewer than 100 deaf-blind children were being served in specialized educational programs, virtually all of which were located at residential schools for blind children. Today, about 6,000 deaf-blind children are being educated in the United States in hundreds of different programs, including those located at schools for deaf children, early childhood developmental centers, vocational training centers, and regular public schools (Dantona, 1986). Deaf-blind students who progress to high school and postsecondary levels are usually integrated into educational programs for students with other disabilities or into programs for nonhandicapped students, with supportive assistance provided by special teachers, intervenors, interpreters, or tutors. Downing and Eichinger (1990) describe instructional strategies to support the education of students with dual sensory impairments in regular classrooms.

Persons with dual sensory impairments have the potential to achieve success and enjoyment in employment and independent living, but they need systematic instruction to facilitate communication, generalization of skills, and development of appropriate social behaviors (Bullis & Bull, 1986).

■ PREVALENCE

Because there is no universally accepted definition of severe handicaps, there are no accurate and uniform figures on prevalence. Estimates of the prevalence of severe handicaps range anywhere from .1% to 1% of the population (Ludlow & Sobsey, 1984). In referring to the group of people served by The Association for Persons with Severe Handicaps, Brown (1990) indicated the "lowest intellectually functioning one percent of [the] population" (p. 1). The number of students with severe handicaps who receive special education services under P.L. 94–142 cannot be determined from data supplied by the U.S. Department of Education, because severe handicaps are not one of the handicapping conditions reported. Students who have severe disabilities are counted among other categories of exceptionality, including mental retardation, multihandi-capped, other health impaired, and deaf-blind.

The difficulty in obtaining accurate prevalence figures indicates the current uncertainties surrounding the definition and classification of students with severe handicaps. The available information, however, shows that this is neither a small nor an isolated population; in fact, the severely handicapped population consists of several different subgroups of students, whose needs are not always the same. Today, most school districts have among their students some children with severe and multiple disabilities.

■ BACKGROUND OF THE FIELD

Little is known about the treatment of individuals with severe handicaps throughout most of history. Because severe handicaps so often occur in conjunction with medical and physical disabilities, many of these children probably did not live past infancy or early childhood. In many earlier societies, abandonment or deliberate killing of children with severe impairments is thought to have been a common practice (Anderson, Greer, & Rich, 1982). A philosophy of "survival of the fittest" prevails in some parts of the world even today.

To say that humane treatment and education of children with severe handicaps did not begin until the 20th century would be an oversimplification. As Scheerenberger's (1983) comprehensive review points out, efforts were made throughout history to understand the causes of severe handicaps and, at times, to provide care and training. In the 19th century, physicians Jean Itard, Edouard Seguin, and Samuel Gridley Howe achieved notable advances in systematically teaching communication and self-help skills to children with severe handicaps. Certainly, many other dedicated teachers, parents, and caregivers sought to help people with severe handicaps; unfortunately, their names have been lost in history.

During the second half of the 19th century, hundreds of state-operated residential institutions were established in the United States. An optimistic philosophy (strongly influenced by the efforts of pioneering physicians) prevailed at the outset, and some individuals with severe disabilities were, in fact, successfully educated and returned to their home communities (Wolfens-berger, 1976).

At first, many institutional programs were called asylums for the feeble-minded. They later came to be called hospitals, state schools, and training centers. But under whatever name, education and training were usually not provided to those residents with the most severe disabilities. Many observers commented on the bleak, unstimulating environments, the lack of adequate care, and the prevailing attitude of pessimism in most large residential institutions. And once placed in an institution, a child with severe handicaps was unlikely to ever leave it. Unless parents were able to provide care and training at home or to afford an expensive private school education, there were virtually no opportunities for children with severe handicaps to learn useful skills or to lead satisfying lives.

Over the last 20 years or so, several judicial decisions and new laws have had important effects on the development of educational services for children with severe handicaps. Particularly significant was the case of *Pennsylvania Association for Retarded Children v. Commonwealth of Pennsylvania* (1972). Before the PARC case, many states had laws allowing public schools to deny educational services to so-called ineducable severely handicapped children. In the PARC case, the court decided against exclusion and noted that education could be useful to severely handicapped individuals.

> Without exception, expert opinion indicates that all mentally retarded persons are capable of benefitting from a program of education. . . . The vast majority are capable of achieving self-sufficiency and the remaining few, with such education and training, are capable of achieving some degree of self-care; that the earlier such education and training begins, the more thoroughly and more efficiently a mentally retarded person will benefit from it and, whether begun early or not, that a mentally retarded person can benefit at any point in his life and development from a program of education. (*PARC v. Commonwealth of Pennsylvania,* 1972)

Many other cases—including *Wyatt v. Stickney* (1971), *Halderman v. Pennhurst State School and Hospital* (1978), *Armstrong v. Kline* (1979), *Irving Independent School District v. Tatro* (1984) and *Homeward Bound, Inc. v. Hissom Memorial Center* (1988)—have since upheld the right of students with severe handicaps to receive a free, appropriate program of education at public expense. The provisions of P.L. 94–142 fully apply to children with severe handicaps: They must have access to an educational program in the least restrictive setting possible, and their parents or guardians must be involved in the development of an appropriate IEP. In addition, the law gives priority to identifying and serving children who have been unserved or underserved, and this provision clearly applies to the severely handicapped population. These legal and judicial developments, coupled with an awareness of the potential of students with severe handicaps, are bringing about a dramatic expansion of educational programs in public schools, vocational facilities, and other community-based settings.

The beginning of the modern era in the education of persons with severe handicaps can be placed in 1975, when a group of 30 people, led by founding President Norris G. Haring of the University of Washington, created The American Association for the Education of the Severely/Profoundly Handicapped. The organization later changed its name to The Association for Persons with Severe Handicaps (TASH). Today TASH has a membership of more than 9,000 educators, parents, and other individuals who are concerned with improving the quality of life for individuals of all ages who have severe handicaps. TASH membership includes many highly creative and productive researchers and teachers who have played leading roles in developing effective educational practices for students with severe handicaps.

The past few years have witnessed a dramatic increase in the number of books, research studies, curricula, and other materials directed at meeting the needs of children and adults with severe handicaps. A strong case could be made that the education of persons with severe handicaps is the most exciting and dynamic area in all of special education today.

Information on TASH can be found at the end of this chapter. The organization's journal, *The Journal of the Association for Persons with Severe Handicaps (JASH),* is a primary source for the latest research and conceptual developments in educating learners who are challenged by severe handicaps.

■ CAUSES

Severe handicaps can be caused by a wide variety of conditions, largely biological, that may occur before, during, or after birth. In most cases, the brain is damaged. A significant percentage of children with severe handicaps are born with chromosomal abnormalities, such as Down syndrome, or with genetic or metabolic disorders that can cause serious problems in physical or intellectual development. Complications of pregnancy—including prematurity, Rh incompatibility, and infectious diseases contracted by the mother—can cause or contribute to severe disabilities. A pregnant woman who uses drugs, drinks excessively, or is poorly nourished has a greater risk of giving birth to a child with severe handicaps. Because their disabilities tend to be more extreme and more readily observable, children with severe handicaps are more frequently identified at or shortly after birth than are children with mild handicaps.

The birth process itself involves certain hazards and complications: Infants are particularly vulnerable to oxygen deprivation and brain injury during delivery. Severe handicaps may also develop later in life from head trauma caused by automobile and bicycle accidents, falls, assaults, or abuse. Malnutrition, neglect, ingestion of poisonous substances, and certain diseases that affect the brain (such as meningitis and encephalitis) can also cause severe handicaps.

Rosen and Gerring (1986) describe educational approaches for head-injured students.

Although hundreds of medically related causes of severe handicaps have been identified, in many cases the cause of a child's disabilities cannot be clearly determined. Severe handicaps are usually considered to be less closely associated with socioeconomic status than are milder handicaps (Snell & Renzaglia, 1986); however, access to good medical care, early identification of disabling conditions, education, and a stimulating home environment may be influenced by a family's level of education, income, and other socioeconomic factors.

■ APPROACHES TO THE EDUCATION OF STUDENTS WITH SEVERE HANDICAPS

How does one go about teaching students whose disabilities are severe? First, three fundamental questions must be considered:

♦ Where should instruction take place?
♦ What skills should be taught?
♦ What methods of instruction should be employed?

Of course, these questions must be asked for all students, but when the learner is a student with severe handicaps, the answers take on enormous importance. During the past decade, major changes and advancements in the education of students with severe handicaps have led to new responses to the questions of placement, curriculum, and teaching methods.

Placement: Where Should Students with Severe Handicaps Be Taught?

What is the least restrictive and most appropriate educational setting for a student with severe handicaps? This question continues to be the subject of much debate and discussion. Some special educators are calling for the abolition of all segregated placements for students with severe handicaps (Brown et al., 1989a; Sailor et al., 1989; Stainback & Stainback, 1991). Lou Brown—an early and consistent advocate for including persons with severe disabilities in normalized, integrated school and community settings and functions—and his colleagues at the University of Wisconsin make a strong case for why students with severe handicaps should attend their "home school" (the school a student would attend if he or she were not disabled).

> The environments in which students with severe intellectual disabilities receive instructional services have critical effects on where and how they spend their postschool lives. Segregation begets segregation. We believe that when children with intellectual disabilities attend segregated schools, they are denied opportunities to demonstrate to the rest of the community that they can function in integrated environments and activities; their nondisabled peers do not know or understand them and too often think negatively of them; their parents become afraid to risk allowing them opportunities to learn to function in integrated environments later in life; and taxpayers assume they need to be sequestered in segregated group homes, enclaves, work crews, activity centers, sheltered workshops, institutions, and nursing homes. (Brown et al., 1989a, p. 1)

For a discussion of 10 challenging issues concerning whether students with severe disabilities should be served in regular or special education classrooms in home schools, see Brown et al. (1989b). One method for helping to integrate students with disabilities into regular classrooms is described on pages 434–437.

Brown and his colleagues offer four reasons they believe home schools should replace segregated and clustered schools. They define a clustered school as "a regular school attended by an unnaturally large proportion of students with intellectual disabilities, but it is not the one any or most would attend if they were not labeled disabled" (1989a, p. 1). First, when students *without* disabilities go to an integrated school with peers who are disabled, they are more likely to function responsibly as adults in a pluralistic society. Second, various sources of information support integrated schools as more meaningful instructional environments. (Hunt, Goetz, and Anderson [1986], for example, compared the IEP objectives for students with severe handicaps who were taught at integrated versus segregated schools. They found the quality of IEP objectives—in terms of age-appropriateness, functionality, and the potential for generalization of what was being taught to other environments—was higher for the students educated in integrated schools.) Third, parents and families have greater access to school activities when children are attending their home schools. Further, and perhaps most convincing, is the argument that there are greater opportunities to develop a wide range of social relationships with nondisabled peers when attending one's home school. Table 10.1 describes and gives examples of 11 kinds of social relationships that might develop between students. Table 10.2 assesses the likelihood that each type of relationship will develop in a home school or in a clustered school.

For detailed information about administrative, curricular, and instructional strategies designed to support the education of students with severe disabilities in regular schools, see Sailor et al. (1989) and Stainback and Stainback (1991).

Research has shown that simply placing students with disabilities into regular schools and classrooms, however, does not necessarily lead to increased positive social interactions (Gresham, 1982; Guralnick, 1980). A wide variety of strategies for promoting desired social relationships has been developed. Some strategies focus on the behavior of students, such as cooperative learning activities (Eichinger, 1990; Putnam, Rynders, Johnson, & Johnson, 1989); other approaches involve changes in the roles and responsibilities of instructional faculty, such as teaching teams (Giangreco, 1991; Thousand & Villa, 1990).

TABLE 10.1

Social relationships that can develop between students with severe disabilities and their nondisabled peers when they attend the same school.

Social Relationship	Example
Peer tutor	Leigh role plays social introductions with Margo, providing feedback and praise for Margo's performance.
Eating companion	Jennifer and Rick eat lunch with Linda in the cafeteria and talk about their favorite music groups.
Art, home economics, industrial arts, music, physical education companion	In art class, students were instructed to paint a sunset. Tom sat next to Dan and offered suggestions and guidance about the best colors to use and how to complete the task.
Regular class companion	A fifth grade class is doing a "Know Your Town" lesson in social studies. Ben helps Karen plan a trip through their neighborhood.
During school companion	"Hangs out" and interacts on social level: After lunch and before the bell for class rang, Molly and Phyllis went to the student lounge for a soda.
Friend	David, a member of the varsity basketball team, invites Ralph, a student with severe disabilities, to his house to watch a game on T.V.
Extracurricular companion	Sarah and Winona prepare their articles for the school newspaper together and then work on the layout in the Journalism lab.
After-school-project companion	The sophomore class decided to build a float for the homecoming parade. Joan worked on it with Maria, a nondisabled companion, after school and on weekends in Joan's garage.
After school companion	On Saturday afternoon, Mike, who is not disabled, and Bill go to the shopping mall.
Travel companion	David walks with Ralph when he wheels from last-period class to the gym where Ralph helps the basketball team as a student manager.
Neighbor	Interacts with student in everyday environments and activities: Parents of nondisabled students in the neighborhood regularly exchange greetings with Mary when they are at school, around the neighborhood, at local stores, at the mall, at the grocery.

Source: From "The Home School: Why Students with Severe Disabilities Must Attend the Schools of Their Brothers, Sisters, Friends, and Neighbors" by L. Brown et al., 1989, *The Journal of the Association for Persons with Severe Handicaps, 14,* p. 4. Adapted by permission.

The education of all students in their home schools, regardless of the challenges presented by their learning and physical disabilities, is today more an ideal than a reality. Sailor and Haring (1988) estimated that 60% to 70% of students with severe handicaps throughout the United States are served in segregated schools. Evidence that successful integration can be achieved, however, mounts each time another student with severe disabilities enters his or her home school.

TABLE 10.2

Feasibility and likelihood of developing and maintaining 11 kinds of social relationships between students with and without disabilities in home and clustered schools.

Social Relationship	Home School				Clustered School			
	Development		Longitudinal		Development		Longitudinal	
	Feasible	Likely	Feasible	Likely	Feasible	Likely	Feasible	Likely
Peer tutor	Yes	Yes	Yes	Yes	Yes	Yes	No	No
Eating companion	Yes	Yes	Yes	Yes	Yes	Yes	No	No
Art, home economics, industrial arts, music, or physical education companion	Yes	Yes	Yes	Yes	Yes	Yes	No	No
Regular class companion	Yes	Yes	Yes	Yes	Yes	Yes	No	No
During school companion	Yes	Yes	Yes	Yes	Yes	Yes	No	No
Friend	Yes	Yes	Yes	Yes	Yes	Yes	No	No
Extracurricular companion	Yes	Yes	Yes	Yes	Yes	No	No	No
After school project companion	Yes	Yes	Yes	Yes	Yes	No	No	No
After school companion	Yes	Yes	Yes	Yes	No	No	No	No
Travel companion	Yes	Yes	Yes	Yes	No	No	No	No
Neighbor	Yes	Yes	Yes	Yes	No	No	No	No

Note. Social relationship refers to a positive personal interaction between a student with severe intellectual disabilities and a peer or other person who is not disabled.

Longitudinal refers to positive personal interactions between a student with severe intellectual disabilities and a peer or others who are not disabled that are developed, maintained, and enhanced across elementary, middle, and high school years.

Home school is the school a student with intellectual disabilities would attend if he or she were not disabled.

Clustered school is a regular school attended by an unnaturally large proportion of students with intellectual disabilities, but it is not the one any or most would attend if they were not disabled.

Feasible refers to a situation in which all the structural resources necessary for a particular kind of social relationship to develop are present.

Likely refers to the probability of a particular kind of social relationship occurring, given the reasonable efforts of parents, guardians, professionals, and others.

Companion is a nondisabled person who accompanies, associates with, or assists a student who is severely intellectually disabled.

(*Source:* From "The Home School: Why students with Severe Disabilities Must Attend the Schools of Their Brothers, Sisters, Friends, and Neighbors" by L. Brown et al., 1989, *The Journal of the Association for Persons with Severe Handicaps, 14,* p. 5. Reprinted by permission.)

Curriculum: What Should Be Taught to Students with Severe Handicaps?

Not long ago, educators focused largely on the so-called mental or developmental ages of their students. Although this approach may be helpful in identifying what skills a student can and cannot perform, it may also detract from the most effective use of instructional time, for it "assumes that those sequences of behavior typical of nonhandicapped students are relevant for the student with severe or profound handicaps" (Brown, 1987, p. 43). Strict reliance on a developmental approach may lead to an emphasis on teaching prerequisite skills that are not really essential for later steps (Ludlow & Sobsey, 1984) and may contribute to the perception of students with severe handicaps as eternal children (Bellamy & Wilcox, 1982). Today, most educators of individuals with severe handicaps consider it important to be familiar with the normal sequences of child development, but they recognize that their students often do not acquire skills in the same way that nonhandicapped students do and that developmental guides should not be the only basis for determining teaching procedures. For example, a 16-year-old student who is just learning to feed and toilet himself should not be taught in exactly the same way or with the same materials as a nonhandicapped 2-year-old child who is just learning to feed and toilet himself. The past experiences, present environments, and future prospects of the two individuals are, of course, quite different, even though their ability to perform certain skills may be similar. Freagon (1982) offers a thoughtful critique of the developmental sequencing strategy.

> When the developmental curricular strategy is employed, severely handicapped students have considerable impediments to achieving a postschool adult life-style that is similar to those of nonhandicapped persons. In the first place, when instructional activities are based on mental, language and social, and gross and fine motor ages, severely handicapped students rarely, if ever, gain more than 1 or 2 developmental years over the entire course of their educational experience. Therefore, 18-year-old students are relegated to performing infant or preschool or elementary nonhandicapped student activities. They are never seen as ready to engage in 18-year-old activities. In the second place, little, if any, empirical evidence exists to support the notion that severely handicapped students need to learn and grow along the same lines and growth patterns as do nonhandicapped students in order to achieve the same goal of education. (p. 10)

Contemporary curriculum content for students with severe handicaps is characterized by its focus on functional skills that can be used in immediate and future domestic, vocational, community, and recreation/leisure environments. Educational programs are future-oriented in their efforts to teach skills and behaviors that will enable students with severe handicaps to be as independent and productive as possible after they leave school.

Functionality

A functional skill is one that is immediately useful to a student and is frequently demanded in her natural environment. The skill should employ real materials and enhance the student's ability to perform as independently as possible. Placing pegs in a pegboard or sorting wooden blocks by color would not be considered functional, because these tasks would not be required in most people's natural environment. Learning to ride a public bus (Robinson, Griffith, McComish, & Swasbrook, 1984) and learning to purchase items from coin-operated vending machines (Sprague & Horner, 1984) are examples of more functional skills.

EVERYONE BELONGS: BUILDING THE VISION WITH MAPS—THE MCGILL ACTION PLANNING SYSTEM

by Marsha Forest and Jack Pearpoint, Directors
Centre for Integrated Education and Community, Toronto, Canada

A shared vision has caught the imagination of parents and educators across Canada: a vision of *all* children—including those with severe disabilities—being educated in regular classrooms alongside their brothers and sisters, friends and neighbors. The movement to integrate children with disabilities into ordinary classrooms is founded on a simple, yet profound philosophy: *Everyone belongs.* MAPS, the McGill Action Planning System, is a systems approach to problem solving that has helped many schools turn vision into reality. MAPS was designed by a team of educators who were searching for ways to help welcome children with disabilities back into regular schools and classrooms. The original MAPS team consisted of the two authors, plus Judith Snow, Evelyn Lusthaus, and John O'Brien.

Miller and friends.

Assumptions of the MAPS Process

1. All people are valuable and can contribute to life on this globe.
2. All people have abilities, talents, and gifts.
3. All people can learn!
4. Disability is a social construct. People are not disabled; systems disable people.
5. There is a real need for support, services, and educators who will reach out and nurture the potential of every child.
6. The only label we recommend is a person's name. Labels hide the fact that we really don't know what to do. After that, we suggest adopting a problem-solving mode that creatively figures out what to do for each unique individual.
7. Common sense is the most important and least common sense.

Who Goes to a MAP?—Friends!

The size of the group that gathers for a MAP session can vary from two to two dozen. The key ingredients for participants are Intimate and Personal Contact with the individual being mapped. A grandmother or neighbor, a friend—all are on equal footing with professionals, who are welcome and needed but as individuals—not as "therapists." Parents and family members usually have the most to offer, if asked. Their perspectives are all welcome in a MAP.

Peer participation is critical. Class/age-mates have enormous untapped energy and creative capacity. Their "straight talk" often empowers teachers with new ideas. Adults must be careful not to constrain or downgrade the participation of peers: They are critical and equal partners in the MAPS process.

There is a delicate question about whether or not the individual who is being "mapped" should be present. It is a judgment call; it works both ways. We hedge toward full participation. People understand an enormous amount—more than we think. Also, a MAP is an "upper," a real boost for an individual who previously has been excluded. Full participation also saves time in trying to explain it all later.

What Happens at a MAP? How Does it Work?

"Mapping" is a collaborative problem-solving process aided by a two-person team of Facilitator and Recorder. The Facilitator, positioned at the open end of a half circle formed by the participants, presents eight key questions to the group. The Facilitator must be skilled in group process and have a problem-solving orientation. Most important, the Facilitator must be committed to building an integrated school community. The information and ideas generated during the session are marked on a large piece of chart paper by the Recorder. Public charting is vital to the MAPS process: It generates "images" that help participants visualize the relationships between and among people and actions, thus promoting the creation of additional problem-solving strategies, and it serves as a permanent record of the plans and commitments made by the group. The Recorder need not be an artist, but it is vital that the MAP be printed or written clearly, using the participants' words. The chart should include contributions from everyone in the group.

MAPS planning typically occurs in one or two sessions, and approximately 3 hours are required to fully address these questions.

1. *What's a MAP?* The Facilitator begins the MAPS process by asking participants, "What is a map?" A recent group gave these answers:

♦ Something that gives direction
♦ A thing that helps you get somewhere
♦ Routes to different places
♦ A way to find a new way
♦ Stops you from getting lost

2. *What is the individual's history?* The participants most intimate with the child being mapped, usually parents and family members, are asked to give a short, 10–15 minute history focusing on key milestones and events in the individual's life.

3. *What is your dream for the individual?* This question is intended to get people, especially parents, to imagine their vision for the child's future. Many parents of children with handicaps have lost their ability to dream about what they really want for their child rather than what they think they can get. The vision of the future

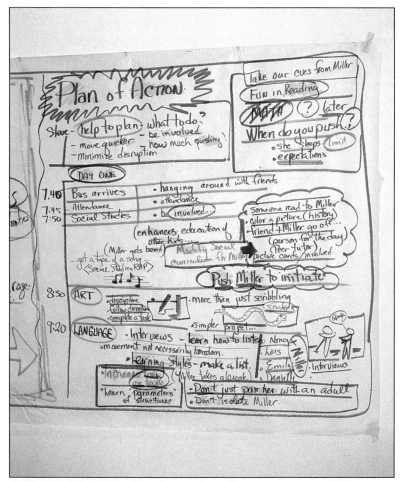

A portion of the MAPS plan of action for Miller.

should not be limited by money or current realities. This question helps the group focus on the direction in which the individual is now heading and encourages concrete action plans for realizing the vision.

4. *What is your nightmare?* This question is the hardest to ask, but very important to get on the table. We must understand the nightmare in order to prevent it. No parent has ever said, "I'm worried that my child won't attend university, won't get an A on the next test, or won't learn to spell." Instead, the nightmare question brings out what is in the heart of virtually every parent of a child with a severe handicap: "We're afraid our child will end up in an institution, work in a sheltered workshop, and have no one to care for her when we die." The MAPS planning must reflect an understanding of the nightmare; preventing the nightmare is one measure of its success.

5. *Who is the individual?* With this question, the MAPS process shifts into a no-holds-barred brainstorming mode. Participants are asked to give words or phrases that describe the person being mapped. The rule is: no jargon, no labels; just describe how you see the person. The image of a unique and distinct personality should emerge. Here are examples from a recent MAP for Miller, a 14-year-old who, to some, is "severely handicapped and mentally retarded."

♦ She has a brother
♦ She gets around in a wheelchair
♦ She's lots of fun
♦ She's active like crazy
♦ She's radical/bad (really means good)
♦ She's temperamental
♦ She likes to touch
♦ She wants to be involved
♦ She looks at you
♦ She can talk some

6. *What are the individual's strengths, abilities, gifts, and talents?* All too often we focus on the things a child with a disability can't do. It's vital to build upon strengths and abilities. This can be a difficult question for parents, who have been struggling with negatives for so long. This question is also intended to produce a brainstormed list from the entire group. Here's part of the list generated for Miller.

♦ She can make us laugh
♦ She moves her arms, can throw a ball
♦ She likes to listen to music
♦ She's persistent, tries real hard
♦ She can count and remember numbers
♦ She enjoys stories and movies

7. *What are the individual's needs?* This too is a brainstorm. Don't let people stop each other, but don't get bogged down either. Keep it short and record people's words and perceptions. Parents, teachers, and peers often have different perceptions about needs. For Miller, it was decided that what she needed most of all was:

♦ A communication system that lets her express her wants and feelings
♦ More independence with dressing and other self-care skills
♦ To be with her own age group
♦ Places to go and things to do after school
♦ Teenage clothes

8. *What is the plan of ACTION?* This is the final, and most important question of all. The MAPS planning group imagines what the individual's

Chronological Age-Appropriateness

Wherever possible, students with severe handicaps should participate in activities that are appropriate for nonhandicapped students of their own chronological age. Severely handicapped adolescents should not use the same materials as young nonhandicapped children—in fact, having handicapped teenagers sit on the floor playing clap-your-hands games or cutting and pasting large snowmen highlights their differences and discourages integration. It is more appropriate to teach recreational skills, such as bowling and tape-recorder operation, or to engage the students in holiday projects, such as printing greeting cards. Teachers of adolescent students with severe handicaps should ideal day at school would look like and what must be done to make it a reality. Step by step, the MAPS group goes through an entire day, envisioning the various environments and activities the individual will experience and what kinds of resources, supports, and adaptations can be created to make the day successful. For example, a peer volunteers to meet the taxi that brings Miller to school each morning and walk with her to the classroom; during language arts period a classmate will help Miller practice with her communication board; and the principle of partial participation will be used on the playground when Miller bats in the softball game and a teammate runs the bases for her.

In addition to describing what a MAP is, we believe it's important to emphasize what MAPS *is not:*

1. *A MAP is not a trick, a gimmick, or a quick-fix solution to complex human problems.* MAPS is not a one-shot session that will provide the magic bullet to blast a vulnerable person into the everyday life and fabric of school and community. MAPS is a problem-solving process; the plans for action are not set in stone,

but must be reviewed and changed as often as needed.

2. *A MAP is not a replacement for an Individualized Education Plan (IEP).* A MAP session may help provide useful information for an IEP, but it is not a substitute for the IEP process and must not be treated as such. A MAPS participant must be personally and/or professionally involved in the individual's life, not simply someone who has tested or given intermittent therapy to the individual.

3. *A MAP is not controlled by experts in order to design a neat program package.* The outcome of a MAP must meet three criteria: (1) the plan must be a personalized plan of action, a one-of-a-kind MAP tailor-made for the person; (2) the person is at the heart of every aspect of the MAP; and (3) the plan brings the person closer and closer into the daily life of the school and community.

4. *A MAP is not a tool to make any segregated setting better.* MAPS was designed to liberate people from segregated settings; it is only for people and organizations trying to figure out together how to get a person fully included in life.

5. *A MAP is not an academic exercise.* It is a genuine, personal approach to problem solving with and on behalf of real individuals who are vulnerable. A MAP produces outcomes that have real implications for how the person will live his or her life.

6. *MAPS is not just talk.* MAPS is talk and action. A MAP gives clear directions and action steps for inclusion.

The metaphor for MAPS is a kaleidoscope, a mysterious and beautiful instrument that changes constantly. We see the kaleidoscope as the outcome of each MAP. It is a medley of people working together to make something unique and better happen. It is more than anyone can do alone.

For additional information and training materials on MAPS, write the Centre for Integrated Education and Community, 24 Thome Crescent, Toronto, Ontario, Canada, M6H 2S5. Two recent journal articles describing the MAPS approach are Forest and Lusthaus (1990) and Vandercook, York, and Forest (1989). ◆

---

avoid decorating classroom walls with child-oriented characters such as Big Bird or Mickey Mouse and should not refer to their students as boys, girls, or kids when young men, young women, or students is clearly more age-appropriate.

It is important to build an IEP for a student with severe disabilities around functional and age-appropriate skills, not only because these are the most needed and desirable skills for the student to learn. Because nonschool settings demand such skills and nondisabled peers exhibit them, functional and age-appropriate behaviors are more likely to be reinforced in the natural environment and, as a result, be maintained in the student's repertoire (Horner, Dunlap, & Koegel, 1988; Stokes & Baer, 1977).

Partial Participation

The principle of partial participation, first described by Baumgart et al. (1982), acknowledges that even though some individuals with severe disabilities are not able to independently perform all the steps of a given task or activity, they can often be taught to do selected components or an adapted version of the task. A nonverbal student, for example, may be able to point to pictures of menu items on a laminated card to place her order at a fast-food restaurant. Snell, Lewis, and Houghton (1989) taught three elementary-aged students with cerebral palsy and mental retardation to perform selected task analysis components of toothbrushing while the teacher performed the steps the students could not do. Both teachers and parents of two of the three students rated the students' partial participation in the toothbrushing activity as "meaningful" in that they appeared "happier and less likely to fuss" when they were participating in dental care rather than having their teeth brushed for them. Follow-up data indicated the toothbrushing skills generalized into the home and were maintained for 19 months following training.

Making Choices

In the past, students with severe handicaps were given few opportunities to make choices and decisions or to express preferences; the emphasis was on establishing instructional control over students. Traditionally, persons with severe handicaps have simply been cared for and taught to be compliant.

> Some caregivers might feel that to complete tasks for persons with disabilities is easier and faster than allowing them to do it for themselves; while others may have the attitude that the person already has enough problems coping with his or her disability. Regardless of the underlying intention, the result can be to overprotect, to encourage learned helplessness, and to deprive the individual of potentially valuable life experiences (Guess, Benson, & Siegel-Causey, 1985, p. 83).

Today, efforts are being made to help students with severe handicaps learn to function more independently and make decisions about matters that will affect them, such as the types of settings in which they will live and work, what foods they will eat, the partners they will socialize with, and whether or not they want to participate in daily routines and activities (Bannerman, Sheldon, Sherman, & Harchik, 1990). Even students who are profoundly handicapped and nonverbal may be able to indicate preferences if given the opportunity. Wacker, Wiggins, Fowler, and Berg (1988) reported the results of three experiments in which students with profound handicaps used preprogrammed microswitches to demonstrate preferences for toys and types of social attention, as well as to make requests.

Shevin and Klein (1984) offer several suggestions for incorporating choice-making activities into the classroom programs of students with severe handicaps. For example, a child might be presented with pictures of two activities and asked to point to the one she would rather engage in. Another child might be asked, "Who would you like for your partner?" Or the teacher might say, "Should we do this again?" Of course, in presenting such choices, the teacher must be prepared to accept whichever alternative the student selects and follow through accordingly.

Communication Skills

There has also been a good deal of research on specialized methods of teaching communication skills to children and youth with severe handicaps. Basic communication skills are highly important for students' successful functioning in vocational and independent living programs (Orlansky, 1986a; Rusch, Chadsey-Rusch, & Lagomarcino, 1987). Many students with severe handicaps are able to learn to understand and produce spoken language; speech is always a desirable goal, of course, for those who can attain it. A student who can communicate verbally is likely to have a wider range of educational, employment, residential, and recreational opportunities than a student who is unable to speak.

Because of sensory, motor, cognitive, or behavioral limitations, some students with severe handicaps may not learn to speak intelligibly even after extensive training. Many systems of augmentative communication have then proven useful—including gestures, various sign language systems, pictorial communication boards, symbol systems, and electronic communication aids. Although these systems are not as widely used as speech in the general community, they do enable many students with severe handicaps to receive and express basic information, feelings, needs, and wants. Sign language and other communication systems can also be learned by a student's teachers, peers, parents, and employers, thus encouraging use outside the classroom. Some students—after learning basic communication skills through sign language, communication boards, or other strategies—are later able to acquire speech skills. Reichle and Keogh (1986) discuss rules for decision making in selecting the most appropriate methods of communication for students with severe handicaps.

Baumgart, Johnson, and Helmstetter (1990) provide an overview of augmentative communication systems and their applicability to students with severe handicaps.

A major focus of Rod's IEP is improving his ability to communicate his needs and choices.

Vocational Training

Vocational and job-related skills are especially important curriculum areas for students with severe handicaps. Much has been learned about methods of training complex vocational skills and about effective procedures to manage inappropriate behaviors. It is now widely believed that even persons with the most severe disabilities have the potential for productive and meaningful work if given the right training and supports (Rusch, 1990).

With each passing month, more evidence accumulates to show that children and adults with severe handicaps are capable of performing useful and remunerative work in a wide variety of settings. Some teachers combine classroom instruction and practical experience in the community for children of school age. Winkler, Armstrong, Moehlis, Nietupski, and Whalen-Carrell (1982) describe a successful program in which students with severe handicaps prepared and delivered classified advertising guides in their community. Most students improved in their ability to attend to tasks such as folding, collating, and packing, and many students learned money management skills with their earnings from the project. Wehman et al. (1982) describe a project in which adults with severe handicaps were placed in community employment—mostly in utility jobs, such as wiping tables in restaurants or sweeping floors. After a 3-year period, 67% of the clients were still employed. Their absenteeism and tardiness rates were generally no worse than those of nonhandicapped workers, and the predominant attitude of co-workers was one of "indifference as long as the client performs his/her job acceptably" (p. 12). The wages and benefits the handicapped workers earned were substantially greater than what they would have earned in sheltered workshops. Rather than being dependent on public financial assistance, these workers were earning money and paying local, state, and federal taxes.

Recreational and Leisure Skills

Most children develop the ability to play and, later, to occupy themselves constructively and pleasurably during their free time. But children with severe handicaps may not learn appropriate and satisfying recreational skills unless they are specifically taught. Teaching appropriate leisure and recreational skills helps severely handicapped individuals interact socially, maintain their physical skills, and become more involved in community activities. A survey by Pancsofar and Blackwell (1986) found that many persons with severe handicaps do not use their unstructured time appropriately; rather than participating in enjoyable pursuits, they may spend excessive time sitting, wandering, or looking at television. A variety of programs to teach recreational and leisure skills have recently been developed; this area is now generally acknowledged as an important part of the curriculum for students with severe handicaps.

Horst, Wehman, Hill, and Bailey (1981) describe how several severely handicapped students, aged 10 to 21, were taught age-appropriate leisure skills. The activities were selected "largely on the basis that many nonhandicapped peers regularly engage in these types of activities" (p. 11). Precise teaching procedures were followed in the assessment and teaching of throwing and catching a Frisbee, operating a cassette tape recorder, and playing an electronic bowling game. All students were able to increase their skills in these activities.

Chapter 15 includes an expanded discussion of school-to-work transition and employment of adults with disabilities.

An integrated aerobic conditioning program was enjoyed by 14 children 6 to 13 years old with moderate to severe disabilities and 25 fifth and sixth grade peers without disabilities (Halle, Gabler-Halle, & Bemben, 1989). Datillo and Mirenda (1987) developed a computerized procedure that enables nonspeaking students with severe handicaps to indicate their preferences and control access to leisure-time activities (e.g., music, action video, slides). Moon and Bunker (1987) and Wehman, Renzaglia, and Bates (1985) provide additional guidelines for selecting and teaching recreational and leisure activities.

Instructional Methods: How Should Students with Severe Handicaps Be Taught?

Care and concern for the well-being of students with severe handicaps and assurance that they have access to educational programs are important. By themselves, however, care and access are not enough. To learn effectively, students with severe handicaps need more than love, care, and classroom placement. They do not acquire complex skills solely through imitation and observation; they are not likely to blossom on their own.

Learning and behavior problems of students with severe handicaps are so extreme and so significant that instruction must be carefully planned and executed. "Precise behavioral objectives, task analysis, and other individualized instructional techniques combine to form a powerful teaching process" for students with severe handicaps (Ludlow & Sobsey, 1984, p. 22). Indeed, structure and precision are essential. The teacher must know what skill to teach, why it is important to teach it, how to teach it, and how to recognize that the student has achieved or performed the skill.

An effective teacher of students with severe handicaps learns to use task analysis (described in Chapter 3), in which skills are broken down into a series of specific, observable steps, and the student's performance of each step is carefully monitored. Table 10.3 breaks down an important self-care skill—washing one's hands—into small, precise steps. Some students may require even more specific steps than the 19 listed here, whereas others might need fewer steps. Before any instruction begins, the teacher needs to accurately assess a student's performance of the task. Judy might be able to perform all the steps up to Step 15 (turning off the water), whereas Sam might not even be able to demonstrate Step 1 (going to the sink). Such assessment helps the teacher determine where to begin instruction. She can gradually teach each required step, in order, until the student can accomplish the entire task independently. Without this sort of structure and precision in teaching, a great deal of time is likely to be wasted.

Careful attention should be given to the following components of an instructional program for a student with severe handicaps.

The student's current level of performance must be precisely assessed. Is Karen able to hold her head up without support? For how many seconds? Under what conditions? In response to what verbal or physical signal? Unlike traditional assessment procedures, which may rely heavily on standardized scores and developmental levels, assessment of children with severe handicaps emphasizes each learner's ability to perform specific, observable behaviors. Assessment

TABLE 10.3

Task analysis for hand washing.

1. Go to bathroom sink.
2. Grasp the cold water faucet.
3. Turn on the water.
4. Wet your hands.
5. Pick up the soap (with the dominant hand).
6. Rub the soap on the other hand.
7. Put the soap down.
8. Rub palms together.
9. Rub back of hand (with palm of opposite hand).
10. Rub back of other hand (with palm of opposite hand).
11. Put hands under water.
12. Rinse palm of hands (until all visible suds removed).
13. Rinse back of hands (until all visible suds removed).
14. Grasp the cold water faucet.
15. Turn off the water.
16. Pick up towel.
17. Dry your palms.
18. Dry the back of your hands.
19. Hang towel over rack.

Source: From *Systematic Instruction of Persons with Severe Handicaps* (3rd. ed.) (p. 75) by M. E. Snell (Ed.), 1987, Columbus, OH: Merrill. Reprinted by permission.

should not be a one-shot procedure but should take place at different times, in different settings, and with different persons. The fact that a severely handicapped student does not demonstrate a skill at one particular time or place does not mean that he is incapable of demonstrating that skill. Precise assessment of current performance is valuable in determining which skills to teach and at what level the instruction can start.

The skill to be taught must be defined clearly. "Ian will feed himself" is too broad a goal for many severely handicapped children. A more appropriate statement might be "When applesauce is applied to Ian's right index finger, he will move the finger to his mouth within 10 seconds." A clear statement like this enables the teacher and other observers to determine whether Ian attains this objective. If, after repeated trials, he has not, it would be advisable to try a different method of instruction.

The skills must be ordered in an appropriate sequence. The teacher must be able to arrange "a relationship between the student and his environment which results in positive experiences for the student and small positive changes in skill acquisition" (Sailor & Haring, 1977, p. 73). This does not imply that severely handicapped students will always acquire skills in exactly the same order as nonhandicapped students, but it is useful to consider that some skills logically come before others, and some groups of skills are naturally taught at the same time.

The teacher must provide a clear prompt or cue to the child. It is important for the child to know what action or response is expected of him. A cue can be verbal; the teacher might say, "Bev, say *apple*," to indicate what Bev must do before she will receive an apple. Or a cue can be physical; the teacher might point to a light switch to indicate that Bev should turn the light on. It may also be necessary for the teacher to demonstrate an activity many times and to physically guide the child through some or all of the tasks required in the activity.

For a review of research on methods of delivering and fading instructional prompts to students with severe handicaps, see Doyle, Wolery, Ault, and Gast (1988) and Wolery and Gast (1984).

The child must receive feedback and reinforcement from the teacher. Students with severe handicaps must receive clear information about their performance, and they are more likely to repeat an action if it is immediately followed by a reinforcing consequence. Unfortunately, it can be quite difficult and time-consuming to determine what items or events a noncommunicative child finds rewarding. Many teachers devote extensive efforts to reinforcer sampling; that is, they attempt to find out which items and activities are reinforcing to a particular child, and they keep careful records of what is and is not effective. Spradlin and Spradlin (1976) describe how a teacher worked with a severely handicapped child for more than 2 years in order to find an effective reinforcer he could use in an instructional program. A total of 57 different items were tried as reinforcers, including praise, hugs, drinks, food, candy, toys, and audio and visual stimuli.

Strategies must be used that promote generalization of learning. It is well known and documented that students with severe handicaps often have difficulty in generalizing the skills they learn. Horner, McDonnell, and Bellamy (1986) explain that "education for students with severe handicaps is relevant only to the extent that the knowledge and behaviors that the students acquire become part of their daily routine" (p. 289). Thus, an effective teacher has students perform tasks in several different settings and with different instructors, cues, and materials before concluding with confidence that the student has acquired and generalized a skill.

Principles and guidelines for facilitating generalization are provided by Baer (1981a); Browder and Snell (1987); Haring (1989); Heward (1987a); and Horner, Dunlap, and Koegel (1988).

The student's performance must be carefully measured and evaluated. Because students with severe handicaps often make progress in very small steps, it is important to measure performance precisely. Careful measurement helps the teacher plan instruction that will be appropriate to the child's needs and evaluate the program's effectiveness. Change in performance is shown most clearly when data on the child's efforts are collected every day. When working on dressing skills, for example, a teacher might measure the number of seconds it takes a child to remove a sock from her right foot when given the cue "Donna, take off your sock." Over a period of time, Donna should perform the task more rapidly. If she does not, some aspect of the instructional program may have to be changed. Accurate information about a child's performance helps the teacher design an appropriate educational program. Some programs keep videotaped records of severely handicapped students' performance on specific tasks. This record can add an important dimension to documenting behavior changes over extended periods.

Increasing Socially Acceptable Behavior

As students with severe disabilities are being increasingly served in integrated school and community settings, there have been notable changes in how teachers manage disruptive, aggressive, or socially unacceptable behaviors. In the recent past, a student who displayed "excess" behaviors, such as stereotypic head-weaving, would likely have been subjected to some unpleasant and undignified procedure, such as having his head restrained or perhaps having a teacher manipulate his head up and down for several minutes (Gast & Wolery, 1987). Some maladaptive behaviors of students with severe handicaps were routinely "treated" with the application of aversive consequences (e.g., being sprayed with water mist) or with an extended time-out from instruction. These were "modes of intervention which most people would reject as absolutely unacceptable if they were used with a person who does not have disabilities" (Center on Human Policy, 1986, p. 4).

With today's emphasis on respect for the individual student and on preparation for independent living, a growing number of educational programs deal with challenging, excessive, or unacceptable behaviors in more functional and dignified ways. Specifically, they attempt to (1) understand the meaning that a behavior has for a student; (2) offer the student a positive alternative behavior; (3) utilize nonintrusive intervention techniques; and (4) use strategies that have been validated and are intended for use in integrated community settings (Center on Human Policy, 1986). Gast and Wolery (1987), LaVigna and Donnellan (1987), and Meyer and Evans (1989) provide more detailed descriptions of such strategies.

Individual or Group Instruction?

Many educational programs for students with severe handicaps conduct instruction largely one-to-one; that is, a teacher works with one student at a time. For many years, most professionals believed that one-to-one teaching was the only effective method for producing changes in the behavior of students with severe handicaps—about 90% of the articles about teaching or modifying the behavior of severely handicapped students described a one-to-one approach (Favell, Favell, & McGimsey, 1978).

More recently, however, a number of researchers have investigated the effectiveness of small-group teaching with students who have severe handicaps. The results of some of these studies are encouraging. Curran (1983) and Orelove (1982a) found that students with severe handicaps were capable of incidental learning of vocabulary; that is, when words were presented to a certain student in a small group, other students in the group could also learn to understand them. Some evidence suggests that small-group instruction can be just as effective as one-to-one teaching (Bourland, Jablonski, & Lockhart, 1987). Edwards (1986) advocates the use of heterogeneous groupings, because the needs of students who require high levels of caretaking are "more easily handled when their presence is in smaller numbers in a classroom" (p. 10).

Group instruction of students with severe handicaps thus appears to be promising, although much research remains to be done. Group instruction allows teachers to use their time more effectively, gives students the benefit of more training time, and encourages the children to socialize. Should research continue to find group instruction effective, future programs of education and

For extended discussion and debate of various viewpoints concerning the use of punishment and aversive consequences with persons with disabilities, see Repp and Singh (1990).

See Polloway, Cronin, and Patton (1986) and Reid and Favell (1984) for reviews of research on group instruction.

training for severely handicapped learners will most likely include a combination of group and one-to-one instructional techniques.

■ THE CHALLENGE AND REWARDS OF TEACHING STUDENTS WITH SEVERE HANDICAPS

The current extension of public education and community-based services to children with severe handicaps is a tremendously important and challenging development. Those people who are providing instruction to students with severe handicaps can rightfully be called pioneers on an exciting new frontier of special education. Professionals who are involved in educating severely handicapped children "can look back with pride, and even awe, at the advances they have made. In a relatively brief period, educators, psychologists, and other professionals have advocated vigorously for additional legislation and funds, extended the service delivery model into the public schools and community, and developed a training technology" (Orelove, 1984, p. 271).

Future research will increase our understanding of the ways students with severe handicaps acquire, maintain, and generalize functional skills. Better techniques of measuring and changing behavior are constantly being developed; these are balanced with a growing concern for the personal rights and dignity of individuals with severe handicaps.

Teaching students with severe handicaps is difficult and demanding. The teacher must be well-organized, firm, and consistent. He must be able to manage a complex educational operation, which usually involves supervising paraprofessional aides, student teachers, peer tutors, and volunteers. The teacher must be knowledgeable about individualized and group instructional techniques and must work cooperatively with other professionals, such as physicians, psychologists, physical therapists, social workers, and language specialists. He must maintain accurate records and must be constantly planning for the future needs of his students. Effective communication with parents (or residential staff), school administrators, vocational rehabilitation personnel, and community agencies is also vital.

Students with severe handicaps sometimes give little or no apparent response, so their teacher must be sensitive to small changes in student behavior. The effective teacher is consistent in designing and implementing strategies to improve learning and behavior (even if some of the students' previous teachers were not). The effective teacher should not be too quick to remove difficult tasks or requests that result in noncompliance or misbehavior. It is better to teach students to request assistance (Durand, 1986) and to intersperse tasks that are easy for the student to perform (Sprague & Horner, 1990).

Some people might consider it undesirable to work with students with severe handicaps because of their serious and multiple disabilities. Yet working with students who require instruction at its best can offer many highly rewarding teaching experiences. There is much satisfaction in teaching a child to feed and toilet herself independently, helping a student make friends with nonhandicapped peers, and assisting a young adult to live, travel, and work independently in the community. The challenge and the rewards of teaching students with severe handicaps are great.

LITTLE CHANGES WITH BIG IMPACTS
Reactions to Progress by Students with Severe Handicaps

Michael F. Giangreco is a special education faculty member at the Center for Developmental Disabilities, University of Vermont. Mike is a nationally recognized leader in helping school districts integrate students with severe and multiple disabilities into regular classes. We asked Mike to share some of his thoughts about the students, teachers, and families with whom he has worked.

Teachers and therapists are people who want to make a difference, people who hope that what they do will improve the quality of life for the students and families with whom they work. Laura is one such teacher. Over the past couple of years, Laura has been working with a heterogeneous group of students with challenging needs at East Middle School. One aspect of its educational program is to teach skills that will allow students to participate more fully in the community with nonhandicapped individuals. Laura has sometimes gotten discouraged because some of her more severely handicapped students' rates of progress have seemed low. She started asking, "Am I really helping? Am I really making a difference?"

One day, Laura received the following letter from a parent regarding her daughter Jackie, a 13-year-old girl with Down syndrome, functioning in the severe range of mental retardation and diagnosed as legally blind.

Dear Laura,
 After school we went grocery shopping, me, Jackie, and Sheldon (the baby). On our way home Jackie said, "Mom, you forgot Italian bread." She was right. I said we would have to go without—I was not hauling the baby out of the car again. Jackie said, "I can buy it myself at P & C." I said, "I don't know, Jackie." "Yes Mom, my teacher helped me." She was so sure she could do it that I didn't want to defeat her—so off to P & C. I pulled up in front with mounting panic. Jackie was still positive she could do it. I explained that the bread was back by the meat and bakery—we had bought it here before, but not recently. Jackie said, "I know—it has a light." I then gave Jackie $2 and let her go. Four minutes later (it seemed like two hours) she was back at the car with her Italian bread in a shopping bag and her change tight in her hand. I couldn't believe it—talk about the taste of success—I think that was the best bread we have ever had! Be proud, teacher—Mom is!

When Laura shared the letter with me, it was clear that this seemingly small achievement had a big impact. It reminded me of a similar experience I had had as a teacher. Tom was one of the most challenging students I had ever encountered. Several years earlier he had suffered a severe brain stem injury in a bicycle-auto accident. The injury left Tom profoundly mentally retarded, severely physically handicapped, and blind. Tom was nonverbal and nonambulatory and had no functional use of his limbs or hands. He slept a lot and seemed alert for only short periods during the day. For a couple of years after his accident, Tom was fed through a plastic tube inserted in his stomach. Tom's family had worked very hard to teach him to eat by mouth again. When I met Tom, he was able to be fed pureed foods by mouth, but he still had the gastrostomy tube in his stomach as a precaution, because he was prone to dehydration during the summer.

In a meeting with Tom's parents to plan his IEP, his dad said, "We'd like him to learn something, anything, so we know that he *can* learn." We agreed that one goal would be to try to teach Tom to follow a simple direction, "Open up," so that he could be fed, have his teeth brushed, and accept medicine. With an instructional procedure called time-delay, Tom began responding to the direction. Although this tiny achievement did little for Tom directly, it had a major impact on the quality of his life indirectly. For the first time in a long time, people at home and at school were encouraged because Tom had learned. This hopeful experience resulted in Tom's receiving more frequent and positive interaction from others.

Seemingly small accomplishments hold the potential for tremendous positive impact. Professionals in schools can make a difference when they work collaboratively with families to select and teach meaningful skills to enhance a student's quality of life at home, at school, and in the community. ◆

SUMMARY

Definition and Characteristics

♦ Despite their limitations, children with severe handicaps can and do learn.

♦ The child with severe handicaps needs instruction in basic self-help, motor, perceptual, social, and communication skills.

♦ Traditional intelligence tests are virtually useless in assessing the child with severe handicaps; instead, the teacher needs to observe the unique abilities and limitations of each child.

♦ Children with severe handicaps frequently show some or all of the following behaviors:

> Little or no communication
>
> Delayed physical and motor development
>
> Frequent inappropriate behavior
>
> Deficits in self-help skills
>
> Infrequent constructive behavior and interaction

♦ These children frequently have multiple disabilities, including physical problems, and usually look and act markedly different from normal children.

♦ Students with dual sensory impairments cannot be accommodated in special education programs for the hearing handicapped or the visually handicapped child. Although the vast majority of children labeled deaf-blind have some functional hearing and/or vision, the dual impairments severely impede learning of communication and social skills.

Prevalence

♦ This population is neither small nor isolated; most communities include some children with severe and multiple handicaps.

Background of the Field

♦ Throughout most of history, many children with severe handicaps probably died in infancy.

♦ State-run custodial institutions were established during the 19th century but offered little in the way of education and training for residents with the most severe handicaps.

♦ Within the last 20 years, numerous court cases and laws have mandated free, public education for all children, regardless of the severity of their disabilities.

Causes

♦ Severe and profound handicaps most often have biological causes, including

> Chromosomal abnormalities
>
> Genetic and metabolic disorders
>
> Complications of pregnancy and prenatal care
>
> Birth trauma
>
> Later brain damage

- The actual cause(s) of a child's severe handicap, however, is often unknown.
- A rubella epidemic caused many cases of deaf-blindness in children born during the mid-1960s.

Approaches to the Education of Students with Severe Handicaps

- Students with severe handicaps must be taught skills that are functional, age-appropriate, and directed toward the community. Interaction with nonhandicapped students should occur regularly.
- Effective instruction requires structure and precision. Skills must be broken down into small steps; current performance must be precisely assessed; the target skill stated clearly; and skills must be taught in an appropriate sequence.
- Students with severe handicaps should be taught choice-making skills.
- Students with severe handicaps should also be taught age-appropriate recreation and leisure skills.
- Small-group instruction has been shown to be effective for some tasks.

The Challenge and Rewards of Teaching Students with Severe Handicaps

- Although the challenge of teaching students with severe handicaps is great, so are the rewards of helping enhance someone's quality of life.

FOR MORE INFORMATION

Journals

The Journal of The Association for Persons with Severe Handicaps (JASH). Published quarterly by The Association for Persons with Severe Handicaps, 7010 Roosevelt Way N.E., Seattle, WA 98115. Publishes articles reporting original research, reviews of the literature, and conceptual or position papers that offer new directions for service delivery and program development and effective assessment and intervention methodologies.

Research in Developmental Disabilities. Published quarterly by Pergamon Press, Macmillian, Maxwell House, Fairview Park, Elmsford, NY 10523. Includes articles on theory and behavioral research related to people "who suffer from severe and pervasive developmental disabilities."

Books

Browder, D. M. (1987). *Assessment of individuals with severe handicaps: An applied behavioral approach to life skills assessment*. Baltimore, MD: Paul H. Brookes.

Brown, F., & Lehr, D. H. (1989). *Persons with profound disabilities: Issues and practices*. Baltimore, MD: Paul H. Brookes.

Goetz, L., Guess, D., & Stremel-Campbell, K. (Eds.). (1987). *Innovative program design for individuals with dual sensory impairments*. Baltimore, MD: Paul H. Brookes.

Horner, R. H., Meyer, L. H., & Fredericks, H. D. B. (Eds.). (1986). *Education of learners with severe handicaps: Exemplary service strategies*. Baltimore, MD: Paul H. Brookes.

Meyer, L., Peck, C., & Brown, L. (Eds.). (1990). *Critical issues in the lives of people with severe disabilities*. Baltimore, MD: Paul H. Brookes.

Orelove, F. P., & Sobsey, D. (1987). *Educating children with multiple disabilities: A transdisciplinary approach*. Baltimore, MD: Paul H. Brookes.

Perske, R., Clifton, A., McLean, B. M., & Stein, J. I. (Eds.). (1986). *Mealtimes for persons with severe handicaps*. Baltimore, MD: Paul H. Brookes.

Repp, A. C., & Singh, N. N. (Eds.). (1990). *Perspectives on the use of nonaversive and aversive interventions for persons with developmental disabilities*. Sycamore, IL: Sycamore Publishing.

Sailor, W., Anderson, J. L., Halvorsen, A. T., Doering, K., Filler, J., & Goetz, L. (1989). *The comprehensive local school: Regular education for all students with disabilities*. Baltimore, MD: Paul H. Brookes.

Snell, M. E. (Ed.). (in press). *Systematic instruction of persons with severe handicaps* (4th ed.). Columbus, OH: Merrill.

Stainback, S., & Stainback, W. (Eds.). (1991). *Teaching in the inclusive classroom: Curriculum design, adaptation and delivery*. Baltimore, MD: Paul H. Brookes.

Wilcox, B., & Bellamy, G. T. (1987). *The activities catalog: An alternative curriculum for youth and adults with severe disabilities*. Baltimore, MD: Paul H. Brookes.

Organizations

ABLENET, 360 Hoover Street, NE, Minneapolis, MN 55413. Offers information and publications on the use of automated learning devices, microswitches, and other technology with persons who have severe handicaps. Has available for purchase a book by Jackie Levin and Lynn Scherfenberg, *Breaking Barriers: How Children and Adults with Severe Handicaps Can Access the World Through Simple Technology*.

The Association for Persons with Severe Handicaps (TASH), 7010 Roosevelt Way N.E., Seattle, WA 98115. "TASH is an organization of professionals in partnership with people with disabilities, their families and others who are dedicated to education, research and advocacy on behalf of individuals of any age who have severe intellectual disabilities and their families, so that these persons may live, learn, work and enjoy life and relationships with dignity, respect and individualized support" (The Association for Persons with Severe Handicaps, 1990, p. 1).

Through its journal and monthly newsletter, disseminates a wide variety of useful information to teachers, parents, administrators, researchers, and others. Through its annual convention, provides the major professional forum for the exchange of new developments relating to the education of persons with severe handicaps. Through its many state and local chapters, also sponsors conferences and activities.

Center on Human Policy, 724 Comstock Avenue, Syracuse, NY 13244. Provides reports and other resources on the integration of people with severe handicaps into community life. Also distributes materials encouraging the development of positive attitudes about persons with disabilities in schools and the media.

Department of Specialized Educational Services, Madison Metropolitan School District, 545 West Dayton Street, Madison, WI 53703. In cooperation with the Department of Studies in Behavioral Disabilities at the University of Wisconsin, has been especially active in developing programs of instruction for severely handicapped children and in seeking to facilitate integration with nondisabled individuals. Has available for purchase a number of curriculum guides and other materials.

Helen Keller National Center for Deaf-Blind Youths and Adults, 111 Middle Neck Road, Sands Point, NY 11050. Offers training programs for persons with impaired vision and hearing and consultation to agencies providing services to this population. Publishes *Directory of Agencies and Organizations Serving Deaf-Blind Individuals,* curriculum manuals, and other informational materials about deaf-blindness.

11

Gifted and Talented Students

Raymond H. Swassing
The Ohio State University

♦ Why and how has the definition of who is gifted and talented changed over the years?

♦ When is special education necessary for gifted and talented children?

♦ What do you think is most important for the development of creativity and talent, nature or nurture?

♦ Do you think IEPs should be required in gifted education?

♦ Where should gifted students be educated: in regular classes, special classes, or special schools?

Our study of exceptional children thus far has focused on children with intellectual or physical disabilities—children who require special methods and materials to derive maximum benefit from their educational programs. Gifted and talented children represent the other extreme on the continuum of academic, artistic, social, and scientific abilities. Gifted and talented children may also find that a traditional curriculum is inappropriate; it may not provide the advanced and unique challenges they require to learn most effectively. They, too, need special educational opportunities if they are to reach their potential.

Although the regular classroom is considered the least restrictive environment for many exceptional children with disabilities, the standard curriculum and usual school activities are often highly restrictive for gifted children. When the school year begins in September, intellectually gifted students may already have all the skills their grade-level peers are supposed to learn during the year. Thus, a school program that does not allow gifted children to explore areas of individual interest or to learn things beyond the basic curriculum would be restrictive. Children with special talents should have opportunities to develop those abilities further; an appropriate education for gifted and talented children must include special curriculum and instruction.

The term *exceptional children* includes both children who experience difficulties in learning and children whose performance is so superior that special education is necessary if they are to fulfill their potential. To reach his or her potential and to succeed fully in school, the gifted and talented child needs specially trained teachers; special instruction, materials, and resources; and perhaps a special classroom placement for part or all of the school day. Issues such as assessment, family involvement, placement, expectations for achievement, and the child's unique abilities are just as important for an effective individualized education program for a gifted and talented student as they are for that of a student with disabilities. Programs tailored to individual needs are beneficial to all exceptional children.

■ DEFINITION AND PREVALENCE OF GIFTED AND TALENTED CHILDREN

Numerous definitions of gifted and talented children have been proposed and debated. Lewis Terman (1925), one of the pioneers in the field, defined the gifted as those who score in the top 2% on standardized tests of intelligence. Witty (1958), recognizing the value of including special skills and talents, described gifted and talented children as those "whose performance is consistently remarkable in any potentially valuable area" (p. 62). Both viewpoints are included within today's most common definitions of gifted and talented children. Federal legislation defines gifted and talented children as those who

> give evidence of high performance capability in areas such as intellectual, creative, specific academic or leadership ability, or in the performing or visual arts, and who by reason thereof require services or activities not ordinarily provided by the school. (P.L. 95–561, sec. 902)

The areas in which children can show outstanding performance or unusual potential to be considered gifted and talented cover almost the full range of human endeavor. Overall intellectual ability and specific academic aptitude are only two areas. General intellectual ability refers to overall performance on intelligence or achievement tests. Children who meet this criterion usually do, or can, perform well in most academic areas. Children with specific academic aptitude have outstanding ability in one or two areas. For example, Reggie, who has specific academic aptitude, performs extremely well in science; however, his work in social studies and English is no better than that of most of his age peers.

Leadership ability has been included in the definition of giftedness only recently. The framers of the current definition were aware of society's need to develop leadership potential. Problems such as pollution, population control, nutrition, and peacekeeping require the efforts not only of scientists and economists but also of those who can bring groups of people together and lead them toward common goals. Scientists may answer pressing problems, and economists may suggest resources, but if we have no leaders to implement scientists' and economists' solutions, the problems will remain at least as critical as when first identified.

The federal definition, essentially unchanged for several years, has received fairly widespread acceptance and has been adopted by many states (Zettel, 1979). Most states limit their definition of giftedness, however, to the three areas of general intellectual ability, creativity, and leadership (Sisk, 1984). Renzulli

An earlier federal definition included a sixth area of giftedness—psychomotor ability. This category included students gifted in the use of gross and fine motor development (e.g., diving, gymnastics), but Congress believed that schools' existing athletic programs served such students adequately.

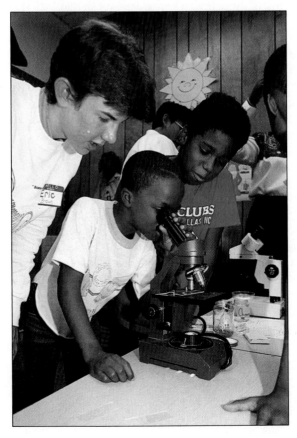

Although only a fourth grader, Reggie is able to quickly understand and synthesize most concepts in the secondary science curriculum.

(1978) has offered an alternative definition that has gained considerable attention:

> Giftedness consists of an interaction among three basic clusters of human traits—these clusters being above average general abilities, high levels of task commitment, and high levels of creativity. Gifted and talented children are those possessing or capable of developing this composite set of traits and applying them to any potentially valuable area of human performance. Children who manifest or are capable of developing an interaction among the three clusters require a wide variety of educational opportunities and services that are not ordinarily provided through regular instructional programs. (p. 184)

Renzulli's definition brings together the three features of ability (actual or potential), task commitment, and creative expression and requires that all three be jointly applied to a valuable area of human endeavor. Like the federal definition, Renzulli's provides a great deal of freedom in determining who is considered gifted and talented, depending on the interpretation of "valuable" human performance.

Prevalence

One way to arrive at the number of students who may be gifted and talented is to make a comparison with normative standards. To be considered gifted or talented for special education programs, a student is often identified as performing in the top 3% to 5% of the school-age population (Marland, 1971). Outstanding ability is based on the performance of the individual as compared to the usual performance of age-mates on a given task or skill.

A more precise estimate of the school age population classified as gifted and talented is the percentage of gifted students enrolled in the schools. Data obtained by the National Center for Education Statistics (1989) indicate that as of 1987, the percentage of gifted and talented students in the total school enrollment ranged across states from 1.2 to 9.9. The median for the 44 states reporting was 3.6%, or nationwide approximately 3.6% of the total school enrollment are classified as gifted and talented.

While the 3.6% figure is consistent with normative data, the percentages reported by the states varies considerably. There are several reasons for the variability. There are great differences across the states in the level of educational development and the fiscal resources allocated to education. In addition, the states vary considerably in their definitions and identification procedures. Students in some states have more accessibility to programs than do students in other states, and therefore more students are identified. The percentage report of 3.6% of the school enrollment, however, is consistent with what would be expected based on normative or normal curve data.

◼ HISTORICAL PERSPECTIVE

Historically, the concept of giftedness has been neither as broad nor as inclusive as current definitions. Early 19th-century works, including a classic study by Sir Francis Galton (1869/1936), focused on the concept of genius. Galton was the first to offer a definition of genius that used observable characteristics or outcomes. His study was based on famous adults, however, and contributed little to the identification and nurturing of potential in children. Furthermore, Galton felt that genius was genetically determined. Despite heavy criticism, Galton's work is recognized as a major contribution to the better understanding of people of genius.

In the United States, special education for gifted and talented children can be traced back as far as 1867, when the St. Louis public schools initiated a plan of flexible promotion. For the next 30 years, schools instituted various plans for promoting high-achieving students at various rates. Around 1900, rapid advancement classes were established, in which children could complete 2 years' worth of academic work in 1 year, or 3 years' work in 2.

One of the earliest enrichment programs for gifted children began in the early 1920s in Cleveland, Ohio. In 1922, a group of "publicly spirited" women organized to promote classes for gifted students. H. H. Goddard (1928), their advisor, published a description of the program. The Cleveland program remains one of the longest-running, continuous programs for gifted children in the United States.

To separate individuals into groups according to intellectual abilities, educators needed effective measuring devices. During the last quarter of the 19th century, several instruments designed to measure intellectual ability were developed. In Paris in 1905, two French psychologists, Alfred Binet and Theophile Simon, published a graduated series of tests called a Measuring Scale of Intelligence. Their system was intended to classify children according to intellectual abilities so as to facilitate their education. The Binet-Simon scale was transported to the United States, where several translations were made. The translation by Terman (1916) at Stanford University became the edition that dominated the field. Known as the Stanford-Binet Intelligence Scale, it was published in 1916 and was most recently revised in 1973 (Thorndike, Hagen, & Sattler, 1986). It has become the scale against which all other measures of intelligence have been compared.

In addition to translating the Stanford-Binet test, Terman conducted a famous long-term study that contributed greatly to our knowledge of the characteristics of gifted individuals. From 1925 through 1959, five volumes of the *Genetic Studies of Genius* were published—periodic reports of a study of approximately 1,500 gifted individuals from childhood into midlife. Terman's colleagues and students have also developed numerous articles and papers, including two that reported on the life satisfaction of some of Terman's original subjects (P. S. Sears, 1979; R. R. Sears, 1977).

For inclusion in the Terman study, a child had to have an intelligence quotient (IQ) of 140 or above, as measured by the 1916 Stanford-Binet. Measures were taken in a number of areas, including social and physical development, achievement, character traits, books read, and play interests. This long-term study refuted certain myths about gifted individuals, including "early ripe, early rot," "genius and insanity go hand in hand," and the stereotype of the gifted child as a little adult.

Leta S. Hollingworth, an educational psychologist, became aware of the needs of the highly gifted when she tested a child with a score of more than 180 on the Stanford-Binet. This was the beginning of a series of case studies Hollingworth conducted with children of extremely high intelligence. In

Children Above IQ 180 (1942, 1975), Hollingworth reported the histories of 12 such children from the New York City area. The children's school histories varied considerably. One factor that differentiated the successful from the unsuccessful in school was early recognition of their superior talents and the willingness of parents and school personnel to act on that awareness. Some of the case studies revealed that these gifted children were frustrated and felt stifled by regular school procedures. Early identification, guidance, personal interest in the children, and special programs contributed to helping the youngsters adjust and accept learning as a rewarding challenge (Hollingworth, 1975). Hollingworth led the way for testing above grade level and differentiated curriculum; she was also an active feminist (Benjamin, 1990).

Although certain myths were dispelled by the early studies, problems were also evident. A narrow view of giftedness, dominated by IQ score, prevailed for many years. It is probable that many children with special gifts and talents were not recognized or given the opportunity to develop fully. IQ score came to be relied on excessively as an identification tool and as a predictor of success in life (Witty, 1930, 1962). Giftedness was restricted to high IQ scores and came to be associated with only the white, urban, middle- and upper-class segments of society (Witty, 1940). In the early 1950s, Guilford, a psychologist noted for his work in the area of analyzing and categorizing mental processes, challenged the field to look beyond traditional conceptions of intelligence and to view the IQ score as a small sample of mental abilities (Guilford, 1956). Since that challenge, the concept of giftedness has developed in several directions to involve many forms of intellectual activity.

During the 1960s, attention turned to creativity and other alternatives to the traditional IQ score for identifying gifted and talented children (Frierson, 1969). Some efforts were initiated to identify and develop talent among the culturally diverse; this movement continued to expand during the 1970s (Torrance, 1977). Also during the 1970s, the need to identify gifted and talented individuals among females and handicapped students came to be more widely recognized (Fox, 1977; Maker, 1977).

Current definitions have grown out of our awareness that IQ alone does not define all the possible areas of giftedness. We have realized that some people have advanced talents in socially valued endeavors that cannot be measured by intelligence tests; intelligence tests are, as Guilford suggested, only a small sample of intellectual activity in limited areas of human endeavor. The concept of giftedness has expanded to include many talents that contribute substantially to the quality of life—for both the individual and society.

Before reading further, see Figure 11.1 to examine your beliefs about students who are gifted and talented.

▓ CHARACTERISTICS OF GIFTED AND TALENTED CHILDREN

Physically, gifted children do not differ substantially from other children their age. The quaint stereotype of the gifted child as a little adult in horn-rimmed glasses, arms laden with volumes of Homer, Plato, Descartes, and Einstein, is not based in reality. Any one gifted child may be taller or shorter than her age-mates.

The concept of giftedness includes many talents that enrich quality of life.

The child may weigh more, about the same, or less than her peers. In other words, a gifted and talented child would not be easily identifiable on a class picnic.

Giftedness is a complex concept covering a wide range of abilities and traits. Some children have special talents. They may not be outstanding in academics, but they may have special abilities in areas such as music, dance, art, or leadership. Other children may have intellectual abilities found only in 1 child in 1,000, or 1 child in 10,000.

Clark (1988) describes the characteristics of gifted children across five domains: cognitive, affective, physical, intuitive, and societal (Table 11.1). She contends that the special education needs of gifted and talented students are a function of the characteristics that differentiate them from typical learners.

> An analysis of those characteristics can provide us with a model for organizing educational programs. Programs that relate clearly to the differentiating characteristics of this population can most effectively meet the educational needs and nurture the high-level abilities of gifted pupils. (Clark, 1988, p. 252–253)

Characteristics that relate to curriculum frequently focus on learning and intellectual skills. Gifted children possess a rich supply of these abilities:

1. The ability to relate one idea to another

2. The ability to make sound judgments

3. The ability to see the operation of larger systems of knowledge than are seen by the ordinary citizen (Gallagher, 1981, p. 137)

4. The ability to acquire and manipulate symbol systems (Gallagher, 1975b, p. 12)

Ability to manipulate symbol systems is a key indicator of intellectual giftedness. Although the most common symbol system is language, there are

FIGURE 11.1

Examine your beliefs.
(*Source:* From *Growing Up Gifted: Developing the Potential of Children at Home and at School* (3rd ed.) (pp. 2–3) by B. Clark, 1988, Columbus, OH: Merrill. Reprinted by permission.)

These questions allow you to look at your beliefs and understandings regarding gifted children. Before each statement place the number that you feel most closely represents your present position. At the end of this exercise the results are discussed. Be as open as you can. You may discover some new insights about yourself.

1—I strongly agree
2—I agree
3—I have no opinion
4—I disagree
5—I strongly disagree

_____ 1 The term *gifted* can mean different things to different people and often causes much confusion and miscommunication.

_____ 2 Intelligence can be developed and must be nurtured if giftedness is to occur.

_____ 3 We seldom find very highly gifted children or children we could call *geniuses;* therefore, we know comparatively little about them.

_____ 4 Thinking of, or speaking of, gifted children as superior people is inaccurate and misleading.

_____ 5 As schools are currently organized, it is not always possible for gifted children to receive appropriate educational experiences without special programs.

_____ 6 Equal opportunity in education does not mean having the same program for everyone, but rather programs adapted to the specific needs of each child.

_____ 7 Gifted children, while interested in many things, usually are not gifted in everything.

_____ 8 Difficulty conforming to group tasks is often the result of the unusually varied interests and curiosity of a gifted child.

_____ 9 Because gifted children have the ability to think in diverse ways, teachers often see them as challenging their authority, disrespectful, and disruptive.

_____ 10 Some gifted children have been found to use their high level of verbal skill to avoid difficult thinking tasks.

_____ 11 The demand for products or meeting of deadlines can inhibit the development of a gifted child's ability to integrate new ideas.

numerous other symbol systems, such as scientific notation, music and dance notation, mathematics, and engineering symbols. These systems can be incorporated into creative endeavors as well as academic and intellectual areas. We must remember that the characteristics we have mentioned here are generalizations about the population of gifted and talented children, not the description of any single individual. We may meet a gifted child who does not neatly match these characteristics. It may be the child's giftedness that makes him unique, and the uniqueness may defy any attempt to categorize it into a neat, well-ordered compartment. We must also realize that many lists of gifted characteristics portray gifted children as having only virtues and no flaws (Gallagher, 1975b). The very attributes by which we identify gifted children,

FIGURE 11.1
continued

_____ 12 Work that is too easy or boring frustrates a gifted child just as work that is too difficult frustrates an average learner.

_____ 13 Most gifted children in our present school system are underachievers.

_____ 14 Commonly used sequences of learning are often inappropriate and can be damaging to gifted learners.

_____ 15 Gifted children, often very critical of themselves, tend to hold lower than average self-concepts.

_____ 16 Gifted children often expect others to live up to standards they have set for themselves, with resulting problems in interpersonal relations.

_____ 17 Gifted children are more challenged and more motivated when they work with students at their level of ability.

_____ 18 Some gifted children may perform poorly or even fail subjects in which they are bored or unmotivated.

_____ 19 The ability of gifted learners to generalize, synthesize, solve problems, engage in abstract and complex thought patterns, and think at an accelerated pace most commonly differentiates gifted from average learners; therefore, programs for gifted students should stress using these abilities.

_____ 20 The persistent goal-directed behavior of gifted children can result in others perceiving them as stubborn, willful, and uncooperative.

_____ 21 If not challenged, gifted children can waste their ability and become mediocre, average learners.

_____ 22 Gifted children often express their idealism and sense of justice at a very early age.

_____ 23 Not all gifted children show creativity, leadership, or physical expertise.

_____ 24 People who work with, study, and try to understand gifted children have more success educating the gifted than those who have limited contact and have not educated themselves as to the unique needs of these children.

_____ 25 I would be pleased to be considered gifted, and I enjoy people who are.

The questionnaire you have just completed should give you some indication of opinions of gifted children that are supportive to their educational growth. The more "1—I strongly agree" answers you were able to give, the more closely your opinions match those who have devoted their energy to understanding gifted children.

however, can cause some problems. High verbal ability, for example, may prompt gifted children to talk themselves out of troublesome situations or to dominate class discussions. High curiosity may give them the appearance of being aggressive or just snoopy as they pursue anything that comes to their attention. The two lists in Table 11.2 describe both positive and not-so-positive aspects of intellectual giftedness. List A describes the positive side; List B identifies some of the problems that may occur as a result of these positive traits.

Awareness of individual differences is also important in understanding gifted students. Like other children, gifted children show both interindividual and intraindividual differences. For example, if three children were given the same reading achievement test and each obtained a different score, we could

TABLE 11.1
Differentiating characteristics of the gifted.

I. The Cognitive Domain	◆ Extraordinary quantity of information; unusual retentiveness ◆ Advanced comprehension ◆ Unusually varied interests and curiosity ◆ High level of language development ◆ High level of verbal ability ◆ High level of visual and spatial ability. ◆ Unusual capacity for processing information ◆ Accelerated pace of thought processes ◆ Flexible thought processes ◆ Comprehensive synthesis ◆ Early ability to delay closure ◆ Heightened capacity for seeing unusual and diverse relationships and overall gestalts ◆ Ability to generate original ideas and solutions ◆ Early differential patterns for thought processing (e.g., thinking in alternatives and abstract terms, sensing consequences, making generalizations) ◆ Early ability to use and form conceptual frameworks ◆ An evaluative approach toward oneself and others ◆ Persistent goal-directed behavior
II. The Affective Domain	◆ Large accumulation of information about emotions that have not been brought to awareness ◆ Unusual sensitivity to the expectations and feelings of others ◆ Keen sense of humor—may be gentle or hostile ◆ Heightened self-awareness, accompanied by feelings of being "different" ◆ Idealism and a sense of justice that appear at an early age ◆ Earlier development of an inner locus of control and satisfaction ◆ Advanced levels of moral judgment ◆ High expectations of self and others, which often lead to high levels of frustration with self, others, and situations ◆ Unusual emotional depth and intensity ◆ Sensitivity to inconsistency between ideals and behavior
III. The Physical Domain	◆ Unusual discrepancy between physical and intellectual development ◆ Low tolerance for the lag between their standards and their physical capacity ◆ Cartesian split—can include neglect of physical well-being and avoidance of physical activity
IV. The Intuitive Domain	◆ Early involvement and concern for intuitive knowing, psychic and metaphysical ideas and phenomena ◆ Open to experiences in this area; will experiment with psi and metaphysical phenomena ◆ Creativity apparent in all areas of endeavor ◆ Acceptance and expression of a high level of intuitive ability, especially with the highly gifted
V. The Societal Domain	◆ Strongly motivated by self-actualization needs ◆ Advanced cognitive and affective capacity for conceptualizing and solving societal problems

Source: From *Growing Up Gifted: Developing the Potential of Children at Home and at School* (3rd ed.) (pp. 253, 260, 264, 268, 271) by B. Clark, 1988, Columbus, OH: Merrill. Reprinted by permission.

speak of interindividual differences in reading achievement. If a child who obtains a high reading achievement score obtains a much lower score on an arithmetic achievement test, we say the child has an intraindividual difference across the two areas of performance.

A graph of any child's abilities would reveal some high points and some lower points; scores would not be the same across all dimensions. The gifted child's *pattern* of performance, however, may be well above the average for that grade and/or age, as we see in Figure 11.2. Leslie's and Jackie's overall abilities are similar. Leslie, however, performs higher in vocabulary and social studies than Jackie does, and Jackie shows higher performance in science and mathematics than Leslie. These are interindividual differences. Each student also has intraindividual differences in scores. For example, Leslie has the vocabulary of an 11th grader, but scores only at a 7th grade equivalent in mathematics; Jackie earned grade equivalents of 10th grade in science and mathematics and 7th grade in writing.

Creativity

Creativity has been called "the highest expression of giftedness" (Clark, 1988, p. 45). There is, however, no universally accepted definition of creativity. The many possible approaches to creativity reflect the complex nature of the concept. Because it is one of the more intriguing aspects of human behavior, creativity

TABLE 11.2
Two sides to the behavior of gifted and talented students.

List A: Positive Aspects	List B: Not-So-Positive Aspects
1. Expresses ideas and feelings well	1. May be glib, making fluent statements based on little or no knowledge or understanding
2. Can move at a rapid pace	2. May dominate discussions
3. Works conscientiously	3. May be impatient to proceed to next level or task
4. Wants to learn, explore, and seek more information	4. May be considered nosey
5. Develops broad knowledge and an extensive store of vicarious experiences	5. May choose reading at the expense of active participation in social, creative, or physical activities
6. Is sensitive to the feelings and rights of others	6. May struggle against rules, regulations, and standardized procedures
7. Makes steady progress	7. May lead discussions "off the track"
8. Makes original and stimulating contributions to discussions	8. May be frustrated by the apparent absence of logic in activities and daily events
9. Sees relationships easily	9. May become bored by repetitions
10. Learns material quickly	10. May use humor to manipulate
11. Is able to use reading skills to obtain new information	11. May resist a schedule based on time rather than task
12. Contributes to enjoyment of life for self and others	12. May lose interest quickly
13. Completes assigned tasks	
14. Requires little drill for learning	

FIGURE 11.2

Profiles of two gifted 10-year-olds. Leslie and Jackie are both 10 years old and are in the fifth grade. For their age and grade placement, they are performing well above what might be expected. Only in social interactions, height, weight, and physical coordination are the two students similar to their average 10-year-old peers.

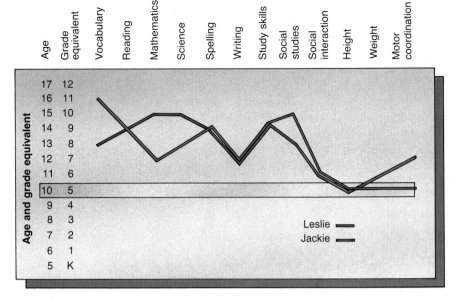

has been studied from several points of view. Gowan (1972) lists five different approaches to understanding creativity:

1. Cognitive, rational, and problem-solving aspects
2. Personality traits, family, and environmental origins
3. Mental health, psychological openness, and self-actualization
4. A Freudian view
5. Existential, psychedelic, and irrational aspects (p. 23)

In addition, we can add the behavior analysis approach to creativity (Glover & Gary, 1976; Goetz, 1982; Goetz & Baer, 1973; Vargas & Moxley, 1979) and Clark's (1988) integrated model, which represents a holistic view of creativity.

Guilford, in his much-cited work "Traits of Creativity" (1959), describes four dimensions of creative behavior.

1. *Fluency*. Many words, associations, phrases and/or sentences, and ideas are produced (p. 145).
2. *Flexibility*. A wide variety of ideas, unusual ideas, and alternative solutions are offered (p. 147).
3. *Originality*. Low probability, unique words and responses are used (p. 148).
4. *Elaboration*. The ability to provide details is evidenced (p. 148).

Another type of creativity is sensitivity, the awareness that a problem exists (Carin & Sund, 1978). And motivation and willingness to work and persevere are personality traits of many creative people. Thus, we could consider creative children as those who can identify problems, come up with a wide variety of ideas and possible solutions (some of them original), examine those ideas, fill out the most likely ones with the necessary details, and then follow through on the most promising.

Creativity is one of the most intriguing and valuable aspects of human behavior.

To be creative, a child must have some knowledge, examine it in a variety of ways, critically analyze the outcomes, and be able to communicate her ideas (Keating, 1980). There are numerous ways to communicate—such as through literature, mathematics, music, poetry, and dance—but the communication skills must be adequate for the idea.

■ IDENTIFICATION

Many educators of gifted and talented children have been critical of the intelligence testing movement, especially because it has led to a one-dimensional concept of giftedness that emphasizes intellectual performance exclusively. It is important to remember, however, that Binet and Simon made a significant contribution to the education of gifted children by developing the first instrument that could predict school success. A standardized objective measure, however crude, makes it possible to identify some children with above-average academic potential. Intelligence tests offered the first means of locating bright children, and plans for meeting their special needs could then be developed.

The use of IQ as the sole criterion for giftedness has been out of favor for many years. After Terman's first report, educators and psychologists raised serious doubts about the ability of an IQ test taken during childhood to predict success in adult life. Far more than IQ is involved in gifted performance. Furthermore, intelligence tests do not always identify gifted persons in all socioeconomic and culturally diverse groups. IQ measures tend to identify giftedness more readily in middle- and upper-middle-class, urban, white populations. During the 1960s, it was recognized that the usual intelligence measures are inappropriate for any child who is not representative of the normative population (Maker, 1977; Torrance, 1977).

Measures of intelligence may be part of the identification process, but no single index or procedure can identify all gifted and talented children. Identification usually involves a combination of procedures, including

♦ Intelligence scores

♦ Creativity measures

♦ Achievement measures

♦ Teacher nomination

♦ Parent nomination

♦ Self-nomination

♦ Peer nomination

Measures and procedures for identification should be determined by the definition of giftedness developed for each program. Knowing what to look for helps to determine where to look and how to recognize it. Test instruments, checklists, observation forms, and other approaches are ultimately tied to the definition of giftedness being used by a given program (Hansen & Linden, 1990).

Linking identification to program goals improves the chances of a good student-to-program match. Students can be assigned to special programs that have objectives consistent with their individual interests and abilities. This approach, however, limits giftedness to those who meet the program's goals; other gifted and talented children may not be identified and adequately served.

One alternative to identification by goals is to develop a comprehensive definition of giftedness and try to identify all the children who are gifted and talented. The school would then try to offer a complete and comprehensive program to meet the needs of all the children identified. Identification by goals has the advantage of allowing for systematic program growth: One set of goals and its respective program can be developed, then another, then another (Swassing, 1985). But until all program goals are developed, some children will remain unidentified and unserved. Comprehensive identification, on the other hand, locates all children who show actual or potential special abilities or talents and then relies on the school, given whatever resources are available, to develop a comprehensive program to serve all the identified gifted and talented students.

In any case, identification procedures should not be used to exclude youngsters from programs for the gifted and talented—that is, any one measure may identify some number of children to be placed in a certain program, but it should not be used to keep everyone else out. A second measure, a third, and so on should be used to include other children in special programs. School districts that provide only one or two programs may not be providing all the children in the system with the appropriate educational experiences. Gifted and

MAKING THE EARTH A BETTER PLACE
Who Said It?

Who do you think made each of these observations? Check your selections with the correct answers found at the bottom.

1. After the strife of war begins the strife of peace.
   A. Napoleon Bonaparte
   B. Carl Sandburg
   C. Dwight Eisenhower
   D. Matthew O'Brien
   E. Abraham Lincoln
2. Global peace is a powerful weapon. If we have it, we can use it to make the earth a better place.
   A. Tom Brokaw
   B. Winston Churchill
   C. Henry David Thoreau
   D. Robert Campbell
   E. Mahatma Ghandi
3. The truth is more important than the facts.
   A. Frank Lloyd Wright
   B. Oscar Wilde
   C. Alyce Jaspers
   D. Albert Einstein
   E. Golda Meir
4. Cooperation is a crucial part of survival. Cooperation is key in human life because humans' needs are so diverse, requiring for their fulfillment more skills, more talents, and more learning than any one individual can possess or acquire.
   A. Lester Brown
   B. Buckminster Fuller
   C. Polao Salori
   D. Andrea Goldberg

E. John Nesbit
5. The only way for earth to even come near perfection is for the people in our society who are in the best position to create a perfect earth to become somewhat competent.
   A. John F. Kennedy
   B. Margaret Mead
   C. John Lennon
   D. Nelson Mandela
   E. Peter Bret Lamphere
6. After much deep thinking and evaluation of those thoughts, I have come to the realization that, without a shadow of a doubt, the most crucial global issue today, and for years to come, is arms reduction.
   A. Edward Kennedy
   B. Mikhail Gorbachev
   C. Roy Stoner
   D. Jimmy Carter
   E. George Bush
7. Change lately has given us humans quite a stir. Berlin wall down, democracy up; Noriega down, taxes up. What a fast changing world we live in.
   A. Barbara Walters
   B. Peter Jennings
   C. Walter Cronkite
   D. Connie Chung
   E. Robert Campbell
8. People should feel obligated to leave the world a little better than they found it.
   A. Pippa Bowde
   B. Carl Sagan

C. Robert Redford
   D. Teddy Roosevelt
   E. Mother Teresa
9. Death in the rain forest used to be a natural part of life. The message was simple: Death was the beginning of a new generation. Now that man has entered the picture, death has come to have a new meaning: An end to birth.
   A. Barry Lopez
   B. Andrea Goldberg
   C. Carl Sagan
   D. Manuel Lujan
   E. Abbie Hoffman
10. If there is no personal concern, nothing happens.
   A. Martin Luther King
   B. Carl Rogers
   C. Benjamin Spock
   D. Thomas Jefferson
   E. Danielle Eckert

Answers: (1) Carl Sandburg, (2) Robert Campbell, Age 10, (3) Frank Lloyd Wright, (4) Andrea Goldberg, Age 9, (5) Peter Bret Lamphere, Age 9, (6) Roy Stoner, Age 9, (7) Robert Campbell, (8) Pippa Bowde, Age 11, (9) Andrea Goldberg, Age 9, (10) Danielle Eckert, Age 9. All of the statements above, other than Nos. 1 and 3, were written by gifted students. We are grateful to Sandy Lethem and Dennis Higgins, Facilitators for the Gifted at the Zuni Elementary Magnet School, Albuquerque, New Mexico, for sharing their students' thoughts on the environment. ◆

talented students who do not have the specific requisite characteristics will be kept from appropriate educational opportunities, a situation that is inconsistent with the concept of equal educational opportunities for all children. For this reason, program planners need to know about their entire school population before they establish hard and fast program goals.

■ CURRICULUM GOALS

The overall goal of educational programs for gifted and talented students should be the fullest possible development of every child's actual and potential abilities. In the broadest terms, the educational goals for these youngsters are no different from those for all children. Feelings of self-worth, self-sufficiency, civic responsibility, and vocational and avocational competence are important for everyone. There are, however, some additional specific educational outcomes that are especially desirable for gifted and talented students.

Gallagher (1981) has classified the educational objectives of programs for gifted students into two areas: (1) mastering the knowledge structure of disciplines and (2) heuristic skills. Knowledge structures include both basic principles and systems of knowledge; heuristic skills include problem solving, creativity, and use of the scientific method. In other words, gifted students need both content knowledge and the abilities to use and develop that knowledge effectively.

Feldhusen and Sokol (1982) refer to gifted students' cognitive, affective, and generative needs. They believe important cognitive skills for gifted students include basic thinking skills, a broad store of knowledge, disciplined and in-depth inquiry, methods of research and analysis, and organizational theories and ideas. In affective terms, gifted students need stimulation through association with peers, interaction with adult models, a strong self-concept, social learning skills, and acceptance of their own abilities. Gifted students also need certain generative characteristics, including an acceptance of their roles as producers of knowledge and creative products, motivation and habits of inquiry and research, creative activity, early and continuous experience in research, and independence in investigation.

Of course, these cognitive and affective skills are appropriate for all students to some degree. The generative skills, however, emphasize the special roles that gifted and talented individuals can play. Not only are gifted and talented students consumers of artistic, scientific, and creative products; they are potential creators of these products, which enrich the lives of all of us (Renzulli, 1977). Generative skills require high levels of motivation and may lead to lifestyles that differ markedly from those of most other people. A glacier geologist may spend months at a time studying ice formations in remote Arctic areas; a cultural anthropologist may spend years living among the inhabitants of remote islands; a concert pianist may spend most of his waking hours practicing.

For gifted and talented students, the three Rs alone do not comprise the basics. Gifted students are about to enter a world where information is transmitted and processed at amazing rates—and where international travel and business will require them to have a wide range of social and language skills in addition to their specialty or profession. Research skills, keyboarding and computer usage, speed reading, at least one foreign language, and interpersonal and affective development should be systematically taught as part of the curriculum. The skills of systematic investigation are fundamental abilities that gifted students use throughout a lifetime of learning. These skills include use of references, use of the library, information (data) gathering, and reporting findings in a variety of ways. These skills may ultimately be used in diverse settings, such as law and medical libraries, museums, chemical and electrical laboratories, theatrical archives, and national parks.

■ CURRICULUM ORGANIZATION—ENRICHMENT AND ACCELERATION

Identification and goal setting mean little if the children in programs for the gifted do not receive appropriate learning opportunities. These experiences can be considered *differentiated education*. Curricula that incorporate higher cognitive concepts should be presented by specially prepared teachers, using strategies that accommodate the students' learning styles. Group arrangements may include special classes, honors classes, seminars, resource rooms, and other flexible approaches to grouping and scheduling. Two widely used approaches to educational programming for gifted students are enrichment and acceleration.

Enrichment experiences are those that let youngsters investigate topics of interest in much greater detail than is ordinarily possible with the standard school curriculum. Topics of investigation may be based on the ongoing activities of the classroom but may permit students to go beyond the limits of the day-to-day instructional offerings.

Enrichment is not a do-your-own-thing approach with no structure or guidance. Children involved in enrichment experiences should not be released

Enrichment activities give students a chance to go beyond the limits of the standard curriculum.

to do a random, haphazard (and thus inefficient) project. A basic framework that defines limits and sets outcomes is necessary. Projects should have purpose, direction, and specified outcomes. A teacher should provide guidance where necessary—and to the degree that is necessary—to keep the youngsters efficient (Renzulli, 1977).

Several administrative or placement options may be followed to implement enrichment programs. There is little evidence to suggest which alternative is best; the decision should be based on the resources and needs of the local school, the community, and the children involved.

Acceleration means providing a child with learning experiences that are usually given to older children; that is, speeding up the usual presentation of content without modifying that content or method of presentation. Approaches to acceleration include

♦ Early admission to school

♦ Grade skipping

♦ Concurrent enrollment in both high school and college

♦ Advanced placement tests

♦ Early admission to college

♦ Content acceleration (giving youngsters the opportunity to move through a particular curricular sequence at their own rates)

One noted educator of gifted children, Sidney Pressey, advocated acceleration because it allows children to reduce the time spent in training and gives more years of productivity. In this way, both society and the individual benefit (Pressey, 1962). Since 1971, the ongoing Study of Mathematically Precocious Youth (SMPY) at Johns Hopkins University has demonstrated the effectiveness of acceleration in mathematics (Stanley, 1991). These students then have the opportunity to enroll in advanced coursework.

Research suggests that wisely practiced acceleration does not cause the problems of social and emotional adjustment often attributed to it (Gallagher, 1975a). Instead,

> It improves the motivation, confidence and scholarship of gifted students. Second, it prevents the development of habits of mental laziness. Third, it allows for earlier completion of professional training, and fourth, it reduces the total cost of education particularly at the collegiate level for parents and for the students themselves. (Van Tassel-Baska, 1986, p. 184)

Neither enrichment nor acceleration will have particular merit if the experiences provided are not appropriate for the gifted and talented children in the program. Kaplan (1986) has suggested the following principles for differentiating curriculum for gifted and talented students.

♦ Present content that is related to broad-based issues, themes or problems.

♦ Integrate multiple disciplines into the area of study.

♦ Present comprehensive, related and mutually reinforcing experiences within an area of study.

♦ Allow for the in-depth learning of a self-selected topic within the area of study.

- Develop independent or self-directed study skills.

- Develop productive, complex, abstract and/or higher level thinking skills.

- Focus on open-ended tasks.

- Develop research skills and methods.

- Integrate basic skills and higher level thinking skills into the curriculum.

- Encourage the development of products that challenge existing ideas and produce "new" ideas.

- Encourage the development of products that use techniques, materials and forms.

- Encourage the development of self-understanding, i.e., recognizing and using one's abilities, becoming self-directed, appreciating likenesses and differences between oneself and others.

- Evaluate student outcomes by using appropriate and specific criteria through self-appraisal, criterion referenced and/or standardized instruments. (p. 183)

Currently, 17 states require IEPs and due process procedures for gifted students (Zirkel & Stevens, 1986). The prescriptive elements of an IEP allow considerable planning flexibility based on the assessed needs of each student. Renzulli and Smith (1979) proposed a detailed model for developing IEPs for gifted and talented students; the model is consistent with Renzulli's (1977) definition of giftedness and incorporates ability, creativity, and task commitment.

Talent Development

The contributions and skill levels of our most talented scientists, artists, musicians, athletes, and political leaders receive much attention. Unfortunately, the interest in their accomplishments far exceeds the research available to guide us in encouraging and nurturing exceptional talent in young people. Two important investigations into the development of highly skilled persons do, however, offer some guidance, and the findings of both studies are clear and consistent. Pressey (1955) studied the careers of musicians, scientists, and Olympic swimmers and identified five common factors in his subjects' backgrounds.

1. Excellent early opportunities for the ability to develop and encouragement from family and friends.

2. Superior early and continuing individual guidance and instruction.

3. The opportunity to frequently and continually practice and extend their special ability and to progress as they were able.

4. Close association with others in the field, which greatly fostered the abilities of all concerned.

5. Many opportunities for real accomplishment, within their possibilities but of increasing challenge; the precocious musician or athlete has had the stimulation of many and increasingly strong success experiences—and his world acclaimed these successes. (p. 124)

Bloom (1985b) studied the development of 120 highly talented individuals in three areas: athletic/psychomotor skills (Olympic swimmers and world class

LITERATURE FOR STUDENTS WHO ARE GIFTED

A common observation of teachers who work with bright students in kindergarten through grade 6 is that many of these youngsters have voracious appetites for recreational reading; they enjoy reading for themselves and being read to. While many classroom teachers have a general awareness of the opportunities for direct and indirect learning present in many books, they are sometimes not as attentive as they could be to specific qualifications of the books they select for able learners.

The following are books that are especially appropriate for gifted students. All of these selections have been used with repeated success by teachers of gifted students. They are organized into four categories that parallel the needs of gifted students as documented in research literature: (1) books that challenge language development, (2) books that encourage creative and imaginative powers, (3) books that provide nonstereotyped role models, and (4) books that provide how-to skill training in a variety of interest areas. Suggested grade levels for readability of content are given in parentheses following most bibliographic entries, representing a consensus of both reviewers and teachers who have used the books with students.

Language Development

The books featured in this section reflect the use of rich vocabulary, sophisticated grammatical construction, fine degrees of subtlety in expression, literary and historical allusions, imagery, and multiple levels of meaning, all of which are vital in a challenging reading program for gifted students (Baskin & Harris, 1980). These books can be used to supplement specific curriculum topics for bright students in the regular classroom or to enrich recreational reading in their areas of interest.

Walther, T. (1978). *A spider might*. New York: Scribner's. (K–3)

Here is precise and accurate scientific information on 20 species of spiders commonly found in urban and suburban habitats. It begins with "spider speculations," which ask the reader to imagine doing the things spiders do (e.g., changing skins). Humorous illustrations accompany each question, and following pages explain in scientific detail, why spiders are the way they are.

Levitt, P. M., Burger, D. A., & Guralnick, E. S. (1985). *The weighty word book*. Longmont, CO: Bookmakers Guild. (4–6)

In this alphabet book, the reader does not discover the word each letter represents until the end of a witty and fanciful story that creates a pun.

Ventura, P. (1986). *There once was a time*. New York: Putnam. (4–6)

For each of eight historical periods, nine special topics are explored. A visual key is used to denote these topics in each chapter so that the reader can choose to track a particular interest (e.g., dress and fashion) from period to period. A wider context for understanding history may be the result.

Wilkes, M. (1986). *The ultimate alphabet*. New York: Holt. (All ages)

Wilkes creates a visual challenge with each of 26 complex paintings created to help viewers see the English language in pictures. For example, the "C" painting contains 433 things beginning with that letter. A workbook accompanying the book will be needed by even the most knowledgeable viewer.

Creative and Imaginative Powers

Bright students have the potential to be very creative, but this potential may not be displayed without deliberate nurturing. The books reviewed in this section can be used to engage students actively in creative problem solving or they can serve as models of the benefits of using one's imagination.

Gardner, B. (1980). *The turn about, think about, look about book*. New York: Lothrop, Lee & Shepard. (All ages)

Each of the appealing, vibrant graphics in this collection challenges the viewer to see something different as the book is turned around. For example, what appears to be a closed eyelid becomes a somersaulting caterpillar and then becomes the view one might have of entering a tunnel.

Small, D. (1985). *Imogene's antlers*. New York: Crown.

This model of creative thinking can be the jumping-off place for reader participation in creating new uses for the antlers that one day appear on Imogene's head. The varied attitudes depicted in the reactions of household members are worth discussing too.

VanAllsburg, C. (1984). *The mysteries of Harris Burdick*. Boston: Houghton Mifflin. (All ages)

Here is a series of 14 pictures with only story titles and picture captions, which begs for imaginative stories to be written.

Caney, S. (1985). *Invention book*. New York: Workman. (4–6)

Caney's stories about 36 exciting inventions provide not only inspiration but positive informational clues about the strategies and mindsets of inventors. The hands-on appeal is Caney's description of items just waiting for invention.

Nonstereotyped Role Models

Positive role models are a critical criterion in the search for good literature for bright students. Both fiction and nonfiction material can help gifted boys and girls gain accurate perspectives on their world.

Konigsburg, E. L. (1967). *From the mixed-up files of Mrs. Basil E. Frankweiler*. New York: Dell. (3–5)

This is the story of Claudia, who runs away and becomes involved in solving the mystery surrounding an exquisite statue at the Metropolitan Museum of Art. Claudia models some notable characteristics of gifted girls: She is bright in a variety of areas, including mathematics; she is sensitive; she is a risk taker; and she is highly stimulated by problems to be solved.

George, J. (1971). *Who really killed Cock Robin?* New York: Dutton. (4–6)

This ecological mystery provides a stimulating example of bright youngsters engaged in investigative study. An especially important true-to-life lesson in perseverance is created in the story when supposedly sure solutions lead to dead ends.

Williams, J. (1969). *The practical princess*. New York: Parents' Magazine Press. (K–3)

This is not the typical fairy tale in which the girl is merely beautiful and passive, waiting to be whisked off by Prince Charming. Bedelia is intelligent as well as practical, and she demonstrates her savvy as she finds and whisks away a prince of *her* choosing.

Riordan, J. (1985). *The woman in the moon and other tales of forgotten heroines*. New York: Dial.

This is an excellent collection of folktales about memorable women from around the world. The heroines exhibit characteristics of independence, imagination, sensitivity, justice, wisdom, bravery, and physical strength.

How-To Skill Training

The goal in selecting how-to-do-it books is to provide students with authentic information about methods used by professionals in their work. The skill development information may deal with some broad categories of skills, such as classifying or sample selection or interviewing, but it should be detailed in the context of the particular discipline in which the student is carrying out an investigation.

James, E., & Barkin, C. (1978). *What do you mean by "average"*. New York: Lothrop, Lee & Shepard. (3–6)

The reader is shown how to take a survey; select an accurate sample; figure means, medians, modes, and percentages; and present data.

Klein, D. (1984). *How do you know it's true?* New York: Scribner's. (6 and up)

This is sophisticated fare aimed at helping students develop an objective and critical viewpoint in analyzing information. An advanced elementary student who is not a novice in data analysis could be challenged by the practices recommended here.

Cooper, K. (1985). *Who put the cannon in the courthouse square?* New York: Walker. (4 and up)

Here is a primer on local history research for the novice. Cast in the perspective of a detective's work, the how-to details are sufficiently detailed but interesting and concise enough to keep a beginner involved.

Webster, D. (1974). *How to do a science project*. New York: Watts. (2–5)

This book provides helpful sections on finding a suitable question or problem and conducting each aspect of the investigation including the presentation of findings. Excerpts from students' projects are useful complements to the text.

Conclusion

A paramount need in a reading program differentiated for gifted students is content that addresses the characteristics and needs of gifted students. Literature that uses rich

professional tennis players); aesthetic/musical/artistic talent (concert pianists and sculptors); and cognitive/intellectual achievement (mathematicians and research neurologists). The study revealed three phases of talent development. The first phase emphasized playful exploration and "messing around," which enticed the learner into further involvement. Instruction was informal, with high rates of personal interaction and reinforcement of the learner's enjoyment of the activity. The second phase emphasized acquisition of skills and attention to detail. Practice became more rigorous, with frequent evaluations based on precision and technique. In the third phase of talent development, a commitment to excellence was made. The learner was almost always taught by a highly vocabulary and attends to style in writing and aptness of expression can challenge the verbal skills of bright learners. Books focusing on an imaginative view of the world can nurture the creative potential of gifted students, while how-to books can provide training in implementing creative, original ideas. Gifted students also profit from literature that includes nonstereotyped role models who solve problems caused by their differentness. Such books can assist gifted students in developing self-understanding.

More Good Books

Alexander, L. (1980). *The high king*. New York: Dell. (5 and up)

Aliki, (1981). *Digging up dinosaurs*. New York: Crowell. (K–2)

Barrett, J. (1985). *Cloudy with a change of meatballs*. New York: Atheneum. (2–5)

Collard, A. (1984). *Two young dancers: Their world of ballet*. New York: Messner. (5 and up)

DeAngelo, M. (1974). *Fiddlestrings*. New York: Doubleday. (3–5)

Denny, N., & Filmer-Sankey, J. (1966). *The Bayeux tapestry*. New York: Atheneum. (4–6)

Fleischman, P. (1985). *I am Phoenix*. New York: Harper and Row. (5 and up)

Fritz, J. (1983). *The double life of Pocahontas*. New York: Putnam. (3–5)

Hahn, M. D. (1983). *Daphne's book*. New York: Clarion. (4–6)

Holt, M. (1975). *Maps, tracks, and the bridges of Konigsberg*. New York: Crowell. (1–3)

Juster, N. (1964). *The phantom tollbooth*. New York: Random House. (3–5)

Lydon, M. (1985). *How to succeed in show business by really trying: A handbook for the aspiring performer*. New York: Dodd. (6 and up)

Mabery, D. L. (1985). *Tell me about yourself: How to interview anyone from your friends to famous people*. New York: Lerner. (4 and up)

Meltzer, M. (1985). *Mark Twain: A writer's life*. New York: Watts. (5 and up)

Merriam, E. (1977). *Ab to Zogg: A lexicon for science-fiction and fantasy readers*. New York: Atheneum. (5 and up)

Most, B. (1979). *If the dinosaurs came back*. New York: Harcourt Brace Jovanovich. (K–3)

Paterson, K. (1977). *Bridge to Terabithia*. New York: Harper and Row. (4–6)

Pinkwater, D. M. (1977). *The big orange splot*. New York: Hastings House. (K–3)

Press, H. J. (1977). *The adventures of the black-hand gang*. Englewood Cliffs, NJ: Prentice-Hall. (3–6)

Siegel, B. (1980). *An eye on the world*. New York: Frederick Warne. (5–6)

Stearns, P. (1976). *Into the painted bear lair*. Boston: Houghton Mifflin.

Tchudi, S. & S. (1984). *The young writer's handbook*. New York: Scribner's. (5 and up)

From "Literature for Students Who Are Gifted" by C. L. Schlichter, 1989, Teaching Exceptional Children, 21*(3), pp. 34–36. Adapted by permission.* ♦

skilled mentor who held high expectations for performance. Practice and instruction were extremely time-consuming and demanded considerable sacrifice. Rewards were infrequent but powerful, such as winning contests, public acclaim, and the acknowledgment of peers.

Teaching-Learning Models

Renzulli (1986) brings together many of the teaching-learning models and systems typically used to guide the development of differentiated education for gifted and talented students. We offer five models as examples of the breadth of available alternatives. A given program may be based on any one or a combination of approaches, depending on the students and the content to be taught. Clark (1988) advised that in combining models, careful attention must be given to making sure the models are consistent with the overall goals of the program and present an integrated total experience.

Bloom's Taxonomy of Educational Objectives

Bloom (1956) developed the Taxonomy of Educational Objectives: Cognitive Domain to provide a hierarchy for writing and classifying learning objectives for testing purposes. Following are the six levels of objectives within the cognitive domain, with examples of items that might be used to test each level.

1. Knowledge:
   "Name the continents."
   "Distinguish between a cross-section and a longitudinal section."
   "Place these seven objects in their proper categories."
   "Name the systems of the human body."

2. Comprehension:
   "Repeat the story."
   "Tell me in your own words."

3. Application:
   "How could you measure this room with 15th-century measuring devices?"
   "Write a short story."

4. Analysis:
   "What are the parts of this problem?"
   "How do the cardiovascular and lymphatic systems relate to each other?"

5. Synthesis:
   "What are some solutions to this problem?"
   "Prepare an article to explain the issues to your readers."

6. Evaluation:
   "Will this new product meet the requirements established for judging its effectiveness?"
   "Tell us about the qualities of this poem that may make it a classic."

Bloom's emphasis on a range of learning beyond reiteration of facts and figures has been the basis of the taxonomy's use in enrichment programs. The taxonomy has been used effectively, for example, in developing learning centers. Some activities in a learning center are appropriate and required for all children in a class; others are intended only for selected students. Children with varying interests and abilities are asked to do individually specified tasks; some tasks may vary according to those interests and abilities, or gifted students may be asked to do only those tasks at the higher levels of the taxonomy.

A classroom learning center on space travel might include activities from all six levels of the taxonomy. All children might be required to read the directions and a preliminary information sheet and to view a slide-tape presentation. Some students might then be asked to answer a series of posttest questions (knowledge level); others might be asked to write a newspaper article (synthesis); still others might be required to read about the Bernoulli principle (regarding objects moving through fluids) and to demonstrate that principle in an experiment (analysis).

The next activity in the learning center might be to examine human energy and nutritional requirements in space. Again, all students would receive the preliminary information—in this case via a NASA videocassette. Some students might be asked to create a display of the basic food groups (comprehension). Some might design a new food capsule for prolonged space exploration (synthesis). Still other students might design meals based on color, texture, and nutritional requirements (evaluation). Using the taxonomy allows a teacher to provide one set of materials but to organize instruction at various levels with tasks appropriate for the students' different ability levels.

Renzulli's Enrichment Triad Model

Renzulli (1977, 1982) developed the Enrichment Triad Model (ETM) to guide the planning of enrichment activities for gifted and talented children. It is based on three levels, or types, of enrichment. General exploratory activities (Type I) are those that let students survey a variety of topics to gain ideas for further study. Students are introduced to a subject and its components, in search of areas of interest. Group training activities (Type II) involve students in exercises to provide the skills, knowledge, and attitudes necessary for future in-depth study; that is, to learn how to learn within the content area of interest. Type III enrichment activities consist of individual and small-group investigations of real problems. Students are to assume the posture of a real investigator in the process of adding to the knowledge base in the selected area of interest. It is considered important that, as true investigators, students address real problems—problems that are not just imposed by the teacher, but that have meaning to the children in light of the subject matter and the circumstances around which the problems have been defined. The teacher must explain that, as fledgling investigators, the students may not be at the forefront of the given area of study, although, as Renzulli pointed out, at times they may actually make discoveries of far-reaching impact.

Reis and Cellerino (1983) use a revolving-door identification model (Renzulli, Reis, & Smith, 1981) that allows all children in a resource room program to participate in Type I and Type II enrichment activities. Only students who show serious interest in a specific topic evolve into Type III investigators. Students are never compelled to begin Type III investigations; it is their option.

When a student does indicate a particular area of interest, the teacher must determine whether the interest is serious enough to warrant launching an in-depth investigation or whether it is only a temporary, superficial interest. Reis and Cellerino (1983) interviewed Michael, a second grade student in their gifted program, who, as a result of Type I and Type II activities, expressed a strong interest in Tchaikovsky. They asked Michael these questions:

1. Michael, will you tell me a little about Tchaikovsky and how you became interested in knowing more about him?
2. Have you read any books about him and his music?
3. How long have you been interested in studying about Tchaikovsky?
4. Do you like looking in different books to find information?
5. Do you have any ideas about what you would like to do with the information you find? (p. 137)

Michael's responses showed his interest in Tchaikovsky to be genuine. After specifying objectives for his research, Michael's teachers helped him set up a management plan for his investigation. Potential sources of information were identified and a timeline developed. Then Michael was encouraged to come up with a specific idea for a product of his investigation and to consider an audience for his product. Michael's product, a children's book of 30 typed pages and an audio-taped version that plays selections of Tchaikovsky's music, is now part of both his school's and his local public library's collection. On the first page of his book, Michael wrote,

> Some of you may wonder why a second grader would want to write a book about Tchaikovsky. People get interested in different things for different reasons. For example, I got interested in Tchaikovsky because I like his music. I play the piano and have a whole book of his music. At Christmas I saw the ballet of the Nutcracker Suite. His music can be both cheerful and sad at the same time. I wondered how music can be both happy and sad at the same time so I decided to learn about Tchaikovsky's life.
>
> I wondered if when he was sad he wrote sad music, and if when he was happy he wrote happy music. In this book you will get to know a little bit more about Tchaikovsky, how he lived and about the music he wrote. (Reis & Cellerino, 1983, p. 139)

Betts's Autonomous Learner Model

The Autonomous Learner Model (Betts, 1986) was developed to guide the gifted and talented to reach their full potential as independent and self-directed (self-actualized) adults, able to accept responsibility for and implement and evaluate their own learning. The model has five major dimensions:

1. *Orientation* helps the students understand themselves, their gifts, and their educational program.
2. *Individual development* guides the students toward autonomous learning through learning the cognitive, social, and emotional skills for independent functioning.
3. *Enrichment activities* to explore areas of interest in new and unique fields.
4. *Seminars* to learn skills necessary for individual and group learning and to become an active participant in the community of learners.
5. *In-depth study* allows students to investigate long-term areas in individual and/or small group study. (pp. 28–31)

The Autonomous Learner Model was originally developed for the high school level. Since its origination however, it has been used at all levels, K–12. It is an exploration of the students themselves and of the life around them, with the goal of helping them become autonomous, and therefore responsible, lifetime learners.

Clark's Integrative Education Model

The Integrative Education Model (IEM) (Clark, 1986) was developed to integrate the four functions of the brain: intuition, feeling, physical sensing, and cognition. The purpose of IEM is to provide experiences that support each of these functions in an integrated learning environment. The model involves seven components:

1. A responsive learning environment, where learning is encouraged.
2. Relaxation and tension reduction, to allow the mind and body to work more cooperatively.
3. Movement and physical encoding, to integrate movement into the learning cycle.
4. Empowering language and behavior, to maintain positive, supportive interactions between teachers and students and among students.
5. Choice and perceived control, to provide values clarification and choice making.
6. Complex and challenging cognitive activity, to challenge learners according to their abilities.
7. Intuition and integration, to foster intuitive thinking and integration of the brain/mind system. (pp. 67–82)

IEM "is a model of learning and teaching that has a highly complex, flexible structure, is decentralized, and is individualized. It allows variation in pace, level, and grouping. The IEM encourages student choice, participation, and involvement." (Clark, 1988, p. 295)

Maker's Integrated Curriculum Model

Maker (1982) analyzed the major contributions of the various teaching-learning models and integrated what she considered the best components of each. Maker's model involves a four-dimensional approach to curriculum modification for gifted and talented students: content, process, product, and environment. To provide enrichment, a teacher can modify any one or more of the four dimensions.

Content modifications emphasize complex, abstract, and varied organization of the ideas, concepts, and facts presented. Process modifications address the method of presentation, emphasizing the higher levels of thinking. Product modifications are aimed at what might be expected of gifted and talented children. The product varies according to the process used to arrive at the product and the intended audience. Environmental modifications focus on the conditions under which learning is to take place, the teacher's role in the activities, and individual students' learning styles. This model emphasizes the teacher as facilitator, complex activities, and open, independent learning environments.

In science, for example, a lesson for the entire class might involve a basic understanding of rain forests—their levels, flora, and fauna. Content modification for the gifted students might encourage them to study the interactions of plants and animals and symbiosis and to draw parallels between plant, animal, and human behavior in a rain forest environment. The learning process might be independent study or inquiry lessons. The products would be real; they might include a slide-tape presentation for the school and/or local library, a newspaper account, a videotaped report, or a presentation to the entire science class. The final modification would be in the learning environment. It must be open, so the students are free to divert from usual procedures. The teacher must be willing to remain in the background, available when needed, ready to encourage and praise, but seldom directive.

Teachers of the Gifted

No instructional theory or approach is more important than the teacher who implements it. One of the first questions most people ask is whether the teacher must be gifted to teach gifted children effectively. The answer is "Not necessarily"—in the sense of giftedness as we use it in this chapter. All teachers should be gifted, regardless of whom they teach—and teachers should be gifted in different ways to teach different children. Nonetheless, teachers of gifted children do need some particular qualities. They must:

♦ Be willing to accept unusual and diverse questions, answers, and projects

♦ Be intellectually curious

♦ Be systematic and businesslike

♦ Have a variety of interests

♦ Appreciate achievement

♦ Be well prepared in instructional techniques

♦ Be well prepared in content area

♦ Want to teach gifted students

♦ Realize that the teacher may not know as much about some topics as the children do, and be comfortable with that situation

■ CURRENT ISSUES/FUTURE TRENDS

Many questions remain in the education of gifted and talented children. We need research in a variety of areas, including the nature of intelligence, learning, creativity, the roles of parents and families, cultural diversity, sex roles, and the impact of high technology on the education and lives of gifted and talented people. Program evaluation, assessing the effectiveness of identification techniques, personnel training, providing better education for the culturally disadvantaged and minority populations, and learning-thinking strategies are crucial issues.

The Jacob K. Javits Gifted and Talented Students Education Act, passed in 1988, has offered substantial support for addressing the research, teacher preparation, and service delivery concerns. This act provided funds for special projects, a national research center, and a position within the U.S. Office of Education with responsibility for the gifted. Twenty-eight projects were funded for 1990 and 13 for 1991.

The center, the National Research Center on the Gifted and Talented (NRC/GT), located at the University of Connecticut, is a collaborative effort of four universities: Connecticut, Georgia, Virginia, and Yale. The center also involves state departments of education and collaborating school districts. Its mission for the first year includes program evaluation, applying theory to identification, teaching and evaluation, giftedness among the economically disadvantaged, and identifying future research needs.

We are rapidly moving from an industrial society to an information-processing, high-technology society. We can no longer remain isolated and self-sufficient as individuals or as a nation. Long-range social goals and instantaneous information based on informal human networks rather than complex political systems are an aspect of social change, personally and politically. Clearly, the future will call for the best human resources available (Naisbitt & Aburdene, 1990). In this vein, we must capitalize on the resources found in special populations—women, people who are handicapped, individuals from culturally diverse groups, and those who are not achieving up to their potential.

The first major issue affecting these groups is the ability of educational planners to identify the gifted and talented individuals among them. The usual testing procedures are often inappropriate or incomplete (Ortiz & Ramirez, 1988). The instruments commonly used (intelligence and achievement tests) seem to penalize anyone who is not like the group that was used to develop the tests' norms. We say that a test or instrument is culturally biased if different groups have different opportunities to learn the skills it measures. For example, do boys and girls have the same opportunities to learn vocabulary? Do children with disabilities have the same opportunities to engage in sequential motor skills or experiences as do nondisabled children? If the opportunities are not the same, the test is biased, and individuals from such special populations may be at a disadvantage when taking the test. The question of cultural bias in intelligence tests has led to much study. Although the evidence of bias is not as substantial as was first expected (Sattler, 1982), the fact remains that, for a given child, the effects of any bias may be enough to preclude that child from being considered for a gifted and talented program.

Cultural barriers, test and social biases, organizational reward systems, sex-role stereotyping, and conflicts between career and marriage and family all continue as external impediments to the advancement of gifted and talented women (Kerr, 1985). In reviewing the topic of gifted women, Silverman (1986) points out that the history of genius and women's roles have been contradictory (eminent contributions cannot be made from a subservient status) and that identification procedures reflect masculine (product-oriented) versus feminine (development-oriented) concepts of giftedness. Silverman (1986, 1988) makes these recommendations for improving the special education of gifted girls:

♦ Hold high expectations for girls.
♦ Believe in their logical and mathematical abilities.
♦ Expose both boys and girls to female role models.
♦ Actively recruit girls for advanced placement math and science classes.
♦ Encourage and deal with girls' multiple interests and talents.
♦ Use nonsexist texts, language, and communication.
♦ Form support groups for girls.
♦ Encourage independence.

Maker (1977) raised a particularly salient point about looking for giftedness among handicapped students, challenging the seeming dichotomy between the concepts of disability and giftedness. When all handicapped children are viewed

A SHORT HISTORY
by Stephen W. Hawking

Stephen W. Hawking is Lucasian Professor of Mathematics and Theoretical Physics at the University of Cambridge in England. He is considered by many to be the foremost theoretical physicist in the world today. His goal is to develop a "grand unifying theory" of the entire universe. Such a theory would encompass all known laws of science and describe how the universe began. While a student in college, he was diagnosed with amyotropic lateral sclerosis (ALS), a degenerative disease of the nervous system sometimes called Lou Gerhig's disease. He uses a wheelchair for mobility and a computer-assisted synthetic speech generator to communicate (see pages 264–265 for a description of his communication system). We asked Professor Hawking to describe a short history of his interests and work as a student and scientist.

I was born on January the 8th, 1942, exactly 300 years after the death of Galileo. However, I estimate that about two hundred thousand other babies were also born that day; I don't know whether any of them was later interested in astronomy.

We lived in Highgate, north London. Our house was damaged by a V2 rocket which landed a few doors away. Fortunately, we were not there at the time. In 1950, we moved to the cathedral city of Saint Albans, 20 miles north of London. My father wanted me to go to Westminster School, one of the main "public," that is to say, private, schools. He, himself, had gone to a minor public school. He felt that this, and his parents' poverty, had held him back, and had led to him being passed over in favor of people with less ability, but more social

graces. However, I was ill at the time of the scholarship exam, and so did not go to Westminster. Instead, I went to the local school, Saint Albans school, where I got an education that was as good as, if not better than, that I would have had at Westminster. I have never found that my lack of social graces has been a hindrance.

I was a fairly normal small boy; slow to learn to read, and very interested in how things worked. I was never more than about half way up the class at school (it was a very bright class). When I was 12, one of my friends bet another friend a bag of sweets that I would never come to anything. I don't know if this bet was ever settled, and, if so, which way it was decided.

My father would have liked me to do medicine. However, I felt that biology was too descriptive, and not sufficiently fundamental. Maybe I would have felt differently if I had been aware of molecular biology, but that was not generally known about at the time. Instead, I wanted to do mathematics, more mathematics, and physics. My father felt, however, that there would not be any jobs in mathematics, apart from teaching. He therefore made me do chemistry, physics, and only a small amount of mathematics. Another reason against mathematics was that he wanted me to go to his old College, University College, Oxford, and they did not do mathematics at that time. I duly went to University College in 1959 to do physics, which was the subject that interested me most, since it governs how the universe behaves. To me, mathematics is just a tool with which to do physics.

Stephen W. Hawking

Most of the other students in my year had done military service, and were a lot older. I felt rather lonely during my first year, and part of the second. It was only in my third year that I really felt happy at Oxford. The prevailing attitude at Oxford at that time was very anti-work. You were supposed to either be brilliant without effort, or to accept your limitations and get a fourth class degree. To work hard to get a better class of degree was regarded as the mark of a gray man, the worst epithet in the Oxford vocabulary.

At that time, the physics course at Oxford was arranged in a way that made it particularly easy to avoid work. I did one exam before I went up, and then had 3 years at Oxford, with just the final exam at the end. I once calculated that I did about 1,000 hours work in the 3 years I was at Oxford, an average of an hour a day. I'm not proud of this lack of work, I'm just describing my attitude of complete boredom and feeling that nothing was worth making an effort for. One result of my illness has been to change all that; when you are faced with the possibility of an early death, it makes one realize that life is worth living and that there are lots of things you want to do.

Because of my lack of work, I had planned to get through the final exam by doing problems in theoretical physics and avoiding any questions that required factual knowledge. However, I didn't sleep the night before the exam, because of nervous tension. So I didn't do very well. I was on the borderline between a first and second class degree, and I had to be interviewed by the examiners to determine which I should get. In the interview, they asked me about my future plans. I replied I wanted to do research. If they gave me a first, I would go to Cambridge. If I only got a second, I would stay in Oxford. They gave me a first.

I felt that there were two possible areas of theoretical physics that were fundamental, and in which I might do research. One was cosmology, the study of the very large. The other was elementary particles, the study of the very small. However, I thought that elementary particles were less attractive, because, although they were finding lots of new particles, there was no proper theory of elementary particles. All they could do was arrange the particles in families, like in botany. In cosmology, on the other hand, there was a well-defined theory, Einstein's General Theory of Relativity.

I had not done much mathematics at school or at Oxford, so I found General Relativity very difficult at first and did not make much progress. Also, during my last year at Oxford, I had noticed that I was getting rather clumsy in my movements. Soon after I went to Cambridge, I was diagnosed as having ALS, amyotrophic lateral sclerosis, or motor neuronic disease, as it is known in England. The doctors could offer no cure or assurance that it would not get worse. The only consolation they could give me was that I was not a typical case.

At first the disease seemed to progress fairly rapidly. There did not seem much point in working at my research, because I didn't expect to live long enough to finish my Ph.D. However, as time went by, the disease seemed to slow down. I also began to understand General Relativity, and to make progress with my work. However, what really made the difference was that I got engaged to a girl called Jane Wilde, whom I had met about the time I was diagnosed with ALS. This gave me something to live for.

If I were to get married, I had to get a job. And to get a job, I had to finish my Ph.D. I therefore started working hard for the first time in my life. To my surprise, I found I liked it. Maybe it is not really fair to call it work.

I applied for a research fellowship at Caius College, pronounced *Keys*. I was hoping that Jane would type my application, but when she came to visit me in Cambridge, she had her arm in plaster, having broken it. I must admit that I was less sympathetic than I should have been. However, it was her left arm, so she was able to write out my application to my dictation, and I got someone else to type it.

I got the fellowship, and have been a fellow of Caius College ever since.

Having got a fellowship, we could get married, which we did in July, 1965.

My research up to 1970 was in cosmology, the study of the universe on a large scale. My most important work in this period was on singularities. Observations of distant galaxies indicate that they are moving away from us: The universe is expanding. This implies that the galaxies must have been closer together in the past. The question then arises: Was there a time in the past when all the galaxies were on top of each other, and the density of the universe was infinite? Or was there a previous contracting phase, in which the galaxies managed to avoid hitting each other? Maybe they flew past each other and started to move away from each other. To answer this question required new mathematical techniques. These were developed between 1965 and 1970, mainly by Roger Penrose and myself. Penrose was then at Birkbeck College, London. Now, he is at Oxford. We used these techniques to show that there must have been a state of infinite density in the past, if the General Theory of Relativity was correct.

This state of infinite density is called the Big Bang singularity. It would be the beginning of the universe. All the known laws of science would break down at a singularity. This would mean that science would not be able to predict how the universe would begin, if General Relativity is correct. However, my more recent work indicates that it is possible to predict how the universe would begin if one takes into account the theory of quantum mechanics, the theory of the very small.

General Relativity also predicts that massive stars will collapse in on themselves when they have exhausted their nuclear fuel. The work that Penrose and I had done showed that they would continue to collapse until they reached a singularity of infinite density. This singularity would be an end of time, at least for the star and anything on it. The gravitational field of the singularity would be so strong that light could not escape from a region around it, but would be dragged back by the gravitational field. The region from which it is not possible to escape is called a black hole, and its boundary is called the event horizon. Anything, or anyone, who falls into the black hole through the event horizon will come to an end of time at the singularity.

I was thinking about black holes as I got into bed one night in 1970, shortly after the birth of my daughter, Lucy. Suddenly, I realized that many of the techniques that Penrose and I had developed to prove singularities could be applied to black holes. In particular, the area of the event horizon, the boundary of the black hole, could not decrease with time. And

when two black holes collided and joined together to form a single hole, the area of the horizon of the final hole would be greater than the sum of the areas of the horizons of the original black holes. This placed an important limit on the amount of energy that could be emitted in the collision. I was so excited that I did not get much sleep that night.

From 1970 to 1974, I worked mainly on black holes. But in 1974, I made perhaps my most surprising discovery: Black holes are not completely black! When one takes the small-scale behavior of matter into account, particles and radiation can leak out of a black hole. The black hole emits radiation as if it were a hot body.

Since 1974, I have been working on combining General Relativity and quantum mechanics into a consistent

theory. One result of that has been a proposal I made in 1983 with Jim Hartle, of Santa Barbara: that both space and time are finite in extent, but they don't have any boundary or edge. They would be like the surface of the Earth, but with two more dimensions. The Earth's surface is finite in area, but it doesn't have any boundary. In all my travels, I have not managed to fall off the edge of the world.

If this proposal is correct, there would be no singularities, and the laws of science would hold everywhere, including at the beginning of the universe. The way the universe began would be determined by the laws of science. I would have succeeded in my ambition to discover *how* the universe began. But I still don't know *why* it began. ◆

as below average, those who are also gifted are cast into a stereotype that disavows their true abilities. Loss of mobility, for example, does not imply reduced intellectual functioning, nor does deafness reduce one's artistic abilities. Recognition of intraindividual differences is important, emphasizing skills rather than deficits. Whitmore and Maker (1985) have identified four obstacles to the identification of gifted handicapped students: stereotypic expectations for disabled persons that restrict the ability to recognize giftedness, developmental delays in specific abilities, incomplete information about these children, and no opportunities for them to display their intellectual abilities or special talents. Maker (1977) suggests using checklists and Meeker's (1969) approaches to testing for identifying the gifted handicapped.

It has been pointed out for some time that there are gifted and talented persons among culturally diverse groups (Frierson, 1965; Torrance, 1977; Witty & Jenkins, 1934). But until recently, identification and development of those individuals received little attention. Work in this important area is now increasing dramatically (Baldwin, Gear, & Lucita, 1978; Maker & Schiever, 1989; and Malone, 1978). Maker (1989) summarizes these recommendations for curricula and teaching strategies for culturally diverse gifted students.

1. Identify student's strengths and plan a curriculum to develop these abilities.

2. Provide for development of basic skills and other abilities students lack.

3. Regard differences as positive, rather than negative, attributes.

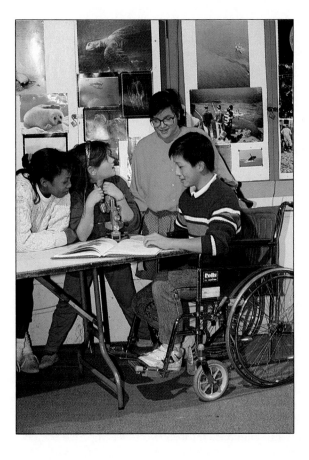

School systems must increase their efforts to identify and serve gifted and talented students who have disabilities or are from culturally diverse groups.

4. Provide for involvement of parents, the community, and mentors or role models.

5. Create and maintain classrooms with a multicultural emphasis. (p. 301)

Underachieving gifted students represent another complex problem. Delisle (1982) described the phenomenon of "learning to underachieve." Some gifted and talented children learn to perform below their potential because

♦ It is socially safe; that is, teachers and peers do not single the child out.

♦ There is nothing to learn that is interesting or challenging.

♦ Peer and parent relationships are not based on expectations of superior achievement.

Whitmore (1980) has described underachievement along two major dimensions, extent and length. The extent of the problem ranges from mild to moderate and moderate to severe. The second dimension, length, may be *situational*—a sudden crisis or problem—or *chronic*—long lasting due to complex causes. Whitmore also discusses the *unknown underachiever*—the child who is performing normally so that no one knows of his hidden exceptional abilities. High aptitude scores with low grades or high standardized achievement scores with low grades may indicate two other kinds of underachievement. Effective remediation involves increasing the child's motivation, working on self-perceptions, and modifying classroom instruction, environment, and curriculum. Guidance and counseling are integral to improved self-concept and self-esteem (Van Tassel-Baska, 1983).

Counseling is an important concern for all gifted children. Gallagher (1990) points out that our "track record" of misunderstanding the gifted leaves us with much work in both research and practice. Blackburn and Erickson (1986) identified a number of predictable crises in the lives of the gifted, including career choice, role expectations (by themselves and others), adolescent female fear of success, having too many choices (multipotentiality), and the possibility of experiencing failure for the first time.

Differences between intellectual, emotional, and physical growth can result in conflicts between cognitive competence and ability to perform, particularly for boys. As mentioned, underachievement is a cause for counseling. Fear of success, particularly for adolescent girls, or meeting failure for the first time can also be ameliorated by appropriate counseling. In addition, because gifted students have so many options, they often need help in sorting through their available choices.

There are other moments when professional counseling may be required (Van Tassel-Baska, 1990). Beyond the stresses of growing up that all children experience, gifted and talented individuals must sometimes deal with conflicts caused by the expectations that they or others hold for their achievement. Conflicting expectations may concern the present—perhaps grades, extracurricular activities, or home life—or they may have to do with future career or lifestyle choices. Gifted students can benefit from guidance and counseling that helps them adjust to their special abilities and how those abilities affect their lives. And finally, as we have seen with other groups of exceptional children, to improve the future for gifted and talented children, we must improve society's attitudes toward them. Many people, including some educators, believe that gifted children, by their very nature, do not need special education—that they can make it on their own. In reality, gifted and talented children do need special education if they are to reach their potential. Too many gifted children are bored and frustrated in school; some even drop out altogether; even more are made to settle for less than they deserve. The quality of our collective future may depend in large measure on our ability to develop this valuable human resource.

SUMMARY

Definition and Prevalence of Gifted and Talented Children

♦ Gifted and talented children have unusual intellectual, creative, artistic, specific academic, or leadership ability, which requires special school services.

♦ To be considered gifted, a student must perform in the top 3% to 5% of the school-age population.

♦ Although some gifted children are outstanding in many areas, others have special talents in only one or two fields.

♦ Gifted children are by no means perfect, and their unusual talents and abilities may make them difficult to manage in the classroom.

Historical Perspective

♦ The concept of giftedness has evolved over the years. The current concept is broader than traditional definitions.

♦ Standardized intelligence tests, beginning with the Stanford-Binet, have been used during most of this century to predict school success and to identify unusually bright children. Reliance on these tests has tended to restrict giftedness to high IQ scores, which are associated with white, urban, middle- or upper-class society.

♦ In the early 1950s, Guilford first suggested that more than IQ should be considered in determining who is gifted.

♦ Since then, the concept of giftedness has expanded to include creativity and other alternatives to traditional IQ scores. We have also come to recognize giftedness among the culturally diverse, among females, and among children with disabilities.

Characteristics of Gifted and Talented Children

♦ Gifted children exhibit negative as well as positive characteristics, and educators must keep in mind their individual differences.

♦ Gifted students need both content knowledge and the abilities to use and develop that knowledge effectively.

♦ Many gifted children are creative. Although there is no universally accepted definition of creativity, we know that creative children have knowledge, examine it in a variety of ways, critically analyze the outcomes, and communicate their ideas.

♦ Guilford includes dimensions of fluency, flexibility, originality, and elaboration in his definition of creativity.

Identification

♦ IQ tests are the first means for locating bright children.

♦ Usual means of identification include a combination of IQ scores; creativity and achievement measures; teacher, parent, and peer nominations; and self-nomination.

Educational Approaches

♦ Two common approaches to educating the gifted are enrichment and acceleration.

♦ Five models for teaching gifted students are Bloom's Taxonomy of Educational Objectives, Renzulli's Enrichment Triad Model, Betts's Autonomous Learner Model, Clark's Integrative Education Model, and Maker's Integrated Curriculum Model.

♦ Teachers of the gifted must be flexible, curious, tolerant, competent, and self-confident.

Current Issues/Future Trends

♦ The importance of identifying gifted and talented children among females, students with disabilities, and diverse cultural groups is now being recognized. We need better procedures for identifying, assessing, teaching, and encouraging these children.

♦ As we have seen with other exceptional children, we must improve society's attitudes toward gifted and talented children if we are to improve their futures.

Journals

Gifted Child Quarterly. Published four times per year by the National Association for Gifted Children, 1155 15th Street N.W., #1002, Washington, DC 20005. Publishes articles by both parents and teachers of gifted children.

Gifted Child Today (formerly *G/C/T*). Published six times per year by GCT, Inc., 350 Weinacker Avenue, Mobile, AL 36604. Publishes articles with ideas aimed at parents and teachers of gifted, talented, and creative youngsters.

Gifted International. Published semi-annually by the World Council for Gifted and Talented Children, Dr. Dorothy Sisk, Secretariate, Lamar University, College of Education, P.O. Box 10034, Beaumont, TX 77710. Devoted to international communication among educators, researchers, and parents.

Journal for the Education of the Gifted. Published quarterly by the Association for the Gifted, the Council for Exceptional Children, 1920 Association Drive, Reston, VA 22091. Presents theoretical, descriptive, and research articles presenting diverse ideas and different points of view on the education of gifted and talented students.

Journal of Creative Behavior, published by Creative Educational Foundation, Inc., State University College, 1300 Elmwood Avenue, Buffalo, NY 14222. Devoted to research reports and program suggestions and designed to understand and enhance creative behavior in children and adults.

Roeper Review. Published quarterly by the Roeper City and Country Schools, 2190 North Woodward, Bloomfield Hills, MI 48013. Publishes articles by teachers, researchers, and students in gifted education.

Books

Barbe, W. B., & Renzulli, J. C. (1981). *Psychology and education of the gifted* (3rd ed.). New York: Irvington.

Clark, B. (1988). *Growing up gifted* (3rd ed.). Columbus OH: Merrill.

Cox, J., Daniel, N., & Boston, B. O. (1985). *Educating able learners: Programs and promising practices*. Austin, TX: University of Texas Press.

Gallagher, J. J. (1985). *Teaching the gifted child* (3rd ed.). Boston: Allyn & Bacon.

Kramer, A. H., Bitan, D., Butler-Or, N., Eryatar, A., & Landau, E. (Eds.). (1981). *Gifted children: Challenging their potential*. New York: World Council for Gifted and Talented Children.

Maker, C. J. (1989). *Critical issues in gifted education: Defensible programs for cultural and ethnic minorities*. Austin, TX: PRO-ED.

Parke, B. N. (1989). *Gifted students in regular classrooms*. Boston: Allyn & Bacon.

Sisk, D. (1987). *Creative teaching of the gifted*. New York: McGraw-Hill.

Swassing, R. H. (Ed.). (1985). *Teaching gifted children and adolescents*. Columbus, OH: Merrill.

Tannenbaum, A. J. (1983). *Gifted children: Psychological and educational perspectives*. New York: Macmillan.

Van Tassel-Baska, J., Feldhusen, J., Seeley, K., Wheatley, G., Silverman, L., & Foster, W. (1988). *Comprehensive curriculum for gifted learners*. Boston: Allyn & Bacon.

Organizations

American Creativity Association, P.O. Box 26068, St. Paul, MN 55126. A new organization that promotes creativity in business, education, the arts, sciences, and social and political decision making.

The Association for the Gifted, The Council for Exceptional Children, 1920 Association Drive, Reston, VA 22091. A growing division of CEC that includes teachers, teacher educators, administrators, and others interested in gifted and talented children.

Gifted Child Society, Suite 6, 190 Rock Road, Glen Rock, NJ 07452. An organization for parents, also offering information and inservice training for educators.

National Association for Gifted Children, 1155 15th Street N.W. #1002, Washington, DC 20005. An organization for parents, professionals, and others interested in the gifted and talented.

World Council for Gifted and Talented Children, Lamar University, P. O. Box 10034, Beaumont, TX 77710. The organization's purpose is to promote worldwide communication on issues related to the education and development of gifted children.

PART III
Cultural, Family, and Life-Span Issues in Special Education

12

Cultural Diversity in Special Education

◆ How do a student's disability and cultural background affect each other?

◆ How are *cultural pluralism, multicultural education, and bilingual special education* related?

◆ If a student cannot speak, read, or write English well enough to progress in the school curriculum, does it make any difference whether the limited English proficiency is caused by cultural differences or by a disability?

◆ Why and how should assessment and placement procedures differ for students from culturally or linguistically different backgrounds?

◆ Does a teacher use different instructional methods with students from each different cultural or linguistic background?

- ◆ "By the turn of the century, it is projected that 40% of public school students will be from ethnically diverse backgrounds." (Ramirez, 1988, p. 45)

- ◆ "Exceptional students, their families, and special educators are first and foremost human beings whose rich diversity of culture, race, ethnicity, religion, geography, economic and social condition, language, and gender must be addressed with respect." (Weintraub, 1986, p. 2)

- ◆ "There is a bitter irony in the fact that an English-speaking student may earn college credit for learning to speak another language, while a language-minority child is encouraged not to use, and therefore lose, the same skill." (Ada, 1986, p. 387)

- ◆ "Many of the teachers of black children have roots in other communities and do not often have the opportunity to hear the full range of their students' voices. I wonder how many of Philadelphia's teachers know that their black students are prolific and 'fluent' writers of rap songs. I wonder how many teachers realize the verbal creativity and fluency black kids express every day on the playgrounds of America as they devise new insults, new rope-jumping chants and new cheers. Even if they did hear them, would they relate them to language fluency?" (Delpit, 1986, p. 383)

These wide-ranging observations suggest some of the challenges special educators face in seeking to provide a relevant, individualized education to exceptional students from culturally diverse backgrounds. Our public school system is based, after all, on a philosophy of equal educational opportunity. The Individuals with Disabilities Education Act (P.L. 94–142) is only one of many significant steps toward implementing equal educational opportunity. Court decisions and legislation, besides prohibiting discrimination in schools because of intellectual or physical disability, have forbidden discrimination in education and employment on the basis of race, nationality, sex, or inability to speak English. Special programs now provide financial support and assistance to schools that serve refugee and migrant students and that provide self-determination in education for Native Americans.

Despite these important efforts, equal educational opportunity for all is not yet a reality (Banks & Banks, in press). Some exceptional students still experience discrimination or receive a less-than-adequate education because of their racial, ethnic, social class, or other differences from the majority. In addressing this issue, we are not implying that belonging to a cultural or linguistic group that differs from the majority culture is a handicap or disability. One of our society's strengths is its cultural diversity; society has benefitted from the contributions of many ethnic groups.

> Ethnic diversity enriches the nation and increases the ways in which its citizens can perceive and solve personal and public problems. This diversity also enriches a society by providing all citizens with more opportunities to experience other cultures and thus to become more fulfilled as human beings. When individuals are able to participate in a variety of ethnic cultures, they are more able to benefit from the total human experience. (Banks, 1977, p. 7)

But even though cultural diversity is a strength of our society, being a member of a minority group too often means discrimination and misunderstanding, closed doors, and lowered expectations.

REASONS FOR CONCERN

Why do students from culturally diverse backgrounds merit special attention? First, the achievement of culturally diverse students typically lags behind that of white, mainstream students. Because the achievement of ethnic minorities such as African-Americans, Hispanics, and Native Americans is similar to white students' in the early grades but falls further behind the longer the students stay in school (Banks, 1989), there is reason for concern over the role our educational system may be playing in limiting the achievement of students from different cultural groups.

Second, data on the prevalence of handicapped students in the United States indicate that a disproportionate number of them come from culturally diverse backgrounds (Salend, Michael, & Taylor, 1984). Kamp and Chinn (1982) report that about one-third of the entire population of students in special education programs in the United States come from multicultural backgrounds. Black students account for more than 28% of students identified as mentally retarded, although the percentage of black students in the overall school population is only about 18%. Black children are also somewhat overrepresented in the emotionally disturbed/behavior disordered category, but to a lesser extent (Wolff & Harkins, 1986). Schildroth (1986) has documented the steadily increasing percentage of black and Hispanic students in residential schools for the deaf concurrent with a "decline in the number of white, non-Hispanic students" (p. 100). Cummins (1986) contends that the currently favored diagnostic category for minority students is "learning disabilities" and that Hispanic students are greatly overrepresented in classes for learning disabled children, despite the absence of "any intrinsic processing deficit unique to Hispanic children" (p. 9).

An influential study of a large California school district, reported by the sociologist Jane Mercer in 1973, is often cited as evidence that race and culture may play an unfair role in determining whether a child is placed in special classes and, if so, what type of services he will receive. Mercer found that black and Mexican-American children were much more likely to be placed in classes for the educable mentally retarded than were Anglo-American children: Only 1.8% of all Anglo-American children in the school district were enrolled in EMR classes, compared to 12.9% of the black children and 18.6% of the Mexican-American children (Mercer, 1973a). These figures can be interpreted to mean that a Mexican-American child was 10 times more likely than an Anglo-American child to receive the EMR label, which at that time led to placement in special classes for much or all of the school day. Another study of racial imbalance in special education classes yielded somewhat different findings, however. Gottlieb, Agard, Kaufman, and Semmel (1976) reported that, although many children in a Texas school district were placed in EMR classes that were "very heavily overrepresented with children of their own race" (p. 212), this situation generally reflected the racial composition of the schools as a whole, rather than bias on the part of school officials.

Many observers maintain that, although culturally diverse children are overrepresented in classes for handicapped students, they are correspondingly underrepresented in programs for gifted and talented students. Chinn and McCormick (1986), for example, point out that "gifted children from minority cultures possess a variety of talents that are valued and nurtured within their own cultures but are often ignored in school" and back up this observation with the fact that ethnic minority students constitute about 27% of the general school population but only about 18% of the students identified as gifted (p. 103).

The fact that culturally diverse children constitute a high percentage of special education students is not, in itself, a problem. Students with special needs should be served in special programs, whatever their ethnic background. However, the presence of large numbers of culturally diverse students raises several important concerns for special educators:

♦ *Adequacy of assessment and placement procedures.* Have students received fair and multifaceted assessments before being placed in special education programs? Is referral based on a child's documented special needs, rather than on value judgments about her background? Are there opportunities for periodic reassessment and for parent and student involvement in program planning? Are culturally diverse students and disabled students included in screenings for gifted and talented children?

♦ *Provision of appropriate supportive services.* Special efforts may help improve the education and adjustment of students from culturally diverse backgrounds; such services may be provided either by the school or by other agencies. Examples of special efforts that may be appropriate include (1) bilingual aides to assist non-English-speaking students in the classroom and to translate correspondence sent home; (2) inservice training for teachers, to encourage sensitivity toward different cultures and to enhance appropriate educational planning; and (3) multiethnic education for students, to increase awareness of their own and others' backgrounds and to reduce the potential for conflict and misunderstanding in the classroom.

♦ *Interactions between school and cultural background.* Schools generally require or expect certain behaviors of students; for example, it is assumed that most children will learn to respond to the teacher's instructions and will be positively motivated by verbal praise. Children are, however, strongly influenced by their early contacts with family members, neighbors, and friends. If the expectations and values of home and school environments are vastly different, children may have serious problems. Many children appear to "think, act, and be motivated appropriately in activities out of school, yet do not demonstrate these same behaviors in school. . . . [M]any school-related problems of minority children seem to be the results of conflict between the hidden curriculum and cultural preparation" (Chan & Rueda, 1979, p. 427). Such conflicts can interfere with a child's learning and behavior and are thus a legitimate concern of special educators.

A Note on Terminology

Many terms have been applied to members of culturally diverse populations. As we have learned elsewhere in this book, it is difficult to use labels effectively. Although labels can sometimes serve a useful purpose in identifying relevant factors, they are just as likely to convey misleading or inaccurate generalizations. This unfortunate effect is especially evident in several terms that have been used to refer to children from different cultural backgrounds.

At first, the term *minority group* seems straightforward enough; its usage has typically meant any racial or ethnic group constituting a recognizable minority in society (Fuchigami, 1980). In many communities and regions of the country, however, "minorities" constitute the predominant population. A black child in Detroit, a Hispanic child in El Paso, or a Navajo child on a reservation in Arizona could be considered part of a "minority" only in respect to the national population, a comparison that would have little relevance to the child's immediate environment. The *majority* of students now enrolled in all but 2 of the 25 largest public school systems in the United States are from ethnically diverse "minority" groups. In addition to suggesting that the population of the group is small, the term *minority group* carries some "negative connotations of being less than other groups with respect to power, status, and treatment" (Chinn & Kamp, 1982, p. 383). For example, Brantliner and Guskin (1985) describe a minority individual as someone who (1) is politically excluded from roles of significance and responsibility in institutions; (2) receives a smaller share of goods, services, and prestige; and (3) is perceived by members of the dominant culture as deviant and inferior (or, if viewed positively, as different or interesting). Although such discriminatory outcomes and perceptions still exist, they are inappropriate.

Terms such as *culturally deprived* and *culturally disadvantaged* have also been used to describe children from various backgrounds. Although these labels recognize the influence of environment on children's education and achievement, they also make the inappropriate suggestion that a background different from that of the majority or of more widely accepted groups is somehow inferior or lacking. A 1966 report, for example, used the terms "deprived" and "disadvantaged" in referring to a population of black preschool children in a southern town. This report also noted, however, that most of the children's families had been in the vicinity for at least three generations and that only 2 of 87 families dropped out of a 3-year-long research and demonstration project (Gray, Klaus, Miller, & Forrester, 1966). Such information strongly suggests the presence, not absence, of a stable cultural environment in the family and community. As Sue (1981) observes, it is now acknowledged that all people inherit a cultural background, and the fact that a culture may differ from white middle-class norms does not mean that it is deviant, impoverished, or in need of reform.

We prefer the term *culturally diverse* when referring to children whose backgrounds are different enough to require, at times, special methods of assessment, instruction, intervention, or counseling. This term implies no judgment of a culture's value and does not equate cultural diversity with disability. We view membership in a cultural group as an opportunity for an enriching experience rather than as a disadvantage.

The Division for Culturally and Linguistically Diverse Exceptional Learners (DDEL) is one of the newest division of CEC.

■ CULTURE, CULTURAL PLURALISM, AND MULTICULTURAL EDUCATION

What must a classroom teacher know to help culturally diverse exceptional students achieve? Are special methods of assessment and instruction necessary to work with students whose cultural heritage differs from the majority? If a classroom contains students from four different cultural groups, does that mean the teacher must use four different ways of teaching? Before a meaningful discussion of these important questions can be attempted, several more fundamental questions must be answered. What is a *culture*? What does membership in a particular social group mean? How do and should members of different cultural groups view and treat one another? What roles and responsibilities do schools have (or should they have) in teaching children from different cultural backgrounds to interact with one another?

Culture

To survive, a social group must adapt to and modify the environments in which it lives. **Culture** can be thought of as the established knowledge, ideas, and skills a social group uses to survive (Bullivant, 1989; Skinner, 1969).

> Culture consists of the shared beliefs, symbols, and interpretations within a human group. Most social scientists today view culture as consisting primarily of the symbolic, ideational, and intangible aspects of human societies. The essence of a culture is not its artifacts, tools, or other tangible cultural elements but how the members of the group interpret, use, and perceive them. (Banks, 1989, p. 7)

A culture, then, is determined by the "world view, values, styles, and above all language" shared by members of a social group (Hilliard, 1980, p. 585). Even though an "outsider" can learn to speak the language of another social group or to use some of its tools, such accomplishments do not confer complete access to or understanding of the group's culture. Although the language, artifacts, and other things associated with a particular group is sometimes presented as its culture, this is only partly accurate. Chopsticks, for example, are an important part of the Chinese culture, but are not culture in and of themselves.

> Unless we know the meaning of and how to use, say, chopsticks, these implements remain just bits of wood, bone, or ivory. We have to acquire the knowledge and ideas about what they mean and what they are used for. . . . If we are members of the social group that uses such implements, we will know the code by virtue of knowing the culture. A stranger in the group would have to watch chopstick-using behavior or ask for instructions. . . . Even then, the stranger might not learn all the subtleties of chopstick use immediately but would have to be acquainted with the social group for a long time before finding out that there are rules of politeness and etiquette surrounding the apparently simple process of eating with chopsticks. (Bullivant, 1989, p. 33)

People who share a particular culture's ideas and values usually interpret events in similar ways. Although membership in a specific cultural group does not determine behavior, members are exposed to (i.e., socialized by) the same set of expectations and consequences for acting in certain ways. As a result, certain types of behavior become more probable (Banks, 1989; Skinner, 1974). It is also important to remember that each student is simultaneously a member of multiple groups according to race, ethnicity, social class, religion, gender, and exceptionality. Each of these groups exerts various degrees of influence on the student's ways of interpreting and responding to the world.

This student's behavior and values are influenced not only by her membership in a specific cultural group, but by her social class, gender, and exceptionality.

Knowledge of the characteristics of groups to which students belong, about the importance of each of these groups to them, and of the extent to which individuals have been socialized within each group will give the teacher important clues to students' behavior. (Banks, 1989, p. 15)

Garcia (1981) outlines three basic concepts of membership in cultural groups that give us a background for considering the special needs of culturally diverse exceptional students.

1. Every person needs to belong to, or have a sense of belonging to, a group. A child's ethnic or cultural group provides a system of values and behaviors and is important in developing self-concept. Group membership should be a source of strength and social sustenance rather than of shame or anxiety.

2. Ethnic groups have both similarities and differences. Students should be encouraged to explore the characteristics of various groups; teachers can strive for cross-cultural communication and understanding. (For example, students can discuss the social implications of racial differences.)

3. Segregated people develop myths, prejudices, and stereotypes about each other. Conflicts can occur when different groups first come into contact. (Students can consider the consequences of separation and integration.)

Stereotyping has been defined as the "arbitrary assigning of certain habits, abilities, and expectations to people solely on the basis of group membership, regardless of their attributes as individuals" (Campbell, 1979, p. 1).

Cultural Pluralism

The United States is a society composed of people from many different cultural groups, and the students in our schools reflect this great diversity. **Cultural pluralism** exists when the cultural differences that make up a society are not only mutually respected by all members of the larger society, but when those differences are fostered and encouraged as well. Cultural pluralism has been defined as

> A state of equal coexistence in a mutually supportive relationship within the boundaries or framework of one nation of people of diverse cultures with significantly different patterns of belief, behavior, color, and in many cases with different languages. (National Coalition for Cultural Pluralism, 1973, p. 149)

Belief in cultural pluralism as a positive value is a recent concept. Throughout most of our country's development, *cultural assimilation* was valued and practiced. This was the so-called *melting pot theory,* wherein all immigrants were expected to relinquish their native language and cultural heritage in exchange for complete adoption of the language, values, and ways of the new "American way of life." During and after World War I, an intensive program of Americanization was put into effect in schools, churches, and the workplace because of concern that some immigrants might support their native countries against the United States (Kopan, 1974).

Even though Americans share an overarching *macroculture* as members of a nation-state, the significant and growing *microcultures* (smaller cultures within the core culture) in the United States are evidence that the melting pot has not been completely successful. As Banks (1989) points out, it is important to distinguish and recognize the various microcultures as different from the macroculture (the larger core culture), because the "values, norms, and characteristics of the mainstream culture are frequently mediated by, as well as interpreted and expressed differently within, various microcultures" (p. 7). The melting pot theory has, nevertheless, had tremendous influence on our society's institutions. Critics contend that one of the undesirable outcomes of attempting to create a monocultural society is an educational system that lacks tolerance for cultural diversity among students.

> America's intolerance of diversity is reflected in an ethnocentric educational system to "Americanize foreigners or those who are seen as culturally different."
> . . . The ill-disguised contempt for a child's language is part of a broader distaste for the child himself and the culture he represents. Children who are culturally different are said to be culturally "deprived." Their language and culture are seen as "disadvantages." (Kobrick, 1972, p. 54)

Unfortunately, some children from cultural backgrounds that are different from white, middle-class America still encounter the institutionalized discrimination that Kobrick described 20 years ago. But there is reason for optimism. Educators are realizing the benefits and necessity, not to mention the ethical and moral correctness, of cultural pluralism. Evidence of this realization is the increasing emphasis on multicultural education.

Currie (1981) recalls a native Canadian parent who likened cultural pluralism to a bouquet that is "more beautiful because of the diversity of flowers, all of which add to the total beauty, and yet, each is beautiful in its own right. . . . It is the differences which must be recognized and accepted instead of being ignored or rejected" (p. 165).

Baca and Cervantes (1989) point out that the term "melting pot" was first used as the title of a Broadway play that debuted in 1908 (Zangwill, 1909).

Multicultural Education

Multicultural education refers to the actualization of cultural pluralism in the schools. According to Grant and Sleeter (1989),

> The multicultural education approach attempts to reform the total schooling process for all children, regardless of whether the school is an all-white suburban school or a multiracial urban school. The curriculum and instructional program are changed to produce an awareness, acceptance, and affirmation of cultural diversity. (p. 53)

James Banks (1989), a leading developer and advocate of multicultural education programs, identifies four major goals of the approach:

1. *To increase the academic achievement of all students.* A major assumption of multicultural education is that the academic achievement of students from diverse groups can be increased if the total school environment is transformed to make it more consistent with their cultures and learning styles.

2. *To help all students develop more positive attitudes toward different cultural, racial, ethnic, and religious groups.* Many children enter kindergarten with misconceptions, negative beliefs, and stereotypes about people. If the school does not help students develop more positive attitudes about various groups, they tend to become even more negative as they grow older. Strategies to reduce prejudice should begin in the earliest grades and be a consistent, ongoing, integral part of the curriculum, not one-shot interventions reserved for special days or celebrations such as "Black History Month."

3. *To help students from victimized groups develop confidence in their ability to succeed academically and to influence societal institutions.* By providing them with opportunities for success, by recognizing and giving visibility to their cultures, and by teaching them decision-making and social action skills, schools can help improve the self-esteem of students from marginal groups.

4. *To help all students learn to consider the perspectives of other groups.* Most of the concepts, events, and issues taught in schools are from the perspective of mainstream, white, middle- and upper-class males. Students are too rarely given the opportunity to view events from the perspectives of women, persons from lower socioeconomic classes, persons with disabilities, and culturally diverse groups. We gain a better view of ourselves when we look at ourselves from the perspectives of other cultures.

The BUENO Center for Multicultural Education at the University of Colorado is an excellent source of materials and information for building cultural awareness in students with disabilities. (See "For More Information" at the end of this chapter.)

Some educators erroneously believe they have incorporated multicultural education into their schools simply by offering various units of study on different cultural groups (e.g., "Scientific Contributions by African-Americans") or by periodically scheduling special cultural awareness events (e.g., "Hispanic Week"). Such activities are an important part of multicultural education, but they are not sufficient. Leaders of the multicultural education movement believe that to truly put the concept into practice, a complete transformation of the school is necessary.

Cultural pluralism is promoted when students teach one another about their ethnic and historical backgrounds.

When I asked one school administrator what efforts were being taken to implement multicultural education in his school district, he told me that the district had "done" multicultural education last year and that it was now initiating other reforms, such as improving the students' reading scores. This administrator not only misunderstood the nature and scope of multicultural education, but he also did not understand that it could help raise the students' reading scores. . . . *The major goal [of multicultural education is] to transform the school so that . . . students from diverse cultural, social-class, racial, and ethnic groups will experience an equal opportunity to learn in school.* (Banks, 1989, p. 20)

◼ SOME CONCERNS OF SPECIFIC CULTURALLY DIVERSE GROUPS

Elsie J. Smith, a counselor who specializes in working with people of diverse cultural backgrounds, finds it helpful to remember the following saying: "Each individual is like all other people, like some other people, and like no other person" (1981, p. 180). We must keep this observation in mind as we consider certain issues that have been of concern to specific cultural groups. The importance of understanding and respecting interindividual and intraindividual differences cannot be stressed too strongly. We hope we have made this clear in our discussion of the widely used categories of exceptionality in special education. We know, for example, that two students affected by Down syndrome may display very different academic abilities, social behavior, and personality traits. We have seen that one blind child may read braille fluently and play the piano well, whereas another blind child does neither. Similarly, two members of the same racial or cultural group may function quite differently in school.

We should always be objective observers of students' behavior and avoid stereotypes based on race or culture; nevertheless, a teacher who is oblivious to the typical values and ideas shared by members of different cultural groups can inadvertently present a lesson that is not only ineffective, but perhaps offensive or embarrassing to a child. We hope to present information that will help teachers and others recognize whether their approaches and interactions with members of diverse cultural groups are as effective as they can be. Understanding and appreciation of different cultures can go a long way toward avoiding misinterpretations of children's behavior.

We cannot make this point too strongly: Each of the cultural groups we discuss is extremely heterogeneous; for example, the term *Native American* describes people from more than 500 tribes with over 200 languages (McDonald, 1989). Asian-Americans are an even more diversified group, coming from more than two dozen countries and speaking over 1,000 languages and dialects (Leung, 1988).

The degree to which a child inherits a distinct cultural background also varies immensely. Remember, a student's cultural group is just one of the social groups that influence his values and behavior.

> For example, a child in the classroom is not just Asian-American, but also male and middle-class. . . . Therefore his view of reality and his actions based on that view will differ from those of a middle-class Asian-American girl or a lower-class Asian-American boy. A teacher's failure to consider the integration of race, social class, and gender could lead at times to an oversimplified or inaccurate understanding of what occurs in schools. (Grant & Sleeter, 1989, p. 49)

African-Americans/Blacks

Americans of African descent currently constitute the largest ethnic minority group in the United States—12.4% of the total population in 1990. And the black population of the United States is growing rapidly, at about double the rate of the white population (*Statistical Abstracts of the United States,* 1990). Cruickshank (1986) believes that black children with disabilities are "doubly handicapped . . . a minority within a minority" and notes the unfairness of some widely held attitudes: "Black cerebral-palsied children . . . have far greater difficulty in receiving equality of service than does the white child similarly handicapped" (p. 18). J. L. Johnson (1976) contends that the black exceptional child has certain special characteristics and that educators should proceed beyond discussions of feelings and implement instruction that will help the black exceptional student achieve important goals.

> The primary task for the black handicapped child is to master the skills of language, eliminate self-destructive behaviors, and understand that he must become

AN ETHNIC FEELINGS BOOK

The self-contained classroom for students with developmental handicaps consisted of 4 boys and 8 girls from 9 to 12 years old. All the children were African-Americans. Their teacher, Charles Jones, was concerned about his students' self-perceptions and levels of self-esteem. Their informal verbal discussions about themselves, their aspirations, and their interpersonal interactions with each other were often negative. When frustrated academically or socially, the students frequently engaged in ethnic name-calling. The name-calling was often associated with skin color and their African heritage (e.g., "You're black"; "I'm not black"; "You're like those dirty Africans"; "My ancestors don't come from Africa!"). Self-deprecating statements, such as "I'm crazy," were also heard. When asked "What do you want to do for a living when you're an adult?" the children's responses typically involved sports, working in a fast-food restaurant, and motherhood, suggesting a limited view of future possibilities.

Collectively, the students did not feel good about themselves, nor did they appear comfortable with their ethnicity. Difficulty in performing academic tasks seemed to reinforce their feelings of inadequacy in general and their negative perceptions of their ethnicity in particular. Working with Bridgie Alexis Ford, a faculty member in special education at the University of Akron, Mr. Jones developed and implemented a cultural awareness project for his students. The project was designed to help the students learn factual information about the historical experiences and contributions of African-Americans. Jones and Ford believed that as a result of learning about their ancestors' experiences and examining their own feelings about those experiences, the students would develop positive feelings about their ethnic heritage. Positive feelings about one's cultural group are an important factor in developing self-esteem and self-confidence.

The cultural awareness unit took about 30 to 45 minutes each day for 10 weeks and revolved around the creation of an ethnic feelings book. The feelings book included both factual information about African-Americans and the students' interpretations of the feelings of their ancestors during various periods. The unit began with the positive aspects of African life prior to the slave-trade era, discussed slavery and segregation, identified actions by African-Americans to create freedom and equal opportunity, and focused on the students' positive characteristics and capabilities. After covering each part of the unit, the students created another section of their feelings book. The emphasis throughout the unit was on highlighting positive aspects and contributions and dispelling negative stereotypes.

a source of knowledge which will improve his community. To do this, black educators must begin to embrace positively results-oriented techniques such as precision teaching. . . . In the case of exceptional black children the major task is to provide them with the adaptive behaviors which will permit normalization of activities of daily living, the release of latent creativity, and provide a set of technical skills which will permit maximum independence in the community. (p. 170)

Much has been written about the unique experiences shared by Americans of African descent. Smith (1981) offers a review of the distinctive cultural and historical perspectives of black Americans, which have sometimes been associated with conflict and misunderstanding in school and other settings. According to Smith, many blacks feel that actions speak louder than words, that

Historical information and personal accounts were presented via low-vocabulary, high-interest, well-illustrated books and filmstrips, recordings, and West African artifacts. African-American leaders from the local community also visited the classroom and discussed their accomplishments and feelings with the students. These were some of the instructional activities that were part of the unit:

Brainstorming. To acquire background information about what the students already knew about their African ancestors.

Adoption of a tribe. Each student adopted one of the tribes portrayed in the books or filmstrips and prepared a report about the tribe. The class selected one of the reports, edited it, and included it in the feelings book.

Discussions about negative terminology and stereotypes assigned to slaves. Ethnic name-calling was also discussed.

Segregation simulation. At the beginning of one school day, half the class tied blue strings around their waists to designate themselves as segregated students (SS). Throughout the rest of that day, these students were treated in a discriminatory manner: They didn't get to use recreational equipment during recess, they could not use the restrooms at the times the non-SS students were using them, and they received no verbal attention or tangible reinforcement during normal class routines. The next day, the students switched roles so that everyone experienced the feelings of segregation.

Identification of positive attributes. Positive characteristics of relatives and community leaders whom the students admired were discussed. The students submitted typed paragraphs describing their talents and interests and indicating the types of jobs they believed they could pursue.

The students exhibited a great deal of enthusiasm and cooperative behavior throughout the project. Name-calling decreased, and when it did occur, the students began to reprimand one another. Multicultural activities are often restricted to a special day or week during the school year; for students with learning handicaps, Ford and Jones believe that an ongoing, systematic approach to cultural awareness is imperative.

From "An Ethnic Feelings Book: Created by Students with Developmental Handicaps" by B. A. Ford and C. Jones, 1990, Teaching Exceptional Children, 22,(4), pp. 36–39. Adapted by permission. ◆

talk is cheap, and that whites beguile each other with verbal discourse. Great importance is attached to people's nonverbal behavior; blacks may spend much time observing others to see "where they are coming from." ﹡

White teachers and counselors generally place a high value on eye contact during interpersonal communication. Many blacks, says Smith, engage in conversation without making eye contact at all times. They may even take part in other activities while still paying attention to a conversation. Smith relates an incident in which a teacher reprimanded a black student for keeping her head down during a swimming lesson; the student insisted she had been paying attention. The teacher then told the student to face her and look her squarely in the eye like the rest of the girls. "So I did," said the student. "The next thing I knew she was telling me to get out of the pool—that she didn't like the way I was looking at her" (p. 155). Communication styles may differ in other ways. Many blacks do not nod their heads or make little "um-hmm" noises during conversation, as whites do, to indicate that they are listening to someone (Hall, 1976). Sensitivity to language and communication practices is important in working with students and parents. However, Smith cautions against trying too hard, noting that blacks often resent white professionals who attempt to use black slang: "Anyone who tries too hard to show you that he understands blacks doesn't understand them at all" (Smith, 1981, p. 169).

The black family in the United States has been the focus of considerable study and interpretation. Norton (1983) describes the black family as a predominantly urban group dependent on the extended family for many support functions and states that "although approximately one-quarter of all black families could be considered in the middle income range, there is an increasing number of black families who are still very poor. The children of these families are growing up in a world that is increasingly separate from most whites, and even from more privileged black children" (p. 192). Poverty and unemployment are facts of life for many black families. Sleeter and Grant (1986), using statistics from the U.S. Department of Commerce, report that the average black family earns only 59% as much as the average white family. Four out of nine black children live in poverty (Kappan Special Report, 1990). The mortality rate for black infants is twice as high as it is for whites, and those surviving black infants have nine times more chance than white infants of being neurologically impaired (Kappan Special Report, 1990).

Smith (1981) contends that black families are basically intact social systems that have served as a source of strength and survival—contrary to the view of the black family as a decaying institution that is the source of many social problems. Smith also challenges the notion that the black family is a matriarchy. Black families with both parents present are similar to white families in their perceptions of power and decision making within the family unit. Many black families include extended relatives who live in or are welcome to drop in at any time. White visitors to the home may have different concepts of privacy and may feel uncomfortable having grandparents, cousins, siblings, and others present when a child's needs are being discussed.

The attitudes of some black parents toward their exceptional children may seem unfamiliar to nonblack professionals. They may be less inclined than whites to blame or punish themselves or to feel guilty for their children's disabilities or behavior problems. Differences in approach, it should be pointed out, are related to parents' economic and educational levels, as well as to their cultural background. More work needs to be done on the special needs of black exceptional children and on ways of improving cross-cultural communication and parent involvement (Olion, 1988).

In one of the few studies to explore racial differences in the perception of exceptionality, Schilit (1977) found that black and white college students held generally similar attitudes toward mental retardation, with two noteworthy exceptions: blacks were "more aware of the inherent dangers that persist in a low socioeconomic environment and what effect they can have on the individual in terms of development" (p. 190), and they held more pessimistic views of the employment potential of people with mental retardation. With respect to the second finding, Schilit conjectured that because the incidence of unemployment

Curriculum goals and instructional methods for children with disabilities, as with all children, should reflect an understanding, respect, and appreciation of each child's cultural and ethnic background.

is high in the black community as a whole, the black students believed that mentally retarded people would have even more difficulty finding employment.

Hispanic Americans

Hispanic refers to persons of different races and countries whose cultural heritage is tied to the Spanish language and the Latino culture (Fradd & Correa, 1989). During the past two decades, the Hispanic population in the United States has risen dramatically, and this growth is projected to continue even more rapidly in the coming years. Hispanic students make up about 15% of the total K–12 enrollment in U.S. schools.

The October 1989 issue of *Exceptional Children* is devoted to the multicultural needs of Hispanic students in special education.

As in virtually all cultures, the family plays a critical role in the early development and socialization of the exceptional Hispanic-American child. Rivera and Quintana Saylor (1977) offer their view of the traditional Spanish-speaking family.

First, the family is considered as the most important social unit, and individual interests or aspirations are subordinate to those of the family. Each member has a unique and responsible role with the father being the head and responsible for providing for his family as well as for their behavior in and out of the home. He has a great degree of freedom to practice his *machismo*, which is done in a strict but gentle manner. The mother devotes herself to her husband and children with her personal interests secondary to those. She has the greatest influence in the family but exercises it in subtle ways. The children are treasured and indulged with great amounts of personal and physical affection. They are not without responsibility, however, and this may take precedence over school or personal attainment. When a disabling condition interrupts this system, it may create a serious crisis. (p. 446)

The concept of *machismo* (maleness) referred to in this description has been the subject of much misinterpretation. Ruiz (1981) cautions against assumptions that Hispanic sex roles are uniform and rigid. Ruiz explains that the term *macho* (male) is used among Hispanics as a flattering term denoting "physical strength, sexual attractiveness, virtue, and potency" (p. 191). It is not meant to imply physical aggressiveness, dominance over women, sexual promiscuity, or excessive use of alcohol. Real masculinity among Hispanics attaches high value to "dignity in conduct, respect for others, love for the family, and affection for children" (Ruiz, 1981, p. 192).

Grossman (1984) describes the Hispanic family as "a fountain of emotional and economic security and support" where children are "brought up to believe that contributing to and sacrificing for the benefit of the group is more important than personal aggrandizement. As a result, they may be highly motivated to do things that have significance for their families, friends, and community. They may prefer to work in groups" (p. 216). Because of their respect for authority, some Hispanic parents "may have difficulty participating in the educational decision-making process as described by P. L. 94–142" (p. 218). They may express agreement with decisions made about their children even if they disagree with the decisions or do not understand them. Other Hispanic parents may be wary of signing documents such as IEPs.

Castaneda (1976) observes that many Mexican-American children work well on cooperative group projects, where they are not compelled to strive for individual gains. They may be reluctant to ask for a teacher's help; they are accustomed to having family members respond to their nonverbal behavior in a way that avoids the embarrassment of requesting help. In general, children and parents are likely to turn to members of the extended family when they need help, rather than rely on schools or agencies, which they regard as impersonal. Different value systems may also affect a child's classroom performance. Many non-Hispanic teachers adopt an objective, impartial attitude in school, in the interest of treating students fairly and equally; however, Hispanic children may take this as a sign of rejection, an indication that the teacher does not care about them. Castaneda (1976) suggests that the teacher of Mexican-American children develop close, personalized relationships with the students and use child-centered, socially reinforcing language, such as "I am proud of you" or "You did that very well."

> The teaching style which is most characteristic in the traditional Mexican-American community is modeling. The child learns to "do it like the teacher" and wants to become like the teacher. It is important, then, that the teacher relate personal anecdotes and be willing to interact with the child outside the classroom. The most effective rewards are those which result in a closer relationship between the child and the teacher. (p. 188)

Ortiz and Garcia (1986) report a recent decline in the percentage of Hispanic students labeled as mildly mentally retarded or as emotionally disturbed. They note that today "approximately 80% of all handicapped Hispanics are served in two language-related categories: learning disabilities and speech handicapped" (p. 10). This situation raises the importance of distinguishing differences from exceptionalities: Assessment procedures should "require evidence that the handicapping condition exists in the primary language, not only in English. . . . If the discrepancy occurs only in English, it is not a learning disability" (p. 11).

Bilingual education will be discussed later in this chapter.

Teachers may find it important to be aware of the nonverbal behaviors of their students and parents from Hispanic backgrounds. The significance of touching provides an illustration. Curt (1984) recalls that when she first came from Puerto Rico to a college in the Northeast, she was struck by the "strange noncontact, nontouching culture" in which students rarely made physical contact with each other. In contrast, "Latins touch to a degree that is outrageous and threatening and oftentimes insulting to most Anglos. . . . If two women of the same age and social status meet, there is hugging, kissing and rubbing of upper parts of bodies in some cases. If men of the same age and social status meet, there is beating of backs, a hug maybe, and the firm shaking of hands" (p. 22). Although non-Hispanic teachers will probably not find it feasible to adopt the nonverbal behaviors of another culture, teacher-student and teacher-parent communication may be enhanced by some knowledge of the different significance attached to touch, interpersonal distance, silence, dress, and gestures.

Asian-Americans

Asian-Americans constitute about 2% of the U.S. population. Exceptional children of Asian descent constitute a sizable and, in many areas, growing population. Some regions, notably Hawaii, California, and New York, have long-established Asian-American communities, and in these and many other states there is a large, recently arrived Asian population. The United States is currently receiving more refugees and immigrants than at any other time in history, and many are from such Asian countries as Cambodia, Korea, Laos, and Vietnam (Scholl, 1986b). Relatively few special education programs, however, have been established to address the particular needs of Asian-American students.

See "Refugee Children from Vietnam: Adjusting to American Schools" on page 509.

Wakabayashi (1977) considers Asian-Americans "the least acknowledged of the national minorities" in the United States (p. 430) and notes that there are widespread misconceptions of Asian-Americans as a monolithic group when, in reality, such cultures as Chinese, Japanese, and Vietnamese are quite different from one another. Leung (1988) reminds us that Asian-Americans are an "extremely diversified conglomerate of various Asiatic ethnicities, sometimes sharing only minority status" (p. 86).

Education is highly valued and is viewed as a means of upward mobility. For many years, teachers and scholars have been revered in China and other Asian countries. For parents influenced by their traditional cultural heritage, no sacrifice is too great to obtain a good education for their children. From the child's viewpoint, scholastic achievement is the highest tribute one could bring to his or her parents and family (Leung, 1988). This philosophy and work ethic has helped many Asian-American students excel in school.

Some educators however, are concerned that a stereotype of Asian students as hard-working, successful, and without problems has given them a "success image" that makes it difficult for many to believe that any Asian-American student may need special education services (Kim & Harh, 1983; Yee, 1988). There are Asian-American students with handicaps, and the combination of cultural differences on the part of their families and misconceptions by educators can hamper their identification and instruction.

Members of certain Asian-American populations may be reluctant to seek out special services for disabled children or adults. Sue (1981) notes that Asian parents emphasize their children's obligations to the family unit, and abnormal or deviant behaviors are handled within the family as much as possible. This suppression of public acknowledgment of disability probably means that there is a largely invisible population of disabled Asian-Americans. In Wakabayashi's (1977) view, the traditions and experiences of many Asian-Americans endow them with "values and attitudes that are often incongruent with the service delivery vehicles that exist in the public sector" (p. 432). Other observers note that it is more acceptable for Asian-Americans to admit to physical problems than to behavioral or psychological difficulties. This tendency may mean that, among Asian-Americans, only people with more severe emotional or behavior disorders seek help from schools, clinics, and other programs.

Special educators must be sensitive to the various ways different cultural groups respond to a disability.

REFUGEE CHILDREN FROM VIETNAM
Adjusting to American Schools

Tam Thi Dang Wei is a school psychologist who is Vietnamese. Wei points out that many Vietnamese refugee children encounter emotional, social, and educational problems in the United States because of different cultural traditions and expectations. The following incidents illustrate some cross-cultural difficulties that have arisen as Vietnamese students and American schools adjust to each other. Wei interprets each incident.

Incident: A Vietnamese girl in the 10th grade in Missouri reportedly refused to go to her gym class. When asked for a valid reason by the gym teacher, she simply said she did not like gym. Only much later did the real reason appear. The girl revealed to a Vietnamese friend that she objected to being seen bare-legged, wearing gym shorts.

Interpretation: Coming from a region of Vietnam where old customs and traditions were still strong and where women, both young and old, were never to be seen bare-legged, this girl confessed to an intense feeling of discomfort when the gym hour occurred. To provide a sense of measure to this interesting case, however, we must also mention the case of two Vietnamese high school girls, one in Georgia and the other in Maryland, who were drum majorettes for their respective high school bands.

Incident: An 8-year-old Vietnamese child in an elementary school in Maryland complained of a stomachache every day after lunch. His teacher was mystified, because the same food and milk did not make any other child in the class sick. The cause was later identified to be the fresh milk, which was perfectly good, but to which the boy's digestive system was not accustomed.

Interpretation: Food habits are different from one culture to the next. Rice is a staple in the Vietnamese diet, whereas bread is a staple in the American diet. Pork is preferred to beef by most Vietnamese; the reverse is true in the United States. Fresh milk is likely to give some Vietnamese an upset stomach. They are used to boiled rather than homogenized milk, and their bodies are said not to produce the necessary enzyme to digest fresh milk.

Incident: A teacher thought his Vietnamese student had an auditory discrimination problem. He found out later that some sounds in the English language do not exist in the Vietnamese language. The student simply could not hear them and thus could not pronounce them correctly. An-

other teacher was surprised to see a Vietnamese child color pictures of eggs brown and cows yellow. The surprise turned into laughter when a Vietnamese friend told the teacher that Vietnamese eggs are brown in color and there are more yellow cows in Vietnam than black or brown cows.

Interpretation: The language problem is still a major handicap for students. It is further complicated by the cultural trait of face-saving, which affects the pride and self-esteem of the Vietnamese and causes them frustration and a loss of motivation. It is important that American teachers understand the consequence of failure for these students.

Refugee children are a unique challenge for educators, not only because they can be misdiagnosed, misclassified, or misunderstood, but also because they may not receive appropriate services when they indeed have handicapping conditions.

From "The Vietnamese Refugee Child: Understanding Cultural Differences" by T. T. D. Wei in The Bilingual Exceptional Child *(pp. 197–212) by D. R. Omark and J. G. Erickson (Eds.), 1983, San Diego: College-Hill. Adapted by permission.* ◆

Brower (1983) observes that some Asian students may find it difficult to speak of their own accomplishments, to ask or answer questions in class, or to voluntarily express opinions, lest they appear to be showing off. Also, "personal matters that embarrass or cause hurt or stress are not usually discussed with anyone except family and very close friends" (p. 114). Some Asian students, Brower suggests, may need to be taught about American expectations and values so they can become more forthright and assertive in educational and employment situations.

"The toughest thing a teacher of Asian students must deal with is the silence; its reasons are complex," observes Fishman (1987, p. 85), who interviewed teachers and students in a largely Asian New York City high school. It may be difficult for a newly arrived student to become accustomed to the typical style of dialogue in American classrooms, in which teachers frequently address students by their first names, ask for their opinions, and seek to recognize individual students for their accomplishments. As one Asian student told Fishman, many of her peers are "afraid of the teacher because we respect the teacher—it's like a god, a mother."

Perhaps because of the tendency of many Asians to deal with exceptionality within the family setting, little has been written about specific approaches for educating disabled or gifted Asian-American students. The following perspectives, offered by Jerry Arakawa (1981), an Asian-American who is blind, may be helpful for educators to keep in mind as they seek to develop such approaches.

> Being disabled and Asian meant having an additional personality trait that can potentially cause shame to the family. Consequently, the disabled Asian youngster has a less outgoing personality and takes risks less willingly. In Western culture, individuality is praised. In Asian culture, anything that breaks homogeneity is troubling. And the disabled Asian knows he is different. The Asian perspective is to minimize the handicap. The emphasis is on adapting and doing as little out of the ordinary as possible. This even means you avoid legal actions against discrimination. To get employment, you tough it out. If buses are inaccessible, you say it doesn't really matter. Consumerism and advocacy are very hard for a disabled Asian to understand. He or she seeks to avoid underscoring a disability and focusing public attention on it. To do otherwise is discomforting. In the last few years, attitudes about disability in the Asian community have become more Western. But the basic values remain: Be a high achiever and transcend your disability. Asians want to excel. They want to be the best. (p. 1)

Native Americans

It is estimated that there are approximately 1,500,000 persons of Native American descent in the United States. About one-half of Native Americans live on or near reservations; the rest are integrated into the general population, mainly in urban areas (Little Soldier, 1990). Many federal, state, tribal, and local agencies provide medical, educational, and social services to Americans of Indian, Eskimo, or other Native ancestry. Information about the prevalence of exceptionality among Native American populations is difficult to obtain, but Ramirez and Johnson (1988) report that the categories of learning disabled and speech impaired accounted for over 80% of the more than 40,000 American Indian students receiving special education in 1986.

As noted earlier, Native Americans are a heterogeneous group. Although a certain cultural heritage and world view are shared by many Native Americans, as Little Soldier (1990) points out, "Tribal differences are very real and tribal affiliations are quite important to Indian people. . . . There is no such thing as a single 'Indian' culture. Navajos are as different culturally from the Siouxs as Canadians are from Mexicans" (pp. 66, 68).

Perhaps to a greater degree than most other cultures, Native Americans often absorb handicapped or disabled children into the family and community without removing them for special services. Non-Native professionals, in fact, often experience difficulty in setting up programs to identify and serve exceptional children on Indian reservations or in Native Alaskan communities (particularly if Native people are not involved in planning and carrying out the programs). Parents may resist having their children removed to be evaluated and educated in distant places.

Anderson and Ellis (1980) suggest that a first step in understanding the Native American's cultural differences is to appreciate the relationship between the individual and the tribe. The "wholeness of the tribe is what gives meaning to the part," they explain. "A flower petal has little beauty by itself but, when it is put together with the other parts of the flower, the whole, which includes the petal, is a thing of great beauty. . . . Indians will judge their worth primarily in terms of whether their behavior serves to better the tribe" (pp. 113–114). The tribe also influences how many Native Americans view knowledge and accomplishment. Unlike the European or Anglo view that promotes a single individual's understanding and achievements as a learning model, "the tribal form emphasizes knowledge after it works its way through the greatest number of community members" (Parent, 1985, p. 137).

Stewart (1977) illustrates the accepting nature of many Native American families toward a handicapped child by noting that it is extremely hard to estimate the deaf population among certain Indian groups. Deaf children frequently become shepherds or learn to perform other useful roles in the community; they are not enrolled in schools or classes for the deaf. Among many Native groups, it is not considered negative or tragic to have a child born with a disability; "it is assumed the child has the prenatal choice of how he wishes to be born and, if handicapped, is so by choice" (Stewart, 1977, p. 439). Indian languages also show a realistic and unemotional recognition of exceptionality. The Ute Indian term *n'kwat* is translated as "can't hear so can't talk," which Stewart considers much more descriptive than the archaic English term "deaf and dumb." Such attitudes of acceptance, however, may not extend to all exceptional children. Several observers have noted that Native Americans with obvious physical impairments and children who have seizures are often teased or regarded with alarm by their peers.

> Contrast this term with the labels discussed in Chapter 1.

Native American students, particularly those from reservations or remote communities, may face special difficulties in making the transition from school to independent and productive adulthood. Kleinfeld (1987) worked in an isolated Alaskan village where people typically supported themselves through a combination of hunting, casual employment, and government assistance programs. Conditions that led many students to drop out of postsecondary education and training programs included "(1) limited knowledge of the system among students and family members, (2) few models of adults who have blended Native and western lifestyles in personally satisfying ways, and (3) great discontinuity between the nurturant world of small, remote villages and the impersonality of a large, modern institution" (p. 553). A special postsecondary counseling program, in which Native students received extensive, personalized assistance in meeting the demands of college and employment, was successful in reducing the dropout rate and improving students' performance.

Sisk (1987) discusses the challenges in identifying and serving Native American students who are gifted and talented. The diversity of this population

Sisk (1987) also provides specific guidelines for identifying gifted children in other culturally diverse groups.

and the varying settings in which Native children are served have been difficult barriers to overcome in developing programs for gifted students. Some educators have found that gifted Native American students tend to have strong skills in observation, visual perception, problem solving, and memory. Activities should emphasize cooperative approaches to problems and deemphasize competition among peers. "The gifted American Indian will not be dominant but will display independence and curiosity in influencing others for the benefit of the group" (Sisk, 1987, p. 234).

Most suggestions for improving the lives of disabled Native Americans focus on broad issues of health, economics, and social development. Richardson (1981) shows that, on the average, the American Indian has a much lower income and shorter life expectancy than other Americans and that there is an extremely high incidence of unemployment, alcoholism, incarceration, and suicide among many Native groups. These problems, of course, merit the attention of the concerned teacher; on a more immediate level, however, researchers offer advice for improving interpersonal communication and classroom instruction with Native students and their families (Pepper, 1976; Richardson, 1981).

♦ Show children expected behaviors by modeling and having them observe, rather than by verbally instructing them.

♦ Don't reward or reprimand a child in front of the class. Quiet, private communication is usually preferable.

♦ Develop the child's self-concept with assuring statements, such as "You can do it." Recognize even partial success at a task.

♦ Social and academic competition among children may lead to problems; use activities in which children can share and work as teams.

♦ Do not overemphasize timed tests and assignments. Many Natives have a flexible attitude toward time and rules.

♦ Do not expect direct eye contact. A Native child may be conveying attention and respect by avoiding eye contact while listening.

♦ Display Native pictures or artifacts in your classroom or office; use materials that depict Native people realistically and with dignity.

♦ American Indians appreciate a gentle handshake, not overly firm. When greeting people, it is considered polite to offer them something, such as a cup of coffee or a glass of water.

♦ Avoid condescending statements and generalizations, such as "I have a good friend who is an Indian" or "Do you Eskimos believe in God?"

♦ Acceptance and restatement of a Native person's views are recommended in counseling situations. Emphasize careful listening. Periods of silence are usually acceptable.

Migrant Students

Migrant students are the children of farm workers who typically live in three or four different locations each year; they are usually Hispanic, but are also black, white, Asian, and Native American children. The migrant lifestyle is characterized by hard, often hazardous work at low wages; poor housing conditions; and

Opportunities to make friends can help develop both self-esteem and language skills.

limited health care. These factors, coupled with the discontinuity of schooling that migrant children experience as they follow the farm crops with their families and the difficulties of trying to cope with an educational system that typically does not use their native language (about 75% of migrants are Spanish-speaking) make migrant students one of the most "at-risk" populations of students in our schools (Salend, 1990).

Extrapolating from the estimated 800,000 migrant students in the United States, Baca and Harris (1988) suggest that about 80,000 migrant students are in need of special education. Yet, according to Perry (1984), only 8,000, or 1%, are receiving special education services, compared to 10% of the general school-age population.

Like other culturally diverse populations, migrant children's educational needs have been widely neglected until recently, when they became mandated and supported by federal and state legislation (notably P.L. 93–380). Procedures now exist to support the identification of migrant children and to help them obtain a free, appropriate program of public education. The U.S. Department of Education operates a national computerized file of information on migrant children, the Migrant Student Record Transfer System (MSRTS), to help schools in the difficult task of maintaining data on students' health, family, and educational performance.

The MSRTS is headquartered in Little Rock, Arkansas. See "For More Information" at the end of this chapter for other organizations that provide educational programming and assistance to migrant students.

Joyce King-Stoops (1980) has compiled a brief guide for teachers of migrant children. Some of her suggestions may also be applicable to other culturally diverse students with special needs. One strategy that has proven useful has been to employ high school or college students with migrant backgrounds (usually bilingual) as part-time aides in classrooms for younger children. This involvement improves the self-concept of both migrant children and aides, facilitates communication with parents, and, at the same time, encourages some young adults from this culture to consider teaching as a profession. Also, the money earned by the aides is generally greatly needed. King-Stoops emphasizes migrant students' need to experience acceptance and success in school, recommending the use of "short tasks that are appropriate and can be accomplished in a reasonable time" (p. 23).

Development of good language and reading patterns is prerequisite to success in school and to employment for most students. King-Stoops presents some activities designed to improve children's listening and speaking skills. Migrant children sometimes speak *pocho,* a mixture of English and Spanish. The teacher should encourage communication by listening first and then modeling standard speech patterns for the child.

> Child: It lunch time. I go walkando.
> Teacher: It's lunch time. We'll all go walking to lunch now. (King-Stoops, 1980, p. 29)

Teachers who work with migrant students often report low levels of self-esteem (Salend et al. 1984). It is understandable that the mobility, poverty, and other conditions inherent in the migrant lifestyle often adversely affect self-concept development. Teaching all students about the migrant lifestyle can reduce the isolation migrant students often experience as well as increase their feelings of self-confidence and worth. For example, a teacher might incorporate these activities into the curriculum (Salend, 1990):

♦ Having migrant students and their parents discuss their experiences and the places where they have lived.

♦ Developing a map that traces the path of a family's migrations.

♦ Establishing a pen-pal system whereby full-year students write to their migrant classmates as they travel around the country.

♦ Discussion of the importance of migrant workers to our society.

♦ Planting and harvesting a class garden. (p. 19)

■ ASSESSING CULTURALLY DIVERSE EXCEPTIONAL CHILDREN

Tests are widely used in special education. But as our review of assessment techniques has shown for virtually every exceptionality, the testing methods used to identify students for special education services represent an inexact science at best and at times little more than guesswork. The likelihood of obtaining valid, accurate, and unbiased assessment results are even less when the student in question is from a culturally diverse background. Figueroa (1989) called the current practice of psychological testing of children from linguistic minorities "random chaos" because it is so fraught with problems.

J. R. Brown (1982) discusses several ways that tests—traditionally standardized on white, English-speaking, middle-class children—may discriminate against those from different cultural backgrounds.

1. The tests use formats and items that are more germane to one group than another. For example, the test may include restrictive time limits, vocabulary tasks that require the child to read the word, items that require a child to read in a task designed to measure listening comprehension ability, and so on.

2. Children have differing amounts of "test wiseness," which is more likely to be a problem with the preschool-aged child than with the school-aged child. For example, white, middle-class preschool-aged children tend to be familiar with question-and-answer formats, with puzzles, and with pointing and naming tasks often included on tests. The same degree of familiarity cannot be assumed when evaluating a disadvantaged child.

3. The skills reflected by the test items may not be relevant to the skills demanded by the disadvantaged and culturally different child's environment. . . . [T]he tests, rather than assessing the disadvantaged child's ability, measure the extent to which such children have assimilated aspects of the dominant culture. (p. 164)

The practice of placing children in special education programs for handicapped or gifted students solely because of their performance on standardized intelligence tests is rapidly disappearing. It is widely believed that, in the past, overreliance on IQ tests resulted in the inappropriate labeling and placement of many students from diverse cultural backgrounds; IQ tests do not present a fair or complete measure of the intelligence of culturally diverse students.

Issues in IQ testing were discussed more fully in Chapter 3.

Hilliard (1975) calls attention to sources of cultural bias in several widely used tests of cognitive ability. These tests appear to be based on the faulty premise that every child comes to the test with a similar background of life experiences. Hilliard cites the following examples of potentially unfair test items:

> On one test, a child must be familiar with such words as *wasp, captain, hive, casserole, shears, cobbler,* or *hydrant.* On another test, a child must know the distance from Boston to London [and] why icebergs melt. . . . The child, in order to get the answers correct, must assume that women are weak and need protection, that policemen are always nice, that labor laws are just. How is the examiner to distinguish ignorance from disagreement? (p. 22)

The Focus feature on pages 522–523 illustrates possible cultural bias in assessment.

Some interesting evidence indicates that a child's performance in testing situations may be heavily influenced by the environment and the examiner. Labov (1975) presents a case study of the verbal behavior of an 8-year-old black child named Leon. When Leon was tested in school by a white interviewer who placed objects on a table and said, "Tell me everything you can about this," his response was minimal, consisting mostly of silence and one-word utterances. It appeared that Leon was functioning well below his age level and perhaps had a serious communication disorder or mental retardation. On another occasion, however, Leon was interviewed by a black examiner who took him to an apartment in a familiar neighborhood, brought along Leon's best friend and a supply of potato chips, and sat down on the floor with the child. In this situation Leon spoke much more fluently; he had a great deal to say to the adult and to his friend. Labov has also performed a detailed linguistic analysis of the nonstandard English used by many black children and has concluded that traditional classroom tests and tasks have little relevance or accuracy. "There is no reason to believe that any nonstandard vernacular is in itself an obstacle to learning" (Labov, 1975, p. 127).

Even though Labov's case study illustrates that one child responded differently to different examiners, it should not be assumed that the race, sex, or age of a teacher or examiner will inevitably affect a child's performance. J. R. Brown (1982) reviewed several studies of the effects of examiner race on the performance of culturally diverse children and concluded that there was no general tendency of black and Hispanic students to score higher or lower when tested by white, black, or Hispanic examiners. Characteristics such as the examiner's "ability to evidence a warm, responsive, receptive, but firm style" were found to be more important than race or ethnic group in motivating children to do their best. "This does not preclude the possibility that ethnic or racial variables can influence performance, but it does suggest that to study race alone—without considering other interactional variables—is likely to be futile" (J. R. Brown, 1982, p. 165).

Mercer (1981) suggests that observation of a child's behavior outside school, in the family and neighborhood, may be more valuable than formal tests in determining abilities and needs and in particular may help differentiate learning disabled from mentally retarded students. If a child is "learning the skills needed to cope intelligently with the nonacademic world, then s/he may be ignorant of the skills needed to succeed in school but is not mentally retarded" (Mercer, 1981, p. 101). Dent (1976) emphasizes the importance of precise descriptions of behaviors—including antecedents and consequences. In certain cultures and settings, loud talking is not always equivalent to boisterous or aggressive behavior. And hitting and name-calling may not be hostile—they may represent a sign of respect or affection (Dent, 1976). Interpretations and value judgments should not be used in reporting children's behavior.

Along with objective recording of behaviors, a child's social and cultural background should be taken into account when assessing performance. What is normal and acceptable in a child's culture may be regarded as abnormal or unacceptable in school and may result in conflict, mislabeling, or punishment. Gallimore, Boggs, and Jordan (1974) offer the example of several native Hawaiian children who sought help from other children on tests and tasks and seemed to pay little attention to the teacher. This behavior was interpreted as cheating and inattentiveness. Closer observation of the children's home and community environments, however, revealed that the Hawaiian children were typically peer-oriented. It was normal for them to share in the responsibility of caring for each other, and they often worked cooperatively on tasks rather than following the directions of an adult.

Cox and Ramirez (1981) report that even though generalizations cannot be made about the learning styles of any group of students, it appears that many black, Hispanic, and other culturally diverse children are more group-oriented, more sensitive to the social environment, and more positively responsive to adult modeling than are white students. Students from certain cultural backgrounds may not learn effectively in highly competitive situations or on nonsocial tasks. They may be uncomfortable with trial-and-error approaches and may not be interested in the fine details of certain concepts and materials.

Nondiscriminatory assessment requires that decisions be based on varied and accurate information. Building rapport with children before testing them; observing their behavior in school, home, and play settings; and consulting with their parents can help teachers and examiners become more aware of cultural differences and reduce the number of students inappropriately placed in special education programs. Paraprofessional personnel or volunteers who are familiar with a child's language and/or cultural background have proven to be valuable assistants in many testing situations (Mattes & Omark, 1984).

As J. R. Brown (1982) notes, limited use of language is not synonymous with limited intellectual ability: "Some culturally different children are virtually silent in the testing situation, and the examiner may need to listen to the child in play with other children to hear a representative sample of the child's language" (p. 170). Standardized tests in English, obviously, are not likely to give an accurate picture of a child's abilities if she comes from a non-English-speaking home. "If the student's primary language is Spanish, Navajo, or Thai, the only justification for testing in English is to determine the student's facility in this second language" (Lewis & Doorlag, 1991, p. 361).

P. L. 94–142 specifies that assessment for the purpose of identifying and placing children with disabilities must be conducted in the child's native language. Figueroa, Fradd, and Correa (1989), however, point out a serious flaw in the way the law can be implemented.

> A curious and perhaps vicious anomaly exists between the law and its regulations. Whereas the actual legislation defines "native language" as the language of the home, . . . the regulations degenerate the intent of the law by defining "native language" as the language normally used by the child in school. Most bilingual children quickly acquire a conversational English that may not support academic development in English. For them, the regulations in P.L. 94–142 preclude any primary language support. As it has turned out, the act's brand of special education for Hispanic children from native language homes has perpetuated preexisting problems. (p. 175)

Unfortunately, when an examiner does wish to use the child's native language, there are not many reliable tests available in languages other than English, and translation or adaptation of tests into other languages poses certain problems (Cummins, 1989). Alzate (1978), for example, reviewed several studies of the performance of Spanish-speaking children on translated versions of English tests and concluded that translated tests are generally unreliable. DeAvila (1976) points out the great variety in language within Hispanic populations and notes that when Mexican-American children were given a test in Spanish that was developed with a population of Puerto Rican children, they performed even more poorly than on an admittedly unfair English test. To illustrate the confusion that may result from inappropriate translations, DeAvila observes that a Spanish-speaking child may use any one of several words to describe a kite, depending on the family's country of origin: *cometa, huila, volantin, papalote,* or *chiringa.* Thus, although translation of tests and other materials into a child's native language may be helpful in many instances, care must be taken to avoid an improper translation that may actually do a disservice to the linguistically different child.

It is not always easy to distinguish between children whose learning and communication problems result from disabilities and those who are solely in need of instruction in English. The high number of language minority students in special education classes, however, implies a need for tests and referral procedures that will "help teachers to distinguish differences from exceptionalities for language minority students" and to accommodate the differences in the least restrictive educational setting (Teacher Education Division, 1986, p. 25).

The law also requires that notice of IEP and placement meetings and other important conferences be given to parents in their native language.

Assessment of children whose native language is not English must be handled with great skill and care.

Ortiz and Yates (1988) recommend the following policies to govern assessment of linguistically different students for eligibility and placement in special education programs.

1. *Assessment of the student's language proficiency must precede assessment of skills in any other area.* These assessments should not be confined to English, but must also include assessment of competence in the student's native language.

2. *To be truly handicapped, a child must be handicapped in his/her native or dominant language, not merely in English.* Policy must be formulated stating that a student who is not handicapped in the native language is not a handicapped student.

3. *Because of the paucity of standardized instruments for students with limited English proficiency and/or bilingual students, adaptations of assessment procedures and instruments are necessary.* All adaptations, however, must be documented and described in the student's records.

4. *It must be recognized that scores obtained for language minority students are most often a minimal, rather than a maximal, indication of abilities.* For a variety of reasons, second language learners will score less than their potential. It is incumbent upon assessment personnel to be sensitive to this fact and to articulate it in both written records and decision-making contexts.

5. *Special educators, parents, and regular educators must insist that assessments are conducted only by personnel fluent in the student's dominant language.*

6. *The traditional concept of an annual review is often inappropriate for language minority students.* These students are continuously enhancing both their English and their native language skills. Results from an initial assessment must lead to a sequence of more frequent follow-up evaluations.

Bias and discrimination can also occur in the referral process, when children's records are reviewed and decisions are made about what type of services to provide. In the opinion of some educators, a child's race, family background, and economic circumstances—rather than actual performance and needs—unfairly influence the label he is likely to receive and the degree to which he will be removed from the regular classroom.

The prereferral process shown in Figure 12.1 was developed by Ortiz and Garcia (1988) as a means of making sure that curriculum and instruction are responsive to the linguistic and cultural needs of Hispanic students who are experiencing difficulty in the regular classroom *before* they are referred for formal assessment to determine special education placement. Although the model was presented in reference to Spanish-speaking students, it is a sound approach to helping improve the quality of regular education for *any* student who is experiencing academic difficulty. By systematically addressing the questions as illustrated in the model, both special and regular educators can work together to improve the student's performance in the mainstream classroom prior to movement to a more restrictive environment.

■ BILINGUAL SPECIAL EDUCATION

The National Center for Educational Statistics estimated that in 1980 there were over 30 million people in the United States whose first language was not English. Today, it is likely that there are more than 10 million school-age children with *limited English proficiency* (LEP) because their first language is not English. Bilingual or language minority children have "been exposed to two languages in natural speaking contexts [and] come from homes where they have made functional use of a language other than that of the dominant culture during interactions with one or more family members" (Mattes & Omark, 1984, p. 2). Some school districts offer programs of *bilingual education*—"the use of two languages as media of instruction for a child or a group of children in part or all of the school curriculum" (Cohen, 1975, p. 18). Bilingual education programs have as their primary goal the academic development of students. That is, the major purpose is not to teach English per se, but to teach LEP students the basic skills, concepts, and knowledge of the school curriculum in the language they know best.

For students who are both linguistically different and disabled, their attempts to succeed in school are especially challenging. Not only must they work to overcome the difficulties posed by their disability, but they must do so in an environment where instruction takes place in a foreign language and

FIGURE 12.1

A prereferral process for preventing inappropriate placements of culturally diverse students in special education. (*Source:* From "A Prereferral Process for Preventing Inappropriate Placements of Culturally Diverse Students in Special Education" by A. A. Ortiz & S. B. Garcia, in *Schools and the Culturally Diverse Exceptional Student: Promising Practices and Future Directions* (p. 9) by A. A. Ortiz and B. A. Ramirez (Eds.), 1988, Reston, VA: Council for Exceptional Children. Reprinted by permission.)

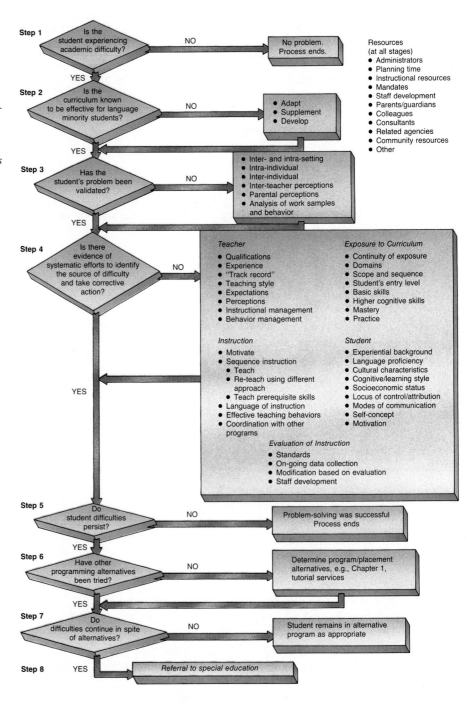

where opportunities to use their native language are too infrequent. For these children, a program of **bilingual special education** may be needed. Baca and Cervantes (1989) define bilingual special education as

the use of the home language and the home culture along with English in an individually designed program of special instruction for the student. Bilingual special education considers the child's language and culture as foundations upon which an appropriate education may be built. The primary purpose of bilingual special education is to help each individual student achieve a maximum potential for learning. (p. 18)

In response to the objection to bilingual special education on the basis that it is too much to ask special educators, who already face the difficult task of teaching basic skills to a child with disabilities, to do so in a second language, Baca and Cervantes (1989) reply that just the opposite is true:

> The imparting of basic skills may be facilitated considerably if one understands that the child's culture and language are the foundations upon which an appropriate education may be built. . . . In short, building on children's acquired repertoires is fundamental to sound educational practice. The English language and Anglo cultural skills are actually the additional materials. (p. 18)

Most bilingual education programs usually emphasize either a transitional or a maintenance approach. In a *transitional* program, the student's first language and culture are used only to the extent necessary to function in the school until English is mastered sufficiently for all instruction. Transitional programs do not teach reading and writing in the native language.

Some educators (e.g., Ada, 1986; Cardenas, 1986) maintain that it is a mistake for a bilingual child to make the transition to English too rapidly and that school instruction should be given in both the native language and in English. "The use of language is imperative to the intellectual development of the child. . . . [R]ather than risk premature restriction of native-language usage and communication capability, I recommend continuation of the use of the native language until there is complete assurance of sufficient mastery of the English language" (Cardenas, 1986, p. 361). Although acknowledging that the development of solid cognitive and linguistic skills in a first language is important, Glenn (1986) points out that "the most critical years of language development have already passed before children come to school. . . . [W]e may be perpetuating and compounding the original linguistic confusion by presenting two languages to children who have enough difficulty with one" (p. 655).

A bilingual program with a goal of *maintenance* encourages children to develop and maintain their native language (including reading and writing) and culture along with English. Cummins (1989) stresses the importance of encouraging children to develop their first-language skills (L1). He cites several studies suggesting that a major predictor of academic success for linguistically different students is the extent to which their native language and culture are incorporated into the school program. Cummins states that even where programs of bilingual education are not offered, schools can encourage and promote children's skills and pride in their first language. He recommends several specific strategies identified by New Zealand educators:

♦ Encourage students to use their L1 around the school.

♦ Provide opportunities for students from the same ethnic group to communicate with one another in their L1.

♦ Recruit people who can tutor students in their L1.

♦ Provide books written in the various languages.

TRY TAKING A CULTURALLY SPECIFIC TEST

Critics have charged that most standardized intelligence and achievement tests are culturally biased. That is, because the tests are developed by and for white, primarily middle-class individuals, some of the items may discriminate against anyone from a different background. To get a feeling for what it might be like to take a culturally specific test, try to answer each of the sample items below. If they appear difficult, confusing, foreign, or unanswerable, then you are beginning to understand how test questions can be inexorably entwined with culture.

The first four test items are taken from "People Ain't Dumb—It's Them Tests!" (compiled by the editors of the *Appalachian Review* at West Virginia University) and are based on Appalachian culture. The last four items are taken from The Hana-Butta Test and are based on Hawaiian culture. Correct answers appear at the end of the test.

1. Blue tick is

   a. an insect
   b. a food stamp
   c. hound dog
   d. NRA sticker

2. Before it is fit to drink, moonshine must be

   a. aged three months
   b. aged three weeks
   c. aged three days
   d. cooled

3. The most successful method for catching catfish is

   a. gigging
   b. setting a trot line
   c. dynamiting
   d. creating electric shock with two pokers and a car battery

4. A gee-haw-whinny-diddle is a

   a. good time
   b. harness for a horse
   c. toy
   d. type of persimmon

- ♦ Incorporate greetings and information in the various languages in newsletters and other school communications.
- ♦ Provide bilingual and multilingual signs.
- ♦ Display pictures and objects of the various cultures in the school.
- ♦ Create study units that incorporate the students' L1.
- ♦ Encourage students to write contributions in their L1 for school newspapers and magazines.
- ♦ Encourage parents to help in the classroom, library, playground, and in clubs.
- ♦ Invite second-language learners to use their L1 during assemblies and other official school functions.

5. If you were at home and someone told you to get "da kine," they would probably mean

   a. a glass of water
   b. a towel
   c. an ash tray
   d. dried fish
   e. any of the above

6. Pakalolo is

   a. salted raw fish and seaweed
   b. whiskey made from ti-root
   c. marijuana
   d. liquor
   e. acid

7. If someone wanted to say dinner was delicious, he would say it was

   a. papa's
   b. kukui
   c. ewa
   d. lola
   e. ono

8. Hana-butta is known statewide as

   a. high butterfat Hana butter
   b. mucus running from the nose of a person with a bad cold
   c. Hana Dairy's margarine
   d. a plain ol' peanut butter sandwich
   e. Toto's Snack Bar's famous peanut butter

Answers: (1) c; (2) d; (3) c; (4) c; (5) e; (6) c; (7) e; (8) d.

From Mental Retardation *(2nd ed.) (p. 124–125) by J. R. Patton, J. S. Payne, and M. Beirne-Smith, 1986, Columbus, OH: Merrill. Reprinted by permission.* ◆

At present, all state and federal laws providing support for bilingual education favor only transitional models. But, as Baca and Cervantes (1989) point out, the laws do not prevent school districts from offering maintenance programs if they desire.

A *restoration* model of bilingual education seeks to restore the language and cultural heritage of the students' ancestors that has been lost or diminished through cultural assimilation. *Enrichment* programs of bilingual education are designed to teach a new language and cultural ways to a group of monolingual students; for example, some school districts now offer language "immersion schools" in which all or most instruction is provided in a second language (Spanish and French are the most common).

Educators disagree about the most effective methods for teaching bilingual students. Former U.S. Secretary of Education William J. Bennett (1986) has written that some children "come from families who encourage their acquisition of English; some run in peer groups where the native language is a matter of pride. Some arrive speaking languages from which the transition to English is relatively easy; others speak languages whose entire structure is perplexingly different from ours" (p. 62). Bennett maintains that the choice of specific methods to teach bilingual children should be a local decision, but he argued strongly that "all American children need to learn to speak, read, and write English as soon as possible" (p. 62). Some professionals and legislators have called for designating English as the "exclusive official language of the United States" (Glenn, 1986). Adopting such a policy, however, would probably discourage schools from offering instruction in students' native languages.

Research in bilingual education has not provided clear guidelines to methodology. There is general agreement, however, that children acquire English most effectively through interactions with teachers, parents, and peers. A child who engages in and talks about interesting experiences will be more likely to develop good English skills than a child who is limited to classroom instruction and teacher correction of errors. Efforts should be made to give bilingual exceptional children a wide variety of opportunities to explore the world through language.

■ GUIDELINES FOR TEACHERS OF CULTURALLY DIVERSE EXCEPTIONAL CHILDREN

How then, does one teach exceptional children from culturally diverse backgrounds? To return to the question posed earlier: Does a teacher with students from four different cultural backgrounds need four different methods of teaching? The answer is both "no" and "yes." For the first answer, it is our view that systematic instructional procedures apply to children of all cultural backgrounds. For the most part, good teaching is good teaching. Indeed, when exceptional students have the additional special need of adjusting to a new or different culture or language, it is even more important for the teacher to plan individualized activities, convey expectations clearly, observe and record behavior precisely, and give the child specific, immediate reinforcement and feedback in response to performance. These procedures, coupled with a helpful and friendly attitude, can help increase the culturally different exceptional child's motivation and achievement in school. But the systematic teacher is, by definition, responsive to changes (or lack of change) in individual students' performance. So it can be argued that the effective teacher needs as many different ways of teaching as there are students in the classroom—regardless of their cultural backgrounds.

We believe this argument is basically true. But it also begs the real question of how cultural and language differences affect a child's *responsiveness* to instruction and, hence, whether those effects warrant different approaches to teaching. So while the basic methods of systematic instruction remain the same, teachers who will be most effective in helping exceptional children from culturally diverse backgrounds achieve will be those who are sensitive to and respectful of their students' heritage and values. A teacher does not have to share his students' culture and native language to serve them effectively, but a teacher will likely be quite ineffective in helping his students achieve in the classroom if he ignores those differences.

Fortunately, multicultural education is becoming a required component in many teacher education programs, and educators are learning how to become more accepting and supportive of cultural differences. As a measure of one's beliefs about culture and its importance to teaching, for example, both practicing and prospective teachers can complete an instrument like the Multicultural Self-Report Inventory (Slade & Conoley, 1989) (Figure 12.2). A low score indicates less multicultural bias; a higher score suggests greater discomfort with the concept. Slade and Conoley (1989) describe several activities that are part of a 2-week module used in a preservice teacher training course designed to develop positive attitudes toward cultural diversity in the classroom.

When developing services to meet the needs of an exceptional child from a culturally diverse background, teachers should obtain as much information as possible about the child, the family, and the cultural group. One useful strategy is to interview parents and others who are familiar with the child and her particular cultural environment. The following questions might be among those asked in an interview:

♦ Why have members of the cultural group left their homeland?
♦ Why have members of the cultural group settled in the local community?
♦ To what extent do members of the cultural group experience poverty?
♦ What is the typical family size?
♦ What roles are assigned to individual family members?
♦ What customs, values, and beliefs in the culture have relevance in understanding children's behavior?
♦ What are the social functions and leisure activities in which members of the cultural group participate?
♦ How do members of the cultural group view education?
♦ How do members of the cultural group view handicapped individuals? (Mattes & Omark, 1984, pp. 43–45)

Information gained from such questions can form a basis for determining appropriate and reinforcing activities. It will also enhance the teacher's understanding of a child's behavior in school and facilitate communication with parents.

The teacher of culturally diverse exceptional children should adopt a flexible teaching style, establish a positive climate for learning, and use a variety of approaches to meet individual student needs. With a caring attitude, careful assessment and observation of behavior, and the use of appropriate materials and community resources, the teacher can do a great deal to help exceptional children from different cultural or language backgrounds experience success in school.

MULTICULTURAL SELF-REPORT INVENTORY							
		SA = Strongly Agree MA = Moderately Agree U = Undecided MD = Moderately Disagree SD = Strongly Disagree				
		SA	MA	U	MD	SD
	1. I am interested in exploring cultures different from my own.	1	2	3	4	5
(−)	2. I have enough experience with cultures different from my own.	1	2	3	4	5
(0)	3. I seem to like some cultures and ethnic groups better than others.	1	2	3	4	5
(−)	4. Part of the role of a good teacher is to encourage children to adopt middle class values.	1	2	3	4	5
(−)	5. I feel that cultural differences in students do not affect students' behavior in school.	1	2	3	4	5
(−)	6. As students progress through school, they should adopt the mainstream culture.	1	2	3	4	5
	7. I am comfortable around people whose cultural background is different from mine.	1	2	3	4	5
	8. I can identify attitudes of my own that are peculiar to my culture.	1	2	3	4	5
	9. I believe I can recognize attitudes or behaviors in children that are a reflection of cultural or ethnic differences.	1	2	3	4	5
	10. I feel I can take the point of view of a child from a different culture.	1	2	3	4	5

FIGURE 12.2

Multicultural Self-Report Inventory. Items marked by a zero (0) have no positive or negative relevance and are included to lessen the probability of giving answers just because they are socially acceptable. Items that are marked with a minus (−) are scored negatively. The lower the score, the more accepting and supportive the person's attitude about cultural differences. (*Source:* From "Multicultural Experiences for Special Educators" by J. C. Slade and C. W. Conoley, 1989, *Teaching Exceptional Children, 22*(1), p. 62. Reprinted by permission.)

■ IN CLOSING: INTERNATIONAL PERSPECTIVES

The principal focus of this chapter is understanding and meeting the needs of exceptional children in our own country who come from diverse ethnic and cultural backgrounds. It is also worth noting that special education, like other fields, is increasingly global in scope. More than 70% of the world's total population of disabled persons is found in the developing countries (Marfo, 1986).

Through international travel, conferences, and publications, American educators have learned about approaches to the education and employment of exceptional individuals in many other countries and in some cases have incorporated aspects of these techniques into their own programs. For example,

		SA	MA	U	MD	SD
(−)	11. It makes me uncomfortable when I hear people talking in a language that I cannot understand.	1	2	3	4	5
(−)	12. Values and attitudes learned in minority cultures keep children from making progress in school.	1	2	3	4	5
(−)	13. Only people who are part of a culture can really understand and empathize with children from that culture.	1	2	3	4	5
(−)	14. I have had few cross-cultural experiences.	1	2	3	4	5
	15. Multicultural education is an important part of a school curriculum.	1	2	3	4	5
(0)	16. I am prejudiced in favor of some ethnic or cultural group or groups.	1	2	3	4	5
(−)	17. Some ethnic groups make less desirable citizens than others.	1	2	3	4	5
	18. Some ethnic groups are more reluctant to talk about family matters than other cultural groups.	1	2	3	4	5
	19. Children from differing ethnic groups are likely to differ in their attitudes toward teacher authority.	1	2	3	4	5
(−)	20. Personally, I have never identified any prejudice in myself.	1	2	3	4	5
(−)	21. I am prejudiced *against* some ethnic or cultural groups.	1	2	3	4	5
(−)	22. In the United States, given equal intelligence and physical ability, every individual has equal access to success.	1	2	3	4	5

FIGURE 12.2
continued

our approaches to normalization—integrating people with disabilities into their own communities—are derived largely from Scandinavian countries. At a time when most Americans with severe mental retardation were in large, impersonal institutions, "the Danish and Swedish institutions and community residences were more like well-kept, comfortable, and pleasant homes" (Goldstein, 1984, p. 80). The concept of the *educateur*—a professional who plays an active, varied role in the education and adjustment of children with emotional disorders—originated in France and has been widely adopted in the United States and Canada. The order, discipline, and academic emphasis in Japanese schools have attracted the interest of many American educators (Ohanian, 1987). Others have studied methods of communication used with deaf and children who are deaf-blind in the Netherlands, approaches to the diagnosis and treatment of learning disabilities in the Soviet Union, and techniques for teaching reading to non-English-speaking native children in Australia and New Zealand.

An international perspective is also evident in the growing number of American special educators who have worked in the developing regions of the world, principally in Africa, Asia, and Latin America. They have assisted host-country colleagues in such tasks as assessing children with disabilities, setting up special education programs, and training teachers and parents. Opportunities for international service can be arranged through governmental agencies—such as the Peace Corps, the Fulbright Scholar program, the Agency for International Development, or the U.S. Department of Education Teacher Exchange Programs—or through private, charitable, or religious organizations.

SUMMARY

Reasons for Concern

♦ Though cultural diversity is a strength of our society, many exceptional students still experience discrimination because of their race, social class, or other differences from the majority. Educators must avoid stereotypes based on race or culture.

♦ About one-third of the children in special education programs are members of culturally diverse groups.

♦ Assessment of students for placement in special education should be fair; referral should be based on each child's needs rather than on background.

Culture, Cultural Pluralism, and Multicultural Education

♦ Special educators should be aware of each child's cultural background in evaluating classroom behaviors.

♦ Multicultural education actualizes cultural pluralism.

♦ As is the case with regular education, the special educator must remember that within each cultural group, students remain heterogeneous.

Some Concerns of Specific Culturally Diverse Groups

♦ Hispanic families often place the interests of the family above the interests of the individual.

♦ Mexican-American children often respond well to close, personalized relationships with teachers.

♦ Classrooms should incorporate the Spanish language and Hispanic culture to facilitate communication with children and their parents.

♦ Native Americans tend to absorb handicapped children into the family and community rather than to segregate them.

♦ Disabled Asian-Americans are a sizable, growing population but may be hard to identify because of the culture's attitudes toward disability and achievement. Asian-Americans often deal with exceptionality within the family, rather than seeking outside services.

♦ Exceptional students from bilingual backgrounds prompt a number of special concerns. Lack of English proficiency should not be confused with a handicapping condition, and assessment in the native language is essential.

♦ Migrant children, many of whom are from culturally diverse backgrounds, are likely to require special instructional programs.

Assessing Culturally Diverse Exceptional Children

♦ Objective, interdisciplinary assessment may help overcome some of the traditional difficulties in assessing culturally diverse children. Assessment should include observing the child outside the school.

♦ Limited English language proficiency use does not indicate limited intellectual ability.

♦ P.L. 94–142 specifies conducting assessment in the child's native language.

Bilingual Special Education

♦ Bilingual special education uses the child's home language and home culture along with English in an individually designed education program.

♦ Most bilingual special education programs take either a transitional or a maintenance approach.

Guidelines for Teachers of Culturally Diverse Exceptional Children

♦ Regardless of their cultural background, all children benefit from good, systematic instruction.

♦ The teacher must, however, be sensitive to the extent to which cultural and language differences affect a child's responsiveness to instruction.

In Closing: International Perspectives

♦ Special education is increasingly global in scope.

♦ The United States' approach to normalization derives from Scandinavian practices.

♦ Many American special educators are working in developing regions of the world.

FOR MORE INFORMATION

Books

Baca, L. M., & Cervantes, H. T. (1989). *The bilingual special education interface* (2nd ed.). Columbus, OH: Merrill.

Banks, J. A. (1988). *Multiethnic education: Theory and practice* (2nd ed.). Boston: Allyn & Bacon.

Banks, J. A., & Banks, C. A. M. (Eds.). (in press). *Multicultural education: Issues and perspectives* (2nd ed.). Boston: Allyn & Bacon.

Cheng, L. L. (1987). *Assessing Asian language performance*. Rockville, MD: Aspen.

Fradd, S. H., & Tikunoff, W. J. (Eds.). (1987). *Bilingual education and bilingual special education: A guide for administrators*. Boston: Little, Brown.

Gollnick, D. M., & Chinn, P. C. (1986). *Multicultural education in a pluralistic society* (2nd ed.). Columbus, OH: Merrill.

Kitano, M. K., & Chinn, P. C. (Eds.). (1986). *Exceptional Asian children and youth*. Reston, VA: Council for Exceptional Children.

Marfo, K., Walker, S., & Charles, B. (Eds.). (1986). *Childhood disability in developing countries: Issues in habilitation and special education*. New York: Praeger.

Mattes, L. J., & Omark, D. R. (1984). *Speech and language assessment for the bilingual handicapped*. San Diego: College-Hill.

Ortiz, A. A., & Ramirez, B. A. (Eds.). (1988). *Schools and the culturally diverse exceptional student: Promising practices and future directions*. Reston, VA: Council for Exceptional Children.

Tiedt, P. L., & Tiedt, I. M. (1986). *Multicultural teaching: A handbook of activities, information, and resources* (2nd ed.). Boston: Allyn & Bacon.

Willig, A. C., & Greenberg, H. F. (1986). *Bilingualism and learning disabilities: Policy and practice for teachers and administrators*. New York: American Library.

Organizations

Division for Culturally and Linguistically Diverse Exceptional Learners (DDEL), Council for Exceptional Children, 1920 Association Drive, Reston, VA 22091. DDEL, one of the newest divisions of CEC, publishes the bi-annual *DDEL Newsletter* and an annual monograph on the needs of culturally diverse exceptional children.

BUENO Center for Multicultural Education, College of Education, University of Colorado, Boulder, CO 80309-0249 (Leonard Baca, Director). The BUENO Center conducts research, implements pre- and inservice teacher training programs, and disseminates information about multicultural education through various publications.

ERIC Clearinghouse on Rural Education and Small Schools, New Mexico State University, Las Cruces, NM 88004. Publishes a directory of organizations and programs involved in the education of migrant students.

Interstate Migrant Education Council, Education Commission of the States, 1860 Lincoln Street, Denver, CO 80203. Acts as forum for development of policy issues and information dissemination about migrant education.

National Association of State Directors of Migrant Education, 200 West Baltimore Street, Baltimore, MD 21201. Information for teachers and parents about delivery of services to migrant students.

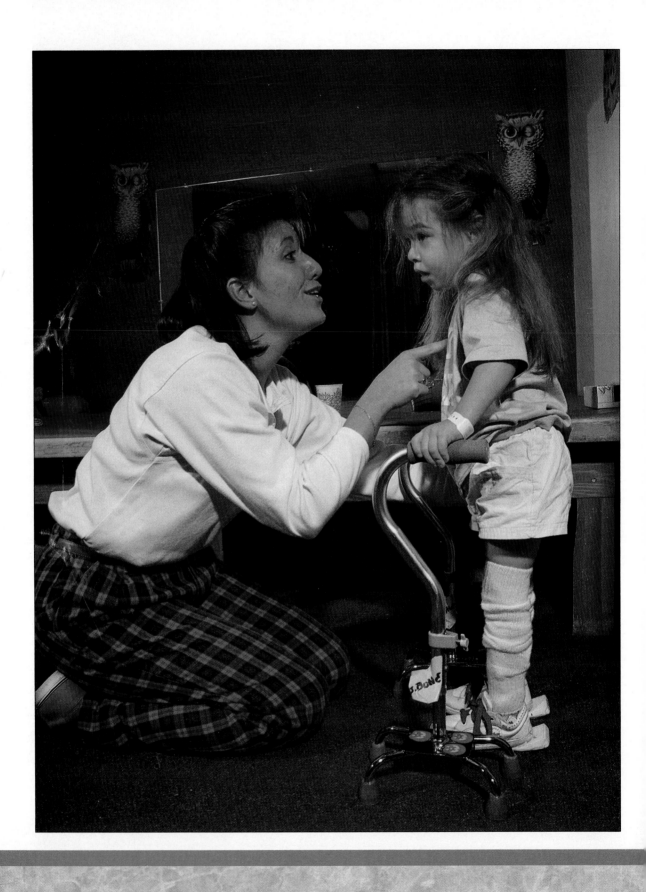

13
Working with Parents and Families

◆ What can a teacher learn from the parents of students?

◆ What information or assistance should the teacher provide to parents?

◆ Does the nature or severity of a student's disability change the importance or objectives of parental and family involvement?

◆ How meaningful can IEP goals and objectives be if the student's parents do not participate in developing them?

◆ At what point are legitimate needs of parents not the proper focus of the special educators' efforts?

A parent is a child's first teacher, the person who is always there giving prompts, encouragement, praise, and corrective feedback. Parents are responsible for helping the young child learn literally hundreds of skills. In many respects, no one ever knows as much about a child as a parent does. And no one else has as much vested interest in that child. These are safe statements, obviously true for the vast majority of parent-child relationships. Yet only recently have special educators begun to understand the primary role of parents and taken these fundamental truths as valuable guidelines for the parent-teacher relationship.

For years, many educators viewed parents as either troublesome (if they asked too many questions or, worse, offered suggestions about their child's education) or uncaring (if they did not jump to attention whenever the professional determined the parent needed something—typically, advice from the professional). Parents, too, have often seen professionals as adversaries. But more recently, parent involvement has received a great deal of attention in special education. Parents and teachers have developed better ways to communicate and work with each other for the common benefit of the exceptional child.

We will explore some of the reasons the parent-teacher relationship has not always been positive and some examples of the progress that has been made. To better understand a parent's perspective, we will look at some of the ways a child's disabilities can affect the family and the roles and responsibilities of parents and siblings. As we describe some of the techniques for communicating with and involving parents in their children's education, you will see that working with parents of exceptional children is among the most important and rewarding skills a teacher can develop.

■ THE PARENT-TEACHER PARTNERSHIP

Parents and teachers who work actively and effectively with one another make a powerful team. A strong parent-teacher partnership is beneficial to the professional, the parent, and the child. According to Heward et al. (1979), a productive parent-professional relationship provides professionals with:

♦ Greater understanding of the overall needs of the child and the needs and desires of the parent.

♦ Data for more meaningful selection of target behaviors that are important to the child in the world outside the school.

♦ Access to a wider range of social and activity reinforcers provided by parents.

♦ More opportunities to reinforce appropriate behaviors in both school and home settings.

♦ Feedback from parents as to changes in behavior that can be used to improve programs being implemented by professionals and parents.

♦ The ability to comply with legislation mandating continuing parental input to the educational process.

A productive parent-professional relationship provides parents with:

♦ Greater understanding of the needs of their child and the objectives of the teacher.

- Information on their rights and responsibilities as parents of an exceptional child.
- Specific information about their child's school program and how they can become involved.
- Specific ways to extend the positive effects of school programming into the home.
- More skills to help their child learn functional behaviors that are appropriate for the home environment.
- Access to additional important resources (current and future) for their child.

And, of most importance, a productive parent-professional relationship provides the child with:

- Greater consistency in her two most important environments.
- More opportunities for learning and growth.
- Access to expanded resources and services. (p. 226)

Barriers to Effective Parent-Teacher Interaction

Let's face it—parents and teachers do not always cooperate. They may sometimes even seem to be on opposite sides, battling over what each feels is best for the child. The child, unfortunately, can never win that battle. He needs to have the people who are responsible for the two places where he spends most of his life—home and school—work together to make those environments consistent. Both home and school must be supportive of his job of learning. Some parents and teachers make assumptions and hold attitudes toward one another that are counterproductive. Parents may complain of

A productive parent-teacher relationship benefits the exceptional child through consistent instruction and feedback at home and school.

professionals who are negative, unavailable, or patronizing. Teachers may complain that parents are uninterested, uncooperative, or hostile.

Roos (1980), a special educator who is the father of a child with mental retardation, blames much of parents' hostility and negative attitudes on what he calls professional mishandling. Many professionals hold negative stereotypes and false assumptions about what parents of children with disabilities face and need (Donnellan & Mirenda, 1984). These attitudes have often led to poor relationships between parents and professionals.

Sonnenschein (1981) describes behaviors of professionals that detract from productive relationships. She examines several attitudes or approaches that create roadblocks to effective partnerships.

- *The parent as vulnerable client.* Professionals who see parents only as helpless souls in need of assistance make a grave mistake. Teachers need parents and what they have to offer as much as parents need teachers.

- *Professional distance.* Most professionals in human services develop some degree of professional distance to avoid getting too involved with a client—supposedly to maintain objectivity and credibility. But aloofness or coldness in the name of professionalism has hindered or terminated many a parent-teacher relationship. Parents must believe the professional really cares about them (Murray, 1990).

- *The parent as patient.* Some professionals make the faulty assumption that having a child with disabilities causes the parent to need therapy. Roos (1978) writes, "I had suddenly been demoted from the role of a professional to that of the 'parent as patient,' the assumption by some professionals that parents of a retarded child are emotionally maladjusted and are prime candidates for counseling, psychotherapy, or tranquilizers" (p. 15).

- *The parent as responsible for the child's condition.* Some parents do feel responsible for their child's disability and, with a little encouragement from a professional, can be made to feel completely guilty. A productive parent-professional relationship focuses on collaborative problem solving, not on laying blame.

- *The parent as less intelligent.* Parents' information and suggestions are given little recognition. Parents are considered too biased, too involved, or too unskilled to make useful observations. Some professionals concede that parents have access to needed information but contend that parents are not able to, or should not, make any decisions based on what they know.

- *The parent as adversary.* Some teachers expect the worst whenever they interact with parents. Even if that attitude can be partially explained by previous unpleasant encounters with unreasonable parents, it is at best a negative influence on new relationships.

- *Tendency to label parents.* As with the students they teach, some professionals seem eager to label parents. If parents disagree with a diagnosis or seek another opinion, they are *denying;* if they refuse a suggested treatment, they are *resistant;* and if parents insist that something is wrong with their child despite test evidence to the contrary, they are called *anxious.* The professional who believes a parent's perception may be the correct one is rare—yet parents often do know best.

Of course, we must be just as careful in generalizing about professionals' behavior as we are with parents. Many teachers do not act in such negative ways toward parents. To the extent that teachers and other special educators believe and behave in these ways, however, it is understandable that parents may feel intimidated, confused, or hostile. But the factors working against positive parent-teacher relationships cannot all be attributed to professional mishandling. Some parents are genuinely difficult to work with or unreasonable.

> The attitudes and behaviors of the parents have also contributed to negative interactions. There is no easy way to tell a mother and father that their child is substantially handicapped. Some parents want to hear the hard truth; others want to be eased into it. Professionals may carefully choose their words with the greatest sensitivity, yet still offend the parents. Sometimes parents are unforgiving and do not realize the difficult position of the professional. They may vent their anger at the professional and discuss the professional's "gross lack of sensitivity" with family and friends. (Turnbull, 1983, p. 19)

> There are situations in which parents fight long and hard for services for their child. After the services are found and the child is receiving an appropriate education, the parents continue their intense advocacy until minor issues with professionals become major confrontations. As one mother stated, "For years I have scrapped and fought for services. Now I come on like gangbusters over issues that are really not that important. I don't like what has happened to me. I've ended up to be an aggressive, angry person." This posture leads to unproductive interactions between parents and professionals. (Bronicki & Turnbull, 1987, p. 10)

The purpose of examining factors that cause friction between parents and teachers is not to determine fault but to identify factors we can change and improve. Professionals who recognize that some of their own behaviors may diminish the potential for productive relationships with parents are in a better position to change their actions and obtain the benefits such relationships can provide. Perhaps the first and most important step for the teacher is to avoid sweeping generalizations about parents of exceptional children and treat them with respect as individuals. After all, isn't that how teachers want to be treated?

Breaking Down Barriers to Effective Parent-Teacher Interaction

Negative interactions between parents and teachers can be related to a mutual lack of awareness and understanding of each other's roles and responsibilities. During recent years, a number of forces have come together to focus national attention on the importance of a parent-teacher partnership based on mutual respect and participation in decision making (Bronicki & Turnbull, 1987). Although many things have contributed to the greater involvement of parents in the education of their exceptional children, three groups are primarily responsible: parents, educators, and legislators.

Parents: Advocates for Change

An *advocate* is someone who speaks for or pleads the case of another. Parents of exceptional children have played that role for many years, but recently they have done so with impressive effectiveness. The first parent group organized for children with disabilities was the National Society for Crippled Children, which began in 1921. The National Association for Retarded Citizens, organized in 1950, and the United Cerebral Palsy Association, organized in 1948, are two national parent organizations that have been largely responsible for making the public aware of their children's needs. The Learning Disabilities Association of America (LDA), another group organized by and consisting mostly of parents, has been instrumental in bringing about educational reform. As we saw in Chapters 1 and 2, parents played a crucial role in bringing about litigation and legislation establishing the rights of handicapped children to education.

More than any other group, parents themselves have been responsible for their greater involvement in special education. They have formed effective organizations that have been the impetus for much educational reform. As individuals, they are learning more about their children's educational needs and are seeing the potential benefits of an effective parent-teacher partnership.

Educators: Striving for Greater Impact

Educators have recognized the necessity of expanding the traditional role of the classroom teacher to meet the special needs of children with disabilities. This expanded role demands a view of teaching as more than delivering the three Rs. Special educators now realize that self-care, social, vocational, and leisure skills are critical to the successful functioning of a student with disabilities. Teachers now attach high priority to developing and maintaining the functional skills that will enable a child or adult with disabilities to be successful in school, home, work, and community settings.

Implementation of this new priority has implications and applications outside the classroom, and teachers have begun to look outside the school for assistance and support. Parents are a natural and necessary resource for expanding educational services to the home and community. At the very least, teachers benefit from information parents provide about their children's success with specific skills outside the classroom.

But parents do much more than just report on behavior change. They can tell what skills their children need to learn and, just as important, which skills they have already acquired. Parents can work with teachers to provide needed extra practice of skills at home and even to teach their children new skills. Research shows that parents can enhance the development of their handicapped children by teaching them at home (e.g., Schumaker & Sherman, 1978; Snell & Beckman-Brindley, 1984; Wedel & Fowler, 1984; Wolery, 1979). Research attesting to the positive outcomes of early intervention with handicapped and at-risk preschoolers also supports the focus on working cooperatively with parents (e.g., Bailey & Wolery, 1984; Odom & Karnes, 1988; Smith & Strain, 1984).

In short, educators are giving up the old notions that parents should not be too involved in their children's educational programs or that they should not try to teach their children for fear of doing something wrong. Teachers now realize parents are a powerful and necessary ally (Kroth, 1978). Only through an effective parent-teacher partnership can everyone's goals—teacher's, parent's, and child's—be fulfilled.

We will examine the effects and methods of early intervention in Chapter 14.

Legislators: Mandates for Involvement

As we have seen, P.L. 94–142 and corresponding state laws mandate parent involvement in the education of children with disabilities. Federal law provides statutory guidelines for parent-professional interaction in regard to a free and appropriate education, referral, testing, placement, and program planning. In addition, the law provides due process procedures if parents believe their child's needs are not being met. Although some educators initially viewed P.L. 94–142 as "the parents' law" and were threatened by the new role it specified for parents, most believe it represents sound educational practice and welcome the parent involvement it encourages.

For a discussion of P.L. 94–142 as it relates to the parent-professional relationship, see Turnbull et al. (1986).

In sum, we can attribute special educators' interest in working effectively with parents of children with disabilities to three related factors:

1. Many parents want to be involved.
2. Research and practice have convinced many educators that their effectiveness can be significantly greater with the assistance and involvement of parents.
3. The law requires it.

◼ EFFECTS OF A CHILD'S DISABILITIES ON PARENTS AND FAMILY

The special educator usually interacts with parents of exceptional children for two primary reasons: (1) to obtain information and suggestions that can help the teacher do a better job in the classroom, and (2) to provide information and assistance to parents for working with their children outside the classroom. The teacher who wants to both seek and provide assistance must be able to communicate effectively with parents. Effective communication is more likely when the educator understands and respects the responsibilities and challenges that parents of exceptional children face.

> All I wanted was a baby and now I've got doctors' appointments, therapy appointments, surgeries, medical bills, a strained marriage, no more free time. . . . When you have a handicapped child, you don't just have to deal with the child and the fact that he's handicapped. You have to adjust to a whole new way of life. It's a double whammy. (Simon, 1987, p. 15)

Parental Reactions to a Child with Disabilities

A great deal has been written about parents' reactions to the birth of a child with disabilities or to the discovery that their child has a learning problem or physical disability. Reviewing the literature describing parental responses to the birth of a handicapped child, Blacher (1984) found a consistent theme suggesting three stages of adjustment. First, parents are said to experience a period of emotional crisis characterized by shock, denial, and disbelief. This initial reaction is followed by a period of emotional disorganization that includes alternating feelings of anger, guilt, depression, shame, lowered self-esteem, rejection of the child, overprotectiveness, and so on. Finally, it is presumed that parents eventually reach a third stage in which they accept their disabled child.

It is not just parents of children with disabilities who go through stages. Any traumatic life event—divorce, death of a family member or friend—requires adjustment (Kubler-Ross, 1969).

There is no question that the birth of a handicapped child or the discovery that a child has a disability is an intense and traumatic event (Turnbull & Turnbull, 1985). And there is evidence that many parents of children with disabilities experience similar reactions and emotional responses and that most go through an adjustment process, trying to work through their feelings (Eden-Piercy, Blacher, & Eyman, 1986; Featherstone, 1980). But we see two problems with emphasizing stages of adjustment as the basis for planning or delivering family services. First, it is easy to assume all parents must pass through a similar sequence of stages and that time is the most important variable in adjustment. In fact, parents react to the arrival of a child with disabilities in many different ways (Allen & Affleck, 1985). For some parents, years may pass and they still are not comfortable with their child; others report that having a child with disabilities has actually strengthened their life or marriage (Schell, 1981; Weiss & Weiss, 1976). The sequence and time needed for adjustment is different for every parent. The one common thread is that almost all parents can be helped during their adjustment by sensitive and supportive friends and professionals (Schlesinger & Meadow, 1976; Turnbull, 1983).

Turnbull and Turnbull (1985) offer a collection of moving personal stories by parents of children with disabilities.

Our second concern is that the various stages of adjustment have a distinct psychiatric flavor, and professionals may mistakenly assume that parents must be maladjusted in some way. As Roos (1978) notes, some educators seem to assume that all parents of handicapped children need counseling.

> It may be that many parents do respond in ways that are well-described by the stage model. But it is dangerous to impose this model on all parents. Those who exhibit different response patterns might be inappropriately judged as "deviant." Parents who do not progress as rapidly through the "stages" might be considered slow to adjust. And those who exhibit emotions in a different sequence might be thought of as regressing. (Allen & Affleck, 1985, p. 201)

As Farber (1975) pointed out, it is a mistake to think of parents of children with disabilities as psychological curiosities; they are more like the parents of normal children then they are different. Parenting any child is a tremendous challenge that produces emotional responses and requires adjustment. Parents of handicapped children, like the parents of nonhandicapped children, must sometimes operate under financial, physical, emotional, and marital stress. Parents of children with disabilities, however, must deal with the additional task of securing and relating to the special services their children need.

Blackstone (1981), himself the parent of a child with disabilities, gives examples of how parents of exceptional children are often viewed and treated differently from other parents.

> The parent of the normal child skips monthly PTA meetings, and his behavior is considered normal. The parent of the exceptional child skips monthly meetings, and he is said to be uncaring and hard to reach.
>
> A couple with normal children divorce. They are said to be incompatible. The couple with an exceptional child divorce, and it is said that the child ruined the marriage.
>
> The parents of a normal child are told that because their child is having reading difficulties, it would be "nice" if they could work with her at home. The parents of the exceptional child are told that if they do not work with their child, she will not learn! (pp. 29–30)

The Many Roles of the Exceptional Parent

Parenthood is an awesome responsibility; parents of children with disabilities face even greater responsibility. Educators who are not parents of a handicapped child cannot know the 24-hour reality of being an exceptional parent. But they should nonetheless try to be aware of the varied and demanding roles these parents must fulfill. Heward et al. (1979) described seven major challenges that parents of exceptional children continue to face today.

1. *Teaching.* Even though all parents are their children's first teachers, most nonhandicapped children acquire a great many skills without their parents' trying to teach them. The child with a disability, however, often does not acquire many important skills as naturally or as independently as his nonhandicapped peers. In addition to systematic teaching techniques, some parents must learn to use, and/or teach their children to use, special equipment such as hearing aids, braces, wheelchairs, and adapted eating utensils.

2. *Counseling.* All parents are counselors in the sense that they deal with their developing children's changing emotions, feelings, and attitudes. But in addition to all the normal joys and pains of helping a child grow up, parents of a child with disabilities must deal with the feelings their child has as a result of his particular disability. "Will I still be deaf when I grow up?" "I'm not playing outside any more—they always tease me." "Why can't I go swimming like the other kids?" Parents play an important role in how the exceptional child comes to feel about himself. They can help develop an active, outgoing child who confidently tries many new things or a withdrawn child with negative attitudes toward himself and others.

3. *Managing behavior.* Even though all children act out from time to time, the range and severity of maladaptive behaviors of some children with disabilities demand more systematic, specialized treatment. Some parents must learn to use behavior management techniques in order to have a good relationship with their children (Snell & Beckman-Brindley, 1984).

4. *Parenting nonhandicapped siblings.* Nonhandicapped children are deeply affected by having a brother or sister with special needs (Powell & Ogle, 1985; Wilson, Blacher, & Baker, 1989). A handicapped child's brothers and sisters often have concerns about their sibling's disability: uncertainty regarding the cause of the disability and its effect on them, uneasiness over the reactions of their friends, a feeling of being left out or of being required to do too much for the handicapped child (Dyson, Edgar, & Crnic, 1989).

See pages 546–547 for the memories and concerns of one woman who grew up with a handicapped brother.

5. *Maintaining the parent-to-parent relationship.* Having a child with disabilities often puts stress on the relationship between husband and wife (Frey, Greenberg, & Fewell, 1989). Particular stress can range from arguing over whose fault the child's disability is, to disagreeing over what expectations should be made for the child's behavior, to spending so much time, money, and energy on the handicapped child that little is left for each other (Cohen, Agosta, Cohen, & Warren, 1989).

6. *Educating significant others.* Grandparents, aunts and uncles, neighbors, even the school bus driver can have an important effect on the development of a child with disabilities. Whereas the parents of a nondisabled child can reason-

Nondisabled brothers and sisters often have special needs and concerns because of their sibling's disability.

George (1988) describes a group therapy program designed to help grandparents and extended family of children with disabilities develop positive and supportive roles toward the child and parents.

ably expect their child to receive certain kinds of treatment from significant others, parents of children with disabilities know they cannot necessarily depend on appropriate interactions. Parents of a child with disabilities must try to be sure that, as much as possible, other people interact with their child in a way that facilitates acquisition and maintenance of adaptive behaviors. Schulz (1978) describes her response to anyone who stares at her Down syndrome son. She looks the person squarely in the eye and says, "You seem interested in my son. Would you like to meet him?" This usually ends the staring and often creates an opportunity to provide information or begin a friendship.

7. *Relating to the school and community*. Although P.L. 94–142 describes specific rights of parents of children with disabilities, it also implies certain responsibilities. Although some involvement in the educational process is desirable for all parents, it is a must for exceptional parents. They need to acquire special knowledge (e.g., understanding what a criterion-referenced test is) and learn special skills (e.g., participating effectively in an IEP planning meeting). In addition, parents of children with disabilities often have other concerns over and above those of most parents; for example, whereas all parents may be concerned about having adequate playgrounds, the parents of a child who uses a wheelchair may also have to work to make the playground accessible.

We could correctly say that these seven areas are things all parents must deal with. But consideration of the requirements of parenting is useful for at least two reasons. First, it shows that exceptional parents are, in fact, more like other parents than they are different. Second, it highlights critical aspects of the job of parenting that can be significantly affected by having a child with disabilities. This kind of analysis helps us understand the responsibilities that parents of handicapped children face and pinpoint specific areas where teachers and other professionals can provide useful services to parents.

Another way to understand how a child's disability affects family members is to examine the likely impact of the child's special needs at various ages. Turnbull et al. (1986) describe the possible issues and concerns parents and nonhandicapped siblings face during four life-cycle stages. Table 13.1 outlines their analysis. A study by Wikler (1986) lends support to the concept that parents and siblings face different challenges at different life-cycle stages of the handicapped child. Wikler's study of 60 families found higher levels of family stress at the onset of adolescence and at the onset of adulthood.

Abuse and Neglect of Children with Disabilities

Child abuse and neglect occur with alarming frequency. In 1987, the American Association for Protecting Children reported over 2 million cases of child abuse, and it is believed that the true incidence is much higher. Because the majority of child abuse and neglect cases are never reported—some professionals believe the number of actual cases is at least twice the number of reported cases (Straus, Gelles, & Steinmetz, 1980)—it is impossible to know the true extent of the problem. Estimates vary considerably, but Harrison and Edwards (1983) believe that as many as 20% of all children may be neglected or physically, sexually, or emotionally abused.

Although the incidence of parental abuse and neglect of children with disabilities is also unknown, Kurtz and Kurtz (1987) state that "a growing body of evidence establishes a convincing connection between child maltreatment and handicapped children" (p. 216). Zirpoli (1987) found that not only were children with disabilities overrepresented in child abuse samples, but they were more likely to be abused for a longer period.

> Whereas the infant with colic may increase family stress for a limited period, the child with cerebral palsy, or any other long-term or permanent handicap, presents a potential long-term family crisis. As a result, children with handicaps are not only at greater risk for abuse, but for longer periods of time. It is no wonder, then, that children with handicaps are disproportionately represented in child abuse samples. (p. 44)

Is a child's handicapping condition the reason she is abused and neglected, as some studies suggest (Fontana, 1971; Milner & Wimberley, 1980)? Or do abuse and neglect produce a disability in an otherwise normally developing child (Brandwein, 1973; Elmer, 1977)?

> In many cases, to ask the question of whether children are abused because they are handicapped, or handicapped because they are abused, is something akin to the old question of which came first—the chicken or the egg. We know this much for certain: some children are abused because they are handicapped, and some children are handicapped because they are abused. (Morgan, 1987, p. 45)

In most instances, however, it would be a mistake to say simply that a child's disability caused the abuse and neglect. Researchers have concluded that child

TABLE 13.1

Possible issues encountered by parents and siblings at different life-cycle stages of an individual with disabilities.

Life Cycle Stage	Parents	Siblings
Early childhood, ages 0–5	Obtaining an accurate diagnosis Informing siblings and relatives Locating services Seeking to find meaning in the exceptionality Clarifying a personal ideology to guide decision making Addressing issues of stigma Identifying positive contributions of exceptionality	Less parental time and energy for sibling needs Feelings of jealousy over less attention Fears associated with misunderstandings of exceptionality
School age, ages 6–12	Establishing routines to carry out family functions Adjusting emotionally to educational implications Clarifying issues of mainstreaming v. special class placement. Participating in IEP conferences Locating community resources Arranging for extracurricular activities	Division of responsibility for any physical care needs Oldest female sibling may be at risk Limited family resources for recreation and leisure Informing friends and teachers Possible concern over surpassing younger sibling Issues of mainstreaming into same school Need for basic information on exceptionality
Adolescence, ages 13–21	Adjusting emotionally to possible chronicity of exceptionality Identifying issues of emerging sexuality Addressing possible peer isolation and rejection Planning for career/vocational development Arranging for leisure time activities Dealing with physical and emotional change of puberty Planning for postsecondary education	Overidentification with sibling Greater understanding of differences in people Influence of exceptionality on career choice Dealing with possible stigma and embarrassment Participation in sibling training programs Opportunity for sibling support groups
Adulthood, ages 21–	Planning for possible need for guardianship Addressing the need for appropriate adult residence Adjusting emotionally to any adult implications of dependency Addressing the need for socialization opportunities outside the family for individual with exceptionality Initiating career choice or vocational program	Possible issues of responsibility for financial support Addressing concerns regarding genetic implications Introducing new in-laws to exceptionality Need for information on career/living options Clarify role of sibling advocacy Possible issues of guardianship

Source: From *Families, Professionals, and Exceptionality: A Special partnership* (pp. 106–107) by A. P. Turnbull, H. R. Turnbull III, J. A. Summers, M. J. Brotherson, and H. A. Benson, 1986. Columbus, OH: Merrill. Reprinted by permission.

abuse and neglect have no single cause, but are the product of the complex interactions of numerous variables, only one of which concerns the child's characteristics (Kurtz & Kurtz, 1987; Zirpoli, 1987, 1990). Just a few of the many factors that have been found to correlate with a higher incidence of child abuse are the parent's own abuse as a child, alcohol or drug dependency, unemployment, poverty, and marital discord. But again, it is important to stress that seldom is any one of these factors the lone cause of child abuse. For example, even though it is true that the lower a family's income, the greater the probability that child abuse and neglect will occur, many children from poor families receive loving and nurturing care. Likewise, the great majority of parents of children with disabilities provide a loving and nurturing environment.

There is a need for greater awareness of the problem of child abuse and neglect throughout society, but especially among professionals who work with children and families. Because teachers see children on a daily basis for most of the year, they are in the best position to identify and report suspected cases of abuse. All states require teachers and other professionals who frequently come into contact with children to report suspected cases of child abuse and neglect. Indeed, many state laws require any citizen who suspects child abuse and neglect to report it. Failure to do so is usually considered a misdemeanor and people who, in good faith, report suspected cases are immune from civil or criminal liability. Reports should be filed with the local child welfare department. All educators should become familiar with the child abuse laws in their states and should learn how to recognize indicators of child abuse and neglect.

> Educators must be willing to get involved. Unfortunately, they and other professionals are frequently unwilling to file a report even when child abuse is highly suspected. Indeed, it may be very difficult for a person to make a child abuse report even anonymously. However, one must consider the possible consequences of not reporting suspected abuse. (Zirpoli, 1987, p. 46)

> Information on detecting signs of child abuse and neglect can be obtained from the National Center on Child Abuse and Neglect. Anyone can and should report a suspected case of child abuse; reports can be filed anonymously. If you do not know the appropriate local agency to contact, call the toll-free number of the National Child Abuse Hotline: 800-422-4453.

■ PARENT-TEACHER COMMUNICATION

Regular two-way communication with parents is the foundation of an effective parent-teacher partnership. Without open, honest communication between teacher and parent, many of the positive outcomes cannot be achieved. The three most-used methods of communication between parents and teachers are conferences, written messages, and the telephone.

> Turnbull et al. (1986) have devised a form that parents can complete to indicate what types of communication they prefer to receive from school personnel.

Parent-Teacher Conferences

Although parent-teacher conferences are as common to school as recess and homework and have been with us for just about as long, conferences are not always the effective vehicle for communication that they should be. Parent conferences often turn out to be stiff, formal affairs, with teachers anxious and parents wondering what bad news they will hear this time. In fact, Bensky et al. (1980) found that teachers ranked communication with parents as a major source of job stress. Fortunately, recognition of the critical role parents play in their child's education and greater parent participation in the schools as a result

ONE SISTER'S STORY

Siblings for Significant Change (823 United Nations Plaza, New York, NY 10017) is a national organization of people with brothers and sisters with disabilities. The organization's director, Gerri Zatlow, dealt with her own need to live a more separate and independent existence by moving out of her mother's apartment at nearly 26 years of age. Now somewhat removed from the situation, her perspectives have altered.

There never was a question of institutionalizing Douglas. From the time we first learned that he was autistic, we resolved to put up a good fight for him . . . not just for his sake, but for ours as well. Doug was clearly an integral part of our family, and nothing would change that. We hoped he would respond to a loving environment—and he did! Doug grew from a silent little boy into the man of 19 he is today. Handsome and tall, he has a distinct personality and a sense of humor. He has particular likes and dislikes. Like all of us, there are traits in his nature that are not always pleasant. He can be stubborn and, when crossed, highly argumentative. And—he remains autistic, for the disability does not melt away with each passing year.

The shaping of Douglas has been well worth the battle. He has made phenomenal strides in an excellent public school special education program. However, if the truth be told, a great deal of his progress has been highly attributable to us . . . his family. The process has been an arduous and unrelenting struggle at great emotional expense. The older Doug gets . . . the harder the fight.

As brother and sister we were always close. The public has a distorted view of the autistic child, one of an aloof and cold being. This image may apply to some of the children, but not to all, and certainly not to Douglas. My brother was warm, affectionate, and quick to respond to my outward displays of love. He still has an uncanny ability to read my moods, making his own jokes when I am in need of a chuckle or a hug when the time is ripe.

We went everywhere together . . . to movies, restaurants, the park. We took countless walks through the city streets, shopped in supermarkets and made joint efforts to clean up at home. We watched an endless series of Saturday morning cartoons together, long after I had outgrown them. We grew together in our different ways. We spent too much time together; I think that was half the problem.

There was no relief from Doug. Day in and day out, his needs had to be tended to regardless of our wants and desires. He always came first. Growing up in a household where only my mother and I were present, the physical responsibility for Douglas was on our shoulders. Much of that burden was mine. Lessening of that responsibility was rare and came in the form of Doug spending a good part of his weekends with my father, and in the summertime when he went to sleep-away camp.

Because Douglas's presence dominated everything, there was no real time for myself. Under these conditions, childhood takes on an uneasy dimension. A sibling is denied the fundamental right of being a child. An opportunity to have friends over did not often materialize because visits were dependent on my brother's moods and behavior. Going out

of IEP planning meetings have enhanced parent-teacher communication skills; parents and teachers are learning to talk to one another in more productive ways.

In a face-to-face meeting, parents and teachers can exchange information and coordinate their efforts to assist the exceptional child at home and in school. Conferences should not be limited to the beginning and end of the school year, but should be scheduled regularly. Special educators should view the parent-teacher conference as a method for planning and evaluating jointly initiated teaching programs.

Preparing for the Conference

Preparation is the key to effective parent-teacher conferences. Stephens, Blackhurst, and Magliocca (1982) recommend establishing specific objectives was governed by my mother's need for my assistance in any way. My mother nicknamed me "the other mother" as I took my responsibility with seriousness and maturity in excess of my young years. Unfortunately, the pattern became a way of life.

I am grateful for the 7 years between us in age. Had I been younger, I do not know whether or not I could have coped with my mysterious brother. I do not know whether I would have accepted gracefully the continual sacrifices made to keep Doug home. I am not sure that I could have handled the immense responsibility that I grew so accustomed to.

In addition to the obvious task of physical care, something must be said about the mental effects on us. Throughout my youth, I was cognizant of the fact that Doug's condition was permanent. He would always be vulnerable and need protection, and he was going to live a full life span as a severely handicapped person. I cannot underestimate the impact of that knowledge, especially to a mother. My mother's frequent melancholy was warranted. Frustrated by his condition in the early days, she feared for his future. What compounded the dilemma was that we were very much alone. Some families have assorted relatives to provide respite . . . to take them out for car rides, spend holidays with, or provide emotional support when the going gets rough. Our family is small. My parents are divorced; and although my father was and is as emotionally and financially supportive as he could possibly be, he was not present during moments of household stress and daily crises. Who did we have? Just each other. Still, that is something. Those single parents without benefit of other children to offer help have it even tougher.

It is inevitable that one day I will lose my parents. I will inherit whatever constitutes their estates, be it money or debts, but their most important legacy will be in the form of my autistic brother. As his future guardian, I will acquire and accept the full responsibility for Douglas. As his only sister, I feel that I have already absorbed too much of this burden. I am hoping that long before my parents' demise, Doug's future will be guaranteed. The only alternative to my becoming his perpetual "other mother" is for him to be settled in a group home offering suitable living conditions.

Douglas is not the boy he was 10 years ago. He has gained many skills over the years, all of which make him a superb candidate for a group home. He is totally competent in areas of self-care. One need never remind him to shower, shampoo, or shave. Actually he is rather vain. When his hair gets to an unruly stage, he will request a trip to the "hair stylist." Doug is helpful in the house as he polishes furniture, makes beds, vacuums, sets the table, and cleans the dishes. He also is proficient at doing laundry.

We have not fought this hard for Douglas to be thwarted by a termination of programs. Personally, I have not given so much of myself and my life to Doug only to see his existence end in despair. Nothing can give me back the years of turbulence and prior sublimation that came out of our circumstances. It was all done for Douglas . . . and I will not see my own effort or that of my family wasted. My brother will have an option.

Without viable alternatives, many of us will have no choice but to remain the ever constant "keepers" . . . denied the opportunity for an independent life. ◆

for the conference, reviewing the student's cumulative progress, preparing examples of the student's work along with a graph or chart showing specific performance, and preparing an agenda for the meeting. Figure 13.1 shows an outline for preparing a parent-teacher conference agenda. After planning the conference agenda, the teacher might examine alternative ways to present delicate issues, perhaps getting feedback from others on her style and manner of speaking (Roberds-Baxter, 1984).

Conducting the Conference

Parent-teacher conferences should be held in the child's classroom because (1) the teacher feels comfortable in familiar surroundings, (2) the teacher has ready access to student files and instructional materials, (3) the classroom itself serves as a reminder to the teacher of things the child has done, and (4) the classroom,

Turnbull et al. (1986) offer guidelines for holding conferences in parents' homes.

ECOBEHAVIORAL TREATMENT OF FAMILIES WITH HISTORIES OF CHILD ABUSE AND NEGLECT

One of the most successful programs for preventing and treating child abuse and neglect is Project 12-Ways, located at the University of Southern Illinois. The guiding philosophy of Project 12-Ways is that family problems can be eased by eliminating stress-producing factors, such as unemployment, and by teaching both children and parents the skills necessary for getting along together without abuse and neglect. Recognizing the multidimensional factors that lead to abuse and neglect and that the entire family must be understood and treated as a dynamic system, the project employs an ecobehavioral approach to treatment. That is, rather than prescribe a standard treatment regimen consisting of one or two components, a thorough assessment of the family's needs and resources is conducted. Following the assessment, the family and a project counselor jointly determine goals. An individualized program of family support services is then implemented; it typically consists of several of the following facets:

♦ *Parent-child training.* Parents are helped to understand their children's behavior and taught positive, nonpunitive forms of child management. Both parents and children are taught how to be more affectionate to one another.

♦ *Basic skills training.* Parents are given hands-on assistance in learning how to deal with important child development areas, such as toilet training, bedwetting, dressing, and language/conversational skills.

♦ *Health maintenance and nutrition.* Behaviors that can cause health problems are addressed. Parents are helped to find medical care for themselves and their family.

♦ *Stress reduction.* Many family conflicts result from a parent's stresses and anxieties. Parents are taught systematic relaxation techniques to control stress (Gierich et al., 1990).

with its desks, chairs, and teaching materials, reminds the teacher and parents that the purpose of the conference is their mutual concern for improving the child's education (Bennett & Hensen, 1977). When conducting parent conferences in their classrooms, however, teachers should not make the mistake of hiding behind their desks, creating a barrier between themselves and the parents, or of seating parents in undersized chairs meant for students.

Stephens and Wolf (1980) recommend a four-step sequence for parent-teacher conferences.

1. *Build rapport.* Establishing mutual trust and the belief that the teacher really cares about the student is important to a good parent-teacher conference. A few minutes should be devoted to relevant small talk. The teacher might begin with something positive about the child or family rather than a superficial statement about weather or traffic.

2. *Obtain information.* Parents can provide teachers with important information for improving instruction. Teachers should use open-ended questions that cannot be answered with a simple yes or no; for example, "Which activities in school has Felix mentioned lately?" is better than "Has Felix told you what we are doing now in school?" The first question encourages the parent to

- *Home safety and cleanliness*. Parents are taught to eliminate safety hazards and to improve home cleanliness and personal hygiene.

- *New parent*. New parents receive training and counseling in preparation for childbirth and infant care. Instruction includes health care during pregnancy, infant development, safety, family planning, and use of leisure time.

- *Family activities*. Families learn to spend free time together engaging in inexpensive activities designed to develop family cohesiveness and positive relations.

- *Problem solving*. Family members are instructed in problem solving, negotiation training, and communication skills as appropriate means of resolving conflicts.

- *Money management*. Training is provided in basic money management, such as saving and budgeting for essential goods and services. Families are also taught how to resolve debts.

- *Self-control*. Parents learn behavioral self-control techniques to control their temper and to meet personal goals such as losing weight or stopping smoking.

- *Self-esteem training*. Self-esteem and assertiveness training gives parents tools for resolving conflicts and asserting their positions within the family without being destructive to others.

- *Job finding*. Unemployed and underemployed parents are given assistance with job-related skills such as interviewing and résumé preparation.

For more information about Project 12-Ways, write: Behavior Analysis & Therapy Rehabilitation Institute, Southern Illinois University, Carbondale, IL 62901. ◆

provide more information—the teacher is trying to build conversation, not preside over a question-and-answer session. Throughout the conference, the teacher should show genuine interest in listening to the parents' concerns, avoid dominating the conversation, and refrain from using comments that judge, threaten, or function as verbal roadblocks to communication (see Table 13.2).

3. *Provide information*. The teacher should give parents concrete information about their child in jargon-free language. The teacher should share examples of schoolwork and data on student performance—what has already been learned and what needs to be learned next. When the student's progress has not been as great as was hoped for, parents and teacher should look together for ways to improve it.

4. *Summarize and follow up*. The conference should end with a summary of what was said. The teacher should review strategies agreed upon during the conference and indicate the follow-up activities either party will do to help carry out those strategies. Some teachers use carbon paper and make a duplicate copy of their conference notes so that parents will also have a record of what was said or agreed upon.

For detailed descriptions of how to plan and conduct parent conferences, see Kroth (1985) and Turnbull et al. (1986).

Conference Outline

Date _2-14-92_   Time _4:30 — 5:00_

Student's Name _Jeremy Wright_
Parents' Name(s) _Barbara and Tom_
Teacher's Name _Tim G._
Other Staff present _None_
Objectives for Conference: _(1) Show graph of J's reading progress, (2) find out about spelling program, (3) get parents' ideas: intervention for difficulties on playground/in gym, (4) share list of books for leisure reading_

Student's Strengths
- _good worker academically, wants to learn_
- _excited about progress in reading fluency_

Area(s) Where Improvement Is Needed:
- _continue w/spelling @ home_
- _arguments & fighting w/other kids_

Questions to Ask Parents:
- _Interactions w/friends while playing in neighborhood?_
- _How would I feel about fdback from classmate re: playground/gym behavior?_
- _Consequences?_

Parent's Responses/Comments:
- _very pleased w/reading — want to build on it._
- _wondering how long w/in-home spelling?_
- _willing to give rewards @ home: playground/gym_

Examples of Student's Work/Interactions:
- _graph of corrects/errors per min: reading_
- _weekly pre- & post test scores: spelling_

Current Programs and Strategies Used by Teacher:
- _reading: silent read, two 1-min. time trials, self-charting comprehension practice_
- _spelling: practice w/tape recorder, self-checking_

Suggestions for Parents:
- _continue spelling games (invite friends)_
- _show interest in/play fantasy games (Dung. & Dragons) w/J_

Suggestions from Parents:
- _Try using some high-interest spelling words (e.g., joust, castle)_
- _Matt & Amin could help with playground/gym program (Agreed to in conf)_

Follow-up Activities:
Parents:
- _Continue to play spelling game 2 nights per week_
- _Take J to library for adventure books_

Teacher:
- _Ask J for high-interest words & use 3-4 in his weekly list._
- _Develop peer intervention strategy w/Matt, Amin & J (group contingency?)_

Date Called for Follow-up and Outcome: _Feb. 28 (Friday)_

FIGURE 13.1

Parent-teacher conference outline. (*Source:* From *Working with Parents of Handicapped Children* (p. 233) by W. L. Heward, J. C. Dardig, and A. Rossett, 1979, Columbus, OH: Merrill. Adapted by permission.)

TABLE 13.2
Communication roadblocks
that professionals should
avoid in their interactions
with parents.

Moralizing:	"You should . . ." "You ought . . ." "It is your responsiblity to . . ."
Lecturing:	"I told you . . ." "Do you realize . . ." "One of these days . . ."
Judging/criticizing:	"You're wrong . . ." "One of your problems is . . ." "That was a mistake . . ."
Prying:	"Why?" "How?" "When?" "Who?"
Providing answers prematurely:	"Here's what you do . . ." "I suggest . . ."
Threatening:	"If you do that I'll . . ." "Unless you take my advice . . ."
Ordering:	"You must . . ." "You will . . ." "You have to . . ."
Consoling/excusing:	"You'll be just fine . . ." "You didn't know any better . . ."
Diagnosing/analyzing:	"You're just going through the stage of . . ." "You're behaving that way because . . ."
Using sarcasm/cynicism:	"You think you've got it bad . . ." "Life's just a barrel of laughs . . ."
Overusing clichés/phrases	"You know . . ." "I mean . . ." "That's neat . . ." "Far out . . ."

Source: From *Families, Professionals, and Exceptionality: A Special Partnership* (p. 150) by A. P. Turnbull, H. R. Turnbull III, J. R. Summers, M. J. Brotherson, and H. A. Benson, 1986, Columbus, OH: Merrill. Reprinted by permission.

Written Messages

Even though much can be accomplished in a parent-teacher conference, the amount of time they require suggests that conferences should not be the sole means of maintaining parent-teacher communication. In a study conducted with 217 parents of exceptional children, Ammer and Littleton (1983) found that most of the parents (69%) preferred to receive regular information in letters from school. Some teachers use frequent written messages to communicate with parents. Although the report card most schools send parents every grading period is a written message, its infrequency and standardized format limit its usefulness as a means of communication.

Many teachers regularly send "happy-grams" home with their students, specifying something positive the student has accomplished and giving parents an opportunity to praise the child at home and stay abreast of activities in the classroom.

Schumaker, Hovell, and Sherman (1977) used a daily report card system (Figure 13.2) with three junior high school boys having serious academic and behavior problems. Different teachers marked a card for each boy in each of six different classes. Parents provided privileges (e.g., snacks, television time, staying up an extra half-hour before bed) based on the teachers' ratings of their child's school performance. All three students improved their adherence to classroom rules and their academic performance.

Parents in this study indicated that their next two preferred vehicles for receiving information from their children's schools were parent-teacher conferences (51%) and telephone calls from teachers (45%). Only 19% of the parents checked home visits, which thus ranked as the least preferred method of establishing or improving home-school communication.

A two-way parent-teacher communication system can be built around a reporting form the child carries between home and school. The form should be simple to use and read, with space to circle or check responses or write short notes. Such an interactive reporting system can be used on either a daily or a weekly basis, depending on the behaviors involved. Several studies have shown that these two-way communication programs can improve both school and home performance (Dickerson, Spellman, Larsen, & Tyler, 1973; Imber, Imber, & Rothstein, 1979).

Similarly, a home-school contract is a behavioral contract that specifies parent-delivered rewards contingent on completion of classroom tasks; for example, for each page of the reading workbook completed, the student might earn a quarter to be used to buy a model airplane (Heward & Dardig, 1978). Home-school contracts use parent-controlled rewards, build in parent recognition and praise of the child's accomplishments, and involve the teacher and parents together in a positive program to support the child's learning.

The class newsletter is another method some teachers use to increase parent-teacher communication. Even though putting together a class newsletter requires a lot of work, in many cases it is worth the effort. Most teachers have access to a mimeograph, and a one- to three-page monthly newsletter can give parents who don't attend meetings or open houses information that is too long or detailed to give over the telephone. A newsletter is also an excellent way to recognize those parents who participate in various activities. By making the newsletter a class project, the teacher can include student-written stories and news items and can create an enjoyable learning activity for the entire class.

Although not used for regular or interactive communication with parents, school handbooks and special-purpose handouts describing policies and procedures, identifying personnel, suggesting parenting tips, and so on are

Playing Nintendo with his sister and friends is one of the rewards Andy chose for his homework contract.

NAME: _____

DATE: _____

TEACHER: _____

	YES	NO	
Did the student . . .			
Come on time?			
Bring supplies?			
Stay in seat?			
Not talk inappropriately?			
Follow directions?			
Raise his hand?			Rules section
Not physically disturb others?			
Clean up?			
Pay attention?			
Speak courteously?			
Were you pleased with his performance today?			Teacher satisfaction section
Points on today's classwork			Classwork section
Grade on test assignment			Grades section
Teacher's initials			

FIGURE 13.2

Daily report card. (*Source:* From "An Analysis of Daily Report Cards and Parent-Managed Privileges in the Improvement of Adolescents' Classroom Performance" by J. B. Schumaker, M. F. Hovell, and J. A. Sherman, 1977. *Journal of Applied Behavior Analysis, 10,* p. 452. Copyright by the Society of the Experimental Analysis, Inc. Adapted by permission.)

another means of using written materials to provide information to parents (Jensen & Potter, 1990).

The Telephone

A brief, pleasant telephone conversation is an excellent way to maintain communication with parents. Regular telephone calls that focus on a child's positive accomplishments let parents and teachers share in the child's success and recognize each other's contributions. Teachers should set aside time on a regular basis so that each child's parent receives a call once every 2 or 3 weeks. Of course, teachers need to find out what times are convenient for parents to receive calls. Keeping a log of the calls helps maintain the schedule and reminds teachers of any necessary follow-up.

Another way teachers can use the telephone is to organize a class telephone "tree." With this system the teacher calls only two or three parents, each of whom calls two or three more, and so on. Telephone trees can be an efficient way to get information to all of the parents associated with a class. And a telephone tree gives parents a way to get actively involved and perhaps to get to know some of the other parents.

Heward and Chapman (1981) used daily recorded telephone messages as a way to increase parent-teacher communication. The teacher of a primary learning disabilities class recorded brief messages on an automatic telephone answering machine. Parents could call 5 nights a week from 5:00 P.M. until 7:00 A.M. the next morning and hear a recorded message like this one:

> Good evening. The children worked very hard today. We are discussing transportation. They enjoyed talking about the airport and all the different kinds of airplanes. The spelling words for tomorrow are train, t-r-a-i-n; plane, p-l-a-n-e; truck, t-r-u-c-k; automobile, a-u-t-o-m-o-b-i-l-e; and ship, s-h-i-p. Thank you for calling. (p. 13)

Figure 13.3 shows the number of telephone calls the teacher received from the parents of the six children in the class each week for the entire school year. The teacher received a total of only five calls for the 32 weeks when the recorded messages were not available (.16 calls per week), compared to 112 calls during the 6 weeks the message system was in operation (18.7 per week). During the nonmessage portions of the study the next day's spelling list was sent home with the children each day, and parents were asked to help their children with the words. Nonetheless, scores on the daily five-word spelling tests improved for all six students when the recorded messages were available.

Teacher-recorded telephone messages can also be used to provide parents with the information and encouragement they need to successfully implement home-based tutoring programs. For an example of how this can be done, see pages 556–557.

There are many ways in which recorded telephone messages can be used to improve parent-teacher communication. Such a system has been used to provide schoolwide and classroom-by-classroom information, good news (such as Citizen of the Month), and suggestions for working with children at home (Heward, Heron, Gardener, & Prayzer, 1991; Minner, Beane, & Prater, 1986; Test, Cooke, Weiss, Heward, & Heron, 1986). Parent callers can also leave messages for the teacher (e.g., a question or a report on how a home-based instructional program is going), enabling the system to be used for two-way communication.

■ PARENT INVOLVEMENT

Parents and the Individualized Education Program

As discussed in Chapter 2, an individualized education program (IEP) must be developed for every child with disabilities. This requirement of P.L. 94–142 is intended to ensure that each child receives special educational services suited to his or her individual needs. Parents are required to be members of the IEP planning team, although they may waive this right by signing a document stating that they do not wish to participate.

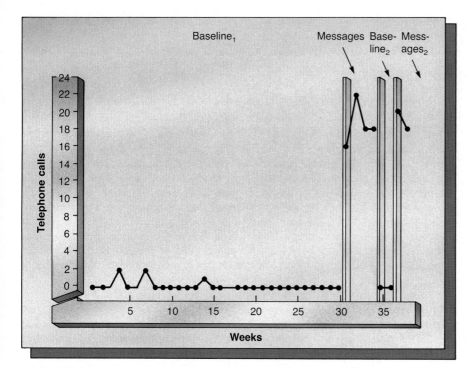

FIGURE 13.3
Graph of telephone calls with and without recorded message. (*Source:* From "Improving Parent-Teacher Communication Through Recorded Telephone Messages: Systematic Replication in a Special Education Classroom" by W. L. Heward and J. E. Chapman, 1981, *Journal of Special Education Technology, 4,* p. 14. Reprinted by permission.)

> The IEP meeting serves as a communication vehicle between parents and school personnel, and enables them as equal participants, to jointly decide what the child's needs are, what services will be provided to meet those needs, and what the anticipated outcomes will be. (*Federal Register,* 1981, p. 5462)

Clearly, the intent is that parents will play an active decision-making role. According to Turnbull and Turnbull (1982), the belief that parents should share the rights and responsibilities of decision making in regard to their child's educational program is based on two assumptions, which may not be valid in all cases.

1. Parents want to be involved in education decision making and, when given the opportunity, will take advantage of it; and
2. Attending the meeting to plan their child's IEP will enable parents to be decision makers. (p. 116)

Turnbull and Turnbull point out, however, that surveys of what parents say they want from special educators and observations of IEP meetings do not necessarily support these assumptions. In interviews conducted with 32 mothers of preschool children with disabilities, Winton and Turnbull (1981) found that, when asked to rank the characteristics of an ideal preschool, the mothers identified parent involvement as the least important factor; the most important factor to the mothers was competent, expert teachers. Lusthaus, Lusthaus, and Gibbs (1981) compiled questionnaire results from 98 parents of students enrolled in self-contained classrooms and resource rooms in eight elementary schools in a middle-class, suburban school district. More than half the parents

THE TELEPHONE

An Underused Method of Home-School Communication

Virtually all parents and educators agree on the importance of regular communication between home and school. How to manage parent-teacher communication most effectively is the question. A face-to-face conference can accomplish much, but parent-teacher conferences demand a great deal of time from both parties and, realistically, can be held only from time to time. Written notes from the teacher; daily, two-way home-school report card systems; and class newsletters can all be excellent means of communication. The time required to prepare and reproduce daily notes or a class newsletter, however, coupled with the uncertainty of student delivery, makes written communications a labor-intensive and unreliable method of parent-teacher communication—at least in terms of communicating with a number of parents on a regular, sustained basis.

Somewhat surprisingly in this burgeoning era of high technology, the telephone—everyday technology that has been with us for decades—has been a relatively unexploited means of parent-teacher communication. Of course, if used in typical fashion, the time required to call and speak individually to the parents of all 15 students enrolled in a resource room program, for example, would place the telephone in the same category as conferences and written messages for regular, sustained communication: a call once a week if you're lucky, but daily communication would most likely be out of the question. Recently, however, teachers have begun to use the telephone in a different way. By recording daily messages on a telephone-answering machine, teachers can provide a great deal of information to parents at relatively little cost. Parents, on the other hand, can call the given number and listen at their convenience, literally 24 hours a day. Parents can also leave messages on the recorder, posing a question, offering a suggestion, and so on.

In addition to information exchange, some studies have begun to explore ways in which teachers can use recorded messages to help parents carry out home-based instruction. One junior high learning disabilities teacher used a telephone-answering machine to manage a summer writing program. Parents of several of her students had indicated their desire to try to help their children maintain or extend some of their academic skills over the summer months. Each day during the 9-week program, the teacher recorded instructions for the session and a story-starter idea. One story starter went like this:

> *Danger on Shore*
> You are going up the river in a boat. You feel safe because the unfriendly natives are on the far shore. Suddenly you notice a leak. . . .

Parent and student called together, the student wrote for 10 minutes on that day's topic, and the parent scored the student's writing according to criteria provided by the teacher. The parents rewarded their children for progress and reported the results after the next day's message. Every few days parents mailed the stories to the teacher.

To get an idea of the results of the program, compare the following stories. Story #8 was written by James before his parents started the program to help him write more action words and adjectives. Story #33 was the sixth story written after his parents began to reward adjectives.

> #8
>
> July 7   James D
>
> First I would go to candy, always thinking of my self. Later I would go to the meet department. After the meat department I would go to wine department

---

> Aug 12 #33 Talking with a Star   James D
>
> I look up from my salad, thick chocolate milk shake, hot golden crisp french fries, and delicious Big Mac with extra pickles.
>
> I glance through shiney, clear glass and see a small, brown creature with a glowing red chest, short legs, long arms, and a large head with big greenish-blue eyes and a smashed-in nose. I grab a white napkin and rush up to him. With the tip of his glowing right index finger he writes...
>
> E.T.

Two stories written by a 13-year-old boy with learning disabilities during an in-home summer program. Story #8 was written during baseline; story #33, when his parents were rewarding the use of adjectives.

From "A Telephone-Managed, Home-Based Summer Writing Program for LD Adolescents" by M. E. Hasset, C. Engler, N. L. Cooke, D. W. Test, A. B. Weiss, W. L. Heward, and T. E. Heron in Focus on Behavior Analysis in Education, *pp. 89–103, by W. L. Heward, T. E. Heron, D. S. Hill, and J. Trap-Porter (Eds.), 1984, Columbus, OH: Merrill. Adapted by permission.* ◆

said they wanted to participate in IEP planning conferences at the level of providing information. The majority were content to let professionals make most decisions. When decisions were to be made about what kinds of records should be kept on their children, what medical services were to be provided, or whether their children would be transferred to other schools, however, more parents wanted to have control over the decisions. Polifka (1981) concluded from a parent survey that parents do want to play an active role in IEP planning.

The research supports what we stated earlier: We should not rely on generalizations that we *assume* to be true for all parents of children with disabilities. Furthermore, we must view this research with the understanding that, for years, most parents were not asked (and in some instances have not wanted) to participate in their children's education; then almost overnight, they are expected, or even virtually required, to do so. It is not surprising that parents have mixed feelings about how much their participation is really desired and how much they really can or should contribute.

Studies on what actually happens during IEP meetings are more conclusive. Parent attendance (mostly mothers) at IEP conferences varies widely across school districts, from less than 50% to as high as 95% (Singer & Butler, 1987). Numerous studies have found that the level of parental participation is more often passive than active (Goldstein, Strickland, Turnbull, & Curry, 1980; Lynch & Stein, 1982; Scanlon, Arick, & Phelps, 1981; Vaughn, Bos, Harrell, & Lasky, 1988). The National Committee for Citizens in Education (1979) surveyed almost 2,300 parents from all over the United States; slightly more than half (52%) of the parents indicated that their children's IEP had been completely written before the meeting. Goldstein et al. (1980) observed IEP meetings for mildly disabled elementary students and found similar results: The average meeting lasted only 36 minutes and consisted mainly of the special education teacher's explaining an already-written IEP to the parent. In another study, observation of 47 IEP conferences revealed the following: (1) in only 6 of the conferences did both mother and father attend, with only mothers attending all others; (2) 28 of the conferences consisted of the special education teacher's explaining an already-completed IEP to the parent(s); (3) approximately one-third of the responses by parents consisted of passive contributions (e.g., head nodding); and (4) the average duration of the meetings was 25 minutes (Vacc et al., 1985).

Although these results appear discouraging, they are not necessarily so. Parents are at least being made aware of what special services their children are receiving and why, and passiveness *may* mean satisfaction with the IEPs (Polifka, 1981). Moreover, many parents do take advantage of the IEP meeting to offer significant input into their children's education programs. In one recent IEP conference,

> The mother of a moderately retarded child questioned why her son was being taught to label prehistoric animals verbally. The parent asked the teachers what type of job they expected the child to have as an adult. The teachers replied that they had never really considered job opportunities for the child, since he was only 10. To the teachers, 10 seemed young; to the parents, 10 meant that almost half his formal education was completed. As the meeting progressed, it was clear that the parents were specifying objectives related to independence as an adult (telling time, reading survival words, sex education) that were different from the

more traditional curriculum proposed by the teachers. Through sharing evaluation data, goals for the child, and special problems, all parties involved created a curriculum that met everyone's approval. (Turnbull, 1983, p. 22)

Parents and professionals are working together to increase the level of parent participation in IEP team meetings. The decision-making process developed by Dardig and Heward (1981b) is one technique for recognizing each team member's input. Turnbull, Strickland, and Brantley (1982) describe group training sessions in which parents learn what goes into an IEP and how to participate more actively in developing it. In one innovative strategy that Goldstein and Turnbull (1982) investigated, school counselors attended the IEP conferences with the parents and served as advocates by introducing the parents, clarifying jargon, directing questions to parents, verbally praising parents for contributing, and summarizing the decisions made at the meeting. The counselors received no formal training; they were simply given a sheet of instructions outlining their five functions. Parents who were accompanied by a counselor-advocate made more contributions. Turnbull et al. (1986) suggest 45 specific steps that school personnel can take before and during the IEP conference to facilitate parent involvement. One suggestion is to learn parents' preferences regarding who will attend the conference, when and where the conference will be held, what special concerns the parents would like to have addressed, and so on. Turnbull et al. have also developed a special form for obtaining preconference information.

Parents as Teachers

All parents are responsible for their children's learning many skills. But as we have pointed out, most of the things children learn from their parents are not the result of systematic teaching procedures. Instead, children acquire many important skills as a natural result of everyday interactions between parent and child. For some children with disabilities, however, the casual routines of everyday home life may not provide enough practice and feedback to teach them important skills. Many parents have responded by systematically teaching their children needed self-help and daily living skills or by providing home tutoring sessions to supplement classroom academic instruction.

Educators do not agree on the role parents should play when it comes to teaching children with disabilities. Some professionals give a variety of reasons why parents should not tutor their children: Parents do not have the teaching skills required for effective tutoring; home tutoring is likely to end in frustration for both parent and child; most teachers do not have the necessary time to guide and support parents' efforts; and home tutoring may give children little rest from instruction (Barsch, 1969; Kronick, 1969; Lerner, 1976). Each of these concerns may represent a legitimate problem in individual situations.

The other perspective—that parents can serve as effective teachers for their children—is supported by numerous reports of research studies and parent involvement projects in which parents have successfully taught their children at home (Barbetta & Heron, 1991; Fay, Shapiro, & Trupin, 1978; Sandler & Coren, 1981; Thurston & Dasta, 1990). The majority of parents who have participated in these home-tutoring programs considered it a positive experience for both the parents and children.

See Wolery (1979) for an annotated bibliography of research on parents as teachers of their handicapped children.

Many parents and children
enjoy home tutoring
sessions.

In most instances in which parents wish to tutor their children at home, they
can and should be helped to do so. Properly conducted, home-based parent
teaching strengthens a child's educational program and gives enjoyment to both
child and parent. It is important, however, for professionals to examine carefully
to what extent parent tutoring is appropriate. Not all parents want to teach their
children at home or have the time to learn and use the necessary teaching
skills—and professionals must not interpret that situation as an indication that
the parents don't care enough about their children.

There are also other circumstances in which parent tutoring is probably
ill-advised.

♦ If parents disagree over whether the child should be tutored
♦ If no quiet, nondistracting place is available in the home
♦ If tutoring might result in neglecting needs of other family members
♦ If either parent resents the time spent tutoring or feels guilty if tutoring
  sessions are skipped or cut short
♦ If tutoring time deprives the child of opportunities to make friends with other
  children or develop necessary social skills (Maddux & Cummings, 1983, p.
  31)

Commenting on the appropriateness of parents teaching a child with severe handicaps at home, Hawkins and Hawkins (1981) write:

> Training and motivating parents to carry out a small number of teaching tasks each day does seem appropriate. These should be tasks that have most of the following characteristics: (1) they are brief, usually requiring no more than three or four minutes each; (2) the ultimate value of them to the parent is obvious (thus self-dressing, but perhaps not block-stacking); (3) they fit the daily routine almost automatically, not requiring a special, noticeable training "session" (thus self-bathing, but not basic communication-board training); (4) they are tasks that cannot be accomplished readily at school alone, either because the opportunities are infrequent or absent (getting up in the morning, toileting), or because training must occur at every opportunity if it is to achieve its objective (mealtime behaviors, walking appropriately with family). (pp. 17–18)

Bristor (1987) and Thurston (1989) describe techniques that teachers can use to help parents who wish to tutor their children at home. Lovitt (1977, 1982) offers four guidelines for parent tutoring.

For a review of research documenting the results of using family members in home-based teaching programs with severely handicapped children, see Snell and Beckman-Brindley (1984).

1. Establish a specific time each day for the tutoring sessions.

2. Keep sessions short. Brief 5- to 10-minute sessions held daily are more likely to be effective than 30- to 40-minute periods, which can produce frustration or will tend to be skipped altogether.

3. Keep responses to the child consistent. Lovitt believes it is particularly important for parents to respond to their child's errors in a consistent, matter-of-fact way. By praising the child's successful responses (materials and activities at the child's appropriate instructional level are a must) and providing a consistent, unemotional response to errors (e.g., "Let's read that word again, together."), parents can avoid the frustration and negative results that can occur when home tutoring is mishandled.

4. Keep a record. A parent, just like a classroom teacher, can never know the exact effects of his teaching unless he keeps a record. A daily record enables both parent and child to see gradual progress that might be missed if subjective opinion is the only basis for evaluation. Most children, disabled or not, do make progress under guided instruction. A record documents that progress, perhaps providing the parent with an opportunity to see the child in a new and positive light.

Parent Education Groups

Education for parenting is not new; educational programs for parents date back to the early 1800s. But as a result of greater parent involvement in the education of children with disabilities, many more programs are offered for and by parents. Parent education groups can serve a variety of purposes—from one-time-only dissemination of information on a new school policy, to make-it-and-take-it workshops in which parents make an instructional material to use at home (e.g., a math facts practice game), to multiple-session programs on participation in IEP planning or child behavior management. Just a few of the many topics that parent education groups address are listed in Table 13.3.

For a review of the literature on parent education programs and research, see Dangle and Polster (1984).

TABLE 13.3
Possible topics for parent education groups.

1. Self-help skills (dressing, brushing teeth, etc.)
2. Leisure-time activities
3. Participation in IEP process
4. Summer reading program
5. Teaching your child responsibility and organization
6. Interacting with peers
7. Preparing for the family vacation
8. Developing and implementing family rules
9. Safety in the home
10. Recreation/physical education activities to do at home
11. Gardening with a child with disabilities
12. Adapting your home for a wheelchair
13. Adapting your home for a blind child
14. Community resources for parents of children with disabilities
15. Eating/mealtime behaviors
16. Shopping skills
17. How to choose/train a baby-sitter
18. Making a home study carrel
19. Cooking skills/activities
20. Speech activities/games
21. Home-school communication systems (notes, telephone)
22. Bicycle safety
23. Interpretation of test results
24. How to help your mainstreamed child adjust/succeed in the regular class
25. Dealing with sibling rivalry
26. Reading to your child at home
27. Dealing effectively with significant others
28. Program for grandparents
29. Fathers-only program
30. Organizing morning activities
31. Home fire safety and escape
32. Helping your disabled child make friends
33. Setting up a parent-run resource room
34. Organizing a summer odd-job program for children
35. Organizing a parent-run respite care exchange system
36. Acceptance and use of prosthetic equipment
37. Preparing for your child's future
38. Dealing with professionals
39. Pets for children with disabilities: selection and care
40. Developing a parent-to-parent support group

There is consistent agreement in the parent education literature on the importance of involving parents in planning and, whenever possible, actually conducting parent groups (Heward et al., 1979; Kroth, 1981; Turnbull et al., 1986). Heward et al. (1979) recommend both open and closed needs assessment procedures to determine what parents want from a parent program. An open-ended needs assessment consists of questions like these:

1. The best family time for my child is when we _____
2. I will never forget the time that my child and I _____
3. When I take my child to the store, I am concerned that he/she will _____
4. People think my child is unable to _____
5. I'm worrying about making a decision about my child's _____

6. Sometimes I think my child will never _____

7. My child is especially difficult around the house when he/she _____

8. I give my child a hug when he/she _____

9. The hardest thing about having a special child is _____

10. I wish I knew more about _____ (p. 240)

Parents' responses to open-ended questions can provide a tremendous amount of information about what kinds of parent training programs might be needed and appreciated.

A closed needs assessment asks parents to indicate, from a list of possibilities, items that they would like to learn more about. For example, parents might be asked to put one check mark by any item of the following topics that is something of a problem and two check marks by any area that is of major interest.

_____ Bedtime behavior	_____ Home chores
_____ Eating behavior	_____ On-task behavior
_____ Interactions with sibling(s)	_____ Leisure activities
_____ Personal cleanliness (dressing, toileting)	_____ Employability skills
_____ Interactions with strangers	_____ Study habits
_____ Compliance with parental requests	_____ Making friends
_____ Interactions with opposite sex	_____ Planning for the future
	_____ Other

Bailey and Simeonsson (1988a) have developed the Family Needs Survey, consisting of 35 items organized into six categories (e.g., needs for information, support, financial needs, family functioning). Because they have obtained different profiles of responses, they recommend that both mothers and fathers complete the needs survey. Bailey and Simeonsson also recommend combining open-ended questions with an overall assessment of family needs. They simply ask parents to list on a piece of paper their "five greatest needs as a family." Turnbull et al. (1986) have developed a comprehensive needs assessment device, the Family Information Preference Inventory, to use as the basis for planning and individualizing parent education and parent involvement programs. By examining the results of needs assessment questionnaires, parents and professionals together can plan parent education groups that are responsive to parents' real needs.

How Much Parent Involvement?

It is sometimes all too easy for professionals to get carried away with a concept, especially one like parent involvement, that has so much promise for positive outcome. But teachers and everyone else involved in providing special education services to exceptional children should not take a one-sided view of parent involvement. Sometimes the time and energy required for parents to participate in home treatment programs or parent education groups cause stress among family members or guilt if the parents cannot fulfill teachers' expectations (Doernberg, 1978; Winton & Turnbull, 1981). The time required to provide additional help to a handicapped child may take too much time and attention away from other family members (Kroth, 1981; Turnbull & Turnbull, 1982).

Kroth (1981) and his colleagues have developed a model guide for parent involvement, the Mirror Model for Parental Involvement, which recognizes that parents have a great deal to offer as well as a need to receive services from special educators. The model assumes that not all parents need everything that professionals have to offer and that no parent should be expected to provide everything. The Mirror Model attempts to give parents an equal part in deciding what services they need and what services they might provide to professionals or other parents. The top half of the model, as illustrated in Figure 13.4, assumes that professionals have certain information, knowledge, and skills that should be shared with parents to help them with their children. The bottom half of the model assumes that parents have information, knowledge, and skills that can help professionals be more effective in helping children.

Cone, Delawyer, and Wolfe (1985) have developed the Parent/Family Involvement Index to objectively measure the 12 types of parent involvement in a special education program.

Professionals must not overlook the importance of leisure time when helping families assess their strengths and needs.

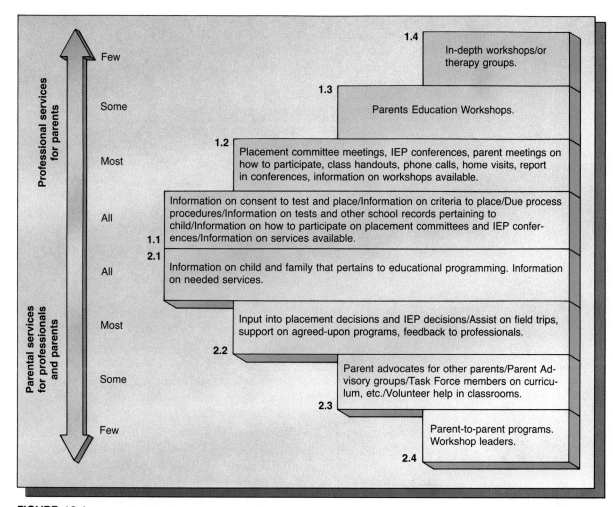

FIGURE 13.4

Mirror model for parent involvement in public schools. (*Source:* From "Involvement with Parents of Behaviorally Disordered Adolescents" by R. Kroth, in *Educating Adolescents with Behavior Disorders* (p. 129) by G. Brown, R. L. McDowell, and J. Smith (Eds.), 1981, Columbus, OH: Merrill. Reprinted by permission.)

■ GUIDELINES FOR WORKING WITH PARENTS OF CHILDREN WITH DISABILITIES

No single approach or set of techniques will be effective, or even appropriate, with every parent. The following suggestions, however, are valuable guidelines for professionals in their interactions with parents.

♦ *Don't assume that you know more about the child, her needs, and how those needs should be met than do the parents.* If you make this assumption, you will often be wrong and, worse, will miss opportunities to get and provide meaningful information.

♦ *Speak in plain, everyday language.* Using educationese does not help a professional communicate effectively with parents (or anyone else, for that matter). Lovitt (1982), a strong believer that we must "junk our jargon," gives us this example from a student's official folder.

> Art shows apraxia due to a vestibular-based deficit. He has laterality, proprioceptive, and sensorimotor dysfunction. Postural ocular deficits are present. He prefers to use right hand but his left hand is more accurate in kinesthesia and proprioception. Nystagmus is depressed during vestibular stimulation. Motor planning activities are difficult for him. (p. 303)

Such a description is of little value to Art's teachers and parents. It would be much better to state clearly what things Art can do now, and what specific things he needs to learn to do.

♦ *Don't let generalizations about parents of children with disabilities guide your efforts.* If you are genuinely interested in what a father or mother feels or needs, ask. Don't assume a parent is in the *x, y,* or *z* stage and therefore needs *a, b,* or *c.*

♦ *Don't be defensive toward or intimidated by parents.* No, you can't really know what it's like to be the parent of a handicapped child unless you are one. But as a trained teacher, you know a great deal about how to help children with disabilities learn; you do it every day, with lots of children. Offer the knowledge and skills you have without apology, and welcome parents' input.

♦ *Maintain primary concern for the child.* If you are a child's teacher, you interact with parents in an effort to improve the child's educational program. In that role you are not a marriage counselor or therapist. Offer to refer parents to professionals who are trained and qualified to provide nonspecial-education services if a parent indicates the need.

♦ *Help parents strive for realistic optimism.* Children with disabilities and their parents benefit little from professionals who are either doom-and-gloom types or who minimize the significance of a disability. Professionals should help parents analyze and prepare for their child's future (Turnbull et al., 1986).

♦ *Start with something parents can be successful with.* Involvement in their child's educational program is a new experience for many parents. Don't punish parents who show an interest in helping their child at home by setting them up to fail by giving them complicated materials, complex instructions, and a heavy schedule of nightly tutoring. Begin with something simple that is likely to be rewarding to the parent.

♦ *Don't be afraid to say, "I don't know."* Sometimes parents ask educational questions that you can't answer or need services that you can't provide. It's OK to say, "I don't know." The mark of a real professional is knowing when you need help, and parents will think more highly of you (Giangreco, Cloninger, Mueller, Yuan, & Ashworth, 1990).

■ CONCLUSIONS/FUTURE TRENDS

We can assume that special educators will strive to continue to develop better ways of working with the families of children with disabilities. These efforts will probably be increasingly driven by values such as those suggested by the Syracuse University Center on Human Policy (1987): (1) families should receive the supports necessary to maintain their children at home; (2) family services should support the entire family; and (3) family supports should maximize the family's control over the services and supports they receive. Thus, we predict that family preservation and family empowerment will increasingly become the goals of working with families with handicapped children. Family-centered services are predicated on the belief that the child is part of a family system and that effective change for the child (who is one part of the system) cannot be achieved without helping the entire family (the whole system) (Cohen et al., 1989). The rationale for family empowerment is based on the belief that families are the primary and most effective social institution, that families cannot be replaced, that parents are and should remain in charge of their families, and that

Family-centered services recognize the child with a disability as part of a whole family system.

RESPITE CARE
Support for Families

"We were really getting worn down. During the first 4 years of Ben's life, we averaged 4 hours of sleep a night. We were wearing ourselves out; I have no doubt we would have completely fallen apart," said Ben's mother, Rebecca Arnett. Ben was born with a neurological condition that produces frequent seizures and extreme hyperactivity. "My husband Roger used his vacations for sleeping in. The respite program came along just in time for us.

"It was hard at first. There's an overwhelming guilt that you shouldn't leave your child. We didn't feel like anyone else could understand Ben's problems. But we had to get away. Our church gave us some money, with orders to take a vacation. It was the first time Roger and I and our 12-year-old daughter, Stacy, had really been together since Ben was born. I was upset at first, calling twice a day to see if everything was all right. But it was wonderful, for everybody.

"Cleo Baker, the respite care worker who stayed with Ben that first time and many times since, is something else. She takes him to McDonald's, shopping, all over. When Ben knows she's coming, he runs for his jacket. He loves her. We've had five or six different respite workers stay with Ben during the year we've used the program, and he likes them all.

"Once parents get over that initial period of letting go, they realize that it's OK to have a life of your own apart from your handicapped child. For us it was a real lifesaver."

Ed Harper, Director of Residential and Family Services for Franklin County, Ohio, explains: "Respite gives families a chance for a more natural lifestyle. Some of the families we serve have gone years without a real break of any kind. Once they try our program and find that a responsible, trained adult can care for their child, it's like a new lease on life.

"At present we are serving about 300 families. Each respite worker completes a 40-hour training program covering feeding techniques, first aid, use of adaptive equipment, leisure-time activities, and so on. We conduct an initial home visit to explain the program and determine the family's special needs. Our workers can be scheduled for any length of time, from 4 hours up to 2 weeks of continuous care. Our respite care is conducted in the family's home or at a respite facility. A sliding fee scale determines the hourly cost according to income and family size."

Respite care can benefit the handicapped family member as well. Susan Clark told of the time she stayed with Stephanie, a 25-year-old mentally retarded woman, so that her mother, who had not had a vacation since her daughter's birth, could go to Florida. "Stephanie and I went everywhere—to the movies, the county fair, out to eat. She did things she had never done in her life. That week was a vacation for her, too."

Another parent, Jean Williams, describes the program this way: "Our son Tom's autism has meant a lot of restrictions in our family life for the past 25 years, bringing with it many problems and much resentment. At last we have been given a no-strings-attached, low-cost way to loosen some of those restrictions. Funny thing is, our Tom is such a nice guy—it's sure good to be able to get far enough away every so often to be able to see that." ◆

the role of professionals is to help parents in their capacity as family leaders (Callister, Mitchell, & Talley, 1986).

Professionals and parents are working to develop and provide a wide range of supportive services for families of children with disabilities. Programs are being implemented to help parents plan effectively for the future, develop problem-solving skills, and acquire competence in financial planning, coping with stress, locating and using community services, and finding time to relax and enjoy life, to name just a few areas of emphasis. In addition, the development and provision of quality respite care services has become a major issue in many communities. Simply defined, respite care is the temporary care of a disabled individual for the purpose of providing relief to the parent and guardian (Salisbury & Intaglia, 1986). Many parents of severely handicapped children identify the availability of reliable, high-quality respite care as their single most pressing need (Grant & McGrath, 1990; Rimmerman, 1989). Fortunately, because of the efforts of parent advocacy groups and concerned professionals, respite services are becoming more and more available throughout the country.

Parents are the most important adults in a child's life. A good teacher should be the next most important adult. Working together, parents and teachers can and do make a difference.

SUMMARY

The Parent-Teacher Partnership

♦ A successful parent-teacher partnership provides benefits for the professional, the parents, and—most important—the child.

♦ Actions of parents, concerned educators, and legislators have all helped to increase parent participation in the special education process.

Effects of a Child's Disabilities on Parents and Family

♦ All parents must adjust to the birth of a handicapped child or the discovery that a child is disabled. This adjustment process is different for each parent, and educators should not make assumptions about an individual parent's stage of adjustment.

♦ A family member's disability is likely to affect parents and nonhandicapped siblings in different ways during the different stages or life cycles.

♦ A disproportionate number of children with disabilities are victims of parental abuse and neglect.

♦ Parents face extra responsibilities in raising children with disabilities, including teaching and counseling the child, managing behavior, dealing with their other nonhandicapped children and other significant people, maintaining the parent-to-parent relationship, and relating to the school and community.

Parent-Teacher Communication

♦ Regular two-way communication is critical to effective parent-teacher partnerships.

♦ Conferences, written messages, and telephone calls are three ways to maintain communication.

Parent Involvement

♦ The extent to which individual parents participate in IEP meetings varies.

♦ Many parents can and should learn to help teach their child with disabilities.

♦ Parents and professionals should be involved in planning and conducting parent education groups.

Guidelines for Working with Parents of Children with Disabilities

♦ Do not assume you know more about a child than do the parents.

♦ Speak in plain, everyday language.

♦ Do not use generalizations as assumptions.

♦ Do not be defensive toward or intimidated by the parents.

♦ Keep concern for the child at the forefront.

♦ Help parents strive for realistic optimism.

♦ Start with something with which parents can be successful.

♦ Do not be afraid to say, "I don't know."

Conclusions/Future Trends

♦ Professionals who work with parents should value family needs and support families in maintaining control over the services and supports they receive.

FOR MORE INFORMATION

Journals

The Exceptional Parent. Published six times per year by the Psy-Ed Corporation, 1170 Commonwealth Ave., Third Floor, Boston, MA 02134. Contains articles for parents and professionals on subjects such as improving parent-professional relationships, maintaining family relationships, and managing financial resources.

Books

Bailey, D. B., & Simeonsson, R. J. (1988). *Family assessment in early intervention*. Columbus, OH: Merrill.

Gallagher, J. J., & Vietze, P. (Eds.). (1988). *Families of handicapped persons: Current research, treatment, and policy issues*. Baltimore, MD: Paul H. Brookes.

Gartner, A., Lipsky, D. K., & Turnbull, A. P. (1990). *Supporting families with a child with a disability*. Baltimore, MD: Paul H. Brookes.

Kroth, R. (1985). *Communicating with parents of exceptional children* (2nd ed.). Denver: Love.

Mullins, J. (1987). Authentic voices from parents of exceptional children. *Family Relations, 36,* 30–33. [This journal article contains a list of 60 books written by parents of children with various handicaps.]

Salisbury, C. L., & Intaglia, J. (1986). *Respite care support for persons with developmental disabilities and their families*. Baltimore, MD: Paul H. Brookes.

Seligman, M. (Ed.). (1983). *The family with a handicapped child: Understanding and treatment*. New York: Grune & Stratton.

Stewart, J. C. (1986). *Counseling parents of exceptional children* (2nd ed.). Columbus, OH: Merrill.

Turnbull, A. P., Turnbull, H. R., III, Summers, J. A., Brotherson, M. J., & Benson, H. A. (1986). *Families, professionals, and exceptionality: A special partnership*. Columbus, OH: Merrill.

Turnbull, H. R., III, & Turnbull, A. P. (1985). *Parents speak out: Then & now* (2nd ed.). Columbus, OH: Merrill.

Organizations

National Center on Child Abuse and Neglect, U.S. Department of Health and Human Services, P. O. Box 1182, Washington, DC 20013. Offers National Child Abuse Hotline with a toll-free number: 800 422-4453.

National Network of Parent Centers, 9451 Broadway Drive, Bay Harbor, FL 33154.

National Parent CHAIN, 515 W. Giles Lane, Peoria, IL 61614. A volunteer organization to establish a national information and education network for handicapped citizens and their families.

Pacer (Parent Advocacy Coalition for Educational Rights) Center, 4701 Chicago Avenue, South, Minneapolis, MN 55407.

Parents Educational Advocacy Center, 116 W. Jones Street, Raleigh, NC 27611.

PEP (Parents Educating Parents) Project, Georgia Association for Retarded Citizens, 1851 Ram Runway, Suite 104, College Park, GA 30337.

14

Early Intervention

◆ Why is it so difficult to measure the effectiveness of early intervention programs?

◆ What are the key differences between an Individualized Education Plan and an Individualized Family Services Plan?

◆ Why is a developmentally-based curriculum not always appropriate for a young child who is exhibiting delays in development?

◆ Why is an interdisciplinary team so critical to effective early intervention?

◆ How can we provide early intervention services for a child whose disability is not yet present?

Most children experience a phenomenal amount of learning during the years from birth to school age. Most children grow and develop in orderly, predictable ways; they learn to move, to communicate, to play. As their ability to manipulate their environment increases, so does their level of independence. Normal rates and patterns of child development contrast sharply with the progress that most children with disabilities experience. If they are to master the basic skills their nonhandicapped peers acquire naturally, many handicapped preschoolers need carefully planned and implemented instruction. But unfortunately, the critical first years of life represent missed opportunities for many children with disabilities.

Not too many years ago, parents who were concerned about deficits in their child's development were often told, "Don't worry. Wait and see. She'll probably grow out of it." As a result, many children with handicaps fell further and further behind their nonhandicapped peers during the early years. Only recently have educators become convinced of the need for early identification and intervention. From a virtual absence of educational programs for infants to school-age children with disabilities 20 years ago, early childhood special education has become one of the most prominent and fastest-growing components in all of education. Virtually every special educator now recognizes the importance of early intervention services, not only for infants and preschoolers with disabilities, but also for young children who are at risk for developing a handicapping condition. Indeed, developing an effective system of early intervention services has become a national priority.

■ IMPORTANCE OF EARLY INTERVENTION

Skeels and Dye (1939) reported the earliest and one of the most dramatic demonstrations of the critical importance of early intervention. Because there was no room at an orphanage, two "hopeless" baby girls, aged 13 and 16 months, had been transferred from an orphanage to a ward of adult women in an institution for persons with mental retardation. "The youngsters were pitiful little creatures. They were tearful, had runny noses, and coarse, stringy, and colorless hair; they were emaciated, undersized, and lacked muscle tone or responsiveness. Sad and inactive, the two spent their days rocking and whining" (Skeels, 1966, p. 5). At the time of their transfer, the two children had IQs estimated between 35 and 46, which classified them in the moderate to severe range of mental retardation. After living with the older women for 6 months, the girls' IQs were measured at 77 and 87, and a few months later, both had IQs in the mid-90s. Such regular intelligence testing was not a common procedure, but because of their unusual placement, the two children were observed closely.

After hearing of the girls' remarkable improvement, Skeels and Dye looked for possible causes. They learned that the children had received an unusual amount of attention and stimulation. Ward attendants had purchased toys and books for the girls, and residents had played and talked with them continuously. Excited by the possibilities, Skeels and Dye convinced the state authorities to permit a most unusual experiment. They selected 13 additional 1- to 2-year-old children. All but two were classified as mentally retarded (average IQ of 64) and, because of a prevailing state law, were judged unsuitable for adoption. The children in this experimental group were removed from the unstimulating orphanage and placed in the one-to-one care of teenage girls with mental retardation who lived at the institution. Each adolescent "mother" was taught how to provide basic care and attention for her baby—how to hold, feed, talk to, and stimulate the child. The children also attended a half-morning kindergarten program at the institution.

A group of 12 children, also under 3 years of age, remained in the orphanage. Children in this contrast group received adequate medical and health services but no individual attention. The children in the contrast group had an average IQ of 86 at the beginning of the study; only two were classified as mentally retarded. Two years later, the children in both groups were retested. The experimental group showed an average gain of 27.5 IQ points, enough for 11 of the 13 children to become eligible for adoption and to be placed in good homes. The children in the contrast group who stayed in the orphanage had lost an average of 26 IQ points.

Twenty-five years later, Skeels (1966) located all the subjects in the original study. What he discovered was even more impressive than the IQ gains originally reported. Of the 13 children in the experimental group, 11 had married; the marriages had produced nine children, all of normal intelligence, and only one of the marriages had ended in divorce. The experimental group's median level of education was the 12th grade, and four had attended college. All were either homemakers or employed outside the home, in jobs ranging from professional and business work to domestic service (for the two who had not been adopted). The story for the 12 children who had remained in the orphanage was less positive. Four were still institutionalized in 1965, and all but one of the noninstitutionalized subjects who were employed were working as unskilled laborers. The median level of education for the contrast group was the third grade. Skeels (1966) concluded his follow-up study with these words:

> It seems obvious that under present-day conditions there are still countless infants with sound biological constitutions and potentialities for development well within the normal range who will become retarded and noncontributing members of society unless appropriate intervention occurs. It is suggested by the findings of this study and others published in the past 20 years that sufficient knowledge is available to design programs of intervention to counteract the devastating effects of poverty, sociocultural, and maternal deprivation. . . . The unanswered questions of this study could form the basis for many life-long research projects. If the tragic fate of the twelve contrast group children provokes even a single crucial study that will help prevent such a fate for others, their lives will not have been in vain. (p. 109)

Although the Skeels and Dye study can be criticized for its lack of tight experimental methodology, it provided a major challenge to the belief that intelligence was fixed and that, therefore, little could be expected from intervention efforts. This classic study served as the foundation and catalyst for many subsequent investigations into the effects of early intervention.

Kirk (1958) reported another often-cited study highlighting the importance of early intervention. This study measured the effects of 2 years of preschool training on the social and cognitive development of 43 children with mental retardation (IQs ranging from 40 to 85). Fifteen of the children in the experimental group lived in an institution and attended a nursery school, while 28 children lived at home and attended a preschool program. Children in the control group—12 in an institution and 26 living at home—did not receive the preschool training. The children who received early intervention gained between 10 and 30 IQ points; the IQ scores of the control group children declined. The differences between the groups were maintained over a period of years.

The Milwaukee Project is another widely-cited effort in early intervention (Garber & Heber, 1973; Heber & Garber, 1971; Strickland, 1971). The project's goal was to reduce the incidence of mental retardation through a program of parent education and infant stimulation for children considered to have a high potential for retarded development because of their mothers' levels of intelligence and conditions of poverty. Mothers with IQs of 70 or less and their high-risk infants were chosen as subjects. The mothers received training in child care and were taught how to interact with and stimulate their children. Beginning before the age of 6 months, the children also participated in an infant stimulation program conducted by trained teachers. By the age of 3½, the experimental children tested an average of 33 IQ points higher than a control group of children who did not participate in the program.

Hailed by the popular media as the "Miracle in Milwaukee," this study is sometimes offered as proof that a program of maternal education and early infant stimulation can reduce the incidence of cultural-familial mental retardation. The Milwaukee Project has, however, also been criticized for its research methods; Page (1972), for example, questions whether bias in sampling and testing was adequately controlled. Nevertheless, according to Garber and Heber (1973),

> Infant testing difficulties notwithstanding, the present standardized test data, when considered along with performance on learning tasks and language tests, indicate an unquestionably superior present level of cognitive development on the part of the experimental group. Also, the first wave of our children are now in public schools. None have been assigned to classes for the retarded. (p. 114)

There have been literally hundreds of studies attempting to determine the effects of early intervention on disadvantaged and handicapped children. White, Bush, and Casto (1986) found that 94% of a sample of 52 previous reviews of the literature concluded that early intervention resulted in substantial immediate benefits for handicapped, at-risk, and disadvantaged children. The immediate benefits included improved cognitive, language, social-emotional, and motor growth and better relationships and functioning with parents and siblings. Analyzing the long-term effects of early intervention, Lazar and Darlington (1982) pooled the data from 12 follow-up studies of children who had participated in preschool programs for socioeconomically disadvantaged children. At the time of the follow-up studies, the children who had participated in the preschool programs were in the 3rd to 12th grades. Fewer of the early intervention children had been placed in special education classes (14% versus 29%), and fewer had been held back to repeat a school year (26% versus 37%).

Although the results reported on the long-term efficacy of early intervention are generally positive, numerous methodological problems make it extremely difficult to conduct this kind of research in a scientifically sound manner

Over a period of 15 years, the Milwaukee Project continued to provide education and family support services to children born of low-IQ mothers. A recent book by Garber (1988), the coordinator of the project's research team, claims significant improvements in intelligence, language performance, and academic achievement for the children who received services compared to a control group of disadvantaged children from mothers of average intelligence.

Reviews of the efficacy of early intervention can be found in Bricker (1986); Dunst, Snyder, and Mankinen (1986); and Smith and Strain (1984).

(Bricker, 1986; Dunst, 1986; Strain & Smith, 1986). Among the problems are the difficulties in selecting meaningful and reliable outcome measures; the wide disparity among handicapped children in the developmental effects of their disabilities; the tremendous variation across early intervention programs in curriculum focus, teaching strategies, length, and intensity; and the ethical concerns of withholding early intervention from some children so that they may form a control group for comparison purposes (Bailey & Wolery, 1984; Casto, 1988; Guralnick, 1988).

In a meta-analysis of 74 studies investigating the efficacy of early intervention with handicapped preschoolers, Casto and Mastropieri (1986) concluded that early intervention produces positive effects and that longer, more intensive programs are generally more effective. They did not, however, find support for two conclusions common to the majority of previous reviews of the literature: They found no evidence that early intervention programs are more effective when begun at an earlier age as opposed to a later age, and they disagreed with previous reviewers who concluded that greater levels of parental involvement are associated with greater effectiveness. Casto and Mastropieri's paper has drawn heavy criticism from other experts on early intervention research, who claim the analysis suffers from conceptual and methodological weaknesses (e.g., Dunst & Snyder, 1986; Strain & Smith, 1986).

In concluding their critique of the Casto and Mastropieri analysis, Strain and Smith (1986), for example, comment on the large but admittedly scientifically questionable body of research that generally indicates positive outcomes of early intervention.

> What do we do then with a data base that is flawed or that offers conflicting results? First, we do not need to apologize for lack of rigor. The methodological weaknesses do not so much reflect poor science or scientists as the reality of field research on complicated questions. The unassailable educational experiment that proves causality once and for all is a myth. Yet, we should not stop trying, with scientific methods, to understand the complexity. . . . Experiments principally designed to determine whether or not early intervention is effective lose their vitality and usefulness. If it looks like a pig, roots, and snorts, it probably is a pig. Similarly, if it looks like we get effects, some weak, some strong, some ambiguous, there probably is a relation between intervention and child outcomes. . . . Policy and program developers have a professional imperative to proceed using the least dangerous assumption that providing appropriate early intervention services is beneficial to handicapped infants, preschoolers, and their families. (pp. 263–264)

Most educators believe that early intervention and preschool services for both handicapped and at-risk children and their families can accomplish the following benefits:

◆ Help produce gains in physical development, cognitive development, language and speech development, social competence, and self-help skills.

◆ Help prevent the development of secondary handicapping conditions.

◆ Reduce family stress and help parents and families support the development of a young child with disabilities.

◆ Reduce the likelihood of social dependence and institutionalization.

Donnellan (1984) suggests that teachers, policy planners, and other human service providers use the criterion of the *least dangerous assumption* when objective data are not available to indicate clearly which placement, program, or procedure is the best or most appropriate. In these instances, decision makers should consider which option will do the least harm to children and their families.

Most educators today believe that early invention is critical for infants and toddlers who are handicapped or at-risk.

♦ Reduce the need for special education services or placement in special classrooms once the child reaches school age.

There is also some evidence that early intervention can save society the costs of higher levels of educational and social services that will be needed later in life if early intervention is not provided. The cost of total services required by a child may be less because of remediation and prevention of developmental problems which would make special services necessary later. Wood (1981) reports an average total cost of cumulative special services through age 18 of $37,273 when intervention begins at birth. This compares favorably with total costs of $46,816 to $53,340 when intervention does not begin until age 6.

■ LEGISLATIVE HISTORY OF EARLY CHILDHOOD SPECIAL EDUCATION

Handicapped Children's Early Education Program

The development and implementation of early intervention services for young children with disabilities have been aided by federal legislation. The first federal law written exclusively for the handicapped preschooler, the Handicapped Children's Early Childhood Assistance Act (P. L. 90–538), was passed in 1968.

This bill created the Handicapped Children's Early Education Program (HCEEP), the purpose of which is to develop model early intervention programs for handicapped children from birth through age 8. HCEEP, often referred to as the First Chance Network, began in 1969 with 24 programs funded for a total of $1 million. By 1985, there were 173 different First Chance Network programs throughout all 50 states and in several U.S. territories; by 1987, over 500 programs had been funded.

HCEEP model projects have collectively developed thousands of print and audiovisual products on early childhood special education, such as screening and assessment devices, curriculum guides, and parent training materials. Many of the products have been purchased and distributed by commercial publishers. Directors of HCEEP model demonstration projects that have been evaluated rigorously and proven worthy of replication can apply for outreach funds to help others set up similar programs elsewhere.

A *model program* evaluates the effectiveness of new assessment, curriculum, instructional procedures, and/or service delivery arrangements (or, as is often the case, a new combination of old techniques) with the hope that, if the model proves effective, it can serve as the basis for developing other similar programs. See Karnes and Stayton (1988) for a review of 96 different HCEEP model programs for infants and toddlers. Suarez, Hurth, and Prestridge (1988) analyzed the characteristics of all 131 HCEEP programs funded during 1982–1986.

Head Start

In 1972, Head Start (a nationwide program begun in 1965 to provide preschool services to children from low-income families) was required by law to reserve at least 10% of its enrollment capacity for children with disabilities. By 1977, 13% of all children enrolled in Head Start programs across the country were handicapped—a total of 36,133 children ("HEW reports," 1978).

The Individuals with Disabilities Education Act (P.L. 94–142)

P. L. 94–142, the Individuals with Disabilities Education Act of 1975 that mandated a free, appropriate public education for all school-age children with disabilities, also included a section on preschool special education. The law required that all children aged 3 to 5 with disabilities were to receive special education services, *if* state law or practice already provided general public education for children in that age group. To stimulate other states to begin programs for handicapped preschoolers, P.L. 94–142 included the incentive grant program that provided funds for establishing or improving preschool programs for children with disabilities. The preschool incentive grants were distributed on the basis of the number of children identified in the state (Cohen, Semmes, & Guralnick, 1979). Although the professionals, parents, and legislators who drafted P.L. 94–142 clearly endorsed the concept of early childhood special education, the incentive grant program was insufficient. In the 1980–81 school year only 16 states provided special education services for the full 3- to 5-year-old range; an additional 22 states required services for preschoolers with disabilities at the age of 4 or 5 (U.S. Comptroller General, 1981).

In 1973, the Division for Early Childhood (DEC) was established within the Council for Exceptional Children. DEC publishes the *Journal of Early Intervention,* a major source of reports of research and innovative practice. For a chronology of the development of early childhood education for both nondisabled and disabled children, see Bailey and Wolery (1984).

P.L. 99–457: The Federal Mandate for Early Childhood Special Education

Since 1975, Congress has enacted three bills reauthorizing and amending P. L. 94–142. The second of the bills, P. L. 99–457, the Education of the Handicapped Act Amendments of 1986, contained two major provisions concerning education of preschoolers with disabilities. Before passage of this law, Congress estimated that states were serving about 70% of the handicapped children aged 3 to 5 under the voluntary provisions of P. L. 94–142; 31 states and territories did not require special education for at least part of that age group (Koppelman, 1986). For handicapped infants and toddlers from birth to age 3, systematic early intervention services were scarce or nonexistent in many states. P.L. 99–457 included a mandatory preschool component for children 3 to 5 years old and a voluntary incentive grant program for early intervention services to infants and toddlers and their families.

Preschool Services for 3- to 5-Year-Olds

P. L. 99–457 requires states to provide preschool services to all children with disabilities ages 3 to 5 years. The regulations governing these programs are similar to those for P.L. 94–142, with these major exceptions:

1. Children do not have to be identified and reported under existing disability categories (e.g., mental retardation, learning disability) in order to receive services.

2. Individualized Education Plans must include a section with instructions/information for parents.

3. Local education agencies may elect to use a variety of service delivery options (home-based, center-based, or combination programs) and the length of the school day and school year may vary.

4. Preschool special eduction programs must be administered by the state education agency; however, services from other agencies may be contracted to meet the requirement of a full range of services.

By the 1991 school year, each state was to show evidence that it was providing a free, appropriate education to all children with disabilities, aged 3 to 5. Failure to comply with these regulations would result in loss of all federal funds for preschool services, and any children who were being served in that age group could not be counted for purposes of receiving that state's funding under P.L. 94–142.

Early Intervention for Infants and Toddlers

All 50 states have elected to pursue federal funds under P.L. 99–457 for the provision of early intervention services to infants and toddlers who are handicapped or at-risk and their families.

The second major change brought about by the passage of P. L. 99–457 was the provision of incentive grants to states for developing and implementing "statewide, comprehensive, coordinated, multidisciplinary, interagency" services of early intervention for handicapped infants and toddlers and their families. The law defines "handicapped infants and toddlers" as individuals from birth through age 2, inclusive, who need early intervention services because they

> (a) are experiencing developmental delays, as measured by appropriate diagnostic instruments and procedures in one or more of the following areas: Cognitive development, physical development, language and speech development, psychosocial development, or self-help skills, or
> (b) have a diagnosed physical or mental condition which has a high probability of resulting in developmental delay.
> Such terms may also include, at a State's discretion, individuals from birth to age 2, inclusive, who are at risk of having substantial delay if early intervention services are not provided. (Section 672)

Special education for 3- to 5-year-olds is now required under federal law.

To receive incentive grant funds, a state must provide services to all infants and toddlers who are experiencing a developmental delay or have an "established risk" (part b, above). Each state's definition of developmental delay must be broad enough to include all disability categories covered by P.L. 94–142. An *established risk* is a diagnosed physical or medical condition that has a high probability of resulting in developmental delays, such as Down syndrome and other chromosomal abnormalities associated with mental retardation, brain or spinal cord damage, sensory impairments, fetal alcohol syndrome, and maternal acquired immune deficiency syndrome (AIDS). Although they are not required to do so, states may also include infants and toddlers who have a *biological* or *environmental risk* in early intervention programs funded by P.L. 99–457. Infants and toddlers may be considered biologically at-risk because of health factors known to produce developmental delays in some children, such as significantly premature birth and low birth weight, and infants of chemically dependent mothers. Young children may be considered environmentally at-risk for developmental disorders because of factors such as being born into extreme poverty or experiencing abuse or neglect.

CEC's Division for Early Childhood issued a position paper suggesting the categories of handicapping, biological and medical, and environmental conditions that should be considered as eligibility criteria for early intervention programs (Smith et al., 1987).

Individualized Family Services Plan

P.L. 99–457 represents a major shift in the focus of educational services. Consistent with current research and understanding of child learning and development, the legislation does not view children as isolated service recipients (Meisels & Provence, 1989). Instead, the law prescribes family-focused early intervention services, delivered according to an Individualized Family Services Plan (IFSP). The IFSP is developed by an interdisciplinary team that includes the child's parents and family. According to P.L. 99–457, each IFSP must contain the following:

♦ A statement of the child's present level of functioning in cognitive, speech and language, psychosocial, motor, and self-help skills.

♦ A statement of the family's strengths and needs relating to the child's development.

♦ A statement of the major expected outcomes to be achieved for the child and family, including criteria, procedures, and time lines for evaluating progress.

♦ A description of the specific early intervention services necessary to meet the unique needs of the child and family, including frequency, intensity, and method of delivering the services.

♦ The projected dates for initiation and expected duration of services.

♦ The name of the case manager from the profession most immediately relevant to the infant's, toddler's, or family's needs who will be responsible for implementation of the plan.

♦ The steps to be taken to support successful transition from early intervention (infant) services to the preschool program.

The IFSP must be evaluated once a year and reviewed with the family at 6-month intervals. Recognizing the critical importance of time for the infant with disabilities, the law allows for initiation of early intervention services before the IFSP is completed, if the parents give their consent. "The IFSP effectively redefines the service recipient as being the family (rather than the child alone)" (Krauss, 1990, p. 388). These are examples of items that IFSPs have included as family goals:

Family will locate reading materials about child's condition.

Grandmother will learn handling techniques with child.

Dad will learn to simplify activities that he enjoys so child can participate.

Parents will make a 2-month medical appointment with the physicians.

Family will integrate the child's developmental goals into the family's daily living activities.

Staff will provide ongoing parent education programs.

Mother will increase time for herself.

Respite care: 5 days, 20 hours provided per month.

Parents will assist child with crawling using reciprocal motion for 10 feet once daily by the end of 8 weeks.

Using "Let's Talk" cards, mother will spend 10 minutes each day talking and playing with child. (Bailey, Winton, Rouse, & Turnbull, 1990, p. 18)

The enactment of P.L. 99–457 formalizes society's recognition of the importance of early intervention both for children who are experiencing handicaps and for those who are at risk for substantial developmental delays in the future. But before early intervention services can begin, the children must be identified.

IDENTIFICATION OF HANDICAPPED AND AT-RISK INFANTS AND PRESCHOOLERS

There is consensus among early childhood experts that the earlier intervention is begun, the better. Child development expert Burton White, who has conducted years of research with nonhandicapped infants and preschoolers at Harvard University's Pre-School Project, believes that the period from 8 months to 3 years is critical to a cognitive and social development. Discussing the development and learning of nonhandicapped children, White (1975) says that "to begin to look at a child's educational development when he is 2 years of age is already much too late" (p. 4).

Smith and Strain (1984) argue that research supports beginning intervention as early as possible in a handicapped child's life. If the first years of life are the most important for children without handicaps, they are even more critical for the handicapped child, who, with each passing month, risks falling even further behind her nonhandicapped age-mates. Hayden and Pious (1979) contend that some interventions may need to begin at or before birth.

> It is simply never too early to intervene, and . . . from the data base we now have, it seems clear that urgently needed interventions should occur long before a child is born. Once a child has arrived, the work necessarily shifts into amelioration, away from prevention—always a second choice for intervention. . . . Beginning at birth is not too soon. (p. 273)

Prenatal Risk Factors

We know more today than ever before about conditions associated with increased probability of the birth of a handicapped baby. We know, for example, that a history of certain disabilities in a family should make us watch for similar risks to any future children. We know that malnutrition during pregnancy can produce severe problems, including retardation, in the baby. And we know that diseases during pregnancy, particularly rubella, can cause serious disabilities in the newborn. Other signs of an at-risk pregnancy include the following:

In the United States, 3 of every 100 babies are born with major birth defects.

♦ Birth of a previous child with a chromosomal abnormality

♦ Alcohol or drug use during pregnancy

♦ Age of the mother over 35 (although women over 35 have only 7% of the babies born, they give birth to more than 33% of all Down syndrome babies)

♦ Two or more congenital malformations in the parents

♦ Mental retardation in the mother

♦ Absence of secondary sex characteristics in the mother

♦ History of several miscarriages for the mother

With widespread genetic counseling, along with greater public awareness of these conditions as predictors of handicaps, many parents or prospective parents can make better decisions, based on more information, about having a child. Likewise, better prenatal care can reduce the incidence of prematurity and low birth weight, both of which are also associated with a higher frequency of handicaps.

We know that drug and alcohol use by pregnant women can have devastating effects on the fetus that result in developmental delays and other handicaps. **Fetal alcohol syndrome (FAS)**, caused by excessive alcohol use during pregnancy, often produces serious physical defects and developmental delays. Drug use during pregnancy, especially cocaine and crack, has reached epidemic proportions and is reported at all economic and educational levels (Williams & Howard, 1990). Miller (1989) reported that, through written surveys, hospitals found 17% of women used cocaine during pregnancy; shocking as this figure is, self-reported use of an illegal substance is almost certain to produce an underestimation. Indeed, Frank et al. (1988) found that 24% of the pregnant women they interviewed failed to report cocaine use that was later verified by urine tests. Hospitals that conduct urine tests on newborns are finding 10% to 15% positive for cocaine (Miller, 1989), yet presence of the drug in the urine of newborns only indicates cocaine use within 48 hours prior to delivery. Cocaine-exposed infants project distress signals such as increased respiration and movement and high-pitched crying, and they often show little ability to interact with caretakers or respond to comforting (Williams & Howard, 1990).

Even with tenfold improvements in public awareness, prenatal care, and early education, however, the possibility of eliminating most handicaps is not likely to be realized in this century. Thus, the need for effective early intervention programs will continue to challenge us.

Screening

As a general rule, the more severe the handicapping condition, the earlier it can be detected. In the delivery room, medical staff can identify certain disabilities, including microcephaly, **cleft palate**, and other physical deformities, as well as most instances of Down syndrome. Within a few days after birth, analysis of a newborn's blood and urine can detect metabolic disorders that will produce mental retardation if not treated within 4 to 12 weeks. Within the first few weeks, other physical characteristics like coma, paralysis, seizures, or rapidly increasing head size can signal possible handicapping conditions (Parmelee & Michaelis, 1971). Within the first months, delays in the development of various critical behaviors can tell a trained observer that an infant is at risk of developing a handicap.

Some handicaps, like learning disabilities or mild retardation, do not show up until a child is in school and his performance in academic subjects is clearly behind that of his peers. But even in those cases, if the child is enrolled in a preschool staffed by experienced professionals, it is possible to note learning problems or lags early.

Even though many measures have been developed to screen for high-risk infants and children, use of the measures is still far from universal. One national effort is the Early and Periodic Screening, Diagnosis, and Treatment (EPSDT) provision of the Social Security Amendments of 1967. Required since 1972, EPSDT was set up to increase the early identification of child health problems and to connect children from low-income families with medical and other related services. But EPSDT has drawn criticism, both for failing to reach more of the children it should serve and for failing to provide as much information as

A DESPERATE LEGACY
by Michael Dorris

At the time I adopted my oldest son in 1971, I knew that his birth-mother had been a heavy drinker, but even the medical textbooks in those days stated that exposure to alcohol could not damage a developing fetus. I knew that he had been born small and premature, had "failed to thrive," and was initially a slow learner, but for 10 years as a single parent, I convinced myself that nurturing, a stimulating environment—and love—could open up life to my little boy.

It wasn't true. At the University of Washington and elsewhere, biochemists and psychologists now confirm that, for some women, even moderate doses of prenatal alcohol can permanently stunt a human being's potential. According to the U.S. Surgeon General, there is no guaranteed "safe" level of alcohol consumption during pregnancy.

My grown son has a full range of physical problems: seizures, curvature of the spine, poor coordination, sight, and hearing; but his most distressing and disabling legacy has to do with his impaired ability to reason. Fetal Alcohol Syndrome (FAS) victims are known for poor judgment, impulsiveness, persistent confusion over handling money, telling time, distinguishing right from wrong.

A majority of full-blown FAS victims are adopted or in state care, but many children, less drastically afflicted by Fetal Alcohol Effect (FAE), remain with their natural parents. Depending on the term of pregnancy in which the harmful drinking occurred, they may look perfectly healthy and test in the normal range for intelligence, yet still, by early adolescence, they show unmistakable signs of comprehension problems or uncontrolled rage. It is currently estimated that in the United States last year, 8,000 babies were born with FAS and another 65,000 with FAE. Nothing will ever restore them to who they might otherwise have been.

At last, thanks to a 1988 act of Congress, liquor-bottle labels must include a warning to pregnant women, and signs posted in many bars proclaim the hazards of alcohol to unborn children. But what happens when public education doesn't work as a deterrent, when a pregnant woman *herself* is a victim of FAS or prenatal crack and therefore cannot understand the long-term disastrous consequences upon the life of another resulting from what she drinks or inhales? It isn't that these women don't love the *idea* of their babies. They just can't foresee the cruel realities.

The conflict of competing priorities—of protecting immediate civil liberties versus preventing future civil strife—is incredibly complex, with no unambiguously right or easy answers. But as a nation it's unconscionable to delay the debate. If we close our eyes, we condemn children not yet even conceived to preordained existences of sorrow and deprivation, governed by prison, victimization, and premature death.

My wife and I think of these issues as we wait for our son to have brain surgery that may reduce the intensity of his seizures, though not eliminate them. At 22, despite all of our efforts and his best intentions, he remains forever unable to live independently, to manage a paycheck or to follow the plot of a TV sitcom. And we worry about the very fabric of society when hundreds of thousands of others with his problems, or worse, become teenagers, become adults, in the year 2000.

Michael Dorris is the author of The Broken Cord *(1989), an award-winning book describing his experiences with his son, an FAS victim. From "A Desperate Crack Legacy" by Michael Dorris,* Newsweek, *June 25, 1990, p. 8. Reprinted by permission.* ◆

---

it could (Margolis & Meisels, 1987). At its best, however, EPSDT is empowered to screen only children who receive Medicaid; no such program is even recommended by the federal or state governments for other children.

Nonetheless, there are promising developments for early identification of handicapped and at-risk infants. For example, the SKI*HI Project at Utah State University, in conjunction with the Utah State Health Department, has developed a statewide screening procedure to detect hearing impairment (Finch, 1985). The procedure involves revisions of Utah's birth certificate format to include

For descriptions of other statewide systems for screening and tracking handicapped and at-risk infants, see Meisels and Provence (1989).

indicators associated with hearing loss. The project coordinates follow-up home visits to every infant in the state who is discovered to be at risk for hearing loss.

One screening procedure performed in almost all hospital delivery rooms in the United States is the Apgar scale, a quick evaluation of five physiological measures in newborn infants (Figure 14.A in "The Apgar Scale"). The scale indicates the degree of **prenatal asphyxia** (oxygen deprivation during the birth process) an infant undergoes during birth. Another widely practiced screening procedure is the analysis of newborn blood and urine samples to detect metabolic disorders, such as PKU, that produce mental retardation. Many hospitals also routinely analyze newborn blood and urine samples to detect the presence of drugs and other toxins.

The most widely used screening instrument for developmental delays is the Denver Developmental Screening Test (DDST) (Frankenburg, Dodds, & Fandal, 1975). The DDST can be administered in 15 to 20 minutes and can be used with children from 2 weeks to 6 years of age. It assesses 107 skills arranged in four developmental areas: gross motor, language, fine motor-adaptive, and personal-social. Each test item is represented on the scoring form by a bar showing at what ages 25%, 50%, 75%, and 90% of normally developing children can perform that skill. The child is allowed up to three trials per item. A delay is noted when the child cannot perform a skill that 90% of younger children can perform. A child's performance is considered abnormal if two of the developmental areas contain two or more delayed items. The child would then be referred for further detailed assessment of her abilities.

The recently published Denver II is a revision and restandardization of the DDST based on the performance of over 2,000 children representing a cross section of the Colorado population (Frankenburg, Dodds, Archer, Shapiro, & Bresnick, 1990). The Denver II differs from the DDST in several ways: (1) the number of items has been increased to 125—most of the new items are in the area of language development; (2) DDST items that had proven difficult to administer and/or interpret were eliminated or modified; (3) items on which there were significant differences in the performance of children from different ethnic groups, maternal education, and/or place of residence (rural, urban, semi-rural) are identified in the Denver II Technical Manual so that the diagnostician can determine if a delay may be due to socio-cultural differences; (4) the test form was modified to fit the schedule of health maintenance visits recommended by the American Academy of Pediatrics. A child's performance on each item is scored as "pass" or "fail" and then interpreted as representing "advanced," "OK," "caution," or "delayed" performance by comparing the child's performance with those of the same age in the standardized population. Figure 14.1 shows the test form for the Denver II.

Many other screening measures are available. The Battelle Developmental Inventory Screening Test (Newborg, Stock, Wnek, Guidubaldi, & Suinicki, 1989) can be administered to handicapped and nonhandicapped children, ages birth through 8. The Battelle has adapted testing procedures for use with children with different disabilities. Several are based on the Gesell Developmental Schedules (Gesell et al., 1940; Knobloch & Pasamanick, 1974), which describe normal motor development, adaptive behavior, language, and personal-social behavior in infants and young children. The Bayley Scales of Infant Development (Bayley, 1969), which evaluate an infant's development from 2 to 30 months, are

THE APGAR SCALE

The Apgar scale is a screening test for newborn infants. Developed in 1952 by Dr. Virginia Apgar, an anesthesiologist, the scale measures the degree of prenatal asphyxia (oxygen deprivation) an infant experiences during birth. The screening is administered to virtually 100% of the babies born in American hospitals. According to Dr. Frank Bowen, director of neonatology at Children's Hospital in Columbus, Ohio, "Every delivery should have a person whose primary interest is the newborn," and it is this person—nurse, nurse anesthesiologist, or pediatrician—who administers the Apgar.

The test administrator evaluates the infant twice on five physiological measures: heart rate, respiratory effort, response to stimulation, muscle tone, and skin color (see the sample rating form in Figure A). On each measure the child is given a score of 0, 1, or 2. The scoring form describes the specific characteristics of each measure so that the results are as objective as possible.

If the newborn receives a low score on the first administration of the test, which is conducted 60 seconds after birth, the delivery room staff takes immediate resuscitation action. The staff's role is to help the infant complete the transition to the world outside the mother's body by establishing strong respiration. This first test measures how the baby fared during the birth process.

The scale is given again 5 minutes after birth. At that point a total score of 0 to 3 (out of a possible 10) indicates severe asphyxia; 4 to 6, moderate asphyxia; and 7 to 10, mild asphyxia. "Some stress is assumed on all births," according to Dr. Bowen. The 5-minute score measures how successful any resuscitation efforts were. Again, a low score calls for continuing action to help the infant.

"A 5-minute score of 6 or less deserves follow-up," says Dr. Bowen, "to determine what is causing the problem and what its long-term consequences will be." The Apgar has been shown to identify high-risk infants—those who have a greater-than-normal chance of developing later problems. Research has shown that oxygen deprivation at birth contributes to neurological impairment, and the 5-minute Apgar score correlates well with eventual neurological outcomes.

Although most newborns are evaluated in terms of gestational weight and age and are screened for certain specific disorders, the Apgar scale is at present the only universally used screening test for high-risk infants. ◆

FIGURE A
Apgar evaluation scale.

			60 sec.	5 min.
Heart rate	Absent	(0)		
	Less than 100	(1)		
	100 to 140	(2)	1	2
Respiratory effort	Apneic	(0)		
	Shallow, irregular	(1)		
	Lusty cry and breathing	(2)	1	1
Response to catheter stimulation	No response	(0)		
	Grimace	(1)		
	Cough or sneeze	(2)	1	2
Muscle Tone	Flaccid	(0)		
	Some flexion of extremities	(1)		
	Flexion resisting extension	(2)	1	2
Color	Pale, blue	(0)		
	Body pink, extremities blue	(1)		
	Pink all over	(2)	0	1
	Total		4	8

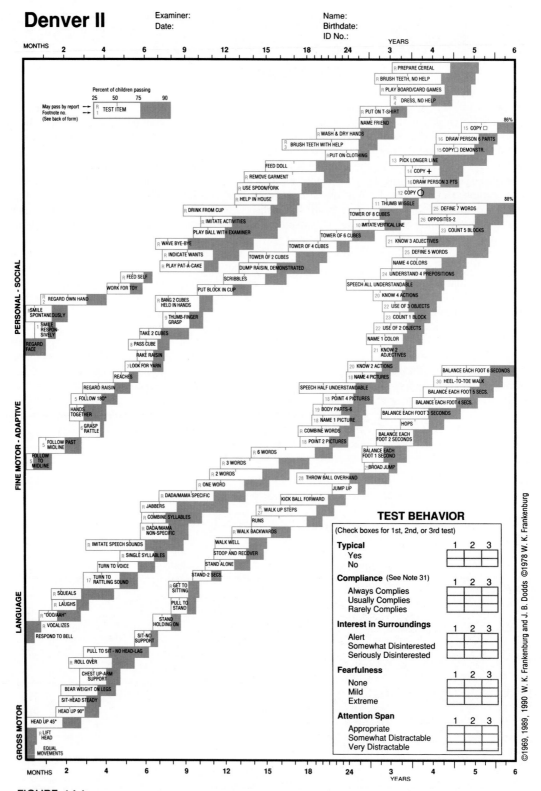

FIGURE 14.1

Test form for the Denver II. (*Source: From The Denver II* by W. K. Frankenburg, J. B. Dodds, P. Archer, H. Shapiro, and B. Bresnick, 1990, Denver: Denver Developmental Materials, Inc.)

standardized adaptations of the Gesell schedules. The Developmental Screening Inventory (Knobloch, Pasamanick, & Sherard, 1966), also based on the Gesell scales, was designed for pediatricians to use in assessing developmental delays in children between 1 and 18 months of age. The Brazelton Neonatal Assessment Scale (Brazelton, 1973) is a more detailed assessment of the newborn.

None of these measures or practices, however, add up to any kind of truly systematic effort to screen all infants. Most state and local screening programs are aimed at older children, especially those about to start school. It is inappropriate to screen children only once during their early years. Developmental screening should occur on multiple occasions between birth and age 6 and should be available throughout the year (Bailey & Wolery, 1989). And it is critical that screening involve multiple sources of information (Meisels & Provence, 1989). For example, a longitudinal study of 268 adolescents with disabilities and an equal number of control group students without disabilities found that, in children from birth to 3 years of age, parental traits such as maternal level of education were more accurate predictors of later involvement in special education than were variables such as the child's rating on developmental screening scales (Kochanek, Kabacoff, & Lipsitt, 1990). Conversely, results from the same study showed that at 4 to 17 years of age, child-centered measures such as developmental competence were more predictive of later problems. Kochanek et al. (1990) concluded that

> Early identification models that focus solely on developmental delay or adverse medical events from birth to 3 years of age are inadequate in fully identifying children eventually judged to be handicapped. While such models will identify youngsters with established conditions, they will ultimately identify only a small segment of the total handicapped population. (p. 535)

Fine motor development and social skills are two important areas of child development.

Identifying high-risk infants and young children most often depends on the experience and concern of the adults who deal with them. Chief among those adults are pediatricians and nurses, social workers, day-care staff, preschool teachers, and, most of all, the child's parents. One study has shown that mothers' estimates of their preschool children's levels of development correlate highly with those that professionals produce using standardized scales (Gradel, Thompson, & Sheehan, 1981).

Not all children who are screened as high risk will necessarily have disabilities. Some grow up to live normal lives, without any special help. The goal of early screening is to identify a possible or likely handicap before it can take its full toll on the child's future. For those who are identified, screening is only the first step. The next step is a careful and detailed assessment of all of the critical areas of development.

Assessment

Assessment in early childhood special education should accomplish three related objectives (McLoughlin & Lewis, 1990). First, assessment should determine whether there is a developmental handicap. Second, information gathered during assessment should reveal the specific nature of the child's needs, the services required, and the instructional objectives. Third, ongoing, systematic assessment serves to monitor the early intervention program and evaluate its effectiveness. Assessment of young children should be guided by a number of criteria (Bailey & Wolery, 1989; McLoughlin & Lewis, 1990; Meisels & Provence, 1989):

♦ Assessments should be conducted in a child's natural environment in a nonthreatening way (Bailey & Wolery, 1984).

♦ Direct observation of behavior is necessary to accurately determine the child's abilities. Checklists and rating scales, although sufficient for targeting general areas of strength and weakness, usually do not pinpoint the specific behaviors that define those areas (Halle & Sindelar, 1982).

♦ Assessments should be repeated over time. It is dangerous to decide that a disability does or does not exist on the basis of one test or observation. Young children's behavior is simply too variable, and the consequences of being wrong too great, to base a decision on one assessment session, no matter how extensive it is (McLoughlin & Lewis, 1990).

♦ Eligibility for services should not be determined by single or limited criteria, but rather by an assessment process that obtains multiple sources of information. For example, Meisels and Provence (1989) describe a 5-month-old infant with Down syndrome who scored in the average range on the Bayley and Vineland Scales used by the early intervention agency to determine eligibility. Because the agency used multiple eligibility criteria (including the diagnosis of Down syndrome, a condition of established risk), the child and his family qualified for services despite the test score in the normal range.

♦ A multidisciplinary assessment should be conducted. It is important that the members of a multidisciplinary assessment team cooperate to determine their respective roles before assessment begins. Intentional overlapping in role assignments helps eliminate gaps in the assessment process (Rose & Logan, 1982).

♦ The assessment process should involve parents and family. Information gathered from interviews with parents and observations of parent-child interactions is extremely important in determining meaningful instructional targets. Not only is the information from parents necessary for a complete assessment, but their cooperation and involvement as active partners throughout the assessment process are desired because parents play a critical role in most early intervention programs (Winton, 1986; Winton & Bailey, 1988). Vincent and her colleagues have developed the Parent Inventory of Child Development in Nonschool Environments, which helps identify skills important to parents and the home (Vincent et al., 1983).

♦ The child should be kept motivated during administration of assessment items, and testing should not continue if the child's attention or performance declines after a time.

♦ Test items and administration should be modified if necessary to allow a child with a disability to display his ability. Bailey and Wolery (1989) recommend that "after following standard administration procedures, assessors should 'test the limits' of children's performance" (p. 61). For example, changing the way a test item is presented (perhaps repeating it and using gestural cues) or even partially assisting a child in responding may provide significantly more useful information about the child's current level of functioning than can be gained by simply marking a score of zero and proceeding to the next item. Although this suggestion goes against the rules of administering standardized tests, the information acquired about the child's abilities and its usefulness in determining appropriate instructional targets is often more important than calculation of a test score (McLean & Snyder-McLean, 1978).

A wide variety of assessment devices are available, including both formal, standardized measures and less formal checklists and rating scales based on observations. Bailey and Wolery (1989) describe and compare numerous formal evaluation instruments for identifying and assessing delayed or abnormal progress in intellectual development, auditory perception, or affective and social development.

As more and more intervention programs for young children with disabilities are started, the number of informal observation checklists, rating scales, and other assessment devices also grows. Most have been developed by federally funded model programs or by locally sponsored centers for young handicapped children. In general, assessment tools seek to measure a child's development in six key areas.

For extensive discussions of screening and assessment of infants and preschoolers, see Bailey and Simeonssen (1988a), Bailey and Wolery (1989), and Meisels (1989).

♦ *Cognitive development* includes such processes as attention, perception, memory, verbal skills, and concept learning; many of the processes are assessed by observing a child's performances in other areas.

♦ *Motor development* includes gross motor skills (like rolling over, crawling, walking, swimming) and fine motor skills (like eye-hand coordination, reaching, touching, grasping).

Assessment should be conducted in natural, nonthreatening environments with the child motivated to do her best.

- *Language development* encompasses all of communication development, including a child's ability to respond nonverbally with gestures, smiles, or actions, and the acquisition of spoken language—sounds, words, phrases, sentences, and so on.
- *Self-help skills* include skills such as feeding, dressing, and using the toilet without assistance.
- *Play skills* include playing with toys, with other children, with games, and in dramatic or fantasy roles.
- *Personal-social skills* include child's social responses to adults and to other children, as well as skills in managing her own behaviors when alone.

Generally, these six areas are broken down into specific, observable tasks and sequenced developmentally; that is, in the order in which most children learn them. Sometimes each task is tied to a specific age at which a child should normally be able to perform it. This arrangement allows the observer to note significant delays or gaps, as well as other unusual patterns, in a high-risk child's development.

Several assessment devices have specific sections to test a child's sensory acuity (hearing and sight, in particular). And many also try to measure a child's readiness for academic learning, with specific tasks related to early reading and math skills. There are also tests designed to measure a child's readiness for school, such as the BRIGANCE K and 1 Screen for Kindergarten and First Grade (Brigance, 1982) and the Metropolitan Readiness Tests (Nurss & McGauvran, 1986). Readiness tests usually include items to assess a child's prereading and premath skills as well as social-emotional development, gross and fine motor performance, and general cognitive development.

A growing number of early intervention programs are moving away from assessments based entirely on developmental milestones and are incorporating curriculum-based assessment. Each item in a curriculum-based assessment relates directly to a skill in the program's curriculum, thereby providing a direct link between testing, teaching, and progress evaluation. But, as Notari and Bricker (1990) note, "although theoretically more appealing, many curriculum-based assessments in fact are drawn from items on standardized tests, thus decreasing their relevance to intervention programming" (p. 118).

See Bagnato, Neisworth, and Capone (1986) for a description and rationale of curriculum-based assessment, as well as a review of 21 assessment measures useful for curriculum-based assessment in early childhood special education programs.

An empirically tested curriculum-based assessment device intended to facilitate the link between assessment, intervention, and evaluation is the Evaluation and Programming System: For Infants and Young Children (EPS-I) (Bricker, Gentry, & Bailey, 1985). Designed for use with children ranging in age from 1 month to 6 years, the EPS-I is divided into six domains: fine motor, gross motor, self-care, cognitive, social-communication, and social. Each domain is divided into strands that group related behaviors and skills considered essential for infants and young children to function independently. All skills selected for inclusion in the EPS-I meet five instructional characteristics:

1. They are functional, in that they enhance the child's ability to cope with daily environmental demands.

2. They are generic, allowing for modifications and adaptations for infants and children with disabilities.

3. They are easily integrated within the classroom or home by teacher or parent.

4. They are observable and measurable, enabling objective determination of performance and progress.

5. They are organized by long-range and short-range goals rather than according to typical developmental sequences.

For further descriptions of the EPS-I and research on its utility, reliability, and validity, see Bricker, Bailey, and Slentz (1990) and Notari and Bricker (1990).

The accuracy and usefulness of the assessment information depend not just on the kind of device or method used. The experience and training of the observer, the number of observations, the settings in which the child is observed, and the care with which the data are interpreted all affect the reliability of an assessment.

DuBose (1981) has noted the particular difficulty posed by evaluating children with severe disabilities. Because there are so few reliable assessment instruments for use with severely impaired children, professionals often must adapt standardized tests and devise informal assessment tasks. DuBose warns that when adaptations must be made, they must be carefully noted and results interpreted with care. The examiner must know why a particular test was given, what it is meant to tap, and what the child's test performances indicate.

Serious dangers can arise from errors in screening or assessment. Children who are disabled but who are not identified may fail to get needed services, and their problems may get worse. On the other hand, children who are not disabled but who are assessed as such may suffer the stigma of an erroneous label. Identification and assessment of young children with disabilities will continue to be a difficult yet extremely important aspect of special education.

EARLY CHILDHOOD SPECIAL EDUCATION PROGRAMS

Early intervention services are usually provided in the child's home, in a center-based facility, or in a combination of both settings.

Home-Based Programs

As the name suggests, a home-based program depends heavily on parental training and cooperation. The parents assume the responsibility of primary caregivers and teachers for their handicapped child. Parent training is usually provided by a teacher or trainer who visits the home regularly to guide the parents, act as a consultant, evaluate the success of intervention, and regularly assess the child's progress. Home visitors (or home teachers or home advisors, as they are often called) in some programs are specially trained paraprofessionals. They may visit as frequently as several times a week, but probably no less than a few times a month. They sometimes carry the results of their in-home evaluations back to other professionals, who may recommend changes in the program.

Perhaps the best known home-based program is the nationally validated Portage Project (Shearer & Shearer, 1972). Operated by a consortium of 23 school districts in south-central Wisconsin, the Portage Project has produced its own assessment materials and teaching activities, The Portage Guide to Early Education. The program is based on 450 behaviors, sequenced developmentally and classified into self-help, cognition, socialization, language, and motor skills. A project teacher normally visits the home one day each week to review the child's progress during the previous week, describe activities for the upcoming week, demonstrate to the parents how to carry out the activities with the child, observe the parent and child interacting and offer suggestions and advice as needed, and summarize where the program stands and indicate what records parents should keep during the next week. The Portage Project has been replicated in hundreds of locations around the country (Shearer & Snider, 1981). A review of outcome studies on the Portage Project states that there is evidence of developmental acceleration in mildly delayed children (Sturmey & Crisp, 1986).

The Transactional Family Systems Model (TFSM) at the University of Washington provides home-based intervention to severely handicapped/medically fragile infants from birth to 2 years and their families (Hedlund, 1989). The program's primary goal is to foster positive interactions between parents and their babies. The TFSM home visitor helps parents become sensitive to their infant's behavioral repertoire and to adjust their interactions to match the baby's needs. Videotaping helps parents learn about the significance of the fleeting and subtle cues these babies often express with their body language. Once parents become sensitive to their babies' behavioral cues, the home visitor helps them adjust their own communication styles accordingly. Parents receive guided practice and encouragement in interactions with their baby. TFSM staff highlight small increments of developmental progress. The ultimate goal of the TFSM program is to give parents a sense of competence and to help them see their child as a developing individual, despite a disability or medical condition.

An early intervention program based in the home has several advantages, especially if the home is the handicapped child's own. First, the home is the child's natural environment, and parents have been the child's first teachers. Other family members—siblings and perhaps even grandparents—have more opportunity to interact with the child, both for instruction and for social contact. These significant others can play an important role in the child's growth and development. Also, home learning activities and materials are more likely to be natural and appropriate. And it is often true that a parent can give more time and attention to the child than even the most adequately staffed center or school. In addition, parents who are actively involved in helping their child learn and develop clearly have an advantage over parents who feel guilt, frustration, or defeat at their seeming inability to help their handicapped child. (Of course, this does not imply that parents of a child in a center-based program cannot or do not take an active role in their child's learning and growth.) Furthermore, in sparsely populated regions, a home-based program allows a child to live at home while receiving an intensive education, without totally disrupting the family's life. Home-based programs can also be less costly to operate without the expenses of maintaining a facility and equipment and transporting children to and from the center (Bailey & Bricker, 1985).

Home-based programs are not without disadvantages. Because the programs place so much responsibility on parents, they are not effective with all families. Not all parents are able or willing to spend the time required to teach their children, and some who try are not effective teachers. Early childhood special education programs must learn to more effectively serve the large and growing number of young children who do not reside in the traditional two-parent family—especially the many thousands of children with teenage mothers who are single, uneducated, and poor. Many of these infants and preschoolers are at risk for developmental delays because of the impoverished conditions in which they live, and it is unlikely that a parent struggling with the realities of day-to-day survival will be able to meet the added demands of involvement in an early intervention program (Turnbull et al., 1986). In addition, because the parent—usually the mother—is the primary service provider, children in home-based programs may not receive as wide a range of services as they would in a center-based program, where they can be seen by a variety of professionals. (It should be noted, however, that the services of professionals such as physical therapists, occupational therapists, or speech therapists can be, and sometimes are, provided in the home.) Another disadvantage of the home-based program is that the child may not receive sufficient opportunity for social interaction with peers.

Bailey and Simeonsson (1988b) provide a detailed discussion of the relative advantages and disadvantages of home-based versus center-based early intervention.

Center-Based Programs

Center-based programs provide early intervention services in a special educational setting outside the home. The setting may be part of a hospital complex, a special day-care center, or a preschool. Some children may attend a specially designed developmental center or training center that offers a wide range of services for children with varying types and degrees of disabilities. One program's setting was an outdoor playground specially built on a New York City rooftop (Jones, 1977). Wherever they are, these centers offer the combined services of many professionals and paraprofessionals, often from several different fields.

Most center-based programs encourage social interaction, and some try to integrate handicapped children with nonhandicapped children in day-care or preschool classes. Some children attend a center each weekday, for all or most of the day; others may come less frequently, although most centers expect to see each child at least once a week. Parents are sometimes given roles as classroom aides or encouraged to act as their child's primary teacher. A few programs allow parents to spend time with other professionals or take training while their child is somewhere else in the center. Virtually all HCEEP model programs and most other effective programs for young children with disabilities recognize the critical need to involve the parents, and they welcome parents in every aspect of the program.

One of the more successful center programs is the Model Preschool Center for Handicapped Children at the University of Washington in Seattle. There, children with a variety of disabilities participate in one of several highly specialized programs: an infant learning program, a communication disorders classroom, a preschool where children with disabilities are integrated with normal children, a program for Down syndrome children, and a program for severely disabled preschoolers. Although all the programs stress parent involvement, most of the children's direct instruction takes place at the center. Instruction consists of rigorously applied behavior analysis: careful screening and initial assessment, pinpointing of target behaviors for instruction, precise instructional planning, and daily assessments of progress. Like that of most centers, the curriculum focuses on key areas of development: gross and fine motor, communication, self-help, social behavior, and preacademic skills. Because of its size and its location at a major university, the center's staff is large and can offer the services of many different specialists in teaching, language and communication disorders, psychology, and medicine. By 1985, the Model Preschool's outreach project had assisted 47 other sites in replicating components of the demonstration model (Assael, 1985).

The Carousel Preschool Program is a center-based early childhood program operated in conjunction with the University of South Florida. The Carousel program operates two integrated preschool classrooms, one serving 4- to 5-year-old children with severe behavior disorders and one serving children considered "at risk" for developing severe behavior problems in the future. Both classrooms provide a regular preschool curriculum to 16 children, half of whom are nonhandicapped same-age peers. Classroom teachers work to engage both the handicapped/at-risk students and nonhandicapped students in the same activities. To ensure the transition to integrated, least restrictive settings, Carousel staff provide a follow-up program and inservice training to the teachers and aides in the children's new schools.

Center-based programs generally offer a number of advantages that are difficult to build into home-based efforts. One important benefit is the opportunity for a team of specialists from different fields—education, physical

At the center-based Carousel Preschool in Florida, children with severe behavior disorders learn to interact with nonhandicapped peers.

and occupational therapy, speech and language pathology, medicine, and others—to observe each child and cooperate in intervention and continued assessment. Some special educators feel that the intensive instruction and related services that can be provided in a center-based program are especially important for children with severe disabilities (Rose & Calhoun, 1990). Many centers hold regular meetings (perhaps once a month) at which all those involved with the child sit down to discuss his progress, his response to the strategies used, and new or revised objectives for him. The opportunity for contact with handicapped and nonhandicapped peers makes center programs especially appealing for some children, and parents involved in center programs no doubt feel some relief at the support they get from the professionals who work with their child and from other parents with children at the same center.

Disadvantages of a center-based program include the expense of transportation, the cost and maintenance of the center itself, and the probability of less parent involvement than in home-based programs.

Combined Home-Center Programs

Many early intervention programs combine center-based activities and home visitation. Few center programs take children for more than a few hours a day, for up to 5 days a week. But because young handicapped children require more intervention than a few hours a day, many programs combine the intensive help of a variety of professionals in a center with the continuous attention and sensitive care of parents at home. Intervention that carries over from center to home clearly offers many of the advantages of the two types of programs and negates some of their disadvantages.

A good example of a home-center program is the PEECH (Precise Early Education of Children with Handicaps) Project at the University of Illinois.

Designed for children aged 3 or older with mild to moderate disabilities, PEECH combines classroom instruction for up to 10 disabled and 5 nondisabled children. A team approach to intervention and parental involvement includes a classroom teacher and a paraprofessional aide, a psychologist, a speech-language pathologist, and a social worker. Children spend 2 or 3 hours in class each day, with some time in large and small groups and in individualized activities. Parents are included in all stages of the intervention, including policy making. The project offers a lending library and toy library for parents to use, as well a parent newsletter. The project's ultimate goal is to successfully integrate youngsters with disabilities into regular classes whenever possible. In 1985, it was reported that 72 replication sites were using components of the PEECH program (Assael, 1985).

The Charlotte Circle Project is a combination home- and center-based early intervention program for infants and toddlers with severe/profound disabilities (Rose & Calhoun, 1990). The project is based on the social reciprocity model, which views the child's behavior as affecting the parent, whose behavior in turn affects the behavior of the child; hence the "circle" in the project's name. Nonresponsiveness, nonvocal behavior, irritability, lack of imitation responses,

At the Charlotte Circle Project in North Carolina, parents learn to identify and increase the frequency of positive behaviors by their handicapped infants such as smiling or imitating.

and need for special health care routines (such as tube feeding and suctioning) all present special challenges to normal infant-parent interactions; behaviors associated with these problems are often viewed negatively. The Charlotte Circle Project attempts to identify and increase the frequency of alternative positive behaviors that will cause parents to want to continue their interactions with their child (Rose & Calhoun, 1990; Rose, Calhoun, & Ladage, 1989).

The center-based component of the project's classroom instruction occurs from 9:00 A.M. to 1:00 P.M. throughout the year. Parents can enroll their children for either a 3-day or 5-day week. The home-based/family services component entails monthly home visits; the visits include family-focused assessment and planning, demonstrations of instructional techniques, and provision of information and other support. Between regularly scheduled home visits, ongoing individualized consultation and collaboration with parents and families are available as needed.

In a survey of 67 HCEEP model programs serving infants and toddlers with disabilities, Karnes and Stayton (1988) found that 70% of the programs offered a home-center combination option, 13% offered home-based services only, and 12% were center-based only. In practice, however, most children (52%) are actually served in centers, compared to 27% who receive all services at home and 15% who participate in a home-center combination. It is probably best to view these choices—home, center, or combined programs—as more alike than different. In fact, they do seem to have more in common than not: carefully sequenced curricula, strong parent involvement, explicit goals and frequent assessment of progress, integration of disabled and nondisabled children whenever possible, and staff teams that consist of specialists in several fields.

■ CURRICULUM IN EARLY CHILDHOOD SPECIAL EDUCATION PROGRAMS

Many early childhood special education programs employ a developmentally based curriculum. That is, the typical gains that nonhandicapped children make in sensorimotor development, language, social skills, academic readiness, and so on are used as a basis for sequencing instructional objectives and evaluating child progress. Developmentally based early intervention programs tend to work with young disabled children when directed at one of five purposes.

1. Remediating—making up for delays or gaps in a child's development, whether in language, motor skills, self-help, or other areas.

2. Teaching basic processes—attention, perception, sensorimotor, language, social skills, and memory.

3. Teaching developmental tasks—skills in a range of areas (motor, language, self-help, social), in sequences that most closely match the order in which normal children learn them.

4. Teaching psychological constructs—self-concept, creativity, motivation, and cognition, assuming that this training will lead to increased learning later.

5. Teaching preacademic skills—in prereading, quantitative concepts (i.e., early math), nature studies, art, music, dance, and so on.

PEER SOCIAL INITIATIONS

A Strategy for Influencing the Social Skills Development of Children with Handicaps

In addition to any deficits in cognitive, motor, language, and other developmental areas, young children with handicaps typically exhibit problems in social skills. When placed in mainstreamed settings, many handicapped preschoolers interact infrequently and incompetently with other children. Strain and his colleagues (Sainato, Goldstein, & Strain, in press; Strain, 1981; Strain & Odom, 1986) have investigated the use of peer social initiations as a means of increasing the social competence of handicapped preschoolers. The procedure involves teaching nonhandicapped peers to direct social overtures to their handicapped classmates. Strain and Odom (1986) recommend that peer intervention agents be taught to make initiations to handicapped children in the form of (1) play opportunities, (2) offers to share, (3) physical assistance, and (4) affection. These initiations are recommended on the basis of naturalistic studies of the social interactions of both nonhandicapped and handicapped preschoolers; the studies showed that such initiations were followed by a positive response more than 50% of the time and that responding to the social bids of others increased a child's social acceptability.

The strategy requires careful arrangement of the classroom environment to encourage greater social interaction. For example, the probability of social interaction can be increased by limiting the number of toys so that, to participate, children must share, and by requiring the children to play within a confined area. The key feature of the procedure, however, is the careful training of the nonhandicapped peers who are chosen to serve as "confederates." Training sessions usually take between 20 and 25 minutes and incorporate teacher modeling and both teacher and confederate role-playing of the desired social initiation. (See the sample script of the first training session in Figure A, in which children learn how to initiate sharing.) Training is followed by daily intervention sessions, in which the teacher arranges an activity for the children that is conducive to social interaction and then prompts and verbally reinforces the confederate for being a good teacher and the target handicapped child for being a good player.

Positive results have been documented using the peer initiation intervention with preschool children handicapped by mental retardation, autism, and behavior disorders. The outcomes include more positive social responses by all target children, more social initiations by some target children, longer social exchanges by target children, and generalization of social interactions by target children to other integrated preschool settings. ◆

Figure A From "Peer Social Initiations: Effective Intervention for Social Skills Development of Exceptional Children" by P. S. Strain and S. L. Odom, 1986, Exceptional Children, 52, 547. *Reprinted by permission.*

FIGURE A

Session 1: Introduction to system—share initiation—persistence.

TEACHER: "Today you are going to learn how to be a good teacher. Sometimes your friends in your class do not know how to play with other children. You are going to learn how to teach them to play. What are you going to do?"

CHILD RESPONSE: "Teach them to play."

TEACHER: "One way you get your friend to play with you is to share. How do you get your friend to play with you?"

CHILD RESPONSE: "Share."

TEACHER: "Right! You share. When you share, you look at your friend and say. 'Here,' and put a toy in his hand. What do you do?" (Repeat this exercise until the child can repeat these three steps.)

CHILD RESPONSE: "Look at friend and say, 'Here,' and put the toy in his hand."

ADULT MODEL WITH ROLE-PLAYER: "Now, watch me, I am going to share with _____. Tell me if I do it right." (Demonstrate sharing.) "Did I share with _____? What did I do?"

CHILD RESPONSE: "Yea! _____ looked at _____, said 'Here _____' and put a toy in his hand."

ADULT: "Right. I looked at _____ and said, 'Here _____' and put a toy in his hand. Now watch me. See if I share with _____." (Move to the next activity in the classroom. This time provide a negative example of sharing by leaving out the "put in hand" component. Put the toy beside the role-player.) "Did I share?" (Correct if necessary and repeat this example if child got it wrong.) "Why not?"

CHILD RESPONSE: "No." "You did not put the toy in _____'s hand."

ADULT: "That's right. I did not put the toy in _____'s hand. When I share, I have to look at _____ and say. 'Here _____' and put the toy in his hand." (Give the child two more positive and two more negative examples of sharing. When the child answers incorrectly about sharing, repeat the example. Vary the negative examples by leaving out different components: looking, saying 'Here,' putting in hand.)

CHILD PRACTICE WITH ADULTS: "Now _____, I want you to get _____ to share with you. What do you do when you share?"

CHILD RESPONSE: "Look at _____ and say. 'Here _____,' and put a toy in his hand."

ADULT: "Now, go get _____ to play with you." (For these practice examples, the role-playing adult should be responsive to the child's sharing.) (To the other confederates:) "Did _____ share with _____? What did she/he do?"

CHILD RESPONSE: "Yes/No. Looked at _____ and said, 'Here _____' and put a toy in his hand."

ADULT: (Move to the next activity.) "Now, _____, I want you to share with _____."

Introduce Persistence

TEACHER: "Sometimes when I play with _____, he/she does not want to play back. I have to keep on trying. What do I have to do?"

CHILD RESPONSE: "Keep on trying."

TEACHER: "Right, I have to keep on trying. Watch me. I am going to share with _____. Now I want you to see if I keep on trying." (Role-player will be initially unresponsive.) (Teacher should be persistent until child finally responds.) "Did I get _____ to play with me?" *CHILD:* "Yes." *TEACHER:* "Did he want to play?" *CHILD:* "No." *TEACHER:* "What did I do?" *CHILD:* "Keep on trying." *TEACHER:* "Right, I kept on trying. Watch. See if I can get _____ to play with me this time." (Again, the role-player should be unresponsive at first. Repeat above questions and correct if necessary. Repeat the example until the child responds correctly.)

These purposes are not mutually exclusive, of course. All use normal development as a yardstick against which to measure each child's individual needs and progress. In other words, a curriculum may try to give a handicapped child instruction in all the processes or skills that a normal child might develop without specific teaching. Or it might try to measure all the skills the child has already learned and then teach only those that are missing. In both instances, the ultimate goal is to help the child develop as many of the behaviors of a normal child of the same age as possible.

The developmental curriculum is not the most appropriate for all young children with disabilities. Bailey and Wolery (1984) remind us that

> The purposes of the early intervention curriculum are to accelerate children's developmental progress and to maximize independent functioning. With some children (e.g., mildly and moderately handicapped children) the primary emphasis is on accelerating developmental progress. With more severely handicapped children, the emphasis is on maximizing independent functioning. (p. 17)

For more severely handicapped or sensorily impaired preschoolers, the objectives suggested by a developmentally based curriculum may be inappropriate. A functionally based curriculum, focusing on skills that will enable immediate improvement in interaction with their environments, may be more appropriate. Laura, for example, is a 5-year-old with multiple disabilities who is unable to dress herself. Because dressing oneself is a functional skill that promotes independent functioning, it might be chosen as an appropriate objective for Laura in a functionally based curriculum. Careful assessment determines what specific steps in dressing Laura cannot perform, and direct instruction in those steps would follow. By contrast, a curriculum that follows typical developmental sequences would focus on the developmental prerequi-

The curriculum in this preschool prepares children for a successful transition to regular kindergarten classrooms.

sites to getting dressed—such as grasping objects, using various gross- and fine-motor movements, and so on.

Early childhood special educators do not have to choose between a strict developmental or functional approach. Many early intervention programs for children with disabilities use a combination of the two approaches, relying on a normal sequence of development as a general guide to the curriculum but applying functional considerations to select specific instructional targets for each child.

Developing Language in Preschoolers with Disabilities

Learning the native language of their community is a major developmental task of children. Most children learn to speak and communicate effectively with little or no formal teaching. By the time they enter school, most children have essentially mastered their native tongue. But children with disabilities often do not acquire language in the spontaneous, seemingly effortless manner of their nonhandicapped peers (Barney & Landis, 1987). And as handicapped children slip further and further behind their peers, their language deficits make social and academic development even more difficult. Preschoolers with disabilities need opportunities and activities directed at language use and development throughout the day.

Eileen Allen and Jane Rieke are two language specialists who, like most of their colleagues, believe that teachers of preschool children must use strategies to help children develop language skills all day long, throughout a total program. They also believe that the basic measure of success of a language intervention should be how much the child talks. Research has shown that the more a child talks, the better the child talks (Hart & Risley, 1975; Rieke, Lynch, & Soltman, 1977). K. E. Allen (1980a) says that good teachers do three things to ensure effective intervention for language-delayed children.

1. They arrange the environment in ways that are conducive to promoting language: by providing interesting learning centers (blocks, housekeeping and dramatic play, creative and manipulative materials); by balancing child-initiated and teacher-structured activities; and by presenting materials and activities that children enjoy.

2. They manage their interactions with children so as to maximize effective communication on the part of each language-impaired child, and use every opportunity to teach "on the fly."

3. They monitor the appropriateness of environmental arrangements; their own behavior; and that of the children in order to validate child progress and thus program effectiveness.

Two models or approaches teachers can use for systematically encouraging and developing language use throughout the school day are the *incidental teaching model* (Hart & Risley, 1968, 1975) and the *mand-model procedure* (Rogers-Warren & Warren, 1980; Warren, McQuarter, & Rogers-Warren, 1984). The essential feature of the incidental teaching model is that when the child wants something from the teacher—help, approval, information, food, or drink—the teacher takes the opportunity to promote language use. In other words, whenever the child initiates an interaction with the teacher, the teacher uses that opportunity to get the best possible language from the child. Allen (1980b) offers the following example of an incidental teaching episode described by Hart.

> A four-year-old girl with delayed language stands in front of the teacher with a paint apron in her hand. The teacher says, "What do you need?" (Teacher does not anticipate the child's need by putting the apron on the child at the moment.)
>
> If the child does not answer, the teacher tells her and gives her a prompt: "It's an apron. Can you say 'apron'?" If the child says "apron," the teacher ties it while giving descriptive praise, "You said it right. It is an apron. I am tying your apron on you." The teacher's last sentence models the next verbal behavior, "Tie my apron," that the teacher will expect once the child has learned to say "apron."
>
> If the child does not say "apron," the teacher ties the apron. No further comments are made at this time. The teacher must not coax, nag or pressure the child. If each episode is kept brief and pleasant, the child will contact the teacher frequently. Thus, the teacher will have many opportunities for incidental teaching. If the teacher pressures the child, such incidental learning opportunities will be lost. Some children may learn to avoid the teacher—they will simply do without; other children may learn inappropriate ways, such as whining and crying, to get what they want.

Through repeated interactions of this type, children learn that language is important; it can get them what they want, and teachers listen when they speak and want to hear more about things of interest to them. An important guideline in incidental teaching is to keep interactions brief and pleasant so that there will be many more opportunities. The child should never be interrogated or put on the spot (K. E. Allen, 1980a).

Warren and Gazdag (1990) combined incidental teaching and mand-model techniques into a milieu instructional approach to teach two 3-year-olds with

This teacher is using a puzzle activity to generate numerous opportunities for incidental teaching of specific language forms both boys need to develop.

developmental delays various language forms during naturalistic play. The authors describe the differences between the two complementary techniques.

> The distinction between the two procedures centers on who (trainer or child) initiates the instructional interaction. With the mand-model the teacher is in the role of facilitator, initiating the interaction by "manding" a target response, typically by asking a target probe questions about the event or activity to which the child is attending. In the incidental teaching procedure, the child initiates the interaction either verbally or nonverbally. The trainer then elicits the target response by prompting a more elaborate response. (p. 70)

Table 14.1 shows examples of instructional episodes using incidental teaching and the mand-model techniques. The methods have much in common. Both view the teacher as (1) an astute and systematic observer and recorder of children's language, (2) a sensitive and willing listener, and (3) a systematic

TABLE 14.1

Examples of language training/prompting episodes using mand-model and incidental teaching procedures.

Example 1	Example 2
Mand Model	
Context: Child is scooping beans with a ladle and pouring them into a pot.	Context: Trainer gives each child a turn to blow bubbles.
Trainer: "What are you doing?" (target probe question)	Trainer: (holds the wand up to the child's mouth) "What do you want to do?" (target probe question)
Child: No response.	Child: "Bubbles."
Trainer: "Tell me." (mand)	Trainer: "*Blow* bubbles." (model)
Child: "Beans."	Child: "Blow bubbles."
Trainer: "Say, *pour beans.*" (model)	Trainer: "OK, you want to blow bubbles. Here you go." (verbal acknowledgement + expansion + activity participation)
Child: "Pour beans."	
Trainer: "That's right, you're pouring beans into the pot." (verbal acknowledgement + expansion)	
Incidental Teaching	
Context: Making pudding activity. Trainer gives peer a turn at stirring the pudding as the subject looks on.	Context: Trainer and subject are washing dishes together in a parallel fashion.
Child: "Me!" (child initiates) and reaches for ladle.	Child: "Wash." (Child initiates with an action-verb, partial target response)
Trainer: "Stir pudding." (model)	Trainer: "Wash what?" (elaborative question)
Child: "Stir pudding."	Child: "Wash" (incorrect response).
Trainer: "All right. You stir the pudding, too." (verbal acknowledgement + expansion + activity participation)	Trainer: "Wash *what*?" (elaborative question)
	Child: "Wash cups."
	Trainer; "That's right. We're washing cups." (verbal acknowledgement + expansion)

Source: From "Facilitating Early Langage Development with Milieu Intervention Procedures" by S. F. Warren and G. Gazdag, 1990, *Journal of Early Intervention, 14,* p. 71. Reprinted by permission.

responder who helps the child "say it better" through differential feedback (K. E. Allen, 1980a).

Developing a Preschool Activity Schedule

Teachers in preschool programs for children with disabilities face the challenge of organizing the 2 to 3 hours of the program day into a schedule that meets each child's individual learning needs. The schedule should include both one-to-one and group instruction, provide children with many learning opportunities throughout the day, and allow easy transition from activity to activity. In short, the schedule should provide a framework for maximizing instruction while remaining manageable and flexible. In addition, how activities are scheduled and organized in integrated programs has considerable effect on the frequency and type of interaction that occurs between handicapped and nonhandicapped children (Burstein, 1986; Strain, 1981) and on the extent to which the mainstreamed children benefit from instruction (O'Connell, 1986).

Lund and Bos (1981) suggest that teachers begin planning a preschool schedule by determining the basic activities and time blocks. Figure 14.2 shows the components that are common to many preschool programs. The next steps

FIGURE 14.2

Typical activities to be considered in planning a preschool schedule. (*Source:* From "Orchestrating the Preschool Classroom: The Daily Schedule" by K. A. Lund and C. S. Bos, 1981, *Teaching Exceptional Children, 14,* p. 121. Copyright by the Council for Exceptional Children. Reprinted by permission.)

Approx. Amount of Time	Components
	Circle—opening exercises that vary in content from day to day or week to week.
	Interactive play—a play area where students interact with peers using teacher-structured materials and activities, e.g., dramatic play centered around a theme, woodworking, kitchen, blockbuilding.
	Movement—gross motor activities in either an indoor or outdoor setting; may also include physical/occupational therapy exercises.
	Snack—fruit juices (natural sugars only), milk, popcorn, dried fruit, granola, etc.
	Bathroom—as scheduled with group or according to individual toileting schedule.
	Activity table—students work at one or several activity tables; activities generally focus on fine motor and preacademic tasks.
	Small groups—students work in small groups on individual and group programs; content of activities varies but usually focuses on communication and preacademic tasks.
	Story—simple picture books, flannel board, hand puppets/finger puppets.
	Music—action songs, finger plays, rhythm band.
	Rest/relax—low lights, mats, listening to soft music, relaxing exercises.
	Flex time—a time when any of the above activities or special experiences (field trips, special guests, etc.) can be planned; activities vary from day to day.
	Special needs therapy—speech/language therapy, occupational therapy, physical therapy, adaptive physical education.

in constructing the schedule are filling in the approximate amount of time to spend on each activity each day, sequencing the components, scheduling children for individual and group instruction, and assigning staff (teachers, aides, and volunteers).

The physical arrangement of the classroom itself must support the planned activities. Lund and Bos (1981) make the following suggestions for setting up a preschool classroom:

♦ Place individual work areas and quiet activities together, away from avenues of traffic, to encourage attending behavior.

♦ Provide a stable area, such as an activity table and rug, where a variety of group programs can be conducted.

♦ Place the activity table within easy access of storage so that materials are readily obtainable.

♦ Place materials used most often close together for accessibility (e.g., clipboard, individual program materials).

♦ Label or color code all storage areas so that aides and volunteers can easily find needed materials.

♦ Arrange equipment and group areas so that the students can move easily from one activity to another. Picture or color codes can be applied to various work areas.

♦ Provide lockers or cubbies for students so they know where to find their belongings. Again, add picture cues to help the students identify their lockers.

O'Connell (1986) offers suggestions for structuring the physical arrangement of small-group learning activities in mainstreamed preschool classrooms.

■ WHO CAN HELP?

Physicians and Other Health Professionals

The success of efforts to prevent disabilities in children and to identify, assess, and intervene with special-needs children as early as possible requires the training and experience of a wide range of professionals. Current "best practice" guidelines for early childhood services call for a transdisciplinary approach to the delivery of related services in which parents and professionals work together in assessing needs, developing the IFSP, providing services, and evaluating outcomes (McDonnell & Hardman, 1988).

No other professional has as great an opportunity to prevent certain disabilities as the obstetrician. Because he knows many of the conditions that predict possible disabilities, the obstetrician can examine the family history and recommend genetic counseling if there appears to be a significant risk. Because he sees an expectant mother several times during pregnancy, he can monitor any possible problems that arise, perform or refer her for amniocentesis if necessary, and generally ensure the kind of prenatal care that reduces the risk of problems at birth. In the delivery room, the doctor's concern for possible birth trauma can contribute to preventing problems or identifying them early.

In the same way, the pediatrician (or perhaps the family doctor) has the chance to see the infant soon after birth and then regularly during the first months of life. Her attention to the Apgar ratings and an immediate postnatal

See McCollum and Hughes (1988) and Woodruff and McGonigel (1988) for discussions of different team models used in early childhood programs. P.L. 99–457 requires that each Individualized Family Service Plan must identify a case manager who will be responsible for seeing that the plan is implemented and coordinating the delivery of services with other agencies and professionals. See Bailey (1989) for a discussion of issues related to case management in early childhood services.

examination of the infant can help prevent problems or identify high-risk infants. Because most moderate to severe disabilities and sensory impairments are recognizable at birth or soon afterward, the pediatrician's role is critical. Other conditions, such as parental neglect or abuse, may also be evident to the attentive physician. For the same reasons, nurses and nurse practitioners can be of enormous help in noting and questioning possible disabilities or conditions in the home that might lead to a disability.

Later, other health professionals also contribute to identification, assessment, or treatment of specific problems that can cause disabilities. An ophthalmologist can detect early vision problems, and he or an optometrist can fit a child with corrective lenses. An audiologist can assess a child's hearing and prescribe a hearing aid or other treatment if there is a loss.

Other Specialists in Early Intervention

Increasingly, early intervention services are being provided to hospitalized newborns and their families. Low-birth-weight and other high-risk newborns who require specialized health care are placed in neonatal intensive care units (NICU). Many NICUs now include a variety of professionals, such as neonatologists who provide medical care for infants with special needs, nurses who provide ongoing medical assistance, social workers or psychologists who help parents and families with emotional and financial concerns, and infant education specialists who promote interaction between parents and infant (Flynn & McCollum, 1989).

A psychologist can evaluate a child's social-emotional skills and cognitive development. Psychologists often participate in a child's initial assessments and frequently administer standardized tests. Staff psychologists often participate in team planning for a child. Although school psychologists have traditionally been trained to provide standardized assessments for school-age students and consultation to classroom teachers, their participation in preschool programs for children with disabilities is likely to increase as the public schools provide more early childhood special education services (Widerstrom, Mowder, & Willis, 1989).

Because so large a portion of mild disabilities are based in social and cultural factors, a social worker can be instrumental in helping children receive much needed services. It is often the social worker who is admitted to many homes in low socioeconomic areas, which correlate with higher incidences of mild retardation and learning problems. The case worker can observe young children whose behavior suggests future problems and refer them for assessment and possible treatment. Later, the social worker may help explain, monitor, or evaluate the progress of a home-based intervention.

A speech-language pathologist is an important part of almost every intervention team. Speech and language specialists usually assess every child referred for services, and they participate in the intervention plans for many children.

For children who have physical or multiple handicaps, a physical therapist is important. Physical therapy can help prevent further deterioration of muscles; it can also be applied to teaching a child gross and fine motor coordination. Likewise, an occupational therapist contributes to the intervention program for children with physical, multiple, or other severe impairments. She provides instruction in movement, self-help skills, and the use of adaptive equipment.

Teachers and other staff in regular preschools and day-care centers may be the first to identify certain delays in development or other problems like mild sensory impairments, social-emotional problems, learning difficulties, or language problems. Prompt referral for special education services can often get these mildly handicapped children the help they need before they fall significantly behind their peers. As more and more children with disabilities are integrated into regular preschools, the role of teachers and paraprofessionals in these settings will become even more critical. Regular preschool and kindergarten teachers also play important roles in supporting a handicapped child's transition into a mainstream setting.

The actual delivery of services, whether in a home or center program, is most often the province of the special teacher, regardless of what title that person has. The special teacher must be the most knowledgeable about a child's instructional goals and objectives, the specific strategies and activities that will accomplish them, and the child's day-to-day progress. That teacher must be well trained in observing, analyzing, selecting, and sequencing learning tasks so that the child overcomes delays rather than falls further behind. The teacher must be imaginative and willing to try new things, but patient enough to give a program a chance once it is begun. Not only must he be able to find what motivates and reinforces a child, but he must also be able to relate to all the other individuals involved in the child's program. In a home-based program, the home teacher or visitor must be able to train parents to take primary responsibility for teaching their child. Even in center-based programs, a large share of the center's parent-training efforts may fall to the special teacher.

A position paper of the Division for Early Childhood recommends specific training and certification requirements for early childhood special educators (McCollum, McLean, McCartan, & Kaiser, 1989).

Parents—Most Important of All

Of all the people needed to make early intervention work, parents are the most important. Given enough information, parents can help prevent many risks and causes of disabilities—before pregnancy, before birth, and certainly before a child has gone months or years without help. Given the chance, parents can become active in determining their children's educational needs and goals. And given some guidance and training, parents can teach their disabled children at home and even at school.

It is no wonder, then, that the most successful intervention programs for young children with disabilities take great care to involve parents. Parents in early intervention programs for handicapped children frequently assume roles as members of advisory councils for the programs, consumers who inform others, staff members, primary teachers, recruiters, curriculum developers, counselors, assessment personnel, and evaluators and record keepers.

Parents are the most frequent and constant observers of their children's behavior. They usually know better than anyone else what their children need, and they can help educators set realistic goals. They can report on events in the home that outsiders might never see—for instance, how a child responds to other family members. They can monitor and report on their children's progress at home, beyond the more controlled environment of the center or preschool. In short, they can contribute to their children's programs at every stage—assessment, planning, classroom activities, and evaluation. Many parents even work in classrooms as teachers, teacher aides, volunteers, or other staff members.

Most early intervention programs focus on the home as the best and most natural learning environment and on the parent as the best and most natural teacher for the child. Even center-based programs rely heavily on parents as teachers who carry the center program into the home. But in our efforts to involve parents, we should heed this warning:

> Early childhood professionals, in their zeal to attain those all-important early developmental gains, should not push parents to the point of burn-out. Early childhood professionals will pass the child on to new programs; their task will be finished when the child reaches school age. But the family will only be beginning a lifetime of responsibility. For early childhood programs, a task equally as important as the achievement of developmental gains is the preparation of families for the long haul. Families must learn to pace themselves, to relax and take time to meet everyone's needs. They must learn that the responsibility of meeting an exceptional child's needs is not a 100-yard dash to be completed in one intensive burst of effort. It is more like a marathon, where slow and steady pacing wins the race (Weyhing, 1983). (Turnbull et al., 1986, p. 93)

And finally, the authors of the curriculum developed by the Macomb 0-3 Project, an HCEEP early intervention program in Macomb, Illinois, remind us that, when all is said and done, we must not forget that early childhood is supposed to be a fun, happy time for children and for the adults who are fortunate enough to work with them.

> Even though the children for whom this curriculum is intended demonstrate behaviors and conditions that may very well make life difficult for them as well as for their families, please do not forget the importance of play, joy and emotional well-being in interactions with these young children. We as professionals who work with young handicapped children sometimes are so serious about the magnitude of our mission that any element of fun, humor or pleasure is absent in our work with both children and their families.
>
> Part of our mission as professionals in the field of early childhood handicapped education is to possess an art of enjoyment ourselves and to help instill it in the young children and families with whom we work.
>
> Early childhood comes but once in a lifetime. . . . Let's make it count! (Hutinger, Marshall, & McCartan, 1983, front matter)

SUMMARY

Importance of Early Intervention

- ♦ Research studies have documented that early intervention results in both intermediate and long-term benefits for handicapped, at-risk, and disadvantaged children. Benefits of early intervention include:
  - — gains in physical development, cognitive development, language and speech development, social competence, and self-help skills.
  - — prevention of secondary handicapping conditions.
  - — reduction of family stress.

- reduced likelihood of social dependence and institutionalization.
- reduced need for special education services or placement during the school year.

♦ Most professionals believe that the earlier in a child's life intervention begins, the better; and that longer, more intensive programs are generally more effective.

Legislative History of Early Childhood Special Education

♦ The first federal legislation written exclusively for the handicapped preschooler—the Handicapped Children's Early Childhood Assistance Act (P.L. 90–538), passed in 1968—provides funding for diverse and innovative approaches to early intervention.

♦ Since 1972, Head Start programs have been required to reserve at least 10% of their enrollment capacity for children with disabilities.

♦ P. L. 99–457, the Education of the Handicapped Act Amendments of 1986, requires that, by 1991, states receiving federal funds for special education of preschool children show evidence of serving all 3- to 5-year-old children with disabilities. The law also provides monetary incentives to states that serve handicapped and at-risk infants and toddlers from birth to age 2.

Identification of Handicapped and At-Risk Infants and Preschoolers

♦ More genetic counseling, better prenatal care, wider screening for metabolic disorders, and public education can help prevent disabilities.

♦ Certain handicapping conditions can be detected during pregnancy, in the delivery room, or soon after birth.

♦ As a rule, the more severe the disability, the earlier it can be detected.

♦ There is no universal system to screen all infants.

♦ Most newborns receive an Apgar rating and a screening for certain metabolic disorders.

♦ Other screening tests based on normal child development are used only when a concerned adult feels an evaluation is necessary.

♦ There are many formal, standardized tests available to assess delayed or abnormal progress in intellectual development, auditory perception, and affective and social development.

♦ Informal checklists, rating scales, and other assessment devices usually measure cognitive development, motor development, language development, self-help skills, play skills, and personal-social skills.

♦ Programs are moving away from assessments based entirely on developmental milestones and are incorporating curriculum-based assessment, in which each item relates directly to a skill included in the program's curriculum—thereby providing a direct link between testing, teaching, and progress evaluation.

Early Childhood Special Education Programs

♦ In home-based programs, a child's parents act as the primary teachers, with regular training and guidance from a teacher or specially trained paraprofessional who visits the home.

♦ In center-based programs, a child comes to the center for direct instruction, although the parents are usually involved. Center programs allow a team of specialists to work with the child and enable the child to meet and interact with other children.

- Many programs offer the advantages of both models by combining home visits with center-based programming.

Curriculum in Early Childhood Special Education Programs

- Curricula may focus on remediating delays or teaching basic processes, developmental tasks, psychological constructs, or preacademic skills.
- These approaches measure each child against a normal developmental standard.
- A functionally based curriculum is more appropriate for more severely disabled preschoolers.
- Many early intervention programs combine developmental and functional curriculum approaches.
- Promoting language development—helping children learn to talk—is a primary curriculum goal for preschoolers with disabilities. The incidental teaching model and the mand-model procedure are two methods for encouraging and developing language use throughout the school day.

Who Can Help?

- A wide range of professionals should be involved in a team that works with young children with disabilities, including obstetricians, pediatricians, nurses, psychologists, social workers, and teachers.
- Parents are the most important people in an early intervention program. They can act as advocates, participate in educational planning, observe their children's behavior, help set realistic goals, work in the classroom, and teach their children at home.

FOR MORE INFORMATION

Journals

Day Care and Early Education. Published bimonthly by Behavioral Publications, 72 Fifth Avenue, New York, NY 10016. Directed at day-care personnel; focuses on innovative ideas for educating preschool children.

Journal of Early Intervention. Published by the Division for Early Childhood, Council for Exceptional Children, 1920 Association Drive, Reston, VA 22091.

Topics in Early Childhood Special Education. Published quarterly by PRO-ED, 5341 Industrial Oaks Boulevard, Austin, TX 78735.

Young Children. Published bimonthly by the National Association for the Education of Young Children, 1834 Connecticut Avenue, N.W., Washington, DC 20009. Spotlights current projects, theory, and research in early childhood education as well as practical teaching ideas.

Books

Bailey, D. B., & Simeonsson, R. J. (1988). *Family assessment in early intervention*. Columbus, OH: Merrill.

Bailey, D. B., & Wolery, M. (1984). *Teaching infants and preschoolers with handicaps*. Columbus, OH: Merrill.

Bailey, D. B., & Wolery, M. (1989). *Assessing infants and preschoolers with handicaps*. Columbus, OH: Merrill.

Bricker, D. D. (1989). *Early intervention for at-risk and handicapped infants, toddlers, and preschool children* (2nd ed.). Palo Alto, CA: Vort Corp.

Cook, R. E., Tessier, A., & Armbruster, V. B. (1987). *Adapting early childhood curricula for children with special needs* (2nd ed.). Columbus, OH: Merrill.

Gallagher, J. J., Trohanis, P. L., & Clifford, R. M. (Eds.) (1989). *Policy implementation and P.L. 99–457*. Baltimore, MD: Paul H. Brookes.

Guralnick, M. J., & Bennett, F. C. (Eds.). (1987). *The effectiveness of early intervention for at-risk and handicapped children*. New York: Academic Press.

Jordan, J. B., Gallagher, J. J., Hutinger, P. L., & Karnes, M. B. (Eds.). (1988). *Early childhood special education: Birth to three*. Reston, VA: Council for Exceptional Children.

Lerner, J. W., Mardell-Czudnowski, C., & Goldenberg, D. (1987). *Special education for the early childhood years* (2nd ed.). Englewood Cliffs, NJ: Prentice-Hall.

Meisels, S. J., & Shonkoff, J. P. (1990). *Handbook of early childhood intervention*. New York: Cambridge University Press.

Neisworth, J. T., & Bagnato, S. J. (1987). *The young exceptional child: Early development and education*. New York: Macmillan.

Odom, S. L., & Karnes, M. B. (Eds.). (1988). *Early intervention for infants & children with handicaps*. Baltimore, MD: Paul H. Brookes.

Thurman, S. K., & Widerstrom, A. H. (1990). *Young children with special needs: A developmental and ecological approach* (2nd ed.). Baltimore, MD: Paul H. Brookes.

Tingey, C. (Ed.). (1989). *Implementing early intervention*. Baltimore, MD: Paul H. Brookes.

Wachs, T. D., & Sheehan, R. (Eds.). (1988). *Assessment of young developmentally disabled children*. New York: Plenum Press.

Organizations

The Division for Early Childhood, Council for Exceptional Children, 1920 Association Drive, Reston, VA 22091.

HCEEP-Funded Early Childhood Research Institutes

Carolina Institute for Research on Early Education of the Handicapped (CIREEH), Frank Porter Graham Child Development Center, University of North Carolina at Chapel Hill, 301 NCNB Plaza, Chapel Hill, NC 27514. Intended to conduct research and develop training materials related to parents and families of moderately and severely handicapped children from birth to 5 years of age.

Early Childhood Research Institute (ECRI), Pittsburgh, PA 15213. Intended to develop procedures for assessing and teaching social and related skills to severely handicapped preschool children so that they can participate successfully in instructional settings with nonhandicapped or less handicapped children.

Early Intervention Research Institute (EIRI), Exceptional Child Center, Utah State University, UMN 68, Logan, UT 84322. Intended to review the findings of previous research on early intervention to determine what is known, what gaps exist, and where future research should focus.

15

Transition to Adulthood

◆ Should special educators in the schools be responsible for the successes and failures of adults with disabilities?

◆ How can the same services, such as sheltered employment programs, that are intended to help an adult with disabilities also limit his participation in life activities?

◆ Does it make sense for society to invest the ongoing resources necessary for a person with severe disabilities to work in the community?

◆ Will there be any large, state-operated institutions in 10 years? 20 years? Should there be?

◆ Why must quality of life be the ultimate outcome measure for special education?

What happens to youths with disabilities when they leave school and enter the adult world? Do graduates of special education programs find work? Where do they live? How do disabled adults' social, recreational, and leisure activities compare to the expectations and experiences of most nonhandicapped citizens? How do adults with disabilities rate their quality of life—are they happy? How can special education programs for school-age children prepare them for adjustment and successful integration into the adult community? What are the most appropriate and effective programs and services for helping adults with disabilities find and keep meaningful work, locate housing, or use community recreation centers? How can special education interrelate its goals and services with those of other human service agencies, such as vocational education and rehabilitation, residential services, and community recreation programs? Many professionals in special education now view the exploration of and solutions to these questions as their highest priority.

A number of follow-up studies of graduates of special education programs and some surveys of adults with disabilities provide enlightening, if not encouraging, information. The findings on the employment status of recent graduates of secondary special education programs are fairly consistent—about 60% to 70% find work after leaving public school; the work, however, is usually part-time, and often at or below minimum wage. As disheartening as these findings are, persons with severe disabilities face a much dimmer prospect of locating competitive employment. Overall, the U.S. Commission on Civil Rights (1983) estimates that between 50% and 75% of all adults with disabilities are unemployed.

Of course, a disability affects more than a person's likelihood of obtaining work. Adults with disabilities face numerous obstacles in day-to-day living that affect where and how they live, how well they can use community resources, and their opportunities for social interaction. Unlike their nondisabled peers, a disproportionate number of adults with disabilities continue to live with their parents after graduation, and many report a high degree of social isolation. A survey conducted by Louis Harris and Associates and reported to the U.S. Congress in 1986 found that 56% of disabled Americans said their handicaps prevented them from moving about the community, attending cultural or sporting events, and socializing with friends outside their homes.

Findings such as these are helping educators focus on what has become perhaps the dominant issue in special education—the transition from school to adult life in the community. No longer can special educators be satisfied with evaluation data that show improved performance on school-related tasks. They must work equally hard to ensure that the preparation students receive during their school years plays a direct and positive role in helping them adjust to successful life in the adult community.

In this chapter, we examine three major life areas—employment, residential alternatives, and recreation/leisure opportunities—in which special educators and other human service professionals are working to help adults with disabilities lead productive, self-sufficient, and rewarding lives in the community.

During the 1987–88 school year, 238,000 teenagers and young adults with disabilities exited from the public schools (U.S. Department of Education, 1990). Approximately 65,000 dropped out; 40,000 left before graduating for other or unknown reasons; and another 6,000 reached the maximum age at which they were eligible for services without graduating.

■ EMPLOYMENT

Work can be defined as using one's physical and/or mental energies to accomplish something productive. Our society is based on a work ethic; we place a high value on work and on people who contribute. Besides providing economic support, work offers opportunities for social interaction and a chance to use and enhance skills in a chosen area. Work generates the respect of others, and it can be a source of pride and self-satisfaction (Terkel, 1974).

All young adults face important questions about what to do with their lives—whether to attend college or technical school, whether to work as a bricklayer or an accountant—but for the nondisabled person, the difficulty involves choosing from a number of options. By contrast, the adult with a disability too often has few, if any, options from which to choose. Occupational choices decrease if the person with disabilities has limited skills; they decrease further, in most cases, because of the nature of the disability; and, needlessly, choices and opportunities are still further limited because of the prejudices and misconceptions about people with handicaps that many employers hold. For most adults with disabilities, obtaining and holding a job is the major rehabilitation goal.

Of the numerous follow-up studies of the employment status of graduates of secondary special education programs, one of the most comprehensive was conducted by Hasazi, Gordon, and Roe (1985), who interviewed 301 young adults who had left secondary special education programs in nine Vermont school districts between 1979 and 1983. The researchers found that only 55% of the former students were employed at the time of the interview, with just two-thirds of those working in full-time positions. A more recent study in Vermont, comparing the employment of youths with and without disabilities

Productive work is a source of pride and self-satisfaction.

YES, I'M STILL LEARNING DISABLED

I grew up in a time when we didn't have all the labels that we have now for disabilities. When I look at my life, I realize I had a bona fide learning disability. When I entered the third grade, I was a nonreader. My auditory memory skills had helped me so much that it had been impossible to catch me before. Everybody thought I was reading from the page, but I was actually reciting, utilizing other cues such as pictures, and getting my buddies to give me the key words that started the sentences. If I got the key word that started the sentence, I could rattle off the rest. But in the third grade, they took the pictures away from the readers. I hadn't started to associate text and topics and sentences with page numbers up in the corner. So I was just lost. But reading was not the only problem I had.

I couldn't do math either. My problem is visual-spatial orientation, and when you put a math problem down on paper, the numbers have to be lined up properly. I knew what it meant to subtract, and to multiply and divide, and I could handle it as long as it was verbal—"7 times 7" or "6 times 3." Basically I learned the problems by heart. But once you get past the two-digit numbers and up into the hundreds, all of a sudden you have to put it down on paper. I couldn't place a number that had to be subtracted beneath the column it had to be subtracted from. Nor could I do problems where you have to carry. I couldn't put the carried-over digits in the right place; they hung all over the place. It was impossible for me to do even a simple sum. When they finally found out it was not the basic operations I had problems with, they modified their approach. I was introduced to little grids that helped me set the problems up, and that countered my visual problems just fine.

I went through all kinds of things. I was in a classroom for the mentally retarded for a while. Yet when I look back on the early years, I did not realize how different I was. When I went to nursery school, at age 5, my mother was still dressing me. I didn't know that other kids could dress themselves.

I was constantly in trouble. The teacher would come over to me and I would start singing, because it would make her so mad that I would get thrown out of the room. If I could just get the teacher to expel me from the room, I could fantasize my whole day away. If I started singing when I wasn't supposed to, by 9:15 I could be out of the room. So I had all of the nonadaptive strategies, things kids learn to do to get out of the mess they're in. And as long as you can get out of the mess, you can have a modicum of self-esteem.

I still consider myself learning disabled, because there are times when I fail because of my problems. As long as there are very specific times when you fail, you still have a learning and perceptual problem.

One example occurred when I was up for my driver's test. I forgot I

Although the overall employment rate of 62% found in the 1989 Vermont study is discouraging, an even more distressing finding was that only 23% of female former special education students were employed 2 years after leaving school as compared to a statewide employment rate of 71% for females without disabilities.

after leaving high school, produced similar results (Hasazi, Johnson, Hasazi, Gordon, & Hull, 1989). One year later, 82% of the youths without disabilities were employed compared to 63% of those with disabilities; a year later, the employment figures were 85% and 62% for the two groups.

A survey of 234 young adults 4 years after they left secondary special education programs in Colorado found 69% working, with only one-third employed full time. (Mithaug, Horiuchi, & Fanning, 1985). Studies of young adults who were classified as learning disabled during high school have found somewhat higher employment rates than those for the population of all previous special education students. Zigmond and Thornton (1985) reported an employment rate of 74%, and Scuccimarra and Speece (1990) found that 78% of a sample of 65 randomly selected youths from a Washington, D.C., metropolitan school system (61 of whom were learning disabled) were employed 2 years after leaving school. Although the employment rate in the Scuccimarra and Speece study was comparable to national and local figures for the same age group, they had to take directions from the policeman. He used "right" and "left," and I didn't know which way to turn. He yelled and screamed at me and took me back and failed me. The second time I went, I told the policeman about my problem. I said, "I'm confused when people say 'right' and 'left,' and I know you'll be telling me to turn right and left. Can I paste these letters on my hands?" He said yes. So I stuck big letters on the backs of my hands where I could see them while holding the wheel. By facing my problem head on, I did fine.

It's almost a daily occurrence. When I have to go places, the first few times I cannot find my way. I build in an extra half-hour whenever I have to go someplace new. I'm OK on the freeway; but if there's any opportunity for failure, I get lost. I still get lost on campus, because there are parts that aren't familiar to me. To hold a map, you have to know where you are and which way you're facing. I go the wrong way anyway. One time I attended a professional meeting in Las Vegas, and I couldn't find anyplace. By the time I got there, the meetings were over. I ended up sitting in my hotel room and crying. I went home three days early.

I've learned to overcome failure by knowing where I need support systems. For example, I'm an author who cannot spell. So I have a secretary who knows what my spelling error patterns are. Without her, I cannot write.

When I travel professionally, I don't rent a car because I'd get lost. So if people want me to speak, they have to pick me up. If I must travel by car, I stay in motels right by major roads. Otherwise, who knows if I'll ever get on the road again? I could be driving in the opposite direction. It's happened often.

Support systems are absolutely essential. I make sure I earn enough to pay for my support systems. Early in my career, my payments for support systems were exorbitant in relation to my salary. But I knew I had to pay to succeed.

Anxiety attacks used to leave me exhausted, like when I got lost and had to go back. These days I say, "So what? I can't find it? They're waiting for me. I'll call and they can come and get me." It's easy in the role of success, but it's totally different for young adults on the way up. Once you've "arrived," you can ask those who want things from you to help you. You don't feel so terrible about not always being quite with it.

My self-esteem has grown with every success, but it took me until I was 40 or older before I had reconciled who I was, and no longer had anxiety attacks and nightmares. Since I reached 40, with every gain toward inner equanimity, I have moved ahead. My growth has been tremendous.

Elisabeth H. Wiig is professor of speech pathology at Boston University. Dr. Wiig is the author of three textbooks, four language assessment tests, and more than 70 research articles dealing with language disorders in children and adolescents. She speaks six languages fluently. We are grateful to Dr. Wiig for her willingness to share some of her experiences with us. ◆

discovered the same pattern of financial instability and dependence upon parents found in previous studies (e.g., Mithaug et al., 1985). The incomes of many individuals hovered near the poverty level, 83% lived with their parents, and one-fourth were dissatisfied with their social lives.

In Virginia, parent interviews concerning the employment status and community integration of 300 young adults with mental retardation who had left four public school special education programs revealed an unemployment rate of 58%, with three-fourths of those employed earning less than $500 per month (Wehman, Kregel, & Seyfarth, 1985a). Analysis of the data for the 117 young adults in the Virginia study with moderate, severe, or profound mental retardation showed that only 25 had jobs (an unemployment rate of 78.6%); of those, 14 had found paid work in the community and 11 were working in sheltered workshops (Wehman, Kregel, & Seyfarth, 1985b). Only 8 of those working earned more than $100 per month.

Competitive Employment

A person who is competitively employed performs work valued by an employer, functions in an integrated setting with nondisabled co-workers, and earns at or above the federal minimum wage (Rusch et al., in press). Wehman and Hill (1985) further specify that a person who is truly competitively employed receives no subsidized wages of any kind. Although the unemployment rate of young adults with mild disabilities is much higher than that of the population in general, many graduates of public school special education programs do find paid employment in the community. A study conducted in 15 school districts in Washington followed 827 learning-disabled or behaviorally disordered young adults who had graduated from public school special education programs or had left because they were too old to meet eligibility requirements. A total of 634 (77%) of these young adults were still employed 1 year after they had left school (Will, 1986); however, only 27% of those working were earning the minimum wage or above. These results and those of the follow-up studies previously mentioned indicate that opportunities for true competitive employment for adults with disabilities have been extremely limited in most communities.

Virtually all special educators who have studied the transition of students with disabilities from school to adult life believe that only through significant revision of the public school curriculum and improved coordination of school and adult vocational habilitation services can the prospect of competitive employment be enhanced for young adults with disabilities (Bellamy & Horner, 1987; Clark & Kolstoe, 1990; Rusch et al., in press; Wehman, Kregel, & Barcus, 1985).

Supported Employment

For adults with handicaps, especially those with severe intellectual or physical disabilities, the opportunity to earn real wages for real work has been almost nonexistent in this country. Only 39% of adults with mental retardation and related developmental disabilities were working for pay in 1987, and of that group, 77% worked in segregated facilities such as sheltered workshops and work activity centers (Lakin, Hill, Chen, & Stephens, 1989). This situation has continued to exist despite numerous demonstrations that persons with severe disabilities can learn meaningful vocational tasks when provided with systematic training and on-the-job support (Bellamy et al., 1979; Gold, 1976; Rusch, 1990). A new type of vocational opportunity has emerged that is aimed at helping individuals with severe disabilities who have historically been unemployed or restricted to sheltered settings. Supported employment enables persons with severe disabilities to participate successfully in integrated work environments.

The supported employment or supported work movement recognizes that many adults with severe disabilities require ongoing, often intensive support to obtain, learn, and hold a job. The incorporation of **supported employment** into P.L. 99–506, the Rehabilitation Act Amendments of 1986, has led to a proliferation of federally assisted supported employment programs throughout the country.

> The amendments defined competitive work in an integrated work setting for individuals with severe handicaps for whom competitive employment has not oc-

Several follow-up studies have found a positive correlation between paid work experiences during high school, including summer jobs, and post-school employment (e.g., Hasazi et al., 1985, 1989; Scuccimarra & Speece, 1990).

Sheltered workshops and work activity centers will be discussed later in the chapter.

curred or for whom competitive employment has been interrupted or intermittent. Accordingly, individuals considered eligible for supported employment services are those who cannot function independently in employment without intensive, ongoing support services and require these ongoing support services for the duration of their employment. These regulations also set at 20 the minimum number of hours a supported employee may work. (Rusch, 1990, p. 9)

Types of Supported Employment

Four distinct placement models have been developed and widely reported in the supported employment literature:

♦ individual placement

♦ work enclave or clustered placement model

♦ mobile work crew

♦ entrepreneurial model

Although other supported employment models have been used and proposed (Kregel & Wehman, in press; Nisbet & Hagner, 1988), over 90% of the 25,000 individuals participating in more than 1,400 supported employment programs in 27 states are served by one of these four models (Wehman et al., 1989). Table 15.1 shows some of the results of a study evaluating the employment outcomes for 1,550 individuals receiving supported employment services in 96 programs in 8 states (Kregel, Wehman, & Banks, 1989). Persons with various types and degrees of disabilities obtained significant increases in earnings, and the individual placement model resulted in the highest hourly and monthly wages.

Wehman and Kregel (1985) describe an *individual placement* model for supported employment that consists of four components:

1. A comprehensive approach to job placement

2. Intensive job-site training and advocacy

3. Ongoing monitoring of client performance

4. A systematic approach to long-term job retention and follow-up

The supported employment specialist is the key to making a supported work program effective. The supported employment specialist, sometimes called a job coach, is a community-based professional who works in a nonprofit job placement program, a public vocational or adult services program, or a secondary special education program. Table 15.2 identifies the major activities and responsibilities of a supported employment specialist in each component of the supported work model. Approximately two-thirds of the specialist's time is spent at the job site, orienting the client to the job, training the client in specific job skills, and advocating for the client with employers, supervisors, and nonhandicapped co-workers (Rehder, 1986). The other one-third of the specialist's time is spent in tasks such as working with the client's parents, planning behavioral intervention programs for the client, and training the client in work-related areas such as transportation, money management, and grooming skills.

Although all clients in supported employment continue to receive support and services as needed, the amount of direct on-the-job assistance the supported employment specialist provides is gradually reduced as the new employee

An *integrated work setting* requires regular contact with nonhandicapped co-workers. In 1986, 9,633 individuals were working in federally assisted Supported Employment Demonstration Projects in 20 states. Just 3 years later, the supported employment movement had grown to almost 25,000 participants in 27 states (Wehman, Kregel, Shafer, & West, 1989). The cumulative wages these workers earned grew from $1.4 million to $12.4 million in less than 2 years in the 15 states that reported earnings data.

The winter 1989 issue of the *Journal of Applied Behavior Analysis* is devoted to research on supported employment. See Rusch (1990) for details on developing supported employment programs.

TABLE 15.1

Supported employment wage outcomes for individuals with various primary disabilities and for individuals in various employment models (N = 1,550).

Primary Disability	Hourly Wage	Hours Worked per Week	Monthly Earnings Prior to Supported Employment	Monthly Earnings During Supported Employment	Percentage Change
Severe/profound mental retardation	$3.09	22.7	$ 45	$286	536
Moderate mental retardation	3.30	26.8	55	372	576
Mild mental retardation	3.15	26.5	95	361	280
Borderline mental retardation	3.27	27.6	80	392	390
Long-term mental illness	3.74	28.0	102	454	345
Physical and sensory disabilities	4.28	29.6	87	556	539

Employment Model	Hourly Wage	Hours Worked per Week	Monthly Earnings Prior to Supported Employment	Monthly Earnings During Supported Employment	Percentage Change
Individual placement	$3.68	26.5	$ 80	$424	430
Enclaves	3.25	28.7	67	301	349
Work crews	2.32	27.6	96	253	164
Small business	1.30	25.4	46	149	224

Source: From "The Effects of Consumer Characteristics and Type of Employment Model on Individual Outcomes in Supported Employment" by J. Kregel, P. Wehman, and P. D. Banks, 1989, *Journal of Applied Behavior Analysis, 22,* pp. 411–412. Reprinted by permission.

For a thought-provoking examination and debate of the issues concerning whether adults with severe disabilities should be permitted to perform meaningful work without pay in community-based integrated work sites while undergoing extended training, see Bellamy et al. (1984) and Brown et al. (1984).

acquires greater competence in completing the job requirements independently (Kregel, Hill, & Banks, 1988; Wehman, Hill, Brooke, Pendleton, & Britt, 1985) (see Figure 15.1).

Wehman, Hill, et al. (1985) report the employment status of 167 adults who were placed in a total of 252 part- and full-time paid jobs with the supported work model. The clients ranged in age from 18 to 66 years old and had a median IQ score of 49.

The great majority (86%) were receiving regular financial aid from the government at the time of placement. In fact, 81% earned under $200 as an annual salary the year prior to placement which indicates the level of economic independence exhibited by these individuals prior to intervention. A total of 71% lived

TABLE 15.2

Responsibilities of supported employment specialist during each component of the supported work model proposed by Wehman and Kregel (1985).

Component	Activities
Job placement	Structured efforts to find jobs for client and matching client strengths to job needs
	Planning of transportation arrangements and/or travel training
	Active involvement with parents to identify appropriate job for client
	Communication with Social Security Administration
Job site training and advocacy	Trained staff provides behavior skill training to improve client's work performance
	Trained staff provides necessary social skill training at job site
	Staff works with employers and co-workers in helping client
Ongoing monitoring	Provides for regular written feedback from employer on client progress
	Utilizes behavioral data related to client work speed, proficiency, need for staff assistance, etc.
	Implements periodic client and parent satisfaction questionnaires
Follow-up and retention	Implements planned effort to reduce staff intervention at job site
	Provides follow-up to employer in form of phone calls and visits to job sites as needed
	Communicates to employer regarding staff accessibility as needed
	Helps client relocate or find new job if necessary

Source: From "A Supported Work Approach to Competitive Employment of Individuals with Moderate and Severe Handicaps" by P. Wehman and J. Kregel, 1985, *The Journal of The Association for Persons with Severe Handicaps, 10,* p. 5. Reprinted by permission.

with their parents or family and 90% lacked skills to use public transportation at the time of their initial placement. (p. 275)

Table 15.3 summarizes the employment outcome measures reported by Wehman, Hill, et al. (1985). A total of 252 job placements, most in entry-level minimum-wage positions, were made with over 100 different employers, representing primarily service occupations, such as cleaning and custodial work in hotels, restaurants, and hospitals. The average length of employment for all 167 of the persons in the study was 19 months. At the time of the report, 72 clients were still employed. The authors note that the 8.1 months of employment during their clients' first year on the job compares favorably with the results of a study by the National Hotel and Restaurant Association (1983) that found more than 2,300 nonhandicapped individuals had retained their comparable entry-level positions for an average of only 5 months. They also point out that the average total cost of $5,255 per client for the supported work program, which resulted in an average of 19 months of paid employment per client, compares favorably with the average annual cost of $4,000 per year for adult day programs (i.e., sheltered workshops and work activity centers). This comparison is especially favorable when one takes into account the total client wages earned and income taxes contributed.

In the *work enclave* or *clustered placement* model of supported employment, a small group of no more than eight persons with disabilities performs work with special training or job supports within a normal business or industry.

FIGURE 15.1

Number of hours of intervention time spent with three clients in a supported work program. (*Source*: From "Competitive Employment for Persons with Mental Retardation: A Follow-Up Six Years Later" by P. Wehman, M. Hill, J. W. Hill, V. Brooke, P. Pendleton, and C. Britt, 1985, *Mental Retardation, 23,* p. 278. Reprinted by permission.)

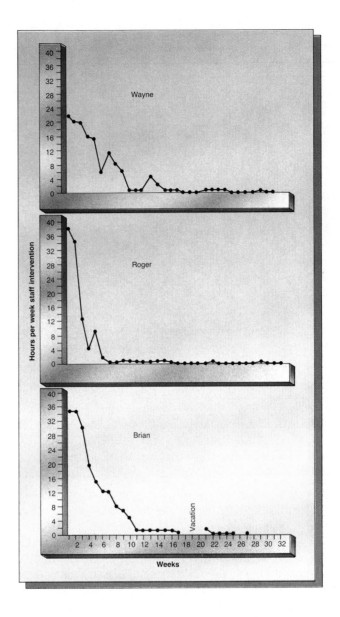

The work enclave provides a useful alternative to traditional, segregated sheltered employment, offering many of the benefits of integrated employment with nondisabled employees as well as the ongoing support necessary for long-term job success.

Rhodes and Valenta (1985) report the preliminary results of a work enclave that resulted in the employment of six persons with severe disabilities. They established a working agreement with Physio Control Corporation of Redmond, Washington, to create a separate production line within the company to employ persons with severe disabilities. Physio Control employs 900 people in its Redmond facility, where it manufactures biomedical equipment, primarily heart defibrillators. A nonprofit organization called Trillium Employment Services was created to provide the employment training and ongoing support the workers

TABLE 15.3
Summary of key
employment outcomes for
persons participating in a
supported work program.

Numbers Placed (median measured IQ = 49)	
1. Number of clients placed October 1978–December 1984	167
2. Number of clients currently working	72
3. Total number of placements	252
Time Employed	
1. Mean months employed for study population	19 months
2. Mean time employed in first year of labor market (two-thirds of all clients were retained in competitive employment beyond six months)	8.1* months
Monetary outcomes	
1. Cumulative client wages earned	$1,069,309
2. Cumulative client taxes contributed	$245,941
Costs	
1. Mean staff intervention hours per client	195
2. Mean cost per client	$5,255
3. Mean cost per placement	$3,483

*Mean length of time nonhandicapped coworkers stayed in job in similar or identical industries = five months (based on National Hotel and Restaurant survey of 2300 nonhandicapped workers in food service industry).

Source: From "Competitive Employment for Persons with Mental Retardation: A Follow-Up Six Years Later" by P. Wehman, M. Hill, J. W. Hill, V. Brooke, P. Pendleton, and C. Britt, 1985, *Mental Retardation, 23,* p. 275. Reprinted by permission.

with severe disabilities needed. The work enclave employees have become part of a production line that does subassemblies of defibrillator components, such as chest paddles and wire harnesses. As much as possible, tasks are selected that are of the same type performed by other employees of the company. The work enclave employees are supervised by Physio Control, although legal employment responsibility rests with the support organization (Trillium) until an individual's 3-month productivity averages 65% of the productivity of other Physio Control employees. At that time, the individual is hired as a Physio Control employee. Work enclave employees receive wages commensurate with their productivity rates. Training and supervision procedures use a behavioral model, incorporating task analysis and direct instruction of specific job skills as well as arrangement of the physical and social aspects of the work environment to encourage improved work rates (Bellamy et al., 1979).

At the end of 1 year, all the enclave employees were producing at or above 50% of the productivity standard of other Physio employees. Total wages earned by all program employees for the first year were $20,207, including $2,425 paid by the employees in federal income tax. Total public costs for the program were $15,945 for the first year, with the majority of those costs incurred during the first 5 months of the program. With respect to interaction with nonhandicapped employees, Rhodes and Valenta (1985) report:

> Managers and supervisors within the assembly area report frequent daily contact between enclave and other employees. These occur within the work environment

as well as during breaks and lunch. Contacts are said to be overwhelmingly positive. Social contacts have also occurred through company-sponsored events such as picnics, dinners, and dances, and through privately initiated events between managers and employees. (p. 15)

In their conclusion, however, the authors warn that

for program developers and industrial managers contemplating this alternative, it will be necessary to insure that employees not become segregated from the rest of the working community (much like the "handicapped wing" of a public school). A balance must be attained in providing the structure to support training interventions, to address low productivity, and insure adaptability to changing work demands, without sacrificing the advantages of a normal industrial environment. (p. 18)

The *mobile work crew* model of supported employment is organized around a small, single-purpose business, such as building or grounds maintenance. Like the enclave model, a mobile work crew involves the ongoing supervision of a small group of supported employees in an integrated community employment setting. A general manager may be responsible for finding and coordinating the work of several small crews of three to eight individuals, with each crew supervised by a supported employment specialist. Mobile work crews are organized as not-for-profit corporations; the extra costs the organizations incur because their employees do not work at full productivity levels are covered by public funds. Such costs are usually less than would be needed to support the work crew employees in activity centers, which provide little or no real work or reimbursement.

Johnson and Rusch (1990) found that the actual number of hours of direct training by employment specialists did not decline over time in clustered or mobile crew supported employment programs, as had been noted with individual placements. They suggest that clustered and mobile crew approaches have been marketed to employers with the promise that the employment specialists will always be present, which may increase the likelihood of unnecessary supervision and inhibit the development of employee independence.

The *entrepreneurial* model provides supported employment for persons with handicaps by establishing a business that takes advantage of existing commercial opportunities within a community. The business hires a small number of individuals with severe disabilities as well as several employees without disabilities. One example of the entrepreneurial model is the Port Townsend Baking Company, a commercial bakery in Port Townsend, Washington.

Another form of supported employment is the *structured employment* model. This model, developed by the Specialized Training Program at the University of Oregon, operates in a small industrial-oriented workshop setting and relies on contract revenues to provide income for employees (Boles, Bellamy, Horner, & Mank, 1984). This model provides intensive training for complex assembly and production contracts. Electronic parts assembly and chain saw assembly are two tasks that have been successfully taught to workers with severe disabilities, who have then been able to earn wages much higher than would have been possible in traditional sheltered workshops. A few nonhandicapped workers may also be employed to integrate the work setting and increase overall productivity.

Learning Independence and Adaptability on the Job

The complexity of competitive and supported work environments requires persons with disabilities to use a wide range of vocational and social skills. Consider the many behaviors covered by this list of work performance measures that can be used to evaluate the independent performance of employees with disabilities.

Performance measures

1. Works independently
2. Completes all assigned tasks
3. Attends to job tasks consistently
4. Meets company standards for quality of work
5. Meets company standards for rate of work performance
6. Follows company procedures
7. Maintains good attendance and punctuality
8. Takes care of equipment and materials
9. Maintains acceptable appearance

Adaptability measures

1. Obtains/returns materials for tasks
2. Adjusts rate of performance according to job demands
3. Works safely
4. Follows a schedule
5. Manages time properly
6. Is able to adjust to changes in routine
7. Solves work-related problems independently

Social skills measures

1. Follows directions
2. Accepts criticism
3. Asks for assistance when necessary
4. Gets along with fellow workers
5. Interacts appropriately with customers (Lagomarcino, Hughes, & Rusch, 1989, p. 143)

To earn high marks for most of these measures, an employee must display some degree of independence and adaptability in the workplace. Successful employees independently solve minor problems (e.g., clear off an obstructed work area before beginning) instead of calling their supervisor. Successful employees are sensitive to stimuli in the work setting that signal changing demands, and they adjust their performance accordingly.

Traditional methods of "job coaching" have relied on direct instruction by an outside agent to teach targeted job tasks or social skills in response to the employer's current standards and expectations. The employment specialist returns to provide more training and intervention whenever the supported employee's productivity slips, the criteria for successful performance on the job change, or other problems arise on the job. Mithaug, Martin, Agran, and Rusch (1988) point out that this approach fosters too much dependence upon the job coach, working against the supported employee's learning how to solve problems on the job and assuming responsibility for his own management.

The belief that individuals with severe disabilities must be taught independence in the workplace has gained widespread acceptance among supported employment professionals and has spawned an exciting and promising area of research. Hughes, Rusch, and Curl (1990) suggest identifying natural stimuli in the work environment that can be used to promote independent performance. For example, clocks or whistles may signal going to a job station; co-workers stopping work and leaving the job station might be the prompt for break time; and a growing pile of dirty dishes should be the cue to increase the rate of dishwashing. The job specialist's role expands from training the employee how to perform various vocational and social skills to teaching the supported employee how to respond independently to the stimuli that occur naturally in the workplace. When naturally occurring stimuli are insufficient to cue the desired behavior, the supported employee can be taught to respond independently to contrived stimuli, such as picture prompts depicting individual steps in a multiple-step task (Wilson, Schepis, & Mason-Main, 1987).

Several recent studies demonstrate that employees with disabilities can learn to self-manage their work performance by providing their own verbal prompts and instructions. Salend, Ellis, and Reynolds (1989) used a self-instructional strategy to teach four adults with severe mental retardation to "talk while you work." Productivity increased dramatically and error rates decreased when the women verbalized to themselves, "Comb up, Comb down, Comb in bag, Bag in box" while packaging combs in plastic bags. Hughes and Rusch (1989) taught two supported employees working at a janitorial supply company how to solve problems by using a self-instructional procedure consisting of four statements:

1. Statement of the problem (e.g., "Tape empty")
2. Statement of the response needed to solve the problem (e.g., "Need more tape")
3. Self-report (e.g., "Fixed it")
4. Self-reinforcement (e.g., "Good")

Each employee was trained to use the self-instructional procedure with five of the problems shown in Table 15.4; no training was provided on the remaining five problem situations. Because the supported employees were able to respond correctly to the five untrained problems only *after* they had learned to use self-instructions for the trained problems, it was shown that they had learned a problem-solving skill they could generalize to other problems.

The Importance of Co-Workers

Social interaction is a natural feature of the workplace. Social interaction provides an important source of support for any employee, with or without disabilities, and it is associated with job performance and job satisfaction (Nisbet & Hagner, 1988). Because of their consistent presence in the work environment, co-workers can be a potentially powerful source of natural support for workers

Research has shown that employees with handicaps can use self-monitoring—observing, counting, recording one's performance—to increase their job productivity and independence (Ackerman & Shapiro, 1984; Joliff, Grossi, Heward, & Sainato, 1991; Wheeler, Bates, Marshall, & Miller, 1988). Additional information on how to increase the independence and adaptability of supported employees can be found in Hughes, Rusch, and Wood (1989), Martin, Mithaug, Agran, and Husch (in press), and Rusch and Hughes (1988).

TABLE 15.4
Work-related problem situations and correct responses used to teach supported employees to solve problems.

Problem Situation	Instruction	Correct Response
1. Paper towel in drain of sink; sink full of water	Instructed by trainer to wring out rag in sink	Remove paper towel; drain sink
2. 5 pieces of trash on table	Instructed by trainer to go to table to begin work	Throw trash in basket located within 2 m of table
3. Radio is unplugged	Instructed by trainer to turn on radio	Plug in radio and turn on
4. Box is on table next to soap dispensing machine	Instructed by trainer to put tray on table	Put box in proper place or seek assistance
5. Bundle on table where work is to be conducted	Instructed by trainer to begin work	Put bundle in proper place
6. Tape dispenser is empty	Instructed by trainer to get tape dispenser	Fill tape dispenser
7. Cardboard pad is in box with chip boards	Instructed by trainer to get more chip boards	Put pad in proper place
8. Chair is in center of work-room	Instructed by trainer to hang rag by sink	Put chair next to table
9. Puddle of soap on table where work is to be conducted	Instructed by trainer to begin work	Wipe up soap with rag
10. Box containing hair nets is in wrong place	Instructed by trainer to get hair net	Put box in proper place

Source: From "Teaching Supported Employees with Severe Mental Retardation to Solve Problems" by C. Hughes and F. R. Rusch, 1989, *Journal of Applied Behavior Analysis, 22,* p. 367. Reprinted by permission.

with disabilities (Rusch & Minch, 1988). Rusch, Hughes, McNair, and Wilson (1990) define a co-worker as an employee who works in the proximity of the supported employee, performs the same or similar duties, and/or takes breaks or eats meals in the same area as the supported employee. The authors describe six different types of co-worker involvement beneficial to the supported employee (Table 15.5). Rusch, Johnson, and Hughes (1990) found fairly extensive involvement with nondisabled co-workers by supported employees working in individual or clustered placements, regardless of the supported employees' level of disability. Supported employees working in mobile work crews, however, experienced far less co-worker involvement. When combined with data showing significantly lower earnings for supported employees working in mobile work crews as compared to those in individual or clustered placements, these results raise the question of whether the mobile work crew should continue to be considered an appropriate supported employment model (Kregel et al., 1989).

In a typical supported employment program, the employment specialist provides direct, on-site job training to the employee with disabilities and serves as the primary source of support and assistance to the supported employee. Although the job coach gradually reduces the time spent in direct, on-site training and support as the supported employee becomes acclimated to the job, this model of "outside assistance" has several inherent drawbacks (Curl, 1990;

TOUCHSTONE CAFE: A GENUINE TEST

On July 10, 1990, Touchstone Cafe opened its doors for business in Columbus, Ohio. This in itself is nothing new in a city where every week new restaurants open amid fanfare and high hopes while recently-opened restaurants quietly go under. What makes Touchstone Cafe different from the more than 600 restaurants in Columbus is its primary purpose—preparing adults with disabilities for jobs in the food service industry.

Two years earlier, Susan Berg, founder and Executive Director of Touchstone Cafe, had watched a television documentary about Eden Express, a San Francisco restaurant with a similar mission. "I was totally intrigued by what I saw, both professionally and personally. I had a little money saved up and I made the decision to invest one year of my life in trying to put this thing together. I went to California for a week and came back determined the concept could work in Columbus." Susan began by taking her idea to state and local government agencies in the developmental disability and human service areas. But she was not able to generate much interest; she was reminded that she was just an ordinary citizen with no experience in either special education or the restaurant business. "My background as a director of development and marketing for a non-profit organization gave me confidence in my skills in organizing people and support around an idea. I wasn't about to give up yet." Susan wrote letters, made telephone calls, and visited Columbus-area restaurant owners, the people who would ultimately have to determine if the concept was sound. She arranged a meeting and sent out invitations. "Almost every one came. Their support was unbelievable."

Joe Drury, Division Vice President of Wendy's International and a member of Touchstone Cafe's Restaurant Advisory Board remembers that first meeting. "The possibilities were obvious. Most people thought, 'Gee, wouldn't it be great?', but they never believed it would happen." With the support of the restaurant owners, Susan then attracted other individuals in the business and human service community to her concept. She then went back to state government and landed a grant from the Ohio Department of Development. That grant and significant contributions of equipment, expertise, and money from several restaurants turned a dream into reality. Susan's goal is to make Touchstone Cafe self-sufficient through its retail restaurant sales within 5 years. "I like the idea of a human service program that actually contributes to the local economy and does not need to be perpetually dependent upon grant support and fund raising."

Trainers with Experience

Touchstone Cafe is a full-service restaurant featuring moderately-priced lunch and dinner menus of American cuisine. The restaurant is staffed by 20 to 25 trainees, each of whom works 15 to 30 hours per week, and 10 to 12 trainers. Trainers know exactly what it is like in the "real world" of restaurant work because they either have worked or still do work in local restaurants as waitpersons, cooks, dishwashers, cashiers, etc. The trainees, who range in age from 18 to 55 years old, all have developmental disabilities or psychiatric disorders and

Susan Berg

no recent history of successful competitive employment. Trainees spend approximately 6 months at Touchstone, where they receive training on a minimum of three different restaurant jobs and instruction on employment-related areas such as transportation, interviewing, social skills, and money management as specified by an individual vocational plan.

Touchstone Cafe's Restaurant Advisory Board includes 20 restaurant professionals who represent more than 150 local restaurants, ranging from fast food chains (Wendy's, White Castle), family-style restaurants (Bob Evans, Tee Jaye's Country Place), and up-scale, white-tablecloth establishments (Rigsby's, Lindey's). They have made commitments to provide employment opportunities to graduates of the program. Mark Emerson, Vice President of Operations for Max &

Erma's Restaurants and a member of the Advisory Board: "The Touchstone concept is long overdue. For us in the restaurant industry it's a welcome approach. We like the idea of hiring workers with the training and experience people at Touchstone receive." But although Emerson and the other professionals give their time, the businesses they represent will neither hire nor keep someone from Touchstone who can't do the job. Touchstone trainees are not guaranteed employment by the participating restaurants. After developing specific job skills, each trainee must interview and be selected for a job. Then he must keep that job just like any other worker—through reliable and satisfactory performance.

But an individual's relationship with Touchstone isn't over when he's employed by a local restaurant. Berg and Teresa Grossi, Touchstone's Director of Training, have developed several follow-along services for their graduates and the restaurants who hire them. One is the Dessert Club, a twice-a-month pie and coffee session in which Touchstone graduates get together to talk of successes, discuss problem-solving strategies, and share the wisdom they've gained from competitive employment with current trainees. Another is a training package designed to assist supervisors and nondisabled co-workers who provide support to the employee with disabilities.

Meeting Competitive Standards

Grossi says that from their first day on the job, trainees begin working toward the goal of competitive employment in another restaurant. "Productivity is a must in the restaurant business, whether you work in the front or the back of the house. When things are hopping during peak hours an employee can't bus tables like he's got all day or decide he'll take a break at the dishwashing station. We determine a competitive standard for each of the job tasks our trainees learn. We do this by observing and measuring the productivity of nondisabled employees in the restaurants where our graduates will likely be working and by measuring the productivity of our trainers here at Touchstone. For example, we know a busperson in a full-service restaurant will take an average of 5 minutes to clear and reset a four-top table. So we don't feel one of our trainees has mastered table bussing until he consistently does tables within a range of 4 to 6 minutes.

"First, we focus on doing the job correctly," Grossi continues. "It doesn't do any good to try to go fast if you're making mistakes or finishing only half of the job. Initially a trainer is right alongside each trainee, modeling the job and providing assistance and prompts as needed. These teaching trials are interspersed with probe trials to find out how the trainee is doing. During a probe trial the trainer stands back and records the trainee's performance on each step of the task analysis for the given job—no help is given. If a customer gets the wrong soup . . . well, natural consequences are usually a pretty good teacher.

"When a trainee demonstrates he can perform the job accurately for five consecutive shifts, we begin working on productivity. For example, Chuck was taking almost 12 minutes to bus a four-person table. I showed him a graph of his times compared to what he'd be expected to do in another restaurant. Chuck was given a stopwatch and taught how to time, graph, and self-evaluate his own performance compared to the competitive standard. It didn't take him long to work consistently at a productivity level equal to what's expected in the workplace."

Risk Taking and Self-Esteem

Susan Berg realizes that in order for the early success to continue, Touchstone Cafe must survive as a restau-

A Touchstone trainee takes an order while his trainer looks on.

rant. "It's always a balancing act between running a restaurant and a training program at the same time. We're a real restaurant, and we have to remember the needs of our customers. While some of our first-time customers come because they're interested, curious, or want to support what we're doing, many who walk through the door don't know anything about our special mission. They come to Touchstone for the same reasons they'd patronize any other restaurant—good food, good value, good service.

"It's our customers who make it real. We don't have to contrive anything in order to 'simulate' community-based instruction. This is it. Nerves get on edge when things get rushed, people are waiting for a table, food gets cold, customers change their minds too many times . . . it's great. Our trainees take risks. What we ask them to do is not easy. But the rewards are tremendous. The biggest reward for me is watching the almost daily growth in self-esteem and confidence in trainees." ◆

Hughes et al., 1990). First, the arrival and presence of the job coach can be disruptive to the natural work setting. Second, the supported employee may perform differently in the presence of his job coach. Third, it is difficult for the employment specialist to be sensitive to the changing demands of the job over time and to provide continued support and training consistent with those changes. Fourth, the cost of providing training and support by an employment specialist who must travel to the job site is higher and the efficiency of the approach is lower than one that takes advantage of the natural interactions of co-workers. Fifth, and perhaps most important, the supported employee may become too dependent upon the job coach, thereby missing the opportunity to develop independence and flexibility. A skilled and friendly co-worker can provide information, answer questions, demonstrate job tasks, provide assistance and repeat instructions as needed, give social praise and feedback for performance, and serve as an important contact point for the supported employee's entry into the social fabric of the workplace.

Although some nondisabled co-workers provide support naturally, observations in the workplace indicate that some formal training is usually necessary

TABLE 15.5

Types of co-worker involvement.

Advocating. A co-worker advocates for a supported employee by *optimizing, backing,* and *supporting* a supported employee's employment status. *Optimizing* refers to encouraging a supervisor to assign high-status and relevant tasks to a supported employee; *backing* refers to supporting a supported employee's rights, for example, by attempting to prevent practical jokes aimed at a supported employee. It also includes speaking up for a supported employee or offering explanations during differences of opinion. *Supporting* relates to providing emotional support to a supported employee in the form of friendship, association, etc.

Associating. A co-worker interacts socially with a supported employee at the workplace.

Befriending. A co-worker interacts socially with a supported employee outside the workplace.

Collecting Data. A co-worker collects data by observing and recording social and/or work performance.

Evaluating. A co-worker appraises a supported employee's work performance and provides (written/oral) feedback to him or her.

Training. A co-worker supports a supported employee by providing on-the-job skill training.

Source: From *Co-worker Involvement Scoring Manual and Index* by F. R. Rusch, C. Hughes, J. McNair, and P. G. Wilson, 1990, Champagne, IL: University of Illinois. Used by permission.

to make co-workers' "help" effective in maintaining successful employment by the disabled worker. For example, one study found that co-workers typically presented over 100 instructions in the first 2 hours of employment training (Curl, Lignugaris/Kraft, Pawley, & Salzberg, 1988)—a frequency likely to overwhelm a newly hired employee with disabilities. Several approaches for co-worker training have been developed recently. Co-workers can be taught how to provide support during brief, 15- to 20-minute sessions during breaks or before or after work. Curl (1990) has developed a program in which co-workers learn to use a simple four-step procedure in which they provide instructions, demonstrate the job task, observe the supported employee performing the same task, and deliver praise and evaluative feedback on the trainee's performance.

A study by Likins, Salzberg, Stowitschek, Lignugaris/Kraft, and Curl (1989) demonstrates the potential of co-workers as job trainers for supported employees. Three women with mental retardation who were employed in the food preparation area of a self-service cafeteria were taught a 19-step sequence by co-workers for preparing a chef salad and how to conduct quality-control checks of their salads.

Sheltered Employment

The **sheltered workshop** is the most common type of vocational setting for adults with disabilities. In 1966, there were 885 certified sheltered workshops in the United States, serving 47,000 clients. By 1975, those numbers had more than doubled, to 2,766 workshops serving more than 117,000 clients (Victor, 1976). However, Whitehead (1979) reported that more than 6 million adults with disabilities were not receiving any kind of vocational or employment services. Sheltered workshops serve clients with a wide variety of handicapping conditions and varying degrees of disability, although about half of all clients are mentally retarded. Sheltered workshops can be classified as providing one or more of three types of programs: evaluation and training for competitive employment in the community (commonly referred to as transitional workshops); extended or long-term employment; and work activities.

Many sheltered workshops offer both transitional and extended employment situations within the same building. Transitional workshops continually try

Co-workers can be a tremendous source of help and encouragement for the supported employee.

to place their clients in competitive employment outside the workshop. Extended employment workshops are operated to provide whatever training and support services are necessary to enable individuals with severe disabilities to work productively within the sheltered environment. The Wage and Hour Division of the U.S. Department of Labor requires that persons working in an extended sheltered workshop receive at least 50% of the minimum wage; they may be paid an hourly wage or a piecework rate.

All sheltered workshops have at least two elements in common. First, they offer rehabilitation, training, and—in some instances—full employment. Second, in order to provide meaningful work for clients, a sheltered workshop must operate as a business. Sheltered workshops—especially extended workshops striving to provide steady, meaningful, paid employment for their clients—generally engage in one of three types of business ventures: contracting, prime manufacturing, or reclamation.

Contracting is the major source of work in most workshops. A contract is an agreement that a sheltered workshop will complete a specified job (e.g., assembling and packaging a company's product) within a specified time for a given price. Most sheltered workshops have one or more professional staff members, called contractors or contract procurement persons, whose sole job is to obtain and negotiate contracts with businesses and industries in the community. Contracts do not come to sheltered workshops as a form of charity or community service. Workshops must bid competitively for each job and therefore must carefully take into account not only the wages paid to workers, but also the equipment needs, training costs, production rate, overhead, and so on.

Prime manufacturing involves the designing, producing, marketing, and shipping of a complete product. The advantage of prime manufacturing over contracting, assuming a successful product is being manufactured, is that the workshops do not have problems with downtime when they are between contracts. They can plan their training and labor requirements more directly. Most sheltered workshops, however, are neither staffed nor equipped to handle the more sophisticated business venture of prime manufacturing.

In a salvage or reclamation operation, a workshop purchases or collects salvageable material, performs the salvage or reclamation operation, and then sells the reclaimed product. Salvage and reclamation operations have proven successful for many sheltered workshops because they require a lot of labor, are low in overhead, and can usually continue indefinitely.

Another kind of sheltered work environment is called the **work activity center**. A work activity center offers programs of activities for individuals whose disabilities are viewed by local decision makers as too severe for productive work in most other settings. Rehabilitation and training revolve around concentration and persistence at a task. Intervals of work may be short, perhaps only an hour long, interspersed with other activities—such as training in social skills, self-help skills, household skills, community skills, and recreation. It is estimated that approximately 100,000 adults with disabilities make use of adult day programs, with about 40,000 being excluded from an opportunity to earn wages (Will, 1986). The remaining 60,000 earn an average of $1.00 per day, or $288 per year.

The average wage of all persons with mental retardation who worked in sheltered employment settings in 1987 was $1.02 per hour (Lakin et al., 1989).

The Problems with Sheltered Workshops

Sheltered workshops and work activity centers have recently come under intense criticism. The theoretical purpose of sheltered workshops is to train individuals in specific job-related skills that will enable them to obtain competitive employment; however, few employees of sheltered workshops are ever placed in jobs in the community. Only about 10% of sheltered workshop employees were placed in community jobs from 1977 to 1987 (U.S. Congress, 1987; U.S. Department of Labor, 1979), and many who are placed do not keep their jobs for long (Brickey, Campbell, & Browning, 1985). By contrast, approximately 50% of all supported employees are still earning wages and paying taxes one year after placement while working alongside nonhandicapped co-workers (Rusch, 1990).

Some professionals believe that the poor competitive employment record of sheltered workshop graduates may be more indicative of limitations inherent in sheltered workshops than of the actual employment potential of persons with disabilities. Whitehead (1979) contends that the only individuals who attained competitive employment in the community were those who did not need skills training. Rusch and Schutz (1981) concluded that "training" in sheltered workshops often consisted of no more than "supervision with vague instructions and occasional prompts to stay on task" (p. 287). After conducting 9,000 hours of observation in a workshop for adults with mental retardation, Turner (1983) found that "the average individual in workshop society spends less than 50% of his or her time on the lines actually working" (p. 153). Turner found that on-task behavior varied tremendously as a function of the availability of subcontracts and that workers decreased their productivity rates to accommodate times when little subcontracted work was available.

Nisbet and Vincent (1986) compared the behavior of employees with moderate and severe mental retardation in sheltered and community work environments. They found that inappropriate behavior (e.g., hostility, aggression, inactivity, self-stimulation) was exhibited 8.8 times more frequently in sheltered environments than in the community work environments.

> In sheltered environments, inactivity accounted for 61% of the inappropriate behavior and in nonsheltered environments, it accounted for 3%. The lack of meaningful work or absence of work altogether due to contract procurement difficulties may, in part, account for the inactivity rather than the inability of the worker with a disability to perform at an acceptable rate over a measurable duration of time. (Nisbet & Vincent, 1986, p. 26)

Brown et al. (1984) are particularly critical of the lack of real work in sheltered workshops and work activity centers.

> Thousands of workers . . . are confined to activity centers and sheltered workshops where they are required to perform "simulated work," "prework," "could be work some day," and "looks like work" year after year. In the process, they are systematically and categorically denied access to the real world of work. (p. 266)

Although the concept of supported work is still relatively new, the positive results produced by a variety of supported work models implemented in both urban and rural communities under various economic conditions cause us to wonder, along with Wehman, Hill, et al. (1985), about the appropriateness of long-term sheltered employment.

> What this report indicates is that many more persons with mental retardation could be working competitively than currently are employed. . . . Furthermore, our data raise some serious questions about the appropriateness of long-term sheltered workshop employment and work activity center placements for individuals that are labeled mentally retarded who could be benefiting from the economic and social benefits of competitive employment. Specifically, one might reasonably ask: why should so many persons be placed in adult activity centers and sheltered workshops if they, in fact, can work competitively under appropriate support conditions? (p. 279)

■ TRANSITION FROM SCHOOL TO WORK

The problems that young people with disabilities experience as they move from school to adult life have demanded the attention of special educators, parents, and legislators. A 1986 survey of the state educational agencies responsible for the education of handicapped students in all 50 states showed that, out of 35 different topics, vocational training and transition was ranked as the highest priority for inservice training (tied with the least restrictive environment) (McLaughlin, Smith-Davis, & Burke, 1986). The topic of secondary curriculum was tied for fourth. When the same survey had been conducted only 4 years before, vocational training had been ranked eighth by the states, and secondary curriculum was not even mentioned. When the parents of 163 high school students with severe disabilities were asked what they perceived to be the most important adult services their children would need after graduation and at 5 years and 10 years thereafter, they ranked a secure vocational placement that offered meaningful work as the first priority for all three points in time (McDonnell, Wilcox, Boles, & Bellamy, 1985).

Congress has also been aware of the difficulties young adults with disabilities face. A major section of P.L. 98–199, the Education for Handicapped Children Amendments of 1983, included funds to support a significant effort in improving secondary special education programs and transitional services. Since passage of P.L. 98–199, the U.S. Department of Education, Office of Special Education and Rehabilitation Services (OSERS) has made transition from school to work a major priority. OSERS proposed a model of transition services encompassing three levels of service, each conceptualized as a bridge between the secondary special education curriculum and adult employment (Will, 1985). The three levels differ in terms of the nature and extent of the services an individual with disabilities would need to make a successful transition from school to work. At the first level are students who require no special transition services. Upon graduation from an appropriate secondary special education curriculum, these young adults, presumably those with mild disabilities, would make use of the generic employment services already available to nonhandicapped people in the community (e.g., job placement agencies). At the second level are persons with disabilities who require the time-limited transitional services offered by vocational rehabilitation or adult service agencies that are specially designed to help individuals with disabilities gain competitive, independent employment. The third level of transitional services consists of ongoing employment services that are necessary if persons with severe disabilities are to enjoy the benefits of meaningful, paid work. The various models of supported employment are examples of ongoing transitional services at this level.

Transition Models

Numerous models for school-to-work transition have been developed. All stress the importance of a functional secondary school curriculum that provides work experience in integrated community job sites, systematic coordination between the school and adult service providers, parental involvement and support, and a written individualized transition plan to guide the entire process (Hasazi & Clark, 1988). Although work-study and vocational training programs for special education students and vocational rehabilitation services for adults with disabilities have existed in every state for a long time, systematic coordination of and communication between schools and community-based adult services have not typically occurred.

For descriptions of various transition education approaches, see Freagon et al. (1986), Hutchins and Renzaglia (1990), McDonnell, Hardman, and Hightower (1989), Rusch et al. (1987), Siegel, Greener, Prieur, Robert, and Gaylord-Ross (1989), and Wehman, Kregel, and Barcus (1985). The addresses of three university-based research institutes devoted to the development and evaluation of methods for school-to-work transition and supported employment are provided at the end of this chapter.

Wehman, Kregel, and Barcus's (1985) model for school-to-work transition involves three stages: the secondary school curriculum, the transition planning process, and placement in meaningful employment (Figure 15.2). Wehman, Kregel, and Barcus consider three characteristics critical to good secondary school programs. First, the curriculum must stress functional skills; that is, students must learn vocational skills that they will actually need and use in local employment situations. Second, school-based instruction must be carried out in integrated settings as much as possible. Students with disabilities must be given ample opportunities to learn the interpersonal skills necessary to work effectively with nonhandicapped workers and peers in integrated work sites. Third, community-based instruction should begin as early as about age 12 for students with severe disabilities and must be used for progressively extended periods as the student nears graduation. While on work sites in the community, students should receive direct instruction in areas such as specific job skills, ways to increase production rate, and transportation to and from employment sites.

> Students should train and work in the community whenever possible. This is not only to expose them to the community and work expectations, but to expose future employers and co-workers to their potential as reliable employees. (Wehman, Kregel, & Barcus, 1985, p. 29)

Development of career awareness and vocational skills should begin in the elementary years for children with severe disabilities. This does not mean, of course, that 6-year-old children must be placed on job sites for training; however, appropriate vocational objectives should be selected at each age level (Freagon et al., 1986; Wehman, 1983). For example, elementary students might sample different types of jobs through classroom responsibilities such as watering plants, cleaning chalkboards, or taking messages to the office. Young children with disabilities might also visit community work sites where adults with disabilities are employed. In addition, assessment and teaching of job

FIGURE 15.2

A three-stage model for helping students with disabilities make a successful transition from school to work. (*Source*: From "From School to Work: A Vocational Transition Model for Handicapped Students" by P. Wehman, J. Kregel, and J. M. Barcus, 1985, *Exceptional Children, 52,* p. 28. Reprinted by permission.)

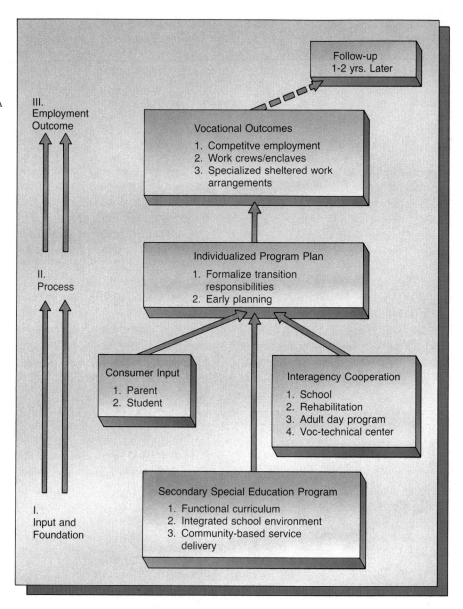

performance skills can be accomplished with elementary-age special education students through prevocational work samples, which provide practice on skills (e.g., counting, packaging, following directions) and which are related to a variety of potentially available jobs in the community (Scott, Ebbert, & Price, 1986). Middle-school students should begin to spend time at actual community job sites, with an increasing amount of in-school instruction devoted to the development of associated work skills, such as being on time, staying on task, and using interpersonal skills (Egan, Fredericks, & Hendrickson, 1985; Sulzbacher, Haines, Peterson, & Swatman, 1987). Secondary students should spend an increasing amount of time receiving instruction at actual community job sites. For example, Test, Grossi, and Keul (1988) describe a procedure for systematically teaching a 19-year-old student with mental retardation janitorial skills in a competitive work setting. The remaining hours of in-school instruction should focus on acquisition of functional skills needed in the adult work, domestic, community, and recreational/leisure environments toward which the student is headed (Brown et al., 1979).

Realizing that the actual number of hours spent at a work site will vary according to a student's age and the particular site, Freagon et al. (1986) suggest the following schedule for students with severe disabilities:

- ◆ Elementary (ages 6–10): ½ hour per week on an in-school job, increasing with age
- ◆ Middle school (ages 11–13): 2 half-days on a community job site
- ◆ High school (ages 14–18): 2 to 3 full days on a community job site
- ◆ High school (ages 19–21): as much time as possible on continuing job sites (i.e., the job the young adult will assume after leaving school)

The second stage of this transition model, the development and implementation of an individualized vocational transition plan for every student with disabilities, is the key element in the transition process. Input from both student and parents and interagency cooperation are critical to an early planning effort that results in a formalized plan identifying school, community, and home responsibilities.

> The plan should include annual goals and short-term objectives which reflect skills required to function on the job, at home, and in the community. Transition services should also be specified, including referral to appropriate agencies, job placement, and on-the-job follow-up. (Wehman, Kregel, & Barcus, 1985, p. 30)

In addition to being individualized and comprehensive, transition plans must be longitudinal. Wehman, Kregel, and Barcus (1985) recommend that an individual transition plan be written 4 years prior to a student's graduation and that the plan be reviewed and modified as necessary at least once each year until the young adult has adjusted successfully to a postschool vocational placement. When a student with disabilities has reached age 16, a transition plan must be included as part of the IEP. After graduation, the transition plan can be a component of the individual written rehabilitation plan if the young adult is served by vocational rehabilitation, or part of an individualized habilitation or service plan if the young adult is served by a community adult services agency (e.g., a county program for people with developmental disabilities). A well-written transition plan ensures that parents are aware of available adult services and employment options in the community, improves the chances that adult services will be available with few disruptions to the graduating student, and provides school and adult-service personnel with a set of procedures and time lines to follow (Rusch et al., 1987).

The third and final stage of the transition model, multiple employment alternatives, must be available if the school-to-work transition effort is to result in meaningful outcomes. Unfortunately, many communities provide little in the way of real employment alternatives for adults with disabilities—perhaps a sheltered workshop offering traditional benchwork for persons with mild or moderate disabilities and an adult activity center for persons with severe

Mithaug, Martin, & Agran (1987) describe a model of school-to-work transitional instruction called *adaptability instruction* designed to help secondary students learn independence in the workplace. Students are taught how to make decisions, perform independently, self-evaluate, and make necessary adjustments the next time they perform the task.

As amended in 1990, P.L. 94-142 now requires that each IEP include include a statement of needed transition services for the student, beginning no later than age 16.

Figure 15.3 is an example of an individualized transition plan. Transition plans, like IEPs, can take many different formats. The important points are that the plan includes all necessary information and is clear to the parties involved.

FIGURE 15.3

Example of an individualized transition plan. (*Source:* From "Preparing Students for Employment" by F. R. Rusch, J. Chadsey-Rusch, and T. Lagomarcino in *Systematic Instruction of Persons with Severe Handicaps* (3rd ed.) by M. E. Snell (Ed.), 1987, p. 488, Columbus, OH: Merrill. Reprinted by permission.)

Student's Name _____	Date of Birth _____	Residence _____	Phone _____
Parent/Guardian _____	Address _____		Phone _____
High School _____	Date of Graduation _____	School year _____	Date of Plan _____
Participants _____			

Issues Related to Vocational Transition	Activities	Product	Date of Initiation	Date of Completion	Personnel Involvement
1.0 Job Placement	1.1 School staff will meet adult-service agency staff and parents to discuss potential employment options for student and discuss level of follow-up services that could be provided after graduation.	Completed job placement plan: includes vocational interests, times available to work, etc.	September 1	September 1	School staff Adult-service agency follow-up staff Parents Student
	1.2 Student will be placed into competitive employment during the fall semester.	Job analysis survey Vocational service plan	September 8	September 1	School staff Employer Student
	1.3 School staff will provide initial on-the-job training.	Task analysis Individualized program plans, graphs Work performance evaluations Job placement logs	November 1	ongoing	School staff Adult-service agency follow-up staff Employer Student
	1.4 School staff will meet with adult-service agency staff and the employer to discuss the transfer of follow-up responsibilities.	Individualized follow-up plan for site: includes time for cooperative programming and gradual fading of school staff involvement	January 15	ongoing	School staff Adult-service agency follow-up staff Employer, student Parent

FIGURE 15.3
continued

2.0 Transportation	2.1 School staff will train student to use the city bus to and from work.	Bus pass Travel training task analysis graph	November 1	November 15	School staff Student
3.0 Income	3.1 Meet with staff from social security office to discuss how employment will affect student's SSI benefits	Written letter from Social Security Office outlining the effects on SSI benefits	September 3	September 3	Social Security staff School staff Adult-service agency case manager Parents
4.0 Recreation-leisure	4.1 Student has time between school and work: has expressed interest in joining fitness center near work.	Membership card	December 1	ongoing	School staff Fitness center staff Student
	Student will go to fitness center on Monday, Wednesday, Friday.	Workout schedule	December 1	December 1	Fitness center staff Student

disabilities, who often have no opportunity to perform meaningful paid work. As we have seen, however, special educators and vocational habilitation specialists are developing an increasing range of true employment options for adults with disabilities, particularly in the area of competitive and supported employment. As more communities and employers implement these alternative models for employment, a successful and meaningful transition from school to the adult world of work will become reality for increasing numbers of young persons with disabilities.

See "For More Information" at the end of this chapter for a list of books on school-to-work transition and supported employment.

■ RESIDENTIAL ALTERNATIVES

Where one lives determines a great deal about how one lives. Where a person lives influences where he can work, what community services and resources will be available, who his friends will be, what the opportunities for recreation and leisure will be, and, to a great extent, what feelings of self and place in the community will develop. It was not long ago that the only place someone who was mentally retarded could live, if he did not live with his family, was a large, state-operated institution. Although he had done no wrong to society, an institution was considered the "best place" for him. There were no other options—no such thing as residential alternatives.

The great majority of adults with disabilities needing residential services are those with mental retardation. A national study, however, found more than 37,000 persons living in the residential facilities who were not labeled mentally retarded but were reported to have other disabilities (Hauber, Bruininks, Hill, Lakin, & White, 1984).

Today, most communities provide a variety of residential options for adults with disabilities. Increased community-based residential services have meant a greater opportunity for adults with somewhat severe disabilities to live in a more normalized setting. Three residential alternatives for adults with mental retardation and related developmental disabilities—group homes, foster homes, and semi-independent apartment living—help to complete a continuum of possible living arrangements between the highly structured and typically segregated public institution and fully independent living. First, however, we will consider the number of persons with mental retardation in large public institutions.

Public Institutions

A national census of large, state-operated residential facilities for persons with mental retardation reported these findings:

About 330,000 persons (including children) with mental retardation/developmental disabilities live in institutions, group homes, foster homes, psychiatric facilities, and nursing homes (Amado, Lakin, & Menke, 1990). This number represents less than .15% of the U.S. population. Using a conservative estimate of 1% of the population with MR/DD, we can estimate that 85% of persons with MR/DD live with their families or on their own without support from the public residential care system.

♦ In 1988, there were 91,582 persons with mental retardation living in 296 large residential facilities.

♦ Although an "institution" is defined as having 16 or more residents, an average of 309 individuals were living in each of the 296 institutions in the United States.

♦ 80% of the persons residing in institutions are classified as severely or profoundly mentally retarded.

♦ Even though the residents have a high prevalence of functional limitations with daily living skills (e.g., only 10% could use the telephone; only 7% could use personal or public transportation to get around the community without assistance), considerable potential for participation in community life is also evident (e.g., 24% could bathe or shower; 30% could dress independently; 66% could feed themselves).

- Only 25% of institutional residents do any work for pay.
- The average daily cost for maintaining a person with mental retardation in an institution was $157.77, or $57,200 per year. (White et al., 1989)

Our nation's residential institutions for persons with mental retardation have come under attack both by professionals (e.g., see Blatt, 1976; Blatt & Kaplan, 1966) and by the courts (e.g., *Homeward Bound v. Hissom Memorial Center,* 1988; *Wyatt v. Stickney,* 1972) as being unable to provide the care and educational services their residents need. Given the principle of normalization, most professionals now view the large residential institution as an inherently inappropriate place for a person with disabilities to live, even if humanistic care and good educational programming are provided.

Many families of institutionalized persons with mental retardation, however, do not feel as negatively about institutions as do those in the professional community. A survey of the parent or nearest relative of 284 residents living in 40 different institutions found that 88% believed the institution provided the kind of services and care their family members with mental retardation needed (Spreat, Telles, Conroy, Feinstein, & Colombatto, 1985). Eighty-seven percent of those who returned the questionnaire considered the staff at the facility to be "very good." When asked whether they would like their family members transferred out of the institution and into a community-based group home, 60% of the respondents indicated they were opposed to such a move; only 23% favored such a transfer. When asked under what conditions they would approve the move of their family members to a group home, 58% said they would never approve such a move.

These results, however, should be interpreted in the context of the respondents' assessment of the ability of the persons with mental retardation to live and work in the community and the respondents' knowledge of community-based residential alternatives. Only half believed their relatives were able to learn more about getting along with others; only 21% believed their relatives could learn to work for pay; 61% considered group homes appropriate only for persons with mild mental retardation; and only 13% strongly agreed with the statement, "I know a lot about group homes and other alternatives to large facilities." Interestingly, several studies have found that parents' views change dramatically after a family member has been transferred from a large institution to a smaller, community-based residence (Braddock & Heller, 1985; Conroy & Bradley, 1985).

Deinstitutionalization—the movement of people with mental retardation out of large institutions and into smaller, community-based living environments, such as foster or group homes—furthers the degree of normalization of persons who have previously resided in institutions. Deinstitutionalization is more than a philosophy or goal of concerned individuals; it has been an active reality over the past 25 years. Evidence of this is the dramatic decline in the number of persons with mental retardation living in large, public institutions, from a high in 1967 of about 195,000 to about 87,000 by 1989

(Amado et al., 1990). Whereas 85% of all people with mental retardation in the residential services system lived in large, state-run institutions in 1967, only 34% were still in institutions by 1988.

In summarizing the findings of their 1982 national census of the nation's MR/DD residential system, Hill, Lakin, and Bruininks (1984) predicted that:

> Public facilities [institutions], which continue to depopulate at a fairly constant rate of 6,000 residents per year, are being replaced by smaller community-based programs that serve individuals with severely/profoundly handicapping conditions. . . . Efforts of this nature [federal and state regulations proposing acceleration of deinstitutionalization], as well as research and testimony, will undoubtedly continue to develop the perception that appropriate care is community-based care and that such a perception is no less true for people who are severely/profoundly retarded than for those who are mildly retarded or nonretarded. While a formal policy of noninstitutionalization may not be imminent, there is considerable longitudinal evidence that through continuing program development efforts of the past few years, that end will be essentially realized by the turn of the century. (p. 249)

Group Homes

Small, community-based group homes of six or fewer residents are the most rapidly growing residential model for adults with mental retardation in the United States. The last published attempt to count the number of group homes was a survey in 1982 that reported 15,700 persons living in 3,557 group homes (Hill & Lakin, 1986). By 1988, there were 80,800 persons with mental retardation and developmental disabilities living in group homes (Amado et al., 1990). Most of the residents who leave state-operated institutions move into group homes.

Group homes provide family-style living for a small group of individuals, usually three to six persons. Most group homes serve adults with mental retardation, although some have residents with other disabilities. Group homes vary as to purpose. Some are principally residential and represent a permanent placement for their residents. In this type of group home, educational programming revolves around developing self-care and daily living skills, forming interpersonal relationships, and learning recreational skills and use of leisure time. During the day, most residents are outside the group home, employed in the community or in a sheltered workshop.

Other group homes operate more as halfway houses. Their primary function is to prepare individuals with disabilities for a more independent living situation, such as a supervised apartment. These transitional group homes typically serve residents who have recently been discharged from institutions, bridging the gap between institutional and community living.

Two key aspects of group homes make them a much more normalized place to live than an institution: their size and their location (Wolfensberger, 1972). Most people grow up in a typical family-sized group, where there is opportunity for personal attention, care, and privacy. Certainly, the 40-beds-to-a-ward, mass-living arrangement common to many institutions cannot be said to be normalized, regardless of the efforts of hardworking, caring staff. By keeping the number of residents in a group home small, there is a greater chance for a family-like atmosphere. Size is also directly related to the neighborhood's ability to assimilate the members of the group home into normal, routine activities

The average per day cost in 1982 for each person in a small group home was $41.22 (Hill et al., 1989).

within the community, which is a key element of normalization. Indeed, there is some evidence that quality of life is better for persons residing in smaller rather than larger group homes (Rotegard, Hill, & Bruininks, 1983).

Although research on the effects of the size of group homes has been inconclusive, operators of community residential programs consistently state that residential settings of three or four individuals are much more likely to have their residents integrated into the community (Cooke, 1981). Bronston (1980) offers four arguments favoring small residential settings: (1) the group and the home do not attract undue attention by being larger than a large family; (2) the smaller the number of different individuals in a group home, the more likely the neighborhood will absorb them; (3) large groups tend to become self-sufficient, orienting inward and thereby resisting movement outward into the community; and (4) in groups larger than six or eight, house parents and advisors can no longer relate properly to individual group members.

The location and physical characteristics of the group home itself are also vital determinants of its ability to provide a normalized lifestyle for its residents. A group home must be located within the community, in a residential area, not a commercially zoned district. It must be in an area where residents have convenient access to shopping, schools, churches, public transportation, and recreational facilities. In other words, a group home must be located in a normal residential area where any one of us might live. And it must look like a home, not conspicuously different from the other family dwellings on the same street. There definitely should not be a sign out front that reads "Elm Street Group Home for the Retarded."

Janicki and Zigman (1984) studied the location and design characteristics of 386 small group homes in New York state. They found that the homes exhibited a wide variety of styles and configurations, were located in all types of residential neighborhoods, and were in close proximity to commercial and recreational resources (e.g., two-thirds of the residences were within one-fourth of a mile of both a corner store and a bus or subway station). Janicki and Zigman concluded that the homes in their study were "normative, homelike dwellings in terms of their structural aspects, and as such they contribute to the physical integration of the residence program within its neighborhood. If this is true, then it is reasonable to assume that these aspects add to the social integration of their occupants as well" (p. 300).

Wolfensberger and Thomas (1983) have developed a method for assessing the degree to which a service setting meets various criteria of normalization. Called Program Analyses of Service Systems (PASS), the assessment produces a quantitative rating. Pieper and Cappuccilli (1980) suggest the following set of questions, based on PASS, as a means of determining how appropriate a given residential setting may be. A group home would be considered a normalized setting if all or most of these questions can be answered yes.

- Did the residents choose to live in the home?
- Is this type of setting usually inhabited by people in the residents' age group?
- Do the residents live with others their own age?
- Is the home located within a residential neighborhood?
- Does the residence look like the other dwellings around it?

- Can the number of people living in the residence be reasonably expected to be assimilated into the community?
- Are community resources and facilities readily accessible from the residence?
- Do the residents have a chance to buy the house?
- Do the managers of the place act in an appropriate manner toward the residents?
- Are the residents encouraged to do all they can for themselves?
- Are the residents encouraged to have personal belongings that are appropriate to their age?
- Are residents encouraged to use community resources as much as possible?
- Are all the residents' rights acknowledged?
- Are the residents being given enough training and assistance to help them grow and develop as individuals?
- Would I want to live in the home? Here is the final test. If the residence appears good enough for you to want to live in it, it will probably be an appropriate living arrangement for persons with special needs. We should demand residential arrangements for persons with special needs that are comparable to those inhabited by most nondisabled citizens.

New group homes are opening almost every day all across the country; however, they continue to run into obstacles. Many communities have been slow to accept group homes into their neighborhoods. Most agencies, service groups, and individuals who have started (or attempted to start) group homes for persons with disabilities have run into harsh resistance (Gelman, Epp, Downing, Twark, & Eyerly, 1989). Convinced that people with mental retardation are dangerous or crazy, that they will have a bad influence on neighborhood children, or that property values will go down if a group home comes into the area, neighborhood associations have too often been effective in keeping group homes from starting.

In 1985, the U.S. Supreme Court unanimously ruled that communities cannot use a discriminatory zoning ordinance to prevent the establishment of group homes for persons with mental retardation in an area already zoned for apartment and other congregate living facilities (*City of Cleburne v. Cleburne Living Center,* 1985). The city of Cleburne, Texas, argued that the nearby presence of a junior high school and the fact that the group home site was located on a 500-year flood plain permitted the city to exclude the group home from that site. The city was also concerned "about the legal responsibility for actions which the mentally retarded might take" and about fire safety, congestion, and the serenity of the neighborhood. In their analysis of the Cleburne decision, the attorneys who prepared a brief on behalf of the group home for the AAMD, CEC, TASH, and four other national disability groups said:

> In each instance, the Supreme Court concluded that the city's purported concerns were a smokescreen for prejudice and unconstitutional discrimination.
>
> Perhaps most significantly, the fears and objections of neighbors were held to be insufficient to support the ordinance because "mere negative attitudes, or fear, unsubstantiated by factors which are properly cognizable in a zoning proceeding, are not permissible bases for treating a home for people with mental

Two studies analyzing real estate transaction data have found that neighborhood property values were not adversely affected by group homes. One study examined the sale prices of 525 homes sold around 13 group homes in and around Omaha, Nebraska (Ryan & Coyne, 1985); the second study analyzed the sale of 388 properties near 19 group homes in the Pittsburgh, Pennsylvania, area (Gelman et al., 1989).

retardation differently from" other uses that the law allows. As the Court observed, "Private biases may be outside the reach of the law, but the law cannot, directly or indirectly, give them effect."

[This case] is a useful precedent for arguments that zoning laws cannot be used as a device to discriminate against the housing needs of people who are mentally retarded, and in particular that the fears and irrational prejudices of neighbors who may be opposed to such a group home will not justify its exclusion from the community. (Ellis & Luckasson, 1985, p. 250)

Foster Homes

When a family opens its home to an unrelated person for an extended period, the term **foster home** applies. Although foster homes have been used for years in providing temporary residential services and family care for children (usually wards of the court), more and more families are now beginning to share their homes with handicapped adults. In return for providing room and board for their new family member, foster families receive a modest financial reimbursement.

For an adult with disabilities, there can be numerous advantages to life in a foster family home. Instead of interacting with paid group home staff, who may or may not actually live at the same address, the person with mental retardation lives in a residence that is owned or rented by individuals or families as their primary domicile. The resident can participate and share in the day-to-day activities of a normal family, receive individual attention from people vitally interested in her continued growth and development, and develop close interpersonal relationships. As part of a family unit, the adult with disabilities also has more opportunities to interact with and be accepted by the community at large. In their survey of small group homes and foster homes, Hill et al. (1989) found that 80% of foster home caregivers perceived residents with disabilities primarily as family members. In contrast, group home staff were more likely to view persons with disabilities as trainees or friends.

> Hill and Lakin (1986) reported that there were 17,147 residents with mental retardation living in 6,587 foster homes in 1982. The average daily cost for foster home placement in 1982 was $16.15 (Lakin, Hill, & Bruininks, 1985).

Apartment Living

Apartment living offers the adult with disabilities an even greater opportunity for integration into the community than group homes do. Whereas the resident of a group home interacts primarily with other handicapped persons, in an apartment-living arrangement (assuming the apartment is in a regular apartment complex), the likelihood of interacting with nonhandicapped persons is greater. Some professionals believe that full integration into the community will be achieved only when all persons with disabilities are in private homes or apartments—that even small group homes are too institutional. Bronston (1980) has even suggested that apartment dwellings could handle the residential needs for all adults with disabilities. Three types of apartment living for adults with disabilities are most common: the apartment cluster, the coresidence apartment, and the maximum-independence apartment.

An apartment cluster consists of a small number of apartments housing persons with disabilities and another nearby apartment for a supervisory person or staff. An apartment cluster is an extremely workable arrangement because it allows for a great deal of flexibility in the amount and degree of supervision

Charles is practicing his laundry skills in preparation for independent community living.

needed by residents in the various apartments. Whereas some residents might require direct help with such things as shopping, cooking, or even getting dressed, others need only limited assistance or suggestions and prompts. Some apartments in an apartment cluster are also occupied by nondisabled persons, which facilitates social integration.

A coresidence apartment is shared by a handicapped and a nonhandicapped person. Although this arrangement is sometimes permanent, most coresidence apartments are used as a step toward independent living. The live-in roommates are often unpaid volunteers.

Two to four adults with disabilities usually cohabit maximum-independence apartments. These adults have all of the self-care and daily living skills required to take care of themselves and their apartment on a day-to-day basis. A supervisory visit is made once or twice a week to help the residents deal with any special problems they may be having.

Salend and Giek (1988) interviewed 25 landlords about their experiences renting to persons with mental retardation. A significant number of the landlords reported problems related to poor independent living skills, failure to maintain the apartment properly, and extreme dependence on the landlord for minor problems. The authors suggest guidelines for promoting the success of apartment living arrangements for adults with mental retardation. Several curricula and training programs for teaching persons with mental retardation housekeeping and other independent living skills are available (Bauman & Iwata, 1977; Crnic & Pym, 1979; Vogelsberg et al., 1980).

See Williams and Cuvo (1986) for an interesting study evaluating task analytic strategies for teaching apartment upkeep skills (e.g., cleaning the refrigerator, operating the air conditioner/heater) to six adults with severe disabilities.

Outcomes and Issues in Residential Services

During the early years of the group home movement, many may have thought that small community-based residences were appropriate only for more highly skilled persons experiencing mild or moderate levels of mental retardation. But in their nationally representative survey of group homes, Hill et al. (1989) found that 41% of the residents were severely or profoundly mentally retarded. The national residential census conducted by Hauber et al. (1984) found that even a small percentage of those persons living in semi-independent apartments are people with severe or profound mental retardation. These data support the notion that community-based living for persons with severe disabilities is feasible. But what about the experiences of those who transfer from large institutions to smaller community residences? Does the quality of their lives improve?

Given the complexity and variety of community residential programs and the many variables that play a part in determining quality of life and developmental progress, answering these important questions in a definitive, scientific manner is nearly impossible. Several studies, however, indicate generally positive outcomes for residents transferred from institutions to group homes. One of the most comprehensive studies was reported by Conroy and Bradley (1985), who monitored over a 5-year period the adjustment of 176 persons with mental retardation who were deinstitutionalized from the Pennhurst State School and Hospital in Pennsylvania and placed in community residences. Measures of the adaptive behavior growth of the individuals placed in the community showed gains 10 times greater than those of a matched comparison group remaining in the institution.

> It is important to note that of the 176 people deinstitutionalized from Pennhurst and followed up by Conroy and Bradley (1985), 81% were labeled severely or profoundly mentally retarded.

Conroy and Bradley also conducted interviews with family members and verbal residents before and after deinstitutionalization. While still in the institution, the residents described themselves as happy and satisfied with their life in the institution. When the same individuals were interviewed again after they had been placed in community-based living arrangements, however, they said they were happier in the community and did not want to return to the institution. Figure 15.4 shows the tremendous turnaround in attitude toward community placement on the part of the individuals' parents and families.

> On the average, the people deinstitutionalized under the Pennhurst court order are better off in every way measured. This is an uncommon, but welcome, situation in social science. More often, evaluative results are mixed, and one must balance gains in one area against losses in another. For the people who have moved from Pennhurst to small community residences, results are not mixed. They are conclusive. (Conroy & Bradley, 1985, p. 322)

> Heller, Bond, & Braddock (1988) also studied the reactions of 335 relatives to the closing of a large, state-operated institution. They found that upon hearing of the closure, 78% of families reported a high level of stress and 81% were unhappy with the closure. As in other studies, dramatic reversals in attitudes occurred over time. One year later, 94% of the families expressed satisfaction with the new placements and reported highly positive attitudes about the change and the concept of normalization.

Larson and Lakin (1989) reviewed 18 studies involving 1,358 persons who moved from large state institutions to small (15 or fewer people) community-based living arrangements. They found that, in all 8 of the experimental group versus contrast group studies and in 5 of the 10 longitudinal studies, moving from the institution to the community was associated with statistically significant improvements in either overall adaptive behavior or in the basic self-help/domestic domain. All 18 studies resulted in at least some improvement for groups moving to the community. Larson and Lakin (1989) concluded that

> The institutionalization of persons who have committed no wrong against society can only be justified in terms of a clear benefit accruing to them from that experience. In the debate about deinstitutionalization, then, objective data showing relative benefits related to either community or institutional settings should play a

FIGURE 15.4
Attitudes of parents and families regarding transfer of a family member with mental retardation from a state institution to a community-based residential setting—before and after deinstitutionalization. (*Source*: From *The Pennhurst Longitudinal Study: A Report on Five Years of Research and Analysis* (p. 179) by J. W. Conroy and V. J. Bradley, 1985, Philadelphia: Temple University Development Disabilities Center. Reprinted by permission.)

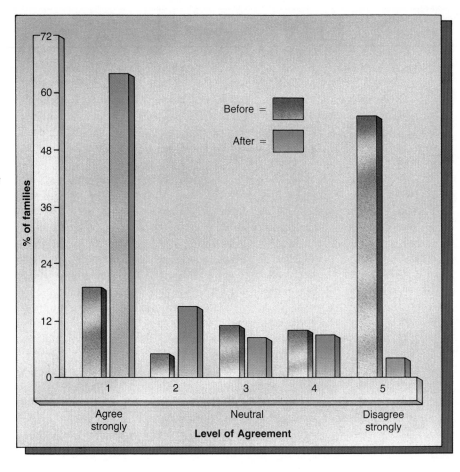

Zirpoli and Wieck (1989) ask, "If the benefits of deinstitutionalization and integration are so overwhelming, why do states continue to spend enormous sums of money maintaining public institutions?" (p. 201). Their analysis of Minnesota's public institutions led them to conclude that the economic and political impact of institutional closure (e.g., loss of jobs, community support for institutions) may be slowing the rate of deinstitutionalization.

prominent role. . . . One must conclude [from the studies we have reviewed] then that available research denies support for the assertion that people obtain greater or even equal benefits in increased adaptive behavior from living in large public institutions. In fact, this research suggests that those benefits very consistently accrue more to the people who leave public institutions to live in small community-based settings. (p. 330)

As encouraging as results such as these are, we know that simply placing a person with disabilities in a small, community-based residence such as a group home does not automatically produce a normalized, adaptive lifestyle. Those responsible for planning and implementing community-based residential services for adults with disabilities face many problems and challenges. Based on her observations of life in various group residential settings in California, Bercovici (1983) concluded that

The circumstances of community placement for many retarded persons are institutional in nature. One prominent fact of this situation is that these retarded individuals have no more control over most facets of their existence than they did in the state hospital. Dependence, passivity, and inability to make decisions are some of the behavioral results of this continuing lack of opportunity for autonomy. (p. 189)

Another kind of problem has to do with what has been called the "relocation syndrome" (Cochran, Sran, & Varano, 1977) or "transition shock" (Coffman & Harris, 1980). One who has just left an institution needs support in the community. In the early days of the deinstitutionalization movement, too many former residents of state institutions were dumped into the community without the necessary skills to cope successfully in their new environment and without easy access to support and follow-up services to see that the transition was successful. Fortunately, we now hear fewer horror stories of institutional residents being released into the community and being victimized or served by the criminal justice system as a result of vagrancy, destitution, or a criminal offense.

The challenge is to provide a flexible system of residential options that truly meets the needs of individuals. Most professionals agree that no one type of residential setting is best for all adults with disabilities—we need a continuum of options. But the continuum-of-services approach, with residential options ranging from most restrictive to least restrictive, is also not without its problems and critics. The typical continuum of residential options does not guarantee that there will be no gaps between one option and the next, nor does it recognize the possibility that there may be other, perhaps more innovative, alternatives that are appropriate for some individuals (Cooke, 1981). Also, continuum-of-service models usually assume that someone moves into the residential service system at the more restrictive end and must earn the right to the least restrictive living arrangement.

> The underlying philosophy of this model is not at all consistent with civil rights decisions in other areas. The Supreme Court ruled in the 1960s that black people had a right to ride in the front of the bus and to go to their neighborhood schools, rights based simply on their citizenship—not rights they had to earn. But with "developmentally disabled" people we have said you must earn the right to live in an integrated setting. You must behave yourself before we'll ever give you this right. This is clearly a basic form of discrimination. (Hitzing, 1980, p. 84)

Several innovative models for residential services for adults with disabilities—based on the belief that residential placements must be adapted to the needs of clients, not vice versa—have been developed (Apolloni & Cooke, 1981; Hitzing, 1980; Provencal, 1980).

A significant problem for any residential option is securing, training, and keeping competent staff. Direct care staff in residential settings must fill a demanding role, often serving as family member, friend, counselor, and teacher to one individual, all in a day's time. The training residential staff members receive varies considerably from one program to another. The more successful residential service programs place tremendous emphasis on staff training, making it mandatory and ongoing. Most training objectives are practical as opposed to theoretical; they stress first aid, fire safety, nutrition, neighborhood relations, behavior management, instruction in daily living skills, and so on (Cooke, 1981).

Wetzel and Hoschouer (1984) offer an excellent model of program development and staff training that they call residential teaching communities. A central concept of their model is that naturally occurring, everyday activities are the most appropriate and effective opportunities for teaching the daily living and interpersonal skills that residents of community-based programs need to learn. For example, Gardner and Heward (1991) used the interactions that occurred naturally in a group home between a man with severe and multiple disabilities and other residents and staff as opportunities to teach appropriate personal interaction/conversational skills (e.g., hands to self, proper distance, ask a question just one time). As they take advantage of such naturally occurring teaching and learning opportunities, however, group home staff and other residential service providers must remember that the residence is first and foremost a home, not a school or training center.

■ RECREATION AND LEISURE

Persons with disabilities must be helped to find a self-satisfying lifestyle, and recreation and enjoyable use of leisure time are primary means to that end. Many of us take our leisure and recreational activities for granted. We benefit from a lifetime of learning how to play or how to enjoy personal hobbies or crafts. But appropriate recreational and leisure-time activities do not come easily for many adults with disabilities; they may not even be available in some communities.

To use community recreational resources, one must have transportation, the physical ability or skills to play the game, and, usually, other willing and able friends to play with. These three variables, alone or in combination, often work together to limit the recreational and leisure-time activities available to the disabled adult. Transportation is not available; her disability does not allow her to swim, bowl, or play tennis; and she has no friends with similar skills and interests and no convenient way to make new friends. Because of these problems, the majority of recreational and leisure activities for adults living in community-based residences are segregated, "handicapped-only" outings.

Providing age-appropriate and otherwise normalized recreational and leisure-time activities is an important facet of extending services to adults with disabilities. Special educators must realize the importance of including training for recreation and leisure in curricula for children with disabilities (Bigge, 1991; Peterson & Gunn, 1984). Professionals must also realize the importance that leisure activities hold for unemployed adults with disabilities (Fain, 1986); often, their so-called leisure activities consist of watching great amounts of television, listening to music in the solitude of their rooms, and spending discretionary time socially isolated (Shannon, 1985). As Bigge (1991) says,

> Choice is the most crucial element. Without choice, activities become simply tasks rather than providing elements of control that lead to leisure satisfaction. If television is the only choice, choice is neglected. Thus, awareness of options through leisure education must precede development of specific recreation-related skills. (p. 429)

Bigge describes how numerous games, hobbies, crafts, and projects can be adapted to become enjoyable, worthwhile leisure-time pursuits for persons with disabilities. Some areas she suggests include raising guinea pigs, music appreciation and study, photography, card games, and nature study. Suggestions are also available for adapting leisure activities for young adults who are

Tom loves to fish. Choice is crucial in anyone's selection of leisure activities.

deaf-blind, such as using permanent tactile prompts (e.g., attaching fabric to the flipper buttons of a pinball machine), adequately stabilizing materials, enhancing the visual or auditory input provided by the materials (e.g., using large-print, low-vision playing cards), and simplifying the requirements of the task (e.g., raising the front legs on a pinball machine, thereby reducing the speed with which the ball approaches the flippers) (Hamre-Nietupski, Nietupski, Sandvig, Sandvig, & Ayres, 1984).

Horseback riding is becoming popular with many physically and mentally handicapped persons. Often called *therapeutic horsemanship* or *equine therapy,* horseback riding has given many persons with disabilities the excitement and thrill of the sport while at the same time improving their gross motor functioning, social skills, and feelings of pride and self-esteem. The National Riding for the Disabled Association, founded in England in 1967 and now associated with groups in many countries, has developed a training program, exercises, and a variety of adaptive equipment to enable persons with just about any kind of disability to ride a horse.

Learning appropriate leisure skills is particularly important for adults with severe disabilities. Most persons with severe disabilities have ample free time but do not use it constructively, often engaging in inappropriate behaviors such

Learning to ride a horse can provide physical, social, and emotional benefits.

as body rocking, hand flapping, or bizarre vocalizations (Wehman & Schleien, 1981). A number of promising studies have been reported in which leisure skills that are age-appropriate have been taught to moderately and severely retarded adults (Johnson & Bailey, 1977; Nietupski & Svoboda, 1982; Schleien, Kiernan, & Wehman, 1981). Schleien, Wehman, and Kiernan (1981) successfully taught three adults with severe and multiple disabilities to throw darts, and Hill, Wehman, and Horst (1982) taught a group of young adults with severe handicaps to play pinball machines. In another study, four teenagers and young adults with severe and profound mental retardation learned to perform a basic dance step (Lagomarcino, Reid, Ivancic, & Faw, 1984).

Therapeutic Recreation

Therapeutic recreation uses recreation services for intervention in some physical, emotional, and/or social behavior to modify that behavior and to promote individual growth and development.

Many communities have therapeutic recreation programs. For example, the Division of Therapeutic Recreation of the Cincinnati Recreation Commission offers a full schedule of recreational activities throughout the year for children and adults with disabilities. Dancing, bicycling, swimming, softball, tennis, soccer, golf, fishing, camping, and hiking are just some of the activities that are offered for citizens with mental retardation, physical disabilities, autism, learning disabilities, and behavioral and emotional problems. One of the goals of the Cincinnati program is to help persons with disabilities move into the recreational mainstream; that is, to participate in integrated activities with nonhandicapped people as much as possible. To help staff evaluate and monitor each participant's progress toward that goal, the Division of Therapeutic Recreation has developed a continuum of five levels.

Going hard for a new personal record.

- Level I consists of activities for persons who require a 1:1 or 1:2 staff-to-participant ratio. Mat activities (such as tumbling), music, crafts, and camping are used to help participants increase their sensorimotor and self-help skills.

- Level II is a program for people who have basic skills (such as running, throwing, or striking) and are able to begin functioning in a group situation. Team sports such as volleyball and softball are used, but the emphasis is on group interaction rather than on specific rules or skills.

- At Level III, teamwork is assumed; the emphasis shifts to learning how to play the game or perform the activity well (e.g., learning to convert spares and to keep score in bowling). Skill improvement is the primary objective in Level III programs.

- At Level IV, activities are held in regular community center facilities and are conducted by the regular staff of those facilities instead of by therapeutic recreation specialists. However, the clients with disabilities still participate as a segregated group.

- Finally, at Level V, individuals with disabilities participate in the recreational programs and activities offered by the Cincinnati Recreation Commission for everyone in the community. Staff from the Division of Therapeutic Recreation monitor and follow up on these mainstreaming efforts, working with regular recreation staff somewhat the same way resource room teachers work with regular classroom teachers to help ease the integration of students with disabilities into the regular classroom.

■ THE ULTIMATE GOAL: A BETTER QUALITY OF LIFE

A continuing problem for many adults with disabilities is lack of acceptance as full members of our society, with all the rights, privileges, and services granted to any citizen. We have made progress in this regard—witness the litigation and legislation on behalf of persons with disabilities that have been discussed throughout this book—but we still have a long way to go. Courts can decree and laws can require, but neither can alter the way individuals feel toward and treat people with disabilities. Individuals with handicaps often "seem to be in the community but not of it" (Birenbaum, 1986 p. 145). As O'Conner (1983) states, "There is precious little evidence that . . . public support of normalization has gone so far that mentally retarded persons would be welcome or even tolerated in most 'nondeviate' social circles" (p. 192).

Handicapism

Most adults with disabilities believe the biggest barriers to full integration into society are not inaccessible buildings or the actual restrictions imposed by their disabilities, but the differential treatment afforded them by nondisabled people. Just as the terms *racism* and *sexism* indicate prejudiced, discriminatory treatment of racial groups and women, the term *handicapism* has been coined to describe biased reactions toward a person with a disability. Those reactions are not based on an individual's qualities or performance, but on a presumption of what the disabled person must feel or must be like because of the disability.

Handicapism occurs on personal, professional, and societal levels. Biklen and Bogdan (1976) describe the following examples of handicapism in personal relations.

> First, there is a tendency to presume sadness on the part of the person with a disability. For example, one woman who has a physical disability, and who, incidentally, smiles a lot, told us of an encounter with a man who said, "It's so good that you can still smile. Lord knows, you don't have much to be happy for."
>
> Second, there is the penchant to pity. You might have heard, "It is a tragedy that it had to happen to her; she had so much going for her." Or people sometimes tell us, "It is so good of you to give up your lives to help the poor souls." Or "My, you must be so patient to work with them. I could never do it."
>
> Third, people without disabilities sometimes focus so intensely on the disability as to make it impossible to recognize that the person with the disability is also simply another person with many of the same emotions, needs, and interests as other people. This attitude is reflected in the perennial questions, "What is it like to be deaf?" "It must be hard to get around in a wheelchair," and "You must really wish you could see sometimes."
>
> Fourth, people with disabilities are often treated as children. Notice for example, that feature films about people with mental retardation and physical handicaps are so frequently titled with first names: "Joey," "Charley," "Larry," and "Walter." We communicate this same message by calling disabled adults by first

names when full names and titles would be more appropriate and by talking in a tone reserved for children.

Fifth is avoidance. Having a disability often means being avoided, given the cold shoulder, and stared at from a distance. The phrases "Sorry, I have to go now," "Let's get together sometime [but not now and not any specific time]," and, "I'd like to talk but I have to run" are repeated too consistently for mere coincidence.

Sixth, we all grow up amidst a rampage of handicapist humor. It must take a psychological toll. "Did you hear the one about the moron who threw the clock out the window?" "There was a dwarf with a sawed-off cane. . . ." "Two deaf brothers went into business with each other . . . and a blind man entered the store."

Seventh, people with disabilities frequently find themselves spoken for, as if they were not present or were unable to speak for themselves. In a similar vein, people without disabilities sometimes speak about people with disabilities in front of them, again as if they were objects and not people.

In terms of personal relations, then, if you are labeled "handicapped," handicapism is your biggest burden. It is a no-win situation. You are not simply an ordinary person.

Only when a man or woman who has a disability is allowed to be simply an ordinary person—given the opportunity to strive and sometimes succeed and allowed the freedom and dignity to strive and sometimes fail—can normalization become a reality. Only then can people with disabilities enjoy a quality of life that citizens without handicaps take for granted.

Quality of Life

Without question, significant strides have been made in the lives of many people with disabilities. Tens of thousands of people who previously were relegated to life in an institution now live in real homes in regular neighborhoods. Thousands who never had an opportunity to learn meaningful job skills go to work each day and bring home a paycheck each week. But living in a community-based residence and having a real job in an integrated setting do not translate automatically into a better life (Bellamy, Newton, LeBaron, & Horner, in press; Landesman, 1986).

What is the quality of life for a young man who lives in a small group home in a residential neighborhood but seldom or never gets to choose what will be served for dinner or when he will go to bed, and whose only "friends" are the paid staff responsible for supervising him on his weekly trip to the shopping mall? One measure of the quality of a person's life is the extent to which he can make choices (Meyer, 1986). The choices we make play a significant role in defining our individual identities—from everyday matters, such as what to eat or wear, to the choices we make on larger matters, such as where to live or what kind of work to do (O'Brien, 1987). Opportunities to make choices for persons living in residential programs, however, "are generally absent from the daily routines" (Bercovici, 1983, p. 42). One study comparing the everyday choices and choice-making opportunities of 24 adults with mental retardation living in group homes with 42 nonretarded adults found the group home residents had significantly fewer choices about fundamental matters of daily living (e.g., what

Little is known about the social contacts of adults with disabilities who live in the community, although research into this important area has begun. For example, Kennedy, Horner, and Newton (1989) presented information on the social contacts over a 2½-year period of 23 adults with severe disabilities who resided in small, community-based residential programs. Social contacts, not counting other residents or paid staff, occurred on the average of once every 2 days.

Normalization becomes reality each time a person with a disability is allowed to be simply an ordinary person.

TV show to watch, whether to make a phone call) (Kishi, Teelucksingh, Zollers, Park-Lee, & Meyer, 1988).

How highly would we rate the quality of life for a woman who always sits alone during lunch and breaks at work because she has not developed a social relationship with her co-workers? Recent research on social interaction patterns in integrated work settings suggests that this is an all-too-common scenario. Several studies have found that the majority of contact between nondisabled and disabled employees involves task performance; disabled workers are less involved in good-natured teasing and joking; and few workers with disabilities are befriended by their co-workers (e.g., Lignugaris/Kraft, Rule, Salzberg, & Stowitscheck, 1988; Rusch, Johnson, & Hughes, 1990; Shafer, Rice, Metzler, & Haring, 1989).

Many advocates and professionals now realize that *placement* of persons with disabilities in community-based residential and work settings is a necessary step, but that the most important outcome measure of human service programs must be improved quality of life. Schalock, Keith, Hoffman, and Karan (1989) believe that "quality of life has recently become an important issue in human services and may replace deinstitutionalization, normalization, and community adjustment as *the* issue of the 1990s" (p. 25).

These authors propose an objective measure of quality of life. Table 15.6 shows the 28 criterion-referenced questions that comprise the Quality of Life Index. The questions are organized under three aspects: control of one's environment, involvement in the community, and social relationships. This approach to assessing the quality of life differs from facility, or program-level, evaluations such as the Program Analysis of Service Systems (Wolfensberger &

TABLE 15.6

The Quality of Life Questionnaire. Each of the 28 questions is answered or scored on a 1- to 3-point scale. A person's Quality of Life Index can range from 28 (low) to 84 (high).

Factor 1: Environmental Control	Factor 2: Community Involvement	Factor 3: Social Relations
1. How many people sleep in your bedroom?	14. Does your job make you feel good?	3. How about your neighbors? How do they treat you?
2. How much control do you have when you go to bed and when you get up?	15. Do you think that your work is important to your employer?	4. How do you like this town?
7. Who plans your meals?	17. How often do you use public transportation? (handibus, taxi, city bus, etc.)	5. How often do you talk with the neighbors, either in the yard or in their home?
8. Who shops for groceries?	18. Do you earn enough money to pay for all the things you need?	6. If there are staff or family where you live, or if you live with another client or spouse, do they eat meals with you?
9. Who chose the decorations in your bedroom?	19. Do you have friends over to vist your home?	10. Do you have any pets?
11. If you have a regular doctor, who chose your doctor?	27. How frequently do you spend time in recreational activities in town?	21. Are there people living with you who have dangerous or annoying behavior problems?
12. If you take medicines, who gives you the medicine?		25. What type of educational program are you involved in at the present time?
13. Who makes your doctor and dentist appointments?		
16. How do you usually get to work?		
20. Do you have a guardian or conservator?		
22. Do you have a key to your house?		
23. How many rooms or areas in your house are locked so that you cannot get in them?		
24. Can you do what you want to do?		
26. Who decides how you spend your money?		
28. When can friends visit your home?		

Source: From "Quality of Life: Its Measurement and Use" by R. L. Schalock, K. D. Keith, K. Hoffman, and O. C. Karan, 1989, *Mental Retardation, 27,* p. 27. Reprinted by permission.

Thomas, 1983). The authors' goal is to "develop an instrument that can be used easily by (re)habilitation personnel to assess, monitor, and improve a person's quality of life" (p. 27). They note the Quality of Life Index is more appropriate for living rather than work environments and that generalizations across all types of living environments is not possible.

Self-Advocacy

Advocacy on the behalf of children and adults with disabilities has had tremendous impact, especially during the past 25 years. Indeed, most of the pervasive changes in education, employment opportunities, and residential services have occurred because of the efforts of advocates. Advocacy for persons with disabilities has traditionally been undertaken by family members, friends, professionals, and attorneys. Bigge (1991), however, is among a growing number of professionals and individuals with disabilities who believe that

> The age of "doing for" a person with a disability is rapidly diminishing. Increasingly, our society is viewing individuals with disabilities as integral and contributing members of the community in which they are a part. Federal and state legislation have provided and supported equal access of individuals with disabilities into all walks of life. . . . Along with the acquisition of these equal rights has come the responsibility for the utilization and protection of these rights. It is now necessary for those with disabilities, as individuals and as groups, to assert themselves as self-advocates. (p. 493)

Persons with disabilities have begun to assert their legal rights, challenging the view that persons with disabilities are incapable of speaking for themselves. Perhaps most conspicuous has been the self-advocacy of individuals with physical disabilities, who have been highly effective in their lobbying as part of the independent living movement. Individuals with sensory impairments have also engaged in self-advocacy. A striking and successful example was the refusal by students at Galludet University to accept the appointment of a hearing president who did not know American Sign Language. Persons with mental retardation, however, have engaged in little self-advocacy, perhaps because many have not learned to recognize when their rights are being violated and because they lack the verbal skills to advocate on their behalf in the natural environment.

Despite the importance of self-advocacy and the efforts of persons with

Self-advocacy: responsibility for the utilization and protection of one's rights.

disabilities to assert their rights, there is little research on how to teach self-advocacy skills. A study by Sievert, Cuvo, and Davis (1988) is a notable exception. They taught eight adults with a variety of mild disabilities (mental retardation, learning disability, cerebral palsy, speech impairment) to discriminate whether or not possible violations of legal rights occurred in up to 200 different hypothetical scenarios involving 30 specific rights (e.g., right to help when voting) across four general areas: personal, community, human services, and consumer. Through role-playing, the participants learned a three-step procedure for redressing a violation that involved (1) asserting their rights directly to the person who violated them, (2) if this person did not resolve the problem, complaining to that person's supervisor, and (3) if the problem remained unsolved, seeking the assistance of a community advocacy agency. Participants were given a handbook describing each of the legal rights and the procedure for redressing violations. With one exception, the participants demonstrated generalization and maintenance of their newly learned self-advocacy skills by responding accurately to simulations and depictions of legal rights violations in natural settings.

Still a Long Way to Go

In general, the quality of life for most adults with disabilities in the 1990s is better than it has ever been. Not only do more adults with disabilities live, work, and play in community-based, integrated environments, but more adults with disabilities have acquired or are acquiring the personal, social, work, and leisure skills that enable them to enjoy the benefits of those settings. But *more* persons with disabilities does not mean *all* persons with disabilities. And individuals don't live life "in general"; they experience specific instances of joy and sadness, success and failure. There is still a long way to go.

True, the quality of life for someone who now has his own bedroom in a group home and works for wages in a segregated sheltered workshop may be appreciably better than it was before he left the institution where he ate and slept communal style and his "work" consisted of an endless series of arts and crafts projects. Does favorable comparison with the unacceptable standards of the past mean a relatively better quality of life today is therefore *good*? Would it be good enough for me or you?

SUMMARY

Employment

♦ Studies of graduates of secondary special education programs report high unemployment rates; most of the young adults who had found competitive employment were working in part-time, low-paying jobs.

♦ Supported employment is a relatively new concept that recognizes that many adults with severe disabilities require ongoing support to obtain and hold a job. Supported employment is characterized by performance of real paid work in regular, integrated work sites; it requires ongoing support from a supported work specialist.

- Many adults with disabilities work in sheltered workshops that provide one, or a combination, of three kinds of programs: training for competitive employment in the community, extended or long-term employment, and work activities.

Transition from School to Work

- Transition from school to life in the community has become perhaps the most challenging issue in special education today. Models for school-to-adult-life transition stress the importance of a functional secondary school curriculum that provides work experience in integrated community job sites, systematic coordination between the school and adult service agencies, parental involvement and support, and a written individualized transition plan to guide the entire process.
- Development of career awareness and vocational skills should begin in the elementary grades for children with severe disabilities.
- Middle school students should begin to spend time on actual community job sites.
- Secondary students should spend more time on actual community job sites, with in-school instruction focusing on the functional skills needed in the adult work, domestic, community, and recreational/leisure environments.

Residential Alternatives

- More community-based residential services mean greater opportunities for adults with severe disabilities to live in more normalized settings.
- Despite *deinstitutionalization*—movement of persons with mental retardation out of large public institutions and into smaller, community-based residences such as group homes—there are still approximately 100,000 persons, mostly adults with severe or profound mental retardation, living in large institutions.
- Foster home placement allows the adult with disabilities to participate in day-to-day activities of family life, receive attention from people interested in his development, and experience close personal relationships.
- Apartment living offers the greatest opportunities for integration into the community and interaction with nonhandicapped people. Three common forms of apartment living for adults with disabilities are the apartment cluster, the coresidence apartment, and the maximum-independence apartment.

Recreation and Leisure

- Learning the skills needed to participate in age-appropriate recreational and leisure activities is necessary for a self-satisfying, normalized life style.
- There are too few community resources and recreation training programs for adults with severe disabilities. Communities are, however, beginning to develop therapeutic recreation programs for children and adults with disabilities.

The Ultimate Goal: A Better Quality of Life

- Adults with disabilities continue to face lack of acceptance as full members of society.
- *Handicapism*—discriminatory treatment and biased reactions toward someone with a disability—occurs on personal, professional, and societal levels. It must be eliminated before normalization can become a reality for every man and woman with a disability.

FOR MORE INFORMATION

Journals

Behavioral Residential Treatment. Published quarterly by John Wiley & Sons, Inc., 605 Third Avenue, New York, NY 10158. Reports of research and descriptions of behavioral treatment programs in residential settings.

Career Development for Exceptional Individuals. Published two times per year by the Division on Career Development, Council for Exceptional Children, 1920 Association Drive, Reston, VA 22091. Focuses on education and other programs for complete life experiences—including vocational, residential, and leisure activities—for children and adults with disabilities.

International Journal of Rehabilitation Research Quarterly. Published by the International Society for Rehabilitation of the Disabled, 432 Park Avenue South, New York, NY 10016.

Journal of Vocational Rehabilitation. Quarterly journal of research and ideas for practitioners published by Andover Medical Publishers, Inc., 80 Montvale Avenue, Stoneham, MA 02180.

Mainstream: Magazine of the Able-Disabled. Published by Exploding Myths, Inc., P.O. Box 370598, San Diego, CA 92137-0598. A monthly magazine of articles about and advertising directed toward persons with disabilities.

Books

Apolloni, T., Cappuccilli, J., & Cooke, T. P. (Eds.). (1980). *Achievement in residential services for persons with disabilities: Toward excellence.* Austin, TX: PRO-ED.

Bercovici, S. M. (1983). *Barriers to normalization: The restrictive management of retarded persons.* Austin, TX: PRO-ED.

Berkell, D. E., & Brown, J. M. (1988). *Transition from school to work for persons with disabilities.* New York: Longman.

Brolin, D. E. (1982). *Vocational preparation of persons with handicaps* (2nd ed.). Columbus, OH: Merrill.

Clark, G. M., & Kolstoe, O. P. (1990). *Career development and transition education for adolescents with disabilities.* Boston: Allyn & Bacon.

Edgerton, R. B., & Gaston, M. A. (1990). *"I've seen it all!" Lives of older persons with mental retardation in the community.* Baltimore, MD: Paul H. Brookes.

Halpern, A. S., Close, D. W., & Nelson, D. J. (1986). *On my own: The impact of semi-independent living programs for adults with mental retardation.* Baltimore, MD: Paul H. Brookes.

Kiernan, W., & Stark, J. (Eds.). (1986). *Pathways to employment for adults with developmental disabilities.* Baltimore, MD: Paul H. Brookes.

Lakin, K. C., & Bruininks, R. H. (Eds.). (1985). *Strategies for achieving community integration of developmentally disabled citizens.* Baltimore, MD: Paul H. Brookes.

Ludlow, B. L., Turnbull, A. P., & Luckasson, R. (Eds.). (1988). *Transitions to adult life for people with mental retardation: Principles and practices.* Baltimore, MD: Paul H. Brookes.

Moon, M. S., Inge, K. J., Wehman, P., Brooke, V., & Barcus, M. (1990). *Helping persons with severe mental retardation get and keep employment.* Baltimore, MD: Paul H. Brookes.

Rusch, F. (1986). *Competitive employment: Issues and strategies*. Baltimore, MD: Paul H. Brookes.

Rusch, F. (1990). *Supported employment: Models, methods, and issues*. Sycamore, IL: Sycamore Publishing.

Schalock, R. L. (Ed.). (in press). *Quality of life: Perspectives and issues*. Baltimore, MD: Paul H. Brookes.

Schwier, K. M. (1990). *Speak-easy: People with mental handicaps talk about their lives in institutions and in the community*. Austin, TX: PRO-ED.

Thomas, C. H., & Thomas, J. L. (1986). *Directory of college facilities and services for the disabled* (2nd ed.). Phoenix, AZ: Oryx Press.

Wehman, P. (Ed.). (1978). *Recreation programming for developmentally disabled persons*. Baltimore, MD: University Park Press.

Wehman, P., Moon, M. S., Everson, J. M., Wood, W., & Barcus, J. M. (Eds.). (1988). *Transition from school to work: New challenges for youth with severe disabilities*. Baltimore, MD: Paul H. Brookes.

Wetzel, R. J., & Hoschouer, R. L. (1984). *Residential teaching communities: Program development and staff training for developmentally disabled persons*. Glenview, IL: Scott, Foresman.

Organizations

American Coalition of Citizens with Disabilities (ACCD), 346 Connecticut Avenue, NW, Washington, DC 20201.

Association on Handicapped Student Service Programs in Post-Secondary Education, P.O. Box 21192, Columbus, OH 43221. A young association devoted to providing accessibility and equal opportunities for disabled college and university students. Includes special interest groups on deafness, learning disabilities, community colleges, and rural institutions.

Clearinghouse on Disability Information, Office of Special Education and Rehabilitation Services, U. S. Department of Education, Room 3132, Switzer Building, Washington, DC 20202-1904.

Disability Rights Education and Defense Funds, Inc., 2212 Sixth Street, Berkeley, CA 94710.

Division on Career Development, Council for Exceptional Children, 1920 Association Drive, Reston, VA 22091. A relatively new division of CEC that focuses on career and lifestyle education for persons with disabilities.

Research Centers on Community Living, Supported Employment, and Transition Education

Center for Residential and Community Services and Research and Training Center on Community Living, Institute on Community Integration, University of Minneapolis, 207 Pattee Hall, 150 Pillsbury Drive, SE, Minneapolis, MN 55455. Robert H. Bruininks, Director.

Rehabilitation Research and Training Center, Virginia Commonwealth University, Box 2011, Richmond, VA 23284-2011. Paul Wehman, Director.

Specialized Training Program, 135 Education Building, University of Oregon, Eugene, OR 97403. Robert H. Horner, Director.

Transition Institute at Illinois, 110 Education Building, College of Education, 1310 S. Sixth Street, University of Illinois, Champaign, IL 61820. Frank R. Rusch, Director.

Postscript

All introductory textbooks contain a great deal of information. In that respect, our book is no different from others. But we hope you have gained more than just some basic facts and information about exceptional learners and special education. We hope you have examined your own attitudes toward and relationships with children and adults with disabilities. At the beginning of the book, we shared seven fundamental beliefs that underlie our personal view of special education, we would like to repeat those beliefs here.

■ OUR PERSONAL VIEW OF SPECIAL EDUCATION

♦ People with disabilities have a fundamental right to live and participate fully in settings and programs—in school, at home, in the workplace, and in the community—that are as normalized as possible. A defining feature of normalized settings and programs is the integration of handicapped and nonhandicapped participants.

♦ Individuals with disabilities have the right to as much independence as we can help them achieve. The ultimate effectiveness of special education should be evaluated in terms of its success in helping students with disabilities maximize their level of independent functioning in normal environments.

♦ Special education must continue to expand and improve its efforts to respond appropriately to all learners with special needs and attributes—the gifted and talented child, the preschooler with a disability, the infant who is at risk for a future learning problem, the exceptional child from a different cultural background, and the adult with disabilities.

♦ Professionals have too long ignored the needs of parents and families of exceptional children, often treating them as patients, clients, or even adversaries instead of partners with the same goals. We have long neglected to recognize parents as their children's first—and in many ways best—teach-

ers. Learning to work effectively with parents is one of the most important skills a special educator can acquire.

♦ Special educators' efforts are most effective when they incorporate the input and services of all of the disciplines in the helping professions. Our primary responsibility as educators is to design and implement effective instruction for personal, social, vocational, and academic skills.

♦ Teachers must demand effectiveness from their instructional approaches. The belief that special educators require unending patience is a disservice to exceptional children and to the teachers whose job it is to help them learn. The special educator should not wait patiently for the exceptional child to learn, but should modify the instructional program to improve its effectiveness.

♦ Finally, the future of exceptional children is optimistic. We have only begun to discover the ways to improve teaching, to increase learning, to prevent handicapping conditions, to encourage acceptance, and to develop technology to compensate for disabilities. We have not come as far as we can in helping exceptional individuals help themselves.

■ A MEMBER OF THE PROFESSION

We ask you, the prospective special educator, to view special education as a *profession* and yourself as a *professional*. View yourself as someone with special skills and knowledge; you are different from people without your special training.

It is commendable that you have a commitment and a desire to help exceptional children. You will probably often be told that you are "wonderful" or "patient" because of this; but desire and commitment are only a beginning. What exceptional children need more than anything is teachers who are *impatient*—impatient with lack of progress, impatient with methods, materials, and policies that do not help their students learn and develop.

Teaching students with disabilities requires systematic instruction. It is demanding work. Prepare yourself for that work the best way you can. Demand relevant, up-to-date information and hands-on practical experiences from your teacher-education program. Continue your education and training throughout your career. Stay on top of the continual developments in special education by reading professional journals, participating in inservice training opportunities, and attending conferences. Even better, experiment with instructional methods and share the results of your research with colleagues through presentations and publications.

Special education is not a grim, thankless business. Quite the opposite—special education is an exciting, dynamic field that offers a personal satisfaction and feeling of accomplishment unequaled in most areas of endeavor. Welcome aboard!

■ A MEMBER OF THE COMMUNITY

The degree of success that a person with disabilities enjoys in the normal routine of daily life does not depend solely on his or her skills and abilities. In large measure, integrating people with disabilities into contemporary society depends on the attitudes and actions of citizens with little knowledge of or experience with exceptional learners. How can people come to accept and support a group they do not know?

Society controls who enters and who is kept out, much as a gatekeeper lets some visitors pass but refuses others. For a particular individual, society's gatekeeper may have been a doctor who urged parents to institutionalize their child or a teacher who resisted having any problem kids in class. It may have been a school psychologist who imposed a label of "trainable mentally retarded" or an employer who had no interest in hiring workers with disabilities. It may have been a social worker, a school board member, a voter. Saddest of all, it may have been a parent whose low expectations kept the gate closed.

How society views people with disabilities influences how individual members of the community respond. Society's views are changing gradually for the better—they are being changed by people who believe that our past principle of exclusion is primitive and unfair. Nowhere can we find a better example of this change that in recent court cases and laws. But to have any meaningful impact, everything we have presented in this book must translate ultimately into personal terms for those of you who will not choose careers in special education. People with disabilities *are* different from nondisabled people, but they are more *like* nondisabled people than unlike them. And the conclusion we hope you have reached is this: Every child and adult with disabilities *must be treated as an individual,* not as a member of a category or a labeled group.

■ IN SUM

Viewing every individual with disabilities first as a *person* and second as a person with disabilities may be the most important step in integrating the individual into the mainstream of community life. But a change in attitude will not diminish the disability. What it will do is give us a new outlook—more objective and more positive—and allow us to see a disability as a set of *special needs*. Viewing exceptional people as individuals with special needs tells us much about how to respond to them—and how we respond is the essence of special education.

Photo Credits

Glossary

Absence seizure A type of epileptic seizure in which the individual loses consciousness, usually for less than half a minute; can occur very frequently in some children.

Acceleration An educational approach that provides a child with learning experiences usually given to older children; most often used with gifted and talented children.

Accommodation The adjustment of the eye for seeing at different distances. Accomplished by muscles that change the shape of the lens to bring an image into clear focus on the retina.

Acquired immune deficiency syndrome (AIDS) A fatal illness in which the body's immune system breaks down. At present there is no known cure for AIDS or a vaccine for the virus that causes it (see human immunodeficiency virus).

Adaptive device Any piece of equipment designed to improve the function of a body part. Examples include standing tables and special spoons that can be used by people with weak hands or poor muscle control.

Adventitious A handicap that develops at any time after birth, from disease, trauma, or any other cause; most frequently used with sensory or physical impairments. Contrasts with congenital handicap.

Advocate Anyone who pleads the cause of a handicapped person or group of handicapped people, especially in legal or administrative proceedings or public forums.

Albinism A congenital condition marked by deficiency in, or total lack of, pigmentation. People with albinism have pale skin; white hair, eyebrows, and eyelashes; and eyes with pink or pale blue irises.

Amblyopia Dimness of sight without apparent change in the eye's structures; can lead to blindness in the affected eye if not corrected.

American Sign Language (ASL) A visual-gestural language with its own rules of syntax, semantics, and pragmatics; does not correspond to written or spoken English. ASL is the language of the deaf culture in the United States and Canada.

Amniocentesis The insertion of a hollow needle through the abdomen into the uterus of a pregnant woman. Used to obtain amniotic fluid in order to determine the presence of genetic and chromosomal abnormalities. The sex of the fetus can also be determined.

Anoxia A lack of oxygen severe enough to cause tissue damage; can cause permanent brain damage and mental retardation.

Aphasia Loss of speech functions; often, but not always, refers to inability to speak because of brain lesions.

Applied behavior analysis "The science in which procedures derived from the principles of behavior are systematically applied to improve socially significant behavior to a meaningful degree and to demonstrate experimentally that the procedures employed were responsible for the improvement in behavior" (Cooper, Heron, & Heward, 1987, p. 14).

Aqueous humor Fluid that occupies the space between the lens and the cornea of the eye.

Articulation The production of distinct language sounds by the vocal organs.

Asthma A chronic respiratory condition characterized by repeated episodes of wheezing, coughing, and difficulty breathing.

Astigmatism A defect of vision usually caused by irregularities in the cornea; results in blurred vision and difficulties in focusing. Can usually be corrected by lenses.

Ataxia Poor sense of balance and body position and lack of coordination of the voluntary muscles; characteristic of one type of cerebral palsy.

Athetosis A type of cerebral palsy characterized by large, irregular, uncontrollable twisting motions. The muscles may be tense and rigid or loose and flaccid. Often accompanied by difficulty with oral language.

At risk A term used to refer to children who are not currently identified as handicapped or disabled but who are considered to have a greater-than-usual chance of developing a handicap. Physicians use the terms at risk or high risk to refer to pregnancies with a greater-than-normal probability of producing a baby with handicaps.

Attention deficit disorder (ADD) See attention deficit-hyperactivity disorder (ADHD).

Attention deficit-hyperactivity disorder (ADHD) Diagnostic category of The American Psychiatric Association for a condition in which a child exhibits developmentally inappropriate inattention, impulsivity, and hyperactivity.

Audiogram A graph of the faintest level of sound a person can hear in each ear at least 50% of the time at each of several frequencies, including the entire frequency range of normal speech.

Audiologist A professional who specializes in the evaluation of hearing ability and the treatment of impaired hearing.

Audiology The science of hearing.

Audiometer A device that generates sounds at specific frequencies and intensities; used to examine hearing.

Auditory canal (external acoustic meatus) Slightly amplifies and transports sound waves from the external ear to the middle ear.

Auditory training A program that works on listening skills to teach hearing impaired persons to make as much use as possible of their residual hearing.

Augmentative communication Nonspeech communication used to supplement whatever naturally acquired speech may be present; may be aided (e.g., computer-based speaking system) or unaided (e.g., signing or gestures), depending upon the individual's cognitive and motor abilities.

Auricle External part of the ear; collects sound waves into the auditory canal.

Autism A severe behavior disorder usually characterized by extreme withdrawal and lack of language and communication skills. Lack of affect, self-stimulation, self-abuse, and aggressive behavior are also common in autistic children.

Baseline A measure of the level or amount of behavior prior to implementation of an instructional procedure that is to be evaluated. Baseline data are used as an objective measure against which to compare and evaluate the results obtained during instruction.

Behavior modification The systematic application of procedures derived from the principles of behavior (e.g., reinforcement) in order to achieve desired changes in behavior.

Behavior observation audiometry A method of hearing assessment in which an infant's reactions to sounds are observed; a sound is presented at an increasing level of intensity until a response, such as head turning, eye blinking, or cessation of play, is reliably observed.

Behavioral disorder A handicapping condition characterized by behavior that differs markedly and chronically from current social or cultural norms and adversely affects educational performance.

Behavioral contract A written agreement between two parties in which one agrees to complete a specified task (e.g., a child agrees to complete a homework assignment by the next morning) and in return the other party agrees to provide a specific reward (e.g., the teacher allows the child to have 10 minutes of free time) upon completion of the task.

Bilingual special education Using the child's home language and home culture along with English in an individually designed program of special education.

Binocular vision Vision using both eyes working together to perceive a single image.

Blind Having either no vision or only light perception; learning occurs through other senses.

Blind, legally See legally blind.

Braille A system of writing letters, numbers, and other language symbols with a combination of six raised dots. A blind person reads the dots with his or her fingertips.

Cataract A reduction or loss of vision that occurs when the crystalline lens of the eye becomes cloudy or opaque.

Catheter A tube inserted into a body to permit injections or withdrawal of fluids or to keep a passageway open; often refers to a tube inserted into the bladder to remove urine from a person who does not have effective bladder control.

Cerebral palsy Motor impairment caused by brain damage, which is usually inflicted during the prenatal period or during the birth process. Can involve a wide variety of symptoms (see ataxia, athetosis, rigidity, spasticity, and tremor) and range from mild to severe. Neither curable nor progressive.

Chorion villus sampling (CVS) A new procedure for prenatal diagnosis of chromosomal abnormalities that can be conducted during the first 8 to 10 weeks of pregnancy; fetal cells are removed from the chorionic tissue, which surrounds the fetus, and directly analyzed.

Cleft palate A congenital split in the palate that results in an excessive nasal quality of the voice. Can often be repaired by surgery or dental appliance.

Cochlea Main receptor organ for hearing located in the inner ear; tiny hairs within the cochlea transform mechanical energy into neural impulses that then travel through the auditory nerve to the brain.

Communication The process by which individuals interact with, transmit, and receive messages by any means, including sounds, symbols, and gestures.

Complex partial seizure A type of epileptic seizure in which an individual goes through a period of inappropriate activity but is not aware of that activity.

Conduct disorder A group of behavior disorders including disobedience, disruptiveness, fighting, and tantrums, as identified by Quay (1975).

Conductive hearing loss Hearing loss caused by obstructions in the outer or middle ear or malformations that interfere with the conduction of sound waves to the inner ear. Can often be corrected surgically or medically.

Congenital Any condition that is present at birth. Contrasts with adventitious handicap.

Continuum of services The range of different placement and instructional options that a school district can use to serve handicapped children. Typically depicted as a pyramid, ranging from the least restrictive placement (regular classroom) at the bottom to the most restrictive placement (institution or hospital) at the top.

Convulsive disorder See epilepsy.

Cornea The transparent part of the eyeball that admits light to the interior.

Cri-du-chat syndrome A chromosomal abnormality resulting from deletion of material from the fifth pair of chromosomes. It usually results in severe retardation. Its name is French for "cat cry," named for the high-pitched crying of the child due to a related larynx dysfunction.

Cued speech A method of supplementing oral communication by adding cues in the form of eight different hand signals in four different locations near the chin.

Cultural-familial mental retardation   Any case of mental retardation for which an organic cause cannot be found; suggests that retardation can be caused by a poor social and cultural environment. (See psychosocial disadvantage.)

Cultural pluralism   The value and practice of respecting, fostering, and encouraging the cultural and ethnic differences that make up society.

Culture   The established knowledge, ideas, values, and skills shared by a society; its program of survival and adaptation to its environment.

Curriculum-based assessment   Evaluation of a student's progress in terms of his performance on the skills that comprise the curriculum of the local school.

Cystic fibrosis   An inherited disorder that causes a dysfunction of the pancreas, mucus, salivary, and sweat glands. Cystic fibrosis causes severe, long-term respiratory difficulties. No cure is currently available.

Deafness   Inability to use hearing to understand speech, even with a hearing aid.

Decibel (dB)   The unit of measure for the relative intensity of sound on a scale beginning at zero. Zero dB refers to the faintest sound a person with normal hearing can detect.

Deinstitutionalization   The social movement to transfer disabled persons, especially persons with mental retardation, from large institutions to smaller, community-based residences and work settings.

Diabetes   See juvenile diabetes mellitus.

Diabetic retinopathy   Type of vision impairment caused by hemorrhages on the retina and other disorders of blood circulation in people with diabetes.

Dialect   A variety within a specific language; can involve variation in pronunciation, word choice, word order, and inflected forms.

Differential reinforcement of other behavior   A behavior modification technique in which any behavior except the targeted maladaptive response is reinforced; results in a reduction of the inappropriate behavior.

Diplegia   Paralysis that affects the legs more often than the arms.

Disability   Technically, refers to the reduced function or loss of a particular body part or organ. In practice, *disability* is often used interchangeably with *handicap*.

Double hemiplegia   Paralysis of the arms, with less severe involvement of the legs.

Down syndrome   A chromosomal anomaly that often causes moderate to severe mental retardation, along with certain physical characteristics such as a large tongue, heart problems, poor muscle tone, and a broad, flat bridge of the nose.

Due process   Set of legal steps and proceedings carried out according to established rules and principles; designed to protect an individual's constitutional and legal rights.

Duration (of behavior)   Measure of how long a person engages in a given activity.

Dyslexia   A disturbance in the ability to read or learn to read.

Echolalia The repetition of what other people say as if echoing them; characteristic of some children with delayed development, autism, and communication disorders.

Electroencephalograph (EEG) Device that detects and records brain wave patterns.

Endogenous Refers to an inherited cause of a disability or impairment.

Enrichment Educational approach that provides a child with extra learning experiences that the standard curriculum would not normally include. Most often used with gifted and talented children.

Epilepsy Convulsive disorder characterized by sudden seizures (see generalized tonic-clonic seizure, complex partial seizure, and absence seizure); can usually be controlled with medication, although the drugs may have undesirable side effects; may be temporary or lifelong.

Equal protection Legal concept included in the 14th Amendment to the Constitution of the United States, stipulating that no state may deny any person equality or liberty because of that person's classification according to race, nationality, or religion. Several major court cases leading to the passage of P.L. 94–142 found that handicapped children were not provided equal protection if they were denied access to an appropriate education solely because they were handicapped.

Etiology The cause(s) of disability, impairment, or disease. Includes genetic, physiological, and environmental or psychological factors.

Evoked-response audiometry A method of testing hearing by measuring the electrical activity generated by the auditory nerve in response to auditory stimulation. Often used to measure the hearing of infants and children considered difficult to test.

Exceptional children Children whose performance deviates from the norm, either below or above, to the extent that special educational programming is needed.

Exogenous Refers to a cause of a disability or impairment that stems from factors outside the body such as disease, toxicity, or injury.

Extinction A behavior modification procedure in which reinforcement for a previously reinforced behavior is withheld. For example, a teacher may ignore a child's disruptive behavior instead of scolding. If the actual reinforcers that are maintaining the behavior are identified and withheld, the behavior will gradually decrease in rate until it no longer, or seldom, occurs.

Fetal alcohol syndrome (FAS) A condition sometimes found in the infants of alcoholic mothers; can involve low birth weight, developmental delay, and cardiac, limb, and other physical defects.

Field of vision The expanse of space visible with both eyes looking straight ahead, measured in degrees; 180 degrees is considered normal.

Fluency The rate and smoothness with which a movement is made. In communication, the rate and ease of speech; the most common speech fluency disorder is stuttering.

Foster home A living arrangement in which a family shares its home with a person who is not a relative. Long used with children who for some reason cannot live with their parents temporarily, foster homes are now being used with disabled adults as well.

Fragile-X syndrome   An chromosomal abnormality associated with mild to severe mental retardation. Thought to be the most common known cause of inherited mental retardation. Affects males more often and more severely than females; behavioral characteristics can be autistic-like. Diagnosis can be confirmed by studies of the X chromosome.

Generalization   Performing a behavior under conditions other than those under which the behavior was originally learned. Stimulus generality occurs when a person performs a behavior in the presence of relevant stimuli (people, settings, instructional materials) other than those that were present originally. For instance, stimulus generality occurs when a child who has learned to label baseballs and beach balls as "ball" identifies a basketball as "ball." Response generality occurs when a person performs relevant behaviors that were never directly trained but are similar to the original trained behavior. For example, a child may be taught to say, "Hello, how are you?" and "Hi, nice to see you," as greetings. If the child combines the two to say, "Hi, how are you?" response generality has taken place.

Generalized tonic-clonic seizure   The most severe type of epileptic seizure, in which the individual has violent convulsions, loses consciousness, and becomes rigid.

Genetic counseling   A discussion between a specially trained medical counselor and persons who are considering having a child about the chances of having a child with a disability, based on the prospective parents' genetic backgrounds.

Glaucoma   An eye disease characterized by abnormally high pressure inside the eyeball. If left untreated, it can cause total blindness, but if detected early most cases can be arrested.

Grand mal seizure   See generalized tonic-clonic seizure.

Group home   A residential arrangement for adults with disabilities, most often persons with mental retardation, in which several residents live together in a house with nonhandicapped supervisors. The residents usually have outside jobs.

Handicap   The problems a person with a disability or behavioral characteristic considered unusual by society encounters when interacting with the environment.

Handicapism   Prejudice or discrimination based solely on a person's disability, without regard for individual characteristics.

Hard of hearing   Level of hearing loss that makes it difficult, although not impossible, to comprehend speech through the sense of hearing alone.

Hearing impaired   Describes anyone who has a hearing loss significant enough to require special education, training, and/or adaptations; includes both deaf and hard-of-hearing conditions.

Hemiplegia   Paralysis of both the arm and the leg on the same side of the body.

Hemophilia An inherited deficiency in blood-clotting ability, which can cause serious internal bleeding.

Hertz (Hz) A unit of sound frequency equal to one cycle per second; used to measure pitch.

Human immunodeficiency virus (HIV) The virus that causes acquired immune deficiency syndrome (AIDS).

Hydrocephalus A condition present at birth or developing soon afterward; involves an enlarged head caused by cerebral spinal fluid accumulating in the cranial cavity; often causes brain damage and severe retardation. Sometimes treated successfully with a shunt.

Hyperactive Describes excessive motor activity or restlessness.

Hyperopia Farsightedness; condition in which the image comes to a focus behind the retina instead of on it, causing difficulty in seeing near objects.

Hypertonia Muscle tone that is too high; tense, contracted muscles.

Hypotonia Muscle tone that is too low; weak, floppy muscles.

Immaturity Group of behavior disorders, including short attention span, extreme passivity, daydreaming, preference for younger playmates, and clumsiness, as identified by Quay (1975).

Impedance audiometry Procedure for testing middle ear function by inserting a small probe and pump to detect sound reflected by the eardrum.

Incidence The percentage of people who, at some time in their lives, will be identified as having a specific condition. Often reported as the number of cases of a given condition per 1,000 people.

Individualized education program (IEP) Written document required by P.L. 94–142 for every child with a disability; includes statements of present performance, annual goals, short-term instructional objectives, specific educational services needed, relevant dates, regular education program participation, and evaluation procedures; must be signed by parents as well as educational personnel.

Individualized family services plan (IFSP) A requirement of P.L. 99–457, Education of the Handicapped Act Amendments of 1986, for the coordination of early intervention services for handicapped infants and toddlers. Similar to the IEP that is required for all school-age handicapped children.

Inflection Change in pitch or loudness of the voice to indicate mood or emphasis.

Inservice training Any educational program designed to provide practicing professionals (such as teachers, administrators, physical therapists) with additional knowledge and skills.

Interdisciplinary team Group of professionals from different disciplines (e.g., education, psychology, speech and language, medicine) who work together to plan and implement a handicapped child's individualized education program (IEP).

Interindividual differences Differences between two or more people in one skill or set of skills.

Intervention All the efforts made on behalf of children and adults with disabilities; may be preventive, remedial, or compensatory.

Intraindividual differences Differences within one individual on two or more measures of performance.

Iris The opaque, colored portion of the eye that contracts and expands to change the size of the pupil.

Juvenile diabetes mellitus A children's disease characterized by inadequate secretion or use of insulin and the resulting excessive sugar in the blood and urine. Managed with diet and/or medication but can be difficult to control. Can cause coma and, eventually, death if left untreated or treated improperly. Can also lead to visual impairments and limb amputation. Not curable at the present time.

Kinesics The study of bodily movement, particularly as it relates to and affects communication.

Language A system of vocal symbols (sounds) that give a group of people who understand the language a way to communicate. Nonverbal languages, such as American Sign Language, use movements and physical symbols instead of sounds.

Least restrictive environment (LRE) The educational setting in which a child with disabilities can receive an appropriate education and which is most like the regular classroom.

Legally blind Visual acuity of 20/200 or less in the better eye after the best possible correction with glasses or contact lenses, or vision restricted to a field of 20 degrees or less. Acuity of 20/200 means the eye can see clearly at 20 feet what the normal eye can see at 200 feet.

Lens The clear part of the eye that focuses rays of light on the retina.

Longitudinal study A research study that follows one subject or group of subjects over an extended period of time, usually several years.

Low-incidence disability A disability that occurs relatively infrequently in the general population; in particular, used to refer to vision and hearing impairments, severe mental retardation, severe behavior disorders such as autism, and multiple handicaps.

Low vision Vision so limited that special educational services are required; nonetheless, permits learning through the visual channel.

Macular degeneration A deterioration of the central part of the retina, which causes difficulty in seeing details clearly.

Magnitude (of behavior) The force with which a response is emitted.

Mainstreaming The return to the regular classroom, for all or part of the school day, of children with disabilities previously educated exclusively in segregated settings.

Meningitis An inflammation of the membranes covering the brain and spinal cord; can cause problems with sight and hearing and/or mental retardation.

Meningocele Type of spina bifida in which the covering of the spinal cord protrudes through an opening in the vertebrae, but the cord itself and the nerve roots are enclosed.

Mental retardation "Significantly subaverage general intellectual functioning resulting in or associated with deficits in adaptive behavior and manifested during the developmental period" (Grossman, 1983, p. 11).

Microcephalus A condition characterized by an abnormally small skull with resulting brain damage and mental retardation.

Minimal brain dysfunction A once-popular term used to describe the learning disability of children with no actual (clinical) evidence of brain damage.

Mobility The ability to move safely and efficiently from one point to another.

Model program A program that implements and evaluates new procedures or techniques in order to serve as a basis for development of other similar programs.

Monoplegia Paralysis affecting one limb.

Morpheme The smallest element of a language that carries meaning.

Multicultural education An educational approach in which the curriculum and instructional methods for all children instill an awareness, acceptance, and appreciation of cultural diversity.

Multifactored assessment Assessment and evaluation of a handicapped child with a variety of test instruments and observation procedures. Required by P.L. 94–142 when assessment is for educational placement of a child who is to receive special education services. Prevents the misdiagnosing and misplacing a student as the result of considering only one test score.

Muscular dystrophy A group of diseases that gradually weakens muscle tissue; usually becomes evident by the age of 4 or 5.

Myelomeningocele A protrusion on the back of a child with spina bifida, consisting of a sac of nerve tissue bulging through a cleft in the spine.

Myopia Nearsightedness; results when light is focused on a point in front of the retina, resulting in a blurred image for distant objects.

Neurologic impairment Any physical disability caused by damage to the central nervous system (brain, spinal cord, ganglia, and nerves).

Normal curve A mathematically derived curve depicting the probability or distribution of a given variable (such as a physical trait or test score) in the general population. Indicates that approximately 68.26% of the population will fall within one standard deviation above and below the mean; approximately 27.18% will fall between one and two standard deviations either above or below the mean; and less than 3% will achieve more extreme scores of more than two standard deviations in either direction.

Normalization The principle of allowing each person's life to be as normal as possible in all aspects, including residence, schooling, work, recreational activities, and overall independence. Similarities between disabled and nondisabled people of the same age are emphasized.

Nystagmus A rapid, involuntary, rhythmic movement of the eyes that may cause difficulty in reading or fixating on an object.

Occupational therapist A professional who programs and/or delivers instructional activities and materials to help children and adults with disabilities learn to participate in useful activities.

Ocular motility   The eye's ability to move.

Operant conditioning audiometry   Method of measuring hearing by conditioning the subject to make an observable response to sound. For example, a child may be taught to drop a block into a box each time a light and a loud tone is presented. Once this response is conditioned, the light is no longer presented and the volume and pitch of the tone are gradually decreased. When the child no longer drops the block into the box, the audiologist knows the child cannot hear the tone. This procedure is used to test the hearing of nonverbal children and adults.

Optic nerve   The nerve that carries impulses from the eye to the brain.

Oral   An approach to education of deaf children that stresses learning to speak as the essential element of integration into the hearing world.

Orientation   The ability to establish one's position in relation to the environment.

Orthopedic impairment   Any disability caused by disorders to the musculoskeletal system.

Ossicles   Three small bones (hammer, anvil, and stirrup) that transmit sound energy from the middle ear to the inner ear.

Osteogenesis imperfecta   A hereditary condition in which the bones do not grow normally and break easily; sometimes called brittle bones.

Otitis media   An infection or inflammation of the middle ear that can cause a conductive hearing loss.

Overcorrection   A behavior modification procedure in which the learner must make restitution for, or repair, the effects of his undesirable behavior and then put the environment in even better shape than it was prior to the misbehavior. Used to decrease the rate of undesirable behaviors.

Paraplegia   Paralysis of the lower part of the body, including both legs; usually results from injury to or disease of the spinal cord.

Paraprofessionals (in education)   Trained classroom aides who assist teachers; may include parents.

Perceptual handicap   A term formerly used to describe some conditions now included under learning disability; usually referred to problems with no known physical cause.

Perinatal   Occurring at or immediately after birth.

Peripheral vision   Vision at the outer limits of the field of vision.

Personality disorder   A group of behavior disorders, including social withdrawal, anxiety, depression, feelings of inferiority, guilt, shyness, and unhappiness, as identified by Quay (1975).

Petit mal seizure   See absence seizure.

Phenylketonuria (PKU)   An inherited metabolic disease that can cause severe retardation; can now be detected at birth and the detrimental effects prevented with a special diet.

Phonemes   The smallest unit of sound that can be identified in a spoken language. There are 45 phonemes, or sound families, in the English language.

Photophobia Extreme sensitivity of the eyes to light; occurs most notably in albino children.

Physical therapist A professional trained to help people with disabilities develop and maintain muscular and orthopedic capability and make correct and useful movement.

Positive reinforcement Presentation of a stimulus or event immediately after a behavior has been emitted, which has the effect of increasing the occurrence of that behavior in the future.

Postlingual Occurring after the development of language; usually used to classify hearing losses that begin after a person has learned to speak.

Postnatal Occurring after birth.

Pragmatics Study of the rules that govern how language is used in a communication context.

Precision teaching An instructional approach that involves pinpointing the behaviors to be changed; measuring the initial frequency of those behaviors; setting an aim, or goal, for the child's improvement; using direct, daily measurements to monitor progress made under an instructional program; graphing results of those measurements; and changing the program if progress is not adequate.

Prelingual Describes a hearing impairment that develops before a child has acquired speech and language.

Prenatal Occurring before birth.

Prenatal asphyxia A lack of oxygen during the birth process usually caused by interruption of respiration; can cause unconsciousness and/or brain damage.

Prevalence The number of people who have a certain condition at any given time.

Projective tests Psychological tests that require a person to respond to a standardized task or set of stimuli (e.g., draw a picture or interpret an ink blot); responses are thought to be a projection of the test-taker's personality and are scored according to the given test's scoring manual to produce a personality profile.

Prosthesis Any device used to replace a missing or impaired body part.

Psychomotor seizure See complex partial seizure.

Psychosocial disadvantage Category of causation for mental retardation that requires evidence of subnormal intellectual functioning in at least one parent and one or more siblings (when there are siblings). Typically associated with impoverished environments involving poor housing, inadequate diets, and inadequate medical care. The term is used, often synonymously with *cultural-familial retardation*, when no organic cause can be identified.

Pupil The circular hole in the center of the iris of the eye, which contracts and expands to let light pass through.

Quadriplegia Paralysis of all four limbs.

Rate (of behavior) A measure of how often a particular action is performed; usually reported as the number of responses per minute.

Refraction   The bending or deflection of light rays from a straight path as they pass from one medium (e.g., air) into another (e.g., the eye). Used by eye specialists in assessing and correcting vision.

Regular education initiative (REI)   A perspective that all students with mild disabilities, as well as some with moderate disabilities, can and should be educated in regular classrooms under the primary responsibility of the general education program.

Rehabilitation   A social service program designed to teach a newly disabled person basic skills needed for independence.

Reinforcement   See positive reinforcement.

Related services   Developmental, corrective, and other supportive services required for a child with disabilities to benefit from special education. Includes special transportation services, speech and language pathology, audiology, psychological services, physical and occupational therapy, school health services, counseling and medical services for diagnostic and evaluation purposes, rehabilitation counseling, social work services, and parent counseling and training.

Remediation   An educational program designed to teach a person to overcome a disability through training and education.

Residual hearing   The remaining hearing, however slight, of a hearing impaired person.

Resource room   Classroom in which special education students spend part of the school day and receive individualized special education services.

Retina   A sheet of nerve tissue at the back of the eye on which an image is focused.

Retinitis pigmentosa (RP)   An eye disease in which the retina gradually degenerates and atrophies, causing the field of vision to become progressively more narrow.

Retinopathy of prematurity (ROP)   A condition characterized by an abnormally dense growth of blood vessels and scar tissue in the eye, often causing visual field loss and retinal detachment. Usually caused by high levels of oxygen administered to premature infants in incubators. Also called *retrolental fibroplasia (RLF)*.

Retrolental fibroplasia (RLF)   See retinopathy of prematurity.

Rigidity   A type of cerebral palsy characterized by increased muscle tone, minimal muscle elasticity, and little or no stretch reflex.

Rubella   German measles; when contracted by a woman during the first trimester of pregnancy, may cause visual impairments, hearing impairments, mental retardation, and/or other birth defects in the child.

Schizophrenic   Describes a severe behavior disorder characterized by loss of contact with one's surroundings and inappropriate affect and actions.

Screening   A procedure in which groups of children are examined and/or tested in an effort to identify high-risk children; identified children are then referred for more intensive examination and assessment.

Self-contained class   A special classroom, usually located within a regular public school building, that includes only exceptional children.

Semantics   The study of meaning in language.

Sensorineural hearing loss   A hearing loss caused by damage to the auditory nerve or the inner ear.

Severe handicaps   Term used to refer to challenges faced by students with severe and profound mental retardation, autism, and/or physical/sensory impairments combined with marked developmental delay. Persons with severe handicaps exhibit extreme deficits in intellectual functioning and need systematic instruction for basic skills such as self-care and communicating with others.

Sheltered workshop   A structured work environment where persons with disabilities receive employment training and perform work for pay. May provide transitional services for some individuals (i.e., short-term training for competitive employment in the community) and permanent work settings for others.

Shunt   Tube inserted in the body to divert fluid from one body part to another; often implanted in people with hydrocephalus to remove extra cerebrospinal fluid from the head and send it directly into the heart or intestines.

Social validity   A desirable characteristic of the objectives, procedures, and results of instruction, indicating their appropriateness for the learner. For example, the goal of riding a bus independently would have social validity for learners residing in most cities, but not for those in small towns or rural areas.

Socialized aggression   A group of behavior disorders, including truancy, gang membership, theft, and delinquency, as identified by Quay (1975).

Spasticity   A type of cerebral palsy characterized by tense, contracted muscles.

Special education   The individually planned and systematically monitored arrangement of physical settings, special equipment and materials, teaching procedures, and other interventions designed to help learners with special needs achieve the greatest possible personal self-sufficiency and success in school and community.

Speech   A system of using breath and muscles to create specific sounds for communicating.

Speechreading   Process of understanding a spoken message by observing the speaker's lips in combination with information gained from facial expressions, gestures, and the context or situation.

Spina bifida   A congenital malformation of the spine in which the vertebrae that normally protect the spine do not develop fully; may involve loss of sensation and severe muscle weakness in the lower part of the body.

Spina bifida occulta   A type of spina bifida that usually does not cause serious disability. Although the vertebrae do not close, there is no protrusion of the spinal cord and membranes.

Standard deviation   A unit used to measure the amount by which a particular score varies from the mean of all scores in the norm sample.

Stereotype An overgeneralized or inaccurate attitude held toward all members of a particular group, on the basis of a common characteristic such as age, sex, race, or disability.

Stereotypic (stereotyped) behavior Repetitive nonfunctional movements (e.g., hand flapping, rocking), characteristic of autism and other severe handicaps.

Stimulus control Occurs when a behavior is emitted more often in the presence of a particular stimulus than it is in the absence of that stimulus.

Strabismus A condition in which one eye cannot attain binocular vision with the other eye because of imbalanced muscles.

Stuttering A complex fluency disorder of speech, affecting the smooth flow of words; may involve repetition of sounds or words, prolonged sounds, facial grimaces, muscle tension, and other physical behaviors.

Supported employment An approach to helping persons with disabilities find, learn, and maintain paid employment at regular work sites in the community. A supported employment specialist assists the disabled worker in performing the job, gradually reducing the amount of on-the-job assistance as the employee's work performance improves over time.

Syntax The system of rules governing the meaningful arrangement of words in a language.

Task analysis Breaking a complex skill or chain of behaviors into smaller, teachable units.

Tay-Sachs disease A progressive nervous system disorder causing profound mental retardation, deafness, blindness, paralysis, and seizures. Usually fatal by age 5. Caused by a recessive gene; blood test can identify carrier; analysis of enzymes in fetal cells provides prenatal diagnosis.

Time-out A behavior management technique that involves removing the opportunity for reinforcement for a specific period of time following an inappropriate behavior; results in a reduction of the inappropriate behavior.

Token economy System of reinforcing various behaviors by delivering tokens (e.g., stars, points, poker chips) when specified behaviors are emitted. Tokens are accumulated and turned in for the individual's choice of items on a "menu" of backup reinforcers (e.g., a sticker, hall monitor for a day).

Topography (of behavior) The physical shape or form of a response.

Total communication An approach to education of deaf students that combines oral speech, sign language, and fingerspelling.

Tremor A type of cerebral palsy characterized by regular, strong, uncontrolled movements. May cause less overall difficulty in movement than other types of cerebral palsy.

Triplegia Paralysis of any three limbs; relatively rare.

Turner's syndrome A sex chromosomal disorder in females, resulting from an absence of one of the X chromosomes. Although not usually a cause of mental retardation, it is often associated with learning problems. It also causes lack of secondary sex characteristics, sterility, and short stature.

Tymphonic membrane (eardrum)   Located in the middle ear, the eardrum moves in and out to variations in sound pressure, changing acoustical energy to sound energy.

Usher's syndrome   An inherited combination of visual and hearing impairments. Usually, the person is born with a profound hearing loss and loses vision gradually in adulthood because of retinitis pigmentosa, which affects the visual field.

Visual acuity   The ability to clearly distinguish forms or discriminate details at a specified distance.

Visual efficiency   A term used to describe how effectively a person uses his vision. Includes such factors as control of eye movements, near and distant visual acuity, and speed and quality of visual processing.

Vitreous humor   The jellylike fluid that fills most of the interior of the eyeball.

Vocational rehabilitation   A program designed to help adults with disabilities obtain and hold employment.

Work activity center   A sheltered work and activity program for persons with severe disabilities; teaches concentration and persistence, along with basic life skills, for little or no pay.

References

Aaronson, D. W., & Rosenberg, M. (1985). Asthma: General concepts. In R. Paterson (Ed.), *Allergic diseases: Diagnosis and management*. Philadelphia: J. B. Lippincott.

Abbott, S. R. (1990). *Effects of self-monitoring on the academic performance and on-task behavior of students with learning disabilities*. Unpublished doctoral dissertation. Columbus, OH: The Ohio State University.

Achenbach, T. M. (1974). *Developmental psychopathology*. New York: Ronald Press.

Achenback, T. M., & Edelbrock, C. S. (1984). *Child Behavior Checklist—Teacher's Report*. Burlington, VT: University Associates in Psychiatry.

Ackerman, A. M., & Shapiro, E. S. (1984). Self-monitoring and work productivity with mentally retarded adults. *Journal of Applied Behavior Analysis, 17,* 403–407.

Ada, A. F. (1986). Creative education for bilingual teachers. *Harvard Educational Review, 56,* 386–394.

Affleck, J. Q., Madge, S., Adams, A., & Lowenbraun, S. (1988). Integrated classroom vs. resource model: Academic viability and effectiveness. *Exceptional Children, 54,* 339–348.

Aiello, B. (1976, April 25). Up from the basement: A teacher's story. *New York Times,* p. 14.

Alber, M. B. (1974). *Listening: A curriculum guide for teachers of visually impaired students*. Springfield, IL: Illinois Office of Education.

Alberto, P. A., & Troutman, A. C. (1990). *Applied behavior analysis for teachers* (3rd ed.). Columbus, OH: Merrill.

Algozzine, B. (1980). The disturbing child: A matter of opinion. *Behavioral Disorders, 5,* 112–115.

Algozzine, B., & Korinek, L. (1985). Where is special education for students with high prevalence handicaps going? *Exceptional Children, 51,* 388–394.

Algozzine, B., & Ysseldyke, J. (1981). Special education services for normal children: Better safe than sorry? *Exceptional Children, 48,* 238–243.

Allen, D. A., & Affleck, G. (1985). Are we stereotyping parents? A postscript to Blacher. *Mental Retardation, 23,* 200–202.

Allen, J. I. (1980). Jogging can modify disruptive behaviors. *Teaching Exceptional Children, 12*(2), 66–70.

Allen, K. E. (1980a). The language impaired child in the preschool: The role of the teacher. *The Directive Teacher, 2*(3), 6–10.

Allen, K. E. (1980b). *Mainstreaming in early childhood education*. Albany, NY: Delmar Pubs.

Allen, T. (1986). Patterns of academic achievement among hearing impaired students: 1974 and 1983. In A. Schildroth & M. Karchmer (Eds.), *Deaf children in America* (pp. 161–206). San Diego: Little, Brown.

Alley, G., & Deshler, D. (1979). *Teaching the learning disabled adolescent: Strategies and methods*. Denver: Love.

Allsop, J. (1980). Mainstreaming physically handicapped students. *Journal of Research and Development in Education, 13*(4), 37–44.

Alzate, G. (1978). Analysis of testing problems in Spanish speaking children. In A. H. Fink (Ed.), *International perspectives on future special education* (pp. 77–79). Reston, VA: Council for Exceptional Children.

Amado, A. N., Lakin, K. C., & Menke, J. M. (1990). *1990 chartbook of services for people with developmental disabilities*. Minneapolis: University of Minnesota, Center for Residential and Community Services.

American Academy of Ophthalmology. (1985). Health alert. *Journal of Visual Impairment and Blindness, 79,* 234.

American Association on Mental Deficiency. (1973). *Rights of mentally retarded persons: An official policy statement of the American Association on Mental Deficiency*. Washington, DC: Author.

American Council on Science and Health. (1979, May). *Diet and hyperactivity: Is there a relationship?* New York: Author.

American Printing House for the Blind. (1987). *Federal quota register*. Louisville, KY: Author.

American Psychiatric Association. (1980). *Diagnostic and statistical manual of mental disorders* (3rd ed.). Washington, DC: Author.

American Psychiatric Association. (1987). *Diagnostic and statistical manual of mental disorders* (3rd ed., revised). Washington, DC: Author.

American Speech-Language-Hearing Association. (1982). *Definitions: Communicative disorders and variations*. Rockville, MD: Author.

American Speech-Language-Hearing Association. (1983). Position paper on social dialects. *ASHA, 25*(9), 23–24.

Ames, L. B. (1977). Learning disabilities: Time to check our roadmaps? *Journal of Learning Disabilities, 10*, 328–330.

Ammer, J. J., & Littleton, B. R. (1983, April). *Parent advocacy: Now more than ever, active involvement in education decisions*. Paper presented at the 61st Annual International Convention of the Council for Exceptional Children, Detroit, MI.

Anderson, E. (1985). A. M. Club. In Council for Children with Behavior Disorders, *Teaching Behavioral Disordered Youth* (Vol. 1) (pp. 12–16). Reston, VA: Author.

Anderson, M. J., & Ellis, R. H. (1980). Indian American: The reservation client. In N. A. Vacc & J. P. Wittmer (Eds.), *Let me be me: Special populations and the helping professional* (pp. 107–127). Muncie, IN: Accelerated Development.

Anderson, R. M., Greer, J. G., & Rich, H. L. (1982). An introduction to severely and multiply handicapped persons. In J. G. Greer, R. M. Anderson, & S. J. Odle (Eds.), *Strategies for helping severely and multiply handicapped citizens* (pp. 1–42). Baltimore, MD: University Park Press.

Anderson-Inman, L. (1986). Bridging the gap: Student-centered strategies for promoting the transfer of learning. *Exceptional Children, 52*, 562–572.

Anderson-Inman, L., Walker, H. M., & Purcell, J. (1984). Promoting the transfer of skills across settings: Transenvironmental programming for handicapped students in the mainstream. In W. L. Heward, T. E. Heron, D. S. Hill, & J. Trap-Porter (Eds.), *Focus on Behavior Analysis in Education* (pp. 17–37). Columbus, OH: Merrill.

Anthony, D. (1971). *Seeing Essential English*. Anaheim, CA: Anaheim School District.

Antonak, R. F., Fiedler, C. R., & Mulick, J. A. (1989). Misconceptions relating to mental retardation. *Mental Retardation, 27*, 91–97.

Apolloni, T., & Cooke, T. P. (Eds.). (1981). *California housing resources for persons with special developmental needs*. Unpublished manuscript, California Institute on Human Services at Sonoma State University.

Arakawa, J. (1981). Minority voices: Neither part of a double disability is the whole person. *Disabled USA, 4*(8), 1.

Armstrong v. Kline, 476 F. Supplement 583 (E.D. PA 1979).

Arnold, K. M., & Hornett, D. (1990). Teaching idioms to children who are deaf. *Teaching Exceptional Children, 22*(4), 14–17.

Arnold, L. E., Christopher, J., Huestis, R. D., & Smeltzer, D. J. (1978). Megavitamins for minimal brain dysfunction: A placebo controlled study. *Journal of the American Medical Association, 240*, 2642–2643.

Arnold, W. R., & Brungardt, T. M. (1983). *Juvenile misconduct and delinquency*. Boston: Houghton Mifflin.

Arter, J. L. (1976). *The effects of metaphor on reading comprehension*. Unpublished doctoral dissertation, University of Illinois, Champaign-Urbana, IL.

Assael, D. (Ed.). (1985). *Directory, 1984–85 edition: Handicapped Children's Early Education Program*. Chapel Hill, NC: University of North Carolina, Technical Assistance Development System.

The Association for Persons with Severe Handicaps. (1990). Draft mission statement, June 27, 1990. *TASH Newsletter, 16*(8), 1.

Atkins, C. P., & Cartwright, L. R. (1982). National survey: Preferred language elicitation procedures used in five age categories. *Journal of the American Speech and Hearing Association, 24*, 321–323.

Baca, L. M., & Cervantes, H. T. (1989). *The bilingual special education interface* (2nd ed.). Columbus, OH: Merrill.

Baca, L., & Harris, K. C. (1988). Teaching migrant exceptional children. *Teaching Exceptional Children, 20*(4), 32–35.

Baer, D. M. (1981a). *How to plan for generalization*. Lawrence, KS: H & H Enterprises.

Baer, D. M. (1981b). A hung jury and a Scottish verdict: "Not proven." *Analysis and Intervention in Developmental Disabilities, 1*, 91–97.

Baer, D. M. (1984). We already have multiple jeopardy; why try for unending jeopardy? In W. L. Heward, T. E. Heron, D. S. Hill, & J. Trap-Porter (Eds.). *Focus on behavior analysis in education* (pp. 296–299). Columbus, OH: Merrill.

Baer, D. M., & Fowler, S. A. (1984). How should we measure the potential of self-control procedures for generalized educational outcomes? In W. L. Heward, T. E. Heron, D. S. Hill, & J. Trap-Porter (Eds.), *Focus on behavior analysis in education* (pp. 145–161). Columbus, OH: Merrill.

Baer, D. M., Wolf, M. M., & Risley, T. R. (1968). Some current dimensions of applied behavior analysis. *Journal of Applied Behavior Analysis, 1*, 91–97.

Bagnato, S. J., Neisworth, J. T., & Capone, A. (1986). Curriculum-based assessment of the young exceptional child: Rationale and review. *Topics in Early Childhood Special Education, 6*, 97–110.

Bailey, D. B. (1989). Case management in early intervention. *Journal of Early Intervention, 13,* 120–134.

Bailey, D. B., & Bricker, D. D. (1985). Evaluation of a three-year early intervention demonstration project. *Topics in Early Childhood Special Education, 5*(2), 52–65.

Bailey, D. B., & Simeonsson, R. J. (1988a). *Family assessment in early intervention.* Columbus, OH: Merrill.

Bailey, D. B., & Simeonsson, R. J. (1988b). Home-based early intervention. In S. L. Odom & M. B. Karnes (Eds.), *Early intervention for infants & children with handicaps* (pp. 199–215). Baltimore, MD: Paul H. Brookes.

Bailey, D. B., Winton, P. J., Rouse, L., & Turnbull, A. P. (1990). Family goals in infant intervention: Analysis and issues. *Journal of Early Intervention, 14,* 15–26.

Bailey, D. B., & Wolery, M. (1984). *Teaching infants and preschoolers with handicaps.* Columbus, OH: Merrill.

Bailey, D. B., & Wolery, M. (1989). *Assessing infants and preschoolers with handicaps.* Columbus, OH: Merrill.

Baker, L., & Lombardi, B. R. (1985). Students' lecture notes and their relation to test performance. *Teaching of Psychology, 12,* 28–32.

Baldwin, A. Y. (1978). Curriculum and methods: What is the difference? In A. Y. Baldwin, G. H. Gear, & L. J. Lucita (Eds.), *Educational planning for the gifted: Overcoming cultural, geographic, and socioeconomic barriers.* Reston, VA: Council for Exceptional Children.

Baldwin, A. Y., Gear, G. H., & Lucita, L. J. (Eds.). (1978). *Educational planning for the gifted: Overcoming cultural, geographic, and socioeconomic barriers.* Reston, VA: Council for Exceptional Children.

Balow, I. H., Farr, R., Hogan, T. P., & Prescott, G. A. (1978). *Metropolitan Achievement Tests: 1978 edition.* New York: Psychological Corp.

Banks, J. A. (1977). *Multiethnic education: Practices and promises.* Bloomington, IN: Phi Delta Kappa Educational Foundation.

Banks, J. A. (1989). Multicultural education: Characteristics and goals. In J.

A. Banks & C. A. M. Banks (Eds.), *Multicultural education: Issues and perspectives* (pp. 2–26). Boston: Allyn & Bacon.

Banks, J. A., & Banks, C. A. M. (Eds.). (in press). *Multicultural education: Issues and perspectives* (2nd ed.). Boston: Allyn & Bacon.

Bankson, N. W. (1982). The speech and language impaired. In E. L. Meyen (Ed.), *Exceptional children and youth* (2nd ed.). Denver: Love.

Bannerman, D. J., Sheldon, J. B., Sherman, J. A., & Harchik, A. E. (1990). Balancing the right to habilitation with the right to personal liberties: The rights of people with developmental disabilities to eat too many doughnuts and take a nap. *Journal of Applied Behavior Analysis, 23,* 79–89.

Barbetta, P. M. (1990a). GOALS: A group-oriented adapted levels system for children with behavior disorders. *Academic Therapy, 25,* 645–656.

Barbetta, P. M. (1990b). Red light-green light: A classwide management system for students with behavior disorders in the primary grades. *Preventing School Failure, 34*(4), 14–19.

Barbetta, P. M. (1991, February). Personal communication.

Barbetta, P. M., & Heron, T. E. (1991). Project SHINE: Summer home instruction and evaluation. *Intervention in School and Clinic, 26,* 276–281.

Barnes, D. M. (1986). Brain function decline in children with AIDS. *Science, 232,* 1196.

Barnett, H. (1989). What teachers should know about their classroom learners. *Foreign Language Annals, 22,* 199–201.

Barnett, W. S. (1986). Definition and classification of mental retardation: A reply to Zigler, Balla, and Hodapp. *American Journal of Mental Deficiency, 91,* 111–116.

Barney, L. G., & Landis, C. L. (1987). Development differences in communication. In J. T. Neisworth & S. J. Bagnato, (Eds.), *The young exceptional child: Early development and education* (pp. 262–296). New York: Macmillan.

Baroff, G. S. (1982). Predicting the prevalence of mental retardation in individual catchment areas. *Mental Retardation, 20,* 133–135.

Barr, M. W. (1913). *Mental defectives: Their history, treatment, and training.* Philadelphia: Blakiston.

Barraga, N. C. (1964). *Increased visual behavior in low vision children.* New York: American Foundation for the Blind.

Barraga, N. C. (1970). *Teacher's guide for development of visual learning abilities and utilization of low vision.* Louisville, KY: American Printing House for the Blind.

Barraga, N. C. (1980). *Source book on low vision.* Louisville, KY: American Printing House for the Blind.

Barraga, N. C. (1983). *Visual handicaps and learning* (rev. ed.). Austin, TX: Exceptional Resources.

Barrera, R. D., & Sulzer-Azaroff, B. (1983). An alternating treatment comparison of oral and total communication training programs with echolalic autistic children. *Journal of Applied Behavior Analysis, 16,* 379–394.

Barsch, R. H. (1969). *The parent-teacher partnership.* Arlington, VA: Council for Exceptional Children.

Barton, L. E., & LaGrow, S. J. (1985). Reduction of stereotypic responding in three visually impaired children. *Education of the Visually Handicapped, 6,* 145–181.

Baskin, B. H., & Harris, K. H. (1980). *Books for the gifted child.* New York: R. R. Bowker.

Batshaw, M. L., & Perret, Y. M. (1986). *Children with handicaps: A medical primer* (2nd ed.). Baltimore, MD: Paul H. Brookes.

Bauman, K. E., & Iwata, B. A. (1977). Maintenance of independent housekeeping skills using scheduling plus self-rewarding procedures. *Behavior Therapy, 8,* 554–560.

Baumgart, D., Brown, L., Pumpian, I., Nisbet, J., Ford, A., Sweet, M., Messina, R., & Schroeder, J. (1982). Principle of partial participation and individualized adaptations in educational programs for severely handicapped students. *Journal of the Association for the Severely Handicapped, 7,* 17–27.

Baumgart, D., Johnson, J., & Helmstetter, E. (1990). *Augmentative and alternative communication systems for persons with moderate and severe disabilities*. Baltimore, MD: Paul H. Brookes.

Bayley, N. (1969). *Bayley Scales of Infant Development*. New York: Psychological Corporation.

Beatty, L., Madden, R., & Gardner, E. (1966). *Stanford Diagnostic Arithmetic Test*. New York: Harcourt Brace Jovanovich.

Becker, W. C. (1964). Consequences of different kinds of parental discipline. In M. L. Hoffman & L. W. Hoffman (Eds.), *Review of child development research* (Vol. 1) (pp. 169–208). New York: Russell Sage Foundation.

Becker, W. C., & Engelmann, S. E. (1976). *Technical report 1976-1*. Eugene, OR: University of Oregon.

Becker, W. C., Engelmann, S., & Thomas, D. R. (1971). *Teaching: A course in applied psychology*. Chicago: Science Research Associates.

Belcastro, F. P. (1989). Use of Belcastro Rods to teach mathematical concepts to blind students. *RE:view, 21*, 71–79.

Belgrave, F. Z., & Mills, J. (1981). Effect upon desire for social interaction with a physically disabled person of mentioning the disability in different contexts. *Journal of Applied Social Psychology, 11*, 44–57.

Bellamy, G. T., & Horner, R. H. (1987). Beyond high school: Residential and employment options after graduation. In M. Snell (Ed.), *Systematic instruction of persons with severe handicaps* (3rd ed.) (pp. 491–510). Columbus, OH: Merrill.

Bellamy, G. T., Horner, R. H., & Inman, D. (1979). *Vocational training of severely retarded adults*. Baltimore, MD: Paul H. Brookes.

Bellamy, G. T., Newton, J. S., LeBaron, N., & Horner, R. H. (in press). Quality of life and lifestyle outcomes: A challenge for residential programming. In R. L. Schalock (Ed.), *Quality of life: Perspectives and issues*. Baltimore, MD: Paul H. Brookes.

Bellamy, G. T., Rhodes, L. E., Wilcox, B., Albin, J. M., Mank, D. M., Boles, S. M., Horner, R. H., Collins, M., & Turner, J. (1984). Quality and equality in employment services for adults with severe disabilities. *The Journal of The Association for Persons with Severe Handicaps, 9*, 270–277.

Bellamy, G. T., & Wilcox, B. (1982). Secondary education for severely handicapped students: Guidelines for quality services. In K. P. Lynch, W. E. Kiernan, & J. A. Stark (Eds.), *Prevocational and vocational education for special needs youth: A blueprint for the 1980s*. Baltimore, MD: Paul H. Brookes.

Benjamin, L. T. (1990). Leta Stetter Hollingworth: Psychologist, educator, feminist. [Special Issue] *Roeper Review, 12*, 145–151.

Benjamin, S. (1989). An ideascape for education: What futurists recommend. *Educational Leadership, 47*, 8–14.

Bennett, L. M., & Hensen, F. O. (1977). *Keeping in touch with parents: The teacher's best friend*. Hingham, MA: Teaching Resources.

Bennett, R. E., & Ragosta, M. (1984). *A research context for studying admission tests and handicapped populations*. Princeton, NJ: Educational Testing Service.

Bennett, W. J. (1986). *First lessons: A report on elementary education in America*. Washington, DC: U.S. Department of Education.

Bensberg, G. J., & Sigelman, C. K. (1976). Definitions and prevalence. In L. L. Lloyd (Ed.), *Communication assessment and intervention strategies*. Baltimore, MD: University Park Press.

Bensky, J., Shaw, S., Gouse, A., Bates, H., Dixon, B., & Beane, W. (1980). Public Law 94–142 and stress: A problem for educators. *Exceptional Children, 47*, 24–29.

Bercovici, S. M. (1983). *Barriers to normalization: The restrictive management of retarded persons*. Austin, TX: PRO-ED.

Berg, F. S. (1986). Characteristics of the target population. In F. S. Berg, J. C. Blair, S. H. Viehweg, & A. Wilson-Vlotman, *Educational audiology for the hard of hearing child* (pp. 1–24). Orlando, FL: Grune & Stratton.

Bergstrom, T., Pattavina, S., Martella, R. C., & Marchand-Martella, N. E. (in press). A number- and color-coded microwave oven and recipe cards for successful meal preparation. *Teaching Exceptional Children*.

Berman, J. L., & Ford, R. (1970). Intelligence quotients and intelligence loss in patients with phenylketonuria and some variant states. *Journal of Pediatrics, 77*, 764–770.

Bernthal, J. E., & Bankson, N. W. (1986). Phonologic disorders: An overview. In J. M. Costello & A. L. Holland (Eds.), *Handbook of speech and language disorders* (pp. 3–24). San Diego: College-Hill.

Betts, G. T. (1986). The autonomous learner model for the gifted and talented. In J. S. Renzulli (Ed.), *Systems and models for developing programs for the gifted and talented* (pp. 27–56). Mansfield Center, CT: Creative Learning Press.

Beukelman, D. (1988, November). Personal communication with S. Blackstone, Editor of *Augmentative Communication News*.

Bierly, K. (1978). Public Law 94–142: Answers to the questions you're asking. *Instructor, 87*(9), 63–67.

Bigge, J. L. (1991). *Teaching individuals with physical and multiple disabilities* (3rd ed.). Columbus, OH: Merrill.

Bijou, S. W. (1966). A functional analysis of retarded development. In N. R. Ellis (Ed.), *International review of research in mental retardation* (Vol. 1). New York: Academic Press.

Bijou, S. W., & Dunitz-Johnson, E. (1981). Interbehavior analysis of developmental disabilities. *Psychological Record, 31*, 305–329.

Biklen, D. (1985). *Achieving the complete school: Strategies for effective mainstreaming*. New York: Teachers College Press.

Biklen, D. (1988). The myth of clinical judgment. *Journal of Social Issues, 44*, 127–140.

Biklen, D., & Bogdan, R. (1976). *Handicapism in America*. Syracuse, NY: WIN.

Bilken, D., & Zollers, N. (1986). The focus of advocacy in the LD field. *Journal of Learning Disabilities, 19*, 579–586.

Birenbaum, A. (1986). Symposium overview: Community programs for people with mental retardation. *Mental Retardation, 24,* 145–146.

Bishop, V. E. (1986). Identifying the components of successful mainstreaming. *Journal of Visual Impairment and Blindness, 80,* 939–946.

Blacher, J. (1984). A dynamic perspective on the impact of a severely handicapped child on the family. In J. Blacher (Ed.), *Severely handicapped children and their families* (p. 3-50). Orlando, FL: Academic Press.

Blackburn, A. C., & Erickson, D. D. (1986). Predictable crises of the gifted student. *Journal of Counseling and Development, 64,* 552–555.

Blackburn, J. A. (1987). Cerebral palsy. In M. L. Wolraich (Ed.), *The practical assessment and management of children with disorders of development and learning.* Chicago: Yearbook Publishers.

Blackstone, M. (1981). How parents can affect communitization, or, what do you mean I'm a troublemaker? In C. H. Hansen (Ed.), *Severely handicapped persons in the community* (pp. 29–52). Seattle: University of Washington, PDAS.

Blackstone, S. W., Cassatt-James, E. L., & Bruskin, D. M. (1988). *Augmentative communication implementation strategies.* Rockville, MD: American Speech-Language-Hearing Association.

Blair, J., Peterson, M., & Viehweg, S. (1985). The effects of mild hearing loss on academic performance of young school-age children. *Volta Review, 87,* 87–93.

Blank, M. (1988). Classroom text: The next state of intervention. In R. L. Schiefelbusch & L. L. Lloyd (Eds.), *Language perspectives: Acquisition, retardation and intervention* (pp. 367–392). Austin, TX: PRO-ED.

Blatt, B. (1976). *Revolt of the idiots: A story.* Glen Ridge, NJ: Exceptional Press.

Blatt, B. (1987). *The conquest of mental retardation.* Austin, TX: PRO-ED.

Blatt, B., & Kaplan, F. (1966). *Christmas in purgatory: A photographic essay on mental retardation.* Boston: Allyn & Bacon.

Bleck, E. E. (1979). Integrating the physically handicapped child. *Journal of School Health, 49,* 141–146.

Bleck, E. E. (1987). *Orthopedic management of cerebral palsy—Clinics in developmental medicine No. 99/100.* Philadelphia: J. B. Lippincott.

Blick, D. W., & Test, D. W. (1987). Effects of self-recording on high school students' on-task behavior. *Learning Disability Quarterly, 10,* 203–213.

Bliton, G., & Schroeder, H. J. (1986). *The new future for children with substantial handicaps: The second wave of LRE.* Bloomington, IN: Indiana University Developmental Training Center.

Bloom, B. S. (Ed.), (1956). *Taxonomy of educational objectives: Handbook I. Cognitive domain.* New York: David McKay Co.

Bloom, B. S. (1985). Generalizations about talent development. In B. S. Bloom (Ed.), Development of talent in young people (pp. 507–549). New York: Ballantine Books.

Bloom, L., & Lahey, M. (1978). *Language development and language disorders.* New York: John Wiley & Sons.

Board of Education of the Hendrick Hudson Central School District v. Rowley, 102 S. Ct. 3034 (1982).

Boatner, M. T., & Gates, J. E. (1966). *A dictionary of idioms for the deaf.* Washington, DC: National Association for the Deaf.

Bogdan, R. (1986). Exhibiting mentally retarded people for amusement and profit, 1850–1940. *American Journal of Mental Deficiency, 91,* 120–126.

Boles, S. M., Bellamy, G. T., Horner, R. H., & Mank, D. M. (1984). Specialized training program: The structured employment model. In S. C. Paine, G. T. Bellamy, & B. Wilcox (Eds.), *Human services that work: From innovation to standard practice* (pp. 181–208). Baltimore, MD: Paul H. Brookes.

Bonvillian, J. D., & Nelson, K. E. (1976). Sign language acquisition in a mute autistic boy. *Journal of Speech and Hearing Disorders, 41,* 339–347.

Book, D., Paul, T. L., Gwalla-Ogisi, N., & Test, D. W. (1990). No more bologna sandwiches. *Teaching Exceptional Children, 22*(2), 62–64.

Boone, D. R. (1977). Our profession: Where are we? *Journal of the American Speech and Hearing Association, 19,* 3–6.

Boothroyd, A. (1978). Speech perception and severe hearing loss. In M. Ross & T. G. Giolas (Eds.), *Auditory management of hearing-impaired children* (pp. 117–144). Baltimore, MD: University Park Press.

Bornstein, H. (1974). Signed English: A manual approach to English language development. *Journal of Speech and Hearing Disorders, 3,* 330–343.

Boshes, B., & Myklebust, H. R. (1964). A neurological and behavioral study of children with learning disorders. *Neurology, 14,* 7–12.

Bostow, D. E., & Bailey, J. (1969). Modification of severe disruptive and aggressive behavior using brief timeout and reinforcement procedures. *Journal of Applied Behavior Analysis, 2,* 31–37.

Bourland, G., Jablonski, E., & Lockhart, D. (1987). Multiple-behavior comparison of group and individual instruction of persons with mental retardation. *Mental Retardation, 26,* 39–46.

Bower, E. M. (1960). *Early identification of emotionally handicapped children in the schools.* Springfield, IL: Charles C. Thomas.

Bower, E. M. (1981). *Early identification of emotionally handicapped children in school* (3rd ed.). Springfield, IL: Charles C. Thomas.

Bower, E. M. (1982). Defining emotional disturbance: Public policy and research. *Psychology in the Schools, 19,* 55–60.

Bower, E. M., & Lambert, N. M. (1962). A process for in-school screening of children with emotional handicaps. Princeton, NJ: Education Testing Service.

Braaten, S., Kauffman, J. M., Braaten, B., Polsgrove, L., & Nelson, C. M. (1988). The Regular Education Initiative (REI): Patent medicine for behavioral disorders. *Exceptional Children, 55,* 21–27.

Braddock, D., & Heller, T. (1985). The closure of mental retardation institutions II: Implications. *Mental Retardation, 23,* 222–229.

Bradley-Johnson, S., & Harris, S. (1990). Best practices in working with students with a visual loss. In A. Thomas & J. Grimes (Eds.), *Best practices in school psychology–II* (pp. 871–885). Washington, DC: National Association of School Psychologists.

Brandwein, H. (1973). The battered child: A definite and significant factor in mental retardation. *Mental Retardation, 11,* 50–51.

Brantliner, E. A., & Guskin, S. L. (1985). Implications of social and cultural differences for special education with specific recommendations. *Focus on Exceptional Children, 18,* 1–12.

Brazelton, T. B. (1973). *Neonatal Assessment Scale.* Philadelphia: J. B. Lippincott.

Bricker, D. D. (1986). An analysis of early intervention programs: Attendant issues and future directions. In R. J. Morris & B. Blatt (Eds.), *Special education: Research and trends* (pp. 28–65). New York: Pergamon Press.

Bricker, D. D., Bailey, E. J., & Slentz, K. (1990). Reliability, validity, and utility of the Evaluation and Programming System: For Infants and Young Children (EPS-I). *Journal of Early Intervention, 14,* 147–158.

Bricker, D. D., Gentry, D., & Bailey, E. J. (1985). *The Evaluation and Programming System: For Infants and Young Children. Assessment level I: Developmentally 1 month to 3 years.* Eugene, OR: University of Oregon.

Brickey, M. P., Campbell, K. M., & Browning, L. J. (1985). A five-year follow-up of sheltered workshop employees placed in competitive jobs. *Mental Retardation, 23,* 67–73.

Brigance, A. (1983). *BRIGANCE Diagnostic Inventory of Basic Skills.* N. Billerica, MA: Curriculum Associates.

Brigance, A. H. (1982). *K & 1 screen for kindergarten and first grade.* N. Billerica, MA: Curriculum Associates.

Brinker, R. P. (1985). Interactions between severely mentally retarded students and other students in integrated and segregated public school settings. *American Journal of Mental Deficiency, 89,* 587–594.

Bristor, V. J. (1987). "But I'm not a teacher." *Academic Therapy, 23,* 23–27.

Brolin, D. E. (1989). *Life centered career education: A competency based approach* (3rd ed.). Reston, VA: Council for Exceptional Children.

Bronicki, G. J., & Turnbull, A. P. (1987). Family-professional interactions. In M. E. Snell (Ed.), *Systematic instruction of persons with severe handicaps* (3rd ed.) (pp. 9–35). Columbus, OH: Merrill.

Bronston, W. (1980). Matters of design. In T. Apolloni, J. Cappuccilli, & T. P. Cooke (Eds.), *Achievements in residential services for persons with disabilities: Toward excellence.* Baltimore, MD: University Park Press.

Browder, D., Lentz, F. E., Knoster, T., & Wilansky, C. (1988). Determining extended school year eligibility: From esoteric to explicit criteria. *The Journal of The Association for Persons with Severe Handicaps, 13,* 235–243.

Browder, D. M., & Snell, M. E. (1987). Functional academics. In M. E. Snell (Ed.), *Systematic instruction of persons with severe handicaps* (3rd ed.) (pp. 436–468). Columbus, OH: Merrill.

Brower, I. C. (1983). Counseling Vietnamese. In D. R. Atkinson, G. Morten, & D. W. Sue, *Counseling American minorities* (2nd ed.) (pp. 107–121). Dubuque, IA: William C. Brown.

Brown v. Board of Education of Topeka. (1954). 347 U.S. 483.

Brown, F. (1987). Meaningful assessment of people with severe and profound handicaps. In M. E. Snell (Ed.), Systematic instruction of persons with severe handicaps (3rd ed.) (pp. 39–63). Columbus, OH: Merrill.

Brown, J. R. (1982). Assessment of the culturally different and disadvantaged child. In G. Ulrey & S. J. Rogers (Eds.), *Psychological assessment of handicapped infants and young children* (pp. 163–171). New York: Thieme-Stratton.

Brown, L. (1990). Who are they and what do they want? An essay on TASH. *TASH Newsletter, 16*(9), 1.

Brown, L., Branston-McClean, M. B., Baumgart, D., Vincent, L., Falvey, M., & Shroeder, J. (1979). Using the characteristics of current and subsequent least restrictive environments in the development of curricular content for severely handicapped students. *AAESPH Review, 4,* 407–424.

Brown, L., Long, E., Udvari-Solner, A., Davis, L., VanDeventer, P., Ahlgren, C., Johnson, F., Gruenewald, L., & Jorgensen, J. (1989a). The home school: Why students with severe disabilities must attend the schools of their brothers, sisters, friends, and neighbors. *The Journal of The Association for Persons with Severe Handicaps, 14,* 1–7.

Brown, L., Long, E., Udvari-Solner, A., Davis, L., VanDeventer, P., Ahlgren, C., Johnson, F., Gruenewald, L., & Jorgensen, J. (1989b). Should students with severe intellectual disabilities be based in regular or in special education classrooms in home schools. *The Journal of The Association for Persons with Severe Handicaps, 14,* 8–12.

Brown, L., Shiraga, B., York, J., Kessler, K., Strohm, B., Rogan, P., Sweet, M., Zanella, K., VanDeventer, P., & Loomis, R. (1984). Integrated work opportunities for adults with severe handicaps: The extended training option. *The Journal of The Association for Persons with Severe Handicaps, 9,* 262–269.

Brown, S. C. (1986). Etiological trends, characteristics, and distributions. In A. N. Schildroth & M. A. Karchmer (Eds.), *Deaf children in America* (pp. 33–54). San Diego: College-Hill.

Bryan, T. H., & Bryan, J. H. (1978). Social interactions of learning disabled children. *Learning Disability Quarterly, 1,* 107–115.

Bryan, W. H., & Jeffrey, D. L. (1982). Education of visually handicapped students in the regular classroom. *Texas Tech Journal of Education, 9,* 125–131.

Bryant, N. D., & McLoughlin, J. A. (1972). Subject variables: Definition, incidence, characteristics, and correlates. In N. D. Bryant & C. E. Kass (Eds.), *Final report, Vol. 1, USOE* contract, leadership training institute in learning disabilities (pp. 5–158). Washington, DC: USOE, Grant No. OEO-0-71-4425 604, Project No. 127145.

Buchanan, L., & Kochar, C. (1989). The right to a free & appropriate public education (for some?): The case of Timothy vs. Rochester School District (Policy Briefs in Special Education, Paper No. 1). Washington, DC: The George Washington University, School of Education and Human Development.

Bulgren, J. A., & Schumaker, J. B. (in press). Learning strategies curriculum: The paired-associates strategy. Lawrence, KS: Institute for Research in Learning Disabilities.

Bull, G. L., & Rushakoff, G. E. (1987). Computers and speech and language disordered individuals. In J. D. Lindsey (Ed.), Computers and exceptional individuals (pp. 83–104). Columbus, OH: Merrill.

Bullis, M., & Bull, B. (1986). Review of research on adolescents and adults with deaf-blindness. Washington, DC: Catholic University of America, DATA Institute.

Bullis, M., & Otos, M. (1988). Characteristics of programs for children with deaf-blindness: Results of a national survey. The Journal of The Association for Persons with Severe Handicaps, 13, 110–115.

Bullivant B. M. (1989). Culture: Its nature and meaning for educators. In J. A. Banks & C. A. M. Banks (Eds.), Multicultural education: Issues and perspectives (pp. 27–45). Boston: Allyn & Bacon.

Burchard, J. D., & Harig, P. T. (1976). Behavior modification and juvenile delinquency. In H. Leitenberg (Ed.), Handbook of behavior modification and behavior therapy (pp. 405–452). Englewood Cliffs, NJ: Prentice-Hall.

Burkhardt, L. J. (1981). Homemade battery powered toys and educational devices for severely disabled children. Millville, PA: Burkhardt.

Burstein, N. D. (1986). The effects of classroom organization on mainstreamed preschool children. Exceptional Children, 52, 525–534.

Bursuck, W. D., Rose, E., Cowen, S., & Yahaya, M. A. (1989). Nationwide survey of postsecondary education services for students with learning disabilities. Exceptional Children, 56, 236–245.

Buss, A. H. (1966). Psychopathology. New York: John Wiley & Sons.

Byers, J. (1989). AIDS in children: Effects on neurological development and implications for the future. The Journal of Special Education, 23, 5–16.

Callister, J. P., Mitchell, L., & Talley, G. (1986). Profiling family preservation efforts in Utah. Children Today, 15, 23–25, 36–37.

Calvert, D. R. (1986). Speech in perspective. In D. M. Luterman (Ed.), Deafness in perspective (pp. 167–191). San Diego: College-Hill.

Campbell, P. B. (1979). Diagnosing the problem: Sex stereotyping in special education. Newton, MA: Education Development Center.

Campbell, V., Smith, R., & Wool, R. (1982). Adaptive Behavior Scale differences in scores of mentally retarded individuals referred for institutionalization and those never referred. American Journal of Mental Deficiency, 86, 425–428.

Cardenas, J. A. (1986). The role of native-language instruction in bilingual education. Phi Delta Kappan, 67(5), 359–363.

Carin, A., & Sund, R. B. (1978). Creative questioning and sensitive listening techniques: A self-concept approach (2nd ed.). Columbus, OH: Merrill.

Carrier, C. A. (1983). Notetaking research: Implications for the classroom. Journal of Instructional Development, 6(3), 19–25.

Carrow, E. (1974). Carrow Elicited Language Inventory. Austin, TX: Author.

Carter, J., & Sugai, G. (1989). Survey on prereferral practices: Responses from state departments of education. Exceptional Children, 55, 298–302.

Cartledge, G., & Milburn, J. F. (1986). Teaching social skills to children: Innovative approaches (2nd ed.). New York: Pergamon Press.

Castaneda, A. (1976). Cultural democracy and the educational needs of Mexican American children. In R. L.

Jones (Ed.), Mainstreaming and the minority child (pp. 181–214). Reston, VA: Council for Exceptional Children.

Casto, G. (1988). Research and program evaluation in early childhood special education. In S. L. Odom & M. B. Karnes (Eds.), Early intervention for infants & children with handicaps (pp. 51–62). Baltimore, MD: Paul H. Brookes.

Casto, G., & Mastropieri, M. A. (1986). The efficacy of early intervention programs: A meta-analysis. Exceptional Children, 52, 417–424.

Cavallaro, C. C., & Poulson, C. L. (1985). Teaching language to handicapped children in natural settings. Education & Treatment of Children, 8, 1–24.

Cavan, R. S., & Ferdinand, T. N. (1975). Juvenile delinquency (3rd ed.). New York: J. B. Lippincott.

Cawley, J. F., & Webster, R. E. (1981). Reading and behavior disorders. In G. Brown, R. L. McDowell, & J. Smith (Eds.), Educating adolescents with behavior disorders (pp. 294–325). Columbus, OH: Merrill.

Center, D. B. (1990). Social maladjustment: An interpretation. Behavioral Disorders, 15, 141–148.

Center on Human Policy. (1986, December). Positive interventions for challenging behavior. The Association for Persons with Severe Handicaps Newsletter, 12(12), 4.

Chalfant, J. C., & Pysh, M. V. D. (1989). Teacher assistance teams: Five descriptive studies on 96 teams. Remedial and Special Education, 10(6), 49–58.

Chan, K. S., & Rueda, R. (1979). Poverty and culture in education: Separate but equal. Exceptional Children, 45, 421–428.

Chaney, C., & Frodyma, D. A. (1982). A noncategorical program for preschool language development. Teaching Exceptional Children, 14, 152–155.

Chapman, E. K. (1978). Visually handicapped children and young people. London: Routledge and Kegan Paul.

Chase, J. B. (1986a). Application of assessment techniques to the totally blind. In P. J. Lazarus & S. S. Strichart (Eds.), Psychoeducational evaluation of children and adolescents with low-incidence handicaps (pp. 75–102). Orlando, FL: Grune & Stratton.

Chase, J. B. (1986b). Psychoeducational assessment of visually-impaired learners. In P. J. Lazarus & S. S. Strichart (Eds.), Psychoeducational evaluation of children and adolescents with low-incidence handicaps (pp. 41–74). Orlando, FL: Grune & Stratton.

Chelser, B. (1982). ACLD Vocational Committee completes survey on LD adult. ACLD Newsbriefs, 5, 20–23.

Chinn, P. C., & Kamp, S. H. (1982). Cultural diversity and exceptionality. In N. G. Haring (Ed.), Exceptional children and youth (3rd ed.) (pp. 371–390). Columbus, OH: Merrill.

Chinn, P. C., & McCormick, L. (1986). Cultural diversity and exceptionality. In N. G. Haring & L. McCormick (Eds.), Exceptional children and youth (4th ed.) (pp. 95–117). Columbus, OH: Merrill.

Ciaranello, R. D., Vandenberg, S. R., & Anders, T. F. (1982). Intrinsic and extrinsic determinants of neuronal development: Relation to infantile autism. Journal of Autism and Developmental Disabilities, 12, 115–146.

Clarizio, H. F. (1990). Assessing severity in behavior disorders: Empirically based criteria. Psychology in the Schools, 27(1), 5–15.

Clark, B. (1986). The integrative education model. In J. S. Renzulli (Ed.), Systems and models for developing programs for the gifted and talented (pp. 57–91). Mansfield Center, CT: Creative Learning Press.

Clark, B. (1988). Growing up gifted: Developing the potential of children at home and at school (3rd ed.). Columbus, OH: Merrill.

Clark, G. M., & Kolstoe, O. P. (1990). Career development and transition education for adolescents with disabilities. Boston: Allyn & Bacon.

Clark, L. A., & McKenzie, H. S. (1989). Effects of self-evaluation training of seriously emotionally disturbed children on the generalization of their classroom rule following and work behaviors across settings and teach-

ers. Behavioral Disorders, 14, 89–98.

Clarke, B., & Leslie, P. (1980). Environmental alternatives for the hearing handicapped. In J. W. Schifani, R. M. Anderson, & S. J. Odle (Eds.), Implementing learning in the least restrictive environment: Handicapped children in the mainstream (pp. 199–240). Baltimore, MD: University Park Press.

Clarke, K. L. (1988). Barriers or enablers? Mobility devices for visually impaired and multihandicapped infants and preschoolers. Education of the Visually Handicapped, 20, 115–132.

Clausen. J. A. (1967). Mental deficiency: Development of a concept. American Journal of Mental Deficiency, 71, 727–745.

Clausen, J. A. (1972). The continuing problem of defining mental deficiency. The Journal of Special Education, 6, 97–106.

Clearinghouse for Offender Literacy Programs. (1975). Literacy: Problems and solutions: A handbook for correctional educators. Washington, DC: American Bar Association.

Cleeland, L. K. (1984). The function of the auditory system in speech and language development. In R. K. Hull & K. I. Dilka (Eds.), The hearing-impaired child in school (pp. 7–17). Orlando, FL: Grune & Stratton.

Clements, S. D. (1966). Minimal brain dysfunction in children (NINDS Monograph No. 3, Public Health Service Bulletin No. 1415). Washington, DC: U.S. Department of Health, Education and Welfare.

Cline, D. H. (1990). Interpretations of emotional disturbance and social maladjustment as policy problems: A legal analysis of initiatives to exclude handicapped/disruptive students from special education. Behavioral Disorders, 15, 159–173.

Cochran, W. E., Sran, P. K., & Varano, G. A. (1977). The relocation syndrome in mentally retarded individuals. Mental Retardation, 15, 10–12.

Coffman, T. L., & Harris, M. C. (1980). Transition shock and adjustments of mentally retarded persons. Mental Retardation, 18, 28–32.

Cohen, A. (1975). A sociolinguistic approach to bilingual education. Rowley, MA: Newbury House.

Cohen, H. L. (1973). Behavior modification and socially deviant youth. In C. E. Thoresen (Ed.), Behavior modification in education. Chicago: University of Chicago Press.

Cohen, S., Agosta, J., Cohen, J., & Warren, R. (1989). Supporting families of children with severe disabilities. The Journal of The Association for Persons with Severe Handicaps, 14, 155–162.

Cohen, S., Semmes, M., & Guralnick, M. J. (1979). Public Law 94–142 and the education of preschool handicapped children. Exceptional Children, 4, 279–285.

Cole, E. B., & Paterson, M. M. (1986). Assessment and treatment of phonologic disorders. In J. M. Costello & A. L. Holland (Eds.), Handbook of speech and language disorders (pp. 93–127). San Diego: College-Hill.

Coleman, M., & Webber, J. (1988). Behavior problems? Try groups! Academic Therapy, 23, 265–274.

Commission on Education of the Deaf. (1988). Toward equality: Education of the deaf, a report to the President and the Congress of the United States, February. Washington, DC: U.S. Government Printing Office.

Condon, M. E., York, R., Heal, L. W., & Fortschneider, J. (1986). Acceptance of severely handicapped students by nonhandicapped peers. The Journal of The Association for Persons with Severe Handicaps, 11, 216–219.

Cone, J. D., Delawyer, D. D., & Wolfe, V. V. (1985). Assessing parent participation: The Parent/Family Involvement Index. Exceptional Children, 51, 417–424.

Cone, T. E., Wilson, L. R., Bradley, C. M., & Reese, J. H. (1985). Characteristics of LD students in Iowa: An empirical investigation. Learning Disability Quarterly, 8, 211–220.

Conley, J. E. (1976). Role of idiomatic expressions in the reading of deaf children. American Annals of the Deaf, 121, 381–385.

Connolly, A., Natchman, W., & Pritchett, E. (1973). KeyMath Diagnostic Arithmetic Test. Circle Pines, MN: American Guidance Service.

Connor, L. E. (1986). Oralism in perspective. In D. M. Luterman (Ed.), *Deafness in perspective* (pp. 116–129). San Diego: College-Hill.

Connors, C. K., Goyette, C., Southwick, D., Lees, J., & Andrulonis, P. (1976). Food additives and hyperkinesis: A controlled double blind study. *Pediatrics, 58,* 154–166.

Conroy, J. W., & Bradley, V. J. (1985). *The Pennhurst longitudinal study: A report on five years of research and analysis.* Philadelphia: Temple University Developmental Disabilities Center.

Cook, P. S., & Woodhill, J. M. (1976). The Feingold dietary treatment of the hyperkinetic syndrome. *Medical Journal of Australia, 2,* 85–90.

Cooke, N. L., Heron, T. E., & Heward, W. L. (1983). *Peer tutoring: Implementing classwide programs in the primary grades.* Columbus, OH: Special Press.

Cooke, N. L., Heron, T. E., Heward, W. L., & Test, D. W. (1982). Integrating a Down syndrome student into a classwide peer tutoring system. *Mental Retardation, 20,* 22–25.

Cooke, T. P. (1981). Your place or mine? Residential options for people with developmental disabilities. In C. L. Hansen (Ed.), *Severely handicapped persons in the community* (pp. 103–145). Seattle: University of Washington PDAS.

Cooper, J. O., Heron, T. E., & Heward, W. L. (1987). *Applied behavior analysis.* Columbus, OH: Merrill.

Corn, A., & Ryser, G. (1989). Access to print for students with low vision. *Journal of Visual Impairment and Blindness, 83,* 340–349.

Corn, A. L. (1986). Low vision and visual efficiency. In G. T. Scholl (Ed.), *Foundations of education for blind and visually handicapped children and youth: Theory and practice* (pp. 99–117). New York: American Foundation for the Blind.

Corn, A. L. (1989). Instruction in the use of vision for children and adults with low vision: A proposed program model. *RE:view, 21,* 26–38.

Cornett, R. O. (1974). What is cued speech? *Gallaudet Today, 5*(2), 3–5.

Cott, A. (1972). Megavitamins: The orthomolecular approach to behavioral disorders and learning disabilities. *Academic Therapy, 7,* 245–258.

Coulter, W. A., & Morrow, H. W. (Eds.). (1978). *Adaptive behavior: Concepts and measurements.* New York: Grune & Stratton.

Council for Children with Behavior Disorders. (1987). Position paper on definition and identification of students with behavioral disorders. *Behavioral Disorders, 12,* 9–19.

Council for Children with Behavior Disorders. (1989). Best assessment practices for students with behavioral disorders: Accommodation to cultural diversity and individual differences. *Behavioral Disorders, 14,* 263–278.

Courson, F. H. (1989). *Comparative effects of short- and long-form guided notes on social studies performance by seventh grade learning disabled and at-risk students.* Unpublished doctoral dissertation. Columbus, OH: The Ohio State University.

Cox, B. G., & Ramirez, M., III. (1981). Cognitive styles: Implications for multiethnic education. In J. A. Banks (Ed.), *Education in the 80's: Multiethnic education* (pp. 61–71). Washington, DC: National Education Association.

Creaghead, N. A., Newman, P. W., & Secord, W. (1989). *Assessment and remediation of articulatory and phonological disorders* (2nd. ed.). Columbus, OH: Merrill.

Cremins, J. J. (1983). *Legal and political issues in special education.* Springfield, IL: Charles C. Thomas.

Crnic, K. A., & Pym, H. A. (1979). Training mentally retarded adults in independent living skills. *Mental Retardation, 17,* 13–16.

Cruickshank, W. M. (1986). *Disputable decisions in special education.* Ann Arbor, MI: University of Michigan Press.

Culton, G. L. (1986). Speech disorders among college freshmen: A 13-year survey. *Journal of Speech and Hearing Disorders, 51,* 3–7.

Cummins, J. (1986). Psychological assessment of minority students: Out of context, out of focus, out of control? In A. C. Willig & H. F. Greenberg (Eds.), *Bilingualism and learning disabilities: Policy and practice for teachers and administrators* (pp. 3–11). New York: American Library.

Cummins, J. (1989). A theoretical framework for bilingual special education. *Exceptional Children, 56,* 111–119.

Curl, R. M. (1990). A demonstration project for teaching entry-level job skills: The Co-worker Transition Model for Youths with Disabilities. *Exceptional News, 13*(3), 3–7.

Curl, R. M., Lignugaris/Kraft, B., Pawley, J. M., & Salzberg, C. L. (1988). *"What's next?" A quantitative and qualitative analysis of the transition for trainee to valued worker.* Manuscript submitted for publication.

Curran, B. E. (1983). *Effects of one-to-one and small-group instruction on incidental learning by moderately/ severely handicapped adults.* Unpublished master's thesis. Ohio State University, Columbus, OH.

Curran, J. J., & Algozzine, B. (1980). Ecological disturbance: A test of the matching hypothesis. *Behavioral Disorders, 5,* 159–174.

Currie, W. (1981). Teacher preparation for a pluralistic society. In J. A. Banks (Ed.), *Education in the 80's: Multiethnic education* (pp. 162–174). Washington, DC: National Education Association.

Curry, S., & Hatlen, P. (1988). Meeting the unique educational needs of visually impaired pupils through appropriate placement. *Journal of Visual Impairment and Blindness, 82,* 417–424.

Curt, C. J. N. (1984). *Non-verbal communication in Puerto Rico* (2nd ed.). Cambridge, MA: Lesley College, Evaluation, Dissemination, and Assessment Center.

Cusick, B. (1991). Therapeutic management of sensorimotor and physical disabilities. In J. L. Bigge, *Teaching individuals with multiple and physical disabilities* (3rd ed.) (pp. 16–49). Columbus, OH: Merrill.

Dale, D. M. C. (1984). *Individualised integration: Studies of deaf and partially-hearing children and students in ordinary schools and colleges.* London: Hodder & Stoughton.

D'Angelo, K. (1981). Wordless picture books and the young language-disabled child. *Teaching Exceptional Children, 14,* 34–37.

Dangle, R. F., & Polster, R. A. (Eds.). (1984). *Parent training: Foundations of research and practice.* New York: Guilford Press.

Dantona, R. (1986). Implications of demographic data for planning of services for deaf-blind children and adults. In D. Ellis (Ed.), *Sensory impairments in mentally handicapped people.* San Diego: College-Hill.

Dardig, J. C., & Heward, W. L. (1981). A systematic procedure for prioritizing IEP goals. *The Directive Teacher, 3,* 6–8.

Datillo, J., & Mirenda, P. (1987). An application of a leisure preference assessment protocol for persons with severe handicaps. *The Journal of The Association for Persons with Severe Handicaps, 12,* 306–311.

Davis, H. (1978). Anatomy and physiology of the auditory system. In H. Davis & S. R. Silverman, *Hearing and deafness* (4th ed.). New York: Holt, Rinehart & Winston.

Davis, H., & Silverman, S. R. (Eds.). (1970). *Hearing and deafness* (3rd ed.). New York: Holt, Rinehart & Winston.

Davis, J. M. (1986). Academic placement in perspective. In D. M. Luterman (Ed.), *Deafness in perspective* (pp. 205–224). San Diego: College-Hill.

Dean, M. *A closer look at low vision aids.* Wethersfield, CT: Connecticut State Board of Education and Services for the Blind, Division of Children's Services.

DeAvila, E. (1976). Mainstreaming ethnically and linguistically different children: An exercise in paradox or a new approach? In R. I. Jones (Ed.), *Mainstreaming and the minority child* (pp. 93–108). Reston, VA: Council for Exceptional Children.

Delisle, J. (1982). Learning to underachieve. *Roeper Review, 4,* 16–18.

Delpit, L. D. (1986). Dilemmas of a progressive black educator. *Harvard Educational Review, 56,* 379–385.

Delquadri, J., Greenwood, C. R., Whorton, D., Carta, J. J., & Hall, R. V. (1986). Classwide peer tutoring. *Exceptional Children, 52,* 535–542.

Dent, N. E. (1976). Assessing black children for mainstream placement. In R. L. Jones (Ed.), *Mainstreaming and the minority child* (pp. 77–91). Reston, VA: Council for Exceptional Children.

Denton, D. M. (1972, August 18). *A philosophical foundation for total communication.* Paper presented at the Indiana School for the Deaf, Preschool Parent Conference, Indianapolis.

Deshler, D. D., Lowrey, N., & Alley, G. R. (1979). Programming alternatives for learning disabled adolescents: A nationwide survey. *Academic Therapy, 14*(4).

Deshler, D. D., Schumaker, J. B., & Lenz, B. K. (1984). Academic and cognitive interventions for LD adolescents: Part I. *Journal of Learning Disabilities, 17,* 108–117.

Dever, R. B. (1989). A taxonomy of community living skills. *Exceptional Children, 55,* 395–404.

Dever, R. B. (1990). Defining mental retardation from an instructional perspective. *Mental Retardation, 28,* 147–153.

Dickerson, D., Spellman, C. R., Larsen, S. C., & Tyler, L. (1973). Let the cards do the talking: A teacher-parent communication program. *Teaching Exceptional Children, 5,* 170–178.

DiFrancesca, S. (1972). *Academic achievement test results of a national testing program for hearing-impaired students* (Series D, No. 9). Washington, DC: Gallaudet University, Center for Assessment and Demographic Studies.

DiGiandomenico, J., & Carey, M. L. (1988). Special approaches for special needs. *Foreign Language News Notes, 4,* 1–2.

Divoky, D. (1978). Can diet cure the LD child? *Learning, 3,* 56–57.

Dobelle, W. H. (1977). Current status of research on providing sight to the blind by electrical stimulation of the brain. *Journal of Visual Impairment and Blindness, 71,* 290–297.

Doernberg, N. L. (1978). Some negative effects on family integration of health and educational services for young handicapped children. *Rehabilitation Literature, 39,* 107–110.

Doll, E. A. (1941). The essentials of an inclusive concept of mental deficiency. *American Journal of Mental Deficiency, 46,* 214–219.

Doll, E. A. (1965). *Vineland Social Maturity Scale.* Circle Pines, MN: American Guidance Service.

Donnellan, A. (1984). The criterion of the least dangerous assumption. *Behavioral Disorders, 9,* 141–150.

Donnellan, A. M., & Mirenda, P. L. (1984). Issues related to professional involvement with families of individuals with autism and other severe handicaps. *The Journal of The Association for Persons with Severe Handicaps, 9,* 6–24.

Downing, J., & Bailey, B. (1990). Developing vision use within functional daily activities for students with visual and multiple disabilities. *RE:view, 21,* 209–221.

Downing, J., & Eichinger, J. (1990). Instructional strategies for learners with dual sensory impairments in integrated settings. *The Journal of The Association for Persons with Severe Handicaps, 15,* 98–105.

Doyle, P. M., Wolery, M., Ault, M. J., & Gast, D. L. (1988). System of least prompts: A literature review of procedural parameters. *The Journal of The Association for Persons with Severe Handicaps, 13,* 28–40.

Drabman, R. S., Spitalnik, R., & O'Leary, K. D. (1973). Teaching self-control to disruptive children. *Journal of Abnormal Psychology, 82,* 10–16.

Dratner, Minor, Addicott, & Sunderland, 1971 p. 417.

DuBose, R. F. (1981). Assessment of severely impaired young children: Problems and recommendations. *Topics in Early Childhood Special Education, 1,* 9–12.

Dudley-Marling, C. C., & Edmiaston, R. (1985). Social status of learning disabled children and adolescents: A review. *Learning Disability Quarterly, 8,* 189–204.

Duffy, F. H., & McAnulty, G. B. (1985). Brain electrical activity mapping (BEAM): The search for a physiological signature of dyslexia. In F. H. Duffy & N. Geschwind (Eds.), *Dyslexia: A neuroscientific approach to clinical evaluation* (pp. 105–122). Boston: Little, Brown.

Dunlap, G., & Koegel, R. L. (1980). Motivating autistic children through stimulus variation. *Journal of Applied Behavior Analysis, 13,* 619–627.

Dunn, L. M. (1965). *Peabody Picture Vocabulary Test.* Circle Pines, MN: American Guidance Service.

Dunn, L. M., & Markwardt, F. C. (1970). *The Peabody Individual Achievement Test.* Circle Pines, MN: American Guidance Service.

Dunst, C. J. (1986). Overview of the efficacy of early intervention programs: Methodological and conceptual considerations. In L. Bickman & D. Weatherford (Eds.), *Evaluating early intervention programs for severely handicapped children and their families.* Austin, TX: PRO-ED.

Dunst, C. J., & Snyder, S. W. (1986). A critique of the Utah State University early intervention meta-analysis research. *Exceptional Children, 53,* 269–276.

Dunst, C. J., Snyder, S. W., & Mankinen, M. (1986). Efficacy of early intervention. In M. Wang, H. Walberg, & M. Reynolds (Eds.), *Handbook of special education: Research and practice* (Vols. 1–3). Oxford, England: Pergamon Press.

Durand, V. M. (1986). Review of strategies for educating students with severe handicaps. *The Journal of The Association for Persons with Severe Handicaps, 11,* 140–142.

Durrell, D. D. (1955). *Durrell Analysis of Reading Difficulty.* New York: Harcourt Brace Jovanovich.

Dykes, M. K., & Venn, J. (1983). Using health, physical, and medical data in the classroom. In J. Umbreit (Ed.), *Physical disabilities and health impairments: An introduction* (pp. 259–280). Columbus, OH: Merrill.

Dyson, L., Edgar, E., & Crnic, K. (1989). Psychological predictors of adjustment by siblings of developmentally disabled children. *American Journal of Mental Retardation, 94,* 292–302.

Eakin, W. M., & McFarland, T. L. (1960). *Type, printing, and the partially seeing child.* Pittsburgh, PA: Stanwix.

Eastman, M. (1978). The Eden express doesn't stop here anymore. *American Pharmacy, 40,* 12–17.

Eden-Piercy, G. V. S., Blacher, J. B., & Eyman, R. K. (1986). Exploring parents' reactions to their young child with severe handicaps. *Mental Retardation, 24,* 285–291.

Edgerton, R. B., & Bercovici, S. M. (1976). The cloak of competence: Years later. *American Journal of Mental Deficiency, 80,* 485–497.

Edmonds, C. (1985). Hearing loss with frequent diving: Deaf divers. *Undersea Biomedical Research, 12,* 315–319.

Edwards, P. L. (1986). *Heterogeneous grouping effects on educational service delivery for students with moderate, severe, and profound retardation.* Unpublished manuscript, Kent State University, Kent, OH.

Egan, I., Fredericks, H. D., & Hendrickson, K. (1985). Teaching associated work skills to adolescents with severe handicaps. *Education & Treatment of Children, 8,* 239–250.

Egel, A. L. (1981). Reinforcer variation: Implications for motivating developmentally disabled children. *Journal of Applied Behavior Analysis, 14,* 3–12.

Eichinger, J. (1990). Effects of goal structure on social interaction between elementary level nondisabled students and students with severe disabilities. *Exceptional Children, 56,* 408–417.

Elliott, B. (1979). Look but don't touch: The problems blind children have learning about sexuality. *Disabled USA, 3*(2), 14–17.

Ellis, E. S. (1985). *The effects of teaching learning disabled adolescents an executive strategy to facilitate self-generation of task-specific strategies.* Unpublished doctoral dissertation. University of Kansas, Lawrence, KS.

Ellis, E. S., Deshler, D. D., & Schumaker, J. B. (1989). Teaching adolescents with learning disabilities to generate and use task-specific strategies. *Journal of Learning Disabilities, 22,* 108–119.

Ellis, J. W., & Luckasson, R. A. (1985). Discrimination against people with mental retardation: A comment on the Cleburne decision. *Mental Retardation, 23,* 249–252.

Ellwood, P. (1971). Prescription of wheelchairs. In F. Krussen, F. Kottke, & P. Ellwood, *Handbook of physical medicine and rehabilitation* (2nd ed.). Philadelphia: W. B. Saunders.

Elmer, E. (1977). A follow-up study of traumatized children. *Pediatrics, 59,* 273–279.

Emerick, L. L., & Haynes, W. O. (1986). *Diagnosis and evaluation in speech pathology* (3rd ed.). Englewood Cliffs, NJ: Prentice-Hall.

Engelmann, S. E., Becker, W. C., Carnine, D., & Gersten, R. (1988). The Direct Instruction Follow Through Model: Design and outcomes. *Education & Treatment of Children, 11,* 303–317.

Englemann, S. E. (1977). Sequencing cognitive and academic tasks. In R. D. Kneedler & S. G. Tarver (Eds.), *Changing perspectives in special education* (pp. 46–61). Columbus, OH: Merrill.

Epilepsy Foundation of America. (1987). *Epilepsy school alert.* Washington, DC: Author.

Epstein, L. G., Sharer, L. R., & Goudsmit, J. (1988). Neurological and neuropathological features of human immunodeficiency virus infection in children. *Annals of Neurology, 23,* 19–23.

Epstein, M. H., Bursuck, W., & Cullinan, D. (1985). Patterns of behavior problems among the learning disabled: II. Boys aged 12–18, girls aged 6–11. *Learning Disability Quarterly, 8,* 123–131.

Epstein, M. H., Cullinan, D., & Lloyd, J. W. (1986). Behavior-problem patterns among the learning disabled: III. Replication across age and sex. *Learning Disability Quarterly, 9,* 43–54.

Epstein, M. H., Cullinan, D., & Rosemier, R. (1983). Patterns of behavior problems among the learning disabled: Boys aged 6–11. *Learning Disability Quarterly, 6,* 305–312.

Epstein, P. B., Detwiler, C. L., & Reitz, A. L. (1985). Describing the clients in programs for behavior disordered children and youth. *Education & Treatment of Children, 8,* 265–273.

Esposito, B. G., & Reed, T. M. (1986). The effects of contact with handicapped persons on young children's attitudes. *Exceptional Children, 54,* 224–229.

Esposito, L., & Campbell, P. H. (1987). Computers and severely and physically handicapped individuals. In J. D. Lindsey (Ed.), *Computers and exceptional individuals* (pp. 105–124). Columbus, OH: Merrill.

Evans, W. H., Evans, S. S., Schmid, R. E., & Pennypacker, H. S. (1985). The effects of exercise on selected classroom behaviors of behaviorally disordered adolescents. *Behavioral Disorders, 11,* 42–51.

Fain, G. S. (1986). Leisure: A moral imperative. *Mental Retardation, 24,* 261–263.

Farber, B. (1975). Family adaptations to severely mentally retarded children. In M. Begab & S. A. Richardson (Eds.), *The mentally retarded and society: A social science perspective* (pp. 247–266). Baltimore, MD: University Park Press.

Favell, J. E., Favell, J. E., & McGimsey, J. F. (1978). Relative effectiveness and efficiency of group vs. individual training of severely retarded persons. *American Journal of Mental Deficiency, 83,* 104–109.

Fay, G., Shapiro, S., & Trupin, E. (1978). Should parents teach reading to their children? Further evidence that they should. In D. Edge, B. J. Strenecky, & S. I. Mour (Eds.), *Parenting learning-problem children: The professional educator's perspective* (pp. 9–15). Columbus, OH: Ohio State University, National Center for Educational Materials and Media for the Handicapped.

Featherstone, H. (1980). *A difference in the family: Living with a disabled child.* New York: Basic Books.

Federal Register. (1977, August 23). Washington, DC: U.S. Government Printing Office.

Federal Register. (1981, January 19). Washington, DC: U.S. Government Printing Office.

Federal Register. (1988). Code of federal regulations. 34: Education: Parts 300–399, revised as of July 1, 1988. Washington, DC: U.S. Government Printing Office.

Fein, D. J. (1983). The prevalence of speech and language impairments. *ASHA, 25,* 37.

Feingold, B. F. (1975a). Hyperkinesis and learning disabilities linked to artificial food flavors and colors. *American Journal of Nursing, 75,* 797–803.

Feingold, B. F. (1975b). *Why your child is hyperactive.* New York: Random House.

Feingold, B. F. (1976). Hyperkinesis and learning disabilities linked to ingestion of artificial food colors and flavorings. *Journal of Learning Disabilities, 9,* 551–559.

Feldhusen, J., & Sokol, L. (1982). Extra school programming to meet the needs of gifted youth: Super-Saturday. *Gifted Child Quarterly, 26,* 51–56.

Feldman, D., Kinnison, L., Jay, R., & Harth, R. (1983). The effects of differential labeling on professional concepts and attitudes toward the emotionally disturbed/behavior disordered. *Behavioral Disorders, 8,* 191–198.

Fellows, R. R., Leguire, L. E., Rogers, G. L., & Bremer, D. L. (1986). A theoretical approach to vision stimulation. *Journal of Visual Impairment and Blindness, 80,* 907–909.

Fernald, G. M. (1943). *Remedial techniques in basic school subjects.* New York: McGraw-Hill.

Ferrari, M., & Harris, S. L. (1981). The limits and motivating potential of sensory stimuli as reinforcers for autistic children. *Journal of Applied Behavior Analysis, 14,* 339–343.

Ferrell, K. A. (1984). A second look at sensory aids in early childhood. *Education of the Visually Handicapped, 16,* 83–101.

Ferrell, K. A. (1985). *Reach out and teach.* New York: American Foundation for the Blind.

Ferrell, K. A. (1986). Infancy and early childhood. In G. T. Scholl (Ed.), *Foundations of education for blind and visually handicapped children and youth: Theory and practice* (pp. 119–135). New York: American Foundation for the Blind.

Fiedler, J. F., & Knight, R. R. (1986). Congruence between assessed needs and IEP goals of identified behavior-

ally disabled students. *Behavioral Disorders, 12,* 22–27.

Figueroa, R. A. (1989). Psychological testing of linguistic-minority students: Knowledge gaps and regulations. *Exceptional Children, 56,* 145–152.

Figueroa, R. A., Fradd, S. H., & Correa, V. I. (1989). Bilingual special education and this special issue. *Exceptional Children, 56,* 174–178.

Finch, T. E. (1985). Introduction. In D. Assael (Ed.), *Directory, 1984–85 edition: Handicapped Children's Early Education Program* (pp. ix–xiii). Chapel Hill, NC: University of North Carolina, Technical Assistance Development System.

Fishman, K. D. (1987). American high: At Seward Park, the melting pot still bubbles. *New York, 20*(9), 78–94.

Fitzgerald, E. (1929). *Straight language for the deaf.* Washington, DC: Alexander Graham Bell Association for the Deaf.

Florence, I. J., & LaGrow, S. J. (1989). The use of a recorded message for gaining assistance with street crossings for deaf-blind travelers. *Journal of Visual Impairment and Blindness, 83,* 471–472.

Flynn, L. L., & McCollum, J. (1989). Support systems: Strategies and implications for hospitalized newborns and families. *Journal of Early Intervention, 13,* 173–182.

Fontana, V. J. (1971). *The maltreated child.* Springfield, IL: Charles C. Thomas.

Ford, B. A., & Jones, C. (1990). An ethnic feelings book: Created by students with developmental handicaps. *Teaching Exceptional Children, 22*(4), 36–39.

Forest, M., & Lusthaus, E. (1990). Everyone belongs with the MAPS Action Planning System. *Teaching Exceptional Children, 22*(2), 32–35.

Fowler, S. A. (1986). Peer-monitoring and self-monitoring: Alternatives to traditional teacher management. *Exceptional Children, 52,* 573–581.

Fox, C. L. (1989). Peer acceptance of learning disabled children in the regular classroom. *Exceptional Children, 56,* 50–59.

Fox, L. H. (1977). Sex differences: Implications for program planning for the academically gifted. In J. C. Stanley, W. C. George, & C. H. Solano (Eds.), *The gifted and creative: A fifty-year perspective*. Baltimore, MD: Johns Hopkins.

Fradd, S. H., & Correa, V. I. (1989). Hispanic students at risk: Do we abdicate or advocate? *Exceptional Children, 56,* 105–110.

Frank, D. A., Zuckerman, B. S., Amaro, H., Aboagye, K., Baucher, H., Cabral, H., Fried, L., Hingson, R., Kayne, H., Levenson, S. M., Parker, S., Reece, H., & Vinvi, R. (1988). Cocaine use during pregnancy: Prevalence and correlates. *Pediatrics, 82,* 888–895.

Frankenburg, W. K., Dodds, J., & Fandal, A. (1975). *Denver Developmental Screening Test*. Denver: LADOCA Project and Publishing Foundation.

Frankenburg, W. K., Dodds, J., Archer, P., Shapiro, H., & Bresnick, B. (1990). *The Denver II—revision and restandardization of the DDST*. Denver: University of Colorado School of Medicine.

Freagon, S. (1982). Present and projected services to meet the needs of severely handicapped children [Keynote address]. In *Proceedings of the National Parent Conference on Children Requiring Extensive Special Education Programming*. Washington, DC: U.S. Department of Education, Special Education Programs.

Freagon, S., Smith, B., Costello, C., Bay, J., Ahlgren, C., & Costello, D. (1986). *Procedures and strategies for program development leading to employment of students with moderate and severe handicaps*. DeKalb, IL: Northern Illinois University.

Fredericks, H. D., & Baldwin, V. (1987). Individuals with sensory impairments: Who are they? How are they educated? In L. Goetz, D. Guess, & K. Stremel-Campbell, (Eds.), *Innovative program design for individuals with dual sensory impairments* (pp. 3–14). Baltimore, MD: Paul H. Brookes.

Frey, K. S., Greenberg, M. T., & Fewell, R. R. (1989). Stress and coping among parents of handicapped children: A multidimensional approach. *American Journal on Mental Retardation, 94,* 240–249.

Friedman, P. R. (1976). *The rights of mentally retarded persons*. New York: Avon.

Friedman, P. R. (1977). Human and legal rights of mentally retarded persons. *International Journal of Mental Health, 6,* 50–72.

Frierson, E. C. (1965). Upper and lower status children: A study of differences. *Exceptional Children, 32,* 83–90.

Frierson, E. C. (1969). The gifted. *Review of Educational Research, 39,* 25–37.

Frostig, M., & Horne, D. (1973). *The Frostig program for the development of visual perception* (rev. ed.). Chicago: Follett.

Frostig, M., Lefever, D. W., & Whittlesey, J. R. B. (1964). *The Marianne Frostig Development Test of Visual Perception*. Palo Alto, CA: Consulting Psychologists Press.

Fuchigami, R. Y. (1980). Teacher education for culturally diverse children. *Exceptional Children, 46,* 634–641.

Fuchs, D., & Fuchs, L. S. (1988a). Evaluation of the Adaptive Learning Environments Model. *Exceptional Children, 55,* 115–127.

Fuchs, D., & Fuchs, L. S. (1988b). Response to Wang and Walberg. *Exceptional Children, 55,* 138–146.

Fuchs, D., Fuchs, L. S., & Bahr, M. W. (1990). Mainstream assistance teams: A scientific basis for the art of consultation. *Exceptional Children, 57,* 128–139.

Fuchs, D., Fuchs, L. S., Bahr, M. W., Fernstrom, P., & Stecker, P. (1990). Prereferral intervention: A prescriptive approach. *Exceptional Children, 56,* 493–513.

Furth, H. G. (1973). *Deafness and learning: A psychosocial approach*. Belmont, CA: Wadsworth Publishing.

Gadow, K. D. (1986). *Children on medication: Volume I. Hyperactivity, learning disabilities, and mental retardation*. San Diego: College-Hill.

Gallagher, J. J. (1975a). Characteristics of gifted children: A research summary. In W. B. Barbe & J. S. Renzulli (Eds.), *Psychology and education of the gifted* (2nd ed.) (pp. 127–150). New York: Irvington.

Gallagher, J. J. (1975b). *Teaching the gifted child* (2nd ed.). Boston: Allyn & Bacon.

Gallagher, J. J. (1981). Differential curriculum for the gifted. In A. H. Kramer, D. Bitan, N. Butler-Por, A. Eryatar, & E. Landau (Eds.), *Gifted children: Challenging their potential* (pp. 136–154). New York: World Council for Gifted and Talented Children.

Gallagher, J. J. (1984). The evolution of special education concepts. In B. Blatt & R. J. Morris (Eds.), *Perspectives in special education: Personal orientations* (pp. 210–232). Glenview, IL: Scott, Foresman.

Gallagher, J. J. (1990). Editorial: The public and professional perception of the emotional status of gifted children. [Special Issue], *Journal for the Education of the Gifted, 13,* 202–211.

Gallaudet Research Institute. (1985). *Gallaudet Research Institute Newsletter*. Washington, DC: Gallaudet University Press.

Gallimore, R., Boggs, J., & Jordan, C. (1974). *Culture, behavior, and education*. Beverly Hills, CA: SAGE Publications.

Galton, F. (1936). Genius as inherited. In A. Rothenberg & C. R. Hausman (Eds.), *The creativity question* (pp. 42–48). Durham, NC: Duke University. (Reprinted from *Hereditary genius: An inquiry into its laws and consequences,* 1869. London: Macmillan.)

Gannon, J. (1981). *Deaf heritage: A narrative history of deaf America*. Silver Spring, MD: National Association of the Deaf.

Ganschow, L., & Sparks, R. (1987). The foreign language requirement. *Learning Disabilities Focus, 2,* 116–123.

Garber, H. L. (1988). *The Milwaukee Project: Preventing mental retardation in children at risk*. Washington, DC: American Association on Mental Retardation.

Garber, H., & Heber, R. (1973). *The Milwaukee Project: Early intervention as a technique to prevent mental retardation* [Technical paper]. Storrs, CT: University of Connecticut.

Garcia, R. L. (1981). *Education for cultural pluralism: Global roots stew.* Bloomington, IN: Phi Delta Kappa Educational Foundation.

Gardner, R., III, (1990a). Life-space interviewing: It can be effective, but don't . . . *Behavioral Disorders, 15,* 111–118.

Gardner, R., III, (1990b). Sincere, but sincerely wrong: A reply to Nicholas Long. *Behavioral Disorders, 15, 125–126.*

Gardner, R., III, & Heward, W.L. (1991). Case study: Improving the social interaction of a group home resident with severe and multiple disabilities. *Behavioral Residential Treatment, 6,* 39–50.

Garreau, B., Parthelmy, D., Sauvage, D., Leddet, I., & LeLord, G. (1984). A comparison of autistic syndromes with and without associated neurological problems. *Journal of Autism and Developmental Disabilities, 14,* 105–113.

Gartner, A., & Lipsky, D. K. (1987). Beyond special education: Toward a quality system for all students. *Harvard Educational Review, 57,* 367–395.

Gast, D. L., & Wolery, M. (1987). Severe maladaptive behaviors. In M. E. Snell (Ed.), *Systematic instruction of persons with severe handicaps* (3rd ed.) (pp. 300–332). Columbus, OH: Merrill.

Gates, A. T., & McKillop, A. S. (1962). *Gates-McKillop Reading Diagnostic Test.* New York: Columbia University, Teachers College, Bureau of Publication.

Gaylord-Ross, R. J., Haring, T. G., Breen, C., & Pitts-Conway, V. (1984). The training and generalization of social interaction skills with autistic youth. *Journal of Applied Behavior Analysis, 17,* 229–247.

Gearheart, B. R., & Litton, F. W. (1975). *The trainable retarded: A foundations approach.* St. Louis, MO: C. V. Mosby.

Geers, A. E. (1985). Assessment of hearing impaired children: Determining typical and optimal levels of performance. In F. Powell, T. Finitzo-Hieber, S. Friel-Patti, & D. Henderson (Eds.), *Education of the hearing impaired child* (pp. 57–83). San Diego: College-Hill.

Geers, A., & Moog, J. (1989). Factors predictive of the development of literacy in profoundly hearing-impaired adolescents. *The Volta Review, 91,* 69–86.

Gelman, S. R., Epp, D. J., Downing, R. H., Twark, R. D., & Eyerly, R. W. (1989). Impact of group homes on the values of adjacent residential properties. *Mental Retardation, 27,* 127–134.

Gentile, A., & DiFrancesca, S. (1969). *Academic achievement test performance of hearing-impaired students. United States, Spring, 1969.* (Series D, No. 1). Washington, DC: Gallaudet University, Center for Assessment and Demographic Studies.

George, J. D. (1988). Therapeutic intervention for grandparents and extended family of children with developmental delays. *Mental Retardation, 26,* 369–375.

Geschwind, N., & Galaburda, A. M. (1987). *Cerebral lateralizaton: Biological mechanisms, associations, and pathology.* Cambridge, MA: MIT Press.

Gesell, A., & Associates. (1940). *Gesell Developmental Schedules.* 1940 Series. New York: Psychological Corp.

Giangreco, M. F. (1991). Curriculum in inclusion-oriented schools: Trends, issues, challenges, and potential solutions. In S. Stainback & W. Stainback (Eds.). *Teaching in the inclusive classroom: Curriculum design, adaptation and delivery.* Baltimore, MD: Paul H. Brookes.

Giangreco, M. F., Cloninger, C. J., & Iverson, V. S. (1990). *C.O.A.C.H.: Cayuga-Onondaga assessment for children with handicaps* (Version 6.0). Stillwater, OK: National Clearinghouse of Rehabilitation Training Materials.

Giangreco, M. F., Cloninger, C. J., Mueller, P. H., Yuan, S., & Ashworth, S. (1990, April). *A quest to be heard: Perspectives of parents whose children are dual sensory impaired.* Paper presented at the annual meeting of the Council for Exceptional Children, Toronto, Canada.

Giangreco, M. F., York, J., & Rainforth, B. (1989). Providing related services to learners with severe handicaps in educational settings: Pursuing the least restrictive option. *Pediatric Physical Therapy, 1*(2), 55–63.

Gierich, K. B., Allison, P. A., Kitchens, C. D., O'Cleirigh, C. M., Danials, M. E., Norman, K. R., & Greene, B. F. (1990, May). *Acquisition of behavioral relaxation technique skills among parents with a history of child abuse and neglect.* Paper presented at the 16th Annual Convention of the Association for Behavior Analysis, Nashville, TN.

Gies-Zaborowski, J., & Silverman, F. H. (1986). Documenting the impact of a mild dysarthria on peer perception. *Language, Speech, and Hearing Services in the Schools, 17,* 143.

Gilgoff, I. S. (1983). Spinal cord injury. In J. Umbreit (Ed.), *Physical disabilities and health impairments: An introduction* (pp. 132–146). Columbus, OH: Merrill.

Gilhool, T. K. (1976). Changing public policies: Roots and forces. *Minnesota Education, 2*(2), 8.

Gillespie, E. B. (1981). Student participation in the development of IEP's. Perspective of parents and students. Unpublished doctoral dissertation, University of North Carolina at Chapel Hill.

Gillham, B. (Ed.). (1986). *Handicapping conditions in children.* London: Croom Helm.

Glavin, J. P., & Annesley, F. R. (1971). Reading and arithmetic correlates of conduct-problem and withdrawn children. *The Journal of Special Education, 5,* 213–219.

Glenn, C. L. (1986). New challenges: A civil rights agenda for the public schools. *Phi Delta Kappan, 67*(9), 653–656.

Glover, J., & Gary, A. L. (1976). Procedures to increase some aspects of creativity. *Journal of Applied Behavior Analysis, 9,* 79–84.

Goddard, H. H. (1928). *School training of gifted children.* New York: World Book.

Goetz, E. M. (1982). A review of functional analyses of preschool children's creative behaviors. *Education & Treatment of Children, 5,* 157–177.

Goetz, E. M., & Baer, D. M. (1973). Social control of form diversity and the emergence of new forms in children's blockbuilding. *Journal of Applied Behavior Analysis, 6*, 209–218.

Gold, M. W. (1976). Task analysis of a complex assembly task by the retarded blind. *Exceptional Children, 43*, 73–85.

Gold, M. W. (1980). An alternative definition of mental retardation. In M. W. Gold (Ed.), *"Did I say that?" Articles and commentary on the Try Another Way System*. Champaign, IL: Research Press.

Golden, G. (1980). Nonstandard therapies in the developmental disabilities. *American Journal of Diseases of Children, 134*, 487–491.

Goldstein, H. (1984). A search for understanding. In B. Blatt & R. J. Morris, *Perspectives in special education: Personal orientations* (pp. 56–100). Glenview, IL: Scott, Foresman.

Goldstein, S., Strickland, B., Turnbull, A. P., & Curry, L. (1980). An observational analysis of the IEP conference. *Exceptional Children, 46*(4), 278–286.

Goldstein, S., & Turnbull, A. P. (1982). The use of two strategies to increase parent participation in the IEP conference. *Exceptional Children, 48*, 360–361.

Gonzales, R. (1980). Mainstreaming your hearing impaired child in 1980: Still an oversimplification. *Journal of Research and Development in Education, 13*(4), 14–21.

Goodenough, F. L., & Harris, D. B. (1963). *The Goodenough-Harris Drawing Test*. New York: Harcourt Brace Jovanovich.

Goodman, J. F. (1989). Does retardation mean dumb? Children's perceptions of the nature, cause, and course of mental retardation. *The Journal of Special Education, 23*, 313–329.

Goodman, L. V. (1976). A bill of rights for the handicapped. *American Education, 12*(6), 6–8.

Gottlieb, J., Agard, J. A., Kaufman, M. J., & Semmel, M. I. (1976). Retarded children mainstreamed: Practices as they affect minority group children. In R. L. Jones (Ed.), *Mainstreaming and the minority child* (pp. 195–214). Reston, VA: Council for Exceptional Children.

Gottlieb, J., & Leyser, Y. (1981). Facilitating the social mainstreaming of retarded children. *Exceptional Education Quarterly, 1*, 57–69.

Gowan, J. C. (1972). *Development of the creative individual*. San Diego: Robert R. Knapp.

Gradel, K., Thompson, M. S., & Sheehan, R. (1981). Parental and professional agreement in early childhood assessment. *Topics in Early Childhood Special Education, 1*, 31–39.

Graden, J. L. (1989). Redefining "prereferral" intervention as intervention assistance: Collaboration between general and special education. *Exceptional Children, 56*, 227–231.

Graden, J. L., Casey, A., & Christenson, S. L. (1985). Implementing a prereferral intervention system: Part I. The model. *Exceptional Children, 51*, 377–384.

Grant, C. A., & Sleeter, C. E. (1989). Race, class, gender, exceptionality, and educational reform. In J. A. Banks & C. A. M. Banks (Eds.), *Multicultural education: Issues and perspectives* (pp. 46–65). Boston: Allyn & Bacon.

Grant, G., & McGrath, M. (1990). Need for respite-care services for caregivers of persons with mental retardation. *American Journal on Mental Retardation, 94*, 638–648.

Gray, S. W., Klaus, R. A., Miller, J. O., & Forrester, D. J. (1966). *Before first grade: The early training project for culturally disadvantaged children*. New York: Teachers College Press.

Gray, W. S. (1963). *Gray Oral Reading Tests*. Indianapolis: Bobbs-Merrill.

Greenwood, C. R., Carta, J. J., Hart, B., Thurston, L. P., & Hall. R. V. (1989). A behavioral approach to research on psychosocial retardation. *Education & Treatment of Children, 12*, 330–346.

Gresham, F. M. (1982). Misguided mainstreaming: The case for social skills training with handicapped children. *Exceptional Children, 48*, 422–433.

Gresham, F. M., & Elliot, S. N. (1989). Social skills deficits as a primary learning disability. *Journal of Learning Disabilities, 22*, 120–124.

Gresham, F. M., & Reschly, D. J. (1986). Social skill deficits and low peer acceptance of mainstreamed learning disabled children. *Learning Disability Quarterly, 9*, 23–32.

Griffing, B. L. (1986). Planning for the future: Programs and services for the blind and visually impaired children. In *Yearbook of the Association for Education and Rehabilitation of the Blind and Visually Impaired* (Vol. 3) (pp. 2–11). Alexandria, VA: Association for Education and Rehabilitation of the Blind and Visually Impaired.

Groht, M. A. (1958). *Natural language for deaf children*. Washington, DC: Alexander Graham Bell Association for the Deaf.

Grossman, H. (1984). *Educating Hispanic students: Cultural implications for instruction, classroom management, counseling and assessment*. Springfield, IL: Charles C. Thomas.

Grossman, H. J. (Ed.). (1973). *Manual on terminology and classification in mental retardation* (1973 rev.). Washington, DC: American Association on Mental Deficiency.

Grossman, H. J. (Ed.). (1977). *Manual on terminology and classification in mental retardation* (1977 rev.). Washington, DC: American Association on Mental Deficiency.

Grossman, H. J. (Ed.). (1983). *Classification in mental retardation*. Washington, DC: American Association on Mental Deficiency.

Grove, N. M. (1982). Conditions resulting in physical disabilities. In J. L. Bigge (Ed.), *Teaching individuals with physical and multiple disabilities* (2nd ed.) (pp. 1–11). Columbus, OH: Merrill.

Guess, D., Benson, H. A., & Siegel-Causey, E. (1985). Concepts and issues related to choice-making and autonomy among persons with severe disabilities. *The Journal of The Association for Persons with Severe Handicaps, 10*, 79–86.

Guess, D., & Mulligan, M. (1982). The severely and profoundly handicapped. In E. L. Meyen (Ed.), *Exceptional children and youth: An introduction* (2nd ed.). Denver: Love.

Guilford, J. P. (1956). The structure of intellect. *Psychological Bulletin, 53*(4), 276–293.

Guilford, J. P. (1959). Traits of creativity. In H. H. Anderson (Ed.), *Creativity and its cultivation* (pp. 142–161). New York: Harper & Brothers.

Guralnick, M. J. (1988). Efficacy research in early childhood intervention programs. In S. L. Odom & M. B. Karnes (Eds.), *Early intervention for infants and children with handicaps: An empirical base* (pp. 75–88). Baltimore, MD: Paul H. Brookes.

Guralnick, M. J. (1990). Social competence and early intervention. *Journal of Early Intervention, 14,* 3–14.

Gustason, G. (1985). Interpreters entering public school employment. *American Annals of the Deaf, 130,* 265–266.

Gustason, G., Pfetzing, D., & Zawolkow, E. (1980). *Signing Exact English.* Los Alamitos, CA: Modern Signs Press.

Halderman v. Pennhurst State School & Hospital, 446 F. Supp. 1295 (E. D. Pa. 1977).

Hall, A., Scholl, G. T., & Swallow, R. M. (1986). Psychoeducational assessment. In G. T. Scholl (Ed.), *Foundations of education for blind and visually handicapped children and youth: Theory and practice* (pp. 187–214). New York: American Foundation for the Blind.

Hall, E. T. (1976). How cultures collide. *Psychology Today, 10*(2), 66–74, 97.

Hallahan, D. P., & Kauffman, J. M. (1976). *Introduction to learning disabilities: A psychoeducational approach.* Englewood Cliffs, NJ: Prentice-Hall.

Hallahan, D. P., & Kauffman, J. M. (1977). Labels, categories, behaviors: ED, LD, and EMR reconsidered. *The Journal of Special Education, 11,* 139–149.

Hallahan, D. P., Keller, C. E., McKinney, J. D., Lloyd, J. W., & Bryan, T. (1988). Examining the research base of the regular education initiative: Efficacy studies and the adaptive learning environment model. *Journal of Learning Disabilities, 21*(1), 29–35, 55.

Halle, J. W., Gabler-Halle, D., & Bemben, D. A. (1989). Effects of a peer-mediated aerobic conditioning program on fitness measures with children who have moderate and severe disabilities. *The Journal of The Association for Persons with Severe Handicaps, 14,* 33–47.

Halle, J. W., & Sindelar, P. T. (1982). Behavioral observation methodologies for early childhood education. *Topics in Early Childhood Special Education, 2,* 43–54.

Ham, R.. (1986). *Techniques of stuttering therapy.* Englewood Cliffs, NJ: Prentice-Hall.

Hammill, D. D. (1976). Defining learning disabilities for programmatic purposes. *Academic Therapy, 12,* 29–37.

Hammill, D. D. (1990). On defining learning disabilities: An emerging consensus. *Journal of Learning Disabilities, 23,* 74–84.

Hammill, D. D., Goodman, L., & Wiederholt, J. L. (1974). Visual-motor processes: Can we train them? *Reading Teacher, 27,* 469–478.

Hammill, D. D., & Larsen, S. (1974). The effectiveness of psycholinguistic training. *Exceptional Children, 41,* 5–15.

Hammill, D. D., & Larsen, S. (1978). The effectiveness of psycholinguistic training: A reaffirmation of position. *Exceptional Children, 44,* 402–417.

Hammill, D. D., Leigh, J. E., McNutt, G., & Larsen, S. C. (1981). A new definition of learning disabilities. *Learning Disability Quarterly, 4,* 336–342.

Hamre-Nietupski, S., Nietupski, J., Sandvig, R., Sandvig, M. B., & Ayres, B. (1984). Leisure skills instruction in a community residential setting with young adults who are deaf/blind severely handicapped. *The Journal of The Association for Persons with Severe Handicaps, 9,* 49–54.

Hansen, J. B., & Linden, K. W. (1990). Selecting instruments for identifying gifted and talented students. *Roeper Review, 13*(1), 10–15.

Haring, N. G. (1988). *Generalization for students with severe handicaps: Strategies and solutions.* Seattle, WA: University of Washington.

Haring, N. G., Lovitt, T. C., Eaton, M. D., & Hansen, C. L. (1978). *The fourth R: Research in the classroom.* Columbus, OH: Merrill.

Harrell, R., Capp, R., Davis, D., Peerless, J., & Ravitz, L. (1981). Can nutritional supplements help mentally retarded children? An exploratory study. *Proceedings of the National Academy of Science, 100,* 29–45.

Harris, J. (1986). *Anatomy and physiology of the peripheral auditory mechanism.* Austin, TX: PRO-ED.

Harris, W. J., & Schutz, P. N. B. (1986). *The special education resource program: Rationale and implementation.* Columbus, OH: Merrill.

Harrison, R., & Edwards, J. (1983). *Child abuse.* Portland, OR: Ednick.

Hart, B., & Risley, T. R. (1968). Establishing the use of descriptive adjectives in the spontaneous speech of disadvantaged preschool children. *Journal of Applied Behavior Analysis, 1,* 109–120.

Hart, B., & Risley, T. R. (1975). Incidental teaching of language in the preschool. *Journal of Applied Behavior Analysis, 8,* 411–420.

Hasazi, S. B., & Clark, G. M. (1988). Vocational preparation for high school students labeled mentally retarded: Employment as a graduation goal. *Mental Retardation, 26,* 343–349.

Hasazi, S. B., Gordon, L. R., & Roe, C. A. (1985). Factors associated with the employment status of handicapped youth exiting high school from 1979 to 1983. *Exceptional Children, 51,* 455–469.

Hasazi, S. B., Johnson, R. E., Hasazi, J. E., Gordon, L. R., & Hull, M. (1989). Employment of youth with and without handicaps following high school: Outcomes and correlates. *The Journal of Special Education, 23,* 243–255.

Hasselbring, T., & Hamlet, C. (1983). *Aimstar: A computer software program.* Portland, OR: ASIEO Education.

Hassett, M. E., Engler, C., Cooke, N. L., Test, D. W., Weiss, A. B., Heward, W. L., & Heron, T. E. (1984). A telephone-managed, home-based summer writing program for LD adolescents. In W. L. Heward, T. E. Heron, D. S. Hill, & J. Trap-Porter (Eds.), *Focus on behavior analysis in edu-*

cation (pp. 89–103). Columbus, OH: Merrill.

Hatlen, P. H. (1976, Winter). Priorities in education programs for visually handicapped children and youth. *Division for the Visually Handicapped Newsletter, 8*–11.

Hatlen, P. H. (1978, Fall). The role of the teacher of the visually impaired: A self-definition. *Division for the Visually Handicapped Newsletter,* 5.

Hatten, J. T., & Hatten, P. W. (1975). *Natural language.* Tucson, AZ: Communication Skill Builders.

Hauber, F. A., Bruininks, R. H., Hill, B. K., Lakin, K. C., & White, C. C. (1984). *National census of residential facilities: Fiscal year 1982.* Minneapolis: University of Minnesota, Center for Residential and Community Services.

Hawkins, R. P. (1984). What is "meaningful" behavior change in a severely/profoundly retarded learner? The view of a behavior analytic parent. In W. L. Heward, T. E. Heron, D. S. Hill, & J. Trap-Porter (Eds.), *Focus on behavior analysis in education* (pp. 282–286). Columbus, OH: Merrill.

Hawkins, R. P., & Hawkins, K. K. (1981). Parental observations on the education of severely retarded children: Can it be done in the classroom? *Analysis and Intervention in Development Disabilities, 1,* 13–22.

Haycock, G. S. (1933). *The teaching of speech.* Stoke-on-Trent, England: Hill & Ainsworth.

Hayden, A. H., & Pious, C. G. (1979). The case for early intervention. In R. York & E. Edgar (Eds.), *Teaching the severely handicapped* (Vol. 4) (pp. 267–287). Seattle: American Association for the Education of the Severely/Profoundly Handicapped.

Haywood, H. C. (1979). What happened to mild and moderate mental retardation? *American Journal of Mental Deficiency, 83,* 427–431.

Heber, R. F. (1961). A manual on terminology and classification in mental retardation (rev. ed.). *Monograph Supplement, American Journal of Mental Deficiency, 64.*

Heber, R. F., & Garber, H. (1971). An experiment in prevention of cultural-familial mental retardation. In

D. A. Primrose (Ed.), *Proceedings of the Second Congress of the International Association for the Scientific Study of Mental Deficiency.* Warsaw: Polish Medical Publishers.

Hedlund, R. (1989). Fostering positive social interactions between parents and infants. *Teaching Exceptional Children, 21*(4), 45–48.

Hegde, M. N. (1986). Treatment of fluency disorders: State of the art. In J. M. Costello & A. L. Holland (Eds.), *Handbook of speech and language disorders* (pp. 505–538). San Diego: College-Hill.

Heinze, T. (1986). Communication skills. In G. T. Scholl (Ed.), *Foundations of education for blind and visually handicapped children and youth: Theory and practice* (pp. 301–314). New York: American Foundation for the Blind.

Heller, T., Bond, M. S., & Braddock, D. (1988). Family reactions to institutional closure. *American Journal on Mental Retardation, 92,* 336–343.

Hemming, H., Lavender, T., & Pill, R. (1981). Quality of life of mentally retarded adults transferred from large institutions to new small units. *American Journal of Mental Deficiency, 86,* 157–169.

Henderson, J. (1986). *Making regular schools special.* New York: Schocken.

Heron, T. E., & Harris, K. C. (1987). *The educational consultant: Helping professionals, parents, and mainstreamed students* (2nd ed.). Austin, TX: PRO-ED.

Heron, T. E., & Heward, W. L. (1988). Ecological assessment: Implications for teachers of learning disabled students. *Learning Disability Quarterly, 11,* 117–125.

Heron, T. E., & Skinner, M. E. (1981). Criteria for defining the regular classroom as the least restrictive environment for LD students. *Learning Disability Quarterly, 4,* 115–121.

Heston, L. L. (1970). The genetics of schizophrenic and schizoid disease. *Science, 167,* 249–256.

HEW reports 13 percent of Head Start children are handicapped. (1978). *Report on Preschool Education, 10.*

Heward, W. L. (1979). Teaching students to control their own behavior:

A critical skill. *Exceptional Teacher, 1,* 3–5, 11.

Heward, W. L. (1987a). Promoting the generality of behavior change. In J. O. Cooper, T. E. Heron, & W. L. Heward, *Applied behavior analysis* (pp. 552–583). Columbus, OH: Merrill.

Heward, W. L. (1987b). Self-management. In J. O. Cooper, T. E. Heron, & W. L. Heward, *Applied behavior analysis* (pp. 515–549). Columbus, OH: Merrill.

Heward, W. L., & Cavanaugh, R. A. (in press). Educational equality for students with disabilities. In J. A. Banks & C. A. M. Banks (Eds.), *Multicultural education: Issues and perspectives* (2nd ed.). Boston: Allyn & Bacon.

Heward, W. L., & Chapman, J. E. (1981). Improving parent-teacher communication through recorded telephone messages: Systematic replication in a special education classroom. *Journal of Special Education Technology, 4,* 11–19.

Heward, W. L., & Dardig, J. C. (1978). Improving the parent-teacher relationship through contingency contracting. In D. Edge, B. J. Strenecky, & S. I. Mour (Eds.), *Parenting learning-problem children: The professional educator's perspective* (pp. 71–78). Columbus, OH: Ohio State University, National Center for Educational Materials and Media for the Handicapped.

Heward, W. L., Dardig, J. C., & Rossett, A. (1979). *Working with parents of handicapped children.* Columbus, OH: Merrill.

Heward, W. L., Eachus, H. T., & Christopher, J. (1974). *Establishment of talking in an elective mute.* Unpublished manuscript, University of Massachusetts.

Heward, W. L., Heron, T. E., & Cooke, N. L. (1982). Tutor huddle: Key element in a classwide peer tutoring system. *Elementary School Journal, 83,* 115–123.

Heward, W. L., Heron, T. E., Gardner, R., III, & Prayzer, R. (1991). Two strategies for improving students' writing skills. In G. Stoner, M. R. Shinn, & H. M. Walker (Eds.), *Interventions for achievement and behav-*

ior problems (pp. 379–398). Silver Spring, MD: The National Association of School Psychologists.

Hewett, F. M. (1964). A hierarchy of educational tasks for children with learning disorders. *Exceptional Children, 31,* 207–214.

Hewett, F. M. (1968). *The emotionally disturbed child in the classroom.* Boston: Allyn & Bacon.

Hewett, F. M., & Forness, S. R. (1977). *Education of exceptional learners* (2nd ed.). Boston: Allyn & Bacon.

Hewett, F. M., & Taylor, F. D. (1980). *The emotionally disturbed child in the classroom: The orchestration of success* (2nd. ed.). Boston: Allyn & Bacon.

Hieronymus, A. N., & Lindquist, E. F. (1978). *Iowa Tests of Basic Skills.* Boston: Houghton Mifflin.

Hill, B. K., & Lakin, K. C. (1986). Classification of residential facilities for mentally retarded people. *Mental Retardation, 24,* 107–115.

Hill, B. K., Lakin, K. C., & Bruininks, R. H. (1984). Trends in residential services for people who are mentally retarded: 1977–1982. *The Journal of The Association for Persons with Severe Handicaps, 9,* 243–250.

Hill, B. K., Lakin, K. C., Bruininks, R. H., Amado, A. N., Anderson, D. J., & Copher, J. I. (1989). *Living in the community: A comparative study of foster homes and small group homes for people with mental retardation.* Minneapolis, MN: Center for Residential and Community Services (Report #28), University of Minnesota.

Hill, E. W., & Jacobson, W. H. (1985). Controversial issues in orientation and mobility: Then and now. *Education of the Visually Handicapped, 17,* 59–70.

Hill, J. W., Wehman, P., & Horst, G. (1982). Toward generalization of appropriate leisure and social behavior in severely handicapped youth: Pinball machine use. *The Journal of The Association for the Severely Handicapped, 6*(4), 38–44.

Hilliard, A. G., III. (1975). The strengths and weaknesses of cognitive tests for young children. In J. D. Andrews (Ed.), *One child indivisible* (pp. 17–33). Washington, DC: National Association for the Education of Young Children.

Hilliard, A. G. (1980). Cultural diversity and special education. *Exceptional Children, 46,* 584–588.

Hingtgen, J. N., & Bryson, C. Q. (1972). Recent developments in the study of early childhood psychoses: Infantile autism, childhood schizophrenia, and related disorders. *Schizophrenia Bulletin* (No. 5), 8–54.

Hirschberg, G., Lewis, C., & Thomas, D. (1964). *Rehabilitation.* Philadelphia: J. B. Lippincott.

Hitzing, W. (1980). ENCOR and beyond. In T. Apolloni, J. Cappuccilli, & T. P. Cooke (Eds.), *Achievements in residential services for persons with disabilities: Total excellence.* Baltimore, MD: University Park Press.

Hobbs, N. (1966). Helping the disturbed child: Psychological and ecological strategies. *American Psychologist, 21,* 1105–1115.

Hobbs, N. (1975). *The futures of children.* San Francisco: Jossey-Bass.

Hobbs, N. (Ed.). (1976a). *Issues in the classification of children* (Vol. 1). San Francisco: Jossey-Bass.

Hobbs, N. (Ed.). (1976b). *Issues in the classification of children* (Vol. 2). San Francisco: Jossey-Bass.

Hobbs, N. (1982). *The troubled and troubling child.* San Francisco: Jossey-Bass.

Hoemann, H. W., & Briga, J. I. (1981). Hearing impairments. In J. M. Kauffman & D. P. Hallahan (Eds.), *Handbook of special education.* Englewood Cliffs, NJ: Prentice-Hall.

Holburn, C. S. (1990). Symposium overview: Our residential rules—have we gone too far? *Mental Retardation, 28,* 65–66.

Holland, A. L., & Reinmuth, O. M. (1982). Aphasia in adults. In G. H. Shames & E. H. Wiig (Eds.), *Human communication disorders: An introduction* (pp. 561–593). Columbus, OH: Merrill.

Hollander, R. (1989). Euthanasia and mental retardation: Suggesting the unthinkable. *Mental Retardation, 27,* 53–61.

Hollingworth, L. (1942). *Children above 180 IQ.* Yonkers-on-Hudson, NY: World Books.

Hollingworth, L. S. (1975). *Children above IQ 180: Stanford-Binet: Origin and development* (reprint ed.). New York: Arno Press.

Homeward Bound, Inc. v. Hissom Memorial Center, U.S. Court of Appeals for the Tenth Circuit, No. 88-1119, 88-1241 (October 3, 1988).

Hoover, J. J. (1989). Study skills and the education of students with learning disabilities. *Journal of Learning Disabilities, 22,* 452–455.

Hops, H., Beickel, S., & Walker, H. M. (1976). *CLASS (Contingencies for Learning Academic and Social Skills): Manual for consultants.* Eugene, OR: University of Oregon, Center at Oregon for Research in Behavioral Education of the Handicapped.

Horner, J. (1986). Moderate aphasia. In J. M. Costello & A. L. Holland (Eds.), *Handbook of speech and language disorders* (pp. 891–915). San Diego: College-Hill.

Horner, R. H., Dunlap, G., & Koegel, R. L. (1988). *Generalization and maintenance: Life-style changes in applied settings.* Baltimore, MD: Paul H. Brookes.

Horner, R. H., McDonnell, J. J., & Bellamy, G. T. (1986). Teaching generalized skills: General case instruction in simulation and community settings. In R. H. Horner, L. H. Meyer, & H. D. B. Fredericks (Eds.), *Education of learners with severe handicaps: Exemplary service strategies* (pp. 289–314). Baltimore, MD: Paul H. Brookes.

Horst, G., Wehman, P., Hill, J. W., & Bailey, C. (1981). Developing age-appropriate leisure skills in severely handicapped adolescents. *Teaching Exceptional Children, 14,* 11–16.

Horton, S. V., & Lovitt, T. C. (1989). Construction and implementation of graphic organizers for academically handicapped and regular secondary students. *Academic Therapy, 24,* 625–640.

Horton, S. V., Lovitt, T. C., & Bergerud, D. (1990). The effectiveness of graphic organizers for three classifications of secondary students in content area classes. *Journal of Learning Disabilities, 23,* 12–22.

Houlihan, M., & Van Houten, R. (1989). Behavioral treatment of hyperactivity: A review and overview. *Education & Treatment of Children, 12,* 265–275.

Howell, K. W., Kaplan, J. S., & O'Connell, C. Y. (1979). *Evaluating exceptional children: A task analysis approach.* Columbus, OH: Merrill.

Howell, K. W., & Morehead, M. K. (1987). *Curriculum based evaluation in special and remedial education.* Columbus, OH: Merrill.

Howell, K. W., & Lorson-Howell, K. A. (1990). What's the hurry? Fluency in the classroom. *Teaching Exceptional Children, 22*(3), 20–23.

Hubbell, R. (1985). Language and linguistics. In P. Skinner & R. Shelton (Eds.), *Speech, language, and hearing: Normal processes and disorders* (2nd ed.). New York: John Wiley & Sons.

Huberty, T. J., Koller, J. R., & Ten Brink, T. D. (1980). Adaptive behavior in the definition of mental retardation. *Exceptional Children, 46,* 256–261.

Huebner, K. M. (1986). Social skills. In G. T. Scholl (Ed.), *Foundations for education for blind and visually handicapped children and youth: Theory and practice* (pp. 341–362). New York: American Foundation for the Blind.

Hughes, C., & Rusch, F. R. (1989). Teaching supported employees with severe mental retardation to solve problems. *Journal of Applied Behavior Analysis, 22,* 365–372.

Hughes, C., Rusch, F. R., & Curl, R. M. (1990). Extending individual competence, developing natural support, and promoting social acceptance. In F. Rusch (Ed.), *Supported employment: Models, methods, and issues* (pp. 181–197). Sycamore, IL: Sycamore Publishing.

Hughes, C., Rusch, F. R., & Wood, C. S. (1989). Workplace independence for students with severe handicaps. *Teaching Exceptional Children, 22*(1), 50–53.

Hull, F. M., Mielke, P. W., Willeford, J. A., & Timmons, R. J. (1976). *National speech and hearing survey* (Final report; Project No. 50978; Grant No. OE-32-15-0050-5010 [607]). Washington, DC: U.S. Department of Health, Education, and Welfare.

Hunsucker, P. F., Nelson, R. O., & Clark, R. P. (1986). Standardization and evaluation of the Classroom Adaptive Behavior Checklist for school use. *Exceptional Children, 53,* 69–71.

Hunt, P., Goetz, L., & Anderson, J. (1986). The quality of IEP objectives associated with placement on integrated versus segregated school sites. *The Journal of The Association for Persons with Severe Handicaps, 11,* 125–130.

Huntze, S. L. (1985). A position paper of the Council for Children with Behavioral Disorders. *Behavioral Disorders, 10,* 167–174.

Hurlbut, B. I., Iwata, B. A., & Green, J. D. (1982). Nonvocal language acquisition in adolescents with severe physical disabilities: Blissymbol versus iconic stimulus formats. *Journal of Applied Behavior Analysis, 15,* 241–258.

Hurvitz, J. A., Pickert, S. M., & Rilla, D. C. (1987). Promoting children's language interaction. *Teaching Exceptional Children, 19*(3), 12–15.

Hutchins, M. P., & Renzaglia, A. M. (1990). Developing a longitudinal vocational training program. In F. Rusch (Ed.), *Supported employment: Models, methods, and issues* (pp. 365–380). Sycamore, IL: Sycamore Publishing.

Hutinger, P. L., Marshall, S., & McCarten, K. (1983). *Core curriculum: Macomb 0-3 regional project* (3rd ed.). Macomb, IL: Western Illinois University.

Idol, L. (1989). The resource/consulting teacher: An integrated model of service delivery. *Remedial and Special Education, 10*(6), 38–48.

Imber, S. C., Imber, R. B., & Rothstein, C. (1979). Modifying independent work habits: An effective parent-teacher communication program. *Exceptional Children, 46,* 218–221.

Iran-Nejad, A., Ortony, A., & Rittenhouse, R. K. (1981). The comprehension of metaphorical uses of English by deaf children. *Journal of Speech and Hearing Research, 24,* 31–36.

Ireland, J. C., Wray, D., & Flexer, C. (1988). Hearing for success in the classroom. *Teaching Exceptional Children, 20*(2), 15–17.

Ireland, W. W. (1900). *The mental affections of children: Idiocy, imbecility, and insanity.* Philadelphia: Blakiston.

Irving Independent School District v. Tatro, 104 S. Ct. 3371, 82 L.Ed. 2d 664 (1984).

Iscoe, I., & Payne, S. (1972). Development of a revised scale for the functional classification of exceptional children. In E. P. Trapp & P. Himelstein (Eds.), *Readings on the exceptional child* (pp. 7–29). New York: Appleton-Century-Crofts.

Itard, J. M. G. (1962). *The wild boy of Aveyron.* (G. Humphrey & M. Humphrey, Eds. and Trans.). New York: Appleton-Century-Crofts. (Original work published 1894)

Janicki, M. P., & Zigman, W. B. (1984). Physical and environmental design characteristics of community residences. *Mental Retardation, 22,* 294–301.

Jastak, J. F., & Jastak, S. R. (1965). *The Wide Range Achievement Test* (rev. ed.). Wilmington, DE: Guidance Associates.

Jastak, J. F., & Wilkinson, G. S. (1984). *The Wide Range Achievement Test—Revised.* Wilmington, DE: Jastak Associates.

Jenkins, J. R., Speltz, M. L., & Odom, S. L. (1985). Integrating normal and handicapped preschoolers: Effects on child development and social interaction. *Exceptional Children, 52,* 7–17.

Jensen, B. F., & Potter, M. L. (1990). Best practices in communicating with parents. In A. Thomas & J. Grimes (Eds.), *Best practices in school psychology—II* (pp. 183–193). Washington, DC: National Association of School Psychologists.

Johnson, B., & Cuvo, A. (1981). Teaching mentally retarded adults to cook. *Behavior Modification, 12,* 69–73.

Johnson, J. L. (1976). Mainstreaming black children. In R. L. Jones (Ed.), *Mainstreaming and the minority child* (pp. 159–180). Reston VA: Council for Exceptional Children.

Johnson, J. R., & Rusch, F. R. (1990). Analysis of hours of direct training provided by employment specialists to supported employees. *American Journal on Mental Retardation, 94,* 674–682.

Johnson, M., & Bailey, J. (1977). The modification of leisure behavior in a halfway house for retarded women. *Journal of Applied Behavior Analysis, 10,* 273–282.

Johnson, T. P. (1986). *The principal's guide to the educational rights of handicapped students.* Reston, VA: National Association of Secondary School Principals.

Johnson, T. S. (1986). Voice disorders: The measurement of clinical progress. In J. M. Costello & A. L. Holland (Eds.), *Handbook of speech and language disorders* (pp. 477–502). San Diego: College-Hill.

Jolliff, G., Grossi, T. A., Heward, W. L., & Sainato, D. M. (1991). *Using self-monitoring and public posting to increase the work productivity of students with developmental handicaps.* Manuscript submitted for publication.

Jonas, G. (1976). *Stuttering: The disorder of many theories.* New York: Farrar, Straus & Giroux.

Jones, M. H. (1977). Physical facilities and environments. In J. B. Jordan, A. H. Hayden, M. B. Karnes, & M. M. Woods (Eds.), *Early childhood education for exceptional children: A handbook of ideas and exemplary practices.* Reston, VA: Council for Exceptional Children.

Jones, M. H. (1983). Cerebral palsy. In J. Umbreit (Ed.), *Physical disabilities and health impairments: An introduction* (pp. 41–58). Columbus, OH: Merrill.

Jose, R. (1983). *Understanding low vision.* New York: American Foundation for the Blind.

Justen, J. E. (1976). Who are the severely handicapped? A problem in definition. *AAESPH Review, 1*(2), 1–12.

Kaiser-Kupfer, M. I., & Morris, J. (1985). Advances in human genetics: The long range impact on blindness and the visually impaired. *Yearbook of the Association for Education and Rehabilitation of the Blind and Visually Impaired* (Vol. 2) (pp. 46–49). Alexandria, VA: Association for Education and Rehabilitation of the Blind and Visually Impaired.

Kameenui, E. J., & Simmons, D. C. (1990). *Designing instructional strategies: The prevention of academic learning problems.* Columbus, OH: Merrill.

Kamp, S. H., & Chinn, P. C. (1982). *A multiethnic curriculum for special education students.* Reston, VA: Council for Exceptional Children.

Kampfe, C. M. (1984). Mainstreaming: Some practical suggestions for teachers and administrators. In R. H. Hull & K. I. Dilka (Eds.), *The hearing-impaired child in school* (pp. 99–112). Orlando, FL: Grune & Stratton.

Kaplan, S. (1986). The Grid: A model to construct differentiated curriculum for the gifted. In J. Renzulli (Ed.), *Systems and models for developing programs for the gifted and talented* (pp. 182–193). Mansfield Center, CT: Creative Learning Press.

Kappan Special Report. (1990, June). *Children of poverty: The status of 12 million young Americans.* Bloomington, IN: Phi Delta Kappan.

Karchmer, M. (1984). Hearing impaired students and their eduction: Population perspectives. In W. Northcott (Ed.), *Introduction to oral interpreting: Principles and practices* (pp. 41–59). Baltimore, MD: University Park Press.

Karmody, C. S. (1986). Otology in perspective. In D. M. Luterman (Ed.), *Deafness in perspective* (pp. 1–13). San Diego: College-Hill.

Karnes, M. B., & Stayton, V. D. (1988). Model programs for infants and toddlers with handicaps. In J. B. Jordan, J. J. Gallagher, P. L. Hutinger, & M. B. Karnes (Eds.), *Early childhood special education: Birth to three* (pp. 67–108). Reston, VA: Council for Exceptional Children.

Katz, L., Mathis, S. L., & Merrill, E. C. (1978). *The deaf child in the public schools* (2nd ed.). Danville, IL: Interstate Printers & Publishers.

Kauffman, J. M. (1977). *Characteristics of children's behavior disorders.* Columbus, OH: Merrill.

Kauffman, J. M. (1980). Where special education for disturbed children is going: A personal view. *Exceptional Children, 48,* 522–527.

Kauffman, J. M. (Ed.). (1981). Special issue: Are all children educable? *Analysis and Intervention in Developmental Disabilities, 1*(1).

Kauffman, J. M. (1982). Social policy issues in special education and related services for emotionally disturbed children and youth. In M. M. Noel & N. G. Haring (Eds.), *Progress of change: Issues in educating the emotionally disturbed. Vol. 1: Identification and program planning* (pp. 1–10). Seattle: University of Washington.

Kauffman, J. M. (1985). An interview with James M. Kauffman. *The Directive Teacher, 7*(1), 12–14.

Kauffman, J. M. (1986). Educating children with behavior disorders. In R. J. Morris & B. Blatt (Eds.), *Special education: Research and trends* (pp. 249–271). New York: Pergamon Press.

Kauffman, J. M. (Ed.). (1989). *Characteristics of behavior disorders of children and youth* (4th ed.). Columbus, OH: Merrill.

Kauffman, J. M., Gerber, M. M., & Semmel, M. I. (1988). Arguable assumptions underlying the regular education initiative. *Journal of Learning Disabilities, 21*(1), 6–11.

Kauffman, J. M., & Krouse, J. (1981). The cult of educability: Searching for the substance of things hoped for; the evidence of things not seen. *Analysis and Intervention in Developmental Disabilities, 1*(1), 53–61.

Kauffman, J. M., & Pullen, P. L. (1989). An historical perspective: A personal perspective on our history of service to mildly handicapped and at-risk students. *Remedial and Special Education, 10*(6), 12–14.

Kaufman, A., & Kaufman, N. (1983). *Kaufman Assessment Battery for Children, interpretive manual.* Circle Pines, MN: American Guidance Service.

Kavale, K. (1981). Functions of the Illinois Test of Psycholinguistic Abilities (ITPA): Are they trainable? *Exceptional Children, 47,* 496–510.

Kavale, K., & Mattson, P. D. (1983). One jumped off the balance beam: Meta-analysis of perceptual-motor training. *Journal of Learning Disabilities, 16,* 165–173.

Keating, D. P. (1980). Four faces of creativity: The continuing plight of the intellectually underserved. *Gifted Child Quarterly, 24,* 56–61.

Keller, W. D., & Bundy, R. S. (1980). Effects of unilateral hearing loss upon educational achievement. *Child Care, Health & Development, 6,* 93–100.

Kelly, D. J., & Rice, M. L. (1986). A strategy for language assessment of young children: A combination of two approaches. *Language, Speech, and Hearing Services in the Schools, 17,* 83–94.

Kelly, R. R. (1987). Computers and sensory impaired individuals. In J. D. Lindsey (Ed.), *Computers and exceptional individuals* (pp. 125–146). Columbus, OH: Merrill.

Kennedy, C. H., Horner, R. H., & Newton, J. S. (1989). Social contacts of adults with severe disabilities living in the community: A descriptive analysis of relationship patterns. *The Journal of The Association for Persons with Severe Handicaps, 14,* 190–196.

Kenney, K. W., & Prather, E. M. (1986). Articulation development in preschool children: Consistency of productions. *Journal of Speech and Hearing Research, 29,* 29–36.

Keogh, B. K. (1988). Improving services for problems learners: Rethinking and restructuring. *Journal of Learning Disabilities, 21*(1), 19–22.

Keogh, B. K. (1990). Narrowing the gap between policy and practice. *Exceptional Children, 57,* 186–190.

Kephart, N. C. (1971). *The slow learner in the classroom* (2nd ed.). Columbus, OH: Merrill.

Kern, L., Koegel, R. L., & Dunlap, G. (1984). The influence of vigorous versus mild exercise on autistic stereotyped behaviors. *Journal of Autism and Developmental Disabilities, 14,* 57–67.

Kerr, B. (1985). Smart girls, gifted women: Special guidance concerns. *Roeper Review, 8*(1), 30–33.

Kerr, M. M., & Nelson, C. M. (1983). *Strategies for managing behavior problems in the classroom.* Columbus, OH: Merrill.

Kerr, M. M., & Nelson, C. M. (1989). *Strategies for managing behavior problems in the classroom* (2nd ed.). Columbus, OH: Merrill.

Kershner, J. R., Cummings, R. L., Clarke, K. A., Hadfield, A. J., & Kershner, B. A. (1986). Evaluation of the Tomatis Listening Training Program with learning disabled children. *Canadian Journal of Special Education, 2,* 1–32.

Kershner, J. R., Cummings, R. L., Clarke, K. A., Hadfield, A. J., & Kershner, B. A. (1990). Two-year evaluation of the Tomatis Listening Training Program with learning disabled children. *Learning Disability Quarterly, 13,* 43–53.

Kershner, J., Hawks, W., & Grekin, R. (1977). Megavitamins and learning disorders: A controlled double-blind experiment. Unpublished manuscript, Ontario Institute for Studies in Education.

Kidd, J. W. (1979). An open letter to the Committee on Technology and Classification of AAMD from the Committee on Definition and Terminology of CEC-MR. *Education and Training of the Mentally Retarded, 14,* 74–76.

Kim, K. C., & Harh, W. M. (1983). Asian Americans and the "success" image: A critique. *Amerasia Journal, 10,* 3–21.

King-Stoops, J. (1980). *Migrant education: Teaching the wandering ones.* Bloomington, IN: Phi Delta Kappa Educational Foundation.

Kirk, S. A. (1958). *Early education of the mentally retarded: An experimental study.* Urbana, IL: University of Illinois.

Kirk, S. A. (1963). Behavioral diagnosis and remediation of learning disabilities. In *Proceedings of the Conference on Exploration into the Problems of the Perceptually Handicapped Child* (Vol. 1). Chicago: Perceptually Handicapped Children.

Kirk, S. A. (1978). Foreword. In D. F. Moores, *Educating the deaf: Psychology, principles, and practices.* Boston: Houghton Mifflin.

Kirk, S. A. (1982). Foreword to the first edition. In D. F. Moores, *Educating the deaf: Psychology, principles and practices* (2nd ed.). Boston: Houghton Mifflin.

Kirk, S. A., & Elkins, J. (1975). Characteristics of children enrolled in the child service demonstration centers. *Journal of Learning Disabilities, 8,* 630–637.

Kirk, S. A., McCarthy, J. J., & Kirk, W. D. (1968). *Illinois Test of Psycholinguistic Abilities* (rev. ed.). Urbana, IL: University of Illinois Press.

Kirsten, I. (1981). *The Oakland picture dictionary.* Wauconda, IL: Don Johnston.

Kishi, G., Teelucksingh, B., Zollers, N., Park-Lee, S., & Meyer, L. (1988). Daily decision-making in community residences: A social comparison of adults with and without mental retardation. *American Journal on Mental Retardation, 92,* 430–435.

Kleinberg, S. (1984). Facilitating the child's entry to school and coordinating school activities during hospitalization. In *Home care for children with serious handicapping conditions* (pp. 67–77). Washington, DC: Association for the Care of Children's Health.

Kleinberg, S. B. (1982). *Educating the chronically ill child.* Rockville, MD: Aspen.

Kleinfeld, J. (1987). Guiding minority students into adulthood. *Phi Delta Kappan, 68*(7), 553–554.

Klima, E., & Bellugi, U. (1979). *The signs of language.* Cambridge, MA: Harvard University Press.

Kline, C. S. (1986). *Effects of guided notes on academic achievement of learning disabled high school students.* Unpublished masters thesis. Columbus, OH: The Ohio State University.

Klinghammer, H. D. (1964). Social perception of the deaf and of the blind by their voices and their speech. In *Report of the proceedings of the International Congress on the Education of the Deaf and of the 41st meeting of the Convention of American Instructors of the Deaf.* Washington, DC: U.S. Government Printing Office.

Kluwin, T. N. (1985). Profiling the deaf student who is a problem in the classroom. *Adolescence, 20,* 863–875.

Kluwin, T. N., & Moores, D. F. (1989). Mathematics achievement of hearing impaired adolescents in different placements. *Exceptional Children, 55,* 327–335.

Knitzer, J. (1982). *Unclaimed children: The failure of public responsibility to children and adolescents in need of mental health services.* Washington, DC: Children's Defense Fund.

Knitzer, J., Steinberg, Z., & Fleisch, B. (1990). *At the school house door: An examination of programs and policies for children with behavioral and emotional problems.* New York: Bank Street College of Education.

Knobloch, H., & Pasamanick, B. (1974). *Gesell's and Amatruda's developmental diagnosis: The evaluation and management of normal and abnormal neuropsychotic development in infancy and early childhood.* Hagerstown, MD: Harper & Row.

Knobloch, H., Pasamanick, B., & Sherard, E. S., Jr. (1966). *Developmental Screening Inventory.* New York: Psychological Corp.

Kobrick, J. W. (1972, April 19). The compelling case for bilingual education. *Saturday Review,* pp. 54, 58.

Kochanek, T. T., Kabacoff, R. I., & Lipsitt, L. P. (1990). Early identification of developmentally disabled and at-risk preschool children. *Exceptional Children, 56,* 528–538.

Koestler, F. (1976). *The unseen minority: A social history of blindness in the United States.* New York: David McKay Co.

Kokaska, C. J., & Skolnik, J. (1986). Employment suggestions from LD adults. *Academic Therapy, 21,* 573–577.

Kolstoe, O. P., & Frey, R. (1965). *A high school work-study program for mentally subnormal students.* Carbondale, IL: Southern Illinois Press.

Kopan, A. (1974). Melting pot—myth or reality? In E. Eppr (Ed.), *Cultural pluralism.* Berkeley, CA: McCutchan.

Koppelman, J. (Ed.). (1986). Reagan signs bill expanding services to handicapped preschoolers. *Report to Preschool Programs, 18*(21), 3–4.

Kraemer, M. J., & Bierman, C. W. (1983). Asthma. In J. Umbreit (Ed.), *Physical disabilities and health impairments* (pp. 159–166). Columbus, OH: Merrill.

Krauss, M. W. (1990). New precedent in family policy: Individualized Family Service Plan. *Exceptional Children, 56,* 388–395.

Kregel, J., Hill, M., & Banks, P. D. (1988). Analysis of employment specialist intervention time in supported competitive employment. *American Journal on Mental Retardation, 93,* 200–208.

Kregel, J., & Wehman, P. (in press). Supported employment for persons with severe handicaps: Promises deferred. *The Journal of The Association for Persons with Severe Handicaps.*

Kregel, J., Wehman, P., & Banks, P. D. (1989). The effects of consumer characteristics and type of employment model on individual outcomes in supported employment. *Journal of Applied Behavior Analysis, 22,* 407–415.

Krim, M. (1969). Scientific research and mental retardation. *President's Committee on Mental Retardation message* (No. 16). Washington, DC: U.S. Government Printing Office.

Kronick, D. (1969). *They too can succeed: A practical guide for parents of learning-disabled children.* San Rafael, CA: Academic Therapy.

Kroth, R. L. (1978). Parents: Powerful and necessary allies. *Teaching Exceptional Children, 10,* 88–90.

Kroth, R. L. (1981). Involvement with parents of behaviorally disordered adolescents. In G. Brown, R. L. McDowell, & J. Smith (Eds.), *Educating adolescents with behavior disorders* (pp. 123–139). Columbus. OH: Merrill.

Kroth, R. L. (1985). *Communicating with parents of exceptional children* (2nd ed.). Denver: Love.

Kubler-Ross, E. (1969). *On death and dying.* New York: Macmillan.

Kugel, R. B., & Wolfensberger, W. (Eds.). (1969). *Changing patterns in residential services for the mentally retarded.* Washington, DC: Superintendent of Documents.

Kuhlman, F. (1924). Mental deficiency, feeble-mindedness, and defective delinquency. *American Association for the Study of the Feeble-Minded, 29,* 58–70.

Kudrjavcev, T., Schoenberg, B. S., Kurland, L. T., et al. (1983). Cerebral palsy—trends in incidence and changes in concurrent neonatal mortality: Rochester, MN, 1950–1976. *Neurology, 33,* 1433–1438.

Kurtz, G., & Kurtz, P. D. (1987). Child abuse and neglect. In J. T. Neisworth & S. J. Bagnato, *The young exceptional child: Early development and education* (pp. 206–229). New York: Macmillan.

Labov, W. (1975). The logic of nonstandard English. In P. Stoller (Ed.), *Black American English: Its background and its usage in the schools and in literature.* New York: Dell.

Lagomarcino, A., Reid, D. H., Ivancic, M. T., & Faw, G. D. (1984). Leisure-dance instruction for severely and profoundly retarded persons: Teaching an intermediate community-living skill. *Journal of Applied Behavior Analysis, 17,* 71–84.

Lagomarcino, T. R., Hughes, C., & Rusch, F. R. (1989). Utilizing self-management to teach independence on the job. *Education and Training of the Mentally Retarded, 24,* 139–148.

LaGrow, S. J., & Mulder, L. (1989). Structured solicitation: A standardized method for gaining travel information. *Journal of Visual Impairment and Blindness, 83,* 469–471.

Lahey, M. (1988). *Language disorders and language development.* New York: Macmillan.

Lakin, K. C., Hill, B. K., & Bruininks, R. H. (Eds.). (1985). *An analysis of Medicaid's Intermediate Care Facility for the Mentally Retarded (ICF-MR) program.* Minneapolis: University of Minnesota, Center for Residential and Community Services.

Lakin, K. C., Hill, B. K., Chen, T., & Stephens, S. A. (1989). *Persons with mental retardation and related conditions in mental retardation facilities: Selected findings for the 1987*

National Medical Expenditure Survey. Minneapolis: University of Minnesota, Center for Residential and Community Services.

Lambert, N. M., & Windmiller, M. (1981). *AAMD adaptive behavior scale, School edition*. Monterey, CA: Publishers Test Service.

Lancaster, J. (1806). *Improvement in education*. London: Collins & Perkins.

Landesman, S. (1986). Quality of life and personal life satisfaction: Definition and measurement issues. *Mental Retardation, 24,* 141–143.

Lane, H. L. (1988). Is there a "psychology of the deaf"? *Exceptional Children, 55,* 7–19.

Lang, H. (1989). Academic development and preparation for work. In M. Wang, M. Reynolds, & H. Walberg (Eds.), *The handbook of special education: Research and practice* (Vol. 3) (pp. 71–93). Oxford, England: Pergamon Press.

Lang, H., & Propp, G. (1982). Science education for hearing-impaired students: State of the art. *American Annals of the Deaf, 127,* 860–869.

Larson, S. A., & Lakin, K. C. (1989). Deinstitutionalization of persons with mental retardation. *The Journal of The Association for Persons with Severe Handicaps, 14,* 324–332.

LaVigna, G. W., & Donnellan, A. M. (1987). *Alternatives to punishment: Solving behavior problems with nonaversive strategies*. Los Angeles: Institute for Applied Behavior Analysis.

Lazar, I., & Darlington, R. (1982). Lasting effects of early education: A report from the consortium for longitudinal studies. *Monographs of the Society for Research in Child Development, 47*(2 & 3, Serial No. 195).

Leonard, L. B. (1982). Early language development and language disorders. In G. H. Shames & E. H. Wiig (Eds.), *Human communication disorders: An introduction* (pp. 291–330). Columbus, OH: Merrill.

Leonard, L. B. (1986). Conversational replies of children with specific language impairments. *Journal of Speech and Hearing Research, 29,* 114–119.

Leone, P., Lovitt, T. C., & Hansen, C. (1981). A descriptive follow-up study of learning disabled boys. *Learning Disability Quarterly, 4,* 152–162.

Lerner, J. (1976). *Children with learning disabilities* (2nd ed.). Boston: Houghton Mifflin.

Leung, E. K. (1988). Cultural and acultural commonalities and diversities among Asian Americans: Identification and programming considerations. In A. A. Ortiz & B. A. Ramirez (Eds.), *Schools and the culturally diverse exceptional student: Promising practices and future directions* (pp. 86–95). Reston, VA: Council for Exceptional Children.

Levin, J., & Scherfenberg, L. (1987). *Selection and use of simple technology in home, school, work, and community settings*. Minneapolis, MN: ABLENET.

Levine, M. N. (1986). Psychoeducational evaluation of children and adolescents with cerebral palsy. In P. J. Lazarus & S. S. Strichart (Eds.), *Psychoeducational evaluation of children and adolescents with low-incidence handicaps* (pp. 267–284). Orlando, FL: Grune & Stratton.

Levitt, E. E. (1957). The results of psychotherapy with children: An evaluation. *Journal of Consulting Psychology, 21,* 189–196.

Levitt, E. E. (1963). Psychotherapy with children: A further evaluation. *Behavior Research and Therapy, 1,* 45–51.

Levitt, H. (1985). Technology and the education of the hearing impaired. In F. Powell, T. Finitzo-Hieber, S. Friel-Patti, & D. Henderson (Eds.), *Education of the hearing impaired child* (pp. 119–129). San Diego: College-Hill.

Lewis, R. B., & Doorlag, D. H. (1991). *Teaching special students in the mainstream* (3rd ed.). Columbus, OH: Merrill.

Liebergott, J., Favors, A., von Hippel, C. S., & Needleman, H. L. (1978). *Mainstreaming preschoolers: Children with speech and language impairments*. (Stock No. 017-092-00033-2). Washington, DC: U.S. Government Printing Office.

Lieberman, L. M. (1982). The nightmare of scheduling. *Journal of Learning Disabilities, 15,* 57–58.

Lieberman, L. M. (1985). Special education and regular education: A merger made in heaven? *Exceptional Children, 51,* 513–516.

Lignugaris/Kraft, B., Rule, S., Salzberg, C. L., & Stowitschek, J. J. (1988). Social-vocational skills of handicapped and nonhandicapped adults at work. *Journal of Employment Counseling, 23,* 20–31.

Likins, M., Salzberg, C. L., Stowitschek, J. J., Lignugaris/Kraft, R., & Curl, R. (1989). Co-worker implemented job training: The use of coincidental training and quality-control checking on the food preparation skills of trainees with mental retardation. *Journal of Applied Behavior Analysis, 22,* 381–393.

Lilly, M. S. (1986). The relationship between general and specific education: A new face on an old issue. *Counterpoint, 6*(1), 10.

Lindfors, J. W. (1987). *Children's language and learning* (2nd ed.). Englewood Cliffs, NJ: Prentice-Hall.

Lindley, L. (1990, August). Defining TASH: A mission statement. *TASH Newsletter, 16*(8), 1.

Lindman, F. T., & McIntyre, J. M. (1961). *The mentally disabled and the law*. Chicago: University of Chicago Press.

Linebaugh, C. W. (1986). Mild aphasia. In J. M. Costello & A. L. Holland (Eds.), *Handbook of speech and language disorders* (pp. 871–889). San Diego: College-Hill.

Ling, D. (1976). *Speech and the hearing-impaired child: Theory and practice*. Washington, DC: The Alexander Graham Bell Association for the Deaf.

Ling, D. (Ed.). (1984). *Early intervention for hearing-impaired children: Total communication options*. San Diego: College-Hill.

Ling, D. (1986). Devices and procedures for auditory learning. *The Volta Review, 88*(5), 19–28.

Lingwell, J. (1982, July 15). Remarks quoted in M. Kelly, Parent's Almanac: Early Stutterers. *Washington Post,* p. D5.

Little Soldier, L. (1990). The education of Native American students: Where makes a difference. *Equity & Excellence, 24*(4), 66–69.

Livingston-White, D., Utter, C., & Woodard, Q. E. (1985). Follow-up study of visually impaired students of the Michigan School for the Blind. *Journal of Visual Impairment and Blindness, 79,* 150–153.

Lloyd, J. W., Kauffman, J. M., & Gansneder, B. (1987). Differential teacher response to descriptions of aberrant behavior. In R. B. Rutherford, C. M. Nelson, & S. R. Forness (Eds.), *Severe behavior disorders of children and youth* (pp. 41–52). Boston: College Hill Press.

Lloyd, L., Spradlin, J., & Reid, M. (1968). An operant audiometric procedure for difficult-to-test patients. *Journal of Speech and Hearing Disorders, 33,* 236–245.

Long, N. (1990). Comment on Ralph Gardner's article on life-space interviewing. *Behavioral Disorders, 15,* 119–125.

Lotter, V. (1966). Epidemiology of autistic conditions in young children—Part 1: Prevalence. *Social Psychiatry, 1*(3), 124–137.

Lovaas, I. O. (1987). Behavioral treatment and normal educational and intellectual functioning in young autistic children. *Journal of Consulting and Clinical Psychology, 55,* 3–9.

Lovaas, O. I., Koegel, R. L., Simmons, J. Q., & Long, J. S. (1973). Some generalization and follow-up measures on autistic children in behavior therapy. *Journal of Applied Behavior Analysis, 6,* 131–166.

Lovaas, O. I., & Newsom, C. D. (1976). Behavior modification with psychotic children. In H. Leitenberg (Ed.), *Handbook of behavior modification and behavior therapy* (pp. 303–360). Englewood Cliffs, NJ: Prentice-Hall.

Lovitt, T. C. (1975a). Applied behavior analysis and learning disabilities—Part I: Characteristics of ABA, general recommendations and suggestions for practitioners. *Journal of Learning Disabilities, 8,* 432–443.

Lovitt, T. C. (1975b). Applied behavior analysis and learning disabilities—Part II: Specific research recommendations and suggestions for practitioners. *Journal of Learning Disabilities, 8,* 504–518.

Lovitt, T. C. (1977). *In spite of my resistance . . . I've learned from children.* Columbus, OH: Merrill.

Lovitt, T. C. (1978). The learning disabled. In N. G. Haring (Ed.), *Behavior of exceptional children* (2nd ed.) (pp. 155–191). Columbus, OH: Merrill.

Lovitt, T. C. (1979). What should we call them? *Exceptional Teacher, 1*(1), 5–7.

Lovitt, T. C. (1982). *Because of my persistence . . . I've learned from children.* Columbus, OH: Merrill.

Lovitt, T. C. (1984). *Tactics for teaching.* Columbus, OH: Merrill.

Lovitt, T. C. (1986). Oh! That this too too solid flesh would melt . . . the erosion of standardized tests. *The Pointer, 30*(2), 55–57.

Lovitt, T. C. (1989). *Introduction to learning disabilities.* Boston: Allyn & Bacon.

Lowell, E. L., & Pollack, D. B. (1974). Remedial practices with the hearing impaired. In S. Dickson (Ed.), *Communication disorders: Remedial principles and practices.* Glenview, IL: Scott, Foresman.

Lowenfeld, B. (Ed.). (1973). *The visually handicapped child in school.* New York: John Day.

Lowenthal, B. (1981). Effect of small-group instruction on language-delayed preschoolers. *Exceptional Children, 48,* 178–179.

Lucey, J., & Dangman, B. (1984). A reexamination of the role of oxygen in retrolental fibroplasia. *Pediatrics, 73,* 82–96.

Ludlow, B. L., & Sobsey, R. (1984). *The school's role in educating severely handicapped students.* Bloomington, IN: Phi Delta Kappa Educational Foundation.

Lund, K. A., & Bos, C. S. (1981). Orchestrating the preschool classroom: The daily schedule. *Teaching Exceptional Children, 14,* 120–125.

Lund, K. A., Foster, G. E., & McCall-Perez, F. C. (1978). The effectiveness of psycholinguistic training: A reevaluation. *Exceptional Children, 44,* 310–319.

Lusthaus, C. S., Lusthaus, E. W., & Gibbs, H. (1981). Parents' role in the decision process. *Exceptional Children, 48,* 256–257.

Luterman, D. M. (Ed.). (1986). *Deafness in perspective.* San Diego: College-Hill.

Lynas, W. (1986). *Integrating the handicapped into ordinary schools: A study of hearing-impaired pupils.* London: Croom Helm.

Lynch, E. W., & Stein, R. (1982). Perspectives on parent participation in special education. *Exceptional Education Quarterly, 3*(2), 56–63.

M.C.E., Inc. (1988). *Be a winner: Set your goals.* Kalamazoo, MI: Microcomputer Education.

MacCarthy, A., & Connell, J. (1984). Audiological screening and assessment. In G. Lindsay (Ed.), *Screening for children with special needs* (pp. 63–85). London: Croom Helm.

MacDonald, L., & Barton, L. E. (1986). Measuring severity of behavior: A revision of Part II of the Adaptive Behavior Scale. *American Journal of Mental Deficiency, 90,* 418–424.

MacFadyen, J. T. (1986). Educated monkeys help the disabled to help themselves. *Smithsonian, 17*(7), 125–133.

Mack, J. H. (1980). *An analysis of state definitions of severely emotionally disturbed.* Reston, VA: Council for Exceptional Children. (ERIC Document Reproduction Service No. ED 201 135)

Macmann, G. M., Barnett, D. W., Lonbard, T. J., Belton-Kocher, E., & Sharpe, M. N. (1989). On the actuarial classification of children: Fundamental studies of classification agreement. *The Journal of Special Education, 23,* 127–149.

MacMillan, D., Jones, R., & Aloia, G. (1974). The mentally retarded label: A theoretical analysis and review of the literature. *American Journal on Mental Retardation, 79,* 241–261.

MacMillan, D. L. (1982). *Mental retardation in school and society* (2nd ed.). Boston: Little, Brown.

MacMillan, D. L. (1989). Mild mental retardation: Emerging issues. In G. A. Robinson, J. R. Patton, E. A. Polloway, & L. R. Sargent (Eds.), *Best practices in mild mental disabilities* (pp. 3–20). Reston, VA: Council for Exceptional Children.

Maddux, C. D., & Cummings, R. E. (1983). Parental home tutoring: Aids and cautions. *The Exceptional Parent, 13*(4), 30–33.

Madle, R. A. (1978). Alternative residential placements. In J. T. Neisworth & R. M. Smith (Eds.), *Retardation: Issues, assessment, and intervention*. New York: McGraw-Hill.

Maestas y Moores, J., & Moores, D. F. (1980). Language training with the young deaf child. In D. Bricker (Ed.), *Early language intervention with handicapped children*. San Francisco: Jossey-Bass.

Maheady, L., Sacca, M. K., & Harper, G. F. (1987). Classwide student tutoring teams: The effects of peer-mediated instruction on the academic performance of secondary mainstreamed students. *The Journal of Special Education, 21,* 107–121.

Maheady, L., Sacca, M. K., & Harper, G. F. (1988). Classwide peer tutoring with mildly handicapped high school students. *Exceptional Children, 55,* 52–59.

Maheady, L., & Sainato, D. M. (1985). The effects of peer tutoring upon the social status and social interaction patterns of high and low status elementary school students. *Education & Treatment of Children, 8,* 51–65.

Maker, C. J. (1977). *Providing programs for the gifted handicapped*. Reston, VA: Council for Exceptional Children.

Maker, C. J. (1982). Teaching models in education of the gifted. Rockville, MD: Aspen.

Maker, C. J. (1989). Programs for gifted minority students: A synthesis of perspectives. In C. J. Maker & S. W. Schiever (Eds.), *Critical issues in gifted education: Defensible programs for cultural and ethnic minorities, Vol. II*. (pp.). Austin, TX: PRO-ED.

Maker, C. J., & Schiever, S. W. (Eds.). (1989). *Critical issues in gifted education: Defensible programs for cultural and ethnic minorities, Vol. II,*. Austin, TX: PRO-ED.

Malone, C. (Ed.). (1978). Disadvantaged and gifted handicapped. *Gifted Child Quarterly, 22*(3).

Mangrum, C. T., & Strichart, S. S. (1988). *College and the learning disabled student* (2nd ed.). Philadelphia: Grune & Stratton.

Manning, A. L., & Wray, D. (1990). Using figurative language in the classroom. *Teaching Exceptional Children, 22*(4), 18–21.

Mansour, S. L. (1985). 1985 ASHA demographic update. *ASHA, 27*(7), 55.

Marbach, W. D. (1982, July 12). Building the bionic man. *Newsweek,* pp. 78–79.

Marfo, K. (1986). Confronting childhood disability in the developing countries. In K. Marfo, S. Walker, & B. Charles (Eds.), *Childhood disability in developing countries: Issues in habilitation and special education* (pp. 3–26). New York: Praeger.

Margolis, L. H., & Meisels, S. J. (1987). Barriers to the effectiveness of EPSDT for children with moderate and severe developmental disabilities. *American Journal of Orthopsychiatry, 57,* 424–430.

Marland, S. P. (1971). *Education of the gifted and talented*. Washington, DC: U.S. Office of Education.

Marshall, A. E., & Heward, W. L. (1979). Teaching self-management to incarcerated youth. *Behavioral Disorders, 4,* 215–226.

Martin, B. (1975). Parent-child relations. In F. D. Horowitz (Ed.), *Review of child development research* (Vol. 4) (pp. 463–540). Chicago: University of Chicago Press.

Martin, J. E., Mithaug, D. W., Agran, M., & Husch, J. V. (in press). Consumer-centered transition and supported employment. In J. L. Matson (Ed.), *Handbook of behavior modification with the mentally retarded* (2nd ed.). New York: Plenum Press.

Martin, R. R., & Lindamood, L. P. (1986). Stuttering and spontaneous recovery: Implications for the speech-language pathologist. *Language, Speech, and Hearing Services in the Schools, 17,* 207–218.

Mastropieri, M. A., Jenne, T., & Scruggs, T. E. (1988). A level system for managing problem behaviors in a high school resource program. *Behavioral Disorders, 13,* 202–208.

Mattes, L. J., & Omark, D. R. (1984). *Speech and language assessment for the bilingual handicapped*. San Diego: College-Hill.

Mayer-Johnson, R. (1986). *The Picture Communications Symbols* (Book 1). Solana Beach, CA: Mayer-Johnson Co.

Mayhall, W., & Jenkins. J. (1977). Scheduling daily or less-than-daily instruction: Implications for resource programs. *Journal of Learning Disabilities, 10,* 150–163.

Mayo, L. W. (1962). A proposed program for national action to combat mental retardation. *Report of the President's Committee on Mental Retardation*. Washington, DC: U.S. Government Printing Office.

McCollum, J. A., & Hughes, M. (1988). Staffing patterns and team models in infancy programs. In J. B. Jordon, J. J. Gallagher, P. L. Hutinger, & M. B. Karnes (Eds.), *Early childhood special education: Birth to three* (pp. 129–146). Reston, VA: Council for Exceptional Children.

McCollum, J. A., McLean, M., McCartan, K., & Kaiser, C. (1989). DEC White Paper: Recommendations for certification of early childhood special educators. *Journal of Early Intervention, 13,* 195–211.

McCormick, L., & Schiefelbusch, R. L. (1990). *Early language intervention: An introduction* (2nd ed.). Columbus, OH: Merrill.

McCracken, K. (1987, October 5). 85 at TSD suspended in sign language dispute. *Knoxville Journal,* pp. 1, 10.

McDonald, D. (1989). A special report of the education of Native Americans: "Stuck in the horizon" [Special Report insert]. *Education Week, 7*(4), 1–16.

McDonald, E. T. (1980). *Using and teaching Blissymbolics*. Toronto: Blissymbolics Communication Institute.

McDonnell, A., & Hardman, M. (1988). A synthesis of "best practice" guidelines for early childhood services. *Journal of Early Intervention, 12,* 328–341.

McDonnell, J. J., Hardman, M. L., & Hightower, J. (1989). Employment preparation for high school students with severe handicaps. *Mental Retardation, 27,* 396–405.

McDonnell, J. J., Wilcox, B., Boles, S. M., & Bellamy, G. T. (1985). Transition issues facing youth with severe disabilities: Parent's perspective. *The Journal of The Association for Per-*

sons with Severe Handicaps, 10, 61–65.

McGreevy, P. (1983). *Teaching and learning plain English* (2nd. ed.). Sarasota, FL: Precision Teaching Materials and Associates.

McIntire, J. C. (1985). The future role of residential schools for visually impaired students. *Journal of Visual Impairment and Blindness, 79,* 161–164.

McKee, M., da Cunha, K., Echols, L., Starr, C., Naskrent, D., & Urbanovsky, J. (1983). *Occupational and physical therapy services in school-based programs: Organizational manual.* Houston, TX: Psychological Services Division, Harris County Department of Education.

McKinney, J. D. (1985). The search for subtypes of specific learning disability. *Annual Progress in Child Psychiatry & Child Development,* 542–559.

McLaughlin, M. J., Smith-Davis, J., & Burke, P. J. (1986). *Personnel to educate the handicapped in America: A status report.* College Park, MD: University of Maryland, Institute for the Study of Exceptional Children and Youth.

McLaven, J., & Bryson, S. E. (1987). Review of recent epidemiological studies of mental retardation: Prevalence, associated disorders and etiology. *American Journal on Mental Retardation, 92,* 243–254.

McLean, J. E., & Snyder-McLean, L. K. (1978). *A transactional approach to early language training.* Columbus, OH: Merrill.

McLoughlin, J. A., & Kelly, D. (1982). Issues facing the resource teacher. *Learning Disability Quarterly, 5,* 58–64.

McLoughlin, J. A., & Lewis, R. B. (1990). *Assessing special students* (3rd ed.). Columbus, OH: Merrill.

McNutt, G., & Heller, G. (1978). Services for the learning disabled adolescent: A survey. *Learning Disability Quarterly, 1,* 101–103.

McReynolds, L. V. (1990). Articulation and phonological disorders. In G. H. Shames & E. H. Wiig, (Eds.), *Human communication disorders* (3rd ed.) (pp. 30–73). Columbus, OH: Merrill.

Meadow, K. P. (1980). *Deafness and child development.* Berkeley, CA: University of California Press.

Meadow-Orlans, K. P. (1985). Social and psychological effects of hearing loss in adulthood: A literature review. In H. Orlans (Ed.), *Adjustment to adult hearing loss* (pp. 35–57). San Diego: College-Hill.

Meehl, P. (1969). Schizotoxia, schizotypy, schizophrenia. In A. Buss (Ed.), *Theories of schizophrenia.* New York: Atherton.

Meeker, M. N. (1969). *The structure of intellect: Its interpretation and uses.* Columbus, OH: Merrill.

Meisels, S. J. (1989). *Developmental screening in early childhood: A guide* (3rd ed.). Washington, DC: National Association for the Education of Young Children.

Meisels, S. J., & Provence, S. (1989). *Screening and assessment: Guidelines for identifying young disabled and developmentally vulnerable children and their families.* Washington, DC: National Center for Clinical Infant Programs.

Mendelsohn, S. R., & Jennings, K. D. (1986). Characteristics of emotionally disturbed children referred for special education assessment. *Child Psychiatry & Human Development, 16,* 154–170.

Menolascino, F. J., & Eyde, D. R. (1979). Biophysical bases of autism. *Behavioral Disorders, 5,* 41–47.

Menolascino, F. L. (1977). *Challenges in mental retardation: Progressive ideology and sources.* New York: Human Services Press.

Mercer, C. D. (1987). *Students with learning disabilities* (3rd ed.). Columbus, OH: Merrill.

Mercer, C. D., King-Sears, P., & Mercer, A. R. (1990). Learning disabilities definitions and criteria used by state education departments. *Learning Disability Quarterly, 13,* 141–152.

Mercer, C. D., & Mercer, A. R. (1989). *Teaching students with learning problems* (3rd ed.). Columbus, OH: Merrill.

Mercer, J. R. (1973a). *Labelling the mentally retarded.* Berkeley, CA: University of California Press.

Mercer, J. R. (1973b). The myth of 3% prevalence. In R. K. Eymon, C. E.

Meyers, & G. Tarjon (Eds.), Sociobehavioral studies in mental retardation, (pp. 1–18). *American Association on Mental Deficiency, No. 1.*

Mercer, J. R. (1981). Testing and assessment practices in multiethnic education. In J. A. Banks (Ed.), *Education in the 80's: Multiethnic education* (pp. 93–104). Washington, DC: National Education Association.

Mesinger, J. F. (1985). Commentary on "A rationale for the merger of special and regular education" or, is it now time for the lamb to lie down with the lion? *Exceptional Children, 51,* 510–512.

Meyen, E. L. (Ed.). (1978). *Exceptional children and youth: An introduction.* Denver: Love.

Meyer, L. H. (1986, June). Creating options and making choices. *TASH Newsletter,* p. 1.

Meyer, L. H., Cole, D. A., McQuarter, R., & Reichle, J. (1990). Validation of the Assessment of Social Competence (ASC) for children and young adults with developmental disabilities. *The Journal of The Association for Persons with Severe Handicaps, 15,* 57–68.

Meyer, L. H., & Evans, I. M. (1989). *Nonaversive intervention for behavior problems: A manual for home and community.* Baltimore, MD: Paul H. Brookes.

Miller, A. D., Hall, S., & Heward, W. L. (1991). *Effects of sequential 1-minute time trials, with and without inter-trial feedback, on regular and special education students' fluency with math facts.* Manuscript submitted for publication.

Miller, A. D., & Heward, W. L. (in press). Do your students *really* know their math facts? Using daily time trials to build fluency. *Intervention in School and Clinic.*

Miller, D. (1979). *Ophthalmology: The essentials.* Boston: Houghton Mifflin.

Miller, J., & Pfingst, B. (1984). Cochlear implants. In C. Berlin (Ed.), *Hearing science* (pp. 309–339). San Diego: College-Hill.

Miller, W. (1989, July). *Obstetrical issues.* Paper presented at Conference on Drugs, Alcohol, Pregnancy and Parenting: An Intervention Model, Spokane, WA.

Miller, W. H. (1985). The role of residential schools for the blind in educating visually impaired students. *Journal of Visual Impairment and Blindness, 79,* 160.

Milner, J. S., & Wimberley, R. C. (1980). Prediction and explanation of child abuse. *Journal of Clinical Psychology, 36,* 875–884.

Minner, S., Beane, A., & Prater, G. (1986). Try telephone answering machines. *Teaching Exceptional Children, 19*(1), 62–63.

Minskoff, E. (1975). Research on psycholinguistic training: Critique and guidelines. *Exceptional Children, 42,* 136–144.

Mitchell, B. (1982). An update on the state of gifted/talented education in the U.S. *Phi Delta Kappan, 64,* 357–358.

Mitchell, D. C. (1983). Spina bifida. In J. Umbreit (Ed.), *Physical disabilities and health impairments: An introduction* (pp. 117–131). Columbus, OH: Merrill.

Mitchell, J. V. (Ed.). (1985). *The ninth mental measurements yearbook.* Lincoln, NE: University of Nebraska Press.

Mitchell, P. B. (Ed.). (1981). *A policymaker's guide to issues in gifted and talented education.* Washington, DC: National Association of State Boards of Education.

Mithaug, D. E., Horiuchi, C. N., & Fanning, P. N. (1985). A report on the Colorado statewide follow-up survey of special education students. *Exceptional Children, 51,* 397–404.

Mithaug, D. W., Martin, J. E., & Agran, M. (1987). Adaptability instruction: The goal of transitional programming. *Exceptional Children, 53,* 500–505.

Mithaug, D. W., Martin, J. E., Agran, M., & Rusch, F. R. (1988). *Why special education graduates fail: How to teach them to succeed.* Colorado Springs, CO: Ascent.

Montgomery, P. A., & Van Fleet, D. (1978). Evaluation of behavioral and academic change through the Re-Ed process. *Behavioral Disorders, 3,* 136–146.

Moon, M. S., & Bunker, L. (1987). Recreation and motor skills programming. In M. E. Snell (Ed.), *Systematic instruction of persons with severe handicaps* (3rd ed.) (pp. 214–244). Columbus, OH: Merrill.

Moore, P. (1982). Voice disorders. In G. H. Shames & E. H. Wiig (Eds.), *Human communication disorders: An introduction* (pp. 183–241). Columbus, OH: Merrill.

Moores, D. F. (1985). Educational programs and services for hearing impaired children: Issues and options. In F. Powell, T. Finitzo-Hieber, S. Friel-Patti, & D. Henderson (Eds.), *Education of the hearing impaired child* (pp. 3–20). San Diego: College-Hill.

Moores, D. F. (1987). *Educating the deaf: Psychology, principles, and practices* (3rd ed.). Boston: Houghton Mifflin.

Moores, D. F., & Kluwin, T. N. (1986). Issues in school placement. In A. N. Schildroth & M. A. Karchmer (Eds.), *Deaf children in America* (pp. 105–123). San Diego: College-Hill.

Moores, D. F., & Maestas y Moores, J. (1981). Special adaptations necessitated by hearing impairments. In J. M. Kauffman & D. P. Hallahan (Eds.), *Handbook of special education.* Englewood Cliffs, NJ: Prentice-Hall.

Morgan, S. R. (1987). *Abuse and neglect of handicapped children.* San Diego: College-Hill.

Morse, W. C. (1975). The education of socially maladjusted and emotionally disturbed children. In W. M. Cruickshank & G. O. Johnson (Eds.), *Education of exceptional children and youth* (3rd ed.) (pp. 557–608). Englewood Cliffs, NJ: Prentice-Hall.

Morse, W. C. (1976). Worksheet on life-space interviewing for teachers. In N. Long, W. Morse, & R. Newman (Eds.), *Conflict in the classroom* (pp. 337–341). Belmont, CA: Wadsworth Publishing.

Morse, W. C. (1985). *The education and treatment of socioemotionally impaired children and youth.* Syracuse, NY: Syracuse University Press.

Morse, W. C., Cutler, R. L., & Fink, A. H. (1964). *Public school classes for the emotionally handicapped: A research analysis.* Washington, DC: Council for Exceptional Children.

Morsink, C. V., Thomas, C. C., & Smith-Davis, J. (1987). Noncategorical special education programs: Process and outcomes. In M. C. Wang, M. C. Reynolds, & H. J. Walberg (Eds.), *The handbook of special education: Research and practice* (pp. 287–311). Oxford, England: Pergamon Press.

Mow, S. (1973). How do you dance without music? In D. Watson (Ed.), *Readings on deafness* (pp. 20–30). New York: New York University School of Education, Deafness Research and Training Center.

Moyer, J. R., & Dardig, J. C. (1978). Practical task analysis for special educators. *Teaching Exceptional Children, 11*(1), 1–16.

Mullins, J. B. (1979). *A teacher's guide to management of physically handicapped students.* Springfield, IL: Charles C. Thomas.

Murray, J. (1990). Best practices in working with parents of handicapped children. In A. Thomas & J. Grimes (Eds.), *Best practices in school psychology—II* (pp. 823–836). Washington, DC: National Association of School Psychologists.

Myers, P. I., & Hammill, D. D. (1990). *Learning disabilities: Basic concepts, assessment practices, and instructional strategies* (3rd ed.). Austin, TX: PRO-ED.

Nagel, D., Schumaker, J. B., & Deshler, D. D. (1986). *The learning strategies curriculum: The FIRST-letter mnemonic strategy.* Lawrence, KS: Excel Enterprises.

Naisbitt, J., & Aburdene, P. (1990). *Megatrends 2000: Ten new directions for the 1990's.* New York: William Morrow.

Napierkowski, H. (1981). The role of language in the intellectual development of the deaf child. *Teaching Exceptional Children, 14,* 106–109.

National Center for Education Statistics. (1989). *Digest of education statistics, 1989.* Washington, DC: U.S. Department of Education, Office of Research and Improvement.

National Center for Health Statistics. (1975). *Prevalence of selected impairments: United States—1971.* (Publication No. [HRA] 75-1526). Washington, DC: Department of Health, Education and Welfare.

National Center for Health Statistics. (1981). *Prevalence of selected impairments: United States—1977.* (Publication No. [PHS] 82-1562). Washington, DC: Department of Health, Education and Welfare.

National Coalition for Cultural Pluralism. (1973). In M. Stent, W. Hazard, & N. Rivlin (Eds.), *Cultural pluralism in education: A mandate for change* (pp. 149–150). New York: Appleton-Century-Crofts.

National Committee for Citizens in Education. (1979). Unpublished manuscript serving as basis for congressional testimony.

National Hotel and Restaurant Association. (1983). Personal communication with Dr. Philip Nelen, Washington, DC.

National Joint Committee on Learning Disabilities (1989, September 18). *Letter from NJCLD to member organizations.* Topic: Modifications to the NJCLD definition of learning disabilities.

National Society for Autistic Children. (1977, September). A short definition of autism. *Newsletter.*

Neef, N. A., Parrish, J. M., Hannigan, K. F., Page, T. J., & Iwata, B. A. (1989). Teaching self-catheterization skills to children with neurogenic bladder complications. *Journal of Applied Behavior Analysis, 22,* 237–243.

Neisworth, J. T., & Smith, R. M. (Eds.). (1978). *Retardation: Issues, assessment, and intervention.* New York: McGraw-Hill.

Nelson, C. M., & Polsgrove, L. (1984). Behavior analysis in special education: White rabbit or white elephant? *Remedial and Special Education, 5*(4), 6–17.

Nelson, C. M., Rutherford, R. B., Jr., & Wolford, B. I. (1987). *Special education in the criminal justice system.* Columbus, OH: Merrill.

Nelson, K. B., & Ellenberg, J.H. (1986). Antecedents of cerebral palsy: Multivariate analysis of risk. *New England Journal of Medicine, 315,* 81–86.

Nelson, R., & Lignugaris/Kraft, B. (1989). Postsecondary education for students with learning disabilities. *Exceptional Children, 56,* 246–265.

Nevin, A., McCann, S., & Semmel, M. I. (1983). An empirical analysis of the regular classroom teacher's role in implementing IEP's. *Teacher Education and Special Education, 6,* 235–246.

Newborg, J., Stock, J., Wnek, J., Guibaldi, J., & Suinicki, J. (1984). *Battelle Developmental Inventory Screening Test.* Allen, TX: DLM Teaching Resources.

Newell, F. (1982). Retrolental fibroplasia. *American Journal of Ophthalmology, 94,* 552–554.

Nietupski, J., Schutz, G., & Ockwood, L. (1980). The delivery of communication therapy services to severely handicapped students: A plan for change. *The Journal of The Association for Persons with Severe Handicaps, 5,* 13–23.

Nietupski, J., & Svoboda, R. (1982). Teaching a cooperative leisure skill to severely handicapped adults. *Education and Training of the Mentally Retarded, 17,* 38–43.

Nihira, K., Foster, R., Shellhaas, M., & Leland, H. (1974). *AAMD Adaptive Behavior Scale* (1974 rev.). Washington, DC: American Association on Mental Deficiency.

Nisbet, J., & Hagner, D. (1988). Natural supports in the workplace: A reexamination of supported employment. *The Journal of The Association for Persons with Severe Handicaps, 13,* 260–267.

Nisbet, J., & Vincent, L. (1986). The differences in inappropriate behavior and instructional interactions in sheltered and nonsheltered work environments. *The Journal of The Association for Persons with Severe Handicaps, 11,* 19–27.

Noonan, M. J., Brown, F., Mulligan, M., & Rettig, M. A. (1982). Educability of severely handicapped persons: Both sides of the issue. *The Journal of The Association for the Severely Handicapped, 7*(1), 3–12.

Norman, C. A., & Zigmond, N. (1980). Characteristics of children labeled and served as learning disabled in school systems affiliated with Child Service Demonstration centers. *Journal of Learning Disabilities, 13,* 542–547.

Norris, C. (Ed.). (1975). *Letters from deaf students.* Eureka, CA: Alinda Press.

Northcott, W. H., & Erickson, L. C. (1977). *The UNISTAPS Project.* St. Paul: Minnesota Department of Education.

Northern, J. L., & Lemme, M. (1982). Hearing and auditory disorders. In G. H. Shames & E. H. Wiig (Eds.), *Human communication disorders: An introduction.* Columbus, OH: Merrill.

Norton, D. G. (1983). Black family life patterns, the development of self and cognitive development of black children. In G. J. Powell (Ed.), *The psychosocial development of minority group children* (pp. 181–193). New York: Brunner/Mazel.

Not disabled—just deaf. (1991). *Let's Talk, 33*(2), 30.

Notari, A. R., & Bricker, D. D. (1990). The utility of a curriculum-based assessment instrument in the development of Individualized Education Plans for infants and young children. *Journal of Early Intervention, 14,* 117–132.

Nurss, J. R., & McGauvran, M. E. (1986). Metropolitan Readiness Test. Cleveland, OH: Psychological Corp.

Oakland, T. (1980). An evaluation of the ABIE, pluristic norms, and estimated learning potential. *Journal of School Psychology, 18,* 3–11.

O'Brien, J. (1971). How we detect mental retardation before birth. *Medical Times, 99,* 103.

O'Brien, J. (1987). A guide to life-style planning: Using the activity catalog to integrate services and natural life support systems. In B. Wilcox & G. T. Bellamy (Eds.), *A comprehensive guide to the activities catalog: An alternative curriculum for youth and adults with severe disabilities* (pp. 175–189). Baltimore, MD: Paul H. Brookes.

O'Connell, J. C. (1986). Managing small group instruction in an integrated preschool setting. *Teaching Exceptional Children, 18,* 166–171.

O'Conner, G. (1983). Presidential address 1983: Social support of mentally retarded persons. *Mental Retardation, 21,* 187–196.

Odom, S. L., & Karnes, M. B. (Eds.). (1988). *Early intervention for infants and children with handicaps: An* empirical base. Baltimore, MD: Paul H. Brookes.

Office of Technology Assessment. (1987). *Technology-dependent children: Hospital v. home care—A technical memorandum*. OTA-TM-H-38. Washington, DC: Author.

Ohanian, S. (1987). Notes on Japan from an American schoolteacher. *Phi Delta Kappan, 68*(5), 360–367.

O'Leary, K. D. (1980). Pills or skills for hyperactive children. *Journal of Applied Behavior Analysis, 13,* 191–204.

Olion, L. (1988). Enhancing the involvement of Black parents of adolescents with handicaps. In A. A. Ortiz & B. A. Ramirez (Eds.), *Schools and the culturally diverse exceptional student: Promising practices and future directions* (pp. 96–103). Reston, VA: Council for Exceptional Children.

Oliver, L. I. (1974). *Behavior patterns in school and youth 12–17 years* (National Health Survey, Series 11, No. 139, U.S. Department of Health, Education and Welfare). Washington, DC: U.S. Government Printing Office.

Oller, D. K., Wieman, L., Doyle, W., & Ross, C. (1975). Infant babbling and speech. *Journal of Child Language, 3,* 1–11.

Olson, J., Algozzine, B., & Schmid, R. E. (1980). Mild, moderate, and severe EH: An empty distinction? *Behavioral Disorders, 5,* 96–101.

Orelove, F. P. (1982). Acquisition of incidental learning in moderately and severely handicapped adults. *Education and Training of the Mentally Retarded, 17,* 131–136.

Orelove, F. P. (1984). The educability debate: A review and a look ahead. In W. L. Heward, T. E. Heron, D. S. Hill, & J. Trap-Porter (Eds.), *Focus on behavior analysis in education* (pp. 271–281). Columbus, OH: Merrill.

Orlansky, J. Z. (1979). *Mainstreaming the hearing impaired child: An educational alternative*. Ann Arbor, MI: University Microfilms International. (Catalog No. AU00322)

Orlansky, M. D. (1986a). The importance of communication for planning transitional programs for persons who are deaf-blind. In *Yearbook of the Association for Education and Rehabilitation of the Blind and Visually Impaired* (Vol. 3) (pp. 35–40). Washington, DC: Association for Education and Rehabilitation of the Blind and Visually Impaired.

Orlansky, M. D. (1986b). Multiply handicapped. In J. V. Van Cleve (Ed.), *Gallaudet encyclopedia of deaf people and deafness* (Vol. 2) (pp. 335–357). New York: McGraw-Hill.

Orlansky, M. D., & Bonvillian, J. D. (1985). Sign language acquisition: Language development in children of deaf parents and implications for other populations. *Merrill-Palmer Quarterly, 31,* 127–143.

Orlansky, M. D., & Heward, W. L. (1981). *Voices: Interviews with handicapped people*. Columbus, OH: Merrill.

Ortiz, A. A., & Garcia, S. B. (1986). Characteristics of limited-English-proficient Hispanic students served in programs for the learning disabled: Implications for policy and practice. *Counterpoint, 7*(1), 10–11.

Ortiz, A. A., & Garcia, S. B. (1988). A prereferral process for preventing inappropriate referrals of Hispanic students to special education. In A. A. Ortiz & B. A. Ramirez (Eds.), *Schools and the culturally diverse exceptional student: Promising practices and future directions* (pp. 6–18). Reston, VA: Council for Exceptional Children.

Ortiz, A. A., & Ramirez, B. A. (Eds.). (1988). *Schools and the culturally diverse exceptional student: Promising practices and future directions*. Reston, VA: Council for Exceptional Children.

Ortiz, A. A., & Yates, J. R. (1988). Characteristics of learning disabled, mentally retarded, and speech-language handicapped Hispanic students at initial evaluation and reevaluation. In A. A. Ortiz & B. A. Ramirez (Eds.), *Schools and the culturally diverse exceptional student: Promising practices and future directions* (pp. 50–62). Reston, VA: Council for Exceptional Children.

Osguthorpe, R. T., & Scruggs, T. E. (1986). Special education students as tutors: A review and analysis. *Reme-*

dial and Special Education, 7(4), 15–26.

Owens, R. E. (1990). Development of communication, language, and speech. In G. H. Shames & E. H. Wiig, (Eds.), *Human communication disorders* (3rd ed.) (pp. 30–73). Columbus, OH: Merrill.

Pados, G. (1989). *A comparison of the effects of students' own notes and guided notes on the daily quiz performance of fifth-grade students*. Unpublished masters thesis. Columbus, OH: The Ohio State University.

Page, E. B. (1972). Miracle in Milwaukee: Raising the IQ. *Educational Researcher, 15,* 8–16.

Pancsofar, E., & Blackwell, R. (1986). *A user's guide to community entry for the severely handicapped*. Albany, NY: State University of New York Press.

Parent, E. A. (1985). Review of between sacred mountains: Stories and lessons from the land. *Harvard Educational Review, 55,* 134–137.

Parham, J. L. (1983). A meta-analysis of the use of manipulative materials and student achievement in elementary school mathematics. (Doctoral dissertation, Auburn University, 1983.) *Dissertation Abstracts International, 96,* 44A.

Parmelee, A. H., & Michaelis, R. (1971). Neurological examination of the newborn. In J. Hellmuth (Ed.), *Exceptional infant* (Vol. 2). New York: Brunner/Mazel.

Patrick, J. L., & Reschly, D. L. (1982). Relationship of state educational criteria and demographic variables to school-system prevalence of mental retardation. *American Journal of Mental Deficiency, 86,* 351–360.

Patterson, G. R. (1980). Mothers: The unacknowledged victims. *Monographs of the Society for Research in Child Development, 45* (5, Serial No. 186).

Patterson, G. R. (1982). *Coercive family process*. Eugene, OR: Castalia Press.

Patterson, G. R. (1986). Performance models for antisocial boys. *American Psychologist, 41,* 432–444.

Patterson, G. R., Cobb, J. A., & Ray, R. S. (1972). Direct intervention in the classroom: A set of procedures for the aggressive child. In F. W. Clark, D. R. Evans, & L. A. Hammerlynch (Eds.), *Implementing behavioral programs in schools and clinics* (pp. 151–186). Champaign, IL: Research Press.

Patterson, G. R., Reid, J. B., Jones, R. R., & Conger, R. E. (1975). *A social learning approach to family intervention: Vol. 1. Families with aggressive children*. Eugene, OR: Castalia Press.

Patton, J. R., Beirne-Smith, M., & Payne, J. S. (1986). *Mental retardation* (2nd ed.). Columbus, OH: Merrill.

Patton, J. R., Beirne-Smith, M., & Payne, J. S. (1990). *Mental retardation* (3rd ed.). Columbus, OH: Merrill.

Paul, P. V., & Quigley, S. P. (1987). Some effects of early hearing impairment on English language development. In F. Martin (Ed.), *Hearing disorders in children: Pediatric audiology* (pp. 49–80). Austin, TX: PRO-ED.

Paul, P. V., & Quigley, S. P. (1990). *Education and deafness*. New York: Longman.

Payne, J., & Quigley, S. P. (1987). Hearing-impaired children's comprehension of verb-particle combinations. *The Volta Review, 89,* 133–143.

Payne, J. S., Patton, J. R., & Patton, F. E. (1986). Adaptive behavior. In J. R. Patton, J. S. Payne, & M. Beirne-Smith, *Mental Retardation* (2nd ed.). Columbus, OH: Merrill.

Peizer, E. (1975). Wheelchairs. In *Atlas of orthotics*. St. Louis, MO: C. V. Mosby.

Pennsylvania Association for Retarded Children v. Commonwealth of Pennsylvania. (1972). 343 F. Supp. 279.

Pepper, F. C. (1976). Teaching the American Indian child in mainstream settings. In R. L. Jones (Ed.), *Mainstreaming and the minority child*. Reston, VA: Council for Exceptional Children.

Perkins, W. H. (1977). *Speech pathology*. St. Louis, MO: C. V. Mosby.

Perlmutter, B. F., & Parus, M. V. (1983). Identifying children with learning disabilities: A comparison of diagnostic procedures across school districts. *Learning Disability Quarterly, 6,* 321–328.

Perry, J. (1984, August). Migrant children may miss special education services. *San Antonio Light,* 17.

Peters, M. T. (1990). Someone's missing: The student as an overlooked participant in the IEP process. *Preventing School Failure, 34*(4), 32–36.

Peterson, C. A., & Gunn, S. L. (1984). *Therapeutic recreation* (2nd ed.). Englewood Cliffs, NJ: Prentice-Hall.

Peterson, R., Benson, D., Edwards, L., Rosell, J., & White, M. (1986). Inclusion of socially maladjusted children and youth in the legal definition of the behaviorally disordered population: A debate. *Behavioral Disorders, 11,* 213–222.

Pfeiffer, S. I. (1982). The superiority of team decision making. *Exceptional Children, 49,* 68–69.

Phelps, D. L. (1981). Retinopathy of prematurity: An estimate of vision loss in the United States—1979. *Pediatrics, 67,* 924–926.

Pieper, B., & Cappuccilli, J. (1980). Beyond the family and the institution: The sanctity of liberty. In T. Apolloni, J. Cappuccilli, & T. P. Cooke (Eds.), *Achievements in residential services for persons with disabilities: Toward excellence*. Baltimore, MD: University Park Press.

Pieper, E. (1983). *The teacher and the child with spina bifida* (2nd ed.). Rockville, MD: Spina Bifida Association of America.

Pogrund, R. L., & Rosen, S. J. (1989). The preschool child *can* be a cane user. *Journal of Visual Impairment and Blindness, 83,* 431–439.

Polifka, J. C. (1981). Compliance with Public Law 94–142 and consumer satisfaction. *Exceptional Children, 48,* 250–253.

Pollio, H. R., Barlow, J. M., Fine, H. J., & Pollio, M. R. (1977). *Psychology and the poetics of growth: Figurative language in psychology, psychotherapy, and education*. Hillsdale, NJ: Erlbaum.

Polloway, E. A. (1984). The integration of mildly retarded students in the schools: A historical review. *Remedial and Special Education, 5*(4), 18–28.

Polloway, E. A., Cronin, M. E., & Patton, J. R. (1986). The efficacy of group

versus one-to-one instruction: A review. *Remedial and Special Education, 7*(1), 22–30.

Potter, M. L., & Wamre, H. M. (1990). Curriculum-based measurement and developmental reading models: Opportunities for cross-validation. *Exceptional Children, 57,* 16–25.

Powell, T. H., & Ogle, P. A. (1985). *Brothers and sisters: A special part of exceptional families*. Baltimore, MD: Paul H. Brookes.

Prasse, D. P. (1986). Litigation and special education: An introduction. *Exceptional Children, 52,* 311–312.

President's Committee on Mental Retardation. (1969). *The six-hour retarded child*. Washington, DC: U.S. Government Printing Office.

President's Committee on Mental Retardation. (1976). *Mental retardation: Century of decision*. Washington, DC: U.S. Government Printing Office.

Pressey, S. L. (1955). Concerning the nature and nurture of genius. *Scientific Monthly, 80,* 123–129.

Pressey, S. L. (1962). Educational acceleration: Occasional procedure or major issue? *Personnel and Guidance Journal,* 12–17.

Prinz, P. M., & Nelson, K. E. (1985). "Alligator eats cookie": Acquisition of writing and reading skills by deaf children using the microcomputer. *Applied Psycholinguistics, 6,* 283–306.

Prinz, P. M., & Prinz, E. A. (1979). Simultaneous acquisition of ASL and spoken English in a hearing child of a deaf mother and hearing father. *Sign Language Studies, 25,* 283–296.

Provencal, G. (1980). The Macomb-Oakland regional center. In T. Apolloni, J. Cappucilli, & T. P. Cooke (Eds.), *Achievements in residential services for persons with disabilities: Toward excellence* (pp. 19–43). Baltimore, MD: University Park Press.

Pruess, J. B., Fewell, R. R., & Bennett, F. C. (1989). Vitamin therapy and children with Down syndrome: A review of research. *Exceptional Children, 55,* 336–341.

Public Law 95–561. Gifted and Talented Children's Education Act. *Congressional Record* (1978, October 10). H-12179.

Pugach, M. C., & Johnson, L. J. (1989). Prereferral interventions: Progress, problems, and challenges. *Exceptional Children, 56,* 217–226.

Putnam, J. W., & Bruininks, R. H. (1986). Future directions in deinstitutionalization and education: A Delphi investigation. *Exceptional Children, 53,* 55–62.

Putnam, J. W., Rynders, J. E., Johnson, R. T., & Johnson, D. W. (1989). Collaborative skill instruction for promoting positive interactions between mentally handicapped and nonhandicapped children. *Exceptional Children, 55,* 550–557.

Quay, H. C. (1968). The faces of educational exceptionality: Conceptual framework for assessment, grouping, and instruction. *Exceptional Children, 35,* 25–31.

Quay, H. C. (1975). Classification in the treatment of delinquency and antisocial behavior. In N. Hobbs (Ed.), *Issues in the classification of children* (Vol. 1) (pp. 377–392). San Francisco: Jossey-Bass.

Quay, H. C. (1986). Classification. In H. C. Quay, & J. S. Werry, (Eds.). (1986). *Psychopathological disorders of childhood* (3rd ed.). New York: John Wiley & Sons.

Quigley, S. P., & Paul, P. V. (1986). A perspective on academic achievement. In D. M. Luterman (Ed.), *Deafness in perspective* (pp. 55–86). San Diego: College-Hill.

Ramirez, B. A. (1988). Culturally and linguistically diverse children. *Teaching Exceptional Children, 20*(4), 45.

Ramirez, B. A., & Johnson, J. J. (1988). American Indian exceptional children: Improved practices and policy. In A. A. Ortiz & B. A. Ramirez (Eds.), *Schools and the culturally diverse exceptional student: Promising practices and future directions* (pp. 128–140). Reston, VA: Council for Exceptional Children.

Raskin, D. (1990). Fast brakes. *American Health, 9*(6), 24.

Raver, S. (1984). Modification of head droop during conversation in a 3-year-old visually impaired child: A case study. *Journal of Visual Impairment and Blindness, 78,* 307–310.

Rawlings, B. W., & King, S. J. (1986). Postsecondary educational opportunities for deaf students. In A. N. Schildroth & M. A. Karchmer (Eds.), *Deaf children in America* (pp. 231–257). San Diego: College-Hill.

Reagan, T. (1985). The deaf as a linguistic minority: Educational considerations. *Harvard Educational Review, 55,* 265–277.

Reed, V. A. (1986). *An introduction to children with language disorders.* New York: Macmillan.

Reger, R. (1974). What does "mainstreaming" mean? *Journal of Learning Disabilities, 7,* 513–515.

Rehder, K. V. (Ed). (1986). *Rehabilitation Research and Training Center Newsletter, 3*(3). Richmond, VA: Virginia Commonwealth University.

Reichle, J., & Keogh, W. J. (1986). Communication instruction for learners with severe handicaps: Some unresolved issues. In R. H. Horner, L. H. Meyer, & H. D. B. Fredericks (Eds.), *Education of learners with severe handicaps: Exemplary service strategies* (pp. 189–219). Baltimore, MD: Paul H. Brookes.

Reid, D. H., & Favell, J. (1984). Group instruction with persons who have severe disabilities: A critical review. *The Journal of The Association for Persons with Severe Handicaps, 9,* 167–177.

Reis, S. M., & Cellerino, M. (1983). Guiding gifted students through independent study. *Teaching Exceptional Children, 15,* 136–139.

Renfrew, C. E. (1972). *Speech disorders in children.* Oxford, England: Pergamon Press.

Renzulli, J. S. (1977). *The enrichment triad model: A guide for developing defensible programs for the gifted and talented.* Weathersfield, CT: Creative Learning Press.

Renzulli, J. S. (1978). What makes giftedness?: Reexamining a definition. *Phi Delta Kappan, 61,* 180–184.

Renzulli, J. S. (1982). What makes a problem real: Stalking the illusive meaning of qualitative differences in gifted education. *Gifted Child Quarterly, 26,* 147–156.

Renzulli, J. S. (1986). *Systems and models for developing programs for the gifted and talented.* Mansfield Center, CT: Creative Learning Press.

Renzulli, J. S., Reis, S. M., & Smith, L. H. (1981). *The revolving door identification model.* Mansfield Center, CT: Creative Learning Press.

Renzulli, J. S., & Smith, L. (1979). *A guidebook for developing individualized educational programs (IEP) for gifted and talented students.* Mansfield Center, CT: Creative Learning Press.

Repp, A. C., & Barton, L. E. (1980). Naturalistic observations of institutionalized retarded persons: A comparison of licensure decisions and behavioral observations. *Journal of Applied Behavior Analysis, 13,* 333–341.

Repp, A. C., & Singh, N. N. (Eds.). (1990). *Perspectives on the use of nonaversive and aversive interventions for persons with developmental disabilities.* Sycamore, IL: Sycamore Publishing.

Reynolds, M. C. (1978). Staying out of jail. *Teaching Exceptional Children, 10,* 60–62.

Reynolds, M. C. (1989). An historical perspective: The delivery of special education to mildly disabled and at-risk students. *Remedial and Special Education, 10*(6), 7–11.

Reynolds, M. C., Wang, M. C., & Walberg, H. J. (1987). The necessary restructuring of special and regular education. *Exceptional Children, 53,* 391–398.

Rhode, G. (1981). *Generalization and maintenance of treatment gains on behaviorally/emotionally handicapped students from resource rooms to regular classrooms using self-evaluation procedures.* Unpublished doctoral dissertation, Utah State University.

Rhode, G., Morgan , D. P., & Young, K. R. (1983). Generalization and maintenance of treatment gains of behaviorally handicapped students from resource rooms to regular classrooms using self-evaluation procedures. *Journal of Applied Behavior Analysis, 16,* 171–188.

Rhodes, L. E., & Valenta, L. (1985). Industry-based supported employment: An enclave approach. *The Journal of*

The Association for Persons with Severe Handicaps, 10, 12–20.

Rhodes, W. C., & Head, S. (Eds.). (1974). *A study of child variance: Vol 3. Service delivery systems.* Ann Arbor, MI: University of Michigan.

Rhodes, W. C., & Tracy, M. L. (Eds.). (1972a). *A study of child variance: Vol 1. Theories.* Ann Arbor: University of Michigan.

Rhodes, W. C., & Tracy, M. L. (Eds.). (1972b). *A study of child variance: Vol 2. Interventions.* Ann Arbor, MI: University of Michigan.

Rhyne, J. M. (1982). Comprehension of synthetic speech by blind children. *Journal of Visual Impairment and Blindness, 76,* 313–316.

Rich, H. L., Beck, M. A., & Coleman, T. W., Jr. (1982). Behavior management: The psychoeducational model. In R. L. McDowell, G. W. Adamson, & F. H. Wood (Eds.), *Teaching emotionally disturbed children* (pp. 131–166). Boston: Little, Brown.

Richardson, E. H. (1981). Cultural and historical perspectives in counseling American Indians. In D. W. Sue, *Counseling the culturally different: Theory and practice.* New York: John Wiley & Sons.

Richardson, S. A. (1978). Careers of mentally retarded young persons: Services, jobs, and interpersonal relations. *American Journal of Mental Deficiency, 82,* 349–358.

Richmond, V. P., & McCroskey, J. C. (1985). *Communication: Apprehension, avoidance, and effectiveness.* Scottsdale, AZ: Gorsuch Scarisbrick.

Rieke, J. A., Lynch, L. L., & Soltman, S. F. (1977). *Teaching strategies for language development.* New York: Grune & Stratton.

Ries, P. (1986). Characteristics of hearing impaired youth in the general population and of students in special educational programs for the hearing impaired. In A. N. Schildroth & M. A. Karchmer (Eds.), *Deaf children in America* (pp. 1–31). San Diego: College-Hill.

Rimland, B. (1964). *Infantile autism.* New York: Appleton-Century-Crofts.

Rimland, B. (1971). The differentiation of childhood psychoses: An analysis for checklists for 2,218 psychotic children. *Journal of Autism and Childhood Schizophrenia, 1,* 161–174.

Rimmerman, A. (1989). Provision of respite care for children with developmental disabilities: Changes in maternal coping and stress over time. *Mental Retardation, 27,* 99–103.

Rincover, A., Cook, R., Peoples, A., & Packard, D. (1979). Sensory extinction and sensory reinforcement principles for programming multiple adaptive behavior change. *Journal of Applied Behavior Analysis, 12,* 221–233.

Ritvo, E. R., Ritvo, E. C., & Brothers, A. M. (1982). Genetic and immunohematologic factors in autism. *Journal of Autism and Developmental Disabilities, 12,* 109–114.

Rivera, O. A., & Quintana Saylor, L. (1977). Unique problems of handicapped individuals with Spanish surnames. In *The White House Conference on Handicapped Individuals* (Vol. 1) (pp. 433–437). Washington DC: U.S. Government Printing Office.

Roberds-Baxter, S. (1984). The parent connection: Enhancing the affective component of parent conferences. *Teaching Exceptional Children, 17*(1), 55–58.

Roberts, F. K. (1986). Education for the visually handicapped: A social and educational history. In G. T. Scholl (Ed.), *Foundations of education for blind and visually handicapped children and youth: Theory and practice* (pp. 1–18). New York: American Foundation for the Blind.

Robins, L. (1966). *Deviant children grown up.* Baltimore, MD: Williams & Wilkins.

Robins, L. N. (1979). Follow-up studies. In H. C. Quay & J. S. Werry (Eds.), *Psychopathological disorders of childhood* (2nd ed.). New York: John Wiley & Sons.

Robinson, D. (1982). The IEP: Meaningful individualized education in Utah. *Phi Delta Kappan, 64,* 205–206.

Robinson, D., Griffith, J., McComish, L., & Swasbrook, K. (1984). Bus training for developmentally disabled adults. *American Journal of Mental Deficiency, 89,* 37–43.

Robinson, N. M., & Robinson, H. B. (1976). *The mentally retarded child:*

A psychological approach (2nd ed.). New York: McGraw-Hill.

Roeser, R., & Yellin, W. (1987). Puretone tests with preschool children. In F. Martin (Ed.), *Hearing disorders in children: Pediatric audiology* (pp. 217–264). Austin, TX: PRO-ED.

Rogers-Warren, A., & Warren, S. F. (1977). *Ecological perspectives in behavior analysis.* Baltimore, MD: University Park Press.

Rogers-Warren, A. K., & Warren, S. (1980). Mands for verbalization: Facilitating the generalization of newly trained language in children. *Behavior Modification, 4,* 320–245.

Rooney, K. J. (1991). Controversial therapies: A review and critique. *Intervention in School and Clinic, 26,* 134–142.

Rooney, T. E. (1982). Signing vs. speech: What's a parent to do? *SEE What's Happening, 1*(1), 6–8.

Roos, P. (1978). Parents of mentally retarded children—misunderstood and mistreated. In A. P. Turnbull & H. R. Turnbull (Eds.), *Parents speak out: Views from the other side of the two-way mirror* (pp. 12–27). Columbus, OH: Merrill.

Roos, P. (1980). The handling and mishandling of parents of mentally retarded persons. In F. Menolascino (Ed.), *Bridging the gap.* New York: John Wiley & Sons.

Rorschach, H. (1942). *Rorschach psychodiagnostic plates.* New York: Psychological Corp.

Rose, E., & Logan, D. R. (1982). Educational and life/career programs for the mildly mentally retarded. In P. T. Cegelka & H. J. Prehm (Eds.), *Mental retardation: From categories to people* (pp. 186–226). Columbus, OH: Merrill.

Rose, T. L. (1978). The functional relationship between artificial food colors and hyperactivity. *Journal of Applied Behavior Analysis, 11,* 439–446.

Rose, T. L., & Calhoun, M. L. (1990). The Charlotte Circle Project: A program for infants and toddlers with severe/profound disabilities. *Journal of Early Intervention, 14,* 175–185.

Rose, T. L., Calhoun, M. L., & Ladage, L. (1989). Helping young children respond to caregivers. *Teaching Exceptional Children, 21*(4), 48–51.

Rosen, C. D., & Gerring, J. P. (1986). *Head trauma: Educational reintegration.* San Diego: College-Hill.

Ross A. O. (1974). *Psychological disorders of children.* New York: McGraw-Hill.

Ross, M. (1981). Review, overview, and other educational considerations. In M. Ross & L. W. Nober (Eds.), *Educating hard of hearing children* (pp. 102–116). Reston, VA: Council for Exceptional Children.

Ross, M. (1986). A perspective on amplification: Then and now. In D. M. Luterman (Ed.), *Deafness in perspective* (pp. 35–53). San Diego: College-Hill.

Rotegard, L. L., Hill, B. K., & Bruininks, R. H. (1983). Environmental characteristics of residential facilities for mentally retarded persons in the United States. *American Journal of Mental Deficiency, 88,* 49–56.

Rothman, E. P. (1977). *Troubled teachers.* New York: David McKay Co.

Rowitz, L. (1981). A sociological perspective on labeling and mental retardation. *Mental Retardation, 19,* 47–51.

Rubin, R. A., & Balow, B. (1971). Learning and behavior disorders: A longitudinal study. *Exceptional Children, 38,* 293–299.

Rubin, R. A., & Balow, B. E. (1978). Prevalence of teacher identified behavior problems: A longitudinal study. *Exceptional Children, 45,* 102–111.

Ruiz, R. A. (1981). Cultural and historical perspectives in counseling Hispanics. In D. W. Sue, *Counseling the culturally different: Theory and practice.* New York: John Wiley & Sons.

Rules for the education of handicapped children. (1982). Columbus, OH: Ohio Department of Education.

Rusch, F. (1990). *Supported employment: Models, methods, and issues.* Sycamore, IL: Sycamore Publishing.

Rusch, F. R., Chadsey-Rusch, J., & Lagomarcino, T. (1987). Preparing students for employment. In M. E. Snell (Ed.), *Systematic instruction of persons with severe handicaps* (3rd ed.)

(pp. 471–490). Columbus, OH: Merrill.

Rusch, F. R., Chadsey-Rusch, J., & Lagomarcino, T. (in press). Preparing students for employment. In M. E. Snell (Ed.), *Systematic instruction of persons with severe handicaps* (4th ed.). Columbus, OH: Merrill.

Rusch, F. R., & Hughes, C. (1988). Supported employment: Promoting employee independence. *Mental Retardation, 26,* 351–355.

Rusch, F. R., Hughes, C., McNair, J., & Wilson, P. G. (1990). *Co-worker involvement scoring manual and instrument.* Champaign, IL: University of Illinois, The Board of Trustees of the University of Illinois.

Rusch, F. R., Johnson, J. R., & Hughes, C. (1990). Analysis of co-worker involvement in relations to level of disability versus placement approach among supported employees. *The Journal of The Association for Persons with Severe Handicaps, 15,* 32–39.

Rusch, F. R., & Minch, K. E. (1988). Identification of co-worker involvement in supported employment: A review and analysis. *Research in Developmental Disabilities, 9,* 247–254.

Rusch, F. R., Rose, T. L., & Greenwood, C. R. (1988). *Introduction to behavior analysis in special education.* Englewood Cliffs, NJ: Prentice-Hall.

Rusch, F. R., & Shutz, R. P. (1981). Vocational and social work behavior: An evaluative review. In J. L. Matson & J. R. McCartney (Eds.), *Handbook of behavior modification with the mentally retarded* (pp. 247–280). New York: Plenum Press.

Russo, D. C., & Koegel, R. L. (1977). A method for integrating an autistic child in a normal public-school classroom. *Journal of Applied Behavior Analysis, 10,* 579–590.

Rutter, M. (1965). Medical aspects of the education of psychotic (autistic) children. In P. T. B. Western (Ed.), *Some approaches to teaching autistic children* (pp. 61–74). Oxford, England: Pergamon Press.

Rutter, M. (1976). *Helping troubled children.* New York: Plenum Press.

Ryan, C. S., & Coyne, A. (1985). Effects of group homes on neighborhood

property values. *Mental Retardation, 23,* 241–245.

Sabornie, E. J., & Kauffman, J. M. (1986). Social acceptance of learning disabled adolescents. *Learning Disability Quarterly, 9,* 55–60.

Sacco, P. R. (1986). The elephant revisited. *Hearsay: Journal of the Ohio Speech and Hearing Association, 1,* 80–83.

Sacks, O. (1986, March 27). Mysteries of the deaf. *New York Review of Books, 33*(5).

Safer, D. J., & Krager, J. M. (1988). A survey of medication treatment for hyperactive/inattentive students. *Journal of the American Medical Association, 260,* 2256–2258.

Sailor, W., Anderson, J. L., Halvorsen, A. T., Doering, K., Filler, J., & Goetz, L. (1989). *The comprehensive local school: Regular education for all students with disabilities.* Baltimore, MD: Paul H. Brookes.

Sailor, W., Gee, K., Goetz, L., & Graham, N. (1988). Progress in educating students with the most severe disabilities: Is there any? *The Journal of The Association for Persons with Severe Handicaps, 13,* 87–89.

Sailor, W., & Guess, D. (1983). *Severely handicapped students: An instructional design.* Boston: Houghton Mifflin.

Sailor, W., & Haring, K. (1988). *Annual Report: Year 1.* San Francisco State University, Department of Special Education, California Research Institute on Placement of Students with Severe Disabilities.

Sailor, W., & Haring, N. G. (1977). Some current directions in education of the severely/multiply handicapped. *AAESPH Review, 2,* 67–87.

Sainato, D. M., Goldstein, H., & Strain, P. S. (in press). Effects of self-evaluation on preschool children's use of social interaction strategies with their autistic peers. *Journal of Applied Behavior Analysis.*

Salend, S. J. (1990). A migrant education guide for special educators. *Teaching Exceptional Children, 22*(2), 18–21.

Salend, S. J., Ellis, L. L., & Reynolds, C. J. (1989). Using self-instruction to teach vocational skills to individuals who are severely retarded. *Education and Training of the Mentally Retarded, 24,* 248–254.

Salend, S. J., & Giek, K. A. (1988). Independent living arrangements for individuals with mental retardation: The landlords' perspective. *Mental Retardation, 26,* 89–92.

Salend, S. J., Michael, R. J., & Taylor, M. (1984). Competencies necessary for instructing migrant handicapped students. *Exceptional Children, 51,* 50–55.

Salisbury, C. L., & Intaglia, J. (1986). *Respite care support for persons with developmental disabilities and their families.* Baltimore, MD: Paul H. Brookes.

Salvia, J., & Ysseldyke, J. E. (1988). *Assessment in special and remedial education* (4th ed.). Boston: Houghton Mifflin.

Sameroff, A. J., & Chandler, M. J. (1975). Reproductive risk and the continuum of caretaking casualty. In F. D. Horowitz (Ed.), *Review of child development research* (Vol. 4) (pp. 187–244). Chicago: University of Chicago Press.

Samuels, S. J. & Miller, N. L. (1985). Failure to find attention differences between learning disabled and normal children on classroom and laboratory tasks. *Exceptional Children, 51,* 358–375.

Sanders, D. M. (1983). *The dimensions of humor: The development of the appreciation and comprehension of humor in deaf children.* Unpublished doctoral dissertation, University of Illinois, Champaign-Urbana, IL.

Sandler, A., & Coren, A. (1981). Integrated instruction at home and school: Parents' perspective. *Education and Training of the Mentally Retarded, 16*(3), 183–187.

Sansone, J., & Zigmond, N. (1986). Evaluating mainstreaming through an analysis of students' schedules. *Exceptional Children, 52,* 452–458.

Saski, J., Swicegood, P., & Carter, J. (1983). Notetaking formats for learning disabled adolescents. *Learning Disability Quarterly, 6,* 265–270.

Sass-Lehrer, M. (1986). Competencies for effective teaching of hearing impaired students. *Exceptional Children, 53,* 230–234.

Sattler, J. M. (1982). *Assessment of children's intelligence and special abilities* (2nd ed.). Boston: Allyn & Bacon.

Scanlon, C. A., Arick, J., & Phelps, N. (1981). Participation in the development of the IEP: Parents' perspective. *Exceptional Children, 47,* 373–374.

Schalock, R. L., Harper, R. S., & Carver, G. (1981). Independent living placement: Five years later. *American Journal of Mental Deficiency, 86,* 170–177.

Schalock, R. L., Keith, K. D., Hoffman, K., & Karan, O. C. (1988). Quality of life: Its measurement and use. *Mental Retardation, 27,* 25–31.

Scheerenberger, R. C. (1983). *A history of mental retardation: A quarter century of promise.* Baltimore, MD: Paul H. Brookes.

Schell, G. C. (1981). The young handicapped child: A family perspective. *Topics in Early Childhood Special Education, 1,* 21–27.

Schenck, S. (1980). The diagnostic/instructional links in individualized education programs. *The Journal of Special Education, 14,* 337–345.

Schildroth, A. N. (1986). Residential schools for deaf students: A decade in review. In A. N. Schildroth & M. A. Karchmer (Eds.), *Deaf children in America* (pp. 83–104). San Diego: College-Hill.

Schilit, J. (1977). Black versus white perception of mental retardation. *Exceptional Children, 44,* 189–190.

Schleien, S. J., Kiernan, J., & Wehman, P. (1981). Evaluation of an age-appropriate leisure skills program for moderately retarded adults. *Education and Training of the Mentally Retarded, 16,* 13–19.

Schleien, S. J., Wehman, P., & Kiernan, J. (1981). Teaching leisure skills to severely handicapped adults: An age-appropriate darts game. *Journal of Applied Behavior Analysis, 14,* 513–519.

Schlesinger, H. S. (1985). Deafness, mental health, and language. In F. Powell, T. Finitzo-Hieber, S. Friel-Patti, & D. Henderson (Eds.), *Education of the hearing impaired child* (pp. 103–116). San Diego: College-Hill.

Schlesinger, H. S., & Meadow, K. P. (1976). Emotional support for parents. In D. L. Lillie & P. L. Trohanis (Eds.), *Teaching parents to teach* (pp. 35–48). New York: Walker.

Schlichter, C. L. (1989). Literature for students who are gifted. *Teaching Exceptional Children, 21*(3) 34–36.

Schneiderman, C. (1984). *Basic anatomy and physiology in speech and hearing.* San Diego: College-Hill.

Scholl, G. T. (Ed.). (1986a). *Foundations of education for blind and visually handicapped children and youth: Theory and practice.* New York: American Foundation for the Blind.

Scholl, G. T. (1986b). Multicultural considerations. In G. T. Scholl (Ed.), *Foundations of education for blind and visually handicapped children and youth* (pp. 165–182). New York: American Foundation for the Blind.

Scholl, G. T. (1987). Appropriate education for visually handicapped students. *Teaching Exceptional Children, 19*(2), 33–36.

Schultz, E., Salvia, J., & Feinn, J. (1974). Prevalence of behavioral symptoms in rural elementary school children. *Journal of Abnormal Psychology, 1,* 17–24.

Schulz, J. B. (1978). The parent-professional conflict. In A. P. Turnbull & H. R. Turnbull (Eds.), *Parents speak out: Views from the other side of the two-way mirror* (pp. 28–36). Columbus, OH: Merrill.

Schumaker, J. B., & Deshler, D. D. (1988). Implementing the regular education initiative in secondary schools: A different ballgame. *Journal of Learning Disabilities, 21,* 43–52.

Schumaker, J. B., Deshler, D. D., Alley, G. R., & Warner, M. M. (1983). Toward the development of an intervention model for learning disabled adolescents. In J. K. Torgeson & B. Y. L. Wong (Eds.), *Learning disabilities: Some new perspectives.* New York: Academic Press.

Schumaker, J. B., Hovell, M. F., & Sherman, J. A. (1977). An analysis of daily report cards and parent-managed privileges in the improvement of adolescents' classroom performance. *Journal of Applied Behavior Analysis, 10,* 449–464.

Schumaker, J. B., & Sheldon, J. (1985). *The learning strategies curriculum: The sentence writing strategy.* (Curriculum material). Lawrence, KS: Institute for Research in Learning Disabilities.

Schumaker, J. B., & Sherman, J. A. (1978). Parent as intervention agent: From birth onward. In R. L. Schiefelbusch (Ed.), *Language intervention strategies* (pp. 237–315). Baltimore, MD: University Park Press.

Scott, M. L., Ebbert, A., & Price, D. (1986). Assessing and teaching employability skills with prevocational work samples. *The Directive Teacher, 8*(1), 3–5.

Scranton, T., & Downs, M. (1975). Elementary and secondary learning disabilities programs in the U.S.: A survey. *Journal of Learning Disabilities, 8,* 394–399.

Scuccimarra, D. J., & Speece, D. L. (1990). Employment outcomes and social integration of students with mild handicaps: The quality of life two years after high school. *Journal of Learning Disabilities, 23,* 213–219.

Sears, P. S. (1979). The Terman genetic studies of genius, 1922–1972. In A. H. Passow (Ed.), *The gifted and the talented: Their education and development* (pp. 75–96). Chicago: University of Chicago Press.

Sears, R. R. (1977). Sources of life satisfaction of the Terman gifted men. *American Psychologist, 32*(2), 119–128.

Secord, W. (1981). *Test of Minimal Articulation Competence.* Columbus, OH: Merrill.

Semel, E. M., & Wiig, E. H. (1980). *Clinical evaluation of language functions.* Columbus, OH: Merrill.

Shafer, M. S., Rice, M. L., Metzler, H. M. D., & Haring, M. (1989). A survey of nondisabled employees' attitudes toward supported employees with mental retardation. *The Journal of The Association for Persons with Severe Handicaps, 14,* 137–146.

Shannon, G. (1985). *Characteristics influencing current recreational patterns of persons with mental retardation.* Unpublished doctoral dissertation, Brandeis University.

Shearer, D. E., & Snider, R. S. (1981). On providing a practical approach to the early education of children. *Child Behavior Therapy, 3,* 78–80.

Shearer, M. S., & Shearer, D. E. (1972). The Portage Project: A model for early childhood education. *Exceptional Children, 39,* 210–217.

Sheerenberger, R. C. (1983). *Public residential services for the mentally retarded.* Madison, WI: National Association of Superintendents of Public Residential Facilities for the Mentally Retarded.

Shepard, L., & Smith, M. L. (1981, February). *Evaluation of the identification of perceptual-communicative disorders in Colorado: Final report.* Boulder, CO: Laboratory of Educational Research.

Shepard, L. A. (1987). The new push for excellence: Widening the schism between regular and special education. *Exceptional Children, 53,* 327–329.

Shevin, M., & Klein, N. K. (1984). The importance of choice-making skills for students with severe disabilities. *The Journal of The Association for Persons with Severe Handicaps, 9,* 159–166.

Shewan, C. M. (1986). Characteristics of clinical services provided by ASHA members. *ASHA, 28*(1), 29.

Shields, J., & Heron, T. E. (1989). Teaching organizational skills to students with learning disabilities. *Teaching Exceptional Children, 21*(2), 8–13.

Shivers, J. S., & Fait, H. F. (1985). *Special recreational services: Therapeutic and adapted.* Philadelphia: Lea & Febiger.

Siegel, S., Greener, K., Prieur, J., Robert, M., & Gaylord-Ross, R. (1989). The Community Vocational Training Program: A transition program for youth with mild handicaps. *Career Development for Exceptional Individuals, 12*(1), 48–64.

Sievert, A. L., Cuvo, A. J., & Davis, P. K. (1988). Training self-advocacy skills to adults with mild handicaps. *Journal of Applied Behavior Analysis, 21,* 299–309.

Silverman, L. K. (1986). What happens to the gifted girls? In C. J. Maker (Ed.), *Critical issues in gifted education: Defensible programs for the gifted.* Rockville, MD: Aspen.

Silverman, L. K. (1988). Gifted and talented. In E. L. Meyen & T. M. Skrtic (Eds.), *Exceptional children and youth* (3rd. ed.) (pp. 281–283). Denver: Love.

Simon, R. (1987). *After the tears: Parents talk about raising a child with a disability.* San Diego: Harcourt Brace Jovanovich.

Singer, J. D., & Butler, J. A. (1987). The Education of All Handicapped Children Act: Schools as agents of social reform. *Harvard Educational Review, 57,* 125–152.

Sirvis, B. (1982). The physically disabled. In E. L. Meyen (Ed.), *Exceptional children and youth: An introduction* (2nd ed.). Denver: Love.

Sisk, D. (1984, October). *A national survey of gifted programs.* Presentation to the National Business Consortium for Gifted and Talented, Washington, DC.

Sisk, D. (1987). *Creative teaching of the gifted.* New York: McGraw-Hill.

Skeels, H. M. (1966). Adult status of children with contrasting early life experiences. *Monographs of the Society for Research in Child Development, 31* (No. 3).

Skeels, H. M., & Dye, H. B. (1939). A study of the effects of differential stimulation on mentally retarded children. *Convention Proceedings, American Association on Mental Deficiency, 44,* 114–136.

Skinner, B. F. (1969). *Contingencies of reinforcement: A theoretical analysis.* New York: Appleton-Century-Crofts.

Skinner, B. F. (1974). *About behaviorism.* New York: Alfred A. Knopf.

Slade, J. C., & Conoley, C. W. (1989). Multicultural experiences for special educators. *Teaching Exceptional Children, 22*(1), 60–64.

Sleeter, C. E., & Grant, C. A. (1986). Success for all students. *Phi Delta Kappan, 68*(4), 297–299.

Slingerland, B. H. (1971). *A multi-sensory approach to language arts for specific language disability children: A guide for primary teachers.* Cambridge, MA: Educators Publishing Service.

Smith, B. J., & Strain, P. S. (1984). *The argument for early intervention.* Reston, VA: ERIC Information Service Digest, ERIC Clearinghouse on Handicapped and Gifted Children.

Smith, B. J., Vincent, L., Toole, A., Garland, C., Dunst, C., McCarten, K., Williamson, G., Jesien, G., McLean, M., Zeitlin, S., Karnes, M. B., McCollum, J., Monohan, R., & Odom, S. (1987, March). *Positon statements and recommendations relating to PL 99–457 and other federal and state early childhood policies.* Reston, VA: Council for Exceptional Children.

Smith, D. D., & Robinson, S. (1986). Educating the learning disabled. In R. J. Morris & B. Blatt (Eds.), *Special education: Research and trends* (pp. 222–248). New York: Pergamon Press.

Smith, E. J. (1981). Cultural and historical perspectives in counseling blacks. In D. W. Sue, *Counseling the culturally different: Theory and practice.* New York: John Wiley & Sons.

Smith, O. S. (1984). Severely and profoundly physically handicapped students. In P. J. Valletutti & B. M. Sims-Tucker (Eds.), *Severely and profoundly handicapped students: Their nature and needs* (pp. 85–152). Baltimore, MD: Paul H. Brookes.

Smith, R. M., & Neisworth, J. T. (1975). *The exceptional child: A functional approach.* New York: McGraw-Hill.

Smith, R. M., Neisworth, J. T., & Hunt, F. M. (1983). *The exceptional child: A functional approach* (2nd ed.). New York: McGraw-Hill.

Smith, S. W. (1990a). Comparison of Individualized Education Programs (IEPs) of students with behavioral disorders and learning disabilities. *The Journal of Special Education, 24*(1), 85–100.

Smith, S. W. (1990b). Individualized Education Programs (IEPs) in special education—From intent to acquiescence. *Exceptional Children, 57,* 6–14.

Smith, S. W., & Simpson, R. L. (1989). An analysis of individualized education programs (IEPs) for students

with behavioral disorders. *Behavioral Disorders, 14,* 107–116.

Smithdas, R. (1981). Psychological aspects of deaf-blindness. In S. R. Walsh & R. Holzberg (Eds.), *Understanding and educating the deaf-blind/severely and profoundly handicapped: An international perspective.* Springfield, IL: Charles C. Thomas.

Snarr, R. W., & Wolford, B. I. (1985). *Introduction to corrections.* Dubuque, IA: William C. Brown.

Snell, M. E. (Ed.). (1987). *Systematic instruction of persons with severe handicaps* (3rd ed.). Columbus, OH: Merrill.

Snell, M. E. (Ed.). (in press). *Systematic instruction of persons with severe handicaps* (4th ed.). Columbus, OH: Merrill.

Snell, M. E., & Beckman-Brindley, S. (1984). Family involvement in intervention with children having severe handicaps. *The Journal of The Association for Persons with Severe Handicaps, 9,* 213–230.

Snell, M. E., Lewis, A. P., & Houghton, A. (1989). Acquisition and maintenance of toothbrushing skills by students with cerebral palsy and mental retardation. *The Journal of The Association for Persons with Severe Handicaps, 14,* 216–226.

Snell, M. E., & Renzaglia, A. M. (1986). Moderate, severe, and profound handicaps. In N. G. Haring & L. McCormick (Eds.), *Exceptional children and youth* (4th ed.) (pp. 271–310). Columbus, OH: Merrill.

Sonnenschein, P. (1981). Parents and professionals: An uneasy relationship. *Teaching Exceptional Children, 14,* 62–65.

Sontag, E., Sailor, W., & Smith, J. (1977). The severely/profoundly handicapped: Who are they? Where are we? *The Journal of Special Education, 11*(1), 5–11.

Sowell, V., Packer, R., Poplin, M., & Larsen, S. (1979). The effects of psycholinguistic training on improving psycholinguistic skills. *Learning Disability Quarterly, 2,* 69–77.

Sowers, J., Jenkins, C., & Powers, L. (1988). Vocational education of persons with physical handicaps. In R. Gaylord-Ross (Ed.), *Vocational edu-*

cation for persons with handicaps (pp. 387–416). Mountain View, CA: Mayfield Publishing.

Spache, G. D. (1963). *Diagnostic Reading Scales.* Monterey, CA: California Test Bureau.

Sparrow, S. S., Balla, D. A., & Cicchetti, D. V. (1984). *Vineland Adaptive Behavior Scales.* Circle Pines, MN: American Guidance Service.

Spenciner, L. J. (1972). Differences between blind and partially sighted children in rejection by sighted peers in integrated classrooms, grades 2–8. Cited in B. W. Tuckman (Ed.), *Conducting educational research.* New York: Harcourt Brace Jovanovich.

Spivak, M. P. (1986). Advocacy and legislative action for head-injured children and their families. *Journal of Head Trauma Rehabilitation, 1,* 41–47.

Spradlin, J. E., & Spradlin, R. R. (1976). Developing necessary skills for entry into classroom teaching arrangements. In N. G. Haring & R. L. Schiefelbusch (Eds.), *Teaching special children* (pp. 232–267). New York: McGraw-Hill.

Sprague, J. R., & Horner, R. H. (1984). The effects of single instance, multiple instance, and general case training on generalized vending machine use by moderately and severely handicapped students. *Journal of Applied Behavior Analysis, 17,* 273–278.

Sprague, J. R., & Horner, R. H. (1990). Preventing challenging behaviors. *Teaching Exceptional Children, 23*(1), 13–15.

Spreat, S., Telles, J. T., Conroy, J. W., Feinstein, C., & Colombatto, J. J. (1985). Attitudes toward deinstitutionalization: A national survey of families of institutionalized mentally retarded persons, *Occasional paper of the NASPRFMR.* Philadelphia: Temple University.

Spring, C., & Sandoval, J. (1976). Food additives and hyperkinesis: A critical evaluation of the evidence. *Journal of Learning Disabilities, 9,* 560–569.

Stainback, S., & Stainback, W. (1987). Integration versus cooperation: A commentary on "Educating children with learning problems: A shared responsibility." *Exceptional Children, 54,* 66–68.

Stainback, S., & Stainback, W. (Eds.). (1991). *Teaching in the inclusive classroom: Curriculum design, adaptation and delivery.* Baltimore, MD: Paul H. Brookes.

Stainback, W., & Stainback, S. (1984). A rationale for the merger of special and regular education. *Exceptional Children, 51,* 102–111.

Stainback, W., Stainback, S., Raschke, D., & Anderson, R. J. (1981). Three methods of encouraging interactions between severely retarded and non-handicapped students. *Education and Training of the Mentally Retarded, 16,* 188–192.

Stanley, J. C. (1991). An academic model for educating the mathematically talented. *Gifted Child Quarterly, 35,* 36–42.

State of the States: Gifted and Talented Educated, 1986–87. (1988). Helena, MT: Council of State Directors of Programs for the Gifted.

Statistical Abstracts of the United States. (1990, January). Current population reports, series P25, No. 1018. Washington, DC: U.S. Department of Commerce.

Stein, L. (1988). Hearing impairment. In V. B. Van Hasselt, P. S. Strain, & M. Hersen (Eds.), *Handbook of developmental and physical disabilities* (pp. 271–294). New York: Pergamon Press.

Stephens, T. M. (1977). *Teaching skills to children with learning and behavior disorders.* Columbus, OH: Merrill.

Stephens, T. M. (1978). *Social skills in the classroom.* Columbus, OH: Cedars Press.

Stephens, T. M., Blackhurst, A. E., & Magliocca, L. A. (1982). *Teaching mainstreamed students.* New York: John Wiley & Sons.

Stephens, T. M., & Wolf, J. S. (1978). The gifted child. In N. G. Haring (Ed.), *Behavior of exceptional children: An introduction to special education* (2nd ed.) (pp. 387–405). Columbus, OH: Merrill.

Stephens, T. M., & Wolf, J. S. (1980). *Effective skills in parent/teacher conferencing.* Columbus, OH: Ohio State University, National Center for Educational Materials and Media for the Handicapped.

Stern, L. M. (1990, July 10). The healthy-child guide: Check-ups, immunizations, diet, safety. *Woman's Day,* p. 549.

Stewart, J. L. (1977). Unique problems of handicapped Native Americans. In *The White House Conference on Handicapped Individuals* (Vol. 1) (pp. 438–444). Washington, DC: U.S. Government Printing Office.

Stocker, C. S. (1973). *Listening for the visually impaired: A teaching manual.* Springfield, IL: Charles C. Thomas.

Stokes, K. S. (1976). Educational considerations for the child with low vision. In E. Faye (Ed.), *Clinical low vision* (pp. 343–353). Boston: Little, Brown.

Stokes, T. F., & Baer, D. M. (1977). An implicit technology of generalization. *Journal of Applied Behavior Analysis, 10,* 349–367).

Stone, W. L., & La Greca, A. M. (1990). The social status of children with learning disabilities: A reexamination. *Journal of Learning Disabilities, 23,* 32–37.

Stowell, L. J., & Terry, C. (1977). Mainstreaming: Present shock. *Illinois Libraries, 59,* 475–477.

Strain, P. S. (1981). Peer-mediated treatment of exceptional children's social withdrawal. *Exceptional Education Quarterly, 1,* 83–95.

Strain, P. S., Guralnick, M. J., & Walker, H. M. (Eds.). (1986). *Children's social behavior: Development, assessment, and modification.* Orlando, FL: Academic Press.

Strain, P. S., & Odom, S. L. (1986). Peer social initiations: Effective intervention for social skills development of exceptional children. *Exceptional Children, 52,* 543–551.

Strain, P. S., & Smith, B. J. (1986). A counter-interpretation of early intervention effects: A response to Casto and Mastropieri. *Exceptional Children, 53,* 260–265.

Straus, M. A., Gelles, R. J., & Steinmetz, S. K. (1980). *Behind closed doors: Violence in the American family.* New York: Anchor Press.

Strickland, B. B., & Turnbull, A. P. (1990). *Developing and implementing individualized education programs* (3rd ed.). Columbus, OH: Merrill.

Strickland, S. P. (1971). Can slum children learn? *American Education, 7*(6), 3–7.

Sturmey, P., & Crisp, A. G. (1986). Portage guide to early education: A review of research. *Educational Psychology, 6*(2), 139–157.

Suarez, T. M., Hurth, J. L., & Prestridge, S. (1988). Innovation in services for young children with handicaps and their families: An analysis of the Handicapped Children's Early Education Program projects from 1982 to 1986. *Journal of Early Intervention, 12,* 224–237.

Sue, D. W. (1981). *Counseling the culturally different: Theory and practice.* New York: John Wiley & Sons.

Sugai, G., & Maheady, L. (1988). Cultural diversity and individual assessment for behavior disorders. *Teaching Exceptional Children, 21,* 28–31.

Sulzbacher, S., Haines, R., Peterson, S. L., & Swatman, F. M. (1987). Encourage appropriate coffee break behavior. *Teaching Exceptional Children, 19*(2), 8–12.

Sulzer-Azaroff, B., & Mayer, G. R. (1986). *Achieving educational excellence.* New York: Holt, Rinehart & Winston.

Sulzer-Azaroff, B., & Mayer, G. R. (1991). *Behavior analysis for lasting change.* Fort Worth, TX: Holt, Rinehart & Winston.

Swallow, R. M. (1978, May). *Cognitive development.* Paper presented at the North American Conference on Visually Handicapped Infants and Preschool Children, Minneapolis, MN.

Swallow, R. M., & Conner, A. (1982). Aural reading. In S. S. Mangold (Ed.), *A teacher's guide to the special educational needs of blind and visually handicapped children* (pp. 119–135). New York: American Foundation for the Blind.

Swassing, R. (1985). The multiple component alternative. *Gifted Child Today, 33,* 10–11.

Syracuse University Center on Human Policy. (1987). *A statement in support of families and their children.* Syracuse, NY: Author.

Tarjan, G., Wright, S. W., Eyman, R. K., & Keeran, C. V. (1973). Natural history of mental retardation: Some aspects of epidemiology. *American Journal of Mental Deficiency, 77*, 396–379.

Tarnowski, K. J., & Drabman, R. S. (1987). Teaching intermittent self-catheterization to mentally retarded children. *Research in Developmental Disabilities, 8*, 521–529.

Tawney, J. W. (1984). The pragmatics of the educability issue: Some questions which logically precede the assumption of ineducability. In W. L. Heward, T. E. Heron, D. S. Hill, & J. Trap-Porter (Eds.), *Focus on behavior analysis in education* (pp. 287–295). Columbus, OH: Merrill.

Taylor, O. L. (1990). Language and communication differences. In G. H. Shames & E. H. Wiig, (Eds.), *Human communication disorders* (3rd ed.) (pp. 126–158). Columbus, OH: Merrill.

Taylor, S. J. (1988). Caught in the continuum: A critical analysis of the principle of the least restrictive environment. *The Journal of The Association for Persons with Severe Handicaps, 13*, 41–53.

Taylor, S. J., Biklen, D., & Searl, S. J. (1986). *Preparing for life: A manual for parents on least restrictive environment*. Boston: Federation for Children with Special Needs.

Teacher Education Division. (1986). *The national inquiry into the future of education for students with special needs*. Reston, VA: Council for Exceptional Children.

Templin, M. C., & Darley, F. L. (1969). *The Templin-Darley Test of Articulation* (2nd ed.). Iowa City: University of Iowa, Bureau of Educational Research and Service, Division of Extension and University Services.

Terkel, S. (1974). *Working: People talk about what they do all day and how they feel about what they do*. New York: Pantheon Books.

Terman, L. M. (1916). *The measurement of intelligence*. Boston: Houghton Mifflin.

Terman, L. M. (1925). *The mental and physical traits of a thousand gifted children*. Stanford, CA: Stanford University Press.

Test, D. W., Cooke, N. L., Weiss, A. B., Heward, W. L., & Heron, T. E. (1986). A home-school communication system for special education. *The Pointer, 30*, 4–7.

Test, D. W., Grossi, T., & Keul, P. (1988). A functional analysis of the acquisition and maintenance of janitorial skills in a competitive work setting. *The Journal of The Association for Persons with Severe Handicaps, 13*, 1–7.

Thomas, A., & Chess, S. (1984). Genesis and evolution of behavioral disorders: From infancy to early adult life. *American Journal of Psychiatry, 141*, 1–9).

Thomas, A., Chess, S., & Birch, H. G. (1968). Temperament and behavior disorders in children. New York: New York University Press.

Thomas, A., & Grimes, J. (Eds.). (1990). *Best practices in school psychology—II*. Washington, DC: National Association of School Psychologists.

Thomas, D. R., Becker, W. C., & Armstrong, M. (1968). Production and elimination of disruptive classroom behavior by systematically varying teachers' behavior. *Journal of Applied Behavior Analysis, 1*, 35–45.

Thomas, G., & Jackson, G. (1986). The whole-school approach to integration. *British Journal of Special Education, 13*(1), 27–29.

Thomas, S. B. (1985). *Legal issues in special education*. Topeka, KS: National Organization on Legal Problems in Education.

Thompson, K. (1984). The speech therapist and language disorders. In G. Lindsay (Ed.), *Screening for children with special needs: Multidisciplinary approaches* (pp. 86–97). London: Croom Helm.

Thorndike, R. L., Hagen, E. P., & Sattler, J. M. (1986). *Technical manual, The Stanford-Binet Intelligence Scale: Fourth edition*. Chicago: Riverside Publishing.

Thousand, J. S., & Villa, R. A. (1990). Sharing expertise and responsibilities through teaching teams. In S. Stainback & W. Stainback (Eds.), *Support networks for inclusive schooling: Interdependent integrated education* (pp. 151–166). Baltimore, MD: Paul H. Brookes.

Thurman, D. (1978). Mainstreaming and the visually impaired: A report from Atlantic Canada. *Education of the Visually Handicapped, 10*, 35–37.

Thurston, L. P. (1989). Helping parents tutor their children: A success story. *Academic Therapy, 24*, 579–587.

Thurston, L. P., & Dasta, K. (1990). An analysis of in-home parent tutoring in children's academic behavior at home and in school and on parents' tutoring behaviors. *Remedial and Special Education, 11*(4), 41–52.

Todd, J. H. (1986). Resources, media, and technology. In G. T. Scholl (Ed.), *Foundations of education for blind and visually handicapped children and youth: Theory and practice* (pp. 285–296). New York: American Foundation for the Blind.

Todis, B., Severson, H. H., & Walker, H. M. (1990). The critical events scale: Behavioral profiles of students with externalizing and internalizing behavior disorders. *Behavioral Disorders, 15*, 75–86.

Tolan, P. H. (1987). Implications of age of onset for delinquency risk. *Journal of Abnormal Child Psychology, 15*, 47–65.

Tomatis, A. (1978). *Education and dyslexia*. France-Quebec: Les Editions.

Tomes, L., & Sanger, D. D. (1986). Attitudes of interdisciplinary team members toward speech-language services in public schools. *Language, Speech, and Hearing Services in the Schools, 17*, 230–240.

Tomlinson-Keasey, C., Brawley, R., & Peterson, B. (1986). An analysis of an interactive videodisc system for teaching language skills to deaf students. *Exceptional Child, 33*(1), 49–55.

Tooze, D. (1981). *Independence training for visually handicapped children*. Baltimore, MD: University Park Press.

Torrance, E. P. (1977). *Discovery and nurturance of giftedness in the culturally different*. Reston, VA: Council for Exceptional Children.

Tredgold, A. F. (1937). *A textbook on mental deficiency*. Baltimore, MD: Wood.

Trief, E., Duckman, R., Morse, A. R., & Silberman, R. K. (1989). Retinopathy of prematurity. *Journal of Visual Impairment and Blindness, 83,* 500–504.

Trybus, R., & Karchmer, M. (1977). School achievement scores of hearing impaired children: National data on achievement status and growth patterns. *American Annals of the Deaf, 122,* 62–69.

Tucker, J. A. (1985). Curriculum-based assessment: An introduction. *Exceptional Children, 52,* 199–204.

Turnbull, A., & Bronicki, G. J. (1986). Changing second graders' attitudes toward people with mental retardation: Using kid power. *Mental Retardation, 24,* 44–45.

Turnbull, A. P. (1983). Parent-professional interactions. In M. E. Snell (Ed.), *Systematic instruction of the moderately and severely handicapped* (2nd ed.) (pp. 18–43). Columbus, OH: Merrill.

Turnbull, A. P., Strickland, B., & Brantley, J. C. (1982). *Developing and implementing individualized education programs* (2nd ed.). Columbus, OH: Merrill.

Turnbull, A. P., & Turnbull, H. R. (1982). Parent involvement in the education of handicapped children: A critique. *Mental Retardation, 20,* 115–122.

Turnbull, A. P., Turnbull, H. R., Summers, J. A., Brotherson, M. J., & Benson, H. A. (1986). *Families, professionals, and exceptionality: A special partnership.* Columbus, OH: Merrill.

Turnbull, H. R. (1986). Appropriate education and Rowley. *Exceptional Children, 52,* 347–352.

Turnbull, K., & Bronicki, G. J. (1989). Children can teach other children. *Teaching Exceptional Children, 21*(3), 64–65.

Turnbull, H. R., III, & Turnbull, A. P. (1985). *Parents speak out: Then & now* (2nd ed.). Columbus, OH: Merrill.

Turner, J. (1983). Workshop society: Ethnographic observations in a work setting for retarded adults. In K. Kernan, M. Begab, & R. Edgerton (Eds.), *Environments and behavior: The adaptation of mentally retarded persons* (pp. 147–171). Austin, TX: PRO-ED.

Tuttle, D. W. (1984). *Self-esteem and adjusting with blindness: The process of responding to life's demands.* Springfield, IL: Charles C. Thomas.

U.S. Commission on Civil Rights (1983, September). *Accommodating the spectrum of individual abilities* [Clearinghouse Publication 81]. Washington, DC: U.S. Government Printing Office.

U.S. Comptroller General. (1981, September 30). *Disparities still exist in who gets special education.* Report to the chairman, Subcommittee on Select Education, Committee on Education and Labor, House of Representatives of the United States.

U.S. Congress. (1987). *Promotion opportunities for blind and handicapped workers in sheltered workshops under the Javitz-Wagner-O'Day act.* Washington, DC: U.S. Government Printing Office.

U.S. Department of Commerce. (1990a). Persons arrested by crime, sex, and age: 1988. In Statistical abstracts of the U.S. p. 177. Washington, DC: Author.

U.S. Department of Commerce. (1990b). *Statistical abstracts of the United States* (110th ed.). Washington, DC: Author.

U. S. Department of Education. (1989). *Eleventh annual report to Congress on the implementation of the Education of the Handicapped Act.* Washington, DC: Author.

U.S. Department of Education. (1990). *Twelfth annual report to Congress on the implementation of the Education of the Handicapped Act.* Washington, DC: Author.

U.S. Department of Health, Education, and Welfare. (1977). *Closer Look.* Washington, DC: Author.

U.S. Department of Justice. (1985). *Uniform crime reports.* Washington, DC: Author.

U.S. Department of Labor. (1979). *Study of handicapped clients in sheltered workshops* (Vol. 2). Washington, DC: Author.

U.S. General Accounting Office. (1981). *Disparities still exist in who gets special education.* Washington, DC: Author.

U.S. Office of Education. (1977a). Implementation of Part B of the Education of the Handicapped Act. *Federal Register, 42,* 42474–42518.

U.S. Office of Education. (1977b). Procedures for evaluating specific learning disabilities. *Federal Register, 42,* 65082–65085.

Ulicny, G. R., Thompson, S. K., Favell, J. E., & Thompson, M. S. (1985). The active assessment of educability: A case study. *The Journal of The Association for Persons with Severe Handicaps, 10,* 111–114.

Ulrey, G. (1982). Assessment considerations with language impaired children. In G. Ulrey & S. J. Rogers (Eds.), *Psychological assessment of handicapped infants and young children* (pp. 123–134). New York: Thieme-Stratton.

Utley, C. A., Lowitzer, A. C., & Baumeister, A. A. (1987). A comparison of the AAMD's definition, eligibility criteria, and classification schemes with state department of education guidelines. *Education & Training in Mental Retardation, 22,* 35–43.

Vacc, N. A., Vallecorsa, A. L., Parker, A., Bonner, S., Lester, C., Richardson, S., & Yates, C. (1985). Parents' and educators' participation in IEP conferences. *Education & Treatment of Children, 8,* 153–162.

Valcante, G. (1986). Educational implications of current research on the syndrome of autism. *Behavioral Disorders, 11,* 131–139.

van den Pol, R. A., Iwata, B. A., Ivancic, M. T., Page, T. J., Neef, N. A., & Whitely, F. P. (1981). Teaching the handicapped to eat in public places: Acquisition, generalization, and maintenance of restaurant skills. *Journal of Applied Behavior Analysis, 14,* 61–69.

Van Dijk, J. (1983). *Rubella handicapped children: The effects of bilateral cataract and/or hearing impairment on behaviour and learning.* Lisse, Netherlands: Swets & Zeitlinger.

Van Dijk, J. (1985). An educational curriculum for deaf-blind multihandicapped persons. In D. Ellis (Ed.), *Sensory impairments in men-*

tally handicapped people (pp. 374–382). San Diego: College-Hill.

Van Houten, R. (1979). Social validation: The evolution of standards of competency for target behaviors. *Journal of Applied Behavior Analysis, 12,* 581–591.

Van Houten, R. (1980). *Learning through feedback: A systematic approach for improving academic performance.* New York: Human Sciences Press.

Van Riper, C. (1972). *Speech correction: Principles and methods* (5th ed.). Englewood Cliffs, NJ: Prentice-Hall.

Van Riper, C., & Emerick L. L. (1984). *Speech correction: An introduction to speech pathology.* Englewood Cliffs, NJ: Prentice-Hall.

Van Tassel-Baska, J. (1983). The teacher as counselor for the gifted. *Teaching Exceptional Children, 15,* 144–150.

Van Tassel-Baska, J. (1986). Acceleration. In C. J. Maker (Ed.), *Critical issues in gifted education: Defensible programs for the gifted.* Rockville, MD: Aspen.

Van Tassel-Baska, J. (Ed.). (1990). *A practical guide to counseling the gifted in a school setting* (2nd. ed.). Reston, VA: Council for Exceptional Children.

Vandercook, T., York, J., & Forest, M. (1989). The McGill Action Planning System (MAPS): A strategy for building the vision. *The Journal of The Association for Persons with Severe Handicaps, 14,* 205–215.

Vanderheiden, G. C., & Lloyd, L. L. (1986). Communication systems and their components. In S. W. Blackstone, & D. M. Brushkin (Eds.), *Augmentative communication: An introduction* (pp. 29–162). Rockville, MD: American Speech-Language-Hearing Association.

Vargas, J. G., & Moxley, R. A. (1979). Teaching for thinking and creativity: The radical behaviorist's view. In A. E. Lawson (Ed.), *The psychology of teaching for thinking and creativity, 1980 AETS Yearbook.* Columbus, OH: Ohio State University.

Vaughn, S., Bos, C. S., Harrell, J. E., & Lasky, B. A. (1988). Parent participation in the initial placement/IEP conference ten years after mandated

involvement. *Journal of Learning Disabilities, 21,* 82–89.

Venn, J., Morganstern, L., & Dykes, M. K. (1979). Checklists for evaluating the fit and function of orthoses, prostheses, and wheelchairs in the classroom. *Teaching Exceptional Children, 11,* 51–56.

Verhaaren, P. R., & Connor, F. P. (1981). Physical disabilities. In J. M. Kauffman & D. P. Hallahan (Eds.), *Handbook of special education.* Englewood Cliffs, NJ: Prentice-Hall.

Vernon, M. (1987). The primary causes of deafness. In E. Mindel & M. Vernon (Eds.), *They grow in silence: Understanding deaf children and adults* (2nd ed.) (pp. 31–38). San Diego: College-Hill.

Vernon, M., & Koh, S. D. (1970). Effects of manual communication of deaf children's educational achievement, linguistic competence, oral skills, and psychological adjustment. *American Annals of the Deaf, 115,* 527–536.

Victor, J. (1976, April). Some selected findings from the Greenleigh Associates study of sheltered workshops. In *The Auburn conference on the Greenleigh study of sheltered workshops.* Auburn, AL: Auburn University, Rehabilitation Services Education Department.

Vihman, M. M. (1986). Individual differences in babbling and early speech: Predicting to age three. In B. Lindblom & R. Zetterstrom (Eds.), *Precursors of early speech* (pp. 95–112). Basingstroke, Hampshire: MacMillan.

Villa, R. A., & Thousand, J. S. (in press). Student collaboration: The essential curriculum for the 21st century. In S. Stainback & W. Stainback (Eds.), *Teaching in the inclusive classroom: Curriculum, design, adaptation, and delivery.* Baltimore, MD: Paul H. Brookes.

Vincent, L., Davis, J., Brown, P., Broome, K., Miller, J., & Grunewald, L. (1983). *Parent inventory of child development in nonschool environments.* Madison, WI: Metropolitan School District Early Childhood Program, Active Decision Making by Parents Grant.

Vitello, S. J. (1986). The Tatro case: Who gets what and why. *Exceptional Children, 52,* 353–356.

Vogelsberg, R. T., Anderson, J., Berger, P., Haselden, T., Mitwll, S., Schmidt, C., Skowron, A. Ulett, P., & Wilcox, B. (1980). Selecting, setting up, and surveying in an independent living situation: An inventory and instructional approach for handicapped individuals. *AAESPH Review, 5,* 38–54.

Vorrath, H. H., & Brendtro, L. K. (1985). *Positive peer culture* (2nd ed.). Hawthorne, NY: Aldine Publishing.

Wacker, D. P., Wiggins, B., Fowler, M., & Berg, W. K. (1988). Training students with profound or multiple handicaps to make requests via microswitches. *Journal of Applied Behavior Analysis, 21,* 331–343.

Wahler, R. G., & Dumas, J. E. (1986). "A chip off the old block": Some interpersonal characteristics of coercive children across generations. In P. S. Strain, M. J. Guralnick, & H. M. Walker (Eds.), *Children's social behavior: Development, assessment, and modification* (pp. 49–91). Orlando, FL: Academic Press.

Wainapel, S. F. (1989). Attitudes of visually impaired persons toward cane use. *Journal of Visual Impairment and Blindness, 83,* 446–448.

Wakabayashi, R. (1977). Unique problems of handicapped Asian Americans. In *The White House Conference on Handicapped Individuals* (Vol. 1) (pp. 429–432). Washington, DC: U.S. Government Printing Office.

Walker, H. M. (1979). *The acting-out child: Coping with classroom disruption.* Boston: Allyn & Bacon.

Walker, H. M., & Buckley, N. K. (1973). Teacher attention to appropriate and inappropriate classroom behavior: An individual case study. *Focus on Exceptional Children, 5,* 5–11.

Walker, H. M., & Hops, H. (1976). Use of normative peer data as a standard for evaluating classroom treatment effects. *Journal of Applied Behavior Analysis, 9,* 159–168.

Walker, H. M., & Severson, H. H. 1990. *Systematic Screening for Behavior*

Disorders. Longmont, CO: Sopris West, Inc.

Walker, H. M., Severson, H., Stiller, B., Williams, G., Haring, N., Shinn, M., & Todis, B. (1988). Systematic screening of pupils in the elementary age range at risk for behavior disorders: Development and trial testing of a multiple gating model. *Remedial and Special Education, 9*(3), 8–20.

Walker, H. M., & Rankin, R. (1983). Assessing the behavioral expectations and demands of less restrictive settings. *School Psychology Review, 12*(3), 274–284.

Walker, L. A. (1986). *A loss for words: The story of deafness in a family.* New York: Harper & Row.

Wallace, G., & McLoughlin, J. A. (1979). *Learning disabilities: Concepts and characteristics* (2nd ed.). Columbus, OH: Merrill.

Wang, M. C. (1980). Adaptive instruction: Building on diversity. *Theory Into Practice, 19,* 122–128.

Wang, M. C., Reynolds, M. C., & Walberg, H. J. (1985, December). *Rethinking special education.* Paper presented at the Wingspread Conference on the Education of Students with Special Needs: Research Findings and Implications for Policy and Practice. Racine, WI.

Wang, M. C., & Walberg, H. J. (1988). Four fallacies of segregationism. *Exceptional Children, 55,* 128–137.

Ward, M. E. (1979). Children with visual impairments. In M. S. Lilly (Ed.), *Children with exceptional needs: A survey of special education* (pp. 320–361). New York: Holt, Rinehart & Winston.

Ward, M. E. (1986). The visual system. In G. T. Scholl (Ed.), *Foundations of education for blind and visually handicapped children and youth: Theory and practice* (pp. 35–64). New York: American Foundation for the Blind.

Warger, C. L., Aldinger, L. E., & Okun, K. A. (1983). *Mainstreaming in the secondary school: The role of the regular teacher.* Bloomington, IN: Phi Delta Kappa Educational Foundation.

Warren, S. F., & Gazdag, G. (1990). Facilitating early language development with milieu intervention procedures. *Journal of Early Intervention, 14,* 62–86.

Warren, S. F., McQuarter, R. J., & Rogers-Warren, A. K. (1984). The effects of teacher mands on the speech of unresponsive language-delayed children. *Journal of Speech and Hearing Research, 49,* 43–52.

Webster, A., & Ellwood, J. (1985). *The hearing-impaired child in the ordinary school.* London: Croom Helm.

Wechsler, D. (1974). *Manual for the Wechsler Intelligence Scale for Children—Revised.* New York: Psychological Corp.

Wedel, J. W., & Fowler, S. A. (1984). "Read me a story, Mom": A home-tutoring program to teach prereading skills to language-delayed children. *Behavior Modification, 8,* 245–266.

Wehman, P. (1983). Toward the employability of severely handicapped children and youth. *Teaching Exceptional Children, 15,* 220–225.

Wehman, P., & Hill, J. W. (Eds.). (1985). *Competitive employment for persons with mental retardation.* Richmond, VA: Virginia Commonwealth University, Rehabilitation Research and Training Center.

Wehman, P., Hill, M., Goodall, P., Cleveland, P., Brooke, V., & Pentecost, J. H. (1982). Job placement and follow-up of moderately and severely handicapped individuals after three years. *The Journal of The Association for the Severely Handicapped, 7*(2), 5–16.

Wehman, P., Hill, M., Hill, J. W., Brooke, V., Pendleton, P., & Britt, C. (1985). Competitive employment for persons with mental retardation: A follow-up six years later. *Mental Retardation, 23,* 274–281.

Wehman, P., & Kregel, J. (1985). A supported work approach to competitive employment of individuals with moderate and severe handicaps. *The Journal of The Association for Persons with Severe Handicaps, 10,* 3–11.

Wehman, P., Kregel, J., & Barcus, J. M. (1985). From school to work: A vocational transition model for handicapped students. *Exceptional Children, 52,* 25–37.

Wehman, P., Kregel, J., & Seyfarth, J. (1985a). Employment outlook for young adults with mental retardation. *Rehabilitation Counseling Bulletin, 5,* 343–354.

Wehman, P., Kregel, J., & Seyfarth, J. (1985b). Transition from school to work for individuals with severe handicaps: A follow-up study. *The Journal of The Association for Persons with Severe Handicaps, 10,* 132–136.

Wehman, P., Kregel, J., Shafer, M., & West, M. (1989). *Emerging trends in supported employment: A preliminary analysis of 27 states.* Richmond, VA: Rehabilitation Research and Training Center, Virginia Commonwealth University.

Wehman, P., Renzaglia, A. M., & Bates, P. (1985). *Functional living skills for moderately and severely handicapped individuals.* Austin, TX: PRO-ED.

Wehman, P., & Schleien, S. J. (1981). *Leisure programs for handicapped persons: Adaptations, techniques, and curriculum.* Baltimore, MD: University Park Press.

Wei, T. T. D. (1983). The Vietnamese refugee child: Understanding cultural differences. In D. R. Omark and J. G. Erickson (Eds.), *The bilingual exceptional child* (pp. 197–212). San Diego: College-Hill.

Weintraub, F. J. (1986). *Goals for the future of special education.* Reston, VA: Council for Exceptional Children.

Weintraub, F. J., & Abeson, A. (1974). New education policies for the handicapped: The quiet revolution. *Phi Delta Kappan, 55,* 526–529, 569.

Weiss, C. E., & Lillywhite, H. S. (1976). *Communicative disorders: A handbook for prevention and early intervention.* St. Louis, MO: C. V. Mosby.

Weiss, H. G., & Weiss, M. S. (1976). *Home is a learning place: A parent's guide to learning disabilities.* Boston: Little, Brown.

Wepman, J. M. (1958). *Wepman Auditory Discrimination Test.* Chicago: Language Research Associates.

Werry, J., & Quay, H. C. (1971). The prevalence of behavior symptoms in younger elementary school children.

American Journal of Orthopsychiatry, 41, 136–143.

West, J. F., & Idol, L. (1990). Collaborative consultation in the education of mildly handicapped and at-risk students. *Remedial and Special Education, 11*(1), 22–31.

Wetzel, R. J., & Hoschouer, R. L. (1984). *Residential teaching communities: Program development and staff training for developmentally disabled persons.* Glenview, IL: Scott, Foresman.

Weyhing, M. C. (1983). Parental reactions to handicapped children and familial adjustments to routines of care. In J. A. Mulik & S. M. Pueschell (Eds.), *Parent-professional partnerships in developmental disabilities* (pp. 125–138). Cambridge, MA: Ware Press.

Wheeler, J. J., Bates, P., Marshall, K. J., & Miller, S. R. (1988). Teaching appropriate social behaviors to a young man with moderate mental retardation in a supported competitive employment setting. *Education & Training in Mental Retardation, 23,* 105–116.

Whelan, R. J. (1981). Prologue. In G. Brown, R. L. McDowell, & J. Smith (Eds.), *Educating adolescents with behavior disorders* (pp. 1–9). Columbus, OH: Merrill.

White, B. L. (1975). *The first three years of life.* Englewood Cliffs, NJ: Prentice-Hall.

White, C. C., Lakin, K. C., & Bruininks, R. H. (1989). *Persons with mental retardation and related conditions in state-operated residential facilities: Year ending June 30, 1988 with longitudinal trends from 1950 to 1988.* (Report No. 30). Minneapolis: University of Minnesota, Center for Residential and Community Services.

White, K. R., Bush, D., & Casto, G. (1986). Let the past be prologue: Learning from previous reviews of early intervention efficacy research. *The Journal of Special Education, 19*(4), 417–428.

White, O., & Haring, N. (1976). *Exceptional teaching.* Columbus, OH: Merrill.

White, O. R. (1986). Precision teaching—precision learning. *Exceptional Children, 52,* 522–534.

White, O. R., & Haring, N. G. (1980). *Exceptional teaching* (2nd ed.). Columbus, OH: Merrill.

White, W. J. (1985). Perspectives on the education and training of learning disabled adults. *Learning Disability Quarterly, 8,* 231–236.

Whitehead, C. W. (1979). Sheltered workshops in the decade ahead: Work and wages, or welfare. In G. T. Bellamy, C. O'Connor, & O. C. Karan (Eds.), *Vocational rehabilitation of severely handicapped persons* (pp. 71–84). Baltimore, MD: University Park Press.

Whitmore, J. R. (1980). *Giftedness, conflict, and underachievement.* Boston: Allyn & Bacon.

Whitmore, J. R., & Maker, C. J. (1985). *Intellectual giftedness in disabled persons.* Rockville, MD: Aspen.

Widerstrom, A. H., Mowder, B. A., & Willis, W. G. (1989). The school psychologist's role in the early childhood special education program. *Journal of Early Intervention, 13,* 239–248.

Wiederholt, J. L. (1974a). Historical perspectives on the education of the learning disabled. In L. Mann & D. Sabatino (Eds.), *The second review of special education.* Philadelphia: JSE Press.

Wiederholt, J. L. (1974b). Planning resource rooms for the mildly handicapped. *Focus on Exceptional Children, 6,* 1–10.

Wiederholt, J. L., & Chamberlain, S. P. (1989). A critical analysis of resource programs. *Remedial and Special Education, 10*(6), 15–37.

Wiederholt, J. L., Hammill, D. D., & Brown, V. (1983). The resource teacher: A guide to effective practice. (2nd ed.). Boston: Allyn & Bacon.

Wiener, W. R., Deaver, K., DiCorpo, D., Hayes, J., Hill, E., Manzer, D., Newcomver, J., Pogrund, R., Rosen, S., & Uslan, M. (1990). The orientation and mobility assistant. *RE:view, 22,* 69–77.

Wiig, E. H., & Semmel, E. (1984). *Language assessment intervention for the learning disabled* (2nd ed.). Columbus, OH: Merrill.

Wikler, L. D. (1986). Periodic stresses of families of older mentally retarded children: An exploratory study. *American Journal of Mental Deficiency, 90,* 703–706.

Wilbur, R. (1987). *American sign langue: Linguistic and applied dimensions* (2nd ed.). Boston: Little, Brown.

Will, M. C. (1986). Educating children with learning problems: A shared responsibility. *Exceptional Children, 52,* 411–415.

Williams, B. F., & Howard, V. F. (1990, May). *Cocaine exposed infants: Current findings and implications.* Paper presented at the 16th Annual Convention of the Association for Behavior Analysis, Nashville, TN.

Williams, G. E., & Cuvo, A. J. (1986). Training apartment upkeep skills to rehabilitation clients: A comparison of task analytic strategies. *Journal of Applied Behavior Analysis, 19,* 39–51.

Williams, J. (1977). The impact and implication of litigation. In G. Markel (Ed.), *Proceedings of the University of Michigan Institute on the Impact and Implications of State and Federal Legislation Affecting Handicapped Individuals.* Ann Arbor, MI: University of Michigan, School of Education.

Williamson, G. G. (1978). The individualized education program: An interdisciplinary endeavor. In B. Sirvis, J. W. Baken, & G. G. Williamson (Eds.), *Unique aspects of the IEP for the physically handicapped, homebound, and hospitalized.* Reston, VA: Council for Exceptional Children.

Willoughby, D. M., & Duffy, S. (1989). *Handbook for itinerant and resource teachers of blind and visually impaired students.* Baltimore, MD: National Federation of the Blind.

Willoughby, D. M. (1980). *A resource guide for parents and educators of blind children.* Baltimore, MD: National Federation of the Blind.

Wilson, J., Blacher, J., & Baker, B. L. (1989). Siblings of children with severe handicaps. *Mental Retardation, 27,* 167–173.

Wilson, P. G., Schepis, M. M., & Mason-Main, M. (1987). In vivo use of picture prompt training to increase independent work at a restaurant. *The Journal of The Association for Per-*

sons with Severe Handicaps, 12, 145–150.

Winer, M. (1978). A course on resources for the newly blind. *Journal of Visual Impairment and Blindness* 72, 311–315.

Winkler, B., Armstrong, K., Moehlis, J., Nietupski, J., & Whalen-Carrell, B. (1982). Ad guide preparation and delivery for severly handicapped students. *Teaching Exceptional Children, 15,* 29–33.

Winter, R. J. (1983). Childhood diabetes mellitus. In J. Umbreit (Ed.), *Physical disabilities and health impairments: An introduction* (pp. 117–131). Columbus, OH: Merrill.

Winton, P. J. (1986). Effective strategies for involving families in intervention efforts. *Focus on Exceptional Children, 19*(2), 1–12.

Winton, P. J., & Bailey, D. B. (1988). The family-focused interview: A collaborative mechanism for family assessment and goal-setting. *Journal of Early Intervention, 12,* 195–207.

Winton, P. J., & Turnbull, A. P. (1981). Parent involvement as viewed by parents of preschool handicapped children. *Topics in Early Childhood Special Education, 1,* 11–19.

Witty, P. A. (1930). A study of one hundred gifted children. *University of Kansas Bulletin of Education, 2*(7).

Witty, P. A. (1940). Contributions to the IQ controversy from the study of superior deviates. *School and Society, 51,* 503–508.

Witty, P. A. (1958). Who are the gifted? In W. B. Henry (Ed.), *Education of the gifted, fifty-seventh yearbook of the National Society for the Study of Education, part II.* Chicago: University of Chicago Press.

Witty, P. A. (1962). A decade of progress in the study of the gifted and creative pupil. In W. B. Barbe & T. M. Stephens (Eds.), *Attention to the gifted a decade later* (pp. 3–7). Columbus, OH: Ohio Department of Education.

Witty, P. A., & Jenkins, M. D. (1934). The educational achievement of a group of gifted Negro children. *Journal of Educational Psychology, 25,* 585–597.

Wolery, M. (1979). *Parents as teachers of their handicapped children: An annotated bibliography.* Seattle: WESTAR.

Wolery, M., & Dyk, L. (1984). Arena assessment: Description and preliminary social validity data. *The Journal of The Association for Persons with Severe Handicaps, 9,* 231–235.

Wolery, M., & Gast, D. L. (1984). Effective and efficient procedures for the transfer of stimulus control. *Topics in Early Childhood Special Education, 4,* 52–77.

Wolery, M., & Haring, T. G. (1990). Moderate, severe, and profound handicaps. In N. G. Haring & L. McCormick (Eds.), *Exceptional children and youth* (5th ed.) (pp. 239–280). Columbus, OH: Merrill.

Wolf, M. M. (1978). Social validity: The case for subjective measurement, or how applied behavior analysis is finding its heart. *Journal of Applied Behavior Analysis, 11,* 203–214.

Wolfe, D., & Rawlings, B. W. (1986). *Hearing impaired students in postsecondary education.* Washington, DC: National Clearinghouse on Postsecondary Education for Handicapped Individuals.

Wolfensberger, W. (1969). The origin and nature of our institutional models. In R. B. Kugel & W. Wolfensberger (Eds.), *Changing patterns in residential services for the mentally retarded* (pp. 59–71). Washington, DC: President's Committee on Mental Retardation.

Wolfensberger, W. (1972). *Normalization: The principle of normalization in human services.* Toronto, Canada: National Institute on Mental Retardation.

Wolfensberger, W. (1976). The origin and nature of our institutional models. In R. B. Kugel & A. Shearer (Eds.), *Changing patterns in residential services for the mentally retarded* (pp. 35–82). Washington, DC: President's Committee on Mental Retardation.

Wolfensberger, W. (1983). Social role valorization: A proposed new term for the principle of normalization. *Mental Retardation, 21,* 234–239.

Wolfensberger, W., & Thomas, S. (1983). *Program Analysis of Service Systems implementation of normalization goals: Normalization criteria and ratings manual. Vol. 2.* Toronto: National Institute on Mental Retardation.

Wolff, A. B. & Harkins, J. E. (1986). Multihandicapped students. In A. N. Schildroth & M. A. Karchmer (Eds.), *Deaf children in America* (pp. 55–81). San Diego: College-Hill.

Wolk, S., & Schildroth, A. N. (1986). Deaf children and speech intelligibility: A national study. In A. N. Schildroth & M. A. Karchmer (Eds.), *Deaf children in America* (pp. 139–159). San Diego: College-Hill.

Wolman, C., Thurlow, M. L., & Bruininks, R. H. (1989). Stability of categorical designation for special education students: A longitudinal study. *The Journal of Special Education, 23,* 213–222.

Wolraich, M. L., Lindgren, S., Stromquist, A., Milich, R., Davis, C., & Watson, D. (1990). Stimulant medications use by primary care physicians in the treatment of attention deficit hyperactivity disorder. *Pediatrics, 86,* 95–101.

Wood, F. H. (1985). Issues in the identification and placement of behaviorially disordered students. *Behavioral Disorders, 10,* 219–228.

Wood, F. H., & Zabel, R. H. (1978). Making sense of reports on the incidence of behavior disorders/emotional disturbance in school-aged populations. *Psychology in the Schools, 15,* 45–51.

Wood, M. E. (1981). Costs of intervention programs. In C. Garland, N. W. Stone, J. Swanson, & G. Woodruff (Eds.), *Early intervention for children with special needs and their families: Findings and recommendations* (pp. 15–32). Westar Series Paper No. 11. Seattle WA: University of Washington. (ERIC Document Reproduction Service No. 207278)

Woodcock, R. (1974). *Woodcock Reading Mastery Tests.* Circle Pines, MN: American Guidance Service.

Woodruff, G., & McGonigel, M. J. (1988). Early intervention team approaches: The transdisciplinary model. In J. B. Jordon, J. J. Gallagher, P. L. Hutinger, & M. B. Karnes (Eds.), *Early childhood special education: Birth to three* (pp. 163–181). Reston,

VA: Council for Exceptional Children.

Wright, C., & Bigge, J. L. (1991). Avenues to physical participation. In J. L. Bigge, *Teaching individuals with multiple and physical disabilities* (3rd ed.) (pp. 132–174). Columbus, OH: Merrill.

Wright, C., & Momari, M. (1985). *From toys to computers: Access for the physically disabled child*. San Jose, CA: Wright.

Wright, J. E., Cavanaugh, R. A., Heward, W. L., & Sainato, D. M. (1991). *Teaching each other Spanish: Evaluation of a classwide reciprocal peer tutoring program for learning disabled and at-risk high school students*. Manuscript submitted for publication.

Wyatt v. Stickney, 344 F. Supp. 387, 344 F. Supp. 373 (M.D. Ala. 1972), 334 F. Supp. 1341, 325 F. Supp. 781 (M.D. Ala. 1971), aff'd sub nom. Wyatt v. Aderholt, 503 F. 2d 1305 (5th Cir. 1974).

Yang, F. M. (1988). *Effects of guided lecture notes on six graders' scores on daily science quizzes*. Unpublished masters thesis. Columbus, OH: The Ohio State University.

Yee, L. Y. (1988). Asian children. *Teaching Exceptional Children, 20*(4), 49–50.

Yell, M. L. (1988). The effects of jogging on the rates of selected target behavior of behaviorally disordered students. *Behavioral Disorders, 13,* 273–279.

Ysseldyke, J., Algozzine, B., Richey, L., & Graden, J. (1982). Declaring students eligible for learning disability services: Why bother with the data? *Learning Disability Quarterly, 5,* 37–44.

Ysseldyke, J. E., & Salvia, J. (1974). Diagnostic-prescriptive teaching: Two models. *Exceptional Children, 41,* 181–186.

Ysseldyke, J. E., Thurlow, M., Graden, J., Wesson, C., Algozzine, B., & Deno, S. (1983). Generalizations from five years of research on assessment and decision making: The University of Minnesota Institute. *Exceptional Education Quarterly, 4*(1), 75–93.

Yurt, R. W., & Pruitt, B. A. (1983). Burns. In J. Umbreit (Ed.), *Physical disabilities and health impairments: An introduction* (pp. 175–184). Columbus, OH: Merrill.

Zangwill, I. (1909). *The melting pot*. New York: Macmillan.

Zawolkow, E., &DeFiore, S. (1986). Educational interpreting for elementary- and secondary-level hearing-impaired students. *American Annals of the Deaf, 131,* 26–28.

Zelski, R. F. K., & Zelski, T. (1985). What are assistive devices? *Hearing Instruments, 36,* 12.

Zetlin, A., & Murtaugh, M. (1990). What ever happened to those with borderline IQs? *American Journal on Mental Retardation, 94,* 463–469.

Zettel, J. J. (1979). Gifted and talented education over half a decade of change. *Journal for the Education of the Gifted, 3,* 14–37.

Zigler, E., Balla, D., & Hodapp, R. (1984). On the definition and classification of mental retardation. *American Journal of Mental Deficiency, 89,* 215–230.

Zigmond, N., & Baker, J. (1987). *Project MELD grant application to OSERS*. Pittsburgh, PA: University of Pittsburgh.

Zigmond, N., & Baker, J. (1990). Mainstream experiences for learning disabled students (Project MELD): Preliminary report. *Exceptional Children, 57,* 176–185.

Zigmond, N., & Miller, S. E. (1986). Assessment for instructional planning. *Exceptional Children, 52,* 501–509.

Zigmond, N., & Thornton, H. (1985). Follow-up of postsecondary age learning disabled graduates and drop-outs. *Learning Disabilities Research, 1,* 50–55.

Zirkel, P. A., & Stevens, P. L. (1986). Commentary: The law concerning public education for the gifted. *West's Education Law Reporter, 34,* 353–367.

Zirpoli, T. J. (1987). Child abuse and children with handicaps. *Remedial and Special Education, 7*(2), 39–48.

Zirpoli, T. J. (1990). Physical abuse: Are children with disabilities at greater risk? *Intervention in School and Clinic, 26–(1), 6–11.*

Zirpoli, T. J., & Wieck, C. (1989). Economic and political factors affecting deinstitutionalization: One state's analysis. *The Journal of Special Education, 23,* 201–211.

Name Index

Haring, N. G., 156, 157, 443
Haring, T. G., 213, 419, 420–421
Harkins, J. E., 493
Harper, G. F., 165
Harper, R. S., 119
Harrell, J. E., 558
Harrell, R., 149
Harris, D. B., 196
Harris, J., 281
Harris, K. C., 67, 74, 166, 513
Harris, L., 616
Harris, M. C., 651
Harris, S., 362–363
Harris, S. L., 213
Harris, W. J., 167
Harrison, R., 543
Hart, B., 124, 603, 604
Hasazi, J. E., 617–618
Hasazi, S. B., 617, 618, 637
Hasselbring, T., 156
Hasset, M. E., 557
Hatlen, P. H., 357, 361, 367
Hatten, J. T., 267
Hatten, P. W., 267
Hauber, F. A., 642, 649
Hawking, S. W., 264–265, 480–482
Hawkins, K. K., 561
Hawkins, R. P., 424, 561
Hawks, W., 149
Haycock, G. S., 246
Hayden, A. H., 22, 583
Haynes, W. O., 240, 248, 254, 258
Haywood, H. C., 105
Head, 217
Heal, L. W., 77
Heber, R. F., 90, 576
Hedge, M. N., 257–258
Hedlund, R., 594
Hegde, M. N., 258
Heinze, T., 357
Heller, G., 172
Heller, T., 643, 649
Helmstetter, E., 439
Hemming, H., 119
Henderson, J., 72
Hendrickson, K., 638
Hensen, F. O., 548
Heron, T. E., 62, 67, 69, 74, 109, 112,
    158–159, 165, 166, 174, 223, 554,
    557, 559
Heston, L. L., 215
Heward, W. L., 34, 61, 69, 74, 109, 112,
    158–159, 114, 174, 176, 210–211,
    216, 218, 221, 223, 352–354, 361,
    443, 541, 550, 552, 554, 557, 559,
    562, 628, 652
Hewett, F. M., 86, 190, 191, 199,
    203–204, 251, 297, 399
Hieronymus, A. N., 151

Hightower, J., 637
Hill, B. K., 620, 642, 644, 645, 647, 649
Hill, D. S., 557
Hill, E. W., 364, 365
Hill, J. W., 440, 620, 622, 624, 625, 654
Hill, M., 622–623, 624, 625, 636
Hilliard, A. G., III, 496, 515
Hingtgen, J. N., 192
Hirschberg, G., 406
Hitzing, W., 651
Hobbs, N., 14, 218
Hochman, R., 167
Hodapp, R., 97–98
Hoemann, H. W., 293, 294
Hoffman, K., 658, 659
Hogan, T. D., 164
Holburn, C. S., 117
Holcomb, R., 308
Holland, A. L., 251
Hollander, R., 87
Hollingworth, L. S., 456
Hoover, J. J., 165
Hops, H., 199, 207
Horiuchi, C. N., 618
Horne, D., 160
Horner, J., 251
Horner, R. H., 110, 433, 437, 443, 445,
    620, 626, 657
Horst, G., 440, 654
Horton, J. V., 165
Hoschouer, R. L., 651–652
Houghton, A., 438
Houlihan, M., 141
Hovell, M. F., 551, 553
Howard, V. F., 584
Howell, K. W., 18, 114, 151, 154, 156
Hubbell, R., 236
Huberty, T. J., 98
Huebner, K. M., 362
Huestis, R. D., 149
Hughes, C., 627, 628, 629, 630–632,
    658
Hughes, M., 607
Hull, F. M., 245
Hull, M., 617–618
Hull, R. K., 284
Hunsucker, P. F., 95
Hunt, F. M., 14
Huntz, P., 430
Huntze, S. L., 190
Hurlbut, B. I., 262
Hurth, J. L., 579
Hurvitz, J. A., 244
Husch, J. V., 628
Hutchins, M. P., 637
Hutinger, P. L., 610

Idol, L., 74
Imber, R. B., 552

Imber, S. C., 552
Inman, D., 110
Intaglia, I., 569
Iran-Nejad, A., 314
Ireland, J. C., 301
Iscoe, I., 18
Itard, J. M. G., 87
Ivancic, M. T., 654
Iverson, V. S., 58, 74
Iwata, B. A., 262, 392–394, 648

Jablonski, 444
Jackson, G., 77
Jacobson, W. H., 364, 365
Janicki, M. P., 645
Jastak, J. F., 151, 164
Jastak, S. R., 151
Jeffrey, D. L., 334
Jenkins, C., 404
Jenkins, J. R., 77, 167
Jenkins, M. D., 482
Jenne, T., 223
Jennings, K. D., 192
Jensen, B. F., 553
Johnson, B., 358
Johnson, D. W., 430
Johnson, J., 439
Johnson, J. J., 509
Johnson, J. L., 501
Johnson, J. R., 626, 629, 658
Johnson, L. J., 71
Johnson, M., 654
Johnson, R. E., 617–618
Johnson, R. T., 430
Johnson, T. P., 34, 52
Johnson, T. S., 257
Jolliff, G., 628
Jonas, G., 248, 249
Jones, C., 502–503
Jones, M. H., 378, 596
Jones, R. R., 208–209
Jordan, C., 516
Jose, R., 351
Justen, J. E., 420

Kabacoff, R. I., 589
Kaiser, C., 609
Kaiser-Kupfer, M. I., 339
Kameenui, E. J., 22
Kamp, S. H., 493, 495
Kampfe, C. M., 318
Kaplan, F., 116, 643
Kaplan, J. S., 154, 156
Kaplan, S., 468
Kappan Special Report, 504
Karan, O. C., 658, 659
Karchmer, M., 293, 318
Karmody, C. S., 324
Karnes, M. B., 538, 579, 599

Subject Index

McGill Action Planning System,
434–437
Medical social workers, 403
Megavitamin therapy, 149
Melting pot theory, 498
Meningocele, 381
Mental retardation
    alternative definitions of, 99–101
    applied behavior analysis and,
        109–115
    assessment of, 90–98
    causes of, 105–106, 126
    civil rights and, 121–123
    classifications of, 101–104, 126
    curriculum goals and, 107–108
    definitions of, 88–90, 126
    educability and, 106, 424–425, 493
    educational strategies for, 106–115,
        126–127
    future trends in, 120, 127
    group homes for, 119
    history of, 86–88
    institutions, residential, and,
        115–119
    measurement of behavioral goals
        and, 111–115
    prevalence of, 104–105, 126
    prevention of, 123–124
    types of, 103–105, 420
Metropolitan Achievement Tests, 164
Metropolitan Readiness Tests, 593
Microcephaly, 584
Microculture, 498
Middle ear, 281
Migrant Student Record Transfer
    System (MSRTS), 513
Migrant students, 512–514
*Mills v. Board of Education of the
    District of Columbia*, 36, 43
Milwaukee Project, 576
Minority group, 495
Mirror Model for Parental Involvement,
    564
Mobile work crews, 626, 629
Model Preschool Center for
    Handicapped Children, 596
Monoplegia, 378
Morpheme, 236
Morphology, 236
MSRTS. *See* Migrant Student Record
    Transfer System
Multicultural education, 499–500, 528
Multicultural Self-Report Inventory,
    525, 526–527
Multidisciplinary teams, 72
Multifactored assessment, 70
Muscular dystrophy, 384, 412
Mutism, selective, 210

Myelomeningocele, 381
Myopia, 337

National Advisory Committee on
    Handicapped Children, 133
National Association for Mental Health,
    194
National Association for Retarded
    Citizens, 538
National Center for Educational
    Statistics, 454, 519
National Center for Health Statistics,
    245
National Coalition for Cultural
    Pluralism, 498
National Committee for Citizens in
    Education, 558
National Hotel and Restaurant
    Association, 623
National Joint Committee on Learning
    Disabilities (NJCLD), 137–138
National Research Center on the Gifted
    and Talented (NRC/GT), 478
National School Boards Association
    (NSBA), 49
National Society for Crippled Children,
    538
National Technical Institute for the
    Deaf (NTID), 321
Native Americans, 501, 509, 511–512
Native languages, 517, 519, 520–521
Nearsightedness, 337
Neurologic impairment, 377, 378, 412
NJCLD. *See* National Joint Committee
    on Learning Disabilities
Nonlinguistic cues, 234
Normalization, 3–4, 124–125
Norm-referenced tests, 151–154
NRC/GT. *See* National Research Center
    on the Gifted and Talented
NSBA. *See* National School Boards
    Association
NTID. *See* National Technical Institute
    for the Deaf
Nystagmus, 335

Oakland Picture Dictionary, The
    (Kirsten), 261
Occupational therapist, 402–403
Ocular motility, 334–335
Office of Special Education and
    Rehabilitation Services (OSERS),
    636
O&M. *See* Orientation and mobility
Operant conditioning audiometry, 286
Operant conditioning model in
    articulation disorders, 256
Optacon, 347

Optical devices, 350–351
Orientation and mobility, 363–365,
    371
Orthopedic impairment, 377, 378, 412
Orthotists, 403
OSERS. *See* Office of Special Education
    and Rehabilitation Services
Ossicles, 281, 283
Osteogenisis imperfecta, 385, 412
OT. *See* Occupational therapist
Otitis media, 297
Outer ear, 281

Paired-Associates Strategy, 164
Paralinguistic phenomenon, 234
Paraplegia, 378
PARC. *See* Pennsylvania Association for
    Retarded Children
Parent Inventory of Child Development
    in Nonschool Environments, 591
Parents
    abuse and neglect by, 543–545,
        548–549
    black families and, 504
    early intervention and, 609–610, 612
    education groups for, 561–563
    emotional responses of, 539–540
    future trends concerning, 566–569
    Hispanic families and, 505–506, 528
    individualized education program
        and, 554–555, 558–559
    parent-teacher communication,
        534–538, 545–554, 556–557,
        565–566
    P.L. 94–142 and, 539, 542
    responsibilities of, 541–543
    tutoring by, 559–561
PASS. *See* Program Analyses of Service
    Systems
Peabody Individual Achievement Test,
    151
Peabody Picture Vocabulary Test, 253
Pearpoint, J., 434–437
PEECH. *See* Precise Early Education of
    Children with Handicaps
Peer social initiations, 600–601
Peer tutoring, 68–69, 106–107, 165,
    174–177
*Pennsylvania Association for Retarded
    Children (PARC)
    v. Commonwealth of
    Pennsylvania*, 36, 37–40, 428
Perkins School for the Blind, 368
Phelps, Winthrop, 399
Phenylketonuria (PKU), 123
Phonation, 236, 248
Phonemes, 236, 238
Phonologic model, 256